P9-CMF-124

THE

WAR OF THE REBELLION:

A COMPILATION OF THE

OFFICIAL RECORDS

OF THE

UNION AND CONFEDERATE ARMIES.

PUBLISHED UNDER THE DIRECTION OF

The Hon. **ELIHU ROOT**, Secretary of War,

BY

BRIG. GEN. FRED C. AINSWORTH,

CHIEF OF THE RECORD AND PENSION OFFICE, WAR DEPARTMENT,

AND

MR. JOSEPH W. KIRKLEY.

SERIES III—VOLUME V.

WASHINGTON:
GOVERNMENT PRINTING OFFICE.
1900.

PREFACE.

The work of preparing the records of the war for public use was begun, under the resolution of Congress of May 19, 1864, by Col. E. D. Townsend, assistant adjutant-general, U. S. Army (then in charge of the Adjutant-General's Office, and subsequently the Adjutant-General), who caused copies to be made of reports of battles on file in his office and steps to be taken to collect missing records.

Under the provisions of joint resolution of July 27, 1866, Hon. Peter H. Watson was appointed to supervise the preparation of the records and to formulate a plan for their publication, but he performed no service under this appointment, which expired July 27, 1868, by limitation. This resolution having also repealed the former one, the project was suspended for the time being.

The first decisive step taken was the act of June 23, 1874, providing the necessary means "to enable the Secretary of War to begin the publication of the Official Records of the War of the Rebellion, both of the Union and Confederate Armies," and directing him "to have copied for the Public Printer all reports, letters, telegrams, and general orders, not heretofore copied or printed, and properly arranged in chronological order." Appropriations have been made from time to time for continuing such preparation. Under this act the preliminary work was resumed by General Townsend.

Subsequently, under meager appropriations, it was prosecuted in a somewhat desultory manner by various subordinates of the War Department until December 14, 1877, when the Secretary of War, perceiving that the undertaking needed the undivided attention of a single head, detailed Capt. Robert N. Scott, Third U. S. Artillery (subsequently major and lieutenant-colonel same regiment), to take charge of the office.

The act of June 23, 1874, enlarged upon the first scheme of publication. On this more comprehensive basis it was determined that the volumes should include not only the battle reports, correspondence, etc., in possession of the War Department, but also "all official documents that can be obtained by the compiler, and that appear to be of any historical value." Colonel Scott systematized the work, and, upon his recommendation, the Secretary of War approved the following order of publication:

The first series will embrace the formal reports, both Union and Confederate, of the first seizures of United States property in the Southern States, and of all military operations in the field, with the correspondence, orders, and returns relating specially thereto, and, as proposed, is to be accompanied by an Atlas.

In this series the reports will be arranged according to the campaigns and several theaters of operations (in the chronological order of events), and the Union reports of any event will, as a rule, be immediately followed by the Confederate accounts. The correspondence, etc., not embraced in the "reports" proper will follow (first Union and next Confederate) in chronological order.

The second series will contain the correspondence, orders, reports, and returns, Union and Confederate, relating to prisoners of war, and (so far as the military authorities were concerned) to state or political prisoners.

The third series will contain the correspondence, orders, reports, and returns of the Union authorities (embracing their correspondence with the Confederate officials) not relating specially to the subjects of the first and second series. It will set forth the annual and special reports of the Secretary of War, of the General-in-Chief, and of the chiefs of the several staff corps and departments; the calls for troops, and the correspondence between the National and the several State authorities.

The fourth series will exhibit the correspondence, orders, reports, and returns of the Confederate authorities, similar to that indicated for the Union officials, as of the third series, but excluding the correspondence between the Union and Confederate authorities given in that series.

The first volume of the records was issued in the early fall of 1880. The act approved June 16, 1880, provided "for the printing and binding, under direction of the Secretary of War, of 10,000 copies of a compilation of the Official Records (Union and Confederate) of the War of the Rebellion, so far as the same may be ready for publication, during the fiscal year;" and that "of said number 7,000 copies shall be for the use of the House of Representatives, 2,000 copies for the use of the Senate, and 1,000 copies for the use of the Executive Departments." Under this act Colonel Scott proceeded to publish the first five volumes of the records.*

---

*All subsequent volumes have been distributed under the act approved August 7, 1882, which provides that:

"The volumes of the Official Records of the War of the Rebellion shall be distributed as follows: One thousand copies to the Executive Departments, as now provided by law. One thousand copies for distribution by the Secretary of War among officers of the Army and contributors to the work. Eight thousand three hundred copies shall be sent by the Secretary of War to such libraries, organizations, and individuals as may be designated by the Senators, Representatives, and Delegates of the Forty-seventh Congress. Each Senator shall designate not exceeding twenty-six, and each Representative and Delegate not exceeding twenty-one, of such addresses, and the volumes shall be sent thereto from time to time as they are published, until the publication is completed. Senators, Representatives, and Delegates shall inform the Secretary of War in each case how many volumes of those heretofore published they have forwarded to such addresses. The remaining copies of the eleven thousand to be published, and all sets that may not be ordered to be distributed as provided herein, shall be sold by the Secretary of War for cost of publication with ten per cent. added thereto, and the proceeds of such sale shall be covered into the Treasury. If two or more sets of said volumes are ordered to the same address, the Secretary of War shall inform the Senators, Representatives, or Delegates who have designated the same, who thereupon may designate other libraries, organizations, or individuals. The Secretary of War shall report to the first session of the Forty-eighth Congress what volumes of the series heretofore published have not been furnished to such libraries, organizations, and individuals. He shall also inform distributees at whose instance the volumes are sent."

Colonel Scott died March 5, 1887. At his death some twenty-six books only had been issued, but he had compiled a large amount of matter for forthcoming volumes; consequently his name as compiler was retained in all the books up to and including Vol. XXXVI, although his successors had added largely to his compilations from new material found after his demise.

The Secretary of War, May 7, 1887, assigned Lieut. Col. H. M. Lazelle, Twenty-third U. S. Infantry, to duty as the successor of Colonel Scott. He had continued in charge about two years, when, in the act approved March 2, 1889, it was provided—

> That hereafter the preparation and publication of said records shall be conducted, under the Secretary of War, by a board of three persons, one of whom shall be an officer of the Army, and two civilian experts, to be appointed by the Secretary of War, the compensation of said civilian experts to be fixed by the Secretary of War.

The Secretary of War appointed Maj. George B. Davis, judge-advocate, U. S. Army, as the military member, and Leslie J. Perry, of Kansas, and Joseph W. Kirkley, of Maryland, as the civilian expert members of said board. The board assumed direction of the publication at the commencement of the fiscal year 1889, its first work beginning with Serial No. 36 of Vol. XXIV.

July 1, 1895, by direction of the Secretary of War, Maj. George W. Davis, Eleventh U. S. Infantry (subsequently lieutenant-colonel Fourteenth U. S. Infantry), relieved Maj. George B. Davis as the military member and president of the Board of Publication. Subsequently Col. Fred C. Ainsworth, Chief of the Record and Pension Office, War Department, was appointed the military member and president of the board, relieving Lieut. Col. George W. Davis June 1, 1898.

December 1, 1898, under the provision of the sundry civil act of July 1, 1898, relative to the War Records Office, the Board of Publication was dissolved, whereupon, by direction of the Secretary of War, the continuance of the work, beginning with Vol. VI, Series II, devolved on Colonel (now Brigadier-General) Ainsworth.

By operation of law (contained in "An act making appropriations for the legislative, executive, and judicial expenses of the Government for the fiscal year ending June 30, 1900," approved February 24, 1899), the War Records Office was merged into the Record and Pension Office, July 1, 1899, and since that date the work of publication has been conducted under the supervision of the chief of that office.

Each volume includes a copious index, and for the further convenience of investigators there will be, in addition, a separate general index to the entire set.

Nothing is printed in these volumes except duly authenticated contemporaneous records of the war. The scope of the compiler's work is to decide upon and arrange the matter to be published; to correct and verify the orthography of the papers used, and, wherever deemed necessary, to add a foot-note of explanation.

CONTENTS.

1865.

	Sunday.	Monday.	Tuesday.	Wednesday.	Thursday.	Friday.	Saturday.
Jan	1	2	3	4	5	6	7
	8	9	10	11	12	13	14
	15	16	17	18	19	20	21
	22	23	24	25	26	27	28
	29	30	31				
Feb				1	2	3	4
	5	6	7	8	9	10	11
	12	13	14	15	16	17	18
	19	20	21	22	23	24	25
	26	27	28				
March				1	2	3	4
	5	6	7	8	9	10	11
	12	13	14	15	16	17	18
	19	20	21	22	23	24	25
	26	27	28	29	30	31	
April							1
	2	3	4	5	6	7	8
	9	10	11	12	13	14	15
	16	17	18	19	20	21	22
	23	24	25	26	27	28	29
	30						
May		1	2	3	4	5	6
	7	8	9	10	11	12	13
	14	15	16	17	18	19	20
	21	22	23	24	25	26	27
	28	29	30	31			
June					1	2	3
	4	5	6	7	8	9	10
	11	12	13	14	15	16	17
	18	19	20	21	22	23	24
	25	26	27	28	29	30	
July							1
	2	3	4	5	6	7	8
	9	10	11	12	13	14	15
	16	17	18	19	20	21	22
	23	24	25	26	27	28	29
	30	31					
August			1	2	3	4	5
	6	7	8	9	10	11	12
	13	14	15	16	17	18	19
	20	21	22	23	24	25	26
	27	28	29	30	31		
Sept						1	2
	3	4	5	6	7	8	9
	10	11	12	13	14	15	16
	17	18	19	20	21	22	23
	24	25	26	27	28	29	30
October	1	2	3	4	5	6	7
	8	9	10	11	12	13	14
	15	16	17	18	19	20	21
	22	23	24	25	26	27	28
	29	30	31				
Nov				1	2	3	4
	5	6	7	8	9	10	11
	12	13	14	15	16	17	18
	19	20	21	22	23	24	25
	26	27	28	29	30		
Dec						1	2
	3	4	5	6	7	8	9
	10	11	12	13	14	15	16
	17	18	19	20	21	22	23
	24	25	26	27	28	29	30
	31						

1866.

	Sunday.	Monday.	Tuesday.	Wednesday.	Thursday.	Friday.	Saturday.
Jan		1	2	3	4	5	6
	7	8	9	10	11	12	13
	14	15	16	17	18	19	20
	21	22	23	24	25	26	27
	28	29	30	31			
Feb					1	2	3
	4	5	6	7	8	9	10
	11	12	13	14	15	16	17
	18	19	20	21	22	23	24
	25	26	27	28			
March					1	2	3
	4	5	6	7	8	9	10
	11	12	13	14	15	16	17
	18	19	20	21	22	23	24
	25	26	27	28	29	30	31
April	1	2	3	4	5	6	7
	8	9	10	11	12	13	14
	15	16	17	18	19	20	21
	22	23	24	25	26	27	28
	29	30					
May			1	2	3	4	5
	6	7	8	9	10	11	12
	13	14	15	16	17	18	19
	20	21	22	23	24	25	26
	27	28	29	30	31		
June						1	2
	3	4	5	6	7	8	9
	10	11	12	13	14	15	16
	17	18	19	20	21	22	23
	24	25.	26	27	28	29	30
July	1	2	3	4	5	6	7
	8	9	10	11	12	13	14
	15	16	17	18	19	20	21
	22	23	24	25	26	27	28
	29	30	31				
August				1	2	3	4
	5	6	7	8	9	10	11
	12	13	14	15	16	17	18
	19	20	21	22	23	24	25
	26	27	28	29	30	31	
Sept							1
	2	3	4	5	6	7	8
	9	10	11	12	13	14	15
	16	17	18	19	20	21	22
	23	24	25	26	27	28	29
	30						
October		1	2	3	4	5	6
	7	8	9	10	11	12	13
	14	15	16	17	18	19	20
	21	22	23	24	25	26	27
	28	29	30	31			
Nov					1	2	3
	4	5	6	7	8	9	10
	11	12	13	14	15	16	17
	18	19	20	21	22	23	24
	25	26	27	28	29	30	
Dec							1
	2	3	4	5	6	7	8
	9	10	11	12	13	14	15
	16	17	18	19	20	21	22
	23	24	25	26	27	28	29
	30	31					

SERIES III.—VOL. V.

CORRESPONDENCE, ORDERS, REPORTS, AND RETURNS OF THE UNION AUTHORITIES FROM MAY 1, 1865, TO THE END.*

GENERAL ORDERS, No. 79. } WAR DEPT., ADJT. GENERAL'S OFFICE, *Washington, May 1, 1865.*

FOR REDUCING THE NUMBER OF GENERAL, FIELD, AND STAFF OFFICERS.

It is ordered by the President that resignations of general, field, and staff officers will be received until the 15th of this month, at which date the Adjutant-General is directed to commence mustering honorably out of service all general, field, and staff officers who are unemployed, or whose service is no longer needed.

By order of the President of the United States:

W. A. NICHOLS,
Assistant Adjutant-General.

WAR DEPARTMENT, ADJUTANT-GENERAL'S OFFICE,
Washington, May 1, 1865.

(For the Honorable Secretary of War.)

OUTLINE OF METHOD FOR THE MUSTER OUT AND DISCHARGE FROM SERVICE OF THE VOLUNTEER ARMIES OF THE UNITED STATES.

I. Army corps, or at least the divisions thereof, to be kept intact and ordered to convenient points, depending upon the armies to which they belong—say, Old Point Comfort, Washington, Cumberland, Nashville, Saint Louis, and such other places as may be designated.

On arrival at said rendezvous a critical inspection of the regimental and company records to be made and the muster-out rolls prepared under the direction of the assistant commissaries of musters for divisions, superintended by the corps commissaries; corps commanders to see that the work is pushed with energy and executed promptly, using to this end division and brigade commanders to superintend it, and their respective staff officers to aid the mustering officers in col-

*For all documents relating to the organization of troops on the Pacific Coast, &c., see Series I, Vol. L.

lecting the data for the muster-out rolls and discharge papers, as well as the preparation of the same.

II. The rolls and other final papers of a regiment completed, said command, with its arms, colors, and necessary equipage, to be placed en route, generally to that point in the State where mustered in, there to be taken charge of by the chief mustering officer of the State, and met by paymasters to make final payments.

Whilst en route to the State a discreet and capable officer to be specially charged by the commissary of musters with the care of the muster-out rolls and regimental records. Immediately on arrival in the State the rolls and records to be turned over to the chief mustering officer or his assistant at the point of rendezvous. After payment of the troops the regimental and company records to be retained and carefully preserved by the State mustering officers, subject to the orders of the Adjutant-General of the Army.

Whilst waiting payment the chief mustering officer to cause subsistence and other authorized supplies to be provided; also to see that the command is kept together and under discipline. As soon as practicable after the arrival of a regiment at the State rendezvous the chief mustering officer to have its arms and other public property turned over to officers of the respective supply departments; said officers to be designated by the departments concerned.

The departure of regiments from the rendezvous where mustered out to be so regulated that regiments will not arrive more rapidly in their respective States than the Pay Department can pay them off.

III. Under the foregoing the following advantages will be secured:

1. The entire force of commissaries and assistant commissaries of musters for troops in the field will be made available for the work, in connection with the chief and other State mustering officers.

2. The most experienced mustering officers and those most familiar with the regimental records will be secured.

3. The records from which the mustering-out data is to be obtained will be readily accessible, and the loss of records (so common through the neglect of regimental officers) whilst regiments are en route from the field to States can be avoided.

4. Regimental officers can be held to a rigid accountability (by the corps, division, and brigade commanders) in preparing the records, and the interest of the enlisted man thus protected.

5. Order and discipline can be maintained whilst troops are en route to States and after arrival therein.

6. Troops can be comfortably cared for up to the moment they are paid off and ready to start for their homes. Dissatisfaction among them will be obviated, and cause for complaint by State authorities and citizens will be removed.

7. All public property can be easily secured and properly accounted for.

8. Regulations of the War Department now in force can be readily adapted to the musters out and discharge of the troops.

Should the foregoing be approved, a general order can be framed, pointing to the necessary regulations and arranging requisite details.

Respectfully submitted.

THOMAS M. VINCENT,
Assistant Adjutant-General.

MEMORANDUM.—Foregoing was for the consideration of the Secretary of War and lieutenant-general commanding Armies of the

United States, at a meeting to which undersigned was called to consult as to disbanding the volunteer armies. Subject was briefly referred to in conversation; paper, however, not read. Secretary concluded by saying: "Send the method to General Grant, and if approved by him issue the order." Time consumed in the consideration of subject did not extend beyond one hour and a half.

T. M. V.

MEMORANDUM.] ADJUTANT-GENERAL'S OFFICE,
May 11, 1865.

Respectfully forwarded to Lieut. Gen. U. S. Grant, commanding Armies of the United States.

This is the proposed method for musters out which I spoke of to the Secretary of War whilst you were conversing with him on the subject.

THOMAS M. VINCENT,
Assistant Adjutant-General.

[Indorsement.]

MAY 11, 1865.

Plan and suggestions within approved.

U. S. GRANT,
Lieutenant-General.

LEXINGTON, KY., *May 1, 1865.*

ORDERS No. 6.]

On and after this date all recruiting of colored men in the Departments of the Missouri and Arkansas and Military Divisions of the Mississippi and West Mississippi will cease. Volunteers will also not be accepted for white regiments within such limits. All recruiting officers will immediately join their respective commands for duty. Orders will subsequently be given for the consolidation of the incomplete colored regiments and the muster out of service of all supernumerary officers.

By order of the Secretary of War:

L. THOMAS,
Adjutant-General.

QUARTERMASTER-GENERAL'S OFFICE,
Washington, D. C., May 2, 1865.

SIR: As it is probable a large number of troops will soon be returning to their homes, the strictest attention should be given to prevent the use of any but perfectly safe transports, under experienced and careful masters, provided with everything necessary for the safety and comfort of troops. Especial care should be taken to see that they are thoroughly clean and that they are not overloaded. The late calamity to the steamer Sultana shows the need of extreme caution which will be expected from all officers in the management of river transportation.

By order of the Quartermaster-General:

Very respectfully,

LEWIS B. PARSONS,
Colonel and Chief of Rail and River Transportation.

WAR DEPARTMENT,
Washington City, May 3, 1865.

ORDER RESCINDING REGULATIONS PROHIBITING THE EXPORTATION OF ARMS, AMMUNITION, HORSES, MULES, AND LIVE-STOCK.

The Executive order of November 21, 1862, prohibiting the exportation of arms and ammunition from the United States, and the Executive order of May 13, 1863, prohibiting the exportation of horses, mules, and live-stock, being no longer required by public necessities, the aforesaid orders are hereby rescinded and annulled.

By order of the President:

EDWIN M. STANTON,
Secretary of War.

CIRCULAR.] WAR DEPT., ADJUTANT-GENERAL'S OFFICE,
Washington, May 3, 1865.

ALL CHIEF MUSTERING OFFICERS OF LOYAL STATES:

Deserters who have reported, or who may yet report, under the President's proclamation, promulgated in General Orders, No. 35, current series, from this office, and not yet forwarded to their proper commands, will be mustered out and discharged the service, with forfeiture of all pay and allowances due at date of desertion, or which may have accrued since. Arrange with rendezvous commanders accordingly. Under the foregoing, care must be taken not to discharge any deserters who have been arrested and delivered up.

Please acknowledge this.

By command:

THOMAS M. VINCENT,
Assistant Adjutant-General.

WAR DEPARTMENT, ADJUTANT-GENERAL'S OFFICE,
Washington, D. C., May 3, 1865.

ALL DEPT. COMMANDERS AND CHIEF MUSTERING OFFICERS:

All soldiers patients in hospitals (except veteran volunteers, veterans of the First Army Corps, Major-General Hancock's, and soldiers of the Regular Army) will, as soon as they shall cease to require medical treatment, be at once mustered out of service in the usual manner. Should the commissary of musters and his assistants be insufficient to perform this duty promptly, you are authorized to appoint such additional assistants as you may consider necessary, and to avail yourself of such mustering officers within the geographical limits of your command as, in the judgment of the chief mustering officer, can be spared from their present duties. The commissary of musters must take especial pains to see that the commanding officers of the regiments and chief mustering officers of the States to which the soldiers belong are each furnished with a copy of the muster-out roll. An extra copy may be made for this purpose, if necessary. Soldiers whose claims for pensions are entitled to consideration should be discharged on the usual surgeon's certificate of disability. Soldiers absent on furlough from hospitals will be notified by the surgeon in charge to report to the nearest chief mustering officer for muster out, and required to acknowledge the receipt of the notification. As soon as their acknowledgment of the notification is received their descriptive lists will be sent to the chief mustering officer to whom they report. Should they return before receiving such notification they will be mustered out as the others. A copy of the muster-out roll of all men will be furnished to the adjutants-general of the States to which the regiments belong. It is expected that department commanders will use every exertion to have this duty performed promptly and correctly.

Acknowledge receipt.

By order of the Secretary of War:

W. A. NICHOLS,
Assistant Adjutant-General.

GENERAL ORDERS, No. 82. } WAR DEPT., ADJT. GENERAL'S OFFICE, *Washington, May 6, 1865.*

FOR REDUCING THE NUMBER OF COMPANY AND STAFF OFFICERS OF VOLUNTEER REGIMENTS.

By direction of the President all company and staff officers of volunteer regiments absent from their commands on account of physical disability, or by virtue of leaves of absence granted them on their return to loyal States as prisoners of war, will be honorably mustered out of the service of the United States of date the 15th instant.

Said officers will immediately apply by letter to the Adjutant-General of the Army for their muster-out and discharge papers. In case of physical disability from disease or wounds, the letter must be accompanied by a medical certificate of the usual form.

The post-office address of the officer must be given with care in all cases.

By order of the Secretary of War:

W. A. NICHOLS,
Assistant Adjutant-General.

ATTORNEY-GENERAL'S OFFICE,
May 8, 1865.

The PRESIDENT:

SIR: I have the honor to acknowledge the receipt of your letter of April 21, 1865.

By the Constitution of the United States (2d Art., sec. 2, cl. 1) the President is vested with the "power to grant reprieves and pardons for offenses against the United States, except in case of impeachment."

By the 13th section of the act of Congress entitled "An act to suppress insurrection, to punish treason and rebellion, to seize and confiscate the property of rebels, and for other purposes," approved July 17, 1862, "the President is authorized, at any time hereafter, by proclamation, to extend to persons who may have participated in the existing rebellion, in any State or part thereof, pardon and amnesty, with such exceptions and at such time and on such conditions as he may deem expedient for the public welfare."

The right and power of the President to pardon and to issue any proclamation of amnesty are derived from the clauses in the Constitution and the act of Congress as quoted above.

By the Constitution and the act of Congress the power to pardon in individual cases and the power of extending, by proclamation, amnesty to classes of individuals are solely in the hands of the President. It is, therefore, needless to discuss the question whether the act of Congress was necessary in order to enable the President lawfully to issue a proclamation of pardon and amnesty.

The power of exercising and extending mercy resides in some department of every well-ordered government. When order and peace reign its exercise is frequent and its influence valuable. Its influence is of value inestimable at the termination of an insurrection so widespread as the one which in our country is just being suppressed. Its appropriate office is to soothe and heal, not to keep alive or to initiate the rebellious and malignant passions that induced, precipitated, and sustained the insurrection. This power to soothe and heal is appropriately vested in the Executive Department of the Government, whose duty it is to recognize and declare the existence of an insurrection, to suppress it by force, and to proclaim its suppression. In order, then, that this benign power of the Government should accomplish the objects for which it was given, the extent and limits of the power should be clearly understood. Therefore, before proceeding to answer the questions propounded in your letter, it would seem to be eminently proper to state some of the obvious principles upon which the power to grant pardons and amnesty rests, and deduce from those principles the limitation of that power.

The words amnesty and pardon have a usual and well-understood meaning. Neither is defined in any act of Congress; the latter is not used in the Constitution.

A pardon is a remission of guilt; an amnesty is an act of oblivion or forgetfulness.

They are acts of sovereign mercy and grace, flowing from the appropriate organ of the Government.

There can be no pardon where there is no actual or imputed guilt. The acceptance of a pardon is a confession of guilt or of the existence of a state of facts from which a judgment of guilt would follow.

A pardon may be absolute and complete or it may be conditional or partial. The whole penalty denounced by the law against an offender may be forgiven, or so much of it only as may seem expedient. The power to pardon is not exhausted by its partial use. A part of the penalty may be forgiven now, and at a future time another part, and so on till the whole is forgiven. This power may be so used as to place the offender upon trial and probation as to his good faith and purposes.

A pardon may be upon conditions, and those conditions may be precedent or subsequent.

The conditions, however, appended to a pardon cannot be immoral, illegal, or inconsistent with the pardon.

If a condition precedent annexed to a pardon be immoral, so that the person in whose favor it is issued should never speak the truth; or illegal, so that he should commit murder; or inconsistent with the pardon, so that he should never eat or sleep, the pardon would never attach or be of avail. On the other hand, if those conditions were subsequent—that is, if it were declared that the pardon should be void if the party ever spoke the truth, or if he did not commit murder, or if he should eat or sleep—the pardon would attach and be valid, and the condition void and of no effect. If a condition subsequent is broken, the offender could be tried and punished for the original offense. The breach of the condition would make the pardon void. Any conditions, precedent or subsequent, may, therefore, be appended that are not immoral, illegal, or inconsistent with the pardon. This great and sovereign power of mercy can never be used as a cover for immoral or illegal conduct.

As a pardon presupposes that an offense has been committed, and ever acts upon the past, the power to grant it never can be exerted as an immunity or license for future misdoing.

A pardon procured by fraud or for a fraudulent purpose, upon the suppression of the truth or the suggestion of falsehood, is void. It is a deed of mercy, given without other fee or reward than the good faith, truth, and repentance of the culprit. On the other hand, as an act of grace freely given, when obtained without falsehood, fraud, and for no fraudulent use, it should be liberally construed in favor of the repentant offender.

A promise to pardon is not a pardon, and may at any time be withdrawn; but a pardon may be offered, and the offer kept open, and thus be continuing, so that the person to whom it is offered may accept it at a future day. After the pardon has been accepted it becomes a valid act, and the person receiving it is entitled to all its benefits.

The principles hereinbefore stated forbid, however, that an offer of pardon be construed as a license or indulgence to commit continuing or future offenses, or as giving immunity from the consequences of such offenses.

After the offender shall have received notice of the offer, or after a reasonable time shall have elapsed within which he must be presumed to have received notice of the offer, he cannot continue his ill-doing and then accept and rely upon the offer of pardon as an indemnity against what he did before and also what he did after notice. Such a construction of the pardoning power would virtually convert it into a power to license crime.

The high and necessary power of extending pardon and amnesty can never be rightfully exercised so as to enable the President to say to offenders against the law, "I now offer you a free pardon for the past; or at any future day when you shall, from baffled hopes, or after being foiled in dangerous and bloody enterprises, think proper to accept, I will give you a pardon for the then past."

When men have offended against the law their appeal is for mercy, not for justice. In this country and under this Government violators of the law have offended against a law of their own making; out of their own mouths they are condemned—convicted by their own judgments—and, under a law of their own making, they cannot appear before the seat of mercy and arrogantly claim the fulfillment of a promise of pardon they have refused and defied.

The excellence of mercy and charity in a national trouble like ours ought not to be undervalued. Such feelings should be fondly cherished and studiously cultivated. When brought into action they should be generously but wisely indulged. Like all the great, necessary, and useful powers in nature or in government, harm may come of their improvident use, and perils which seem past may be renewed, and other and new dangers be precipitated. By a too extended, thoughtless, or unwise kindness the man or the government may warm into life an adder that will requite that kindness by a fatal sting from a poisonous fang.

Keeping in view these obvious and fundamental principles that fix and limit the powers of pardon and amnesty under the Constitution and the law, I will proceed to consider the questions propounded by you on the proclamations dated, respectively, on the 8th day of December, 1863, and on the 26th day of March, 1864, commonly called the amnesty proclamations.

You ask my opinion, first, as to the proper construction and effect of those proclamations upon the citizens and residents of rebel States who have taken the oath of amnesty prescribed therein.

These two proclamations must be read together and regarded as one instrument. That must, at least, be so from the date of the last proclamation, March 26, 1864. No doubt many persons did, betwixt the 8th of December, 1863, and the 26th of March, 1864, take the oath who could not have done so had the original proclamation contained the exceptions set forth in the second. What the rights are of those who took the oath in that intermediate space of time, and who could not have taken it after the 26th of March, 1864, is purely a judicial question. The facts in such cases are accomplished, and the rights arising out of those facts have attached and become vested. If not improper, it would be, at least, idle in me to express an opinion on those cases. The Judicial Department of the Government must determine the law in those cases when they are properly presented before the courts.

For all practical purposes, so far as the Executive Department of the Government is concerned, both proclamations may therefore be regarded as of the date the 26th of March, 1864. From that point of view their proper operation and effect are now to be considered.

It is plainly stated on the face of the second proclamation that its objects "were to suppress the insurrection, and to restore the authority of the United States, and with reference to these objects alone." In the midst of a gigantic effort on the part of traitors to dismember our country and overthrow our Government, the President, in the legitimate exercise of his great powers, invoked the healing influences of charity and forgiveness. His great heart but responded to the desire of the American people to win back this misguided people to their allegiance, and to peace and order, by gentleness, rather than to compel obedience by the dread powers of war.

It must not be supposed that in giving expression to and making a law of this noble wish of his heart, and the heart of the people whom he represented, it was intended to give license and immunity to crime and treason for the then future. His expressed object was "to suppress the insurrection, and to restore the authority of the United States, and that alone."

His object was made still more manifest when he said that the person "shall voluntarily come forward" and take the said oath, with the purpose of restoring peace and establishing the national authority.

The reluctant, unrepentant, defying persons who, in their hearts, desired the success of the rebellion and the overthrow of the Government, were not invited to take the oath; and if any such should take it they would but add perjury—a God-defying sin—to that of treason; and if that fact can be shown to a judicial tribunal, it seems to me that they should take no benefit from the pardon and amnesty. A mind and heart unpurged of treason were not invited by the amnesty proclamation to add thereto the crime of perjury.

It seems to me, then, that all the citizens and residents of the rebel States not excepted from the amnesty, who did, after the issuing of the proclamation, or after notice thereof, or within a reasonable time within which it must be supposed they had notice, refrain from further hostilities, and take the oath of amnesty voluntarily, with the purpose of restoring peace and establishing the national authority, being at the time free from arrest, confinement, or duress, and not under bonds, are entitled to all the benefits and rights so freely and benignly given by a magnanimous Government. Where the oath has been taken without the purpose of restoring peace and establishing the national authority, though taken promptly, it seems to me that the amnesty and pardon do not attach. This, however, is a judicial question, which the courts may decide contrary to my opinion. I ought not, perhaps, to express any.

In giving this construction to the amnesty proclamation, I have been constantly impressed by a paragraph in the last annual message of the President of the United States. It reads as follows:

> A year ago general pardon and amnesty, upon specified terms, were offered to all, except certain designated classes; and it was, at the same time, made known that the exempted classes were still within contemplation of special clemency. During the year many availed themselves of the general provision, and many more would, only that the signs of bad faith in some led to such precautionary measures as rendered the practical process less easy and certain. During the same time, also, special pardons have been granted to individuals of the excepted classes, and no voluntary application has been denied. Thus, practically, the door has been for a full year open to all, except such as were not in condition to make a free choice; that is, such as were in custody or under constraint. It is still open to all. But the time may come—probably will come—when public duty shall demand that it be closed, and that, in lieu, more rigorous measures than heretofore shall be adopted.

A profound respect for the opinions of that great and good man, Abraham Lincoln, late President of the United States, induces me to ponder long and well before I can venture to express an opinion differing even in a shade from his. But all who had the good fortune to know him well must feel and know that, from his very nature, he was not only tempted but forced to strain his power of mercy. His love for mankind was boundless, his charity was all-embracing, and his benevolence so sensitive that he sometimes was as ready to pardon the unrepentant as the sincerely penitent offender. Clearly and pointedly does the above paragraph show to the world that such was his nature. He says:

> During the whole year that special pardons have been granted to individuals of the excepted classes, no voluntary application has been denied.

The door of mercy to his heart was, we know, ever open; and yet he closes the paragraph with this significant sentence:

> But the time may come—probably will come—when public duty shall demand that it be closed, and that, in lieu, more rigorous measures than heretofore shall be adopted.

It is probably fair to infer that the late President understood his proclamation of amnesty as giving pardon to all, no matter how long they had refused, and whether they had offended after notice of the offer or not. Whether his powers extended so far is, to say the least, a doubtful question.

I am clear and decided in my conviction that the President has no power to make an open offer of pardon which could be relied upon as a protection for offenses committed after notice of the offer. This opinion is induced from principle, and independently of the language of the proclamation.

The language of the first proclamation is, however, consonant with this opinion. It is addressed "to all persons who have participated in the existing rebellion"—words referring to the past.

If I am right in this construction of the proclamation—and I am satisfied in my own mind that I am—another proclamation should be issued. Persons should not be invited to take an oath and to comply with terms under which they cannot obtain firm legal rights. It is especially due to those who have heretofore and would now avail themselves, in good faith, of the benefits of pardon and amnesty, that another proclamation should be substituted covering the now past. Persons who have been constantly engaged in rebellion should know distinctly what they are to do, when and how they are to do it, to free themselves from punishment, in whole or in part, or to reinstate themselves as before the rebellion. Such as have been affected merely by their treasonable associations should be absolutely forgiven. Appropriate conditions should be appended to the pardons of many. The grace and favor of the Government should now be large and generous, and the operation and effect of its proper mercy should not be left uncertain.

The second question you ask is as to the rights of the citizens and residents of the rebel States who have not taken, nor offered to take, the oath and comply with the terms of the proclamation.

Here, again, we meet trouble and uncertainty.

The expressed objects of the proclamation are to suppress the insurrection and restore the authority of the United States. Can any one be permitted to take the oath and comply with the terms prescribed in the proclamation in a State or a community where the civil and military power of the insurrection has been destroyed and the rebellion suppressed, and the authority of the United States is re-established without let or hindrance? Or does the insurrection continue, in legal contemplation, though not in fact, until the Executive Department of the Government shall, by proclamation, declare that it has been suppressed? And would this proclamation of pardon and amnesty continue and be open after proclamation that the rebellion had been suppressed?

It would seem from the proclamation that the amnesty was extended to those who were willing to aid in suppressing, as well as restoring; and yet it may and doubtless will be contended, and with much force and show of reason, that all who have stood by and clung to the insurrection till its organization and power, both civil and military, were gone, have, nevertheless, a right to take all the benefits of the amnesty, because they will lend a reluctant aid in restoring an authority which they hate. Amnesty is proffered for aid in suppressing and restoring; amnesty is demanded for the work of restoration; full reward is required for less than half of the service that is needed.

As a measure to aid in the suppression of the rebellion, the late proclamation has done its full and complete office. Now, one is desired to aid in restoring order and reorganizing society in the rebellious States. Reconstruction is not needed; that word conveys an erroneous idea. The construction of this Government is as perfect as human wisdom can make it. The trial to which its powers and capacities have been subjected in this effort at revolution and dismemberment proves with what wisdom its foundations have been laid. Ours is a task to preserve principles and powers clearly and well defined, and that have carried us safely through our past troubles. Ours is not a duty to reconstruct or change. Society in the rebel States has not been and is not now in a normal condition, nor in harmony with the principles of our Government. That society has rebelled against them, and made war upon the principles and powers of our Government. In so doing it has offended, and stands a convicted culprit. Mercy must be largely extended. Some of the great leaders and offenders only must be made to feel the extreme rigor of the law—not in a spirit of revenge, but to put the seal of infamy upon their conduct. But the mercy extended to the great mass of the misguided people can and should be so used as to reorganize society upon a loyal and freedom-loving basis. It is manifestly for their good, and the good of mankind, that this should be done. The power of pardon and mercy is adequate to this end. Such conditions, precedent and subsequent, can legally and properly be appended as will root out the spirit of rebellion and bring society in those States into perfect accord with the wise and thoroughly tried principle of our Government.

If this power of pardon is wisely used, peace will be established upon a sure and permanent basis.

On these grounds, in addition to what has before been said, I am of the opinion that another and a new offer of amnesty, adapted to the existing condition of things, should be proclaimed.

I do not conceive that it is in place just now, even if I were prepared to do so, which I am not—because not sufficiently advised of the temper of those in rebellion—for me to say what should be the terms of the suggested proclamation.

I have the honor to be, sir, very respectfully, your obedient servant,

JAMES SPEED,
Attorney-General.

GENERAL ORDERS, No. 83. } WAR DEPT., ADJT. GENERAL'S OFFICE, *Washington, May 8, 1865.*

FOR REDUCING THE VOLUNTEER CAVALRY FORCES OF THE ARMY.

I. Immediately upon receipt of this order by commanding generals of armies and departments all volunteer soldiers of the cavalry arm whose terms of service will expire prior to October 1, 1865, will be mustered out and discharged the service of the United States. In discharging the said troops the following will be observed:

1. The musters out will be made, in accordance with existing regulations, by the commissaries of musters of divisions, under the directions of commissaries of musters of corps or departments.

2. Army and department commanders will forthwith ascertain the number of men within their respective commands to be discharged, and report the same direct to the Paymaster-General of the Army, forwarding a duplicate of the report to the Adjutant-General. Said report must specify the number for each regiment, or company, if an independent one.

3. The Paymaster-General will arrange to make immediate payment to the men discharged; said payments to be made in the armies or departments in which the men may be serving at date of muster out.

II. All cavalry remaining in service after the aforesaid discharges have been made will be immediately consolidated into complete maximum regimental organizations, and as follows:

1. Army and department commanders will select and designate the organizations to be consolidated.

2. Organizations from the same State will be consolidated with each other.

3. All supernumerary commissioned and non-commissioned officers will be mustered out of the date the consolidation of their respective commands is made.

4. The commissioned and non-commissioned officers to be retained, not exceeding the legal number, will be selected by army and department commanders.

5. The proper commissaries of musters and their assistants will be charged, under existing regulations, with the prompt execution of the details.

III. Corps and department commanders will see that the work is pushed with energy, and executed accurately and promptly, using to this end division and brigade commanders to superintend it, with their respective staff officers, to aid the mustering officer in collecting the necessary data for the transfer rolls (see Circular No. 64, series of 1864, Adjutant-General's Office), muster-out rolls, and other necessary discharge papers, as well as the preparation of the same.

IV. Horses and other public property rendered surplus by the reduction in the forces will be turned over to and cared for by the proper officers of the supply departments concerned.

V. Regimental and company records, rendered no longer necessary, will be taken charge of by the proper commissary of musters and forwarded to the Adjutant-General of the Army. The records of each company or regiment must be arranged by themselves, and the package containing them marked distinctly with the contents.

VI. Commissaries of musters and their assistants will be held responsible that the necessary rolls are delivered and forwarded to their destination without unnecessary delay.

By order of the Secretary of War:

E. D. TOWNSEND,
Assistant Adjutant-General.

GENERAL ORDERS, No. 84. } WAR DEPT., ADJT. GENERAL'S OFFICE, *Washington, May 8, 1865.*

BALANCES OF BOUNTIES PAYABLE TO VOLUNTEERS WHEN HONORABLY MUSTERED OUT AND DISCHARGED, ON ACCOUNT OF THE GOVERNMENT NO LONGER REQUIRING THEIR SERVICES.

I. Veterans who enlisted under the provisions of General Orders, No. 191, series of 1863, from this office, and the extensions thereof (General Orders, Nos. 324 and 387, of 1863; 20 and 92, of 1864), and recruits (not veterans) who enlisted for three years or the war, under the provisions of the circular letter of October 24, 1863, from the Provost-Marshal-General's Bureau, and its modifications, are, on their honorable muster out and discharge from the service of the United States before the expiration of their respective terms of enlistment, entitled to the unpaid balances of the bounties promised them by the orders and laws under which they enlisted.

II. A volunteer accepted and mustered into service under the act of July 4, 1864 (General Orders, No. 224, Adjutant-General's Office, 1864), whether for the term of one, two, or three years, is, on muster out of service before the expiration of the term of service for which he enlisted, entitled only to receive the proportion of the bounty allowed by the act cited, whether one-third or two-thirds thereof, which had actually accrued before the date of his discharge.

For instance, if the soldier volunteered for two years and is mustered out before the expiration of the first year of his service, he cannot claim either the second or third installments of the bounty of $200, which would have been payable to him had he continued in the service till the expiration of the two years for which he enlisted.

Only the volunteer who at the time of his discharge has completed one-half the term of service for which he enlisted is entitled to the second installment of one-third the amount of bounty given to him by the act, and he is entitled to no more of that bounty. If he is discharged on the next day after the expiration of one-half of his term of enlistment, the second installment of the bounty is due and payable to him, but the discharge precludes him from receiving a third installment, that being due only to a volunteer who may have served his entire term of enlistment.

III. In discharging men from service mustering officers will note the balances of bounties due on the muster-out rolls opposite the names of the soldiers respectively. Great care must be exercised in doing this. Prior to payment paymasters will carefully re-examine the rolls, with the view of detecting errors in amounts thereon noted.

By order of the Secretary of War:

E. D. TOWNSEND,
Assistant Adjutant-General.

WAR DEPARTMENT, ADJUTANT-GENERAL'S OFFICE,
Washington, May 8, 1865.

ALL DEPT. COMMANDERS AND CHIEF MUSTERING OFFICERS:

The Veteran Reserve Corps is excepted from the operations of the telegram of the 3d instant, discharging patients in hospitals, &c.

THOMAS M. VINCENT,
Assistant Adjutant-General.

WAR DEPT., PROVOST-MARSHAL-GENERAL'S BUREAU,
Washington, D. C., May 8, 1865.

Bvt. Col. W. H. SIDELL,
Actg. Asst. Provost-Marshal-General, Louisville, Ky.:

The Secretary of War directs that recruiting be continued until June 1, 1865, for the following regiments of colored troops: The Seventy-second, One hundred and nineteenth, One hundred and twentieth, One hundred and twenty-first Colored Infantry, the Sixth Colored Cavalry, and the Fourth and Thirteenth Colored Artillery, none of these regiments, however, to be recruited beyond the maximum authorized by law. Require weekly reports to be made of the number of men obtained under this authorization.

JAMES B. FRY,
Provost-Marshal-General.

EXECUTIVE CHAMBER,
Washington City, May 9, 1865.

Ordered:

1. That all acts and proceedings of the political, military, and civil organizations which have been in a state of insurrection and rebellion

within the State of Virginia against the authority and laws of the United States, and of which Jefferson Davis, John Letcher, and William Smith were late the respective chiefs, are declared null and void. All persons who shall exercise, claim, pretend, or attempt to exercise any political, military, or civil power, authority, jurisdiction, or right, by, through, or under Jefferson Davis, late of the city of Richmond, and his confederates, or under John Letcher or William Smith and their confederates, or under any pretended political, military, or civil commission or authority issued by them, or either of them, since the 17th day of April, 1861, shall be deemed and taken as in rebellion against the United States, and shall be dealt with accordingly.

2. That the Secretary of State proceed to put in force all laws of the United States the administration whereof belongs to the Department of State applicable to the geographical limits aforesaid.

3. That the Secretary of the Treasury proceed without delay to nominate for appointment assessors of taxes and collectors of customs and internal revenue, and such other officers of the Treasury Department as are authorized by law, and shall put in execution the revenue laws of the United States within the geographical limits aforesaid. In making appointments the preference shall be given to qualified loyal persons residing within the districts where their respective duties are to be performed. But if suitable persons shall not be found residents of the districts, then persons residing in other States or districts shall be appointed.

4. That the Postmaster-General shall proceed to establish post-offices and post routes, and put into execution the postal laws of the United States within the said State, giving to loyal residents the preference of appointment; but if suitable persons are not found, then to appoint agents, &c., from other States.

5. That the district judge of said district proceed to hold courts within said State in accordance with the provisions of the act of Congress. The Attorney-General will instruct the proper officers to libel and bring to judgment, confiscation, and sale property subject to confiscation, and enforce the administration of justice within said State, in all matters civil and criminal within the cognizance and jurisdiction of the Federal courts.

6. That the Secretary of War assign such assistant provost-marshal-general and such provost-marshals in each district of said State as he may deem necessary.

7. The Secretary of the Navy will take possession of all public property belonging to the Navy Department within said geographical limits, and put in operation all acts of Congress in relation to naval affairs having application to the said State.

8. The Secretary of the Interior will also put in force the laws relating to the Department of the Interior.

9. That to carry into effect the guarantee by the Federal Constitution of a republican form of State government, and afford the advantage and security of domestic laws, as well as to complete the re-establishment of the authority and laws of the United States and the full and complete restoration of peace within the limits aforesaid, Francis H. Peirpoint, Governor of the State of Virginia, will be aided by the Federal Government, so far as may be necessary, in the lawful measures which he may take for the extension and administration of the State government throughout the geographical limits of said State.

In testimony whereof I have hereunto set my hand and caused the seal of the United States to be affixed.

[L. S.] ANDREW JOHNSON.

By the President:

W. HUNTER,
Acting Secretary of State.

GENERAL ORDERS, No. 86. } WAR DEPT., ADJT. GENERAL'S OFFICE, *Washington, May 9, 1865.*

LISTS TO BE MADE OF VOLUNTEER OFFICERS.

For the information of the War Department, lists will at once be prepared and forwarded of all officers in the volunteer service, made out separately for each arm of the service and each branch of the staff, showing the relative merit of the officers in their regiments or departments, as determined by boards of officers, to be appointed for the purpose by corps and other independent commanders. The reports of the boards will include the names of all officers belonging to a particular command, whether present or absent; and in the cases of the absent officers the reports will be based upon the best information attainable. The reports will also state what officers, in the opinion of the boards, should be discharged.

These lists will be forwarded through the prescribed channel, and the several commanders through whom they may be transmitted will indorse thereon their recommendations, based on their own knowledge of the character of the officers.

The lists will specify the rank and arm for which the officer is deemed competent, and whether he desires to remain in the military service. For all officers below the grade of colonel these lists will be consolidated and arranged by brigade, division, and corps commanders (or independent commands of less than a corps), so as to include all officers in the corps.

The lists of colonels, generals, and staff officers will also be consolidated at army or department and military division headquarters.

In addition to the lists thus furnished through the ordinary military channels, the chiefs of staff departments at Washington will at once obtain from their subordinates similar lists, conveniently consolidated, and forward them to this Department.

By order of the Secretary of War:

E. D. TOWNSEND,
Assistant Adjutant-General.

GENERAL ORDERS, No. 87. } WAR DEPT., ADJT. GENERAL'S OFFICE, *Washington, May 9, 1865.*

CONCERNING ENGINEER PROPERTY AND LABOR ON FIELD-WORKS.

Army and department commanders will at once cause to be collected and stored, at convenient depots, all tools, siege material, bridge equipage, and other engineer property not absolutely needed for immediate service with troops, and have inventories of property so collected forwarded to the Chief Engineer of the Army, with recommendation for its disposal. The latter will give the necessary instructions.

All labor on construction and repairs of field-works should now be done by troops; hired labor will not, therefore, be so employed, unless specially authorized from these headquarters or the Engineer Department; and no further purchases of engineer material for field-works will be made without similar authority, except in cases of urgent necessity.

By order of the Secretary of War:

E. D. TOWNSEND,
Assistant Adjutant-General.

CIRCULAR.] WAR DEPT., ADJUTANT-GENERAL'S OFFICE,
Washington, May 9, 1865.

ALL ARMY AND DEPARTMENT COMMANDERS:

Upon receipt hereof you are authorized to cause the immediate muster out and discharge from service of all officers and soldiers of your commands whose terms of service will expire prior to May 31, 1865.

In discharging the said troops the following will be observed:

1. The musters out will be made, in accordance with existing regulations, by the commissaries of musters of divisions, under the directions of commissaries of musters of corps or departments.

2. Army and department commanders will forthwith ascertain the number of men within their respective commands to be discharged, and report the same direct to the Paymaster-General of the Army, forwarding a duplicate report to the Adjutant-General. Said report must specify the number for each regiment, or company, if an independent one.

3. The Paymaster-General will arrange to make immediate payment to the men discharged, said payments to be made in the armies or departments in which the men may be serving at the date of muster out.

By order of the Secretary of War:

E. D. TOWNSEND,
Assistant Adjutant-General.

GENERAL ORDERS, No. 29. } QUARTERMASTER-GENERAL'S OFFICE,
Washington City, May 9, 1865.

I. For the purpose of securing a uniform system in the transportation of public property, the annexed forms* for requisitions and bills of lading will hereafter be adopted and the accompanying instructions strictly observed. No other forms will be used except in cases of emergency, when the prescribed forms cannot be procured, and then the reasons for using others will be stated upon the same.

II. The bill of lading should state where the freight is to be paid, and if the transportation is by water, or under contract varying from Government rates, the rates should be specifically stated in the bill of lading, otherwise it should state that payment is to be made at Government rates. Bills of lading issued for shipments to be forwarded on boats belonging to or in the service of the Quartermaster's Department, or on railroads operated by the Government, should state that no payment will be made on the bills of lading.

---

*Omitted.

III. Officers ordering transportation of wagons, ambulances, cannon, caissons, gun carriages, &c., will be particular to state in the bill of lading whether they are to be transported whole or taken apart. In shipments by rail, the number of animals, bales of hay and their weight, of pieces of lumber and measurement thereof, should be expressed in the bill of lading in numbers, in addition to the same in car-loads. The weight of different descriptions of goods must be given separately. When, in an invoice covering a variety of articles, or a number of packages, the total weight only is expressed, the officer receiving the property must, in certifying to its correctness, write out the weight delivered in words as well as in figures.

IV. Erasures, interlineations, or alterations in bills of lading must be explained thereon by the issuing or other competent officer.

V. Officers making shipments will at the time of shipping furnish the carrier with the original bill of lading, which upon the delivery of the property will be receipted by the officer receiving the same, and returned to the carrier with such indorsement as may be necessary to insure settlement for the service. The original bill of lading, receipted, alone will be received in settlement, and in no case will a second original bill of lading be issued for the same shipment.

VI. Duplicate and triplicate copies of the bill of lading will be promptly transmitted by mail to the consignee, and upon the receipt of the property the duplicate will be receipted and returned by mail to the officer making the shipment. The triplicate will be retained by the officer receiving the property. A copy, or quadruplicate, will be retained in book form by the consignor for his information.

VII. In the absence or failure of any officer to receipt for property consigned to him, the officer signing should make a full explanation over his signature, showing that he is duly authorized to receive and receipt for the same, and why the consignee does not receipt therefor. Agents or clerks are not authorized to receipt bills of lading.

VIII. Loss and damage to Government property will be deducted in settlement from the voucher issued to the carrier, and officers receipting for property must indorse on the bill of lading the kinds of property lost or damaged, and its full value, including transportation. When the amount of the damage to property cannot be readily ascertained, the receiving officer should promptly call a board of survey on the same, and duly notify the carrier that he may, if he desires, be present with witnesses to protect his interest. The bill of lading should not be signed until the amount of damage is decided upon by the report of the board of survey, when an indorsement of their decision should be made upon the bill of lading.

IX. Quartermasters will be governed in the settlement of claims for transfer and ferriage by existing instructions and decisions of the Quartermaster-General.

X. Bills of lading for through shipments will only be settled with the last carrier entitled to payment. Quartermasters should exercise care that no second claim is presented by roads performing part of the through transportation. The last carrier will be held responsible for all loss or damage, and such loss or damage will be deducted in making settlement for the service.

XI. The distance by the shortest practicable route, whether over one or many roads, will govern the rate charged. Transportation by water being generally the cheapest should be used when consistent with the interest of the service, and all transportation should be furnished by the shortest practicable route, unless a different one is designated in the order. When transportation is specifically demanded by a proper officer by a longer route, the reason must be given in the bill of lading, and payment will be made according to the length of the route designated, the officer being held to a strict accountability for his requisition.

XII. Quartermasters will be governed in the settlement of claims for transportation by railroad by the rates and classification of the circular of the Quartermaster-General dated May 1, 1862, and all transportation must be settled at the points designated in General Orders, No. 18, Quartermaster-General's Office, March 16, 1865.

By order of the Quartermaster-General:

LEWIS B. PARSONS,
Brig. Gen. and Chief of Rail and River Transportation.

BY THE PRESIDENT OF THE UNITED STATES OF AMERICA:

A PROCLAMATION.

Whereas, the President of the United States by his proclamation of the nineteenth day of April, one thousand eight hundred and sixty-one, did declare certain States therein mentioned in insurrection against the Government of the United States; and

Whereas, armed resistance to the authority of this Government in the said insurrectionary States may be regarded as virtually at an end, and the persons by whom that resistance, as well as the operations of insurgent cruisers, was directed, are fugitives or captives; and

Whereas, it is understood that some of these cruisers are still infesting the high seas, and others are preparing to capture, burn, and destroy vessels of the United States:

Now, therefore, be it known that I, Andrew Johnson, President of the United States, hereby enjoin all naval, military, and civil officers of the United States diligently to endeavor, by all lawful means, to arrest the said cruisers and to bring them into a port of the United States, in order that they may be prevented from committing further depredations on commerce, and that the persons on board of them may no longer enjoy impunity for their crimes.

And I do further proclaim and declare that if, after a reasonable time shall have elapsed for this proclamation to become known in the ports of nations claiming to have been neutrals, the said insurgent cruisers and the persons on board of them shall continue to receive hospitality in the said ports, this Government will deem itself justified in refusing hospitality to the public vessels of such nations in ports of the United States, and in adopting such other measures as may be deemed advisable toward vindicating the national sovereignty.

In witness whereof I have hereunto set my hand and caused the seal of the United States to be affixed.

Done at the city of Washington this tenth day of May, in the year of our Lord one thousand eight hundred and sixty-five, and of the Independence of the United States of America the eighty-ninth.

[L. S.] ANDREW JOHNSON.

By the President:

W. HUNTER,
Acting Secretary of State.

GENERAL ORDERS, No. 91. } WAR DEPT., ADJT. GENERAL'S OFFICE, *Washington, May 12, 1865.*

ORDER ORGANIZING BUREAU OF REFUGEES, FREEDMEN, AND ABANDONED LANDS.

I. By direction of the President, Maj. Gen. O. O. Howard is assigned to duty in the War Department as Commissioner of the Bureau of Refugees, Freedmen, and Abandoned Lands, under the act of Congress entitled "An act to establish a bureau for the relief of freedmen and refugees," to perform the duties and exercise all the rights, authority, and jurisdiction vested by the act of Congress in such commissioner. General Howard will enter at once upon the duties of Commissioner specified in said act.

II. The Quartermaster-General will without delay assign and furnish suitable quarters and apartments for the said Bureau.

III. The Adjutant-General will assign to the said Bureau the number of competent clerks authorized by the act of Congress.

By order of the President of the United States:

E. D. TOWNSEND,
Assistant Adjutant-General.

Act referred to in General Orders, No. 91 (A. G. O.), 1865.

AN ACT to establish a bureau for the relief of freedmen and refugees.

Be it enacted by the Senate and House of Representatives of the United States of America in Congress assembled, That there is hereby established in the War Department, to continue during the present war of rebellion, and for one year thereafter, a Bureau of Refugees, Freedmen, and Abandoned Lands, to which shall be committed, as hereinafter provided, the supervision and management of all abandoned lands, and the control of all subjects relating to refugees and freedmen from rebel States, or from any district of country within the territory embraced in the operations of the Army, under such rules and regulations as may be prescribed by the head of the Bureau and approved by the President. The said Bureau shall be under the management and control of a commissioner to be appointed by the President, by and with the advice and consent of the Senate, whose compensation shall be three thousand dollars per annum, and such number of clerks as may be assigned to him by the Secretary of War, not exceeding one chief clerk, two of the fourth class, two of the third class, and five of the first class. And the Commissioner, and all persons appointed under this act, shall, before entering upon their duties, take the oath of office prescribed in an act entitled "An act to prescribe an oath of office, and for other purposes," approved July second, eighteen hundred and sixty-two; and the Commissioner and chief clerk shall, before entering upon their duties, give bonds to the Treasurer of the United States, the former in the sum of fifty thousand dollars, and the latter in the sum of ten thousand dollars, conditioned for the faithful discharge of their duties, respectively, with securities to be approved as sufficient by the Attorney-General, which bonds shall be filed in the office of the First Comptroller of the Treasury, to be by him put in suit for the benefit of any injured party upon any breach of the conditions thereof.

SEC. 2. *And be it further enacted*, That the Secretary of War may direct such issues of provisions, clothing, and fuel as he may deem needful for the immediate and temporary shelter and supply of destitute and suffering refugees and freedmen and their wives and children, under such rules and regulations as he may direct.

SEC. 3. *And be it further enacted*, That the President may, by and with the advice and consent of the Senate, appoint an assistant commissioner for each of the States declared to be in insurrection, not exceeding ten in number, who shall, under the direction of the Commissioner, aid in the execution of the provisions of this act; and he shall give a bond to the Treasurer of the United States, in the sum of twenty thousand dollars, in the form and manner prescribed in the first section of this act. Each of said commissioners shall receive an annual salary of two thousand five hundred dollars in full compensation for all his services. And any military officer may be detailed and assigned to duty under this act without increase of pay or allowances. The Commissioner shall, before the commencement of each regular session of Congress, make full report of his proceedings, with exhibits of the state of his accounts, to the President, who shall communicate the same to Congress, and shall also make special reports whenever required to do so by the President or either House of Congress; and the assistant commissioners shall make quarterly reports of their proceedings to the Commissioner, and also such other special reports as from time to time may be required.

SEC. 4. *And be it further enacted*, That the Commissioner, under the direction of the President, shall have authority to set apart, for the use of loyal refugees and freedmen, such tracts of land within the insurrectionary States as shall have been abandoned, or to which the United States shall have acquired title by confiscation or sale, or otherwise; and to every male citizen, whether refugee or freedman as aforesaid, there shall be assigned not more than forty acres of such land, and the person to whom it was so assigned shall be protected in the use and enjoyment of the land for the term of three years at an annual rent not exceeding six per centum upon the value of such land as it was appraised by the State authorities in the year eighteen hundred and sixty for the purpose of taxation; and in case no such appraisal can be found, then the rental shall be based upon the estimated value of the land in said year, to be ascertained in such manner as the Commissioner may by regulation prescribe. At the end of said term, or at any time during said term, the occupants of any parcels so assigned may purchase the land and receive such title thereto as the United States can convey, upon paying therefor the value of the land as ascertained and fixed for the purpose of determining the annual rent aforesaid.

SEC. 5. *And be it further enacted*, That all acts and parts of acts inconsistent with the provisions of this act are hereby repealed.

Approved March 3, 1865.

GENERAL ORDERS, No. 94. } WAR DEPT., ADJT. GENERAL'S OFFICE, *Washington, May 15, 1865.*

The following regulations are announced, and will be observed in discharging from service such volunteers as are hereafter to be mustered out with their regimental or company organizations:

I. Army corps, or at least the divisions thereof, will be kept intact, and immediately upon receipt of an order directing any portion of the forces to be mustered out commanding generals of armies and departments will order the said troops (if not already thereat) to one of the following rendezvous, viz:

1. Middle Military Division, and troops of other armies or departments arriving therein: Defenses of Washington, D. C.; Harper's Ferry, Va., and Cumberland, Md.

2. Military Division of the James: Richmond and Old Point Comfort, Va.

3. Department of North Carolina: New Berne and Wilmington.

4. Department of the South: Charleston, S. C., and Savannah, Ga.

5. Military Division of West Mississippi: Mobile, Ala.; New Orleans, La., and Vicksburg, Miss.

6. Military Division of the Missouri: Little Rock, Ark.; Saint Louis, Mo., and Fort Leavenworth, Kans.

7. Department of the Cumberland: Nashville, Knoxville, and Memphis, Tenn.

8. Department of Kentucky: Louisville.

9. Middle Department: Baltimore, Md.

Commanding generals of armies and departments are authorized to change the aforesaid places of rendezvous should the public interest so demand.

For the Departments of the East, Pennsylvania, Northern, Northwest, New Mexico, and Pacific, such special orders will be given from the Adjutant-General's Office relative to the troops therein serving as may be demanded by circumstances as the time for discharge is approached.

II. In case of one or more regiments of a division being mustered out—the division remaining in the field—said regiment or regiments will be mustered out at the place where found serving at the time, and then placed en route to the State, as hereinafter directed.

III. The Adjutant-General of the Army will designate places of rendezvous in the respective States, to which the regiments, after muster out, will be forwarded for payment.

IV. Upon arrival at the rendezvous where the musters out are to take place, a critical examination of the regimental and company records, books, &c., will be made; and in case of omissions, the proper commanders will be made to supply them, and make all the entries as enjoined by the Army Regulations. At the same time the muster-out rolls will be commenced and prepared in accordance with existing regulations, under the direction of the assistant commissaries of musters of divisions, superintended by the corps commissaries. Corps and department commanders will see that the work is pushed with energy and executed promptly, using to this end division and brigade commanders to superintend it, and their respective staff officers to aid the mustering officers in collecting the data for the muster-out rolls and discharge papers, as well as the preparation of the same. In framing the rolls particular care must be exercised in stating balances of bounty payable. (See General Orders, No. 84, current series, from this office.)

V. So soon as the rolls of a regiment are completed, the said command, with its arms, colors, and necessary equipage, will be placed en route to its State, and to the rendezvous therein at or nearest which it was mustered in.

En route, and after arrival in the State, the following will be observed:

1. Immediately on arrival at the State rendezvous the regiment will be reported to and taken control of by the chief mustering officer for

the State, or his assistant at the point. The said officers will lend all needful assistance in their power to the paymasters, with the view to prompt payment of the troops.

2. The regimental officers will be held to a strict accountability for the discipline of their commands and preservation of public property.

3. The commissary of musters of the division to which the regiment belonged in the field will take possession of the copies of muster-out rolls intended for the field and staff, companies, and paymaster; also the company and regimental records, with all surplus blank rolls, returns, discharges, &c., in possession of regimental and company commanders, or other officers, and after boxing them up place them, whilst en route, under the special charge of a discreet and responsible officer of the regiment. The sole duty of said officer will be to care for and preserve said rolls and records whilst en route, and on arrival at the State rendezvous where payment is to be made to turn them over to the chief mustering officer or his assistant at that place.

4. Paymasters will be designated by the Pay Department to meet regiments at the designated State rendezvous and there make final payments, obtaining for that purpose the rolls from the mustering officer thereat.

5. Whilst troops are awaiting payment supplies will be furnished by the respective supply departments, on the usual requisitions and returns, countersigned by the chief mustering officer or his assistant.

6. Until after payment and the final discharge of the troops the chief mustering officer will look to their being kept together and under discipline.

7. The chief mustering officer will, under regulations to be established by himself, take possession of and carefully preserve the regimental and company records, also the colors with the respective regiments, and hold them subject to orders from the Adjutant-General of the Army.

8. As soon as practicable after arrival at the State rendezvous the chief mustering officer or his assistant will see that the arms and other public property brought to the State by the troops are turned over to the proper officer of the supply department thereat.

VI. In preparing the muster-out rolls, corps, department, division, and brigade commanders will hold regimental officers to a strict accountability, in order to insure accurate and complete records of the enlisted men, and the better to establish the just claims of the non-commissioned officers and privates who have been wounded, or of the representatives of those who have died from disease or wounds, or been killed in battle.

VII. Prior to the departure of regiments from the rendezvous where mustered out, all public property (except arms, colors, and equipage required en route) will be turned over to and cared for by the proper officers of the supply departments concerned.

VIII. What is prescribed in the foregoing for a regiment will be applicable to a battery of artillery or an independent company.

IX. At the respective State rendezvous the following is ordered, viz:

1. The Paymaster-General will be prepared to have a sufficient force of paymasters to insure prompt payments.

2. The Quartermaster-General and Commissary-General of Subsistence will be prepared to have a suitable number of officers of their respective bureaus to provide supplies, transportation, &c., and receipt for public property.

3. The Chief of Ordnance will arrange to have a suitable number of officers of his Bureau to receive the arms, accounterments, &c.

X. The attention of commanding generals of armies and departments is directed to the importance of regimental and company officers having their records so completed and arranged that at any time the muster-out rolls may be prepared without delay.

By order of the Secretary of War:

E. D. TOWNSEND,
Assistant Adjutant-General.

CIRCULAR No. 18. } WAR DEPT., ADJUTANT-GENERAL'S OFFICE,
Washington, May 15, 1865.

After the receipt of this commissaries of musters for army corps and departments will render tri-monthly a report of troops mustered out of service under their direction. The first report will embrace all troops mustered out since the 1st instant.

To this end assistant commissaries of musters for divisions will forward corresponding reports to the corps or department commissaries, and these, after consolidation with such musters out as that officer may have made during the same period, will be forwarded to the Adjutant-General of the Army on the 10th, 20th, and last days of each month.

The corps (or department) commissary of musters will forward the consolidated report, which must be in accordance with the following form, viz:

Tri-monthly report of troops mustered out of the service of the United States from ——— to ———, 186—, by ——— ———, commissary of musters.

State to which troops belong.	Designation of regiment or organization.	Date of muster out.	Strength or number mustered out.		Remarks.
			Commissioned officers.	Enlisted men.	
Ohio	56th Volunteer Infantry	May 31	25	605	NOTE.—Envelope containing report will be addressed to Bvt. Col. T. M. Vincent, assistant adjutant-general, Adjutant General's Office, Washington, D. C.
New York	7th Volunteer Cavalry	June 2	6	200	
Massachusetts	3d Volunteer Artillery	June 3	17	425	
Total			48	1,230	

A ——— B ———,
Captain, Twenty-sixth New York Cavalry, Commissary of Musters, Twenty-fourth Corps.

Station: ——— ———.
Date: ——— ———.

Official.

E. D. TOWNSEND,
Assistant Adjutant-General.

GENERAL ORDERS, No. —. } MIL. DIV. OF THE MISSISSIPPI,
CHIEF ENGR.'S OFFICE, U. S. MIL. R. RS.,
New Berne, N. C., May 15, 1865.

By order of the director and general manager of the U. S. Military Railroads the Construction Corps in the Department of North Carolina is disbanded, and the number of employés on the military railroads reduced to a force barely sufficient to keep in repair and operate the Morehead City and Raleigh and the Wilmington-Goldsborough lines.

All men discharged under this order will be furnished free transportation by water from here to Fortress Monroe, or some other Northern port, and those who have served for three months or longer will be furnished transportation from there to their homes.

Good order and discipline are enjoined upon the members of Construction Corps while en route to their homes, and I sincerely trust that all will conduct themselves worthy of the high reputation which this organization has justly acquired.

You leave the service because your work is done. The cause of the Union is triumphant and the rebellion virtually crushed.

Many of you have served long and faithfully in the military railroad service, and you now leave it with the proud consciousness of having done your part to make our cause successful.

Not only does General Sherman bear testimony to the value of the services of the Construction Corps in opening and keeping open his lines of communication and supplies, and thus enabling him to make his long and damaging marches into the enemy's territory, but even his formidable opponent, the rebel leader General Johnston, gives his testimony to the same effect.

With such a record you may be well satisfied.

W. W. WRIGHT,
Chief Engr. Military Railroads, Mil. Div. of the Mississippi.

CIRCULAR No. 19. WAR DEPT., ADJUTANT-GENERAL'S OFFICE,
Washington, May 16, 1865.

I. Under paragraph III, General Orders, No. 94, May 15, current series, from this office, the following State rendezvous, to which troops mustered out will be forwarded for payment, are announced, viz:

Maine: Augusta, Portland, and Bangor.

New Hampshire: Concord and Manchester.

Vermont: Montpelier, Brattleborough, and Burlington.

Massachusetts: Boston (Readville and Gallupe's Island).

Rhode Island: Providence.

Connecticut: Hartford and New Haven.

New York: New York City (Hart's Island), Albany, Elmira, Buffalo, Rochester, Syracuse, Sackett's Harbor, Plattsburg, and Ogdensburg.

New Jersey: Trenton.

Pennsylvania: Philadelphia, Harrisburg, and Pittsburg.

Delaware: Wilmington.

Maryland: Baltimore and Frederick.

West Virginia: Wheeling.

Ohio: Cincinnati (Camp Dennison), Cleveland (Camp Cleveland), Columbus (Camp Chase and Tod Barracks).

Indiana: Indianapolis.

Illinois: Springfield and Chicago.

Michigan: Detroit and Jackson.

Wisconsin: Madison and Milwaukee.

Minnesota: Fort Snelling.

Iowa: Davenport and Clinton.

Kansas: Lawrence and Leavenworth.

Missouri: Saint Louis (Benton Barracks).

Kentucky: Louisville, Lexington, and Covington.

II. When the muster out of a regiment has been completed, and it is ready to start for the State (see paragraph V, General Orders, No. 94, current series, Adjutant-General's Office), the assistant commissary of musters for the division to which it belongs will immediately report (by telegram when practicable) to the Paymaster-General of the Army, Washington, D. C., its numerical designation, number of commissioned officers, number of enlisted men, and rendezvous in the State where ordered to for payment and final discharge.

By order of the Secretary of War:

E. D. TOWNSEND,
Assistant Adjutant-General.

WAR DEPARTMENT, ADJUTANT-GENERAL'S OFFICE,
Washington, May 16, 1865.

The Secretary of War directs that the provisions of General Orders, No. 77, current series, be extended to include all patients who, although requiring further medical treatment, are able to travel and desire to be discharged (with the exceptions heretofore made). Also all men yet in hospitals, recently transferred to the Veteran Reserve Corps, as soon as the interest of the public service will permit. The order for the discharge from hospitals should be liberally interpreted. The word "patients" in telegram of May 3 was intended to include all enlisted men who were in hospital, except the guards and nurses belonging to the Veteran Reserve Corps.

SAMUEL BRECK,
Assistant Adjutant-General.

WAR DEPARTMENT, ADJUTANT-GENERAL'S OFFICE,
May 18, 1865.

Col. J. A. WILCOX,
Chief Mustering Officer, Columbus, Ohio:

All volunteer organizations of white troops in General Sherman's army and the Army of the Potomac whose terms of service expire prior to October 1 next, have been ordered mustered out.

The musters out are to be made in the vicinity of this city, and thereafter regiments and companies sent to State for payment. (See regulations promulgated in General Orders, No. 94, of 15th instant.)

The troops for muster out will be:

First. The three-years' regiments mustered into service under call of July 2, 1862, and prior to October 1 of that year.

Second. Three-years' recruits mustered into service for old regiments between the same dates.

Third. One-year's men for new and old organizations who entered the service prior to October 1, 1864.

Your records, or those of the State adjutant-general, will furnish the number of troops and particular regiments to be discharged, as herein indicated. You should arrange a list accordingly, so that you will be prepared to receive and care for the troops on their arrival in State.

Furnish Governor with copy of this and acknowledge receipt.

By order of Secretary of War:

THOMAS M. VINCENT,
Assistant Adjutant-General.

(Copy for the following chief mustering officers: Brigadier-General Pitcher, Indiana; Brigadier-General Oakes, Illinois; Lieutenant-Colonel Grier, Iowa; Colonel Alexander, Missouri; Lieutenant-Colonel Lovell, Wisconsin; Lieutenant-Colonel Hill, Michigan; Colonel Ely, New Jersey; Major Austine, Vermont; Major Silvey, New Hampshire; Lieutenant-Colonel Neide, Rhode Island; Lieutenant-Colonel Gilbert, Connecticut; Major Clarke, Massachusetts; Lieutenant-Colonel Littler, Maine.)

QUARTERMASTER-GENERAL'S OFFICE,
Washington City, May 19, 1865.

Hon. E. M. STANTON,
Secretary of War:

SIR: I have the honor to inclose certain papers* relative to the Orange and Alexandria Railroad.

The Governor of Virginia, Hon. F. H. Peirpoint, asks that this road be placed in possession of certain gentlemen appointed by the Board of Public Works to receive it. His letter is addressed to the Secretary of War.

Mr. John S. Barbour, president of the Orange and Alexandria Railroad for many years, incloses to Major-General Augur, commanding the Department of Washington, an order of Major-General Ord, placing him in charge of that part of the railroad in the Department of Virginia not in use by the military authorities.

He asks authority to take possession of the property of the company in the city of Alexandria. He states that he has complied with the regulations, *i. e.*, taken the amnesty oath, and that he has held no military office under the rebel Government while governing the road during the last four years of rebellion. He claims to represent the stockholders. I have been advised that there are stockholders, loyal men of the North, whose property was seized four years ago, and who have not been allowed any voice in the control of the affairs of the road or in the election of its president or directors. I doubt whether taking the amnesty oath re-establishes any person elected by disloyal votes as the legal or equitable president of a railroad from which all loyal men have been excluded during the past four years.

The State of Virginia has a Board of Public Works, charged with the general supervision of railroads and other public works of the State. I am advised that the State holds an interest of three-fifths in all the railroads and canals and turnpikes. Mr. John S. Barbour, however, informs me that the Orange and Alexandria Railroad is an exception to this rule; that it is the property almost entirely, if not entirely, of private parties; others deny this.

The question of the disposition of the railroads in the States lately in rebellion is a large one, and after reflection I have the honor to advise that the following principles be established to govern the action of the Quartermaster's Department and of the military authorities in disposing of all of them:

First. The United States will, as soon as it can dispense with the military occupation and control of any road of which the Quartermaster's Department is now in charge, turn it over to the parties asking to receive it who may appear to have the best claim and be able to operate it in such manner as to secure the speedy movement of all

---

*Omitted.

military stores and troops. The Quartermaster-General, upon the advice of the military commander of the department, to determine when this can be done, subject to the approval of the Secretary of War.

Second. No charge to be made against the railroad for expense of material or expense of operation.

Third. All materials for permanent way used in the repair and construction of the road and all damaged material of this class which may be left along its route, having been thrown there during the operations of destruction or repair, to be considered as part of the road and given up with it.

Fourth. No payment or credit to be given to the railroad for its occupation or use by the United States during the continuance of the military necessity which compelled the United States to take possession of it by capture from the public enemy. The recovery of the road from the public enemy and its return to loyal owners, with the vast expenditure of defense and repair, are a full equivalent for its use.

Fifth. All movable property, including rolling-stock of all kinds, the property of the United States, to be sold at auction, after full public notice, to the highest bidder.

Sixth. All rolling-stock and material, the property before the war of railroads, and captured by the forces of the United States, to be placed at the disposal of the roads which originally owned it, and to be given up to these roads as soon as it can be spared and they appear by proper agents authorized to receive it.

Seventh. When a State has a board of public works able and willing to take charge of its railroads, the railroads in possession of the Quartermaster's Department to be given up to this board of public works, leaving it to the State authorities and to the judicial tribunals to regulate all questions of property between rival boards, agents, or stockholders.

Eighth. Roads not being operated by the U. S. Quartermaster's Department not to be interfered with unless under military necessity, such roads to be left in possession of such persons as may now have possession, subject only to the removal of every agent, director, president, superintendent, or operative who has not taken the oath of allegiance to the United States, which rule should be rigidly enforced.

Ninth. When the superintendents in actual possession decline to take such oath, some competent person to be appointed as receiver of the railroad, who shall administer the affairs of the road and account for its receipts to the board of directors who may be formally recognized as the legal and loyal board of managers. This receiver to be appointed, as in the case of other abandoned property, by the Treasury Department.

Tenth. I recommend that the Governor of the State of Virginia be informed that the War Department will interpose no obstacle to the Board of Public Works of the State taking possession of all the railroads in the State not in use and occupation of the military forces of the United States by the Quartermaster's Department, and that as soon as the military occupation of any of these roads can be safely dispensed with the road will be transferred to the charge of the Board of Public Works.

In some of the States the State is a large bondholder in the roads, and though there may be in such States no board of public works, it is probable that the State authorities will be willing to receive and take charge of the roads. If not, receivers should be appointed by the Treasury Department, upon application of the War Department, to take charge of them as abandoned property.

I have the honor to be, very respectfully,

M. C. MEIGS,
Quartermaster-General and Brevet Major-General.

HEADQUARTERS ARMIES OF THE UNITED STATES,
Washington, D. C., May 19, 1865.

Brig. Gen. B. W. BRICE,
Paymaster-General of the Army:

GENERAL: The lieutenant-general desires to know about what time the troops in and around Richmond, and the armies commanded respectively by Generals Sherman and Meade, and now in the vicinity of Washington, will be paid.

Will you please furnish the desired information?

Very respectfully, your obedient servant,

JNO. A. RAWLINS,
Brigadier-General and Chief of Staff.

WAR DEPARTMENT, PAYMASTER-GENERAL'S OFFICE,
Washington, May 20, 1865.

General JOHN A. RAWLINS,
Chief of Staff, &c.:

SIR: Yours of yesterday this moment received, and I have the honor to reply:

All the efforts of the Treasury have been directed for the past two weeks to the means necessary for the final payment of troops ordered to be mustered out, amounting, according to the Adjutant-General's lists, to about 123,000 men, all told. The payment of these, with the large arrears due, the large bounties due, and three months' extra to officers, will require about $50,000,000.

These payments will be met promptly and without peradventure, the Treasury having very nearly, if not quite, met the emergency.

It will depend upon the ability of the Treasury entirely as to the time when the payments about which you inquire can be made. I will have an early conference with the officers of that Department and endeavor to give you an early response.

In addition to the forces named, I regret to say that General Thomas' command, in the West, is yet unpaid since August 31 last. The Army of the Potomac and troops about Richmond have been paid to December 31. Therefore, after Sherman's army, paid to August 31, Thomas' should be next paid. All these payments you will readily perceive will require a very large sum of money to be yet provided.

I have the honor to be, very respectfully, your obedient servant,

B. W. BRICE,
Paymaster-General U. S. Army.

WAR DEPARTMENT, ADJUTANT-GENERAL'S OFFICE,
May 20, 1865.

GOVERNOR OF MAINE:

Under the regulations established by the Secretary of War and the orders from this office based thereon, troops about to be discharged should go out of service promptly, be properly cared for, and their interests fully protected in every respect. Should delinquencies on the part of officers charged with execution of details come to your notice, I will thank you to advise me of the same at once, giving name of neglectful parties, so that a remedy may be applied.

THOMAS M. VINCENT,
Assistant Adjutant-General.

(Same to Governors of New Hampshire, Vermont, Massachusetts, Rhode Island, Connecticut, New York, New Jersey, Delaware, Pennsylvania, Maryland, West Virginia, Ohio, Indiana, Illinois, Iowa, Michigan, Wisconsin, Minnesota, Kansas, Missouri, and Kentucky.)

MILITARY DIVISION OF THE MISSISSIPPI,
CHIEF ENGINEER'S OFFICE U. S. MILITARY RAILROADS,
New Berne, N. C., May 20, 1865.

General D. C. MCCALLUM,
Mil. Director and Genl. Manager Railroads, United States:

GENERAL: I have the honor to submit the following report of operations on the U. S. military railroads under my charge since the date of my last report, November 1, 1864.*

After General Sherman's army was fully supplied at Atlanta he cut loose from his railroad line of supply and we fell back with all rolling-stock and other portable railroad property to Chattanooga, stopping long enough, however, to take up the track between Resaca and Dalton, a distance of eighteen miles, and bring to Chattanooga all the iron rails, including those damaged by the enemy in his last attack on the road. The Construction Corps was then distributed over the lines of military railroads still held by our forces, and employed at various necessary jobs of construction and repairs and in preparing material to reconstruct any portion of the tracks and structures that might again be destroyed. This work was continued until the rebel army under General Hood had advanced so far north of the Tennessee River that it became evident most, if not all, our lines would fall into their hands. The greater part of the corps was then concentrated at certain points from which they could operate to the best advantage when we should again get possession of the roads. One division of trackmen was sent to Louisville to lay additional tracks to hold the large number of cars and engines which we were sending there for safety. On the 15th of December the battle of Nashville commenced, and by the 18th General Thomas had thoroughly defeated Hood and driven his shattered army as far as Franklin. On that day he directed all the damaged railroads to be rebuilt. On the 19th I had four strong working parties at this work—one working from Nashville toward Decatur and following the army as rapidly as possible; another working from Nashville toward Stevenson; a third working from Stevenson toward Nashville, and the fourth working from Stevenson toward Decatur. These lines were all opened up, except a portion of the Nashville and Decatur line, by the 28th of December, the day I received your order to take one division of the Construction Corps and proceed to Savannah to join General Sherman. Orders were immediately given on the receipt of

---

*See Inclosure B to report of General McCallum of November 27, 1864, Vol. IV, this series, p. 957.

your dispatch for the Second Division to prepare for the journey, and they left Nashville on the 4th of January for Baltimore, fully equipped for any kind of railroad work. Arriving in Baltimore on the 10th, there was a delay of eight days before a vessel could be furnished to take them to Savannah. On the 28th they arrived at Hilton Head, but were not disembarked there. On the 29th General Sherman gave me orders to proceed with my men to Morehead City, N. C., and "prepare to make railroad connection to Goldsborough by the middle of March."

We left Hilton Head on the 3d and arrived off Morehead City on the 5th of February. The men and railroad supplies brought with us were landed next day. We found the railroad in running order from Morehead City to Batchelder's Creek, a distance of forty-four miles. The track, however, was in bad condition, and the sidings were entirely inadequate to the business about to be thrown upon the road. The wharf at Morehead City had not half the capacity required for unloading vessels, and there was not fifty cords of wood on the whole road for railroad use. The equipment of the road consisted of sixty-two cars and three locomotives in running order, and nine cars and two locomotives unfit for use without repairs. I appointed J. B. Van Dyne, esq., superintendent of transportation and William Cessford master mechanic, and they went to work at once to organize their respective departments. The Construction Corps, under Mr. Smeed, division engineer, was put to work repairing main track and extending old sidings and laying new ones where required; preparing cross-ties, bridge timber, saw logs, piles, and wharf timber; building and repairing water-tanks, and other necessary work preparatory to an extension of the road and conducting a large business. Arrangements were made for an ample supply of wood. I found Mr. McAlpine on the road with a small construction force; they had repaired a few hundred yards of track and almost completed the bridge over Batchelder's Creek. He had been sent here by order of General Grant, but as soon as we arrived he considered himself relieved and returned at once to Virginia with his men. Mr. McAlpine had brought some little railroad iron and a few cross-ties with him from Virginia, but with this exception we found the road destitute of materials and tools necessary for construction and repairs and for operating it. Accordingly requisitions for the necessary amount of these supplies, together with the probable additional amount of rolling-stock that would be required, were sent at once to your office. Having received orders on the 17th of February to build a new wharf of considerable dimensions at Morehead City, I also made requisition for two steam pile drivers and such material for this purpose as could not be procured here. On the 3d of March General Cox (who was in command of the column that moved from here) commenced his advance toward Goldsborough. He was poorly supplied with wagon transportation, and therefore had to depend upon the railroad almost entirely. The construction of the railroad kept pace with the advance of the troops, and the supplies were moved by rail from camp to camp and unloaded from the main track as the troops marched up the road. Of course track laying could not advance so rapidly under such circumstances as if the track had been kept clear for construction purposes; but still the progress was very satisfactory. This mode of advance and movement of supplies was continued until we reached a point on the railroad opposite the battle-field of Wise's Cross-Roads. Here we made a temporary depot, and (a supply of wagon transportation having arrived) stores were hauled in wagons to Kinston, to which point General Schofield (who had arrived and taken command) pushed forward with his army immediately after the battle. From a short distance beyond Batchelder's Creek we had found the track thus far taken up and the rails carried away and all the bridges and water stations destroyed. An examination of the road beyond showed it to be in the same condition as far as Kinston.

The enemy having fallen back to or beyond Goldsborough, and General Couch's command having arrived from Wilmington, General Schofield desired to accumulate the necessary supplies as rapidly as possible so as to enable him to push forward and make the prearranged junction with General Sherman's army at Goldsborough by the "middle of March." It became, therefore, a matter of utmost importance to push forward the work on the railroad with utmost rapidity (at least as far as the Neuse River), and the Third Division of the Construction Corps having arrived, I was enabled from this time to keep the work going night and day. Most of the cross-ties used up to this time in the new track had been cut alongside the railroad and carried onto the road bed. It became necessary to cut these ties because we had not cars and engines to spare from hauling army supplies to bring up the stock previously prepared at points back on the railroad, and they had to be carried to the place where used because our ox teams could not cross the deep and wide ditch, mostly full of water, on both sides of the road bed. Not having men enough to cut and carry ties as fast as we could put down the rails, I applied to General Schofield for a detail of soldiers to assist. He ordered the detail made, and they worked two days, in that time getting out and bringing to the road 5,400 ties. We reached Neuse River with the track on the 20th of March, and the same day commenced running supplies to that point with all the cars and engines we had. The Neuse River bridge was completed on the 23d, and the track between it and Kinston having been laid while the bridge was building, the construction force moved forward, and, building two bridges and doing some other work by the way, reached Goldsborough late in the night of the 24th, but, in consequence of having to repair a small piece of track at the edge of town, did not reach the depot until 3 a. m. on the 25th. General Sherman's army had all reached the place of meeting on the previous day. The construction force was now sent forward to open up the road to Wilmington, while the whole energies of the transportation department were concentrated in an effort to supply the present wants of the large army which had assembled in and around Goldsborough after its long march from Savannah, and in addition to accumulate supplies by the 10th of April for the contemplated movement on that day. Of course until the Wilmington line could be opened we had to depend upon the Morehead City line alone.

Knowing General Sherman's punctuality, I was much concerned for fear that with the small amount of rolling-stock on hand it would be impossible to accomplish the work required of us within the time named; but by good management and good luck I am happy to state that on the evening of the 9th the chief quartermaster and the chief commissary of subsistence informed me that the whole army was supplied with everything required for the movement next day. I attribute the result partly to good luck, because, although every wheel we had was kept turning night and day during this period, we were so fortunate as not to have a single accident. The disabling of a single locomotive or a few cars would have been an irreparable loss. It seems almost incredible that this work was done; that about 150 car-loads in excess of enough supplies for Sherman's army were moved in fourteen days from Morehead City and New Berne to Goldsborough with only eighty-seven cars and five engines up to April 1, and same number of cars and six engines after that date. The repairs to the Wilmington road were completed on the 4th of April; the trains commenced running the same day. The few cars and the two engines that had arrived at Wilmington up to this date were used in supplying General Terry's command, which lay along this road pending the movement on Raleigh.

On the 10th of April the work of reconstruction commenced on the Goldsborough and Raleigh line. This was found to be much heavier than was anticipated, for the enemy, having obtained information, probably, of the direction in which Sherman was going to move, had within a day or two previous torn up and destroyed about eight miles of track and filled up some of the cuts with trees, brush, logs, rocks, and earth. We were until the 19th in repairing this damaged track and in rebuilding the Little River and Neuse River bridges. On the evening of that day we ran into Raleigh with the construction trains, followed closely by two train-loads of supplies. During the armistice our trains were kept going day and night bringing forward full supplies for the army, either for a resumption of hostilities or a march homeward. On the 25th, when General Sherman informed me that "the army moves to-morrow against the enemy in the direction of Greensborough and Salisbury," the wagons were again fully loaded, and there was, in addition, a considerable accumulation of stores at Raleigh. The addition of our rolling-stock received from the North, together with some captured stock that was serviceable, enabled us to get forward the stores with comparative ease now, and also carry on construction and repairs. It was a great relief to know that we had the means to do our work, and feel that an accident to one train would not necessarily disarrange the whole plans of the campaign. But, although we had rolling-stock enough for present use, we had not enough should the army advance on Greensborough and Salisbury. I therefore, on the 21st of April, went out to Cedar Creek, on the Raleigh and Gaston Railroad, twenty-five miles from Raleigh, to meet the president of that company and see if we could borrow some stock from them. By direction of General Sherman I agreed with him to rebuild the bridge over Cedar Creek for the use of four locomotives and forty cars for as long a time as they might be required for military purposes. We built the bridge, but the surrender of Johnston and the arrival of more stock from the North made it unnecessary to call on that company for the fulfillment of their part of the contract. The rebuilding of Cedar Creek bridge completed the railroad connection between Raleigh and the Roanoke River at Gaston and also at Weldon. During the suspension of hostilities we operated the North Carolina Railroad to Durham's Station, twenty-five miles from Raleigh.

Immediately upon Johnston's surrender I was ordered to rebuild the Flat Creek bridge, some ten miles beyond Durham, which opened the road to Salisbury. And our army being fully supplied, a large amount of stores were sent up the North Carolina Railroad for use of the force which had just surrendered during the time required to parole the men. Sherman's army having marched north, and Johnston's army having been disbanded, there was left in this department only General Schofield's command to supply. Compared with the business which we had been doing, this was but a small thing, and, in accordance with your order, arrangements were at once made to reduce the force employed in the transportation and machine departments to the smallest numbers possible to do the work. Also in accordance with your orders the Construction Corps was disbanded, and the force employed on maintenance of way and structures much reduced. Under these orders about two-thirds of all the railroad employés in this department were discharged and expenses reduced accordingly. It is with no little regret that I part with the Construction Corps, which I have taken such pains to organize and train for military railroad service; but at the same time that I feel this regret I rejoice that the necessity for this organization and their services no longer exist, and that having done their work they can now be disbanded and go home. Since landing at Morehead City, on the 6th of February, we have, in addition to keeping up the superstructure, bridges, water stations, and other work connected with maintenance of way, built about thirty-three miles of new track, including sidings and track laid for the reception of the wide-gauge stock that was to have been sent here.

We have built the following-named bridges:

	Length (feet).
Batchelder's Creek, Morehead City, Goldsborough and Raleigh Railroad	70
Core Creek, Morehead City, Goldsborough and Raleigh Railroad	100
Southwest Creek, Morehead City, Goldsborough and Raleigh Railroad	85
Neuse River, No. 1, Morehead City, Goldsborough and Raleigh Railroad	863
Falling Water Creek, Morehead City, Goldsborough and Raleigh Railroad	70
Bear Creek, Morehead City, Goldsborough and Raleigh Railroad	100
Little River, Morehead City, Goldsborough and Raleigh Railroad	150
Neuse River, No. 2, Morehead City, Goldsborough and Raleigh Railroad	314
Neuse River, No. 3, Wilmington and Goldsborough Railroad	235
Northeast River, Wilmington and Goldsborough Railroad	372
Cedar Creek, Raleigh and Gaston Railroad	532
Flat Creek, North Carolina Railroad	100
Total	2,991

The timber consumed in the construction of these bridges is as follows:

	Feet, B. M.
Batchelder's Creek	10,500
Core Creek	15,000
Southwest Creek	12,750
Neuse River, No. 1	146,710
Falling Water Creek	10,500
Bear Creek	15,000
Little River	25,500
Neuse River, No. 2	62,800
Neuse River, No. 3	39,950
Northeast River	111,600
Cedar Creek	319,200
Flat Creek	10,000
Total	779,510

The new wharf at Morehead City was completed in time to be of much service in discharging vessels. There is room now for seven or eight vessels to lie at these wharves at the same time, and any vessel that can cross the bar can come to the wharf. The depth of water on the bar is fourteen and one-half feet. The area of the new wharf is 53,682 square feet, or very nearly one acre and a quarter. The cost of labor in its construction amounted to $32,086. The amount of timber consumed, 700,000 feet, board measure. The following summary of timber consumed in the different structures on the roads is given. All other materials, except cross-ties and railroad iron, is, or should be, accounted for in the store-house report:

Timber and lumber consumed.

	Feet, B. M.
Bridges	779,510
Water-tanks	26,100
Crib-work (Morehead City)	66,000
Wharf	700,000
Buildings	32,000
Total	1,603,610

The total number of cross-ties used in new track and on repairs was 111,100.

For information in regard to the timber, wood, cross-ties, &c., now on hand, see Exhibit B (report of J. M. Lindley, wood and tie agent), attached to this report.* Not having been furnished with an account of the railroad iron sent here, I cannot make an accurate report of the amount consumed. For the new track laid we straightened and used a great deal of damaged iron. In many cases we had to lay without chairs, because those sent with the iron did not fit it. Your attention is called to Exhibit A, attached tc this report (the store-house report signed by Captain Starkweather).* It purports to give the amount of stores and materials received, consumed, and remaining on hand. The report is evidently inaccurate in regard to lumber and some other items. It is also proper to state that many of the tools and other articles reported as on hand are worn out and worthless. Exhibit C contains accurate plans of all bridges built, together with a plan of the wharves at Morehead City.* Below please find tabular statements of cars and engines on the military railroads in this department. And here I take occasion to say that nearly all the captured stock is worthless. Very little of it is worth even temporary repairs. Of course the best was run off to escape capture, but since the "rebellion has been crushed," and the different railroad companies have commenced operating their roads again, much of this has made its appearance, and we have thus had a good opportunity to judge of the condition of the rolling-stock in the "Confederacy." It was nearly worn out. A tabular statement is also given of the loaded cars moved on the military railroads in this department during seventy-four days ending May 1, 1865.

List of engines on Morehead City and Goldsborough Line (U. S. military railroad stock).

No.	Name.	Builder.	Condition.	When received.
1	Blue Bird	Baldwin	Running order	Mar. 19
2	Union	do	do	Apr. 1
3	Vulcan	do	do	Apr. 26
4	Governor Nye	Norris	do	May 2
5	Reindeer	do	Need repairs	Feb. 9
6	Secretary	Taunton	Running order	Apr. 26
7	Grape Shot	do	do	Apr. 14
8	Chief	do	Need repairs	Feb. 9
9	Scout	Jersey City	do	Feb. 9
10	Commodore	Smith & Jackson	Good order	May 1
11	Lion	do	do	Apr. 14
12	Colonel Webster	Manchester	Need repairs	Feb. 25
13	Ancient	Norris	do	Feb. 9

* Omitted.

Captured on Goldsborough and Raleigh Line.

No.	Name.	Builder.	Condition.	When received.
1	Halifax	Norris	Need repairs	Apr. 19
2	Tornado	....do	Worthless	Apr. 19
3	Raleigh	....do	Need repairs	Apr. 19

NOTE.—Engine Ancient on Morehead City and Goldsborough Line not fit for road is used at Morehead City. Engines Halifax and Raleigh are only serviceable as switch engines and are used in that capacity at Raleigh.

Statement of cars on U. S. military railroads.

MOREHEAD CITY AND GOLDSBOROUGH LINE (U. S. MILITARY RAILROAD STOCK).

Number.	Description.	Condition.	When received.
3	Passenger-cars	Running order	Feb. 9
11	Box-cars	....do	Feb. 9
12	Rack-cars	....do	Feb. 9
35	Flat-cars	....do	Feb. 9
10	....do	Bad order	Feb. 9
25	....do	Running order	*a* Mar. 19
15	....do	....do	*b* Apr. 4
50	....do	....do	*c* Apr. 26

a At Morehead City. *b* From Wilmington and Goldsborough. *c* At New Berne.

WILMINGTON AND GOLDSBOROUGH LINE (CAPTURED STOCK).

Number.	Description.	Condition.	When received.
4	Passenger-cars	Bad order	Apr. 4
3	....do	Unserviceable	Apr. 4
2	Baggage-cars	Bad order	Apr. 4
6	Box-cars	....do	Apr. 4
7	Flat-cars	....do	Apr. 4

Raleigh and Gaston Railroad (captured stock of different roads).

Number.	Description.	Condition.	When received.
2	Passenger-cars	Bad order	Apr. 22
1	Baggage-car	....do	Apr. 22
37	Box-cars	....do	Apr. 22
14	....do	Unserviceable	Apr. 22
1	Rack-car	Bad order	Apr. 22
24	Flat-cars	....do	Apr. 22

List of captured engines on the Wilmington and Goldsborough Line.

No.	Name.	Builder.	Condition.	When received.
1	Wilmington	Manchester	Running order	Mar. 26
2	Perseverance	Baldwin	....do	Mar. 26
3	Goldsborough	Manchester	Need repairs	Mar. 26
4	Orange	....do	Being repaired	Mar. 26
5	Governor Ellis	Baldwin	....do	Mar. 26
6	President	Norris	Worthless	Mar. 26
7	Quickstep	....do	....do	Mar. 26
8	Job Terry	Hinkley	....do	Mar. 26
9	Stonewall Jackson	Norris	....do	Mar. 26
10	Brunswick	....do	....do	Mar. 26
11	North Carolina	Baldwin	....do	Mar. 26
12	Tarborough	Anderson	....do	Mar. 26
13	Unknown	Manchester	....do	Mar. 26

NOTE.—Nos. 1, 2, and 3 are in use, but not considered serviceable.

Statement of loaded cars forwarded and received from February 15 to May 1, 1865.

FORWARDED.

From—	To—	Number.	Contents.
Morehead City	Front	1,841	Stores.
New Berne	do	850	Do.
Wilmington	do	110	Do.
Morehead City	do	400	Troops.
Total		3,201	

RECEIVED.

At—	From—	Number.	Contents.
New Berne	Front	773	Unknown.
Morehead City	do	299	Do.
Wilmington	Goldsborough.	83	Do.
New Berne	Various stations.	300	Wood.
Do	Front	300	Baggage, &c.
Total		1,755	

NOTE.—Two hundred cars stores from dock to Morehead City; 1,541 cars construction material moved an average distance of thirty miles.

RECAPITULATION.

Sent to the front	3,201
Received at New Berne	1,373
Received at Morehead City	299
Received at Wilmington	83
Construction material	1,541
Transferring stores	200
Total number loaded cars forwarded and received	6,697

The following statement of cost of labor is taken from the pay-rolls and embraces the whole time since the Second Division left Nashville until the Construction Corps was disbanded; that is, from January 1 to May 15, 1865:

Cost of labor on U. S. military railroads, Military Division oj the Mississippi, in the Department of North Carolina, 1865.

	January.	February.	March.	April.	May.
Construction and maintenance	$92,083.01	$128,377.69	$191,131.11	$176,433.86	$48,028.05
Machine department	4,799.69	8,568.86	17,336.07	27,697.21	6,431.84
Transportation department	5,023.00	5,972.55	15,116.98	14,582.48	3,423.00
Total	101,905.70	142,919.10	223,584.16	218,713.55	57,882.89

Total, $745,005.40.

Names of U. S. military railroads, Department of North Carolina.

	Miles.
Morehead City and Goldsborough line	85
Wilmington and Goldsborough line	95
Goldsborough and Raleigh line	48
North Carolina, Raleigh to Hillsborough	40
Raleigh and Gaston, Raleigh to Cedar Creek	25
Total	293

In closing this report it gives me great pleasure to again bear testimony to the hearty and effective co-operation of the chief quartermaster and the chief commissary of subsistence Military Division of the Mississippi, Generals L. C. Easton and A. Beckwith, in all our operations. We have worked together for so long a time, under such a variety of circumstances, and over such an extent of territory, that we have learned how to supply a large army by railroad. Nothing but this knowledge and perfect harmony of action enabled us, with our limited railroad facilities, to make operations in this department a success. To my assistants great credit is due for this success. J. B. Van Dyne, superintendent of transportation, has shown good tact, skill, and untiring industry in his department. E. C. Smeed, division engineer, has ably assisted me in the maintenance of way and construction department. William Cessford, master mechanic, by his mechanical skill and indefatigable efforts to keep in repair our hard-worked rolling-stock, did excellent service. I commend the services of these gentlemen, together with many others holding subordinate positions, which the limits of this report preclude me from naming, to your consideration.

Exhibit D shows the present organization in the military railroads in this department.*

I have the honor to be, very respectfully, your obedient servant,

W. W. WRIGHT,

Chief Engineer Military Railroads, Div. of the Miss.,
In charge Military Railroads, Dept. of North Carolina.

GENERAL ORDERS, No. 99. WAR DEPT., ADJT. GENERAL'S OFFICE, *Washington, May 28, 1865.*

I. In order to recruit the ranks of the regular regiments as soon as practicable, the Adjutant-General will open recruiting stations at such points as offer a reasonable prospect of enlisting good men.

II. Volunteers honorably discharged from the U. S. service who enlist in the Regular Army within ten days from date of discharge will be allowed a furlough of thirty days before joining their regiments. They will be paid all pay and allowances to which they may be entitled on being discharged from the volunteer service.

By order of the Secretary of War:

E. D. TOWNSEND,
Assistant Adjutant-General.

[MAY 29, 1865.—For amnesty proclamation of the President, and circular of Department of State establishing rules and regulations for administering and recording the amnesty oath, see Series II, Vol. VIII, p. 578.]

BY THE PRESIDENT OF THE UNITED STATES OF AMERICA:

A PROCLAMATION.

Whereas, the fourth section of the fourth article of the Constitution of the United States declares that the United States shall guarantee

---

* Omitted.

to every State in the Union a republican form of government, and shall protect each of them against invasion and domestic violence; and whereas, the President of the United States is, by the Constitution, made Commander-in-Chief of the Army and Navy, as well as chief civil Executive officer of the United States, and is bound by solemn oath faithfully to execute the office of President of the United States, and to take care that the laws be faithfully executed; and whereas, the rebellion which has been waged by a portion of the people of the United States against the properly constituted authorities of the Government thereof, in the most violent and revolting form, but whose organized and armed forces have now been almost entirely overcome, has, in its revolutionary progress, deprived the people of the State of North Carolina of all civil government; and whereas, it becomes necessary and proper to carry out and enforce the obligations of the United States to the people of North Carolina, in securing them in the enjoyment of a republican form of government:

Now, therefore, in obedience to the high and solemn duties imposed upon me by the Constitution of the United States, and for the purpose of enabling the loyal people of said State to organize a State Government, whereby justice may be established, domestic tranquillity insured, and loyal citizens protected in all their rights of life, liberty, and property, I, Andrew Johnson, President of the United States and Commander-in-Chief of the Army and Navy of the United States, do hereby appoint William W. Holden Provisional Governor of the State of North Carolina, whose duty it shall be at the earliest practical period to prescribe such rules and regulations as may be necessary and proper for convening a convention, composed of delegates to be chosen by that portion of the people of said State who are loyal to the United States, and no others, for the purpose of altering or amending the constitution thereof; and with authority to exercise, within the limits of said State, all the powers necessary and proper to enable such loyal people of the State of North Carolina to restore said State to its constitutional relations to the Federal Government, and to present such a republican form of State government as will entitle the State to the guaranty of the United States therefor, and its people to protection by the United States against invasion, insurrection, and domestic violence: *Provided*, That in any election that may be hereafter held for choosing delegates to any State convention as aforesaid no person shall be qualified as an elector or shall be eligible as a member of such convention unless he shall have previously taken and subscribed the oath of amnesty, as set forth in the President's proclamation of May twenty-ninth, in the year of our Lord one thousand eight hundred and sixty-five, and is a voter qualified as prescribed by the constitution and laws of the State of North Carolina in force immediately before the twentieth day of May, in the year of our Lord one thousand eight hundred and sixty-one, the date of the so-called ordinance of secession; and the said convention when convened, or the legislature that may be thereafter assembled, will prescribe the qualification of electors, and the eligibility of persons to hold office under the constitution and laws of the State, a power the people of the several States composing the Federal Union have rightfully exercised from the origin of the Government to the present time.

And I do hereby direct—

First. That the military commander of the department, and all officers and persons in the military and naval service, aid and assist the said Provisional Governor in carrying into effect this proclamation, and they are enjoined to abstain from in any way hindering, impeding, or discouraging the loyal people from the organization of a State government as herein authorized.

Second. That the Secretary of State proceed to put in force all laws of the United States, the administration whereof belongs to the State Department, applicable to the geographical limits aforesaid.

Third. That the Secretary of the Treasury proceed to nominate for appointment assessors of taxes, and collectors of customs and internal revenue, and such other officers of the Treasury Department as are authorized by law, and put in execution the revenue laws of the United States within the geographical limits aforesaid. In making appointments the preference shall be given to qualified loyal persons residing within the districts where their respective duties are to be performed. But if suitable residents of the districts shall not be found, then persons residing in other States or districts shall be appointed.

Fourth. That the Postmaster-General proceed to establish post-offices and post routes, and put into execution the postal laws of the United States within the said State, giving to loyal residents the preference of appointment; but if suitable residents are not found, then to appoint agents, &c., from other States.

Fifth. That the district judge for the judicial district in which North Carolina is included proceed to hold courts within said State in accordance with the provisions of the act of Congress. The Attorney-General will instruct the proper officers to libel, and to bring to judgment, confiscation, and sale, property subject to confiscation, and enforce the administration of justice within said State in all matters within the cognizance and jurisdiction of the Federal courts.

Sixth. That the Secretary of the Navy take possession of all public property belonging to the Navy Department within said geographical limits, and put in operation all acts of Congress in relation to naval affairs having application to the said State.

Seventh. That the Secretary of the Interior put in force the laws relating to the Interior Department applicable to the geographical limits aforesaid.

In testimony whereof I have hereunto set my hand and caused the seal of the United States to be affixed.

Done at the city of Washington this twenty-ninth day of May, in the year of our Lord one thousand eight hundred and sixty-five, and of the Independence of the United States the eighty-ninth.

[L. S.] ANDREW JOHNSON.

By the President:

WILLIAM H. SEWARD,
Secretary of State.

(Same, *mutatis mutandis*, issued for the State of Mississippi, June 13, 1865; for the States of Georgia and Texas (separate proclamations) June 17, 1865; for the State of Alabama, June 21, 1865; for the State of South Carolina, June 30, 1865, and for the State of Florida, July 13, 1865.

William L. Sharkey was appointed Provisional Governor of Mississippi, James Johnson for Georgia, Andrew J. Hamilton for Texas, Lewis E. Parsons for Alabama, Benjamin F. Perry for South Carolina, and William Marvin for Florida.)

WAR DEPARTMENT,
Washington City, May 29, 1865.

Hon. EDWIN M. STANTON,
Secretary, &c.:

SIR: I have the honor to report that I have examined the subject of the disposition to be made of the railroads in the States lately in rebellion, referred to me in connection with the report of the Quartermaster-General, and the rules which he has recommended to be established.* The second rule proposed by the Quartermaster-General provides that no charge shall be made against railroad for expense of materials or expense of operation while it has been in the hands of the military authorities of the United States. In other words, he proposes to restore every railroad to its claimants without any special consideration from them for any improvements which the United States may have made upon it. It is true that in his fourth rule he includes past expenditures of defense and repair as an equivalent for the use of the road while it has been in the public service, but in many cases this does not appear to me to be sufficient. Our expenditures upon some of these roads have been very heavy. For instance, we have added to the value of the road from Nashville to Chattanooga at least $1,500,000. When that road was recaptured from the public enemy it was in a very bad state of repair. Its embankments were in many places partially washed away, its iron was what is known as the U-rail, and was laid in the defective old-fashioned manner, upon longitudinal sleepers, without cross-ties. These sleepers were also in a state of partial decay, so that trains could not be run with speed or safety. All these defects have now been remedied. The road bed has been placed in first-rate condition. The iron is now a heavy T-rail, laid upon new ties throughout the entire length of the line. Extensive repair shops have also been erected, well furnished with the necessary tools and machinery. I do not conceive that it would be just or advisable to restore this road, with its improved track and these costly shops, without any equivalent for the great value of these improvements other than the use we have made of it since its recapture. The fact that we have replaced the heavy and expensive bridges over Elk, Duck, and Tennessee Rivers, and over Running Water Creek, should also not be forgotten in deciding this question.

The above general remarks are also applicable to that portion of the Orange and Alexandria Railroad between the Potomac and the Rapidan. Very extensive repair shops have been erected at Alexandria and furnished with costly machinery for the use of this road, and I understand that the iron and the road bed are now much better than when the Government began to use it.

The same is still more the case with the road between City Point and Petersburg. When that road was recaptured from the public enemy not only was the road bed a good deal washed away and damaged, but neither rails nor sound ties were left upon it. Now it is in the best possible condition. Can any one contend that it ought to be restored to its claimants without charge for the new ties and iron?

The case of the railroad from Harper's Ferry to Winchester is no less striking. It was a very poor road before the war and was early demolished by the rebels. Not a pound of iron, not a sound tie, was to be found upon the line when we began its reconstruction in Decem-

*See May 19, p. 26.

ber last. We have spent about $500,000 in bringing it into its present condition, and I have no doubt our improvements could be sold for that sum to the Baltimore and Ohio Company, should they obtain the title to the road bed from the proper authorities of Virginia. Why, then, should we give them up for nothing?

On the Morehead City and Goldsborough Railroad we have rebuilt twenty-seven miles of the track and furnished it with new iron, and laid new ties on many miles more since February last. These views also hold good, unless I am much misinformed, with regard to the railroads leading into New Orleans, the Memphis and Little Rock Railroad, the Memphis and Charleston Railroad, and the Mobile and Ohio Railroad. They have all been improved at great expense while in our hands.

In the third rule proposed by the Quartermaster-General it is provided that all materials for permanent way used in the repair and construction of any road, and all damaged materials of this class which may be left along its route, having been thrown there during operations of destruction and repair, shall be considered as part of the road, and given up with it, also without compensation. If this means to give up any new iron that we have on the line of any road, it seems to me to concede to the parties to whom the roads are to be surrendered more than they have a right to claim. For instance, there is now lying at Alexandria, on the line of the Orange and Alexandria road, iron sufficient to lay thirty miles of track. It seems manifest to me that this iron should not be surrendered to that road without being paid for. In my judgment it is also advisable to establish the principle that the Government will not pay for the damages done to any road in the prosecution of active hostilities, any more than it will pay for similar damages done by the enemy. With these exceptions the principles proposed by the Quartermaster-General appear to be correct.

In accordance with these observations I would recommend that the rules be determined upon to govern the settlement of this matter:

First. The United States will, as soon as it can dispense with the military occupation and control of any road of which the Quartermaster's Department is in charge, turn it over to the parties asking to receive it who may appear to have the best claim, and to be able to operate it in such a manner as to secure the speedy movement of all military stores and troops, the Quartermaster-General, upon the advice of the military commander of the department, to determine when this can be done, subject to the approval of the Secretary of War.

Second. Where any State has a loyal board of public works, or other executive officers charged with the supervision of railroads, such roads shall be turned over to such board or officers, rather than to any corporations or private parties.

Third. When any railroad shall be so turned over a board of appraisers shall be appointed, who shall estimate and determine the value of any improvements which may have been made by the United States, either in the road itself or in its repair shops and permanent machinery, and the amount of such improvements shall be a lien upon the road.

Fourth. The parties to whom the road is turned over shall have the option of purchasing at their value any tools, iron, or other materials for permanent way which have been provided by the United States for the improvement of the road but have not been used.

Fifth. All other movable property, including rolling-stock of all kinds, the property of the United States, to be sold at auction after full public notice to the highest bidder.

Sixth. All rolling-stock and materials of railroads captured by the forces of the United States, and not consumed, destroyed, or permanently fixed elsewhere, as, for instance, when captured iron has been laid upon other roads, shall be placed at the disposal of the roads which originally owned the same, and shall be given up to these roads as soon as it can be spared, and they appear by proper agents authorized to receive it.

Seventh. No payment or credit shall be given to any railroad recaptured from the public enemy for its occupation or use by the United States during the continuance of the military necessity which compelled the United States to take possession of it; but its capture and restoration shall be deemed a sufficient consideration for all such use; nor shall any indemnity be paid for injuries done to the property of any road by the forces of the United States during the continuance of the war.

Eighth. Roads which have not been operated by the U. S. Quartermaster's Department not to be interfered with unless under military necessity, such roads to be left in possession of such persons as may now have possession, subject only to the removal of every agent, director, president, superintendent, or operative who has not taken the oath of allegiance to the United States.

Ninth. When superintendents in actual possession decline to take the oath, some competent person shall be appointed as receiver of the road, who shall administer its affairs and account for its receipts to the board of directors, who may be formally recognized as the legal and loyal board of managers; the receiver to be appointed by the Treasury Department, as in the case of abandoned property.

I am, sir, very respectfully, your obedient servant,

C. A. DANA,
Assistant Secretary of War.

WAR DEPARTMENT, ADJUTANT-GENERAL'S OFFICE,
May 29, 1865.

GOVERNOR OF MAINE:

Referring to my telegram of May 18, I have the honor to inform you that the order for muster out of volunteer white troops (except Veteran Reserve Corps) whose terms expire prior to October 1 next has been extended to include all armies and departments.

THOMAS M. VINCENT,
Assistant Adjutant-General.

(Same to Governors of New Hampshire, Vermont, Massachusetts, Rhode Island, Connecticut, New York, New Jersey, Delaware, Pennsylvania, Maryland, West Virginia, Ohio, Indiana, Illinois, Iowa, Michigan, Wisconsin, Minnesota, Missouri, and Kentucky.)

WAR DEPARTMENT, ADJUTANT-GENERAL'S OFFICE,
Washington, May 29, 1865.

DEPARTMENT COMMANDERS:

Please announce that General Orders, No. 36, of 1862, with the three notes attached relating to discharge of the sick, will be applied in all similar cases, as, for instance, in the case of discharges under General Orders, No. 77, of 1865. There appears to be some misunderstanding in regard to it. This does not change regulations and orders as to who shall be mustered out and who discharged for disability, but only applies General Orders, No. 36, of 1862, to partial payments, descriptive lists, transportation, &c., of men discharged under General Orders, No. 77, current series, and similar orders.

SAMUEL BRECK,
Assistant Adjutant-General.

(Copy to chief mustering officers.)

GENERAL ORDERS, No. 101. } WAR DEPT., ADJT. GENERAL'S OFFICE, *Washington, May 30, 1865.*

RETENTION OF ARMS BY SOLDIERS ON BEING HONORABLY DISCHARGED FROM SERVICE.

Upon an honorable muster out and discharge from the service of the United States, all volunteer soldiers desiring to do so are hereby authorized to retain their arms and accouterments on paying therefor their value to the Ordnance Department.

The payments will be made, under the regulations of the Ordnance Department, to the officer or representative thereof at the rendezvous in the State to which the troops are ordered for payment and final discharge.

By order of the Secretary of War:

E. D. TOWNSEND,
Assistant Adjutant-General.

WAR DEPARTMENT, ADJUTANT-GENERAL'S OFFICE,
May 30, 1865.

GOVERNOR OF MAINE:

An order has been issued directing all volunteer artillery in the Armies of the Potomac, Tennessee, and Georgia to be immediately mustered out and discharged the service of the United States.

THOMAS M. VINCENT,
Assistant Adjutant-General.

(Copy for the Governors of New Hampshire, Vermont, Massachusetts, Rhode Island, Connecticut, New York, New Jersey, Pennsylvania, Delaware, Maryland, West Virginia, Ohio, Indiana, Kentucky, Illinois, Missouri, Iowa, Minnesota, Wisconsin, Michigan, and Kansas.)

GENERAL ORDERS, No. 102. } WAR DEPT., ADJT. GENERAL'S OFFICE, *Washington, May 31, 1865.*

Department, district, post, and other commanding officers will make such temporary details of officers and soldiers as may be required by assistant commissioners of the Bureau of Refugees, Freedmen, and Abandoned Lands, and render them, or other officers of said Bureau, any aid that may be required by them in the discharge of their official duties.

By order of the Secretary of War:

E. D. TOWNSEND,
Assistant Adjutant-General.

WAR DEPARTMENT, ADJUTANT-GENERAL'S OFFICE,
May 31, 1865.

Maj. Gen. JOHN A. DIX,
Commanding Department of the East:

The Secretary of War directs that all volunteer organizations of white troops of your command (except the Veteran Reserve Corps) whose terms of service expire prior to October 1 next be immediately mustered out of service.

The organizations to be discharged will be ordered to report to the rendezvous in their respective States at or nearest which mustered in, there to be mustered out under the direction of the chief mustering officer of the State.

Should your command be reduced prejudicially to the service by this order, you are authorized to suspend it in whole or in part, promptly notifying and stating reasons to the Adjutant-General of the Army, with a view to receiving further instructions. Please acknowledge this.

THOMAS M. VINCENT,
Assistant Adjutant-General.

(Same to Maj. Gen. Joseph Hooker, commanding Northern Department, Cincinnati, Ohio.)

CHATTANOOGA, *June 1, 1865.*

A. ANDERSON,
Chief Superintendent and Engineer
Military Railroads of the United States:

SIR: I have the honor to submit the following report of operations of the Construction Corps, U. S. Military Railroads, Division of the Mississippi, from the date I was placed in charge, February 10, to June 1, 1865. Upon the completion of the work assigned me by Col. W. W. Wright, chief engineer, previous to his departure for Savannah, the rebuilding of the bridges on the Nashville, Decatur and Stevenson line, destroyed by Hood in his retreat from Nashville, amounting in the aggregate to 6,000 feet (linear), I reported to you at Nashville. On the 17th of February received orders from General McCallum to send forward a division of the Construction Corps to Baltimore. I selected the Third Division, composed of Speers' and Bones' subdivisions of carpenters and workmen, comprising about 400 men, who, in charge of William McDonald, assistant engineer, left Nashville on February 25, with orders to proceed to Baltimore, and upon arrival there reporting to General McCallum at Washington, D. C. This division I recalled from the East Tennessee and Virginia Railroad, where they had been sent a few days before, General Thomas deciding not to prosecute the work any further at that time. Upon the withdrawal of this division I organized the Seventh Division of trackmen, detaching a part of the Fourth Division of carpenters as a bridge force. The Second Division having been transferred to North Carolina some time previous, and the Fifth and Sixth Divisions employed upon the Nashville and Northwestern and Nashville and Clarksville lines, left us on the 1st of March with the First, Fourth, and Seventh Divisions, amounting in all to about 2,000 men.

On the 1st of March, by your order, I transferred the Fifth and Sixth Divisions of the Construction Corps, engaged in the construction and maintenance of the Northwestern and Clarksville lines, to the transportation department, they taking entire control of the roads from that date.

February 16 sent the First Division of trackmen, who had been assisting the bridge force on the Nashville, Decatur and Stevenson line, to Chattanooga, and returned the bridge-builders of the First Division, by order of General Thomas, to Columbia, to erect a permanent turnpike bridge across Duck River at that point. I directed Mr. Rozelle, superintendent in charge, to put up a Howe truss of three spans, 112 feet each, using the bolts and castings of bridges destroyed on the railroad. The bridge was finished the latter part of May, having been built at intervals when the division was not otherwise employed. It is a strong and permanent structure of 350 feet in length, costing about $50 per foot (linear), which I would respectfully suggest charging the turnpike company or corporation of Columbia with.

On the 25th of February we were visited by a freshet, almost unprecedented, which destroyed or injured to a greater or less extent all the bridges on the Nashville, Decatur and Stevenson line, on the Northwestern, five on the Chattanooga and Atlanta line between Chattanooga and Dalton, and two on the Clarksville line. The repairs of the roads were commenced at once by the First Division, the permanent bridge force of the various lines, and a large force of Nagle's men furnished by the transportation department. The bridges on the Chattanooga and Atlanta line were at the same time commenced by the Fourth Division, in charge of C. Latimer, division engineer, who upon their completion repaired with his force to the Elk River bridge on Nashville, Dacatur and Stevenson line, and continued working from that end of the line until joined by Rozelle, working south.

On the 3d of March we had another freshet, almost as disastrous as the former one, destroying again nearly all the bridges we had rebuilt, and this time washing out three bridges on the Nashville and Chattanooga line and throwing four others out of line. Large forces of men were immediately put to work, and after an interruption of one week communication was again established with Chattanooga on the Northwestern and Nashville, Decatur and Stevenson lines. Communication was not fully restored until the 28th. Owing to the destruction in part of the Red River bridge the Clarksville line west of Springfield was abandoned.

On March 12 received orders from General Thomas to reopen the East Tennessee and Virginia Railroad from Strawberry Plains to Bull's Gap, and put it in condition to sustain as heavy a business as was done upon the Chattanooga and Atlanta line last summer. I accordingly directed Mr. Latimer, division engineer, with the track force of the First Division and a carpenter force from the Fourth Division, to proceed at once to Strawberry Plains for that purpose. We commenced work at that point on the 14th. From thence to New Market the road was destroyed in patches for one mile and a half, including five cattle guards, two bridges of thirty feet span each, and tank at Friend's Station. The road was repaired and opened to New Market the 18th. From New Market to Morristown the track was burnt in patches to the extent of one mile and a quarter. Twenty cattle guards, bridge at Mossy Creek (150 feet in length), and one at Morristown (24 feet span) were destroyed. At this point erected two tanks and extended side track for 1,500 feet. From Morristown to Rogersville Junction, or Bull's Gap, the track was destroyed to the extent of three-fourths of a mile. Three bridges of 24 feet span, one of 40 feet span, and one at Russellville of 150 feet span were also destroyed. The line was opened to Bull's Gap on the 25th. Upon reaching that point I received further orders from General Thomas to open the road to Carter's Station, on the Watauga River, twenty miles west of Bristol, which we reached on the 29th of April. From Bull's Gap to Greeneville the mechanical work on the road was very heavy, and all destroyed. Rebuilt a bridge of 100 feet span and renewed 300 feet of trestle-work at Bull's Gap. From thence to Lick Creek the track was uninjured. The bridge and trestle-work at Lick Creek, 900 feet in length, was burnt and the track totally destroyed for seven miles, extending to a point two miles east of Blue Spring. The extensive trestle-work at Swan Pond, two miles east of Lick Creek, 1,400 feet in length and from 9 to 17 in height, was likewise destroyed.

I would here take occasion to express my acknowledgment of the valuable service rendered by Major-General Stanley, commanding Fourth Army Corps, who furnished all the transportation required and large details of men for cutting ties and wood, loading timber, &c.

The laying of the track between Lick Creek and Blue Spring was much retarded by the incessant rains occurring at that time. East of Blue Spring we erected two water-tanks. Between this point and Greeneville we rebuilt three bridges across the Chucky of 140 feet, 100 feet, and 180 feet, respectively; the track was only destroyed to the extent of one-fourth of a mile. Between Greeneville and Carter's Station, which we reached on the 29th of April, there were three bridges destroyed of 245 feet, 137 feet, and 235 feet in length, respectively. Having reached the point to which we were ordered to open the road, the men were set to work cutting timber and ties, surfacing track, &c., whilst awaiting further orders. During the progress of the work upon the main line another force of trackmen were employed at Knoxville in laying a side track 3,000 feet in length to the commissary building in course of erection on the old Charleston railroad. Another large force were engaged lengthening the sidings on the main line to facilitate the passing of trains. The operations of the Fourth Division, of carpenters, and part of the Seventh Division, of trackmen, under charge of John F. Burgin, division engineer, were confined chiefly to the erection of buildings, though frequently employed upon bridges and repairs of track. The rolling-mill was completed and went into successful operation the latter part of March; a report of operations up to the 1st of June I herewith append.

Report of iron manufactured at rolling-mill U. S. military railroads, at Chattanooga, Tenn., to June 1, 1865.

Articles.	Received.	Expended.	Manufactured.	Issued.	Balance.
Old iron ....pounds..	2, 603, 968	2, 603, 986	....	....	....
New railroad iron ....pounds..	....	....	2, 264, 320	916, 026	1, 348, 294
Coal ....bushels..	59, 092	42, 262	....	....	16, 830

There has been a track graded west of the rolling-mill, and an extensive trestle and coal-bin erected. Fourteen small mess-houses have been built, and three large buildings, in course of erection at date of last report, finished. A large force of the Seventh Division have been constantly employed at the mill up to this date digging a well, unloading cars, &c. Another force of upward of 100 men of the Seventh Division have been employed upon repairs of the Nashville and Chattanooga Railroad up to this date. About eighty men have been constantly employed in the quarry near Chattanooga, getting out stone for foundations, sewers, and ballast. The most of the foundations for the roundhouse are in, and the greater part of the lumber intended for it cut and delivered. A double track was graded from the main track outside the depot yard, running to the roundhouse, and from thence extended almost to the Crutchfield House, with the design ultimately of connecting with the tracks in the street. There has been erected also extensive barracks and officers' quarters for the depot guard, and a large building for officers of the transportation department, and extensive mess-houses for their men. At Knoxville there has been erected one large office building, two large mess-houses, and a blacksmith shop of fifty by eighty feet. Also depot buildings at Charleston, Athens, and Sweet Water. We have had five saw-mills in operation, which have cut the last three months 1,200,000 feet of lumber, board measure, and 500,000 shingles, a large amount of which we have on hand.

On the 6th of May I received your order directing the reduction of the Construction Corps to the lowest practicable limit. I at once suspended operations on the roundhouse and in the stone quarry, and ordered a suspension of the saw-mills, after cutting up the stock on hand. From the Fourth and Seventh Divisions and saw-mill department I have discharged 1,000 men since the receipt of your order, making the available force of the Construction Corps at the present time 1,200 men. A further reduction of the force was arrested by an order from General Thomas directing the relaying of the track between Dalton and Resaca and rebuilding of the bridge across the Oostenaula. Commencing the track at Dalton on the 10th of May, I sent forward part of the bridge force of the First Division to Resaca to rebuild the bridge, five spans of which had been destroyed. This they accomplished and laid one mile of track south of it by the time we reached there, the 24th of May. From thence to Kingston we rebuilt three bridges, two tanks, and repaired sidings at Calhoun and Adairsville; the rest of the track was in comparatively good order. Reached Kingston on the 26th, and the following day turned the road over to the transportation department. Between Kingston and Etowah three more bridges and two tanks were destroyed. The track was unimpaired. Reached the Etowah on the 29th, when I received further orders from General Thomas to open the line to Atlanta, at which all the force of the corps at the present time are employed. I omitted to state we had built an engine-house and a large reservoir adjoining the machine-shop at Chattanooga of a capacity of 80,000 gallons. The shops in the yard, as well as the locomotives, are now amply supplied with water from the works built by the U. S. Engineer Department. We have, in connection with their tubs on Cameron Hill, erected a tank of a capacity of 50,000 gallons, and have laid about 5,000 feet of main pipe and 4,000 of branch to the commissary building, store and mess houses.

In conclusion, I take pleasure in testifying to the efficient and valuable services of John F. Burgin and C. Latimer, division engineers, who have on all occasions manifested an untiring zeal in the prosecution of work committed to their charge.

Summary of work done on the East Tennessee and Virginia Railroad from March 15 to April 29, 1865: Ninety-four miles of track opened and repaired; 12 miles of track rebuilt; 4,400 linear feet of bridging; 20,000 cross-ties cut and delivered; 57,000 cubic feet of timber cut for bridging; 19 switches put in; 18 frogs put in; 5 water-tanks erected.

Summary of work done on the Chattanooga and Atlanta line from May 10 to May 31, 1865: Eighteen miles of track relaid; 1,000 linear feet of bridging; 6 frogs and switches put in; 4 tanks erected.

Ten miles of the above track were laid with burnt iron, which we straightened; five miles with the U-rail taken from the Nashville and Chattanooga line, and three miles with new iron.

I have the honor to be, very respectfully, your obedient servant,

L. H. EICHOLTZ,
Acting Chief Engineer, Government Railroads,
Military Division of the Mississippi.

WAR DEPT., PROVOST-MARSHAL-GENERAL'S BUREAU,
Washington, D. C., June 1, 1865.

Major-General SAXTON,
Supt. Recruiting for Colored Troops, Beaufort, S. C.:

The Secretary of War directs that all enlistment of colored troops be immediately discontinued throughout the United States.

Acknowledge receipt of this order.

JAMES B. FRY,
Provost-Marshal-General.

(Same to Major-General Palmer, Louisville, Ky.; Major-General Gillmore, Hilton Head, S. C.; Major-General Wilson, Macon, Ga.; Col. W. H. Sidell, Louisville, Ky.; Capt. Leslie Smith, Hilton Head, S. C.)

WAR DEPARTMENT,
Washington, D. C., June 2, 1865.

RESTRICTIONS ON TRADE.

Ordered, That any and all military restrictions upon trade in any of the States or Territories of the United States, except in articles contraband of war, shall cease from and after the present date.

By order of the President:

EDWIN M. STANTON,
Secretary of War.

GENERAL ORDERS, No. 105. } WAR DEPT., ADJT. GENERAL'S OFFICE,
Washington, June 2, 1865.

REDUCTION OF VOLUNTEER ARTILLERY.

Department commanders will at once reduce their batteries of volunteer light artillery to the number absolutely required under existing circumstances by the necessities of the service in their respective departments.

The companies thus relieved will be sent to Washington, Louisville, or Cairo, as may be most convenient, for final payment and muster out.

All artillery horses that may become surplus under the operation of this order will be sold in the department where they now are, and the guns of the companies that are to be discharged will be retained for the present within the department.

The number of public animals retained in service, both for artillery and transportation purposes, will be reduced, as far as possible, throughout the country, and all surplus animals will be sold.

By command of Lieutenant-General Grant:

E. D. TOWNSEND,
Assistant Adjutant-General.

GENERAL ORDERS, No. 106. } WAR DEPT., ADJT. GENERAL'S OFFICE, *Washington, June 2, 1865.*

Department commanders will immediately, on the receipt of this order, relieve all general and staff officers whose services can be dispensed with within their respective commands, and order them to proceed without delay to their respective places of residence, and from there report by letter to the Adjutant-General of the Army.

Department commanders will report the names of all officers relieved by them under this order to the Adjutant-General of the Army.

By command of Lieutenant-General Grant:

E. D. TOWNSEND,
Assistant Adjutant-General.

GENERAL ORDERS, No. 107. } WAR DEPT., ADJT. GENERAL'S OFFICE, *Washington, June 2, 1865.*

REMOVAL OF RESTRICTIONS ON TRADE.

Ordered, That all military restrictions upon trade in any of the States or Territories of the United States, except in articles contraband of war—to wit, arms, ammunition, gray cloth, and all articles from which ammunition is manufactured; locomotives, cars, railroad iron, and machinery for operating railroads; telegraph wires, insulators, and instruments for operating telegraphic lines—shall cease from and after the present date.

By order of the President of the United States:

E. D. TOWNSEND,
Assistant Adjutant-General.

HARRISBURG *June 2, 1865.*

Hon. E. M. STANTON,
Secretary of War:

I was under the impression when I left Washington that the troops would be paid up to the date of their discharge. The paymasters here pay from the date of muster out. The One hundred and forty-first Regiment Pennsylvania Volunteers arrived here on the 30th ultimo and has not been paid. They were mustered out on the 28th and left Washington on the 29th. I learn it is proposed to pay them until and including the 27th. If it can at all be done, I wish much it could be. It would add so much to the satisfaction of the officers and men going out of service. I only arrived in the night, and have not learned the reason of the delay in the payment. There are now seven regiments here, and I fear that it will be some time before they will be paid off.

A. G. CURTIN.

WAR DEPARTMENT,
Washington City, June 2, 1865.

His Excellency Governor A. G. CURTIN,
Harrisburg, Pa.:

The Paymaster-General reports that he has this day instructed his chiefs of districts that troops mustered out under General Orders, No. 94, are to be paid to the date they arrive at the designated State rendezvous, and that all mustered-out troops at all points are being paid as rapidly as possible.

EDWIN M. STANTON,
Secretary of War.

CIRCULAR No. 21. } WAR DEPT., ADJUTANT-GENERAL'S OFFICE,
Washington, June 3, 1865.

Before the accounts with commanding officers of organizations are settled, mustering officers should satisfy themselves that the rolls and returns, as required by Army Regulations for their organization, have been forwarded to this office.

E. D. TOWNSEND,
Assistant Adjutant-General.

WAR DEPARTMENT,
Washington, D. C., June 5, 1865.

DISCHARGE OF VOLUNTEERS.

The Adjutant-General will issue an order for the immediate discharge of—

First. All dismounted cavalry in every military department.

Second. All cavalry force in General Dix's department.

Third. All volunteer infantry in General Dix's department (except Veteran Reserves) whose services can in the judgment of the commander of the department be dispensed with.

Fourth. All volunteer infantry in General Hooker's department (except Veteran Reserves) whose services are in the opinion of the commander of the department no longer required.

EDWIN M. STANTON,
Secretary of War.

CIRCULAR No. 23. } WAR DEPT., ADJUTANT-GENERAL'S OFFICE,
Washington, June 5, 1865.

Volunteer soldiers entitled to discharge, and wishing to enlist in the Regular Army, under the terms of General Orders, No. 99, current series, will be forthwith mustered out at their several commands, receive their discharges, and will not be sent to rendezvous under the provisions of General Orders, No. 94, current series, but on enlistment in the Regular Army will receive final payments under the requirements of paragraph 3, General Orders, No. 83, current series.

The attention of commanding officers of regiments, batteries, and detached commands of the Regular Army is called to the immediate necessity of appointing recruiting officers for their several commands, in order to obtain the advantages of General Orders, No. 99, current series. In designating these officers, commanding officers will be governed by the requirements of paragraphs 986, 987, and 988, Revised Regulations for the Army, governing regimental recruiting service.

E. D. TOWNSEND,
Assistant Adjutant-General.

GENERAL ORDERS, No. 110. | WAR DEPT., ADJT. GENERAL'S OFFICE, *Washington, June 7, 1865.*

The following order of the President of the United States (in relation to the transfer of abandoned lands, funds, and property set apart for the use of freedmen) to the Bureau of Refugees, Freedmen, and Abandoned Lands is published for the information and guidance of all concerned:

EXECUTIVE MANSION,
Washington, D. C., June 2, 1865.

Whereas, by an act of Congress approved March third, eighteen hundred and sixty-five, there was established in the War Department a Bureau of Refugees, Freedmen, and Abandoned Lands, and to which, in accordance with the said act of Congress, is committed the supervision and management of all abandoned lands, and the control of all subjects relating to refugees and freedmen from rebel States, or from any district of country within the territory embraced in the operations of the Army, under such rules and regulations as may be prescribed by the head of the Bureau and approved by the President; and whereas, it appears that the management of abandoned lands and subjects relating to refugees and freedmen, as aforesaid, have been, and still are, by orders based on military exigencies, or legislation based on previous statutes, partly in the hands of military officers disconnected with said Bureau, and partly in charge of officers of the Treasury Department: It is therefore

Ordered, That all officers of the Treasury Department, all military officers, and all others in the service of the United States, turn over to the authorized officers of said Bureau all abandoned lands and property contemplated in said act of Congress, approved March third, eighteen hundred and sixty-five, establishing the Bureau of Refugees, Freedmen, and Abandoned Lands, that may now be under or within their control. They will also turn over to such officers all funds collected by tax or otherwise, for the benefit of refugees or freedmen, or accruing from abandoned lands, or property set apart for their use, and will transfer to them all official records connected with the administration of affairs which pertain to said Bureau.

ANDREW JOHNSON.

By order of the Secretary of War:

E. D. TOWNSEND,
Assistant Adjutant-General.

CHICAGO, *June 8, 1865.*

Hon. E. M. STANTON,
Secretary of War:

Pursuant to your orders I have given directions for the immediate discharge of all volunteer troops in the Northern Department except the Eighty-eighth and One hundred and twenty-eighth Ohio Volunteers and the Veteran Reserve Corps. The Eighty-eighth is stationed at Camp Chase and the One hundred and twenty-eighth at Johnson's Island. The interest of the service requires that these regiments shall be retained a few weeks longer.

JOSEPH HOOKER,
Major-General, Commanding.

GENERAL ORDERS, No. 111. } WAR DEPT., ADJT. GENERAL'S OFFICE,
Washington, June 10, 1865.

The annexed opinions of the Attorney-General relative to the amounts of bounty payable to certain soldiers and the proper construction of section 4 of the Army appropriation act of March 3, 1865 (General Orders, No. 45, Adjutant-General's Office, March 21, 1865), concerning the allowance of "three months' pay proper" to certain volunteer officers continuing in the service "to the close of the war," are published for the information and guidance of all concerned:

ATTORNEY-GENERAL'S OFFICE,
May 6, 1865.

Hon. EDWIN M. STANTON,
Secretary of War:

SIR: I have considered the several questions presented by the Paymaster-General and the Adjutant-General of the Army in their respective communications of May 3 and May 4, instant, relative to the amounts of bounty payable to the soldiers of certain military organizations now being mustered out of service, and also the point suggested in those communications relative to the proper construction of the fourth section of the Army appropriation act of March 3, 1865 (13 Stat., 497), concerning the allowance of extra pay (as it may be called) to certain volunteer officers continuing in the service "to the close of the war."

The first question is, whether veterans who re-enlisted and persons who enlisted in the regular or volunteer forces of the United States for three years or during the war, under the regulations and orders referred to in the communication of the Paymaster-General, issued by the Secretary of War, and by the Provost-Marshal-General with the approval of the Secretary, and who may be honorably mustered out the service by reason of the Government no longer requiring their services, before the expiration of their term of enlistment, are respectively entitled, on being so mustered out, to the unpaid balances of the bounties promised to them by the orders under which they were enlisted.

I am of opinion that they are so entitled, by the operation of the joint resolutions of Congress, approved respectively January 13, 1864, and March 3, 1864, which give the force and effect of law to the regulations and orders of the War Department just referred to, providing for the payment of bounties to the classes of soldiers above named. These regulations and orders, in terms, promise and declare that "if the Government shall not require these troops for the full period of three years, and they shall be mustered honorably out of the service before the expiration of their term of enlistment, they shall receive, upon being mustered out, the whole amount of bounty remaining unpaid, the same as if the full term had been served."

The second question relates to soldiers who entered the service pursuant to and under the provisions of the act of July 4, 1864, promulgated by your Department in General Orders, No. 224; and it is whether they are respectively entitled to receive, on being thus mustered out of the service before the expiration of their respective terms of enlistment, the whole amounts of bounty to which they would have been entitled if they had continued in the service throughout their respective periods of enlistment, or only those proportions or installments of the several bounties which may have actually accrued to them at the dates of their respective discharges.

I am of opinion that a volunteer accepted and mustered into the service under the statute of July 4, 1864, whether for a term of one year, or of two years, or of three years, if he is mustered out of the service, for the reason mentioned, before the expiration of the term of service for which he enlisted, is entitled to receive only the proportion of the bounty allowed him by the statute, whether one-third or two-thirds thereof, which had actually accrued before the date of his discharge. If, for instance, he volunteered for two years, and is mustered out before the expiration of the first year of his service, he cannot claim either the second or the third installment of the bounty of $200 which would have been payable to him had he continued in the service till the expiration of the two years for which he enlisted. The volunteer only who, at the time of his discharge, has completed one-half of the term of service for which he enlisted, is entitled to the second installment of one-third of the amount of bounty given to him by the act; and he is entitled to no more of that bounty. If he is discharged on the next day after the expiration of one-half of his term of enlistment, the second installment of the bounty is due and payable to him. The Government cannot reclaim it if it has been paid, nor withhold it if it remain unpaid. But the discharge precludes him from receiving the third installment; that only is due to a volunteer who may have served through the whole term for which he enlisted. I confess that there is some obscurity in the act, and that there is a little difficulty in determining its meaning. But, on the whole, I am of opinion that the Paymaster-General has arrived at the true construction of the statute.

The third question is, whether commissioned officers of volunteers below the rank of brigadier-general, whom the Government may now muster out of service because their services are no longer required, are entitled respectively to receive, on their leaving the service, "three months' pay proper," under the provisions of the fourth section of the act of March, 1865.

The right of these officers to receive that allowance depends upon the determination of the point whether they have continued in the service "to the close of the war" within the meaning of the statute of 1865. I am of opinion if such an officer continue in the Army till he is honorably mustered out, because his military services are no longer needed, and till the Government thus declares that it no longer requires him to perform any duty on its behalf under his commission, that he is within the provision of the statute, and in its contemplation he has continued in the military service "to the close of the war." The war, so far as he is concerned in his capacity as an officer, has closed. He has performed his duty—his entire duty—to the Government and the cause for which he drew his sword. When his country, by its appropriate organ, commands him to return his sword to the scabbard, and retires him honorably from its service, I know not how we can, with respect to that officer, say that the war has not closed. I am of opinion that an officer of the class named in the statute now, and thus mustered out of service, is entitled to receive "three months' pay proper."

I am, sir, most respectfully, your obedient servant,

JAMES SPEED,
Attorney-General.

By order of the Secretary of War:

E. D. TOWNSEND,
Assistant Adjutant-General.

WAR DEPARTMENT, ADJUTANT-GENERAL'S OFFICE,
June 10, 1865.

COMMANDING GENERALS OF DEPARTMENTS AND ARMIES:

Under General Orders, No. 101, May 30, current year, from this office, soldiers honorably mustered out, who desire to do so, are authorized to retain their arms and accouterments on paying therefor their value. To this end soldiers who desire to take advantage of the said order must signify their intention before leaving the field, so that the prices may be entered on their muster-out rolls.

The prices fixed by the Ordnance Department are as follows: Muskets, all kinds, with or without accouterments, $6; Spencer carbines, $10; all other carbines, $8; sabers and swords, with or without belts, $3.*

Please promulgate this order for the guidance of commissaries of musters and all others concerned.

E. D. TOWNSEND,
Assistant Adjutant-General.

* Also announced in Circular No. 24, Adjutant-General's Office, June 10, 1865.

WAR DEPARTMENT, ADJUTANT-GENERAL'S OFFICE,
June 13, 1865.

GOVERNOR OF MAINE:

Under instructions of the Secretary of War, chief mustering officers have been ordered to turn over to Your Excellency the colors in their charge, under paragraph V of General Orders, No. 94, current series, at such time as you may designate.

Please to communicate your wishes to the said officers.

THOMAS M. VINCENT,
Assistant Adjutant-General.

(Same to Governors of New Hampshire, Vermont, Massachusetts, Rhode Island, Connecticut, New York, New Jersey, Pennsylvania, Delaware, Maryland, West Virginia, Ohio, Indiana, Kentucky, Illinois, Missouri, Iowa, Minnesota, Wisconsin, Michigan, Kansas.)

GENERAL ORDERS, No. 113. } WAR DEPT., ADJT. GENERAL'S OFFICE, *Washington, June 15, 1865.*

ORDER IN RELATION TO SALE OF UNSERVICEABLE QUARTERMASTER'S PROPERTY.

I. Chief quartermasters of military departments, the chief of the inspection division, and the regularly assigned inspectors of the Quartermaster's Department will immediately cause to be made and forwarded to the Quartermaster-General invoices of such articles of clothing, camp and garrison equipage, and quartermaster's stores as, on personal inspection, they may find unserviceable or worthless to the Government; and also of such articles as it would be more economical to the Government to sell than to ship to other points. The latter invoices will be separate from the former. The sale of the property embraced in these invoices having been approved by the Quartermaster-General, they will be submitted to the Secretary of War for his orders. All proceedings subsequent to any order of sale that may be given will be conducted according to the Regulations, by due advertisement, &c.

II. No sale of public buildings, barracks, quarters, stables, &c., will be made except on an order of the Quartermaster-General, approved by the Secretary of War, indorsed upon a report to be made in each case in the usual form.

By order of the Secretary of War:

E. D. TOWNSEND,
Assistant Adjutant-General.

GENERAL ORDERS, No. 114. } WAR DEPT., ADJT. GENERAL'S OFFICE, *Washington, June 15, 1865.*

Soldiers honorably discharged will be permitted to retain, without charge, their knapsacks, haversacks, and canteens.

By order of the Secretary of War:

E. D. TOWNSEND,
Assistant Adjutant-General.

GENERAL ORDERS, No. 115. } WAR DEPT., ADJT. GENERAL'S OFFICE, *Washington, June 15, 1865.*

The payment of all U. S. bounties to men enlisting in the military service will cease from and after July 1, 1865.

By order of the Secretary of War:

E. D. TOWNSEND,
Assistant Adjutant-General.

CIRCULAR No. 25. } WAR DEPT., ADJUTANT-GENERAL'S OFFICE, *Washington, June 15, 1865.*

Officers or enlisted men who may hereafter be commissioned (under first appointments) by the Governors of States to regiments or companies of volunteers serving in Texas will be furnished with free transportation on Government transports to the respective stations of their regiments or companies. Existing regulations are amended accordingly.

The presentation of a Governor's commission will be sufficient to secure a transportation order from the proper officer of the Quartermaster's Department.

By order of the Secretary of War:

E. D. TOWNSEND,
Assistant Adjutant-General.

HDQRS. STATE OF ARKANSAS, ADJT. GEN.'S OFFICE,
Little Rock, June 15, 1865.

HON. EDWIN M. STANTON,
Secretary of War, Washington, D. C.:

SIR: I am requested by His Excellency the Governor of the State to ask that the citizens of Arkansas now serving in the regiments of other States be mustered out of the service. There is a large class of this class of soldiers on duty in the Department of Arkansas and elsewhere in regiments from Missouri and Kansas, and somewhat from Iowa and Illinois. Many of their families are in the State in the most destitute condition, while others are refugees and equally requiring their assistance. It is also a matter of very great importance in the maintenance of law and order, and the restoration of peace and quiet throughout the State, that they should be permitted to return to their homes at the earliest possible moment to secure that preponderance of tried loyal sentiment so necessary in the present emergency.

I have the honor to remain, very respectfully, your obedient servant,

A. W. BISHOP,
Adjutant-General.

GENERAL ORDERS, No. 116. } WAR DEPT., ADJT. GENERAL'S OFFICE, *Washington, June 17, 1865.*

Enlisted men of the Veteran Reserve Corps who, if they had remained in the volunteer regiments from which they were transferred to the Veteran Reserves, would, under existing orders, now be entitled to muster out of service, will be so discharged, provided that no man shall be mustered out who desires to serve his full term.

By order of the Secretary of War:

E. D. TOWNSEND,
Assistant Adjutant-General.

CIRCULAR No. 26. } WAR DEPT., ADJUTANT-GENERAL'S OFFICE, *Washington, June 17, 1865.*

ORDERS AND INSTRUCTIONS RELATIVE TO THE MUSTER OUT AND DISCHARGE OF CERTAIN VOLUNTEER TROOPS.

White troops (except Veteran Reserve Corps) whose terms expire prior to October 1, 1865; artillery in the Armies of the Potomac (including Ninth Corps), Tennessee, and Georgia; dismounted cavalry in all armies and departments; all cavalry in the Department of the East, and certain infantry in the Northern Department and Department of the East.

TELEGRAM.] WAR DEPARTMENT, ADJUTANT-GENERAL'S OFFICE, *Washington, May 17, 1865.*

Maj. Gen. GEORGE G. MEADE,
Commanding Army of the Potomac:

The Secretary of War directs that all volunteer organizations of white troops in your command whose terms of service expire between this date and September 30 next, inclusive, be immediately mustered out of service.

The musters out will be made with existing regimental and company organizations, and under the regulations promulgated in General Orders, No. 94, of the 15th instant, from this office.

All men in the aforesaid organizations whose terms of service expire subsequent to October 1, 1865, will be transferred to other organizations from the same State; to veteran regiments when practicable, and when not practicable to regiments having the longest time to serve.

It is proper to add that this order will discharge as follows:

First. The three-years' regiments that were mustered into service under the call of July 2, 1862, and prior to October 1 of that year.

Second. Three-years' recruits mustered into service for old regiments between the same dates.

Third. One-year's men for new and old organizations, who entered the service between May 17 and October 1, 1864.

Please acknowledge receipt of this.

THOMAS M. VINCENT,
Assistant Adjutant-General.

NOTE.—Orders and instructions, as in the foregoing, were applied to the Army of the Tennessee and Army of Georgia, under the command of Major-General Sherman, June 18, 1865.

TELEGRAM.] WAR DEPARTMENT, ADJUTANT-GENERAL'S OFFICE, *Washington, May 18, 1865.*

Maj. Gen. GEORGE G. MEADE,
Commanding Army of the Potomac:

In connection with the telegram order of yesterday, relative to the discharge of troops whose terms expire prior to October 1, and referring to paragraph IV, General Orders, No. 94, current series, I am directed to say that it is of importance that the muster-out rolls should be ready in the shortest time possible.

Extra clerks should be detailed to assist the commissaries of musters and their assistants.

In the absence of rooms for use as offices, hospital and wall tents should be provided for the use of mustering officers in making out the necessary papers. All other proper facilities at command should also be afforded.

The attention of corps, division, and brigade commanders should be particularly directed to what is required of them under paragraph IV, General Orders, No. 94.

Assistant inspectors-general should be directed to frequently visit regiments and companies, to see in person if the data for the rolls and other papers are promptly and accurately furnished by regimental and company officers, conferring with the commissaries of musters and their assistants with the view of correcting at once any delinquencies they may find to exist.

THOMAS M. VINCENT,
Assistant Adjutant-General.

NOTE.—The foregoing instructions were applied to the Army of the Tennessee and Army of Georgia, May 18, 1865, and to other armies and departments, except Department of the East, Northern Department, Departments of the Pacific and New Mexico, June 2, 1865.

WAR DEPARTMENT, ADJUTANT-GENERAL'S OFFICE,
Washington, May 29, 1865.

TELEGRAM TO COMMANDING GENERALS OF ALL ARMIES AND DEPARTMENTS, EXCEPT ARMIES OF THE POTOMAC, TENNESSEE, AND GEORGIA, AND DEPARTMENTS OF THE EAST, PACIFIC, NEW MEXICO, AND NORTHERN DEPARTMENT.

The Secretary of War directs that all volunteer organizations of white troops in your command whose terms of service expire between this date and September 30 next, inclusive, be immediately mustered out of service.

The musters out will be made with existing regimental and company organizations, and under the regulations promulgated in General Orders, No. 94, of the 15th instant, from this office.

All men in the aforesaid organizations whose terms of service expire subsequent to October 1 will be transferred to other organizations from the same State; to veteran regiments when practicable, and when not practicable to regiments having the longest time to serve.

It is proper to add that this order will discharge as follows:

First. The three-years' regiments that were mustered into service under the call of July 2, 1862, and prior to October 1 of that year.

Second. Three-years' recruits mustered into service for old regiments between the same dates.

Third. One-year's men for new and old organizations who entered the service prior to October 1, 1864.

Should your command be reduced prejudicially to the service by this order, you are authorized to suspend it in whole or in part, promptly notifying the Adjutant-General of the Army, with a view to receiving further instructions.

Please acknowledge receipt of this.

THOMAS M. VINCENT,
Assistant Adjutant-General.

TELEGRAM.] WAR DEPARTMENT, ADJUTANT-GENERAL'S OFFICE,
Washington, May 29, 1865.

Maj. Gen. GEORGE G. MEADE,
Commanding Army of the Potomac.
Maj. Gen. JOHN G. PARKE,
Commanding Ninth Army Corps:

CIRCULAR TO COMMANDING GENERALS ARMIES OF GEORGIA AND TENNESSEE, THROUGH HEADQUARTERS MILITARY DIVISION OF THE MISSISSIPPI.

The Secretary of War directs that all the volunteer artillery of your command (army) be immediately mustered out and discharged.

For this arm of the service General Orders, No. 94, current series, from this office, is so modified as to allow said troops to be sent to their respective States, there to be mustered out under the direction of the chief mustering officer of the State.

Prior to their departure all public property will be turned over to the proper officers of the supply departments concerned for the command with which they may be serving.

The troops should be placed en route with the least practicable delay, and forwarded to the respective rendezvous in their States at or nearest which they were mustered in.

Please acknowledge receipt of this.

THOMAS M. VINCENT,
Assistant Adjutant-General.

WAR DEPARTMENT, ADJUTANT-GENERAL'S OFFICE,
Washington, June 5, 1865.

TELEGRAM TO COMMANDING GENERALS OF ALL ARMIES AND DEPARTMENTS, EXCEPTING DEPARTMENTS OF THE EAST AND THE NORTHERN.

The Secretary of War directs that all dismounted volunteer cavalry of your command be immediately discharged the service.

The musters out will be made by commissaries of musters and their assistants, and the troops afterward forwarded to their respective States for payment.

The general principles of General Orders, No. 94, current series, from this office, will be applied in executing this order.

Please acknowledge receipt of this by telegram and report the number of men to be discharged.

THOMAS M. VINCENT,
Assistant Adjutant-General.

MEMORANDA.

1. See General Orders, No. 105, of June 2, for the discharge of certain batteries of artillery.

2. Telegram from this office of June 5, 1865, to Major-General Dix, commanding Department of the East, directed all volunteer cavalry in that department to be discharged; organizations to be sent to their respective States for muster out under the direction of the chief mustering officers thereof.

3. Telegram from this office of June 5, 1865, to Major-General Dix, commanding Department of the East, and Major-General Hooker, commanding Northern Department, directed all volunteer infantry (except Veteran Reserve Corps) in said departments whose services were no longer required to be discharged; organizations to be sent to their respective States for muster out under the direction of the chief mustering officers thereof.

4. Telegram from this office of June 16, 1865, to Major-General McDowell, commanding Department of the Pacific, directed all volunteer troops in that department whose terms expire prior to October 1, 1865, to be immediately discharged. Should the order reduce the command prejudicially to the service, authority was given to suspend it, in whole or in part, until the receipt of further orders through the Adjutant-General of the Army.

E. D. TOWNSEND,
Assistant Adjutant-General.

CONFIDENTIAL CIRCULAR.] WASHINGTON, *June 22, 1865.*

All department commanders commanding in States where martial law prevails will immediately put detectives upon the watch for gambling-houses, especially faro banks, and at the appropriate time make a descent upon them all simultaneously, arresting all disbursing officers of the Government who may be found gambling in them, or visitants therein at the time, and who it can be proven had previously gambled at such places. The gambling institutions will be completely broken up and their money and stock confiscated, and the owners or proprietors of such gambling institutions be made to disgorge and refund all money they have won from U. S. disbursing officers. The officer so taken will be imprisoned and tried immediately. The same proceedings will be taken by department commanders in the North within their respective commands in the cities where disbursing officers may be located, except that instead of confiscating the money and stock of the gambling establishments, or compelling by military action the owners and proprietors of the same to disgorge or refund any moneys they may have won from disbursing officers of the Government, they will be immediately reported to the civil authorities for their action. This will be kept strictly confidential, except so far as it may be necessary to communicate it to those who are to carry it into execution.

U. S. GRANT,
Lieutenant-General.

(Sent to all military division and department commanders in cipher.)

MEMORANDUM.] WAR DEPT., PAYMASTER-GENERAL'S OFFICE,
Washington, D. C., June 22, 1865.

All veteran volunteers in batteries of volunteer artillery mustered out as organizations from Armies of Potomac, Tennessee, and Georgia, under recent orders, are mustered out "on account of their services being no longer required," and are entitled to balance of veteran bounty.

Heavy artillery follows the general rule, not that for field artillery.

SPECIAL ORDERS, No. 328. } HDQRS. OF THE ARMY, ADJT. GEN.'S OFFICE,
Washington, June 23, 1865.

* * * * * * *

5. Bvt. Maj. Gen. J. D. Webster, U. S. Volunteers, is hereby temporarily detached from the staff of Maj. Gen. W. T. Sherman, and will proceed without delay on a tour of inspection of the railroads of the Southern States, reporting upon their present condition and their ability to transport the U. S. mails.

In his report he will consider all the subjects mentioned in the letter of instructions which will be given him, and such other matters pertaining to the Southern railroads as in his investigations may suggest themselves.

General Webster is authorized to employ and take with him an experienced railroad man.

Upon the execution of this order General Webster will report to Major-General Sherman for duty.

By command of Lieutenant-General Grant:

E. D. TOWNSEND,
Assistant Adjutant-General.

WAR DEPARTMENT, ADJUTANT-GENERAL'S OFFICE,
Washington, June 23, 1865.

Maj. Gen. G. M. DODGE,
Saint Louis, Mo.:

The Secretary of War directs that all troops belonging to the Missouri State Militia, authorized by General Orders, No. 96, of 1861, and yet remaining in service, be immediately discharged.

The musters out will be made under the regulations promulgated in General Orders, No. 94, current series, from this office.

THOMAS M. VINCENT,
Assistant Adjutant-General.

WAR DEPARTMENT, ADJUTANT-GENERAL'S OFFICE,
June 25, 1865.

CHIEF MUSTERING OFFICERS UNITED STATES:

On the 22d instant the following additional reductions of the effective volunteer infantry forces present were ordered, viz: Army of the Potomac, 18,000 men; Army of the Tennessee, 15,000 men; Middle Military Division, 7,000. The reductions will be made by the muster out of entire organizations of veteran regiments having the shortest time to serve, including all recruits and additions to said regiments from other sources; also all absentees. The total reduction will be about 70,000. General Orders, No. 94, current series, from this office, will govern the musters out and payments.

Please furnish the Governor with a copy of this.

THOMAS M. VINCENT,
Assistant Adjutant-General.

CIRCULAR }
No. 27. }

WAR DEPT., ADJUTANT-GENERAL'S OFFICE,
Washington, June 26, 1865.

The necessity for the services of the invalid companies of the Regular Army, authorized by paragraph 5 of General Orders, No. 245, of 1863, having ceased, the organizations will be discontinued. Commanding officers of depots will at once cause a careful medical examination to be made of the enlisted men composing them. All men who are not now, or who are not likely to become in a reasonable time, capable of performing field duty will at once be discharged on the usual medical certificates. The remainder will be forwarded to their companies as rapidly as their condition will permit.

E. D. TOWNSEND,
Assistant Adjutant-General.

WAR DEPARTMENT, ADJUTANT-GENERAL'S OFFICE,
Washington, June 26, 1865.

TELEGRAM TO DEPARTMENT COMMANDERS.

Please cause an immediate investigation as to the expiration of service of all men on detached duty, in confinement, &c., within your department, that all entitled to discharge may be forwarded to the chief mustering officer of their respective States for muster out, or to be otherwise disposed of, as required by existing orders. Applications from the friends of this class of persons for their discharge are being constantly received at this Department.

SAMUEL BRECK,
Assistant Adjutant-General.

WASHINGTON, *June 28, 1865.*

Hon. E. M. STANTON,
Secretary of War:

I understand there is a great delay in carrying out orders for the muster out of troops in hospitals throughout the North arising principally from neglect of officers forwarding with sick men their descriptive rolls. In many instances the organizations to which sick men belong have been mustered out, leaving no way to get at their descriptive rolls further than their record is kept in the Adjutant-General's Office.

I would recommend that a circular be sent to all hospitals directing promptness in carrying out existing orders so far as they apply to men supplied with the requisite papers to enable them to do so, and report to the Adjutant-General the name, regiment, &c., of all men who should be mustered out but are not supplied with descriptive rolls.

U. S. GRANT,
Lieutenant-General.

CIRCULAR } WAR DEPT., ADJUTANT-GENERAL'S OFFICE,
No. 28. } *Washington, June 28, 1865.*

ORDERS AND INSTRUCTIONS RELATIVE TO THE MUSTER OUT OF VOLUNTEER TROOPS.

Certain veteran regiments in the Armies of the Potomac, Tennessee, and Middle Military Division, and certain infantry, cavalry, and artillery in various armies and departments.

I. Veteran regiments.

TELEGRAM.] WAR DEPARTMENT, ADJUTANT-GENERAL'S OFFICE,
Washington, June 22, 1865.

COMMANDING GENERAL ARMY OF THE POTOMAC:

The Secretary of War directs that the effective infantry force present of the Army of the Potomac be reduced by the discharge of 18,000 men.

The musters out will be by entire organizations of veteran regiments, to be selected from those having the shortest time to serve, including all recruits and additions thereto from other sources; also, absentees belonging to them. The absentees to be an additional reduction of the effective force.

The musters out and discharges will be made under the regulations promulgated in General Orders, No. 94, current series, from this office.

Please forward to this office without delay a list of the regiments you may select under this order, giving therein for each the strength, present and absent, respectively.

Acknowledge the receipt of this.

THOMAS M. VINCENT,
Assistant Adjutant-General.

NOTE.—Similar orders sent June 22 to the commanding general Army of the Tennessee for the discharge of 15,000 men from that army, and to the commanding general Middle Military Division for the discharge of 7,000 from that division.

II. Regiments of cavalry, artillery, and infantry (whose services are no longer required) ordered mustered out of service under special instructions, of dates set opposite the organizations respectively.

Connecticut.—First Battery, May 29, 1865.

Illinois.—Eighty-second Infantry, June 12, 1865.

Indiana.—One hundred and first Infantry, June 12, 1865; Ninety-first Infantry, June 15, 1865.

Maine.—Three unassigned companies infantry, June 16, 1865; three companies Coast Guard, June 16, 1865.

Maryland.—First Potomac Home Brigade Infantry, May 29, 1865; Second Potomac Home Brigade Infantry, May 29, 1865; Third Potomac Home Brigade Infantry, May 29, 1865; First Potomac Home Brigade Cavalry, June 23, 1865.

Massachusetts.—First Cavalry, June 17, 1865.

Michigan.—Twenty-sixth Infantry, June 2, 1865.

Missouri.—Forty-eighth Infantry, June 13, 1865; Missouri State Militia (about 2,200, authorized under General Orders, No. 96, Adjutant-General's Office, 1861), June 23, 1865.

New Jersey.—Thirty-ninth Infantry, June 5, 1865.

New York.—One hundred and fiftieth Infantry, May 29, 1865; Batteries A, K, and F, First Artillery, June 5, 1865; First Engineers, June 5, 1865; Fifteenth Engineers, June 5, 1865; Fiftieth Engineers, June 5, 1865; Second Cavalry (Harris Light), June 17, 1865; Eighth Cavalry, June 17, 1865; Nineteenth Cavalry (First Dragoons), June 17, 1865; First Cavalry (Lincoln), June 18, 1865; Twenty-fifth Cavalry, June 20, 1865; One hundred and fifty-first Infantry (battalion), June 22, 1865.

Ohio.—One hundred and tenth Infantry, June 16, 1865; One hundred and eighteenth Infantry, June 16, 1865; One hundred and twenty-second Infantry, June 16, 1865; One hundred and twenty-sixth Infantry, June 16, 1865; First Heavy Artillery, June 25, 1865.

Pennsylvania.—One hundred and fiftieth Infantry, June 10, 1865; Two hundred and first Infantry, June 15, 1865; Independent Battery G, June 7, 1865.

Tennessee.—Eighth Infantry, June 22, 1865.

West Virginia.—First Cavalry, June 17, 1865; Second Cavalry, June 17, 1865; Third Cavalry, June 17, 1865; Sixth Infantry, May 13, 1865; Company A, First Virginia (exempts) Infantry, May 8, 1865; Fourteenth Infantry, June 23, 1865; Seventeenth Infantry, June 23, 1865.

U. S. Volunteers.—First Infantry, June 2, 1865; Second Infantry, June 2, 1865; Third Infantry, June 2, 1865; Fourth Infantry, June 2, 1865; Fifth Infantry, June 2, 1865; Sixth Infantry, June 2, 1865.

MEMORANDA.—*June 23, 1865.*—The order of June 5 relative to dismounted volunteer cavalry (see Circular No. 26, current series) was revoked for the Middle Military Division and Major-General Sheridan's command, and instead it was ordered: That a limited number of cavalry regiments having the shortest time to serve be dismounted and mustered out by entire organizations (under General Orders, No. 94, current series, from this office), and the horses thus obtained taken to mount the dismounted cavalrymen of regiments having the longest terms to serve. The number of regiments to be dismounted to be determined by the number of dismounted men of the long-termed organizations.

A like revocation was also ordered for other armies and departments, provided the said order of June 5 had not been executed.

E. D. TOWNSEND,
Assistant Adjutant-General.

GENERAL ORDERS, No. 119. } WAR DEPT., ADJT. GENERAL'S OFFICE, *Washington, June 29, 1865.*

PENALTIES FOR NEGLECT OF DUTY AND DISOBEDIENCE OF ORDERS ON THE PART OF COMMISSIONED OFFICERS IN CHARGE OF TROOPS ABOUT TO BE DISCHARGED THE SERVICE.

In many instances delays have resulted in paying mustered-out troops in consequence of regimental and company officers allowing their men to disband, in violation of orders, prior to their commands being reported for payment and final discharge to the chief mustering officer or his assistant, after arrival at the designated State rendezvous. In other cases there has been delay from company and regimental officers neglecting to furnish full data relative to the enlisted men, thus rendering the muster-out rolls imperfect and necessitating corrections.

With the arrangements of the War Department, as now completed, there need be no delay, and consequently no hardship or inconvenience to the enlisted men, if full data for the rolls be furnished in the field, and if, after arrival in their respective States, as well as during transit thereto, commissioned officers look closely after the comfort and interests of their men and remain constantly with them, so as to enforce orders and control them.

It is therefore ordered that chief mustering officers and their assistants report by telegram the names of all neglectful officers, with the charges against them, to the Adjutant-General of the Army (withholding in the meantime their final payments and honorable discharges), with a view to their summary and dishonorable dismissal from the service with forfeiture of all pay. The report by telegraph will be sent promptly upon cases of neglect being brought to notice, and at the same time the facts in full will be reported by mail.

Governors of States are requested to report delinquencies coming to their notice to the chief mustering officer of the State and to the Adjutant-General of the Army, so that a prompt remedy may be applied.

By order of the Secretary of War:

E. D. TOWNSEND,
Assistant Adjutant-General.

OFFICE ENGINEER AND SUPT. MILITARY RAILROADS,
DEPARTMENTS OF THE TENNESSEE AND ARKANSAS,
Memphis, Tenn., June 30, 1865.

Bvt. Brig. Gen. D. C. MCCALLUM,
Director and General Manager
Military Railroads United States, Washington, D. C.:

GENERAL: I herewith submit a report of the operations of the military railroads under my charge for the year ending June 30, 1865:

At the close of the last fiscal year the Memphis and Charleston Railroad was in operation from Memphis to Grand Junction, fifty-two miles. On the 2d of August following we ran through to Holly Springs, on the Mississippi Central road, twenty-five miles south of Grand Junction. On August 6 we ran to Waterford and Tallahatchie River, 100 miles from Memphis. We moved Maj. Gen. A. J. Smith and command to that point. We continued to run to that point until the 18th day of August, when we abandoned the Mississippi Central road. On the 22d day of August an order was received to open it again. We did so in two days, but there being no guards upon the road the bridges were destroyed, and we did not run the road after the 23d of August. On the 29th day of August I received an order to evacuate the Memphis and Charleston road, and on the 6th day of September we ran to White's Station, ten miles from Memphis, to the headquarters of the cavalry division. The road was kept open that distance until the middle of October, when we abandoned the road altogether and did not open it again until the 20th of December. We repaired the road to Collierville, twenty-four miles, and kept it open until the 1st day of January, 1865, when we again evacuated. Between the opening and closing of the road at different times the bridge force was getting out timber, ties, &c., and framing bridges preparatory to another move.

I received another order on the 28th day of February to open the road again. We repaired it a distance of fifteen miles, took out forage and supplies for an expedition, and evacuated on the 4th of March. Remained to close up until the 20th of March, when an order was received to again open the road. Found the road badly damaged. We had it opened to Collierville, twenty-four miles, on the 24th of March; to La Fayette, thirty-one miles, on the 2d of April. We found heavy work to be done between La Fayette and Moscow. Heavy rains at this time, and water so high that no work could be done for several days. Road open to Moscow, thirty-nine miles, on the 13th day of May; to La Grange, forty-nine miles, on the 14th day of May; to Grand Junction, fifty-two, on the 20th day of May. Regular trains run to Grand Junction only until the 1st day of July, when road was opened to Pocahontas, seventy-five miles distance from Memphis, to which point we are now running regularly. The opening and closing of the line was so frequent that we could do hardly anything else. Each time the road was badly damaged, everything in the way of bridges, trestles, cattle guards, &c., being destroyed, together with several miles of track burned or thrown from the road bed. The uncertainty of what use we might have for the road, or when we would be called upon to repair it, caused me to keep considerable of a force ready at all times that could not all the time be advantageously employed. The machine-shops have been running throughout the year. Since the 1st of July, 1864, we have rebuilt five locomotives, three of which had hardly any machinery on them, nothing but the frames and boilers and part of the cylinders; no trucks or driving wheels, and nothing but the iron for the tanks. I sent to the Rogers Works, Norris & Sons, and to Lancaster, Pa., for the duplicate machinery. They are now first-class locomotives. We also gave a general overhauling and repairing to four others, which are now in fine order and running. We have thirteen altogether in running order, eleven of which are No. 1, one of the remaining two needing heavy repairs, the other light repairs. Three more in the shops being rebuilt, one of which will be out about the 1st of August; the other two, perhaps, one month later. We have built ten new box-cars and four hand-cars. A large majority of the cars on this road were in bad order and have all been repaired.

The Mobile and Ohio Railroad from Columbus, Ky., has not been in operation during the year until May 15, 1865, when the road was opened to Union City, twenty-six miles. A small force was retained during the year and one large trestle near Columbus repaired. Cars and engines were repaired. Some bridge timber and a few cross-ties were provided. I can get no data of the Memphis and Little Rock Railroad prior to the date that I took charge, May 1, 1865. Work has been done on this road at a great disadvantage owing to the want of proper facilities for keeping road and stock in repair. No machine-shops, engine-houses, or other buildings until recently. I have finished one engine-house with ten stalls and machine-shop attached, a carpenter's shop for repairs of cars, &c., and several other small buildings used for storing, offices, &c. They were partly finished when I took charge, and most of the material was on hand for finishing. Heavy work was necessary on road bed and track to make it safe. It is now in good order. Sickness prevails there to a large extent, rendering it imperative to keep a much larger number of employés than would otherwise be necessary in order to have well ones enough to operate the road. At times fully one-half of our force are unable for duty.

Very respectfully, yours, &c.,

A. F. GOODHUE,

Engineer and Superintendent Military Railroads,

Departments Tennessee and Arkansas.

WASHINGTON, *July 1, 1865.*

Hon. E. M. STANTON,
Secretary of War:

From present indications I think it perfectly safe to muster out of service the remaining veteran regiments of the Army of the Potomac and of the Army of the Tennessee. I would therefore respectfully recommend that orders be issued for such muster out.

U. S. GRANT,
Lieutenant-General.

GENERAL ORDERS, No. 121. } WAR DEPT., ADJT. GENERAL'S OFFICE, *Washington, July 1, 1865.*

The assignment of medical officers as medical directors, assistant medical directors, and acting medical inspectors of armies, army corps, and divisions is discontinued.

Medical directors will be assigned to the headquarters of military geographical departments only, and by the order of the Secretary of War.

Owing to the reduction of the Army, the act of Congress approved February 25, 1865, becomes inoperative, and no increase of rank, pay, or emoluments pertains to such assignment.

By order of the Secretary of War:

E. D. TOWNSEND,
Assistant Adjutant-General.

CIRCULAR No. 30. } WAR DEPT., ADJUTANT-GENERAL'S OFFICE, *Washington, July 1, 1865.*

ORDERS AND INSTRUCTIONS RELATIVE TO THE MUSTER OUT OF VOLUNTEER WHITE TROOPS.

Surplus troops—infantry, cavalry, and artillery—in all departments and armies, exclusive of the Department of the Gulf, Army of the Tennessee, Provisional Corps Army of the Potomac, First Army Corps, and command in Texas.

I. Surplus troops.

TELEGRAM AND CIRCULAR. } WAR DEPARTMENT, ADJUTANT-GENERAL'S OFFICE, *Washington, June 30, 1865.*

The Secretary of War directs that the strength of your command be immediately reduced, for all arms, to the minimum necessary to meet the requirements of the service, and all surplus troops mustered out.

The musters out will be by entire organizations, including all additions thereto by recruits and from other sources. In selecting the organizations for discharge, preference will be given to veteran regiments having the shortest time to serve.

The musters out and discharges, except for artillery, will be made under the regulations promulgated in General Orders, No. 94, current series, from this office. Troops of the artillery arm will be forwarded to the designated State rendezvous in the respective States (see Circular No. 19, current series, from this office), there to be mustered out under the direction of the chief mustering officer for the State.

Please forward to this office without delay a list of the regiments, batteries, and independent companies you may select for discharge under this order, giving therein, for each, the strength, present and absent, respectively.

So soon as the list is completed, inform me by telegram of the number present and absent for the respective States.

Acknowledge receipt of this.

THOMAS M. VINCENT,
Assistant Adjutant-General.

(To commanding generals of all armies and departments, except the Department of the Gulf, Army of the Tennessee, Provisional Corps Army of the Potomac, First Army Corps, and troops in Texas.)

NOTE.—For the Departments of the East, Pennsylvania, Northwest, New Mexico, Pacific, and Northern Department, the foregoing stands modified so as to send all the organizations selected for discharge to their respective States, there to be mustered out under the direction of the chief mustering officer for the State.

II. Regiments of cavalry and infantry (whose services are no longer needed) ordered mustered out of service under special instructions of dates set opposite the organizations, respectively.

Minnesota.—Eighth Infantry, June 30, 1865.

New Hampshire.—First Cavalry, July 1, 1865.

New York.—First Provisional Cavalry, July 1, 1865; Ninth Cavalry, July 1, 1865.

Pennsylvania.—Two hundred and fifteenth Infantry, June 30, 1865; First Provisional Cavalry, July 1, 1865.

E. D. TOWNSEND,
Assistant Adjutant-General.

OFFICE CHIEF ENGINEER AND GENERAL SUPT.
MILITARY RAILROADS OF VIRGINIA,
Alexandria, Va., July 1, 1865.

Brig. Gen. D. C. MCCALLUM,
Director and General Manager
Military Railroads United States, Washington, D. C.:

GENERAL: I have the honor to submit a report of operations in the U. S. Military Railroad service, Department of Virginia, from July 1, 1864, to June 30, 1865. My superintendency of this department did not commence until November 11, but to render this a complete record of main events, I commence with the fiscal year, July 1, 1864. During the year the following roads have been operated in this department: Washington and Alexandria; Orange and Alexandria and Manassas Gap; Alexandria, Loudoun, and Hampshire; City Point and Army Line and South Side; Petersburg and Richmond and Clover Hill Branch; Norfolk and Petersburg; Seaboard and Roanoke; Richmond and Danville; Winchester and Potomac. Accompanying this report you will find sundry tabular statements, as follows:

Table No. 1 gives a statement of the number of railroads with their length and the number of miles in use from July 1 to June 30.

Table No. 2 shows number of persons employed each month during the year (classified).

Table No. 3 shows distribution of labor and material during the year.

Table No. 4 is a list of locomotive engines with cost of maintenance and repairs; also shows the number of miles run, and cost per hundred miles of each engine.

Table No. 5 shows the number of cars hauled, miles run, and tonnage.

Table No. 6 shows number of passengers carried.

Table No. 7 shows receipts for passage and freight.

Table No. 8 shows amount of material received and used.

Table No. 9 gives estimated value of property on military railroads of Virginia June 30, 1865.

Table No. 10 shows gradients, alignments, elevations, &c.

Table No. 11 shows number of miles of track laid during the year.

Table No. 12 shows number of feet of trestle-work built during the year.

I will proceed to give a detailed account of my operations on each road separately, and propose to commence with the

WASHINGTON AND ALEXANDRIA RAILROAD.

The track on this important connection is in the best possible condition, it having been ballasted with gravel its entire length. We experienced great difficulty in keeping the old Long Bridge secure for the passage of trains. August 22 the draw south end of bridge was nearly destroyed by a tug with schooner in tow running into it. The damage was immediately repaired, and navigation was interrupted for only a few days. February 18 engine Minot, drawing wood train to Washington, broke through south span of bridge, the entire span being wrecked. The length of time necessary to repair the old bridge, and the importance of having railroad communication between Washington and Alexandria kept open (in accordance with your order February 19), the new Long Bridge was taken possession of and track laid on it. We commenced running regular trains over it February 21. Since that date we have experienced no difficulty in operating the road. An average of three passenger trains each way have been run over this road, in addition to the large number of freight trains run for the movement of troops, hauling wood for Quartermaster's Department, &c. (Please find accompanying this report a detailed statement of operations on this road, giving number of trains, stores carried, &c.)

ORANGE AND ALEXANDRIA AND MANASSAS GAP RAILROADS.

From June 30 to September 27 the Orange and Alexandria Railroad was very little used. Occasionally trains would be run to Edsall and Springfield Stations for the purpose of procuring fuel and supplying detachments of troops stationed at points along the line. An order was received from you July 17 for the construction at car shops in Alexandria of 100 flat-cars (5-feet gauge) for the use of military railroads in the Division of the Mississippi; work was immediately commenced on them, under the supervision of Mr. B. P. Lamason, master car-builder, and pushed forward with all vigor. Some delay occurred in procuring car wheels, axles, and other iron-work, but by the 1st of November fifty-six cars had been built. The whole number, 100, not being required for the military railroads in the Division of the Mississippi, the remaining forty-four were completed for use of the Virginia department. In compliance with an order received from you July 10, a force of conductors, brakemen, engineers, and firemen were sent from Alexandria for temporary service on the Philadelphia and Reading Railroad. This arrangement was made necessary by the employés of that road striking for higher wages, thereby stopping the running of the trains and delaying the shipment of coal for Government use. The regular employés soon came to terms and commenced work, and our whole party returned to this place July 21. Orders were received from you September 28 to repair and put in running order the road from Alexandria to Rappahannock River, a distance of fifty miles. A construction force was immediately dispatched supplied with all necessary material. All the bridges on the road were destroyed, with the exception of those across Cedar and Kettle Runs, which were badly damaged. By the evening of October 2 the track was repaired; bridges, water stations, &c., rebuilt, and the road in complete running order to Rappahannock River. At 8 p. m. October 2 a telegram was received from Major-General Halleck ordering us to cease work on Orange and Alexandria Railroad south of Manassas and repair railroad to Piedmont and Front Royal, on the Manassas Gap Railroad. In obedience, all men and material at Rappahannock were loaded and sent to Manassas Junction. The repairs were commenced from that point October 3. The bridges were all destroyed; the track as far as Piedmont had not been disturbed to any great extent, but the cross-ties were badly decayed and all needed replacing. Beyond Piedmont the bridges were all destroyed, track torn up, and iron removed. Working parties and troops guarding them were very much annoyed by the operations of guerrillas; trains were fired into, and, in several instances, thrown from the track. On the 10th of October a train drawn by two engines was thrown from the track near White Plains by guerrillas. They removed a rail, thereby precipitating the train down a steep embankment, and causing the death of Mr. M. J. McCrickett, superintendent; E. J. Bolt and G. W. Fuller, conductors; Charles Brooks and Richard Cowhig, firemen. This sad accident created a deep gloom in the department. Mr. McCrickett was a young man of fine promise; his untiring energy and the skillful and urbane manner in which he discharged his duties had won for him the esteem and love of all who knew him. Messrs. Bolt, Fuller, Brooks, and Cowhig were valuable and trustworthy men. The record left by them shows a long and faithful service. Mr. P. McCallum, formerly in charge of military railroads at Norfolk, was appointed October 12 superintendent of military railroads diverging from Alexandria, the position made vacant by the death of Mr. McCrickett. The road was repaired October 11 to Piedmont, distant thirty-four miles from Manassas Junction, and sixty-one from Alexandria. The first regular train ran through October 12. From that date the construction force was kept busily engaged putting in sidings, turn-tables, erecting water stations, &c., and rebuilding road beyond Piedmont, with the intention of opening it to Front Royal, seventeen miles farther. An order was received October 26 to abandon the road and take up the iron from Piedmont to Manassas Junction. This was completed November 10. Most of this iron was sent direct to Winchester and Potomac Railroad, via Alexandria, and Baltimore and Ohio Railroad, without change of cars, and was used by a large construction force then at work on that line relaying it.

From November 10 until June 27 the Orange and Alexandria Railroad was operated only to Fairfax Station, sixteen and a half miles from Alexandria. A turn-table was put in at that station and platforms built to facilitate the proper working of the road. One regular train was run each way per day, and an average of two wood trains daily for use of Quartermaster's Department. May 20, built large platform at Edsall Station and commenced running supplies to that point for use of General Sherman's army. From this date considerable business was done moving troops from along the line to Washington en route home. June 27, in accordance with your order, the Orange and Alexandria Railroad was turned over to Messrs. Quigley and Jamieson, agents of Board of Public Works of Virginia.

A large force of men had to be employed in the different departments doing work for quartermasters. Sixty-eight vessels were repaired for the post quartermaster at Alexandria during the year. Sidings and wharves were built at Point Lookout and Giesborough Point. Wharves built and repaired at Alexandria and Sixth street, Washington, and sidings laid at Bladensburg. In all cases we furnished men, pile-drivers, and material. A force of men had to be employed constantly at our railroad wharf, shipping and receiving material. (Accompanying this report please find detailed report of our railroad wharf operations.) Since the consolidation of our storehouses at Alexandria the business in this branch has been attended to in a prompt and efficient manner, under the directions of Mr. A. Roeloss, store-keeper. Monthly reports have been furnished you showing amount of material received and issued. Our printing office has done good service, and without it we would have experienced serious delay in many instances.

ALEXANDRIA, LOUDOUN AND HAMPSHIRE RAILROAD.

This road is in complete running order to Vienna Station, a distance of fifteen miles from Alexandria. The bridges are all substantial and durable and have been kept in good repair. Nothing toward construction has been done on this road with exception of building a turn-table at Vienna and laying a side track at Arlington Mills Station, five miles from Alexandria. During July, August, and September but few trains were run beyond Falls Church Station, distant ten miles from Alexandria. During October a force of troops were advanced to Vienna, and that post held up to the time of disbanding the armies. A regular train has been run daily each way for the purpose of carrying mails, supplies, &c., for troops stationed at that point along the line of road and Convalescent Camp three and a half miles from Alexandria. A large number of wood trains were run to transport the wood cut by Quartermaster's Department. A large portion of this was sent direct to Washington over the Alexandria and Washington Railroad. A large quantity of supplies were sent to Arlington Mills and Convalescent Camp during May and June for the Army of the Potomac, then camped near these stations, previous to being mustered out of service. This road has been operated in connection with Alexandria and Washington and Orange and Alexandria Railroads, and all accounts, &c., up to June 30 are included in Alexandria railroad. By your order the road was turned over to Lewis McKenzie, esq., agent of Board of Public Works of Virginia, August 8.

CITY POINT AND ARMY LINE.

After taking up the track of the Richmond and York River Railroad, and removing all the material of value (June 13, 1864), Mr. C. L. McAlpine, engineer of construction and repairs, was ordered to proceed to City Point with part of the Construction Corps and adequate material, in anticipation of an order to build the wharves at that place and reopen the City Point and Petersburg Railroad. The expedition was delayed nearly four days on account of a pontoon bridge stretched across the James River, about twenty-five miles below City Point, upon which the Army of the Potomac was crossing to the south bank of the river. Immediately on the arrival of the construction force at City Point (June 18, 1864) orders were received to rebuild the City Point and Petersburg Railroad; also to construct wharves and buildings for the use of the army in unloading and receiving supplies. An examination was made of the road, and it was ascertained that the bridges were gone, track taken up, and the iron removed for a distance of four miles. From there on to within two miles and a half from Petersburg the track had not been disturbed, but the ties were very much decayed and the gauge needed changing from five feet to four feet eight and one-half inches. By the 5th of July the bridges were all rebuilt, track repaired, and the road was in complete running order for a distance of seven miles from City Point. By the time the repairs were completed a full equipment of engines and rolling-stock had been received, and regular trains commenced running July 7, 1864. A large force was kept constantly employed in building wharves, warehouses, and all other improvements asked for by Quartermaster's Department.

Orders were received July 22 to make a preliminary survey of a branch line of railroad from a point near Pitkin Station (distant five miles and a half from City Point) to the headquarters of the Fifth Army Corps, on the Weldon railroad at Yellow House. The survey was made (without instruments) and everything got in readiness for the proposed extension. An explosion occurred on the 9th of August, caused by the accidental ignition of ammunition stored in an ordnance boat lying at the wharf at City Point. The force of the explosion completely demolished some 400 feet of warehouse just completed and a large portion of the wharves in the vicinity; also a large quantity of supplies accumulated for shipment to the front. The damage to railroad property was very slight, and only a few of our men were injured. July 26 a force of trackmen equipped with tools were sent to Deep Bottom to report to General Sheridan, for the supposed purpose of destroying the track of the railroad connecting Petersburg with Richmond. They returned July 30 without effecting anything of importance. Again, August 13 another party in charge of John Morgan, assistant engineer, was ordered to report to General Hancock for the purpose of destroying the track on the Weldon railroad. Nine miles and a quarter of track were destroyed, and the iron made useless by heating and then bending the rails.

Orders were received August 30 to commence building Army Line from Pitkin Station to Yellow Tavern, on the Weldon railroad. Work was commenced September 1, and by the 10th of September the new line was completed a distance of nine miles from Pitkin Station and fourteen miles and a half from City Point. The grading on the new line was comparatively light, but some very extensive trestle-works were constructed. For quite a distance the rebel batteries had full range of the track, and trains passing and our Construction Corps were much annoyed by the constant fire kept up on them. This difficulty, however, was obviated by the construction of a line of earth-works about half a mile in length, completely protecting the road.

Extensive tracks for the accommodation of the hospitals and bakeries were built; also very large warehouses for the storage of quartermaster, commissary, and ordnance stores. Substantial and roomy wharves were built for a distance of nearly one mile at City Point;

also wharves at Bermuda Hundred and Light-House Point. An extension wharf was built on the Appomattox River for the accommodation of the hospitals. Water tanks and steam pumping engines were also furnished to keep up an adequate supply of water. The construction of hospital buildings on a very large scale for the several army corps was ordered October 8. After most of the lumber and other material had arrived at City Point the plans were changed. They concluded to build them more temporary than was at first proposed. One hundred and ten of these buildings were constructed during the fall and winter. While this work for the accommodation of the army was being done the various improvements to facilitate the operations of the road were not neglected. The road bed was put in first-rate order, and the track would compare favorably with any first-class road. During the month of October the yard at City Point was enlarged, switches and sidings were put in, turn-tables were constructed at all necessary points, a substantial and convenient engine-house was built capable of accommodating nine locomotive engines; also shops with all the requisite machinery for the repairs of engines and cars. At all the stations on the line sidings were laid and station-houses built. An average of nine trains, exclusive of specials, were run each way daily, amply supplying the wants of the army. The amount of rolling-stock for the working of the road was increased from time to time, as the demands for transportation became more heavy. Orders were received October 22 to proceed with the extension of the City Point and Army Line from General Warren's headquarters at the Yellow House to the Peebles house, a distance of two miles and a quarter.

The work on this extension (now called the Patrick Branch) did not commence until November 2 on account of an engagement that took place near where the proposed line was to run. It was completed with all the necessary sidings November 9. The grading was not very heavy on account of our conforming to the surface of the ground. The grades are heavy (a maximum of 228 feet). Eight hundred and fifty feet of trestle-work, averaging twenty feet in height, was built. During its construction the weather was very unfavorable, it raining nearly all the time, making it almost impossible to do any work on track.

From November 10 to December 19 the construction force were busily engaged in constructing hospital buildings, repairing wharves, laying additional side tracks, and building quarters for the Quartermaster's Department and railroad employés. A large clothing warehouse and extensive commissary buildings were then built; also distribution barracks for the accommodation of the troops passing through City Point. The coal wharf at City Point and a large wharf at Bermuda Hundred were also completed. Trains continued to run on good time without accidents, business constantly increasing. Some days fifteen trains were run over the road each way. Work was commenced December 21 on a branch line of road running from Hancock Station, on the main Army Line, to Fort Blaisdell, on the Jerusalem plank road. It was completed December 29, but trains did not run over it for some days after on account of the very wet weather, which made it impossible to get the track in good order. January 2 orders were received to extend this branch line still farther, to the headquarters of General Crawford, who commanded one division of the Fifth Army Corps, a distance of two miles and a quarter from Hancock Station. Work was immediately commenced, but owing to the inclement weather progress was not very rapid.

The track was laid, 1,040 feet of trestle-work 18 feet high was built, and the line opened by January 20. Station-houses, platforms, and water-stations were built.

This line is called the Gregg Branch of the City Point and Army Line. During January a plank road, extending the whole length of the wharves at City Point, was built. Orders were received from Lieutenant-General Grant January 25 to send a construction force (with materials) to Beaufort, N. C., to repair railroad running inland as far as Winton. In obedience, I dispatched Mr. C. L. McAlpine, principal assistant engineer, in charge of a force of carpenters and trackmen, with tools, camp equipage, and material, from City Point for that place, January 26, on steamers Detroit, Rebecca Barton, and Charles Barton. The whole force reached New Berne without any serious detention January 30. They immediately went to work relaying track, getting out cross-ties, and rebuilding bridges. By February 2 the track was repaired to Batchelder's Creek bridge, and bridge rebuilt. February 5 Col. W. W. Wright, chief engineer, with his construction force, arrived at Morehead City. Our party kept at work till February 8, when they were relieved by Colonel Wright's force and embarked for City Point the same day. The whole force arrived at City Point February 12, in time to take part in the extension of the Army Line. From January 25 to February 12 the construction force remaining at City Point were engaged in constructing quarters, offices, &c., for the Quartermaster's Department, repairing and extending wharves, and building a large wharf at Deep Bottom, on the James River, and keeping the track of the City Point and Army Line and branches in good repair. Our forces made an advance to the left of Petersburg February 5, and after three days' fighting succeeded in gaining and holding a position on the Vaughan road, a distance of about five miles in advance of their former line.

An order was received February 8 to extend the Army Line. The proposed extension was located the 12th. The line, leaving Warren Station, ran down the old bed of the Weldon railroad about two miles, then, diverging to the right, across the most favorable ground to the Cummings house, on the Vaughan road, a distance of five miles from Warren Station. Work was commenced February 13 and completed to the Cummings house (Humphreys Station) on the 24th. We also furnished all the necessary sidings, buildings, platforms, water stations, and Y for the proper working of the road. During the progress of this work the weather was very unfavorable, raining almost without intermission, making the ground so soft that it was almost impossible to do any work or get the teams over it with material. Two thousand seven hundred and eighty-one feet of trestle-work was built on this extension, averaging twenty-five feet high. Most of the timber was cut in the woods and hauled to the work with teams detailed for that purpose. A number of hospital cars were fitted up for the purpose of moving the sick and wounded from the front and along the line to City Point. These were kept in almost constant use. Trains were running regularly and amply supplying all the wants of the army. In addition to the regular freight business two passenger trains were run each way daily for the accommodation of mails, officers, and others, to and from the front. At the time of building the Army Line many of the officers of the Army of the Potomac, together with the regular Engineer Corps, denounced this location, declaring that it would be impossible for an engine alone to ascend the heavy grades; and as for furnishing the necessary supplies for the army over it, they considered it altogether out of the question. It was discovered, however, that engines hauled an average of fifteen loaded cars per train, and in many cases twenty-three loaded cars, with one of our ordinary engines, thus demonstrating the practicability of supplying a large army over a temporary road constructed in this manner. The total length of track laid on Army Line, branches, and sidings was 21 miles 3,955 feet, and total length of trestle work, 1 mile 1,393 feet, an average of twenty-one feet high.

Not much of note in railroad affairs occurred from February 28 to April 3. The construction department was kept busy making additional improvements wherever needed, and building a wharf at City Point in the gap between the quartermaster's and railroad wharves. I also increased our force and made heavy additions to our rolling-stock, iron, timber, and other material in anticipation of a movement of our army. April 3, immediately after the successful advance of our forces, we abandoned the Army Line and commenced relaying the track taken up on the South Side Railroad to Petersburg, our troops having taken possession of that place on the morning of the 3d. The road was opened and in running order to Petersburg April 4. A large force was set to work changing the gauge of side-tracks and switches in yard at Petersburg from five feet to four feet eight and a half inches, to suit our rolling-stock. We also commenced changing the gauge on main line of South Side Railroad and completed it to Burkeville, sixty-two miles from City Point, April 11, and trains commenced running through with supplies to that point. The road was found to be in wretched condition. The ties were decayed and worthless, and most of the iron nearly worn out. For two or three days it was with the greatest difficulty that trains could be got over the road; but very soon the condition of it was improved by placing a large construction force at work renewing ties, relaying and repairing the track. Trains commenced to run regularly and on time without any accident of a serious nature, and easily filling all requisitions for transportation. We also opened the Petersburg and Richmond Railroad, and regular trains commenced running from City Point to Manchester (opposite Richmond), via Petersburg, April 7. On the 24th of April orders were received through General Ingalls to make the necessary repairs on the Richmond and Danville Railroad and open communication with Danville, and also to advance on the South Side Railroad and rebuild the High Bridge near Farmville, seventy-six miles from City Point. I sent a large force with material to this bridge, but before the work was fairly under way the order was countermanded. April 30 an order was received from you to suspend all work on repairs or rebuilding railroads in Virginia, and only finish such improvements as had been commenced and were nearly completed. In compliance, immediate steps were taken to reduce the expenses in the different departments. As soon as the men could be spared the greater part of the Construction Corps and transportation departments were sent to Alexandria and discharged.

By the 1st of June all the force that possibly could be spared had been discharged, and only a sufficient number retained to insure the successful operation of the roads. Twenty-four new locomotive engines and about 275 new box-cars (all 5-feet gauge) arrived at City Point, loaded on a fleet of about ninety vessels. By your directions this stock was sent to Manchester (opposite Richmond) and there unloaded. A wharf had to be built, long sidings laid, and connections made with the Richmond and Danville road for the purpose of storage.

Possession was taken of the machine-shops at Manchester belonging to Richmond and Danville road, and a force engaged to put the engines and cars in proper condition before they were sold. Most of the stock had been on board vessels for nearly three months, exposed to all kinds of weather, and was in bad condition when received.

During the month of June the Army Line Railroad was taken up and material brought to City Point. All property not in use was collected from the lines of the several roads and brought to City Point for shipment. Regular trains were run on the South Side and Richmond and Petersburg roads, connecting with trains on Richmond and Danville road, amply supplying all the troops along the lines. A large number of discharged troops were brought to City Point, and transportation furnished a large number of rebel troops returning to their homes.

July 3 the Petersburg and Richmond Railroad was turned over to the company, and the Richmond and Danville road was turned over July 4. All material and rolling-stock that could be spared had in the meantime been shipped to Alexandria. We continued running the South Side Railroad from City Point to Burkeville, transporting supplies and large numbers of troops en route north from North Carolina, until July 24. At this date the road was turned over to the company, which closed up our operations of military railroads at City Point. The whole force (with the exception of some sixteen men left to take charge of property, &c.) were brought to Alexandria and discharged. All the property has been removed from City Point, with the exception of some material which will remain there until sold. Mr. C. L. McAlpine, principal assistant engineer, in charge of construction department, and G. M. Huntington, superintendent, in charge of transportation department on this line, were persevering in the discharge of their varied and arduous duties. May 15 Mr. McAlpine having resigned his position, Mr. T. D. Hays was then appointed "in charge" of all our railroad operations at City Point; and to him I am indebted for valuable assistance rendered.

PETERSBURG AND RICHMOND RAILROAD AND CLOVER HILL BRANCH.

When Petersburg and Richmond were abandoned by the enemy, April 3, and during the time we were changing the gauge and making an advance on South Side Railroad, orders were received to open communication with Richmond. A trestle bridge 400 feet long and 12 feet high had to be built, connecting with bridge over the Appomattox River at Petersburg. The road was opened April 7. Two regular passenger trains were run each way daily from City Point to Manchester (opposite Richmond), by way of Petersburg. No freight business of any note was done until the last of April, when orders were received to establish a depot at Manchester in order to provide the Army of the Potomac and General Sherman's army with supplies previous to their march to Alexandria and Washington. Sidings and platforms were built and large quantities of supplies sent forward from City Point. All orders on us for transportation were filled promptly. In connection with this road we operated the Clover Hill Branch, a coal road diverging from the main line nine miles from Petersburg, and running up to coal mines, a distance of eighteen miles. This became necessary on account of the scarcity of coal in Richmond and Petersburg. One train daily was run, carrying all the coal that was loaded in cars at the mines. After the armies moved from Manchester but little business was done on these roads. Application having been made by Governor Peirpoint to have the road transferred to the company, by your order it was turned over July 3, and all material, &c., removed to City Point.

RICHMOND AND DANVILLE RAILROAD.

On the evacuation of Richmond, and during the time our army was advancing, it became necessary to rebuild a number of the railroads that had been used by the enemy during the war. By orders received from you April 20 I made an examination of this road. It was found to be in good order, with the exception of the bridges over Appomattox and Staunton Rivers, and about 2,000 feet of track were destroyed. The officers of the Richmond and Danville Railroad ran all their rolling-stock then in running order south of the bridges, and subsequently concentrated it at Clover Station, as a point midway between our two grand armies, and it was then captured by the Sixth Army Corps on its advance to Danville. April 24, I received orders, through General Ingalls, to make the necessary repairs and open communication with Danville; work was commenced on Staunton River bridge April 26, and it was completed May 2. The bridge is 600 feet long and 40 feet high. All the timber used in constructing it was cut in the surrounding woods, and hauled to the bridge by teams detailed for that purpose. During the progress of the work trains were run between the river and Danville for transportation of supplies. Twenty cars of subsistence stores received from wagon trains were taken to Danville, and the First Brigade, First Division, Sixth Army Corps, brought from Danville to the bridge to await the completion for further transportation. On completion of the bridge, May 2, four trains of troops were sent to Burkeville. Transportation of balance of First Division commenced at once and was completed May 5; the entire division of 8,000 men employing 253 cars, in twenty-one trains. May 6 commenced transportation of captured ordnance, ordnance stores, arsenal machinery, &c., from Danville to Burkeville; thence by way of South Side Railroad to City Point, amounting in all to 360 car-loads, in thirty trains; finished May 15. May 10 commenced moving balance of Sixth Army Corps, numbering about 18,000 men, with usual baggage, officers' horses, &c., from Danville to Manchester, 140 miles. This work employed forty-five trains, or 468 cars, and was finished May 22. In addition to this business was transportation of supplies for the Sixth Army Corps while at Danville. Crowds of negroes and paroled prisoners going north and south. After passage of Sixth Corps to June 15 but little business was done, consisting principally of transportation of mails, supplies, &c., for posts at Danville, Keysville, and Amelia Court-House; occasional regiments for points on line, some from Lynchburg by way of Burkeville Junction to Richmond. June 15 commenced transportation of large numbers of paroled prisoners to Danville, which continued until surrendering the road to Board of Public Works of Virginia, at the rate of 864 per day, and total of 15,600. June 22 commenced transportation of troops arriving at Danville from North Carolina for the north, by way of Burkeville and City Point; this continued until surrender of the road July 4, amounting to 7,250 soldiers, 115 horses, and 15 cars baggage. The cars on this road were found in very bad condition and many set aside. The locomotives were eighteen in number, belonging as follows: To Richmond and Danville road, ten; East Tennessee and Virginia road, five; Nashville and Chattanooga road, two; and Norfolk and Petersburg road, one. We also recaptured U. S. Military Railroad engine Colonel McCallum; this one had been captured from us at Bristoe Station, on Orange and Alexandria road, in 1862, during General Pope's retreat, taken south to Danville road, changed to 5-feet gauge, and is now called Pocahontas. All these were in bad order, but by hard labor kept up and caused to do good service. Mr. O. H. Dorrance, formerly of the Winchester and Potomac line, was superintendent of this road, and conducted affairs with his usual ability. In consequence of the uncertainty of our operations I did not enter upon a thorough organization. The old operatives of this road were retained, considerable reduction from U. S. Military Railroad rates made in their pay, as satisfactory to them, a point of economy, and that men just from rebellion did not deserve to be rated with old military railroad employés and loyal men. As City Point was considered the base of all supplies this is called one of the connecting roads, and the accounts are included in the tabular statements opposite City Point and connecting roads.

NORFOLK AND PETERSBURG RAILROAD.

During the year the business of this road has been only nominal. A large amount of wood has been hauled in from the line of the road to Norfolk for use of the quartermaster at the post. A flag-of-truce train was run to Suffolk about once in two weeks, or whenever called upon. The track is in good condition to Suffolk, a distance of twenty-three miles; it is laid with iron, sixty-four pounds to yard, and is decidedly the best road in Virginia. October 12 Mr. H. F. Woodward was appointed assistant superintendent and engineer of the Norfolk and Petersburg and Seaboard and Roanoke Railroads, vice Mr. P. McCallum, appointed to the superintendency of military railroads diverging from Alexandria. April 1 Mr. Phin. B. Tompkins was appointed superintendent in charge, and Mr. Woodward transferred to City Point. This road was operated in connection with the Seaboard and Roanoke road and rolling-stock used on either road as occasion demanded, a connection having previously been made at Suffolk between the two roads. Possession of this road was given to the company June 30 and ended our operations at Norfolk and Portsmouth, with the exception of a small force left in charge of material.

SEABOARD AND ROANOKE RAILROAD.

This road has been in use to Suffolk, distance eighteen miles from Portsmouth. One daily train, exclusive of specials, has been run to that point. Only a small number of troops were stationed on line of this road and at Suffolk, consequently the demands for transportation have not been very pressing. A large number of cross-ties have been cut along the line of road and hauled to Portsmouth; from there they have been shipped to the several points where military railroads have been opened and extended. Fifteen thousand nine hundred and ninety-two ties were sent to North Carolina for use of roads running inland from Beaufort. By your directions, April 6, the new 5-feet-gauge rolling-stock was ordered to Norfolk, with the intention of landing it at that point, the object being to open communication with Weldon and use this stock on the road. The order was afterward countermanded by you, on account of the cessation of hostilities, and all the rolling-stock ordered to Manchester (opposite Richmond), there to be stored until sold. We abandoned this road June 30 and turned it over to the company, leaving a small force to take charge of Government property until sold or removed to Alexandria.

WINCHESTER AND POTOMAC RAILROAD.

In obedience to an order received from you August 12 to repair and put in working order this road from Harper's Ferry to Halltown (a distance of six miles), a construction force with material was sent to Harper's Ferry. Repairs were commenced August 14, and regular trains commenced running through to Halltown August 19. From that date the road was not used to any great extent, and only a limited amount of freight was transported until October 29, at which date you ordered the extension of the road to Winchester. November 2 a detachment of our Construction Corps commenced rebuilding the road from Halltown. Track was completed to Charlestown (ten miles from Harper's Ferry) on the 5th; Summit Point (eighteen miles from Harper's Ferry) on the 14th, and Stephenson's (twenty-eight miles from Harper's Ferry) on the 24th. I received orders from General Sheridan to make this the terminus of the road, establish depot grounds, lay the necessary sidings, and prepare for a heavy business. Our rolling-stock consisted of thirteen engines and about seventy-five cars, all in good condition. Our railroad employés numbered about 600 men. December 12 Mr. O. H. Dorrance was appointed superintendent of this line, relieving Mr. Beggs, who was ordered to report to Alexandria. The old strap rail was removed from line of road and sent to Alexandria, engine-house and machine-shops built at Harper's Ferry, and a number of extensive platforms built at Harper's Ferry and Stephenson's for the shipping of quartermaster's and commissary stores. I also frequently employed a portion of our construction force unloading cars at Stephenson's. This was done on account of the large amount of freight kept in the cars by quartermasters, they not having sufficient force to unload it. During the months of January, February, March, and April business continued to be done promptly and without any serious accident. April 29 I ordered Mr. Dorrance, superintendent, to City Point, for the purpose of taking charge of the Richmond and Danville Railroad, leaving Mr. D. T. Shaw, dispatcher, in charge of Winchester and Potomac line.

In May business began to slack off. On the 21st the Opequon bridge, one of the largest on the road, was swept off by a freshet, interfering with operations for a few days. During the month of June I reduced the rolling-stock to five engines and about sixty cars, and the force employed on the road to about 175 men, thus carrying out your previous order. A total of 3,294 feet of trestle-work, an average of 12½ feet high, was built on main track and sidings on this road. This ends the report of operations up to this date. I might add, however, that all railroad material used in construction of this road had to be sent from Alexandria to Harper's Ferry over the Baltimore and Ohio road. Most of the railroad iron was shipped direct from the Manassas Gap Railroad, where a large force was engaged in removing the track from Piedmont to Manassas Junction; the same cars being used in distributing the iron on Winchester road as were in loading it not forty-eight hours previous on Manassas Gap road. It is a fact worthy of note that during a business extending but little over seven months, in which time 2,238 trains passed over the road, carrying nearly 200,000 persons, but one accident of any consequence occurred and but one man was killed. The advantages resulting from the completion of this line were observable, not only in furnishing supplies to the Army of the Shenandoah, but in rapidity with which troops could be moved. At the time of moving the Sixth Army Corps, the First Division arrived at City Point by way of Washington in forty-four hours after leaving Stephenson's, and the Second Division in fifty-two hours, saving at least thirty hours by having this short line open. Please see tabular statements for further information. This sums up the report of my operations in the Department of Virginia during the fiscal year ending June 30, 1865.

I desire to express my thanks to superintendents, engineers, agents, and other employés on the different lines for the manner in which they have discharged their varied and arduous duties. Always diligent and faithful, they have never been found wanting when called on. It is with pleasure I acknowledge the services of Mr. J. M. Pitkin, principal assistant, in charge of all business appertaining to my duties; his untiring energy and faithful services cannot be too highly appreciated.

Respectfully submitted.

J. J. MOORE,

Chief Engr. and Genl. Supt. Military Railroads of Virginia.

[Table No. 1.]

Schedule of military railroads operated in the Department of Virginia during fiscal year.

Road.	From—	To—	Length.	Operated during the year.	In use June 30, 1865.
				Miles.	*Miles.*
Washington and Alexandria	Washington	Alexandria	7½	7½	7½
Orange and Alexandria	Alexandria	Gordonsville	88	50	15
Alexandria, Loudoun and Hampshire.	....do	Leesburg	41	15	15
Manassas Gap Railroad	Manassas	Strasburg	62	34	......
Winchester and Potomac	Harper's Ferry	Stephenson's	28	28	28
Norfolk and Petersburg	Norfolk	Petersburg	80	23	23
Seaboard and Roanoke	Portsmouth	Weldon	80	17	17
City Point and Army	City Point	Humphreys	18½	18½	18½
South Side	....do	Lynchburg	131	62	62
Richmond and Petersburg	Manchester	Petersburg	22	22	22
Richmond and Danville	....do	Danville	140	140	140
Total			698	417	348
Richmond and Petersburg (Clover Hill Branch.)			18	18	18

[Table No. 2.]

U. S. MILITARY RAILROADS.

Number of persons employed each month during fiscal year ending June 30, 1865.

Month.	Chief engineer and general superintendent.	Superintendents.	Engineers.	Fuel agents.	Clerks.	Printers.	Agents, &c.	Draughtsmen.	Supervisors.	Store-keepers.	Timber inspectors.	Conductors.	Brakemen.	Enginemen.	Firemen.	Switchmen.	Wipers.
July	1	3	3	1	22	1	15	1	4	1	1	60	121	61	74	10	40
August	1	3	3	1	17	1	9	1	10	2	1	29	63	51	30	5	29
September	1	4	3	1	17	1	11	1	11	2	1	33	78	47	40	4	37
October	1	4	4	1	17	1	12	2	10	2	1	39	125	70	64	6	60
November	1	4	3	1	16	1	16	2	14	2	2	55	149	83	78	6	50
December	1	4	3	1	19	1	19	1	10	2	2	56	149	86	79	12	55
January	1	4	3	1	20	1	19	1	11	2	2	60	166	77	78	16	62
February	1	4	3	1	20	2	18	1	11	2	2	53	151	75	66	16	62
March	1	6	4	1	20	2	21	2	13	2	2	55	151	74	81	22	64
April	1	5	4	1	23	2	22	2	15	1	2	75	209	89	89	31	66
May	1	4	4	....	22	2	22	1	14	1	2	43	129	48	56	17	45
June	1	4	3	....	19	1	24	1	13	1	2	39	113	52	49	16	46
Total	12	49	40	10	232	16	208	16	136	20	20	597	1,604	813	784	161	616

Month.	Commissaries.	Carpenters.	Car department.	Machinists.	Blacksmiths.	Stationary engineers.	Pattern makers.	Copper and tin smiths.	Messengers.	Teamsters.	Pile drivers.	Painters.	Laborers.	Watchmen.	Photograph department.	Boiler makers.	Total.
July	76	569	92	101	69	11	5	18	12	3	9	13	1,069	36	....	10	2,512
August	64	572	74	83	48	13	5	11	8	3	9	12	914	25	....	6	2.103
September	82	728	77	82	54	14	5	12	15	3	21	10	932	30	....	12	2,369
October	92	735	70	99	58	16	5	13	16	3	20	10	884	27	1	11	2,479
November	89	978	99	76	58	41	5	16	11	3	22	9	1,480	28	....	14	3,412
December	103	986	98	95	66	15	5	16	13	3	19	9	1,260	37	3	13	3,241
January	117	761	100	102	73	17	5	16	15	3	19	8	1,345	33	3	11	3,152
February	117	813	113	101	72	20	5	18	16	4	11	10	1,490	33	3	13	3,327
March	128	972	138	116	80	22	5	18	17	3	12	7	1,841	33	2	11	3,926
April	145	990	135	136	81	22	5	20	18	3	11	7	2,278	40	2	12	4,542
May	109	913	71	79	32	12	2	9	23	1	10	7	1,954	25	4	12	3,674
June	111	433	75	73	32	7	2	10	14	2	10	7	781	29	3	10	1,983
Total	1,233	9,450	1,142	1,143	723	210	54	177	178	34	173	109	16,228	376	21	135	36,720

[Table No. 3.]

U. S. MILITARY RAILROADS.

Distribution of labor and material during fiscal year ending June.

Account.	Freight and cartage.	Labor.	Material.	Total.
Alexandria railroads	....	$685,099.30	$474,350.74	$1,159,450.04
City Point railroads	....	648,371.90	400,053.94	1,048,425.84
Winchester and Potomac Railroad	....	305,586.69	129,606.75	435,193.44
Norfolk railroads	....	39,353.91	25,548.82	64,904.73
Virginia railroads	$12,523.89	79,653.67	17,675.83	109,853.39
North Carolina railroads	....	2,631.33	331,278.01	333,909.34
Savannah railroads	....	139.38	9,208.54	9,347.92
Baltimore and Ohio Railroad	....	....	1,300.00	1,300.00
Quartermaster's Department	....	198,035.58	182,617.46	380,653.04
Photograph department	....	3,292.53	3,271.14	6,563.67
Telegraph department	....	306.86	225.43	532.29
Total	12,523.89	1,962,473.15	1,575,136.66	3,550,133.70

[Table No. 4.]

U. S. MILITARY RAILROADS OF VIRGINIA.

Schedule of engines, with cost of maintenance and repairs.

Builders and names of engines.	Weight.	Diameter drivers.	Size of cylinder.	Cost.	Value.	Expenses.	Miles run.	Cost per 100 miles.
Baldwin & Co.:	*Pounds.*	*In.*	*Inches.*					
S. S. Post	66,000	48	18 x 22	$10,303.00	$22,000.00	$3,800.39	6,597	$57.61
C. Vibbard	59,000	56	16 x 24	11,845.00	22,000.00	4,318.78	5,709	75.64
Geo. A. Parker	59,000	60	16 x 24	9,500.00	21,000.00	3,256.53	11,084	29.38
Union	59,000	60	16 x 24	9,500.00	21,000.00	11,467.80	897	1,278.46
General Dix	59,000	60	16 x 24	9,500.00	21,000.00	6,136.62	16,766	36.60
Vulcan	57,000	60	15 x 24	9,250.00	20,000.00	3,513.21	3,892	90.26
Blue Bird	55,000	60	16 x 22	5,500.00	6,000.00	4,289.64	4,611	93.00
Humming Bird	55,000	60	16 x 22	6,000.00	6,000.00	5,664.21	7,057	80.26
Norris & Son:								
E. M. Stanton	59,850	48	18 x 22	9,500.00	22,000.00	4,362.19	6,384	68.33
Romeo	58,000	48	16 x 24	9,500.00	21,000.00	4,271.20	6,751	63.27
Fire Fly	57,910	56	16 x 24	8,900.00	20,000.00	5,196.66	9,129	56.91
Manfred	57,910	56	16 x 24	10,990.00	21,000.00	3,828.66	10,743	35.63
May Queen	57,910	56	16 x 24	10,990.00	21,000.00	4,053.74	8,733	46.42
Governor Nye	57,910	60	16 x 24	12,875.00	21,000.00	4,550.73	9,396	48.42
Hiawatha	57,910	56	16 x 24	10,990.00	21,000.00	4,487.16	7,910	56.92
Pickwick	57,910	56	16 x 24	10,990.00	21,000.00	4,320.16	12,207	35.39
General Meigs	57,910	60	16 x 24	12,875.00	21,000.00	3,650.81	18,565	19.66
Colonel Beckwith	57,910	60	16 x 24	12,875.00	21,000.00	3,825.68	14,130	27.07
President	....	54	12½ x 24	....	....	1,645.81	2,780	59.02
William Mason:								
W. H. Whiton	55,000	60	16 x 22	9,300.00	21,000.00	4,381.30	7,087	61.82
General Robinson	55,000	60	16 x 22	9,300.00	21,000.00	8,580.30	16,071	53.39
General Sickles	55,000	60	16 x 22	11,845.00	22,000.00	3,944.92	9,804	40.23
H. L. Robinson	55,000	60	16 x 22	11,845.00	22,000.00	2,899.50	10,759	26.85
Clarke	54,000	60	15 x 22	....	21,000.00	4,870.64	10,108	48.18
E. L. Wentz	54,000	60	15 x 22	9,350.00	21,000.00	4,440.57	10,534	42.15
Taunton Locomotive Co.:								
General Meade	56,000	60	16 x 22	12,875.00	22,000.00	4,902.52	8,330	58.50
General Couch	56,000	60	16 x 22	12,875.00	22,000.00	3,873.09	10,605	36.52
Grape Shot	56,000	60	16 x 22	10,969.00	22,000.00	2,307.92	3,322	69.47
Secretary	55,000	60	15 x 24	9,000.00	20,000.00	4,070.49	5,691	71.52
New Jersey Locomotive Works:								
D. H. Rucker	56,000	60	16 x 24	13,000.00	22,000.00	3,740.19	1,522	244.74
Chas. Minot	56,000	60	16 x 24	13,000.00	22,000.00	5,768.29	1,130	510.47
Commodore	56,000	60	16 x 24	13,000.00	22,000.00	2,848.17	4,795	59.40
General McClellan	56,000	60	16 x 24	10,500.00	21,000.00	2,542.13	12,442	20.43
Col. D. C. McCallum	56,000	60	16 x 24	10,500.00	21,000.00	4,303.79	18,516	23.24
Zebra	56,000	56	16 x 24	11,845.00	21,000.00	4,558.79	9,821	46.42
Tiger	56,000	56	16 x 24	11,845.00	21,000.00	4,604.60	13,706	33.59
Lion	56,000	56	16 x 24	12,491.00	22,000.00	3,983.62	4,060	98.11
Fred Leach	56,000	56	16 x 24	10,500.00	21,000.00	4,945.32	8,814	56.10
J. H. Devereux	52,000	60	15 x 22	9,660.00	20,000.00	5,835.38	8,869	65.79
Rogers Locomotive Works:								
Osceola	51,300	56	15 x 22	9,000.00	20,000.00	3,225.67	13,043	24.73
Buffalo	51,300	56	15 x 22	11,330.00	20,000.00	3,299.63	16,516	19.97
W. W. Wright	51,300	56	15 x 22	12,088.00	21,000.00	2,650.80	12,226	21.68
U. S. Military Railroads:								
Lieut. General Grant	51,300	66	$15\frac{5}{16}$ x 22	....	20,000.00	3,613.30	18,222	21.72
General Sheridan	58,000	52	17 x 26	....	22,000.00	8,921.69	60	....
Rapidan	....	48	16 x 22	....	20,000.00	4,483.10	6,019	74.48
Jersey City Locomotive Works: General Geary	54,000	56	16 x 22	8,750.00	20,000.00	9,068.94	5,867	154.57
J. Souther:								
Hoosac	54,000	56	16 x 20	7,000.00	15,000.00	6,709.88	12,935	51.87
Monitor	54,000	56	16 x 20	7,000.00	15,000.00	2,960.95	7,414	39.53
Miscellaneous:								
Senator	56,000	60	15 x 24	6,800.00	7,000.00	5,484.62	6,567	83.51
Sentinel	55,000	56	16 x 20	5,300.00	5,000.00	6,756.12	3,897	173.36
Dover	46,000	56	15 x 20	4,500.00	5,000.00	2,975.59	4,274	69.62
Contest	44,000	69	14 x 20	4,750.00	5,000.00	....	....	....
Victor	50,000	69	16 x 20	4,750.00	5,000.00	....	....	....
Vidette	50,000	69	16 x 20	9,000.00	15,000.00	2,372.99	6,579	36.07
Epping	50,000	60	15 x 20	5,000.00	3,000.00	126.59		
Romulus	24,000	48	10 x 18	....	2,500.00	....	....	....
						236,691.38	562,946	42.04

[Table No. 5.]

U. S. MILITARY RAILROADS.

Tons carried and miles run during fiscal year.

Road.	Subsistence stores.	Quartermaster's stores.	Ordnance stores.	Medical stores.	Miscellaneous freight.	Railroad material.	Total.	Cars hauled.	Miles run by cars.
	Tons.	*Tons.*	*Tons.*	*Tons.*	*Tons.*	*Tons.*	*Tons.*		
Alexandria	39,541	113,078	851	64	1,788	13,839	169,161	54,370	656,507
Winchester and Potomac.	44,452	51,631	760	240	5,084	665	102,832	22,664	632,912
City Point and connecting roads.	162,506	193,652	76,540	9,665	75,370	21,579	539,312	97,200	2,322,800
Norfolk	22,598	26,311	364	61	2,258	561	52,153	6,517	69,903
Total	269,097	384,672	78,515	10,030	84,500	36,644	863,458	180,751	3,682,122

[Table No. 6.]

U. S. MILITARY RAILROADS.

Number of passengers carried July 1, 1864, to June 30, 1865.

Road.	July	Aug.	Sept.	Oct.	Nov.	Dec.
Alexandria	13,496	11,845	14,684	16,785	14,596	17,591
City Point	35,370	46,150	43,440	66,766	63,451	59,781
Winchester and Potomac	1,368	1,271	2,125	2,206	17,255	24,666
Norfolk	2,645	3,158	4,647	3,741	3,963	4,767
Total	52,879	62,424	64,896	89,498	99,265	106,805

Road.	Jan.	Feb.	March.	April.	May.	June.	Total.
Alexandria	16,963	25,041	18,954	21,334	6,135	6,692	184,116
City Point	57,841	66,845	64,345	97,467	96,560	87,965	785,981
Winchester and Potomac	36,765	38,644	21,652	20,854	18,676	7,778	193,260
Norfolk	3,968	3,673	4,861	3,239	2,671	2,784	44,117
Total	115,537	134,203	109,812	142,894	124,042	105,219	1,207,474

[Table No. 7.]

U. S. MILITARY RAILROADS.

Receipts for freight and passengers during fiscal year ending June 30.

Receipts.	July.	Aug.	Sept.	Oct.	Nov.	Dec.
Passengers	$89.10	$51.70	$88.50	$260.40	$425.70	$2,237.45
Freight	30.00	5.00	366.00	2,472.75	2.565.00	3,623.29
Total	119.10	56.70	454.50	2,733.15	2,990.70	5,860.74

Receipts.	Jan.	Feb.	March.	April.	May.	June.	Total.
Passengers	$2,639.30	$3,917.40	$2,335.30	$2,803.95	$12,181.06	$18,156.73	$45,186.59
Freight	3,830.60	3,184.90	6,029.20	2,266.70	4,335.32	7,368.82	36,077.58
Total	6,469.90	7,102.30	8,364.50	5,070.65	16,516.38	25,525.55	81,264.17

[Table No. 8.]

U. S. MILITARY RAILROADS.

Amount of material received and used July 1, 1864, to June 30, 1865.

Month.	On Hand.	Received.	Used.	On Hand.
July	$371, 479. 59	$86, 834. 93	$136, 243. 41	
August		117, 223. 67	77, 244. 93	
September		116, 786. 39	142, 395. 72	
October		124, 429. 01	63, 038. 64	
November		348, 706. 10	98, 953. 12	
December		219, 772. 71	80, 722. 27	
January		90, 626. 80	149, 825. 13	
February		97, 441. 39	122, 932. 82	
March		173, 833. 42	162, 670. 32	
April		436, 152. 83	454, 427. 86	
May		54, 541. 11	45, 492. 48	
June		36, 435. 51	53, 049. 36	$687, 267. 40
	371, 479. 59	1, 902, 783. 87	1, 586, 996. 06	687, 267. 40

[Table No. 9.]

Estimated value of property on military railroads, State of Virginia, June 30, 1865.

Description.	Alexandria railroads.	Winchester and Potomac Railroad.	City Point railroads.	Norfolk railroads.	Total.
Machine-shops and additions	$6, 150. 00	$600. 00	$2, 500. 00	$8, 000. 00	$17, 250. 00
Engine-houses	34, 500. 00	1, 200. 00	3, 100. 00	29, 000. 00	67, 800. 00
Car-shops and additions	28, 950. 00	45. 00	2, 650. 00	4, 000. 00	35, 645. 00
Depot buildings, &c	2, 500. 00	1, 139. 00	811. 28	1, 560. 00	6, 010. 28
Bridge shops, &c	1, 800. 00	223. 00	1, 250. 00	650. 00	3, 923. 00
Store-house buildings	3, 500. 00	180. 00	866. 00	150. 00	4, 696. 00
Offices	2, 350. 00	250. 00	900. 00		3, 500. 00
Quarters and dwelling-houses	6, 500. 00	611. 00	14, 689. 05	2, 070. 00	23, 870. 05
Commissary buildings	3, 500. 00	630. 00	450. 00		4, 580. 00
Wharves and fixtures	8, 000. 00		14, 820. 00		22, 820. 00
Baggage and switch-houses	400. 00	106. 00	220. 00		726. 00
Water stations	1, 650. 00	275. 00	560. 00	430. 00	2, 915. 00
Locomotive engines	602, 300. 00	68, 000. 00	125, 000. 00	84, 000. 00	879, 300. 00
Box-cars	280, 350. 00	51, 450. 00	44, 100. 00	17, 850. 00	393, 750. 00
Flat-cars	159, 800. 00		27, 200. 00	23, 800. 00	210, 800. 00
Stock-cars	11, 700. 00	12, 600. 00	1, 800. 00		26, 100. 00
Passenger-cars	16, 450. 00	16, 450. 00	11, 750. 00	2, 350. 00	47, 000. 00
President's and wreck car	14, 000. 00				14, 000. 00
Hand-cars	625. 00	250. 00	250. 00	625. 00	1, 750. 00
Pile-drivers	5, 000. 00		2, 500. 00		7, 500. 00
Stationary engines	5, 900. 00	2, 500. 00	3, 000. 00	2, 600. 00	14, 000. 00
Pumping engines	10, 000. 00	2, 500. 00	7, 500. 00	2, 100. 00	22, 100. 00
Printing department	1, 542. 00				1, 542. 00
Commissary department	1, 719. 67	976. 00	1, 807. 68	476. 00	4, 979. 35
Iron, railroad	107, 840. 00	1, 280. 00	352, 920. 00	12, 480. 00	475, 520. 00
Iron and steel	59, 300. 00	5, 325. 00		9, 375. 00	74, 000. 00
Chairs	(*a*)	24. 48	5, 798. 40	15. 36	5, 838. 24
Spikes, railroad	(*a*)	21. 90	8, 712. 00	27. 00	8, 760. 90
Machinery in machine department	24, 043. 00	2, 450. 00	9, 795. 00	13, 725. 00	50, 013. 00
Machinery in car department	4, 101. 00	465. 00	153. 00	2, 175. 00	6, 894. 00
Material in machine and car department.	8, 895. 60	7, 415. 00	5, 310. 00	25, 310. 00	46, 930. 60
Tools in machine department	18, 913. 21	3, 243. 00	4, 760. 00	2, 142. 00	29, 058. 21
Tools in car department	3, 471. 43	1, 761. 05	895. 00	1, 761. 00	7, 888. 48
Office furniture	1, 488. 00	187. 50	222. 00	452. 00	2, 349. 50
Tools, &c., in construction department.	23, 690. 84	3, 621. 00	5, 676. 00	1, 851. 60	34, 839. 44
Lumber	(*a*)	1, 960. 00	20, 997. 23	4, 083. 00	27, 040. 23
Miscellaneous property	27, 080. 00	5, 321. 00	4, 176. 00	11, 571. 00	48, 148. 00
Store-house report	687, 267. 40				687, 267. 40
Total	2, 175, 277. 15	193, 059. 93	688, 138. 64	264, 628. 96	3, 321, 104. 68

a Store-house sheet.

[Table No. 10.]

U. S. MILITARY RAILROADS.

*Gradients, alignments, elevations, &c.**

[Table No. 11.]

MILITARY RAILROADS OF VIRGINIA.

Track laid from July 1, 1864, to June 30, 1865.

	Miles.	Feet.
Army Line:		
Main line from Pitkin Station to Humphreys Station	13	3,100
Sidings, from Pitkin Station to Humphreys Station	2	4,705
Gregg Branch, from Hancock Station to Crawford Station	2	1,200
Sidings, from Hancock Station to Crawford Station	--	2,960
Patrick Branch, from Warren Station to Patrick Station	2	1,000
Sidings, from Warren Station to Patrick Station	--	1,550
Total length of track in main line, branches, and sidings	21	3,955
South Side Railroad, from City Point to Burkeville:		
Main line relaid	10	320
Hospital, bakery, and other sidings	4	2,800
Total	14	3,120
Petersburg and Richmond Railroad:		
Siding laid at Manchester	--	1,520
Richmond and Danville Railroad:		
Main line, near Appomattox bridge	--	2,000
Siding at Manchester, storage of cars	2	2,430
Total	2	4,430
Seaboard and Roanoke Railroad:		
Main line, fifteen miles from Portsmouth	--	5,210
Alexandria and Washington Railroad:		
Across Long Bridge and approaches	1	200
Alexandria, Loudoun and Hampshire Railroad:		
Siding at Arlington Mills	--	800
Orange and Alexandria Railroad:		
First siding south of Alexandria	--	1,620
Main track on Accotink bridge	--	140
Track over Pope's Head bridges Nos. 1, 2, 3, 4, and 5	--	580
Track over Bull Run bridge	--	150
Track over Broad Run bridge	--	240
Track over Kettle Run bridge	--	80
Track over Cedar Run bridge	--	175
Total	--	2,985
Manassas Gap Railroad:		
Main line near Piedmont	--	3,980
Sidings at Piedmont	--	1,990
Sidings at Salem	--	770
Sidings at Rectortown	--	300
Total	1	1,760
Baltimore and Ohio Railroad:		
Siding at Bladensburg	--	1,350
Point Lookout, Md.:		
Siding and tracks for quartermaster	--	840

*Omitted.

Winchester and Potomac Railroad:	Miles.	Feet.
Main track, from Harper's Ferry to Stephenson's	28	400
Sidings, from Harper's Ferry to Stephenson's	2	4,640
Total	30	5,040
Total track laid during the year	74	140

[Table No. 12.]

MILITARY RAILROADS OF VIRGINIA.

Trestle bridges built during year ending June 30.

	Length.	Height.
	Feet.	*Average feet.*
Army Line:		
Pitkin Station to Humphreys Station	4,483	15
Patrick Branch	850	20
Gregg Branch	1,040	18
Total length	6,373	
South Side Railroad:		
City Point to Burkeville	325	27
Petersburg and Richmond Railroad:		
Connection at Petersburg	400	12
Richmond and Danville Railroad:		
Manchester to Danville	1,030	39
Seaboard and Roanoke Railroad:		
Sixteen miles from Portsmouth	100	35
Winchester and Potomac Railroad:		
Total length	3,294	12½
Alexandria and Washington Railroad:		
Approaches to new Long Bridge	248	4½
Orange and Alexandria and Manassas Gap Railroads:		
Total length	1,263	27
Total trestle-work built during the year	13,033	
Average		21

[JULY 1, 1865.]

Bvt. Brig. Gen. D. C. McCALLUM,
General Manager U. S. Military Railroads:

GENERAL: As general superintendent of military railroads, Division of the Tennessee, I have the honor to submit the following report:

I succeeded Maj. E. L. Wentz as general superintendent military railroads, Military Division of the Mississippi in May, 1865. He succeeded A. Anderson in the same position in November, 1864; so that I am the third general superintendent who has had charge of operations in this department during the fiscal year ending June 30, 1865. Not having access to all the annals of my predecessors in office, I shall find it almost impossible to make a report as minute and complete as is desirable.

1, 2, 3. On the 1st day of July, 1864, the length of railroads then in operation which came afterward under my direction was as follows:

Title of railroad.	Prior to the war.			Now used as U. S. military railroad lines.	
	Original owners	Terminal stations.	Length.	Terminal stations.	Length.
			Miles.		*Miles.*
Nashville and Chattanooga.	Nashville and Chattanooga R. R. Co.	Nashville—Chattanooga.	151	The whole road	151
Nashville and Decatur.	Tennessee and Alabama R. R. Co.; Central Southern R. R. Co.; Tennessee and Alabama Central R. R. Co.	Nashville—Decatur.	120	.....do	120
Nashville and Northwestern.	Nashville and Northwestern R. R. Co.	Nashville—Hickman, Ky.	......	Nashville—Johnsonville.	78
Nashville and Kentucky.	Edgefield and Kentucky R. R. Co.	Nashville—State Line.	47	Nashville—Clarksville.	61
Western and Atlantic.	State of Georgia	Chattanooga, Tenn.—Atlanta, Ga.	138	Chattanooga, Tenn.—Big Shanty, Ga.	107
Kingston Branch	.....do	Kingston, Ga.—Rome, Ga.	17	Kingston, Ga.—Rome, Ga.	17
East Tennessee and Georgia.	East Tennessee and Georgia R. R. Co.	Chattanooga, Tenn.—Knoxville.	112	Chattanooga, Tenn.—Knoxville.	112
Dalton Branch	.....do	Cleveland, Tenn.—Dalton, Ga.	27	Cleveland, Tenn.—Dalton, Ga.	27
East Tennessee and Virginia.	East Tennessee and Virginia R. R. Co.	Knoxville, Tenn.—Bristol, Va.	130	Not in use	......
Rogersville Branch	.....do	Junction—Rogersville.	15	.....do	......
Memphis and Charleston.	Memphis and Charleston R. R. Co.	Memphis, Tenn.—Stevenson.	271	Decatur Junction—Stevenson, Ala.	81

During July and August, 1864, the advance of General Sherman's army gave us the remainder of the Western and Atlantic Railroad from Big Shanty, 107 miles from Chattanooga, to Atlanta, 138 miles from Chattanooga, to which place we ran early in September, 1864. Some of the roads in use at the beginning of the fiscal year were abandoned as they became useless for military operations, and others from time to time added, until the end of the year, June 30, 1865, found us in possession and operating the following roads, viz:

Title of railroad.	Prior to the war.			Now used as U. S. military railroad lines.	
	Original owners.	Terminal stations.	Length.	Terminal stations.	Length.
			Miles.		*Miles.*
Nashville and Chattanooga.	Nashville and Chattanooga R. R. Co.	Nashville—Chattanooga.	151	The whole road	151
Nashville and Decatur.	Tennessee and Alabama R. R. Co.; Central Southern R. R. Co.; Tennessee and Alabama Central R. R. Co.	Nashville—Decatur.	120	.....do	120
Nashville and Northwestern.	Nashville and Northwestern R. R. Co.	Nashville—Hickman, Ky.	......	Nashville—Johnsonville.	78
Nashville and Kentucky.	Edgefield and Kentucky R. R. Co.	Nashville—State Line.	47	Nashville—Springfield.	28
Western and Atlantic.	State of Georgia	Chattanooga—Atlanta, Ga.	138	Chattanooga—Atlanta.	138
Kingston Branch	.....do	Kingston—Rome, Ga.	17	Kingston—Rome	17

Title of railroad.	Prior to war.			Now used as U. S. military railroad lines.	
	Original owners.	Terminal stations.	Length.	Terminal stations.	Length.
			Miles.		*Miles.*
East Tennessee and Georgia.	East Tennessee and Georgia R. R. Co.	Chattanooga—Knoxville.	112	Chattanooga—Knoxville.	112
Dalton Branch	do	Cleveland—Dalton, Ga.	27	Cleveland—Dalton	27
East Tennessee and Virginia.	East Tennessee and Virginia R. R. Co.	Knoxville—Bristol	130	Knoxville—Carter's Station.	110
Rogersville Branch	do	Junction — Rogersville.	15	Junction — Rogersville.	15
Memphis and Charleston.	Memphis and Charleston R. R. Co.	Memphis — Stevenson.	271	Decatur—Stevenson	81

As a general summary of this item of report it will be sufficient to say that there were in use July 1, 1864, 754 miles of road, and at the end of the fiscal year 877 miles, showing a gain of 123 miles during the year.

4. To meet the demand for the increased necessities of the army of General Sherman and supply the parts depending upon the military railroads for supplies, and to forward the great accession of troops in this department and transport to the rear the sick and wounded, and near the close of the fiscal year to transport the immense army back on their way to points of muster out, and send the refugees who during the winter had been dispatched to the rear again over our roads to their former homes, we have purchased from manufacturers sixty-two new engines and captured from the enemy three, adding thus sixty-five efficient engines to the number in use at the close of the last fiscal year.

SUMMARY.

Locomotives reported June 30, 1864	150
Purchased during the fiscal year	62
Captured from the enemy	3
Total June 30, 1865	215

5. There were purchased during the same period 989 box-cars and 397 flat-cars, thus adding 1,386 freight-cars to those in use June 30, 1864.

SUMMARY.

Freight-cars reported June 30, 1864	1,452
Added during fiscal year	1,386
Total	2,838

6. I submit herewith the report of the auditor,* showing that the average number of men employed in the entire department during the fiscal year was 13,043, at an average expense of $779,644.85 per month, making the total expense for employés in the entire department $9,355,738.21.

7. The report of the auditor of all accounts audited and prepared for payment during each month of the fiscal year is herewith submitted: Average amount, $940,734.95; total, $11,288,819.78.

* Omitted.

Stores and troops were transported from Nashville at the following rate per month:

Month.	Cars, stores.	Cars, troops.	Cars, empty.	Total cars.	Stores.	Number of troops.
					Tons.	
July	3,208	300	....	3,508	25,664	18,000
August	3,166	325	282	3,773	25,328	19,100
September	2,698	144	1,081	3,923	21,584	10,297
October	3,698	563	1,699	5,960	29,584	31,150
November	1,671	1,249	1,307	4,227	13,368	65,450
December	360	137	783	1,280	2,880	6,850
January	2,420	346	479	3,245	19,360	17,300
February	2,415	399	854	3,668	19,320	19,950
March	2,169	588	195	2,952	17,352	24,400
April	2,639	330	738	3,707	21,112	16,500
May	1,935	406	1,020	3,361	15,480	20,300
June	2,677	886	244	3,807	21,416	34,419
Total	29,056	5,673	8,682	43,411	232,448	283,716

The foregoing is the business ordered by Capt. S. B. Brown, and embraces nothing of the large business done by the Quartermaster's Department in Chattanooga, Huntsville, Knoxville, and Atlanta, sending the army over portions of our road and finally dispatching it back to Nashville when mustered out of service.

During the fiscal year the following monthly report will show the actual number of cars moved upon the roads centering in Nashville:

Month.	Year.	Forwarded.	Received.	Total.	Month.	Year.	Forwarded.	Received.	Total.
July	1864	4,618	4,493	9,111	February	1865	4,710	4,718	9,428
August	1864	4,781	4,744	9,525	March	1865	3,990	4,349	8,339
September	1864	4,384	4,058	8,442	April	1865	5,110	5,331	10,441
October	1864	6,225	6,031	12,256	May	1865	4,113	4,584	8,697
November	1864	4,764	5,569	10,333	June	1865	4,437	4,793	9,230
December	1864	1,754	1,622	3,376					
January	1865	4,571	4,271	8,842	Total	......	53,457	54,563	108,020

Making a total of 108,020 cars actually forwarded and received at this station. The order of General Sherman of April 10, 1864, stopping all travel on private account over military roads was in full force until December, 1864.

In December, 1864, and again in March, 1865, these orders were so far modified as to allow passengers and freight to be carried when not interfering with the business of the Government. The receipts from the express company, private freights, and passengers during the fiscal year are as follows, viz:

Month.	Express service.	Freight.	Passengers.	Total.
1864.				
July	$17,389.22	....	....	$17,389.22
August	11,756.52	$2,062.11	....	13,818.63
September	7,381.44	235.60	....	7,617.04
October	7,578.06	2,800.00	....	10,378.06
November	7,975.53	6,041.80	....	14,017.33
December	3,246.64	....	....	3,246.64

Month.	Express service.	Freight.	Passengers.	Total.
1865.				
January	$16,748.98	$4,670.34	$4,719.40	$26,138.72
February	25,278.30	570.15	25,250.50	51,098.95
March	17,604.09	99.65	18,042.75	35,746.49
April	17,373.99	9,885.33	20,231.00	47,490.32
May	17,228.04	15,792.88	44,146.65	77,167.57
June	27,675.41	27,321.96	56,150.67	111,148.04
Total	177,236.22	69,479.82	168,540.97	415,257.01

CARE OF ROAD.

The repairs of the 877 miles of road was continued from last year. The Nashville and Chattanooga line has been made new for its whole length—cross-ties and T-iron substituted for the U-iron and stringers—so that from one of the worst and least available it has become one of the best under my control. Large additions have been made to the yard at Nashville, at Decherd, and Stevenson. Side-tracks to lumber yard, Government saw-mills, &c., have rendered the work of keeping all the different departments of the railroad service in efficient operation much easier. To complete and keep in repair the track upon this long line of road there has been purchased 777,879 cross-ties, 104,100 feet switch timber, and 38½ sets switch ties, the total cost of which, delivered upon the lines of road where needed, has been $414,727.15. During the year the number of tons of new iron has been 7,833.3. This has been distributed as follows:

	Tons.
Upon the Nashville and Chattanooga line	3,922.9
Tennessee and Alabama line	445.9
Edgefield and Kentucky line	113.4
Nashville and Northwestern	25.8
Memphis and Charleston	67.8
Yard, Nashville and Decherd	26.7
Shipped to Captain Starkweather, assistant quartermaster, for use below Chattanooga	1,674.7
Shipped to W. W. Wright	1,484.7
Shipped to Captain Parks, Memphis	71.4
Total	7,833.3

CARE OF BRIDGES.

On the Nashville and Decatur Railroad line 8,000 feet of trestle bridges have been constructed during the year. With the exception of the high trestle-work in Nashville, the high waters of 1864 carried out all the bridges once, and many of them twice; while in Hood's movements upon Nashville in December, 1864, they were destroyed by fire the same number of times. In addition to this temporary rebuilding of these bridges with trestle-work, 2,145 feet of bridges upon this line have been permanently built by contractors—Post, Skidmore & Co. and Boomer & Co.—with Howe's truss and McCallum bridges.

NASHVILLE AND CHATTANOOGA.

On the Nashville and Chattanooga Railroad line 4,259 feet of bridges have been built in a temporary manner, yet intended to be permanent.

In September, 1864, Wheeler destroyed by fire bridge No. 7, 300 feet long. In December, in Hood's raid, bridges Nos. 1, 2, 3, 4, 5, 6, and 12 were destroyed by fire, and these have been permanently rebuilt. By high water and the enemy the bridges named have been destroyed, some twice and some three times, and as often rebuilt.

WATER-TANKS.

On the Nashville and Decatur line nine water-tanks were constructed complete. On the Nashville and Chattanooga line forty-five water-tanks were constructed. There has been laid nearly five miles of new water pipe to make the water stations complete. The exact figures are 24,660 feet. On the Chattanooga and Knoxville, Chattanooga and Atlanta, and Knoxville and Bristol lines twenty-five new and complete water stations have been built, and nine of these are fitted with water wheels, which render them self-acting and complete in every respect. On the Nashville and Chattanooga line near 115 miles of main line and side-tracks have been relaid with new ties, new iron, and ballast.

CONSTRUCTION OF BUILDINGS.

The large machine, pattern, and repair shops alluded to in the last yearly report and the roundhouse for the large number of engines then projected have been completed during the year. R. H. Nagle, master carpenter, has built two machine-shops.

Number.	Kind of buildings.	Length.	Width.	Height.
		Feet.	*Feet.*	
1	Machine-shop	195	88	2 stories.
1	.....do	80	65	Do.
1	Pattern shop	100	48	Do.
1	Blacksmith and boiler shop	450	62	1 story.
1	Roundhouse	*a* 27	*b* 85	Do.
1	Carpenter shop	200	40	Do.
1	Tin shop	65	40	Do.
1	Copper shop	60	27	Do.
1	Store-house	150	35	Do.
1	.....do	175	36	Do.
8	Hospital buildings	705	201	Do.
1	Quatermaster's office	72	40	2 stories.
1	Office for auditor	56	20	Do.
1	Office master machinist	90	25	3 stories.
1	Office master carpenter	38	18	1 story.
1	U. S. printing office	45	36	2 stories.

a Stalls. *b* Long.

In addition to these buildings, sixty-nine mess-houses, fitted with bunks, benches, and tables for the comfort of the men employed, were erected. In addition to the various platforms along the line of the Nashville and Northwestern Railroad, and at Nashville, for the convenient loading of freight and troops and animals, there were built at Decherd one roundhouse with twelve stalls 60 feet long; one blacksmith shop 60 by 30 feet; one car shop 66 by 35 feet, besides fifteen buildings used as mess-houses, offices, and depot buildings, varying from 20 by 40 to 20 by 80 feet. In addition to these buildings all the desks, cases, &c., needed by all the officers of the military railroads were constructed by this department. To complete this work there were used 4,216,203 feet of lumber; 1,312 kegs of nails; 1,442 locks, with the hinges, screws, &c., to make the work complete. In addition to the above work the carpenter force under Mr. Nagle has assisted in all emergencies in rebuilding bridges, getting out bridge and block-house timbers, &c., building 4,500 feet of bridges on the various lines, and hewing and preparing in the woods 1,000,519 feet of square timber suitable for bridges and buildings. The construction of these buildings for offices and mess-houses and accommodations for the men employed upon the railroad work was rendered indispensable by the impossibility of procuring any accommodations at all for the large number of men thus brought together in Nashville in the Government service. In the last annual report it was stated that until February, 1864, no provisions had been made for the repairs of cars. This department had to be created. Under the thorough and efficient supervision of George Herrick the necessary buildings were begun and completed which has rendered this one of the most perfect establishments in the country. The buildings so completed during the fiscal year are one car shop, 202 by 77 and 23 high, with skylights above the square throughout its whole length; one machine and blacksmith shop, 126 by 47 and 23 high, with skylights and blinds through its whole length. There is a wing to this shop 55 by 35 and 17 high with ventilator and boiler room attached, 35 by 18; one paint shop, 112 by 47 and 23 high, with skylights similar to those before mentioned; one brick dry-house, 40 by 15 and 17 high, which has been partially rebuilt a second time; one coal house, 20 by 35 and 8 high; one iron store-house, 14 by 20 and 16 high; one house for oil, waste, and tools, 18 by 40 and 8 high; one building, 20 by 50, for storage of coke and sand; eight mess-houses, fitted with bunks and all complete for the men, have also been erected. This, as before stated, was indispensable, as no accommodations could possibly be secured for the men. The necessary masonry, grading, and ballasting the grounds, yards, and track, through the repair-shop grounds, has been a large but necessary part of the work of preparing these shops for efficient service.

At Decatur Junction houses and shops were erected suitable to work 100 men. During Hood's raid upon the city in December, 1864, these were all nearly destroyed by our own forces, and had to be replaced by this department. At Johnsonville provision was made for shops, mess-houses, &c., to work twenty-five to forty men. At Taylor depot, cn Broad street, accommodations were provided to work twenty-five to fifty men. The shops at Chattanooga have been made efficient, an engine house erected, and other necessary improvements made. The same has been done at Knoxville and Stevenson. In the machine shop at Nashville 916 men have been employed on the average monthly during the fiscal year. During that year 5,571 orders have been filled for light repairs on engines, involving many hours' work of skillful mechanics. Fifty-four engines were received in the shop for general repairs; three engines were completed that were being rebuilt. Ten thousand six hundred and ten days of common labor were performed in the shops and yards; 4,035 days of machinist's labor were performed upon shops, tools, &c.; 1,914 on track and bridge repairs; 369 on setting up new engines, while 620 days of common labor was employed during the same time upon setting up new engines. In December 979 men worked twelve days upon the fortifications, while the city was threatened by General Hood. During the fiscal year the shops in Nashville have been entirely built. Two powerful engines, with all the shafting necessary to drive the tools used, have been set up. Room to house twenty-seven engines for repairs, erecting shop large enough to rebuild twenty engines, room to house forty-five engines, with pattern shops, blacksmith shops, carpenter shops, and offices in proportion—all these have been made new and complete in every respect. The grading of the yards and assistance in erecting these structures has been done by the common laborers in the numbers above enumerated.

CAR REPAIRS.

The work accomplished in the car repair department has been large and thorough. Mr. Herrick perfected a wrecking car which enabled him to clear and pick up a wrecked train very speedily. This train has picked up 530 wrecked freight-cars and 16 wrecked engines since January 1, 1865, and brought them to Nashville for repairs. During the remainder of the fiscal year nearly as many more were also saved. During the same period this train has picked up and brought in from trains destroyed by fire, 294 car-loads of wheels, axles, bridge irons and railroad iron along the lines of road centering in Nashville. Most of these wrecks were caused by guerrillas placing obstructions upon the track or displacing rails. The car department has worked an average force of nearly 800 men per month during the year. This force, in addition to the buildings erected and completed during the fiscal year before described, have repaired and rebuilt during the last six months of the year at Nashville, Chattanooga, Huntsville, Stevenson, Johnsonville, and Clarksville, 13,429 cars, and during the first six months more than half as many more, making a total of 20,000 cars repaired, rebuilt, and fitted for hospital and troop cars during the year. The amount of material cast in the iron and brass foundry during the last six months of the year was 1,053,945 pounds iron castings, 46,139 pounds brass castings, making an average per month of 175,000 pounds of iron and 7,500 pounds of brass castings. This is too large an average for the whole fiscal year, though it is believed that 225,000 pounds of iron and 10,000 pounds of brass castings per month will not be too large. It is impossible to condense and specify the amount of work done upon the long lines of roads centering in Nashville so as to show what has actually been done. The emergencies of military service have often allowed no time for proper orders of transportation of troops, stores, refugees, prisoners, &c., to be issued, so that many hundred trains have been run and many thousands of troops and refugees carried for which we have no credit. The work has been done in the midst of war, running through a country filled with enemies, so that the ordinary risks of railroad management have been enormously increased and the expenses largely extended. But in the midst of all this danger the coolness, bravery, and daring of the men in every department, from the highest official to the humblest laborers, have been worthy of praise. At the close of this fiscal year it gives me great pleasure to state that throughout the whole length of the lines of military railroads controlled and operated by me there is every facility to perform well and efficiently every duty that may be required. The roads are in first-rate order, the bridges for the most part are permanent structures of the best description, and the water stations in perfect order. The amount of rolling-stock is sufficient for all work required, and in good order. The machine-shops and repair-shops are as complete as could be desired.

I cannot close this imperfect and desultory report without expressing my obligations to the following gentlemen for the zeal, fidelity, and intelligence with which they have co-operated with me on all occasions in their departments of duty: J. B. Van Dyne, assistant superintendent; George H. Hudson, superintendent; A. W. Dickerson, W. R. Gifford, A. J. Cheeney, W. W. Tuttle and A. Watts, in the freight department; Col. John C. Meginnis, general engineer district; Stephen Hobbs, engine dispatcher; J. W. Wallace, engine dispatcher; John Trenbath, auditor; GeorgeHerrick, superintendent car repairs; R. H. Nagle, master carpenter; H. Elliott, master machinist; Messrs. Hebard, Nash, Lyman, Caryl, Craig, Gardiner, Jones, Kingsley, and Jenkins, in the road repair and bridge repairs. With F. J. Crilly, the efficient and gentlemanly chief quartermaster of military railroads, my relations have been most pleasant, while the co-operation of Major-General Thomas, General Donaldson, and Capt. S. B. Brown has been always harmonious with the railroad authorities.

All of which is respectfully submitted.

W. J. STEVENS,
Superintendent, &c.

GENERAL ORDERS, No. 122. } WAR DEPT., ADJT. GENERAL'S OFFICE, *Washington, July 8, 1865.*

REGIMENTAL OFFICERS OF VOLUNTEERS ON DETACHED SERVICE TO JOIN THEIR PROPER COMMANDS.

I. With the exceptions hereinafter enumerated, the following is ordered:

1. All commissioned officers of volunteers, for both white and colored regiments or independent companies, now absent on detached service from their commands and not on duty within their proper armies or departments, will proceed forthwith to join their respective regiments and companies.

2. Hereafter no commissioned regimental officer of volunteers will be placed on duty or transferred thereon out of the army or department in which his regiment may be serving.

The exceptions authorized under the foregoing are as follows:

1. Officers on duty mustering out and discharging the volunteer forces.

2. Aides-de-camp to general officers on duty commanding troops.

3. Officers on courts-martial or military commissions and those on duty in the Bureau of Refugees, Freedmen, and Abandoned Lands under direct orders from the War Department, Adjutant-General's Office.

II. All enlisted men absent on detached service from their regiments or companies and outside the armies or departments in which the same may be serving will at once be sent to join their respective commands, unless they are absent therefrom by orders from the headquarters of a military division or superior authority.

III. Commanding generals of departments and armies are charged with the prompt execution of this order, and upon its provisions being fully complied with will report the fact to the Adjutant-General of the Army.

IV. No commissioned officer or enlisted man absent in violation of this order will be paid outside of the army or department in which his regiment or company may be serving.

By order of the Secretary of War:

E. D. TOWNSEND,
Assistant Adjutant-General.

CIRCULAR } No. 31. } WAR DEPT., ADJUTANT-GENERAL'S OFFICE,
Washington, July 8, 1865.

ORDERS AND INSTRUCTIONS RELATIVE TO THE MUSTER OUT OF CERTAIN VOLUNTEER WHITE TROOPS.

Veterans in the Army of the Tennessee, and Provisional Corps, Army of the Potomac, and, thereafter, all remaining volunteers in the said commands.

WAR DEPARTMENT, ADJUTANT-GENERAL'S OFFICE,
Washington, July 1, 1865.

Maj. Gen. JOHN A. LOGAN, U. S. Volunteers,
Commanding Army of the Tennessee, Louisville, Ky.:

The Secretary of War directs that the remaining veteran regiments of your command be mustered out under the same conditions and regulations as the 15,000 men ordered discharged by the telegraphic instructions from this office of the 22d instant. (See circular No. 28, current series.)

Please acknowledge receipt of this and forward without delay a list of the additional regiments, giving therein, for each, the strength, present and absent, respectively.

THOMAS M. VINCENT,
Assistant Adjutant-General.

CIRCULAR.] WAR DEPARTMENT, ADJUTANT-GENERAL'S OFFICE,
Washington, July 1, 1865.

Maj. Gen. H. G. WRIGHT,
Commanding Provisional Corps, Army of the Potomac:

The Secretary of War directs that all veteran regiments of your command be mustered out of service. The muster out will be by entire organizations, including all additions by recruits and from other sources. The musters out, discharges, and payments will be made under the regulations promulgated in General Orders, No. 94, current series, from this office.

Please acknowledge receipt of this and forward without delay a list of the regiments, giving therein, for each, the strength, present and absent, respectively.

THOMAS M. VINCENT,
Assistant Adjutant-General.

TELEGRAM.] HEADQUARTERS ARMIES OF THE UNITED STATES,
Washington, July 6, 1865.

Major-General LOGAN,
Louisville, Ky.:

Under the last order you may muster out of service all that remains of the Army of the Tennessee remaining under your command.

U. S. GRANT,
Lieutenant-General.

WAR DEPARTMENT, ADJUTANT-GENERAL'S OFFICE,
Washington, July 7, 1865.

Maj. Gen. JOHN A. LOGAN,
Commanding Army of the Tennessee, Louisville, Ky.:

In discharging the remainder of your army, as directed by the telegraphic orders of yesterday from Lieutenant-General Grant, the musters out, discharges, and payments will be made under the regulations promulgated in General Orders, No. 94, current series, from this office.

Please forward to this office without delay a list of the regiments and independent companies to be discharged under the order, giving therein, for each, the strength, present and absent, respectively. So soon as the list is completed inform me by telegraph of the number, present and absent, for the respective States.

Please acknowledge receipt of this.

By order of the Secretary of War:

THOMAS M. VINCENT,
Assistant Adjutant-General.

WAR DEPARTMENT, ADJUTANT-GENERAL'S OFFICE,
Washington, July 7, 1865.

Maj. Gen. H. G. WRIGHT, U. S. Volunteers,
Commanding Provisional Corps:

GENERAL: The Secretary of War directs that all the remaining volunteer troops of your command be mustered out of service. The musters out, discharges, and payments will be made under the regulations promulgated in General Orders, No. 94, current series, from this office.

Please acknowledge the receipt of this and forward without delay a list of the organizations, giving therein, for each, the strength, present and absent, respectively.

I have the honor to be, very respectfully, your obedient servant,

THOMAS M. VINCENT,
Assistant Adjutant-General.

MEMORANDA.—See General Orders, No. 116, of June 17, for the discharge of certain enlisted men of the Veteran Reserve Corps.

E. D. TOWNSEND,
Assistant Adjutant-General.

WASHINGTON, *July 17, 1865.*

Maj. Gen. GEORGE G. MEADE,
Eighteenth and Delancy Place:

Send staff officers to each, Virginia, North Carolina, and South Carolina, and direct the muster out of all cavalry that can be dispensed with, and the sale of their horses when dismounted. When it is necessary to retain cavalry for want of other troops, dismount them and have their horses sold, except the actual number of mounted men required. A few hundred mounted men in each State I would think the greatest abundance. Order also the muster out of all cavalry possible to dispense with in the other departments of your command. The horses to be turned over to quartermasters and reported to the Quartermaster-General. Request department commanders to report the number of men and horses disposed of under this order.

U. S. GRANT,
Lieutenant-General.

CIRCULAR No. 33.

WAR DEPT., ADJUTANT-GENERAL'S OFFICE,
Washington, July 18, 1865.

REGULATIONS UNDER WHICH OFFICERS OF MUSTERED-OUT REGIMENTS CAN RECEIVE FINAL PAYMENTS.

(Extracts from telegrams and circulars to chief mustering officers of States.)

I. Officers of mustered-out regiments can be paid on the certificate of the mustering officer that they have rendered all required returns and accounts, and on their affidavits that they are not indebted to the Government.

In the absence of other evidence (certificates or statements from the supply departments concerned, retained papers, &c.) relative to the rendition of the said papers, the War Department has authorized the affidavit of the mustered-out officer concerned to be received as evidence, and mustering officers can base thereon their certificates relative to the rendition of returns and accounts.

II. Mustering officers are not required to examine accounts of officers and give them certificates of non-indebtedness. The settlement of accounts belongs to the Treasury Department.

E. D. TOWNSEND,
Assistant Adjutant-General.

GENERAL ORDERS, No. 127. } WAR DEPT., ADJT. GENERAL'S OFFICE, *Washington, July 21, 1865.*

Ordered, That a bureau be organized in the Adjutant-General's Office for the collection, safe-keeping, and publication of the rebel archives that have come into possession of this Government, the bureau to consist of one chief, with the pay of a colonel of cavalry, and one assistant, with the pay of a lieutenant-colonel of cavalry, and such number of clerks, to be detailed by the Adjutant-General, as may be found necessary for the speedy collection of the archives. Dr. Francis Lieber is hereby appointed chief of said bureau, and the Quartermaster-General is directed to furnish suitable apartments and buildings for the collation and custody of the archives mentioned.

By order of the Secretary of War:

E. D. TOWNSEND,
Assistant Adjutant-General.

[JULY 22, 1865.—For General Grant's official report covering operations from March, 1864, to May, 1865, see Series I, Vol. XXXVI, Part I, p. 12.]

CIRCULAR No. 35. } WAR DEPT., ADJT. GENERAL'S OFFICE, *Washington, July 22, 1865.*

ORDERS AND INSTRUCTIONS RELATIVE TO THE MUSTER OUT OF CERTAIN VOLUNTEER CAVALRY IN THE DEPARTMENT OF VIRGINIA, DEPARTMENT OF NORTH CAROLINA, AND MIDDLE DEPARTMENT; ALSO CERTAIN VOLUNTEER INFANTRY AND ARTILLERY IN OTHER DEPARTMENTS.

I. Cavalry.

TELEGRAM.] WAR DEPARTMENT, ADJUTANT-GENERAL'S OFFICE, *Washington, July 21, 1865.*

Maj. Gen. A. H. TERRY, U. S. Volunteers,
Commanding Department of Virginia, Richmond, Va.:

The Secretary of War directs that the volunteer cavalry forces in your department be reduced to two regiments of maximum strength. The musters out of the surplus will be by entire regiments, and the said musters, discharges, and payments made under the regulations promulgated in General Orders, No. 94, current series, from this office.

Please forward to this office without delay a list of the regiments you may select for discharge under this order, giving therein for each the strength, present and absent, respectively.

THOMAS M. VINCENT,
Assistant Adjutant-General.

NOTE.—Similar orders sent to the commanding general Department of North Carolina to reduce the cavalry in that department to one regiment, and to the commanding general Middle Department to reduce the cavalry in West Virginia to one regiment.

II. Infantry and artillery (whose services are no longer needed) ordered mustered out under special instructions, of dates set opposite the organizations respectively:

Pennsylvania.—Two hundred and second Infantry, July 20.
Delaware.—Ahl's Independent Battery, July 20.
Tennessee.—Fourth Infantry, July 20, 1865.

E. D. TOWNSEND,
Assistant Adjutant-General.

CIRCULAR No. 36. } WAR DEPT., ADJUTANT GENERAL'S OFFICE,
Washington, July 25, 1865.

By an act of the Legislature of the State of Minnesota, approved September 27, 1862, the right to vote for certain State officers is given to volunteers or soldiers from that State in the military service of the United States, and provision is made for the appointment of commissioners to the regiments of Minnesota Volunteers for the purpose of carrying out this act. It is hereby ordered that all such duly accredited commissioners from Minnesota be furnished with proper facilities for visiting the volunteers from that State, and allowed access to them for the purpose indicated.

By order of the Secretary of War:

E. D. TOWNSEND,
Assistant Adjutant-General.

CIRCULAR No. 39. } WAR DEPT., ADJUTANT-GENERAL'S OFFICE,
Washington, August 2, 1865.

ORDERS AND INSTRUCTIONS RELATIVE TO THE MUSTER OUT OF CERTAIN VOLUNTEER WHITE TROOPS, VIZ, INFANTRY, CAVALRY, AND ARTILLERY, IN THE DEPARTMENT OF TEXAS, AND ARTILLERY AND CAVALRY IN OTHER DEPARTMENTS.

I. Troops in Department of Texas.

TELEGRAM.] WAR DEPARTMENT, ADJUTANT-GENERAL'S OFFICE,
Washington, August 1, 1865.

Maj. Gen. P. H. SHERIDAN, U. S. Army,
Commanding Military Division of the Gulf, New Orleans, La.:

You are authorized by the Secretary of War to cause all volunteer white troops—cavalry, infantry, and artillery—serving in the Department of Texas, that you think can be dispensed with, to be mustered out of service.

The musters out will be by entire organizations, including all additions thereto by recruits and from other sources. In selecting the organizations for discharge preference should ge given to veteran regiments having the shortest time to serve.

The musters out, discharges, and payments will be made under the regulations promulgated in General Orders, No. 94, current series, from this office, except that officers and men who desire to receive their discharges and payments at the rendezvous where mustered out will be permitted to do so.

Please forward to this office without delay a list of the regiments and independent companies you may select for discharge under this order, giving therein for each the strength, present and absent, respectively. So soon as the list is completed, inform me by telegraph of the number, present and absent, for the respective States.

Separate lists of those who may desire to receive their discharges and payments at the rendezvous for muster out should be placed in the hands of the chief paymaster, so that he can at once make arrangements for payments.

Acknowledge receipt of this.

THOMAS M. VINCENT,
Assistant Adjutant-General.

II. Cavalry and artillery (whose services are no longer needed) ordered mustered out under special instructions, of dates set opposite the organizations respectively:

New York.—Seventh Artillery (Battalion), July 24, 1865; Second Provisional Cavalry, July 23, 1865.

Pennsylvania.—Second Provisional Cavalry, July 23, 1865; One hundred and eighty-seventh Infantry, July 24, 1865.

E. D. TOWNSEND,
Assistant Adjutant-General.

STATE OF IOWA, ADJUTANT-GENERAL'S OFFICE,
Clinton, August 9, 1865.

Col. T. M. VINCENT,
Assistant Adjutant-General, Washington, D. C.:

COLONEL: I have the honor to transmit you exhibit of men furnished by Iowa for three-months' term of service (4,816), for which as yet the State has not been allowed credit. All the men raised for the term of one and two years, except drafted and substitutes, have been heretofore reported on the regular monthly exhibits forwarded from this office.

In addition to the 4,816 three-months' men now reported, the State has furnished men for which no credit has been given, as follows:

Not allowed on report of July 30, 1865	779
Not allowed reported from this office from October 1, 1864, to May 20, 1865	172
Not allowed men in Wisconsin regiments	100
Not allowed men in Dakota regiments	16
Not yet reported to your office:	
Men in Illinois regiments	465
Men in Kansas regiments	186
Men in Nebraska regiments	177
Total three-years' men	1,895
Total two-years' men embraced in reports of January, February, and March, 1864	5
One-year's men reported from October 1, 1864, to May 20, 1865, not yet acknowledged	7,495
Equal to 2,397 three-years' men not yet allowed.	

This statement is based on the assumption that all the men acknowledged by your Department were counted as for three-years' term, and is exclusive of drafted men and substitutes, which class has not yet been reported to this office by the acting assistant provost-marshal-general of the State. I have the honor to request that the necessary instructions may be issued directing such a report furnished with a view to completion of the records of this office and a final adjustment of quotas and credits.

With great respect, I have the honor to be, truly, yours,

N. B. BAKER,
Adjutant-General of Iowa.

MEMORANDUM.] WAR DEPT., ADJT. GENERAL'S OFFICE,
Washington, August 12, 1865.

It has been decided that the men of the Signal Corps shall be considered, as regards payment of balance of bounty, on the same footing as volunteers.

They will therefore be entitled to receive the balance of bounty in the same way as volunteers under the recent orders for discharge on account of their services being no longer required.

SAML. BRECK,
Assistant Adjutant-General.

CIRCULAR No. 41. WAR DEPT., ADJUTANT-GENERAL'S OFFICE,
Washington, August 15, 1865.

ORDERS AND INSTRUCTIONS RELATIVE TO THE MUSTER OUT OF CERTAIN VOLUNTEER WHITE TROOPS.

Infantry and heavy artillery in the Middle Department, and Departments of Washington, Virginia, North Carolina, Kentucky, and Mississippi. Also certain infantry, cavalry, and artillery in various armies and departments.

I. Infantry and heavy artillery in Middle and other departments.

TELEGRAM.] WAR DEPARTMENT, ADJUTANT-GENERAL'S OFFICE,
Washington, August 14, 1865.

Maj. Gen. A. H. TERRY, U. S. Volunteers,
Commanding Department of Virginia, Richmond, Va.:

The Secretary of War directs that the volunteer white troops—infantry and heavy artillery—in your department be reduced immediately by the discharge of 5,000 men. The musters out will be by entire organizations, including all additions thereto by recruits and from other sources. Organizations having the shortest time to serve will be selected for discharge. The musters out, discharges, and payments will be made under the regulations promulgated in General Orders, No. 94, current series, from this office.

Please forward to this office without delay a list of the regiments and independent companies you may select for discharge under this order, giving therein for each the strength, present and absent, respectively.

So soon as the list is completed inform me by telegraph of the number, present and absent, for the respective States.

Acknowledge receipt of this.

THOMAS M. VINCENT,
Assistant Adjutant-General.

NOTE.—Similar orders, dated August 14, were sent the commanding generals of the following departments for the discharge of the number of men set opposite them, respectively, viz: Middle, 6,000; Washington, 8,000; Kentucky, 5,000; North Carolina, 8,000; Mississippi, 2,000.

II. Regiments of infantry, cavalry, and artillery (whose services are no longer required) ordered mustered out of service under special instructions, of dates set opposite them respectively:

New York.—Fifteenth Heavy Artillery, August 8, 1865; Fifth Infantry, August 9, 1865; Sixty-second Infantry, August 14, 1865; Sixty-sixth Infantry, August 14, 1865.

Pennsylvania.—One Hundred and eighty-sixth Infantry, August 8, 1865.

Indiana.—Ninth Cavalry, August 10, 1865; Tenth Cavalry, August 10, 1865.

MEMORANDA.—*August 3, 1865.*—The order of August 2 (Circular No. 39, current series, Adjutant-General's Office), relative to discharge of troops in the Department of Texas, was extended to include the Department of Louisiana.

E. D. TOWNSEND,
Assistant Adjutant-General.

CHATTANOOGA, TENN., *August 15, 1865.*

Brig. Gen. D. C. MCCALLUM,
Director and General Manager Military Railroads of the United States:

GENERAL: In compliance with your order of the 31st ultimo, I herewith transmit a report of operations of the Construction Corps, U. S. Military Railroads, Division of the Tennessee, from June 1, 1865 (the date of my last report), to August 1, 1865. At the date of my former report we had an effective force of 1,200 men, composed of the First, Seventh, and part of the Fourth Divisions, all of whom were employed in the reconstruction of the Chattanooga and Atlanta Railroad, which had been opened at that time to the Etowah River. From thence to Atlanta, forty-five miles, the road had been totally destroyed by General Sherman prior to his evacuation of the city. Upon the completion of the bridge across the Etowah, three spans of which had been destroyed, the whole of the carpenter force was distributed along the line and employed in cutting and hauling out cross-ties. One division of trackmen were employed laying the iron, whilst another division was clearing off the debris and surfacing up track, thereby allowing the use of the road as fast as the iron was laid. I had at the same time a large force of the Seventh Division of trackmen at Chattanooga straightening crooked rails, which were used exclusively in laying the track between Etowah to Marietta. We crossed the Etowah bridge June 5, having been four days rebuilding it, and reached Allatoona on the morning of the 15th. Upon reaching this point I sent the bridge force of the First Division ahead to Allatoona Creek, who by the time we reached it with the track had the bridge, 200 feet in length, including a truss of 50 feet, completed and ready for crossing. Reached Acworth on the 20th and turned the road over to the transportation department, who commenced operating it at once to that point. Again sent forward the carpenter force to Big Shanty and points south of it, and whilst a part were getting out ties another party commenced laying track northward, thus enabling us to close up the gap of six miles in four days, reaching the latter point on the 24th. Rebuilt water-tank and frame and put up a pump at Moon Station, two miles north of Big Shanty. Between Big Shanty and Marietta there was laid by colored troops, under the direction of General Winslow, commanding at Atlanta, about three miles of iron which they had gathered up and straightened. It was laid without chairs, and owing to the scarcity of spike only about one-fourth spiked. Put up a tank, frame, and pump at Kenesaw Mountain, and reached Marietta on the 29th. From Marietta to Atlanta, which point we reached on the morning of July 4, the track had been laid, with the exception of about three miles, by parties under the direction of General Winslow. There was but little of it spiked, and few or no chairs on, excepting from the Chattahoochee to Atlanta. They also built the Chattahoochee bridge, a structure 725 feet in length and 90 feet in height, and a trestle 400 feet in length around a break in the high embankment near Vining's, caused by the destruction of a culvert. The expense incurred in building the Chattahoochee bridge, the trestle at Vining's, and laying some eighteen miles of track, in addition to the labor of troops, was as follows:

Cost of bridge, as per settlement of General Winslow with Grant & Co., builders, and approved by General Wilson:

725 feet (lineal) of bridging, at $11 per foot	$7,975
Amount due for track laying, as per check rolls, approved as above	7,167
Amount of work done at culvert near Vining's, approved as above	528
Total amount	15,670

The above amount ($15,670) I think is justly chargeable to construction, and would therefore respectfully recommend its payment. The work was done by order of Major-General Wilson, commanding Cavalry Corps in Georgia, and at a cost less perhaps than we could have done it ourselves, besides very materially expediting the completion of the road.

At Atlanta we have put down extensive side-tracks, amounting in the aggregate to over three miles, and have erected a large freight platform 400 feet in length by 30 in width, with a shed roof over part of it. Upon the completion of the road to Atlanta, and after having put the track in a thorough condition, I again commenced a reduction of the corps, which at this date amounts to but little over 200 men. With the small bridge force retained, I am putting the Howe truss bridge, ordered for Allatoona Creek a year ago, and stored at Chattanooga, across the chasm in the bank, near Vining's, produced by the destruction of the culvert before alluded to. The break is upward of 100 feet in width and gradually increasing, and the trestle around it on so insecure a foundation I have thought it advisable to substitute it with a bridge. The balance of my track force are gathering up the crooked iron on the Chattanooga and Atlanta road. Below please find a recapitulation of work done in June and July, expenditure of material, amount of iron manufactured at rolling-mill, and amount of pay-rolls for June and July, exclusive of wages paid at rolling-mill.

Summary of work done on the Chattanooga and Atlanta Railroad during June and July, 1865: 28 miles of track relaid; 41 miles of track surfaced and repaired; 525 feet (lineal) of bridging; 42,000 cross-ties cut and delivered; 3,000 cubic feet of timber cut; 5 water-tanks erected; 20 switches and frogs put in.

Expenditure of material: 14,794 iron rails (20 feet long), 18,000 chairs, 1,140 kegs railroad spike, 60 kegs bridge spike, 20 frogs and switches, 5 water-tanks (complete), 3,000 cubic feet timber, 42,000 cross-ties.

Cost of labor in June and July: Amount of pay-roll for June, $117,866.91; for July, $76,361.

Report of iron manufactured at U. S. Military Railroad rolling-mill at Chattanooga, Tenn., up to July 31, 1865.

Date.	Articles.	Manufactured.	Issued.	On hand.
		Pounds.	*Pounds.*	*Pounds.*
To June 1, 1865	Iron rails	2,264,320	916,026	1,348,294
To June 30, 1865	do	1,156,292		2,504,586
To July 31, 1865	do	1,365,100	28,492	3,841,194
Total		4,785,712	944,518	

	Tons.
Manufactured to date	2,136
Issued to date	421
On hand to date	1,715

Plans and drawings of the rolling-mill, with an estimate of its cost, were forwarded to A. Anderson, esq., chief superintendent and engineer, ten days ago.

I have the honor to be, very respectfully, your obedient servant,

L. H. EICHOLTZ,
Acting Chief Engineer Government Railroads Division of the Tennessee.

QUARTERMASTER-GENERAL'S OFFICE,
Washington, D. C., August 21, 1865.

Hon. E. M. STANTON,
Secretary of War, Washington, D. C.:

SIR: I have the honor to transmit herewith letter of Brevet Major-General Webster, dated July 23, 1865, referred for report.

The Quartermaster-General is fully impressed with the importance of restoring the Southern railroads to civil control. Paragraph II, General Orders, No. 77, War Department, April 28, 1865, directed that all purchases for railroad construction and transportation be stopped.

This paragraph the Quartermaster-General republished in his General Orders, No. 24, April 29, 1865, calling special attention thereto, and directed (paragraph VI) that all railroad construction and repairs, except those needed on lines by which troops are still supplied or by which troops may be marching, will cease.

The Quartermaster-General, on the 19th of May, 1865, made report recommending a basis for transfer of railroads to their owners, and in this report anticipated most of the considerations presented by General Webster. Reference is respectfully made to that report.*

Orders have been given to the general manager U. S. Military Railroads for the relinquishment of the railroads under his control in Virginia and North Carolina and in the Southwest; and on the 1st of August, 1865, a recommendation was forwarded to the War Department that two roads, reported by General McCallum as the only ones in his control of which the transfer had not been ordered, should be also ordered to be turned over.

The railroads in the Military Division of the Gulf not having been under control of General McCallum, the chief quartermaster of that division has been instructed to turn these over to parties approved by the general commanding.

Orders, therefore, have been given for the transfer to their companies of all railroads in military possession as soon as parties qualified and willing to assume charge of them present themselves.

Specific instructions from the Secretary of War or from the lieutenant-general to the military commanders of departments and districts urging upon them the importance of transferring all these railroads to their civil managers, and directing them to communicate with the civil authorities and endeavor to effect this transfer in all cases, would probably hasten the event.

Upon return from a short absence on duty in Missouri the Quartermaster-General found that the great lines of railroads diverging from Nashville, though ordered to be turned over under authority of the Secretary of War dated July 21, 1865, were still under Government control, and he is informed that no responsible parties have as yet

---

* See p. 26.

qualified themselves to take charge of them. Probably Major-General Thomas, if his attention is directed to the urgent importance of the subject by the Secretary of War or by the lieutenant-general, may be able to induce the representatives of the owners of the roads to qualify themselves to take charge of them.

Schedules of all rolling-stock and railroad equipment the property of the United States are being prepared with a view to their sale.

The sale of much railroad property in Virginia and at several other points has been already advertised.

Very respectfully, your obedient servant,

M. C. MEIGS,
Quartermaster-General, Brevet Major-General.

[Inclosure.]

MACON, GA., *July 23, 1865.*

Lieut. Gen. U. S. GRANT,
Comdg. Armies of the United States, Washington, D. C.:

GENERAL: I deem it my duty to earnestly recommend that the railroads now operated by the United States be turned over to their respective companies so soon as (1) those companies shall elect officers and directors who can be relied on as thoroughly loyal to the Government, and (2) the accounts between the railroads and the Government can be properly adjusted.

Although, as I have heretofore said, the roads might be economically and advantageously operated by the Government, it is yet not likely that, as a matter of fact, they will be so operated, and consequently they should be given up at the earliest moment that the two above specified conditions can be fulfilled.

In the meantime, the United States ought not to be at the expense of putting the roads in thorough repair merely for the benefit of the companies. All work on track or bridges beyond what is absolutely necessary for the safety of trains should be discontinued. All repairs to locomotives and cars to which the companies have any claim should be stopped at once, as should also the running of the rolling-mill at Chattanooga.

The proper adjustment of accounts between the Government and the roads will require a good deal of consideration. Some of the roads have been put by the Government in a much better condition than they were before it took possession. It will not be right to give them, without pay, the advantage of thorough repairs, new iron, permanent bridges, &c. If they claim compensation for the use of their roads, it is sufficient to answer that in the early stages of the war they voluntarily and zealously aided the enemy, furnishing them not only with the great "interior lines" of communication and supply, of which all have heard so much, but with knowing heads and ready hands to operate them. Their able railroad men were of more service to the rebels than many of their general officers. No claim of theirs for pay or damages should be entertained a moment. It is only necessary to find out how much they are fairly indebted to the United States. To do this, the disbursing officers should be called on for reports of expenditures for permanent improvements.

Of course it will be necessary, previous to relinquishing the roads, to make agreements as to future transportation of troops and supplies, mails, and such other matters as the convenience of the Government may require.

The points herein noticed may have been already fully considered and decided upon, but as they are included in the letter of my instructions for my present duty, I make the suggestions, with a strong impression of the importance of early action in the matter.

I am, very respectfully, general, your most obedient servant,

J. D. WEBSTER,
Brevet Major-General.

GENERAL ORDERS, No. 137. } WAR DEPT., ADJT. GENERAL'S OFFICE, *Washington, August 31, 1865.*

The following proclamations of the President of the United States in relation to restrictions on trade are published for the information and guidance of all concerned:

I. *August 29, 1865.*—Removing restrictions on articles contraband of war.

BY THE PRESIDENT OF THE UNITED STATES OF AMERICA:

A PROCLAMATION.

Whereas, by my proclamations of the thirteenth and twenty-fourth of June, one thousand eight hundred and sixty-five, removing restrictions, in part, upon internal, domestic, and coastwise intercourse and trade with those States recently declared in insurrection, certain articles were excepted from the effect of said proclamations as contraband of war; and whereas, the necessity for restricting trade in said articles has now, in a great measure, ceased: It is hereby ordered that on and after the first day of September, one thousand eight hundred and sixty-five, all restrictions aforesaid be removed, so that the articles declared by the said proclamations to be contraband of war may be imported into and sold in said States, subject only to such regulations as the Secretary of the Treasury may prescribe.

In testimony whereof I have hereunto set my hand and caused the seal of the United States to be affixed.

Done at the city of Washington this twenty-ninth day of August, in the year of our Lord one thousand eight hundred and sixty-five, and of the Independence of the United States of America the eighty-ninth [ninetieth].

[L. S.]

ANDREW JOHNSON.

By the President:

WILLIAM H. SEWARD,
Secretary of State.

II. *June 13, 1865.*—Removing restrictions on trade east of the Mississippi River, and declaring insurrection suppressed in Tennessee, and certain disabilities in that State removed.

BY THE PRESIDENT OF THE UNITED STATES OF AMERICA:

A PROCLAMATION.

Whereas, by my proclamation of the twenty-ninth of April,* one thousand eight hundred and sixty-five, all restrictions upon internal, domestic, and commercial intercourse, with certain exceptions therein specified and set forth, were removed "in such parts of the States of Tennessee, Virginia, North Carolina, South Carolina, Georgia, Florida, Alabama, Mississippi, and so much of Louisiana as lies east of the Mississippi River as shall be embraced within the lines of national military occupation;"

And whereas, by my proclamation of the twenty-second of May, one thousand eight hundred and sixty-five, for reasons therein given, it was declared that certain ports of the United States which had been previously closed against foreign commerce should, with certain specified exceptions, be reopened to such commerce on and after the first day of July next, subject to the laws of the United States, and in pursuance of such regulations as might be prescribed by the Secretary of the Treasury;

And whereas, I am satisfactorily informed that dangerous combinations against the laws of the United States no longer exist within the State of Tennessee; that the insurrection heretofore existing within said State has been suppressed; that within

---

*Executive order; see p. 105.

the boundaries thereof the authority of the United States is undisputed, and that such officers of the United States as have been duly commissioned are in the undisturbed exercise of their official functions:

Now, therefore, be it known, that I, Andrew Johnson, President of the United States, do hereby declare that all restrictions upon internal, domestic, and coastwise intercourse and trade, and upon the removal of products of States heretofore declared in insurrection, reserving and excepting only those relating to contraband of war, as hereinafter recited, and also those which relate to the reservation of the rights of the United States to property purchased in the territory of an enemy, heretofore imposed in the territory of the United States east of the Mississippi River, are annulled, and I do hereby direct that they be forthwith removed; and that, on and after the first day of July next, all restrictions upon foreign commerce with said ports, with the exception and reservation aforesaid, be likewise removed; and that the commerce of said States shall be conducted under the supervision of the regularly appointed officers of the customs provided by law; and such officers of the customs shall receive any captured and abandoned property that may be turned over to them, under the law, by the military or naval forces of the United States, and dispose of such property as shall be directed by the Secretary of the Treasury. The following articles contraband of war are excepted from the effect of this proclamation: Arms, ammunition, all articles from which ammunition is made, and gray uniforms and cloth.

And I hereby also proclaim and declare that the insurrection, so far as it relates to and within the State of Tennessee, and the inhabitants of the said State of Tennessee as recognized and constituted under their recently adopted constitution and reorganization, and accepted by them, is suppressed; and therefore, also, that all the disabilities and disqualifications attaching to said State and the inhabitants thereof consequent upon any proclamations issued by virtue of the fifth section of the act entitled "An act further to provide for the collection of duties on imports, and for other purposes," approved the thirteenth day of July, one thousand eight hundred and sixty-one, are removed.

But nothing herein contained shall be considered or construed as in any wise changing or impairing any of the penalties and forfeitures for treason heretofore incurred under the laws of the United States, or any of the provisions, restrictions, or disabilities set forth in my proclamation bearing date the twenty-ninth day of May, one thousand eight hundred and sixty-five, or as impairing existing regulations for the suspension of the habeas corpus, and the exercise of military law in cases where it shall be necessary for the general public safety and welfare during the existing insurrection; nor shall this proclamation affect, or in any way impair, any laws heretofore passed by Congress, and duly approved by the President, or any proclamations or orders issued by him during the aforesaid insurrection, abolishing slavery, or in any way affecting the relations of slavery, whether of persons or [of] property; but, on the contrary, all such laws and proclamations heretofore made or issued are expressly saved and declared to be in full force and virtue.

In testimony whereof I have hereunto set my hand and caused the seal of the United States to be affixed.

Done at the city of Washington this thirteenth day of June, in the year of our Lord one thousand eight hundred and sixty-five, and of the Independence of the United States of America the eighty-ninth.

[L.S.] ANDREW JOHNSON.

By the President:

WILLIAM H. SEWARD,
Secretary of State.

III. *June 24, 1865.*—Removing restrictions on trade west of the Mississippi River.

By the President of the United States of America:

A PROCLAMATION.

Whereas, it has been the desire of the General Government of the United States to restore unrestricted commercial intercourse between and in the several States, as soon as the same could be safely done in view of resistance to the authority of the United States by combinations of armed insurgents;

And whereas, that desire has been shown in my proclamations of the twenty-ninth of April, one thousand eight hundred and sixty-five; the thirteenth of June, one thousand eight hundred and sixty-five; and the twenty-third of June, one thousand eight hundred and sixty-five;

And whereas, it now seems expedient and proper to remove restrictions upon internal, domestic, and coastwise trade and commercial intercourse between and within the States and Territories west of the Mississippi River:

Now, therefore, be it known that I, Andrew Johnson, President of the United States, do hereby declare that all restrictions upon internal, domestic, and coastwise intercourse and trade, and upon the purchase and removal of products of States and parts of States and Territories heretofore declared in insurrection, lying west of the Mississippi River (excepting only those relating to property heretofore purchased by the agents or captured by or surrendered to the forces of the United States, and to the transportation thereto or therein, on private account, of arms, ammunition, all articles from which ammunition is made, gray uniforms and gray cloth), are annulled, and I do hereby direct that they be forthwith removed; and also, that the commerce of such States and parts of States shall be conducted under the supervision of the regularly appointed officers of the customs, [who] shall receive any captured and abandoned property that may be turned over to them, under the law, by the military or naval forces of the United States, and dispose of the same in accordance with instructions on the subject issued by the Secretary of the Treasury.

In testimony whereof I have hereunto set my hand and caused the seal of the United States to be affixed.

Done at the city of Washington this twenty-fourth day of June, in the year of our Lord one thousand eight hundred and sixty-five, and of the Independence of the United States of America the eighty-ninth.

[L. S.] ANDREW JOHNSON.

By the President:

W. HUNTER,
Acting Secretary of State.

IV. *April 29, 1865.*—Executive order removing restrictions on trade, except in articles contraband of war, in certain States.

EXECUTIVE CHAMBER,
Washington, April 29, 1865.

Being desirous to relieve all loyal citizens and well-disposed persons residing in insurrectionary States from unnecessary commercial restrictions, and to encourage them to return to peaceful pursuits, it is hereby ordered:

I. That all restrictions upon internal, domestic, and coastwise commercial intercourse be discontinued in such parts of the States of Tennessee, Virginia, North Carolina, South Carolina, Georgia, Florida, Alabama, Mississippi, and so much of Louisiana as lies east of the Mississippi River as shall be embraced within the lines of national military occupation, excepting only such restrictions as are imposed by acts of Congress and regulations in pursuance thereof, prescribed by the Secretary of the Treasury and approved by the President, and excepting also from the effect of this order the following articles contraband of war, to wit, arms, ammunition, all articles from which ammunition is manufactured, gray uniforms and cloth, locomotives, cars, railroad iron, and machinery for operating railroads, telegraph wires, insulators, and instruments for operating telegraph lines.

II. All existing military and naval orders in any manner restricting internal, domestic, and coastwise commercial intercourse and trade with or in the localities above named be, and the same are hereby, revoked; and that no military or naval officer in any manner interrupt or interfere with the same, or with any boats or other vessels engaged therein, under proper authority, pursuant to the regulations of the Secretary of the Treasury.

ANDREW JOHNSON.

V. *May 22, 1865.*—Reopening of ports, except four in Texas, disallowing belligerent rights in certain cases, and removing certain restrictions on trade.

BY THE PRESIDENT OF THE UNITED STATES OF AMERICA:

A PROCLAMATION.

Whereas, by the proclamation of the President of the eleventh day of April last, certain ports of the United States therein specified, which had previously been subject to blockade, were, for objects of public safety, declared, in conformity with previous special legislation of Congress, to be closed against foreign commerce during the national will, to be thereafter expressed and made known by the President; and whereas, events and circumstances have since occurred which in my judgment render it expedient to remove that restriction, except as to the ports of Galveston, La Salle, Brazos de Santiago (Point Isabel), and Brownsville, in the State of Texas:

Now, therefore, be it known that I, Andrew Johnson, President of the United States, do hereby declare that the ports aforesaid, not excepted as above, shall be open to foreign commerce from and after the first day of July next; that commercial intercourse with the said ports may from that time be carried on subject to the laws of the United States, and in pursuance of such regulations as may be prescribed by the Secretary of the Treasury. If, however, any vessel from a foreign port shall enter any of the before-named excepted ports in the State of Texas, she will continue to be held liable to the penalties prescribed by the act of Congress approved on the thirteenth day of July, eighteen hundred and sixty-one, and the persons on board of her to such penalties as may be incurred, pursuant to the laws of war, for trading or attempting to trade with an enemy.

And I, Andrew Johnson, President of the United States, do hereby declare and make known that the United States of America do, henceforth, disallow to all persons trading, or attempting to trade, in any ports of the United States in violation of the laws thereof, all pretense of belligerent rights and privileges; and I give notice that, from the date of this proclamation, all such offenders will be held and dealt with as pirates.

It is also ordered that all restrictions upon trade heretofore imposed in the territory of the United States east of the Mississippi River, save those relating to contraband of war, to the reservation of the rights of the United States to property purchased in the territory of an enemy, and to the twenty-five per cent. upon purchases of cotton, be removed. All provisions of the internal revenue law will be carried into effect under the proper officers.

In witness whereof I have hereunto set my hand and caused the seal of the United States to be affixed.

Done at the city of Washington this twenty-second day of May, in the year of our Lord one thousand eight hundred and sixty-five, and of the Independence of the United States of America the eighty-ninth.

[L. S.] ANDREW JOHNSON.

By the President:

W. HUNTER,
Acting Secretary of State.

VI. *June 23, 1865.*—Rescinding the blockade as to all ports of the United States, including that of Galveston.

BY THE PRESIDENT OF THE UNITED STATES OF AMERICA:

A PROCLAMATION.

Whereas, by the proclamations of the President of the nineteenth and twenty-seventh of April, eighteen hundred and sixty-one, a blockade of certain ports of the United States was set on foot; but whereas, the reasons for that measure have ceased to exist:

Now, therefore, be it known that I, Andrew Johnson, President of the United States, do hereby declare and proclaim the blockade aforesaid to be rescinded as to all the ports aforesaid, including that of Galveston and other ports west of the Mississippi River, which ports will be open to foreign commerce on the first of July next, on the terms and conditions set forth in my proclamation of the twenty-second of May last.

It is to be understood, however, that the blockade thus rescinded was an international measure for the purpose of protecting the sovereign rights of the United States. The greater or less subversion of civil authority in the region to which it applied, and the impracticability of at once restoring that in due efficiency, may, for a season, make it advisable to employ the Army and Navy of the United States toward carrying the laws into effect, wherever such employment may be necessary.

In testimony whereof I have hereunto set my hand and caused the seal of the United States to be affixed.

Done at the city of Washington this twenty-third day of June, in the year of our Lord one thousand eight hundred and sixty-five, and of the Independence of the United States of America the eighty-ninth.

[L. S.] ANDREW JOHNSON.

By the President:

W. HUNTER,
Acting Secretary of State.

VII. *April 11, 1865.*—Closing certain ports.

BY THE PRESIDENT OF THE UNITED STATES OF AMERICA:

A PROCLAMATION.

Whereas, by my proclamations of the nineteenth and twenty-seventh days of April, one thousand eight hundred and sixty-one, the ports of the United States in the States of Virginia, North Carolina, South Carolina, Georgia, Florida, Alabama, Mississippi, Louisiana, and Texas were declared to be subject to blockade; but whereas, the said blockade has, in consequence of actual military occupation by this Government, since been conditionally set aside or relaxed in respect to the ports of Norfolk and Alexandria, in the State of Virginia; Beaufort, in the State of North Carolina; Port Royal, in the State of South Carolina; Pensacola and Fernandina, in the State of Florida, and New Orleans, in the State of Louisiana;

And whereas, by the fourth section of the act of Congress approved on the thirteenth of July, eighteen hundred and sixty-one, entitled "An act further to provide for the collection of duties on imports, and for other purposes," the President, for the reasons therein set forth, is authorized to close certain ports of entry:

Now, therefore, be it known that I, Abraham Lincoln, President of the United States, do hereby proclaim that the ports of Richmond, Tappahannock, Cherrystone, Yorktown, and Petersburg, in Virginia; of Camden (Elizabeth City), Edenton, Plymouth, Washington, New Berne, Ocracoke, and Wilmington, in North Carolina; of Charleston, Georgetown, and Beaufort, in South Carolina; of Savannah, Saint Mary's, and Brunswick (Darien), in Georgia; of Mobile, in Alabama; of Pearl River (Shieldsborough), Natchez, and Vicksburg, in Mississippi; of Saint Augustine, Key West, Saint Mark's (Port Leon), Saint John's (Jacksonville), and Apalachicola, in Florida; of Teche (Franklin), in Louisiana; of Galveston, La Salle, Brazos de Santiago (Point Isabel), and Brownsville, in Texas, are hereby closed, and all right of importation, warehousing, and other privileges shall, in respect to the ports aforesaid, cease, until they shall have again been opened by order of the President; and if, while said ports are so closed, any ship or vessel from beyond the United States, or having on board any articles subject to duties, shall attempt to enter any such ports, the same, together with its tackle, apparel, furniture, and cargo, shall be forfeited to the United States.

In witness whereof I have hereunto set my hand and caused the seal of the United States to be affixed.

Done at the city of Washington this eleventh day of April, in the year of our Lord one thousand eight hundred and sixty-five, and of the Independence of the United States of America the eighty-ninth.

[L. S.] ABRAHAM LINCOLN.

By the President:

WILLIAM H. SEWARD,
Secretary of State.

VIII. *April 11, 1865.*—Port of Key West to remain open.

BY THE PRESIDENT OF THE UNITED STATES OF AMERICA:

A PROCLAMATION.

Whereas, by my proclamation of this date the port of Key West, in the State of Florida, was inadvertently included among those which are not open to commerce:

Now, therefore, be it known that I, Abraham Lincoln, President of the United States, do hereby declare and make known that the said port of Key West is and shall remain open to foreign and domestic commerce upon the same conditions by which that commerce has there hitherto been governed.

In testimony whereof I have hereunto set my hand and caused the seal of the United States to be affixed.

Done at the city of Washington this eleventh day of April, in the year of our Lord one thousand eight hundred and sixty-five, and of the Independence of the United States of America the eighty-ninth.

[L. S.] ABRAHAM LINCOLN.

By the President:

WILLIAM H. SEWARD,
Secretary of State.

By order of the Secretary of War:

E. D. TOWNSEND,
Assistant Adjutant-General.

CIRCULAR No. 44.

WAR DEPT., ADJUTANT-GENERAL'S OFFICE,
Washington, September 9, 1865.

ORDERS AND INSTRUCTIONS RELATIVE TO THE MUSTER OUT OF CERTAIN VOLUNTEERS, VIZ, ORGANIZATIONS OF COLORED TROOPS ENLISTED IN NORTHERN STATES, AND CERTAIN WHITE TROOPS IN VARIOUS ARMIES AND DEPARTMENTS.

I. Organizations of colored troops enlisted in Northern States.

TELEGRAM.]

WAR DEPARTMENT, ADJUTANT-GENERAL'S OFFICE,
Washington, September 8, 1865.

COMMANDING GENERAL DEPARTMENT OF NORTH CAROLINA,
Raleigh, N. C.:

The Secretary of War directs that all organizations of colored troops in your department which were enlisted in the Northern States be mustered out of service immediately. The musters out will be by entire organizations, including all additions thereto by recruits and from other sources. The musters out, discharges, and payments will be made under the regulations promulgated in General Orders, No. 94, current series, from this office.

Please forward to this office without delay a list of the regiments and independent companies to be discharged under this order, giving therein for each the strength, present and absent, respectively.

Acknowledge receipt of this.

THOMAS M. VINCENT,
Assistant Adjutant-General.

NOTE.—Orders similar to the foregoing, dated September 8, were sent to the commanding generals of the Departments of Virginia, Florida, Texas, Louisiana, and Arkansas.

II. White troops in various departments—services no longer required.

MEMORANDA.

1. *August 21, 1865.*—Major-General Reynolds, commanding Department of Arkansas, was directed to muster out 3,000 additional troops of his command.

2. *August 24, 1865.*—Major-General Hooker, commanding the Department of the East, was directed to cause the two remaining "Independent companies, Maine Coast Guards," to be mustered out.

3. *September 1, 1865.*—Major-General Hooker was directed to relieve from duty for muster out Companies A and B, New Hampshire Heavy Artillery, and Company D, First Battalion Massachusetts Heavy Artillery.

4. *September 8, 1865.*—Major-General Augur, commanding Department of Washington, was ordered to reduce the volunteer force in his command to 6,000 commissioned officers and enlisted men, of all arms.

E. D. TOWNSEND,
Assistant Adjutant-General.

WAR DEPT., PROVOST-MARSHAL-GENERAL'S OFFICE,
Washington, D. C., September 11, 1865.

[Hon. E. M. STANTON,
Secretary of War:]

Under the general orders of the War Department I, sometime since, discharged all the employés in the different districts who could be spared, so that now there is in a district only a provost-marshal and one clerk, and they are engaged in closing up old business. Some districts have been consolidated, and one provost-marshal is acting for two or more consolidated districts. The arrest of deserters by this Bureau cannot therefore be effected, unless it is deemed best by the Secretary of War to order that provost-marshals employ and pay suitable persons for that purpose, or that a reward be allowed for the arrest and delivery of deserters to provost-marshals, the reward being made large enough to induce outsiders to engage in the business. Section 21 of the act approved March 3, 1865, is as follows:

SEC. 21. *And be it further enacted*, That, in addition to the other lawful penalties of the crime of desertion from the military or naval service, all persons who have deserted the military or naval service of the United States, who shall not return to said service, or report themselves to a provost-marshal, within sixty days after the proclamation hereinafter mentioned, shall be deemed and taken to have voluntarily relinquished and forfeited their rights of citizenship and their rights to become citizens; and such deserters shall be forever incapable of holding any office of trust or profit under the United States, or of exercising any rights of citizens thereof; and all persons who shall hereafter desert the military or naval service, and all persons who, being duly enrolled, shall depart the jurisdiction of the district in which he is enrolled, or go beyond the limits of the United States, with intent to avoid any draft into the military or naval service, duly ordered, shall be liable to the penalties of this section. And the President is hereby authorized and required forthwith, on the passage of this act, to issue his proclamation setting forth the provisions of this section, in which proclamation the President is requested to notify all deserters returning within sixty days as aforesaid, that they shall be pardoned on condition of returning to their regiments and companies, or to such other organization as they may be assigned to, until they shall have served for a period of time equal to their original term of enlistment.

To make this law operative the fact of desertion should be established and announced in each case, if possible. The undertaking, however, would be one of magnitude. Two hundred and sixty thousand three hundred and thirty-nine men have been reported to this office as deserters from the Army. I estimate that 25 per cent. of these are not deserters in fact, but are men who became absentees unintentionally or unavoidably, and afterward returned to duty. Adopting this estimate, the total number of desertions appears to be 195,255 from the ranks of the Army. Seventy-six thousand two hundred and fifty-three deserters have been arrested by this Bureau, as required by the seventh section of the enrollment act, approved March 3, 1863, which is still in force and is as follows:

SEC. 7. *And be it further enacted*, That it shall be the duty of the provost-marshals to arrest all deserters, whether regular, volunteer, militiamen, or persons called into the service under this or any other act of Congress, wherever they may be found, and to send them to the nearest military commission or military post.

Only 1,755 deserters surrendered themselves under the President's proclamation of March 11, 1865, offering pardon to all who would return to duty. There are therefore still at large 117,247 deserters from the ranks of the Army. This number does not include the non-reporting drafted men, who are deemed deserters by the law; of this class there are, by the reports, 161,286. It may be estimated that 30 per cent. of these are excusable, some having entered the service after having been drafted, others were absent at sea, and for various other causes the absence of many was unavoidable and excusable. Making the reduction of 30 per cent. gives 112,901 as the number of non-reporting drafted men who are deemed deserters, which, added to the number of deserters from the ranks, makes the total number of deserters still at large 230,148.

JAMES B. FRY,
Provost-Marshal-General.

[Inclosure.]

Colonel John Ely, acting assistant provost-marshal-general, Trenton, N. J., May 27, 1865, refers for instructions a communication from Capt. William M. Shipman, provost-marshal Third District of New Jersey, stating that many men drafted in his district in May and July, 1864, who fled to Canada and other parts unknown after being drafted, are now returning home, much to the dissatisfaction of the loyal portion of the community. Desires to know if they are to be arrested as deserters, and if so, what means are to be taken to secure their arrest, as he has no officers and no authority to employ any, and no guards to send in charge of them should they be arrested by citizens.

F. C. Reed, of Clyde, Wayne County, New York, July 31, 1865, states that the citizens of that section of country are apprehensive that their private property is insecure from the large number of sneaks and deserters who have recently come among them, and who threaten the good order of the community. He desires to know the status of this class of persons, and if they are subject to arrest as deserters. If they are, he asks for the appoinment of a suitable person to apprehend and deliver them to the proper authorities.

Bvt. Lieut. Col. R. I. Dodge, acting assistant provost-marshal-general for New York City, N. Y., August 2, 1865, recommends that the usual reward of $30 be paid for the apprehension and delivery of all deserters from the Regular Army to the proper officers, as there are large numbers of these deserters who show themselves with impunity in New York and Brooklyn, relying upon the absence of reward to secure them from arrest.

Bvt. Lieut. Col. R. M. Littler, acting assistant provost-marshal-general for Maine, August 12, 1865, forwards a communication from Capt. Elijah Low, provost-marshal, Fourth District of Maine, representing that his district is overrun with deserters from the Army and draft; that they are insolent and abusive to soldiers who have endured the hardships and perils of war, and many of whom are crippled by wounds or disease and are entitled to protection. He fears that as the only disability put upon deserters is disfranchisement by the United States Government, and as each State regulates the qualification of its own voters, they will have the right to vote under existing State laws. He asks permission to appoint suitable persons as deputy marshals to assist in executing the laws in his district.

Colonel Littler states that the same complaints of deserters returning and taunting soldiers who have lost limbs in service are made from all parts of the State, but are more numerous from the Fourth and Fifth Districts, and asks instructions as to committing deserters and payment of expenses. The majority of those lately arrested have been discharged by orders from headquarters Department of the East, with forfeiture of pay and allowances.

Stephen Miller, Governor of Minnesota, August 19, 1865, states that he learns from good citizens that many of the poltroons who fled from Minnesota to Canada and elsewhere either prior to or immediately subsequent to the draft to avoid military duty are now returning, and as they should in some way be held to a strict accountability for their infamous conduct, he hopes the War Department will take the matter in hand, as the laws of Minnesota make no provision for their punishment.

Brig. Gen. E. W. Hinks, Harrisburg, Pa., June 9, 1865, refers communication from provost-marshal Eighteenth District, Pa., representing that a large number of deserters who had previously absconded are now returning; requests to be informed if it is the desire of the Government to make special efforts for the arrest of deserters.

Lieut. Col. William N. Grier, Harrisburg, Pa., July 3, 1865, refers communication from provost-marshal Twentieth District, Pa., in reference to the number of deserters at large, and his inability, under the present arrangements, to arrest them.

Lieut. Col. William N. Grier, acting assistant provost-marshal-general for Harrisburg, Pa., August 24, 1865, forwards a communication from Capt. J. W. Kirker, provost-marshal Twenty-third District of Pennsylvania, who suggests the propriety of restoring the reward for the arrest of deserters and non-reporting drafted men, so that the assistance of civil officers and citizens may be obtained to apprehend and arrest this class of criminals, the deputy provost-marshals and special officers having been discharged.

Bvt. Brig. Gen. James Oakes, acting assistant provost-marshal-general for Illinois, forwards for instructions a communication from Capt. William H. Collins, provost-marshal Twelfth District of Illinois, who states that a number of deserters from the Army and the draft are reported to be within the limits of his district. Under existing arrangements, without guards, or rewards to secure the co-operation of citizens, he is powerless to make arrests, although good men inform him in regard to this class of persons, and asks that the Government punish them, in justice to those who have not evaded service; suggests that measures be taken to make the records of his offices permanently accessible to every county in the district, to prevent deserters from voting, and requests information on this point from the proper authorities. General Oakes says the preparation of a record of deserters for each county, as suggested by Captain Collins, would, if possible to be done at all with sufficient fullness and accuracy as to be of practical value for the purpose designated, be a work requiring much time and labor. He suggests that printed lists of deserters be prepared from the records of each district.

Lieut. Col. Charles S. Lovell, Madison, Wis., May 6, 1865, refers communication relative to the state of affairs in the town of Benton, Lafayette County, which is infested with disloyal men and returned deserters. The provost-marshal Third District of Wisconsin says the town has been in open rebellion against the Government since the war broke out, and that this is the second time he has been called upon for aid, but is unable to do anything in the matter, owing to the discharge of the special officers.

Brig. Gen. T. G. Pitcher, Indianapolis, Ind., July 3, 1865, refers communication with regard to returning deserters from the draft, and asks if it is desirable to arrest them; if so, suggests that provost-marshal be authorized to employ one deputy special agent for that purpose.

Brig. Gen. T. G. Pitcher, Indianapolis, Ind., July 20, 1865, refers for instructions communication from provost-marshal Sixth District of Indiana, stating that several deserters from the draft have returned from Canada, and asking if he shall arrest them, and if so, what disposition shall be made of them.

Bvt. Maj. William Silvey, Concord, N. H., May 31, 1865, says he is almost daily receiving information concerning the presence, in various places in the State, of deserters, and having no deputies or special agents, desires to know in what manner the arrest of these men is to be accomplished.

Col. James A. Wilcox, Columbus, Ohio, August 5, 1865: Relative to arresting deserters from the draft, their assignment, and urging that some reasonable reward be allowed to facilitate arrests. * * *

Maj. George E. Scott, Veteran Reserve Corps, August 28, 1865, forwards an extract from the report of Capt. A. D. Bean, provost-marshal Fifth District of Maine, of August 20, recommending that a list of absentees and deserters from the several drafts be furnished to the municipal authorities of the towns in his district for the purpose of enforcing the provisions of section 21 of act of Congress approved March 3, 1865, disfranchising deserters.

Exhibit of volunteers and militia mustered into the U. S. service from November 1, 1864, to April 13, 1865, the date when recruiting of troops by voluntary enlistments was stopped.

State.	New organizations.								
	3-years.			2-years.			1-year.		
	Infantry.	Cavalry.	Artillery.	Infantry.	Cavalry.	Artillery.	Infantry.	Cavalry.	Artillery.
Connecticut									
	1						1		8
Delaware									
Illinois									
	171			10			14,062		
Indiana									
	2						13,781		12
Iowa									
Kansas			58						
			6						5
Kentucky	3,211	159	255	519		2	93		
	202	4		53			1,857		
Maine									
	535			31			2,373		
Maryland							23		
		10	1				209	21	
Massachusetts									
	391	82	144				1,492	807	1
Michigan									
	3						869		
Minnesota									
	2						647		1,189
Missouri	117						101		
	37	1					2,123		
New Hampshire	25								
	7						2		3
New Jersey									
							16		
New York	94	16					40	7	
	2,862			51			1,750	515	
Ohio	1								
	26			10			14,478		
Pennsylvania	9			3		2	690		
	10					3	3,997		
Rhode Island									
							85		
Vermont									
								201	
West Virginia									
							1		
Wisconsin							23		
	121		3	351			6,831		60
District of Columbia *a*									
							2		
Grand total	3,457	175	313	522		4	970	7	
	4,370	97	154	506		3	64,576	1,544	1,278

a Up to March 31, 1865.

Exhibit of volunteers and militia mustered into the U. S. service, &c.—Continued.

State.	Old regiments.									Unassigned.		Total by States.
	3-years.			2-years.			1-year.					
	Infantry.	Cavalry.	Artillery.	Infantry.	Cavalry.	Artillery.	Infantry.	Cavalry.	Artillery.	New.	Old.	
Connecticut	77			1			3					1,488
	696	374	293				17	16	1			
Delaware	1						89	15				105
Illinois	14	1		11			282		74		29	23,426
	89	116	3	14	12	1	4,718	3,573	242			
Indiana	5						245				37	17,375
	9	7	2				2,484	218	336	7	230	
Iowa	1						26					869
	2	2	1	1	5		493	321	14		3	
Kansas	2			1			62		5			475
	11	123	5	1	16		11	128	1			
Kentucky												8,097
		8								603		
Maine	11	1					3					4,216
	139	17	12	2	2	1	918	39	50	82		
Maryland	32			2			136					1,522
	7	2		166			790	50	6		24	
Massachusetts	9											5,365
	828	410	359	10	3	4	305	173	356			
Michigan							68					6,006
	164	53		6	2		3,052	1,770	8		2	
Minnesota							9				5	2,362
		2		1	2		195	209	101			
Missouri	3						34				132	*b*6,184
	15	715	34		10	2	254	25	38	77	2,466	
New Hampshire												931
	252	101	47	1			339	112	37			
New Jersey	36						82					2,824
	529	25	3	4	1	1	2,081	42	4			
New York	128	16		16			40				2	13,629
	2,897	1,708	292	80	54	21	1,759	971	176	2	97	
Ohio	3	1					282				503	20,014
	59	18	5	72	6	1	2,292	2,095	127	21	9	
Pennsylvania	14			1			81				137	18,306
	453	357	23	4	13		4,327	2,522	76	3,086	2,498	
Rhode Island									3			1,074
	81	39	101	5	4	3	240	167	344		1	
Vermont	3						5					1,012
	107	39	5	4		2	635	3	5		3	
West Virginia	4						29					1,583
	4	12			4		877	650	2			
Wisconsin												8,620
	19	4			1		935	236	6	28	1	
District of Columbia*a*	4						20					40
	6						5			3		
Grand total	346	19		32			1,408		82		845	145,523
	6,368	4,132	1,185	371	135	36	26,816	13,335	1,830	3,909	5,334	

a Up to March 31, 1865. *b* 636 infantry and 20 cavalry for 20 months not included.

[NOTE.—The first line of figures inclosed in braces indicates colored troops; the second line represents white troops. In the original the figures for colored troops appear in red ink.]

RECAPITULATION.

	White.	Colored.	Total.	Aggregate.
New:				
Three-years	4,621	3,945	8,566	77,976
Two-years	509	526	1,035	
One-year	67,398	977	68,375	
Old:				
Three-years	11,685	414	12,099	56,293
Two-years	542	32	574	
One-year	42,081	1,539	43,620	

RECAPITULATION—Continued.

	White.	Colored.	Total.	Aggregate.
Unassigned:				
New	3, 909	1, 166	....	5, 075
Old	5, 334	845	....	6, 179
Grand total	....	....	....	145, 523

NOTE.—I am quite sure that some recruits for colored regiments were not, as the regulations direct, reported to the chief mustering officers of the States, and therefore some do not appear on this exhibit. To correct this I have directed the chief of the Bureau for Colored Troops to report direct to you the number mustered. Should his number exceed those herein, the excess should be added to my totals. I have omitted from this the musters from rebel States, as they will be furnished in the report above referred to.

THOMAS M. VINCENT,
Assistant Adjutant-General.

WAR DEPARTMENT, ADJUTANT-GENERAL'S OFFICE,
September 13, 1865.

Exhibit of the number of troops—volunteers (white and colored) and regulars—that will remain in service after the musters out, as already ordered, shall have been completed.a

Department.	For the orders directing reductions to the numbers below enumerated, see Circulars Nos. 22, 26, 28, 30, 31, 35, 39, 41, and 44, Adjutant-General's Office, 1865.		
	White.	Colored.	Total.
East	3, 999	....	3, 999
Middle	7, 026	....	7, 026
Washington	6, 000	....	6, 000
Ohio	5, 173	....	5, 173
Kentucky	....	10, 196	10, 196
Missouri	11, 400	....	11, 400
Virginia	18, 483	....	18, 483
North Carolina	4, 516	2, 530	7, 046
South Carolina	5, 732	4, 620	10, 352
Georgia	13, 376	3, 789	17, 165
Mississippi	3, 806	10, 500	14, 306
Arkansas	5, 300	2, 932	8, 232
Alabama	14, 400	4, 000	
	4, 000	2, 695	
	10, 400	6, 695	17, 095
Florida	3, 591	3, 638	7, 229
Louisiana	6, 700	16, 816	23, 516
Texas	24, 000	9, 363	33, 363
Tennessee	2, 000	16, 000	
	....	4, 000	
	....	12, 000	14, 000
California Columbia	12, 030	....	12, 030
Total	143, 532	83, 079	226, 611

a By the 1st of October the muster out of 8,598 white troops in the Department of Washington and 24,200 colored in other departments should be completed, and then the forces in the respective departments, except Missouri and Alabama, will

Since the foregoing was made up General Sheridan, by telegraph of September 21, reports the following numbers (approximate) of white troops ordered mustered out:

Texas	7,500
Louisiana	2,000
Florida	800
Total	10,300
Thus left remaining	216,311

THOMAS M. VINCENT,
Assistant Adjutant-General.

WAR DEPARTMENT, ADJUTANT-GENERAL'S OFFICE,
September 14, 1865.

STATE OF OHIO, EXECUTIVE DEPARTMENT,
Columbus, September 16, 1865.

Hon. E. M. STANTON,
Secretary of War, Washington, D. C.:

SIR: We have had, and are almost daily receiving in various forms, a great number of petitions and complaints from our volunteers against their detention in the service.

Passing without comment their murmuring as to their food, exposures, diseases, &c., as being in fact unavoidable incidents to all military service, and perhaps in habit of all volunteer soldierings, I beg leave in accordance with repeated promises to them thus to call the attention of the Department and of the President to their case.

They complain bitterly, not only against their detention in the service as a matter of right on the part of the National Government, or of duty and obligation upon theirs as a class, but also on account of their own special and peculiar calamity in being thus kept in an arduous and painful service, wholly unanticipated by them, whilst their friends and late comrades have been discharged and are living happy and useful at home. Of course the latter complaint (derived from a comparison of their fortunes with those of others), though natural enough, can constitute by itself no sound reason for their discharge—since in any army it may well become the policy and duty of the Government to discharge one part before another and before their legal term may have expired.

But after all the consideration I can give this case and the questions which underlie it, it does seem to me that their first, the general complaint, that all and any of the volunteers who are detained beyond the period of actual war and the time necessary in the mere processes of their discharge are unlawfully and unjustly detained, is well founded. I can see no legal authority in keeping up that army or any part of it for any other service or services than those specified in the laws and in the proclamations of the President. And it seems to me, too, that the proceeding is inequitable and hard in its operation, and it is unlawful; and this wholly irrespective of the question whether the other ends of detaining them shall be good, wise, and practicable, or the contrary. These were not a part of their obligations and duties when they enlisted in contemplation of either party, probably, and

---

stand as indicated by the figures herein. Missouri, General Pope reports, will be completed by October 15. General Thomas has ordered five regiments of black troops, say 4,000, from Department of Tennessee to Department of Alabama to replace an equal number of white troops in that department with view to their muster out. The white troops thus relieved should be mustered out by October 10.

certainly not of the volunteers. And assuredly the class of citizens who so enlisted (whether we judge them by their individual worth, or by the cause in which they periled their all, or by the services they have performed) is not a class that deserves illegal, harsh, or even doubtful estimate or treatment at the hands of the Nation they have saved.

Doubtless you have considered all these and more like matters in this connection. I know, too, the infinite embarrassments of mere detail as well as of the complicated questions of principle which beset an administration or department in the closing of a war so stupendous as this, and therefore I would neither show nor encourage in others a spirit of fault-finding and impatience. Nevertheless, whilst so frequently implored to endeavor to rescue them from what I myself do believe to be an unjust and undeserved hardship, and yet acquiescing in the propriety of your request that the State Executive should not add to your embarrassments by transmitting special complaints and applications for discharge, I have thought it to be my official duty thus to present my reasons in behalf of the right of all to their discharge at the close of hostilities. If, as is possible, these opinions as to the law and justice of the case agree with those of the Department this communication may do good by its urgency of more dispatch in the process of discharging them. If, as is probable, they may be in some essential particular in conflict with those of the national authorities, then I respectfully beg leave to ask for them such a consideration or reconsideration as the rights and merits of these volunteers and my own strength and sincerity of convictions deserve.

Very respectfully,

CHARLES ANDERSON,
Governor of Ohio.

Exhibit showing the number of colored recruits enlisted in the service of the United States, for old and new regiments, where enlisted, and where credited, from November 1, 1864, to date in 1865, when enlistments ceased.

State.	Alabama.	Arkansas.	Connecticut.	Delaware.	District of Columbia.	Florida.	Georgia.	Illinois.	Indiana.	Iowa.	Kansas.	Kentucky.	Louisiana.	Maine.	Maryland.	Massachusetts.	Michigan.
Alabama	2,970												1			11	
Arkansas		172															
Connecticut			77														
Delaware				34													
District of Columbia			1		163			1						1			1
Florida			7			8							4				
Georgia			181				2,170	1								19	
Illinois								530									
Indiana									187								
Iowa										29							
Kansas											178						
Kentucky									1			5,909					
Louisiana													828	1			
Maine														36			
Maryland															563		
Massachusetts																135	
Michigan																	166
Minnesota																	
Mississippi								18					10			754	
Missouri								2									
New Hampshire																	
New Jersey																	

Exhibit showing the number of colored recruits enlisted in the service of the United States, &c.—Continued.

State.	Alabama.	Arkansas.	Connecticut.	Delaware.	District of Columbia.	Florida.	Georgia.	Illinios.	Indiana.	Iowa.	Kansas.	Kentucky.	Louisiana.	Maine.	Maryland.	Massachusetts.	Michigan.
New York																	
North Carolina			36											27		91	
Ohio																	
Pennsylvania																	
Rhode Island																	
South Carolina			353											1		203	
Tennessee	2	18					1	4				11	1	1		6	
Vermont																	
Virginia			123		1									12	2	87	
Wisconsin																	
West Virginia																	
Total number credited	2,972	190	778	34	164	8	2,171	556	188	29	178	5,920	844	79	565	1,306	167

State.	Minnesota.	Mississippi.	Missouri.	New Hampshire.	New Jersey.	New York.	North Carolina.	Ohio.	Pennsylvania.	Rhode Island.	South Carolina.	Tennessee.	Vermont.	Virginia.	Wisconsin.	West Virginia.	Total number enlisted.
Alabama																	2,982
Arkansas																	172
Connecticut																	77
Delaware																	34
District of Columbia				1		4			5				1				178
Florida																	19
Georgia						331						5					2,707
Illinois																	530
Indiana																	187
Iowa																	29
Kansas																	178
Kentucky																	5,910
Louisiana		30															859
Maine																	36
Maryland																	563
Massachusetts																	135
Michigan																	166
Minnesota	25					109		20									25
Mississippi		501															1,412
Missouri			1,083														1,085
New Hampshire				31													31
New Jersey					262												262
New York						416											416
North Carolina						248	1,379										1,781
Ohio								774									774
Pennsylvania									1,067								1,067
Rhode Island										59							59
South Carolina						600					858			1			2,015
Tennessee						3	1	5				2,443					2,497
Vermont													1				1
Virginia					43	62	5		10	6				364			715
Wisconsin															26		26
West Virginia																33	33
Total number credited	25	531	1,083	32	305	1,773	1,385	799	1,082	65	858	2,448	2	365	26	33	26,961

THOMAS M. VINCENT,
Assistant Adjutant-General.

WAR DEPARTMENT, ADJUTANT-GENERAL'S OFFICE,
September 20, 1865.

[SEPTEMBER 28, 1865.—For report of Bvt. Maj. Gen. Rufus Ingalls, U. S. Army, chief quartermaster of Armies operating against Richmond, of operations during the fiscal year ending June 30, 1865, see Series I, Vol. LI, Part I, p. 251.]

WASHINGTON, D. C., *October 5, 1865.*

Hon. EDWIN M. STANTON,
Secretary of War:

SIR: Your special instructions to me dated March 25, 1863, require that I should proceed to the Mississippi River and inspect the troops operating in the field against the rebel forces, to examine into all operations in cotton connected with the troops, and to announce to the army the policy of the General Government respecting the negro race held in bondage in the States in rebellion.

I reported to you from time to time the condition of the troops and their determination to meet and beat the enemy. On the 23d of June I reported to you in relation to operations in cotton, showing what frauds I had detected, and the difficulties I had to contend with in obtaining correct information whereby the guilty persons might be brought to trial. My operations in this respect were of little practical value, and I only excited opposition; and I discovered that this opposition acted injuriously upon the third and most important part of my duties—your instructions respecting the blacks. The present report is intended to give the results in the organization of colored troops. You undoubtedly recollect that the determination to send me on this duty was a sudden one, and the purpose was only unfolded to me the day prior to the date of the instructions, and you urged expedition in the matter. The subject was new to me, and I entered upon the duty by no means certain of what I might be able to effect. Still, as more of my military service was performed in the slave States, and I was perfectly familiar with plantation life—I felt that I knew the peculiarities of the colored race—I could, with the blessing of Divine Providence, at least do something to alleviate the condition of the numerous thousands who would come within our military lines for protection.

At Cairo, Ill., I first came in contact with what were then called contrabands—over 1,500 men, women, and children huddled together in insufficient quarters, the helpless drawing rations from the Government, and the able-bodied men employed in the various departments of the Government as laborers to the extent they were required. Compensation, $10 per month and one ration per day. I found the mortality of the place had been very great, especially among the children—measles, diarrhea, and pneumonia being the prevailing diseases—and this subsequently I found to be the case at all other points visited by me where large numbers were collected. Cairo was not a proper place for them, and they were soon removed to Island No. 10, in the Mississippi River, below this place. March 29 I reviewed the troops and announced to some extent the policy of the Government, and having up to the 1st of April carefully considered the whole subject, I on that day communicated to you my views. These views were subsequently enlarged as I came in more immediate contact with large bodies of troops and thousands of negroes. With but very few exceptions I had the troops paraded, and after a review had them brought together in mass and announced the purpose of my mission.

I then requested the body of the troops to call on such of their commanders as they might desire to make an address on the policy I had announced. In this way the views and opinions of many general and other officers were communicated directly to the troops. With a single exception (the regiment from Chicago, Ill.) the policy was most enthusiastically received by the troops. The prejudice against colored troops was quite general, and it required in the first instance all my efforts to counteract it; but finally it was overcome, and the blacks themselves subsequently by their coolness and determination in battle fought themselves into their present high standing as soldiers.

I found the treatment of the blacks varied very materially at the different military stations and by the operating columns. Some commanders received them gladly, others indifferently, whilst in very many cases they were refused admission within our lines and driven off by the pickets. They were thus obliged in numerous cases to return into slavery. This resulted from the fact that no policy in regard to them had been made known, but as soon as I had announced by your authority the views of the President and yourself, all opposition to their reception ceased. In this connection I may state that the general-in-chief of these armies (Lieutenant-General Grant) early took steps to provide for the welfare of this unfortunate race, and detailed humane clergymen as superintendents of contrabands to see to their welfare. The general on all occasions gave me his hearty support, and was ever ready to second my views. The policy, as I announced it, was that all officers and enlisted men were required to treat the blacks kindly and encourage their seeking the protection of the troops, to be fed and clothed as far as possible until they could be able to provide for themselves; the able-bodied men to be organized into regiments, except such laborers as were required in the several staff corps and departments—cooks for the troops and servants for the officers. I also distinctly announced that if any officer should stand in the way or oppose this policy I would not hesitate to dismiss him from the service of the United States.

April 2 I addressed the troops at Columbus, Ky. April 4 explained the plan to Major-General Hurlbut, commanding at Memphis, Tenn., and at his request authorized him to raise six companies of artillerists to man the heavy guns in position at that place; also to organize contrabands for work in the Quartermaster's Department. April 6 addressed some 7,000 troops at Helena, Ark., commanded by Major-General Prentiss. April 9 addressed Generals McArthur's and Logan's divisions, of Major-General McPherson's corps. April 12, at Milliken's Bend, La., joined the headquarters of the commanding general (Lieutenant-General Grant). At this time, as we had possession of the west bank of the Mississippi River, and could collect the negroes, I became satisfied that 20,000 troops could be organized if necessary, and first made arrangements for 10,000 and afterward for another 10,000. In cases where I could not personally visit troops operating at a distance I invariably made known to the generals in command by communications what was desired, and urged upon them the utmost zeal in carrying out the policy of the Government. In regard to officering these regiments, I authorized commanding generals of corps and divisions to assemble boards of officers to examine applicants desiring commissions, and to be particularly careful to select none but those whose hearts were in the work, and who would devote themselves to elevate the blacks and endeavor to early bring them into a high state of discipline. These generals were then desired to furnish rosters for regiments on which I would issue appointments and give the necessary authority to raise the troops. I also authorized the first sergeants of companies to be whites, but I soon found that soldiers only took these positions to obtain promotion, and if not made in a very short time dissatisfaction was the consequence. I therefore changed the rule and urged colonels to select intelligent blacks and instruct them. This system worked admirably, and I have seen colored sergeants drill their squads as well as white sergeants could. The best class of officers, as a general thing, did not offer themselves, owing to the prejudice existing against colored troops and a number merely wanted higher positions; still, some good and zealous officers were obtained. Afterward, when the prejudice against this species of troops had been overcome, a higher class of officers presented themselves, and in larger numbers than could be appointed. By means also of frequent inspections by myself and two officers of my staff, the careless and indifferent officers were gotten rid of and more zealous ones appointed.

I remained with the troops until they crossed the Mississippi River at Bruinsburg, Miss., May 1, and afterward visited the army on the Big Black River May 5, and then returned up the river to Memphis, Tenn., to visit the corps of Major-General Hurlbut. Visited the portions of his corps as far as Corinth by a circuitous route by railroad of some 160 miles, and addressed the troops at seven different stations on the first day, twice to the troops and contrabands at Corinth second day, and to the troops at six different stations on the third day, returning to Memphis. The weather was excessively hot, and the exposure and exertion, together with previous exposure, prostrated me with sickness, and I was ordered by my physician to leave the country. After several days of sickness at Memphis I proceeded to Louisville, Ky., where I was compelled to remain in hospital over two weeks. Before leaving Louisville (June 13) I authorized Col. William A. Pile to raise troops under my instructions in the State of Missouri. He rendered good service, and was subsequently rewarded by the appointment of brigadier-general. Also, June 15 I addressed a communication to Major-General Rosecrans, commanding Department of the Cumberland, at Murfreesborough, Tenn., and urged him to carry out the views of the Government, which I fully set forth to him.

August 2, having measurably recovered my health, I left for the Southwest, and at Cincinnati, Ohio, August 5, authorized Major-General Burnside, commanding Department of the Ohio, on his entering Tennessee, to organize colored troops. Likewise gave similar authority to Major-General Schofield, who was about starting on an expedition into Arkansas. After the fall of Vicksburg I accompanied the commanding general to New Orleans, La., to organize troops in the Department of the Gulf, commanded by Major-General Banks. I found, however, that the regiments of the Corps d'Afrique, twenty-nine in number, had been organized on the basis of 500, and, except to authorize one regiment of cavalry, I directed that the regiments should be filled up to the maximum standard of 1,000 before other regiments would be authorized. This will account for there being no additional regiments raised in that department except the one referred to. The recruits obtained now brought these regiments up to that standard. Maj. George L. Stearns, assistant adjutant-general, having been ordered to Nashville, Tenn., to superintend the organization of colored troops, reported to me. I found that he entered into the duty with great zeal and rendered good service.

In the middle of December I was compelled to leave the Mississippi River in consequence of sickness. The year's operations may be summed up as follows:

	Officers.	Enlisted men.	Aggregate.
1 regiment of cavalry	22	390	412
4 regiments of heavy artillery	151	3,956	4,107
4 batteries of light artillery	11	385	396
24 regiments of infantry	745	15,767	16,512
1 independent company	3	93	96
Total	932	20,591	21,523

The above numbers are taken from returns in the Adjutant-General's Office, and are below the number actually enlisted, as the loss in battle, by death, and by desertion could not have been less than 5,000. This may seem a large estimate, but it is known that raw troops early contract disease, especially the measles, and it is further known that when the blacks become sick, not having the vitality of the white race, they sink under disease, and the percentage of mortality is very great. The able-bodied men were largely employed in the several staff departments, especially at the principal depots; also by the troops themselves as cooks and servants, and some commanders organized them into pioneer parties without being mustered into the service of the United States. Many, induced by high wages, took employment on the transports; others, again, readily found employment as wood-choppers, also as laborers in the towns on the river. Admiral Porter stated to me that in the naval fleet under his command he had 1,000 negroes. I state these facts to show why a larger number of colored men were not enlisted.

Col. A. Cummings, Nineteenth Regiment Pennsylvania Cavalry, by your directions, reported to me in Philadelphia January 4, 1864, for duty, and I ordered him to Little Rock, Ark., to superintend the recruiting service in that State. He exerted himself, but as the negroes had to a great extent been sent to Texas, comparatively few were obtained; still, some regiments were organized. He was subsequently made a brigadier-general.

While at Louisville, Ky., in the month of January, 1864, I satisfied myself that from 5,000 to 7,000 negroes of Kentucky had passed the border of that State into Ohio, Indiana, Illinois, and Tennessee, and that many of them had enlisted into various organizations, some into regiments being raised in the Eastern States; also that the entire slave population of the State was in a state of ferment. This induced me to proceed to Frankfort, the capital, to present my views to Governor Bramlette. This I did, and fully set forth my opinions, urging them with what ability I possessed. I represented that slavery was forever at an end, to which the Governor assented, and that as the negroes were constantly passing the borders of the State, and it could not be prevented, I urged that I might take the able-bodied men and organize them into troops, whereby the owners of the negroes would receive certificates of their muster and the State receive credit on the quota for the draft. The Governor, while generally assenting to my positions, urged that I would not establish recruiting stations in the State, but desist from my purpose, stating that the subject was one of peculiar delicacy to the people of Kentucky; that they did not desire the General Government to interfere, and that as they desired to manage the institution in their own way, he especially deprecated any agitation at that time, stating, also, that Kentucky would come up to the measure of her duty in this respect, and by legal enactment provide for the extinction of slavery. I remarked that under their present laws some four or five years would be necessary to fully accomplish this measure. I conversed with most, and perhaps nearly, all the members of the Legislature, which was then in session, all of whom took the ground advocated by the Governor, and some of them even requested that I should remove my recruiting stations in Tennessee on the borders of Kentucky to a distance, which of course I refused to do. Finding this feeling so prevalent in the State, I withdrew from it without then doing anything. My action in this case I reported to you from Louisville under date of February 1. The first recruiting in Kentucky commenced at Paducah under Second Lieut. J. Cunningham, Second Illinois Artillery, in February, pursuant to a request made to you by the member of Congress from the First District, in which Paducah is situated. The lieutenant was authorized to raise a regiment of artillery to man the works at that place.

Brigadier-General Chetlain reported to me, and I assigned him as superintendent of the recruiting service in West Tennessee; afterward in the entire State. He proved a most valuable officer, for I found him to possess intelligence and zeal, with a rare qualification for the organization of troops. He never failed on any duty to which he was assigned, either as a superintendent or as an inspector, to which latter duty I also assigned him, and I am gratified that he was subsequently rewarded by the brevet of major-general.

February 9, Major Stearns having relinquished his position in Tennessee as superintendent of the recruiting service, I appointed Capt. R. D. Mussey, who had acted as his assistant. The superintendent was subsequently made the colonel of the One hundredth Regiment of Colored Troops, and continued to perform the duties of superintendent until recruiting had ceased, and he rendered most efficient service. He, too, has been properly rewarded by having conferred upon him the brevet of brigadier-general.

Having returned to Louisville, Ky., in June, I became satisfied that the time had fully arrived for the organization of colored troops in that State, as the negroes were rapidly coming to our military stations (my purpose of doing so I mentioned to you in Washington and received your verbal sanction). Accordingly the 13th of June, by my Order No. 20 of that date, I directed that recruiting should commence throughout the entire State, and designated a camp of reception in each Congressional district where the negroes would be received and organized into regiments. I designated Brigadier-General Chetlain as the superintendent, who entered upon the duty, and continued in its performance until July 6, when he was relieved at the request of Major-General Burbridge, commanding in Kentucky, made both to you and myself, who desired the superintendence, as he had, as I well knew, taken special interest in this measure, advocating it on all proper occasions, and with benefit to the service, as he was then the owner of many blacks.

Under these circumstances it was perfectly proper that the change should be made, but I nevertheless regretted it, believing that his higher duties of commander in Kentucky would prevent his personal attention to the superintendency. The result proved as I had anticipated, for he very soon delegated the duties to another officer; first to Lieutenant-Colonel Hammond, and afterward to Colonel Brisbin, the latter of whom I placed at the head of the Fifth U. S. Colored Cavalry. The reports of these officers came to me through Major-General Burbridge, but they had nothing to do with the establishment of the system, but only carried out what had been ordered.

At this time I found it next to impossible to obtain the necessary medical officers for the colored regiments. The grade of surgeon could readily be filled by the promotion of assistant surgeons of volunteers, but few, except an occasional contract medical officer, would take the position of assistant surgeon. As the sanitary condition of the men required a greater number of medical officers, I ordered on the 8th of July Surg. B. W. Sargent, on my staff, to proceed to the Eastern States and endeavor to procure from the graduates of the medical schools as many physicians as possible, the number then required being some 120. By his energy and activity he procured quite a number, who, having passed the medical board at Boston and elsewhere, were duly appointed, and the service was greatly benefited by this measure.

July 16 Brigadier-General Pile was relieved as superintendent in Missouri and assigned to duty in the field, and Brig. Gen. Thomas Ewing, jr., stationed at Saint Louis, was charged with the duty, who performed it satisfactorily and with ability.

May 1, 1865, pursuant to your instructions, I directed the discontinuance of all recruiting of colored men in the Deparments of the Missouri and Arkansas and the Military Divisions of the Mississippi and West Mississippi, and also consolidated some of the incomplete regiments, thus discontinuing three regiments in Kentucky, one in Tennessee, and two in Arkansas. Before this order could be received by the troops operating in the field three additional regiments were organized from the negroes gathered by Major-General Wilson on his march through Georgia under the standing instructions, and these regiments were retained in service.

Very many of the regiments were filled to the maximum standard, and others to the minimum of 800, when ordered to stations on the Mississippi River and elsewhere, or sent to the field; but as recruiting for them was continued, and nearly all received recruits after organization, it is proper to estimate their numbers at the maximum standard, up to which in mass they undoubtedly came.

The whole of my operations in the West and Southwest in the organization of colored troops may be given as follows:

Forces.	Officers.	Enlisted men.	Aggregate.
Missouri:			
1 regiment of infantry	36	1,000	1,036
Kentucky:			
5 regiments of infantry	180	5,000	5,180
2 regiments of cavalry	84	2,400	2,484
1 battery of light artillery	5	100	105
3 regiments of heavy artillery	204	5,040	5,244
Tennessee:			
13 regiments of infantry	468	13,000	13,468
3 batteries of light artillery	15	300	315
3 regiments of heavy artillery	204	5,040	5,244
14 regiments of infantry	504	14,000	14,504

Forces.	Officers.	Enlisted men.	Aggregate.
Alabama:			
4 regiments of infantry	144	4,000	4,144
Georgia:			
3 regiments of infantry	108	3,000	3,108
Mississippi:			
1 regiment of cavalry	42	1,200	1,242
2 regiments of heavy artillery	136	3,360	3,496
6 regiments of infantry	216	6,000	6,216
Arkansas:			
1 battery of light artillery	5	100	105
5 regiments of infantry	180	5,000	5,180
Louisiana:			
1 regiment of cavalry	42	1,200	1,242
3 batteries of light artillery	15	300	315
1 regiment of heavy artillery	68	1,680	1,748
6 regiments of infantry	216	6,000	6,216
Total	2,804	76,040	78,844

Two regiments were organized in Kansas from negroes, I understood, obtained from Arkansas, though not under my superintendence.

It may be proper to state that, while each State named above is credited with certain regiments, the men did not always come from there, and the companies of a regiment were sometimes made up in two different States. A regiment of 1,000 men was recruited at Evansville, Ind., from Kentucky negroes, and the latter State received credit for them on her quota of the draft. This regiment is not enumerated in the tabular statement.

RECAPITULATION.

Regiments.	Officers.	Enlisted men.	Aggregate.
4 regiments of cavalry	168	4,800	4,968
8 batteries of light artillery	40	800	840
9 regiments of heavy artillery	612	15,120	15,732
57 regiments of infantry	2,052	57,000	59,052
Total	2,872	77,720	80,592

I have the honor to be, very respectfully, your obedient servant,

L. THOMAS,
Adjutant-General.

GENERAL ORDERS, No. 141. } WAR DEPT., ADJT. GENERAL'S OFFICE, *Washington, October 7, 1865.*

I. Commanding generals of military departments and districts will be allowed the following staff officers, and no others:

Generals commanding military departments.—One assistant adjutant-general, one assistant inspector-general, one chief quartermaster, one chief commissary of subsistence, one medical director, one judge-advocate, two aides-de-camp, to be selected from officers of their commands.

Generals commanding districts.—Two aides-de-camp, to be selected from officers of their commands.

II. General officers without military command are not allowed aides-de-camp or other staff officers.

III. All officers serving on the staff of general officers not included in the above allowance will be immediately relieved from such duty. The officers of the regular and volunteer regiments so relieved will be ordered to join their regiments without delay, and the staff officers of volunteers will be ordered to their homes to report thence by letter to the Adjutant-General for instructions.

By order of the Secretary of War:

E. D. TOWNSEND,
Assistant Adjutant-General.

GENERAL ORDERS, No. 146. | WAR DEPT., ADJT. GENERAL'S OFFICE, *Washington, October 9, 1865.*

The allowance of means of transportation at all posts east of the Mississippi and immediately west of the Mississippi will be—

For posts garrisoned by one company, and for every two companies at a post, one four-mule wagon.

All other public animals, wagons, spring wagons, and ambulances will be immediately turned in and disposed of by the Quartermaster's Department.

By command of Lieutenant-General Grant:

E. D. TOWNSEND,
Assistant Adjutant-General.

GENERAL ORDERS, No. 149. | WAR DEPT., ADJT. GENERAL'S OFFICE, *Washington, October 14, 1865.*

BY THE PRESIDENT OF THE UNITED STATES OF AMERICA:

A PROCLAMATION.

Whereas, by a proclamation of the fifth day of July, one thousand eight hundred and sixty-four, the President of the United States, when civil war was flagrant, and when combinations were in progress in Kentucky for the purpose of inciting insurgent raids into that State, directed that the proclamation suspending the privilege of the writ of habeas corpus should be made effectual in Kentucky, and that martial law should be established there, and continue until said proclamation should be revoked or modified; and whereas, since then the danger from insurgent raids into Kentucky has substantially passed away:

Now, therefore, be it known that I, Andrew Johnson, President of the United States, by virtue of the authority vested in me by the Constitution, do hereby declare that the said proclamation of the fifth day of July, one thousand eight hundred and sixty-four, shall be, and is hereby, modified in so far that martial law shall be no longer in force in Kentucky from and after the date hereof.

In testimony whereof I have hereunto set my hand and caused the seal of the United States to be affixed.

Done at the city of Washington this twelfth day of October, in the year of our Lord one thousand eight hundred and sixty-five, and of the Independence of the United States of America the ninetieth.

ANDREW JOHNSON.

[L. S.]
By the President:

W. HUNTER,
Acting Secretary of State.

By order of the President of the United States:

E. D. TOWNSEND,
Assistant Adjutant-General.

GENERAL ORDERS, No. 152. } WAR DEPT., ADJT. GENERAL'S OFFICE, *Washington, October 17, 1865.*

Hereafter no person shall be arrested as a deserter for having failed to report under any draft, or for any other non-compliance with the enrollment act or the amendments thereto. Any and all persons of this class now held will be immediately discharged.

By order of the Secretary of War:

E. D. TOWNSEND,
Assistant Adjutant-General.

HEADQUARTERS ARMIES OF THE UNITED STATES,
Washington, October 20, 1865.

Hon. E. M. STANTON,
Secretary of War:

SIR: I have the honor to submit the following report of the reduction of the Army, and to make some suggestions for the reorganization of the Regular Army. The surrender of the rebel armies and the collapse of the rebellion rendered a large part of our military force unnecessary, and immediate steps were taken to reduce it by stopping enlistments, discharging non-effectives, and the muster out of men and regiments whose terms of service expired before given dates.

By the 1st of July, 1865, the spirit in which the results of the war were accepted by the South was known. Already two months have passed without a collision of any importance between the soldiers of the rebel army returned to their homes and our troops. Everywhere submission was perfect, and all that was asked by them was permission to resume the ordinary pursuits of civil life. The reduction of the Army was now made by organizations, and during the month of July the two most important armies in the country—that of the Potomac and of the Tennessee—returned to the people from whom they had come four years before. Since that time the reduction of troops left in the Southern States to secure order and protect the freedmen in the liberty conferred on them has been gradually going on in proportion as continued quiet and good order have justified it.

On the 1st of May, 1865, the aggregate of the military force of the United States was 1,000,516 men.* On October 20th this had been reduced, as it is estimated, to 210,000, and further reductions are still being made. These musters out were admirably conducted, 800,000 men passing from the Army to civil life so quietly that it was scarcely known, save by the welcomes to their homes received by them. The ordinary process was to muster out the regiments in the field or wherever they might be, transport them as organizations to the States from which they came, and there pay them off and discharge them from service.

The apprehensions felt by some, of disturbance and disorder at so vast a force being suddenly thrown upon the country to resume the occupations of civil life after having been so long absent from them, proved entirely unfounded, the soldiers showing by their conduct that devotion to their country in the field is no disqualification for devotion to it at home.

At the beginning of the war our small Regular Army was barely adequate to protect our overland routes and our Indian frontier and

---

*But see Vol. IV, of this series, p. 1283, for a later official compilation showing an aggregate of 1,052,038.

garrison our sea-coast works. At its close we practically had no Indian frontier, as the mines of the Rocky Mountains had scattered settlements at numerous points along their slopes, and the force employed in protecting these settlements and the overland routes was double that of the whole Regular Army at the beginning of the war. In view of the vast extent of our country, the recent hostile condition of a portion of it, with the possibility of future local disturbances arising from ill-feeling left by the war or the unsettled questions between the white and black races at the South, I am of the opinion that a Regular Army of 80,000 men is needed, and would recommend the following legislation.*

Very respectfully, your obedient servant,

U. S. GRANT,
Lieutenant-General.

WAR DEPARTMENT, ADJUTANT-GENERAL'S OFFICE,
Washington, October 20, 1865.

Hon. EDWIN M. STANTON,
Secretary of War:

SIR: I have the honor to submit the following report of the operations of this department for the past year:

RECRUITING FOR THE REGULAR ARMY.

From October 31, 1864, to October 1, 1865, the number of recruits enlisted, for all arms, is 19,555. (Statement A.)

The recruiting service for the Regular Army is progressing favorably. The regiments suffered so severely in their many battles that they were left at the termination of active hostilities, almost without exception, reduced to mere skeleton organizations. They have now been distributed to stations and are rapidly filling up, thus enabling the department to relieve volunteer regiments as fast as they can be transported to their homes and paid.

There are two principal depots for the general recruiting service, one at Fort Columbus, New York Harbor, for infantry, and one at Carlisle Barracks, Pa., for mounted troops. The officers detailed from the several regiments for recruiting duty are stationed in such localities as give promise of success, and their recruits are sent in parties to the depots, whence they are forwarded to the regiments to which they may be assigned. Besides this, the several regiments recruit their own ranks, as far as practicable, from the country adjacent to their posts.

AUTHORIZED STRENGTH AND ORGANIZATION OF THE REGULAR ARMY.

The authorized strength of the regular regiments of the Army, supposing each company full, is as follows:

	Officers.	Men.
6 regiments of cavalry (72 companies)	264	7,248
5 regiments of artillery (60 companies)	273	4,890
10 regiments of infantry, single battalion (100 companies)	340	8,360
9 regiments of infantry, each 3 battalions of 8 companies (216 companies)	693	21,321
Total	1,570	41,819

*Remainder of this letter (here omitted) relates to the reorganization of the Regular Army.

This calculation is made on the basis of forty-two privates to a company at all but frontier posts. The total strength, upon the basis of 100 enlisted men to a company, would be 1,570 officers, 45,751 men.

By existing acts of Congress the strength of companies is limited to the following number of private soldiers:

The ten old regiments of infantry and four old regiments of artillery—forty-two privates per company (act of August 23, 1842), except when serving on the Western frontier, or at remote and distant stations, when the allowance is seventy-four privates per company. (Act June 17, 1850.)

The nine new regiments of infantry, three battalions each of eight companies—eighty-two privates per company. (Act July 29, 1861.)

Eight light artillery companies—sixty-four privates per company. (Act June 17, 1850.)

Twelve companies of the Fifth Artillery—122 privates per company. (Act July 29, 1861.)

Six regiments of cavalry, each twelve companies—seventy-eight privates per company. (Act July 17, 1862.)

There is no good reason for such dissimilarity in the several organizations, and much inconvenience really arises from it. A company of forty-two privates is not sufficient for the ordinary duties of a garrison, and 122 privates are not needed except for a battery of six pieces serving in the field. It is recommended that all companies of the Regular Army be allowed 100 enlisted men as the maximum standard, leaving to the War Department to regulate the strength of companies within that limit as may be demanded by the nature of the service at the various stations. It is not probable that this maximum would often be reached, but emergencies sometimes arise when it becomes a matter of great importance, and also of economy, to have large companies instead of mere platoons for immediate active duty.

STATIONS OF THE REGULAR ARMY.

The following is the present disposition of the regular artillery regiments:

SECOND U. S. ARTILLERY.

On the Pacific coast.

THIRD U. S. ARTILLERY.

Fort Sullivan, Eastport, Me., one company.

Fort Preble, Portland, Me., one company.

Fort Constitution, Portsmouth, N. H., one company.

Fort Warren, Boston, Mass., the regimental headquarters and three companies.

Fort Independence, Boston, Mass., one company.

Fort Adams, Newport, R. I., three companies.

One light battery, C, Division of the Mississippi.

One light battery, E, Department of North Carolina.

Detachments from some of these companies will be placed at the unfinished forts and batteries along the coast near their stations.

FIRST U. S. ARTILLERY.

Fort Trumbull, New London, Conn., one company.

Fort Schuyler, N. Y., three companies.

Fort Lafayette, New York Harbor, one company.

Fort Hamilton, New York Harbor, the regimental headquarters and two companies.

Fort Richmond and Batteries Hudson and Morton, New York Harbor, two companies.

Sandy Hook, N. J., one company.

One light battery } Division of the Gulf.
One light battery }

FOURTH U. S. ARTILLERY.

Fort Delaware, Del., two companies.

Fort McHenry, Baltimore, Md., two companies.

Fort Washington, Md., the regimental headquarters and one company.

Fort Foote, Md., one company.

Forts around Washington, four companies.

One light battery } Division of the Mississippi.
One light battery }

FIFTH U. S. ARTILLERY.

Fort Monroe, Old Point Comfort, Va., the regimental headquarters and four companies.

Fort Taylor, Key West, Fla., two companies.

Fort Jefferson, Dry Tortugas, Fla., four companies.

One light battery, F, Department of Virgina.

One light battery, G, Division of the Mississippi.

All the companies, except two of each regiment of artillery, have been dismounted, and their horses and batteries turned over to the proper staff departments. The dismounted companies have been assigned to permanent fortifications on the sea-board. The two batteries in each regiment are retained under the provisions of the acts of March 2, 1821, and March 3, 1847.

All sea-coast forts south of Fort Monroe, except Forts Taylor and Jefferson, Fla., are to be garrisoned by colored troops.

OF THE CAVALRY REGIMENTS.

The First, Fourth, and Sixth Regiments are assigned to the Division of the Gulf in the Southwest.

The Second and Third Regiments to the Division of the Missouri.

The Fifth Regiment is divided between the Departments of Washington, the Middle Department, and the Division of the Tennessee.

The single-battalion infantry regiments are assigned as follows:

FOURTH U. S. INFANTRY.

Fort Brady, Sault Ste. Marie, Mich., two companies.

Fort Wayne, Detroit, Mich., the regimental headquarters and two companies.

Fort Niagara, N. Y., one company.

Fort Ontario, Oswego, N. Y., one company.

Madison Barracks, Sackett's Harbor, N. Y., two companies.

Rouse's Point, N. Y., two companies.

The First Regiment U. S. Infantry is in the Department of Louisiana.

The Second in the Department of Kentucky.
The Third and Tenth are in the Division of the Missouri.
The Fifth is in New Mexico.
The Sixth in the Department of South Carolina.
The Seventh in the Department of Florida.
The Eighth in the Middle Department.
The Ninth on the Pacific Coast.
The three battalion regiments of infantry are assigned as follows:
The Eleventh and Seventeenth Regiments are recruiting and organizing preparatory to assignment.
The Twelfth Regiment is assigned to the Department of Virginia.
The Thirteenth, Eighteenth, and Nineteenth Regiments are assigned to the Division of the Missouri.
The Fourteenth is on the Pacific Coast.
The Fifteenth and Sixteenth Regiments are in the Division of the Tennessee.

ENLISTMENT OF MINORS AS MUSICIANS.

The act of July 4, 1864, section 5, and the act of March 3, 1864, section 18, make it an offense to enlist any minor under the age of sixteen years. It is recommended that this act be modified so far as to authorize a limited number, say 100, of boys, not under twelve years, as musicians, provided the consent of parent or guardian is previously obtained. Until the passage of the act referred to a detachment of boys was kept under instruction at each of the recruiting depots. They were not only carefully trained as young soldiers and musicians—*i. e.*, drummers, fifers, and buglers—but were well taught in the common school branches at the post school. Many of these boys have turned out good scholars and excellent soldiers, reaching, as their age matured, to the grades of non-commissioned, and even of commissioned officers.

DEDUCTION OF PAY FROM OFFICERS ON LEAVE.

By section 31, act of March 3, 1863, and section 11, act of June 20, 1864, it is provided that officers on leave of absence for a longer period than thirty days in one year shall receive only half of the pay and allowances prescribed by law, and no more. It is recommended that this provision be now repealed. It operates to the serious disadvantage of valuable officers who have earned a longer respite from duty than thirty days, and who probably, through a series of years, may have been absent in all less than thirty days. At the same time it places no restriction on those who serve little with their regiments, but habitually report on surgeon's certificate of ill-health.

SERGEANTS FOR SUPERINTENDENTS OF CEMETERIES.

There are now in existence some forty National Cemeteries, sad monuments of mortality among our soldiers during the war. It is recommended that an act of Congress shall provide for the enlistment of a disabled soldier as a superintendent for each cemetery, who shall have the same pay and allowances as an ordnance-sergeant, and be charged with the care and preservation of the grounds and all their appurtenances. An analogy to this proposed measure may be found in the ordnance-sergeants of the Army, appointed under the act of April 5, 1832, for the care of ordnance stores at posts.

REPORTS OF BATTLES.

Much attention and labor has been expended upon the preparation of the documents relating to the rebellion, required to be printed by resolution of May 19, 1864. Eight volumes, with maps and indexes, have been completed and sent to the Public Printer. The greater part of the other reports of battles, marches, &c., have been copied and arranged, but await the receipt of some important reports, which, though repeatedly called for, have not been furnished, and are requisite to preserve the chronological order.

REGISTER OF VOLUNTEERS.

The Register of Volunteer Officers called for by resolution approved June 30, 1864, will be completed by the time Congress assembles, and all the manuscript will by that time be in the hands of the Public Printer. As will be seen by examination, it is a work of considerable magnitude, embracing some 200,000 names of officers. No pains have been spared to make it a full and accurate record of every volunteer regiment received into the U. S. service during the war.

VOLUNTEER SERVICE.

The accompanying statement, marked B, will show the number of volunteer recruits, drafted men, and substitutes forwarded to the field (aggregate 202,117), and of volunteers, drafted men, and militia mustered out and discharged (aggregate 61,000), under the direction of this office, from November 1, 1864, until April 30, 1865.

When the work came of disbanding the large armies no longer required by the exigencies of the service, the plan suggested by experience, which had been successful with small bodies, was continued. The same machinery of mustering officers and depots which had been employed in recruiting has been used in discharging. As many regiments as could be at one time furnished with means of transportation and funds for paying them off, have been sent home with their organization entire, from time to time as they could be spared from the department in which they were serving, beginning with those whose terms of service would soonest expire. The regiments have been mustered out of service on rolls carefully prepared to exhibit the dues from the Government to each soldier. The rolls, boxed up and sent under charge of an officer, have arrived at the State rendezvous simultaneously with the regiments. The officers of each regiment have been held to a strict accountability, under pain of forfeiture of an honorable discharge and pay, for the good behavior of the enlisted men until all were finally paid their dues and furnished with discharges within a few miles of their homes. With rare exceptions the conduct of these gallant regiments, coming from every part of the North, has been most admirable in maintaining the strict discipline which made them successful in battle, until they were released from military restraint and had separated, each to his home and his civil avocation. Too much praise cannot be given the numerous corps of mustering officers and paymasters, whose fidelity is attested by the large numbers (800,963) of men discharged and paid within a brief period, as shown in the annexed statement B. Nor can the extraordinary facilities offered by the several railroad companies for transporting such large bodies of men fail to attract attention. No apology is made for alluding to these matters in this report, for they are facts of the utmost significance in connection with the military power and resources of this country. Statement C shows the force in service May 1, 1864, and March 1, 1865, respectively.

COLORED TROOPS.

For statistics and information in regard to the colored troops, reference is invited to the accompanying report of the able chief of the Bureau for Colored Troops, attached to this office. The number at present retained in service is about 85,024, out of 186,097, the whole number, officers and men, mustered in since it was first decided to employ them.

The general orders and circulars annexed to this report will give useful information concerning movements of the Army.*

By systematic classification of the varied duties of this department, the officers intrusted with each branch have been able promptly and successfullv to accomplish all that could in reason be expected of them, and they, together with the admirable clerks—mostly taken from the armies—by whom they were so ably assisted, are entitled to the warmest commendation.

The officers of the Adjutant-General's Department are employed as follows:

One brigadier-general on special service.

One colonel in charge of the Adjutant-General's Office, War Department.

One colonel and six majors, assistants in the Adjutant-General's Office.

One lieutenant-colonel and one major, on duty at the Headquarters of the Army.

One lieutenant-colonel and two majors, on duty at headquarters of military divisions and departments.

One lieutenant-colonel, Provost-Marshal-General.

One lieutenant-colonel and one major awaiting orders.

One major on duty in the Provost-Marshal-General's Bureau.

One major on leave of absence.

One major on duty in the War Department.

I have the honor to be, sir, very respectfully, your obedient servant,

E. D. TOWNSEND,
Assistant Adjutant-General.

---

*See General Orders, Nos. 101, 105, 106, 114, 119, 121, 141, and 146, and Circulars Nos. 19, 26, 28, 30, 31, 35, 39, 41, 44, and 46, pp. 43, 48, 49, 54, 62, 65, 124, 125, 24, 56, 61, 65, 93, 95, 96, 98, 108, 156, respectively.

A.—*Statement of the number of enlistments and re-enlistments in the Regular Army from October 31, 1864, to October 1, 1865.*

(Compiled from reports forwarded to this office by recruiting officers.)

General service	4,698	7th Infantry	64
Mounted service	3,033	8th Infantry	115
1st Cavalry	131	9th Infantry	241
2d Cavalry	16	10th Infantry	13
3d Cavalry	6	11th Infantry	953
4th Cavalry	24	12th Infantry	694
5th Cavalry	42	13th Infantry	742
6th Cavalry	37	14th Infantry	1,752
1st Artillery	149	15th Infantry	1,208
2d Artillery	7	16th Infantry	804
3d Artillery	357	17th Infantry	761
4th Artillery	182	18th Infantry	852
5th Artillery	155	19th Infantry	698
1st Infantry	44	Engineer Corps	237
2d Infantry	859	Ordnance Corps	209
3d Infantry	9	Military Academy	260
4th Infantry	30		
5th Infantry	33	Total	19,555
6th Infantry	140		

E. D. TOWNSEND,
Assistant Adjutant-General.

WAR DEPARTMENT, ADJUTANT-GENERAL'S OFFICE,
Washington, November 14, 1865.

B.—*Exhibit of recruits—volunteers, drafted, and substitutes—for old and new organizations, forwarded to the field; volunteers, drafted men, and militia mustered out and discharged from the service of the United States under the direction of the Adjutant-General's Office, from November 1, 1864, to November 15, 1865.*

FORWARDED TO FIELD.

State.	Volunteers for 1, 2, and 3 years.					Drafted men and substitutes.	Total.
	Old organizations.	New organizations.					
		Regiments.	Companies.*a*	Batteries.	Strength.		
Alabama	*b* 2,982						2,982
Arkansas	*b* 172						172
California	251						251
Colorado							
Connecticut	1,457			1	130	1,307	2,894
Delaware	(*c*)					765	765
Florida	*b* 19						19
Georgia	*b* 2,707						2,707
Illinois	8,829	10	66		15,380	5,304	29,513
Indiana	3,710	15			12,554	6,987	23,251
Iowa	1,046					1,480	2,526
Indian Territory							
Kansas	525					65	590
Kentucky	*b* 7,565	2			1,857	1,264	10,686
Louisiana	*b* 859						859
Maine	1,260		30		2,808	1,590	5,658
Maryland	918					2,180	3,098
Massachusetts	2,336		8		800	109	3,245
Michigan	4,439		4		318	1,686	6,443
Minnesota	549		16		1,967	598	3,114

a Assigned to old regiments in which there were vacancies for companies.
b Includes new organizations (colored).
c The number opposite Maryland includes those forwarded from Delaware.

B.—*Exhibit of recruits—volunteers, drafted, and substitutes, &c.*—Continued.

FORWARDED TO FIELD—Continued.

State.	Volunteers for 1, 2, and 3 years.					Drafted men and substitutes.	Total.
	Old organizations.	New organizations.					
		Regiments.	Companies.*a*	Batteries.	Strength.		
Mississippi	*b* 1,412						1,412
Missouri	1,254	2			2,183	2,575	6,012
New Hampshire	648		2		176	797	1,621
New Jersey	2,190		3		278	3,614	6,082
New York	9,414	2	6		2,795	6,228	18,437
North Carolina	*b* 1,781						1,781
Ohio	5,097	14			14,371	2,846	22,314
Pennsylvania	7,690	8	62		8,907	9,271	25,868
Rhode Island	655		2		172	32	859
South Carolina	*b* 2,015						2,015
Tennessee	*b* 2,497						2,497
Texas							
Vermont	839		2		206	68	1,113
Virginia	*b* 715						715
West Virginia	210		4		363	447	1,020
Wisconsin	1,710	5	13		5,541	3,272	10,523
District of Columbia	170					905	1,075
Rendezvous for volunteers							
U. S. volunteers							
Veteran Reserve Corps							
Unclassified							
Total	77,921	58	218	1	70,806	53,390	202,117

a Assigned to old regiments in which there were vacancies for companies.
b Includes new organizations (colored).

MUSTERED OUT AND RETURNED TO THEIR HOMES.

State.	From Nov. 1, 1864, to April 30, 1865.				From May 1, 1865, to Nov. 15, 1865.					Total.
	Regiments.	Companies.	Batteries.	Strength.*a*	Regiments.	Companies.	Batteries.	Strength.	Officers under G. O. 79 and 82, A. G. O., series of 1865.	
Alabama					1			622	2	624
Arkansas					6		1	4,688	1	4,689
California										
Colorado					1			566		566
Connecticut	1	1		212	21		3	13,992	26	14,230
Delaware	1			712	5		1	2,943	6	3,661
Florida									1	1
Georgia										
Illinois	1	5		1,498	102	2	26	68,922	150	70,570
Indiana	1	11	3	2,220	99		25	60,083	65	62,368
Iowa		5		416	34		2	23,515	22	23,953
Indian Territory					3			2,139		2,139
Kansas		16	1	677	15		1	7,631	2	8,310
Kentucky	17	29	2	9,466	21		3	12,124	14	21,604
Louisiana					2	1		1,156		1,156
Maine	4	1		677	19	4	7	15,576	31	16,284
Maryland		1		261	15	2	3	11,765	10	12,036
Massachusetts	7	11		5,523	42	17	15	34,003	64	39,590
Michigan			1	223	34	1	10	27,835	47	28,105
Minnesota				57	11		1	8,640	17	8,714

a Including individual musters out.

B.—*Exhibit of recruits—volunteers, drafted, and substitutes, &c.*—Continued.

MUSTERED OUT AND RETURNED TO THEIR HOMES—Continued.

States.	From Nov. 1, 1864, to April 30, 1865.				From May 1, 1865, to Nov. 15, 1865.					
	Regiments.	Companies.	Batteries.	Strengh. *a*	Regiments.	Companies.	Batteries.	Strength.	Officers under G. O. 79 and 82, A. G. O., series of 1865.	Total.
Mississippi	......	......	......	....	1	......	......	426	....	426
Missouri	......	......	......	9,342	23	......	8	13,214	15	22,571
New Hampshire	2	......	......	326	16	......	1	9,018	10	9,354
New Jersey	1	......	......	247	21	......	5	18,770	15	19,032
New York	13	5	1	4,358	153	1	35	117,206	191	121,755
North Carolina	......	......	......	....	3	......	......	2,248	1	2,249
Ohio	4	10	5	1,686	122	4	30	81,704	106	83,496
Pennsylvania	10	12	......	7,500	118	1	14	102,450	116	110,066
Rhode Island	......	......	......	....	6	......	6	4,795	4	4,799
South Carolina	......	......	......	....	......	......	......	....	....	....
Tennessee	......	......	......	1,944	23	......	5	14,588	8	16,540
Texas	......	......	......	....	1	......	......	853	....	853
Vermont	1	......	......	310	12	1	2	9,492	25	9,827
Virginia	......	......	......	....	......	1	......	98	....	98
West Virginia	1	......	......	851	16	4	4	12,104	2	12,957
Wisconsin	4	2	1	1,556	40	......	15	30,004	32	31,592
District of Columbia	......	......	......	....	4	......	......	2,699	....	2,699
Rendezvous for volunteers	......	......	......	*b*10,938	......	......	......	....	....	10,938
U. S. volunteers	......	......	......	....	10	3	3	10,075	2	10,077
Veteran Reserve Corps	......	......	......	....	......	......	......	25,087	....	25,087
Unclassified	......	......	......	....	......	......	......	48,947	....	48,947
Total	68	109	14	61,000	1,000	42	226	799,978	985	861,963

a Including individual musters out.

b Drafted substitutes and volunteers.

RECAPITULATION.

Forwarded to field	202,117
Mustered out and returned to their homes	861,963
Total	1,064,080

REMARKS.

The rapidity with which the work of mustering out and disbanding the Volunteer Army was executed will be apparent from the following, showing the numbers mustered out to the dates set opposite them, respectively, viz:

Aug. 7, 1865	640,806
Aug. 22, 1865	719,338
Sept. 14, 1865	741,107
Oct. 15, 1865	785,205
Nov. 15, 1865	800,963

The command of Major-General Sherman (Army of the Tennessee and Army of Georgia) and the Army of the Potomac were the first to complete their musters out entirely. Regiments commenced leaving General Sherman's command—then numbering, present and absent, 116,183 officers and men—from the rendezvous near this city on the 29th of May, and on the 1st of August the last one of the regiments mustered out left Louisville, Ky., to which point the command (after the musters out therefrom were partly completed) was transferred and the armies composing it merged into one, called the Army of the Tennessee. The work of mustering out the troops was not continuous, it having been interrupted and delayed by the transfer of the two armies from this city to Louisville, and their subsequent consolidation. Regiments commenced leaving the Army of the Potomac (then numbering, including Ninth Corps, 162,851 officers and men, present and absent) from the rendezvous near this city on the 29th of May, and about six weeks thereafter (July 19) the last regiment started for home. During the interval the work, like that for General Sherman's command, was not continuous, it being interrupted and delayed by the movement of the Sixth Corps from Danville, Va., to this city and the consolidation, by orders of June 28, of the remaining portion of the army into a provisional corps, numbering, present and absent, 22,699 officers and men. Thus, for the two commands in question, and between the 29th of May and the 1st of August (two months), 279,034 officers and men, present and absent, were mustered out and placed en route to their homes. Including other armies and departments, the number was increased by August 7 (two months and seven days) to 640,806 officers and men. From the foregoing it is seen that the mass of the forces discharged were mustered out by September 14, or within two months and a half from the time the movements of troops homeward commenced. The average per month during that time is 296,442.

THOMAS M. VINCENT,
Assistant Adjutant-General.

WAR DEPARTMENT, ADJUTANT-GENERAL'S OFFICE,
November 15, 1865.

C.—*Exhibit of the forces of the United States on the 1st of May, 1864.*

Army or department.	Aggregate present available for duty.*
Department of Washington	42,124
Army of the Potomac	120,384
Department of Virginia and North Carolina.	59,130
Department of the South	18,169
Department of the Gulf	61,865
Department of Arkansas	23,666
Department of the Tennessee	74,170
Department of the Missouri	15,775
Department of the Northwest	5,296
Department of Kansas	4,798
Headquarters Military Division of the Mississippi.	476
Department of the Cumberland	119,948
Department of the Ohio	35,416
Northern Department	9,546
Department of West Virginia	30,782
Department of the East	2,828
Department of the Susquehanna	2,970
Middle Department	5,627
Ninth Army Corps	20,780
Department of New Mexico	3,454
Department of the Pacific	5,141
Total	a 662,345

Summary.	Aggregate.
Brought forward—present available for duty.	662,345
Present, sick in field hospitals or unfit for duty.	a 41,266
Absent on detached service	109,348
Absent with leave, including prisoners of war.	b 66,290
Absent, in general hospitals and on sick leave at home.	b 75,978
Absent without authority	b 15,483
Grand aggregate, present and absent.	970,710

a Taken from monthly returns. b Taken from tri-monthly returns.

*An examination of the orignal returns for April 30, 1864 (from which the numbers in this column were compiled), shows that all officers and men reported as "present for duty," "on extra or daily duty," and "in arrest or confinement," are here included under the head of "aggregate present available for duty."

C.—*Exhibit of the forces of the United States on the 1st of March, 1865*—Cont'd.

(Made up from tri-monthly returns.)

Army or department.	Aggregate present available for duty.*	Summary.	Aggregate.
Army of the Potomac	103,273	Brought forward—present available for duty.	602,598
Headquarters Military Division of the Mississippi.	17	Present, sick in field hospitals or unfit for duty.	35,628
Department of the Cumberland	62,626	Absent on detached service	132,538
Department of the Tennessee	45,649	Absent with leave, including prisoners of war.	31,695
Left Wing, Army of Georgia	31,644	Absent, in general hospitals and on sick leave at home.	143,449
Cavalry Corps, Military Division of the Mississippi.	27,410	Absent without authority	19,683
Headquarters Military Division of West Mississippi.	24	Grand aggregate, present and absent.	*a* 965,591
Reserve Brigades Military Division of West Mississippi.	13,748		
Department of the Gulf	35,625		
Department of Arkansas	24,509		
Department of the Mississippi	24,151		
Sixteenth Army Corps	14,395		
Headquarters Military Division of the Missouri.	12		
Department of the Missouri	18,557		
Department of the Northwest	4,731		
Headquarters Middle Military Division	841		
Cavalry Forces Middle Military Division	12,980		
Nineteenth Army Corps	6,612		
Middle Department	2,089		
Department of Washington	26,056		
Department of West Virginia	15,517		
Department of Pennsylvania	820		
Department of the East	7,462		
Department of Virginia	45,986		
Department of North Carolina	34,945		
Department of the South	11,510		
Department of Kentucky	10,655		
Northern Department	11,229		
Department of the Pacific	7,024		
Department of New Mexico	2,501		
Total	602,598		

a By the 1st of May, 1865, the aggregate number (965,591) was increased to 1,000,516 by additional enlistments.†

THOMAS M. VINCENT,
Assistant Adjutant-General.

WAR DEPARTMENT, ADJUTANT-GENERAL'S OFFICE,
November 18, 1865.

[Inclosure.]

ADJT. GEN.'S OFFICE, BUREAU FOR COLORED TROOPS,
Washington, D. C., October 20, 1865.

GENERAL: To the 101,950 colored soldiers in the service of the United States at the date of my last report, the following additions have been made during the year, namely:

17 regiments of infantry, aggregate strength	16,201
2 regiments of heavy artillery, aggregate strength	2,703
2 batteries light artillery, aggregate strength	251
1 regiment of cavalry, aggregate strength	1,255
Recruits, drafted men, and substitutes sent to old regiments	29,099
Total gain	49,509

*An examination of the original returns for February 28, 1865 (from which the numbers in this column were compiled), shows that all officers and men reported as "present for duty," "on extra or daily duty," and "in arrest or confinement," are here included under the head of "aggregate present available for duty."

†But see a later official compilation for April 30, 1865 (Vol. IV, this series, p. 1283), which gives an aggregate of 1,052,038.

Four thousand two hundred and forty-four recruits were enlisted at the rendezvous established in the disloyal States and credited to loyal States under section 3 of the act of Congress approved July 4, 1864.*

On the 15th of July, 1865, the date on which the last organization of colored troops was mustered in, there were in the service of the United States—

	Aggregate.
120 regiments of infantry	98,938
12 regiments heavy artillery	15,662
10 batteries light artillery	1,311
7 regiments cavalry	7,245
Total	123,156

The foregoing is the largest number of colored troops in service at any one time during the war.

The entire number of troops, commissioned and enlisted, in this branch of the service during the war is 186,097.

The States in which this force was recruited or drafted are as follows, namely:

Maine	104	Ohio	5,092
New Hampshire	125	Indiana	1,537
Vermont	120	Illinois	1,811
Rhode Island	1,837	Missouri	8,344
Massachusetts	3,966	Minnesota	104
Connecticut	1,764	Iowa	440
New York	4,125	Wisconsin	165
New Jersey	1,185	North Carolina	5,035
Pennsylvania	8,612	South Carolina	5,462
Delaware	954	Georgia	3,486
Maryland	8,718	Florida	1,044
District of Columbia	3,269	Kansas	2,080
Virginia	5,723	Texas	47
West Virginia	196	Colorado Territory	95
Alabama	4,969	State or Territory unknown	5,896
Mississippi	17,869		
Louisiana	24,052	Total enlisted	178,975
Arkansas	5,526	Officers	7,122
Tennessee	20,133		
Kentucky	23,703	Aggregate	186,097
Michigan	1,387		

The loss during the war, from all causes except muster out of organizations in consequence of expiration of term of service or because service was no longer required, is 68,178.

The number of colored troops already mustered out, or under orders for muster out, is as follows, namely:

	Aggregate strength.
32 regiments of infantry	28,354
2 independent companies and band	172
2 regiments of heavy artillery	3,007
4 batteries of light artillery	571
1 regiment of cavalry	1,130
Total	33,234

*This number was subsequently changed to 5,052. See Vol. IV, this series, p. 1270.

The number of organizations discontinued during the war, by consolidation or transfer, and their strength when discontinued, is as follows, namely:

	Aggregate strength.
27 regiments of infantry	9,337
1 regiment of heavy artillery	607
Total	9,944

The aggregate of colored troops remaining in service, after the execution of all orders to this date for muster out of organizations, is as follows, namely:

	Aggregate strength.
83 regiments of infantry	66,073
9 regiments of heavy artillery	12,394
6 light batteries of artillery	701
6 regiments of cavalry	5,856
Total	85,024

There have been received at this office since June 1, 1863—

Applications for appointment	9,019
Candidates examined by the Board	3,790
Candidates rejected by the Board	1,472
Candidates appointed	2,318
Total number of appointments and promotions	3,573
Provisional appointments made by department commanders confirmed at this office	481
White soldiers discharged to accept appointment	1,767

For further details respecting examinations, appointments, resignations, and matters of a kindred nature, attention is respectfully invited to appendix marked B,* in which will also be found an exhibit of the organizations discontinued by consolidation, muster out, and those remaining in service.

The reputation of the organization for efficiency, good conduct, and reliability has steadily advanced; and the reports of officers of the Inspector-General's Department, so far as they have come to the knowledge of this office, are very satisfactory as to its present condition.

The commission appointed for the State of Delaware, under the provisions of section 24 of the act of Congress approved February 24, 1864, having been dissolved, there is at this time in session, under the provisions of the act referred to, only the commission or board for the State of Maryland, which has been in session since October, 1864.

The whole number of claims for compensation on account of the enlistment of slaves in the service of the United States, filed with the boards in both the above States, is 3,971.

Compensation, varying in amount, was awarded upon 733 of these claims; 294 have been rejected by the commissions as not being well founded, and the remainder are still before the Board. The total

* Omitted.

amount of compensation awarded loyal owners is $213,883. Twenty-five claims have been paid, amounting in the aggregate to $6,900, leaving 708 claims unpaid, amounting to $206,983. Ninteen thousand nine hundred and thirty dollars and forty cents have been expended in salaries of members of boards and to defray the current expenses of the same, including rent of rooms, purchase of fuel, stationery, &c., making the total expenditures to this date $26,830.40.

In closing this report it affords me pleasure to acknowledge the important services rendered the Bureau by Maj. F. W. Taggard, assistant adjutant-general of volunteers, in charge of rolls and returns, and Maj. A. F. Rockwell, assistant adjutant-general of volunteers, general assistant and disbursing officer. To their efficient and cordial co-operation may be attributed whatever of success has been attained in the management of the Bureau.

The employés of the office, all originally detailed from the volunteer service, have zealously and faithfully discharged the duties assigned them.

I have the honor to be, very respectfully, your obedient servant,

C. W. FOSTER,

Assistant Adjutant-General Volunteers.

Bvt. Brig. Gen. E. D. TOWNSEND,

Assistant Adjutant-General, U. S. Army, Washington, D. C.

WAR DEPARTMENT, ORDNANCE OFFICE,

October 20, 1865.

Hon. E. M. STANTON,

Secretary of War:

SIR: I submit the following report of the principal operations of the Ordnance Department during the fiscal year ended June 30, 1865, with such remarks and recommendations as the interests of that branch of the military service seem to require:

The fiscal resources and the disbursements of the department during the year were as follows, viz:

Amount of appropriations remaining in the Treasury June 30, 1864	$4,978,791.97
In the Government depositories, to the credit of disbursing officers, on same date	1,797,387.16
Amount of appropriations from June 30, 1864, to June 30, 1865, including the fixed annual appropriation for arming and equipping the militia	38,800,000.00
Received since June 30, 1864, on account of damages to arms in hands of troops, from sales of arms to officers, and of condemned stores, and from all other sources not before mentioned	207,476.97
Total	45,783,656.10
Amount of expenditures since June 30, 1864	43,112,531.27
In the Government depositories, to the credit of disbursing officers, June 30, 1865	2,671,124.83
Amount of appropriations remaining in the Treasury same date	
Total	45,783,656.10

The estimates for the next fiscal year call for appropriations only for continuing the armament of our permanent fortifications, and for the work already begun for increasing the manufacturing and storage capacity of the arsenals, including a distinct provision for the proper storage and care of gunpowder. These are all measures not cónfined to the necessities of war, but requisite for keeping up a suitable preparation for any contingency and for preserving the large and valuable munitions of war which the country now possesses.

The manufacturing capacity of the arsenals was steadily increased from the date of my last report until May, when the sudden termination of hostilities made it apparent that the immediate demand for munitions of war beyond the supply then on hand and contracted for had ceased.

Measures were promptly taken to reduce the manufacture and purchase of supplies, and to provide for necessary storage, and for preserving the vast quantities of ordnance and ordnance stores which had been issued to the armies and captured from the enemy. Extensive temporary buildings have been erected at some of the principal arsenals, and much of this property has already been received and securely stored in them.

Large and commodious fire-proof workshops are now being erected at Allegheny, Watervliet, and Frankford Arsenals; and so much of these buildings as will not be required in time of peace for manufacturing purposes can be advantageously used as store-houses, of which the want of an adequate supply is now manifest.

It is in contemplation to erect extensive fire-proof workshops at Washington Arsenal, which is considered an eligible position for a first-class arsenal. A portion of these shops can likewise be used for storing the large quantities of ordnance supplies which are now necessarily kept in insecure temporary buildings at that arsenal. Money for this object has already been appropriated by Congress.

The importance to the country of having the armaments placed in the forts as rapidly as they can be prepared to receive them is so evident that I have caused the manufacture of sea-coast gun carriages to be continued as rapidly as practicable at the two arsenals which possess the proper facilities for making them; and orders have been given to the several founders, who have been engaged in making heavy guns for this department, for as many guns as carriages can be made for.

I have been informed by the chief engineer that he will be prepared to receive guns in the forts faster than carriages can now be made, and it is in contemplation to increase the capacity for manufacturing sea-coast carriages.

Experimental wrought-iron field and siege gun carriages have also been made and tested, with results so satisfactory as to render it certain that these carriages may be advantageously substituted for the wooden carriages, and it is proposed to make no more gun carriages of wood.

The smooth-bore cannon of large caliber, which have been used during the war, have given satisfaction, and are regarded as perfectly reliable. The great importance of having reliable rifled guns of large caliber is universally admitted, and the attention of this Government and of the nations of Europe has been directed to that object, but so far, it is believed, without entire success in its accomplishment.

The many failures, by bursting, of the celebrated Parrott guns in the land and naval service have weakened confidence in them, and make it the imperative duty of this department to seek elsewhere for a more reliable rifle gun.

Mr. Horatio Ames, of Falls Village, Conn., invented a plan of making wrought-iron guns, which many believe would possess those qualities which are so very desirable for guns of heavy caliber, and although the cost of these guns was necessarily very great in comparison with the cost of cast-iron guns, a conditional order was given to Mr. Ames to manufacture fifteen of them for the Government, the condition being that the guns should be superior to any rifled guns in the service. One of these guns was fired under the direction of a board of officers, who unanimously expressed the opinion that the "Ames wrought-iron guns possess, to a degree never before equaled by any cannon of equal weight offered to our service, the essential qualities of great lateral and longitudinal strength, and great powers of endurance under heavy charges; that they are not liable to burst explosively and without warning, even when fired under very high charges, and that they are well adapted to the wants of the service generally, but especially whenever long ranges and high velocities are required." The Board also expressed the opinion that the fifteen Ames 7-inch guns possessed sufficient weight and strength to receive an 8-inch bore, and recommended that the gun which had been fired under their direction should be reamed up to eight inches and subjected to further trial.

They further decided that Mr. Ames had fulfilled the obligation incurred by him in his contract to furnish the gun, and that so many of the guns as should endure a proof of ten rounds with the service charge, and pass the proper inspection, should be accepted and paid for.

Two of the fourteen guns burst in proof, exhibiting serious defects in their manufacture—defects in welding—which I had been apprehensive could not be avoided. The guns which endured the proof of ten rounds were accepted and paid for by this Department.

The gun which was fired under the direction of the Board was bored up to eight inches and fired twenty-four times with service charges, when it burst, exhibiting the same defects that were developed in the other guns which burst. The failures in subsequent firing indicate that these guns cannot be relied upon, and that no more of them ought to be made for the department.

Believing that, with our present knowledge of the properties of metals and our skill in working them, reliable rifle guns of large caliber can be made of cast-iron, I have, with your sanction, caused a pair of 8-inch rifle guns of the supposed proper model and weight to be made. These guns are now at Fort Monroe undergoing extreme proof, and should their endurance be satisfactory it is proposed to have other guns like them made.

NATIONAL ARMORY.

The capacity of this establishment for the manufacture of muskets was not increased after the date of my last report, and upon the conclusion of hostilities, in view of the large number of muskets on hand of a model which will probably become obsolete very soon, the manufacture was reduced as rapidly as it could be done with economy; and at present no new muskets are being assembled. Only those parts which were in different stages of advancement are being finished.

In my last report I stated that it was in contemplation to change the manufacture at the National Armory as soon as the best model for a breech-loading musket could be established, and that details for effecting this measure would receive the early attention of this Bureau. Extensive experiments have been made by a board of officers, and also under my direction and supervision, to effect that object; but as yet no arm has been presented which I have been willing to recommend for adoption. The selection of a proper model is considered so important a measure that I have preferred to act slowly and with great care in its selection rather than take a false step and have to retrace it. I hope to be able very soon to recommend a model for your approval.

A plan for altering the muzzle-loading musket into efficient breech-loaders has been devised by the master armorer at Springfield Armory, which appears to be superior to any other that I have seen. I have taken measures to have 5,000 muskets altered according to it, and will have some of them issued to troops for trial as soon as the alterations can be made.

The muskets of the prescribed pattern which have been turned in by the troops are being cleaned and repaired.

The number of Springfield muskets on hand and suitable for issue will reach nearly one million, while the number of foreign and captured muskets will exceed half a million. As none of the latter class will probably be required for issue, and as the care and preservation of them will be attended with considerable expense, they should be sold whenever suitable prices can be obtained for them. This recommendation will apply to other ordnance stores of a perishable nature, which are in excess of the wants of the department.

In my last annual report I called your attention to the danger of keeping large quantities of gunpowder at our arsenals, which are generally in the vicinity of closely populated districts, and recommended that a suitable site for a depot capable of storing at least 100,000 barrels of gunpowder should be acquired. The conclusion of the war has left this department with vast supplies of gunpowder and prepared ammunition on hand, all of which has to be stored at the arsenals, and much of it in buildings which are entirely unfit for the purpose, thereby endangering the safety of the arsenals, and in some cases of private property in the vicinity. This evil cannot be corrected too soon, and I earnestly call your attention to the necessity of obtaining from Congress authority to purchase a suitable site for a powder depot.

In my annual estimate I have asked for an appropriation for the purchase of a site and the erection of magazines. Only so much powder as may be necessary to supply the current wants of the Army should be kept at the arsenals.

The military reserve at Jefferson Barracks, Mo., being a suitable position for a powder depot for supplying the Mississippi Valley, and a portion of it having some years ago been assigned to this department for the erection of powder magazines, I have taken measures to have three magazines capable of containing 5,000 barrels each erected on it, and two of them will be finished this fall.

In my last annual report I stated that, in pursuance of the provisions of the act of Congress approved April 19, 1864, possession had been taken of Rock Island for the purpose of building and maintaining thereon an arsenal for the construction, deposit, and repairs of arms and munitions of war. The United States has not yet acquired a title to the property which has been taken possession of. It is important that the provisions of the act of Congress above referred to should be carried into effect and a complete title to all of Rock Island acquired by the United States before any permanent buildings are commenced. I recommend that this be done with as little delay as practicable. Evidences of title to the land, of which possession has been taken, have been forwarded to you for examination by the Attorney-General, as is required by the act above referred to.

Adjacent to Rock Island and connected with it by a dam is a small island known as Benham's Island, of which possession has not been taken. It appears to have been the intention of Congress in passing the act above referred to that the United States should have full and complete possession and control of Rock Island for military purposes. Should Benham's Island or any other small islands or accretions in the river lying between Rock Island and the shores of Illinois and Iowa be held by private parties, with the right of way across the island, as is now claimed by the owner of Benham's Island, the principal object of the law will be thereby defeated.

If additional legislation is necessary to give the United States full possession and control of the whole of Rock Island, including the adjacent island, I recommend that it be asked of Congress.

The buildings erected as a prison and barracks on Rock Island have been turned over to the Ordnance Department and are now used as store-houses, &c.

Several of the Southern arsenals have been reoccupied, and it is the intention of the department to reoccupy all of them, except the Fayetteville Arsenal, in North Carolina, which was destroyed.

An extensive powder mill at Augusta, Ga., and a large armory (unfinished) and a laboratory at Macon, Ga., which were built by the rebel government, have fallen into possession of this department. The necessary measures for preserving the property have been taken.

The number of permanent U. S. arsenals and armories, exclusive of temporary depots established for war purposes, most of which have been and all of which will soon be discontinued, is now twenty-eight. In addition to the command and supervision of these, the officers of this department are charged with the inspection of materials and manufacture of ordnance, gunpowder, and such small-arms and equipments as are made for the Government at the foundries, powder mills, and other private establishments. These duties furnish constant employment for all the officers of the ordnance corps now authorized by law, the total number of which is sixty-four. The arsenals alone require, as a minimum number in time of peace, fifty-six, and the Bureau and inspection duties at least eight more. During the late rebellion the want of a greater number of regular ordnance officers educated for and experienced in their peculiar duties was seriously felt; and the necessity, arising from the inadequate provision in this respect, of the frequent employment of acting ordnance officers caused much embarrassment and confusion, and was detrimental to the public service and interest. These now require that the additional offices of the Ordnance Department authorized temporarily by sections 4 and 12 of the act of March 3, 1863, shall be continued as part of the military peace establishment.

The tabular statement accompanying this report shows in detail the ordnance, arms, and other ordnance supplies which have been procured and issued through this department during the past fiscal year. The armies in the field were amply and well supplied in this respect. The permanent fortifications have had their armaments kept in order, and strengthened and increased by the addition of guns of heavy caliber and great efficiency.

Very respectfully, your obedient servant,

A. B. DYER,

Brigadier-General and Chief of Ordnance.

Statement of ordnance, arms, ammunition, and other ordnance stores procured and supplied to the Army, and the quantity remaining on hand at the close of the fiscal year ending June 30, 1865.

Articles.	On hand June 30, 1864.	Purchased, fabricated, and turned in by the Army during the year ending June 30, 1865.	Issued to the Army and expended in manufacture during the year ending June 30, 1865.	On hand June 30, 1865.
Field guns of different calibers	875	1,235	354	1,756
Siege guns and mortars of different calibers	346	424	32	738
Sea-coast guns and mortars of different calibers	812	612	593	831
Cannon-balls, shells, and other projectiles for field guns.	278,324	969,130	676,815	570,639
Cannon-balls, shells, and other projectiles for siege guns and mortars.	193,297	332,305	14,779	510,823
Cannon-balls, shells, and other projectiles for sea-coast guns and mortars.	469,619	317,658	178,235	609,042
Artillery carriages for field service	618	725	448	895
Artillery carriages for siege service	134	131	109	156
Artillery carriages for sea-coast forts	790	545	797	538
Mortar beds	142	329	7	464
Caissons	616	639	307	948
Traveling forges	70	116	87	99
Battery wagons	67	97	42	122
Muskets and rifles	1,167,405	426,571	398,404	1,195,572
Carbines	22,616	142,201	99,051	65,766
Pistols	34,821	70,744	37,503	68,062
Swords and sabers	80,645	112,067	64,692	128,020
Infantry accouterments ... sets	355,434	336,130	271,925	419,639
Cavalry accouterments ... do	68,428	127,850	93,281	102,997
Horse equipments ... do	26,958	142,497	95,030	74,425
Artillery harness for two horses ... do	3,029	4,069	1,255	5,843
Saddle blankets	79,829	238,388	197,940	120,277
Ammunition for field guns ... rounds	793,455	702,156	286,925	1,208,686
Ammunition for siege guns and mortars ... do	53,009	42,738	15,236	80,511
Ammunition for sea-coast guns and mortars, rounds.	4,805	54,465	4,631	54,639
Ammunition for small-arms ... rounds	209,315,880	261,636,538	188,784,530	282,167,888
Percussion-caps	150,931,237	178,211,512	238,063,778	91,078,971
Friction-primers	1,251,842	2,242,900	1,583,640	1,911,102
Fuses	980,854	1,300,012	719,678	1,561,188
Powder ... pounds	2,329,230	6,619,925	5,582,330	3,366,825
Niter ... do	8,120,240	....	21,254	8,098,986
Sulphur ... do	622,054	....	213,122	408,932
Lead ... do	30,668,929	19,743,668	10,751,494	39,661,103
Lead balls ... do	6,128,502	11,295,637	11,906,208	5,517,931

A. B. DYER,
Brigadier-General and Chief of Ordnance.

ORDNANCE OFFICE,
October 20, 1865.

OFFICE COMMISSARY-GENERAL OF SUBSISTENCE,
Washington City, D. C., October 20, 1865.

HON. EDWIN M. STANTON,
Secretary of War:

SIR: In compliance with the special instructions of the War Department of October 7, addressed to chiefs of bureaus, I have the honor to submit the following report of the operations of the Subsistence Department during the past year:

The subsistence stores required for distribution to the several armies in the field have during the year been purchased, as was done during the earlier years of the war, in the principal markets of the Northern States. The facilities and cost of transportation to the various points where they were required for issue, the relative prices in the different markets, and a due regard to the general commercial interests of the country, have governed this department in apportioning these purchases among the several market centers of the country. New Orleans, gradually resuming a healthy commercial condition, already enables this department—and in further aid of such resumption—to obtain in that market a considerable portion of the supplies required for distribution from that point. Although the present general condition of the Southern States is not such as to afford a large amount of supplies for the troops on duty therein, still, the officers of this department are able in some parts of those States to enter into contracts for beef-cattle and slaughtered beef, as also to some extent to purchase therein other articles. The principal purchasing officers of the Subsistence Department have performed their duties with great fidelity to the interests of the country and with much mercantile ability, and also, as I am frequently assured, to the general satisfaction of the commercial men of the country with whom they have transacted the business of this department.

So far as has been practicable, subsistence stores have been obtained by advertising for and receiving sealed proposals for their delivery. During the past six months 402 such advertisements have been received and placed on file in this office.

The principal commissaries immediately responsible for the subsistence of the several armies in the field have performed the important and often difficult duties of receiving, protecting, and distributing the supplies forwarded to them with commendable efficiency and success. They have also, by great energy, been able, to a considerable extent, to subsist the troops upon the resources of the country in which the armies were operating or through which they were passing.

It is believed that during the entire war no campaign, contemplated movement, or expedition has failed on account of the inability of the Subsistence Department to meet its proper requirements. It is also believed that the troops, wherever stationed or operating, have, with rare exceptions, been supplied with rations in good and wholesome condition.

While the Subsistence Department has furnished a constant, timely, and adequate supply of subsistence for the several large armies occupying widely different fields of operations, as also for the troops at all the separate positions occupied throughout the entire country, it is due to the Quartermaster's Department that its vast labors in the transportation of these supplies be recognized as having been performed with a readiness and efficiency worthy of the highest commendation. As a single item indicating the amount of these labors, I instance the fact that during the year 1863 the Quartermaster's Department shipped from the port of New York an average of 7,000 packages of subsistence stores per day for every working day of the year, and for the year 1864, 6,727 packages per day.

The sudden close of the war, and the consequent immediate muster out of a large part of the Army, unavoidably left on hand in some of the depots an excessive supply of subsistence stores. This excess has been sent to other points, where stores were required, instead of meeting such requirements by further purchases. By this course a considerable part of these supplies have been, or will be, economically disposed of. Surplus and damaged stores are in process of being disposed of by sale. A considerable quantity of hard bread, surplus or too old for issue to troops, remains to be disposed of. A sufficient quantity of this and other surplus articles have been held back from an earlier sale with the view of meeting, in an economical manner, the urgent wants of those people, white and colored, who have, by the events of the war, been reduced to a suffering condition; to whom it has been deemed an act of charity, due from the Government, to make limited issues of food.

I have the honor to report that under your orders of June 29, 1865, directing the discontinuance of the whisky ration, and the sale of the whisky on hand, the issue of that article was at once stopped. The sale has already taken place at many points, and will soon be completed.

During the past year, as in the previous years of the war, a very considerable income has been derived from the sale of the hides, tallow, and other parts of beef cattle not issuable as beef to the troops. The total amount of such sales has not been ascertained. At the Washington and Alexandria depots alone they amount to \$344,468.98½ for the year ending 30th of September, 1865, and to \$1,377,875.93 during the four years ending at that date.

Under the able and judicious management of Bvt. Brig. Gen. William Hoffman, U. S. Army, Commissary-General of Prisoners, the prisoners of war, held under his charge at thirty-two forts, prison barracks, camps, and hospitals, have been well and humanely subsisted, having received a sufficient portion and variety of the ration to insure health, leaving in the hands of the several issuing commissaries, as "savings," that portion of the ration not deemed necessary for persons living in entire idleness. The pecuniary value of these "savings" has constituted a prison fund, available, under the instructions of the Commissary-General of Prisoners, for the purchase of articles necessary for the prison barracks and hospitals, and for meeting other necessary expenses of the prisoners. General Hoffman has already, under your instructions, transferred to the Subsistence Department a "savings" credit of the amount of \$1,507,359.01, and reports that there remains yet to be transferred an amount not less than \$337,766.98, making a total amount of \$1,845,125.99.

The discharge of volunteer forces, and the consequent reduction of the expenses of this department, will enable it to meet all demands without exhausting the appropriation for the current fiscal year.

The current work of this Bureau is, habitually, up to date. The examination of the money and property accounts is nearly as close up to date as it is practicable to have it. It would, however, facilitate the prompt examination of the money and property accounts of the officers of the Subsistence Department if the law permitted the former, as well as the latter, to be sent, by the officers rendering them, direct to this Bureau for its administrative action before going to the accounting officers of the Treasury. I do not doubt that the Third Auditor is of the same opinion.

Under section 3 of the act of July 4, 1864, authorizing the claims of loyal citizens in States not in rebellion, for subsistence actually furnished to the Army of the United States, and receipted for by the proper officer receiving the same, or which may have been taken by such officers without giving such receipt, to be submitted to the Commissary-General of Subsistence, and making it his duty to cause each claim to be examined, there have been submitted as follows:

Whole number	1,470
Approved for payment	50
Disallowed	413
Awaiting explanations, &c	650
Awaiting examination	357

With your approval it is proposed to ascertain and exhibit, in a tabular form, the total quantity of each article of subsistence stores purchased for use of the Army during each year of the war, from 1861 to 1865, inclusive. Such a statement would form an interesting addition to the mercantile statistics of the country.

Under the act of March 3, 1865, for the better organization of the Subsistence Department, authorizing, during the continuance of the rebellion, the selection and assignment of commissaries of subsistence of the volunteer and regular service to geographical military divisions, to separate armies in the field, to military departments, to principal subsistence depots, and to the office of the Commissary-General of Subsistence as assistants, with the rank, pay, and emoluments of a colonel of the Subsistence Department, there have been so selected and assigned nine commissaries of subsistence; one from the regular service and eight from the volunteer service. There have also been selected and assigned, under authority of the same act, to inspection or other special duty, two commissaries of subsistence with the rank of lieutenant-colonel; one from the volunteer and the other from the regular service. Also, to divisions, two commissaries of subsistence with the rank of major; both from the volunteer service.

During the past year two vacancies have occurred in the regular service of the Subsistence Department; one by the brief sickness and death, after much zealous and efficient field service, of Maj. John Kellogg, and the other by resignation of Capt. Edward R. Hopkins, a valuable officer. Both of these vacancies were filled by selections and appointments from the volunteer branch of the Subsistence Department.

The Subsistence Department at the commencement of the war contained but twelve officers of all grades. It had reached this number by small additions, authorized by law, from time to time, as the Army was increased and the territory occupied by it extended; the several additions subsequent to the act of April 14, 1818, by which a commissary-general of subsistence was originally authorized, being as follows: By the act of March 2, 1820, two commissaries; by the act of July 5, 1838, five commissaries; by the act of September 20, 1850, four commissaries. Since the commencement of the rebellion there have been added as follows: By the act of August 3, 1861, twelve commissaries; by the act of February 9, 1863, five commissaries, making a total of twenty-nine officers of all grades. A further increase is not recommended until it shall be made to appear that the present number of officers is inadequate to the service required of the department.

The officers of this department, regulars and volunteers, have, with but few exceptions, performed their duties with signal fidelity and success. Some of them have been held from serving with troops in the field, much against their choice and ambition.

To the able senior assistant commissary-general of subsistence, and to the other officers on duty in this Bureau, is largely due the credit of the general good condition of the affairs of the Subsistence Department which I am enabled to report.

I have the honor to be, very respectfully, your obedient servant,

A. B. EATON,

Commissary-General of Subsistence.

WAR DEPARTMENT, SURGEON-GENERAL'S OFFICE,
Washington, D. C., October 20, 1865.

Hon. E. M. STANTON,
Secretary of War:

SIR: I have the honor to submit the following statement of finances and general transactions of the Medical Department for the fiscal year ending June 30, 1865:

RECEIPTS.

Balance in the Treasury July 1, 1864	$914,135.10
Balance in the hands of the disbursing officers	324,061.65
Balance remaining of appropriation for artificial limbs for soldiers and seamen, per act of July 16, 1862, chapter 182, section 6	4,265.00
Annual appropriation for the year ending June 30, 1865, by act of June 15, 1864, chapter 124, section 1	8,930,640.00
Deficiency appropriation for the current fiscal year, by act of March 2, 1865, chapter 73, section 8	3,251,000.00
Annual appropriation for the year ending June 30, 1866, by act of March 3, 1865, chapter 81, section 1, required for disbursement during the present fiscal year, and placed to the credit of the Medical Department for that purpose March 22, 1865	6,000,000.00
Amount drawn from appropriation made by joint resolution of April 29, 1864, to cover expenditures for medical attendance and medicine for 100-day's volunteers	300,000.00
Amount refunded by the Subsistence Department for board of sick and wounded soldiers in private hospitals	64,293.40
Amount refunded for medical attendance and supplies furnished prisoners of war	140,506.08
Amount received for subsistence of officers in hospitals	286,281.04
Amount disallowed in account of Ebenezer Swift, U. S. Army, for June, 1863, and refunded from appropriation for pay of volunteers	17,762.91
Proceeds of sales of condemned and unserviceable hospital property	59,671.41
Proceeds of sales of ice not required for hospital use	12,352.25
Value of books and surgical instruments sold to medical officers and private physicians	8,311.30
Received for hospital property sold to the Quartermaster's Department	7,003.61
Received for medicines, &c., issued to refugees and freedmen	554.73
Recovered for hospital property lost or damaged in transportation	534.45
Recovered of Actg. Asst. Surg. J. S. Geltner, U. S. Army, for property and moneys illegally disposed of	1,000.00
Amount received for care of patients belonging to the U. S. Navy	283.00
Amount received from all other sources	446.20
Total credits for the year	20,323,102.13
Amount over-expended by disbursing officers	166,578.34
	20,489,680.47

DISBURSEMENTS DURING THE YEAR.

For medical and hospital supplies	$15,204,497.20
For pay of private physicians	1,865,821.82
For pay of hospital employés	949,462.46
For expenses of purveying depots	683,830.33
For care of sick soldiers in private hospitals	240,476.11
For artificial limbs for soldiers and seamen *a*	126,538.00
Expenses of hospitals for officers	243,876.37
Miscellaneous expenses of the Medical Department	13,996.94
	19,328,499.23
Balance in the Treasury June 30, 1865	1,161,181.24
	20,489,680.47

a Furnished during the year—artificial legs, 1,388; arms, 1,121.

The ample provision for sick and wounded existing at the date of my last annual report was increased during the ensuing months until a maximum of 204 general hospitals, with a capacity of 136,894 beds, was reached. Field hospitals, hospital transports and cars, ambulance corps, and the purveying depots were kept in condition to meet all possible requirements, and General Sherman's army was met at Savannah by four first-class sea-going steamers, thoroughly equipped as hospital transports, with extra stores and supplies for 5,000 beds, should it have become necessary to establish large hospitals upon his line of operations.

Upon the receipt of General Orders, No. 77, dated War Department, Adjutant-General's Office, April 28, 1865, immediate measures were taken to reduce the expenses of this department. Of the 201 general hospitals opened on January 1, 1865, 170 have been discontinued. Three of the four sea-going hospital transports have been discharged; the fourth is now constantly engaged in the transfer of sick and wounded from Southern ports to the general hospitals in New York Harbor. All of the river hospital boats have been turned over to the Quartermaster's Department, and but a single hospital train is retained in the Southwest.

The vast amount of medicines and hospital supplies becoming surplus through the reduction of the Army have been carefully collected at prominent points and are being disposed of at public auction, most of the articles bringing their full value, and in some instances their cost price.

Since April, 1861, there have been appointed 547 surgeons and assistant surgeons of volunteers; mustered into service, 2,109 volunteer regimental surgeons and 3,882 volunteer regimental assistant surgeons; employed as acting staff surgeons, 75; as acting assistant surgeons, 5,532.

As far as returns have been received during the war 34 officers of the medical staff have been killed or died of wounds received in action, 24 wounded, and 188 have died from disease or accident incurred in the service; 1 died in a rebel prison; 6 of yellow fever. A completed record will increase this number.

Two hundred and fourteen surgeons and assistant surgeons of volunteers, reported as supernumerary, have been mustered out.

In compliance with the act of Congress hospital chaplains have been reported for muster out when the hospitals to which they were attached have been discontinued. Of the 265 appointed during the war 29 are still in commission.

The business of this office has been largely increased by the necessity for immediate examination and settlement of the accounts of staff and regimental medical officers mustered out of service, while the number of applications from the Pension Bureau for "official evidence of cause of death" now averages 1,550 a month, the number received and acted upon in the last fiscal year being over 19,000. Other official inquiries requiring reference to records and hospital registers are very numerous.

The returns of sick and wounded show that of white troops 1,057,423 cases have been treated in general hospitals alone from 1861 to July 1, 1865, of which the mortality rate was 8 per cent. In addition to the alphabetical registers of dead, not yet fully completed, the records of the Medical Department contain 30,000 special reports of the more important forms of surgical injuries, of disease, and of operations. These reports, with statistical data and a pathological collection numbering 7,630 specimens, furnish a mass of valuable information which is being rapidly arranged and tabulated as a medical and surgical history of the war, for the publication of the first volumes of which an appropriation will be asked.

In this connection and as illustrating more in detail the importance of this work the Army Medical Museum assumes the highest value. By its array of indisputable facts, supported and enriched by full reports, it supplies instruction otherwise unattainable and preserves for future application the dearly-bought experience of four years of war. Apart from its great usefulness it is also an honorable record of the skill and services of those medical officers whose contributions constitute its value and whose incentive to these self-imposed labors has been the desire to elevate their profession. A small appropriation has been asked to continue and extend this collection.

During the fiscal year ending June 30, 1865, an Army Medical Board was appointed to meet in Cincinnati, Ohio, on the 18th day of October, 1864, for the examination of candidates for the medical staff of the Army and of assistant surgeons of that corps for promotion. Nine applicants for admission into the medical staff were invited to present themselves before this board. Of this number two were fully examined and approved, one withdrew before his examinations were concluded, two were rejected as unqualified, and four failed to appear. Six assistant surgeons were examined for promotion and found qualified. Two assistant surgeons were reported for re-examination. Of the approved candidates two have been appointed assistant surgeons.

Boards have been in session at New York; Washington, D. C.; Hilton Head, S. C.; New Orleans, La.; Memphis, Tenn.; Little Rock, Ark., and Cincinnati, Ohio, for the examination of candidates for appointment in the volunteer medical staff. One hundred and fifty-two candidates were invited before these boards, fifty-eight of whom passed satisfactory examinations and were appointed accordingly. The remainder were rejected, failed to appear, or withdrew before examination was completed. These boards were discontinued in June, 1865.

The casualties in this corps since June 30, 1864, are as follows: Appointed, 96; promoted, 40; restored, 2; resigned, 32; declined, 1; died, 7; dismissed, 3; discharged, 3; dropped, 1; mustered out, 19; canceled, 7.

Boards for the examination of candidates for appointment as medical officers to colored troops have been in session permanently at Boston, New York, Washington, Philadelphia, Cincinnati, Saint Louis, and at such other points from time to time as the necessities of the service demanded.

In nearly all sections of the country the health of the troops has been fully equal to that of the preceding years, though military movements of unprecedented magnitude have been pushed to successful termination without regard to seasons. An epidemic of yellow fever prevailed in New Berne, N. C., in September, October, and November, 1864, causing 278 deaths among the troops stationed there, of whom 571 were attacked. The released or exchanged prisoners arriving at Wilmington, N. C., from rebel prisons suffered from an epidemic of typhoid fever, which, however, was arrested by strict attention to hygienic rules and prompt transfer to Northern hospitals. With these exceptions no serious epidemics have appeared, and it is interesting to note that quarantine regulations strictly enforced by military authority have proven, during the occupation of Southern sea-ports and cities by our troops, to be an absolute protection against the importation of contagious or infectious diseases. In view of the apprehensions entertained in regard to the Asiatic cholera, now devastating the shores of the Mediterranean, this becomes a significant fact.

For recommendations of measures tending to the greater efficiency of the Medical Department you are respectfully referred to the special report from this office called for by circular dated War Department, Adjutant-General's Office, October 7, 1865.

In conclusion, I desire to bear testimony to the ability, courage, and zeal manifested throughout the war by the officers of the Medical Department under all circumstances and upon all occasions. With hardly an exception they have been actuated by the highest motives of national and professional pride, and the number who have been killed and wounded bears most honorable testimony to their devotion to duty on the field of battle.

To the medical directors of armies in the field and of military geographical departments especial praise is due for the successful execution of their arduous and responsible duties.

I am, sir, very respectfully, your obedient servant,

JOS. K. BARNES,
Surgeon-General, Brevet Major-General, U. S. Army.

OFFICE OF THE SIGNAL OFFICER,
Washington, October 20, 1865.

Hon. E. M. STANTON,
Secretary of War, Washington, D. C.:

SIR: In answer to your communication of the 7th instant, I have the honor to submit the following annual report of the operations of the Signal Corps for the year ending October 20, 1865:

On the 1st of November, 1864, the corps was represented in the field by the following detachments, thoroughly equipped, active, and energetic, to wit:

Detachment.	Officers of Signal Corps.	Acting officers.	Non-commissioned officers.	Privates.
Office of the Signal Officer	3		2	9
Department of Washington	6	1	5	66
Signal Camp of Instruction	16	4	3	86
Army of the Potomac	12	3	13	167
Department of Virginia and North Carolina	15	8	14	137
Department of the South	7		13	39
Department of the Cumberland	9	10	10	87
Department of the Tennessee	6	7	7	140
Department of the Ohio	4	4	1	42
Military Division of West Mississippi	10	15	10	210
Department of Kansas	2	5	2	51
Middle Military Division	8	8	2	168
Department of the Susquehanna	4	1	2	64
Total	102	66	84	1,266
	168		1,350	

Such was the disposition of the corps, and the following, in general terms, the nature of services performed:

The duties of the corps during the past year were better understood than in previous years, which gave to it more tone and character, and enabled it to approximate in most of the military departments to its true position.

In one—the Department of the Gulf—it combined all the branches of the corps of information which it was designed, and of right ought, to be. Here it added to aerial telegraphing, telescopic reconnoitering, and general scouting, the entire secret service department, thus having all information usually gathered from these sources flow into one common center, where it was compared, classified, reduced to logical form, and then laid before the commanding general to be acted upon. The advantage arising from thus concentrating these services is specially apparent in the fact that particular reports and doubtful information could be thoroughly sifted, and tested in two, three, or more different modes by the one officer having control of the several means for collecting knowledge of the enemy's movements and designs.

In other military departments, as I have stated, the corps only approximated to this more perfect system of economy. But as the value of concentration in military organizations was being daily more and more recognized, these duties, if the war had continued, would undoubtedly have been eventually assigned to the corps wherever a detachment of it would have been placed upon duty.

In the Army of the Potomac our duties were limited to signal communication, observing and reporting the changes and movements of the enemy, and such aide duty as we were called upon to perform.

In the armies operating under Major-General Sherman the signal detachment added to signaling and telescopic reconnoitering, general scouting, courier, guide, and aide duty.

The detachment in the Department of the South was limited to keeping communication open between the several military posts along the coast, and between the land and naval forces, when operating in conjunction.

Upon the plains a detachment operated with the various expeditions against the Indians, keeping open communication between detached parties and the main body of the army.

In the Department of Pennsylvania the signal detachment was employed in watching the crossings of the Potomac, as well as doing general outpost duty, with instructions to give timely information to the commanding general of any threatening danger, that it might be met upon the threshold of the department, and overcome before any injury could be done to the community.

In the Department of Virginia and North Carolina, in addition to communicating by signals between portions of the army, and the observing of the movements of the enemy, the detachment was beneficially employed in various expeditions and operations of the army and navy combined, connecting the commanders of the two forces so immediately as to make their several efforts harmonize in such manner that their blows fell with double effect upon the strongholds and battalions of the enemy.

The insurrectionary armies having been, at the opening of the spring campaign, forced to surrender, and the power of the Government having been re-established to its rightful extent, the great work of disbanding and returning to the conditions of peace the military force of the United States was commenced. The Signal Corps of the Army having been organized by an act of Congress—which in some of its provisions had a view to permanency, but gave to the corps only an organization for the term of the rebellion—was, by various orders from the War Department, materially reduced, until all that portion of it on duty east of the Mississippi River was mustered out and discharged.

There now remain the detachment in the Military Division of the Mississippi, numbering 9 officers, 2 non-commissioned officers, and 35 enlisted men, and the detachment in the Military Division of the Gulf, numbering 15 officers, 13 non-commissioned officers, and 86 enlisted men. These detachments are operating with the troops upon the plains, and throughout Texas, and along the Southwestern boundary.

OFFICE OF THE SIGNAL OFFICER.

The office of the Signal Officer is three-fold in its character. It is, first, the headquarters of the corps, where the records are collected, completed, and filed, and has advisory superintendence and control of the special duties of the corps, and of all assignments of officers and men to signal duty; second, a purchasing and disbursing office, from which supplies of signal stores and equipments are issued to the various detachments of the corps in the field; third, an office for the examining of the signal accounts and returns of signal stores of all officers responsible to Government for such property.

Connected with this office are two clerks of "class two," to wit, Messrs. Simeon White and Alexander Ashley, appointed in 1863. To the ability and faithful exertions of these persons is owing much of the degree of system and perfection attained in the records of the office.

EXPENDITURES, ETC.

There were expended during the year ending September 30, 1865, of the sums appropriated for the fiscal year ending June 30, 1865, $8,537.06, leaving a balance which, added to that yet remaining of former appropriations and to the amount appropriated for the fiscal year ending June 30, 1866, makes the sum of $248,062 still available.

SPECIAL SERVICES.

Having thus given a general view of the corps, its strength, duties, and expenses, I propose, without entering into a detailed statement of the constant and various acts of service performed, which were part and parcel of every battle fought and campaign made during the year, and which played in each a more or less important function, to merely place upon record, through the War Department, several instances where the operations of the corps were of such vital importance that all who read must acknowledge that the Signal Corps was a valuable adjunct to the Army, and rendered such material service in the great contest just closed that its members can view with pride and infinite self-satisfaction a substantial record, made in the face of the difficulties that usually attend the introduction of a new element into any old-established system.

The first instance of the kind referred to which I shall mention occurred in October, 1864, and just previous to the commencement of the great campaign of General Sherman from the northern part of

Georgia to the sea-coast. That great leader, whose military genius never allowed him to overlook any visible means to aid in securing success, or guard against any and all possible occurrences to endanger his plans, in whatever enterprise undertaken, seeing the liability of his telegraph wires communicating with his depot of supplies at Allatoona being cut, he established in addition a line of signal communication through which he afterward, when the enemy obtained a lodgment in his rear and cut his telegraph wires, as was foreseen, transmitted his orders and instructions that saved from capture Allatoona, its garrison, and stores of supplies, the value of which at that time and place cannot be computed, as without them it can well be doubted whether the great campaign, which exposed the great weakness of the enemy and propagated the seeds of the coming dissolution of the rebellion, could have been executed for months later. In connection with this transaction General Sherman states:

In several instances this corps (Signal Corps) has transmitted orders and brought me information of the greatest importance that could not have reached me in any other way. I will instance one most remarkable case. When the enemy had cut our wires and actually made a lodgment on our railroad about Big Shanty, the signal officers on Vining's Hill, Kenesaw, and Allatoona sent my orders to General Corse at Rome, whereby General Corse was enabled to reach Allatoona just in time to defend it. Had it not been for the services of this corps on that occasion I am satisfied we should have lost the garrison at Allatoona and a most valuable depository of provisions there, which was worth to us and the country more than the aggregate expense of the whole Signal Corps for one year.

This will serve to evince the important character of the services of the corps at times when operating with the army alone. The following account will demonstrate its eminent usefulness where the army and navy operated in conjunction. In the expedition organized to attack Fort Fisher in the month of January of this year, an army signal officer was with Admiral Porter, commanding the fleet, and others with General Terry, commanding the land forces, who by means of signals placed these commanding officers in such immediate communication that the fire of the navy, which otherwise must have slackened after the assault commenced upon the part of the army, was kept up without cessation as the enemy was driven from traverse to traverse. In this connection Admiral Porter, in a communication to the Secretary of the Navy, which induced the latter to tender the thanks of the Navy Department to the War Department for this efficient agency, states:

Through Mr. Clemens (signal officer) I was in constant communication with General Terry, even during the assault on Fort Fisher, and was enabled to direct the fire of the New Ironsides to the traverses occupied by the enemy, without fear of hurting our own people, from my complete reliance on him.

Thus, through this mobile system of visual telegraphing, the army and navy are made to act as a unit. During the war there were more forcible instances of this kind than the above, when, in most important crises, it would have been impossible for the navy to have rendered the necessary assistance save through the aid of army signals, by means of which its fire was directed to unseen points with almost as much facility and certainty as could have been done if the gunners would have had the object of their aim in view. I would also state here that improvements were made during the year in the simple cipher apparatus used by the corps in sending secret messages which, if they did not absolutely defy deciphering, were of such an intricate and complex character that messages sent thereby cannot possibly be interpreted by the uninitiated within such period as to be of any service to the enemy, even should the messenger fall into his hands.

With these references to special transactions of the corps, and having accorded to its members the merit and thanks so well earned by earnest patriotism, by zealous, faithful, and constant exertion to render services throughout the war to their country, and by the success achieved, and having conceded to them the claim that no class of the military was more anxious to be useful, or welcomed with more satisfaction additional duties, we will conclude this report by calling attention to the necessity for additional action, in order to afford in the future to the Army the requisite signal service.

As experience has clearly demonstrated the eminent advantage of having a signal officer attached to garrisons and posts liable to be besieged, in order to secure communication over the heads of an enemy, should occasion arise, and of having a sufficient number of signal officers as a nucleus that would be immediately available in the event of future wars, it is submitted that such action should be taken by the authorities as would secure for such contingencies the properly instructed officers. This can be done in two modes: Either by continuing a small permanent organization with specifically defined duties, or by detailing a certain number of officers from other branches of the service, and directing them to report to the Signal Officer of the Army to be instructed, with a view to their being assigned to such garrisons and posts as it may be deemed necessary to provide with means of signal communication.

If the former mode be adopted it is recommended that a board of officers, more or less acquainted with the past services of this department, be appointed to report the form of the required organization, and to define, as far as practicable, the specific duties to be assigned it, to avoid in the future the great stumbling-block which was left in the way in the past organization, and which, in many instances, crippled the usefulness of the corps by its not being properly understood what it could do or was expected to do.

It is presumed that no argument need be presented in favor of a new organization, as it is self-evident greater interest would be taken in the service, and greater perfection attained in it, than in a simply acting corps.

I have the honor, sir, to be, very respectfully, your obedient servant,

B. F. FISHER,

Chief Signal Officer and Colonel, U. S. Army.

CIRCULAR No. 46.

WAR DEPT., ADJUTANT-GENERAL'S OFFICE,
Washington, October 20, 1865.

ORDERS AND INSTRUCTIONS RELATIVE TO THE MUSTER OUT OF VOLUNTEER TROOPS, VIZ, ALL CAVALRY (WHITE) EAST OF THE MISSISSIPPI, AND CERTAIN VOLUNTEERS IN VARIOUS ARMIES AND DEPARTMENTS.

I. Cavalry east of the Mississippi.

Under paragraph V, General Orders, No. 144, Adjutant-General's Office, October 9, 1865, the following regiments of volunteer cavalry —all of that arm remaining in service east of the Mississippi River—

were ordered mustered out. (Telegram to department commanders from Adjutant-General's Office, dated October 16, 1865.)

Alabama.—First (ten companies).

Florida.—First and Second.

Illinois.—Sixth, Seventh, and Ninth.

Indiana.—Thirteenth.

Massachusetts.—Fourth.

Missouri.—Fourth.

Michigan.—Tenth.

New York.—Second Veteran and Fourth Provisional.

New Jersey.—Second.

Ohio.—Fifth and Twelfth.

Pennsylvania.—Third Provisional.

Rhode Island.—Third.

District of Columbia.—First (squadron).

II. Troops in various armies and departments—services no longer required.

MEMORANDA.

1. October 9, 1865.—Major-General Halleck, commanding Military Division of the Pacific, was directed to muster out all volunteers on the Pacific Coast, as many as possible immediately, the remainder on the arrival of the last battalion of the Fourteenth U. S. Infantry.

2. October 10, 1865.—Major-General Pope, commanding the Department of the Missouri, was directed to order all California Volunteers in New Mexico to their State at once for muster out. Also, to relieve as soon as possible all New Mexican Volunteers, one regiment thereof to be mustered out immediately, the remainder on the arrival of certain regular troops.

3. Regiments of cavalry, infantry, and artillery ordered mustered out under special instructions of dates set opposite the organizations, respectively:

Ohio.—Infantry: Eighteenth, September 29, 1865.

Pennsylvania.—Artillery: Third Heavy, October 9, 1865 (General Orders, No. 144).

New York.—Infantry: One hundred and sixty-first (battalion), October 9, 1865 (General Orders, No. 144).

Kentucky (*U. S. Colored Troops*).—Infantry: One hundred and twenty-third, One hundred and twenty-fourth, and One hundred and thirty-fifth, October 2, 1865. Artillery: Twelfth Heavy (Thirteenth Heavy since substituted), October 2, 1865.

E. D. TOWNSEND,
Assistant Adjutant-General.

WAR DEPARTMENT, ADJUTANT-GENERAL'S OFFICE,
Washington, October 20, 1865.

Adjt. Gen. N. B. BAKER,
Clinton, Iowa:

GENERAL: Referring to your letter of August 9, inclosing exhibit of three-months' men, and referring to certain other troops as not credited, I have the honor to state that all men duly and legally reported to this office "on report of July 30, 1864," and from "October 1, 1864, to May 20, 1865," have been reported to the Provost-Marshal-General of the United States.

In regard to Iowa men in regiments from other States, I would refer to the correspondence heretofore had with your headquarters on the subject, and in which the principle was enunciated that no such credits could be allowed, except on an adjustment between the Governors of the States concerned. All troops regularly reported from October 1, 1864, to May 20, 1865, have been duly credited, and the records of the acting assistant provost-marshal-general of the State should bear evidence of the fact. Your letter of August 9, with a copy of this, has been referred to the Provost-Marshal-General of the United States for his action.

I am, general, very respectfully, your obedient servant,

THOMAS M. VINCENT,
Assistant Adjutant-General.

List of volunteer organizations which have been, or are ordered to be, mustered out of service, not included in previous circulars.

WAR DEPARTMENT, ADJUTANT-GENERAL'S OFFICE,
Washington, October 24, 1865.

Connecticut.—Infantry: Twenty-ninth (Colored).

District of Columbia.—Cavalry: First.

Florida.—Cavalry: First. Second and First East, consolidated with First Cavalry.

Illinois.—Infantry: Fifty-fourth. Cavalry: Sixth, Seventh, Ninth. Men of Ninety-fifth Infantry remaining in service, transferred to Forty-seventh Infantry—latter still in service.

Indiana.—Cavalry: Thirteenth.

Kansas.—Cavalry: Companies L and M, Fifth. This completes the muster out of the regiment.

Missouri.—Cavalry: Fourth, Fifteenth, Sixteenth.

Michigan.—Cavalry: Tenth.

Massachusetts.—Cavalry: Fourth, Fifth (Colored).

New York.—Infantry: One hundred and fifty-sixth, One hundred and sixtieth, One hundred and sixty-first, and One hundred and seventy-third. Cavalry: Second Veteran, Fourth Provisional.

New Jersey.—Cavalry: Second.

Ohio.—Infantry: One hundred and ninety-fourth. Cavalry: Fifth and Twelfth.

Pennsylvania.—Artillery: Third Heavy. Cavalry: Third Provisional.

Rhode Island.—Cavalry: Third.

U. S. Colored Troops.—Infantry: Second, Third, Eighth, Twenty-second, Twenty-third, Twenty-fourth, Twenty-fifth, Twenty-eighth, Twenty-ninth, Thirty-first, Forty-first, Forty-second, Forty-third, Forty-fifth, Seventy-third, Seventy-fourth, Seventy-seventh, One hundred and sixth, One hundred and twenty-third, One hundred and twenty-fourth, One hundred and twenty-seventh, One hundred and thirty-fifth. One company Pioneers. Artillery: Thirteenth Heavy.

NOTE.—Seventy-third Infantry has been heretofore reported consolidated with Ninety-sixth U. S. Colored Troops. Seventy-seventh Infantry has been heretofore reported consolidated with the Tenth U. S. Colored Heavy Artillery. One hundred and sixth Infantry has been heretofore reported consolidated with Fortieth U. S. Colored Troops.

GENERAL ORDERS, No. 155. } WAR DEPT., ADJT. GENERAL'S OFFICE, *Washington, October 26, 1865.*

ORDER FOR DISCHARGING CERTAIN OFFICERS AND MEN OF THE VETERAN RESERVE CORPS.

In view of the very numerous and pressing applications for discharge by members of the Veteran Reserve Corps, department commanders will cause all organizations of that corps within the geographical limits of their command to be paraded before a general or general staff officer as soon after the receipt of this order as practicable.

Any general or general staff officer on duty within the limits of the department whose services can be spared may be detailed for this purpose. The officer will question each officer and enlisted man so paraded as to whether he wishes to be discharged or to remain in the service, and will make out separate lists of those who wish a discharge and of those who wish to remain in service. Each list will then be read before the officers and men, who will have an opportunity to correct it, so that it will be a true expression of their wishes on the subject. The officer will visit all those who may be absent from the parade, and in a similar manner obtain their wishes and enter their names on the proper rolls.

The rolls of officers and men who wish to be discharged will then be turned over to the proper commissary of musters, who will immediately muster out of service those whose names are on the rolls of such as desire discharge. He will obtain from regimental officers the necessary data, and complete the rolls of those who desire to remain in service, so as to exhibit their rank and degree of disability. These rolls, when completed, will be forwarded to the Adjutant-General.

Names of officers and men belonging to different companies or regiments will not be borne on the same rolls in any of the above cases. The rolls of those who wish to remain in service, as well as those who wish for discharge, will be made on the prescribed blanks for muster and descriptive rolls, and will contain full information according to the form of the blank.

Department commanders will see that this order is executed with promptness.

By order of the Secretary of War:

E. D. TOWNSEND,
Assistant Adjutant-General.

CIRCULAR No. 47. } WAR DEPT., ADJUTANT-GENERAL'S OFFICE, *Washington, October 26, 1865.*

The credit of recruits and re-enlisted men of the Regular Army to the quota of the States, Territories, and the District of Columbia, required to be made by Circular No. 7, February 16, 1865, from this office, will be discontinued from and after November 1, 1865, and all reports required by said circular to be forwarded to this office, and to the Governors and assistant provost-marshals-general of States and Territories, will cease to be rendered from and after that date.

E. D. TOWNSEND,
Assistant Adjutant-General.

HDQRS. KENTUCKY VOLS., ADJT. GENERAL'S OFFICE,
Frankfort, October 26, 1865.

Bvt. Col. THOMAS M. VINCENT,
Assistant Adjutant-General, Washington, D. C.:

COLONEL: I have the honor to acknowledge the receipt of your telegram of the 20th instant, and as requested I inclose herein a statement of the designation, date of organization, and numerical strength of troops raised under the authority of the act of Congress approved February 7, 1863. These regiments and batteries were for twelve months' service, and organized for the better defense of Kentucky. At that time (1863) all the Federal forces were required at the front, and Kentucky was left in comparatively a defenseless position. As the communication with our army, then occupying Tennessee, was a matter of great importance, the term of service of these troops was fixed at twelve months to induce a speedy organization, as they were intended to keep open that communication. They rendered good and efficient service both in Kentucky and elsewhere, and many of them availed themselves of the privilege allowed by the War Department and re-enlisted. If you desire a statement of the expenses incurred by the State in organizing these troops I will willingly forward same and any other definite information you may desire appertaining thereto.

Very respectfully, your obedient servant,

D. W. LINDSEY,
Adjutant-General of Kentucky.

[Inclosure.]

A list of regiments and batteries raised under the act of Congress approved February 7, 1863, authorizing the State of Kentucky to raise a force not exceeding 20,000 men for one year's service.

Numerical designation of organization.	Date of muster into the U. S. service.	Number mustered into service.
30th Kentucky Infantry	Feb. 19 to April 5, 1863	831
35th Kentucky Infantry	Sept. 16 to Oct 2, 1863	823
37th Kentucky Infantry	Sept. 4, 1863, to Jan. 4, 1864	867
40th Kentucky Infantry	July 30 to Sept. 29, 1863	823
45th Kentucky Infantry	Oct. 10, 1863, to Feb. 4, 1864	842
47th Kentucky Infantry	Oct. 5 to Dec. 29, 1863	754
48th Kentucky Infantry	Oct. 26, 1863	836
49th Kentucky Infantry	Sept. 19 to Oct. 7, 1863	847
52d Kentucky Infantry	Oct. 16, 1863, to March 3, 1864	760
Total		7,383
CAVALRY.		
13th Kentucky Cavalry	Dec. 23, 1863	1,157
ARTILLERY.		
3d Kentucky Battery (C) *a*	Sept. 10, 1863	141
4th Kentucky Battery (D) *a*	Oct. 6, 1863	99
Total		240

a Re-enlisted for three years.

D. W. LINDSEY,
Adjutant-General of Kentucky.

STATE OF OHIO, EXECUTIVE DEPARTMENT,
Columbus, October 27, 1865.

Hon. EDWIN M. STANTON,
Secretary of War, Washington, D. C.:

SIR: I inclose an application of Maj. L. G. Marshall, commanding Eleventh Regiment Ohio Volunteer Cavalry, to have his regiment mustered out of the U. S. service.*

I have already, by my letter of the 16th ultimo, expressed so fully my views of this whole case—the detention of volunteers in a service not contemplated by themselves when they enlisted, nor yet authorized by the acts of Congress—that I do not think it now necessary to repeat my reasons for these opinions and their consequent demand.

I should have been pleased to have been informed of the views and intentions of your Department in regard to the Ohio Volunteers now in the service, in order to have conformed my own action, if consistent with duty to these citizens, to the designs and convenience of your Department. As it is, having failed apparently in procuring an assent to my demand for the prompt discharge of all, I can only forward their applications in detail.

Very respectfully,
CHARLES ANDERSON,
Governor of Ohio.

BY THE PRESIDENT OF THE UNITED STATES OF AMERICA:

A PROCLAMATION.

Whereas, it has pleased Almighty God, during the year which is now coming to an end, to relieve our beloved country from the fearful scourge of civil war, and to permit us to secure the blessings of peace, unity, and harmony, with a great enlargement of civil liberty;

And whereas, our Heavenly Father has also during the year graciously averted from us the calamities of foreign war, pestilence, and famine, while our granaries are full of the fruits of an abundant season;

And whereas, righteousness exalteth a nation, while sin is a reproach to any people:

Now, therefore, be it known that I, Andrew Johnson, President of the United States, do hereby recommend to the people thereof that they do set apart and observe the first Thursday of December next as a day of national thanksgiving to the Creator of the universe for these great deliverances and blessings.

And I do further recommend that on that occasion the whole people make confession of our national sins against His infinite goodness, and with one heart and one mind implore the Divine guidance in the ways of national virtue and holiness.

In testimony whereof I have hereunto set my hand and caused the seal of the United States to be affixed.

Done at the city of Washington this twenty-eighth day of October, in the year of our Lord one thousand eight hundred and sixty-five, and of the Independence of the United States of America the ninetieth.

[L. S.]
ANDREW JOHNSON.

By the President:

WILLIAM H. SEWARD,
Secretary of State.

---

* Omitted.

ENGINEER DEPARTMENT,
Washington, October 30, 1865.

Hon. E. M. STANTON,
Secretary of War, Washington, D. C.:

SIR: I have the honor to present the following report upon the several branches of the public service committed to the care of this department for the year ending on the 30th of June, 1865:

CORPS OF ENGINEERS.

Duties of the officers during the year.—The Corps of Engineers consisted of eighty-five officers, the Military Academy, its officers and professors, and the battalion of engineer soldiers of five companies.

Of the eighty-five officers of engineers embraced in the corps, fifty-four were on detached duty commanding army corps, divisions, and other military organizations; on staff duty and as engineers and assistant engineers with armies operating against the rebels; in command of the pontoon-bridge service, and in command of the troops of the engineer battalion; and thirty-one on duty superintending sea-coast defenses, lake surveys, lake and sea-coast harbor improvements, Military Academy, and assisting the Chief Engineer in connection with all these duties.

Every officer of the corps has been on continued and uninterrupted duty during the entire year, and four of its members have died in service.

The loss in officers killed and who have died in service from wounds and other causes during the rebellion is fourteen.

Twenty-one of the members of the corps still remain on detached service performing important duties growing out of the rebellion, which prevent their returning to engineer duty.

The value and estimation in which the military talents and practical knowledge of the officers of the corps are held have, by contributing to the command of the armies and for staff service, together with the loss of those who have given their lives to the defense of their country, greatly reduced its numbers and efficiency for the many duties devolving upon it. Many of those of highest rank and experience are still on detached service, and the vacancies from casualties have necessarily been filled by junior members, recent distinguished graduates of the Military Academy.

Although the legal strength of the corps is sufficient to perform the proper functions of its members, the present assignment of its officers renders it impracticable to meet the numerous demands upon the department.

For a comprehensive knowledge of the duties of the engineers, a recurrence to the general objects of the campaign is necessary. (See plans Nos. 1 and 11.*)

It will be recollected that by descending the Shenandoah and crossing the Potomac above Harper's Ferry the rebel army in 1864 threatened Washington, Baltimore, Pittsburg, and even Philadelphia, as also intermediate cities. Washington City had become the great depot for immense supplies for all arms of service for months in advance. An extensive ordnance depot, a navy-yard, the general hospitals, the archives of the Nation, its Executive and judiciary, with the public edifices for all national purposes, was the rich prize,

*Plate LXXXIX, Map 1, and Plate C, Map 1 (revised), of the Atlas.

to gain possession of which the rebel authorities directed their efforts, as well as to divert our armies from the attack on Richmond. At Antietam and South Mountain they had been defeated and driven back into the Valley of the Shenandoah. Again they made a powerful effort and were defeated at Gettysburg and driven across the Potomac and up the valley. In July, 1864, after the lieutenant-general had forced the rebel armies concentrated under Lee from Todd's Tavern, through Spotsylvania and Cold Harbor, into Richmond and Petersburg, they made another effort to divert the lieutenant-general by detaching Early on another expedition down the Valley of the Shenandoah and across the Potomac, threatening Baltimore by moving on the Monocacy, where a small body of our troops were repulsed, thus jeopardizing both Baltimore and Washington. The attention of the lieutenant-general was given to these efforts of his adversary to divert him from his main object—the defeat and capture of Lee's army—and, while withdrawing part of the garrison to re-enforce the armies operating against Richmond, he held the command of his rear and Washington by being enabled to transport from before Petersburg as large a force as Lee could detach to operate in the valley and on Washington. Many thousands of wounded and sick occupied the hospitals in Washington, and the troops fit for duty did not suffice to man the armaments of the forts around the city. The engineers had previously constructed a system of detached redoubts and forts around the city on a circuit of upward of thirty-five miles. Early, after his success at Monocacy, moved directly upon the defenses of Washington between the Potomac and the Eastern Branch. (See plan No. 1.*) Colonel Alexander, of the Corps of Engineers, was the only officer of the corps whose personal attention could be given to these defenses. Colonel Woodruff and Major Kurtz, of the Corps of Engineers, and assistants of the Chief Engineer, were first ordered to these defenses. Subsequently all the officers on the sea-coast, north and east of this city, were detached from their labors of constructing sea-coast batteries (then threatened by rebel iron-clads building in Europe, as another effort to divert our armies in the field), and were ordered to the defenses of Baltimore and Washington—Major Prime, Captain Robert, and Lieut. J. A. Smith to the aid of Colonel Brewerton at Baltimore, and Colonel Macomb, Major Blunt, Major Casey, and Captain Tardy to the aid of Colonel Alexander at Washington. The rebel blow was aimed at Washington. The wise foresight of the Secretary of War had caused all the employés of the several bureaus of his Department to be organized and drilled as infantry troops. The necessity for the withdrawal of the Sixth Army Corps from Petersburg and of the Nineteenth from New Orleans had also been foreseen, and orders sent to them to proceed to this city to meet the blow that was threatened. The Veteran Reserves and convalescents from the hospitals were also ordered to garrison the defenses. Requisitions were made upon the Governors of States to furnish troops, but with little success. The Sixth and Nineteenth Corps arrived at the most opportune moment. Early directed his efforts upon Fort Stevens, but finding the garrison re-enforced, and even moving out of the defenses to meet him, he suddenly retreated across the Potomac and up the Valley of the Shenandoah. The engineers were then ordered to their former stations on the sea-board.

---

*Plate LXXXIX, Map 1, of the Atlas.

Early was pursued by Sheridan with his cavalry and the troops that drove him from Washington up the Shenandoah, defeating him and his re-enforcements, and eventually annihilating his army. For this expedition Major Stewart, Captain Gillespie, and Lieutenant Meigs, of the Corps of Engineers, were assigned. In the death of Lieutenant Meigs, while reconnoitering in the neighborhood of Winchester, the corps lost one of its most meritorious and valued members. Captain Gillespie accompanied Sheridan's expedition to the James River, destroying the rebel communications on that river and all others west and north of Richmond, and finally joined the lieutenant-general before Petersburg.

With the investment of Petersburg commenced a series of laborious and difficult engineering operations by the Army of the James and the Army of the Potomac. The narratives collated from the reports of Colonel Michler and General Michie give the details of these operations.* A reference to plan No. 12 will explain the extent of the defenses about Petersburg and Richmond and the labors of our engineers about Petersburg and the rebel defenses on the north side of the James River.†

The rebels after being defeated by the army under Lieutenant-General Grant and driven from their intrenchments around Petersburg, extending to the Hatchie [Hatcher's Run?], evacuated that city on the 2d of April, 1865. The evacuation of Richmond followed on the 3d of April, when the rebel army under Lee retreated, and was closely pursued and pressed to Appomattox Court-House, where it yielded to the superior prowess and skill of the armies of the United States, on the 9th of April, 1865, thus breaking up all semblance of rebel authority, leaving Sherman to end it by the capture of Johnston on the 23d of April. A map of this campaign is in progress, awaiting information yet to be collected to perfect it as an historical record of these ever-memorable military operations which resulted in restoring the power and union of a nation.

After the evacuation of Richmond the rebel chief and his advisers, who devised this most unjust and unwarrantable scheme to destroy a nation, sought safety in flight toward Georgia. Their movements had been foreseen, and were provided for by a brilliant campaign of a cavalry force under General James H. Wilson (captain of the Corps of Engineers), who posted his troops with great discrimination and judgment, and succeeded in capturing the leader at Irwinton [Irwinville] on the 10th of May, 1865.

From Atlanta the grand army of the West, commanded by Sherman, commenced moving for the sea-coast, while Thomas occupied Tennessee and Kentucky. The rebels under Hood on evacuating Atlanta operated on Sherman's previous line of march.

The labors of the engineers at Chattanooga under Colonel Merrill, and the volunteer engineers, had rendered this important position as well as Knoxville impregnable; and Hood retrograded toward the Tennessee River with a force so far superior to Thomas' as to cause the latter to fall back gradually upon Nashville. The labors of the engineers in fortifying Franklin, on the Harpeth River, did not suffice, with a single army corps under Schofield, to hold those intrenchments. Our army fell back to Nashville, where much labor and the skill of the engineers had previously been bestowed in fortifying it by General

---

*For reports of Michler and Michie, see Series I, Vols. XXXVI, XL, XLII, XLVI, and LI.

†Plate C, Map 2, of the Atlas.

Morton, Colonel Merrill, Captains Barlow and Burroughs, and other junior officers of the Corps of Engineers, together with volunteer engineers. In September, 1864, Major Tower, Corps of Engineers (brevet major-general of volunteers), took charge of these defenses, and perceiving the great importance of Nashville as a depot of supplies, as well as other important strategic advantages, commenced to add to and perfect the fortifications (see plan No. 4*), on which he continued unremittingly until Hood's advance and investment of the place on the 15th and 16th of December, 1864 [*sic*].

During the few days preceding Hood's arrival before Nashville, Thomas had concentrated his several available army corps within the fortifications of Nashville, the plan of which is given on plate No. 4.*

The importance of these defenses was mainly in enabling Thomas to concentrate his army at a depot well stored with munitions of war, and to hold his enemy, flushed with his successful march from Atlanta, in check until he was ready to take the field.

The accompanying plan of the fortifications (No. 4*) by General Tower and annexed extracts from his report explain more fully the successes of this most important advance of Thomas, resulting in the demolition and annihilation of the rebel power in Tennessee.

During the same eventful period the fortifications that had been constructed by the engineers at Murfreesborough were successfully held and defended by a part of Thomas' army.

Colonel Merrill, captain of engineers, with the volunteer engineers, had during the year given special attention to fortifying all the important points on the railroads in Tennessee and part of Kentucky, while Lieutenant-Colonel Simpson, Corps of Engineers, had fortified Cincinnati, Ohio; Covington and Newport, Frankfort and Louisville, Ky., and the lines of the Louisville, Nashville and Kentucky Central Railroads, thus covering Thomas' rear and defending his lines of communication.

Such is a general outline of the labors of the engineers in Tennessee.

The march of the grand army of the West under Sherman (see plan No. 3†) did not call for offensive or defensive fortifications.

The labors of the engineers, Captain Poe (brevet brigadier-general, U. S. Army), Captain Reese (brevet brigadier-general, U. S. Army), Lieutenant Stickney (brevet major, U. S. Army), Lieutenant Ludlow (brevet major, U. S. Army), and Lieutenant Damrell, were most advantageously bestowed upon the roads and bridges, and reconnoitering the enemy's movements and positions. (See annexed narratives.)

The pontoon trains under charge of these officers were indispensable to the success of the army, They consisted of canvas boats, which proved serviceable for the march of this army from the Tennessee to its final disbandment in Washington City in 1865. The advantages of these light trains, their frequent use during the campaign proving their adaptation to our country, are fully developed in the narrative collated from Poe's and Reese's reports.

In September, 1863, Knoxville was captured by our force, and in November of the same year Chattanooga was occupied by our army. At the latter point Sherman concentrated his supplies and moved in force against the rebels, driving them through Ringgold, Tunnel Hill, Dalton, Resaca, Allatoona, and Kenesaw, to Atlanta.

---

* Plate LXXII, Map 2, of the Atlas.
† Plate LXXVI, Map 2, of the Atlas.

At this latter place the rebel army was strongly intrenched. The place was first invested by our army on the north and east, when, its strength being fully ascertained, Sherman marched his army to the south, defeating the rebels at Jonesborough and Lovejoy's, thus investing it on the south and compelling Hood to evacuate this stronghold.

The annexed narrative, collated from the report of Brevet Brigadier-General O. M. Poe, U. S. Army, captain of engineers, gives the important incidents connected with its capture, and furnishes plans of the rebel defenses. (See plan No. 2*; see narrative annexed.)

While these movements and successes of the armies under Thomas and Sherman were in progress, General Grant ordered a division of his army under General Terry to co-operate with the navy in the reduction of the defenses of the mouth of Cape Fear River in January, 1865.

Captain Comstock, of the Corps of Engineers (lieutenant-colonel, aide-de-camp, brevet brigadier-general of volunteers), had charge of the engineer operations of this expedition.

Fort Fisher, situated at and commanding the northern entrance of this river, was found to be the key of the position. Plans Nos. 5 and 6† give the details of the defenses constructed by our army to cover its landing and its rear while operating on Fort Fisher.

A bombardment by the fleet, resulting in dismounting many of the guns on the land front of the work, as well as cutting the electric wires for exploding a formidable system of mines on the same front, preceded a successful assault by the troops under General Terry.

The accompanying plans Nos. 5 and 6, with extracts from General Comstock's report, give the details of the rebel fortifications and those thrown up by our troops. (See General Comstock's report, annexed.)

Later in the season General Canby concentrated the troops under his command and moved to the attack of the city of Mobile, having the co-operation of the navy. The labors of the engineers under Captain McAlester (brevet major, U. S. Army), Captain Palfrey (brevet lieutenant-colonel, U. S. Army), Lieutenant Burnham (brevet major, U. S. Army), and others, were here called into requisition.

Blakely (see plan No. 7 ‡) was invested, batteries constructed and opened upon the formidable rebel batteries covered by strong intrenchments, with abatis surrounding their entire position, with its flanks resting on the Blakely River.

Plan No. 7, with extracts from the report of Major McAlester, gives the details of the operations, final assault and destruction of the rebel defenses on the 8th of April, 1865. (See McAlester's report, annexed.)

Spanish Fort was at the same time invested by our army, and the more formidable siege operations of a first and second parallel with approaches and enfilading batteries became necessary, and resulted finally in the capture of the rebel defenses by assault, on the 8th and 9th of April, 1865. (See plan No. 8.§)

These defenses and approaches are given in detail on plans Nos. 7 and 8, which, with extracts from Major McAlester's report, will explain and illustrate this well-designed and skillfully executed siege.

---

* Plate LXXXVIII, Map 1, of the Atlas.
† Plate LXXV, Maps 1 and 2, of the Atlas.
‡ Plate LXXI, Map 14, of the Atlas.
§ Plate LXXIX, Map 7, of the Atlas.

The fall of Blakely and Spanish Fort caused the rebel army under Taylor, Gardner, and Maury to evacuate Mobile, and retreat to the north.

Plan No. 9* gives the formidable rebel defenses of the city of Mobile, surrounding it with three lines of detached forts and connecting intrenchments, with the flanks resting on Mobile River. The skillful labors of the rebel engineers about this city were very extensive and the system exceedingly strong.

The determination of the commanding general to turn these works, by first reducing Blakely and Spanish Fort, proved successful, and the character of the works as shown on the plan forcibly illustrates the saving of lives and treasure in not first attempting to reduce these powerful defenses.

Plan No. 10† gives the position of the entire and connected system of rebel defenses that succumbed to the skill and talent of Canby.

While these important operations were in progress in Tennessee and Alabama, Sherman, with the grand army of the West, and Lieutenant-General Grant, with the combined Armies of the Potomac and the James, together with the garrison of Washington City, were simultaneously leading the national forces to strike a final blow to rebel power, and enforce the restoration of national authority from the Atlantic to the Pacific. (See plan No. 3.‡)

Sherman's army reached the sea-coast, by first capturing Fort McAllister, on the 13th of December, 1864, by Hazen. The strong rebel intrenchments at Savannah were then invested, and the rebel General Hardee driven from them across the Savannah River. The department has as yet received no plans of Fort McAllister or of the defenses of Savannah. The labors of the engineers of Sherman's army (see Poe's narrative) were again bestowed principally in reconnoitering the enemy's positions, and maneuvering the canvas pontoon trains to cross the army over the several rivers between Savannah and the last water-course crossed in pursuit of rebels. The success of these bridge trains is given in the extracts from Generals Poe's and Reese's reports. The city of Charleston fell into our power on the 18th of February, 1865, after its evacuation by the rebels in consequence of Sherman's movements in its rear, and cutting off its supplies from the interior, while it was already blockaded by our fleet and invested by land by our army.

Schofield, after the reduction of the entire defenses of Smithville, moved upon Raleigh, and united his forces with those of Sherman. The engineer operations on this line were in reconnoitering and maneuvering the pontoon-bridge trains for the passage of the rivers, under Lieutenant Stickney (brevet major, U. S. Army), of the Corps of Engineers. (See Stickney's narrative.) After obstinately contested combats at Averasborough and Bentonville, the rebel power under Johnston was finally overcome and subdued by the capture of his entire command on the 23d [26th] of April, 1865; after which, by easy marches, the grand army of the West repaired to Washington City. (See plans Nos. 1, 11, and 12.§)

The momentous campaign of the armies under the command of the lieutenant-general, with the purpose of capturing Richmond, and

* Plate CV, Map 1, of the Atlas.
† Plate LXXI, Map 13, of the Atlas.
‡ Plate LXXVI, Map 2, of the Atlas.
§ Plates LXXXIX, Map 1; C, 1 and C, 2, of the Atlas.

overthrowing the rebel authorities holding the semblance of Confederate power in that city, was commenced on the Rapidan in May, 1864. The battles of Todd's Tavern, on the 7th of May; of Spotsylvania, on the 14th and 19th, and passage of the North Anna, on the 24th; of Cold Harbor, on the 31st of May and 1st of June; the march thence and passage of the James River on the 16th, 17th, and 18th, with the investment of Petersburg on the 3d of July, 1864, constitute a brilliant series of grand battles and maneuvers that do not come within the scope of engineer reports.

The annexed narrative and information from the report of Colonel Michler, dated October, 1865, give more specifically the labors of the officers of the Engineer Corps during the progress of this campaign.

SEA-COAST AND LAKE DEFENSES.

While most of the officers of the Corps of Engineers have been actively engaged in the field, as heretofore stated, others have given their attention to the important labor of sea-coast defenses.

Against predatory expeditions of rebel cruisers and iron-armored vessels, built in foreign ports claiming to be neutral, it was necessary to construct batteries to mount rifle artillery and smooth-bored ordnance of heavier calibers than heretofore used. Colonel Macomb, Major Blunt, Major Casey, of the Corps of Engineers, were employed in thus fortifying thirteen harbors on the Eastern coast. At the same time progress on the permanent sea-coast defenses was continued at all the harbors from Maine to Hampton Roads, inclusive, at Key West and Tortugas, and at San Francisco; and repairing the permanent works on the Gulf of Mexico that were taken from the rebels, which had been more or less injured by them and by our attacks, to restore them to the Union. On the Northern and Eastern works, as also on the California coast, the main object has been so to direct the operations as soonest to mount the contemplated armaments, which, at this time, are required to be of such penetrating and crushing power as will in all probability insure the destruction of any iron-armored vessels that can combat them. The introduction of these increased calibers and this power of artillery has made it necessary to renew most of the gun platforms heretofore constructed, which were designed for no larger caliber than 42-pounders. At the present time no smaller gun is prepared for the sea-coast batteries than 100-pounder rifle guns, and ten to fifteen inch rifled and smooth-bored guns.

The further construction of the sea-coast batteries has been retarded by the necessity which now exists of so covering part of our guns and gunners as to render them secure against any advantage that an attacking power in iron-armored ships opposed to them shall possess. So far as we have yet progressed, preparations for guns of large caliber have been perfected, and the guns mounted to throw, collectively, 147,150 pounds of metal at a single discharge, which is an addition during the year of 40,651 pounds of metal that can be so thrown against an enemy.

Continuing to increase the armament on our sea-coast in the same ratio for a reasonable time will render the harbor defenses exceedingly difficult for any maritime power to overcome, and, in combination with other auxiliary means of defense, will carry the cost and time requisite to subdue them beyond the means of foreign powers, provided we hold our works in a perfect condition for both land and sea attacks.

Boards of engineers have been detailed to consider what modifications are necessary at each and every work along our sea-coast to adapt them to resist the powerful armaments that European fleets, singly or combined, may be enabled to bring across the Atlantic, over the bars of our ports and harbors, to attack them.

The details of the operations during the year at the several works on the Atlantic, Gulf of Mexico, Lake and Pacific Coasts, derived mostly from the reports of the superintending engineers, are annexed.

PRISON DEPOTS.

The prison depots also called for the labors of engineer officers. Point Lookout, at the mouth of the Potomac, was subject to sudden attack from marauding parties and detached cavalry from armies operating against Baltimore and Washington, which, with the immense body of prisoners, made it necessary to fortify the position against attempts to liberate them by forts commanding both the interior and exterior. Major Stewart, assisted by Lieutenant Cantwell, and afterward Colonel Brewerton, constructed these defensive works.

THE PRISON DEPOT AT JOHNSON'S ISLAND.

Cleveland Harbor, Lake Erie, had to be defended against attempts of the prisoners, and succor by water from expeditions organized in the friendly and neutral territories of Great Britain in Canada. Major Casey and Captain Tardy were assigned to and performed this service, constructing a water battery at the mouth of the harbor, against a force approaching by water, and temporary field forts on Johnson's Island.

SURVEYS, MAPS, AND TOPOGRAPHY.

The surveys for the armies in the field, embracing the topography of the country passed over and particular sites occupied, have been referred to in other parts of this report.

The extent of the labors performed by the officers on duty in the Bureau has been the engraving, lithographing, photographing, and issuing 24,591 sheets for officers in the field and various branches of the service requiring this information, leaving still on hand a few copies of each publication for reference and the calls of the War Department.

The survey of the northwestern lakes has been in progress for several years, to obtain for the commerce of the States whose industry is promoted by that extended interior navigation the safety that a perfect and correct knowledge of the shores and bottom alone can attain. It is being conducted under the direction of Major Raynolds, of the Corps of Engineers, upon the same scientific principles and with the same care and accuracy that has been bestowed upon the coast survey and other national geodetic surveys. During the year two maps have been prepared from the field-notes published and issued to the navigators of the lakes. One gives the west end of Lake Superior and the other the northeastern part of Lake Michigan. Three others have been prepared and are now ready for engraving, giving the Portage River and the Bay of L'Anse, on Lake Superior, and a third giving the north end of Green Bay.

Two thousand eight hundred and twenty sheets of the maps of the lake surveys have been issued for commercial, harbor improvement, and military purposes during the year, making the whole number of maps called for and issued since these surveys were commenced 27,411 sheets.

Special surveys have also been made during the year, maps issued and forwarded for the use of the department, of Niagara River, Erie, Conneaut, Ashtabula, Grand River, Cleveland, Black River, Sandusky, Saint Joseph's, Grand Haven, Chicago, Racine, and Sheboygan.

SURVEYS.

The principal labors of the parties engaged in these surveys during the year are comprised in the measurement of 269½ miles of shoreline, 164½ square miles of topography, 187 miles of soundings, and 1,200 square miles of offshore hydrography on 1,586 miles of lines of soundings; the measurement of a base line of 4,173 feet in length; difference of longitude between several distant points by electric observations, and observations by flashing lights; also astronomical observations for the latitude of eight points.

Recommendation.—These surveys are called for by numerous parties and individuals, as well as by commercial men, for private as well as for public use. It is indispensable that some rules and system be established to keep the issue of these valuable maps within such limits as will insure the great objects of the survey, the diffusion of this information to promote national industry, at the same time to prevent them falling into the hands of persons collecting for other purposes than the public good. I recommend that the department be therefore authorized to issue these maps, after supplying the wants of the Government, at the cost of paper and printing, as is now and for years past has been authorized for distributing the Coast Survey maps. This will prevent an improper use, and enable all persons capable of using them to obtain copies.

The estimate for carrying on the work for the next year is $184,604.42, which exceeds the amount appropriated for last year's operations about $60,000. It is proper to say that this increase of estimate does not contemplate any advance in the wages of assistants, but is simply due to the increased cost of materials and supplies.

On our Pacific Coast Major Williamson, of the Corps of Engineers, has explored and reconnoitered parts of Northern California and Southern Oregon, giving the topography of its roads, and continues observations for barometric correction of altitudes, having also in view an investigation of the formula for determining heights by this instrument. He has traversed and explored the heights of the Nevada Range in Northern California, said to be 10,000 to 11,000 feet above the level of the sea, and the military roads between the coast and this range of mountains to facilitate the military operations of the commanding general. During the year he also examined the various sites on Admiralty Inlet and Puget Sound, that might hereafter become useful for military purposes, and selected such as should be reserved from sale by the Land Office.

PRESERVATION AND REPAIR OF ATLANTIC HARBORS AND SEA-WALLS.

An appropriation was made in 1864 for renewing the construction of the sea-walls in Boston harbor to preserve the headlands from further destruction by the ocean waves, and, as a consequence, injury to the harbor for commercial use, while at the same time it preserves important sites that hereafter will be occupied by batteries bearing on the channel leading to the city of Boston. The following narratives of the operations on these islands are drawn from the report of Colonel Graham, the superintending engineer. The same officer was charged with the application of the appropriation of $100,000 for the preservation and repair of the harbors on the Atlantic. The accompanying summary gives his views on this subject in relation to the Susquehanna River below Havre de Grace, dredging the Patapsco River, Portland Harbor breakwater, navigation of the Hudson River below Troy, and Delaware Breakwater. Colonel Graham recommends additional appropriations for the Atlantic harbor improvements.*

MILITARY ACADEMY.

During the past year sixty-eight cadets completed their studies and military exercises at the Academy, and were commissioned as lieutenants in the Army. This is the most numerous class that has ever graduated at the institution since its organization in 1802. For many years the number of graduates has not sufficed to fill the annual vacancies in the Army.

The number of officers in the several branches of the staff, and of regiments now comprising the Regular Army, has greatly increased from time to time, while the number of cadets authorized by law has remained unaltered since 1843. The result is that neither the staff corps, nor regiments of artillery, cavalry, and infantry, can be furnished with the numbers to perfect their company organizations, and military science and art cannot be disseminated throughout the country in proportion to the increase of population and national interests to be protected. The total number of cadets now at the Academy is 235, and the total number authorized by existing laws is 293. From various incidents to which the appointments are subject, this ratio does not materially alter from year to year.

The average cost of the institution for the last twenty years has been $160,711.83. The cost during the past academic year was $201,217. These sums include the pay of cadets, officers, and professors, and all contingencies.

The annual average appropriation for twenty years is $166,684.63, and for the present year is $257,505. This excess arises from the increase of the pay of cadets, and for increase cost of forage for artillery and cavalry horses, &c.

Recommendations.—To meet the wants of the military service, and to diffuse a knowledge of the science and art of war more extensively throughout our widely extended domain, I recommend at this time an increase in the total number of cadets of two additional appointments from each State and Territory and the District of Columbia, thus making the number of appointments to be authorized under the law to be one from each Congressional district and Territory and the District of Columbia, ten from "at large" annually by the President's selection, and two in addition from each State and Territory and the District of Columbia.

The difficulties that have been experienced for years past in training the minds and bodies of the young gentlemen sent to the Academy

*For portion of this report relating to river and harbor improvements, here omitted, see Executive Document No. 1, House of Representatives, Thirty-ninth Congress, first session, Vol. II, pp. 921-925, of said document.

to prepare them for usefulness as members of the military profession arise mainly from the qualifications of the candidates being so exceedingly limited. While at the present time it may not be expedient to increase the standard for admission, I do urgently recommend that a selection from at least five candidates to be nominated for each appointment may be authorized by law, when every section of the country would more certainly have its due proportion of graduates entering the Army annually. Should this principle be authorized by law, the examination of the candidates could be ordered in several sections of the country at convenient military posts, and thus save a great annual expense now incurred by partially educating and returning deficient cadets to their distant homes, insure a much greater proportion of members who could master the course of studies, and avoid the numerous and frequent discharges from the Academy for inability to acquire the requisite information and proficiency for a graduate of this institution.

FINANCES.

During the year ending June 30, 1865, the expenditures of the department for fortifications on the Atlantic, Gulf of Mexico, Pacific Coast, and on the Northern Lakes, including bridge trains, intrenching tools, and for all other military purposes, amounted to	$5,174,335.23
For civil works, as lake harbors, harbors on the Atlantic, survey of the lakes, they amounted to	218,400.00
And for the Military Academy, not including the pay of professors and cadets	86,685.00
Making a total annual expenditure of	5,479,420.23

The accounts of the disbursing officers of the department have been regularly forwarded from month to month. These accounts had accumulated in the department during the past four years beyond the means allotted to the financial branch to examine, correct, and forward to the Treasury Department for final settlement.

During the year 1,203 monthly accounts, amounting to $11,834,308.35, have been thus examined and forwarded to the Auditor for final settlement, and there remain on hand at this time 398 monthly accounts to be examined, amounting to $4,492,964.85. At the rate of progress made during the past year in the examination of these accounts the work in a short time will be brought up to the months in which they are received from the officers. No defalcation or losses in any way exist in the disbursements and accountability of the officers of the department.

At the present time all property purchased for the armies in the field, either worn or of a perishable character, is being sold, and the avails will be returned to the Treasury. The amount of sales to this date is $34,123.12. The residue of this property is being stored in engineer depots for further use, at the Jefferson Barracks depot, Mo., and at the Willets Point depot, N. Y., under charge of engineer officers and troops of the Engineer Battalion.

The property of the department in the hands of its agents is accounted for quarterly, and the returns examined in this Bureau.

The number of returns examined during the year is	220
And remaining to be examined	43
Making the number of property returns rendered by officers	263

RICHD. DELAFIELD,
General and Chief of Engineers U. S. Army.

*Narrative collated from the reports of Col. N. Michler.**

* * * * * * *

Upon the explosion of the mine [July 30, 1864] and failure of the assault the troops engaged were directed on the following day to resume their previous positions to a great extent, some few changes being ordered for the purpose of reducing their fronts and establishing reserves for ulterior movements. The plan of the siege by regular approaches having been abandoned, Colonel Michler was directed at the same time to "make such a disposition of the lines then occupied by the corps as would enable them to be held by a diminished force," and therefore determined to select an interior line, to consist of some few detached, inclosed works, subsequently to be connected by lines of infantry parapets. The first line selected was one lying on very commanding ground, and extending from the present Fort Sedgwick to the Rushmore house, immediately opposite Fort Clifton, one of the enemy's works on the Appomattox, at the head of navigation for large sea-going vessels, passing near the Avery, Friend, Dunn, and Jordan houses. This being considered too far to the rear of the then advanced position, and apparently yielding too much ground, for the possession of which such desperate fighting had taken place, he finally chose an intermediate one, and sites for Forts Rice, Meikel, Morton, Haskell, Stedman, and McGilvery were selected, and the intervening batteries and lines located. It had also been decided to enlarge and strengthen the lunette, the site of which is now occupied by Fort Sedgwick. By direction of Lieutenant-General Grant the supervision of the line in front of the Eighteenth Corps had also been placed under his direction. The construction of these different works was pushed rapidly forward by night, under the immediate charge of Captains Gillespie and Harwood and Lieutenants Howell, Benyaurd, and Lydecker, as much so as the sparsity of officers, the extreme heat of the weather, and the heavy and constant artillery fire of the enemy would permit.

Several officers of the Corps of Engineers, including Captains Mendell, Turnbull, and Farquhar, had been ordered away from the army on other duty, and some of the lieutenants were absent on sick leave. By the 20th of August the works were so near completion as to be in readiness for the contemplated movement on the Petersburg and Weldon Railroad. After the successful advance and holding of that most important thoroughfare he was directed to select positions for large works on or near that road for the protection of the left flank of the army, and also to connect them, by a system of redoubts, with Fort Sedgwick. On the 26th of August, in connection with the disposition of troops then made, orders were given him to "proceed at once to the construction of the redoubts proposed for the left of the line on the Weldon railroad, and of the works at the Burnt chimney and the Strong house," now designated Forts Dushane, Wadsworth, Howard, and Alexander Hays.

The construction of these works and intermediate batteries, connected by infantry parapets, was immediately commenced, under the more immediate charge of Lieutenants Howell, Benyaurd, and Lydecker, and was afterward turned over to Captains Folwell and McDonald, Fiftieth New York Volunteer Engineers. Owing to the

*The portion of this narrative here omitted is covered by full reports published in Series I, Vols. XXXVI and XL. See also Series I, Vols. XLII, XLVI, and LI, for reports of later operations.

bad condition of the roads during the late move, the commanding general directed that a line should be selected for a military railroad from the depot at City Point to the intersection of the Weldon railroad, at or near the Yellow Tavern, for the more certain and rapid transportation of supplies. The laying of this road was placed in charge of the construction corps of the chief quartermaster of the Armies operating against Richmond. The soil contains a great quantity of sand, and at times becomes almost impassable.

By the 7th of September the interior portions of the works last referred to were well advanced, sufficiently so to be occupied in case of an attack by the enemy, and obstructions, consisting of wire entanglements, abatis, fraises, and slashing generally of the timber along the entire front, had been prepared. Many miles of corduroy roads and bridges had been built by the Fiftieth New York Volunteer Engineers for the convenience of and more direct communication between the different corps of the army.

During the first few days of September he also selected sites for different works, and traced a line from the bastion works (Fort Dushane) on the Weldon railroad to the rear of the camps of the armies operating against Petersburg, its left resting on the Blackwater Swamp, near Fort Bross. These were designed to guard against any movement of the enemy on the three large and important thoroughfares—the Jerusalem plank, the Norfolk stage, and Halifax roads. The several redoubts then laid out and commenced were subsequently named Davison, McMahon, Stevenson, Blaisdell, and Kelly.

In his report for the week ending on the 17th of September he reported that along every portion of the line, from the Appomattox River, below Petersburg, to the Weldon railroad, and thence back to the Blackwater Swamp, work was progressing rapidly. The length of the line at that time was over sixteen miles, and along it had been constructed, or were in course of construction, nineteen forts and redoubts and forty-one batteries. In addition to the labor on these works, including the obstructions in their front, bombproofs, magazines, and drainage in the interior, nearly 2,000 yards of roads and one-third of the covered ways had been "corduroyed," and 6,700 square feet of substantial bridging built. The old intrenched lines were also being leveled. These labors were continued during the following week, the officers and men of the regular battalion of engineers and of the Fiftieth New York Volunteer Engineers having the construction of them. At the same time his attention, under instructions from the commanding general, was directed to the examination of the country in reference to a defensive line from Blackwater Swamp, near Prince George Court-House, north toward Old Court-House, on Bailey's Creek, the latter a deep, impassable stream, emptying within a few miles of that point into the James River.

This line, in connection with that already in course of construction, completed the chain of works from the Appomattox, below Petersburg, to the Weldon railroad, and thence back to the James River, adding nine miles to its length, making twenty-five miles in all, the flanks resting on the two rivers, and with them entirely encircling the Army of the Potomac. (See plan No. 12.*)

The sites of five works were traced, and work commenced upon three of them. At the same time he was directed to confer with Lieutenant-Colonel Benham, Corps of Engineers (brigadier-general of volunteers), in command of the immediate defenses of City Point, in regard to a

* Plate C, map 2, of the Atlas.

short line extending from the Court-House, on Bailey's Creek, north toward the Appomattox, to cover and protect against any sudden attack of cavalry the depot at that point.

On the 21st a circular from headquarters Army of the Potomac directed that "the armaments and garrisons designated for the forts be regarded as permanent, to be moved only when specially directed."

By the 26th the military railroad was completed, opened for travel, and placed in charge of the provost-marshal-general of the army.

On the 28th, in company with the chief of artillery, he made a general inspection of the whole line and found the work progressing most satisfactorily. During the evening of the same day orders were issued for certain dispositions and arrangements of the troops to be made, and that the whole army should be in readiness to move before daylight on the following morning. The corps commanders were directed to "hold in view the contingency of the withdrawal of their troops from the rifle-pits connecting the inclosed works, leaving the line from the Appomattox to Fort Davison to be held by the redoubts and inclosed batteries, and the further contingency of withdrawing entirely from the intrenchments."

In consequence of this projected movement, instructions were immediately given to the officers of engineers to suspend all operations on the different field-works in course of construction, and to hold their commands and the pontoon trains in readiness to obey further instructions.

The active operations of the army were successfully advanced some few miles to the left or west of the Weldon railroad during the 29th and 30th of September and 1st and 2d of October, causing a corresponding extension of the lines. On the morning of the latter, after the repulse of the enemy in his final attack, it having been determined to hold on to the position, he was ordered to select a new line to connect the advanced point near the Pegram house with Fort Wadsworth, and locate the necessary intermediate works. The tracing, profiling, and construction of them was immediately commenced.

Before daylight on the morning of the 4th, by direction of the commanding general, he made a reconnaissance for the purpose of selecting a line to be refused from the left flank toward the rear, and to be connected with Fort Dushane. The sites of several new redoubts were established, the connecting lines traced, and with large details their construction immediately commenced.

By this extension to the west of the Weldon railroad eleven additional inclosed works—Keene, Urmston, Conahey, Fisher, Welch, Gregg, Cummings, Sampson, Emery, Siebert, and Clarke—and several batteries were linked with the already formidable cordon that surrounded the army. The length of this portion of the line is nearly seven miles, making a continuous stretch of twenty-three miles of earth-work from the right, on the Appomattox, to the left, on the Blackwater Swamp. Adding to this the section from the latter to the James River, the line measures more than thirty-two miles, comprising thirty-six forts and fifty batteries. In addition to these, there were eight other inclosed works along the inner line of the defense of City Point.

The incredibly short time in which those to the west of the Jerusalem plank road were built surprised the officers of our own army. The sites of the works were only selected on the 2d and 4th of the month; still, the weekly report of the 8th states that they were already nearly completed.

To the officers of the Corps of Engineers then present, under his orders—Harwood, Gillespie, Howell, Benyaurd, Lydecker, and Phillips—and to those of the Fiftieth New York Volunteer Engineers, under the immediate command of Lieut. Col. I. Spaulding, and to the men of their respective detachments, must be given the credit for the immense amount of work accomplished.

The works were well constructed and finished, and the infantry parapets are as strong as they could be made to answer a useful purpose. The artificial strength of the line was to a great extent increased by the naturally strong position chosen to resist any attack or assault by the enemy.

On the 4th of the same month, notwithstanding the few officers of the corps that remained on duty, he was compelled to send Lieutenant Phillips to report to General Benham to assist in constructing the line in front of City Point; the latter was about three miles in length, comprising eight small redoubts.

On the 12th the commanding general directed Colonel Michler to make an examination of that part of the line extending between Forts Hays and Fisher, to ascertain whether said line could be shortened, and to furnish a written report for Lieutenant-General Grant's information. As no particular advantage could be gained and a considerable amount of work would be required, he reported unfavorably.

The weekly report dated October 22 informs the General-in-Chief "that the whole line occupied by the Army of the Potomac was entirely constructed and in a defensible condition. Some minor details still required attention. Additional obstacles, palisades, and fraises in connection with the abatis and wire entanglements had been rapidly pushed forward every night to strengthen it." In consequence of reports that the enemy were driving galleries at different points to undermine several works, he directed shafts to be sunk within them and listening galleries to be run out as precautionary measures, although no indications were found to exist after a most careful personal examination.

On the 16th, accompanied by Captain Gillespie and Lieutenant Benyaurd, he examined critically the ground between Fort McGilvery and a point opposite Fort Clifton, to ascertain the strength of the enemy's position, and whether any new works were in course of construction, as well as to decide upon the possibility of forcing a passage of the river and severing his communication by rail with Richmond.

On the 20th, by direction of the commanding general, he visited City Point in company with the medical director of the army for the purpose of selecting the ground for a general field hospital. An advantageous place was found on the bluff overlooking the James, between the railroad and Bailey's Creek. Besides the convenience of locality, it possessed the advantage of retirement and security, as well as that of health. Fine springs burst forth here and there from the banks sufficient to supply every want.

The names of the different works of the line to the west of the Weldon railroad and of that in front of City Point were selected from among those of the many distinguished officers who were killed in action during the recent campaigns, nobly fighting their country's battles, and so given in plan No. 12.*

---

*Plate C, map 2, of the Atlas.

On the morning of the 24th of October two new redoubts were ordered to be thrown up at points he had previously selected, the one between the Norfolk road and the Avery house, the other near the Friend house, from both of which positions command was had over the main line of works. These were sufficiently far advanced for the movement ordered to commence on the afternoon of the 26th. The latter, in which the greater part of the army participated, continued through the 27th and 28th, extending west across Hatcher's Run, and reaching along and south of it as far as the Boydton plank road where the latter crosses the stream at Burgess' Mill.

During the afternoon of the last day the different commands returned to their old camps. The engineer troops were then engaged along the entire line, in repairing damages, adding obstructions, driving galleries, and in every conceivable way rendering the line as strong as possible.

On the 7th of November he was directed by the major-general commanding the Army of the Potomac "to furnish General Benham, commanding defenses of City Point, with the project of the line of intrenchments from Prince George Court-House to Old Court-House, and also to indicate what was necessary to be done to connect the right of that line with the rear intrenchments resting on the Blackwater."

In consequence of a contemplated movement he had been compelled to suspend work upon that section of the defensive line, and its construction was subsequently turned over to the above-named officer.

By the 12th of the same month, the lines being completed, both as regards their external and internal arrangements, the following extract from Special Orders, No. 306, headquarters Army of the Potomac, of the same date, was issued for the information of all concerned:

The attention of corps commanders is called to the necessity of preserving, in good order, the intrenchments front and rear, with the abatis, slashings, and other defenses.

*　　*　　*　　*　　*　　*　　*

The chief engineer officer will inspect the lines, both front and rear, from time to time, and report to these headquarters any failure to keep the same in good order, or any destruction of the defenses.

From this time forward the engineer troops were principally occupied during the winter in attending to the needed repairs of the forts and batteries, in keeping in order the several corduroy roads, in overhauling and placing in good condition the pontoon trains, in constructing huts for winter quarters, and in building stabling for the large number of animals required for the transportation of the tool and bridge trains.

The temporary quiet of the army was again interrupted for several days. On the 6th of December, by direction of the commanding general, an engineer officer, with a battalion of engineer troops and 150 feet of canvas bridging, was directed to accompany the Fifth Corps during the movement of the latter south along the Weldon railroad, and subsequently all, both regular and volunteer, were called upon to be under arms to take part in the same operation. Orders were issued at the same time that all camps located, as well as huts, corrals, or other structures erected in the vicinity of the lines of defense, either in front or rear, which, in the judgment of the engineer, interfered with the proper defense of the works, should be immediately removed. Preparations were also made to move, if necessary, all surplus property and the sick in hospitals to within the lines of City Point. Arrangements in regard to the further disposition of troops were directed in the event of a general move; those not previously designated for holding the intrenched lines to be formed into a movable column, under the immediate orders of the commanding officer of the Second Corps. All work not necessary for the defense of the position held by the army was suspended. The movement had scarcely commenced when, in consequence of severe storms of rain, accompanied with sleet, the army was finally compelled to return to its old position, some considerable damage having been effected along the line of the railroad.

Comparative quiet again reigned throughout the army, with the exception of the attempt of the enemy's iron-clads to come down the James River on the 24th of January, 1865, until the 4th of February, when a movement of the cavalry was ordered for the following day, to be supported by the Fifth and Second Corps. The cavalry successfully captured a small train of the enemy on the Boydton plank road and entered Dinwiddie Court-House. In consequence of the destruction of a bridge over Hatcher's Run, the Fifth Corps was detained for several hours in crossing, and the former, not being supported, fell back. A severe attack was made upon the Second Corps, but was repulsed, and little more was effected on that day. On the following morning (6th) the Fifth Corps was ordered to pass the stream at the crossing on the Vaughan road and take up position to the left of the Second, the cavalry protecting its flank.

Some severe fighting took place during the day. Early on the same morning he had been sent to select a line between Fort Sampson and Armstrong's Mill, and choose sites for works to hold and command the crossing at the latter place and the one on the Vaughan road. On the 7th orders were issued to intrench the line, but on the following day were so modified as to cause the line to be run direct from Fort Sampson to the Vaughan road crossing. The length of this addition to the intrenched line is nearly four miles, making the front line from the Appomattox to Hatcher's Run fifteen miles of continuous earthworks. Heavy storms of rain and sleet again disturbed this movement.

With the exception of the attack on Fort Stedman on the 25th of March, and its temporary occupancy by the enemy, no event of importance occurred until the inauguration of the campaign on the 28th of the same month. The distance from Battery No. 10, adjoining Fort Stedman, to the point of the enemy's line (Colquitt's salient), immediately opposite, is only 613 feet between the main works, the shortest distance between the two at any point, excepting at Elliott's salient (the locality of the mine). The picket-lines of the two armies were only 435 feet apart, those of the enemy only a few feet in front of his main works. One of the advanced Union pickets was only separated 205 feet from his opposite neighbor, a narrow boyau leading to his pit from the main line. Without the exercise of the most untiring vigilance on the part of the picket and the garrison, any sudden dash at the first early dawn of the morning might prove momentarily successful; but a position so well flanked by adjacent batteries, and commanded by others in its rear, proved so untenable as to cause the enemy to be most severely punished for his temerity, and to compel him to relinquish the object of an attack for which no reasonable explanation can be made.

Before proceeding further he calls attention to the topographical department of the Army of the Potomac.

Owing to the limited degree of information which could be obtained, either from published maps or inquiries made of the inhabitants—the latter generally being averse and in most cases unable from ignorance to impart it, even in relation to the particular localities in which they lived—his assistants had a laborious although an interesting duty. They have not only been constantly engaged in following up every movement, and in most cases acting as guides to the different columns of troops, thereby obtaining a most reliable knowledge of the country by actual experience, but have been compelled to anticipate the geographical wants of a large army ever in motion by constant and careful researches.

In order to be able to furnish the necessary data upon which to base the different military combinations, and thereby being made responsible to a great extent for the information upon which the commanding general was able to hypothecate a reasonable degree of success in the execution of his plans, the department had necessarily to be ever active and always exact.

The Engineer Bureau has been furnished from time to time with the many maps supplied the officers of armies operating against Richmond and Petersburg, including those of the campaigns from the Rapidan to the Appomattox; that of the carefully surveyed plan of the lines occupied during the siege of Petersburg; the several sheets representing the country adjacent to the latter city, and also about Richmond, comprising the several lines of the enemy for the defense of the capital; and also copies of those prepared in anticipation, and upon which were based the movements which terminated so successfully and gloriously the last grand campaign of April, 1865.

On the 27th of March certain movements of the several corps of the Army of the Potomac were ordered to commence at an early hour of the 29th. On the 28th the instructions of the previous day were somewhat modified, but at the appointed time the several columns were in motion.

A pontoon train accompanied the Fifth Corps to enable it to cross Hatcher's Run, and subsequently remained there for the passage of the general trains. The Second Corps, which had been replaced by a portion of the Twenty-fourth along the intrenched line heretofore occupied by it, crossed by the bridge on the Vaughan road. The cavalry passed over by a bridge still farther down, at Malone's Crossing, and moved toward Dinwiddie Court-House.

In gaining their position but little opposition was encountered; one division of the Fifth had a spirited engagement on the Quaker road, and handsomely repulsed the enemy.

On the 30th the Second and Fifth Corps advanced their lines to beyond the junction of the Quaker and Boydton plank roads, driving the enemy into his main works; the two lines were within easy artillery range; the right of the Second now rested on Hatcher's Run, near the Crow house. A division of the Twenty-fourth Corps crossed the run and connected the right of the Second with the tête-de-pont on the Vaughan road; both lines were intrenched.

During the night previous and throughout the whole of this day the rain poured down in torrents. The roads had become impassable for wagons and artillery, and the engineer troops were engaged in corduroying them and in rebuilding bridges over Hatcher's and Gravelly Runs.

The wagon train stuck fast in the mud. The cavalry had to be sent back by divisions to the terminus of the military railroad to replenish their supplies of rations, the wagons not being able to come up to them.

During the night of the 30th the Second Corps extended its front to the left along the Boydton plank road, resting its flank on Gravelly Run. On the morning of the following day an unsuccessful effort was made by the Fifth Corps to drive the enemy from the White Oak road; subsequently, upon being re-enforced, the attack was renewed and possession gained of that road.

Toward evening the cavalry had repulsed and held in check, in front of Dinwiddie Court-House, a superior force of the enemy. During the night of that day, the 31st, the Fifth Corps was sent to the assistance of the cavalry. From the commencement of the movement he had accompanied the commanding general over different parts of the field, in readiness to execute such instructions as might be given, and on the 1st of April, by his direction, rode along and inspected the lines from Hatcher's Run toward the west. The evening of that day witnessed a most brilliant engagement on the left, in which both the cavalry and the Fifth Corps participated, the enemy along that immediate front having been completely routed.

This glorious news was communicated throughout the army, and orders were issued that a simultaneous attack should be made at different points along the entire length of the intrenched line at 4 o'clock on the following morning. The grand assault of the 2d of April was made, and the exterior line of the enemy's works penetrated and possession gained of the larger portion of them.

The enemy having been pierced at his center and divided, one portion was driven within an interior line of works immediately encircling the city, and the other moved off from the White Oak along the Claiborne road, rapidly pursued by a division of the Second Corps. The line of the army extended at noon of that day from the Appomattox, above Petersburg, to the Appomattox below, the two flanks resting on the river.

Colonel Michler was at that time ordered to rectify this line if necessary, and later in the day to select a site for a pontoon bridge across the river, and positions for batteries to command the crossing and protect passage of the army in the event of the retreat of the enemy.

Early on the morning of the 3d it was ascertained that the enemy had evacuated the city of Petersburg, and orders of march were immediately issued to the different corps to follow in pursuit. The roads were found in wretched condition, and a great deal of corduroying and bridging had to be done. About noon on the 5th he was ordered to proceed in advance of the Second and Sixth Corps to report to General Sheridan, who had arrived with the cavalry and Fifth Corps at Jetersville on the previous evening, to consult with him in regard to the position to be taken by the army in anticipation of an expected attack by the enemy, it being reported that his whole force was concentrating at Amelia Court-House. His line of retreat toward Danville had been cut off, and it was presumed he would venture a heavy battle to regain it. In company with the general he rode over the line, and by the direction of the general the troops were posted as they arrived. A part of the line of battle had been previously intrenched, and work was commenced on other portions; the anticipated fight, however, did not take place.

On the following day (6th) the Army of the Potomac was put in motion in three parallel columns toward Amelia Court-House to attack the enemy, but the cavalry having early ascertained that he was endeavoring to escape by Deatonsville toward Farmville, the direction of the line of march was immediately changed; the Second moved directly on the former place and in a short time came upon and commenced a brisk skirmish with the retreating force and continued to drive him until night closed the operation; the Fifth Corps was shifted to the right flank and took the road to Paineville.

Colonel Michler was directed to report the change of movement and explain its object to the commanding officer of the Sixth Corps. His column was countermarched and thrown from the right to the left flank. After retracing its steps through Jetersville and passing some two miles beyond the village, it left the main turnpike and followed a road which he had found leading toward the northwest, and by which the troops moving along it were absolutely certain of striking the flank of the retreating army. The entire cavalry force was operating on the same flank.

By night the battle of Sailor's Creek was fought, which will long be remembered as one of the most brilliant and successful affairs of the war. It was, in fact, the last desperate engagement between these two armies.

On the 7th of April the pursuit was continued. The enemy having succeeded in crossing the Appomattox at Farmville and High Bridge, he succeeded in destroying all the bridges at the former place, but failed in his efforts to damage the common road bridge at the latter crossing; three spans of the railroad bridge (Richmond and Danville road) were burnt; this structure is 2,400 feet long and 125 feet high. The enemy made some slight resistance at both these places and also on the Lynchburg plank road at a point about four miles beyond Farmville.

The naturally very strong position at High Bridge was rendered additionally so by several redoubts which had been built there sometime previous for the protection of the bridge against cavalry raids.

On the 8th the Second and Sixth Corps followed along the Stage road to Lynchburg, whilst the Fifth, Twenty-fourth, and Cavalry Corps pursued the one by Hampden Sidney College and Prospect Stations toward Appomattox Court-House.

During the day he returned to Farmville to hasten the construction of some additional pontoon bridges and rejoined the major-general commanding on the main road. On the previous evening Lieutenant-General Grant had demanded the surrender of General Lee to avoid the further effusion of blood. No skirmishing had taken place during the day, although the one army was close on the rear of the other.

About noon on the 9th, in consequence of the negotiations in regard to the surrender which were pending and exchanged under flags of truce between the generals commanding the respective armies, the advance of the Army of the Potomac, still engaged in pursuit, when within three miles of Appomattox Court-House was ordered to halt and await the issue of the proceedings. The other column had, by rapid marching, succeeded in passing around and confronting the head of that of the enemy at the latter place.

The few hours of anxious suspense were happily compensated by the glorious tidings which were soon proclaimed throughout the army announcing "the surrender of the Army of Northern Virginia."

On the following day the army commenced a retrograde movement toward Burke's Station, where it remained in camp until ordered to take up its final march toward Washington, D. C.

On the 14th of April Colonel Michler was detached from the staff of the commanding general of the Army of the Potomac, and directed, in conformity with instructions from Lieutenant-General Grant, to proceed to Petersburg, in order to examine and direct military surveys of the respective intrenched positions held by the two opposing armies during the siege and prepare plans of the same, combined with a detailed and accurate topographical map of the adjacent country; also to assume charge of the surveys of the different battle-fields and lines of operations from the James River to Appomattox Court-House.

By the 30th of June, the termination of the fiscal year for which this report is called, the field-work had been far advanced, but in consequence of the necessity of continuing during favorable weather the survey of the several hundred square miles through which it extends, little or no office duty was accomplished—only sufficient drawing to answer necessary purposes at the time; and consequently the maps at that time were not sufficiently far advanced, and could not exhibit the large amount and the nature of the work accomplished.

—

Narrative collated from reports of Major Mendell.

PONTOON TRAINS.

The companies of the U. S. Engineer Battalion with the Army of the Potomac were under the immediate command of Major Mendell, of the Corps of Engineers, with Captain Turnbull, Lieutenants Mackenzie, Benyaurd, Howell, Cuyler, and Heap, whose services, with the men under their command, are given in Major Michler's reports.

The pontoon trains for service in the field, and to accompany the several army corps, were under the command of Lieutenant-Colonel Spaulding, of the Fiftieth New York Volunteers. The services rendered by this branch of the Engineer Department were indispensable to the success of the army. Without these transportable bridges the armies could not have moved through a country intersected with numerous rivers, wide and deep, and oftentimes with rapid currents, as well as ebb and flood tides. The material of this branch of our service is modeled from the French wooden trains and the Russian canvas trains. These trains, particularly that with light canvas boats, have, during this war, for the first time been proved advantageous and efficient and adapted to our country. They have been very generally used by the armies in the West and South, as well as the armies in the East. The officers having charge of these trains and their construction have devised and adopted many useful modifications in the details. Lieutenant-Colonel Spaulding has added much to these modified improvements. The accompanying tabular statement from his report will exemplify the use and value of this indispensable branch of the engineer service.*

From the above statement it appears that the total number of pontoon bridges built was thirty-eight, and their aggregate length 6,458 feet.

During the whole time covered by this report he believes the pontoon trains have been promptly on time when ordered, the bridges rapidly and skillfully built, and all other engineering operations of the command faithfully performed.

---

*See Series I, Vol. XXXVI, Part I, p. 316.

Whatever credit may be awarded to this is mainly due to the energy and skill of the officers in immediate charge of the several works, and to the zealous and faithful co-operation of the men under their command.

Narrative from the report of Lieut. P. S. Michie, Corps of Engineers, brevet brigadier-general of volunteers, to General Delafield, Chief Engineer U. S. Army, dated October 10, 1865.

(See plans 11 and 12.*) The Army of the James, consisting of the Tenth and Eighteenth Army Corps (and subsequently of the Twenty-fourth and Twenty-fifth), commanded by Maj. Gen. B. F. Butler, occupied a defensive position across the peninsula of Bermuda Hundred on a line 6,058 yards long, its right resting on the James River about one mile below the Howlett house, and its left on the Appomattox River, on the high ground across the creek, from and on the high ground overlooking Port Walthall.

This defensive line, from its position, was unusually strong. With its flanks resting on and protected by two rivers, and its front of attack being diminished to about one-fourth of its length, because of impassable ravines, it was capable of being held by a much inferior force than the enemy were required to keep in its front. But it had also its disadvantages; for the enemy intrenched on a line approaching not nearer than 800 yards, with flanks as secure as ours, and a front made unassailable by means of all the obstacles known to field defense, and thus effectually closed to our forces there every avenue to do damage to the railroad and turnpike, which were the lines of communication to the wings of the rebel army and the avenues to their capital. The position of the two lines is given below in the sketch.

In addition to the line above described there was a strong work thrown up on Spring Hill, on the south side of the Appomattox River, just opposite Point of Rocks, and also strong works at Wilson's Wharf and Fort Powhatan, on the James River, all of which were constructed and garrisoned by detachments from this army.

These latter commanded the channel of the river at very important points, and on their occupation depended the uninterrupted supply of the "Armies operating against Richmond."

Brig. Gen. Godfrey Weitzel, U. S. Volunteers, captain U. S. Engineers, was the senior engineer of this army until October, 1864, but in consequence of his illness, in August, the duties of his office devolved upon General Michie.

July.—No engineering operations of any importance were carried on during this month. Attention was principally directed to strengthening the lines already laid out, in building water batteries for 100-pounder guns for the defense of Trent's Reach, and in general repairs to the line. During this month there was constant picket firing all along the front, constant surprises on the part of both forces of the picket-lines, and attempts to gain ground toward each other.

A signal tower 120 feet high was built at Point of Rocks, from the top of which could be seen the Richmond and Petersburg Railroad and turnpike. This gave us the means of obtaining a great deal of information, and must have impressed the enemy with this idea, for they established a casemated battery of three Whitworth rifled field

---

* Plate C, Maps 1 and 2, of the Atlas.

guns for the special purpose of firing at this tower. But one shot of all fired at it struck it, and that only splintered one of the posts without damaging the tower itself.

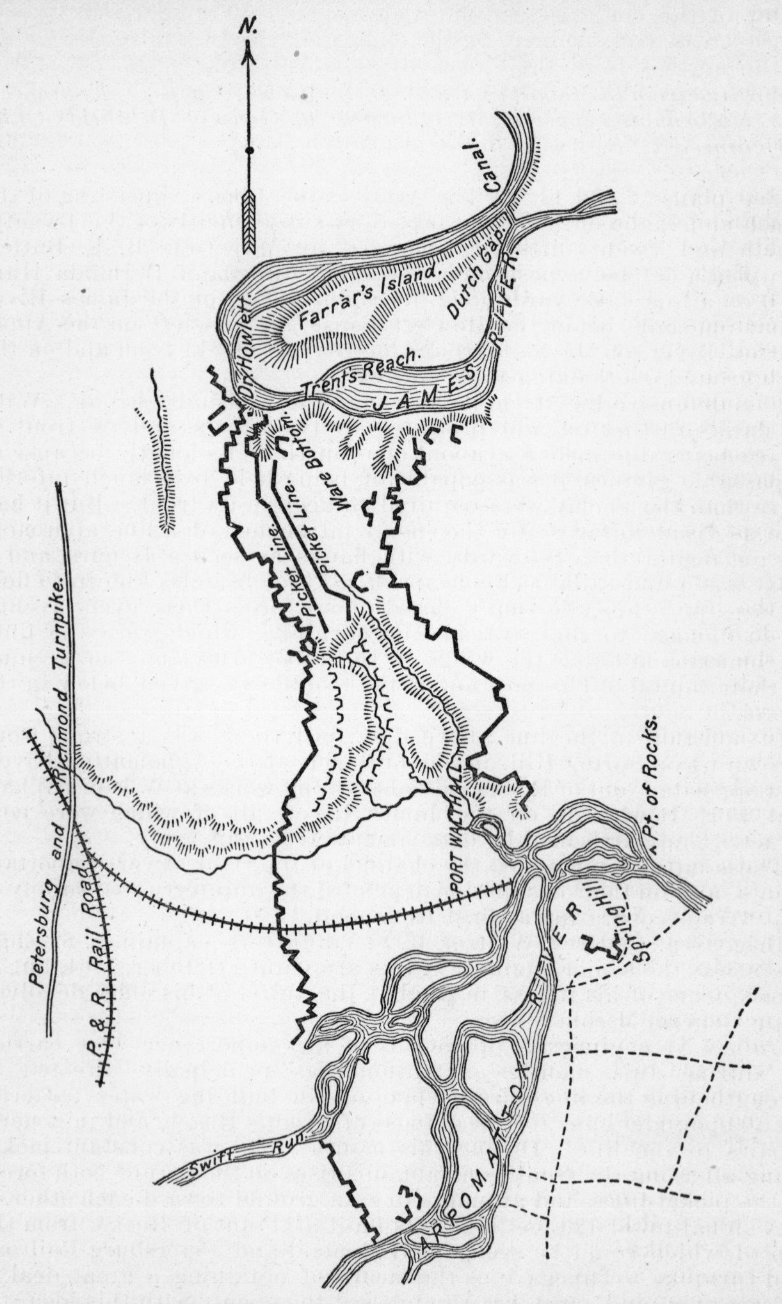

August.—On the 3d of August a pontoon bridge 560 feet long was built on the Appomattox River at Broadway Landing for the passage of the Second Army Corps.

A second signal tower 126 feet high, and capable of being made 40 feet higher, was built on the right flank of the line, on the high bluff known as "Crow's Nest," James River, opposite Aiken's. From the top of this could be seen the Richmond and Petersburg turnpike and the cross-roads connecting the main roads which ran to Richmond on the north side of the James River. A lookout constantly stationed here gave information of the enemy's movements.

Major-General Butler having conceived the idea of cutting a canal across the peninsula known as Dutch Gap, to pass iron-clads and other war vessels through to avoid Trent's Reach and the Howlett Battery, and the idea receiving the warm support of the then commander of the navy in the river, a survey of the locality was made by his direction.

From the sketch given below it will be seen that the river widens from 400 feet at the Howlett house to 2,700 at Trent's Reach. As a consequence, at the latter place the channel becomes narrower and shallower, and at ordinary high water vessels drawing twelve feet ten inches of water can pass under favorable circumstances, but the channel was effectually blocked by the powerful battery (Dantzler) at the Howlett house, which had a plunging fire upon the whole channel from Trent's Reach up to within a few hundred yards of the Howlett house. This battery had also embrasures cut to look up the river, to give a fire in rear in case any vessel was successful in passing the heavy fire of its front.

The survey of Dutch Gap showed a center section line 522 feet long, from a point in the channel on the south to a point in the channel on the north, 15 feet deep. The highest point on this center line was 38.5 feet above high-water mark, and the lowest 4 feet, which was at the south mouth. On a line 60 feet from this center line, on either side, the ground rose to 42.8 feet at the north mouth, and to 11.4 feet on the south. The difference of water level was 10.1 inches, taken at extreme low tide, thus showing the natural fall of the river between these points to be 2.13 inches to the mile. To all appearances the soil offered no insuperable difficulties for excavation, although it was rumored that the James River granite, which outcropped a mile above the lower mouth and a mile and a half below, would be met with beneath the upper strata and cause a complete failure.

The strata met with were as follows, viz: Yellow Virginia brick clay for twelve feet; layer of coarse sand and gravel, two to four feet; half an inch to two inches bog-iron ore; layer of pebbles and large gravel, two feet; then hard blue clay, or hardpan, containing a large quantity of sulphuret of iron or iron pyrites. This latter stratum was never exhausted, and the bottom and sides of the canal were chiseled out of this, presenting as smooth and compact a surface as if built with masonry. In round numbers, there were about 48,000 cubic yards to be excavated—the canal to be sixty feet wide at high water, forty feet wide at bottom, and fifteen feet deep.

It is a question whether this project—one of the simplest in civil engineering—would have been of any advantage other than to bring our navy a few miles farther up the river; for after it was commenced it was well known that other and nearly as powerful batteries lined both banks of the James River, commanding almost impassable obstacles, and ready to do their share in disputing the passage to the rebel capital. And besides, it was an ascertained fact that the river was filled with torpedoes of the most delicate construction, most painful evidence of which we had in the destruction of three of our vessels in reaching the position then occupied. If any advantage could have accrued to us from this canal in a military point of view, it would be a maximum only by keeping it a profound secret.

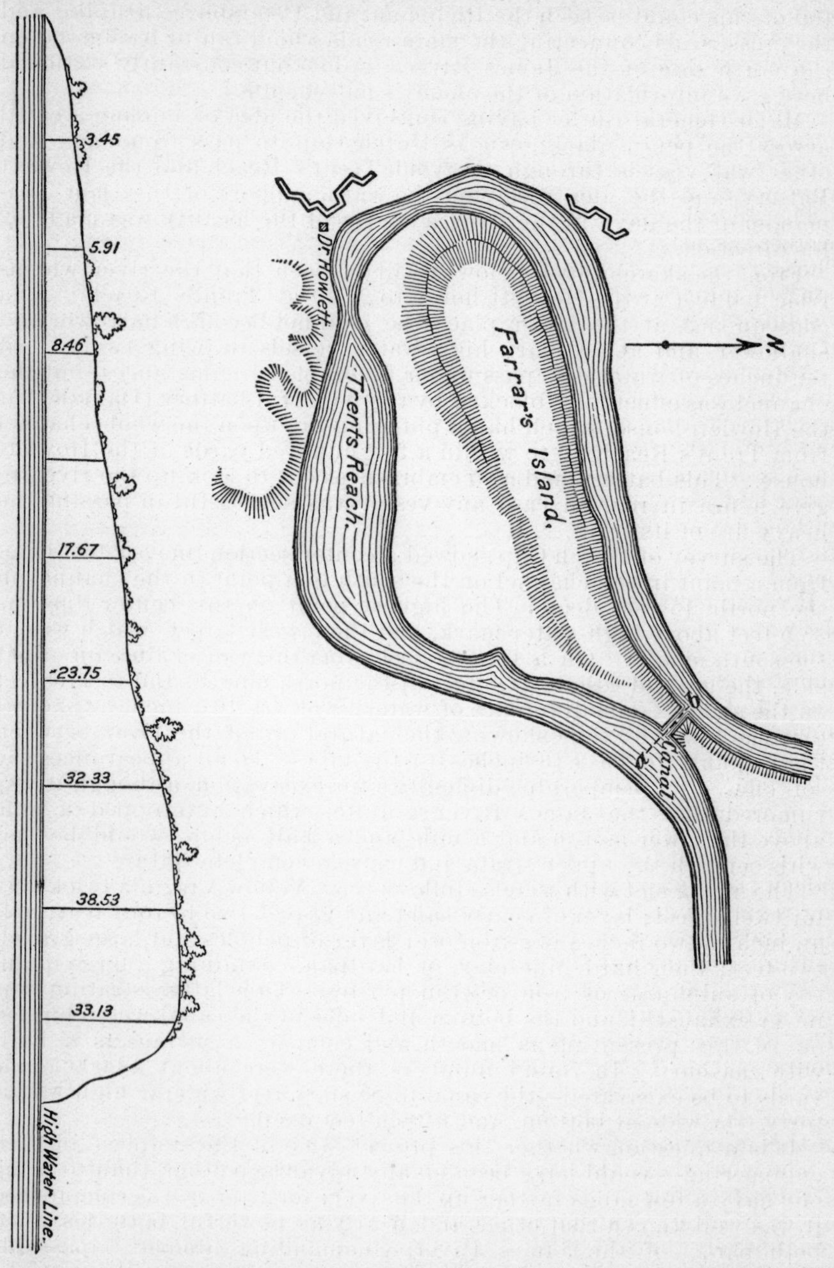

The excavation being ordered to proceed, ground was broken on the 9th of August, and immediately thereafter the enemy began the constant annoyance with their rifle and mortar batteries, which ended only with the suspension of labor on the canal, January 1, 1865. There were thrown in the vicinity of the working parties over 20,000 shells during the whole period of the work. The canal was excavated mainly by soldiers and partly by dredges. The latter were old and almost worn out, and were worked by civilians, who did not come up to their promises, being driven off and frightened by the enemy's shells. Not more than 6,000 to 7,000 cubic yards were removed by the dredges, which were promised to remove 400 cubic yards every ten hours. They worked from the south mouth 200 feet up into the canal, where an embankment separated the part on which the soldiers were working from the lower half.

The whole canal, except an embankment at the north mouth to protect against direct firing, was excavated to the required dimensions. The soil was very favorable below high-water mark. It was the "hard-pan" of miners—a hard, stiff, blue clay, perfectly impervious to and insoluble in water. Whatever leakage took place through the strata of sand and gravel was removed by a steam pump.

About the middle of December the mines which had been made in the embankment were nearly completed. This embankment was much larger than was intended to be blown out with powder, for it had been General Michie's endeavor to reduce it far below what would have been almost certain to be removed, but during his absence the water had been let into the excavated part and up to the embankment without orders. It would have required a greater amount of labor and length of time to remove it than we were warranted to use at this period.

It remained then only to do the best to blow out the mass between the water in the river and that in the canal; and the problem became to use an amount of powder large enough to remove the embankment and disturb its foundation so that it would be easy to remove afterward and, at the same time, not so much as to disturb and cave down the walls of the canal in the vicinity. Twelve thousand pounds of powder were divided among five mines—one of 4,000 and four of 2,000 each—distributed as follows: Three mines were placed at a depth of fifteen feet below high water, one of 4,000 being on the center line of the canal and thirty-five feet from the face of the embankment, and two of 2,000 each were placed on the same level ten feet on each side of the center line and twenty-five feet from the face. Two remaining were at a depth of twenty-five feet below high-water mark, or ten feet lower than the three first, and twenty feet farther out than the central mine toward the channel on the north side.

Toward the time of charging and tamping the mines the water leaked in very rapidly and the pumps were kept going night and day. The powder in the four smaller mines was in tin cans holding 125 pounds each. In the larger mine the powder was in four large rubber bags holding 800 pounds, all opening into a water-tight box which contained 800 pounds, and in the center of which was the point of fusion of this mine.

The method of exploding the mines was by means of the Gomez fuse, a quick-burning composition said to be instantaneous for distances under 100 feet. This method proved defective, and the results showed conclusively that all of the powder did not burn, and will not when ignited in the center of large mines. The effect would, in General Michie's opinion, have been several times greater if centers of fusion could have been made for every hundred pounds of powder, which can be done now with an electric apparatus.

In the method used, in the center of each charge was placed the end of a length of Gomez fuse, cut at different points to allow the flame to ignite the powder in several places. This fuse was then grafted to an equal length in the same level running to the other mine. The three mines in the upper level were joined in the same way and, finally, the two lines were grafted together and joined to the end of a piece of slow-match cut to burn twenty minutes. The grafts had been tried repeatedly before being finally determined on, and had always been successful.

On exploding the mine the embankment was thrown down and a current commenced running through the canal. Excavation by means of discharging cans of powder under water deepened and widened the channel, aided by strong freshets, so that at high water six and a half feet of water is on the embankment. General Butler having been relieved from the department about this time, work was discontinued by order.

The canal at present is used by the steamer O. S. Pierce and others of that class, which save by this way about five miles and a half of travel. A few days' work to clear up the disturbed mass and to widen and deepen the north mouth would make this the usual traveled route by all vessels navigating the river. The current and tide partly flow through this way, but their action is unimportant in clearing it out, because the debris consists of large lumps of cemented gravel and hard blue clay. The above embraces all the data of interest in this much-talked-of project, and is given complete to avoid referring to it in the account of each month's labor.

September.—During this month a line of works was built and a post established at Harrison's Landing. The defensive works consisted of a redoubt of four embrasures, with a stockaded gorge commanded by the gun-boats in the river, and infantry breast-works running from the flanks to the river. The length of the whole line is 1,412 yards. A canvas pontoon bridge of twenty-three boats was built on the Appomattox River September 19. The pontoniers who built it, having no experience with these boats, were twelve minutes in building the first and three minutes in building the last, the average time being seven minutes and a half for each boat. Owing to the river being affected by the tide, the claw balks had to be lashed to the saddle piece, or they would slip up or down, according as the tide was ebb or flow. Often this bridge had to be covered with manure to deaden the sound of travel when troops crossed. In these cases the dust of the manure falling into the canvas boats would rot the threads of the canvas and cause more or less leakage. It was noticed that some of the canvas coverings would leak as much as six inches of water at night and none the following day. Teams heavily loaded would often sink these boats to within four inches of the gunwale. These were among the most prominent things noticed in the use of these boats in a permanent bridge, a use, however, for which they were never intended.

During the night of September 28 a pontoon bridge 1,320 feet long was built on the James River at Aiken's Landing. With 100 pontoniers the bridge was finished in six and a half hours, so quietly as not to disturb the enemy's pickets on the opposite side of the river.

The army began to cross at 3 a. m. September 29 in two columns, one on the bridge above spoken of and the other on the bridge at Deep Bottom. A successful advance was made; Fort Harrison, the key point of the outer line of Richmond defense, carried by assault, and the line of works extending to the Darbytown road occupied by our army. It having been determined to remain in the position thus carried, the rebel works from Fort Harrison to the New Market road were occupied by our troops and their front turned during the night and following day. Shortly afterward a line was thrown up, with batteries at appropriate intervals, extending from our left flank, at Fort Harrison, to the James River, where it rested on a large work at a point a little above Cox's Landing. This work, called Fort Brady, was on the site on which the rebels had commenced the erection of a powerful rifled battery to command the mouth of the canal. We armed the work with three 100-pounder Parrott guns and several 4½-inch Rodman rifles, constructed a large bombproof for the protection of the garrison, and surrounded it by strong lines of abatis. The line from this work to Fort Harrison afforded a secure defense in case of a flank attack on the left, as it subjected the attacking party to a chance of being defeated, cut off, and captured, or driven into the river, after leaving their own lines.

October.—Efforts were early made to strengthen the right flank by a strong line and redoubts, but the work was stopped by order from the then commander of the Tenth Army Corps. A strong attack on this flank was made by the enemy in force on the 7th of October, which the cavalry who guarded this flank were unable to withstand, and which at one time threatened to be very disastrous to this army.

Terry's division, of this corps, with the artillery under Jackson, checked and finally drove back the enemy, and then the work of securing the flank was pushed rapidly along.

About 400 yards east of the New Market road a strong redoubt fifty yards square was built, and formed a salient from which the whole country within 600 yards was commanded, and from its right flank an infantry parapet of strong profile, well protected from assault by abatis, ran toward the New Market road, where it rested, about the vicinity of the Four-Mile Church. From this point to near the mouth of Four-Mile Creek strong isolated redoubts were built and manned with troops and artillery, so placed as to mutually support each other. Along New Market Heights the most salient points were taken and occupied by strong closed works, and in their front for 1,000 and 1,500 yards the woods were "slashed," thus making a continuous abatis in their front to the limit of the range of their artillery. Works were also placed to flank the valleys and sides of these hills.

As there was some possibility of moving the greater part of this army to a new field of operations, leaving but a small force behind, a line of interior works, some 3,400 yards long, was built but for such a contingency. The right rested on Four-Mile Creek, and the left on the marsh below Aiken's Landing. The details of construction were the same as generally belong to field defenses, the stronger batteries being placed so as to command the most important roads or the most probable points from which an attack would be made, with infantry parapets four to six feet thick on top joining them.

In front were ditches from eight to twelve feet wide and six feet deep, and in advance of these a line of good abatis. This line was well indicated, the batteries completed, and infantry parapet two-thirds finished, the remaining work to be done after the troops occupied the line. Often the greatest difficulty has been in getting an army to take up a proper and exact line of defense at first, each regiment, company, and man digging where they find their spades, without reference to the fitness of things, indicating the necessity of more engineer officers.

As detached works to this line, it was intended to hold those on New Market Heights and Camp Holly, which would have given us the command of New Market, Kingsland, and Darbytown roads. The necessity for this line never occurring, it was never occupied by troops.

After the occupation of Fort Harrison and the rebel captured lines, the enemy began the construction of a new line of defense joining their water batteries on the river at Chaffin's farm with Fort Gilmer, and running thence easterly to join on to that portion of the captured line which we could not occupy at the Charles City road, and so on to New Bridge on the Chickahominy.

The line that our forces occupied was made as strong as possible, and possessed the advantage of having but a short part exposed to an attack of the enemy, which part was strongly manned and guarded.

On the 27th a movement was made on the Darbytown and Williamsburg roads with no other result than to keep the enemy from sending re-enforcements to the right of their army at Petersburg, which was then being attacked by the Army of the Potomac. During this movement General Weitzel's troops fought on the same ground in advance of Seven Pines on which the Army of the Potomac fought in 1862.

November.—Details of both engineers and infantry were constantly employed during this month in repairing the works of defense and perfecting and completing those alluded to. During this season the roads used by the supply trains from the wharves and bridges became much cut up, and corduroying was commenced. Wharves for the quartermaster, ordnance, commissary, and medical departments were built at suitable places on the river. Frequent rumors arriving at Fort Harrison that the enemy were mining the work, in order to allay the fears of the garrison well holes were dug on the glacis to serve for listening galleries. As the nearest approach of the rebel works was 800 yards, and a valley twenty feet deep had to be crossed before reaching the work, but little attention was paid to these rumors.

While attention was paid to the defensive operations we also found time to collect, repair, and put in working order three saw-mills, which were located in a splendid forest in the Bermuda woods. By these mills from 7,000 to 10,000 feet of lumber were sawed per day, the greater portion of which was used in the construction of a permanent hospital at Point of Rocks. Sufficient was obtained, however, to stock the engineer depot and build platforms and magazines in all the batteries, wharves, and bridges on the river.

Below is a report of the engineer force of the army, and how employed, which may be taken as a fair standard of each day's detail during the period of quiet:

Two officers, 80 men, building redoubts and corduroying roads; 2 officers, 66 men, repairing Tenth Army Corps front; 2 officers, 90 men, repairing Eighteenth Army Corps front; 1 officer, 30 men, bombproof to dredge Dutch Gap and Fort Brady; 1 officer, 50 men, corduroying roads; 2 officers, 30 men, engineer depots at Bermuda and Fortress Monroe; 2 officers, 143 men, various small details, &c.—12 officers, 489 men. First New York Volunteer Engineers—four officers, 105 men, on duty at saw-mills, building wharf, pontoon bridges, repairing wagons, &c.

December.—This month's labor was a continuation of the last, and the principal roads of supply were ready for winter use quite early in the month. Whatever damages had been done to the defenses were repaired. Timber for a permanent pile bridge was prepared in the woods, which bridge was to be built in January. A detachment of engineer troops accompanied the expeditionary force to Fort Fisher.

January.—As the enemy frequently opened a heavy mortar fire from in front of his works opposite Fort Harrison, and as the artillerymen were unable to stand to their guns during its continuance, it was deemed advisable to make protection to the guns on the front of Fort Harrison. The mortars used by the enemy were Coehorns, placed outside of their works and behind the line of picket reserves, protected in their front by a strong line of abatis. It was designed to bombproof the whole front of the work and put in casemates enough, constructed somewhat on the Hoxo plan, for the guns on the front. There was a banquette for infantry on top, reached by broad, wide stairs in rear, which gave the infantry good cover and enabled them to see perfectly every point in advance. The ditch was deepened and widened and a fraise placed in the scarp to prevent scaling. But four of these casemates were constructed, and two bombproofs, a sketch of which is shown on the opposite page.

There were also three strong lines of abatis and wire entanglement placed in front of the ditch, making the whole work quite formidable and easy to hold.

In order to save sand-bags, which at this time became very expensive, Lieutenant King, Engineer Corps, designed some loop-holes for riflemen and for use in the picket-lines, which proved admirably well adapted for their purpose, and being prepared at slight cost at the saw-mills, were used on all the works and rifle-pits. They were constructed of boards, and of the form shown in the diagram. They presented a smaller target for the enemy's sharpshooters and at the same time gave a large field of fire. They were not easily discernible at any distance and could easily be removed and replaced.

NOTE.—The rebel device for the same purpose consisted in placing logs of various lengths, ten to fourteen inches in diameter, hewn on two sides, with notches cut in the lower side once in about six feet along the interior crest of the parapet, and banking these logs in front with earth. The notches which formed the loop-holes were tapering toward the outside, similar to our own, and where there was much sharpshooting the orifice was still further reduced by a plate of thin boiler iron eight or ten inches square, with a hole in the center but little larger than the barrel of a musket. These plates were spiked to the front side of the logs (covering the notches), and in some cases were found with fifteen to twenty bullet marks upon them, many of which were so near the edge of the opening that the bullets probably went through, and it is quite likely that all the bullets that struck the plate would have struck the man in the rear of it had ordinary sand-bag loop-holes been used.

The engineer may at times find this expedient worthy his attention, observing that the logs near the crest of the parapet are not suitable where artillery can be used against them.

The permanent pile bridge was finished after a little more than two weeks' labor, being 1,368 feet long. It became necessary as a substitute for the pontoon bridge owing to the great freshets in the river, the floating ice, and the driftwood that came down the river at this time. It was a pile bridge, each pier consisting of three piles driven firmly into the bed of the river and connected by a cap piece, and the piers joined by strong pieces to form bays each fifteen feet wide. An inclined log was attached to each pier to ward off drift and ice. This

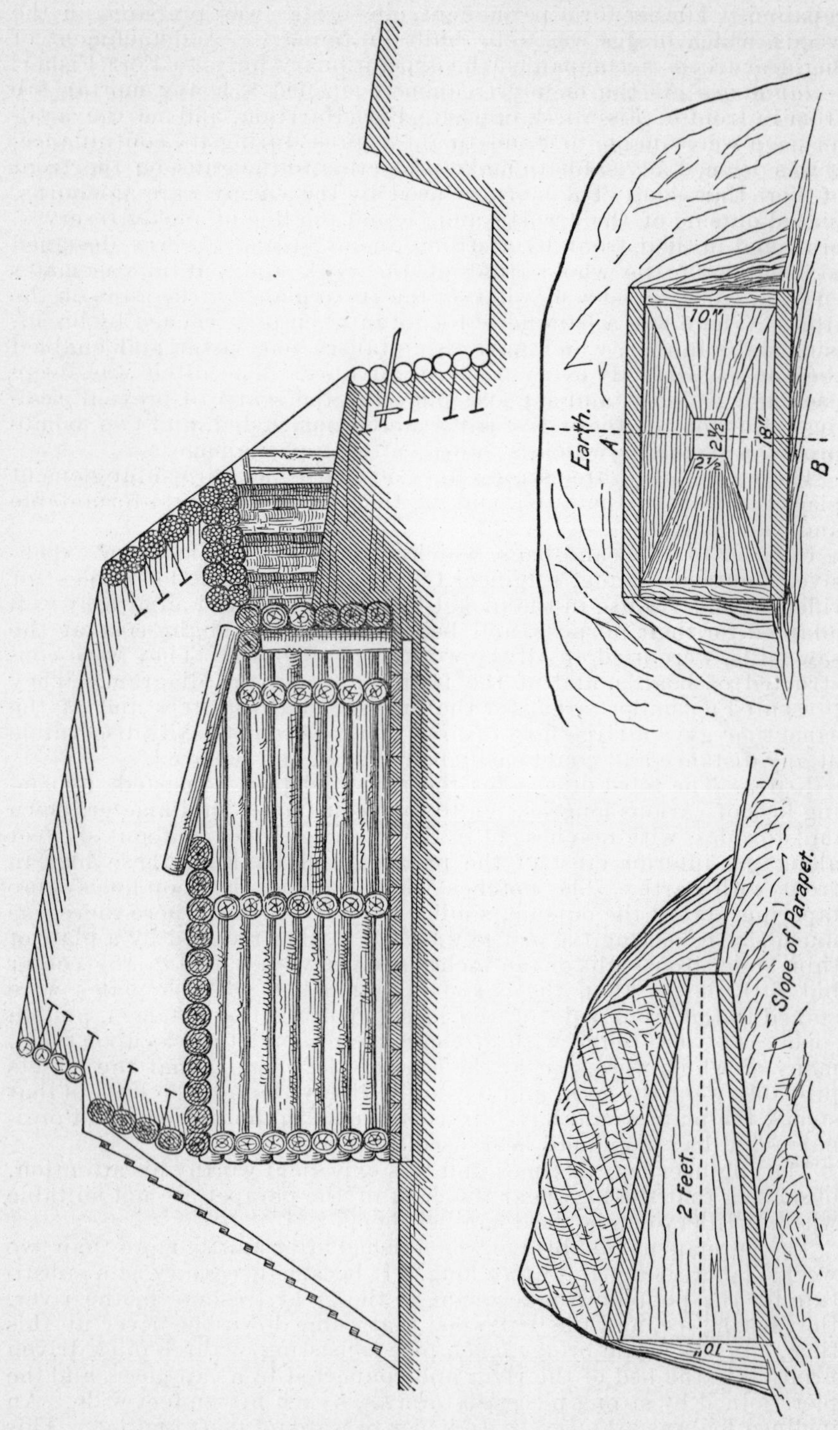
10"
2½
2½
18"
Earth.
A
B
Slope of Parapet.
2 Feet.
10"

was securely attached to a pile driven a short distance above and in the prolongation of the pier, which pile was nearly sawed off. When driven by the pile-drivers sufficiently it was broken off, and the end of the inclined pile thus anchored to the bottom; the other was spiked to the pier, as shown in the sketch below.

The river deepens to 16 feet about 1,000 feet from the north shore, and then to 30 feet for a distance of nearly 180 feet, and then decreases rapidly to the shore-line. At the channel a draw of pontoon-boats was made 180 feet wide. The lumber which was used in the construction of this bridge was obtained from the engineer depot saw-mills.

February.—There were additional river batteries on the south side of the James, constructed and armed with 100-pounder guns, as an additional protection against another rebel raid of iron-clads. During this month and early in March the engineer force of the army decreased rapidly, owing to the expiration of their term of service.

March.—There were at this time less than 300 effective men for duty, and but a small number of these were engineer soldiers proper. Repairs of the batteries were constantly going on. To obviate the effects of winter weather, platforms were relaid, magazines drained,

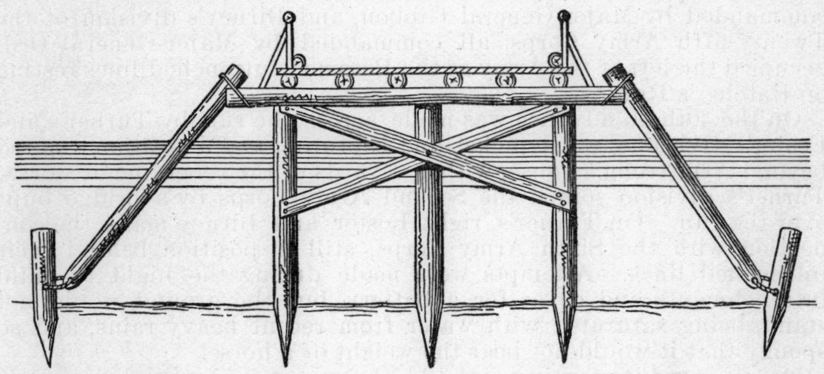

and their cover renewed and thickened, and generally the lines of the army put in good defensible condition.

The mules belonging to the pontoon train were worked continuously at the saw-mills during the winter, and only relieved when directed by Major-General Barnard, the engineer of the combined armies operating against Richmond, to be used in preparing four pontoon trains for active service and marching. New mules were obtained, and every effort made to break them to harness in time. The whole artisan force was put at work to repair and strengthen the wagons and boats. Finally orders were issued to take a train of but fifteen canvas boats, which was ready for the march on the day specified. The engineer force was divided; one part under Bvt. Maj. W. R. King, U. S. Engineers, remained with General Weitzel's forces, and entered the city of Richmond with his command. They began and continued the erection of a defensive line until the news of Lee's surrender reached the city. They also built a pontoon bridge joining Richmond and Manchester 2,400 feet long, upon which afterward the Armies of the James, the Potomac, Sherman's army, and Sheridan's cavalry crossed. The engineer force with the moving column consisted of six companies of engineers and one of pontoniers.

A tool train of ten wagons moved with the pontoon trains; the latter consisted of thirty-two wagons, carrying forage, spare chess, and 380 feet of bridge material. The weight, drawn by eight mules, was ascertained by weighing a pontoon wagon with its material two weeks after the campaign closed, and was found to be as follows:

	Pounds.
Two boats of canvas and box	305
Transoms	470
Claw balks	1,440
Saddle balks	244
Boat sides	224
Anchor lines	175
Anchors	310
Wagon load	3,168
Wagon	1,278
Weight drawn	4,446

During the march there were rains, which would increase the weight. On the 29th of March the moving column of the Army of the James, consisting of Turner's division of West Virginia troops, of the Twenty-fourth Army Corps, and Foster's (First) division of the same corps, commanded by Major-General Gibbon, and Birney's division of the Twenty-fifth Army Corps, all commanded by Major-General Ord, occupied the left of the Army of the Potomac, intrenched lines resting on Hatcher's Run.

On the 30th an advance was made across the run by Turner's and Foster's divisions, rebel picket-line captured, and a position secured beyond Armstrong's house, with 800 yards of the rebel line of works. Turner's division joined the Second Army Corps by a bridge built over the run. On Turner's right Foster and Birney made the connection with the Sixth Army Corps, still in position behind their intrenched lines. Attempts were made during the night to build intrenchments and cover for a battery, but the ground would not stand, being saturated with water from recent heavy rains, and so spongy that it would not bear the weight of a horse.

April.—On the morning of the 2d, the successful assault being made and rapidly followed up by an attack on Fort Gregg, which was taken after some desperate fighting, the troops occupied a position entirely surrounding Petersburg. During the night everything was got in readiness for a rapid march in the morning. Starting at 5 a. m., and taking the Cox road, our army made a rapid march toward Burkeville; a part of the engineer force moved ahead to repair roads and bridges; the pontoon trains followed headquarters, to be in readiness in case of necessity. Burkeville was reached on the night of the 5th and occupied during the next day. A small force being sent out to burn the High Bridge at Farmville was met by the rebel advance and captured, after desperate fighting. The troops moved in that direction on the 6th, and engaged a portion of the advance of the enemy, while the cavalry headed them off on the Prince Edward Court-House road. On the afternoon of the 7th the troops entered Farmville, the enemy burning the bridges at this place and retreating across the river. The pontoon train of our army having been well kept up to the front, notwithstanding its overloaded condition, was fortunately able to be used to pass over the artillery and trains of the Sixth and Second Army Corps and enable them to follow in rapid pursuit of the enemy that night. The pontoons were relieved by those of the Army of the Potomac before daybreak, and once more in position for a new march.

At daylight on the 8th the Twenty-fourth Army Corps moved from Farmville, taking the road running nearly with the South Side Railroad, and made a forced march of nearly thirty-three miles before midnight, resting for a few hours on the railroad where Sheridan had captured several cars loaded with bacon and corn. At 3.30 a. m. on the 9th the infantry moved again, and at 8 a. m. were in action on the extreme left of the army. The leading brigade of Foster's division, of the Twenty-fourth Army Corps, went into action on the double-quick, and delivered the volley which staggered and drove back the advance of the enemy, who had at that moment gained some temporary advantage over the cavalry. The action lasted until 10 a. m., when a truce was granted preliminary to the surrender.

May.—During this month a bridge was built at Fredericksburg. Surveys were made, by direction of Major-General Barnard, of the detached works surrounding the city, and orders were afterward received to continue the survey of the intrenched lines and country adjacent to Richmond.

June.—Brevet Major King was intrusted with the charge of rebuilding a bridge, called Mayo's Bridge, connecting Richmond and Manchester. The following is an extract from his report on the completion of the bridge. The plan adopted for the bridge is represented by the accompanying drawing, page 45 [195].

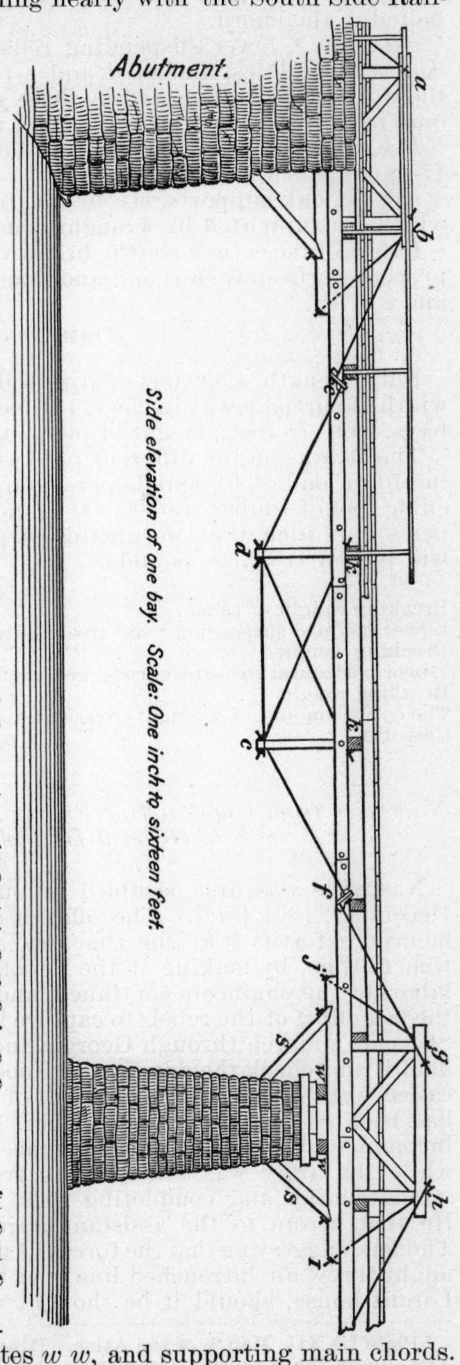

Side elevation of one bay. Scale: One inch to sixteen feet.

DESCRIPTION.

c f i, main chords made of four pieces, four by twelve inches, breaking joints, and forming continuous beams the entire length of the bridge.

j i, corbels, fourteen by sixteen inches, resting on wall plates *w w*, and supporting main chords.

a b g h, &c., straining beams, ten by twelve inches, oak, supported by posts and struts.

b c g f, &c., main suspending rods in pairs, secured at *b* and *g* by wrought-iron plates, and at *c* and *f* by cast-iron connecting plates bolted to the chord.

c d and *e f*, lower suspending rods, secured at *c* and *f* to cast-iron connecting plates, and at *d* and *e* to horizontal wrought-iron bars; these bars being connected by three small rods *d e*, *d k*, and *e k*, diagonal iron braces, to prevent vertical undulations.

k k, floor girders, ten by fourteen inches, supporting 4-inch by 12-inch joists and 3-inch plank.

d k e k, oak supports, six by ten inches, resting in cast-iron shoes, which are supported by wrought-iron bars *d* and *e*.

Lateral braces (not shown in drawing) connect the floor girders to prevent horizontal swaying, and diagonal braces steady the posts *d k* and *e k*.

DIMENSIONS.

Entire length, 1,396 feet; entire width, including sidewalks, 31 feet; width of carriage-way in clear, 19½ feet; number of bays, 18; width of bays, 69 to 78 feet; height of piers at low water, 20 feet.

The strains on the different rods were computed as follows: Allowing for a load of 40 pounds per square foot of roadway, 40 pounds per cubic foot of timber, and 60,000 pounds as the breaking weight of iron per square inch, then the greatest strain on the upper suspension rods will be nearly 32,500 pounds.

	Pounds.
Breaking weight of same	90,000
Lower inclined suspension rods, greatest strain	16,000
Breaking weight	46,500
Lower horizontal suspension rods, greatest strain	10,200
Breaking weight	26,000
The entire amount of wrought-iron used, including bolts, plates, &c., was	44,068
Cast-iron	13,586

Narrative from General Tower's reports of February 1 and March 31, 1865, to General Delafield, Chief Engineer.

Nashville was first occupied by our army on the 15th and 16th of December, 1864 [*sic*]. The officers of the Corps of Engineers commenced to fortify it at that time, and as its importance increased from time to time, by making it the depot for the armies of the West, the labors of the engineers continued, and were not relaxed to the date of the last effort of the rebels to capture it, and thus endeavor to frustrate Sherman's march through Georgia and the Carolinas to Virginia. To hold it and check the advance of Hood through Kentucky to the Ohio called forth all the zeal and talent of the engineers. General Tower had been sent thither in September, 1864, and labored to perfect the incomplete defenses. On the advance of the rebel General Hood, and while the army was falling back from Franklin, the necessity for strengthening and completing these defenses became more urgent. He then wrote to the assistant adjutant-general of Major-General Thomas, suggesting that the forces of the Quartermaster's Department might throw an intrenched line over the high hills in advance of the Lorenz house, should it be thought expedient. (See plan No. 4.*)

*Plate LXXII, Map 2, of the Atlas. It appears that the map published in the Atlas omits the numbers designating the hills herein mentioned. For the map containing these numbers, see Executive Document No. 1, House of Representatives, Thirty-ninth Congress, first session, Vol. II.

At 12 m. General Thomas visited Fort Morton and informed him that about 5,000 men would report at 1 o'clock. To his question, "Shall they intrench the Lorenz Hills?" he replied, "No; let them construct your interior line connecting with the forts. The army will hold the hills and intrench them."

He therefore gave Captain Jenney, who was assisting him, directions to run the line of infantry intrenchments from Fort Morton around the Taylor house to hill 210. Captain Jenney was assisted by Major Powell, of the Tennessee Army reserve artillery. Major Dickson, inspector of artillery of the Army of the Tennessee, superintended assiduously the construction of the large and important battery on hill 210. Captain Barlow, of the Corps of Engineers, took charge of the line from the Cumberland River to the Chattanooga railroad, south side of the city.

A portion of the line from hill 210 to Hyde's Ferry was laid out by Captain Barlow and himself, the rest by Major Willett. During the fifteen days preceding the battles before Nashville more than seven miles of infantry parapet and rifle-pit intrenchments were thus constructed by the quartermaster's and railroad forces. This gave a continuous line (see plan No. 4*) in advance of all the hospitals, store-houses, and other structures, except the scattered houses of the suburbs in front of College Hill, and held the elevated positions which looked upon the buildings within range. It is the line indicated in his report of October, 1864. It is just as long a line as that occupied by the army over the hills, but the shortest that would effectually secure the hospitals and other important structures. The line over the hills was the best army line, but deriving no support from Forts Morton, Houston, Gillem, and Hyde's Ferry, could not be held by the usual forces occupying Nashville.

It would have required a large number of redoubts of expensive construction, owing to the rocky nature of the soil, to have fortified the line of hills, but such line would hold an enemy well away from the city, covering it effectually. It was his opinion that completing the works already described, and strengthening the principal batteries at intermediate points, would make Nashville secure with its usual garrison, aided by the quartermaster's organized forces. Hill 210 must be strengthened, as it is a key position, and the Taylor house knoll should be supported by a keep. Small block-houses in batteries, like the construction for Battery Donaldson, are a good arrangement when well covered by the parapets. Unfortunately, wood constructions are the most difficult of accomplishment. Embrasures, magazines, and block-house bombproofs cause the great delay in making forts and batteries. A great deal, however, has been accomplished during the past three months in spite of extremely unfavorable weather, mud, and muddy roads. It has rained more than half the time.

When General Sherman appointed him inspector-general of fortifications for his military division he requested him to look well to the defenses of Nashville. He also called his attention to Murfreesborough and Columbia, the line of defense for the army falling back. Murfreesborough was known to be well defended. Columbia was the position on Duck River which would have been held by our army had

*Plate LXXII, Map 2, of the Atlas. It appears that the map published in the Atlas omits the numbers designating the hills herein mentioned. For the map containing these numbers, see Executive Document No. 1, House of Representatives, Thirty-ninth Congress, first session, Vol. II.

the corps from Missouri arrived a week sooner. As things occurred, Nashville was the threatened point, and he gave his attention to its defenses, using all his personal influence to get aid from every source possible. The plans submitted will show works devised by him for the defense of this depot and alterations in original works. He had to thank the railroad department for much assistance rendered, and especially the quartermaster's department for aid in laborers and material. These laborers were mostly organized as brigades, and turned out as such and guarded two miles of the interior line during the battles of the 15th and 16th of December, 1864, and in case of an attack on the city would doubtless be an efficient assistance to this garrison.

Captain Barlow understands this position well, and would doubtless do everything in his power to forward its defenses. Waiting for plans has delayed this synopsis of engineer operations at Nashville.

He was getting up a plan of the magnificent battles of December 15 and 16, gained by the U. S. army commanded by Major-General Thomas over the rebel forces under General Hood. (See plan No. 4.*)

Having accompanied the commanding general during these fights, it was his special request that he should direct the survey and drawing of the plan illustrating them.

Captain Barlow, U. S. Engineers, in immediate charge of the defenses of Nashville since the middle of December, had much improved his department and heartily responded to his efforts to push forward the defensive line. Captain Jenney, aide-de-camp on General Sherman's staff, in charge of topographical office there, had voluntarily assisted and had done excellent service superintending at Forts Houston and Gillem, and in the construction of infantry line of intrenchments.

He has sent the map (see plan No. 4*) of the battles of Nashville, which shows the dispositions of troops before and during the battles, and which, with the exception of sections, seems clear and complete. By a little attention it will be perceived how admirably the battle was planned. Its execution was in accordance with the plan.

X was the turning point on which the army wheeled as on a pivot. From that point to the river on the left the lines were held by new troops under General Steedman, while the three infantry corps, commanded by Generals Wood, Smith, and Schofield, and the Cavalry Corps under General Wilson, were hurled upon the enemy's center and left. Our army, thus in position, formed nearly a straight line, of which the left, far refused (made up of new troops), held lines supported by works and covered by a brilliant dash of General Steedman with a small force in advance toward the enemy's right. The right was the old fighting army, which, though requiring much time to swing into position (about 40,000 strong), necessarily broke the enemy's left and drove him from his main line.

The second day the rebel general had concentrated his forces; but the moral effect of his first day's fight, his losses, especially in artillery, together with our superiority of cavalry, which dismounted and attacked his left rear, all contributed to his defeat; and the left of his line was broken about 4 o'clock by a dash of General Smith's corps. The battle is worthy of study.

---

*Plate LXXII, Map 2, of the Atlas.

*Narrative from the report of Bvt. Brig. Gen. O. M. Poe to the Chief Engineer, dated October 8, 1865.**

—

Narrative collated from the report of Lieutenant and Brevet Captain Stickney, Corps of Engineers, June 3, 1865, to General Richard Delafield, Chief Engineer U. S. Army. (See plans Nos. 3 and 11.†)

While remaining in Goldsborough, from March 24 to April 10, the pontoon train was put in complete repair as far as material at hand would admit. Thirty new canvas boat covers were received and all but ten of the old covers sent to New Berne.

April 10 the army moved out from Goldsborough toward Raleigh, arriving at the latter place on the 14th. The next day the Fifteenth Army Corps proceeded to Morrisville and the Seventeenth Army Corps to Jones' Station, at which places they were halted on account of the negotiations for the surrender of the enemy's army. None of the bridges over the streams between Goldsborough and Raleigh were destroyed, but the planks were in most cases thrown off and were soon replaced, causing no delay of any consequence. The roads were in very bad condition between Goldsborough and Pineville, the Fifteenth Army Corps being obliged to build 214 feet of wagon bridges over sloughs, 175 feet of foot bridges, and 13,196 yards of corduroy. The Seventeenth Army Corps made 426 feet of bridges and 16,918 yards of corduroy. The army remained in the vicinity of Raleigh till April 29, when, the rebel army having surrendered, it started on its homeward march toward Petersburg, where it arrived May 6. The roads were in excellent condition and bridges standing over all the rivers except the Neuse and Roanoke. The army arrived at Robinson's Ferry, on the Roanoke, May 3, the pontoon train being in advance. This river is 740 feet wide at the point at which the army crossed, and the depth of water from five to ten feet. The pontoon train contained only 580 feet of bridging, but they found four large wooden boats on the river, which were rigged up with centerpieces, made four trestles, and the bridge was ready for crossing by 8 a. m. on the 4th, after a hard night's work. After remaining two days at Petersburg the army moved to Manchester.

The major-general commanding informed Captain Stickney that from Manchester up they would find bridges over all streams, as they were to be left for them by the Army of the Potomac, which preceded them; consequently he did not think it necessary to procure more chesses.

On the 12th of May the Seventeenth Army Corps started for Alexandria, the Fifteenth Army Corps on the following day, and arrived there on the 19th. The roads were generally good all the way from Raleigh to Alexandria, and the army moved with surprising celerity. He was disappointed, however, about the bridges, there being none over the Pamunkey or Occoquan Rivers. The former was very much swollen, the water overflowing the southern bank to the depth of about two feet and a half when they first arrived, the morning of May 13, and continued to rise during the day and following night.

The pontoon bridge was laid and some trains passed over that afternoon, but before the next morning the water rose so high that it became necessary to build a kind of trestle bridge about thirty

*Here omitted in view of the full report published in Series I, Vol. XXXVIII, Part I, p. 127; Vol. XLIV, p. 58, and Vol. XLVII, Part I, p. 169.

†Plate LXXVI, Map 2, and Plate C, Map 1, of the Atlas.

yards in length to approach the pontoons. This was done by the First Michigan Engineers and Seventeenth Army Corps pioneers.

Lieut. Col. William Tweeddale, with his regiment, the First Missouri Engineers, had charge of the pontoon train.

The pontoon train has most of the time been divided into two sections—one section moving with each army corps and each section being accompanied by a portion of the First Missouri Engineers.

The First Michigan Engineers moved with the Seventeenth Army Corps, but were under Captain Stickney's orders only on the occasion at the Roanoke River.

Following is a statement of places where pontoon bridges were laid:

April 14, over Neuse River, at Battle's Bridge, 160 feet.

April 29, over Neuse River, at Powell's Bridge, 200 feet.

May 3, over Roanoke River, at Robinson's Ferry, 740 feet.

May 13, over Pamunkey River, at Littlepage's Bridge, 200 feet.

May 18, over Occoquan River, at Occoquan, 280 feet.

—

*Narrative collated from the report of Lieutenant-Colonel and Brevet Brigadier-General Comstock, of the Corps of Engineers, of the 27th of January, 1865, addressed to General Terry, and copy to General Delafield, Chief Engineer.**

WAR DEPARTMENT, PAYMASTER-GENERAL'S OFFICE,
Washington, October 31, 1865.

Hon. EDWIN M. STANTON,
Secretary of War:

SIR: I have the honor to submit a report of the official transactions of the Pay Department of the Army for the fiscal year ending June 30, 1865.

The tabular statements herewith presented exhibit the details from which the following statement in gross is made:†

Balance in hands of paymasters and unissued requisitions in Treasury at beginning of fiscal year (July 1, 1864)	$86,039,808.87
Received from the Treasury during the fiscal year (including unissued requisitions in Treasury on June 30, 1865)	337,200,000.00
Received by paymasters from other sources, exclusive of sums transferred among themselves	6,815,137.50
Total to be accounted for	430,054,946.37
Accounted for as follows:	
Disbursements to the Regular Army	7,839,225.47
Disbursements to the Military Academy	153,099.11
Disbursements to the volunteers	300,738,635.95
Total disbursement	308,730,960.53
Amount of unissued requisitions in the Treasury on June 30, 1865	65,900,000.00
Balance actually in hands of paymasters on June 30, 1865	55,423,985.84
	430,054,946.37

This large amount in the hands of paymasters at the end of the fiscal year was an unavoidable necessity from the fact that at that

---

*Here omitted in view of the publication of full report in Series I, Vol. XLVI, Part I, p. 406.

†Tabular statements omitted in view of the general summary following.

precise period of time the department was everywhere throughout the country under the greatest pressure of payments to mustered-out troops, and money in large sums had to be kept thus distributed.

From the above it will be seen that the sum actually disbursed during the fiscal year and in process of disbursement at the end thereof was $430,054,946.37.

Since the beginning of the current fiscal year, besides the above sums in the hands of paymasters and the unissued requisitions stated, $94,000,000 have been disbursed and distributed for disbursement, making a total expenditure of $524,054,946.37 during the last fiscal year and the present one to this date.

Of this large sum more than one-half ($270,000,000) has been paid to disbanded volunteer troops mustered out of service.

From the early days of June to the present time this department has made final payment to more than 800,000 officers and men. The number paid cannot be definitely stated for the want of time for full official returns to be received from the many various and distant points of payment throughout the country, especially as these payments are still continuing. Enough, however, is known with certainty to establish the fact that the figures stated are not in excess.

This is an extraordinary exhibit of work performed chiefly within the three months of June, July, and August—$270,000,000 of money paid to 800,000 individual men. When the manner of these payments is observed, with a knowledge of the particularity required in each case—the accounts varying in amounts, each to be separately computed in its several items of pay, clothing, bounty, &c., with such stoppages as may be chargeable deducted; the final amount stated and the signature of each officer and man to be appended in duplicate to the receipt rolls—a just appreciation may be formed of the stupendous labor involved. No similar work of like magnitude, regarding its immensity both as to men and money and the small limit of time in which it has been performed, has, it is believed, any parallel in the history of armies.

The troops for discharge were, under the orders from the Adjutant-General's Office, transported to their respective State rendezvous as rapidly as the proper officers of the various organizations could dispatch the duty of mustering out.

This department engaged to prepare with funds officers at all the sixty different places of designated rendezvous throughout the States, and to make prompt payment in the shortest practicable time on the arrival of each organization, so as substantially to avert delays, with all their evil consequences, at the places of rendezvous. How far this pledge on our part has been redeemed the country can answer. The facts of record in the War Department show no delays of moment occurring in any quarter; none, at least, chargeable to this department. The work is mainly accomplished, satisfactorily accomplished, beyond the most sanguine anticipations of those who could understand and properly measure the vastness of the undertaking.

For this result the country is indebted largely to the zeal, intelligence, and sleepless industry of a corps of experienced paymasters who signalized themselves in this the closing act of their military staff service by a faithfulness and devotion which reflects the highest honor upon them as a body and as individual officers. To them, under the skillful management of their supervising district chiefs, this department owes its success; and I take occasion, as the head of the department, in this public official communication to render to them the homage of my grateful acknowledgments. The credit is theirs, for without their experience and cordial co-operative efforts not all the powers of the Government combined could have wrought so favorable a solution of a difficult problem.

It becomes my duty also to notice here, in most favorable terms, the valued services of the officers and clerks connected immediately with this office. They appreciated the emergency and bent themselves to the difficult work which, for a time, pressed upon the office with almost overwhelming weight. With payments simultaneously progressing at sixty different points, widely separated, with the necessity of keeping each one supplied with funds from day to day, and a necessity also that each should have no more than required for immediate disbursement—drawing from the Treasury at the rate of $20,000,000 per week and compelled to make close estimate and careful watch of its daily distribution, so that the demand at each given point should be surely supplied and yet no more than supplied; telegrams and letters continually pouring in noting the movement and destination of troops, and repeating these notices to the proper points of rendezvous; applications and appeals constantly arriving requiring immediate answers; new questions arising and referred to this office for instructions, &c.—kept our thoughts, our pens, our press, and the telegraph in constant requisition by day and by night. Mid all this I am happy to bear testimony that every one labored with cheerful alacrity—in some instances, indeed, during the heated season, even beyond their strength. It may be said of these, as I have said of the paymasters in the field—but for their willing efforts, rendered with self-denying devotion, the work could not have been a success.

The unstinted facilities extended, sir, by your authority and orders, in the free use of the military telegraph, the printing press, and all other agencies that could be profitably applied to the end, together with the liberal confidence which you were pleased to repose in this office, leaving to it an almost unrestricted discretion to manage, without hindrance, its own details; your concurrence in and support of its acts and orders—these reveal the vital secret of a result so favorable.

I cannot close this branch of my subject without a grateful expression of indebtedness to the officers of the Treasury Department for the courteous and zealous attention with which, during the trying exigency, they always entertained the importunate demands of this office. What often seemed as hopeless impossibilities obstructing the financial path were, by their fervent efforts, readily dispelled, and thus all our requisitions were met with most satisfactory promptness.

At the date of my last annual report, besides the small number of officers constituting the Pay Department of the Regular Army (and which is without casualty or change since), there were in the service 409 additional paymasters, contingent appointments under the law of July, 1838. Afterward, up to March 3, 38 others were appointed and confirmed, making a total of 447, accounted as follows: Resigned, 89; commission declined, 1; dismissed, 4; appointments canceled, 21; dropped, 2; died of disease, 5; lost at sea, 1; killed by guerrillas, 2; died while prisoner of war, 1; mustered out, 111; total casualties, 237; remaining in service, 210.

This reduction may still continue, following with even pace, as their services can be spared and their accounts be rendered, the progress of the reduction of the Army.

The sudden disbandment of our volunteer hosts, besides their final payment on the ordinary forms of muster-out rolls and other discharge papers, has devolved upon this department an inordinate accumulation of "referred claims" transmitted for adjustment and payment. These have arisen from various causes, but chiefly from the inability of the officers charged with the execution of the muster-out papers to reach a complete history as to pay, clothing, bounty, &c., of large numbers of enlisted men, so as to enable a final settlement at the time of discharge. To all such certificates of discharge are furnished, upon which are indorsed the fact of non-payment, and the holders are directed to forward the same, as the basis of their claim, to the Paymaster-General for adjustment.

Such magnitude has this demand attained that it has been found necessary to organize a special division of paymasters as an attachment of this Bureau to take exclusive cognizance of this class of claims.

This "division of referred claims" is now composed of a chief supervising paymaster of much intelligence, judgment, and experience, with twelve other paymasters; also competent officers of experience and a corps of sixty-four active clerks. The peculiar labors of this division could not be near so well performed under any other organization, having, as this does, enlightened paymasters to supervise every branch of the work, each being responsible for his own.

Every claim sent to this division requires for its elucidation a careful and laborious search through all the previous rolls on file in this and the Second Auditor's Office, besides constant reference to the Adjutant-General's Office, to trace out through the past records all the facts touching the case, the charges, stoppages, forfeitures, &c., that it may be stated with accuracy the balance due the claimant. This done, vouchers in form covering that balance are filled out and transmitted to the claimant for his signature, which returned to the paymaster, the latter remits a check for the amount. From this it will be seen how tedious is the work of this division, what careful industry it demands, and how inevitable are the delays complained of by impatient claimants.

The clerical force of this Bureau is without material change since the date of my last annual report.

For months past, in anticipation of an early permanent reduction of that force, I have refrained from recommending new appointments to fill such vacancies as have occurred by resignation and other casualties.

This course, I apprehend, may continue without injury or material inconvenience to the public service. Such, however, is the sudden accumulation of the business of the Bureau, by reason of the present influx for examination of rolls and other classes of vouchers, resulting from the recent and continued large payments to disbanded troops already adverted to, that but a very slight reduction in the number of clerks employed will be practicable for some months to come.

I need hardly urge the unqualified conviction that the compensation allowed by the Government to this indispensable class of public agents is quite inadequate in view of the present exorbitant cost of the necessaries of life. The clerks of this Bureau as a body are highly meritorious and deserving public servants. None, I am sure, better than they have by faithful industry earned just title to favorable consideration. It becomes my duty, therefore, respectfully, but urgently, to recommend a reasonable increase of the rates of compensation now by law fixed for the clerks employed in this Bureau. Especially is this demanded by every consideration of the public interest, of enlightened public economy, for the clerks of the higher grades and for the chief clerk. I feel sure I have only to present this subject to your attention to insure your influence in the furtherance of a consummation so proper.

In another paper communicated to you, dated the 11th instant, I have had the honor to submit for your consideration a plan for the better organization and a permanent increase of the Pay Department of the Army, to which I respectfully invite your attention in connection with this report.

The entire of the Regular Army and the volunteer forces of every description retained in service, and not embraced in orders for muster out, have been paid, or are provided for and in process of payment, to the end of the last fiscal year (to 1st of July last).

Many organizations have been paid to the later date of September 1.

All discharged troops have been paid in full, and all being discharged or under orders for discharge are provided for, and will be paid as fast as they arrive at their respective places of rendezvous.

Paymasters are held in readiness to make another payment to the troops who shall be continued in the service, whenever the needful funds for that purpose may be available.

In conclusion, I beg to present to your attention the following remarkable summary statement of the results in this department during the past four years of war:

The total of money disbursed by the department from July 1, 1861, to the present date is $1,029,239,000.

Total defalcations in the department for same period, supposing that nothing is made from sureties (it is believed that more than one-half will be collected from these sources)	$541,000
Total expenses for disbursements, including pay and allowances to paymasters and their clerks, mileage, and traveling expenses, &c., an average of 350 paymasters and 400 clerks for the term of four years and four months (a large average)	6,429,600
Total defalcations and expenses	6,970,600

Thus it is seen that the total of every character of expense to the Government arising from the disbursement of the pay to the armies during the period stated is less than seven-tenths of 1 per cent. of the sum disbursed.

Surely this is a cost most wonderfully cheap for the execution of duties so important and responsible. It is much questioned if there is another instance on record of public disbursement so cheaply performed.

Respectfully submitted.

B. W. BRICE,
Paymaster-General U. S. Army.

PROVOST-MARSHAL-GENERAL'S OFFICE,
Washington, D. C., November 1, 1865.

Brig. Gen. JAMES B. FRY,
Provost-Marshal-General of the United States:

GENERAL: In obedience to instructions I have the honor to submit the annual report of the operations of the Disbursing Branch of the

Provost-Marshal-General's Bureau for the year ending November 1, 1865:

Upon assuming the duties of this branch in March, 1865, it was not deemed necessary to make any changes in the system then in operation, which was fully described in the last annual report. No material change in the status of the employés of this Bureau had occurred up to the 31st day of March, 1865, from that shown in the annual report dated November 7, 1864, the number of persons employed and the salaries paid them being nearly alike at both dates. Since that time the number of employés and all expenditures have been reduced as rapidly as circumstances and the interests of the public service would permit.

The following exhibit of the employés of this Bureau as they stood on the 1st day of November, 1864, will, on comparison with the statement given on the succeeding page, show the relative status at the two dates:

State.	Number of districts.	Deputies.	Special agents.	Clerks.	Temporary clerks.	Assistant surgeons.	Janitors.	Civil guards.	Interpreters.	Watchmen.	To draw tickets.	Total.
Maine	5	14	25	17	46	5	4	......	....	....	1	112
New Hampshire	3	9	3	12	7	3	1	......	....	....	....	35
Vermont	3	7	3	11	3	2	1	......	....	....	....	27
Massachusetts	10	16	23	33	62	1	7	1	....	....	....	143
Rhode Island	2	4	10	6	2	2	1	......	....	....	....	25
Connecticut	4	3	5	11	13	3	4	......	....	....	....	39
New York	31	67	89	99	178	22	25	55	1	3	5	544
New Jersey	5	20	12	14	55	11	4	2	....	....	....	118
Pennsylvania	24	70	80	93	130	14	24	31	....	....	1	443
Delaware	1	8	7	3	8	1	1	......	....	....	....	28
Maryland	5	19	17	22	12	2	5	......	....	....	3	80
West Virginia	3	14	12	10	6	1	4	......	....	....	....	47
Kentucky	9	85	26	25	19	5	7	......	....	....	1	168
Ohio	19	60	58	63	153	15	11	19	....	....	4	383
Michigan	6	17	35	19	40	5	3	......	....	....	1	120
Indiana	11	59	23	28	68	7	3	7	....	....	....	195
Illinois	13	39	48	41	77	14	7	......	....	1	....	227
Iowa	6	52	15	16	16	6	7	......	....	....	1	113
Minnesota	2	25	8	9	14	2	3	......	....	....	1	62
Wisconsin	6	40	37	19	44	7	1	......	....	....	....	148
Missouri	9	57	22	22	2	8	4	......	....	....	....	115
District of Columbia	1	......	7	6	3	2	......	......	....	....	....	18
Kansas	2	4	4	7	......	1	......	......	....	....	....	16
Nebraska Territory	1	1	2	1	......	......	......	......	....	....	....	4
Colorado Territory	1	1	......	1	......	......	......	......	....	....	....	2
Dakota Territory	1	1	2	2	......	......	1	......	....	....	....	6
Nevada Territory	1	......	......	1	......	1	......	......	....	....	....	2
Washington Territory	1	2	......	2	......	......	1	......	....	....	....	5
California	3	4	4	6	......	......	2	......	....	....	....	16
Oregon	1	......	......	1	......	......	1	......	....	....	....	2
Total	189	698	577	600	958	140	132	115	1	4	18	3, 243

The subjoined statement will show the number and classification of all employés on duty in the offices of provost-marshals and acting assistant provost-marshals-general at this date:

State.	Number of districts.	Deputies.	Special agents.	Clerks.	Temporary clerks.	Assistant surgeons.	Janitors.	Civil guards.	Interpreters.	Watchmen.	To draw tickets.	Total.
Maine	5			5	1		1					7
New Hampshire	3			5								5
Vermont	3			5								5
Massachusetts	10			12			4					16
Rhode Island	2											
Connecticut	4			5			1					6
New York	31			42			11					53
New Jersey	5			7			3					10
Pennsylvania	24			25	1		10					36
Delaware	1			1			1					2
Maryland	5			7			1					8
District of Columbia	1			1								1
West Virginia	3			5			2					7
Kentucky	9			13	1		3					17
Missouri	9			11	1		4					16
Ohio	19			24			2					26
Indiana	11			13			5					18
Illinois	13			15			7					22
Michigan	6			8			1					9
Iowa	6			8			4					12
Wisconsin	6			8			2					10
Minnesota	2			4			1					5
Kansas	2			4			2					6
Nebraska Territory	1											
Colorado Territory	1											
Dakota Territory	1											
Oregon Territory	1											
Washington Territory	1											
California	3			6			3					9
Nevada	1											
Total	189			234	4		68					306

The number of clerks, messengers, and watchmen at present employed in the Disbursing Branch is as follows:

Office of—	Clerks.					Messengers, general service.	Messengers.	Watchmen.	Total.
	Fourth class.	Third class.	Second class.	First class.	Unclassified.				
Maj. H. R. Rathbone	1	2	3	7	1	2		2	18
Capt. R. Lodor, First and Second Divisions			3	3			1		7
Capt. S. Dana, Third and Fourth Divisions			4	6		1		1	12
Total	1	2	10	16	1	3	1	3	37

As rapidly as the number of employés was reduced and expenses curtailed it became necessary to reduce and consolidate the divisions of this branch, the first consolidation going into effect on the 1st day of June, 1865, at which date Capt. F. H. Barroll, disbursing officer in charge of Third Division, was relieved, and his duties transferred to Capt. S. Dana, in charge of Fourth Division, both divisions being consolidated in one.

The continued reduction of the business of this branch necessitated a still further consolidation, which took effect September 4, 1865, Bvt. Lieut. Col. J. McL. Hildt, disbursing officer in charge of First Division, being relieved on that date, and his duties transferred to Capt. R. Lodor, disbursing officer in charge of Second Division, both divisions being consolidated in one.

The number of letters received, letters sent, and indorsements made during the year ending November 1, 1865, is as follows:

Letters received	25,820
Letters sent	4,625
Indorsements made	3,830

The amount of funds received, disbursed, and turned over during the year ending November 1, 1865, on account of "enrollment and draft" is as follows:

Capt. James McMillan, formerly in charge of the First Division, received, disbursed, and turned over from November 1, 1864, to December 19, 1864 (the date at which he was relieved), the following amounts:

On hand November 1, 1864		$204,618.27
Received since		430,219.42
Total		634,837.69
Disbursed	$251,865.75	
Turned over	382,971.94	
Total disbursed and turned over		634,837.69

Capt. H. R. Rathbone, who succeeded Capt. James McMillan in charge of the First Division, received, disbursed, and turned over from December 20, 1864, to March 23, 1865 (the date at which he was relieved by Capt. J. McL. Hildt), the following amounts:

Received from Captain McMillan		$357,929.54
Received since		450,034.50
Total		807,964.04
Disbursed	$435,088.18	
Turned over	372,875.86	
Total disbursed and turned over		807,964.04

Capt. J. McL. Hildt, who succeeded Capt. H. R. Rathbone in charge of the First Division, received, disbursed, and turned over from March 23, 1865, to August 31, 1865 (the date at which he was relieved from duty in the Provost-Marshal-General's Bureau), the following amounts, viz:

Received from Capt. H. R. Rathbone		$267,875.86
Received since		450,302.99
Total		718,178.85
Disbursed	$436,905.18	
Turned over	281,273.67	
Total disbursed and turned over		718,178.85

Capt. R. Lodor, in charge of Second Division, has received, disbursed, and turned over from November 1, 1864, to November 1, 1865, the following amounts:

On hand October 31, 1864		$168,072.65
Received since		1,373,035.39

Received from Bvt. Lieut. Col. J. McL. Hildt September 1, 1865		$145,013.82
Total		1,686,121.86
Disbursed	$1,168,253.87	
Turned over	353,300.00	
Total disbursed and turned over		1,521,553.87
Balance on hand November 1, 1865		164,567.99

Capt. F. H. Barroll, formerly in charge of the Third Division, received, disbursed, and turned over from November 1, 1864, to June 1, 1865 (the date at which he was relieved from duty in the Provost-Marshal-General's Bureau), the following amounts, viz:

On hand November 1, 1864		$41,450.99
Received since		104,833.08
Total		146,284.07
Disbursed	$129,259.17	
Turned over	17,024.90	
Total disbursed and turned over		146,284.07

Capt. Samuel Dana, in charge of the Fourth Division, has received, disbursed, and turned over from November 1, 1864, to November 1, 1865, the following amounts:

On hand November 1, 1864		$84,881.44
Received since		575,659.45
Total		660,540.89
Disbursed	$588,213.45	
Turned over	14,000.00	
Total disbursed and turned over		602,213.45
Balance on hand November 1, 1865		58,327.44

Maj. T. C. English, Fifth U. S. Infantry, acting assistant provost-marshal-general for Portland, Oreg., has received, disbursed, and turned over from November 1, 1864, to August 31, 1865 (the date of his last report), the following amounts, viz:

On hand November 1, 1864	Nothing.
Received since	$51,000.00
Disbursed	27,418.26
Balance on hand August 1, 1865	23,581.74

Brig. Gen. John S. Mason, formerly acting assistant provost-marshal-general for San Francisco, Cal., received, disbursed, and turned over from November 1, 1864, to March 28, 1865 (the date of the transfer of the funds to Capt. H. B. Fleming, his successor), the following amounts, viz:

On hand November 1, 1864		$42,297.60
Received since		60,935.00
Total		103,232.60
Disbursed	$21,826.48	
Transferred	81,406.12	
Total disbursed and transferred		103,232.60

Capt. H. B. Fleming, Ninth U. S. Infantry, acting assistant provost-marshal-general for San Francisco, Cal., has received, disbursed, and turned over from March 28, 1865, to September 1, 1865 (the date of his last return), the following amounts, viz:

Received from Brigadier-General Mason		$55,406.12
Disbursed	$10,507.60	
Transferred	25,000.00	
Total disbursed and transferred		35,507.60
Balance on hand September 1, 1865		19,898.52

The amount of funds received, disbursed, and turned over during the year ending October 31, 1865, on account of incidental expenses, Quartermaster's Department, is as follows, viz:

Capt. F. H. Barroll, in charge of Third Division, has received, disbursed, and turned over from November 1, 1864, to June 1, 1865 (the date at which he was relieved), the following amounts, viz:

On hand November 1, 1864		$36,863.13
Received since		12,132.40
Total		48,995.53
Disbursed	$11,937.46	
Turned over	37,058.07	
Total disbursed and turned over		48,995.53

Capt. Samuel Dana, in charge of Fourth Division, has received, disbursed, and turned over from June 1, 1865, to November 1, 1865, the following amounts, viz:

On hand June 1, 1865		$37,058.07
Disbursed	$51.00	
Turned over	8.50	
Total disbursed and turned over		59.50
Balance on hand October 31, 1865		36,998.57

Capt. Hugh B. Fleming, Ninth U. S. Infantry, acting assistant provost-marshal-general for San Francisco, Cal., has received, disbursed, and turned over from March 28, 1865, to August 31, 1865 (the date of his last return), the following amounts, viz:

On hand	$500.00
Disbursed	170.12
Balance	329.88

Capt. S. Dana has received, disbursed, and turned over on account of the fund for sick and wounded soldiers during the past year the following amounts:

Received	$30,000.00
Disbursed	9,300.00
Balance on hand November 1, 1865	20,700.00

Total amount disbursed on account of enrollment and draft during the present year	3,175,744.06
Total amount disbursed on account of incidental expenses of Quartermaster's Department during the present year	12,158.58
Total amount disbursed in refunding commutation money to non-combatants, from the fund for "sick and wounded soldiers"	9,300.00

The amount of commutation money received by receivers thereof (collectors of internal revenue) and deposited by them to the credit of the Treasurer of the United States, from November 1, 1864, to November 1, 1865, is as follows:

On account of draft and substitutes		$317,130.00
On account of sick and wounded soldiers	$337,500.00	
There was also deposited to the credit of the Treasurer on account of sick and wounded soldiers by the Provost-Marshal-General, being funds turned over to him by the ex-Governor of Ohio	3,487.53	
		340,987.53
Total		658,117.53

There has been disbursed on account of the commutation fund the following amounts, as follows:

PERCENTAGE.

Amount disbursed to receivers in payment of the percentage allowed them in conformity with the rates established November 4, 1863, is from November 1, 1864, to November 1, 1865	$42,781.62
Amount reimbursed to receivers and paid to others for expenses of stationery, blanks, express charges, exchange, postage, &c., from November 1, 1864, to November 1, 1865	2,440.98

REFUNDED.

Amount refunded to persons who had paid commutation money and furnished substitutes and afterward were exempted for various causes, from November 1, 1864, to November 1, 1865:	
By disbursing officers of this branch	$39,970.00
By disbursing officers C., D., and O. Branch	10,500.00
Total	50,470.00

Thinking that a résumé of all transactions relating to the commutation fund would be more satisfactory, a statement is herewith appended showing the entire amounts received, disbursed, and turned over:

Amount of commutation money received—	
Prior to November 1, 1863	$10,518,000.00
From November 1, 1863, to October 31, 1864	15,188,699.25
Amount received from November 1, 1864, to November 1, 1865	657,817.53
Total commutation money received from July 22, 1863, to October 31, 1864	26,364,516.78
Amount deposited to credit of Provost-Marshal-General from July 22 to October 31, 1863	10,518,000.00
Provost-Marshal-General from November 1, 1863, to October 31, 1864	4,945,800.00
Amount deposited to credit of the Treasurer of the United States—	
From February 23, 1864, to October 31, 1864	10,242,599.25
From November 1, 1864, to November 1, 1865	658,117.53
Total deposits	26,364,516.78
Amount deposited on account of—	
Appropriation for draft and substitutes	25,902,029.25
Sick and wounded	462,487.53
Total	26,364,516.78
Amount of commutation money deposited by receivers to credit of the Treasurer of the United States	10,900,716.78
Balance in the hands of the Provost-Marshal-General deposited to the credit of the Treasurer in compliance with the joint resolution of Congress	7,439,035.20

Amount deposited to credit of the Treasurer of the United States by Capt. J. McL. Hildt	$270.00
Total	18,340,021.98
Amount of commutation money deposited to the credit of the Provost-Marshal-General	15,463,800.00
Amount donated	900.00
Amount left by deserters	742.50
Amount of tax	33.45
Amount turned over by mustering and disbursing officers	200,000.00
Total	15,665,475.95
Amount disbursed and turned over to mustering and disbursing officers by Provost-Marshal-General	8,226,440.75
Amount turned over to Treasurer of the United States by Provost-Marshal-General	7,439,035.20
Total	15,665,475.95

At the date of the last annual report the total number of officers and employés of the Provost-Marshal-General's Bureau was 4,716, at a cost per month of $311,868.60. The number now on duty and in the employ of the Bureau is 383, at a cost per month of $35,050.32. It is thought that no further requisitions for funds need be made by this branch.

I am, general, very respectfully, your obedient servant,

H. R. RATHBONE,
Major and Asst. Adjt. Gen., in Charge Disbursing Branch.

WAR DEPARTMENT, ADJUTANT-GENERAL'S OFFICE,
Washington, November 3, 1865.

His Excellency CHARLES ANDERSON,
Governor of Ohio, Columbus:

SIR: I have the honor to acknowledge the receipt of your letter of the 27th ultimo relative to the muster out of Ohio regiments, and in which you refer to your letter of September 16 past, giving in full your views on the subject.

The attention of the Secretary of War has this date been invited to both communications, and in reply I have the honor to inform you that your letter of the 16th of September was received during the absence of the Secretary and was not then considered by him, but referred to the General-in-Chief for his information and retained at his headquarters until receipt of your recent letter. No reply to it was sent you, but the views expressed, taken in connection with similar ones from authorities of other States, were duly considered, and no means have been spared to hasten the muster out of volunteer organizations as rapidly as their services could be dispensed with.

Since the letter of September 16 many Ohio organizations have been discharged, and of the eighteen (seventeen regiments and one battery) yet reported as in service thirteen regiments are in Texas. Major-General Sheridan has recently ordered the discharge of some additional troops, and it is believed that some from your State will be embraced, although the organizations selected have not yet been reported. All volunteer troops are being relieved in the field and mustered out as rapidly as the public interest will permit; but as from necessity some organizations have to be retained longer than others, an order for the discharge of all at the same time cannot be given.

The attention of the commanding general of the Department of the Missouri has been invited to the discharge of the Eleventh Ohio Cavalry, specially referred to in your letter of the 27th ultimo.

I have the honor to remain, sir, very respectfully, your obedient servant,

THOMAS M. VINCENT,
Assistant Adjutant-General.

WASHINGTON, *November 6, 1865.*

Maj. Gen. G. G. MEADE,
Commanding Military Division of the Atlantic:

In view of the peaceful condition of the South, I think now the number of interior posts held may be materially reduced in number, and where regular troops are used they can generally be one and two company posts. In this way you may be enabled to discharge from service most of the white volunteers still remaining within your command.

I wish you would send one or more of your staff officers through the Southern States of the command with full instructions to designate the posts to be held [and] the garrisons to be put in them. Let all surplus troops then be mustered out of service. Instruct your inspectors to see that all previous orders for the reduction of transportation and expenses in every way be carried out. Let them also report all public property which in their judgment may be removed or sold with advantage to the public service.

Property is many times so scattered as to make a large force necessary for performing guard duty alone, where, but for the public property to be cared for, but few troops would be necessary. Let this subject receive attention also.

U. S. GRANT,
Lieutenant-General.

QUARTERMASTER-GENERAL'S OFFICE,
Washington, November 8, 1865.

Hon. EDWIN M. STANTON,
Secretary of War:

SIR: I have the honor to submit the annual report of operations of the Quartermaster's Department during the fiscal year ending 30th of June, 1865:

On the 1st of July, 1864, the balance of appropriation in the Treasury undrawn was	$8,699,768.16
Appropriation for fiscal year ending 30th of June, 1865	199,250,000.00
Deficiency bill, March 2, 1865	83,181,137.00
Appropriation for fiscal year ending 30th of June, 1866	168,500,000.00
Total	459,630,905.16
Requisitions on Treasury in fiscal year ending 30th of June, 1865	431,706,057.44
Balance remaining 30th of June, 1865	27,924,847.72

A financial statement in detail will be found in a table at the end of this report.

This department is charged with the duty of providing means of transportation by land and water for all the troops and for all the material of war. It furnishes the horses for artillery and cavalry, and the horses and mules of the wagon trains; provides and supplies tents, camp and garrison equipage, forage, lumber, and all materials for camps and for shelter of the troops. It builds barracks, hospitals, and store-houses; provides wagons and ambulances, harness, except for cavalry and artillery horses; builds or charters ships and steamers, docks, and wharves; constructs and repairs roads, railroads, and their bridges; clothes the Army, and is charged generally with the payment of all expenses attending military operations not assigned by law or regulation to some other department.

While the Ordnance Department procures and issues arms and ammunition, and the Subsistence Department supplies provisions, and the Medical Department medical and hospital stores, the Quartermaster's Department is called upon to transport the stores of all these departments from the depots to the camps, upon the march, and to the battle-field, where they are finally issued to the troops.

These duties have been efficiently performed during the year.

In the last, as in former years of the war, under the energetic and liberal administration of the War Department, the wants of the troops have been regularly supplied, their comfort, health, and efficiency have been amply and regularly provided for. The Army itself does justice to the wise and enlarged administration which has enabled it to move successfully in a field of warfare constantly widening.

Atlanta, the key of the rebel defense, was secured after a campaign involving a line of operations of 300 miles in length, maintained for months through a hostile country so effectually as to enable an army of 90,000 men, with over 40,000 animals, to subsist not only while advancing, but, what is much more difficult, while laying siege for weeks to that advanced position.

The enemy's army, driven from Atlanta, but still formidable in numbers and in courage, threw itself upon this long line of operations—two slender rods of iron, crossing wide rivers, winding through mountain gorges, plunging under the mountain ranges, and everywhere exposed to the raids of an enterprising enemy, favored by the thick forests which bordered the railroad throughout nearly its whole extent.

The guards of the posts upon the line of communication did their duty, and the Railroad Construction Corps of this department, thoroughly organized, strong in numbers, in skill, and in discipline, repaired broken bridges and railroads. New engines from the workshops of the North replaced those which torpedoes or broken rails threw from the track. Trains loaded with timber, with iron, with water and fuel for the engines, preceded the trains of subsistence and ammunition, and scarce was the communication broken before it was re-established.

The conquering army followed the desperate garrison of Atlanta and drove him off the lines of communication. The railroad was worked night and day to its full capacity; supplies for a new campaign for an army of 90,000 men were poured into Atlanta. All surplus stores, all sick and all enfeebled men were sent by railroad to the rear, and the army of General Sherman, with its 3,000 wagons full loaded with every material of war, accompanied by droves of many thousand beef-cattle, re-enforced by the return of those who, disabled in the earlier events of the campaign, had been recruited in the hospitals of Nashville, 300 miles to the rear, and forwarded by railroad to resume their places in its ranks, marched out of Atlanta, blew up that depot, destroyed all the railroads which made that city of value in the war, and bent its steps toward the ocean.

In no other country have railroads been brought to perform so important a part in the operations of war. Scarce in any other country could be found the workmen to perform the feats of construction which have illustrated this campaign.

At no time during the march from Chattanooga to Atlanta were the railroad trains five days behind the general commanding.

The reconstruction of the bridges over the Etowah and the Chattahoochee are unparalleled feats of military construction.

The Etowah bridge, 625 feet long, 75 feet high, was burned by the rebels, and was rebuilt by the labor of 600 men of the Construction Corps in six days.

The Chattahoochee bridge, six miles from Atlanta, is 740 feet long and 90 feet high, and was built in four and a half days by 600 men of the Construction Corps.

The army under General Sherman moved southeast from Atlanta; it plunged into the forests and sands of Georgia and was lost to our view. The rebel army moved into Tennessee and advanced upon Nashville, to be dashed in pieces against the army of Major-General Thomas, and thus perished the last great army of the rebellion in the central South and West, east of the Mississippi.

The rebel press reported defeats, disasters, repulses to the army, with which we had no communication. No anxiety as to their fate oppressed the minds of those who had in the War Department directed the measures and provisions for their equipment for this bold and decisive march. A bare possibility that, by the abandonment of all eastern positions, the rebel Army of Virginia might throw itself across Sherman's path, induced the department to order supplies to Pensacola, to relieve any immediate wants should the army be obliged to move southward; but the great work of preparation to meet and refit this army upon the southeastern Atlantic Coast was at once commenced and steadily prosecuted. While a few vessels went to Pensacola to await orders, a great fleet of transports was collected at Port Royal, laden with everything that experience indicated as necessary to repair the consumption and the losses of this adventurous march. Clothing, shoes, shelter tents, forage, provisions, spare parts of wagons, wagons complete, harness, leather, wax, thread, needles, and tools for all the trades which were plied on the march and in the camp were collected in the harbor of Hilton Head.

All this was done in the dead of winter. Light-draft, frail river steamers trusted themselves, under daring Yankee captains and crews, to the storms of the stormiest coast of the world, and all arrived safely at their destination. And here let me pay a tribute to those gallant seamen of the merchant shipping of the Nation, who in war entered its transport fleet. No service has been so difficult or so tedious—none so dangerous as to discourage or to daunt them.

No call for volunteers has ever failed to meet a ready response, whether to tempt the shoals and storms of a tempestuous coast, the hidden and mysterious dangers of the dark bayous of the South, strewn with torpedoes by the devilish ingenuity of deserters from our own military and naval service, or to run in frail river steam-boats the batteries of the Potomac, the James, and the Pamlico, or the still more formidable works of Vicksburg. Urged by the spirit of adventure, supported by the patriotism of freemen, they have always stood ready, and have cheerfully obeyed every order, incurred every risk.

On the 13th of December Fort McAllister fell before the assault of General Sherman's veterans. The transport fleet was ordered at once to the mouths of the Ogeechee and of the Savannah. The city of Savannah was carried within a few days, and a wrecking party, then employed upon the coast of Florida, with all the ingenious equipment which modern science has contrived for submarine operations, was towed by a steamer to the Savannah River and set to work to remove the formidable obstacles to its navigation. These for four years seemed to have employed all the ingenuity and mechanical skill of the people, who had torn up the pavements of their commercial streets to supply material to obstruct the channels of their harbor.

In a few days a passage was cleared, and the steamers and vessels of the transport fleet discharged their cargoes at the long-disused and dilapidated wharves of Savannah, and sailed for the North richly freighted with captured cotton.

On the 22d of January General Sherman again moved northward.

A division of the Railroad Construction Corps had been ordered from the Tennessee to the Savannah to meet him. It had crossed the Alleghanies in midwinter and was promptly at the rendezvous with men and officers and all tools, materials, and machinery for rebuilding the railroads of the coast.

It was decided not to operate directly against Charleston, the great stronghold of the rebellion, which had for four years defied our ships and the forces we could spare for the siege. The wiser and more daring plan of marching inland, cutting off its means of supply, capturing the capital, and devastating the agricultural portion of the State, was pursued.

Charleston soon fell and the Construction Corps was moved to Morehead City, there to open up the railroad from the harbor of Beaufort, N. C., toward Kinston, at which point General Sherman, when I parted from him in January—his army reclad, reshod, supplied, and ready to resume its march—told me to look out for him next.

His chief quartermaster, General Easton, who had accompanied the army in its march from Chattanooga to Savannah, remained on the coast, taking charge of the fleet loaded with supplies. The fleet and supplies were transferred to the harbor of Beaufort. Fort Fisher fell in January and the Cape Fear River was opened to our transports. The troops which had captured, with the aid of the navy, the defenses at the mouth of this river, re-enforced by the Twenty-third Army Corps, which in January was transferred from the Tennessee to the Atlantic, captured Wilmington and advanced toward Goldsborough. The two railroads, each ninety-five miles in length, from Wilmington and from Morehead City to Goldsborough, were repaired by the Construction Corps. They were stocked with cars and engines, and when the Right Wing of General Sherman's army entered Goldsborough on the 22d of March it met supplies of provisions brought by the railroads from the transport fleet on the coast, and found Goldsborough occupied by a corps which on the 15th of January had been encamped on the banks of the Tennessee.

Again was the army supplied with full equipment of clothing, shoes, and of all the various articles of necessity for itself and its trains, worn out in the long march from Savannah, and by the 10th of April, the appointed day, fully equipped, it moved against the enemy at Raleigh.

Upon the surrender of the rebel armies in Virginia and North Carolina the armies of General Sherman and of Lieutenant-General Grant marched for Washington, where they were reviewed by the President and Cabinet, after which they went into camp on the heights surrounding the capital, and the preparations for their transfer to other fields of operation and for their disbandment were made.

While the coast was the scene of the efforts of the department to support and supply the army of General Sherman, the armies in front of Richmond also required a vast expenditure. These armies were stronger in numbers than General Sherman's. Their equipment for march as well as for siege was constantly kept in the highest state of efficiency. The country in which they lay furnished no supplies, and food and forage and all stores were brought by rail and by sea from the North and Northwest. The shipments of forage alone to the armies on the James averaged over $1,000,000 per month throughout the winter.

The tables at the end of this report give information as to the strength of the fleet and the magnitude of the operations involved in the supply from distant ports of an army over 100,000 in strength, with at times over 5,000 wagons to keep in repair and over 65,000 animals, horses, and mules to be fed.

From the depots in the West, under the general direction of Bvt. Maj. Gen. Robert Allen, senior quartermaster in the Mississippi Valley, the wants of the armies on the Tennessee, the Cumberland, the Mississippi, the Missouri, the Arkansas, and the Gulf of Mexico were supplied.

The Northwest was the store-house from which were drawn subsistence, forage, and all other material which, by steam-boats and railroad trains, were distributed to the posts.

Lists of steamers employed on the Atlantic, upon the Gulf, and upon the Western rivers are attached to this report.

The transport fleet exceeded 1,000 vessels of every variety of construction, impelled by sail or steam. Details of this fleet and its cost will be found in another part of this report.

Great movements of troops continued to be made. The army of General Thomas, having dispersed the rebel army in the campaign which culminated in the battle of Nashville, on the 15th and 16th of December, 1864, and the pursuit which followed it, was divided. The Twenty-third Corps, under General Schofield, 15,000 strong, was in January, as hereinafter detailed, transported to the coast of North Carolina to co-operate with General Sherman, expected at Kinston. The Sixteenth Corps, under General A. J. Smith, 17,000 strong, with artillery and baggage trains, was sent to New Orleans to co-operate with the troops then under General Canby in the reduction of Mobile.

The cavalry, under Major-General Wilson, was refitted, remounted, equipped, and launched into the interior of Alabama to capture the principal interior cities of Alabama and Georgia. Selma, Montgomery, Columbus, and Macon fell before them.

In all these movements the troops were kept well supplied with the necessary material. Horses, forage, food, and clothing were promptly delivered at the appointed rendezvous and depots, and steamers were ready on river and coast to move the troops and their supplies promptly.

During the whole year—I believe I may say during the whole war—no movement was delayed, no enterprise failed, for want of means of transportation or the supplies required from the Quartermaster's Department.

The close of hostilities made even greater exertions on the part of this department necessary. Two hundred and thirty-three thousand men were distributed from Washington alone to their homes in the North—carried to every hamlet and village, camps of discharge being established in every State, at which the regiments rendezvoused until paid off, when the men dispersed.

Sixty thousand men of the army of General Sherman were moved from Washington to Louisville, from which place, after a short time, they were put in motion for their homes and discharged. Twenty-five thousand men were moved from the James River to the Rio Grande. Seven thousand were sent from the Potomac to Savannah. Sixty thousand prisoners of war, released, were sent to their homes in the Southern States.

Regiments were brought from the Gulf and South Atlantic coasts and sent to their States to be discharged. Their places were in some cases supplied by the transfer to the South of the regiments which had longer to serve. A large force of cavalry was moved from the Potomac to the Arkansas and to the Western plains.

The activity of the transportation branch of this department has never been greater than since the cessation of hostilities, its duty embracing the transportation to their homes of the greater part of an army of a million men, the collection and transportation to depots, for storage or for sale, of the animals and stores surplus from the rapid reduction in the forces employed.

Officers were sent to inspect the various depots and posts to report what stores should be sold and what preserved. Stringent orders were issued directing reductions in purchases, in lists of persons employed, ordering the sale of surplus material, the reduction of the strength of the trains, the sale of all surplus animals of the cavalry, artillery, and trains, and the discharge or sale of transports not needed for the returning troops. Reports in detail herewith contain such information as to these operations as can be collected at this time and embraced within the limits of this report.

The examination, collation, and analysis of the records of this department are not complete. The material is abundant, and I propose, with your approbation, to establish a board of officers whose business it shall be to collect from the official reports full statistics of the vast operations which, during the last four years, have taxed the fullest energies of every officer of ability and experience in this department.

The work has been accomplished, the record is in possession of the office, but the labors of execution have not left leisure for that examination and comparison of the records which is necessary for a full statistical report of operations of this department during the four years of war.

In the last annual report I had the honor to make nominal report of the officers who held the most important and responsible positions in this department during the previous year, and to call attention to their merits and their worth. Many of these officers have received the promotion which they have so well deserved, and which they so highly prize as the recognition by their Government of faithful service. I am grateful for the recognition of the service and success of the department under my control thus given to its officers.

The general distribution of duties has not materially varied during the year. The officers had, in the course of three years of active service, generally found the positions in which their respective qualities made them of the greatest service to their country.

Bvt. Maj. Gen. Robert Allen continued to exercise the authority and control with which he had been invested as senior and supervising quartermaster in the Valley of the Mississippi. His duties have remained the same as during the previous years. His annual report is herewith. Had it been more full in detail it would have given a better idea of the magnitude of his responsibilities, his labors, and his merits. There passed through his hands during the fiscal year $33,933,646.45.

Bvt. Maj. Gen. Rufus Ingalls continued in the field to control the service of the quartermaster's department with the armies operating under Lieutenant-General Grant against Richmond.

The admirable manner in which the duties of his post were performed is shown in the efficiency of the operations which supplied the troops during the long siege and the rapid marches which, after the enemy was driven from his works, resulted in the capture of his entire army. The disbursements have been (under his direction) $1,636,759.08, principally for wages of workmen. The supplies for this army were purchased under direction of this office and shipped to it from the depots at the North, as required.

Bvt. Maj. Gen. D. H. Rucker has continued in charge of the great depot of Washington, the depot through which a great part of the supplies of the armies before Richmond and upon the Atlantic Coast passed. Here the animals and the clothing for these armies were collected. To this point their worn-out and disabled animals and equipment were returned for recuperation or repair, or to be disposed of and replaced.

Upon this depot, after the fall of Richmond, 250,000 troops were concentrated, and here were made all the arrangements for their transportation to the West and North before their final dispersion. The expenditures of the year under his direction have been $8,822,065.33.

Bvt. Maj. Gen. James L. Donaldson has continued in charge of the great base of supplies of the armies of Sherman and Thomas. He is now supervising quartermaster of the Military Division of the Tennessee, and is engaged in the supply of the troops still quartered in the South and in returning them as discharged to their homes, and in disposing of the vast accumulation of stores no longer needed since the cessation of hostilities and consequent reduction of the Army. He has controlled the expenditure of $24,821,005.79.

Bvt. Brig. Gen. Thomas Swords, senior quartermaster in the Department of the Ohio, assisted by Colonel Moulton, has been in charge of the operations of the department at the important depot of Cincinnati, which has furnished nearly one-third of the clothing for the armies of the United States. He has received and distributed to other officers or disbursed during the year $17,402,501.95.

Bvt. Brig. Gen. G. H. Crosman, who had been on duty in Philadelphia from the 30th of August, 1861, to the 24th of August, 1864, in charge of the Philadelphia depot and the providing of clothing and equipage, was then temporarily relieved by Col. A. J. Perry, chief of the division of clothing and equipage. He has since been engaged in preparing a manual of the service of the Quartermaster's Department, intended to fix the forms, sizes, and construction and qualities of the various articles of equipment which are supplied by the Quartermaster's Department, in order that the experience gained in all these details may not be lost, but may be at hand to instruct the officers of the department in future operations. The records and details of these models should be preserved. They have enabled our armies to make unexampled marches with less suffering, privation, sickness, and loss than we find recorded in the history of the campaigns of other nations. His disbursements have been during the year $6,274,278.55.

Bvt. Brig. Gen. D. H. Vinton has continued at the head of the depot of clothing and equipage at New York. No officer has more thoroughly and efficiently performed his duty. He has received and expended $34,637,511.11.

Bvt. Brig. Gen. L. C. Easton, chief quartermaster of the army of General Sherman, accompanied that army in its campaign from Chattanooga, and during the siege of Atlanta superintended its outfit for and accompanied its march to the sea. At Savannah he took charge of the transport fleet and of the stores sent to meet the army on the coast, conducted them to the coast of North Carolina, and sent forward the supplies which, by the 10th of April, enabled it again to march against the rebels at Raleigh. After the dispersion and reduction of the army he was assigned to duty as chief quartermaster at the headquarters of the major-general commanding the Military Division of the Mississippi, with his post at Saint Louis, where he exercises a general supervision and control. He has received and accounted for $981,822.27.

Bvt. Brig. Gen. Charles Thomas, assistant quartermaster-general, has aided me in the management of the business of this office, having charge of the finances and accounts of the office.

Bvt. Brig. Gen. William Myers, as chief assistant to General Robert Allen in the Mississippi Valley, has been in charge of the depot at Saint Louis. His responsibilities have been great and have been met to the satisfaction and approbation of his senior officers. General Allen, in his report, speaks of him in the highest terms. He reports the receipt and expenditure or transfer of $49,871,975.35.

Bvt. Brig. Gen. Stewart Van Vliet has continued at New York in charge of the operations of the department at that important post. His disbursements and transfers during the year have reached the sum of $20,170,162.60.

Col. C. W. Moulton has been, during a portion of the fiscal year, in charge of the clothing and equipage depot at Cincinnati. He reports the receipt and expenditure of $31,287,324.49.

Bvt. Brig. Gen. George S. Dodge, chief quartermaster of the Army of the James, accompanied the naval and military expedition which reduced Fort Fisher, on the coast of North Carolina. He displayed great energy and skill in disembarking upon an open coast men and material for the siege and assault of that formidable work, and was specially rewarded by brevet promotion for signal services on that occasion. He has since been actively employed in extensive inspections, both North and South, which have been most efficiently performed and have aided this department in enforcing great reductions of expenditure. He is a most deserving officer.

Col. William W. McKim, for some time in charge of the depot of Cincinnati, has been in charge of the depot at Philadelphia, including the operations of the great depot of clothing and equipage at the Schuylkill Arsenal, since the 15th of February last. He is a most efficient and deserving officer. He reports an expenditure during the year of $24,986,188.16.

The depot of Baltimore has been in charge of Col R. M. Newport since the 24th of September, 1864. In the earlier part of the fiscal year it was under charge of Maj. C. W. Thomas, Quartermaster's Department. Colonel Newport's expenditures and transfers are reported at $8,167,971.73.

Col. S. B. Holabird has continued on duty at New Orleans, where his long experience and his business capacity have made his service most valuable. He accompanied the army of General Banks to Louisiana when that officer first assumed command in the Southwest, and has always been zealous and successful in the discharge of the heavy duties which have been imposed upon him. His receipts, transfers, and expenditures during the year were $15,290,396.67.

Col. C. G. Sawtelle, as chief quartermaster of the command, first of General Canby, and lately of the troops and military division under Major-General Sheridan, has rendered most valuable service. As chief quartermaster of General Canby's army, he directed the operations of the quartermaster's department in the movements against Mobile. After the fall of Mobile, and the assignment of Major-General Sheridan to command in the Southwest, he was attached to his staff as chief quartermaster of the military division, and forwarded the army which was sent from New Orleans to Texas, including the later movements of the Twenty-fifth Army Corps, which, embarking on the James, rendezvoused on the northern coast of the Gulf of Mexico, before proceeding to Texas. He reports the receipt, transfer, and expenditure during the fiscal year of $684,857.45.

The principal disbursements in the command to which he is attached have been made by officers at depots.

The limits of this report will not permit me to notice here all the officers of the department who have held important positions during the extended operations of the last year of this most active and eventful war. I mention the names merely of some of the officers whose merits have promoted them to most important positions.

Lists of officers of the Quartermaster's Department who have served as chief quartermasters of armies, of great territorial divisions, and in charge of important depots, and of those who have been specially noted in the records received at this office for good service, are attached to this report.

The officers who have been my personal assistants in charge of the several divisions of this office are noticed in referring to the branches of the service in which they have had special control.

HORSES AND MULES.

The purchase and supply of the animals of the Army pertains to the First Division of this office, of which Bvt. Brig. Gen. James A. Ekin, of the Quartermaster's Department, has charge. He reports:

Purchases of cavalry horses during the year ending June 30, 1865	141,632
Total from January 1, 1864, to May 9, 1865, at which time purchases ceased	193,388
Of artillery horses, from September 1, 1864, to June 30, 1865, purchases having ceased May 9	20,714
Of mules, from July 1, 1864, to June 30, 1865, purchases having ceased May 9	58,818

The earlier purchases of horses delivered in Washington at the beginning of the war were at $125. Subsequently, for a time, horses were delivered here as low as $100. The price gradually advanced until the close of the war.

The prices of cavalry horses during the last fiscal year have varied from	$144 to $185
Of artillery horses	161 to 185
Of mules	170 to 195

There have been sold at the depots since January 1, 1864, of cavalry horses	40,070
There have died at these depots	38,277
Artillery horses reported as having died at the depots, September 1, 1864, to June 30, 1865	434
Mules sold September 1, 1864, to June 30, 1865	13,479
Died in depots in same time	7,336

The deaths reported occurred at depots principally among animals sent in from the field as broken down and unserviceable.

The destruction in the field was greater, probably nearly equaling the number supplied by purchase and capture, as neither the trains nor the cavalry of the armies have been materially increased during the last year of the war, and the purchases have been almost entirely to supply losses.

The issues of cavalry horses to the Army of the Shenandoah, actively engaged under Major-General Sheridan, have been at the rate of three remounts per annum. The service of a cavalry horse under an enterprising commander has therefore averaged only four months.

Of the animals which are sent to the depots for recuperation about 60 per cent. recovered, and, becoming serviceable, have again been issued.

SALES.

There have been sold, so far as reported, to October 17, and since May 8, 1865, and in accordance with General Orders, No. 28, of the Quartermaster-General's Office, dated May 8, 1865, 53,794 horses and 52,516 mules, for the sum of $6,107,618.14. It is probable that when the full returns are received the total amount of sales from May 8 to October 17 will prove to exceed $7,000,000.

With few exceptions these sales have been made by persons employed at fixed daily rates by the Quartermaster's Department. In a few cases officers who have failed to receive the general order of the Quartermaster-General prescribing this mode of sale have employed local auctioneers at various rates of compensation. The results in most cases have been less satisfactory than when the sales have been made in the first mode, and such sales have given rise to some complaints of excessive fees. All the officers of the department now, it is believed, have received General Orders, No. 42, Quartermaster-General's Office, 1865, and understand their duty in this respect.

General Ekin names the officers who have acted under his orders in the business of providing and disposing of animals of the Army, and bears testimony to their good service, for which I respectfully refer to his report, herewith.

He reports the expenditures of the fiscal year as follows:

On hand July 1, 1864, and received during the fiscal year		$8,501,078.84
Expended	$3,719,070.13	
Transferred to officers	4,295,963.72	
		8,015,033.85
Remaining to his credit June 30, 1865		486,044.99

Estimates of quartermasters for purchase of horses, submitted to and approved by him during the year:	
For horses	23,600,456.66
For mules	6,434,637.66
Total	30,035,094.32

CLAIMS FOR ANIMALS.

Under the law of July 4, 1864, 4,174 claims for animals have been filed in the First Division of the Quartermaster-General's Office; of these 2,792 have been acted on, leaving 1,382 not acted on. This business is increasing rapidly.

General Ekin states, succinctly, some of the difficulties attending just decisions upon these claims. Generally when the animals have been taken by officers of this department, reference to the official records shows that they have been properly reported and accounted for.

But when officers' papers have been captured by the enemy or destroyed, and where the seizure has been made by officers not of the Quartermaster's Department, as many of the officers have been discharged from the service, it is difficult to communicate with them by letter, and to ascertain whether the signatures and memorandum receipts offered in evidence are true or forged. To arrive at certain conclusions upon evidence entirely *ex parte*, and without cross-examination, is impossible, and this department will be unable to arrive at that conviction necessary to enable it to report many claims, some of them no doubt just, without some further action. It may, after a time, become expedient to create boards of officers to visit the localities in which most of these claims originate, and there take testimony as to the facts, the truth of the documentary evidence presented, and especially as to the loyalty of the claimants and witnesses. Judging from the papers presented with these claims, there are few persons unable to present certificates of loyalty.

Copies of the more important orders regulating the mode of purchasing and disposing of public animals accompany this report.

They are the result of the experience gained during a great war, in which the consumption of horses and mules has been very large. The specifications have been amended from time to time as experience has shown defects.

Under the system which these orders and regulations set forth the Army has been well supplied with animals adapted to the military service. The order, regularity, and abundance of supply, the correctness and clearness of the record of this branch of the service, since the organization of the First Division of this office, are most creditable to Bvt. Brig. Gen. James A. Ekin, who has been at its head.

CLOTHING AND EQUIPAGE.

The clothing and equipage of the Army are provided by contract, by purchase, and by manufacture at the several principal depots, which during the fiscal year have been:

New York depot, under charge of Bvt. Brig. Gen. D. H. Vinton, Quartermaster's Department.

Philadelphia depot, under charge, successively, of Bvt. Brig. Gen. G. H. Crosman, Col. A. J. Perry, Col. and Bvt. Brig. Gen. H. Biggs, and Col. W. W. McKim, who is still in charge.

Cincinnati depot, under charge of Bvt. Brig. Gen. Thomas Swords, Col. C. W. Moulton, Col. W. W. McKim, who, on his transfer to Philadelphia, was relieved by Col. C. W. Moulton.

Saint Louis depot, under charge of Bvt. Brig. Gen. William Myers, Quartermaster's Department.

There are several branch depots established at points at which the war had collected many destitute women, either of the families of refugees or of soldiers, whom employment in making up army clothing relieved from dependence upon public charity.

These depots were supplied with material from the three principal depots of New York, Philadelphia, and Cincinnati, and their operations were confined to the making up of such material into garments.

Such depots are established at Quincy, Ill., and Steubenville, Ohio.

The quality of the clothing and equipment furnished to the Army has been excellent; very few complaints of inferior quality have been made, considering the immense quantity of material which has been issued to the troops. The marches made from Atlanta to Savannah, and from Savannah to Goldsborough, by armies which during their marches had no opportunity to replace articles of equipment worn out, are evidence of the good quality of the shoes and clothing with which the Army is supplied.

Of the principal articles of clothing and equipage the following quantities have been purchased and manufactured at the three principal depots during the fiscal year ending June 30, 1865:

Article	Quantity	Article	Quantity
Uniform coats	311,597	Blouses	2,617,374
Uniform jackets	410,667	Shoes ....pairs	1,688,017
Uniform trousers	3,463,858	Boots ....do	959,543
Drawers	3,708,393	Stockings ....do	5,684,572
Shirts, flannel	3,268,166	Hats	442,832
Greatcoats	873,289	Caps	1,151,948
Blankets:		Knapsacks	958,287
Woolen	1,746,034	Haversacks	1,066,647
Waterproof	625,624	Guidons	1,293
Canteens	1,163,347	Picks	42,446
Hospital tents	10,265	Axes	108,196
Wall-tents	8,412	Spades and shovels	150,931
Wedge or common tents	1,412	Hatchets	88,054
Shelter tents	698,187	Mess-pans	169,296
Bedsacks	19,610	Camp-kettles	73,895
Regimental colors	1,321	Bugles	3,795
Camp colors	4,167	Drums	16,330
National colors	760	Fifes	1,400
Flags	4,185		

The stock on hand ready for issue on the 30th of June, 1865, but not transferred to the armies for issue, was:

Article	Quantity	Article	Quantity
Uniform coats	462,105	Camp-kettles	106,417
Uniform jackets	504,811	Knapsacks	868,578
Uniform trousers	1,185,234	Haversacks	522,621
Drawers	1,166,541	Canteens	845,209
Shirts, flannel	1,542,294	Hospital tents	6,121
Greatcoats	929,725	Wall-tents	15,672
Blankets:		Wedge or common tents	53,902
Woolen	1,009,106	Shelter tents	791,254
Waterproof	384,975	Bedsacks	167,037
Blouses	1,410,059	Regimental colors	789
Shoes ....pairs	1,582,156	Camp colors	7,270
Boots ....do	435,032	National colors	609
Stockings ....do	1,803,719	Flags	7,697
Hats	397,595	Guidons	2,039
Caps	926,922	Picks	103,228
Axes	90,548	Bugles	3,893
Spades and shovels	152,523	Trumpets	3,869
Hatchets	111,247	Drums	5,865
Mess-pans	364,086	Fifes	11,747

For further details of the supply of clothing, camp and garrison equipage, during the fiscal year, and during the whole war, I respectfully refer to the tables accompanying this report. They give information as to the quantities of the various materials purchased, as well as of the articles manufactured therefrom, or purchased ready made, in a compact form and with greater precision than is possible in this narrative.

There have been purchased during the fiscal year—

Cloth and other materials to the value of	$21,416,858.84
Clothing	70,087,282.20
Equipage	13,515,301.09
The expenditure for all objects relating to clothing and equipage, including payment of rents, compensation to workmen, clerks, and others, at the principal depots, has been during the year ending June 30, 1865	105,019,406.13

Two of the tables herewith give approximately the quantities of material and of ready-made articles of clothing and equipage, which the three principal depots have supplied during the war.

At the commencement of the war the department had but one depot for the supply of clothing and equipage, the Schuylkill Arsenal, at Philadelphia. This was organized for the equipment of an army of 13,000 men. The material was purchased by contract from manufactories, and the clothing, shoes, &c., were made up at the arsenal.

The sudden increase of the Army made it necessary to greatly enlarge the operations of this depot and to establish new ones, and also to accept the aid of State authorities in providing the clothing of the numerous regiments of volunteers organizing in every district in the country. Eight thousand or 10,000 work-people were employed in Philadelphia in the manufacture of clothing and equipage. The new depots established at New York and Cincinnati went into operation early in 1862, under energetic and able officers. Contracts were made for the supply of clothing ready made. The manufacturers of the loyal States were urged to turn their machinery upon army goods. The clothing merchants who had before the war supplied the Southern markets made contracts with the department for the supply of army clothing, and in a few months the industry and manufacturing power of the country were turned into the new channel, and the difficulties at first experienced in procuring a sufficient supply for the immense army which sprang into being ceased.

The only domestic branch of manufacture which has not shown capacity to supply the Army is that of blankets. The department has been obliged throughout the war to use a considerable proportion of army blankets of foreign manufacture.

The condition of the property stored at the Schuylkill Arsenal at Philadelphia is a source of apprehension. About $20,000,000 of property are in store there, and it is recommended that alterations and additions be made in the buildings, or within the walls, to enable the department to remove much valuable property now stored in temporary sheds and exposed to danger from fire into proper fireproof buildings.

The prices of clothing and equipage have constantly advanced during the war. A table of the lowest and highest prices paid accompanies this report. It will be seen that toward the termination of the war the prices of many important articles had more than doubled; of some articles the price has quadrupled.

The Second Division of this office has charge of the provision and distribution of clothing and equipage. It has been under the charge of Col. A. J. Perry, of the Quartermaster's Department, who has in this office had charge of this branch of its business since the commencement of the war. He is an officer of rare merit, and I have taken occasion heretofore to ask that he receive promotion as a testimony that his services have been recognized and appreciated by his country as they are by the chief of this department.

Although in the active operations of the past four years, and especially during the unprecedented movements of the last year, very heavy demands have been made upon this branch of the department, it has been able to place the material needed at the right places and at the right moment.

During the last year large armies have changed their bases. The army of General Sherman from the Tennessee and Ohio to the Atlantic Coast at Savannah; then again to the harbor of Beaufort, N. C., several hundred miles distant. Yet at each of these new bases this army, from 70,000 to 100,000 strong, found the supplies for a complete new outfit ready for issue. Most of the clothing and equipage for this purpose was sent from New York. Details of the operation are found elsewhere in this report.

So armies of 15,000 to 25,000 men have been during the past year suddenly moved from the Tennessee to the Atlantic; from the Tennessee to the Gulf Coast; from the James to the Rio Grande; but from none of these new fields and bases of operation, in the midst of these sudden and gigantic movements, has the complaint been made of suffering for want of any of the supplies which it is the duty of this department to provide or to transport.

OCEAN TRANSPORTATION.

Col. George D. Wise, in charge of the Third Division of this office, reports that during the first month of the fiscal year the office work of the division—that of ocean and lake transportation—was embarrassed by the absence of most of the clerks and officers, who were called to active service in the field during the demonstration and attack on the capital by the rebel army under Early and Breckinridge. During this time, however, the necessary steamer transportation was assembled at City Point and moved to Washington and Baltimore the Sixth Army Corps in time to meet the advancing enemy at the battles of the Monocacy and the attack on Washington. The Nineteenth Army Corps was also brought from the Chesapeake, where it was arriving by sea from New Orleans, and reached Washington in time to take part in the operations for its defense and in the pursuit of the baffled enemy.

During the month of July, also, the army of Major-General Canby was moved by sea from New Orleans to Mobile Bay, co-operating with the navy in the reduction of the fortifications at its entrance.

From August to December no great movements of troops by sea were made, but a large fleet was constantly employed in supplying the armies before Richmond and the troops at the various stations along the coast from the Chesapeake to New Orleans.

In the inclement month of December the approach of General Sherman's army to the coast required a large fleet to be employed in readiness to supply and refit that army after its long march from Atlanta.

Transports were dispatched to Pensacola with supplies to await the arrival of the troops, should unexpected opposition compel General Sherman to change his course to the south.

The greater part of the stores intended for his use, however, were sent direct to Port Royal Harbor, there to await his arrival at some point on the coast of the Carolinas or Georgia.

When he appeared in rear of Savannah, and capturing Fort McAllister by a *coup de main*, communicated with the naval squadron, the transports were sent round to the mouths of the Ogeechee and Savannah Rivers, and light-draft steamers, fitted for river and bay service, which had been dispatched upon the first news of his approach, arrived in time to transfer to the river landings the clothing, camp and garrison equipage, quartermaster's stores, and forage and provisions which had been of necessity sent in seagoing vessels, both sail and steam, and which were of too heavy draft to enter the Ogeechee or pass through the opening first made in the artificial obstructions of the Savannah.

The army was quickly reclothed, reshod, and refitted; its wagons filled with rations and forage.

A large portion of the army was transferred by steamers from the Savannah to Beaufort, S. C., or Port Royal Harbor, at which place the vessels of heavy draft could land their stores without the labor of transshipment.

After a short and much-needed rest, the army, re-equipped, left the coast, and the transports and fleet of light-draft steamers repaired to the harbor of Morehead City, where they awaited the arrival of the troops, who, after a march of 500 miles through a hostile country, without communication with their base of supplies, depending solely upon the stores in their wagons and the resources of the enemy's country for their subsistence, were certain to arrive in a condition to require an entire renewal of their clothing and shoes and a new supply of provisions.

When I parted with General Sherman at Savannah on the 19th of January he told me to look out for him at Kinston, and also to be prepared for him lower down the coast should the rebel Army of Virginia, abandoning Richmond, unite with the troops in the Carolinas and succeed in preventing his passage of the Santee.

During the month of December, also, an expedition was embarked at City Point and Fortress Monroe, which made an unsuccessful attempt, in co-operation with the navy, upon Fort Fisher, at the mouth of Cape Fear River. The troops failing to attack were re-embarked and returned to Hampton Roads. The transportation by sea, the landing and return, were successfully performed.

In January the expedition was re-embarked with a larger force and successfully landed above Fort Fisher, which place, with the aid of a naval bombardment unexampled in severity, they carried by assault.

The troops of the Twenty-third Army Corps, under General Schofield, having borne their part in the campaign in Georgia and Tennessee, after the battle of Nashville, which took place on the 15th and 16th of December, and the termination of the pursuit of the rebel army on the Tennessee, were moved by rail and river to Washington and Baltimore, where, amid many difficulties from the severity of the season, ice entirely suspending for a time the navigation of the Potomac, they were embarked on ocean steamers and dispatched to the Cape Fear River and to Beaufort, N. C., to move, in co-operation with the victors of Fort Fisher, upon Wilmington and Kinston, N. C.

In anticipation of the arrival of General Sherman's army, I had ordered to Savannah a portion of the Military Railroad Construction Corps. Two divisions of the corps, as organized, with tools and materials and officers, were brought from Nashville to Baltimore by railroad. At Baltimore they were re-enforced and embarked on ocean steamers and were promptly at the rendezvous.

As the army moved, however, without depending upon railroad communication, destroying instead of repairing railroads in its march, the Construction Corps was transferred to Wilmington and Beaufort Harbor, and the railroads which, starting from Wilmington and Morehead City, meet at Goldsborough were repaired and stocked with engines and cars, either captured or sent from the North.

Two hundred miles of railroad were thus repaired and stocked under the protection of the troops of Generals Schofield and Terry; and when, after the battle of Bentonville, the Right Wing of General Sherman's army, under Howard, marched into Goldsborough, on the 22d of March, ragged from their struggles with the thickets and swamps, and blackened by the smoke of the burning forests of Carolina, they met these railroad trains from the Atlantic loaded with three days' rations for their immediate wants. I met General Sherman at Morehead City on the 25th of March, when he advised me that he desired to move again on the 10th of April.

This army of nearly 100,000 men needed to be entirely reclad and reshod; the troops were to be fed while resting, for as soon as the army ceased its march it ceased to supply itself by foraging, and depended upon the supplies from the coast. Nevertheless, on the 7th of April I was able to inform General Sherman that the necessary supplies were in his camps.

Every soldier had received a complete outfit of clothing and had been newly shod. The wagons were loaded with rations and forage, and each of the 3,000 wagons, whose canvas covers had been torn on the march from Chattanooga, was supplied with a new cover. The army moved on the appointed day against the enemy, interposing between it and the Army of the Potomac, then holding the principal rebel army fast behind the lines of Richmond.

A tug-boat of this department, under the command of Captain Ainsworth, had reached Fayetteville by the Cape Fear River on the 12th of March, and first bore greeting to the Army of the West from their comrades whom they had left on the banks of the Tennessee, and who, joined with others of the Army of the Potomac, were then forcing a communication with them from the new base which they sought on the Atlantic Coast.

The demands upon the department at this time compelled it to take into its service not only the fleet which it had gradually acquired by purchase, but nearly every new steam vessel that had been built in the United States to navigate the ocean.

A fleet of powerful propellers, vessels of 900 to 1,100 tons, swift and staunch, burning twelve to sixteen tons of coal per day, with a speed of eight to ten knots, had been created during the war, and nearly the whole of them were at this time in the service of the department.

Large sailing ships were also employed, loaded with forage and subsistence, and compelled to anchor on the exposed coast of Carolina, where they rode out the winter storms.

A large quantity of railroad engines and cars were shipped to Beaufort Harbor for the railroads in North Carolina, most of which were on the termination of hostilities sent to the James River to be sold.

To aid in the rapid supply of General Sherman while at Goldsborough and relieve the railroad, and also to enable the department to supply him at Winton by the shallow waters of North Carolina in his northern march, a large number of canal-boats and barges was sent to New Berne. Some of them were used in the Trent River carrying supplies to Kinston bridge, but the greater part of them were released from service by the surrender of the rebel armies and have been returned to the Chesapeake and to their owners or sold.

In all the active movements by sea during the fiscal year, employing a fleet in which nearly all the seagoing steamers of the country have been employed, but three vessels have been lost while in the service of this department.

The North America, a chartered side-wheel steamer of the first class, perfectly new, went down in a gale off Cape Hatteras, the General Lyon was burned, and the Admiral Du Pont was run down at sea.

After the surrender of the rebel armies orders were given to discharge all the chartered steamers and to sell those which were the property of the department as fast as they could be spared. Very heavy movements, however, ordered before much progress in the reduction was made, have delayed the discharge and sale of some of the transports.

In May the Twenty-fifth Army Corps was ordered from City Point to Texas. The corps numbered about 25,000 men, with artillery and baggage. Its guns, ambulances, wagons, and harness, subsistence and ammunition, went with it. About 2,000 horses and mules also accompanied it. The greater part of its artillery, cavalry, and team horses were left behind. This movement required a fleet of fifty-seven ocean steamers, one of which made two voyages. The entire tonnage of the fleet was 56,987 tons. The vessels were all provided for a twelve-days' voyage, consuming 947 tons of coal and 50,000 gallons of water daily. The daily expense of this fleet amounted to $33,311. The vessels were fitted with bunks for the troops, and with stalls for 2,139 horses and mules, which formed part of the expedition. The vessels were all rigidly inspected before sailing, and all reached their destination in safety. No accident to any of them has been reported. A list of the vessels accompanies this report.

While this expedition of 25,000 troops was afloat another, of 7,000 troops, was sent by sea from Washington to Savannah, and 3,000 rebel prisoners were sent from Point Lookout, on the Chesapeake, to Mobile. Besides this large numbers of convalescent and discharged men were then returning from the Southern ports, and recruits were forwarded to the regiments on the coast.

There were, therefore, more than 30,000 troops and prisoners afloat upon the ocean in steam transports at the same time.

The last annual report of this department gives information as to the army transport fleet owned and employed on the 15th of October, 1864.

This list omitted to give the names of the Western river steamers, of which the department then owned a large number.

There were in the employment of the department of ocean and lake transportation, in the spring of 1865, owned by the department—steamers, 106; steam-tugs, 29; sailing vessels, 15; barges, 21; total, 171 vessels, with a tonnage of 49,358 tons. The department also had under charter at that time—steamers, 275; tugs, 91; sailing vessels, 75; barges, 171; with a tonnage of 191,149 tons.

Total number of vessels employed, 783; tonnage, 240,507 tons. Average daily expense of this fleet, $97,500.

On the 1st of July, 1865, the fleet owned consisted of—steamers, 115; tugs, 23; sail-vessels, 12; barges, 20; tonnage, 55,496 tons.

The chartered fleet consisted of—steamers, 177; tugs, 69; sail-vessels, 74; barges, 100; tonnage, 138,440 tons.

Total number of vessels, 590; tonnage, 193,936 tons; daily cost, $82,400.

During the fiscal year the average size of the transport fleet was—

	Number.	Tons.
Steamers	351	171,081
Steam-tugs	111	13,262
Sail-vessels	89	17,738
Barges	168	22,903
Total	719	224,984

Its average daily cost was $92,414.

The report of Colonel Wise, who is in charge of this branch of the Quartermaster-General's Office, contains some important observations upon the construction and management of steam ocean transports.

At the beginning of the war the department was imposed upon. Officers and agents had little experience, and inferior vessels were sometimes chartered, and excessive prices were paid for steamers chartered from the regular trade, not then entirely and hopelessly broken up by the war.

Stringent measures of reform were adopted; a scale of prices for the different classes of vessels was fixed by the order of the Quartermaster-General. The examination and audit of all accounts for charter of vessels was brought to this office. All charters contained provisions to enable the United States to purchase the vessels at a reasonable price, provided that should prove advantageous, and system, order, and regularity were introduced into the service.

This branch of the service, on the reorganization of this office under the law of the 4th of July, 1864, was assigned to the Third Division of the office, under the direction of Col. G. D. Wise. The safety, efficiency, dispatch, and punctuality with which its affairs have been conducted do him high honor.

At one time 40,000 men have been afloat. The fleet has averaged 719 vessels of all classes, with a burden of 225,000 tons. But three vessels have been lost during the year, though the greatest and most important movements were made during the inclement months of the winter—from January to May.

Very full tables which accompany this report give details in reference to the transport fleet and the operations of the department upon the ocean and upon the waters of the coast.

RAIL AND RIVER TRANSPORTATION.

The service of transportation upon the Western rivers has been under the direction of the Fourth Division of this office.

Col. L. B. Parsons, who had been placed in charge of the Western river transportation in 1863, just before the preparations for the campaign of Atlanta commenced, was upon the organization of the division of rail and river transportation in this office called to its head. He has conducted the service with great efficiency and economy. Of some of the more important movements his report gives details. When he took charge of this service the Mississippi had been opened and the merchants of the West were in condition to establish lines of steamers to all parts of its navigable waters. The system of time-charter of steamers was as fast as possible abandoned, and contracts were made on public advertisement with the lowest responsible bidders to move the stores of the department at fixed rates per pound. The rapid accumulation at Nashville and at other points of supplies, which enabled General Sherman to move successfully into Georgia, have been detailed in the last annual report of this office.

WESTERN RIVER TRANSPORTATION.

In the course of the war a considerable fleet of river steamers and other vessels had become the property of the department upon the Mississippi and its tributaries, by purchase, by construction, or by capture. A list of the steamers accompanies the report. It contains the names of—

Side-wheel steamers	34	
Stern-wheel steamers	37	
Center-wheel steamers	3	
Ferry-boats	1	
Screw-tugs	16	
Total steam-boats		91

Of other vessels the department owned upon those rivers—

Steam-boat hulls		2
Model barges	74	
Gunwale barges	226	
Small wood barges	26	
Box barges	3	
Barges not classified	23	
Total barges		352
Wharf-boats	18	
Canal-boats	3	
Coal-boats	60	
Yawl-boats	56	
Sail-boats	1	
Metallic boats	1	
Total boats		139
Skiffs		9
Sectional docks		3
Small flats		2
Floating docks		1
Total boats and barges of all kinds		599

Nearly all of these have been advertised for sale. Those which have been constructed or purchased by the department have been or will be sold. Those which have been captured or seized will be turned over to the Treasury Department, to be disposed of under the law, or will be returned to their original owners, if pardoned, and, if so ordered, upon full consideration of their claims.

RAILROAD TRANSPORTATION.

The agreement made early in the war with a convention of railroad companies has continued in force through all the changes in values which the war has brought. The railroad officers have responded to every demand of the transportation department of the Government, and by their cordial co-operation with the officers of the Quartermaster's Department have made these great movements of troops easy of execution and unexampled in dispatch.

To Brig. Gen. L. B. Parsons, who has been in charge of the Fourth Division of this office, and to Bvt. Col. Alexander Bliss, his assistant, and frequently, in his absence, in charge of the office, and the officers at the various posts and depots, charged with the duty of transportation, great credit is due for the safety, order, and speed with which this immense business has been conducted.

There have been filed in the office of the Fourth Division since its organization 442 claims, amounting to $268,545.02; 202 have been allowed, amounting to $68,712.34; 92 have been referred to the Third Auditor or to disbursing officers for examination and settlement, amounting to $87,462.30; 99 have been rejected, amounting to $60,138.34; 48 await action, amounting to $16,891.04; 1 has been withdrawn, amounting to $5,341.

From the imperfect reports yet received at the office of the Fourth Division the number of passages granted to prisoners and refugees who have been transported by the division during the fiscal year is 356,541, costing over $1,300,000.

General Schofield's movement from Clifton, on the Tennessee, by the Tennessee River, the Ohio, and the Baltimore and Ohio Railroad, to the Potomac, and thence to the coast of North Carolina, was accomplished in the midst of a very severe winter, during which the navigation of the Ohio and the Potomac was at times interrupted by ice. Within five days after the movement was decided on in Washington the troops upon the Tennessee, nearly 1,400 miles distant, were embarking. The movement to Washington occupied an average time of only eleven days. It took place during the month of January.

The special report of Colonel Parsons, of the Quartermaster's Department, who was dispatched by the War Department to attend to it personally, accompanies this report; it is an interesting detail of the difficulties overcome, and of the success with which they were surmounted.

On the conclusion of the campaign in Tennessee, while the Twenty-third Corps, under General Schofield, was ordered across the Alleghanies, by Washington, to the coast of North Carolina, to co-operate with General Sherman, the Sixteenth Corps, under Maj. Gen. A. J. Smith, was ordered to New Orleans to co-operate with General Canby in the reduction of Mobile. A fleet of forty steamers was promptly assembled at Eastport, on the Tennessee, below the Muscle Shoals. The entire command, including a brigade of artillery and the Seventh Division of the Cavalry Corps, was embarked on the fleet. It consisted of 17,314 men, 1,038 horses, 2,371 mules, 351 wagons, 83 ambulances. The embarkation began on the 5th of February, 1865, and was completed on the 8th. The fleet sailed on the 9th, and the command arrived at New Orleans on the 23d, having been moved in thirteen days 1,330 miles.

DISPERSION OF THE ARMIES CONCENTRATED AT WASHINGTON.

The armies of the West and of the Potomac, after the fall of Richmond and the surrender of the eastern rebel armies, marched through Washington, were reviewed by the President and Cabinet, and encamping upon the heights surrounding the capital, prepared for their final dispersion and disbandment.

During the forty days between the 27th of May and the 6th of July 233,200 men, 12,838 horses, and 4,300,850 pounds of baggage were moved from Washington by the Washington Branch Railroad to the Relay House, where a large portion of them turned westward. The remainder passed through Baltimore, dividing at that city into two streams, one of which moved north through Harrisburg, the other northeast through Philadelphia.

The general instructions of the Quartermaster-General, preparing for this movement, will be found among the papers attached to this report. They designate the routes and prescribe certain precautions and preparations for the comfort and safety of the troops moving by rail.

Of the troops there were returning home for discharge from service 161,403 men, with 4,630 horses, and 1,828,450 pounds baggage, distributed as follows:

To the Northeastern States, 28,803 men, 1,307 horses, 287,000 pounds baggage.

To the Middle States, 100,309 men, 2,323 horses, 907,000 pounds baggage.

To the Western States, 32,291 men, 1,000 horses, 634,450 pounds baggage.

The Army of the Tennessee, ordered to move to Louisville, from which place they were, in a few weeks, sent to their homes for discharge from service, 60,904 men, 2,657 horses, 2,424,000 pounds baggage.

Cavalry ordered West for active service, 10,893 men, 5,757 horses, 308,000 pounds baggage.

Total number in forty days, over the Washington Branch Railroad and the various railroads diverging from the Relay House and from Baltimore, 233,200 men, 12,838 horses, and 4,300,850 pounds baggage.

The Army of the Tennessee, the troops ordered West for active service, and a portion of those ordered to their Western homes for discharge, passed over the Baltimore and Ohio Railroad to Parkersburg, its western terminus, on the Ohio River, where boats were provided for their march to Louisville, Lawrenceburg, Camp Dennison, and Cincinnati. Between May 27 and July 6, within forty days, during twelve of which no troops arrived at Parkersburg from Washington, there were moved from that place:

To—	Men.	Horses.
Louisville	78,450	5,855
Saint Louis	7,082	3,314
Lawrenceburg, Ind	8,424	153
Camp Dennison, Ohio	1,479	29
Cincinnati	1,361	545
Total	96,796	9,896

In this movement by water ninety-two steam-boats were employed an average of seventeen days and a fraction for each boat, at an average compensation of $175 per day each. Each boat consumed on an average 200 bushels of coal per day.

The total service of all the boats was 1,601 days, costing for charter $280,175, and consuming 320,200 bushels of bituminous coal, $48,030.

Total cost of transportation from Parkersburg by water to various points on the Ohio and to Saint Louis of 96,796 men and 9,896 horses, $328,205.

The same movement if performed by railroad, at the reduced rates at which the railroads serve the Government, would have cost $746,964.

Thus 96,000 men and 10,000 horses were, in the short space of forty days, moved from Washington, on the Potomac, across the Alleghanies and, descending the Ohio and ascending the Mississippi, were placed in the several positions to which they had been ordered.

During these same forty days 233,000 men in all were moved by railroad from Washington, 96,000 of them to the posts above named; the others were distributed to every hamlet and village of the States north of the Potomac and Ohio Rivers, and restored to their homes, the labor of war over, to return to the pursuits of peaceful industry which they had left at the call of their country in her hour of need.

In all these movements there have been few accidents, and the safety and economy of the service are not less noticeable than its speed.

Had the armies marched to their several places of destination the pay of the men, the subsistence of men and animals, the maintenance of the immense trains which would have accompanied them, considering the time which the march would have consumed, would have far exceeded the cost of this rapid movement by rail and river.

It is understood that since the close of the war 800,000 men have been safely brought back from the rebellious districts, transported by this department to the several camps of discharge established in every loyal State, and finally sent to their homes. Many of these men came from Texas and the Gulf Coast; others from the territories of all the lately rebellious States.

Such a movement is unexampled. It illustrates the resources of the country for the operations of war, and the great advantages it possesses in its system of navigable rivers and its 40,000 miles of railroads.

MILITARY RAILROADS.

In the winter of 1863, when the rebel armies were driven back from Chattanooga, the immediate repair and almost total reconstruction of the track of the railway from Nashville to Chattanooga became an imperative necessity.

The positions taken up by the troops along the line of the Tennessee River, for the winter, required for their supply that the railroads from Nashville to Decatur, and from Decatur to beyond Knoxville, should also be repaired and equipped. Bridges were rebuilt; new and heavier iron was laid down upon the road from Nashville to Chattanooga; locomotives and cars in great numbers were manufactured at the North and transported to the scene of active operations.

As the Louisville and Nashville Railroad proved insufficient for the heavy traffic thrown upon it, and was sometimes cut by guerrillas, the Nashville and Northwestern Railroad, from Nashville to Johnsonville, on the Tennessee River, was repaired, completed, and opened to trade. This afforded a new avenue by which the products of the Northwest were transported to the base of operations at Nashville, the Tennessee River being navigable for light-draft boats from the Ohio to Johnsonville.

Seventeen hundred and sixty-nine miles of military railways were at one time repaired, maintained, stocked, and operated by the agents of this department, under the energetic supervision of Bvt. Brig. Gen. D. C. McCallum, general manager of military railways of the United States.

In the repair of so many miles of railway great quantities of iron, burned and twisted by the contending forces, both of which, on occasion, destroyed railroads which they were obliged to abandon, came into our possession.

To make this iron serviceable in the repair of the railroads toward Atlanta and to the Gulf, should the same stubborn resistance be offered beyond Atlanta as was met with on the advance to that place, I directed the completion of an unfinished rolling-mill captured at Chattanooga.

For local military reasons Major-General Thomas required that the mill should be constructed within the intrenchment of the city of Chattanooga, instead of on the foundations of the mill, some two miles from that town. A rolling-mill capable of rerolling fifty tons of railroad iron per day was constructed and put in operation. It utilized a large quantity of iron taken from the lines of Southern railroads, and was of important aid in restoring the railroad communication between Chattanooga and Atlanta, broken up by order of General Sherman when, in the fall of 1864, he destroyed the latter city and set forth on his adventurous march to the sea.

The termination of the war having relieved the War Department of the duty of repairs and reconstruction of railroads, this rolling-mill was advertised and sold at a satisfactory price. It will be of great advantage to the Southwestern railroads, on all of which the iron is much worn by constant use during the war, with little means of renewal.

Most of their iron will require rerolling, and this mill is now in full operation upon the work.

General McCallum reports 1,769 miles of railroad as operated during the fiscal year, with an equipment of 365 engines and 4,203 cars either in use or in reserve, and an expenditure of $22,000,000. His report is among the papers submitted herewith.

The force employed in the repair, construction, and operation of the military railways has been very large. A table herewith shows the strength at several different periods. In April, 1865, the number employed in this branch of the service was 23,533.

TRANSFER OF MILITARY RAILROADS.

As soon as the surrender of the rebel armies and the cessation of hostilities made it possible, efforts were made to induce the railroad companies of the rebellious territories to reorganize by the election of loyal directors and managers, and to resume the charge of the lines which had fallen into the hands of this department and been repaired and used for the supply of our armies.

At this date nearly all the roads have been transferred, either to the presidents and directors or to boards of public works of the States in which they are situated. In the Atlantic States the policy pursued has been to deliver up the roads in whatever condition they were left by the fortune of war at the moment of transfer.

Questions of ownership, claims to material of the road tracks transferred either by rebel or by U. S. authority from one road to another, are left for decision of the courts. The United States merely retires, leaving the lawful owners to resume their property. Such material as had been collected for repair or construction and not used, and such as was in depot, has been sold to the companies at a fair valuation, and upon credit of greater or less extent, as circumstances seemed to require.

The department does not propose to charge the railroads for expenditures or repairs, or for materials actually used on the roads; nor does it propose to allow any charge against it for the use and profits of the roads while occupied as military routes, nor for damages done by its troops or agents under the pressure of military operations.

A railroad is an engine of war more powerful than a battery of artillery, subject to capture and to use; and there is, it would seem, as little reason for paying damages or rent for its occupation and use as there would be for a captured battery.

The rolling-stock and movable machinery have been hired to the railroads desiring their use until arrangements could be made for a sale. Most of that collected in the Atlantic States has at this date been disposed of at public auction, either for cash or in payment of debts for transportation due by the department to railroads.

In the Southwest the rolling-stock belonging to the United States, some 220 engines and 3,000 cars, was all of the wide gauge, fitted for the Southern roads. It could not be used without expensive alterations upon the Northern railroads, and these could not be expected, therefore, to purchase it at prices approaching its value.

The railroads and the territory of the Southwest were too much impoverished by the events of the unsuccessful rebellion to be able to purchase for cash the rolling-stock and machinery which had cost this department several millions of dollars.

The reconstruction of the Southwestern railroads and their operation were of the greatest importance to the pacification, restoration, and prosperity of the country, and on the 8th of August an Executive order was issued prescribing the terms upon which these railroads should be restored to their lawful owners.

Difficulties having arisen in carrying this into full effect, additional orders were issued on the 14th of October, 1865.

Under these orders the railroads and the railroad property of the department in the Southwest are being disposed of. Copies of the orders, as published by this department for the information and guidance of its officers, accompany this report; they are General Orders of the War Department, No. 276, 1863, and Quartermaster-General's Office, Nos. 56 and 62, 1865.

This branch of the service has been a very costly one, but its expenditures have accomplished their objects. They have supplied our armies, and have enabled them to move and accomplish in weeks what without them would have required years, or would have been impossible.

Of the skill and ability of General D. C. McCallum, director and general manager of the U. S. Military Railroads, and of the able body of engineers, superintendents, and assistants, who have enabled the department to repair, to build, and to manage the railroads during these great operations, it is impossible to speak too highly.

The commanding generals of armies as well as the Quartermaster-General recognize their courage and devotion, their services, and their merits.

TELEGRAPH.

The Military Telegraph has continued to be a most important instrument in the conduct of military operations. Its officers have shown the same fidelity and devotion as in former years.

Col. Anson Stager has been chief of the Military Telegraph, and Maj. Thomas T. Eckert, assistant quartermaster, has been assistant superintendent, on duty at the War Department, and in charge of all telegraph lines in the Departments of the Potomac, Virginia, North Carolina, and the South.

The funds for the support of the Military Telegraph are furnished from the appropriations of the Quartermaster's Department, and are disbursed under the direction of the chief of Military Telegraphs, whose reports, with those of his assistants, are submitted herewith.

The duties of these officers have brought them more directly under the notice of the Secretary of War than of the Quartermaster-General, and their merits are well known to the War Department.

Expenditures during the year were $300,000 for material and supplies, of which about $130,000 was expended for purchase of 285 miles of submarine telegraph cable for use in case of necessity upon the coast and bays. The greater part of this is still on hand.

Referring to Colonel Stager's report, herewith, it appears that the estimated cost of supplying and maintaining and operating military lines now in use is $75,000 per month:

	Land.	Sub-marine.	Aggre-gate.
	Miles.	*Miles.*	*Miles.*
Military telegraph in operation July 1, 1864	4, 955¼	52¾	
Constructed during the year	3, 246½	68¾	
Total in operation during the fiscal year ending June 30, 1865	8, 201¾	121½	8, 323¼
Taken down or abandoned during the year	2, 049	46¼	
Total in operation June 30, 1865	6, 152¾	75¼	6, 228

During the rebellion there have been constructed and operated about 15,000 miles of military telegraph.

The cost of the Military Telegraph from May 1, 1861, to December 1, 1862, was about $22,000 per month.

During the year 1863 it averaged $38,500 per month.

In 1864 the telegraph was greatly extended, and the cost reached $93,500 per month.

The total expenditure during the year ending June 30, 1865, has been $1,360,000.

The total expenditure from May 1, 1861, to June 30, 1865, $2,655,500.

Upon the fall of the rebellion the telegraph lines throughout the South were taken possession of by the Government. The telegraph companies were called upon to repair their lines and put them in good working order, furnishing all labor and material therefor, the United States to be at no outlay beyond the expense of maintaining purely military lines and military stations. An account of Government business is kept, subject to future consideration or settlement.

FORAGE, FUEL, AND REGULAR SUPPLIES.

From the records in this office it appears that the armies in the field required, under the organization prevailing during the third year of the war, for the use of cavalry, artillery, and for the trains, one-half as many horses and mules as they contained soldiers.

The full ration of forage for a horse is fourteen pounds of hay and twelve pounds of grain daily, twenty-six pounds in all. The gross weight of a man's ration of subsistence is three pounds; the forage for an army therefore weighs, when full rations are supplied, about four and a half times as much as the subsistence stores. The forage, probably, exceeds the subsistence as much in bulk as in weight.

With armies marching in the field, the forage is in great part gathered along the line of march.

Thus the army of General Sherman, on its march through the Southern States, supplied itself with abundant forage. The moment that the army halted, as at Savannah and at Goldsborough, large shipments of grain and hay were necessary to keep the animals alive.

So the army which operated in the vicinity of Nashville, and General Sherman's army during its slow progress from Nashville [Chattanooga?] to Atlanta, and during the siege of that city, drew immense quantities of grain and hay from the Ohio River at vast expense.

The armies operating against Richmond during the past fiscal year occupied a fixed position in the lines of their fortified camps, and drew all their supplies from the North by sea.

The animals of the Army have been well supplied throughout the year, notwithstanding the extent of the territory over which they have been scattered, and the sudden and great changes of base, and consequently of lines of supply.

When General Sherman's army reached Savannah, and before the opening of the obstructed channels leading to that city permitted the approach of the fleet which had been dispatched to Port Royal, laden with forage and other stores, there was for a short time a scarcity of forage. The rice straw and rice which alone the country about Savannah furnished were soon consumed, and I am informed that some artillery horses perished. But the opening of the river soon enabled the department to deliver ample supplies, and his army moved north with abundance of animals and of food.

Col. S. L. Brown was placed in charge of the purchase and supply of forage to the armies on the Atlantic Coast in December, 1863, and upon the organization of the Fifth Division of this office was transferred to its head. His administration has been successful, and his reports record a business of magnitude and importance seldom equaled. Between the 8th of December, 1862, and the 30th of June, 1865, he purchased and shipped to the depots and armies 2,787,758 bushels of corn, 20,997,289 bushels of oats, 43,311 bushels of barley, 269,814 tons of hay, 8,243 tons of straw; the cost of which was $31,308,563.98. The grain was purchased at certain points, under the direction of Colonel Brown, and transported to Portland, Boston, New York, and Philadelphia by rail, canal, river, and lake, making 8,567 car-loads, 560 barge-loads by canal, and 49 schooner, 29 bark, and 20 propeller cargoes on the lakes. The hay, purchased upon the line of railroad, was transported to the coast in 5,555 car-loads. The whole was reshipped from the above-named ports to the depots of the armies on the coast in 2,570 cargoes. The freight paid to these vessels was $2,576,152.14.

Daily reports from the depots of the various armies, when daily mail or telegraphic communication was open, have been required, and have kept this office advised of the state of supply. Contracts made at a distance have been subjected to a careful examination by Colonel Brown himself, and every effort made to correct and prevent extravagance and fraud, both in the purchase and consumption of forage.

The loss by wastage, fire, and the perils of the sea upon shipments of forage amounting to $25,000,000, has been less than seven-eighths of one per cent.—about eighty-three hundredths of one per cent. That there has been waste is undeniable; but in the handling of 30,000,000 bushels of grain, and its daily distribution to the manger or nose-bag of every horse or mule in the public service, over a country of 2,000 miles in width, this was unavoidable.

The abstracts with the report of the Fifth Division show, as approximate results, that during the fiscal year there have been supplied to the Army:

Articles.	Quantity.	Value.
Corn .... bushels..	5,902,273	$8,558,296
Oats .... do....	23,794,930	23,794,930
Barley .... do....	43,311	64,967
Hay .... tons..	407,799	13,049,568
Straw .... do....	10,665	213,300
Feed .... do....	146	219
Fodder .... do....	614	304
Forage		45,681,584

Fuel for the troops has, generally, in the field, been cut by themselves. At positions held for some time and not in the enemy's territory, it is supplied by contract, the labor of troops being employed in different degrees, according as the exigencies of military duty, in the view of commanding generals, will permit.

Fuel for steam-vessels is procured by contract, principally at Philadelphia and Pittsburg.

The reports in the Fifth Division show an aggregate of supplies of fuel during the fiscal year of—

Fuel.	Quantity.	Value.
Wood .... cords..	336,169	$1,680,840
Coal .... tons..	832,452	8,324,520

These numbers, however, are imperfect and subject, probably, to important increase upon a complete examination and analysis of the records and reports and accounts of officers.

The reports from the depot of Washington show the issue during the war of—

Corn	bushels..	4,500,000
Oats	do....	29,000,000
Hay	tons..	490,000
Straw	do....	15,000
Coal	do....	392,000
Wood	cords..	210,000

Capt. E. D. Chapman, forage officer at Saint Louis, reports the purchase of forage at that depot during the war of—

Corn	bushels..	3,847,480
Oats	do....	17,403,778
Hay	tons..	213,216
Straw	do....	3,206

But I am of opinion that there have been many purchases of which Captain Chapman cannot have knowledge, and that the quantity actually purchased at that depot is considerably greater than above stated.

Imperfect analyses of contracts and reports in this office indicate a supply of forage during the war exceeding—

Articles.	Quantity.	Value.
Corn ....bushels..	22,816,271	$29,879,314
Oats ....do....	78,663,799	76,362,026
Hay ....tons..	1,518,621	48,595,872
Straw ....do....	21,276	425,520
Total estimated cost of forage during the war, so far as ascertained from reports analyzed in this office.	....	155,262,732

But vast quantities of forage were purchased and issued at remote or subordinate posts, the accounts of which cannot be made up without a complete analysis of the vouchers of disbursing officers. Much was purchased or taken on the march by officers subsequently killed or disabled, or by officers not reporting to this department. For much of this memorandum receipts were given; and these are among the claims continually reaching this office under the law of July 4, 1864.

The total quantity of fuel reported as furnished is—

	Quantity.	Value.
Wood ....cords..	551,436	$2,757,180
Coal ....tons..	1,620,910	13,777,735

The wood was generally used near the place of purchase. The coal has been transported, at the expense of the department, from the market in which it was purchased to all the Atlantic, Gulf, and Western river ports between Saint Louis and Pittsburg.

CLAIMS FOR REGULAR SUPPLIES.

To the Fifth Division is intrusted the examination of claims for fuel, forage, and other regular supplies, irregularly taken by the armies, and not accounted for or imperfectly reported by officers of this department. Such of these as appear to be just and equitable are referred to the Third Auditor of the Treasury, with a recommendation for settlement, under the law of July 4, 1864.

A copy of General Orders, No. 35, which contains the rules for examination of these claims, accompanies this report.

These claims are examined as to the actual use of the supplies by the Army, as to the past and present loyalty of the claimants and witnesses, and as to the genuineness of the signatures. Information as to loyalty is sought from provost-marshals; and a very large number of claims is rejected upon evidence of disloyalty of both claimants and witnesses.

There have been received and referred to the Fifth Division, from January 1 to October 16, 1865, 4,245 packages, containing 14,455 claims, vouchers given by officers of the Quartermaster's Department, and claims presented under the act of July 4, 1864, and General Orders, No. 35.

HOSPITALS AND BARRACKS.

During the fiscal year hospitals of importance have been erected at Indianapolis, at an estimated cost of	$30,000
At Newark, N. J	70,000

Worcester, Mass., conversion of the Eclectic College into a hospital	$36,800
Manchester, N. H	30,000
Hicks Hospital, Baltimore	75,000
Nashville	25,000
Hilton Head hospital, extended	30,000

At the commencement of the fiscal year the capacity of the hospitals of the Army was 120,521 beds. The capacity of the principal hospitals erected during the fiscal year is 7,300 beds.

By the pitching of hospital tents adjacent to the wooden hospitals, great additions to their capacity have been made.

Hospital buildings are erected and hospital tents are furnished by the Quartermaster's Department. The hospitals, after being constructed, are turned over to the Medical Department, to be administered under direction of the Surgeon-General. Repairs and extensions are made upon his requisition, approved by the War Department, as they become necessary.

When the hospitals are vacated they are returned to this department, to be sold or otherwise disposed of.

The hospitals throughout the country (and during the war they have been located in almost every State) have been built by the Quartermaster's Department upon plans generally prepared or suggested by the Surgeon-General.

They are temporary structures built of wood with a view to economy, but from their magnitude some of them have been costly.

The Mower General Hospital, at Chestnut Hill, Philadelphia, with a capacity for nearly 4,000 patients; the hospital at Davids Island and that at Willets Point, N. Y.; the Jarvis and the Patterson Park Hospitals, at Baltimore; the general hospital at Jeffersonville, Ind.; the several hospitals in the District of Columbia and adjacent thereto; the hospitals at Fortress Monroe and at City Point, on the James River, and the hospitals at Nashville and at Chattanooga, Tenn., are among the largest and most expensive which have been constructed by this department.

The material (wood) used in these hospitals is cheaper than any other, cheaper even than tents; but to provide for the cooking, warming, ventilating, and purification of such numbers of sick men requires at all these great general hospitals very expensive and costly arrangements for cooking, for laundries, and for supplying water in great abundance. Many of them are heated by steam; some are supplied with water from the pipes of city water-works, at others special provisions have been made for an independent water supply. Most of them have steam machinery for washing and for pumping. At one of these hospitals the daily consumption of water has exceeded 100,000 gallons.

The principal barracks erected during the year have been barracks for draft rendezvous.

Spring Mills, near Philadelphia	$84,000
Slocum, N. Y	25,000
Johnson's Island, for guard of prisoners of war, Sandusky, Ohio	15,000

A depot for prisoners of war was also constructed on Hart's Island, N. Y.

Necessary repairs have been made from time to time upon these and upon the numerous other barracks scattered throughout the country.

As the reduction of the Army and cessation of enlistments have vacated the various barracks, they have been inspected and reported to the War Department, most of them with recommendation for sale.

Very large numbers of buildings erected as hospitals, store-houses, offices, and barracks have already been sold, and others are now being advertised for sale. These sales are at public auction to the highest bidder. The materials generally bring fair prices, and a considerable sum will be realized from this source.

The Sixth Division of this office, which has charge of hospitals and barracks, is also charged with the records and reports of interments. Under General Orders, No. 40, of July 3, 1865, which on the conclusion of the war called upon officers of this department for special reports of the number of interments registered during the war, reports have been received from officers in seventeen States, including the District of Columbia.

They report the interments registered in their offices at 116,148. Of these there were—whites, 95,803; colored, 20,345; loyal, 98,827; disloyal, 12,596; refugees, 600; contrabands, 4,125. These include few of the interments made immediately after battles, which are made by details of troops, and are reported by the commanding generals in the lists of killed in battle.

These are the records of those who die in hospitals, camps, and barracks, for whose burial there is time to make decent and orderly provision under the general orders and regulations. They do not include the numerous victims of skirmishes and of assassination by bushwhackers and robbers under the guise of guerrillas, whose remains bleach by the waysides and in the woodland paths of the South. They do include, however, the 12,912 victims of the barbarities of Andersonville, Ga., and the 1,500 whose graves were marked this spring upon the battle-fields of Spotsylvania and the Wilderness.

The National Soldiers' Cemetery, at Arlington, continues to be used for the interment of the victims of the rebellion who die in Washington or its vicinity. It contains the remains of 5,291 persons. The cemetery at the Military Asylum contains 5,211; Harmony Cemetery, 388; Battle Cemetery, 40; Alexandria Cemetery, 3,600. These cemeteries have been carefully tended and decorated. A cemetery has been constructed, under order of Maj. Gen. G. H. Thomas, at Chattanooga, within the walls of which it is intended to collect the remains of all who fell in battle or died in the hospital in that vicinity.

Capt. J. M. Moore, assistant quartermaster, was by your order, immediately upon the opening of communication, dispatched in a steamer loaded with materials, with workmen, and clerks to identify and mark in a suitable manner the graves of those who died at Andersonville. With the aid of a detail furnished by Major-General Wilson this duty was performed.

The grounds in which 12,912 of our comrades had been buried in trenches were inclosed; the bodies where the earth had been washed from them by rains were again covered. Head-boards, painted white, were placed over each, bearing the name, rank, regiment, and State, with date of death, as ascertained from the captured hospital records.

Twelve thousand four hundred and sixty-one were identified, and upon 451 graves Captain Moore was compelled to place the inscription "Unknown U. S. soldier." His report is herewith.

The names of those who have been interred in the military cemeteries of the District of Columbia and of Washington have by your authority been published in a general order, which has been distributed to State authorities, public libraries, and to newspapers which publish official advertisements. The list is thus made accessible to the friends of those who have fallen.

The lists of interments at Spotsylvania and the Wilderness and of those who died at Andersonville are being printed. As other lists are received at this office they will be submitted to you for publication.

It is reported unofficially that several thousand of our dead are buried at Florence, S. C., and at other prison camps of the South. As soon as arrangements can be made for the purpose proper and decent attention will be given to their remains. Orders have been given for inspection of the cemeteries of other prison camps and of battle-fields. It is hoped that most of them can in time be inclosed and preserved.

SIXTH DIVISION—CLAIMS.

There have been presented to the Sixth Division 2,479 claims under the law of July 4, 1864. The amount claimed was $1,587,181.47. Seven hundred and fifty-one of these claims, amounting to $183,452.30, have after examination been referred to the Third Auditor, with recommendation for settlement under the law; 1,054 have been rejected, amounting to $446,163.32. Claims amounting to $957,565.85 still await examination and final action in this division.

The Sixth Division has since its organization been under charge of Col. J. J. Dana, of the Quartermaster's Department, an officer who has in various positions during the war displayed signal intelligence and devotion to his duties. As chief of transportation at the great depot of Washington, as chief quartermaster of the First Army Corps during the campaign of Chancellorsville and Gettysburg, and as assistant in this office, and after its organization chief of the Sixth Division, he has won the approval and esteem of his commanders.

MILITARY TRAINS.

The officer in charge of the division of military trains reports from the returns of officers of the department, so far as received, that during the fiscal year ending June 30, 1864, there were purchased 14,549 wagons, 1,229 ambulances, 1,279 carts, 58,144 sets wheel harness, 87,480 sets lead harness, 5,255 sets irregular harness, 335 sets artillery harness, 1,702 sets cart harness, 60 traveling and 824 portable forges. There were captured from the rebels during the same fiscal year 1,541 wagons, 468 ambulances, 245 carts, 6 carriages, 6,661 sets wheel harness, 6,906 sets lead harness, 797 sets irregular harness, 119 sets artillery harness, 406 sets cart harness, 3 traveling and 73 portable forges. There were expended, lost, and sold during the year 2,372 wagons, 277 ambulances, 96 carts, 5 carriages, 17,907 sets wheel harness, 16,732 sets lead harness, 3,453 sets irregular harness, 393 sets artillery harness, 133 sets cart harness, 3 traveling and 229 portable forges.

During the fiscal year ending June 30, 1865, there were purchased 4,762 wagons, 1,436 ambulances, 247 carts, 13,215 sets wheel harness, 18,961 sets lead harness, 2,588 sets irregular harness, 4 sets artillery harness, 328 sets cart harness, 34 traveling and 890 portable forges. There were manufactured in the repair and other shops of the department 1,443 wagons, 79 carts, 14,152 sets wheel harness, 20,767 sets lead harness, 929 sets irregular harness, 34 sets artillery harness, and 173 sets cart harness. There were captured 1,599 wagons, 174 ambulances, 108 carts, 6,228 sets wheel harness, 7,770 sets lead harness, 867 sets irregular harness, 65 sets artillery harness, and 46 portable forges. There were expended, lost, and sold 2,211 wagons, 679 ambulances, 97 carts, 18,325 sets wheel harness, 23,254 sets lead harness, 1,583 sets irregular harness, 12 traveling and 432 portable forges.

The trains of the Army had been brought to a high state of efficiency by the 30th of June, 1864, and they were probably not increased in magnitude during the year, the purchase and manufacture serving only to keep them in a complete and efficient state. Much of the harness and many of the wagons having been purchased early in the war, and in continual use, are worn and of little value.

The army of General Sherman and the Army of the Potomac uniting at Washington, after four years of active campaign, in which the former had marched from the Mississippi to the Potomac, brought together in the District of Columbia army wagons of the regulation pattern which had been used at the first battle of Bull Run on the 21st of July, 1861, some of which had made all the campaigns of each army since.

The baggage wagons and harness, the general equipment of the trains of our armies, are probably of models which cannot be improved. They have borne the rough usage of war in the hands of men of little experience at first, and not willing to take that care of them which can be expected from and enforced upon the veteran soldier.

The experience of this war has convinced all officers of this department that for the army trains mules are much superior to horses, and of late the horses have almost entirely disappeared from the trains, being transferred to the cavalry or artillery and replaced by mules.

A copy of Special Orders, No. 44, headquarters Armies of the United States, City Point, Va., June 28, 1864, accompanies this report. It sets forth in detail and clearly the organization and size of the trains of an active army as perfected by four years' experience in the field.

With this report are several reports from officers of this department giving information as to the movement and management of the trains of armies in campaigns. This information is seldom available to the military student. It is of great value and should be printed for reference and use hereafter.

SEVENTH DIVISION—CLAIMS.

During the fiscal year ending June 30, 1865, and from the termination of that year to October 10, 1865, there were presented and referred to the Seventh Division of this office 11,494 claims, amounting to $2,316,361.53. Four thousand three hundred and thirty-seven were passed, amounting to $1,239,872.23; 5,867 were rejected, amounting to $950,455.66; 1,290 remain on file for further action, amounting to $126,033.64.

The Seventh and Ninth Divisions of this office have been in charge of Col. B. C. Card, whose intelligent and prompt discharge of the duties assigned to him have met my entire approbation. I have named him with others to you for the promotion which he richly merits.

TRANSPORTATION OVER THE PLAINS.

The troops operating on the great Western plains and in the mountain regions of New Mexico, Colorado, Utah, and Idaho are supplied principally by the trains of the Quartermaster's Department from depots established on the great routes of overland travel, to which depots supplies are conveyed by contract. The contractors are the freighters or merchants of the overland trade. This department has not statistics to show the extent of this traffic, but it has of late years increased with the development of the mines of the central region of the continent until it has become a most important interest. Travelers by the stage from Denver to Fort Leavenworth, a distance of 683 miles, in the month of July, 1865, were never out of sight of wagon trains, belonging either to emigrants or to the merchants who transport supplies for the War Department, for the Indian Department, and for the mines and settlers of the central Territories.

Cost of transportation of a pound of corn, hay, clothing, subsistence, lumber, or any other necessary from Fort Leavenworth to—

Fort Riley	$0.0246
Fort Union, the depot for New Mexico	.1435
Santa Fe, N. Mex	.1685
Fort Kearny	.0644
Fort Laramie	.1410
Denver City, Colo	.1543
Salt Lake City, Utah	.2784

The cost of a bushel of corn purchased at Fort Leavenworth and delivered at each of these points is as follows:

Fort Riley	$2.79
Fort Union	9.44
Santa Fé	10.84
Fort Kearny	5.03
Fort Laramie	9.26
Denver City	10.05
Salt Lake City	17.00

To this last point none is now sent.

The expenses of this department will be reduced by the advance of the Pacific railroads, two of which are rapidly moving westward, one from Leavenworth toward Fort Riley and the other from Omaha toward Fort Kearny.

The present general mode of transport is by heavy wagons, each drawn by ten oxen. The loads of these wagons average 5,500 pounds each. Lighter freight and passengers are carried by express in lighter wagons, drawn by mules, which animals are almost exclusively used in the winter when the grass is covered with snow.

The heavy trains in dry weather move readily over the prairie roads, which outside the limits of the settlements follow the best routes, and can make wide detours to avoid sloughs or wet places in the prairies. The progress of settlement injures these roads. No laws appear to exist reserving the road bed on these great overland routes to the public. The lines of survey of the public lands cross the trail at all angles, and each farmer is at liberty to fence in his tract according to the unyielding lines of his rectangular boundaries.

These overland trails, now well-beaten wagon tracks, were originally located upon the high and dry swells of the prairie, the most desirable land for agricultural purposes. They followed the best routes and sought the easiest crossings of the streams, low grounds, and swamps. Near Leavenworth the progress of inclosure is driving them into the wet grounds, and greatly increases the difficulties of travel.

It is much to be desired that in all future land sales the great and long-established trails, the highways across the continent, should be reserved from sale and be devoted forever as public highways. A certain width on each side of them should be marked out by actual survey and reserved for this purpose. Wagon roads across the continent will always be needed, even when the railroads are completed.

The following is an estimate of the cost of transportation of military stores westward across the plains by contract during the fiscal year ending June 30, 1865:

I. Northern and western route:		
To Utah and posts on that route		$1,524,119.00
II. Southwestern route:		
To Fort Union, N. Mex., and posts on that route	$1,301,400	
Posts in the interior of New Mexico	138,178	
		1,439,578.00
Cost of the transportation of grain on above routes, where the grain was delivered by contractors and the transportation entered into the price paid, same year—		
1. Utah route	$2,526,727,68	
2. New Mexico route	697,101.69	
		3,223,829.37
Cost of transportation of military stores across the plains same year by Government trains—		
1. Utah route	$34,600	
2. New Mexico route	166.730	
		201,330.00
Total by contract and Government trains		6,388,856.37

This expenditure would be reduced by the opening of railroads by a sum which would aid materially in paying interest upon the cost of their construction.

The present season has been a very wet one upon the plains. In wet weather the heavy wagons are generally compelled to go into camp and wait patiently till dry weather makes the roads practicable. Any effort to move exhausts the animals and destroys the wagons, while the progress of such a train would not average in bad weather over many portions of the roads one mile a day. Trains from Fort Leavenworth to Denver City have this year occupied from forty-five to seventy-four days in the march.

DIVISION OF INSPECTION.

The Eighth Division of this office is the division of inspection. Its duties are delicate and difficult. It receives, registers, analyzes, and prepares for action of the Quartermaster-General all reports of the regular inspectors, or of officers acting as inspectors under orders of the Quartermaster's Department, and all reports of inspections of that department by the Inspector-General of the Army which may be referred to this office for action.

It keeps the roster of the officers of the Quartermaster's Department, and keeps a careful and minute record of the service of all officers as reported to this office. It also prepares and records the general and special orders of the department and its nominations for assignment to duty.

The organization of the inspectors of the Quartermaster's Department provides for six inspectors, with the rank of colonel, and a chief of the division of inspection. Other officers of the department are placed on inspection duty from time to time, as their services are needed.

Since the cessation of hostilities a number of officers have been thus employed to collect the information necessary to compel great and necessary reductions in the establishment, which had been created during the war.

The report of Col. G. V. Rutherford, chief of the division of inspection, which is herewith, gives in detail the operations of the office.

During the fiscal year 216 reports were received from the inspectors. Over 11,000 inventories and reports of inspection of property recommended for sale or condemnation and 293 reports of boards of survey were received and acted on.

A record of the appointment, movements, services, and duties of each officer of the Quartermaster's Department, and of reports of commanding officers and inspectors in relation to his performance of duty has been kept. Five hundred and ninety-one annual reports of officers were rendered during the fiscal year, and 340 such reports have been received since its termination. From the information given in these reports, tables of quantities and of expenditures by officers have been prepared, which accompany this report.

Several boards for examination of officers of this department have been in session during the year. Two hundred and forty-three officers have been examined, of whom forty-nine were reported by the boards as disqualified and 194 as qualified.

On the 30th of June, 1865, there were in the Qartermaster's Department:

Regular officers	67
Military store-keepers	11
	78
Assistant quartermasters of volunteers	488
Total, including eleven military store-keepers	566

Many of these officers have, for distinguished services during the war, received brevet promotion beyond their lineal rank. Many have been assigned to important positions, to which, under the law, increased, though temporary, rank is attached.

The report of the inspection division gives details as to the number of officers who have won such distinction. For the names I must refer to the tables accompanying this report, in which most of them are mentioned, and to the Army Register. During the fiscal year there were appointed 5 assistant quartermasters of the Regular Army, 145 assistant quartermasters of the Volunteer Army, and 2 military store-keepers.

During the fiscal year there retired from the service 5 assistant quartermasters of the Regular Army and 203 assistant quartermasters of volunteers. Since the termination of the fiscal year, and to the 1st of October, 1 assistant quartermaster of regulars, 1 military store-keeper, and 172 assistant quartermasters of volunteers have retired from the service, resigned, dismissed, or honorably mustered out.

The reduction is still going on rapidly, as troops are discharged and posts abandoned, and the services of these officers can be dispensed with. Three hundred and eighty-two officers in all left the service of the Quartermaster's Department between the 1st of July, 1864, and the 1st of October, 1865.

The distribution of general orders to officers of the Quartermaster's Department is part of the duty of the inspection division. It distributed during the fiscal year 177,289 copies of general orders, of which 124,177 were general orders of the Adjutant-General's Office.

Colonel Rutherford's vigilance and promptness in the discharge of his duties have been most important aids in the supervision of the extended operations of this department, and I am happy to acknowledge the recognition which they have met from the Secretary of War.

ACCOUNTS FOR MONEY AND PROPERTY.

The assistant quartermaster-general has charge of the examination of the accounts of disbursing officers and of officers responsible for public property (other than property accounts of clothing, camp and garrison equipage, which latter accounts are examined in the division of clothing and equipage).

The chief of the Ninth Division reports that there were received at this office in the fiscal year ending June 30, 1862, 7,094 accounts, all of which have been examined and transmitted to the Treasury for settlement.

In the year ending June 30, 1863, there were received 29,153, all of which have been examined and transmitted to the Treasury.

In the year ending June 30, 1864, there were received 67,856 accounts; of these there have been examined and transmitted to the Treasury 14,588. There remain to be examined 53,268.

In the year ending June 30, 1865, there were received 72,299 accounts; of these there have been examined and transmitted to the Treasury 12,424. There remain to be examined 59,875.

During the four years, July 1, 1861, to June 30, 1865, there were received in all 176,402 accounts; examined and sent to the Treasury 63,259; remaining to be examined 113,143.

These are not single vouchers, but accounts, many of which contain hundreds, and some of them thousands, of single vouchers. They represent the expenditure of over one thousand millions of dollars in money, and the use and application of the property purchased therewith. The delay in their final settlement is injurious alike to the officer and to the Government, and it is of great importance that their settlement be expedited by all the means in the power of the Government. It is from the final examination and discussion of these accounts that the statistical information necessary to a proper understanding of the cost of the great war, now happily ended, is to be obtained. These accounts record the purchases of materials; the cost of movements by rail, river, and sea; the application of the materials purchased; the distance men and material were transported; the cost and extent of the hospitals, barracks, store-houses, and camps which have covered the country with buildings and canvas.

Reports made by officers are often imperfect; their accounts for purchases must be complete; and these accounts record the actual cost and the time of purchase of every article provided by the Quartermaster's Department during the war, from the ocean steamer of 2,500 tons to the saddler's or tent-maker's needle and thread.

In the last annual report of this department attention was called to the inadequate force provided by law for the prompt examination of officers' accounts, and a recommendation was made for the increase of that force by the addition of 170 clerks, classified as follows: 70 of class one, 60 of class two, 30 of class three, and 10 of class four. Another year's experience makes more urgent the necessity of this increase, and I repeat the recommendation of the last annual report.

MILITARY ORGANIZATION OF EMPLOYÉS OF THE QUARTERMASTER'S DEPARTMENT.

In the last annual report of this office I had the honor to report the services rendered in the field, as soldiers, at Nashville, at Johnsonville, and at Washington City, by the Quartermaster's Volunteers, a military organization under your sanction, of the clerks, agents, and operatives of the Quartermaster's Department at the principal depots. Since that report was written the Quartermaster's Volunteers at Nashville, under the command of Bvt. Brig. Gen. J. L. Donaldson, have again had the opportunity to render important service. Two brigades of these troops, 4,500 strong, were assigned a position in the operations of the 15th and 16th of December, 1864, the days of the decisive battle of Nashville, and so conducted themselves as to merit and receive the approval of their commanders.

The surrender of the rebel armies having made their services no longer necessary, the several brigades and regiments have been disbanded, and most of their members have, in the general reduction of the force employed, been discharged from service. The arms and equipments have been returned to the Ordnance Department.

Colored men continued to the close of the war to be employed in connection with the trains of the Quartermaster's Department as laborers at depots, as pioneers with the marching columns. In all these positions they have done good service and materially contributed to that final victory which confirmed their freedom and saved our place among nations.

I cannot close this report without calling your attention to the services rendered by the officers and agents of this department. Some of these officers had at the beginning of the war the advantage of previous experience in the Quartermaster's Department during former wars, but by far the greater part of them were taken from the occupations of civil life, without military training or experience. Many of them as the war went on were promoted from the ranks of the volunteers. A very few have proved unfaithful, but the great body of them have served laboriously and zealously, successfully and honorably.

Whether in the field or at the depot, there is no intermission to the labor and the responsibility of a quartermaster. In the field he is expected to overcome the difficulties of the road cut up by the passage of troops and artillery, and to run the gauntlet of a hostile population in the rear of the armies—a population exasperated by the loss of property taken by foragers. Often insufficiently guarded, upon his vigilance and energy depend the safety of his train and of the indispensable supplies which it bears. Long after the troops are at rest in their camps the quartermaster is upon the road.

At the depot of an army the reception, care, and distribution of the immense supplies of food, ammunition, and clothing, and all other equipment, all of which pass through the hands of the quartermaster, tax him night and day. He is held to strict accountability for every item of the stores which pass through his hands.

In the greater depots which have been during the war the centers at which the business of providing for the Army has been concentrated, the officers in charge have borne the responsibility of disbursing millions of dollars, collecting, auditing, and settling the vouchers issued by officers at smaller depots and in the field, and purchasing the stores to be distributed to armies through wide districts. Some of these officers have transacted business to the amount of millions monthly. From officers of every rank, from those in charge of the great centers of manufacture and purchase at the principal cities, from those to whom has been committed only the care of the property and trains of a single brigade, I have received and I recognize cordial support and assistance in the business committed to this department.

It is well understood among soldiers that upon the efficiency and integrity of the supply branches of the service depends, in a great degree, the power to make long marches, the health and efficiency of the troops.

I have imperfectly set forth in this report some of the more important operations of the Quartermaster's Department during the past year. I hope at a future time to be able to present to you more complete and detailed information of the extent of the resources, in material and men and money, which under your administration of the War Department have been applied to support and sustain the armies in every part of the wide field of operation during the past four years of war.

This information properly digested, if published, will stand before the world as an example and a warning of the power and resources of a free people for any contest into which they heartily enter, and from it the soldier and statesman will be able to draw valuable lessons for use in case it ever again becomes necessary for this Nation to put forth its strength in arms.

The merits and services of many of the officers of the department have been presented to you by myself, or by the generals under whom they have served in the field. I acknowledge the kindness with which their claims and my recommendations have been considered, and thank you for the recognition which has been given by their promotion of the services of the department which I have had the honor to control.

I transmit herewith reports of officers, with many tables, giving in detail information of value in relation to the operations of the department. To these I respectfully call your attention.*

All of which is respectfully submitted.

M. C. MEIGS,

Brevet Major-General, U. S. Army, Quartermaster-General.

No. 1.

On June 30, 1864, the termination of the preceding fiscal year, the balances in the hands of officers (after deducting the disbursements ascertained from accounts which had passed the required administrative examination of this office) amounted, as stated in the last annual report, to			$296,968,869.36
From which there is to be made a further deduction of the amount of disbursements, ascertained from accounts for periods prior to and of the fiscal year ending June 30, 1864, which had been received and registered, but of which the required administrative examination had not been made, viz:			
Prior to the fiscal year	$26,096,345.50		
During the fiscal year	201,064,148.97		
		$227,160,494.47	
Less amount shown to have been received from sales of property, rent of buildings, &c		5,820,943.99	
			221,339,550.48
Leaving an outstanding balance due June 30, 1864, of			75,629,318.88

* Such of these reports and tables as are here omitted will be found in Executive Document No. 1, House of Representatives, Thirty-ninth Congress, first session, Vol. I, unless otherwise indicated as appearing in Series I, or elsewhere in this series.

Which was made up as follows, viz:

1. Amount of requisitions drawn during the fiscal year 1864, the accounts for disbursement of which had not been received at this office	$31,317,806.00	
A large portion of this, although remitted during the fiscal year, could not have been received before its termination, and could not, therefore, be accounted for during that fiscal year; the greater portion had doubtless been accounted for direct to the proper accounting officer of the Treasury Department, as required by the act of Congress approved July 17, 1862.		
2. Amount in the hands of officers, to be accounted for hereafter	44,311,512.88	
		$75,629,318.88

Of this latter amount the sum of $3,378,279.87 was amount of requisitions drawn during the fiscal years 1862 and 1863 in favor of officers, not taken up in their accounts received at this office, viz:

In the fiscal year 1862	$1,579,471.87	
In the fiscal year 1863	1,798,799.00	
		3,378,270.87
The sum of $24,336,849.80 was amount in hands of officers unaccounted for (as ascertained from balances found due the Government upon examination of the last accounts received and from receipts for advances made to officers for disbursement during the fiscal year 1864) by officers whose accounts had been rendered		24,336,849.80
Of this amount the sum of $20,895,967.70 was the amount of balances found due the Government upon examination of the last accounts received in the fiscal year 1864	$20,895,967.70	
The balance, $3,440,882.10, was the amount of the receipts for advances made to officers for disbursements during the fiscal year 1864, not taken up in the accounts received at this office, as before stated	3,440,882.10	
The greater portion of this had probably been accounted for direct to the proper accounting officers of the Treasury Department, as required by the act of Congress before referred to. The remainder was distributed among the officers disbursing at the various posts and stations and in the field, and was applicable to the payment of debts contracted during the year. It was		16,596,392.21
Total amount, as above		44,311,512.88
Balance for which the accounts had not received the required administrative examination of this office, as above reported		296,968,869.36
To which are to be added:		
1. Remittances in July, 1864	$38,584,250.00	
Remittances in August, 1864	32,976,611.00	
Remittances in September, 1864	25,476,722.41	
Remittances in October, 1864	24,151,957.00	
Remittances in November, 1864	35,704,491.00	
Remittances in December, 1864	41,124,342.60	
Remittances in January, 1865	7,466,063.10	
Remittances in February, 1865	600,000.00	
Remittances in March, 1865	90,341,901.94	
Remittances in April, 1865	49,813,329.76	
Remittances in May, 1865	59,880,447.72	
Remittances in June, 1865	25,585,940.91	
		431,706,057.44
2. Proceeds of sales of property, rents of buildings, &c		3,620,997.88
Total to be accounted for		732,295,924.68

From which are to be deducted the disbursements by officers, ascertained from accounts which have passed the required administrative examination of this office, viz:

Prior to the fiscal year (the accounts for which had not passed the required administrative examination in time for the last annual report)	$167,746,758.97	
In the month of July, 1864	12,815,518.03	
In the month of August, 1864	16,971,042.31	
In the month of September, 1864	11,254,975.51	
In the month of October, 1864	8,062,686.55	
In the month of November, 1864	2,553,155.61	
In the month of December, 1864	3,176,591.08	
In the month of January, 1865	853,742.04	
In the month of February, 1865	1,367,986.64	
In the month of March, 1865	480,870.03	
In the month of April, 1865	263,275.35	
In the month of May, 1865	369,061.42	
In the month of June, 1865	203,698.70	
		$226,119,362.24
Balance due June 30, 1865		506,176,562.44

From which there is to be made a further deduction of the amount of disbursements, as ascertained from accounts for periods prior to and in the fiscal year ending June 30, 1865, which have been received and registered, but of which the required administrative examination has not been made, viz:

Amount prior to the fiscal year 1865	$82,446,154.51	
Amount in the fiscal year 1865	375,932,744.71	
Total	458,378,899.22	
Less amount shown to have been received from sales of property, rent of buildings, &c	12,005,976.93	
		446,372,922.29
Leaving an outstanding balance due June 30, 1865, of		59,803,640.15

Which is made up as follows, viz:

1. Amount of requisitions drawn in favor of officers and not taken up in their accounts received at this office, viz:

In the fiscal year 1862	$996,287.87	
In the fiscal year 1863	417,988.00	
In the fiscal year 1864	447,916.00	
In the fiscal year 1865	8,528,557.99	
Total		10,390,749.86

2. Amount of advances made to officers for disbursements not taken up, as ascertained from the accounts received at this office, viz:

In the fiscal year 1864	$615,660.55	
In the fiscal year 1865	4,176,717.71	
Total		4,792,378.26

3. Amount in the hands of officers and agents, accounted for as balances due the Government, ascertained upon examination of their last accounts received 44,620,512.03

The amounts paid during the fiscal year ending June 30, 1865 (including those for purchases made and services rendered in the preceding fiscal year, and not included in the last annual report), as ascertained from the accounts which passed the required administrative examination of this office, were, viz:

1. For regular supplies, viz:

Fuel	$3,159,423.61	
Forage	50,584,487.59	
Straw	191,175.28	
Stationery	618,688.65	
		54,553,775.08

2. For incidental expenses of the Army, viz:		
Postage	$150,379.92	
Expenses of courts-martial	203,836.79	
Express and escorts	21,650.46	
Burial expenses	128,940.12	
Guides, interpreters, and spies	167,262.43	
Clerks and agents	1,883,582.07	
Pay of wagon and forage masters	4,116.61	
Laborers	4,012,721.91	
Soldiers on constant labor	378,428.22	
Hire of veterinary surgeons	28,041.01	
Office furniture	90,961.54	
Medicines for horses and other animals	107,522.79	
Forges, blacksmiths' and shoeing tools	131,740.55	
Horse and mule shoes, nails, iron, and steel, for shoeing	1,580,337.68	
Picket rope	457.36	
Apprehension of deserters	450,202.16	
		$9,340,181.62
3. Cavalry and artillery horses		10,749,054.35
4. Transportation and supply of prisoners, &c		156,240.39
5. Telegraph for military purposes, and expenses in operating the same		245,420.27
6. Barracks and quarters, viz:		
For rent	$1,562,140.28	
For repairs and construction	5,778,531.51	
		7,340,671.79
7. Mileage—transportation of officers and baggage		258,073.94
8. Transportation, viz:		
Of clothing	$268,588.38	
Of subsistence	1,620,087.39	
Of ordnance	476,235.38	
Of troops and supplies	80,776,781.72	
		83,141,692.87
9. Purchase of stoves		309,623.71
10. For material for and amount expended in the purchase and preparation of clothing, camp and garrison equipage		59,307,028.77
11. Collecting, drilling, and organizing volunteers		9,292.08
12. For the construction and maintenance of the gun-boat fleet proper		295,177.91
13. For the purchase, construction, and maintenance of steam rams		190,918.25
14. Special expenditures for other departments, and under special appropriations, viz:		
For Medical Department	$86,881.86	
For Ordnance Department	27,921.63	
For Pay Department	9,937.14	
For Subsistence Department	2,449.53	
For Engineer Department	30,675.33	
For Adjutant-General's Department	2,564.50	
For Army contingencies	89,515.15	
For Provost-Marshal-General's Department	4,220.46	
For Signal Service	175.88	
		60,366,382.20
		226,151,492.51
Less amount of errors, &c., ascertained in officers' accounts		32,130.27
Total		226,119,362.24

From the above statement it will be seen that during the past year accounts to the amount of $226,119,362.24 have passed the official examination of this office, prior to transmission to the Treasury for final examination and settlement. They number 7,066; and 12,189 accounts remain in this office to be examined, relating to disbursements, amounting to $458,378,899.22.

During the year preceding the last annual report from this office the accounts examined and transmitted to the Treasury covered disbursements to the amount of $284,809,697.72.

Abstract of appropriations for the Quartermaster's Department for the fiscal years 1862–1866, including arrearages for 1861.

Heads of appropriations.	Appropriation for the fiscal year ending June 30, 1862, including arrearages for 1861.	Jan. 15, war warrant.	Appropriation March 18, war warrant, act of Feb. 25, 1862.	Appropriation March 27, war warrant, act of Feb. 25, 1862.
Quartermaster's Department	$14, 265, 059. 37			$13, 000, 000. 00
Incidental expenses of the Quartermaster's Department.	7, 666, 666. 00			6, 000, 000. 00
Purchase of horses	10, 514, 500. 00		$1, 661, 040. 00	5, 000, 000. 00
Barracks, quarters, &c	1, 500, 000. 00			500, 000. 00
Transportation of the Army	16, 220, 954. 00		14, 881, 000. 00	22, 000, 000. 00
Transportation of officers' baggage	500, 000. 00			
Clothing of the Army	13, 416, 037. 02		12, 173, 546. 77	29, 000, 000. 00
Military telegraph				
Transportation of prisoners				1, 000, 000. 00
Appropriation for stoves				
Collecting, organizing, and drilling volunteers.		$5, 000, 000. 00		
Construction, &c., of steam rams				
Gun-boats for Western rivers	1, 000, 000. 00			
Contingencies of the Army	200, 000. 00			
Total	65, 083, 216. 39	5, 000, 000. 00	28, 715, 586. 77	76, 500, 000. 00

Heads of appropriations.	Appropriation for the fiscal year ending June 30, 1863.	Deficiency bill for the fiscal year ending June 30, 1863.	Appropriation for the fiscal year ending June 30, 1864.	Deficiency bill for the fiscal year ending June 30, 1864.
Quartermaster's Department	$36, 912, 000. 00	$6, 000, 000. 00	$67, 217, 791. 00	$18, 500, 000. 00
Incidental expenses of the Quartermaster's Department.	20, 836, 750. 00		19, 125, 000. 00	2, 000, 000. 00
Purchase of horses	5, 400, 000. 00	11, 000, 000. 00	23, 189, 375. 00	17, 500, 000. 00
Barracks, quarters, &c	4, 234, 000. 00	1, 730, 000. 00	8, 000, 000. 00	3, 500, 000. 00
Transportation of the Army	40, 000, 000. 00	25, 000, 000. 00	56, 500, 000. 00	30, 000, 000. 00
Transportation of officers' baggage	1, 291, 600. 00		1, 000, 000. 00	100, 000. 00
Clothing of the Army	39, 322, 513. 25	27, 136, 000. 00	76, 281, 911. 54	7, 000, 000. 00
Military telegraph	500, 000. 00		500, 000. 00	
Transportation of prisoners	3, 373, 728. 00		1, 500, 000. 00	
Appropriation for stoves	90, 000. 00		140, 000. 00	
Collecting, organizing, and drilling volunteers.				
Construction, &c., of steam rams	580, 000. 00	450, 000. 00		
Gun-boats for Western rivers	2, 560, 000. 00			
Contingencies of the Army	500, 000. 00		600, 000. 00	
Total	155, 100, 591. 25	71, 316, 000. 00	253, 454, 077. 54	78, 600, 000. 00

Abstract of appropriations for the Quartermaster's Department for the fiscal years 1862–1866, including arrearages for 1861—Continued.

Heads of appropriations.	Appropriation for the fiscal year ending June 30, 1865.	Deficiency bill for the fiscal year ending June 30, 1865.	Appropriation for the fiscal year ending June 30, 1866.	Total.
Quartermaster's Department	$60,000,000.00	$20,000,000.00	$50,000,000.00	$285,894,850.37
Incidental expenses of the Quartermaster's Department.	13,000,000.00	1,000,000.00	10,000,000.00	79,628,416.00
Purchase of horses	21,000,000.00	7,600,000.00	21,000,000.00	123,864,915.00
Barracks, quarters, &c	5,000,000.00	2,000,000.00	5,000,000.00	31,464,000.00
Transportation of the Army	40,000,000.00	19,856,137.00	30,000,000.00	294,458,091.00
Transportation of officers' baggage	700,000.00	....	500,000.00	4,091,600.00
Clothing of the Army	58,000,000.00	30,000,000.00	50,000,000.00	342,330,008.58
Military telegraph	275,000.00	725,000.00	500,000.00	2,500,000.00
Transportation of prisoners	900,000.00	2,000,000.00	1,000,000.00	9,773,728.00
Appropriation for stoves	100,000.00	....	100,000.00	430,000.00
Collecting, organizing, and drilling volunteers.	....	....	....	5,000,000.00
Construction, &c., of steam rams	275,000.00	....	....	1,305,000.00
Gun-boats for Western rivers	....	....	....	3,500,000.00
Contingencies of the Army	400,000.00	....	400,000.00	2,100,000.00
Total	199,250,000.00	83,181,137.00	168,100,000.00	1,184,300,608.95
Special appropriation entered May 23, 1864, for clothing, &c., of 100-days' volunteers.	....	....	....	5,000,000.00

NOTE.—Appropriations for contingencies of the Army, though included in the annual estimates of the Quartermaster-General, have not of late years been expended under his direction; they are not, therefore, included in the summing up of the appropriations for the Quartermaster's Department in this table.

No. 2.

QUARTERMASTER-GENERAL'S OFFICE, FIRST DIVISION,
Washington, D. C., October 17, 1865.

Bvt. Maj. Gen. M. C. MEIGS,
Quartermaster-General U. S. Army, Washington, D. C.:

GENERAL: In compliance with General Orders, No. 39, Quartermaster-General's Office, dated July 1, 1865, I have the honor to submit the following annual report, embracing the operations of this division for the fiscal year ending June 30, 1865, together with general statements of operations up to the present date, as required by circular from the Quartermaster-General of the 24th of July, 1865:

My annual report for the fiscal year ending June 30, 1864, was forwarded to the Quartermaster-General, from this division, on the 27th of September, 1864.

During the last fiscal year, and up to the present time, I have been stationed at Washington, D. C., continuing to perform the duties of chief quartermaster of the Cavalry Bureau, to which I had been assigned, by order of the War Department, on the 27th of December, 1863, relieving Lieut. Col. C. G. Sawtelle. In addition to these duties I have, since the 2d of August, 1864, performed those pertaining to the office of colonel and brevet brigadier-general in charge of the First Division of the Quartermaster-General's Office, having been assigned, by order of the War Department, to these duties at the date just mentioned, under the act of Congress of July 4, 1864, to provide for the better organization of the Quartermaster's Department.

As chief quartermaster of the Cavalry Bureau I was charged with the purchase and supply of all animals required for the cavalry branch of the service, under the immediate orders of Maj. Gen. H. W. Halleck, chief of staff, and subsequently under those of Lieutenant-General Grant. As the officer in charge of the First Division of the Quartermaster-General's Office, I was charged with the purchase, procurement, and disposition of horses and mules for cavalry, artillery, wagon and ambulance trains, and all other purposes for which horses and mules may be procured for the armies of the United States. The duties of both these assignments I still continue to discharge.

It is a source of great satisfaction to me that during the great campaigns immediately preceding the downfall of the rebellion, as indeed in preceding operations against the enemy, the Cavalry Bureau and this division were enabled, with the energetic co-operation of the various quartermasters and assistant quartermasters at the several purchasing depots under my direction, to meet promptly all requisitions for the supply of public animals to our gallant armies in the field. The animals thus furnished were generally of a very good quality, owing to the rigid character of the inspection made by the inspecting officers, who were governed in their actions by General Orders, No. 43, of the Quartermaster-General, series 1864. As the war progressed those furnished to the Armies of the Potomac and James, especially, were so superior as to elicit the commendation of Bvt. Maj. Gen. Rufus Ingalls, chief quartermaster, from whose indorsement of November 30, 1864, forwarding estimate of public animals required for these armies for the month of December, 1864, the following is an extract:

> The supply (of animals) is already very good, and it is proper to state that the artillery and cavalry horses sent to these armies during the past three months have been the best we have received during the war.

Testimonials of a similar character were received during the past year from chief quartermasters in the armies of the South and Southwest.

The business of my office does not require the rendition of either of the statements called for in paragraphs 3, 5, 6, 7, 8, 9, 10, and 11, of General Orders, No. 39, Quartermaster-General's Office, current series.

It will be seen by statement herewith that under the immediate direction of the several officers in charge of purchasing depots within the control of the Cavalry Bureau and First Division, Quartermaster-General's Office, there were purchased as follows, viz:

CAVALRY HORSES.

From January 1, 1864, to June 30, 1864, per last report		48,719
From January 1, 1864, to June 30, 1864, per reports subsequently received		3,037
Total from January 1, 1864, to June 30, 1864		51,756
From June 30, 1864, to December 31, 1864	98,555	
From January 1, 1865, to May 9, 1865, when purchase ceased	43,077	
Total purchased during the year ending June 30, 1865		141,632
Total purchased from January 1, 1864, to May 9, 1865		193,388

ARTILLERY HORSES.

From September 1, 1864, to December 31, 1864	12,453
From January 1, 1865, to May 9, 1865	8,261
Total purchased from September 1, 1864, to May 9, 1865	20,714

MULES.

From September 1, 1864, to December 31, 1864	20,711
From January 1, 1865, to May 9, 1865	25,210
Total purchased from September 1, 1864, to May 9, 1865	45,921

There are no records on file in this office by which the number of animals purchased by the Cavalry Bureau prior to January 1, 1864, can be determined.

Reports to this office of purchases of artillery horses and mules date from September 1, 1864.

During the fiscal year ending June 30, 1865, the prices paid for cavalry horses ranged from $144 per head (the lowest contract price) to $185 per head (the highest market price). From September 1, 1864, to June 30, 1865, the prices paid for artillery horses ranged from $161 to $185 per head, and during the latter period the prices paid for mules ranged from $170 to $195 per head. The average (approximate) prices are given in the tabular statement herewith.

The following is a statement of the number of public animals sold and died at the several depots since the 1st of January, 1864, viz:

CAVALRY HORSES.

Sold from January 1, 1864, to June 30, 1864	5,845
Sold from June 30, 1864, to December 31, 1864	8,598
Sold from January 1, 1865, to June 30, 1865	25,627
Total sold from January 1, 1864, to June 30, 1865	40,070
Died from January 1, 1864, to June 30, 1864	8,434
Died from June 30, 1864, to December 31, 1864	13,662
Died from January 1, 1865, to June 30, 1865	16,181
Total died from January 1, 1864, to June 30, 1865	38,277

ARTILLERY HORSES.

Of artillery horses none were reported as sold from September 1, 1864, to June 30, 1865.

Died from September 1, 1864, to December 31, 1864	176
Died from January 1, 1865, to June 30, 1865	258
Total died from September 1, 1864, to June 30, 1865	434

MULES.

Sold from September 1, 1864, to December 31, 1864	287
Sold from January 1, 1865, to June 30, 1865	13,192
Total sold from September 1, 1864, to June 30, 1865	13,479
Died from September 1, 1864, to December 31, 1864	1,230
Died from January 1, 1865, to June 30, 1865	6,106
Total died from September 1, 1864, to June 30, 1865	7,336

Of unserviceable stock received at depots for recuperation, the returns to this office are not sufficiently complete to enable me to pronounce the exact proportion restored to ability for service. Observations made at several depots during limited periods indicate 60 per cent. as about the proportion so restored. It is a matter of regret that, although several attempts have been made by this office to procure returns of the destruction of animals in the field, such returns have not been obtained. Without doubt this destruction has been very great, especially in the army operating in the Shenandoah Valley under General Sheridan. The issues of cavalry horses to this force were at the rate of three remounts per annum.

Following this is the report of animals purchased and issued at the several depots referred to and also statement of quartermasters' property, marked A.

*Report of the purchase and issue of cavalry horses at depots under direction of the Cavalry Bureau during the six months ending December 31, 1864.**

SUMMARY TO FOREGOING TABLE.

On hand at depots July 1, 1864	17,507	Issued to departments	121,521
Purchased July 1 to December 31, 1864	98,555	Sold	8,598
Received from sundry sources	60,050	Lost, destroyed, and died	13,662
Received from artillery (transferred)	1,545	Transferred to artillery	4,014
		On hand December 31, 1864	29,862
Total	177,657	Total	177,657

*Report of the purchase and issue of cavalry horses at depots under direction of the First Division, Quartermaster-General's Office, during the six months ending June 30, 1865.**

SUMMARY.

On hand at depots January 1, 1865	29,862	Issued to departments	59,835
Purchased from January 1 to May 9, 1865	43,077	Sold	25,627
Received from sundry sources	42,424	Lost, destroyed, and died	16,181
Received from artillery (transferred)	2,827	Transferred to artillery	1,630
		On hand June 30, 1865	14,917
Total	118,190	Total	118,190

*Report of the purchase and issue of artillery horses at depots under direction of the First Division, Quartermaster-General's Office, from September 1, 1864, to June 30, 1865.**

SUMMARY TO FOREGOING TABLE.

On hand at depots September 1, 1864	346	Issued to departments	15,683
Purchased from September 1, 1864, to May 9, 1865	20,714	Lost, destroyed, and died	434
Received from sundry sources	890	Transferred to cavalry	4,372
Received from cavalry (transferred)	2,014	On hand June 30, 1865	3,475
Total	23,964	Total	23,964

NOTE.—Average price only approximate. Number shown on report of cavalry as transferred to artillery, 5,644; number shown on report of artillery as received from cavalry, 2,014; difference, 3,630. Explained thus: Artillery horses sent to Giesborough were received as cavalry and afterward transferred to artillery.

*Report of the purchase and issue of mules at depots under direction of the First Division, Quartermaster-General's Office, from September 1, 1864, to June 30, 1865.**

SUMMARY TO FOREGOING TABLE.

On hand at depots September 1, 1864	15,885	Issued to departments	61,911
Purchased September 1, 1864, to June 30, 1865	45,921	Sold	13,479
Received from sundry sources	57,089	Lost, destroyed, and died	7,336
		On hand at depots June 30, 1865	36,169
Total	118,895	Total	118,895

A.—*Statement of quartermaster's property for the fiscal year ending June 30, 1865.* †

SALES OF PUBLIC ANIMALS.

As far as returns to this office indicate, there has been sold since the 8th of May last, in accordance with General Orders, No. 28, Quartermaster-General's Office, current series, the following number

* Omitted, except the "Summary." See foot-note (*), p. 249.

† Omitted. See pp. 134, 135 of the Executive Document referred to in foot-note (*) p. 249.

of animals, viz, 53,794 horses and 52,516 mules, for which the sum of $6,107,618.14 was received. It is probable that when full returns shall have been received the total amount of sales of animals from the 8th of May last up to the present time will be found to be upward of seven millions of dollars.

As required by the provisions of General Orders, No. 42, Quartermaster-General's Office, current series, these sales, with one or two exceptions, have been conducted by employés of this department, and this course has in all cases proved more advantageous to the Government than the employment of the professional auctioneers of any one locality for sales in that locality. The prices obtained by employés are generally greater than those secured by local auctioneers.

The success of this division in supplying the armies in the field has been mainly attributable to the zeal and fidelity of the officers acting under its orders, among whom I would mention—

Bvt. Col. C. H. Tompkins, assistant quartermaster, U. S. Army, Washington, D. C.

Capt. Ingham Coryell, assistant quartermaster, late in charge at Saint Louis, Mo.

Capt. L. Loury Moore, assistant quartermaster, New York City.

Capt. George T. Browning, assistant quartermaster, Giesborough, D. C.

Capt. E. C. Wilson, assistant quartermaster, Buffalo, N. Y.

Capt. J. L. Trumbull, assistant quartermaster, Saint Louis, Mo.

Capt. C. Hay, assistant quartermaster, Washington, D. C.

Capt. D. W. McClung, assistant quartermaster, Cincinnati, Ohio.

Capt. E. C. Reichenbach, assistant quartermaster, Harrisburg, Pa.

Capt. J. M. Bradshaw, assistant quartermaster, late at Chicago, Ill.

Capt. H. A. Du Puy, assistant quartermaster, Syracuse, N. Y.

Capt. C. H. Gallagher, assistant quartermaster, Wilmington, Del.

In the claim department I have had the valuable assistance of Bvt. Maj. J. T. Powers, assistant quartermaster.

All these have served faithfully and energetically, and I take pleasure in bearing this testimony to the Quartermaster-General.

The following is a statement of public moneys received and disbursed by me during the fiscal year ending June 30, 1865:

On hand July 1, 1864		$3,254,732.42
Received from officers during the year		373,888.75
Received from Treasury Department		4,851,800.00
Received from sales of property, &c		20,657.67
Total		8,501,078.84
Expended	$3,719,070.13	
Transferred to officers	4,295,963.72	
		8,015,033.85
Remaining on hand June 30, 1865		486,044.99
Deposited as follows:		
First National Bank, Washington		483,192.28
On hand		2,852.71
		486,044.99

Estimates made by various quartermasters for the purchase of animals during the fiscal year approved by me:

For the purchase of horses	$23,600,456.66
For the purchase of mules	6,434,637.66
Total	30,035,094.32

CLAIMS.

The business in the claim branch of this division has been increasing rapidly since the passage of the act of Congress of July 4, 1864.

During the fiscal year ending June 30, 1865, the whole number of claims, regular and miscellaneous, filed amounts to 4,174.

Number acted on	2,792
Number not acted on	1,382
Total	4,174

Very little progress has been made in the adjustment of these claims, as previous to January 1, 1865, only 800 had been filed, 3,374 having been filed during the last six months.

Considering the many disadvantages under which officers of this department labored in the discharge of their duties in the field, and the necessity of intrusting important positions to acting quartermasters, I find claims for animals taken for public use by them to be comparatively easy of adjustment, as, with but few exceptions, the proper accountability has been rendered except in cases where records and papers have been captured or destroyed by the enemy; hence the great mass of claims filed is for property taken by unauthorized officers of the Army, not accountable to this department.

The following difficulties are met with in the adjudication of these claims, viz:

First. Where memoranda receipts are given and the signatures of the officers certifying are unknown, and the only evidence the claimants can furnish that the officers took the property are the receipts themselves, great difficulty and embarrassment result from not being able to determine the genuineness of the signatures. Before the muster out of service of the troops it was the practice to communicate by letter with the officers themselves. The number of receipts given by irresponsible and unknown parties in the name of officers has attached suspicion to many claims, no doubt just and equitable, which I do not feel satisfied to pass upon without the verification of the officer's signature.

Second. Where memoranda receipts have not been given I am of opinion that the interests of the Government cannot be sufficiently protected by adjudicating these claims upon the *ex parte* evidence, which under present regulations can only be procured. As a general rule, just and equitable decisions cannot be given upon evidence presented by claimants unless the department can adopt some practice of examining witnesses in the locality where the claims originate.

Proof of loyalty seems to be so easily procured that from the records of this division it would seem that few have ever been disloyal, and I respectfully suggest that an additional guard be thrown around this kind of evidence; at least to require officers and witnesses to state their reasons for believing the claimants to have been loyal at the dates the claims originated.

The kind and character of evidence furnished in support of the great mass of these claims are insufficient to satisfy me that the property has been "actually received or taken for the use of and used by" the U. S. Army. As the act is now construed a very limited number of the claims on file will be allowed, and if a more liberal construction is given in regard to the phrase "proper officer," I would respectfully suggest that a board of officers be appointed in each military department to examine and report upon these claims.

In closing this report I cannot but express to the Quartermaster-General my high appreciation of the uniform kindness and courtesy he has extended toward me in the discharge of my official duties, and I feel grateful to that Providence who chooses the bounds of our habitations for having assigned me, during the prevalence of the great slaveholders' rebellion, to a department of mammoth proportions and of great responsibility, under the guidance and direction of an officer of distinguished ability, with whom I have had such delightful personal and official intercourse.

I am, general, very respectfully, your obedient servant,

JAMES A. EKIN,
Bvt. Brig. Gen., in Charge First Division, Q. M. G. O.

No. 3.

Statement of claims (regular and miscellaneous) filed in the First Division of the Quartermaster-General's Office during the fiscal year ending June 30, 1865, and from July 1, 1865, to October 20, 1865, showing the number paid, referred, and recommended for settlement, the number rejected and suspended, and the number not acted on, with their respective amounts.

Date.	Claims filed.		Paid, referred, and recommended for settlement.		Rejected and suspended.		Not acted on.	
	Number.	Amount.	Number.	Amount.	Number.	Amount.	Number.	Amount.
From July 1, 1864, to Dec. 31, 1864.	800	$248,472.60	694	$211,150.60	79	$15,272.00	27	$22,050.00
From Jan. 1, 1865, to June 30, 1865.	3,374	1,097,100.00	981	356,750.00	1,038	211,231.00	1,355	529,119.00
Total during the fiscal year.	4,174	1,345,572.60	1,675	567,900.60	1,117	226,503.00	1,382	551,169.00
From July 1, 1865, to Oct. 20, 1865.	3,781	1,357,486.00	210	74,514.00	31	11,047.00	3,540	1,271,925.00
Total	7,955	2,703,058.60	1,885	642,414.60	1,148	237,550.00	4,922	1,823,094.00

Many claims entered in the column of "rejected and suspended" have been rejected for want of evidence or accountability for the property, and may come before the department again; hence the impossibility of discriminating between "rejected" and "suspended."

Many of the claims entered in the column of "not acted on" are under investigation.

Respectfully submitted.

JAMES A. EKIN,
Bvt. Brig. Gen., in Charge First Division, Q. M. G. O.

FIRST DIVISION, QUARTERMASTER-GENERAL'S OFFICE,
November 8, 1865.

No. 4.

QUARTERMASTER-GENERAL'S OFFICE,
Washington, D. C., October 19, 1865.

Maj. Gen. M. C. MEIGS,
Quartermaster-General U. S. Army, Washington, D. C.:

GENERAL: In response to the circular of the Quartermaster-General of July 24, 1865, requiring reports of the operations of the several divisions of the office during the fiscal year ending June 30, 1865, I have the honor to submit the following tabular statements collected from the tables submitted to this office, in conformity with orders therefrom based upon the circular above referred to:

1. Statement of number of articles on hand and not transferred to the armies for issue June 30, 1864, showing the points at which they were stored.

2. Statement of quantity of material purchased during the fiscal year ending June 30, 1865, showing the quantity and cost of each kind and where purchased; also total quantity and cost of all.

3. Statement of number of articles of clothing and equipage purchased and manufactured during the fiscal year ending June 30, 1865, showing the quantity and cost of each kind, where purchased or manufactured; also total quantity and cost of all.

4. Statement of number of articles on hand and not transferred to the armies for issue, June 30, 1865, showing the points at which they were stored.

5. Statement showing the aggregate expenditure for the purchase of clothing, equipage, and material at the purchasing depots of New York, Philadelphia, and Cincinnati during the fiscal year ending June 30, 1865.

6. Statement showing quantity of material purchased at the depots of New York, Philadelphia, and Cincinnati since May, 1861.

7. Statement showing the number of principal articles of clothing and equipage purchased at the depots of New York, Philadelphia, and Cincinnati since May, 1861.

8. Statement showing the highest and lowest prices paid by the department for articles of clothing and equipage during the past four years of war.

These tables present in compact form the operations of the clothing and equipage division during the fiscal year ending June 30, 1865, and, as far as the reports that have been received to date will permit, the operations during the last four years of war.

The clothing and equipage supplied to the Army during the last fiscal year have been procured by purchase and manufacture at the principal depots of Philadelphia, New York, and Cincinnati, and in relatively small quantities at Saint Louis, Quincy, Ill., Steubenville, Ohio, and at Milwaukee, where the work was distributed among the needy relatives of soldiers in the ranks of the Union Army.

The material required for the manufacture of these large supplies has been drawn from our own markets, and has generally been made from native products.

Although very large demands have been made on the department during the past year, they have in no case exceeded its ability to produce and issue with promptitude the supplies required for the Army in its most extended operations. Perhaps the most prominent instance of the kind was the successful supply of Sherman's army after its triumphant march through the Southern States to the sea-coast, where it found at the right time and in the right places everything needed in this branch of the department.

The articles were shipped principally from the depot at New York upon short notice, and it is due to your own foresight and the promptness and energy of the officers in charge of the clothing and the transportation branches at New York that the success was so complete.

The tabular statements herewith will afford more precise knowledge upon the points referred to than could be given in narrative. The results are that there has been produced during the year material amounting to $21,416,818.84; equipage, $13,515,305.09; clothing, $70,087,282.20—making the expenditures for all objects, including payment of rents, compensation to employés, &c., more than $105,019,406.13.

The commencement of the war found the department prepared only for the supply of the old Army—a force on paper of about 13,000 men, with an actual strength seldom exceeding 10,000. The supplies of clothing and equipage for this force had been drawn entirely from the Schuylkill Arsenal, at Philadelphia, where they were manufactured under the supervision of the officers in charge from materials purchased for the purpose.

The sudden expansion of this small army to the great armies called into existence to quell the rebellion rendered necessary corresponding changes in the administration and operations of the clothing branch of the Quartermaster's Department. The manufacturing of clothing was increased to the greatest limit possible, employing from 8,000 to 10,000 operatives at once. Yet this force was found unequal to the task before it, and it was soon evident that other sources must be called upon to assist in meeting the demands made upon the department.

Two other principal depots were established in the summer of 1861, at New York and Cincinnati, respectively, and under the charge of energetic and skillful officers enabled the department to furnish supplies nearly as rapidly as required.

Both the manufacture and purchase by contract of the various articles required were pursued at Philadelphia, New York, and Cincinnati, the manufacture alone not being of itself a sufficient source of supply.

Many of the regiments called into service were clothed and equipped through the agency of their State authorities. In some cases where authority had been given them by the War Department the States were reimbursed through the Quartermaster's Department, after the examination of each account and its reference to the proper disbursing officer for settlement, as in the case of his own purchases. In other cases States were reimbursed by the United States through the Treasury Department under a special act of Congress to that effect.

The necessity of resorting to this method of partial supply soon passed away with the more perfect organization of the department, and since the first year of the war the department has been able to meet with alacrity every call made upon it.

Depots for the manufacture and purchase of army clothing and equipage, in addition to that at Schuylkill Arsenal, have been established during the war at New York, under General Vinton; at Cincinnati, under Capt. J. H. Dickerson, but since his resignation it has been under the charge of Col. W. W. McKim and Col. C. W. Moulton; at Quincy, Ill., for the benefit of suffering Union refugees and relatives of Union soldiers, under the charge of Capt. N. Flagg, assistant quartermaster; and for similar objects at Steubenville, Ohio, under Capt. Alexander Conn, assistant quartermaster. Saint Louis, Mo., was also at an early date made a prominent point for the manufacture of clothing, to give relief to impoverished operatives, friends of the Union cause in that city.

Purchases, except when specially authorized to be made in small quantities at other points, have only been made at the three depots of New York, Philadelphia, and Cincinnati. At all others the articles manufactured have been made from material sent from one of the three last named, generally from Philadelphia.

The object for which these smaller depots were established seems to have been fully accomplished, and the department has been well and economically provided with good serviceable garments near the points at which they were wanted for issue.

The smaller depots above mentioned have, since the termination of hostilities in the field, been broken up, in compliance with orders from the Secretary of War, and the garments moved to the central depots of Saint Louis and Cincinnati.

Col. W. W. McKim, in charge of the Schuylkill Arsenal, calls the attention of the department to the importance of substituting fire-proof buildings for the wooden structures now in use as store-houses at that depot.

The value of the property now stored there is about $20,000,000, and is in constant danger from fire. Locomotives pass along the entire length of the wall on the northern side many times every day and night. Colonel McKim reports that he has rearranged the stores, endeavoring to place the most valuable in the brick buildings; but much of it still remains in the wooden sheds, put up under pressing emergencies during the war.

I respectfully recommend that the brick buildings at present composing the permanent store-houses of the arsenal be enlarged and altered, so that they may be of sufficient dimensions to meet the increased wants of the service in this particular. No purchase of land would be necessary—simply the enlargement of the present buildings as they now stand, on ground owned by the Government.

It is not deemed necessary to submit details, unless the general plan shall be adopted. The matter, however, is one of much importance, and I hope it will meet with due consideration by the department.

The experience of the past war has developed the fact that exact uniformity of texture and quality of material and articles are in some respects not altogether practicable. The department will, however, from that experience, be enabled to arrive at exactly what the markets of the country can afford, and thereby determine such standards as are attainable by the majority of dealers, and at the same time equal to the requirements of the case. I recommend such modifications where they are necessary.

The quantity of clothing and equipage reported on hand June 30, 1865, being nearly the full supply preparatory to any demand that might possibly have been made during the past summer, is large in view of the much reduced forces. I am of the opinion, though, that were these articles forced upon the market for sale, being of that description for which there is no demand outside of the Army, the sacrifice would be greater than any loss that may result from damage while in store.

As to the material, much of it I believe might be sold to advantage, and I shall submit special reports recommending such disposition to be made of it.

The prices of clothing and equipage during the war were constantly advancing, and kept pace with the fluctuations of the Government currency. I have submitted in illustration of this fact a statement showing the highest and lowest prices paid from the beginning to the end of the war. It will be observed that the prices of many important articles have more than doubled, and in some instances they have even quadrupled their former value.

The complaints received from the armies as to the inferior quality of clothing and equipage have been very few, and have principally been confined to articles of equipage, especially knapsacks and haversacks, which, being manufactured from painted cloth, are from their nature subject to great deterioration, particularly when packed together, as they necessarily must be for transportation and economy of storage. It is generally conceded that the supplies have been of the most serviceable quality, and furnished in plentiful quantities.

The tabular statements submitted herewith do not include the purchases made by State authorities, the accounts for which have generally been settled by the Treasury Department under act of Congress, and from appropriation therefor not estimated for by this department.

They will give, however, in condensed form, full information as to the operations of the division of clothing and equipage during the last fiscal year, as well as interesting information concerning its operations during the last four years of war.

Respectfully submitted.

ALEX. J. PERRY,
Colonel, Quartermaster, in Charge Second Division.

No. 5.

*Monthly statement of clothing reported on hand at the various clothing depots for June 30, 1864.**

No. 6.

Monthly statement of camp and garrison equipage reported on hand at the various clothing depots for June 30, 1864.

---

*Omitted. This statement and No. 6 (following) are printed in Vol. IV, this series, pp. 907-912.

No. 7.

Statement of quantity of material purchased during the fiscal year ending June 30, 1865.

Articles.	Philadelphia.			New York.		
	Number or quantity.	Average cost.	Total value purchased.	Number or quantity.	Average cost.	Total value purchased.
Alpaca, black ....yards..	16, 573$\frac{1}{4}$	\$0. 51	\$8, 452. 35	......	......	......
Bunting, red, white, and blue ....pieces..	1, 174	17. 90	21, 015. 00	......	......	......
Burlaps ....yards..	150, 166	. 34$\frac{1}{2}$	51, 808. 11	......	......	......
Buckles, pantaloon ....gross..	2, 405	. 52$\frac{11}{12}$	1, 273. 55	......	......	......
Buttons ....do...	208, 694	. 32$\frac{3}{7}$	67, 739. 15	......	......	......
Braid, $\frac{1}{8}$-inch, scarlet ....yards..	42, 192	. 01$\frac{1}{25}$	439. 42	......	......	......
Crayons, tailors' ....boxes..	1, 000	. 60	600. 00	......	......	......
Cloth:						
Dark blue, $\frac{6}{4}$ ....yards..	356, 627$\frac{1}{2}$	5. 25$\frac{1}{2}$	1, 874, 077. 51	......	......	......
Dark blue, $\frac{3}{4}$ ....do...	43, 358$\frac{1}{2}$	3. 40	147, 418. 90	......	......	......
Scarlet facing, $\frac{6}{4}$ ....do...	1, 385$\frac{1}{2}$	4. 00	5, 542. 00	......	......	......
White facing, $\frac{3}{4}$ ....do...	82$\frac{3}{4}$	5. 83	482. 42	......	......	......
S. B. facing, $\frac{6}{4}$ ....do...	1, 313$\frac{3}{4}$	5. 17$\frac{5}{12}$	6, 793. 25	......	......	......
Cord, tent lacing ....pounds..	7, 310$\frac{1}{2}$	. 38	2, 777. 98	......	......	......
Cotton, sewing ....spools..	83, 400	. 10$\frac{7}{8}$	9, 069. 75	......	......	......
Duck, cotton ....yards..	22, 535$\frac{1}{2}$	. 71$\frac{1}{4}$	16, 064. 40	......	......	......
Drilling, cotton, $\frac{3}{4}$ ....do...	666, 029$\frac{1}{4}$	. 51	339, 669. 79	......	......	......
Flannel:						
Canton, $\frac{3}{4}$ ....do...	654, 513	. 52$\frac{1}{2}$	344, 033. 04	......	......	......
Gray twilled, $\frac{3}{4}$ ....do...	2, 120, 096	. 51$\frac{5}{7}$	1, 097, 066. 84	......	......	......
Blue wool, $\frac{6}{4}$ ....do...	193, 959	1. 91$\frac{9}{11}$	372, 048. 62	......	......	......
Blue wool, $\frac{3}{4}$ ....do...	1, 892, 823	. 95$\frac{10}{11}$	1, 815, 389. 33	......	......	......
Opera ....do...	......	......	......	......	......	......
Hooks and eyes ....gross..	3, 000	. 23$\frac{1}{5}$	696. 00	......	......	......
Kerseys:						
Sky-blue, $\frac{6}{4}$ ....yards..	353, 777$\frac{1}{2}$	2. 48$\frac{1}{2}$	879, 137. 08	......	......	......
Sky-blue, $\frac{3}{4}$ ....do...	3, 687, 827$\frac{3}{4}$	1. 59$\frac{3}{4}$	5, 891, 304. 83	......	......	......
Dark, $\frac{3}{4}$ ....do...	2, 525$\frac{1}{4}$	2. 19	5, 530. 29	......	......	......
Linings ....do...	899, 696	. 61$\frac{1}{2}$	533, 600. 09	......	......	......
Linen, brown ....do...	13, 876$\frac{1}{2}$	. 66	9, 159. 80	......	......	......
Lace:						
Worsted ....do...	2, 160, 458	......	94, 159. 68	16, 000	......	\$976. 20
Silk ....do...	36, 149	......	10, 784. 04	......	......	......
Leather:						
Wax upper ....feet..	530, 275$\frac{3}{4}$	. 31$\frac{5}{8}$	167, 699. 69	......	......	......
Sole ....pounds..	416, 100$\frac{1}{2}$	. 55	228, 800. 27	......	......	......
Welt ....do...	28, 107$\frac{1}{4}$	. 51	14, 553. 53	......	......	......
Muslin delaine, light-blue ....yards..	1, 012	. 69	698. 28	......	......	......
Muslin:						
Bleached, $\frac{4}{4}$ ....do...	524$\frac{1}{2}$	. 27	141. 61	......	......	......
Unbleached ....do...	683, 981$\frac{1}{4}$	. 46	314, 328. 25	......	......	......
Padding, canvas ....do...	119, 726$\frac{1}{2}$	. 21$\frac{1}{2}$	25, 671. 34	......	......	......
Rope:						
Baling ....pounds..	13, 843	. 12$\frac{7}{8}$	1, 761. 40	......	......	......
Yarn ....do...	5, 002	. 15	750. 30	......	......	......
Bolt ....do...	5, 645$\frac{1}{2}$	. 30	1, 693. 65	......	......	......
Silesia, black ....yards..	88, 992$\frac{1}{2}$	. 30$\frac{1}{4}$	26, 895. 02	......	......	......
Silk, yellow floss ....pounds..	10	15. 95	159. 50	......	......	......
Thread ....do...	69, 644$\frac{7}{8}$	3. 14$\frac{1}{2}$	219, 033. 12	......	......	......
Twine ....do...	5, 729$\frac{1}{4}$	......	2, 752. 71	......	......	......
Twine, cotton ....dozen..	811$\frac{1}{2}$	. 27$\frac{1}{6}$	1, 367. 25	......	......	......
Tent line, manila ....pounds..	2, 577$\frac{1}{2}$	1. 68$\frac{1}{2}$	700. 20	......	......	......
Wadding ....dozen..	16, 500	. 85$\frac{1}{3}$	14, 175. 00	......	......	......
Webbing ....yards..	783, 622	. 04$\frac{5}{6}$	37, 828. 85	......	......	......
Webbing, linen, 1$\frac{1}{2}$ ....do...	11, 232$\frac{1}{2}$	. 03$\frac{3}{4}$	421. 20	......	......	......

No. 7.—*Statement of quantity of material purchased during the fiscal year ending June 30, 1865*—Continued.

Articles.	Cincinnati.			Total number or quantity purchased.	Total value of material purchased.
	Number or quantity.	Average cost.	Total value purchased.		
Alpaca, black ....yards..	2, 187$\frac{1}{2}$	\$0. 79$\frac{2}{5}$	\$1, 740. 46	18, 760$\frac{3}{4}$	\$10, 192. 81
Bunting, red, white, and blue ...pieces..				1, 174	21, 015. 00
Burlaps ....yards..	102, 603$\frac{1}{2}$	. 32$\frac{1}{5}$	33, 016. 42	252, 769$\frac{1}{2}$	84, 824. 53
Buckles, pantaloon ....gross..				2, 405	1, 273. 55
Buttons ....do...	78, 322		28, 338. 63	287, 016	96, 077. 78
Braid, $\frac{1}{8}$-inch, scarlet ....yards..	*a* 16, 306	1. 07$\frac{1}{10}$	17, 464. 30		17, 903. 72
Crayons, tailors' ....boxes..				1, 000	600. 00
Cloth:					
Dark blue, $\frac{6}{4}$ ....yards..				356, 627$\frac{1}{2}$	1, 874, 077. 51
Dark blue, $\frac{3}{4}$ ....do...	406, 561	2. 07$\frac{2}{5}$	843, 295. 33	449, 919$\frac{1}{2}$	970, 714. 23
Scarlet facing, $\frac{6}{4}$ ....do...				1, 385$\frac{1}{2}$	5, 542. 00
White facing, $\frac{3}{4}$ ....do...	249	4. 95	1, 233. 75	331$\frac{25}{28}$	1, 716. 17
S. B. facing. $\frac{6}{4}$ ....do...				1, 313$\frac{3}{4}$	6, 793. 25
Cord, tent lacing ....pounds..				7, 310$\frac{1}{2}$	2, 777. 98
Cotton, sewing ....spools..				83, 400	9, 069. 75
Duck, cotton ....yards..	1, 493, 131	1. 30	1, 887, 675. 01	1, 515, 666$\frac{1}{2}$	1, 903, 739. 41
Drilling, cotton, $\frac{3}{4}$ ....do...	905, 341$\frac{1}{3}$	. 46$\frac{4}{5}$	424, 721. 22	1, 571, 370$\frac{7}{12}$	764, 391. 01
Flannel:					
Canton, $\frac{3}{4}$ ....do...	1, 990, 325$\frac{1}{2}$	. 46$\frac{4}{5}$	930, 283. 56	2, 644, 838$\frac{1}{2}$	1, 274, 316. 60
Gray twilled, $\frac{3}{4}$ ....do...	1, 842, 023$\frac{2}{3}$	. 58$\frac{2}{3}$	1, 080, 118. 45	3, 962, 119$\frac{2}{3}$	2, 177, 185. 29
Blue wool, $\frac{6}{4}$ ....do...				193, 959	372, 048. 62
Blue wool, $\frac{3}{4}$ ....do...	574, 945$\frac{1}{3}$	. 90$\frac{3}{10}$	519, 018. 47	2, 467, 768$\frac{1}{3}$	2, 234, 407. 80
Opera ....do...	1, 517$\frac{1}{2}$	. 90	1, 365. 74	1, 517$\frac{1}{2}$	1, 365. 74
Hooks and eyes ....gross..	1, 152	. 35	403. 20	4, 152	1, 099. 20
Kerseys:					
Sky-blue, $\frac{6}{4}$ ....yards..				353, 777$\frac{1}{2}$	879, 137. 08
Sky-blue, $\frac{3}{4}$ ....do...	416, 213$\frac{1}{3}$	1. 29$\frac{1}{10}$	537, 466. 67	4, 104, 041$\frac{1}{12}$	6, 428, 771. 50
Dark, $\frac{3}{4}$ ....do...				2, 525$\frac{1}{4}$	5, 530. 29
Linings ....do...				899, 696	533, 600. 09
Linen, brown........do...				13, 876$\frac{1}{2}$	9, 159. 80
Lace:					
Worsted ....do...	1, 109, 092		44, 124. 20	3, 285, 550	139, 260. 08
Silk ....do...				36, 149	10, 784. 04
Leather:					
Wax upper ....feet..				530, 275$\frac{3}{4}$	167, 699. 69
Sole ....pounds..				416, 100$\frac{1}{2}$	228, 800. 27
Welt ....do...				28, 107$\frac{1}{4}$	14, 553. 53
Muslin delaine, light-blue ....yards..				1, 012	698. 28
Muslin:					
Bleached, $\frac{4}{4}$ ....do...	1, 090	. 26$\frac{4}{5}$	292. 00	1, 614$\frac{1}{2}$	433. 61
Unbleached ....do...	455, 975$\frac{2}{3}$	. 38$\frac{1}{2}$	175, 501. 39	1, 139, 956$\frac{11}{12}$	489, 829. 64
Padding, canvas........do...	90, 839$\frac{1}{2}$	. 28$\frac{9}{10}$	26, 288. 57	210, 566	51, 959. 91
Rope:					
Baling........pounds..				13, 843	1, 761. 40
Yarn........do...				5, 002	750. 30
Bolt........do...				5, 645$\frac{1}{2}$	1, 693. 65
Silesia, black........yards..				88, 992$\frac{1}{2}$	26, 895. 02
Silk, yellow floss ....pounds..	461	11. 45$\frac{3}{5}$	5, 281. 50	471	5, 441. 00
Thread........do...	41, 337		80, 187. 05	110, 981$\frac{7}{8}$	299, 220. 17
Twine........do...	11, 281$\frac{1}{2}$		21, 439. 69	17, 010$\frac{3}{4}$	24, 192. 40
Twine, cotton........dozen..				811$\frac{1}{2}$	1, 367. 25
Tent line, manila ....pounds..	191, 788	. 31$\frac{1}{10}$	58, 829. 10	194, 365$\frac{1}{2}$	59, 529. 30
Wadding ....dozen..	9, 510	. 94$\frac{7}{10}$	9, 002. 73	26, 010	23, 177. 73
Webbing........yards..	20, 160	. 02$\frac{7}{10}$	546. 00	803, 782	38, 374. 85
Webbing, linen, 1$\frac{1}{2}$ ....do...	40, 320	. 05$\frac{2}{5}$	2, 170. 00	51, 552$\frac{1}{2}$	2, 591. 20

a Binding.

Respectfully submitted to the Quartermaster-General.

ALEX. J. PERRY,
Colonel, Quartermaster's Department.

QUARTERMASTER-GENERAL'S OFFICE, SECOND DIVISION,
October 21, 1865.

No. 8.

Statement of number of articles of clothing and equipage purchased and manufactured during the fiscal year ending June 30, 1865.

Articles.	Philadelphia.						New York.	
	Purchased.		Manufactured.		Total purchased and manufactured.	Total value of all articles purchased and manufactured.	Purchased.	
	Number or quantity.	Total value purchased.	Number or quantity.	Total value manufactured.			Number or quantity.	Total value purchased.
Boots:								
Pegged	22,777	$63,547.83			22,777	$63,547.83	131,915	$420,074.95
Sewed	251,379	1,135,918.85	26,577	$140,054.98	277,956	1,275,973.83	162,500	716,145.00
Bootees:								
Sewed	469,353	1,311,059.37	120,953	452,515.41	590,306	1,763,574.78	240,000	625,965.00
Pegged	30,557	47,814.05			30,557	47,814.05	190,640	342,626.72
Blankets:								
Wool	577,434	3,010,355.92			577,434	3,010,355.92	441,000	2,755,100.00
Irregular	22,028	89,465.46			22,028	89,465.46		
Caps:								
Forage	401,748	201,593.37			401,748	201,593.37	300,000	312,000.00
Irregular	1,000	500.00			1,000	500.00		
Coats:								
Great, mounted	164,287	2,526,734.06	672	10,584.00	164,959	2,537,318.06	50,000	798,300.00
Great, foot	182,780	2,278,352.70	34,393	463,273.71	217,173	2,741,626.41	150,000	1,954,500.00
Artillery, uniform	24,973	304,171.14	12,683	187,962.06	37,656	492,133.20	19,000	268,830.00
Infantry, uniform	50,000	639,000.00	36,217	536,735.94	86,217	1,175,735.94	85,500	1,148,575.00
Lined, sacks	355,031	1,592,905.75	319,727	1,467,546.93	674,758	3,060,452.68	577,200	2,748,652.00
Unlined, sacks	148,157	526,625.81	215,912	792,397.04	364,069	1,319,022.85	140,600	552,540.00
Chevrons			170,595	63,145.90	170,595	63,145.90		
Crossed cannon, brass	50,065	998.66			50,065	998.66	19,850	496.25
Crossed sabers	50,002	999.03			50,002	999.03	50,700	1,014.00
Castles							9,700	1,697.50
Drawers	1,418,115	1,673,188.10	69,778	78,151.36	1,487,893	1,751,339.46	1,408,000	2,147,490.00
Eagles	50,000	850.00			50,000	850.00		
Greatcoat straps	59,315	4,448.62			59,315	4,448.62	200,000	17,660.00
Hats, uniform	200,054	443,129.06			200,054	443,129.06		
Hat bugles	50,000	795.00			50,000	795.00		
Hat cords and tassels:								
Infantry	78,900	13,207.85			78,900	13,207.85		
Artillery	40,000	7,040.00			40,000	7,040.00		
Cavalry	40,000	6,992.00			40,000	6,992.00		
Jackets:								
Cavalry	80,004	735,736.72	30,824	332,282.72	110,828	1,068,019.44		
Light artillery	15,000	138,600.00	29,760	320,812.80	44,760	459,412.80	10,000	99,400.00

No. 8.—*Statement of number of articles of clothing and equipage purchased and manufactured, &c.*—Continued.

Articles.	Philadelphia.						New York.	
	Purchased.		Manufactured.		Total purchased and manufactured.	Total value of all articles purchased and manufactured.	Purchased.	
	Number or quantity.	Total value purchased.	Number or quantity.	Total value manufactured.			Number or quantity.	Total value purchased.
Jackets:								
Veteran Reserve Corps			29,966	$194,779.00	29,966	$194,779.00	5,000	$31,750.00
Zouave			461	4,075.24	461	4,075.24	800	5,752.00
Letters								
Leggings	65	$109.85			65	109.85	9,900	7,322.00
Mittens, woolen							2,000	585.00
Numbers	246,100	1,111.14			246,100	1,111.14		
Overalls			3,640	6,806.80	3,640	6,806.80		
Ponchos:								
India rubber	164,967	1,011,278.48			164,967	1,011,278.48	27,000	133,380.00
Gutta-percha	10,000	73,000.00			10,000	73,000.00		
Shirts, flannel and knit	495,847	728,895.09	467,644	752,906.84	963,491	1,481,801.93	1,062,800	2,538,096.00
Stockings	1,849,935	786,222.37			1,849,935	786,222.37	2,001,500	920,925.00
Sashes	880	1,443.20	350	413.00	1,230	1,856.20		
Stable frocks								
Trousers:								
Footmen, S. B	278,239	1,237,236.08	669,949	3,262,651.63	948,188	4,499,887.71	506,080	2,501,390.00
Mounted, S. B	135,148	764,937.68	188,873	1,195,566.09	324,021	1,960,503.77		
Irregular	7,242	23,489.20			7,242	23,489.20		
Blankets:								
Vulcanized india rubber	375,624	1,567,598.20			375,624	1,567,598.20	190,000	919,000.00
Gutta-percha	35,000	162,250.00			35,000	162,250.00		
Axes:								
Pick	11,833	16,802.86			11,833	16,802.86	29,000	44,190.00
Felling	55,020	77,908.32			55,020	77,908.32	30,400	53,876.00
Ax-handles:								
Pick	29,671	4,129.20			29,671	4,129.20	22,916	4,583.20
Felling	50,346	6,934.89			50,346	6,934.89	20,000	3,600.00
Ax slings	15,795	16,245.34			15,795	16,245.34		
Bugles, extra mouthpieces	96	218.88			96	218.88	850	2,672.50
Bedsacks, single and double			20	86.00	20	86.00		
Books, company and regimental, &c	4,947	12,487.62			4,947	12,487.62	(sets) 50	1,650.00
Bugle cords and tassels:								
Artillery	150	104.25			150	104.25		
Cavalry	1,184	917.60			1,184	917.60		
Canteens, complete	303,847	99,887.98			303,847	99,887.98	366,000	261,540.00
Canteen corks and straps	10,000	279.00	321,400	6,428.00	331,400	6,707.00	10,000	1,530.00

Colors:								
Regimental infantry	282	19,127.20			282	19,127.20	200	15,000.00
Regimental artillery	25	1,500.00			25	1,500.00	50	3,750.00
Regimental cavalry								
National artillery	5	221.75			5	221.75		
National infantry	182	10,844.13			182	10,844.13	250	11,500.00
Camp	665	1,030.75			665	1,030.75	2,000	3,340.00
Color belt and sling	406	1,404.76			406	1,404.76		
Drums, complete	2,700	18,435.00			2,700	18,435.00	1,500	9,300.00
Drumheads:								
Batter	710	585.10			710	585.10	12,500	14,000.00
Snare	2,281	752.73			2,281	752.73	12,500	3,975.00
Drum snares, sets	4,000	1,070.00			4,000	1,070.00		
Drumsticks and carriages							5,000	1,600.00
Flags:								
General hospital	61	512.40	12	72.00	73	584.40		
Post and field	205	1,168.50	9	31.50	214	1,200.00		
Ambulance and staff	1,000	1,650.00			1,000	1,650.00		
Designating corps, division, and brigade	316	2,451.10			316	2,451.10		
Garrison			202	15,352.00	202	15,352.00	150	16,700.00
Storm			384	9,600.00	384	9,600.00	160	5,352.00
Recruiting							400	3,360.00
Flag halliards								
Fifes							1,400	546.00
Guidons, cavalry	736	6,740.00			736	6,740.00	300	2,775.00
Hatchets	27,054	13,541.24			27,054	13,541.24	35,000	23,650.00
Hatchet handles	7,061	220.65			7,061	220.65	20,000	1,800.00
Hatchet slings	16,109	9,537.92			16,109	9,537.92		
Haversacks, strapped	443,246	402,792.11	284	85.20	443,530	402,877.31	232,400	221,920.00
Knapsacks, strapped	223,840	614,844.42			223,840	614,844.42	379,000	1,109,910.00
Kettles, camp	18,909	17,188.17			18,909	17,188.17	25,000	31,550.00
Mess-pans	31,971	10,861.49			31,971	10,861.49	29,000	14,380.00
Pots, iron	400	694.46			400	694.46		
Spades and shovels	37,731	43,944.27			37,731	43,944.27	38,000	48,910.00
Spade slings	53	73.67			53	73.67		
Tents:								
Hospital and flies	1,827	362,979.33			1,827	362,979.33	1,650	366,843.50
Hospital	2,000	214,460.00	3	$450.00	2,003	214,910.00		
Tent flies, hospital	2,610	110,686.67	3	150.00	2,613	110,836.67	100	6,932.00
Tents, wall	3,327	169,677.00	3	186.00	3,330	169,863.00		
Tent flies, wall	3,270	49,278.90	3	72.00	3,273	49,350.90		
Tents:								
Common	1,400	27,769.00	3	88.50	1,403	27,857.50		
Shelter	343,694	2,782,576.36	3	20.25	343,697	2,782,596.61	270,000	2,140,600.00
Tent-poles:								
Hospital	3,059	22,290.00			3,059	22,290.00	200	772.00
Wall	1,086	1,433.52			1,086	1,433.52	1,000	1,980.00
Common	3,236	4,854.00			3,236	4,854.00		
Tent-pins	638,249	14,611.72			638,249	14,611.72	295,000	5,140.00

No. 8.—*Statement of number of articles of clothing and equipage purchased and manufactured, &c.*—Continued.

Articles.	Cincinnati.						Total number purchased and manufactured at Philadelphia, New York, and Cincinnati.	Total value of all articles purchased and manufactured at Philadelphia, New York, and Cincinnati.
	Purchased.		Manufactured.		Total purchased and manufactured.	Total value of all articles purchased and manufactured.		
	Number or quantity.	Total value purchased.	Number or quantity.	Total value manufactured.				
Boots:								
Pegged	364, 395	$1, 360, 124. 11			364, 395	$1, 360, 124. 11	519, 087	$1, 843, 746. 89
Sewed							440, 456	1, 992, 118. 83
Bootees:								
Sewed	27, 998	62, 049. 20			27, 998	62, 049. 20	858, 304	2, 451, 588. 98
Pegged	608, 516	1, 374, 770. 00			608, 516	1, 374, 770. 00	829, 713	1, 765, 210. 77
Blankets:								
Wool	705, 572	4, 611, 390. 00			705, 572	4, 611, 390. 00	1, 724, 006	10, 376, 845. 92
Irregular							22, 028	89, 465. 46
Caps:								
Forage	449, 200	409, 312. 00			449, 200	409, 312. 00	1, 150, 948	922, 905. 37
Irregular							1, 000	500. 00
Coats:								
Great, mounted	41, 256	482, 911. 74	33	$319. 77	41, 289	483, 230. 51	256, 248	3, 818, 848. 57
Great, foot	249, 050	2, 714, 033. 50	818	7, 850. 08	249, 868	2, 721, 883. 58	617, 041	7, 418, 009. 99
Artillery, uniform	2, 800	28, 588. 00	3, 000	27, 332. 50	5, 800	55, 920. 50	62, 456	816, 883. 70
Infantry, uniform	76, 314	797, 516. 30	1, 110	10, 173. 15	77, 424	807, 689. 45	249, 141	3, 132, 000. 39
Lined, sacks	489, 922	2, 150, 469. 11	142, 371	649, 217. 06	632, 293	2, 799, 686. 17	1, 884, 251	8, 608, 790. 85
Unlined, sacks	174, 235	513, 478. 30	54, 219	188, 833. 02	228, 454	702, 311. 32	733, 123	2, 573, 874. 17
Chevrons	14, 649	1, 857. 19			14, 649	1, 857. 19	185, 244	65, 003. 09
Crossed cannon, brass	50, 000	1, 030. 50			50, 000	1, 030. 50	150, 065	2, 029. 16
Crossed sabers	54, 968	1, 120. 35			54, 968	1, 120. 35	155, 670	2, 119. 38
Castles							9, 700	1, 697. 50
Drawers	86, 700	87, 567. 00	726, 800	872, 733. 99	812, 500	960, 300. 99	3, 708, 393	4, 859, 130. 45
Eagles	151, 981	2, 887. 12			151, 981	2, 887. 12	201, 981	3, 737. 12
Greatcoat straps	200, 000	18, 079. 99			200, 000	18, 079. 99	459, 315	40, 188. 61
Hats, uniform	242, 778	455, 833. 42			242, 778	455, 833. 42	442, 832	898, 962. 48
Hat bugles	154, 500	3, 085. 49			154, 500	3, 085. 49	204, 500	3, 880. 49
Hat cords and tassels:								
Infantry	41, 074	8, 259. 19			41, 074	8, 259. 19	119, 974	21, 467. 04
Artillery	18, 040	3, 608. 00			18, 040	3, 608. 00	58, 040	10, 648. 00
Cavalry	18, 028	3, 389. 06			18, 028	3, 389. 06	58, 028	10, 381. 06
Jackets:								
Cavalry	39, 793	272, 378. 74	103, 872	829, 909. 95	143, 665	1, 102, 288. 69	254, 493	2, 170, 308. 13
Light artillery			64, 503	510, 397. 02	64, 503	510, 397. 02	119, 263	1, 069, 209. 82
Veteran Reserve Corps			684	3, 040. 04	684	3, 040. 04	35, 650	229, 569. 04
Zouave							1, 261	9, 827. 24

Letters	300,000	2,250.00			300,000	2,250.00	300,000	2,250.00
Leggings							9,965	7,435.85
Mittens, woolen							2,000	585.00
Numbers	350,000	1,809.50			350,000	1,809.50	596,100	2,920.64
Overalls			8,094	29,138.40	8,094	29,138.40	11,734	35,945.20
Ponchos:								
India rubber	509,012	2,295,369.65			509,012	2,295,369.65	700,979	3,440,028.13
Gutta-percha							10,000	73,000.00
Shirts, flannel and knit	679,436	1,627,277.93	562,439	1,071,346.26	1,241,875	2,698,624.19	3,268,166	6,718,522.12
Stockings	1,833,137	754,417.81			1,833,137	754,417.81	5,684,572	2,461,565.18
Sashes	2,499	6,872.25			2,499	6,872.25	3,729	8,728.45
Stable frocks	30,000	66,900.00			30,000	66,900.00	30,000	66,900.00
Trousers:								
Footmen, S. B	963,232	4,574,150.20	64,402	217,749.48	1,027,634	4,791,899.68	2,481,902	11,793,177.39
Mounted, S. B	295,408	1,590,321.83	35,877	153,690.13	331,285	1,744,011.96	950,714	3,704,515.73
Irregular	10,000	24,000.00			10,000	24,000.00	31,242	47,489.20
Blankets:								
Vulcanized india rubber							565,624	2,486,598.20
Gutta-percha	25,000	135,000.00			25,000	135,000.00	60,000	297,250.00
Axes:								
Pick	1,613	1,524.28			1,613	1,524.28	42,446	62,517.14
Felling	22,776	39,751.98			22,776	39,751.98	108,196	171,536.30
Ax-handles:								
Pick	10,197	1,274.62			10,197	1,274.62	62,784	9,987.02
Felling	66,346	13,843.42			66,346	13,843.42	73,946	24,378.31
Ax slings							15,795	16,245.34
Bugles, extra mouthpieces	2,849	9,162.40			2,849	9,162.40	3,795	12,053.78
Bedsacks, single and double			19,590	67,707.23	19,590	67,707.23	19,610	67,793.23
Books, company and regimental, &c	16,035	30,635.79			16,035	30,635.79	21,032	44,773.41
Bugle cords and tassels:								
Artillery							150	104.25
Cavalry							1,184	917.60
Canteens, complete	493,500	249,220.25			493,500	249,220.25	1,163,347	610,648.23
Canteen corks and straps							341,400	8,237.00
Colors:								
Regimental infantry	280	18,889.00			280	18,889.00	762	53,016.20
Regimental artillery	72	3,687.75			72	3,687.75	147	8,937.75
Regimental cavalry	412	6,530.20			412	6,530.20	412	6,530.20
National artillery							5	221.75
National infantry	323	19,535.91			323	19,535.91	755	41,880.04
Camp	1,502	2,913.88			1,502	2,913.88	4,167	7,284.63
Color belt and sling							406	1,404.76
Drums, complete	12,130	105,094.32			12,130	105,094.32	16,330	132,829.32
Drumheads:								
Batter	3,650	3,577.00			3,650	3,577.00	16,860	18,162.10
Snare	549	205.87			549	205.87	15,330	4,933.60
Drum snares, sets	2,179	641.60			2,179	641.60	6,179	1,811.61
Drumsticks and carriages							5,000	1,600.00
Flags:								
General hospital							73	584.40
Post and field	28	274.40			28	274.40	242	1,474.40
Ambulance and staff	50	90.00			50	90.00	1,050	1,740.00

No. 8.—*Statement of number of articles of clothing and equipage purchased and manufactured, &c.*—Continued.

Articles.	Cincinnati.						Total number purchased and manufactured at Philadelphia, New York, and Cincinnati.	Total value of all articles purchased and manufactured at Philadelphia, New York, and Cincinnati.
	Purchased.		Manufactured.		Total purchased and manufactured.	Total value of all articles purchased and manufactured.		
	Number or quantity.	Total value purchased.	Number or quantity.	Total value manufactured.				
Flags—Continued.								
Designating corps, division, and brigade	41	$639.00					357	$3,090.10
Garrison	100	12,500.00			100	$12,500.00	452	44,552.00
Storm	383	14,169.50					927	29,121.50
Recruiting	1	8.40			1	8.40	401	3,368.40
Flag halliards	756	4,202.75			756	4,202.75	756	4,202.75
Fifes							1,400	546.00
Guidons, cavalry	257	2,301.21			257	2,301.21	1,293	11,816.21
Hatchets	26,000	23,120.00			26,000	23,120.00	88,054	60,311.24
Hatchet handles	20,027	751.00			20,027	751.00	47,088	2,771.65
Hatchet slings							16,109	9,537.92
Haversacks, strapped	390,717	313,507.60			390,717	313,507.60	1,066,647	938,304.91
Knapsacks, strapped	355,447	1,030,026.05			355,447	1,030,026.05	958,287	2,754,780.47
Kettles, camp	29,986	25,085.40			29,986	25,085.40	73,895	73,823.47
Mess-pans	108,325	40,810.37			108,325	40,810.37	169,296	66,051.86
Pots, iron							400	694.46
Spades and shovels	75,200	107,014.49			75,200	107,014.49	150,931	199,868.76
Spade slings							53	73.67
Tents:								
Hospital and flies							3,477	729,822.83
Hospital	1,065	165,452.27	3,720	$560,432.91	4,785	725,885.18	6,788	940,795.18
Tent flies, hospital	1,065	72,404.62	3,719	245,335.74	4,784	317,780.36	7,497	435,549.03
Tents, wall	2,010	115,436.00	3,072	228,464.61	5,082	343,900.61	8,412	513,763.61
Tent flies, wall	2,010	50,671.00	3,073	101,251.38	5,083	151,922.38	8,356	201,273.28
Tents:								
Common			9	164.88	9	164.88	1,412	28,022.38
Shelter			84,490	420,665.15	84,490	420,665.15	698,187	5,343,861.76
Tent-poles:								
Hospital	3,000	7,350.00			3,000	7,350.00	6,259	30,412.00
Wall	4,500	7,425.00			4,500	7,425.00	6,586	10,838.52
Common							3,236	4,854.00
Tent-pins	856,780	18,923.68			856,780	18,923.68	1,790,029	38,675.40

No. 8.—*Statement of number of articles of clothing and equipage purchased and manufactured, &c.*—Continued.

Articles.	Saint Louis, Mo.				Quincy, Ill.		Steubenville.		Total number or quantity purchased and manufactured at Saint Louis, Quincy, and Steubenville.[a]
	Purchased.		Manufactured.		Manufactured.		Manufactured.		
	Number or quantity.	Total value.	Number or quantity.	Total value.	Number or quantity.	Total value.	Number or quantity.	Total value.	
Drawers, flannel ....number	11,640	$15,248.40			31,246				42,886
Blankets, woolen ....do	504	3,024.00							504
Caps, forage ....do	1,500	685.00							1,500
Hat cords and tassels ....do	1,920	230.40							1,920
Trousers:									
Mounted ....do			172,922	$999,489.16			13,931		186,853
Footmen ....do			218,098	1,005,431.78	76,337		51,300		345,735
Jackets:									
Cavalry ....do			79,120	786,935.20					79,120
Artillery ....do			13,603	135,485.88					13,603
Uniform coats, infantry ....do			9,627	113,784.57					9,627
Greatcoats, cavalry ....do			3	41.76					3
Chevrons ....do			148	52.00					148
Shirts ....do					26,351				26,351
Sack coats, lined ....do							13,652		13,652
EQUIPAGE.									
Boxes, packing ....number	6,234	14,129.59							6,234
Camp-kettles ....do	12,931	11,957.30							12,931
Colors, regimental and national ....do	2	100.00							2
Drumheads, batter ....do	395	300.30							395
Tent-poles:									
Hospital ....sets	26	109.20							26
Wall ....do	372	430.80							372
Shelter ....do	140,000	10,500.00							140,000
Common ....do	120	84.00							120
Tent-pins, hospital and common ....number	18,610	288.00							18,610
MATERIAL.									
Beeswax ....pounds	165	132.40							165
Buttons, tent ....number	6,231	52.79							6,231
Brush, varnish ....do	1	.90							1½
Camphor ....pounds	1,001½	1,852.77							1,001

a Manufactured from material furnished by the principal depots.

No. 8.—*Statement of number of articles of clothing and equipage purchased and manufactured, &c.*—Continued.

Articles.	Saint Louis, Mo.				Quincy, Ill.		Steubenville.		Total number or quantity purchased and manufactured at Saint Louis, Quincy, and Steubenville. a
	Purchased.		Manufactured.		Manufactured.		Manufactured.		
	Number or quantity.	Total value.	Number or quantity.	Total value.	Number or quantity.	Total value.	Number or quantity.	Total value.	
Checks, inspectors' .... number..	18,000	$22.50	....	....	....	....	....	....	18,000
Duck .... yards..	6,742½	8,154.58	....	....	....	....	....	....	6,742½
Gum .... pounds..	2	1.50	....	....	....	....	....	....	2
Kersey:									
Sky-blue, 6/4 .... yards	31,923¼	95,066.33	....	....	....	....	....	....	31,923¼
Sky-blue, 3/4 .... do...	1,755¼	2,286.57	....	....	....	....	....	....	1,755¼
Lampblack .... pounds..	1	.30	....	....	....	....	....	....	1
Muslin, 4/4 .... yards..	13,184	6,565.85	....	....	....	....	....	....	13,184
Pattern paper .... pounds..	29	10.15	....	....	....	....	....	....	29
Plates, sheet-iron .... number..	1,100	11.00	....	....	....	....	....	....	1,100
Rope .... pounds..	5,210	831.98	....	....	....	....	....	....	5,210
Rivet and burr .... do...	1	1.00	....	....	....	....	....	....	1
Rings, tent-pole .... number..	500	15.00	....	....	....	....	....	....	500
Slides .... do...	10,853	196.58	....	....	....	....	....	....	10,853
Tags, printed .... do...	240,000	204.00	....	....	....	....	....	....	240,000
Twine .... pounds..	2,001	472.08	....	....	....	....	....	....	2,001
Thread .... do...	6	14.75	....	....	....	....	....	....	6
Twills .... yards..	514½	565.68	....	....	....	....	....	....	514½
Tape .... pieces..	600	35.00	....	....	....	....	....	....	600
Varnish .... gallons..	4	20.00	....	....	....	....	....	....	4

a Manufactured from material furnished by the principal depots.

Respectfully submitted to the Quartermaster-General.

ALEX. J. PERRY,
Colonel, Quartermaster's Department.

QUARTERMASTER-GENERAL'S OFFICE, SECOND DIVISION,
October 21, 1865.

No. 9.

Monthly statement of clothing reported on hand at the various clothing depots on June 30, 1865.

Articles of clothing.	New York.	Philadelphia.	Cincinnati.	Saint Louis.	Washington.	Boston.	New Orleans.	Baltimore.
Uniform coats:								
Engineers'	3,925	2,344	1,000	....	....	....	5,100	....
Ordnance	386	1,784	....	....	34	8	3	....
Artillery	3,712	29,295	2,400	484	15,836	5,942	9,085	4,275
Infantry	59,080	69,609	82,334	15,486	25,094	5,782	781	4,983
Uniform jackets:								
Cavalry	40,994	70,921	86,280	25,534	9,462	1,573	2,547	6,599
Artillery	1,862	16,116	44,165	2,653	27,578	1,074	5,619	3,584
Infantry	....	....	....	....	....	....	....	....
Zouave	....	....	855	....	....	....	373	21
Knit	2,238	....	....	....	....	....	....	....
Invalid Corps	1,666	28,703	2,780	2,545	2,924	1,828	3,631	70
Uniform trousers:								
Footmen	85,467	27,889	368,116	57,232	38,913	17,274	4,559	12,903
Horsemen	64,186	77,483	92,407	21,783	8,915	4,253	....	22,453
Zouave	....	....	653	....	....	....	214	16
Knit	....	....	....	....	....	....	....	....
Cotton-duck trousers	....	....	....	....	....	....	....	....
Zouave vests	....	....	....	....	....	....	....	....
Overalls	6,410	790	5,335	9,790	15	....	4,932	265
Drawers	154,363	322,023	262,241	73,639	30,754	23,910	3,466	40,294
Shirts:								
Flannel	33,313	364,230	365,834	29,254	13,902	38,411	....	45,503
Knit	143,470	54,200	....	85,083	84,768	7,444	....	....
Zouave, gray	17,644	....	....	....	....	....	40	3
Greatcoats:								
Footmen	103,252	122,744	146,111	46,456	34,607	11,430	32,736	7,282
Horsemen	45,279	71,871	42,738	23,416	21,267	3,926	10,216	5,891
Straps for greatcoats	131,090	120,259	225,584	83,660	141,855	10,223	60,416	22,064
Blankets:								
Woolen	232,741	103,335	311,745	23,118	99,784	19,430	40,013	19,182
Rubber and painted	22,521	....	150,278	25,947	66,018	8,088	17,257	8,797
Ponchos	....	....	115,719	13,856	41,178	4,688	8,889	9,488
Talmas	....	....	....	....	....	....	....	....
Sack coats:								
Lined	200,384	138,224	242,661	44,315	123	12,368	5,286	18,747
Unlined	168,819	179,415	155,596	44,107	13,296	2,279	....	12,083
Knit	....	....	....	....	....	....	21,070	48
Bootees	287,730	203,999	319,791	33,114	258,303	31,298	36,398	13,962
Boots	93,058	83,310	52,373	34,744	13,897	4,156	45,969	15,627
Leggings	3,241	8,065	....	....	9,446	....	1,178	380
Stockings	711,085	269,797	315,797	114,405	40,626	32,648	....	53,666
Stocks, leather	154,247	36,097	28,559	7,832	18,685	20,066	5,657	1,506
Uniform hats:								
Trimmed	10,371	122,967	42,383	7,037	42,802	20,397	943	8,001
Untrimmed	....	....	....	58,201	....	....	....	....
Uniform caps	154	744	....	....	....	....	1,500	....
Forage caps	195,763	118,892	304,514	43,933	35,461	32,387	....	21,573
Zouave caps	....	3,180	....	....	....	....	373	3
Cap covers	....	44,085	34,446	121	....	2,630	....	1,163
Stable frocks	62,114	1,780	34,506	8,096	3,016	1,133	2,204	1,359
Sashes	6,523	372	2,456	1,219	85	302	2,051	185
Gloves	....	....	....	....	....	....	....	....
Mittens	....	....	26,824	....	1,877	....	....	....
Knapsacks	211,579	86,379	248,353	49,168	62,085	23,613	42,465	11,866
Haversacks	111,744	82,207	40,101	58,987	3,336	16,596	27,056	9,219
Canteens	225,749	123,433	194,147	57,689	25,003	18,544	19,869	9,923
Brogans	57,663	....	11,983	....	....	....	9,747	....
Leather gaiters	2,084	....	....	....	....	....	....	....
Waterproof blankets:								
Horsemen	....	115,243	....	....	....	....	....	....
Footmen	....	87,021	....	....	....	....	....	....

No. 9.—*Monthly statement of clothing reported on hand at the various clothing depots on June 30, 1865*—Continued.

Articles of clothing.	Fort Monroe.	Harrisburg.	Indianapolis.	Columbus.	Fort Leavenworth.	Quincy.	Pittsburg.	Detroit.
Uniform coats:								
Engineers'					120			
Ordnance					67			2
Artillery	8,218				464			
Infantry	12,113	131	1,040	6,457	944	560	14,847	6,167
Uniform jackets:								
Cavalry	9,343	158	1,113	3,924	4,086		4,144	537
Artillery	10,930	42	191	1,266	773		765	638
Infantry	3,185		2,246	86		136		
Zouave								
Knit		51						
Invalid Corps	1,688	484		426		129		400
Uniform trousers:								
Footmen	48,785	436	5,363	23,512	5,464	5,461	6,476	3,529
Horsemen	25,658	204	4,198	1,359	2,421	6	2,310	1,710
Zouave								
Knit								
Cotton-duck trousers								
Zouave vests								
Overalls	2,694				20			
Drawers	47,590	543	2,462	20,859	7,301	5,360	11,523	4,027
Shirts:								
Flannel	55,668	921	6,378	27,866	9,657	4,962	10,663	4,475
Knit	13,227	22						
Zouave, gray								
Greatcoats:								
Footmen	9,141	392	5,750	14,500	12,189	149	5,176	3,332
Horsemen	3,355	12	83	930	14,021	19	2,992	1,367
Straps for greatcoats	23,521	3,535	1,142		50,797		10,959	6,506
Blankets:								
Woolen	29,147	348	4,272	19,073	12,154	272	5,386	3,245
Rubber and painted	26,592	930	1,958	4,425	7,903			2,164
Ponchos		58		363			1,648	7
Talmas								
Sack coats:								
Lined	23,076	489	5,876	10,327	20	363	1,143	3,300
Unlined	8,669	475		10,000	38	116	6,038	
Knit	752							
Bootees	76,333	648	2,725	16,179	9,017	307	7,867	6,609
Boots	44,520	136	141	1,353	3,152	52	2,355	1,194
Leggings	5,158							
Stockings	93,332	1,866		2,448	2,469	973	12,357	7,079
Stocks, leather	26,861		5,179		22,373		3,985	2,296
Uniform hats:								
Trimmed	5,982	6	722	739	1,851		2,163	17
Untrimmed								
Uniform caps	1,000							
Forage caps	17,922	796	6,828	17,991	9,348	58	9,631	3,272
Zouave caps	19							
Cap covers				15,717			7,550	
Stable frocks	1,096	32	77	1,955	4,697		3,199	2,140
Sashes	686	213	164	174	58		31	48
Gloves				200				
Mittens	166				10,967			
Knapsacks	6,756	4,615	12,190	7,783	6,772		5,516	3,923
Haversacks	26,705	4,941	18,477	6,485	7,643		6,641	3,658
Canteens	29,420	3,713	20,369	7,384	2,771	144	3,236	3,584
Brogans								
Leather gaiters								
Waterproof blankets:								
Horsemen								455
Footmen								

No. 9.—*Monthly statement of clothing reported on hand at the various clothing depots on June 30, 1865*—Continued.

Articles of clothing	Louisville.	Davenport.	Chicago.	New Berne.	City Point.	Saint Paul.	Cairo.	Memphis.	Norfolk.
Uniform coats:									
Engineers'									
Ordnance		13							
Artillery	153			2,365	165			2,066	75
Infantry	7,652	1,646	1,704	2,375	69	7,742		7,822	585
Uniform jackets:									
Cavalry	4,389	213	2,450	4,770	12	699	493	9,484	111
Artillery	4,159		1,743	2,441	126	80	291	459	188
Infantry	1,373								2,284
Zouave									
Knit	8,631		3,985						
Invalid Corps			4,911						
Uniform trousers:									
Footmen	29,552	1,539	9,259	11,757	522	1,229	1	18,595	17
Horsemen	8,909	275	2,272			700	227	5,384	181
Zouave									
Knit									
Cotton-duck trousers									
Zouave vests									
Overalls	898		126					12	
Drawers	84,836	2,032	12,105	426		1,400	1,249	23,589	378
Shirts:									
Flannel	25,452	9,287	19,687	6,130		1,708	506	18,729	290
Knit					79		465	3,219	61
Zouave, gray									
Greatcoats:									
Footmen	51,716	1,008	8,559	2,558	40	3,639		13,142	39
Horsemen	8,269		2,474	2,717	106	1,387	40	7,488	268
Straps for greatcoats	10,286	1,749	14,341	2,691	819	65		6	1,297
Blankets:									
Woolen	5,789	7,336	11,213	8,704	375	626	98	26,050	4,165
Rubber and painted	721		8,129	9,362	310	36			579
Ponchos	2,506		25	7,505	15	1,042	66		
Talmas	4								
Sack coats:									
Lined	10,640	1,837	7,202	3,270		1,066	517		41
Unlined	42		4,950	2,843	1,421	582	666	15,831	274
Knit									
Bootees	53,794	8,642	12,662	27,647	83	13,889	279	47,624	2,706
Boots	3,409	319	2,335	5,849	167	540	455	12,677	454
Leggings									
Stockings	22,877	2,496	23,071	12,324		2,400	1,133	18,740	613
Stocks, leather	9,010	914	9,510	2,374	97	1,218		3,254	102
Uniform hats:									
Trimmed	286	1,974	12,621	13,771		2,451	198	28,173	87
Untrimmed									
Uniform caps									
Forage caps	6,506	4,171	12,690	9,109	32	6,734		248	110
Zouave caps									
Cap covers	31,540			14,975		1,000			
Stable frocks	79		2,994	127	20	1,400		3,040	156
Sashes		116	115	208	14	18		607	
Gloves									
Mittens						1,936		233	
Knapsacks	14,571	13,298	17,484	8,806	21	1,865	175	2,783	65
Haversacks	13,945	11,320	20,872	9,647	462	1,899	459	19,620	84
Canteens	7,074	8,075	16,463	27,142	10	2,000	260	17,516	192
Brogans									
Leather gaiters									
Waterproof blankets:									
Horsemen								6,500	
Footmen								7,359	

No. 9.—*Monthly statement of clothing reported on hand at the various clothing depots on June 30, 1865*—Continued.

Articles of clothing.	Prairie du Chien.	Keokuk.	Madison.	Augusta.	Wheeling.	Hilton Head.	Trenton.	Total.
Uniform coats:								
Engineers'						1,129		13,618
Ordnance			4					2,301
Artillery			74			1,025		85,634
Infantry	319	1,009	7,280	2,251	1,711	925	12,054	360,552
Uniform jackets:								
Cavalry		200	1,835	530	1,885	2,803		297,089
Artillery			1,496	282	500	2,065	4	131,090
Infantry					356			7,666
Zouave							3	1,252
Knit						24		14,929
Invalid Corps							500	52,785
Uniform trousers:								
Footmen	152	1,246	20,323	540	3,456	6,117	8,068	823,763
Horsemen	89	300	526	314	951	9,943	2,089	361,509
Zouave						79		962
Knit								
Cotton-duck trousers								
Zouave vests								
Overalls						2,323		33,610
Drawers	187	1,286	9,678	972	3,354	9,205	5,492	1,166,541
Shirts:								
Flannel	27	1,311	10,547	1,115	3,043	11,042	10,541	1,130,482
Knit					18	2,069		394,125
Zouave, gray								17,687
Greatcoats:								
Footmen	55	69	6,428	2,856	2,604	2,535	1,069	651,564
Horsemen		209	2,207	444	1,827	2,531	820	278,161
Straps for greatcoats		921	13,722	1,175	577	6,918	3,055	949,233
Blankets:								
Woolen	215	475	9,254	548	5,342	4,603	1,041	1,009,106
Rubber and painted			7,855	526	1,138	13,431		384,975
Ponchos			1,739	103	510	1,500		210,905
Talmas								4
Sack coats:								
Lined	404	120	8,098	522	117	6,830	4,108	751,544
Unlined		99	185		1,233	7,588		636,645
Knit								21,870
Bootees	282	1,809	11,525	5,475	3,626	1,479	4,877	1,500,679
Boots	100	200	205	458	1,616	7,351	2,860	435,032
Leggings				993				28,461
Stockings	359	1,545	10,135	3,686	5,751	33,114	5,963	1,803,719
Stocks, leather		1,907	7,558	739	4,442	13,768	7,486	386,952
Uniform hats:								
Trimmed		1,153	272		1,591	5,592	5,044	339,394
Untrimmed								58,201
Uniform caps								33,098
Forage caps	200	2,219	10,130	1,179	2	13,079	5,471	890,248
Zouave caps								3,575
Cap covers				2,810	3,877	64	5,000	164,987
Stable frocks				577	133	2,140		138,070
Sashes		3	65	8	89	210	43	16,063
Gloves								200
Mittens			5,310					47,313
Knapsacks		899	5,247	2,684	1,389	11,342	4,886	868,578
Haversacks	200	188	5,285	2,860	1,488	5,464	5,032	522,621
Canteens	200	651	6,190	2,890	2,406	4,806	4,350	845,209
Brogans								79,393
Leather gaiters								2,084
Waterproof blankets:								
Horsemen								122,198
Footmen								94,380

No. 10.

Monthly statement of camp and garrison equipage reported on hand at the various clothing depots on June 30, 1865.

Articles of equipage.	New York.	Philadelphia.	Cincinnati.	Saint Louis.	Washington.	Boston.	New Orleans.	Baltimore.
Hospital tents	480	813	1,875	850	625	13	52	387
Wall-tents	4,295	2,537	3,716	775	4	....	580	220
Sibley tents	....	6	2	30	89	....	3	26
Common tents	20,799	3,677	325	1,988	7,659	....	470	4,166
Shelter tents	80,653	152,041	124,241	62,206	15,794	2,675	30,187	10,800
Frémont and Bell tents	....	....	39	4	....	....	....	....
Tent stoves	3,074	2,016	45	893	955	....	....	254
Bedsacks, single	62,642	1,363	....	12,975	3,467	1,661	8,486	714
Bedsacks, double	3,006	26,692	....	4,043	4,566	1,646	2,338	185
Mosquito bars	29,575	9,511	....	10,472	27	....	15,522	....
Regimental colors	291	109	170	73	6	10	17	17
Camp colors	3,426	448	1,502	132	546	64	238	31
National colors	204	87	126	46	7	3	10	11
Standards	449	108	536	40	23	....	....	24
Storm flags	74	136	75	15	66	17	39	10
Garrison flags	52	99	36	28	62	3	13	9
Recruiting flags	1,085	302	282	38	18	50	106	15
Guidons	445	231	221	418	5	25	386	57
Pickaxes	23,539	7,209	14,145	10,960	18,596	2,586	1,130	1,199
Axes	17,041	15,216	8,946	4,208	21,965	1,853	65	2,135
Spades	21,972	8,786	18,254	12,047	17,043	3,415	....	1,067
Shovels	354	8,594	12,740	8,804	7,105	462	298	1,101
Hatchets	31,419	13,312	10,452	9,806	13,925	1,203	2,997	2,025
Mess-pans	39,518	80,742	76,163	24,512	22,810	4,403	18,649	5,069
Iron pots	371	719	....	16	107	....	225	....
Camp-kettles	17,250	23,254	26,521	4,896	611	125	2,462	1,327
Bugles	345	67	441	1,336	302	369	55	237
Trumpets	492	720	839	748	57	17	30	175
Drums	1,315	1,688	651	801	42	138	52	143
Fifes	2,975	2,097	1,165	1,634	633	382	339	243
General-hospital flags	47	48	128	....	41	....	69	27
Post and field flags	52	209	1	208	145	....	190	83
Ambulance flags	....	833	1,628	....	150	....	....	76
Mosquito nets (pieces)	38,164	....	....	....	....	....	....	....
Books:								
Company order	1,911	955	2,650	465	205	67	629	163
Company clothing account.	1,809	290	2,515	472	314	89	957	238
Company descriptive	1,837	440	2,553	448	262	74	867	204
Company morning report	2,561	532	2,754	458	341	60	954	218
Post order	981	3,100	1,011	70	165	57	507	115
Post morning report	935	3,595	1,035	57	224	65	521	103
Post letter	889	3,000	1,364	83	229	72	544	104
Post guard	634	2,026	603	117	45	67	553	166
Regimental general order	543	254	215	69	103	26	83	120
Regimental letter	303	3	474	62	229	19	90	101
Regimental descriptive	310	5	493	65	141	23	153	132
Regimental index	488	244	382	66	212	19	90	170
Regimental order	253	97	169	64	197	24	77	226
Target Practice	1,953	42	449	....	50	....	45	50
Consolidated morning report.	....	....	....	....	....	....	....	....
Inspectors' report books	....	....	....	....	....	....	....	....
Brigade letter books	32	106	....	21	....	....	....	....
Brigade letters-received books.	34	103	....	21	....	....	....	....
Brigade order books	3	49	....	15	....	....	....	....
Indorsement and memorandum books.	35	37	....	16	....	....	....	....

No. 10.—*Monthly statement of camp and garrison equipage reported on hand at the various clothing depots on June 30, 1865*—Continued.

Articles of equipage.	Fortress Monroe.	Harrisburg.	Indianapolis.	Columbus.	Fort Leavenworth.	Quincy.	Pittsburg.	Detroit.
Hospital tents	170	35	43	16	227		7	2
Wall-tents	294	179	353	876	288		19	12
Sibley tents		2	1		75			
Common tents	2, 451	2, 148	496	367	1, 714			
Shelter tents	11, 104	2, 843	11, 205		25, 278		6, 633	
Frémont and Bell tents			88		6			
Tent stoves	860	329	375		529			42
Bedsacks, single	1, 124	202		22	15, 413			4, 233
Bedsacks, double	1, 084	70	659	10	1, 032	200	40	902
Mosquito bars	109				68			
Regimental colors		6	2	2	9		1	2
Camp colors	101	80		3	44		18	52
National colors		6	5		6		10	2
Standards		4						
Storm flags	57	4		3	30	2	3	
Garrison flags	58	5	1	2	21			4
Recruiting flags	17	6		2	31			16
Guidons	28	18	4		8		2	
Pickaxes	2, 542	65	2, 935	1, 749	2, 888	7	661	846
Axes	1, 948	162	556	644	3, 257		254	716
Spades	1, 558	175	2, 632	828	2, 871	16	316	601
Shovels	2, 209	259	112	161	1, 490			
Hatchets	5, 584	489	644	1, 340	2, 747	11	843	669
Mess-pans	12, 826	500	7, 960	1, 101	3, 541	10	5, 109	1, 270
Iron pots	57				25			
Camp-kettles	2, 452	121	3, 097		1, 859		2, 081	501
Bugles	58	50	32	99	91		7	11
Trumpets	47	19		10	199		9	
Drums	90	51	107	128	94		17	15
Fifes	713	34	365	147	29		20	42
General-hospital flags	4	3		4	18		4	
Post and field flags	13			8	30			
Ambulance flags					200			
Mosquito nets (pieces)								
Books:								
Company order	333		75	41	134		38	30
Company clothing account.	338	6	73	86	82		28	43
Company descriptive	321	6	67	81	162		30	42
Company morning report.	338		78	64	117		20	37
Post order	83		12		43			5
Post morning report	81		23	25	23			
Post letter	71		14	4	40			
Post guard	138		12	2	10		1	3
Regimental general order.	106		8	10	20		4	6
Regimental letter	100		18	1	48		3	
Regimental descriptive	139		13	1	51		4	4
Regimental index	121		19		58		3	1
Regimental order	107		11	5	58		4	5
Target Practice					52			
Consolidated morning report.								
Inspectors' report books.								
Brigade letter books	39							
Brigade letters-received books.	32							
Brigade order books	52							
Indorsement and memorandum books.	27							

No. 10.—*Monthly statement of camp and garrison equipage reported on hand at the various clothing depots on June 30, 1865*—Continued.

Articles of equipage.	Louisville.	Davenport.	Chicago.	New Berne.	City Point.	Saint Paul.	Cairo.	Memphis.	Norfolk.
Hospital tents	240	....	40	186	10	....	7	....	6
Wall-tents	....	6	608	23	26	....	1	413	131
Sibley tents	....	....	5	....	....	....	....	....	....
Common tents	306	5	253	387	25	....	461	1,653	535
Shelter tents	9,902	362	5,558	9,285	262	100	....	218,931	310
Frémont and Bell tents	225	....	....	....	....	....	....	1	....
Tent stoves	25	....	571	438	....	....	....	45	....
Bedsacks, single	724	192	1,003	1,032	....	370	....	29	20
Bedsacks, double	....	214	1,026	....	....	657	76	31	....
Mosquito bars	....	....	....	....	....	....	102	86	257
Regimental colors	6	13	28	....	6	....	2	7	....
Camp colors	8	74	295	....	34	4	....	47	....
National colors	16	16	27	....	7	....	2	5	....
Standards	....	2	4	....	5	....	....	32	....
Storm flags	18	....	129	10	8	1	2	10	6
Garrison flags	....	2	74	4	8	3	2	1	2
Recruiting flags	19	....	86	2	....	....	....	9	....
Guidons	20	13	19	33	....	....	....	66	....
Pickaxes	3,071	....	1,295	1,605	45	428	5	1,353	93
Axes	....	1,947	2,607	1,980	88	167	205	1,978	134
Spades	3,248	1,911	1,709	1,751	17	346	210	1,223	398
Shovels	....	....	7	826	250	....	41	2,499	....
Hatchets	543	1,968	2,874	2,205	20	515	91	2,284	177
Mess-pans	16,232	3,290	5,370	8,683	120	884	302	4,886	732
Iron pots	....	....	80	78	....	....	....	....	....
Camp-kettles	162	1,058	1,906	326	177	167	60	3,652	370
Bugles	34	50	86	40	23	....	5	33	9
Trumpets	....	23	70	150	9	20	4	70	....
Drums	16	72	85	....	8	43	7	124	22
Fifes	....	....	110	234	86	3	17	154	....
General-hospital flags	22	....	....	74	....	....	....	16	....
Post and field flags	....	....	....	....	....	....	....	7	....
Ambulance flags	....	....	....	....	....	....	....	....	....
Mosquito nets (pieces)	....	....	....	....	....	....	....	....	....
Books:									
Company order	224	91	79	69	8	11	18	490	4
Company clothing account	287	82	90	81	15	21	19	430	1
Company descriptive	346	84	77	114	10	18	23	450	1
Company morning report	224	55	117	50	7	17	6	534	1
Post order	....	....	....	15	27	7	....	6	2
Post morning report	36	....	....	17	26	7	....	6	....
Post letter	....	....	....	15	26	10	....	2	2
Post guard	85	2	....	13	44	8	....	....	....
Regimental general order	26	5	9	34	2	....	6	106	....
Regimental letter	53	10	18	28	11	....	8	77	....
Regimental descriptive	45	9	19	17	1	1	11	179	....
Regimental index	81	11	8	17	1	4	10	111	....
Regimental order	54	7	18	21	26	1	9	47	....
Target Practice	....	....	....	5	....	....	....	....	....
Consolidated morning report.	....	....	....	....	....	....	....	....	....
Inspectors' report books	....	....	....	....	....	....	....	....	....
Brigade letter books	....	....	....	....	....	....	....	....	....
Brigade letters-received books.	....	....	....	....	....	....	....	....	....
Brigade order books	....	....	....	....	....	....	....	....	....
Indorsement and memorandum books.	....	....	....	....	....	....	....	....	....

No. 10.—*Monthly statement of camp and garrison equipage reported on hand at the various clothing depots on June 30, 1865*—Continued.

Articles of equipage.	Prairie du Chien.	Keokuk.	Madison.	Augusta.	Wheeling.	Hilton Head.	Trenton.	Total on hand.
Hospital tents	...	...	25	...	...	10	2	6,121
Wall-tents	...	...	32	8	23	222	31	15,672
Sibley tents	...	...	...	...	...	1	...	240
Common tents	...	...	...	226	1,235	2,374	185	53,902
Shelter tents	...	...	2,762	2,059	310	4,897	856	791,254
Frémont and Bell tents	...	...	...	...	...	...	...	363
Tent stoves	...	...	20	...	1,066	2	...	11,639
Bedsacks, single	...	150	27	492	200	274	...	116,815
Bedsacks, double	...	...	937	30	500	...	278	50,222
Mosquito bars	...	...	...	...	...	545	...	66,274
Regimental colors	...	...	7	1	...	...	4	789
Camp colors	...	...	32	9	57	13	12	7,270
National colors	...	...	7	2	...	...	4	609
Standards	...	...	2	...	...	5	...	1,234
Storm flags	...	...	2	5	...	21	5	748
Garrison flags	...	...	1	1	...	6	...	497
Recruiting flags	...	...	3	19	...	...	...	2,103
Guidons	...	...	2	19	...	19	...	2,039
Pickaxes	12	190	1,233	285	1,267	979	310	103,228
Axes	7	255	1,402	96	250	170	296	90,548
Spades	7	98	1,405	123	500	...	605	105,132
Shovels	...	...	61	...	18	...	...	47,391
Hatchets	24	188	1,191	178	498	716	309	111,247
Mess-pans	...	229	3,682	1,440	2,849	8,925	2,279	364,086
Iron pots	...	...	...	...	...	...	...	1,678
Camp-kettles	...	71	1,161	693	327	8,624	1,106	106,417
Bugles	...	7	...	18	2	77	9	3,893
Trumpets	...	...	...	...	3	47	2	3,869
Drums	...	6	63	22	29	6	30	5,865
Fifes	...	4	102	21	77	80	51	11,747
General-hospital flags	...	...	4	...	2	...	...	511
Post and field flags	...	...	6	...	...	...	...	951
Ambulance flags	...	...	...	...	...	...	...	2,887
Mosquito nets (pieces)	...	...	...	...	...	...	...	38,164
Books:								
Company order	...	10	30	30	53	18	37	8,858
Company clothing account.	...	10	35	12	73	35	40	8,571
Company descriptive	...	10	31	13	...	49	38	8,658
Company morning report	...	10	35	13	58	27	33	9,749
Post order	...	...	...	...	...	50	...	6,256
Post morning report	...	...	...	...	...	50	...	6,829
Post letter	...	...	1	...	...	50	...	6,511
Post guard	...	1	8	...	...	105	4	4,647
Regimental general order	...	1	...	1	...	14	1	1,772
Regimental letter	...	...	6	18	...	20	1	1,701
Regimental descriptive	...	1	7	...	...	11	3	1,848
Regimental index	...	1	6	24	...	13	...	2,160
Regimental order	...	1	4	20	...	13	3	1,521
Target Practice	...	...	...	...	...	62	...	2,708
Consolidated morning report.	...	...	...	...	...	...	...	...
Inspectors' report books	...	...	...	...	...	...	...	...
Brigade letter books	...	...	...	...	...	9	...	207
Brigade letters-received books.	...	...	...	...	...	8	...	198
Brigade order books	...	...	...	...	...	10	...	129
Indorsement and memorandum books.	...	...	...	...	...	6	...	121

Respectfully submitted to the Quartermaster-General.

ALEX. J. PERRY,
Colonel, Quartermaster's Department.

QUARTERMASTER-GENERAL'S OFFICE, SECOND DIVISION,
October 21, 1865.

No. 11.

Statement showing the aggregate expenditure for the purchase of clothing, equipage, and material during the fiscal year ending June 30, 1865, at the purchasing depots at New York, Philadelphia, and Cincinnati.

	Philadelphia.	New York.	Cincinnati.	Total.
Clothing	$20, 297, 473. 96	$23, 340, 040. 42	$26, 449, 767. 82	$70, 087, 282. 20
Equipage	7, 992, 255. 65	3, 105, 147. 20	2, 417, 902. 24	13, 515, 305. 09
Material	14, 678, 464. 21	976. 20	6, 737, 378. 43	21, 416, 818. 84
Total	42, 968, 193. 82	26, 446, 163. 82	35, 605, 048. 49	105, 019, 406. 13

Respectfully submitted to the Quartermaster-General.

ALEX. J. PERRY,
Colonel, Quartermaster's Department.

QUARTERMASTER-GENERAL'S OFFICE, SECOND DIVISION,
October 21, 1865.

No. 12.

Statement showing the quantity of material purchased at the depots at New York, Philadelphia, and Cincinnati since May, 1861.

Articles.	Philadelphia.	New York.	Cincinnati.	Total.
Woolen cloths and kerseys:				
$\frac{6}{4}$ dark-blue cloth (uniform coat) ... yards	588, 496	290, 000	822, 516	1, 701, 012
$\frac{3}{4}$ dark-blue cloth (uniform coat) ... do	1, 630, 839	166, 000		1, 796, 839
$\frac{6}{4}$ dark-blue cloth (forage cap) ... do	4, 820	23, 250		28, 070
Canteen (covering) ... do	109, 487			109, 487
$\frac{6}{4}$ sky-blue kersey ... do	772, 341	138, 000		910, 341
$\frac{3}{4}$ sky-blue kersey ... do	11, 760, 168	802, 000	1, 503, 943	14, 066, 111
$\frac{6}{4}$ dark-blue kersey ... do	60, 736	884, 000		944, 736
$\frac{3}{4}$ dark-blue kersey ... do	459, 826	25, 000		484, 826
$\frac{6}{4}$ green facing-cloth ... do	929			929
$\frac{6}{4}$ scarlet facing-cloth ... do	3, 028			3, 028
$\frac{6}{4}$ sky-blue facing-cloth ... do	12, 405	10, 100		22, 505
$\frac{3}{4}$ sky-blue facing-cloth ... do	90			90
Irregular cloth ... do	330, 255			330, 255
Cotton duck:				
Hospital tents, 30-inch, 22½-ounce ... do	11, 265			11, 265
Hospital-tent flies, 30-inch, 15½-ounce ... do			25, 022	25, 022
Wall and Sibley tents, 28½-inch, 15-ounce ... do	152, 155			152, 155
Wall-tents, 24-inch, 12¼-ounce ... do			893, 784	893, 784
Wall-tent flies, 28½-inch, 10-ounce ... do	184, 588		3, 845, 409	4, 029, 997
Common tents, 22-inch, 11-ounce ... do	14, 516			13, 516
Common tents, 22-inch, 9-ounce ... do	46, 722			46, 722
Tent frills and baling, 28½-inch, 8-ounce ... do	21, 092		200, 162	221, 254
Tent frills and baling, 33-inch, 10-ounce ... do	8, 111			8, 111
Flannels:				
$\frac{3}{4}$ Canton flannel ... do	3, 220, 219		2, 312, 510	5, 532, 729
Gray ... do	4, 818, 994	1, 081, 250	2, 414, 648	8, 314, 892
$\frac{3}{4}$ blue ... do	333, 969	680		334, 649
$\frac{6}{4}$ blue wool (sack coat) ... do	310, 886	680, 510		991, 396
$\frac{3}{4}$ blue wool (sack coat) ... do	2, 562, 119	770, 246	1, 094, 776	4, 427, 041
Black silesia ... do	337, 992	139, 700		477, 692
Muslin twills and corset jeans ... do	6, 334	257, 117		263, 452
$\frac{4}{4}$ muslin twills, unbleached ... do	2, 029, 747	78, 500	261, 316	2, 369, 559
$\frac{3}{4}$ cotton drilling ... do	2, 395, 100	600, 000		2, 995, 100
$\frac{4}{4}$ cotton drilling ... do	231, 789			231, 789
Cotton, sewing, spools ... number	413, 448	16, 900	493, 500	923, 848
Russia sheeting ... yards	109, 057			109, 057
Alpaca ... do	197, 873	19, 000	2, 167	219, 040
Brown linen ... do	146, 303		72, 243	218, 546
Canvas padding ... do	596, 903		78, 278	675, 181
Linings ... do	2, 720, 104			2, 720, 104
Webbing, cotton, 1-inch ... do		3, 000	20, 160	23, 160
Tape ... pieces	182, 607	128, 000	14, 400	325, 007
Webbing, cotton, 1½-inch ... yards	20, 118		40, 320	
Flax, bagging ... do	6, 986			6, 986
Pasteboard ... pounds	5, 785			5, 785

No. 12.—*Statement showing the quantity of material purchased at the depots at New York, Philadelphia, and Cincinnati since May, 1861*—Continued.

Articles.	Philadelphia.	New York.	Cincinnati.	Total.
Bunting:				
Red .... pieces..	1,783	19,000	....	20,783
White .... do...	1,546	17,000	....	18,546
Blue .... do...	737	8,000	....	8,783
Worsted lace:				
1½-inch .... yards..	399,653	....	150,100	449,753
½-inch .... do...	1,844,768	....	300,000	2,144,768
⅜-inch .... do...	4,572,205	....	1,018,360	5,590,565
Silk lace, ½-inch .... do...	78,562	....	....	78,562
Silk, sewing .... ounces..	42,544	6,000	....	48,544
Burlaps .... yards..	271,540	6,000	111,805	389,345
Standard drills .... do...	....	....	3,011,797	3,011,797
Luster .... do...	....	....	3,527	3,527
Thread .... pounds..	189,871	....	13,427	203,298
Buttons:				
Coat .... gross..	83,825	28,650	....	112,475
Vest .... do...	148,591	16,670	29,765	195,026
Shirt .... do...	223,601	33,350	13,212	276,163
Suspender .... do...	196,067	33,350	19,080	248,497
All kinds .... do...	....	....	21,988	21,988
Buckles:				
⅝-inch, roller .... do...	13,640	....	....	13,640
¾-inch, roller .... do...	3,531	....	....	3,531
1-inch, roller .... do...	2,241	....	....	2,241
1½-inch, roller .... do...	4,806	....	....	4,806
Flax sewing twine .... pounds..	2,323	....	1,051	3,374
Hooks and eyes .... gross..	25,184	13,900	3,136	42,220
Baling rope .... pounds..	40,631	....	....	40,631
Cotton twine .... do...	....	....	39,670	39,670
Flag thimbles .... do...	3,526	....	....	3,526
Chin-strap slides .... number..	222,180	....	....	222,180
Leather:				
Buckskins .... do...	2,117	....	....	2,117
Sheep, morocco, skins .... sides..	3,247	....	....	3,247
Black, bridle .... do...	15,981	....	....	15,981
Russet, bridle .... do...	2,599	....	....	2,599
Wax, upper .... feet..	529,875	....	....	529,875
Sole .... pounds..	1,895,982	....	....	1,895,982
Welt .... do...	158,263	....	....	158,263
Stock .... sides..	652	....	....	652
Visor .... feet..	13,872	....	....	13,872
Chin straps .... do...	3,857	....	....	3,857
Split, for knapsacks .... pounds..	24,958	....	....	24,958
Cap leathers, complete .... sets..	41,663	....	....	41,663
Tent buttons .... number..	2,442,056	....	1,903,200	4,345,256
line, large .... pounds..	40,894	....	....	40,894
twine, cotton, sewing .... do...	16,000	....	....	16,000

Respectfully submitted to the Quartermaster-General.

ALEX. J. PERRY,
Colonel, Quartermaster's Department.

QUARTERMASTER-GENERAL'S OFFICE, SECOND DIVISION,
October 21, 1865.

No. 13.

Statement showing the number of the principal articles of clothing and equipage purchased at the depots of Philadelphia, New York, and Cincinnati since May, 1861.

(NOTE.—This statement includes only articles purchased already made up. It is exclusive of the articles manufactured from material purchased, for which see Statement No. 6.)

Articles.	Philadelphia.	New York.	Cincinnati.	Total.
Uniform coats	948,904	587,000	345,823	1,881,727
jackets	591,125	343,400	169,646	1,104,161
trousers, foot	2,398,772	2,195,674	1,473,603	6,068,049
trousers, horse	607,997	553,420	527,329	1,688,746
Vests	3,844	....	....	3,844
Overalls	5,001	26,000	....	31,001

No. 13.—*Statement showing the number of the principal articles of clothing and equipage purchased at the depots of Philadelphia, New York, and Cincinnati since May, 1861*—Continued.

Articles.	Philadelphia.	New York.	Cincinnati.	Total.
Drawers	4,697,300	3,408,900	2,632,165	10,738,365
Shirts	4,349,656	4,391,634	2,350,349	11,091,639
Greatcoats:				
Foot	1,062,258	1,063,600	677,661	2,803,519
Horse	437,835	312,300	273,396	1,023,531
Straps for greatcoats	1,705,753	....	398,530	2,104,283
Blankets:				
Woolen	1,920,902	2,380,053	1,609,104	5,910,059
Rubber and painted	959,307	723,700	210,000	1,893,007
Ponchos rubber and painted	532,279	254,525	809,755	1,596,559
Talmas	25,451	6,259	3,000	34,710
Sack coats:				
Lined	1,031,139	1,459,000	1,195,616	3,685,755
Unlined	594,451	842,150	372,669	1,809,270
Knit	....	530,144	....	530,144
Bootees:				
Sewed	3,231,647	2,759,900	90,750	6,082,297
Pegged	....	363,880	1,835,459	2,199,339
Brogans	....	124,920	....	155,580
Boots:				
Sewed	909,016	559,532	....	1,468,548
Pegged	....	341,900	731,166	1,073,066
Leggings	145,138	27,000	5,169	177,307
Stockings	7,901,546	7,429,596	4,988,754	20,319,896
Stocks, leather	276,254	419,000	50,560	745,814
Uniform hats	701,566	990,618	682,340	2,347,524
caps	6,287	....	....	15,738
Forage caps	2,163,522	1,644,280	958,298	4,766,100
Cap covers	100,143	394,200	180,243	674,586
Stable frocks	....	109,000	45,000	154,000
Sashes	19,618	....	6,099	25,717
Gloves	74,570	....	....	74,570
Mittens	95,675	22,000	92,000	209,675
Knapsacks	1,208,627	1,430,310	944,387	3,583,324
Haversacks	1,714,319	1,841,400	1,008,889	4,564,608
Canteens	1,979,797	1,903,260	1,317,557	5,200,614
Hospital tents	16,243	7,605	1,265	25,113
Wall-tents	39,541	28,625	2,783	70,949
Sibley tents	21,572	15,099	165	36,836
Common tents	128,037	124,868	3,142	256,047
Shelter tents	998,326	866,900	334,140	2,199,366
Bell tents	....	....	1,287	1,287
Tent stoves	24,777	19,500	1,175	45,452
Bedsacks, single	32,748	147,000	....	179,748
Bedsacks, double	49,275	30,000	....	79,275
Mosquito bars	9,580	124,000	....	133,585
Regimental colors	765	1,021	564	2,350
Camp colors	1,819	7,800	1,502	11,121
National colors	890	917	500	2,307
Standards	286	225	700	1,211
Storm flags	308	759	430	1,497
Garrison flags	25	557	180	762
Recruiting flags	357	2,670	500	3,527
Guidons	4,189	4,551	1,476	10,216
Pickaxes	79,448	114,910	62,522	256,280
Axes	276,095	183,000	139,258	568,353
Spades	107,910	121,700	84,379	313,989
Shovels	63,887	23,931	60,536	148,354
Hatchets	137,760	135,389	70,174	343,323
Mess-pans	446,542	298,300	281,422	1,026,264
Iron pots	1,398	1,700	....	3,098
Camp-kettles	232,655	141,000	152,548	526,203
Bugles	9,717	7,700	4,010	21,427
Trumpets	8,238	4,610	2,010	14,858
Drums	19,154	13,840	4,502	37,496
Fifes	15,533	12,420	4,687	32,640
Hospital flags:				
General	261	101	200	562
Post and field	698	201	....	899
Ambulance flags	2,500	401	1,750	4,651
Books:				
Company order	12,414	16,660	8,631	37,705
Company clothing	14,692	17,200	8,629	40,521
Company descriptive	14,349	16,960	8,631	39,940
Company morning report	13,311	16,460	8,631	38,402
Post order	1,994	3,000	1,151	6,145
Post morning report	2,000	3,000	1,313	6,313

No. 13.—*Statement showing the number of the principal articles of clothing and equipage purchased at the depots of Philadelphia, New York, and Cincinnati since May, 1861*—Continued.

Articles.	Philadelphia.	New York.	Cincinnati.	Total.
Books—Continued.				
Post letter	2,000	3,000	1,506	6,506
Post guard	1,560	3,000	955	5,515
Regimental general order	2,170	2,056	750	4,976
Regimental letter	2,471	2,156	1,251	5,878
Regimental descriptive	2,118	1,956	1,250	5,324
Regimental index	1,914	1,556	1,300	4,770
Regimental order	2,763	2,056	1,249	6,068
Target Practice	398	....	500	898
Consolidated morning report	....	....	....	....

Respectfully submitted to the Quartermaster-General.

ALEX. J. PERRY,
Colonel, Quartermaster's Department.

QUARTERMASTER-GENERAL'S OFFICE, SECOND DIVISION,
October 21, 1865.

No. 14.

Statement showing the highest and lowest prices paid by the department for articles of clothing and equipage during the past four years of war.

Articles.	Lowest price.	Highest price.	Articles.	Lowest price.	Highest price.
Uniform hat	$1.62	$2.18½	Shirts:		
Uniform hat feather	.08½	.15½	Flannel	$0.45	$3.01
cord and tassel	.10½	.16	Knit	.69	2.34
eagle	.00½	.02	Drawers:		
castle	.08	.19	Flannel	.37	1.90
shell and flame	.04	.04	Knit	.72	1.78
crossed sabers	.01⅘	.03	Stockings	.22½	.52½
crossed cannon	.01⅘	.02½	Bootees:		
bugle	.00 69/100	.02	Sewed	1.71	3.24
letters	.00 1/10	.01¾	Pegged	1.33	2.45
numbers	.0087½	.01¾	Boots:		
Forage caps	.35	1.04	Sewed	3.00	4.83
Forage-cap covers	.07½	.12½	Pegged	1.45	4.08⅓
Uniform coats	4.08	14.67	Greatcoats:		
jackets	4.25	9.94	Footmen's	6.50	13.17
Chevrons:			Horsemen's	7.74	16.11
N. C. S ....pair	.30	.45	Blankets:		
First sergeant's ....do	.18	.35	Woolen	2.18¾	7.75
Sergeant's ....do	.19½	.27	Rubber	2.00	5.00
Corporal's ....do	.12¼	.18	Painted	1.99	2.35
Caduceus	.35	.80	Ponchos:		
Shoulder scales:			Rubber	1.87	5.60
N. C. S ....pair	.35	.80	Painted	1.83	2.35
Sergeant's ....do	.33	.80	Leather stocks	.08	.13
Private's ....do	.25	.60	leggings	1.12½	2.00
Trousers:			Cotton leggings	.74	1.25
Footmen's	2.05	5.40	Overalls	1.31	2.06
Horsemen's	3.31½	5.89	Stable frocks	.62	2.23
Sash	1.98	2.50	Hospital tents and flies	56.40	227.61
Flannel sack coat:			Wall-tents and flies	23.50	55.00
Lined	2.10	5.09	Common tents	9.87	25.00
Unlined	1.87½	4.37½	Shelter tents	1.93	10.74

Respectfully submitted to the Quartermaster-General:

ALEX. J. PERRY,
Colonel, Quartermaster's Department.

QUARTERMASTER-GENERAL'S OFFICE, SECOND DIVISION,
October 21, 1865.

No. 15.

Statement of claims received in the Second Division of the Quartermaster-General's Office during the fiscal year ending June 30, 1865.

	Number.	Amount.
Received	34	$98, 274. 65
Reported to Third Auditor and referred to officers for settlement	16	66, 662. 22
Disallowed (in their present condition)	10	8, 682. 65
Not acted on	8	22, 929. 78

Respectfully submitted.

A. G. ROBINSON,
Capt. and A. Q. M., for Col. Alexander J. Perry, in Charge Second Division.

QUARTERMASTER-GENERAL'S OFFICE,
Washington, D. C., November 4, 1865.

Statement of claims received in the Second Division of the Quartermaster-General's Office from July 1, 1865, to present date.

	Number.	Amount.
Received	17	$4, 515. 90
Reported to Third Auditor and referred to officers for settlement	1	10. 25
Disallowed (in their present condition)	7	2, 484. 40
Not acted on	9	2, 021. 25

Respectfully submitted.

ALEXANDER J. PERRY,
Colonel, Quartermaster's Department, in Charge Second Division.

QUARTERMASTER-GENERAL'S OFFICE,
Washington, D. C., November 6, 1865.

No. 16.

QUARTERMASTER-GENERAL'S OFFICE,
Washington, D. C., August 31, 1865.

Bvt. Maj. Gen. M. C. MEIGS,
Quartermaster-General U. S. Army, Washington, D. C.:

GENERAL: I have the honor to report for the fiscal year ending June 30, 1865, relative to the operations of the Third Division, in charge of the ocean and lake transportation of the War Department, as follows:

During the first month of the year the office work of the division was nearly suspended by most of the employés being called into active service in the field to assist in repelling the rebel raid on Washington; nevertheless, sufficient steamers were promptly on hand at City Point for the transportation of the Sixth Army Corps to Washington and Baltimore, rendering efficient service in driving back the invading force.

Also, in this month, the army of General Canby was moved from New Orleans to Mobile Bay, co-operating with the navy in the reduction of the forts.

From August to December no large army movements requiring water transportation were made, but a great number of steamers were used to forward the supplies for the armies before Richmond.

In December the approach of General Sherman's army to the Atlantic Coast taxed the resources of the department to the utmost extent.

The precise point of his advent was not known; it was a stormy season of the year, and only reliable ocean steamers could be used, with a proper regard for the lives of the passengers and the property on board.

At this time some 300,000 men, including the armies of Grant and Sherman, were dependent entirely for their supplies upon water transportation. The winter was unusually severe; storms swept the ocean, and ice blocked the bays and rivers. Notwithstanding, the troops were kept well supplied, and stores and forage were sent as far south as Pensacola, and a large number of light-draft river steamers and tugs were sent to Hilton Head, S. C., to be on hand for the navigation of the shoal rivers of the Southern coast, all of which, fortunately, arrived in safety and rendered efficient service after the fall of Savannah and Charleston.

When General Sherman's army left Savannah, in continuation of its victorious march through the Southern States, a part was transported by sea to Beaufort, N. C., while the light fleet of steamers followed along the coast, ready again to meet and co-operate with the army at Wilmington and Morehead City. A large number of canal barges were sent via the Chesapeake and Albemarle Canal to carry supplies up the North Carolina rivers.

On the 24th of this month (December), an eventful one in our history, the first attack on Fort Fisher was made, and ocean transportation was provided for the land forces from City Point, Va., and, when the expedition proved unsuccessful, brought the troops back to Fortress Monroe. In January another and successful expedition was sent to the Cape Fear River, resulting in the fall of Fort Fisher and the evacuation of Wilmington, N. C., by the rebels.

The department was much embarrassed at this time by the difficulty of procuring ocean steamers whose draft of water would allow them to enter Cape Fear River, and at Morehead City, which were not safe to attempt with a greater draft than twelve feet. Steamers had to lie at anchor on an open coast in midwinter and discharge their cargoes in small vessels.

In this connection I would state, as worthy of remark, that during the last fiscal year only three vessels in the service of the War Department have been lost at sea. One of them, the North America, was a new, first-class steamer; another, the General Lyon, took fire and was burned; and the third one, the Admiral Du Pont, collided with a ship at sea and was sunk. These were all chartered steamers, and the loss of life and property was not great.

From January to the surrender of General Lee, in April, the water transportation department continued faithfully to supply the two great armies of Grant and Sherman, and nearly every ocean steamer of any capacity in the country was employed.

After the surrender of the rebel armies in the Atlantic States, and the virtual close of the war, every exertion was made to reduce the expenses of the department, and vessels belonging to the Government were sold and chartered ones discharged as fast as the service would allow.

Of the first class it is not supposed the Government will realize a sum from their sale in proportion to their original cost. The requirements of the service were such that they were always under a severe strain, and, notwithstanding frequent repairs, the close of the war found most of them in bad condition. Many ships were yet required to carry back the returning veterans, and, in addition, transportation had to be furnished for thousands of our own released prisoners, and for rebel released prisoners, refugees, and freedmen, to the points nearest their homes.

In May a requisition was made upon the department for ocean transportation for the Twenty-fifth Army Corps from City Point, Va., to Texas. This corps numbered about 25,000 men.

The inclosed tabular list will enable you to form an idea of the requirements necessary for a large ocean expedition.

It comprised fifty-seven ocean steamers (one of which made two voyages), making the entire tonnage of the vessels employed amount to 56,987 tons.

They were all provided for a twelve-days' voyage, allowing for the consumption of coal, per day, 947 tons, and for water, 50,000 gallons.

While all the vessels were employed the expense of the expedition amounted to $33,300.91 per day.

Each vessel was fitted up suitably for the cargo to be carried. Bunks were constructed for the troops, and stalls for 2,139 animals, being part of the expedition.

The vessels were supplied with an ample quantity of coal and water and were thoroughly inspected, so that in case of disaster no blame would attach to the department for sending unseaworthy vessels. They all arrived safely at their destination, no accident of any kind having been reported.

At the same time the Texas expedition was under way, 7,000 troops were sent by sea from Washington to Savannah, and 3,000 released rebels from Point Lookout and Fort Delaware to Mobile.

With this closes the work of the ocean and lake transportation division for the fiscal year ending June 30, 1865.

No mention has been made of transportation on the lakes, as none was required except one small steamer used for the convenience of the prisoners on Johnson's Island, between that and the main.

The inclosed tabular list of transportation employed by the division shows the number of vessels in service during the year, from which it appears the average daily expense of the division, for the fiscal year, amounts to $92,414.

The average number of steamers employed, owned, and chartered, 351; tugs, 111.

The average amount of tonnage of the above, 171,081; tonnage of tugs, 13,262.

The average number of sail vessels employed, 89.

The average amount of tonnage of the above, 17,738.

The average number of barges employed, 168.

The average amount of the tonnage of the above, 22,903.

The total number of vessels employed, 719.

The total amount of tonnage employed, 224,984.

In closing my report, I would respectfully make some remarks relative to the duties of my division, and the transportation, by water, of the United States.

At the beginning of the rebellion we were found wanting in nearly every material preparation for the war, except an ample supply of ships and steamers, the importance of which was very great in a country like ours, penetrated in every direction by navigable rivers, and indented on the coast by deep and sheltered harbors.

Nothing contributed more to the success of our cause than this, enabling us, with the assistance of the Navy, to concentrate rapidly and secretly large bodies of troops upon the weak points of the enemy, and in this way New Orleans, Hilton Head, Fort Fisher, City Point, Mobile, and the great Mississippi Valley were cleared of the rebels. That they fully appreciated this is evident from their desperate and frantic efforts to destroy our shipping by the torch of the incendiary, torpedoes, or the more open attack by armored vessels.

In the first rush of troops to the war, by the inexperience of quartermasters, or the unfaithfulness of Government agents, and not over-patriotic shipowners, many unsuitable vessels were employed for the service and paid at high prices. This was remedied as soon as possible by the Quartermaster-General, and a scale of prices fixed per ton for the guidance of quartermasters, and stringent orders issued that no vessel should be sent with troops to sea unless she had been properly constructed for such purpose.

All charters were made allowing the department to take possession of the vessel by paying 33 per cent. profit on the valuation, and the running expenses and repairs, and be credited with the amount paid for charter. By this means a large number of vessels became the property of the Government, and the higher the rate of charter the sooner the vessel would pay for herself. The valuation was fixed by one or more officers of the Navy duly detailed for that duty.

It is important that quartermasters should inform themselves of the kind of steamers suitable to carry troops by sea.

If a side-wheel steamer, in order that the paddle wheels may be secure from the action of the waves, the projection in the side, called the sponsing, should be carried up so as to make that portion as solid as any other part of the ship. This is to be done by carrying timbers, curved according to the form necessary for admitting the water to the paddles, from the floor of the ship to the very outermost projection as well as within the paddles, deviating very little from what would be the regular form of a sailing vessel.

According to the best authorities, the following parts of a vessel of this kind should be increased in actual strength by one-fourth, viz: The keel, stern, apron or inner stern, futtocks, floor timbers, deadwood, stern post, transom, inner post, frame timbers, and filling timbers abreast of the engine, as should also the wales, the rudder, and the rudder fastenings. The steamer should be provided with sufficient masts and sails, in case of accident to her motive power, which should not be less than a fore-and-aft sail to each mast, set upon a gaff, these being intended for the usual wants of the vessel; while there should also be a trysail to each mast, to be set in storms.

The weight of machinery should be well below the water-line; and quartermasters should not be deceived into employing as ocean steamers river or lake vessels boxed up to resemble a sea vessel, but having broad guards only a few feet from the water, and which the first storm at sea is liable to send to the bottom.

Steamers for the transportation of troops by sea should be high between decks, and well ventilated by hatches, wind-sails, and side-lights. Water-closet arrangements and temporary bath fixtures can easily be made, which contribute greatly to the health and comfort of troops on shipboard. Dampness can be obviated by the use of drying stoves.

I would respectfully recommend that the arms, baggage, and knapsacks of the troops be taken, as they embark, and stowed in a convenient place, to be returned when about to leave the ship. Soldiers from seasickness, want of use to the motion of the ship, are unable to take care of their arms, which might be damaged without the possibility of their preventing it.

When a steam vessel comes alongside of a wharf or other vessel care should be taken that the gang boards are properly fixed and attended by seamen before the troops are allowed to step on them, and they ought to be made to march with regularity.

The senior officer in command of troops on board should cause a careful inspection to be made twice a day relative to their condition, and if any symptoms of a contagious disease should appear among the men, they should be immediately separated from their comrades until the character of the disease is known.

While a well-regulated ship is remarkable for health, one where proper precautions are not observed soon becomes a floating pest-house. A steamer for the transportation of troops should be well provided with boats ready to lower away at a moment's notice. She should be fitted with sufficient life buoys, ready to be shipped or cast away if a person should fall overboard.

The troops on board should on no account be allowed to interfere with the management of the ship, and arrangements should be made in case of accidents to prevent a rush to the boats.

If a boat is to be lowered, it should be done by the people of the ship, and not by soldiers unaccustomed to that kind of service, which often causes loss of life.

The commanding officer on board should only under extraordinary circumstances oblige the captain to put to sea, or cross a dangerous bar, to go into port, if the captain should protest against it as incurring risk of life and property. For the more particular guidance of quartermasters in charge of transportation I would refer to the excellent instructions embodied in the Revised Army Regulations of the War Department, page 20, article 37.

I have the honor to be, very respectfully, your obedient servant,

GEO. D. WISE,
Colonel, in Charge Ocean and Lake Transportation.

No. 17.

*Statement of vessels chartered or employed in the Quartermaster's Department (on ocean and lake service) during the fiscal year ended June 30, 1865.**

RECAPITULATION.

Side-wheel steamers	97
Screw steamers	80
Screw tugs	53
Barks	4
Brigs	6
Schooners	76
Pilot-boats	3
Canal-barges	95
Total	414

GEO. D. WISE,
Colonel, in Charge of Ocean and Lake Transportation.

*Omitted, except the "Recapitulation."

No. 18.

*List of vessels owned by the United States and employed on ocean and lake service for the fiscal year ending June 30, 1865.**

RECAPITULATION.

Side-wheel steamers	75
Propellers	40
Tugs	28
Schooners	12
Canal-barges	22
Grand total	177

GEO. D. WISE,
Colonel, in Charge Third Division, Ocean and Lake Transportation.

No. 19.

Vessels owned and chartered January 1, 1865.

(Ocean and Lake Division, Colonel Wise.)

Class.	Owned.			Chartered.		
	Number.	Tons.	Expense per month, victualing and manning.	Number.	Tons.	Expense per month.
Steamers	106	41,822	$151,066.75	275	140,822	$1,930,849.02
Tugs	29	3,496	23,475.50	91	11,426	182,673.70
Sailing vessels	15	1,559	4,589.00	75	15,236	67,505.21
Barges	21	2,481	2,580.00	171	23,665	69,834.18
Total	171	49,358	181,711.25	612	191,149	2,250,862.11

RECAPITULATION.

Total number of vessels chartered and owned	783
Total amount of tonnage of vessels chartered and owned	240,507
Total cost per month, victualing and manning owned vessels	$181,711.25
Total cost per month, vessels chartered	2,250,862.11
Estimated cost per month, coaling owned and chartered vessels—say 50,000 tons of coal, at $8 per ton	400,000.00
Estimated repairs, &c	90,000.00
Total monthly expenses	2,922,573.36
Daily expenses	97,419.11

Vessels owned and chartered July 1, 1865.

Class.	Owned			Chartered.		
	Number.	Tons.	Expense per month, victualing and manning.	Number.	Tons.	Expense per month.
Steamers	115	48,175	$192,244.00	177	99,780	$1,463,850.00
Tugs	23	2,978	21,181.00	69	6,964	133,950.00
Sailing vessels	12	1,938	7,570.00	74	17,686	88,851.00
Barges	20	2,405	2,480.00	100	14,010	42,049.00
Total	170	55,496	223,475.00	420	138,440	1,728,700.00

*Omitted, except the "Recapitulation."

RECAPITULATION.

Total number of vessels chartered and owned	590
Total amount of tonnage of vessels chartered and owned	193, 936
Total cost per month, victualing and manning owned vessels	$223, 475. 00
Total cost per month, vessels chartered	1, 728, 700. 00
Estimated cost per month, coaling owned and chartered vessels—say 40,000 tons of coal, $8 per ton	320, 000. 00
Estimated repairs, &c	200, 000. 00
Total monthly expenses	2, 472, 175. 00
Daily expenses	82, 405. 00

Estimated average expenses for the year, $92,414 per day.

Average number of vessels, with the tonnage, employed by the Third Division, Quartermaster-General's Department, during the fiscal year ending June 30, 1865.

	Number.	Tonnage.
Steamers	351	171, 081
Tugs	111	13, 262
Sailing vessels	89	17, 738
Barges	168	22, 903
Total	719	224, 984

No. 20.

*List of vessels in service of Quartermaster's Department supplying General Sherman's army.**

SUMMARY.

Steamers	73
Tugs	8
Ships	2
Brigs	1
Schooners	12
Pilot-boats	2
Total	98

GEORGE D. WISE,
Colonel, in Charge Third Division.

No. 21.

QUARTERMASTER-GENERAL'S OFFICE,
Washington, D. C., November 8, 1865.

Maj. Gen. M. C. MEIGS,
Quartermaster-General:

GENERAL: From the best information that we have in my office, we had in service, supplying the armies of General Grant before Richmond in the spring of 1865, 190 steamers chartered and owned; 60 tugs chartered and owned; 40 sailing vessels chartered and owned; 100 barges chartered and owned; in all, 390 vessels, 120,000 tons, at a daily expense of $48,000.

Very respectfully, your obedient servant,

GEO. D. WISE,
Colonel, in Charge of Ocean and Lake Service.

No. 22.

WASHINGTON, D. C., *August, 1865.*

Bvt. Maj. Gen. M. C. MEIGS,
Quartermaster-General:

GENERAL: In accordance with your orders I came to this city in November last to undertake the organization of the Fourth Division of

*Omitted, except the "Summary."

your office, charged with the general management of rail and river transportation under the recent law of Congress.

Finding in addition to present current duties that there was thrown upon the division millions of dollars of complex, unadjusted accounts for services rendered in the early years of the war, and discovering that not only were Government creditors justly complaining of delay in the settlement of their claims, but that these arrears were greatly interfering with the regular business of the office, I gave the subject prompt attention, and I am glad to report that by the vigilant efforts of the division not only have these arrears of business been brought up, but by my request all transportation accounts have been transferred from the general accounting office and are now being regularly audited in the Fourth Division. This change will, I think, in securing a more prompt and efficient investigation by experts, result in a decided improvement.

To perform this service properly, however, the clerical force should be so increased that an examination of all the accounts may be had within a month after their return, and thus errors be promptly detected, instead of continuing for months or years without a remedy.

Until recently, as you are aware, there has been no uniform system in the mode of procuring transportation, in the forms used, or in settling for the same, each quartermaster acting independently, adopting such as best suited his views or convenience, some being good and others materially defective, in furnishing no proper checks, and resulting in irregularity, confusion, and much loss to the Government.

Perceiving this, and convinced that a uniform system in a business so complex and important, even if not perfect, was better than none, or than many various and conflicting ones, and seeing no reason why such uniformity was not attainable and applicable to every section of the country, also satisfied that in no other way could the Government be protected from loss or its officers made familiar with their duties, it became a primary object with me to secure such system as, while it should remedy patent defects, would at the same time be satisfactory to the transportation interests of the country.

This end has been, I think, to a great extent attained by General Orders, No. 17, March 16, 1865, in reference to passenger transportation; by General Orders, No. 29, May 9, 1865, as to freight transportation, and by General Orders, No. 18, March 16, 1865, in reference to the settlement of accounts, copies of which are herewith transmitted, together with the forms and blanks adopted and used under such orders. The system is now in general operation with most satisfactory results, and I believe meets not only with the general approbation of Government officers, but also of railroad companies and others furnishing Government transportation.

There are still some defects which can only be corrected by a change in the Regulations, which will probably be made whenever a revision occurs. Experience will also doubtless suggest further improvements which should be adopted as their importance becomes obvious.

A table of distances between all important points in the country has been prepared and other improvements made, which will result in a large saving of labor and expense.

For such particular tabular statements as you may desire I beg leave to refer to my successor in charge of the division, as at the present time the required reports of various officers of the department have not been returned to enable me to collect and furnish the same.

In conclusion, I believe the duties of the division are being satisfactorily performed, and am pleased to report that the officers and clerks have labored not only harmoniously, but with the most commendable zeal and fidelity for the public interest. Some of them, I think, are fully entitled to advancement, which I trust may be given them. To Mr. Wallace, chief clerk of the railroad division, I am indebted for many suggestions and valuable improvements. His observation and experience in railroad business, combined with his energy and devotion to his duty, render him a valuable assistant.

Very respectfully,

LEWIS B. PARSONS,
Brig. Gen. and Chief of Fourth Div., Q. M. General's Office.

No. 23.

RAIL AND RIVER TRANSPORTATION, FOURTH DIVISION.

*List of steamers and other vessels at Mobile and on the Mississippi River and tributaries belonging to the United States June 30, 1865.**

RECAPITULATION.

Side-wheel steamers	34	
Stern-wheel steamers	37	
Center-wheel steamers	3	
Screw tugs	16	
Ferry-boats	1	
Total steamers		91
Steam-boat hulls		2
Model barges	74	
Gunwale barges	226	
Small wood barges	26	
Box barges	3	
Barges not classified	23	
Total barges		352
Wharf-boats	18	
Canal-boats	3	
Coal-boats	60	
Yawl-boats	56	
Sail-boats	1	
Metallic boats	1	
Total boats		139
Skiffs		9
Floating docks		1
Small flats		2
Sectional docks		3
Total		599

ALEXANDER BLISS,
Bvt. Col. and A. Q. M., in Charge Fourth Div., Q. M. General's Office.

No. 24.

OFFICE DIRECTOR AND GENERAL MANAGER
MILITARY RAILROADS OF UNITED STATES,
Washington, D. C., October 31, 1865.

Bvt. Maj. Gen. M. C. MEIGS,
Quartermaster-General U. S. Army, Washington, D. C.:

GENERAL: I have the honor to submit the following brief statement of operations of U. S. Military Railroads for the year ending June 30, 1865:

A more full and comprehensive report will be made as soon as the necessary statistics can be compiled.

These operations were conducted in six different fields, as follows:

I. Virginia.

*Omitted, except the "Recapitulation."

II. Military Division of the Mississippi.
III. Georgia.
IV. North Carolina.
V. Missouri.
VI. Arkansas.

I.—VIRGINIA.

The following lines were in operation July 1, 1864:

Name of line.	Terminal station. From—	Terminal station. To—	Length.
			Miles.
Alexandria and Washington	Alexandria	Washington	7
Alexandria, Loudoun and Hampshire	do	Vienna	10
Orange and Alexandria	do	Springfield	8
Norfolk and Petersburg	Norfolk	Suffolk	23
Seaboard and Roanoke	Portsmouth	do	18
City Point and Petersburg	City Point	Near Petersburg	8
Winchester and Potomac	Harper's Ferry	Halltown	6
Total			80

During the year the railroads from Alexandria and Norfolk have not borne a prominent part in extended military operations, but were used almost entirely for local purposes.

In the vicinity of Petersburg thirteen miles of new railroad were built to supply the army of General Grant during his siege of that place.

Upon the surrender of Petersburg, Richmond, and the army of General Lee, the Richmond and Petersburg Railroad, twenty-one miles long, was immediately opened; also the line from Petersburg to Burkeville, fifty-two miles.

Statement of total number of miles operated during year ending June 30, 1865.

Name of line.	Terminal station. From—	Terminal station. To—	Length.
			Miles.
Alexandria and Washington	Alexandria	Washington	7
Alexandria, Loudoun and Hampshire	do	Vienna	15
Orange and Alexandria	do	Rappahannock	51
Manassas Gap	Manassas	Piedmont	34
Norfolk and Petersburg	Norfolk	Suffolk	23
Seaboard and Roanoke	Portsmouth	do	18
City Point and Army	Pitkin Station	Humphreys	13
South Side	City Point	Burkeville	62
Richmond and Danville	Manchester	Danville	140
Winchester and Potomac	Harper's Ferry	Stephenson's	28
Richmond and Petersburg	Petersburg	Manchester	21
Clover Hill Branch	Clover Hill Station	Coal Mines	18
Total			430

Excepting the Winchester and Potomac Railroad, which is still operated by this department, all these roads were turned over to the original owners or to the Board of Public Works during or previous to the month of August last.

The largest number of persons employed in any month during the year was 4,489, in April, 1865; and the least number per month was 3,268.

The expenses during the year amounted to $4,900,000.

II.—MILITARY DIVISION OF THE MISSISSIPPI.

At the commencement of the year the lines in operation were as follows:

Name of line.	Terminal station.		Length.
	From—	To—	
			Miles.
Nashville and Chattanooga	Nashville	Chattanooga	151
Nashville, Decatur and Stevenson	do	Stevenson	200
Nashville and Northwestern	do	Tennessee River	78
Chattanooga and Knoxville	Chattanooga	Knoxville	112
Chattanooga and Atlanta	do	Big Shanty	107
Cleveland and Dalton	Cleveland	Dalton	27
Rome Branch	Kingston	Rome	17
Memphis and Charleston	Memphis	Grand Junction	52
Total			744

In August and September, 1864, the Nashville and Clarksville Railroad, sixty-two miles long, was opened, by order of Major-General Sherman, to reach another line of water supply for the depot of Nashville.

By the capture of Atlanta, in August, the entire Chattanooga and Atlanta line, 136 miles long, was opened, and for a short time trains were run a few miles south of Atlanta on the road toward Macon, Ga.

Upon the advance of General Sherman toward Savannah, in November, the Chattanooga and Atlanta line was abandoned south of Dalton, Ga., until after the surrender of General J. E. Johnston's army, when it was reopened by order of Major-General Thomas.

Some forty miles of this road were destroyed by General Hood in his great raid of October, 1864, and about the same distance by order of General Sherman, upon his leaving Atlanta. All this damage was repaired by the Construction Corps, as well as that caused during the December campaign to the railroad near Nashville, amounting in the aggregate to about 130 miles of new track.

The Knoxville and Bristol line was opened in the spring of 1865 to Carter's Station, 110 miles from Knoxville and to within twenty miles of the Virginia line.

In West Tennessee the railroad was extended from Grand Junction to Tallahatchie River, 100 miles southeast from Memphis, in August, 1864.

This line was abandoned, partially reopened, again abandoned, and again reopened, and still once more abandoned and reopened, until, on the 20th day of May, 1865, it was finally reopened to Grand Junction, and June 30 to Pocahontas, seventy-five miles east of Memphis.

The Mobile and Ohio road was opened in May, 1865, from Columbus, Ky., to Union City, Tenn., twenty-six miles.

The following table shows the lines and distances upon each operated during the year:

Name of line.	Terminal station. From—	To—	Distance.
			Miles.
Nashville and Chattanooga	Nashville	Chattanooga	151
Nashville, Decatur and Stevenson	do	Stevenson	200
Nashville and Northwestern	do	Johnsonville	78
Nashville and Clarksville	do	Clarksville	62
Shelbyville Branch	Wartrace	Shelbyville	9
Chattanooga and Knoxville	Chattanooga	Knoxville	112
Knoxville and Bristol	Knoxville	Carter's Station	110
Cleveland and Dalton	Cleveland	Dalton	27
Chattanooga and Atlanta	Chattanooga	Atlanta	136
Rome Branch	Kingston	Rome	17
Atlanta and Macon	Atlanta	Rough and Ready	11
Memphis and Charleston	Memphis	Pocahontas	75
Mississippi Central	Grand Junction	Tallahatchie River	48
Mobile and Ohio	Columbus, Ky	Union City, Tenn	26
Total			1,062

The expenditures during the year for these roads, including labor, materials, and supplies, in round numbers, were $17,000,000.

All the lines embraced in this military division, since merged in the Military Division of the Tennessee, were turned over in September, 1865, to the companies owning them before the war, in obedience to the Executive order of August 8, 1865.

III.—GEORGIA.

In December a force of the Construction Corps with some transportation men were ordered from Tennessee to Savannah, Ga., to operate such roads as General Sherman should require.

Before this force reached Savannah, General Sherman had left on his march to North Carolina, and it was turned back from Hilton Head about the 1st of February and sent to New Berne, N. C.

A few miles of railroad at Savannah were operated until July for local military purposes, when they were surrendered to the companies by order of the department commander.

IV.—NORTH CAROLINA.

The first installment of railroad operatives arrived at Morehead City on the 6th of February, 1865. At that date the railroad toward Goldsborough was in running order forty-four miles. At various times, as the country was occupied by the Union armies, the roads were opened, and on the 19th of April trains entered Raleigh. At that date there were in operation as military railroad lines the following:

	Miles.
Morehead City to Goldsborough	85
Wilmington to Goldsborough	95
Goldsborough to Raleigh	48
Total	228

In rebuilding these lines 2,991 linear feet of bridging was constructed, consuming 779,510 feet, B. M., of timber.

A wharf was built at Morehead City at a cost of $32,086, with an area of 53,682 square feet, and employing 700,000 feet, B. M., of timber.

All the railroads in this State have been returned to the original owners.

The expenditures in North Carolina from February 6 to June 30, 1865, amounted to $967,847.53.

V.—MISSOURI.

In October, 1864, orders were received to have the bridges rebuilt which had been destroyed by the rebels on the main line of the Pacific Railroad of Missouri and its southwestern branch. This work was completed April 1, 1865, at a cost of $170,564.65.

VI.—ARKANSAS.

The only line used in this State for military purposes is a portion of the Memphis and Little Rock Railroad, between Devall's Bluff, on White River, and Little Rock, forty-nine miles long.

This did not come under control of this office until May 1, 1865. At that time it was in exceedingly bad order, and required large expenditures to make it capable of doing the work required of it. At this date it is still operated as a military railroad line.

In the foregoing statements it is shown there was in operation within the last fiscal year the following aggregate number of miles of military railroad lines:

	Miles.
In Virginia	430
In Military Division of the Mississippi	1,062
In North Carolina	228
In Arkansas	49
Total	1,769

On these lines was the following quantity of rolling-stock, including that captured from the enemy:

Division or State.	Locomotives.		Cars.	
Virginia		52		631
Military Division of the Mississippi:				
Nashville	216		2,424	
Memphis	21		200	
Columbus	2		37	
		239		2,661
North Carolina		29		262
Arkansas		10		98
Total		330		3,652

The above does not include the locomotives and cars built in the fall and winter of 1864, which, owing to the close of the war, were never sent to the roads, but sold at the manufacturers' or at points where stored.

Of these, there were 35 locomotives and 492 cars of five-feet gauge, designed for the Military Division of the Mississippi and North Carolina; 50 cars of four feet eight and a half inch gauge, for Virginia and North Carolina; and 9 cars of same gauge used on the Western railroads to transport five-foot cars from the makers to the Ohio River, making in all 551 cars.

Very respectfully, your obedient servant,

D. C. McCALLUM,

Bvt. Brig. Gen., Director and Gen. Man. Mil. Railroads, U. S.

Per H. K. COOPER, *in Charge.*

No. 25.

Statement showing the number of employés in U. S. Military Railroad Department from December, 1864, to April, 1865, taken from the officers' reports of persons hired for the months given, which are on file in this office.

Station.	Officers.	December, 1864.	January, 1865.	February, 1865.	March, 1865.	April, 1865.
Chattanooga, Tenn	Capt. W. R. Hopkins	4,350	4,613	4,622	5,198	5,662
Do. / New Berne, N. C	Capt. F. T. Starkweather	1,036	1,339	2,127	2,843	3,318
Nashville, Tenn	W. J. Stevens			9,176	7,744	8,831
Do	Capt. F. J. Crilly	29	68	2,386	1,263	73
Do	L. H. Eicholtz			1,196	1,009	
Memphis, Tenn	Capt. John Parks	373		263	302	391
Little Rock, Ark	Capt. J. H. Pratt		640	479	1,036	774
Virginia	J. J. Moore	2,956	3,301	3,458	4,082	4,489
Total		8,744	9,961	23,707	23,477	23,538

ALEXANDER BLISS,
Bvt. Col. and A. Q. M., in Charge Fourth Div., Q. M. General's Office.

No. 26.

Statement of claims received and disposed of in the Fourth Division, Quartermaster-General's Office, from November 1, 1864, to June 30, 1865.

Nature of service.	Number of claims.	Examined and referred for payment to disbursing officers, and to the Third Auditor for settlement.	Rejected.	Awaiting action.	Withdrawn.	Total amount of claims.
Employés on the U. S. Military Railroads.	203	$17,105.58	$1,391.39	$7,176.27		$25,673.24
Employés on U. S. steamers, gun-boats, &c.	87	25,442.52	28,715.79	494.92		54,653.23
Use of vessels, barges, &c	101	62,063.09	26,138.60	39,038.19		127,239.88
Materials furnished for use of U. S. Military Railroads.	7	9,721.31	2,275.00			11,996.31
Transporting troops and Government supplies by rail and stage.	1,464	4,575,479.68	889.21	1,112,935.59	$5,341.00	5,694,645.48
Lithographing transportation orders.	1	2,469.00				2,469.00
Advertising army transportation and proposals.	5	442.13				442.13
Employés in Quartermaster's Department.	10	324.61	628.35	76.08		1,029.04
Supplies furnished Quartermaster's Department.	4	68.00				68.00
Telegraphing	4	164.54		105.58		270.12
Employés on U. S. military telegraph lines.	4	274.36				274.36
Materials furnished for use of military telegraph.	1		100.00			100.00
Services in the Army	2					
Total		4,693,554.82	60,138.34	1,159,826.63	5,341.00	5,918,860.79
Total number of claims.	1,893	1,454	99	339	1	

ALEXANDER BLISS,
Brevet Colonel and Assistant Quartermaster, in Charge of Fourth Division.

No. 27.*

No. 28.†

No. 29.‡

No. 30.§

No. 31.‖

No. 32.

Accounts division, Section C.

QUARTERMASTER-GENERAL'S OFFICE,
Washington, D. C., October 31, 1865.

The following is a statement of the amounts paid Epifanio Aguirre during the months from July 1, 1864, to June 30, 1865, as taken from the money accounts of Maj. H. M. Enos for that period, viz:¶

BENJAMIN C. CARD,
Colonel, Quartermaster's Dept., in Charge of Ninth Division.

No. 33.

QUARTERMASTER-GENERAL'S OFFICE,
Washington, D. C., May 10, 1865.

Bvt. Brig. Gen. D. C. McCALLUM,
Director and General Manager Military Railroads, United States:

(Through Colonel Parsons, Division of Rail and River Transportation.)

GENERAL: A very large number of troops will be sent within the next twenty days from this vicinity to their respective States to be there mustered out of service. The several railway companies should be advised to prepare for the movement.

Troops for the West and Southwest will probably move by the Baltimore and Ohio Railroad to the Ohio River, which will be used as far as possible for transportation by steam-boat of troops destined for the country bordering on the Ohio and for points south of the Ohio.

Troops for Saint Louis, Mo., and Kansas will probably go down the Ohio to Lawrenceburg, and then take the Ohio and Mississippi Railroad west.

Troops for Central Ohio, Indiana, and Illinois will go by Bellaire, Columbus, Indianapolis, and so on west.

Troops for the Northwest, by Harrisburg, Pittsburg, Chicago, or Cleveland, Lake Erie, and Detroit.

Troops for Central Pennsylvania and New York, by the Northern Central Railway to Harrisburg and Elmira.

Troops for Eastern New York, New Jersey, and New England, by

---

*For special report of Col. L. B. Parsons of the transportation of the Twenty-third Army Corps from the Tennessee to the Potomac (here omitted), see Series I, Vol. XLVII, Part II, p. 214.

†For report of Col. L. B. Parsons of movements on the Western rivers and railroads during the war (here omitted), see Series I, Vol. LII, Part I, p. 704.

‡For General Orders, No. 17, Quartermaster-General's Office, March 16, 1865 (here omitted), see Vol. IV, this series, p. 1239.

§For General Orders, No. 18, Quartermaster-General's Office, March 16, 1865 (here omitted), see Vol. IV, this series, p. 1241.

‖For General Orders, No. 29, Quartermaster-General's Office, May 9, 1865 (here omitted), see p. 16, *ante*.

¶Details omitted. The total amount was $138,177.89.

Baltimore, Philadelphia, New York, Albany, or New Haven, Hartford, and Springfield.

The sound and river boats should be used wherever possible, as affording a relaxation and rest to the troops crowded in cars, and as being cheaper generally than railroad transportation.

Troops for the Northeast will go by way of New York, and the most direct routes thence to their respective destinations.

It is important that in this movement, which will be large and continue for some time, every possible precaution to insure the safety and comfort of the men should be observed.

For this purpose you will put yourself in communication with the several railroad lines. You will insist upon the orders of this department, requiring cars used for transportation of troops to be carefully fitted up and provided with water and other necessary conveniences, being fully observed and enforced.

Halts of the trains at proper points, to enable the soldiers to attend to the calls of nature, should be arranged.

Proper stoppages for meals; in short, everything should be done to enable those soldiers who have survived the dangers of four years of warfare to reach their homes with the least inconvenience, fatigue, suffering, and danger.

A copy of memorandum of routes is with this.* Orders for the movement will be given by the military commanders. It is desired that it be as rapid as is consistent with safety.

I have recommended that troops going north and northeast be marched to Baltimore, believing that the single railroad from this point to Baltimore will be fully occupied with the movement of troops going west from the Relay House, and that for any large body of troops the quickest movement for forty miles will be made on foot.

I am, very respectfully, your obedient servant,

M. C. MEIGS,
Quartermaster-General, Brevet Major-General.

QUARTERMASTER-GENERAL'S OFFICE,
Washington, D. C., May 27, 1865.

Brig. Gen. E. D. TOWNSEND,
Assistant Adjutant-General, Washington, D. C.:

GENERAL: The necessary general arrangements for the transportation of the troops of the armies of the Potomac and General Sherman to the points indicated by Circular 19, Adjutant-General's Office, 1865, have been made.

In order, however, to avoid delay and confusion in this city, and insure prompt forwarding to destination, I request that the commanders of regiments, and larger commands, upon receiving orders to move, shall make their requisition at once upon Brigadier-General Rucker, leaving their commands in camp until such time as, upon conference with General Rucker, shall be fixed for departure.

Five thousand men for any one section of the country are as many as should go together; 10,000 can go from here to Relay House per day, if necessary.

It is requested that a list of the commands ordered to move may be each day, and as early as possible, furnished this office.

Very respectfully, your obedient servant,

M. C. MEIGS,
Quartermaster-General, Brevet Major-General.

---

* See p. 303, *post*.

QUARTERMASTER-GENERAL'S OFFICE,
Washington, D. C., May 27, 1865.

Brig. Gen. D. H. RUCKER,
Depot Quartermaster, Washington, D. C.:

GENERAL: Inclosed are copies of General Orders, No. 94, and Circular No. 19, Adjutant-General's Office, an estimate of troops to be mustered out of the armies of the Potomac and of General Sherman;* also memoranda giving the routes to be taken by the troops of the several States to their points of destination, respectively.

The troops will begin to move at once. Colonel Moulton, at Cincinnati, is prepared to provide river transportation from Parkersburg for those indicated to go by that route.

Please give him timely notice of movements thither as they occur, that he may have boats ready.

General Van Vliet, at New York, has been instructed to provide water transportation where practicable for forwarding from New York New England troops.

The troops of Michigan and Wisconsin will take boats at Cleveland for Detroit, and those for Wisconsin again at Grand Haven for Milwaukee.

The quartermaster at these points especially should receive timely notice of departure of troops to go by those routes, and at all points on the lines of railroads where change of cars must be made ample notice should be given to the quartermasters and railroad companies concerned, that they may be prepared to receive and forward the troops at once.

Very respectfully,
M. C. MEIGS,
Quartermaster-General, Brevet Major-General.

[Inclosure.]

Routes of troops returning home.

Trocps of Missouri and Kansas: Baltimore and Ohio Railroad to Bellaire or Parkersburg, Ohio River to Lawrenceburg, Ohio and Mississippi Railroad to Saint Louis, thence rail to points of destination.

Troops of Kentucky, Tennessee, and Northern Alabama: Baltimore and Ohio Railroad to Bellaire or Parkersburg, Ohio River to Covington and Louisville, and thence rail to destination.

Troops for Arkansas: Baltimore and Ohio Railroad to Bellaire or Parkersburg, Ohio River, Memphis, Devall's Bluff, Little Rock.

Troops for Middle and Southern Illinois: Baltimore and Ohio Railroad to Wheeling, Ohio River to Lawrenceburg, Ohio and Mississippi and Illinois Central Railroads, or Indianapolis, Terre Haute, and La Fayette, according to points of destination.

Troops for Nebraska. Baltimore and Ohio Railroad to Bellaire or Parkersburg, Ohio River to Lawrenceburg, Ohio and Mississippi Railroad to Saint Louis, thence by river or rail, according to circumstances.

Troops for Michigan: Baltimore, Harrisburg, Pittsburg, Cleveland, Lake Erie, and Detroit.

Troops for Northern Ohio and Northern Indiana: Baltimore, Harrisburg, Pittsburg, Pittsburg, Fort Wayne and Chicago Railroad and connecting lines.

Troops for Central Ohio: Baltimore and Ohio Railroad, Bellaire, Columbus.

---

* For General Orders, No. 94 and Circular No. 19 (here omitted), see pp. 20 and 24, *ante.*

Troops for Northern Illinois: Baltimore, Harrisburg, Pittsburg, Fort Wayne and Chicago, and connecting roads to points of destination.

Troops for Wisconsin: Baltimore, Harrisburg, Pittsburg, Cleveland, Lake Erie to Detroit, Grand Rapids, Milwaukee, and thence to different points of destination.

Troops for Iowa: Baltimore, Harrisburg, Pittsburg, Pittsburg, Fort Wayne and Chicago Railroad to Chicago, thence by rail to Prairie du Chien, Dubuque, Fulton, Burlington, Keokuk, thence to points of destination.

Troops for Minnesota: Baltimore, Harrisburg, Pittsburg, Pittsburg, Fort Wayne and Chicago Railroad to Chicago, thence by rail to nearest points of destination on the Mississippi River, thence by steamer.

Troops for Pennsylvania: Baltimore, Harrisburg, Pittsburg, or Baltimore and Philadelphia and connecting roads.

Troops for West Virginia: Baltimore and Ohio Railroad.

Troops for New Jersey: Baltimore, Philadelphia, and Trenton.

Troops for New York: Baltimore, Philadelphia, New York, Albany, or Baltimore, Harrisburg, and Elmira, to points of destination.

Troops for New England: Baltimore, Philadelphia, New York, thence by rail or water to points nearest their destination.

In case of delay for want of boats at Bellaire or Parkersburg, troops to be sent so far as necessary by rail via Cincinnati.

A special officer to be detailed for Bellaire or Parkersburg. Quartermasters at other important points to be immediately advised of contemplated movements and instructed to make full preparation.

Troops for the North and East to march to Baltimore, thence take rail to Harrisburg or Philadelphia.

Troops for the Baltimore and Ohio Railroad to take the cars at Alexandria and go through by rail to the Ohio River.

Estimate of troops in Army of the Potomac (including Sixth Corps) and General Sherman's army whose terms will expire prior to October 1, and now under orders for muster out.

States.	Number of 3-years' regiments, 1862.	Strength.	Number of 3-years' recruits, 1862.	Number of 1-year's regiments, 1864.	Strength.	Number of 1-year's recruits, 1864.	Aggregate.
Connecticut	2	800	200	*a* 1	140	295	1,435
Delaware	2	800	50			300	1,150
Illinois	15	6,000	1,000				7,000
Indiana	13	5,200	2,000				7,200
Iowa	5	2,000					2,000
Maine	6	2,400	400			934	3,734
Maryland	2	800	500			400	1,700
Massachusetts	6	2,400	2,000			4,004	8,404
Michigan	9	3,600	1,000			1,500	6,100
Missouri	5	2,000					2,000
New Hampshire	2	800	200	1	500	1,045	2,545
New Jersey	5	2,000	300	2	1,200	4,378	7,878
New York	32	12,800	6,000	6	4,000	15,000	37,800
Ohio	11	4,400	1,000				5,400
Pennsylvania	14	5,600	4,000	13	9,000	2,000	20,600
Rhode Island	1	400	300			141	841
Vermont	2	800	700			1,723	3,223
Wisconsin	7	2,800	500				3,300
Total	139	55,600	20,150	23	14,840	31,720	122,310

a Battery artillery.

RECAPITULATION.

139 three-years' regiments of 1862, each regiment 400	55,600
Three-years' recruits, 1862	20,150
22 one-year's regiments, 1864, and 1 battery	14,840
One-year's recruits, 1864	31,720
Total	122,310

WAR DEPARTMENT, ADJUTANT-GENERAL'S OFFICE,
May 18, 1865.

Exhibit of all volunteer troops in the service of the United States whose terms will expire prior to October 1, 1865, now under orders to be mustered out of service.

States.	Number of 3-years' regiments, 1862.	Strength.	Number of 3-years' recruits, 1862.	Number of 1-year's regiments, 1864.	Strength.	Number of 1-year's recruits, 1864.	Aggregate
Connecticut	7	2,800	308	*a* 1	140	155	3,403
Delaware	2	800	60	*b* 4	240	314	1,414
Illinois	50	20,000	1,200	2	1,600	....	22,800
Indiana	26	10,400	2,500	....	....	889	13,789
Iowa	15	6,000	15	....	....	339	6,354
Kansas	3	1,200	....	....	....	4	1,204
Kentucky	2	800	700	....	....	44	1,544
Maine	5	2,000	451	*b* 4	240	739	3,430
Maryland	4	1,600	618	....	....	909	3,127
Massachusetts	8	3,200	3,921	*c* 16	1,880	2,129	11,130
Michigan	10	4,000	1,400	....	....	2,864	8,264
Minnesota	5	2,000	726	1	600	1,247	4,573
Missouri	3	1,200	592	8	4,800	....	6,592
New Hampshire	6	2,400	431	*d* 8	480	570	3,881
New Jersey	5	2,000	350	2	1,200	3,335	6,885
New York	42	16,800	9,000	6	4,000	18,173	47,973
Ohio	32	12,800	3,200	6	4,000	4,627	24,627
Pennsylvania	18	7,200	5,000	17	12,630	7,928	32,758
Rhode Island	1	400	500	*b* 1	60	81	1,041
Vermont	4	1,600	1,300	....	....	1,723	4,623
West Virginia	2	800	300	....	....	1,313	2,413
Wisconsin	7	2,800	1,000	4	2,600	2,017	8,417
Total	257	102,800	33,572	*e* 80	34,470	49,400	220,242

a Battery.
b Companies.
c Twelve companies of artillery and four companies of infantry.
d Seven companies of artillery and one company of infantry.
e One battery, thirty-three companies, and forty-six regiments.

NOTE.—This includes the Army of the Potomac and General Sherman's army. The number from these two armies is 122,310. See estimate of May 18, 1865 [next, *ante*].

RECAPITULATION.

257 three-years' regiments, 1862, each 400 men	102,800
Three-years' recruits, 1862	33,572
46 regiments, 33 companies, and 1 battery, one-year's men, 1864	34,470
One-year's recruits, 1864	49,400
Total	220,242

WAR DEPARTMENT, ADJUTANT-GENERAL'S OFFICE,
May 30, 1865.

No. 34.

DIVISION OF REGULAR SUPPLIES,
QUARTERMASTER-GENERAL'S OFFICE,
Washington, D. C., October 16, 1865.

Maj. Gen. M. C. MEIGS,
Quartermaster-General U. S. Army, Washington, D. C.:

GENERAL: In compliance with instructions received from the Quartermaster-General, per circular July 24, 1865, I have the honor to submit the following report:

I was appointed as chief of the division of regular supplies of the

Quartermaster-General's Office, September 7, 1864, at which time I was on duty in the city of New York as purchasing officer of forage for the entire armies of the East, together with depots on the sea-coast as far south as Mobile, Ala., and in part the depot of New Orleans.

The importance of prompt supplies to the armies and depots above alluded to was deemed sufficient to justify my remaining in New York until January 1, 1865, at which time I assumed personally the supervision of the business of this division.

From the date of my appointment as chief of this division until January 1, 1865, Bvt. Brig. Gen. Charles Thomas supervised the examination of contracts, and Col. B. C. Card the examination of claims connected therewith.

Upon entering on duty in this office I at once opened record books of all existing contracts, carefully examining and entering all contracts made since, comparing prices therein with the market value of supplies at posts where the contracts were made, and directing the places at which contracts should be made, as the large demands upon certain markets rendered this necessary to prevent holders of supplies from taking advantage of the wants of the Government.

Records have been kept of the quantities delivered upon contracts from month to month, canceling each contract at time of its expiration.

Daily reports have been required from the principal depots of supply, and weekly reports from all others, showing the quantities on hand, afloat to be received, and quantities due on contracts, keeping this office constantly informed relative to the state of supplies at all posts; enabling the Quartermaster-General to prevent the accumulation of large supplies when posts might be abandoned.

The establishing of purchasing and contracting depots at prominent points where supplies are produced, or large accumulations are thrown upon the market, has greatly concentrated the business of this division, and the withdrawal of so many purchasing officers, destroying the competition created by them when seeking supplies in the same market, has been of great advantage to the interests of the Government.

CLAIMS.

The records of this division show that from January 1, 1865, to date there have been received 6,852 claims, which have been acted on as follows:

	Number.	Amount.
Settled	1,266	$319,336.36
Rejected	1,379	552,623.95
Suspended awaiting evidence	541	428,649.07
Not acted on	3,666	1,248,842.37
Total	6,852	2,549,451.75

The examination of these claims, especially those presented under act of July 4, 1864, has been critical in relation to the following points:

First. As to the actual use by the Army of stores for which payment is claimed.

Second. As to the past and present loyalty of the claimants and witnesses.

Third. Whether the signatures of the certifying officers were genuine.

After the above points have been considered the claims have been generally referred to the provost-marshals of the districts where the claimants reside for all additional information which was thought auxiliary to a just decision in each case.

A very large number have been rejected on account of ascertained disloyalty of both claimants and witnesses.

The procurement of supplies for the fiscal year has been made principally by contract at all depots of supplies, except those procured at New York City, up to January 1, 1865, where the quantities required under the exigencies of the service were such as to render it necessary to purchase in open market.

Many purchases have been made by the officers in the field to supply the demand on the march, of which this division has no information, nor can this information be obtained except by examination of all the official returns forwarded to the Quartermaster-General.

The quantities of stationery purchased and used by the Army it is impossible to obtain, as all contracts for the same show only the prices of articles, the quantities in all cases to be delivered as required. The official reports of officers receiving the stationery, which are too numerous for examination, are the only data by which it can be gained.

The schedule annexed shows the quantities of forage and fuel delivered on contract, in which the deliveries are specified, and purchases made in open market, not including those made by officers in the field, for the fiscal year ending June 30, 1865.

The contracts at all large purchasing depots have been made, in most cases, for quantities to be delivered as required, at prices named. The quantity received on this class of contracts cannot be ascertained from the contracts at present, but the aggregate must be much greater than that arrived at in Schedule A.

The reason for making contracts of this kind was the impossibility of knowing what quantity would be required for the Army, depending on the place of purchase, as well as to prevent the accumulation of supplies at posts which could be supplied to advantage from other points.

Since the close of the war this mode of contracting has been adopted almost entirely, to prevent the accumulation of supplies at posts which would soon be abandoned.

Very respectfully, your obedient servant,

S. L. BROWN,

Colonel, in Charge Regular Supplies.

REGULAR SUPPLIES.

A.—*Consolidated report of deliveries of forage and fuel on contracts specifying quantities, purchases in open market reported, and official reports received at Quartermaster's Department for fiscal year ending June 30, 1865.*

	Corn.	Oats.	Barley.	Hay.	Straw.	Feed.	Fodder.	Wood.	Coal.
	Bushels.	*Bushels.*	*Bushels.*	*Tons.*	*Tons.*	*Tons.*	*Tons.*	*Cords.*	*Tons.*
Received on contracts specifying amount to be delivered.	4,681,247	9,979,829	33,311	296,675	3,196	......	......	225,796	176,889
Purchased in open market.	1,221,026	11,759,402	10,000	111,124	2,442	146	614	110,373	655,563
Amounts reported received by officers for fiscal year ending June 30, 1865, not included in the above.	....	3,055,699	....	....	5,027	......	......	....	....
Total............	5,902,273	23,794,930	43,311	407,799	10,665	146	614	336,169	832,452

Approximate valuation of articles.

Corn	$8,558,296
Oats	23,794,930
Barley	64,967
Hay	13,049,568
Straw	213,300
Feed	219
Fodder	307
Wood	1,680,845
Coal	8,324,520
Total	55,686,952

No. 35.

DIVISION OF REGULAR SUPPLIES,
QUARTERMASTER-GENERAL'S OFFICE,
Washington, D. C., October 17, 1865.

Bvt. Maj. Gen. M. C. MEIGS,
Quartermaster-General U. S. Army, Washington, D. C.:

GENERAL: In compliance with General Orders, No. 39, Quartermaster-General's Office, July 1, 1865, I have the honor to submit the following as my personal report for the year ending June 30, 1865:

My report for the fiscal year ending June 30, 1864, was transmitted to the Quartermaster-General November 28, 1864.

At the commencement of the fiscal year of 1864–'65 I was on duty in the city of New York, under my commission as captain and assistant quartermaster, engaged in the purchase, procurement, and shipment of forage.

September 7, 1864, in accordance with the law of July 4, 1864, reorganizing the Quartermaster's Department, I was assigned to duty in charge of the Fifth Division of the Quartermaster-General's Office, with the rank of colonel, to date from August 2, 1864.

September 8, 1864, Special Orders, No. 298, Adjutant-General's Office, directed that I should turn over my property and duties in New York City, under such instructions as might be given me by the Quartermaster-General, and report in person to him and enter upon my duties as chief of the Fifth Division of the Quartermaster-General's Office.

The fact that I was supplying forage for the entire armies of the East and the Atlantic and Gulf sea-coast depots, and the importance of keeping up the supply, in the opinion of the Quartermaster-General, justified my remaining in New York and giving my personal attention to these shipments until January 1, 1865, at which time I reported in person to the Quartermaster-General and entered upon my duties as chief of the division of regular supplies of the Quartermaster-General's Office.

Preparatory to my departure from New York City, Capt. E. D. Chapman, assistant quartermaster, was, by Special Orders, No. 395, Adjutant-General's Office, November 12, 1864, directed to repair at once to New York City—this order relieving him from duty at Saint Louis, Mo.—and relieve me from my duties as forage officer; and I was by the same order directed, on being relieved, to report to the Quartermaster-General in person.

December 20, 1864, I turned over to Captain Chapman all the quartermaster's property for which I was responsible, and, as before stated, entered upon my duties in charge of the Fifth Division of the Quartermaster-General's Office, where I still remain.

The Schedules A, C, CC, D, and G, and the statement of public moneys called for by General Orders, No. 39, are hereto attached.

No clothing or camp and garrison equipage having been in my possession during the fiscal year, the Schedule B has not been prepared. Schedules E and F, of property captured from the enemy, are not furnished, no such property having come under my control.

My entire business as forage officer has been conducted by myself personally, no officer having ever been detailed to assist me.

Very respectfully, your obedient servant,

S. L. BROWN,
Colonel, Quartermaster's Department.

No. 36.

Statement of public moneys for the fiscal year ending June 30, 1865.

On hand July 1, 1864	$835,369.46
Received from officers during the year	260,719.52
Received from Treasury Department during the year	19,515,000.00
Received from sales of property and other sources during the year	30,462.32
Total	20,641,551.30
Expended during the year	19,544,351.44
Transferred to officers during the year	850,500.00
Remaining on hand June 30, 1865	246,699.86
Total	20,641,551.30
Balance on hand is deposited as follows:	
U. S. Treasury certificates	204,371.20
Cash	39,341.61
National Bank of Commerce	2,665.76
First National Bank of Washington, D. C	321.29
Total	246,699.86

I certify that the above statement is correct.

S. L. BROWN,
Colonel, Quartermaster's Department.

No. 37.

C.—*Statement of amount paid on account of rail, river, stage, and wagon transportation by Col. S. L. Brown, Quartermaster's Department, during the fiscal year ending June 30, 1865.*

	Transportation.			
	Railroads.	Steam-boats, barges, &c.	Stages.	Wagons, &c.
Passengers—civilians	$1,883.10			
Freight	248,774.76	$1,910,090.64		$21,061.96
Total	250,657.86	1,910,090.64		21,061.96
Expenditures	1,624.58	9,710.00		
Grand total	252,282.44	1,919,800.64		21,061.96

Aggregate $2,193,145.04.

I certify that the above statement is correct.

S. L. BROWN,
Colonel, Quartermaster's Department.

No. 38.

CC.—*Statement of amount paid on account of ocean and lake transportation by Col. S. L. Brown, Quartermaster's Department, during the fiscal year ending June 30, 1865.*

Freight	$1,890,109.46
Expenditures	9,710.00
Total	1,899,810.46

I certify that the above statement is correct.

S. L. BROWN,
Colonel, Quartermaster's Department.

No. 39.

D.—*Statement of all troops and stores transported by Col. S. L. Brown, Quartermaster's Department, during the fiscal year ending June 30, 1865.*

Kinds of transportation.	Passengers, civilians.	Quartermaster's stores.	
Not owned or run by Government:		*Tons.*	*Lbs.*
Railroads	1,773	81,503	
Steam-boats, barges, &c		273,545	799
Stages			
Wagons, &c		123,475	1,301
Total not owned or run by Government	1,773	478,524	
Owned or run by Government:			
Railroads			
Steam-boats, barges, &c			
Total owned or run by Government			
Grand total	1,773	478,524	

I certify that the above statement is correct.

S. L. BROWN,
Colonel, Quartermaster's Department.

No. 40.

Report of quantity and approximate valuation of forage shipped to armies on the James River during the winter of 1864–'65.

Month.	Corn.	Oats.	Hay.	Straw.	Approximate valuation.
1864.	*Bushels.*	*Bushels.*	*Tons.*	*Tons.*	
September	76,087	1,237,972	9,641.12	410.90	$1,877,336.92
October	166,902	505,156	5,515.00	452.18	1,048,234.77
November	118,355½	540,645	5,341.13	139.17	964,261.00
December	41,780	455,836	8,290.80	119.20	933,511.39
1865.					
January	21,259	736,586	5,084.60	76.40	1,154,628.03
February	35,235	683,546	3,756.15	111.13	989,153.91
March	63,583	489,018	5,800.00	147.16	976,894.28
April	38,829	595,359	11,011.11	239.00	1,229,513.70
Total	562,030½	5,244,118	54,441.50	1,696.19	9,173,534.00

And 90,547 tons of coal, costing $1,099.21

I certify that the above report is correct.

S. L. BROWN,
Colonel, in Charge Division of Regular Supplies.

QUARTERMASTER-GENERAL'S OFFICE,
Washington, D. C., October 25, 1865.

No. 41.

Statement of the cost of transportation of grain delivered at stations on the plains by contractors, and the transportation being a part of the price.

From Fort Leavenworth to—	Distance.	Grain.	Cost of transportation per 100 pounds per 100 miles.		Total cost.	
			Route No. 1.	Route No. 2.		
	Miles.	*Pounds.*				
Olathe	63	3,360,000	....	$2.05	$43,394.40	
Paoli	94	3,360,000	....	2.05	64,747.20	
Fort Scott	125	5,360,000	....	2.05	137,600.00	
Fort Zarah	252	996,800	....	2.05	51,494.69	
Fort Lyon	510	1,848,000	....	2.05	193,208.40	
Fort Larned	287	280,000	....	2.05	16,473.80	
Camp Fillmore	630	1,008,000	....	2.05	190,183.20	
						a 697,101.69
Omaha	....	840,000	(*b*)	(*b*)		
Fort Kearny	286	1,120,000	$2.26	....	72,392.32	
Cottonwood	376	1,120,000	2.26	....	95,549.12	
Julesburg	486	1,120,000	2.26	....	123,016.32	
Valley Station	526	1,120,000	2.26	....	133,141.12	
Collins	693	560,000	2.26	....	87,706.08	
Fort Laramie	620	2,520,000	2.26	....	353,102.40	
Fort Halleck	750	560,000	2.26	....	94,915.00	
Denver	683	8,120,000	2.26	....	1,253,386.36	
Cañon City	698	336,000	....	2.05	55,058.24	
Camp Sanborn	*c* 198	1,680,000	....	2.05	240,391.20	
Dakota City	*c* 109	448,000	....	2.05	10,010.56	
Pawnee Agency	*c* 117	336,000	....	2.05	8,058.96	
Lawrence	....	840,000	(*d*)	(*d*)	....	
						e 2,526,727.68
Total	....	36,932,800	....	....	3,223,829.37	

a Route No. 2.
b No transportation; corn delivered at $26,250.
c Estimated distance.
d No transportation; corn delivered at $29,700.
e Route No. 1.

A true exhibit.

S. L. BROWN,
Colonel, in Charge of Fifth Division.

No. 42.

DIVISION OF REGULAR SUPPLIES,
QUARTERMASTER-GENERAL'S OFFICE,
Washington, D. C., October 30, 1865.

Maj. Gen. M. C. MEIGS,
Quartermaster-General, Washington, D. C.:

GENERAL: As requested in your circular of July 24, 1865, I have the honor to submit the following report of the operations of the Quartermaster's Department in the procurement of regular supplies during the past four years of war:

To obtain a complete statement of the quantity of forage, fuel, and stationery purchased it will be necessary to make an analysis of the returns of all officers of the Quartermaster's Department, which cannot be done at present.

Reports have been received from some of the most prominent officers engaged in the purchase of forage and fuel.

The purchases of other officers by contract, where quantities to be delivered are stated, have been collected from the contracts on file.

The material thus obtained is collated in Schedule A, of which the following is a brief summary:

	Quantity.	Cost.
Corn .... bushels..	22,816,271	$29,879,314.01
Oats .... do...	78,663,799	76,362,026.83
Hay .... tons..	1,518,621	48,595,872.00
Straw .... do...	21,276	425,520.00
Wood .... cords..	551,436	2,757,180.00
Coal .... tons..	1,620,910	13,777,735.00
Stationery (approximate)	....	2,571,200.00
Total	....	174,368,847.84

Although this is an immense quantity of supplies, it does not cover the full consumption, as many contracts, especially for straw, wood, and coal, call for deliveries "as required;" hence quantities purchased under these contracts are not included in Schedule A, nor are the quantities of forage and fuel purchased on the march included.

The stationery purchased could not be ascertained, and nothing but its approximate cost is stated in the schedule.

To show the operations of a single depot, the reports of General D. H. Rucker, showing issues of the depot of Washington during the war, are inclosed, marked B and C, from which it appears that the issues of that depot from May 1, 1861, to October 1, 1865, were: Corn, 241,633,972 pounds, or 4,314,892 bushels; oats, 924,273,963 pounds, or 28,883,500 bushels; mixed grain, 19,049,151 pounds, or 432,935 bushels; hay, 982,163,849 pounds, or 491,081 tons; straw, 30,681,907 pounds, or 15,349 tons; coal, 877,992,141 pounds, or 391,900 tons; wood, 209,846 cords.

Very respectfully, your obedient servant,

S. L. BROWN,
Colonel, in Charge Regular Supplies.

No. 43.

A.—*Approximate statement of purchases of regular supplies during four years of war ending June 30, 1865.*

Names of purchasing officers.	Corn.	Oats.	Hay.	Straw.	Wood.	Coal.
	Bushels.	*Bushels.*	*Tons.*	*Tons.*	*Cords.*	*Tons.*
Maj. Gen. D. H. Rucker	1,646,486	10,530,482	226,501	3,864	134,587	35,301
Maj. Gen. R. Allen	8,864,173	26,234,423	377,518	....	....	....
Brig. Gen. S. Van Vliet	96,112	1,732,628	32,074	....	....	158,342
Col. S. L. Brown *a*	1,750,922	17,929,990	269,814	6,193	....	....
Col. James Belger	1,229,385	2,815,287	66,063	2,202	35,317	59,627
Capt. E. D. Chapman *b*	321,086	3,025,457	31,097	1,280	....	....
Capt. S. D. Burchard	191,081	2,023,863	40,634	1,612	....	....
Capt. C. W. Holt	....	201,059	5,004	....	....	....
Captains McClung and Phelps, Cincinnati, Ohio.	2,084,673	2,388,722	66,846	....	....	....
Col. W. W. McKim	....	....	....	....	....	838,533
Capt. James Brooks	....	....	....	....	....	238,193
Other officers, as per contracts on file in Quartermaster-General's Office.	6,632,353	11,781,888	403,070	6,125	381,532	290,914
Total	22,816,271	78,663,799	1,518,621	21,276	551,436	1,620,910

a This does not include purchases made by Colonel Brown under General Rucker's orders.
b This does not include purchases made by Captain Chapman under General Allen's orders.

APPROXIMATE VALUATION.*

I certify that the above statement is correct.

S. L. BROWN,
Colonel, Quartermaster's Department.

* Omitted. Embodied in Brown to Meigs, next, *ante*.

No. 44.

B.—*Summary statement of the amount of forage received, issued, and transferred at the depot of Washington by assistant quartermasters since May 1, 1861.*

RECEIVED.

Station, and names of officers.	Abstract D.				
	Corn.	Oats.	Mixed grain.	Hay.	Straw.
Washington, D. C.	*Pounds.*	*Pounds.*	*Pounds.*	*Pounds.*	*Pounds.*
Capt. E. L. Hartz	2,362,880	11,166,354	....	17,642,141	1,059,278
Capt. J. J. Dana	....	....	....	....	....
Capt. J. M. Robinson	....	....	....	....	....
Capt. S. L. Brown	44,461,524	80,978,466	....	127,041,522	3,119,883
Capt. E. S. Allen	889,896	27,724,384	....	20,843,644	1,885,523
Capt. S. B. Lauffer	....	....	....	1,636,247	702,711
Alexandria, Va.					
Capt. C. B. Ferguson	15,204,887	27,101,388	....	46,187,230	462,192
Capt. W. Stoddard	20,498,258	167,617,644	10,365,320	217,829,822	460,141
Capt. J. G. C. Lee	....	....	....	63,660	....
Capt. T. G. Whytal	8,785,822	22,387,194	3,709,014	21,758,086	40,000
Capt. I. N. Buck	....	....	....	....	....
Total	92,203,267	336,975,430	14,074,334	453,002,352	7,729,728

Station, and names of officers.	Abstracts E and N.				
	Corn.	Oats.	Mixed grain.	Hay.	Straw.
Washington, D. C.	*Pounds.*	*Pounds.*	*Pounds.*	*Pounds.*	*Pounds.*
Capt. E. L. Hartz	5,296,273	19,963,120	....	25,067,955	1,229,553
Capt. J. J. Dana	*a*47,583,867	*a*77,757,578	....	*a*110,408,661	*a*4,983,018
Capt. J. M. Robinson	....	....	....	....	....
Capt. S. L. Brown	11,177,749	14,320,999	....	24,362,526	1,574,601
Capt. E. S. Allen	41,235,407	212,550,942	1,350,933	148,017,617	7,236,192
Capt. S. B. Lauffer	10,153,626	90,241,846	....	97,722,649	3,970,782
Alexandria, Va.					
Capt. C. B. Ferguson	9,126,706	10,112,177	....	9,309,641	49,790
Capt. W. Stoddard	6,838,686	10,071,056	....	5,268,405	61,516
Capt. J. G. C. Lee	5,834,421	29,274,634	97,657	29,073,406	498.950
Capt. T. G. Whytal	12,479,909	118,978,664	3,526,227	65,115,394	1,702,892
Capt. I. N Buck	1,969,132	28,446,361	....	17,849,231	502,778
Total	151,695,776	611,717,377	4,974,817	532,195,485	21,810,072

a Abstracts D, E, and N.

No. 44.—B.—*Summary statement of the amount of forage received, issued, and transferred at the depot of Washington by assistant quartermasters since May 1, 1861*—Continued.

ISSUED.

Station, and names of officers.	Abstracts G, H, L, and M.				
	Corn.	Oats.	Mixed grain.	Hay.	Straw.
Washington, D. C.	*Pounds.*	*Pounds.*	*Pounds.*	*Pounds.*	*Pounds.*
Capt. E. L. Hartz	7, 659, 153	31, 129, 474	....	42, 740, 096	2, 288, 831
Capt. J. J. Dana	47, 583, 867	77, 757, 578	....	110, 408, 661	4, 983, 018
Capt. J. M. Robinson	....	....	....	....	....
Capt. S. L. Brown	57, 317, 155	96, 857, 127	....	158, 125, 984	7, 220, 329
Capt. E. S. Allen	42, 125, 303	239, 285, 326	1, 350, 933	168, 861, 261	9, 121, 715
Capt. S. B. Lauffer	10, 118, 796	84, 388, 138	....	96, 831, 754	3, 557, 323
Alexandria, Va.					
Capt. C. B. Ferguson	24, 331, 593	36, 893, 075	....	55, 163, 613	516, 175
Capt. W. Stoddard	27, 336, 944	177, 688, 700	10, 365, 320	223, 098, 227	521, 657
Capt. J. G. C. Lee	5, 519, 870	25, 208, 105	97, 657	24, 233, 470	465, 558
Capt. T. G. Whytal	18, 731, 316	133, 405, 307	7, 235, 241	86, 876, 030	1, 742, 892
Capt. I. N. Buck	909, 975	21, 661, 133	....	15, 824, 753	264, 409
Total	241, 633, 972	924, 273, 963	19, 049, 151	982, 163, 849	30, 681, 907

RECAPITULATION.

Abstracts.	Corn.	Oats.	Mixed grain.	Hay.	Straw.
Received:	*Pounds.*	*Pounds.*	*Pounds.*	*Pounds.*	*Pounds.*
Abstract D	92, 203, 267	336, 975, 430	14, 074, 334	453, 002, 352	7, 729, 728
Abstracts E and N	151, 695, 776	611, 717, 377	4, 974, 817	532, 195, 485	21, 810, 072
Total	243,899, 043	948, 692, 807	19, 049, 151	985, 197, 837	29, 539, 800
Issued: Abstracts G, H, L, and M	241, 633, 972	924, 273, 963	19, 049, 151	982, 163, 849	30, 681, 907

I certify that the above statement is as correct a compilation as can be made from reports received at this office and papers which are now accessible at the depot.

D. H. RUCKER,
Brevet Major-General and Chief Quartermaster, Depot of Washington.

No. 45.

C.—*Consolidated statement of the quantity of fuel received, issued, and transferred at the depot of Washington by assistant quartermasters since May 1, 1861.*

Station, and names of officers.	Received.				Issued and transferred.	
	Abstract D.		Abstracts E and N.		Abstracts F, L, and M.	
	Coal.	Wood.	Coal.	Wood.	Coal.	Wood.
Washington, D. C.	*Pounds.*	*Cords.*	*Pounds.*	*Cords.*	*Pounds.*	*Cords.*
Capt. E. L. Hartz	27, 551, 787	78, 031	204, 111, 902	52, 741	231, 663, 689	130, 772
Capt. James M. Moore	33, 151, 680	8, 150	80, 546, 510	7, 572	113, 698, 190	14, 722
Alexandria, Va						
Capt. C. B. Ferguson	14, 230, 116	48, 406	167, 345, 949	8, 082	174, 408, 065	40, 400
Bvt. Lieut. Col. J. G. C. Lee	2, 349, 330	....	386, 239, 815	29, 679	358, 222, 197	23, 952
Total	77, 282, 913	134, 587	838, 244, 176	98, 074	877, 992, 141	209, 846

No. 45.—C.—*Consolidated statement of the quantity of fuel received, issued, and transferred at the depot of Washington by assistant quartermasters since May 1, 1861*—Continued.

RECAPITULATION.

Abstracts.	Coal.	Wood.
Received:	*Pounds.*	*Cords.*
Abstract D	77,282,913	134,587
Abstracts E and N	838,244,176	98,074
Total	915,527,089	232,661
Issued: Abstracts F, L, and M	877,992,141	209,846

I certify that the above statement is as correct a compilation as can be made from reports received at this office and papers which are now accessible at the depot.

D. H. RUCKER,
Brevet Major-General and Chief Quartermaster, Depot of Washington.

No. 46.

QUARTERMASTER-GENERAL'S OFFICE,
Washington, D. C., October 16, 1865.

Bvt. Maj. Gen. M. C. MEIGS,
Quartermaster-General U. S. Army:

GENERAL: In compliance with your circular of July 24, 1865, desiring reports of the operations of the several divisions of this office during the fiscal year ending June 30, 1865, &c., I have the honor to report as to the Sixth Division:

That the most costly structures which have been erected by the Quartermaster's Department during the period above mentioned were for hospital purposes. The most important are hospitals at Indianapolis, Ind.; Newark, N. J.; Worcester, Mass.; Manchester, N. H.; Baltimore, Md.; Nashville, Tenn., and enlargement of hospital at Hilton Head, S. C.

Under provisions of General Orders, No. 24, Quartermaster-General's Office, April 29, 1865, construction and extension of all barracks, hospitals, and other buildings ceased. But few special cases were reported in which continuance of work was ordered under paragraph VII of above-mentioned order.

With the reduction of the troops, hospitals, barracks, &c., were from time to time reported upon as vacant by the chief quartermasters of departments or by duly authorized inspectors. Recommendations to the Secretary of War for the sale of such public buildings as were no longer required for the service have been made, and, when authorized, the buildings have been sold at public sale after due notice by advertisement. I proposed to present a tabular statement of the original cost and of the amount received from the sales of public buildings erected during the war, but at present this office does not possess the requisite data to prepare such a statement.

The attention of the chief quartermasters of military divisions has been called to the failure on the part of some of their subordinates to comply with the requirements of General Orders, No. 3, Quartermaster-General's Office, 1864, and it is hoped that the material for a satisfactory and complete report of all hospitals, barracks, storehouses, &c., may soon be collected, from which an accurate statement of the number, cost, and proceeds of sale of such structures, as also of the amount of rents paid for buildings used for the public service, may be prepared. It was proposed to obtain this information in part from the investigations of the officers recommended to examine the accounts of officers of this department at the Treasury.

The work connected with the consideration of claims and questions arising from the occupation of grounds and buildings for the purposes of the military service occupies the attention of my assistant, Bvt. Col. J. B. Howard, U. S. Volunteers, and of four of the five clerks acting under my supervision. Since the organization of the Sixth Division 2,479 claims of this character have been presented, amounting to $1,587,181.47, of which 751 have been referred to the Treasury or to officers of this department for settlement, amounting to $183,452.30; 1,054 have been rejected, amounting to $446,163.32, and claims (674) to the amount of $957,565.85 still await examination and final action.

Apart from the cost of construction and proceeds of sales of public buildings the operations of this division can hardly be tabulated. The correspondence incident to its operations is extensive and varied, and the want of office room only prevents me from applying for, or employing on my own report of persons, several additional clerks for the more speedy disposition of current business.

The examination of reports of officers of this department relative to payment of commutation of fuel and quarters should, I think, be made in this division, as decisions on the validity of orders entitling officers to such allowance, together with the questions incident thereto, demand special investigation.

A statement of the number of interments registered during the war, white and black, loyal and disloyal, so far as reports have been received at this office under General Orders, No. 40, Quartermaster-General's Office, 1865, is respectfully submitted herewith.

Very respectfully, your obedient servant,

J. J. DANA,
Colonel, Quartermaster's Department, U. S. Army.

GENERAL ORDERS, No. 40. } QUARTERMASTER-GENERAL'S OFFICE,
Washington, D. C., July 3, 1865.

Officers of the Quartermaster's Department on duty in charge of the several principal posts will report to this office without delay the number of interments registered during the war, white and black, loyal and disloyal, to be separately enumerated.

All officers of the Quartermaster's Department who have made interments on battle-fields during the war will report the number of the same, giving the localities, dates of battles, and dates of interments.

M. C. MEIGS,
Quartermaster-General, Brevet Major-General.

No. 47.

Statement of the number of interments registered during the war, white and black, loyal and disloyal, so far as reports have been received at this office under General Orders, No. 40, Quartermaster-General's Office, 1865.

States.	Reports to—	Report of interments to—	White.	Black.	Loyal.	Disloyal.	Refugees.	Contrabands.	Total.
	1865.	1865.							
Missouri	Sept. 14	Aug. 5	10,695	837	10,150	1,382	.....	627	12,159
Illinois	Sept. 4	Aug. 1	11,718	219	5,776	6,161	360	1,482	13,779
Indiana	Aug. 30	Aug. 1	6,005	67	2,925	3,147	.....	.....	6,072
Ohio	Aug. 19	Aug. 1	1,338	3	1,121	220	.....	.....	1,341
Michigan	Sept. 19	Aug. 1	149	.....	149	.....	.....	.....	149
Pennsylvania	Aug. 15	Aug. 1	355	.....	342	13	.....	.....	355
Massachusetts	Aug. 15	Aug. 1	238	43	281	.....	.....	.....	281
District of Columbia	July 31	July 19	12,347	5,620	17,493	474	.....	.....	17,967
Maryland	Aug. 16	July 26	5,555	250	5,576	229	10	.....	5,815
Kentucky	Aug. 15	Aug. 1	6,778	2,059	8,536	301	.....	.....	8,837
Louisiana	Aug. 29	Aug. 1	7,441	5,786	12,951	276	.....	.....	13,227
New York	Aug. 7	Aug. 1	3,140	71	3,000	211	.....	.....	3,211
Connecticut	July 28	June 30	222	64	285	1	.....	.....	286
Rhode Island	Aug. 9	Aug. 1	333	26	353	6	.....	.....	359
Virginia	July 27	July 1	3,803	308	4,075	36	35	59	4,205
South Carolina	Aug. 14	Aug. 1	649	681	1,325	5	.....	.....	1,330
Tennessee	Sept. 6	Aug. 14	10,025	186	10,077	134	195	1,957	12,363
Reinterments.									
Andersonville	Oct. 21	Oct. —	12,912	.....	12,912	.....	.....	.....	12,912
Spotsylvania / Wilderness	Oct. 21	Oct. —	1,500	.....	1,500	.....	.....	.....	1,500
Total	.....	.....	95,203	16,220	98,827	12,596	600	4,125	116,148

Total number of whites interred 95,803
Total number of blacks interred 20,345

I certify that the foregoing is a correct abstract of reports received at this office under General Orders, No. 40, Quartermaster-General's Office, 1865, and on special reports of Captain Moore.

J. J. DANA,
Colonel, Quartermaster's Department.

No. 48.

Extract from annual report of Capt. J. M. Moore, assistant quartermaster, U. S. Army, for the year ending June 30, 1865.

WASHINGTON, D. C.

* * * * * * *

The charge of the National Cemeteries and burial of deceased soldiers and others dying in the service of the United States in hospitals in and about Washington is under the jurisdiction of this office, and is probably the most important of my specialties. It was deemed advisable at the expiration of the burial contract, December 31, 1863, for the Government to manufacture all the coffins required for interments in the National Cemeteries, as well as those needed for shipment to distant points. The coffins now issued cost less than one-half the price paid by contract and are far superior. The hearses used for transportation to the graves are covered ambulances, painted black, and are well suited for the purpose. The tablets or head-boards are principally of white pine, with the exception of some 4,000 of black walnut, purchased more than two years ago. They are painted in white and lettered in black, with the name, company, regiment, and date of death. I would here remark that unless tablets are painted before lettering the wood will absorb the oil in the paint and the rain soon wash off the lead in the lettering.

By much pains and labor I have succeeded in preparing a mortuary record for future reference, giving a succinct history of the deceased, every page of which has been compared with the records of hospitals, and up to the present date believed to be the most reliable register of the dead extant. Information is daily furnished to numerous friends respecting deceased soldiers, and frequently before it can be obtained elsewhere, as the record is always kept up to date, no matter how great may be the mortality.

In accordance with Special Orders, No. 132, headquarters Middle Military Division, Washington, D. C., June 7, 1865, I proceeded to the battle-fields of the Wilderness and Spotsylvania Court-House for the purpose of superintending the interments of the remains of Union soldiers yet unburied and marking their burial places for future identification. This work was commenced on the 12th and completed on the 24th of that month. Careful search was made over the above-mentioned battle-fields, and the remains of all soldiers, both Union and rebel, interred, and headboards, with name, rank, and regiment, placed at each grave (with some exceptions in cases of rebels) when it was possible to identify the deceased. The words "Unknown U. S. soldiers, killed May 10, 1864," on a neat tablet, mark the remains of our own soldiers that could not be identified.

On the battle-ground of the Wilderness two cemeteries are laid out, inclosed by a paling fence. Cemetery No. 1 is on the Orange Court-House turnpike, about two miles from the Wilderness Tavern, and contains the remains of 108 men. Cemetery No. 2 is on the Orange Court-House plank road, about two miles and a half from the junction of the Orange Court-House turnpike, and contains 534 men. The sites are well adapted for the resting-places of those who fell in the vicinity, having been selected where the carnage appeared to be the greatest.

It was no unusual occurrence to observe the bones of our men close to the abatis of the enemy; and in one case several skeletons of our soldiers were found in their trenches. The bones of these men were gathered from the ground where they fell, having never been interred, and by exposure to the weather for more than a year all traces of their identity were entirely obliterated.

On the battle-field of Spotsylvania but few men were found unburied, many of them having been interred by a Mr. Sanford, who resides at Spotsylvania Court-House, in compliance with an agreement to that effect with General Sherman while on his march to Washington City. Over 700 names were found in this battle-field, and tablets erected in memory of the deceased.

It was my intention to remove those partly buried to a suitable site for a cemetery, but the weather being exceedingly warm, and the unpleasant odor from decayed animal matter was so great as to make the removal impracticable. They were, however, carefully recovered with earth and entirely hidden from view.

Hundreds of graves on these battle-fields are without any mark whatever to designate them, and so covered with foliage that the visitor will be unable to find the last resting-places of those who have fallen until the rains and snows of winter wash from the surface the light covering of earth and expose their remains.

The work on the cemetery in the vicinity of Old Soldiers' Home has been completed, the ground refenced, a neat and handsome lodge erected, a garden laid out, the graves sodded, the walks graveled, and choice flowers and trees planted.

Great care and attention have also been paid to the Harmony Burial Ground, where all soldiers dying of infectious diseases, and contrabands, are interred.

The improvement of the National Cemeteries has been a source of great gratification to all who visit them, and entirely dissipates the prevailing opinion of those living remote from Washington that soldiers were irreverently or carelessly buried.

At Arlington Cemetery a new road has been made by leveling, in part, the hill on the south side of the mansion, by bridging small streams and by grading and ditching from the mansion, where it commences, to the new lodge on the Alexandria road, where it ends. A large number of well-selected shade trees and choice flowers have been planted, the gardens on both sides of the mansion improved and refenced, and the graves sodded; indeed, the place so transformed as hardly to be recognized by persons who had previously visited it.

* * * * * * *

*Number of deaths reported from August 1, 1864, to June 30, 1865.**

[JULY 1, 1865.—Report of Capt. James M. Moore of burials on the battle-fields of the Wilderness and Spotsylvania (here omitted) is embodied in the extract from his annual report, p. 318.]

Graves of Union prisoners at Andersonville.—Report of Captain Moore.

WASHINGTON, *Wednesday, October 18, 1865.*

The following report of Capt. J. M. Moore, assistant quartermaster, who was sent to Andersonville, Ga., to mark the graves of Union prisoners for future identification, contains valuable information, in which the people are interested, and will doubtless be appreciated by the relatives and friends of those who have given their lives to their country:

ASST. QUARTERMASTER'S OFFICE, DEPT. OF WASHINGTON,
Washington, D. C., September 20, 1865.

Bvt. Maj. Gen. M. C. MEIGS,
Quartermaster-General U. S. Army, Washington, D. C.:

GENERAL: In accordance with Special Orders, No. 19, Quartermaster-General's Office, dated June 30, 1865, directing me to proceed to Andersonville, Ga., for the purpose of marking the graves of Union soldiers for future identification and inclosing the cemetery, I have the honor to report as follows:

I left Washington on the 8th of July last with mechanics and materials for the purpose above mentioned.

On my arrival at Savannah I ascertained that there was no railroad communication whatever to Andersonville, the direct road to Macon being broken and that from Augusta via Atlanta also in the same

*For statement (here omitted) see pp. 259–262, of Executive Document No. 1, to which reference is made in foot-note (*) p. 249.

condition. I endeavored to procure wagon transportation, but was informed by the general commanding the Department of Georgia that a sufficient number of teams could not be had in the State to haul one-half of my stores, and as the roads were bad and the distance more than 400 miles, I abandoned all idea of attempting a route through a country difficult and tedious under more propitious circumstances.

The prospect of reaching Andersonville at this time was by no means favorable, and nearly one week had elapsed since my arrival at Savannah. I had telegraphed to Augusta, Atlanta, and Macon almost daily, and received replies that the railroads were not yet completed.

At length, on the morning of the 18th of July, the gratifying telegram from Augusta was received announcing the completion of the Augusta and Macon road to Atlanta, when I at once determined to procure a boat and proceed to Augusta by the Savannah River. The desired boat was secured, and in twenty-four hours after the receipt of the telegram alluded to was on my way with men and material for Augusta. On my arrival there I found the railroad completed to Macon, and that from Macon to Andersonville having never been broken, experienced little difficulty in reaching my destination, where I arrived July 25, after a tiresome trip, occupying six days and nights.

At Macon, Major-General Wilson detailed one company of the Fourth U. S. Cavalry and one from the One hundred and thirty-seventh Regiment U. S. Colored Troops to assist me. A member of the former company was killed on the 5th of August at a station named Montezuma, on the Southwestern Railroad.

The rolling-stock of all the roads over which I traveled is in a miserable condition, and very seldom a greater rate of speed was obtained than twelve miles an hour. At the different stations along the route the object of the expedition was well known, and not unfrequently men wearing the garb of rebel soldiers would enter the cars and discuss the treatment of our prisoners at Andersonville, all of whom candidly admitted it was shameful, and a blot on the escutcheon of the South that years would not efface.

While encamped at Andersonville I was daily visited by men from the surrounding country, and had an opportunity of gleaning their feelings toward the Government, and with hardly an exception found those who had been in the rebel army penitent and more kindly disposed than those who have never taken a part, and anxious to again become citizens of the Government which they fought so hard to destroy.

On the morning of the 26th of July the work of identifying the graves, painting and lettering the headboards, laying out the walks, and inclosing the cemetery was commenced, and on the evening of August 16 was completed, with the exceptions hereafter mentioned.

The dead were found buried in trenches, on a site selected by the rebels, about 300 yards from the stockade. The trenches were from two to three feet below the surface, and in several instances, where the rains had washed away the earth, but a few inches. Additional earth was, however, thrown on the graves, making them of still greater depth.

So close were they buried, without coffins or the ordinary clothing to cover their nakedness, that not more than twelve inches was allowed to each man; indeed, the little tablets marking their resting-place, measuring hardly ten inches in width, almost touching each other.

U. S. soldiers while prisoners at Andersonville had been detailed to inter their companions, and by a simple stake at the head of each grave, which bore a number corresponding with a similar-numbered name upon the Andersonville hospital record, I was enabled to identify and mark with a neat tablet, similar to those in the cemeteries at Washington, the number, name, rank, regiment, &c., and date of death, of 12,461 graves, there being but 451 which bore the inscription "Unknown U. S. soldiers."

One hundred and twenty thousand feet of pine lumber was used in these tablets alone.

The cemetery contains fifty acres, and has been divided by one main avenue, running through the center, and subdivided into blocks and sections in such a manner that, with the aid of the record, which I am now having copied for the superintendent, the visitors will experience no difficulty in finding any grave.

A force of men is now engaged in laying out walks and clearing the cemetery of stumps, preparatory to planting trees and flowers.

I have already commenced the manufacture of brick, and will have a sufficient number by the 1st of October to pave the numerous gutters throughout the cemetery, the clay in the vicinity of the stockade being well adapted for the purpose of brickmaking.

Appropriate inscriptions are placed through the ground, and I have endeavored, as far as my facilities would permit, to transfer this wide, unmarked, and unhonored grave-yard into a fit place of interment for the Nation's gallant dead.

At the entrance the words "National Cemetery, Andersonville, Ga.," designate the city of the dead.

On the morning of the 17th of August, at sunrise, the Stars and Stripes were hoisted in the center of the cemetery, when a national salute was fired and several national songs sung by those present.

The men who accompanied me and to whom I am indebted for the early completion of my mission worked zealously and faithfully from early in the morning until late at night, although suffering intensely from the effects of heat. Unacclimated as they were, one after another was taken sick with the fever incident to the country, and in a brief period my force of mechanics was considerably lessened, obliging me to obtain others from the residents in different parts of the State. All my men, however, recovered, with the exception of Mr. Eddy Watts, a letterer, who died on the 16th of July of typhoid fever, after a sickness of three weeks. I brought his body back with me and delivered it to his family in this city.

Several of the U. S. cavalry detailed by General Wilson died of the same fever shortly after joining their command at Macon.

Andersonville is situated on the Southwestern Railroad, sixty miles from Macon. There is but one house in the place, except those erected by the so-called Confederate Government as hospitals, officers' quarters, and commissary and quartermaster's buildings. It was formerly known as Anderson, but since the war the "ville" has been added.

The country is covered mostly with pines and hemlocks, and the soil is sandy, sterile, and unfit for cultivation, and unlike the section of country a few miles north and south of the place, where the soil is well adapted for agricultural purposes. Cotton, as well as corn, is extensively raised.

It is said to be the most unhealthy part of Georgia, and was probably selected as a depot for prisoners on account of this fact. At midday the thermometer, in the shade, reaches frequently 110°, and in the sun the heat is almost unbearable.

The inhabitants of this sparsely settled locality are, with few exceptions, of the most ignorant class, and from their haggard and sallow faces the effects of chills and fever are distinctly visible.

The noted prison pen is 1,540 feet long and 750 feet wide, and contains twenty-seven acres. The dead-line is seventeen feet from the stockade, and the sentry boxes are thirty yards apart. The inside stockade is eighteen feet high, and the outer one twelve feet high, and the distance between the two is 120 feet.

Nothing has been destroyed. As our exhausted, emaciated, and enfeebled soldiers left it, so it stands to-day as a monument to an inhumanity unparalled in the annals of war.

How men could survive as well as they did in this pen, exposed to the rays of an almost tropical sun by day and drenching dews by night without the slightest covering, is wonderful.

The ground is filled with the holes where they had burrowed in their efforts to shield themselves from the weather, and many a poor fellow, in endeavoring to protect himself in this manner, was smothered to death by the earth falling in upon him.

A very worthy man has been appointed superintendent of the grounds and cemetery, with instructions to allow no buildings or structures of whatever nature to be destroyed—particularly the stockade surrounding the prison pen.

The stories told of the sufferings of our men while prisoners here have been substantiated by hundreds, and the skeptic who will visit Andersonville, even now, and examine the stockade, with its oozy sand, the cramped and wretched burrows, the dead-line, and the slaughter-house, must be a callous observer indeed if he is not convinced that the miseries depicted at this prison pen are no exaggerations.

I have the honor to be, general, your obedient servant,

JAMES M. MOORE,
Captain and Assistant Quartermaster, U. S. Army.

No. 49.

QUARTERMASTER-GENERAL'S OFFICE, SEVENTH DIVISION,
Washington, D. C., October 12, 1865.

Bvt. Maj. Gen. M. C. MEIGS,
Quartermaster-General U. S. Army:

GENERAL: I have the honor to submit herewith a report of the wagons, ambulances, carts, harness, &c., pertaining to the U. S. Quartermaster's Department, purchased, captured, lost, and expended during the fiscal years ending on the 30th of June, 1864, and 30th of June, 1865, so far as shown by the reports received at this office up to the present date.

I am, general, very respectfully, your obedient servant,

BENJ. C. CARD,
Colonel, Quartermaster's Department, in Charge of Division.

Report of wagons, ambulances, carts, harness, &c., pertaining to the U. S. Quartermaster's Department, purchased, captured, lost, and expended during the fiscal years ending on the 30th of June, 1864, and the 30th of June, 1865, as shown by reports received at the Quartermaster-General's Office up to the 12th of October, 1865.

I.—FISCAL YEAR COMMENCING JULY 1, 1863, AND ENDING JUNE 30, 1864.

How received or expended.	Army wagons.	Two-horse wagons.	Spring wagons.	Irregular wagons.	Ambulances.	Carts.	Carriages.	Wheel harness.	Lead harness.	Irregular harness.	Artillery harness.	Cart harness.	Traveling forges.	Portable forges.
Purchased...	13,989	156	66	338	1,229	1,279	1	58,144	87,480	5,355	335	1,702	60	824
Captured, &c.	1,347	81	71	42	468	245	6	6,661	6,956	797	119	406	3	73
Expended, lost, and sold.	2,021	154	106	91	277	96	5	17,907	16,732	3,453	393	133	3	229

II.—FISCAL YEAR COMMENCING JULY 1, 1864, AND ENDING JUNE 30, 1865.

How received or expended.	Army wagons.	Two-horse wagons.	Spring wagons.	Irregular wagons.	Ambulances.	Carts.	Carriages.	Wheel harness.	Lead harness.	Irregular harness.	Artillery harness.	Cart harness.	Traveling forges.	Portable forges.
Purchased...	4,524	24	127	27	1,436	247	....	13,215	18,961	2,588	4	325	34	890
Fabricated...	322	54	32	35	....	79	....	14,152	20,767	929	34	173	....	....
Captured, &c.	1,135	126	20	318	174	108	....	6,228	7,770	867	65	......	....	46
Expended, lost, and sold.	1,351	516	83	261	679	97	....	18,325	23,254	1,583	....	......	12	432

No. 50.

QUARTERMASTER-GENERAL'S OFFICE, SEVENTH DIVISION,
Washington, D. C., October 12, 1865.

Bvt. Maj. Gen. M. C. MEIGS,
Quartermaster-General U. S. Army:

GENERAL: I have the honor to submit herewith a statement of the number and amount of claims received, acted upon, and remaining on file in the Seventh Division of this office during the fiscal year ending June 30, 1865, and also from July 1, 1865, to October 10, 1865:

	Presented.		Approved.		Rejected.		On file for further action.	
	Number.	Amount.	Number.	Amount.	Number.	Amount.	Number.	Amount.
Fiscal year ending June 30, 1865.	9,211	$2,059,939.50	3,410	$1,172,327.22	4,778	$817,525.87	1,023	$70,086.41
From July 1 to October 10, 1865.	2,283	256,422.23	927	67,545.01	1,089	132,929.79	267	55,947.23
Total.........	11,494	2,316,361.53	4,337	1,239,872.23	5,867	950,455.66	1,290	126,033.64

Very respectfully, your obedient servant,

BENJ. C. CARD,
Colonel, Quartermaster's Department, in Charge of Division.

No. 51.*

*For Special Orders, No. 44, Headquarters Armies of the United States, June 28, 1864, prescribing means of transportation, &c., see Series I, Vol. XL, Part I, p. 40.

No. 52.

QUARTERMASTER-GENERAL'S OFFICE, EIGHTH DIVISION,
Washington, D. C., October 10, 1865.

Bvt. Maj. Gen. M. C. MEIGS,
Quartermaster-General U. S. Army, Washington, D. C.:

GENERAL: In consequence of my continued absence on inspection duty your circular of the 24th of July, 1865, requiring from the chief of each division a full report of the operations of his division during the fiscal year ending June 30, 1865, was not brought to my notice until yesterday, but I hope to be able to furnish all the important data in time to be embodied in your annual report to the Honorable Secretary of War.

The act of Congress approved July 4, 1864, for the better organization of the Quartermaster's Department, was promulgated by the War Department in General Orders, No. 231, July 18, 1864.

Section 1 of the act referred to sets forth that "the Eighth Division shall have charge of all inspections of the Quartermaster's Department and all reports made by officers assigned to inspection duty, analyzing and preserving the reports as received, and communicating through the Quartermaster-General to the chief of the proper division such portions of the reports as may be necessary for their information and use," with provisions for subsequent action upon such references.

On the 23d of July, 1864, the Quartermaster-General submitted to the Adjutant-General a list of names of officers for assignment to duty under the aforesaid act.

On the 6th of August following officers were assigned as chiefs of the divisions in the Quartermaster-General's Office, with two exceptions, the Seventh and Eighth Divisions. Subsequently, on the 24th of August, 1864, I was assigned as chief of the Eighth (inspection) Division.

Previous to this assignment I had had charge of the annual reports of officers, the duties connected with the assignment of officers of the Quartermaster's Department to duty, the duties connected with their changes of station, the transmission of remarks on the accounts of officers, personal reports, and the distribution of orders and blanks.

Subsequent to my assignment as chief of the inspection division I was relieved of the transmission of remarks on accounts of officers and examination of monthly reports. The other duties referred to I still continue to perform.

Immediately after my assignment as above, to wit, on the 26th of August, 1864, I was ordered on special inspection duty for the War Department, and was absent from the Quartermaster-General's Office from that date until the 1st of October, 1864, when I was ordered to return to duty in the Quartermaster-General's Office.

During my absence Col. H. Biggs, inspector, Quartermaster's Department, acted as chief of the inspection division.

On the 14th of October, 1864, I received verbal instructions from the Secretary of War to make a series of inspections in the Department of Washington. I accordingly entered upon and continued upon this duty until the 20th of October, 1864, at the same time performing the duties of my division of the Quartermaster-General's Office.

About the last of October, 1864, I was ordered to resume my inspection under orders of the War Department; was absent about twenty days and returned to duty in the Quartermaster-General's Office.

During this absence Col. J. D. Bingham, inspector, Quartermaster's Department, was in charge of the Eighth Division.

On the 19th of April, 1865, I left Washington on a leave of absence for thirty days. After enjoying ten days of my leave I noticed in a newspaper General Orders, No. 77, of the War Department, for the prompt reduction of expenses, &c., in view of which, and believing my services would be more important at that than at any other time, I telegraphed the Quartermaster-General, proposing to enter upon duty at once, if required, and avail myself of the remainder of my leave some other time. He immediately ordered me upon inspection duty in the Northern Department with a view to curtailing expenses.

I was engaged upon inspection duty and investigations from that time until the 20th of August, 1865, when I returned to duty in charge of the inspection division.

During this absence Colonel Bingham officiated in charge of the inspection division.

On the 20th of September, 1865, I was again ordered upon inspection duty in the Department of the East. I returned to duty in the Quartermaster-General's Office on the 7th of October, 1865.

Of the six inspectors provided for by act of Congress approved July 4, 1864, only four of the officers nominated by the Quartermaster-General on the 23d of July, 1864, for assignment to duty as inspectors of the Quartermaster's Department, were so assigned on the 6th of August, 1864. These four were Colonels Biggs, Bingham, Cruttenden, and Owen. As soon as they were relieved from duty where they were serving at the time of such assignment three of these were ordered upon inspection duty, and a large number of inspections have been made in different parts of the United States, resulting most beneficially to the department. Concerning these inspections I shall remark more in detail hereinafter.

Colonel Biggs was not ordered on inspecting duty, as he was detailed for other duty until the tender of his resignation.

Upon my return to the Quartermaster-General's Office, October 1, 1864, Colonel Biggs was assigned to duty as depot quartermaster at Philadelphia, which position he held until February 15, 1865, when he was relieved, and shortly after tendered his resignation.

It was unofficially communicated to this office that his resignation had been accepted, and he was not therefore assigned to duty. It was subsequently ascertained that his resignation had not been formally accepted. The attention of the War Department was called to the matter and information sought as to his status, whereupon his resignation was accepted on the 11th of October, 1865.

On the 24th of August, 1864, Capt. Gilbert A. Pierce was assigned as an inspector of the Quartermaster's Department, with the rank of colonel.

He made several inspections in the Departments of the South and the Gulf. * * * He was relieved from an assignment as an inspector of the Quartermaster's Department on the 13th of May, 1865.

On the 30th of August, 1864, Capt. John C. Crane, assistant quartermaster, was assigned to duty as an inspector, Quartermaster's Department, with the rank of colonel, but he has never performed inspection duty under orders of the Quartermaster-General.

On April 30, 1865, Capt. J. F. Rusling, assistant quartermaster, was assigned to duty as an inspector, Quartermaster's Department, with the rank of colonel.

He made inspections in the Department of the Tennessee and an investigation at Chicago, Ill., after which, August 2, 1865, he was granted a leave of absence of thirty days, at the expiration of which time he was ordered by the Quartermaster-General to return to Nashville on inspection duty, which order was revoked by order of the President September 8, 1865, and Colonel Rusling ordered to report to him. The latter order is still in force so far as this office is advised.

On the 24th of June, 1865, Capt. R. Brinkerhoff, assistant quartermaster, was assigned to duty as an inspector, Quartermaster's Department, but on the 24th of August was ordered to report to the Secretary of War for special duty, upon which he is still engaged.

The following summary will show briefly the nature of the duties performed by these inspectors:

Col. J. D. Bingham, inspector, Quartermaster's Department, transmitted to this office his first inspection report on the 10th of November, 1864, at which time he was engaged in certain investigations in the Department of the East. Subsequently he returned to Washington and was placed temporarily in charge of the inspection division during my absence on special duty.

On the 27th of November, 1864, he was ordered West in connection with certain investigations, and was engaged on important duties there until the 20th of April, 1865, when he returned to Washington, and was again placed temporarily in charge of the Eighth Division during my absence West.

On my return he was ordered to make inspections at Boston and New York City.

On the 24th of September he returned to the Quartermaster-General's Office and assumed temporarily the duties of the Seventh and Ninth Divisions, Quartermaster-General's Office, during the absence of Col. B. C. Card, in charge of those divisions.

Upon Colonel Card's return he resumed his inspection duty in the Department of the East, and is now engaged upon these duties.

During the fiscal year he transmitted to this office reports of eight inspections, and since the 1st of July, 1865, he has transmitted to this office the reports of four inspections.

The reports of Colonel Bingham have been complete, full, and satisfactory, and the prompt, thorough, and intelligent manner with which he has performed the duties allotted to him is in the highest degree creditable to him as an officer of this department.

Col. J. D. Cruttenden, inspector, Quartermaster's Department, was directed on the 17th of September, 1864, to proceed to Devall's Bluff, Ark., and enter upon a series of inspections in the Departments of Arkansas, Missouri, Kentucky, Tennessee, Kansas, and Colorado.

He was continuously employed upon such duties until August 30, 1865, when he was granted a leave of absence by the War Department for fifteen days.

On the 20th of September, 1865, he was directed to proceed upon another tour of inspections comprising the District of the Plains and Utah.

The total number of reports received from him during the fiscal year is fifteen, and since the close of said year seven; total, twenty-two.

* * * * * * *

Col. G. A. Pierce while upon inspection duty transmitted to this office reports of seventeen inspections.

* * * * * * *

Col. W. H. Owen was relieved from his assignment as inspector, Quartermaster's Department, February 16, 1865. He made inspections in the Departments of Missouri, Ohio, and the Middle Department. He transmitted to this office sixteen reports.

* * * * * * *

Col. James F. Rusling, inspector, Quartermaster's Department, has made three reports, one of them during the fiscal year, the other two since the 1st of July, 1865.

Those reports are very voluminous, numbering in the aggregate 452 pages.

* * * * * * *

During the fiscal year I transmitted to the Quartermaster-General's Office reports of seventeen inspections and investigations, and since the 1st of July, 1865, have added thirty-two to that number—in all, forty-nine.

These inspections and investigations have been made in the Northern Department, in Kansas, Missouri, and in the Department of the East. * * *

In addition to the inspectors regularly assigned, and whose duties have been briefly stated above, other officers of the Quartermaster's Department have been temporarily assigned to inspection duty as the necessities of the service required. Particularly since active operations have ceased it has been necessary to call into requisition the services of such, and in many cases the results have been highly satisfactory and productive of the greatest good in connection with the retrenchment and reduction of force and expense.

The following list indicates the number of reports rendered by each of the officers who have been thus temporarily assigned during the fiscal year ending June 30, 1865:

Lieut. Col. J. G. Chandler, assistant quartermaster of volunteers	2	
Capt. J. V. Furey, assistant quartermaster of volunteers	3	
Col. S. B. Holabird, aide-de-camp	1	
Lieut. Col. J. H. Stokes, assistant quartermaster of volunteers	23	
Lieut. Col. A. L. Thomas, assistant quartermaster of volunteers	1	
Capt. T. R. Dudley, assistant quartermaster of volunteers	1	
Lieut. Col. C. W. Tolles, assistant quartermaster of volunteers	4	
Capt. P. T. Turnley, assistant quartermaster, U. S. Army	1	
Capt. George P. Webster, assistant quartermaster of volunteers	3	
Capt. M. D. Wickersham, assistant quartermaster of volunteers	3	
Capt. C. H. Deane, assistant quartermaster of volunteers	1	
Capt. George Q. White, assistant quartermaster of volunteers	1	
Capt. Charles Worms, assistant quartermaster of volunteers	1	
Capt. E. D. Chapman, assistant quartermaster of volunteers	8	
Lieut. Col. G. A. Shallenberger, assistant quartermaster of volunteers	1	
		54
Since July 1, 1865:		
Bvt. Brig. Gen. George S. Dodge, assistant quartermaster of volunteers	21	
Capt. H. A. Royce, assistant quartermaster of volunteers	3	
Capt. Newton Flagg, assistant quartermaster of volunteers	2	
Capt. T. C. Bowles, assistant quartermaster of volunteers	1	
		27
Aggregate to October 1		81

RECAPITULATION.

Number of inspection reports received in the Eighth Division, Quartermaster-General's Office, during the fiscal year ending June 30, 1865:

Col. George V. Rutherford, inspector, Quartermaster's Department	17	
Col. J. D. Bingham, inspector, Quartermaster's Department	8	
Col. J. D. Cruttenden, inspector, Quartermaster's Department	15	
Col. W. H. Owen, inspector, Quartermaster's Department	16	
Col. J. F. Rusling, inspector, Quartermaster's Department	3	
Col. G. A. Pierce, inspector, Quartermaster's Department	17	
By temporary inspectors	54	
Received from various sources	86	
		216
Number received since July 1, 1865:		
Col. George V. Rutherford, inspector, Quartermaster's Department	32	
Col. J. D. Bingham, inspector, Quartermaster's Department	4	
Col. J. D. Cruttenden, inspector, Quartermaster's Department	7	
By temporary inspectors	27	
		70
Grand total		287

Two hundred and sixteen inspection reports rendered by officers of the Quartermaster's Department, under orders of the Quartermaster-General, have been entered in the inspection division during the fiscal year ending June 30, 1865. Many of these reports contain 240 pages of foolscap paper. All of them have been thoroughly and carefully examined and extracts made and sent to the several divisions to which they had reference.

There have been received and entered in the inspection division during the same time 579 communications referring to inspections, investigations, and the official character of officers of the Quartermaster's Department.

The entries in the inspection book are in fact briefs of the original papers, and not merely skeletons. Every name of a person, however insignificant, occurring in these papers is alphabetically entered, so that one name being recollected, all the facts pertaining to the transaction can be at once ascertained.

INVESTIGATIONS.

Investigations involving the conduct of officers have generally been conducted by officers of this department with great thoroughness and efficiency, but some mistakes have been made in the mode of investigating by a want of shrewdness and propriety of action.

It was intended to give a summary of the recommendations by the several officers assigned to inspection duty for reductions, and the amount saved to the Government by these inspections; but my protracted absence and the little time now left precludes the possibility of carrying out this design.

INVENTORY AND INSPECTION REPORTS.

The number of inventory and inspection reports rendered by officers in compliance with paragraph 1023, Revised Regulations, received from June 30, 1864, to July 1, 1865, is	11,193
All of which have been acted upon.	
Received, entered, and acted upon since July 1 to October 1, 1865	6,302
Total	17,495

BOARDS OF SURVEY.

The number of reports of boards of survey received, entered, and acted upon from June 30, 1864, to July 1, 1865, is	293
Received, entered, and acted upon since July 1, 1865	136
Total	429

OFFICERS' RECORD.

An officers' record has been compiled, comprising all officers of the Quartermaster's Department, each officer occupying one page, showing at one view a condensed record of his appointment, movements, services, changes, recommendations, &c. For this purpose the books of the office have been consulted for over three years back. In proportion as this division has become more thoroughly organized this record has been made more minute, and is kept up daily—almost hourly.

ANNUAL REPORTS.

The annual reports received during the fiscal year ending June 30, 1865, appertaining to the fiscal year ending June 30, 1864, were 591.

From July 1, 1865, to the present the number of annual reports received appertaining to the fiscal year ending June 30, 1865, is 340.

From the latter tables have been prepared for the annual report of the Quartermaster-General showing the amount of supplies on hand July 1, 1864, received, purchased, manufactured, captured, &c., during the fiscal year; also the amount of public moneys received and expended during the fiscal year.

Extracts have been made from the narratives of officers giving all the valuable information contained in them for the information of the Quartermaster-General.

The tables and statements referred to do not comprise all the operations of the Quartermaster's Department, because of the fact that a large number of the officers have failed to render their reports as required by general orders; but these exceptions are officers whose duties were light, and if their reports had been rendered they would not swell to any great extent the lists prepared.

OFFICIAL BONDS.

Number on file July 1, 1864	415
Number received during the fiscal year	219
Number received since July 1 to October 1, 1865	20
Total number received	654
Number approved by the Secretary of War and sent to the Second Comptroller U. S. Treasury for file during the fiscal year	490
Number approved and sent since July 1, 1865, to October 1, 1865	34
Total number approved and sent for file	524

The balance of the bonds (130) have been found to be imperfect, and are now being corrected and perfected as required by law and regulations.

The total number of bonds on file July 1, 1864, and since received represent the sum of $6,540,000, a sum considerably less than that frequently confided to the care and disposition of one officer of the Quartermaster's Department.

BOARDS OF EXAMINERS.

The following is a summary of the operations of the several boards for the examination of officers of the Quartermaster's Department:

1. The Examining Board for the Departments of the Cumberland, Tennessee, and Ohio, was organized by Special Orders, No. 317, Adjutant-General's Office, September 23, 1864, and was composed of the following officers: Lieut. Col. W. G. Le Duc, chief quartermaster Twentieth Army Corps; Lieut. Col. A. J. Mackay, chief quartermaster Fourteenth Army Corps; Lieut. Col. H. Hayes, chief quartermaster Fourth Army Corps.

Lieutenant-Colonel Mackay's arduous duties in the field rendered it impracticable for him to serve upon the Board. He applied to be relieved from such assignment, and by Special Orders, No. 57, Adjutant-General's Office, February 4, 1865, he was relieved by Col. R. C. Webster, chief quartermaster Department of Virginia.

By Special Orders, No. 173, Adjutant-General's Office, April 17, 1865, Lieut. Col. W. G. Le Duc, chief quartermaster Twentieth Army Corps, was relieved by Capt. J. F. Rusling, assistant quartermaster volunteers, and Colonel Le Duc ordered to join his proper command.

By Special Orders, No. 222, Adjutant-General's Office, May 11, 1865, Capt. J. F. Rusling, inspector, Quartermaster's Department, was relieved by Capt. E. B. Carling, assistant quartermaster, U. S. Army, and Captain Rusling ordered upon inspection duty.

By Special Orders, No. 309, Adjutant-General's Office, June 16, 1865, Capt. E. B. Carling was relieved as a member of the Board, and as no officer had been assigned to fill the vacancy no officers have since been examined by this Board.

Number of officers examined by this Board to July 1, 1865	50
Number reported qualified	41
Number reported disqualified	9
Number mustered out by reason of disqualification	8
Number not acted upon	1
Number of officers examined by this Board since July 1, 1865	9
Number reported qualified	3
Number reported disqualified	6
Number mustered out by reason of disqualification	3
Number of resignations	1
Total	4
Total number examined by this Board	59
Total number reported qualified	44
Total number disqualified	15
Total number mustered out by reason of disqualification	11
Total number resigned by reason of disqualification	1
Total number not acted upon	3
	15

The Examining Board for the Departments of Arkansas and the Gulf, convened by Special Orders, No. 317, Adjutant-General's Office, September 23, 1864, was composed of the following officers:

Lieut. Col. Alexander Bliss, assistant quartermaster, U. S. Army; Maj. M. S. Miller, assistant quartermaster, U. S. Army; Capt. S. E. Rundle, assistant quartermaster of volunteers.

After completing their duties in the above departments this Board was transferred to the Departments of Washington and the East, by Special Orders, No. 137, Adjutant-General's Office, March 21, 1865.

By Special Orders, No. 202, Adjutant-General's Office, May 3, 1865, Captain Rundle was relieved and Maj. Nelson Plato, assistant quartermaster of volunteers, assigned to duty in his stead.

By Special Orders, No. 440, Adjutant-General's Office, August 15, 1865, Lieutenant-Colonel Bliss was relieved from his assignment as lieutenant-colonel, by which change the Board was practically dissolved, and no officers have since been examined by it.

Number of officers examined by the Board to July 1, 1865	73
Number reported qualified	45
Number reported disqualified	28
Number resigned by reason of disqualification	13
Number mustered out by reason of disqualification	10
Number not acted upon	5
	28
Number of officers examined since July 1, 1865	31
Number reported qualified	19
Number reported disqualified	12
Number not acted upon	12
Total number of officers examined by this Board	104
Total number reported qualified	64
Total number reported disqualified	40
Total number mustered out by reason of disqualification	10
Total number resigned by reason of disqualification	13
Disapproved and not acted upon	17
Grand total	40

The Examining Board for the district comprising armies operating against Richmond, convened and organized by Special Orders, No. 317, Adjutant-General's Office, September 23, 1864, was composed of the following officers: Col. R. N. Batchelder, chief quartermaster Army of the Potomac; Lieut. Col. L. H. Peirce, chief quartermaster Ninth Army Corps; Maj. G. A. Shallenberger, chief quartermaster Second Division, Second Army Corps.

Colonel Batchelder's services being required with the army by Special Orders, No. 109, Adjutant-General's Office, May 2, 1865, Col. R. N. Batchelder was relieved by Maj. W. H. D. Cochrane, chief quartermaster First Division, Second Army Corps.

By Special Orders, No. 219, Adjutant-General's Office, May 10, 1865, Major Cochrane was relieved, and no officers have since been examined.

Total number of officers examined by this Board to July 1, 1865	42
Number reported qualified	36
Number reported disqualified	6
Number mustered out by reason of disqualification	4
Number of resignations	1
Not acted upon	1
	6

The Examining Board for the Departments of Kansas, Missouri, and Northern and Northwest, convened by Special Orders, No. 317, Adjutant-General's Office, September 23, 1864, was composed of the following officers: Col. C. H. Hoyt, chief quartermaster Northern Department; Lieut. Col. J. B. Howard, chief quartermaster Eighteenth Army Corps; Lieut. Col. F. Myers, quartermaster, U. S. Army, aide-de-camp.

By Special Orders, No. 95, Adjutant-General's Office, February 25, 1865, Lieut. Col. J. B. Howard was relieved, and by Special Orders, No. 151, Adjutant-General's Office, March 29, 1865, Capt. W. H. Owen, assistant quartermaster of volunteers, was assigned to duty in his stead.

By Special Orders, No. 232, Adjutant-General's Office, May 16, 1865, the Quartermaster-General was authorized to adjourn the Board until further notice, which was done. The Board has not been reassembled.

Total number officers examined by this Board to July 1, 1865	78
Number reported qualified	72
Number reported disqualified	6
Number mustered out by reason of disqualification	3
Number of resignations	3
	6

RECAPITULATION.

Total number of officers of the Quartermaster's Department examined by the several boards during the fiscal year ending June 30, 1865, is	243
Total number reported qualified	194
Total number reported disqualified	49
Total number mustered out by reason of disqualification	25
Total number resigned by reason of disqualification	17
Total number disapproved or not acted upon	7
	49
Total number of officers of the Quartermaster's Department examined by the several boards since the 1st of July, 1865	40
Total number reported qualified	22
Total number reported disqualified	18
Total number mustered out by reason of disqualification	3
Total number resigned by reason of disqualification	1
Total number disapproved and not acted upon	14
	18

GRAND TOTAL.

Number examined to date (October 1, 1865)	283
Number reported qualified	216
Number reported disqualified	67
Number mustered out by reason of disqualification	28
Number resigned by reason of disqualification	18
Number disapproved and not acted upon	21
	67

The number of officers still in service who have not been examined is 245.

Owing to the present status of the boards constituted by the orders above cited, it will be impossible to proceed with the examinations until further orders are issued by the Secretary of War in the premises.

On the 1st of July, 1864, there were in the Regular Army 76 officers of the Quartermaster's Department, as follows:

Brevet major-general	1
Colonels	3
Lieutenant-colonels	4
Majors	12
Captains	47
Military store-keepers	9
Total	76

Of the lieutenant-colonels there was: Colonel and aide-de-camp, 1.

Of the majors there were: Brigadier-generals of volunteers, 3; brevet lieutenant-colonel, 1; not on duty in the Quartermaster's Department, but a major-general of volunteers, 1; assigned to duty as lieutenant-colonel and chief quartermaster in accordance with an act approved July 17, 1862, 1.

Of the captains there were: Colonels and aides-de-camp, 2; lieutenant-colonel and aide-de-camp, 1; not on duty in the Quartermaster's Department, but brigadier-generals of volunteers, 3; not on duty in the Quartermaster's Department, but colonels of volunteers, 2; assigned to duty as lieutenant-colonels and chief quartermasters of corps under act of July 17, 1862, 6.

Awaiting orders: Lieutenant-colonel, 1; captain 1.

The effective force of the regular corps of the Quartermaster's Department was on the 1st of July, 1864, 68.

On the 1st of July, 1864, there were assistant quartermasters of volunteers, 549. Of these there were: Colonels and aides-de-camp, 2; major and aide-de-camp, 1; assigned to duty as lieutenant-colonels and chief quartermasters of corps under the act of July 17, 1862, 9; not on duty in the Quartermaster's Department, 1; not on duty in the Quartermaster's Department, but colonels of volunteers, 2; unknown, never having reported nor replied to communications from this office, 41.

The effective force, therefore, of officers in the Quartermaster's Department of the volunteer service was, July 1, 1864, 505.

On the 30th of June, 1865, there were 78 officers of the Quartermaster's Department belonging to the regular corps, as follows:

Brevet major-general	1
Brevet brigadier-generals	2
Colonel	1
Lieutenant-colonels	4
Majors	11
Captains	48
Military store-keepers	11
Total	78

Of the lieutenant-colonels there were: Colonel and aide-de-camp, 1; assigned to duty as colonel under act approved July 4, 1864, 1.

Of the majors there were: Brigadier-generals of volunteers, 3; not on duty in the department, but a brevet major-general of volunteers, 1; awaiting orders, 1; assigned to duty as colonels under the act approved July 4, 1864, 3; lieutenant-colonel and aide-de-camp, 1.

Of the captains there were: Brigadier-generals of volunteers not on duty in the Quartermaster's Department, 3; colonels, 3; brevet brigadier-generals, 2; colonels and aides-de-camp, 2; assigned to duty as colonels under the act approved July 4, 1864, 12; assigned to duty as lieutenant-colonels under the act approved July 17, 1862, 5; not subject to orders, 2.

The effective force of the regular corps on the 30th of June, 1865, was 67.

On the 1st of July, 1865, the number of assistant quartermasters of volunteers was 488. Of these there were: Brigadier-general, 1; brevet brigadier-general, 1; colonel and aide-de-camp, 1; colonels assigned under act approved July 4, 1864, 25; lieutenant-colonels assigned under act approved July 17, 1862, 13; brevet colonels, 5; brevet lieutenant-colonel, 1; majors assigned under act approved July 4, 1864, 26; brevet majors, 3; major and aide-de-camp, 1.

Of the above colonels there are:

In charge of departments	9
Inspectors	4
In charge of divisions of the Quartermaster-General's Office	3
In charge of depots	5
Chief quartermasters of armies	4
Total	25

Of these there were: Colonels (regulars), 16; colonels (volunteers), 25; majors (regulars), 2; majors (volunteers), 27.

Effective force:	
Regulars	67
Volunteers	488
Total	555

On the 1st of October, 1865, there were officers of the Quartermaster's Department in the Regular Army as follows:

Brevet major-general	1
Colonels	3
Lieutenant-colonels	4
Majors	11
Captains	47
Total	66

Of the colonels there are: Brevet brigadier-generals, 2.

Of the lieutenant-colonels there are: Brevet brigadier-general, 1; colonel and aide-de-camp, 1; colonels assigned under the act of July 4, 1864, 2.

Of the majors there are: Brevet brigadier-generals, U. S. Army, 6; brevet major-generals of volunteers, 3; colonels assigned under act of July 4, 1864, 2.

Of the captains there are: Brevet major-generals not on duty in the department, 3; brevet brigadier-generals of volunteers, 3; colonels and aides-de-camp, 2; colonels assigned under act of July 4, 1864, 10; brevet lieutenant-colonels, U. S. Army, 8; lieutenant-colonel assigned under act of July 17, 1862, 1; major assigned under act of July 4, 1864, 1; military store-keepers, 10.

The colonels assigned under act of July 4, 1864, are on duty as follows: Inspectors, 2; depot quartermasters, 3; divisions of the

Quartermaster-General's Office, 4; chief quartermasters of departments, 5. The effective force of the Quartermaster's Department, regular officers, October 1, 1865, were 63.

On the 1st of October, 1865, there were in service as assistant quartermasters of volunteers	370
Under arrest	1
Awaiting orders	28
Total	399

Of the above officers there are: Brigadier-general, 1; brevet brigadier-generals, 3; brevet colonels, 7; brevet lieutenant-colonels, 3; brevet majors, 10; colonel and aide-de-camp, 1.

Colonels assigned under act of July 4, 1864, 22, as follows:

Inspectors	5
Depot quartermasters	4
Chief quartermasters of departments	10
Chiefs of divisions of the Quartermaster-General's Office	3
Total	22

Majors assigned under act of July 4, 1864, 2; major and aide-de-camp, 1; lieutenant-colonel assigned under act of July 17, 1862, 1.

Effective force:	
Regulars	63
Volunteers	370
Total	433

Of the assignment of colonels under the act of July 4, 1864, there are—regulars, 14; volunteers, 22; excess regulars, 3.

During the fiscal year there were appointed assistant quartermasters—in the Regular Army, 5; in the Volunteer Army, 145; military store-keepers, 2.

Since the 30th of June to the 1st of October, 1865, there have been appointed in the Regular Army—assistant quartermaster, 1; military store-keeper, 1.

During the fiscal year ending June 30, 1865, officers of the Quartermaster's Department went out of service as follows:

	Regulars.	Volunteers.
Resigned	2	92
Mustered out	....	26
Honorably discharged	....	4
Died	....	13
Appointments vacated	2	2
Appointments revoked	....	9
Appointments declined	....	2
Appointments canceled	....	43
Dismissed	....	12
Dropped from rolls	1	....
Total	5	203
Aggregate	....	208

Since the 30th of June to the 1st of October, 1865, officers of the Quartermaster's Department have gone out of service as follows:

	Regulars.	Volunteers.
Assistant quartermasters:		
Resigned	1	13
Appointments vacated	....	1
Mustered out	....	136
Appointments canceled	....	21
Dismissed	....	1
Military store-keeper resigned	1	....
Total	2	172
Aggregate	....	174

RECAPITULATION.

July 1, 1864, to October 1, 1865, resigned, assistant quartermasters of the Regular Army	3	....
Appointments vacated, assistant quartermasters, Regular Army	2	....
Dropped from rolls, Regular Army	1	....
Assistant quartermasters, volunteers:		
Resigned	....	105
Mustered out	....	162
Appointments vacated	....	3
Appointments canceled	....	64
Appointments revoked	....	9
Appointments declined	....	2
Dismissed	....	13
Honorably discharged	....	4
Died	....	13
Military store-keepers resigned	1	....
Total	7	375
Aggregate	....	382

During the fiscal year there were 460 assignments of officers of the Quartermaster's Department to duty by orders of the War Department, of which we have record; and from July 1, 1865, to October 1, 1865, there were 70 such assignments; in all, 530, including changes of station.

PERSONAL AND CONSOLIDATED MONTHLY REPORTS.

Personal reports for the past year have been rendered more promptly. Also consolidated monthly reports have been rendered by the chief quartermasters of the different departments of all officers serving in the Quartermaster's Department under their direction, as required by circular from this office, dated January 18, 1865.

From these reports much valuable information has been derived. They give the stations of officers and the various duties in which they have been engaged during the previous month, and exhibit all the changes and transfers within the departments during the month, accompanied by copies of department orders pertaining to the Quartermaster's Department.

DISTRIBUTION OF ORDERS.

This division has experienced much difficulty in supplying officers of the Quartermaster's Department with the orders of the War Department and of the Quartermaster-General's Office. Though they have been promptly and regularly sent to the chief quartermasters in quantities sufficient to supply their subordinates, the failure to receive them was frequently made the excuse for neglect of duty. To remedy to some extent this evil a system was adopted to require a receipt from the officer to whom orders were transmitted. Had this been devised and adopted earlier, and had it been made a point to retransmit orders to officers doing important duties when receipts were not forthcoming, no doubt much irregularity in the rendering of accounts and in the general management of business would have been obviated.

COMPILATION OF ORDERS, ETC.

A very general desire has been expressed that all the orders relating to this department should be collected, revised, and published in convenient form, and a reference made to the laws and regulations bearing upon the subject; the decisions of the Quartermaster-General since the commencement of this war to be embodied in the same work. This should be done under the sanction of the Quartermaster-General, and published by authority of the War Department. The publication of any treatise of this kind without this sanction and authority would not meet the wants of the department.

The several works which have lately appeared, though no doubt prompted by a commendable spirit, fail to meet the requirements, inasmuch as the subjects are not properly collated; and besides, an officer would hesitate to base a heavy disbursement upon a decision contained in an unofficial digest. The Book of Decisions of the Second Comptroller of the Treasury Department is the best I have seen, though some of his decisions as given are contrary to the Regulations. I will cite as instances Article 1234, Decisions of Second Comptroller, *versus* Paragraph 1142 and Form 20 to Abstract B, Revised Army Regulations; and the last clause of Article 1265 and Article 1266, Decisions of Second Comptroller, *versus* Paragraphs 1082 and 1083, Revised Army Regulations, and laws of Congress.

COMMUNICATIONS SENT AND RECEIVED.

The number of letters received and entered in this division is as follows:

From—	Principal entries.	Cross entries.	Total.
January 1 to June 30, 1865	2,204	4,161	6,365
July 1 to September 30, 1865, inclusive	1,178	1,743	2,921
Total	3,382	5,904	9,286

The number of communications (exclusive of correspondence in reference to annual and personal reports, the transmission of printed orders, and printed circular letters) forwarded from this division from January 1 to June 30, 1865, inclusive, is as follows:

To the Secretary of War	140
To the Adjutant-General	410
Miscellaneous	1,266
Total	1,816

And from July 1, 1865, to September 30, 1865, inclusive:

To the Secretary of War	79
To the Adjutant-General	384
Miscellaneous	837
Total	1,300

Total number from July 1, 1864, to September 30, 1865, as follows:

To the Secretary of War	219
To the Adjutant-General	794
Miscellaneous	2,103
Total	3,116

GENERAL ORDERS.

Estimated number of general orders received and issued during the year:

	During the year.		July 1, 1865, to October 1, 1865.		July 1, 1864, to September 30, 1865.	
	Received.	Issued.	Received.	Issued.	Received.	Issued.
Adjutant-General's orders	124,800	124,177	220,000	10,460	344,800	134,637
Quartermaster-General's orders	75,000	53,121	28,800	11,699	103,800	64,820
Total	199,800	177,298	248,800	22,159	448,600	199,457

THE RANK OF OFFICERS OF THE QUARTERMASTER'S DEPARTMENT NOT COMMENSURATE WITH THE IMPORTANT SERVICE THEY HAVE RENDERED IN THIS WAR.

It is now a conceded fact that commanding generals owe much of their success to the untiring zeal and determined energy of officers of the Quartermaster's Department.

At the eleventh hour they were ready to accord to officers of this department their just meed of praise for the faithful discharge of onerous and often difficult duties.

Congress to this time has been unmindful of this indispensable enginery to the success of armies and has made no provision for proper reward. The distribution of "brevets," which has been judiciously done by the Honorable Secretary of War, was all that was left for those who have taken or will soon take their places again as citizens. These marks of recognition of their services, if promptly ratified by the coming Congress, will cause great gratification and create the thought that those who have remained at home—in the rear—to enjoy the fruits of peace and plenty vouchsafed by victory, while it was being achieved by their constituents, under privations and hardships in the field—at the front—are not wholly incapable of appreciating the relative position of citizen and soldier.

OFFICERS ON DUTY IN THIS DIVISION.

Before closing this report I would respectfully invite the attention of the Quartermaster-General to the merits of Capt. H. A. Royce, assistant quartermaster of volunteers, my assistant in this division. He is a civil engineer by profession, and first entered the service July 20, 1861, as a quartermaster-sergeant Twenty-first Massachusetts Volunteers. He was commissioned regimental quartermaster Twenty-second Massachusetts Volunteers November 29, 1861, and served with his regiment, subject to various details, till October 12, 1864, when he was mustered out of the service. He was appointed assistant quartermaster of volunteers March 11, 1865, received his commission May 6, 1865, and was assigned to duty in the Eighth Division of the Quartermaster-General's Office May 20, 1865. Captain Royce has a liberal education. His general qualifications for business, his excellent judgment and discrimination, and extensive experience in the field in the Quartermaster's Department eminently fit him to render, and he has rendered, most valuable services in this division. He is industrious, efficient, and possessed of all the elements requisite for the prompt discharge of official duties. Though he has served but a short time as an assistant quartermaster of volunteers, his services during the war in the Quartermaster's Department entitle him to consideration and to promotion by brevet, a compliment which can be bestowed without money and without price. I recommend him for appointment to the rank of lieutenant-colonel by brevet.

Capt. John V. Furey, assistant quartermaster of volunteers, has had in charge under my direction the annual reports of officers, personal reports, the distribution of orders, &c. In the discharge of these and other duties he has proved himself faithful, efficient, and worthy of the kind consideration of the Quartermaster-General, to which I commend him, and recommend that he be appointed a major by brevet.

*　*　*　*　*　*　*

CLERKS.

The clerks on duty in this division having access to and employed upon the books and papers—many of which are confidential—are gentlemen of a high order of qualification, morally and educationally. They are punctual in their attendance and observe the utmost decorum during office hours. They have proved themselves worthy of the confidence and commendation of the Quartermaster-General.

All of the foregoing is respectfully submitted.

I have the honor to be, very respectfully, your obedient servant,

GEO. V. RUTHERFORD,
Colonel, Quartermaster's Department.

No. 53.

*Statement of clothing and camp and garrison equipage on hand July 1, 1864, purchased, manufactured, captured, gained, taken up, sold, lost, expended, and remaining on hand in the Quartermaster's Department during the fiscal year ending June 30, 1865.**

---

* For this statement (here omitted) see pp. 287–295 of Executive Document No. 1, to which reference is made in foot-note (*) p. 249. It "embraces reports received from 368 officers out of over 700 officers who were in service during the fiscal year and who had reports to render." The same remark applies to No. 54 next, *post*, which also appears in House Executive Document No. 1, Thirty-ninth Congress, first session, Vol. I, pp. 296, 297.

No. 54.

*Statement of the principal articles of quartermaster's property, means of transportation, &c., on hand July 1, 1864, purchased, manufactured, captured, gained, taken up, sold, died, lost, expended, and remaining on hand in the Quartermaster's Department during the fiscal year ending June 30, 1865.**

No. 55.

Statement of vessels owned by Government and in the employ of the Quartermaster's Department during the fiscal year ending June 30, 1865.†

RECAPITULATION.

Steam-boats	74	Sloops	4
Steam tugs	12	Steam dredge	1
Steam rams	5	Barges	33
Steamer	1	Lighter	1
Ferry-boats	2*	Canal-boats	3
Propellers	8	Wharf-boat	1
Army gun-boats	2	Wrecks	2
Steam water-boat	1		
Schooners	5	Total vessels	155

No. 56.

Statement of vessels chartered, impressed, or employed by the Quartermaster's Department during the fiscal year ending June 30, 1865.†

RECAPITULATION.

Total earnings		$9,274,017.38
Amount paid	$5,443,991.72	
Amount remaining unpaid	3,810,469.25	
Deductions	19,556.41	
		9,274,017.38
Of the above amount were paid for demurrage		168,235.36

CLASSIFICATION OF VESSELS EMPLOYED.

Steamers	25	Brigs	123
Steam-boats	603	Barks	69
Propellers	71	Schooners	1,282
Steam barges	8	Sloops	27
Steam tugs	281	Barges	738
Water-boats	4	Transports, classification not specified	24
Canal-boats	399		
Ferry-boats	6	Total vessels	3,693
Ships	33		

No. 57.

FROM OFFICERS' ANNUAL REPORTS.

Statement of property captured from the enemy during the fiscal year ending June 30, 1865.†

RECAPITULATION.

CLOTHING, CAMP AND GARRISON EQUIPAGE.‡

Total value reported	$543,569.60

RECAPITULATION OF QUARTERMASTER'S STORES.‡

Total value reported	$593,387.58
Clothing, camp and garrison equipage	543,569.60
Quartermaster's stores	593,387.58
Grand total	1,136,957.18

* See explanatory foot-note, p. 339.

† Omitted, except the "Recapitulation." See Executive Document No. 1, referred to in foot-note (*) p. 249.

‡ Details omitted.

No. 58.

*Statement of property captured or destroyed by the enemy during the fiscal year ending June 30, 1865.**

RECAPITULATION.

CLOTHING, CAMP AND GARRISON EQUIPAGE.†

Total value reported $48,649.21

RECAPITULATION OF QUARTERMASTER'S STORES.†

Total value reported $140,828.76

Total clothing, camp and garrison equipage	48,649.21
Total quartermaster's stores	140,828.76
Grand total	189,477.97

NOTE.—This statement is compiled from the annual reports of officers for the past fiscal year. The estimated value is inserted as far as stated, but it does not show the full value of the property by at least one-third of the amount reported.

In addition to the above statement Brevet Major-General Donaldson reports the total loss and destruction of public property in the Department of the Cumberland during the past year by fire, by freshet, captured, abandoned, or destroyed, to prevent its falling into the hands of the rebels, at $3,500,000.

No. 59.

Summary statement of transportation furnished during the fiscal year ending June 30, 1865.

TRANSPORTATION ORDERS OR SINGLE PASSAGES.

Kind of transportation.	Officers and men under orders.	Soldiers on furlough.	Prisoners of war.	Civilians.	Total.
Railroads	1,557,655	169,969	80,351	71,392	1,879,367
Steam-boats, barges, &c	207,369	15,900	24,247	21,136	268,652
Stages	5,840	473	1	99	6,413
Wagons	1,412	....	16	1	1,429
Ocean and lake	44,387	48	1,930	2,500	48,865
Total not owned or run by Government	1,816,663	186,390	106,545	95,128	2,204,726
Railroads	589,034	10	13,162	16,986	619,192
Steam-boats, barges, &c	896,669	14,706	109,986	36,515	1,057,876
Ocean and lake	73,644	....	27,000	....	100,644
Total owned or run by Government	1,559,347	14,716	150,148	53,501	1,777,712
Grand total	3,376,010	201,106	256,693	148,629	3,982,438

*Omitted, except the "Recapitulation." See Executive Document No. 1, referred to in foot-note (*) p. 249.

†Details omitted.

No. 59.—*Summary statement of transportation furnished during the fiscal year ending June 30, 1865*—Continued.

MOVEMENTS OF ANIMALS.

Kind of transportation.	Horses.	Mules.	Cattle.	Total.
Railroads	223, 608	58, 382	15, 023	297, 013
Steam-boats, barges, &c	47, 266	19, 029	76, 775	143, 070
Stages				
Wagons				
Ocean and lake	25		4, 131	4, 156
Total not owned or run by Government	270, 899	77, 411	95, 929	444, 239
Railroads	57, 663	27, 855	6, 134	91, 652
Steam-boats, barges, &c	79, 286	18, 182	81, 864	179, 332
Ocean and lake			1, 197	1, 197
Total owned or run by Government	136, 949	46, 037	89, 195	272, 181
Grand total	407, 848	123, 448	185, 124	716, 420

MOVEMENTS TO VARIOUS DISTANCES OF STORES.

Kind of transportation.	Subsistence stores.		Quartermaster's stores.		Ordnance stores.	
	Tons.	*Lbs.*	*Tons.*	*Lbs.*	*Tons.*	*Lbs.*
Railroads	2, 837, 893	932	2, 409, 450	552	291, 773	658
Steam-boats, barges, &c	381, 751	1, 480	570, 428	268	376, 948	420
Stages						
Wagons	12, 085	459	19, 413	454	9, 626	1, 781
Ocean and lake	65, 788	200	293, 991	1, 025	7, 448	737
Total not owned or run by Government	3, 297, 518	1, 071	3, 293, 283	299	685, 796	1, 596
Railroads	105, 385	329	156, 189	1, 016	9, 569	956
Steam-boats, barges, &c	726, 790	1, 164	313, 532	1, 273	641, 053	300
Ocean and lake	6, 948	000	4, 269	415	1, 220	000
Total owned or run by Government	839, 123	1, 493	473, 991	704	651, 842	1, 256
Grand total	4, 136, 642	564	3, 767, 274	1, 003	1, 337, 639	852

Kind of transportation.	Medical stores.		Miscellaneous stores.		Total of all kinds of stores.	
	Tons.	*Lbs.*	*Tons.*	*Lbs.*	*Tons.*	*Lbs.*
Railroads	58, 784	1, 924	16, 635	408	5, 614, 537	474
Steam-boats, barges, &c	14, 280	170	15, 716	1, 041	1, 359, 124	1, 379
Stages						
Wagons	6, 064	1, 691	53	451	47, 243	836
Ocean and lake	1, 089	533	1, 064	000	369, 381	495
Total not owned or run by Government	80, 219	318	33, 468	1, 900	7, 390, 286	1, 184
Railroads	4, 047	620	79, 447	1, 000	354, 638	1, 921
Steam-boats, barges, &c	3, 922	759	14, 398	1, 547	1, 699, 697	1, 043
Ocean and lake	1, 758	000	53	000	14, 248	415
Total owned or run by Government	9, 727	1, 379	93, 899	547	2, 068, 584	1, 379
Grand total	89, 946	1, 697	127, 368	447	9, 458, 871	563

No. 60.

Recapitulation of amounts paid for transportation during the fiscal year ending June 30, 1865.

Kind of transportation.	Passengers.			
	Officers and men.	Prisoners of war.	Civilians.	Total.
Railroads	$6,955,247.56	$212,680.92	$200,489.44	$7,368,417.92
Steam-boats, barges, &c.*a*	1,081,876.05	3,018.56	1,183.66	1,086,078.27
Stages	88,355.86	....	885.07	89,240.93
Wagons	10,680.92	9.00	82.00	10,771.92
Ocean and lake	168,633.50	375.00	713.00	169,721.50
Grand total	8,304,793.89	216,083.48	203,353.17	8,724,230.54

Kind of transportation.	Freight.	Total.	Expenditures.	Grand total.
Railroads	$3,423,471.60	$3,423,471.60	$8,377,451.67	$19,169,341.19
Steam-boats, barges, &c.*a*	7,808,857.11	7,808,857.11	6,264,410.40	15,159,345.78
Stages	75.40	75.40	....	89,316.33
Wagons	1,053,310.29	1,053,310.29	252,449.80	1,316,532.01
Ocean and lake	9,113,606.63	9,113,606.63	3,473,269.07	12,756,597.20
Grand total	21,399,321.03	21,399,321.03	18,367,580.94	48,491,132.51

a The amount paid for transportation on Western rivers, as abstracted from above report, is as follows:

For passengers	$1,009,546.97
For freight	5,554,854.03
For expenditures	6,238,365.07
	12,792,766.07

The amount paid for transportation on ocean and lake does not include Western rivers. Under the head of expenditures are included all expenses incurred in repairing, supplying, and running railroads operated by Government; also all steam-boats, &c., owned or chartered by Government.

No. 61.

List of officers of the Quartermaster's Department in charge of divisions, Quartermaster-General's Office, during the fiscal year ending June 30, 1865.

Divisions.	Names and rank.	Remarks.
First	Bvt. Brig. Gen. James A. Ekin, assistant quartermaster, U. S. Army	
Second	Col. Alexander J. Perry, assistant quartermaster, U. S. Army	
Third	Col. George D. Wise, assistant quartermaster, volunteers	
Fourth	Brig. Gen. Lewis B. Parsons, assistant quartermaster, volunteers	
	Lieut. Col. Alexander Bliss, assistant quartermaster, brevet colonel, U. S. Army.	Acting.
Fifth	Col. S. L. Brown, assistant quartermaster, volunteers	
Sixth	Col. J. J. Dana, assistant quartermaster, U. S. Army	
Seventh	Col. B. C. Card, assistant quartermaster, U. S. Army	Do.
Eighth	Col. George V. Rutherford, assistant quartermaster, volunteers	
Ninth	Col. B. C. Card, assistant quartermaster, U. S. Army	

No. 62.

List of officers who have been assigned as inspectors, Quartermaster's Department, during the fiscal year ending June 30, 1865.

Col. Gilbert A. Pierce, assistant quartermaster, volunteers (out of service); Col. James F. Rusling, assistant quartermaster, volunteers; Col. J. D. Cruttenden, assistant quartermaster, volunteers; Col. J. C. Crane, assistant quartermaster, volunteers; Col. J. D. Bingham, assistant quartermaster, U. S. Army; Col. R. Brinkerhoff, assistant quartermaster, volunteers; Col. H. Biggs, assistant quartermaster, U. S. Army; Col. W. H. Owen, assistant quartermaster, volunteers.

No. 63.

List of officers who served as chief quartermasters of armies during the fiscal year ending June 30, 1865.

Armies.	Names and rank.	Remarks.
Armies operating against Richmond.	Brig. Gen. Rufus Ingalls, quartermaster, U. S. Army, brevet major-general, volunteers.	
With Sherman	Bvt. Brig. Gen. L. C. Easton, quartermaster, U. S. Army.	
Cumberland	Col. A. J. Mackay, assistant quartermaster, volunteers.	
Potomac	Col. R. N. Batchelder, assistant quartermaster, U. S. Army, brevet brigadier-general, volunteers.	
	Bvt. Maj. Gen. Rufus Ingalls, quartermaster, U. S. Army.	
With Sheridan	Lieut. Col. C. W. Tolles, assistant quartermaster, volunteers.	Acting; dead.
	Lieut. Col. Henry Page, assistant quartermaster, volunteers.	Acting.
	Col. C. G. Sawtelle, assistant quartermaster, U. S. Army.	
Tennessee	Col. J. T. Conklin, assistant quartermaster, volunteers.	
James	Col. J. B. Howard, assistant quartermaster, volunteers.	
Georgia	Col. H. M. Whittelsey, assistant quartermaster, volunteers.	
Army of the Ohio	Lieut. Col. J. F. Boyd, assistant quartermaster, volunteers.	
With Butler	Col. George S. Dodge, assistant quartermaster, volunteers, brevet brigadier-general.	

List of officers who have acted as chief quartermasters of army corps during the fiscal year ending June 30, 1865.

Corps.	Names and rank.	Remarks.
First	Lieut. Col. William Painter, assistant quartermaster, U. S. Volunteers.	Out of service.
	Bvt. Col. C. H. Tompkins, assistant quartermaster, U. S. Army.	
Second	Lieut. Col. R. N. Batchelder, assistant quartermaster, volunteers.	Afterward chief quartermaster Army of the Potomac.
	Lieut. Col. G. A. Shallenberger, assistant quartermaster, volunteers.	
Third	Lieut. Col. J. B. Howard, assistant quartermaster, volunteers.	
Fourth	Lieut. Col. H. C. Ransom, assistant quartermaster, U. S. Army.	
	Lieut. Col. Hiram Hayes, assistant quartermaster, U. S. Volunteers.	
	Capt. Thomas Palmer, assistant quartermaster, volunteers.	Acting during absence (in April, 1865) of Lieutenant-Colonel Hayes on board of examination.
Fifth	Lieut. Col. W. H. Owen, assistant quartermaster, volunteers.	Afterward inspector, Quartermaster's Department.
	Lieut. Col. A. L. Thomas, assistant quartermaster, volunteers.	Out of service.
Sixth	Lieut. Col. C. W. Tolles, assistant quartermaster, volunteers.	Dead.
	Lieut. Col. S. H. Manning, assistant quartermaster, volunteers.	
Seventh	Lieut. Col. B. O. Carr, assistant quartermaster, volunteers.	
	Lieut. Col. C. A. Henry, assistant quartermaster, volunteers.	
Eighth	Lieut. Col. Alexander Bliss, assistant quartermaster, U. S. Army, brevet colonel.	
	Capt. C. R. Tyler, assistant quartermaster, volunteers.	Acting during absence of Lieutenant-Colonel Bliss on board of examination.
	Capt. G. S. Blodgett, assistant quartermaster, U. S. Army.	Acting temporarily.
Ninth	Lieut. Col. L. H. Peirce, assistant quartermaster, U. S. Army.	
Tenth	Lieut. Col. C. E. Fuller, assistant quartermaster, volunteers.	
	Lieut. Col. G. W. Bradley, assistant quartermaster, volunteers.	

No. 63.—*List of officers who have acted as chief quartermasters of army corps during the fiscal year ending June 30, 1865*—Continued.

Corps.	Names and rank.	Remarks.
Eleventh	Lieut. Col. W. G. Le Duc, assistant quartermaster, volunteers.	
Twelfth	Lieut. Col. Charles Hopkins, assistant quartermaster, volunteers.	
Thirteenth	Lieut. Col. A. N. Shipley, assistant quartermaster, U. S. Army.	
Fourteenth	Lieut. Col. A. J. Mackay, assistant quartermaster, volunteers.	
	Lieut. Col. J. E. Remington, assistant quartermaster, volunteers.	
Fifteenth	Lieut. Col. G. L. Fort, assistant quartermaster, volunteers.	
Sixteenth	Lieut. Col. Elias Nigh, assistant quartermaster, U. S. Army.	
	Capt. C. K. Drew, assistant quartermaster, volunteers.	Acting.
Seventeenth	Lieut. Col. E. M. Joel, assistant quartermaster, volunteers.	
Eighteenth	Lieut. Col. J. B. Howard, assistant quartermaster, volunteers.	Afterward chief quartermaster Twenty-fourth Army Corps.
Nineteenth	Lieut. Col. J. G. Chandler, assistant quartermaster, U. S. Army.	
Twentieth	Lieut. Col. W. G. Le Duc, assistant quartermaster, volunteers.	
Twenty-first	....	Consolidated with the Fourth Army Corps. No officer ever appointed.
Twenty-second	Lieut. Col. E. M. Greene, assistant quartermaster, volunteers.	
Twenty-third	Lieut. Col. J. F. Boyd, assistant quartermaster, volunteers.	
	Capt. J. B. Campbell, assistant quartermaster, volunteers.	Acting temporarily.
Twenty-fourth	Lieut. Col. J. B. Howard, assistant quartermaster, volunteers.	Afterward chief quartermaster Army of the James.
	Lieut. Col. A. B. Lawrence, assistant quartermaster, volunteers.	
Twenty-fifth	Lieut. Col. H. B. Blood, assistant quartermaster, volunteers.	

No. 64.

List of officers who served as chief quartermasters of departments during the fiscal year ending June 30, 1865.

Departments.	Names and rank.	Remarks.
Valley of the Mississippi	Bvt. Brig. Gen. R. Allen, quartermaster, U. S. Army, brevet major-general, volunteers.	
Cumberland	Bvt. Brig. Gen. J. L. Donaldson, quartermaster, U. S. Army, brevet major-general, volunteers.	
East	Bvt. Brig. Gen. S. Van Vliet, quartermaster, U. S. Army.	
Missouri	Capt. William Myers, assistant quartermaster, U. S. Army, colonel, aide-de-camp, brevet brigadier-general.	
Pacific	Lieut. Col. E. B. Babbitt, deputy quartermaster-general, U. S. Army.	
Middle	Lieut. Col. Alexander Bliss, assistant quartermaster, U. S. Army, brevet colonel, U. S. Army, chief quartermaster Eighth Army Corps.	Acting.
Washington	Col. E. M. Greene, assistant quartermaster, volunteers.	Out of service.
	Col. J. A. Elison, assistant quartermaster, volunteers.	
	Col. M. I. Ludington, assistant quartermaster, volunteers.	
Northern	Col. C. H. Hoyt, assistant quartermaster, volunteers, brevet brigadier general.	
Susquehanna	Col. J. G. Johnson, assistant quartermaster, volunteers.	Do.
Tennessee	Col. J. D. Bingham, assistant quartermaster, brevet colonel, U. S. Army, now inspector, Quartermaster's Department.	
	Col. M. C. Garber, assistant quartermaster, volunteers.	
Virginia and North Carolina	Col. H. Biggs, assistant quartermaster, U. S. Army, brevet brigadier-general, volunteers.	

No. 64.—*List of officers who served as chief quartermasters of departments during the fiscal year ending June 30, 1865*—Continued.

Departments.	Names and rank.	Remarks.
Virginia and North Carolina	Col. R. C. Webster, assistant quartermaster, volunteers.	
West Virginia	Capt. J. G. Farnsworth, assistant quartermaster, volunteers.	
	Capt. A. V. Barringer, assistant quartermaster, volunteers.	Out of service.
South	Capt. C. W. Thomas, assistant quartermaster, brevet major, U. S. Army.	
Virginia	Col. W. L. James, assistant quartermaster, volunteers.	
Gulf	Capt. S. B. Holabird, assistant quartermaster, U. S. Army, colonel, aide-de-camp.	
Northwest	Maj. Frederick Myers, quartermaster, U. S. Army, lieutenant-colonel, aide-de-camp.	
New Mexico	Col. J. C. McFerran, quartermaster, U. S. Army.	
North Carolina	Col. G. S. Dodge, assistant quartermaster, volunteers.	
	Col. J. F. Boyd, assistant quartermaster, volunteers.	
Arkansas	Col. B. O. Carr, assistant quartermaster, volunteers.	Do.
	Col. H. T. Noble, assistant quartermaster, volunteers.	
Kentucky	Col. H. Howland, assistant quartermaster, volunteers.	
Pennsylvania	Col. J. G. Johnson, assistant quartermaster, volunteers.	Do.
	Col. George W. Bradley, assistant quartermaster, volunteers.	

No. 65.

List of principal depots, with the names of officers in charge during the fiscal year ending June 30, 1865.

Depots.	Names of officers.	Remarks.
New York, N. Y	Bvt. Brig. Gen. D. H. Vinton, deputy quartermaster-general.	
Philadelphia, Pa	Col. A. J. Perry, assistant quartermaster, U. S. Army.	Acting for a time.
	Col. H. Biggs, assistant quartermaster, U. S. Army.	At different dates.
	Col. W. W. McKim, assistant quartermaster, U. S. Army.	Assigned.
Washington, D. C	Bvt. Maj. Gen. D. H. Rucker, quartermaster, U. S. Army, brevet major-general, volunteers.	
Baltimore, Md	Col. R. M. Newport, assistant quartermaster, volunteers.	Do.
Chicago, Ill	Col. J. A. Elison, assistant quartermaster, volunteers.	Do.
Fort Leavenworth, Kans	Col. J. A. Potter, assistant quartermaster, U. S. Army.	Do.
Detroit, Mich	Col. G. W. Lee, assistant quartermaster, volunteers.	Do.
Saint Louis, Mo	Capt. William Myers, assistant quartermaster, U. S. Army, colonel, aide-de-camp.	
Louisville, Ky	Col. G. F. Clark, assistant quartermaster, volunteers.	Do.
Cincinnati, Ohio	Col. W. W. McKim, assistant quartermaster, U. S. Army.	
	Col. C. W. Moulton, assistant quartermaster, U. S. Army.	Do.
Columbus, Ohio	Col. Raymond Burr, assistant quartermaster, volunteers.	Do.
City Point, Va	Col. P. P. Pitkin, assistant quartermaster, volunteers.	Out of service. Assigned.
	Col. G. W. Bradley, assistant quartermaster, volunteers.	Assigned.
New Orleans, La	Capt. C. K. Mark, assistant quartermaster, volunteers.	
Fort Monroe, Va	Bvt. Maj. W. L. James, assistant quartermaster, volunteers.	

No. 66.

List of officers serving at depots other than principal depots during the fiscal year ending June 30, 1865.

Depots.	Names of officers.
Alexandria, Va	Bvt. Lieut. Col. J. G. C. Lee, assistant quartermaster, U. S. Army.
Boston, Mass	Capt. J. W. McKim, assistant quartermaster, volunteers.
Brattleborough, Vt	Capt. F. O. Sawyer, assistant quartermaster, volunteers.
Covington, Ky	Capt. J. R. Webster, assistant quartermaster, volunteers.
Chattanooga, Tenn	Capt. W. R. Hopkins, assistant quartermaster, volunteers.
Cairo, Ill	Capt. A. C. Woolfolk, assistant quartermaster, U. S. Army.
Concord, N. H	Capt. A. Norton, acting assistant quartermaster and commissary of subsistence.
Camp Dennison, Ohio	Capt. Ralph Plumb, assistant quartermaster, volunteers.
Davenport, Iowa	Capt. E. Corning, assistant quartermaster, volunteers.
Giesborough, D. C	Capt. L. L. Moore, assistant quartermaster, volunteers.
	Capt. George T. Browning, assistant quartermaster, volunteers.
Harrisburg, Pa	Capt. E. C. Reichenbach. assistant quartermaster, volunteers.
Indianapolis, Ind	Capt. James Wilson, assistant quartermaster, volunteers.
Lexington, Ky	Capt. J. B. Campbell, assistant quartermaster, volunteers.
Memphis, Tenn	Lieut. Col. R. E. Clary, deputy quartermaster-general, U. S. Army.
New Haven, Conn	Capt. D. D. Bullock, assistant quartermaster, volunteers.
Pittsburg, Pa	Lieut. Col. O. Cross, deputy quartermaster-general, U. S. Army.
Portland, Me	Capt. H. Inman, assistant quartermaster, U. S. Army.
Rock Island, Ill	Capt. J. J. McDermid, assistant quartermaster, volunteers.
San Francisco, Cal	Maj. R. W. Kirkham, quartermaster, U. S. Army.
Quincy, Ill	Capt. Newton Flagg, assistant quartermaster, volunteers.

No. 67.

Names of officers of the Quartermaster's Department who have been specially mentioned to the Quartermaster-General for good service.

Names.	Rank.	Remarks.
REGULARS.		
M. S. Miller	Major	
J. C. McFerran	do	Colonel under act of July 4, 1864.
J. D. Bingham	Captain	Do.
Augustus Boyd	do	Resignation accepted Oct. 11, 1864. Special Orders, No. 341, Adjutant-General's Office.
H. C. Hodges	do	
J. A. Potter	do	Colonel under act of July 4, 1864.
C. H. Tompkins	Captain and brevet colonel	Lieutenant-colonel under act of July 17, 1862.
A. N. Shipley	Captain	Do.
E. B. Carling	Captain and brevet lieutenant-colonel.	
F. J. Crilly	Captain	
Alexander Bliss	Captain and brevet colonel	Lieutenant-colonel under act of July 17, 1862.
A. C. Woolfolk	Captain	
L. H. Peirce	do	Do.
J. G. C. Lee	Captain and brevet lieutenant-colonel.	
J. M. Moore	Captain	
E. B. Grimes	do	Appointed May 16, 1865.

No. 67.—*Names of officers of the Quartermaster's Department who have been specially mentioned to the Quartermaster-General for good service*—Continued.

Names.	Rank.	Remarks.
VOLUNTEERS.		
Allen, E. S	Captain	
Burr, Raymond	do	Colonel under act of July 4, 1864.
Bradley, G. W	do	Do.
Bailhache, W. H	do	Resigned. Resignation accepted June 5, 1865.
Brinkerhoff, R	do	Colonel under act of July 4, 1864.
Brooks, James	do	
Bowles, T. C	do	
Burr, A. G	do	
Bowman, Henry	do	Major under act of July 4, 1864.
Bliven, C. E	do	Appointed Oct. 24, 1864.
Browning, G. T	do	
Belcher, J. H	do	Appointed Oct. 14, 1864.
Bean, S. B	do	Major under act of July 4, 1864.
Conklin, J. T	Captain and brevet brigadier-general.	Colonel under act of July 4, 1864.
Cruttenden, J. D	Captain	Do.
Cochrane, W. H. D	do	Major under act of July 4, 1864.
Chapman, E. D	do	
Cox, T. J	do	
Carlile, T. J	do	
Cumming, Alex. M	do	
Cadwalader, G. B	do	
Colburn, W. J	do	Appointed Sept. 19, 1864.
Crowell, J. H	do	
Cilley, John K	do	
Chamberlain, H. S	do	
Currie, William	do	
Campbell, John B	do	
Daniels, W. H	Captain and brevet major	Major under act of July 4, 1864.
Del Vecchio, James R	Captain	
Dunton, A. T	do	
Drew, C. K	do	
Dexter, J. B	do	
Elwell, J. J	do	
Edwards, Arthur	Captain and brevet colonel	
Elwell, Jos. S	Captain	Appointed Feb. 2, 1865; appointment canceled June 6, 1865.
Fort, G. L	do	Lieutenant-colonel under act of July 17, 1862.
Flagg, Newton	Captain and brevet major	
Farnsworth, J. G	Captain	
Farnsworth, H. J	do	Appointed July 8, 1864.
Forsyth, L. Cass	do	
Finney, C. G	do	Major under act of July 4, 1864.
Furey, John V	do	
Farnum, E. J	do	
Farr, E. P	do	Appointed March 6, 1865.
Garber, M. C	do	Colonel under act of July 4, 1864.
Goodridge, M. H	do	
Goldie, William	do	
Gleason, James	Captain and brevet major	Major under act of July 4, 1864.
Garvens, H	Captain	
Gear, Alonzo S	do	
Grierson, John C	do	Appointed Feb. 11, 1865.
Hayes, Hiram	do	Lieutenant-colonel under act of July 17, 1862.
Hopkins, W. R	do	
Holden, William	do	
Hibbard, G. B	do	
Hamill, S. R	do	
Hunt, T. B	do	
Hutchings, W. V	do	Resignation accepted May 29, 1865.
Howell, W. T	Captain and brevet lieutenant-colonel	
Jennings, John R	Captain	
Jones, J. E	do	
Johnson, H. W	do	Appointed June 1, 1865. Major under act of July 4, 1864.
Kimball, A. S	do	
Kelly, John L	do	
Kerr, Thomas J	do	
Kirk, E. B	do	
Kelley, B. F	do	
Lawrence, A. B	do	Lieutenant-colonel under act of July 17, 1862.
Lee, George W	do	Colonel under act of July 4, 1864.
Lacey, H. A	do	
Mackay, A. J	do	Do.
Morford, W. E	do	
McClung, D. W	do	
Morgan, R. C	do	
Metcalf, L. S	do	

No. 67.—*Names of officers of the Quartermaster's Department who have been specially mentioned to the Quartermaster-General for good service*—Continued.

Names.	Rank.	Remarks.
Morse, E. A	Captain	
McKim, John W	do	
Manning, S. H	Captain and brevet major	Lieutenant-colonel under act of July 17, 1862.
McDermid, J. J	Captain	
Newport, R. M	do	Colonel under act of July 4, 1864.
Noble, H. T	do	Do.
Norton, G. A	do	
Owen, W. H	do	Colonel under act of July 4, 1864. Honorably mustered out June 19, 1865.
Owen, R. B	do	
Parsons, L. B	Colonel, aide-de-camp	Brigadier-general of volunteers.
Plumb, Ralph	Captain	
Plato, Nelson	do	Major under act of July 4, 1864.
Perkins, F. W	do	
Peugnet, E	do	
Parker, G. L	do	
Powers, Jos. T	Captain and brevet major	
Parsons, Charles	Captain	Resignation accepted July 5, 1864.
Parks, John	do	
Poor, L. A	do	
Pitkin, P. P	do	Resignation accepted Nov. 7, 1864. Colonel under act of July 4, 1864.
Rusling, J. F	do	Colonel under act of July 4, 1864.
Rundle, S. E	do	
Restieaux, E. B. W	do	
Reichenbach, E. C	do	
Rutherford, John P	do	
Remington, J. E	do	Lieutenant-colonel under act of July 17, 1862.
Rutherford, R. C	do	Appointed Dec. 20, 1864.
Royce, H. A	do	Appointed March 11, 1865.
Stinson, Daniel	do	
Stager, Anson	do	Colonel and aide-de-camp.
Shallenberger, G. A	do	Lieutenant-colonel under act of July 17, 1862.
Smith, C. K	do	
Stubbs, Jos. D	do	
Staples, Robert G	do	
Strang, E. J	Captain and brevet colonel	
Summers, Moses	Captain	
Smith, H. M	do	
Tighe, J. H	do	
Tolles, C. W	do	Lieutenant-colonel under act of July 17, 1862. Died Nov. 11 [8], 1864.
Tucker, A. M	do	
Tredway, J. D	do	Appointed Nov. 12, 1864.
Van Vliet, L. S	do	
Van Ness, W. W	do	
Webster, R. C	do	Colonel under act of July 4, 1864.
Wagner, C. B	do	
Wing, C. T	do	
Webster, G. P	do	
Wilson, E. C	do	
Welch, D. N	do	
Wilson, James	do	
Wilson, Thomas P	do	
Winslow, G. C	do	
Whitman, E. B	do	
Woods, J. L	do	
Wright, Samuel I	do	
Wainwright, W. A	do	
Watson, Charles T	do	Appointed August 20, 1864.
Wickersham, M. D	do	
Walbridge, C. E	Captain and brevet major	
Wills, A. W	do	
Whittelsey, H. M	Captain	Colonel under act of July 4, 1864.

No. 68.

List of officers of the Quartermaster's Department who have been promoted (by brevet) for faithful and meritorious services during the war.

Names.	Rank.	Remarks.
REGULARS.		
M. C. Meigs	Brevet major-general	
Charles Thomas	Brevet brigadier-general	
Thomas Swords	do	
George H. Crosman	do	
D. H. Vinton	do	
Robert Allen	do	Brevet major-general of volunteers.
J. L. Donaldson	do	Do.
L. C. Easton	do	
S. Van Vliet	do	
D. H. Rucker	do	Do.
R. N. Batchelder	Brevet colonel	Brevet brigadier-general of volunteers.
S. B. Holabird	do	
J. C. McFerran	do	
J. J. Dana	do	
C. W. Moulton	do	
E. B. Babbitt	do	
J. A. Potter	do	
Benjamin C. Card	do	
Judson D. Bingham	do	
William Myers	do	Do.
W. W. McKim	do	
H. M. Enos	do	
Alexander Bliss	do	
C. G. Sawtelle	do	
Alexander J. Perry	do	
Rufus Saxton	do	Brevet major-general of volunteers.
R. O. Tyler	do	Do.
A. C. Gillem	do	Do.
Charles H. Tompkins	do	
George B. Dandy	do	
James A. Ekin	do	Brevet brigadier-general of volunteers.
Herman Biggs	do	Do.
C. W. Thomas	Brevet lieutenant-colonel	
John G. Chandler	do	
H. C. Hodges	do	
L. H. Peirce	do	
Alexander N. Shipley	do	
H. C. Ransom	do	
W. L. Lothrop	do	
E. B. Carling	do	
J. G. C. Lee	do	
A. C. Woolfolk	Brevet major	
F. J. Crilly	do	
A. G. Robinson	do	
G. S. Blodgett	do	
James M. Moore	do	
VOLUNTEERS.		
George V. Rutherford	Brevet brigadier-general	
George D. Wise	do	
H. M. Whittelsey	do	
A. J. Mackay	do	
J. F. Boyd	do	
J. T. Conklin	do	
S. L. Brown	do	
George S. Dodge	do	
C. H. Hoyt	do	
H. T. Noble	Brevet colonel	
M. I. Ludington	do	
J. F. Rusling	do	
Raymond Burr	do	
George W. Lee	do	
J. D. Cruttenden	do	
J. B. Howard	do	
R. C. Webster	do	
W. L. James	do	
L. S. Metcalf	do	
Charles T. Wing	do	
J. G. Farnsworth	do	
G. W. Bradley	do	
R. M. Newport	do	
M. C. Garber	do	
Henry Page	do	
A. P. Blunt	do	
Arthur Edwards	do	

No. 68.—*List of officers of the Quartermaster's Department who have been promoted (by brevet) for faithful and meritorious services during the war*—Cont'd.

Names.	Rank.	Remarks.
VOLUNTEERS.		
C. H. Irvin	Brevet colonel	
John H. James	do	
H. L. Robinson	do	
Ingham Coryell	Brevet lieutenant-colonel	
G. L. Fort	do	
G. A. Shallenberger	do	
E. M. Joel	do	
J. E. Remington	do	
A. B. Lawrence	do	
M. D. Wickersham	do	
W. H. D. Cochrane	do	
E. S. Allen	do	
Hiram Hayes	do	
William Goldie	do	
A. T. Dunton	do	
S. H. Manning	do	
H. B. Blood	do	
G. B. Cadwalader	do	
Gilbert E. Dunbar	do	
E. J. Strang	do	
G. A. Pierce	do	
W. T. Howell	do	
Hanson Rasin	Brevet major	
E. C. Reichenbach	do	
E. B. Kirk	do	
Thomas B. Hunt	do	
W. M. Kimball	do	
George W. Johnes	do	
H. B. Lacey	do	
Benjamin Burton	do	
C. B. Wagner	do	
Henry Howland	do	
R. C. Morgan	do	
Thomas J. Cox	do	
J. F. Hazelton	do	
A. Austin	do	
W. H. Daniels	do	
M. H. Mandeville	do	
G. W. Davis	do	
H. F. Gerrish	do	
M. H. Alberger	do	
C. W. Folsom	do	
W. H. Brown	do	
H. C. King	do	
F. Lyon	do	
W. H. Lambert	do	
E. P. Farr	do	
H. C. Lawrence	do	
C. B. Whittemore	do	
Harry Brownson	do	
B. C. Carter	do	
H. M. Smith	do	
J. E. Jones	do	
Alexander Conn	do	
Fred. Crain	do	
Charles G. Finney	do	
J. D. Tredway	do	
C. M. Sampson	do	
T. J. Carlile	do	
C. K. Smith	do	
James Gleason	do	
J. K. Cilley	do	
P. Hiestand	do	
J. C. Mann	do	
S. B. Bean	do	
O. O. Potter	do	
E. D. Chapman	do	
T. C. Bowles	do	
Newton Flagg	do	
Daniel Stinson	do	
E. M. Camp	do	
G. A. Flagg	do	
Joseph T. Powers	do	
A. Webster	do	
A. W. Wills	do	
John R. Craig	do	
C. E. Walbridge	do	
C. S. McEntee	do	
Q. I. Drake	Brevet captain	Lieutenant, 12th Illinois Volunteers.

No. 69.*

RECAPITULATION.

	Money accounts.	Property accounts.	Company accounts.	Total.
Received from July 1, 1861, to June 30, 1865	28,378	103,063	44,961	176,402
Examined and sent to Treasury	16,189	34,112	12,958	63,259
On hand to be examined	12,189	68,951	32,003	113,143

The total number of accounts received in each of the last four fiscal years is as follows:

Year commencing July 1, 1861, and ending June 30, 1862	7,094
Year commencing July 1, 1862, and ending June 30, 1863	29,153
Year commencing July 1, 1863, and ending June 30, 1864	67,856
Year commencing July 1, 1864, and ending June 30, 1865	72,299

In order to bring up the arrears in the examination of these accounts, I have the honor respectfully to recommend that there be employed, temporarily, 150 clerks. If this additional force is authorized, an additional building for their accommodation will be required.

Very respectfully, &c.,

BENJ. C. CARD,
Colonel, Quartermaster's Department, in Charge of Division.

Bvt. Maj. Gen. M. C. MEIGS,
Quartermaster-General U. S. Army.

No. 70.†

No. 71.‡

No. 72.§

No. 73.

GENERAL ORDERS, No. 24. | QUARTERMASTER-GENERAL'S OFFICE, *Washington, D. C., April 29, 1865.*

I. In carrying out the provisions of General Orders, No. 77, from the War Department, Adjutant-General's Office, dated 28th of April, 1865,‖ so far as relates to the Quartermaster's Department, all char-

*Report of the Ninth Division, Quartermaster-General's Office, dated October 12, 1865, omitted, except the "Recapitulation." See Executive Document No. 1, referred to in foot-note (*), p. 249.

†For General Orders, No. 35, Quartermaster-General's Office, August 29, 1864 (here omitted), publishing "rules and regulations to govern the submission and examination of claims to be presented to the Quartermaster-General and to the Commissary-General of Subsistence, respectively," under the act of July 4, 1864, see p. 475 of Executive Document No. 1, referred to in foot-note (*), p. 249.

‡For General Orders, No. 43, Quartermaster-General's Office, September 23, 1864 (here omitted), promulgating "rules and regulations relating to the purchase, procurement, and disposition of horses and mules for the Army," see p. 477 of Executive Document No. 1, referred to in foot-note (*), p. 249.

§For General Orders, No. 276, War Department, Adjutant-General's Office, August 8, 1863 (here omitted), see Vol. III, this series, p. 638.

‖See Vol. IV, this series, p. 1280.

tered steamers, both ocean and river, which, under the new military situation, can be spared, will be discharged immediately.

II. Ocean steamers at distant ports will be loaded with the supplies which are no longer needed at such ports and returned either to the depots of New York or of Washington.

III. Troops under orders to return North will be transported in the returning steamers or in the steamers which are the property of the department.

IV. The chiefs of divisions of this office and the chiefs of the principal depots will immediately report to the Quartermaster-General the extent of the reduction which they are able to make in the force of laborers, operatives, clerks, and agents under their command.

V. It is understood that troops will be made available for most of the work at the depots, and that thus very large reductions in the rolls of employés will be possible.

VI. All railroad construction and repairs, except those needed on lines by which troops are still supplied or by which troops may be marching, will cease.

VII. Construction and extension of all barracks, hospitals, and other buildings will cease, unless authorized upon special report, which, in all cases of necessity, should be made immediately by telegraph.

VIII. Property returns of all property on hand on the 30th of April should be made up immediately and forwarded to this office, with recommendations as to the dispositions to be made thereof, whether to be stored or to be sold, and where to be stored or sold in each case.

IX. The efforts of all officers of this department will be directed to the greatest possible reduction of expenditure consistent with the efficiency and comfort of the troops now about to be withdrawn from active operations in the field.

X. Attention of all officers of the Quartermaster's Department is specially called to paragraphs II and IX, of General Orders, No. 77, which are herewith republished as follows:

II. That the Quartermaster-General discharge all ocean transports not required to bring home troops in remote departments. All river and inland transportation, except that required for necessary supplies to troops in the field. Purchases of horses, mules, wagons, and other land transportation will be stopped; also purchases of forage, except what is required for immediate consumption. All purchases for railroad construction and transportation will also be stopped.

IX. The chiefs of the respective bureaus will immediately cause property returns to be made out of the public property in their charge, and a statement of the property in each that may be sold upon advertisement and public sale without prejudice to the service.

M. C. MEIGS,
Quartermaster-General, Brevet Major-General.

No. 74.

GENERAL ORDERS, No. 25. } QUARTERMASTER-GENERAL'S OFFICE, *Washington, D. C., April 29, 1865.*

The chief of the inspection division will direct the inspectors to visit all depots and posts within their respective districts, and report the reductions which may be possible in expenditure, and make such suggestions therefor as may seem to them necessary.

Officers not on duty in the field or at important posts will also be selected, to be placed temporarily on inspection duty, in order that this inspection may be the more general and speedy.

M. C. MEIGS,
Quartermaster-General, Brevet Major-General.

No. 75.

GENERAL ORDERS, No. 28. } QUARTERMASTER-GENERAL'S OFFICE, *Washington, D. C., May 8, 1865.*

All horses and mules on hand in the Quartermaster's Department not fit for immediate issue will be advertised and sold at public sale as soon as the necessary public notice can be given.

Brevet Brigadier-General Ekin, chief of the First Division of the Quartermaster-General's Office, will telegraph the necessary instructions to each depot of animals.

Sales should be commenced within one week and continued at regular intervals until all unserviceable animals are disposed of.

They should be sold at the depots at which or near which they are kept at the time the order is received.

M. C. MEIGS,
Quartermaster-General, Brevet Major-General.

No. 76.

GENERAL ORDERS, No. 42. } QUARTERMASTER-GENERAL'S OFFICE, *Washington, D. C., July 15, 1865.*

Large quantities of property belonging to the Quartermaster's Department of the U. S. Army are now being sold by order of the War Department. Special reports of such sales will be made and sent to the Quartermaster-General at Washington.

These reports will state the kind of articles sold and the amount realized by said sale, according to the annexed form.

They will be forwarded to the Quartermaster-General's Office daily, so long as the sales continue.

These reports are not intended to supersede the regular accounts of the sales of public property to be sent with officers' accounts and returns, as required by the Army Regulations, which must be sent as heretofore.

The first reports after the receipt of this order will embrace all sales made since the 1st of May last.

Sales should be made at auction by persons employed for that purpose by the officers of this department or by clerks already employed who may be competent.

The compensation to be allowed to persons specially employed to make such sales should be a reasonable daily or monthly salary, not a commission or percentage on the amount sold.

M. C. MEIGS,
Quartermaster-General, Brevet Major-General.

FORM OF REPORT.

Abstract of sales of public property made at ——, under the direction of ——, on the —— of ——, 186—.

Date of sale.	Description of property.	Amount.		Total.	
		Dollars.	Cts.	Dollars.	Cts.
	REGULAR SUPPLIES.				
	Fuel				
	Forage and straw				
	BARRACKS AND QUARTERS.				
	Barracks, quarters, hospitals				
	Material for ditto				
	TRANSPORTATION OF THE ARMY.				
	Ships, brigs, and other sail vessels				
	Steamers				
	Horses and mules, draft				
	Harness of all kinds				
	Wagons, carts, drays, ambulances, &c				
	INCIDENTAL EXPENSES.				
	Forages, horse and mule shoes and nails, &c				
	Iron, steel, blacksmiths' tools, &c				
	Cavalry horses				
	Artillery horses				
	Mules				
	Clothing, and camp and garrison equipage				
	Total amount				

No. 77—A.

GENERAL ORDERS, No. 56. } QUARTERMASTER-GENERAL'S OFFICE, *Washington, D. C., September 28, 1865.*

The following order by the President of the United States, in relation to the relinquishment of the Government's control over all railroads in the State of Tennessee and their continuations in adjoining States, now occupied by the U. S. military authorities and no longer needed for military purposes, is published for the information of all officers and agents of the Quartermaster's Department.

M. C. MEIGS,
Brevet Major-General, U. S. Army, Quartermaster-General.

WAR DEPARTMENT,
Washington, August 8, 1865.

Maj. Gen. GEORGE H. THOMAS,
Comdg. Military Division of the Tennessee, Nashville, Tenn.:

GENERAL: It having been determined by the Government to relinquish control over all railroads in the State of Tennessee and their continuations in adjoining States that have been in charge of and are now occupied by the U. S. military authorities and no longer needed for military purposes, you are hereby authorized and directed to turn over the same to the respective owners thereof at as early a date as practicable, causing in all cases of transfer as aforesaid the following regulations to be observed and carried out:

1. Each and every company will be required to reorganize and elect a board of directors whose loyalty shall be established to your satisfaction.

2. You will cause to be made out in triplicate, by such person or persons as you may indicate, a complete inventory of the rolling-stock, tools, and other materials and property on each road.

3. Separate inventories will be, in the same manner, made of the rolling-stock and other property originally belonging to each of said roads, and that furnished by and belonging to the Government.

4. Each company will be required to give bonds satisfactory to the Government that they will, in twelve months from the date of transfer as aforesaid, or such other reasonable time as may be agreed upon, pay a fair valuation for the Government property turned over to said companies, the same being first appraised by competent and disinterested parties at a fair valuation, the United States reserving all Government dues for carrying mails and other service performed by each company until said obligations are paid; and if at the maturity of said debt the amount of Government dues retained as aforesaid does not liquidate the same the balance is to be paid by the company in money.

5. Tabular statements will be made of all expenditures by the Government for repairing each road, with a full statement of receipts from private freights, passage, and other sources; also a full statement of all transportation performed on Government account, giving the number of persons transported, and amount of freight, and the distance carried in each case; all of said reports or tabular statements to be made in triplicate, one each for the Secretary of War, the military headquarters of the department, and the railroad company.

6. All railroads in Tennessee will be required to pay all arrearages of interest due on the bonds issued by that State prior to the date of its pretended secession from the Union, to aid in the construction of said roads, before any dividends are declared or paid to the stockholders thereof.

7. Buildings erected for Government purposes on the line of railroads, and not valuable or useful for the business of said companies, should not form a legitimate charge against such companies; nor should they be charged for rebuilding houses, bridges, or other structures which were destroyed by the Federal Army.

8. You are authorized to give any orders to quartermasters within your division which you may deem necessary to carry into execution this order.

By order of the President:

EDWIN M. STANTON,
Secretary of War.

No. 77—B.

GENERAL ORDERS, No. 62. | QUARTERMASTER-GENERAL'S OFFICE, *Washington, D. C., October 23, 1865.*

The following order by the President of the United States, in relation to Executive order of 8th of August, 1865, extending the provisions and benefits of the same to all railroads within the limits of the Military Division of the Tennessee desiring to purchase railroad rolling-stock and material from the United States for the purpose of repairing the losses of the war, is published for the information of all officers and agents of the Quartermaster's Department.

M. C. MEIGS,
Brevet Major-General, U. S. Army, Quartermaster-General.

WAR DEPARTMENT,
Washington, D. C., October 14, 1865.

Maj. Gen. GEORGE H. THOMAS,
Comdg. Mil. Div. of the Tennessee, Hdqrs., Nashville, Tenn.:

GENERAL: The provisions and benefits of the Executive order of 8th of August are hereby extended to all railroads within the limits of your command desiring to purchase railroad rolling-stock and material from the United States for the purpose of repairing the losses of the war.

You are also authorized to direct the sale to any such railroads of rolling-stock now within the limits of your command and not needed by the United States for actual use, upon the following conditions, if they are preferred to the terms of the order of 8th of August, and the individual security required by you under that order.

You will take care that this property is distributed among the several roads in proportion to their actual needs, and that none is sold to any railroad in excess of the reasonable requirements of its business, or to be used for purposes of speculation, sale, or hire to other roads.

You will require from all such railroad companies satisfactory bonds, in the form herewith inclosed, binding them to the payment to the United States of the full appraised value of the property sold to them, in equal monthly installments, with interest at the rate of 7.3 per cent. per annum, within two years, credit being allowed to them on the first of each month for any service of military transportation rendered by them during the preceding month, at the established rates now allowed to Northern railroads for such service.

Full reports of all sales under this order will be made to the War Department from time to time, as required by existing orders.

The serviceable railroad iron in possession of the Quartermaster's Department at Chattanooga and Nashville is excepted. It will be sold only for cash at the prices fixed by the War Department.

By order of the President:

EDWIN M. STANTON,
Secretary of War.

BOND.

Know all men by these presents, that the —— railroad company, duly incorporated by the act of the ——, of the State of ——, by ——, its president, acting for and in behalf of said railroad company, do hereby acknowledge itself and its successors held and firmly bound unto the United States of America, in the full and just sum of —— dollars, lawful money of the United States, for which payment, well and truly to be made to the disbursing quartermaster of the United States Military Railroads, at his office in Nashville, or to such other disbursing quartermaster as may be designated by the War Department, within two years from the date of these presents, the said railroad company, by its president, hereby binds itself and its successors firmly by these presents.

Sealed with its corporate seal, attested by the signature of its president, and affixed by the express authority of its directors, this —— day of ——, in the year of our Lord one thousand eight hundred and sixty —— (186—).

The nature of the above obligation is such, that whereas the above-bounden railroad company has purchased and received, or shall receive, from the War Department of the United States, rolling-stock, iron rails, cross-ties, chairs, spikes, timber, and other materials for repairing and operating its railroad, in quantities, at prices, and to an amount and value which shall be evidenced by the receipts given for the same by the said railroad company to the proper officer of the said

War Department, upon a credit of two years from the date of these presents, payable in equal monthly installments, with interest at the rate of 7 3-10 per cent. per annum, within the said two years, either in cash to the disbursing quartermaster of the United States Military Railroads, at his office in Nashville, or to such other disbursing quartermaster as may be designated for this purpose by the War Department, or in transportation of the troops or military supplies of the United States, under the orders of the proper military authorities, at the rates of fare and tolls allowed for such service to Northern railroads; and whereas, the said railroad company desires, and by these presents intends, to secure to the United States the complete and punctual payment as aforesaid of the amounts which may be due for the said materials received or to be received by it from the United States:

Now, therefore, if the said railroad company shall well and truly pay as aforesaid, either in cash, in equal monthly installments, or in transportation as aforesaid, to the United States, within two years from the date of these presents, all that shall be due as aforesaid to the United States on account and in payment for all the materials received as aforesaid from the United States, then this obligation shall be void and of no effect.

But if the said railroad company shall fail to pay to the United States all or any portion of what may be due to the United States, on account of the said materials received from the United States, within two years from the date of these presents, either in cash as aforesaid, or in transportation as aforesaid, or shall fail to pay any of the monthly installments aforesaid punctually when due, then this obligation shall remain in full force and effect to the extent that may be necessary to fully repay to the United States for the full amount which may be due on account of the said materials so received as aforesaid, and all loss or damage which may have been incurred by the United States by reason of the said railroad company's failure to pay for the same, what shall be due therefor, when the same shall be due.

And as a further security for such payment and indemnity to the United States, the United States shall have a lien upon the property sold to said company; and in default of such complete and punctual payment of all moneys which may be due on account of the aforesaid purchase of materials, be fully authorized to take possession of and sell said property, and also to place in charge and control of the said company's railroad an agent of the said United States, who shall be fully empowered, and by these presents is fully empowered, in case of such default as aforesaid, to collect all the revenues of the said company, and apply the same to the payment to the United States of all the moneys which shall be due at the times of such application of such revenues to the United States for any such materials which shall have been delivered by the United States to the said railroad company, or by reason of any loss or injury to the United States resulting from such default in payment of the same. And the said company shall have no authority to sell or convey out of its possession, without the consent of the United States, first in writing obtained, any of the property referred to in this agreement, but shall hold and retain the same to the exclusive use of said company, in carrying on the business of transportation of persons and property over its line of road, until the whole is fully paid for as aforesaid.

In witness whereof the corporate seal of said railroad company is affixed hereto, by authority of its directors, and attested by its president.

——— ———.

Witness: ——— ———.

NOTE.—The amount of this bond to be double the valuation of the property sold and delivered. Internal revenue stamps should be affixed to the amount of fifty cents for every thousand dollars.

No. 78.

*Annual report of Col. Anson Stager, chief U. S. Military Telegraphs, for the fiscal year ending June 30, 1865.**

CLEVELAND, OHIO, *September 15, 1865.*

Maj. Gen. M. C. MEIGS,

Quartermaster-General U. S. Army, Washington, D. C.:

GENERAL: In obedience to General Orders, No. 39, Quartermaster-General's Department, Washington, D. C., July 1, 1865, I have the

* Another report, containing substantially the same information, was addressed to the Secretary of War September 15, 1865.

honor to submit my annual report of the operations and condition of U. S. Military Telegraphs for the fiscal year ending June 30, 1865, &c. I have the honor to hand you also herewith the reports of such of the officers serving under me as have been received up to this time. That of Capt. J. C. Van Duzer, marked A; Capt. R. C. Clowry, B; Capt. W. G. Fuller, C; Capt. W. L. Gross, D; Capt. J. R. Gilmore, E; Capt. S. G. Lynch, F. The report of Maj. Thomas T. Eckert has not yet reached me.* My annual report for 1864 was forwarded to your department in the latter part of October, 1864, accompanied by the reports of the several officers acting as assistant superintendents and assistant quartermasters, attached to this branch of the public service.

It has been my duty during the past year to act as chief officer of U. S. Military Telegraphs, having a general superintendence over all the lines, providing the necessary funds, and supervising the purchase of material required for the operation and construction of the same. I have been very ably and energetically assisted in the discharge of my duties as general superintendent of U. S. Military Telegraphs by the several officers acting as assistant superintendents in the various military departments, and I desire to accord to them the greater portion of whatever merit attaches to this branch of the public service. I have the honor to call attention to the reports of those officers, herewith transmitted, and to ask the consideration of the department to the merits of the officers respectively.

The demands of the proper military authorities for telegraphic communication have always been promptly answered, and, I believe, fully satisfied. The military telegraph, under the immediate charge of the several assistant superintendents thereof, has kept company with our armies wherever they have gone and upon all important expeditions, and it is a well-established fact that the mobility of the Army has been greatly accelerated by its usefulness and assistance.

The military telegraph has been an invaluable assistant in the construction and operation of the various military railroads. Trains have been run and many of the roads operated almost exclusively by telegraph. The military railroads and the military telegraph have been great auxiliaries to the gigantic and successful efforts of the Government in suppressing the rebellion.

The military telegraph has operated frequently in the field in conjunction with the Signal Corps, and has rendered efficient aid in this respect by diffusing information from advanced signal stations simultaneously to the headquarters of the commanding general and the different corps headquarters. The military telegraph could be made the means of establishing the Signal Corps of the Army for active operations upon a much more useful basis than heretofore. The telegraph depends not upon the atmosphere nor the weather, but flashes its thoughts alike unheeded, through storm or sunshine, darkness or light. I am, however, of the opinion that the field telegraph, which we have operated independently, as well as in connection with the Signal Corps, could be so perfected and operated as to completely and advantageously supplant the use of a signal corps for military operations.

In May, 1865, it was decided by the War Department that all commercial telegraph lines throughout the Southern States, lately in armed resistance to the U. S. authorities, should be supervised and controlled by the officers of the U. S. Military Telegraph, subject to

*But see Series I, Vol. LI, Part I, p. 261.

specified conditions favorable to the different telegraph companies, which privileges, however, were to be ignored under certain circumstances. Previous to cessation of hostilities these lines had been operated to a great extent by the rebel authorities, making it necessary, therefore, on account of the morale of the former employés and the peculiar power of the telegraph for public good or evil, for the Government to exercise its prerogative in regard to the operations of the lines referred to. Under the present arrangement the telegraph companies are called upon to repair their lines and put them in good working order, furnishing all labor and material therefor, the United States to be at no outlay beyond the expense of maintaining purely military lines and military stations. An account is to be kept of all Government business passing over the lines. The account, however, is not assumed as an indebtedness by the Government, but is left open for future consideration or settlement.

The amount of supplies which will be required for future operations of the military telegraph, so far as I am at present informed, will be such as is necessary only for maintaining the lines at present in use. It is supposed that the Government will require no more lines constructed, unless, perhaps, in Texas, or upon the Western frontier.

The amount of money expended during the year ending June 30, 1865, for the purchase of material and supplies required for the U. S. Military Telegraph was about $300,000. One hundred and thirty thousand dollars of this amount, however, was for the purchase of 285 miles of English submarine cable, the greater portion of which is still on hand. Probably not more than from $1,000 to $1,500 per month will hereafter be required for the purchase of necessary material and supplies.

So long as the military telegraph lines in present use are needed by the Government it will require about $75,000 per month to supply, maintain, and operate the same. As the usefulness of some of these telegraph lines to Government shall cease from time to time, and the lines are taken down or otherwise disposed of, the expenditures for maintaining the U. S. Military Telegraph will be proportionately reduced. A considerable revenue to Government will probably be derived from the sale of the material now on hand so soon as the same shall be of no further use to the Government. Such of the lines as may be located most advantageously for commercial purposes can undoubtedly be disposed of to the owners of the "telegraph right of patent" within the territory through which the lines pass and at a reasonable consideration. The less important lines can be taken down and the material sold.

The number of miles of land and submarine U. S. Military Telegraph lines in operation July 1, 1864, was, after deducting error in former report, as follows:

	Land.	Submarine.	Aggregate.
	Miles.	*Miles.*	*Miles.*
July 1, 1864	4,955¼	52¾	
Constructed during the year	3,246½	68¾	
In operation within the year	8,201¾	121½	8,323¼
Taken down or abandoned during the year	2,049	46¼	
In operation June 30, 1865	6,152¾	75¼	6,228

The 3,315¼ miles of line constructed during the year were built under the supervision of the following officers and within the departments specified, viz:

Maj. Thomas T. Eckert, assistant quartermaster, Department of the Potomac	1,217¾
Capt. J. R. Gilmore, assistant quartermaster, Department of the South	86¼
Capt. W. G. Fuller, assistant quartermaster, Department of the Gulf	228¼
Capt. J. C. Van Duzer, assistant quartermaster, Departments of Kentucky, Tennessee, and Mississippi	1,476
Capt. R. C. Clowry, assistant quartermaster, Departments of Missouri, Kansas, and Arkansas	307
Total	3,315¼

The lines in operation June 30, 1865, were under charge of the following officers, and located as mentioned, viz:

Location.	Name of officer.	Land.	Submarine.
		Miles.	*Miles.*
Department of the Potomac	Maj. Thomas T. Eckert	1,824¼	53½
Department of the South	Capt. J. R. Gilmore	140	13¼
Department of the Gulf	Capt. W. G. Fuller	56	5
Department of West Virginia	Capt. S. G. Lynch	303	½
Departments of Kentucky, Tennessee, and Mississippi	Capt. J. C. Van Duzer	2,127½	1¼
Departments of Missouri, Kansas, and Arkansas	Capt. R. C. Clowry	1,702	1¾
		6,152¾	75¼
Total		6,228	

It is estimated that from the commencement of the rebellion up to June 30, 1865, there has been constructed and operated about 15,000 miles of U. S. military telegraph—land, submarine, and field lines.

From May 1, 1861, up to December 31, 1862, $22,000 per month sufficed to construct and maintain U. S. military telegraphs. For the year 1863 about $38,500 per month was required for the same purpose. During the year 1864 the military telegraph was greatly extended and required about $93,500 per month. From May 1, 1861, to June 30, 1865, $2,655,500 has been received by me from the U. S. Treasury, and disbursed or transferred by me for the construction, maintenance, and operation of U. S. military telegraphs.

Herewith please find statement of public moneys received during the year, and Form A, embracing all the articles of property received by me during the same period. I have no occasion to use Forms B, C, CC, D, E, F, nor G.

I have the honor to be, general, very respectfully, your obedient servant,

ANSON STAGER,
Colonel and Chief U. S. Military Telegraph.

Statement of public moneys in possession of Col. A. Stager, assistant quartermaster, chief of U. S. Military Telegraphs, during the fiscal year ending June 30, 1865.

On hand July 1, 1864	$1,360,000.00	
Received from Treasury Department during the year	....	
Total received		$1,360,000.00
Expended during the year	149,304.72	
Transferred to officers during the year	1,210,695.28	
Remaining on hand June 30, 1865	....	
Total		1,360,000.00

Statement of quartermaster's property received by Col. A. Stager, chief quartermaster U. S. Military Telegraphs, for the fiscal year ending June 30, 1865.

English submarine cable purchased during the year ending June 30, 1865, 284 miles and 1,070 yards.

English submarine cable transferred during the year ending June 30, 1865, 284 miles and 1,070 yards.

A.*

No. 79.

Annual report of Maj. Thomas T. Eckert, assistant quartermaster and assistant superintendent U. S. Military Telegraph, for the fiscal year ending June 30, 1865.†

Statement of public moneys received and disbursed during the year ending June 30, 1865, by Maj. Thomas T. Eckert, assistant quartermaster, Washington, D. C.

On hand July 1, 1864	$3,306.82
Received from officers during the year	228,000.00
Total	231,306.82
Expended during the year	185,035.04
Transferred to other officers during the year	24,523.08
Remaining on hand June 30, 1865	21,745.70
Total	231,306.82

The balance on hand is deposited in the U. S. Treasury.

Statements embraced in Forms C, CC, D, E, F, and G do not "come under the scope of my duties."

Statement of U. S. military telegraph lines in operation July 1, 1864, and constructed and taken down during the year ending June 30, 1865, by direction of Thomas T. Eckert, major and assistant superintendent.

Between what points.	In operation during the year.	Taken down during the year.	In operation July 1, 1865.	Land line.	Submarine cable.
In operation July 1, 1864.	*Miles.*	*Miles.*	*Miles.*	*Miles.*	*Miles.*
Washington depot and Alexandria	9		9	9	
Washington depot and Harper's Ferry via Point of Rocks	75		75	75	
Washington depot and Fort Corcoran, six wires	15		15	15	
Washington City wires, 8, 2½, 2, 4	16½		16½	16½	
Washington City and Point Lookout, Md	100		100	100	
Georgetown Aqueduct and Tennallytown, two wires	3		3	3	
Georgetown Aqueduct and water station, six wires	3		3	3	
Alexandria City wires, 4, 2, 3	9		9	9	
Alexandria and Manassas Junction via Court-House	32		32	32	
Alexandria and Fort Corcoran, two wires	14		14	14	
Fort Corcoran and Seminary	9	2	7	7	
Wilmington, Del., and Cherrystone Point, Va	158		158	158	
Crossing streams on Eastern Shore line (cable)	1¾		1¾		1¾
Cherrystone Point and Back Creek Light-House (cable)	23		23		23
Back Creek Light-House and Fort Monroe	7		7	7	
Fort Monroe and Yorktown	27		27	27	
Yorktown and Fort Magruder	12		12	12	
Fort Magruder and Jamestown Island	10	10			
Jamestown Island and Swan's Point (cable)	2½	2½			
Swan's Point and Fort Powhatan	25		25	25	
Fort Powhatan and Bermuda Hundred	23		23	23	
Loop at City Point	4		4	4	

* For Van Duzer's report (here omitted), see Series I, Vol. LII, Part I, p. 694.

† Here omitted, but see Series I, Vol. LI, Part I, p. 261.

Statement of U. S. military telegraph lines in operation July 1, 1864, and constructed and taken down during the year ending June 30, 1865, &c.—Cont'd.

Between what points.	In operation during the year.	Taken down during the year.	In operation July 1, 1865.	Land line.	Submarine cable.
In operation July 1, 1864—Continued.	*Miles.*	*Miles.*	*Miles.*	*Miles.*	*Miles.*
City Point and headquarters Ninth Army Corps	12	8	4	4	....
Former headquarters of General Gillmore to headquarters of General Foster.	8½	....	8½	8½	....
Loop at Newport News	9	....	9	9	....
Newport News and Sewell's Point (cable)	4	....	4	....	4
Sewell's Point and Portsmouth	11	....	11	11	....
Portsmouth and Suffolk	17	....	17	17	....
Wilmington and Middletown, Del	25¾	....	25¾	25¾	....
Port Tobacco and Maryland Point	28	....	28	28	....
Beaufort and Batchelder's Creek, N. C	42	....	42	42	....
Constructed during the fiscal year 1865.					
Pitkin Station and City Point	8	....	8	8	....
Jamestown Island and Fort Powhatan (cable)	22	22	....	....	....
Field line in Army of the Potomac	20	20	....	....	....
Pitkin Station and General Warren's headquarters	10	10	....	....	....
Across Appomattox River (cable)	¼	....	¼	....	¼
Cedar Level and headquarters Army of the Potomac	14	14	....	....	....
Deep Bottom and New Market road	10	3	7	7	....
Alexandria and Catlett's Station	39	39	....	....	....
Manassas Junction and Piedmont	25	25	....	....	....
Warren Station and Patrick Station	5	....	5	5	....
Headquarters Army of the James and Fort Harrison	4	....	4	4	....
Harper's Ferry and Winchester	31	....	31	31	....
Winchester and General Sheridan's headquarters	4	4	....	....	....
Field wire in Army of the Potomac	8	8	....	....	....
Pitkin Station and Petersburg, two wires	10	....	10	10	....
Jones' Landing and headquarters Army of the James	3½	....	3½	3½	....
Berlin, Md., and Lovettsville, Va	8	8	....	....	....
Warren Station and headquarters Second Army Corps	11	....	11	11	....
Field wire in Army of the Potomac	10	10	....	....	....
Patrick Station and Petersburg	6	....	6	6	....
Field wire in Army of the Potomac	40	40	....	....	....
Wilmington, N. C., and Fort Fisher	22	....	22	22	....
Wilmington, N. C., and Nine-Mile Station	9	....	9	9	....
Batchelder's Creek and Kinston, N. C	24	....	24	24	....
Petersburg and Weldon	65	....	65	65	....
Richmond and Petersburg	22	....	22	22	....
Manchester and Petersburg (railroad wire)	22	....	22	22	....
Kinston and Greensborough, N. C	180	....	180	180	....
Goldsborough and Northeast Station	75	....	75	75	....
Richmond and Washington via Fredericksburg	130	....	130	130	....
Richmond and Danville	140	....	140	140	....
Richmond and Burkeville	55	....	55	55	....
War Department and Soldiers' Home	5	....	5	5	....
Alexandria and Richmond	120	....	120	120	....
Richmond and Williamsburg	60	....	60	60	....
Williamsburg and Fort Magruder	1	....	1	1	....
Total	1,954¾	225½	1,729¼	1,700¼	29

B—No. 80.

Report of Capt. R. C. Clowry, assistant quartermaster, for the fiscal year ending June 30, 1865.

U. S. MIL. TELEGRAPH, ASST. QUARTERMASTER'S OFFICE,
Saint Louis, Mo., July 31, 1865.

Col. ANSON STAGER,
Assistant Quartermaster, Chief U. S. Military Telegraph:

COLONEL: I have the honor to transmit herewith my annual report for the fiscal year ending June 30, 1865, comprising—

A statement of public money received, expended, and transferred.

A statement of quartermaster's property on hand, received from officers, purchased, manufactured, captured, taken up, &c., issued and transferred, sold, died, lost, expended, &c.

A statement of clothing, camp and garrison equipage, ditto, ditto.

A statement of the number of miles of land and submarine telegraph line constructed, repaired, abandoned, &c., and a statement of the number of telegrams transmitted over said line.

Since my last annual report I have been on duty as assistant quartermaster and assistant superintendent U. S. Military Telegraph from June 30, 1864, to September 30, 1864, in charge of lines in Department of Arkansas, and from October 1, 1864, to June 30, 1865, in charge of lines in Departments of Missouri, Kansas, and Arkansas, as per your orders.

My monthly and annual "line and cable reports" give a detailed statement of the number of miles of line constructed, repaired, abandoned, &c.

Although the lines under my control for the last nine months of the year ending June 30, 1865, embrace a large territory, we have managed to keep them almost constantly in operation, day and night, to the full satisfaction of all officers from the division to the post commanders.

As the country became more settled and peaceable I gradually reduced my expenses, and, although I have always had sufficient force for emergencies, I have rarely permitted a man to be idle a single day.

Since I have had charge of the lines in Missouri, Kansas, and Arkansas (1,702 miles) I have operated, constructed, and repaired them at about an average cost of $15,000 per month, and I am weekly reducing expenses without detriment to the service.

When it is taken into consideration that these lines are all single—that is, one wire on one set of poles (which requires twice as many operators and repairers as double wires)—and that the country has been full of thieving, wire-cutting guerrillas, while U. S. troops have been "few and far between," I think that my expense account will compare favorably with any other telegraphic department in the United States.

Very respectfully, your obedient servant,

R. C. CLOWRY,

Capt., A. Q. M., and Asst. Supt. U. S. Military Telegraphs, Missouri, Kansas, and Arkansas.

Statement of public moneys received, transferred, and expended during the fiscal year ending June 30, 1865, by Capt. R. C. Clowry, assistant quartermaster and assistant superintendent U. S. Military Telegraphs, Departments of Missouri, Kansas, and Arkansas.

On hand July 1, 1864	$4,984.40
Received from officers during the year	135,986.72
Received from sales of clothing	123.56
Received for transmission of private telegrams in Department of Arkansas.	3,809.50
Total	144,904.18
Expended during the year	130,929.06
Transferred to other officers during the year	856.22
Remaining on hand June 30, 1865	13,118.90
Total	144,904.18

The balance on hand is deposited in my safe at Little Rock, Ark.

I certify that the above statement is correct.

R. C. CLOWRY,

Captain and A. Q. M., Asst. Superintendent U. S. Military Telegraphs.

A.—*Statement of quartermasters' property for the fiscal year ending June 30, 1865, by Capt. R. C. Clowry, assistant quartermaster and assistant superintendent U. S. Military Telegraphs.**

B.—*Statement of clothing and camp and garrison equipage for the fiscal year ending June 30, 1865, by Capt. R. C. Clowry, assistant quartermaster and assistant superintendent U. S. Military Telegraphs.**

Statement of the number of miles of land and submarine telegraph line constructed in the Departments of Missouri, Kansas, and Arkansas, during the fiscal year ending June 30, 1865, by Capt. R. C. Clowry, assistant quartermaster and assistant superintendent U. S. Military Telegraphs.

	Miles.
Lines in operation July 1, 1864	211
Lines received during the year	1,320
Lines constructed and repaired during the year	290
Total	1,821
Deduct lines abandoned during the year	119
	1,702
Lines in operation June 30, 1865:	
From Saint Louis, Mo., to Fort Smith, Ark	403
From Saint Louis, Mo., to New Madrid, Mo	207
From Bloomfield, Mo., to Cape Girardeau, Mo	45
From Pilot Knob, Mo., to Patterson, Mo	28
From Saint Louis, Mo., to Macon, Mo	168
From Jefferson City, Mo., to Syracuse, Mo	43
From Allen via Boonville and Weston to Saint Joseph, Mo	296
From Fort Leavenworth, Kans., to Fort Scott, Kans	120
From Saint Louis, Mo., to City Lines, Mo	10
From Little Rock, Ark., to mouth of White River, Ark	152
From Little Rock, Ark., to Pine Bluff, Ark	45
From Little Rock, Ark., to Fort Smith, Ark	185
Total	1,702
Cable on hand June 30, 1864	1¼
Cable received during the year ending June 30, 1865	1
Cable laid and recovered during the year ending June 30, 1865	
Total	2¼
Cable lost during the year ending June 30, 1864, to be deducted	½
Cable in operation June 30, 1865	1¾
Cables in operation June 30, 1865:	
From Ferry Landing, Mo., to Saint Charles, Mo	1
From Boonville, Mo., to opposite shore, Missouri River	¾
Total	1¾

R. C. CLOWRY,
Captain and Assistant Quartermaster.

No. 81.

Second annual report of Capt. W. G. Fuller, assistant quartermaster of volunteers.

NEW ORLEANS, LA., *July 25, 1865.*

The close of the fiscal year ending June 30, 1864, found me in charge of military telegraph lines in the Department of the Tennessee, with headquarters at Memphis, Tenn.

*Omitted.

July 20, 1864, I received orders from Col. Anson Stager, chief of Military Telegraphs, to proceed to New Orleans, La., and relieve Capt. C. S. Bulkley, assistant quartermaster and assistant superintendent of Military Telegraphs, in the Military Division of West Mississippi. After transferring the portions of lines under my charge lying in the District of Cairo to Capt. S. Bruch, of Louisville, Ky., and three days at home on leave, I proceeded to New Orleans, and received the transfer from Captain Bulkley on the 1st day of August, 1864. During the month of August, 1864, by order of Major-General Washburn, a line of telegraph was constructed from Grand Junction, Tenn., to Abbeville, Miss., forty-five miles; about half of the poles of an old line were used, and all new wire.

September 5 received an order from Major-General Canby to lay a submarine cable between Forts Morgan and Gaines, Mobile Bay. September 8 left New Orleans in person with the cable. September 11 succeeded in laying the cable between Forts Morgan and Gaines, using 23,530 feet of No. 9 iron wire cable, galvanized armor. During the month of September General Washburn's forces fell back from Abbeville, Miss., toward Memphis, abandoning the lines from Abbeville to Grand Junction, and from Saulsbury, Tenn., to White's Station, Tenn. Ninety-seven miles of wire was lost, it being operated until the last moment, and Forrest's forces advancing as fast as General Washburn's fell back.

In October, 1864, constructed a line from Fort Morgan, Ala., to Pilot Town, Ala., four miles. The submarine cable across Pass Chef Menteur, at Fort Macomb, La., failed and could not be resuscitated. A new cable 800 feet long was laid.

In November, 1864, constructed a line from headquarters, Memphis, Tenn., to outpost stations, five miles; repaired the New Orleans and Fort Pike line, putting up a large number of new poles, and abandoned the line from White's Station to Memphis, Tenn.; also received orders from Major-General Canby to survey a route for a telegraph line from New Orleans to Ship Island, and thence to Forts Gaines and Morgan, Mobile Bay; made the survey in person on tug Blossom.

December 6, 1864, made report to General Canby that the route for a line from New Orleans to Ship Island and Fort Morgan could be made available for temporary purposes, but was too difficult a route for a permanent line; that it would require eleven submarine crossings between New Orleans and Ship Island, over twenty-three miles in length in all.

December 9 received orders from General Canby to proceed with the construction of the line from New Orleans to Ship Island. Constructed a loop in Baton Rouge line to Plaquemine, La., ten miles long, and laid 150 feet of cable across Taliaferro Canal, on Balize line.

December 15 received twenty miles of "Red Sea" submarine cable, but was unable to pass a current through it. After testing it in about a dozen places the imperfect spot was discovered. No sign of imperfection could be seen in the armor wires, but the conductor was parted at least two inches and the gutta-percha covering whittled. But very little progress was made upon the Ship Island line during December for want of water transportation.

In January, 1865, reconstructed the line from Memphis, Tenn., to Collierville, Tenn., twenty-four miles, and abandoned it again after a few days' operations, by order of General Washburn.

January 7 the cable between Forts Morgan and Gaines was broken by a bark dragging her anchors over it in a gale.

January 18, repaired the cable in person. Constructed line from Fort Macomb to Cat Island, forty-five miles. This line was built across marshes which overflow at high tide, and poles had to be rafted along the shore, water being too shallow for steamers. A very difficult line to construct.

In February, 1865, transferred the Memphis, Tenn., and outpost lines to Capt. S. Bruch, assistant quartermaster, Louisville, Ky.; completed the land portion of line from Ship Island across Horn Island, Petit Bois Island, Hurricane Island, and Dauphin Island, to Fort Gaines, forty-five miles, and laid the following submarine cables: Across Lake Borgne, nine miles in length; across Bayous Catharine, Biloxi, Little Cable, Dixon, False Bay, Nine-Mile Bayou, Boudreau, Three-Mile Bayou, Lagoon Jones, Grand Pass, Blind Bay, Johnson's, Dead Man's Bayou, and the pass between Isle du Pied and Cat Island, four miles and a half in length, and between Cat and Ship Islands, six miles and a half; total, 23 miles 1,540 feet. The cable used was "Red Sea" cable for the long crossings, and cable prepared from old core at New Orleans, armored with worthless wire taken down from abandoned lines.

In March, 1865, extended line from Navy Cove, Mobile Bay, to Fish River, thirty-five miles, which was soon after abandoned, and a field line constructed between each headquarters, surrounding Spanish Fort and Fort Blakely, fifteen miles. These lines were run with the pack-mule train, and did valuable service. Constructed a line from New Orleans to Hickox Landing, eight miles, and laid submarine cables from Ship Island to Horn Island, twelve miles, and from Horn Island to Petit Bois Island, four miles. This exhausted all the submarine cable on hand that could be made available. The laying of these cables was very much delayed by hard and continuous southeasterly gales, and the "Red Sea" cable proved too frail for the strong currents and quicksands of these island passes. In "dead" water, across Lake Borgne, it worked perfectly; and when first laid across the island passes it worked clear and fine, but the "three-day storms," such as frequent this coast, destroyed the cable ends with each recurrence in spite of all the wrappings and preventives that could be placed upon them with the means at hand. I risked the lives of myself and men several times in the surf in endeavoring to keep the cables in working order and make them perform the designed mission. I have the consciousness that everything was done that promised success to accomplish the work of keeping New Orleans and the army advancing up Mobile Bay in telegraphic communication, but the frail nature of the armor wires covering the "Red Sea" cable and the action of the currents and quicksands in the island passes could not be overcome, nor could the constant and severe southeasterly gales, which prevailed to a very unusual extent during this season, be avoided. To these causes alone can the slow progress of the work and final failure of the scheme be attributed.

The cable across the Mississippi River at New Orleans was destroyed this month by the sloop-of-war Portsmouth dragging her anchors across it.

In April, 1865, constructed a line from Mobile, Ala., to Spring Hill, eight miles, and repaired the line from Mobile to Spanish Fort, and from Mobile to Citronelle, and took down the lines from Navy Cove to Fish River, and surrounding Forts Spanish and Blakely. Laid a new cable across the Mississippi River at New Orleans, which was a second time destroyed by the sloop-of-war Portsmouth dragging her anchors.

In May, 1865, constructed lines from Mobile, Ala., to Fort Pike, La., 130 miles, all new line, and from Baton Rouge to Clinton, La., forty-three miles, all new line, and repaired lines throughout Mississippi and Alabama, using about 150 miles of new wire upon them; also took up lines from Mobile to Spanish Fort, and from Fort Macomb, La., to Fort Gaines, Ala. Much of the line from Baton Rouge, La., to the mouth of Red River, upon the west bank of the Mississippi, was washed away by extensive crevasses. Much of the wire was saved and coiled up for future use. During the month eleven cables were laid upon the line between Fort Pike and Mobile, upward of thirteen miles in length, and most of the cable between Fort Macomb and Mobile Bay was taken up and saved.

In June, 1865, 725 miles of line in Texas were repaired and put in operation, mostly by their former managers, under the direction of my agents sent to Galveston, Houston, and Shreveport. The necessary material was ordered and the work commenced upon a line extending from Shreveport, La., to Vicksburg, Miss., and also upon a line extending from Houston, Tex., via Hempstead, Brenham, La Grange, Bastrop, Austin, San Marco, New Brunfels, to San Antonio. Upon the completion of these lines, which are being pushed forward rapidly, nearly all the important sections of Texas will be in direct communication with the other States of the Union. I give a general summary of the work performed during this fiscal year, as follows:

Lines in operation July 1, 1864:	Miles.
From Cairo, Ill., to Paducah, Ky	60
From Memphis, Tenn., to outposts and Saulsbury	62
From Cairo, Ill., to Moscow, Ky	42
Total	164

Cables in operation July 1, 1864:	Feet.
From Cairo, Ill., to Kentucky shore	3,500
From Paducah, Ky., to Illinois shore	3,300
Total	6,800

Men employed July 1, 1864:	
Operators	34
Foreman	1
Laborers	19
Clerk	1
Repairers	16
Total	71

Lines constructed during the year:	Miles.
From Grand Junction, Tenn., to Abbeville, Miss	45
From Fort Morgan, Ala., to Pilot Town, Ala	4
From Memphis, Tenn., to outposts	5
Loop from Morganza line to Plaquemine, La	10
From Fort Macomb, La., to Cat Island	45
From Ship Island to Fort Gaines	45
From Navy Cove, Ala., to Fish River	35
From Stark's Landing, Ala., to Fort Blakely	15
From New Orleans, La., to Hickox Landing	8
From Mobile, Ala., to Spring Hill, Ala	8
From Mobile, Ala., to Fort Pike, La	130
From Baton Rouge, La., to Clinton, La	43
Total	393

Lines reconstructed and repaired during the year:	Miles.
From Memphis, Tenn., to Collierville, Tenn	24
From Mobile, Ala., to Spanish Fort, Ala	18
From Mobile, Ala., to Citronelle, Ala	35
From Citronelle, Ala., to Corinth, Miss	293
From Meridian, Miss., to Vicksburg, Miss	140
From Pass Manchac, La., to Grand Junction	356
From Grenada, Miss., to Senatobia, Miss	80
From Osyka, Miss., to Woodville, Miss	70
From Mobile, Ala., to Montgomery, Ala	162
From Montgomery, Ala., to West Point, Ga	88
From Opelika, Ala., to Columbus, Ga	30
From West Point, Ga., to Atlanta, Ga	87
From Meridian, Miss., to Montgomery, Ala	136
From Selma, Ala., to Talladega, Ala	75
From Camden, Ark., to Shreveport, La	110
From Shreveport, La., to Houston, Tex	335
From Galveston, Tex., to Houston, Tex	80
From Houston, Tex., to Orange, Tex	200
Total	2,319

Lines abandoned and taken down during the year:	Miles.
From Grand Junction, Miss., to Abbeville, Miss	45
From Saulsbury, Tenn., to White's Station, Tenn	52
From Memphis, Tenn., to White's Station, Tenn	5
From Memphis, Tenn., to Collierville, Tenn	24
From Navy Cove, Ala., to Fish River, Ala	35
From Stark's Landing, Ala., to Fort Blakely, Ala	15
From Mobile, Ala., to Spanish Fort, Ala	18
From Baton Rouge, La., to the mouth of Red River	77
From Fort Morgan, Ala., to Pilot Town, Ala	4
From Mobile, Ala., to Spring Hill, Ala	8
From Fort Macomb, La., to Fort Gaines, Ala	90
From Baton Rouge, La., to Port Hudson, La., on the west bank of the river	25
Total	398

Lines transferred to other officers during the year:	Miles.
From Cairo, Ill., to Paducah, Ky	60
From Cairo, Ill., to Moscow, Ky	42
From Memphis, Tenn., to outposts	10
Total	112

Cables laid and recovered during the year:	Miles.	Feet.
Two cables across Southwest Pass of Mississippi River		4,500
From Fort Morgan, Ala., to Fort Gaines, Ala		23,530
Across Chef Menteur Pass at Fort Macomb, La		1,200
Across Taliaferro Canal, La		150
From Fort Macomb, La., to Ship Island	23	1,540
From Ship Island to Horn Island	12	
From Horn Island to Petit Bois Island	4	
From New Orleans, La., to Algiers, La	1	
From Fort Pike to Mobile, Ala	13	560
Total	58	5,080

Cables lost and destroyed during the year:		
Two cables across Southwest Pass of Mississippi River		4,401
Across Chef Menteur Pass at Fort Macomb, La		800
From New Orleans, La., to Algiers, La	1	
From New Orleans, La., to Algiers, La	1	
Between Fort Macomb, La., and Petit Bois Island	5	640
Total	8	561

	Miles.	Feet.
Cables transferred during the year:		
From Cairo, Ill., to Kentucky shore		3,500
From Paducah, Ky., to Illinois shore		3,300
Total	1	1,520
Cables taken up during the year:		
From Fort Macomb, La., to Petit Bois Island	34	900

RECAPITULATION.

		Miles.
Lines in operation July 1, 1864		164
Lines constructed during the year		393
Lines repaired during the year		2,319
Lines received from officers		615
		3,491
Lines abandoned and taken down during the year	398	
Lines transferred during the year	112	
		510
Lines in operation June 30, 1865		2,981

	Miles.	Feet.
Cables in operation July 1, 1864	1	1,520
Cables laid and recovered during the year	58	5,080
Cables received from officers	6	4,438
	67	478
Cables lost and destroyed	8	561
Cables taken up	34	900
Cables transferred	1	1,520
	43	2,981
Cables in operation June 30, 1865	23	2,777

Monthly average of men employed during the year:	
Operators	59
Clerks	4
Teamsters	6
Laborers	67
Boatmen	4
Messengers	5
Foremen	5
Repairers	19
Artisans	5
Total	174

I have the honor to be, most respectfully, your obedient servant,

W. G. FULLER,

Capt. and Asst. Q. M. Vols., Asst. Supt. U. S. Mil. Telegraphs.

Statement of public moneys on hand, received, and disbursed during the fiscal year ending June 30, 1865, by Capt. W. G. Fuller, assistant quartermaster.

Amount on hand July 1, 1864	$2,139.63	
Amount received from officers during the year	97,356.71	
Total amount on hand and received during the year		$99,496.34
Amount expended during the year	99,450.09	
Total amount expended and transferred during the year		99,450.09
Balance remaining on hand June 30, 1865		46.25

I certify that the above is a true and correct statement, and that the balance on hand is deposited in my office.

W. G. FULLER,
Captain and Assistant Quartermaster Volunteers.

*Statement of quartermaster's property for the fiscal year ending June 30, 1865.**

*Statement of clothing, camp and garrison equipage for the fiscal year ending June 30, 1865.**

No. 82.

HDQRS. U. S. MIL. TEL., MIL. DIV. OF THE GULF,
New Orleans, August 23, 1865.

Maj. Gen. M. C. MEIGS,
Quartermaster-General U. S. Army, Washington, D. C.:

GENERAL: In obedience to General Orders, No. 39, dated at your office July 1, 1865, I have the honor to submit the following detailed report of my official action during the fiscal year ending June 30, 1865, and to inclose herewith a statement of public moneys in the prescribed form, together with Statements A and B, which are all that are required by the operations of my office:

My annual report for the fiscal year ending June 30, 1864, was mailed from Danville, Ky., October 13, 1864, in which will be found a detailed account of my official action prior to July 1, 1864, from the time last above mentioned until June 22, 1865. I continued on duty as assistant superintendent U. S. Military Telegraph, headquarters at Danville, Ky., my jurisdiction embracing Central and Eastern Kentucky and East Tennessee. With the exception of a few insignificant guerrilla raids, the lines under my control have not been molested by the enemy during the year.

The following U. S. military telegraph lines were in operation under my charge July 1, 1864:

	Miles.
From Mount Sterling, via Lexington and Danville, to Camp Burnside, Ky	127
From Lebanon, Ky., via Danville and Cumberland Gap, to Knoxville, Tenn	216
From Lebanon, Ky., via Columbia, to Burkesville, Ky	67
Total in operation July 1, 1864	410

During the year the following lines have been constructed and repaired:

	Miles.
From Lexington, Ky., to Richmond, Ky	26
Connecting fortifications in and around Knoxville, Tenn	4
From Columbus, Ky., to Burkesville, Ky	30
Total constructed and repaired	60

During the year the following lines have been abandoned:

	Miles.
From Camp Burnside, Ky., to Somerset, Ky	7
From Burkesville, Ky., to Columbia, Ky	30
Connecting fortifications in and around Knoxville, Tenn	4
Total abandoned	41

The following U. S. military telegraph lines were in operation at the close of the year, June 30, 1865:

*Omitted.

	Miles.
From Mount Sterling, Ky., via Lexington and Danville, to Somerset, Ky	120
From Lebanon, Ky., via Danville and Cumberland Gap, to Knoxville, Tenn	216
From Lebanon, Ky., to Burkesville, Ky	67
From Lexington, Ky., to Richmond, Ky	26
Total in operation June 30, 1865	429

RECAPITULATION.

	Miles.
Lines in operation June 30, 1864	410
Lines constructed and repaired during the year	60
Total	470
Deduct lines abandoned during the year	41
Total in operation June 30, 1865	429

My headquarters have been during the entire year at Danville, Ky. Have engaged in no marches, battles, sieges, or skirmishes. Beyond the steady, uniform assistance I was able to afford the military authorities by supplying them with a quick, reliable means of communication, but little has been required within my jurisdiction. My operation on the lines of the enemy in the months of December, 1864, and January, 1865, in Southwestern Virginia, however, are deserving of mention.

Mr. E. T. Chapman, under my instructions, accompanied Major-General Stoneman on his celebrated raid in the capacity of cipher clerk and operator. The truly valuable assistance he rendered the expedition was duly acknowledged by the second officer in command, Maj. Gen. S. G. Burbridge. Indeed, there can be little doubt that the entire success of the expedition resulted from the invaluable information as to the position and numbers of the enemy which Mr. Chapman obtained while he held the telegraph office at Bristol. For several hours he held the office while dispatches were passing to and from General Breckinridge and his subordinates, which he carefully copied and laid before General Stoneman. By causing the regular operator at that place, whom he captured in his office, to manipulate the instrument, and dictating to him what should be said, Mr. Chapman was enabled to deceive the operators at Lynchburg and Richmond, and received a long press report from Richmond and gathered much valuable information.

The general condition of the lines under my control was much better at the close than at the commencement of the year. A great deal of pains has been taken in their repairs, and for steady, constant working through all kinds of weather I challenge comparison with any military telegraph lines. One thing in particular I desire to call the department's attention to, and that is the very small cost of maintaining so extended a district as that under my control. Not a man was employed that could be dispensed with nor a dollar expended unnecessarily. When, therefore, the general orders for retrenchment were received I was unable to operate the lines at a less cost than I had been doing.

On the 22d of June, 1865, I received an order from Col. Anson Stager, chief of the U. S. Military Telegraph Corps, directing me to turn over my public property and employés to Capt. John C. Van Duzer, assistant quartermaster and assistant superintendent U. S. Military Telegraphs, Nashville, Tenn., and to relieve Capt. W. G. Fuller, assistant quartermaster and assistant superintendent U. S. Military Telegraphs, New Orleans, La., and assume the control of the lines in charge of that officer. From the 22d of June to the 30th of

June, 1865, I was engaged in making the transfer to Captain Van Duzer.

All of which is respectfully submitted.

Very respectfully, general, your obedient servant,

W. L. GROSS,

Capt. and A. Q. M., and Asst. Supt. U. S. Military Telegraphs.

Statement of public moneys for the fiscal year ending June 30, 1865, by Capt. W. L. Gross, assistant quartermaster and assistant superintendent U. S. Military Telegraphs, at New Orleans, La.

On hand July 1, 1864	$4,388.68
Received from officers during the year	71,881.21
Total	76,269.89
Expended during the year	61,168.24
Remaining on hand June 30, 1865	15,101.65
Total	76,269.89

The amount remaining on hand June 30, 1865, was in my possession, there being at that time no available depository of public moneys at hand.

I certify that the above statements are correct.

W. L. GROSS,

Capt. and Asst. Q. M., and Asst. Supt. U. S. Military Telegraphs.

*Statement of quartermaster's property for the fiscal year ending June 30, 1865, in the possession of Capt. W. L. Gross, assistant quartermaster and assistant superintendent U. S. Military Telegraphs at New Orleans, La.**

*Statement of clothing and camp and garrison equipage for the fiscal year ending June 30, 1865, by Capt. W. L. Gross, assistant quartermaster and assistant superintendent U. S. Military Telegraphs at New Orleans, La.**

No. 83.

OFFICE A. Q. M. AND ASST. SUPT. U. S. MIL. TEL.,
HEADQUARTERS DEPARTMENT OF SOUTH CAROLINA,
Hilton Head, S. C., August 12, 1865.

Col. ANSON STAGER,
A. Q. M. and Asst. Supt. U. S. Military Telegraphs:

COLONEL: In compliance with General Orders, No. 39, Quartermaster-General's Office, Washington, D. C., July 1, 1865, I have the honor to report as follows:

On the 28th of July, 1862, I was mustered into the service of the United States as a private in Company A, One hundred and twenty-sixth regiment Pennsylvania Volunteers, First Brigade, Third Division, Fifth Army Corps.

December 23, 1862, reported to Maj. Thomas T. Eckert, assistant quartermaster and assistant superintendent U. S. Military Telegraphs, in compliance with Special Orders, No. 397, War Department, Adjutant-General's Office, series of 1862; was assigned to duty as operator at Hagerstown, Md. February 13, 1863, in compliance with orders from Maj. T. T. Eckert, reported for duty as operator at Fortress Monroe, Va. May 14, 1863, in compliance with orders from Maj. T. T. Eckert, reported to L. F. Sheldon, assistant superintendent U. S. Military Telegraphs, Department of the South, and was assigned to duty as chief operator of the department. June 14, 1863, in compliance with orders from L. F. Sheldon, assistant superintendent, I proceeded to New Berne, N. C., and constructed a line from that city to the headquarters of the various sub-districts

*Omitted.

of the District of North Carolina, remaining in charge of said line until November 3, 1864, when I was appointed as assistant quartermaster of volunteers, with the rank of captain, and ordered to report to Maj. T. T. Eckert, assistant quartermaster and assistant superintendent U. S. Military Telegraphs. December 5, 1864, in compliance with orders from Major Eckert, I relieved Capt. L. F. Sheldon, assistant quartermaster and assistant superintendent U. S. Military Telegraphs, and took charge of the lines in this department. By order of Maj. Gen. John G. Foster, commanding Department of the South, I immediately proceeded to construct a line of telegraph from Deveaux's Neck to the headquarters of Brigadier-General Hatch, commanding Provisional Brigade, to facilitate operations against the enemy at Pocotaligo, S. C. December 18, 1864, by order of Major-General Foster, I reported to Major-General Sherman, at his headquarters near King's Bridge, Ga., to build such lines as he might require in his operations against Savannah, Ga. By order of Major-General Sherman I repaired, constructed, and operated lines from his headquarters in Savannah to the headquarters of General Hazen, near Fort McAllister, to the headquarters of General Kilpatrick, on the Ogeechee road, and to Fort Pulaski, Ga., and from Port Royal Ferry to Pocotaligo, S. C. The building and operation of these and other lines in this department, extending, as they do, through forest, swamp, and river, was attended with almost insurmountable difficulties, and the work was greatly retarded by the troops, who frequently destroyed the lines for miles, using the poles for firewood.

In May last, in compliance with orders from Maj. Thomas T. Eckert, I assumed control of all telegraph lines in the States of South Carolina and Georgia, north to Charlotte, N. C., and west to Montgomery, Ala. Most of these lines had been destroyed by General Sherman's army in its march through the country, and the railroads along which they were built having been destroyed at the same time, the repair and reconstruction of the lines has been a difficult and laborious work. It is progressing, however, as rapidly as circumstances will permit, and it is hoped that before the 1st of September next all the lines in these States will be in reliable working order.

Referring to the annexed statements as an exhibit of their extent, &c.

I have the honor to be, colonel, very respectfully, your obedient servant,

JAMES R. GILMORE,

Capt. and A. Q. M., and Asst. Supt. U. S. Military Telegraphs.

Statement of the number of miles of telegraph lines, to and from what points constructed or repaired and operated, under my control since May 1, 1865, not borne on Form A.

	Miles.
From Wilmington, N. C., to Columbia, S. C	196
From Charlotte, N. C., to Columbia, S. C	109
From Charleston, S. C., to Darlington, S. C	112
From Charleston, S. C., to Kingsville, S. C	105
From Charleston, S. C., to Savannah, Ga	104
From Augusta, Ga., to Savannah, Ga	132
From Augusta, Ga., to Macon, Ga	164
From Macon, Ga., to Atlanta, Ga	103
From Atlanta, Ga., to Montgomery, Ala	175
From Macon, Ga., to Opelika via Columbus	128
From Tallahassee, Fla., to Jacksonville, Fla	175
Total	1,503

Statement of public moneys for fiscal year ending June 30, 1865.

Received from officers during the year	$11,118.68
Expended during the year	11,038.50
Remaining on hand June 30, 1865	80.18

The balance on hand is deposited as follows:

Eighty dollars and eighteen cents deposited in a safe in my office at Hilton, Head, S. C.

A.—*Statement of quartermaster's property for the fiscal year ending June 30, 1865.**

E.—*Statement of clothing and camp and garrison equipage for the fiscal year ending June 30, 1865.**

No. 84.

Annual report of Capt. S. G. Lynch, assistant quartermaster and assistant superintendent of U. S. Military Telegraphs, Department of West Virginia, for the fiscal year ending June 30, 1865.

CLEVELAND, OHIO, *September 1, 1865.*

Maj. Gen. M. C. MEIGS,
Quartermaster-General U. S. Army, Washington, D. C.:

GENERAL: I have the honor to submit to your department, through Col. A. Stager, chief, &c. (pursuant to General Orders, No. 39, Quartermaster-General's Department), my annual report for the fiscal year ending June 30, 1865. My annual report for 1864 was rendered to your department through Col. A. Stager, chief of U. S. Military Telegraphs, in the latter part of October, 1864.

It has been my duty during the past year to act as assistant superintendent of U. S. Military Telegraphs within the Department of West Virginia and the State of Ohio, and to be chief purchasing officer for the supplies required by the different officers connected with this branch of the public service for the operation and construction of U. S. military telegraphs within the several departments. My headquarters have been at Cleveland, Ohio.

Military operations have not been extensively active within the Department of West Virginia during the last year, and, with the exception of two or three important movements, the operations have been confined to maintaining a line of military posts adjacent to the Baltimore and Ohio Railroad and along the Kanawha River.

Whenever our troops have been dispatched upon expeditions or raids within the enemy's lines cipher operators have generally been furnished to accompany such movements. The expedition of Major-General Crook in May, 1864, was not referred to in my report for that year, and allusion to the same is therefore made herein. A portion of General Crook's command, comprising three brigades of infantry and about 300 cavalry, left Fayetteville, W. Va., during the first week of May and proceeded to Lexington, where they destroyed the camp and garrison equipage of two rebel regiments which had been left in charge of rebel guards. On the evening of the 8th the expedition arrived at Shannon's Cross-Roads, ten miles from Dublin Depot. At Shannon's Cross-Roads a rebel telegraph line was intercepted by the cipher operator accompanying the expedition, but owing to the pre-

* Omitted.

caution of the rebel operators but little information of interest to our forces was obtained beyond the fact that a considerable rebel force was posted at Cloyd's Mountain, on our line of march. On the morning of the 9th our forces reached Cloyd's Mountain, five miles from Dublin Depot, and General Crook at once made an attack upon the rebels, who were protected by earth-works; but after two hours' determined resistance the enemy fled in utter confusion, leaving their dead and wounded. During this engagement the telegraph operator acted as aide-de-camp to the general, and received a complimentary notice from that officer in his official report of the affair. General Crook pushed on for Dublin Depot, and when within three miles of the town met a force of Morgan's men, numbering about 1,000, who had come from Saltville to re-enforce the rebels at Cloyd's Mountain, but were not in time to effect a junction. After a skirmish the rebels retreated, and our forces entered Dublin Depot, on the Virginia and Tennessee Railroad, about 3 p. m. on the 9th. The depot buildings, rebel government property, and telegraph office here were destroyed, and General Crook pushed on to destroy the long railroad bridge ten miles from Dublin Depot, which, after an engagement of two hours, was accomplished. The object of the expedition having been attained, the command started upon its return via Salt Pond and Peter's Mountain, through Union, across Greenbrier River to Meadow Bluff, reaching there May 23, having marched about 300 miles. At Meadow Bluff we were in telegraphic communication, and cipher messages detailing operations, &c., were forwarded to headquarters, Washington, D. C.

On the 1st of June following General Crook started with his command for Staunton, Va., via Lewisburg, Hot and Warm Springs, through Panther Gap, into Augusta Valley. At Panther Gap a soldier in rebel uniform was captured, claiming to belong to Imboden's command, but upon being brought to headquarters was found to be the bearer of cipher messages from General Hunter ordering General Crook to join him at Charlottesville. The order, however, was afterward countermanded, and our forces joined the other command at Staunton. From Staunton the expedition moved via Lexington and Buckhannon, crossing the Blue Ridge at the foot of Peaks of Otter via Liberty, for Lynchburg. On arriving in the vicinity of Lynchburg we encountered the rebel force and whipped it during the first day's engagement. At night the rebels were re-enforced by troops under General Early. After successfully resisting the rebel attack on the second day our forces fell back under cover of the night and started for the Shenandoah Valley; but finding that the rebels were pursuing actively, and that probably we could not get out in the direction taken, our column turned toward the Kanawha Valley and marched out via Salem, Sweet Springs, and Lewisburg to Gauley Bridge. At the latter place orders were received to move the troops on to Charleston, where they took transports for Parkersburg, and from thence by railroad to Martinsburg, Va. From Martinsburg the troops were ordered to Harper's Ferry and into Maryland after General Early, who had come down the Shenandoah Valley and crossed the Potomac into Maryland. At Hillsborough it was ascertained that Early had fallen back, going toward Snicker's Gap and Winchester, Va. Near Hillsborough the Sixth Corps joined us and the command moved to Snicker's Gap. The Sixth Corps moved from here to Washington and General Crook's forces for Winchester. At Kernstown, three miles from Winchester, General Crook fought General Early on the 24th of July. Crook was defeated and at night retreated to Bunker

Hill. The cipher operator was employed all night in putting the general's official dispatches into cipher for transmission from the nearest telegraph station to Washington and other points. Next morning we marched from Bunker Hill to Williamsport, through Shepherdstown to Pleasant Valley, and from there to Frederick, and thence to Harper's Ferry and up the Shenandoah Valley to Strasburg, but again fell back to Halltown. After remaining at Halltown five days the command again moved up the valley to Berryville, at which place the cipher operator received orders to return to the Department of West Virginia.

On the 26th of September, 1864, the military telegraph line from Clarksburg, Va., to Weston was intercepted at Weston by a rebel operator, who, under the pretense of being the regular U. S. military telegraph operator stationed at that post, transmitted a telegram in the name of the commandant of that post, addressed to the commandant of the post at Clarksburg, stating that 3,000 rebels under General Basil Duke were advancing on Weston, and asking how many troops were at Clarksburg and how many could be sent to Weston. The military operator at Clarksburg felt satisfied from the peculiarity of the manipulation of the telegraph key at Weston that the telegram was a fraud and that it had been transmitted by a rebel operator, and so informed Colonel Wilkinson, then in command at Clarksburg. This suspicion, however, was kept from the rebel operator, and an answer regularly transmitted to Weston stating that 2,000 troops had just arrived by railroad and that more were expected during the night. Subsequent facts proved that the rebels were under command of Colonel Witcher, 900 strong, who retreated after plundering Weston and its inhabitants, although the original intention of the rebels had been to capture Clarksburg and destroy the large amount of Government property at that depot, which they could very easily have accomplished, only two companies of troops being stationed at Clarksburg at that time. Whether the subterfuge resorted to on our part was the means of saving Clarksburg and its supplies or not is unknown.

On the morning of September 27, 1864, the rebels under Colonel Witcher, about 900 strong, captured the town of Buckhannon, burned bridges and several dwellings, and plundered the inhabitants. Most of the small garrison stationed at this place eluded capture.

On the morning of October 29, 1864, a force of rebel infantry, 300 strong, under Captain Hill, attacked the Federal forces at Beverly, Va., but after a sharp contest were repulsed. After the rebels had retreated, the military telegraph repairer stationed at Beverly, having a thorough knowledge of the country, took the lead of our pursuing force, and, by taking a short by-road, got to the front of the rebels, when a charge was made, driving the rebels across a creek, taking 93 prisoners and recapturing about 40 of our own men taken in the attack on Beverly. The telegraph employé was complimented in the official report of the affair.

At about 11 a. m. November 28 the rebels, in U. S. uniform, under General Rosser, surprised the Federal force at New Creek, Va., and took possession of the place. The rebel force consisted of a division of cavalry. Much Government property was destroyed. The military telegraph office was seized so quickly that the operator had not time to escape and was carried off by the retreating rebels. He was robbed of his valuables and clothing, compelled to march barefoot to Harrisonburg, given nothing to eat until the third day of his captivity, and then merely three-quarters of a pound of fresh beef, which had to suffice until the evening of the fifth day, was confined in Castle Thunder, Richmond, and by sharing the blanket of a prison companion was kept from freezing.

On the 11th of January, 1865, at about 5 o'clock in the morning, a rebel force of about 600, under command of General Rosser, surprised and captured the picket-post at Beverly, Va.; passed quietly toward the Federal camp, surprised it, and captured the whole force, numbering some 800 men, under command of Colonel Youart, Eighth Ohio Volunteer Cavalry. A very humiliating affair.

Herewith will be found my property statement A, embracing all the property which has come into my possession during the year.

I have nothing to report on Form B.

Herewith will also be found my statement of public moneys received, &c., during the year. Out of the total amount expended, $149,799.76 was applied to purchases, and $124,564.76 to service account.

Have nothing to report on Forms C, CC, nor D.

Herewith will be found Form E, showing the articles of property which the enemy has captured during the year while in my possession, and the estimated value thereof.

Have no use for Form F, nothing having been captured from the enemy and come into my possession.

The following U. S. military telegraph land and submarine lines were in operation July 1, 1864, under my supervision in the Department of West Virginia and the State of Ohio:

	Miles.
From Hamden, Ohio, to Fayette, Va	151
From Gallipolis, Ohio, to South Point, Ohio	45
From Clarksburg, Va., to Beverly, Va	58
From Clarksburg, Va., to Bulltown, Va	49
From Green Spring, Va., to Springfield, Va	7
	310
Submarine line from Point Pleasant to Ohio shore	1/8
Total	310 1/8
The line from Green Spring to Springfield was necessarily abandoned in July, 1864	7
Leaving	303 1/8

Number of lines in operation June 30, 1865, as follows:

	Miles.
From Hamden, Ohio, to Fayette, Va	151
From Gallipolis, Ohio, to South Point, Ohio	45
From Clarksburg, Va., to Beverly, Va	58
Prom Clarksburg, Va., to Bulltown, Va	49
Cable from Point Pleasant to the Ohio shore	1/8
Total	303 1/8

I have nothing to report upon Form G.

Very respectfully, your obedient servant,

S. G. LYNCH,

Captain and Asst. Quartermaster, Asst. Superintendent.

Statement of public moneys for fiscal year ending June 30, 1865.

On hand July 1, 1864	$557.06
Received from officers during the year	285,695.28
Total	286,252.34

Expended during the year	$274,364.52
Transferred to other officers during the year	10,000.00
Remaining on hand June 30, 1865	1,887.82
Total	286,252.34

The balance on hand is deposited in my safe.

*Statement of property captured and destroyed by the enemy from Capt. S. G. Lynch, assistant quartermaster, and its estimated value, during the fiscal year ending June 30, 1865.**

Statement of quartermaster's property for the fiscal year ending June 30, 1865.†

No. 85.

OFFICE OF THE CHIEF QUARTERMASTER,
Louisville, Ky., October 19, 1865.

Maj. Gen. M. C. MEIGS,
Quartermaster-General U. S. Army, Washington, D. C.:

GENERAL: I have the honor to transmit herewith a retrospective report of the transactions of the department under my direction for the period commencing October 1, 1861, and ending June 30, 1865.‡ I regret that I have been unable to make it more complete. I am sensible that it is only an outline, and conveys a very inadequate idea of the actual amount of labor performed.

I inclose, also, a statement of receipts and disbursements of public moneys for the fiscal year ending on the 30th of June, 1865.

Please acknowledge the receipt.

Very respectfully, your obedient servant,

ROBT. ALLEN,
Brevet Major-General and Chief Quartermaster.

Statement of public moneys received and disbursed by Bvt. Maj. Gen. Robert Allen, quartermaster, U. S. Army, for the year ending on the 30th of June, 1865.

On hand July 1, 1864	$628,003.57
Received from officers during the year	1,238,594.28
Received from Treasury Department during the year	37,018,955.25
Total	38,885,553.10
Expended during the year	5,420,101.22
Transferred to other officers during the year	28,513,545.23
Remaining on hand June 30, 1865	4,951,906.65
Total	38,885,553.10
The balance due the United States is deposited as follows:	
Central National Bank at New York	1,607,549.28
U. S. depository at Louisville, Ky	3,047,837.78
First National Bank in Philadelphia in $7\frac{3}{10}$ bonds	291,477.41
Office safe, in gold and Treasury notes	5,042.18
Total	4,951,906.65

I certify that the above statement is correct.

ROBT. ALLEN,
Brevet Major-General and Chief Quartermaster, Valley of the Mississippi.

---

*Details omitted. The estimated value of the property was $502.

†Omitted.

‡See Series I, Vol. LII, Part I, p. 690.

No. 86.*

HEADQUARTERS ARMIES OF THE UNITED STATES,
Washington, D. C., September 28, 1865.

Bvt. Maj. Gen. M. C. MEIGS,
Quartermaster-General U. S. Army, Washington, D. C.:

GENERAL: I have the honor to submit my annual report for the fiscal year ending June 30, 1865, called for in your General Orders, No. 39, of July 1, of the present year.

By reference to my report of last year, rendered on the 28th of August, 1864, and which you did me the honor to publish with your own, together with my report for the previous fiscal year, and the Chancellorsville campaign, it will be observed that on the 1st of July, 1864, I was on duty at City Point, Va., at the headquarters of the lieutenant-general commanding the Armies of the United States, as chief quartermaster Armies operating against Richmond. These armies were composed of the Army of the Potomac and Army of the James, and our lines extended from the north side of the James River, near Richmond, to the southeast of Petersburg, a distance of over twenty-five miles, along the whole length of which was almost constant skirmishing night and day. Several attempts had been made before the 1st of July to carry the enemy's works, and to find and turn his flanks, sometimes bringing on severe conflicts, but without material success on our side. I refer to the attacks of the 16th, 17th, 18th of June, and to Generals Wilson's and Kautz's expedition to Reams' Station, June 22 to 28, more particularly. It became manifest that the defense of Richmond and Petersburg would be as protracted and stubborn as the resources and ability of the rebel commander could render it. I proceeded, therefore, under the written orders of the lieutenant-general to create suitable depots for receiving, storing, and issuing necessary supplies for the armies. The principal depot was established at City Point, on the James, at the mouth of the Appomattox, and was made one of the most convenient, commodious, economical, and perfect ever provided for the supply of armies. I have already rendered you a special report, on the 24th of June last, of this depot, showing amount of wharfage, store-houses, railroad shops, tracks, &c., with a recommendation how to dispose of the same. A secondary depot was kept up at Bermuda Hundred, and a still lesser one at Deep Bottom, more especially for the Army of the James. There was an average of some 40 steam-boats of all sorts, including tugs, 75 sail vessels, and 100 barges daily in the James River engaged in the transportation of supplies and plying between that river and the Northern ports. With such facilities an army of 500,000 men could have been fully supplied within any reasonable distance of our base. I do not know the whole number of vessels employed in our supply. A daily line of boats was established between City Point and Washington for mail and passenger service. Besides this, our transport fleet was constantly engaged in bringing cavalry and artillery horses, mules, clothing, ammunition, subsistence, &c., and in carrying back to Washington broken-down animals and other unserviceable property. The depot was placed under the charge of Col. P. P. Pitkin, who held the position of chief quartermaster of the depot until November 7, 1864, when he resigned to accept the position of quartermaster-general of the State of Vermont, and was suc-

*Portions of this report having been inadvertently omitted from Series I, Vol. LI, Part I, p. 251, the whole document is here printed.

ceeded by Col. George W. Bradley. Both of the gentlemen were highly experienced, vigorous, and accomplished officers, and performed their very arduous and responsible duties with great credit to themselves and advantage to the service.

The chief quartermaster at the principal depot always kept direct charge of the water transportation in James River. The other branches of the department, however, such as employés, forage, clothing, and railroad transportation, were in charge of subordinate quartermasters, selected for peculiar fitness, subject to the supervision of the chief depot quartermaster, who was required to report to me in writing every day, such as arrivals and clearances of shipping, receipts and issues of clothing, forage, &c. The chief quartermaster of each army was required to render, on or before the 25th of every month, a detailed consolidated estimate, revised and approved by the army commander, of the supplies required for issue to the army the month following. Upon this data I prepared and submitted my estimate for the combined forces on or before the 1st of each month. This method had very many good results. It compelled all interested to ascertain the real wants of the troops and to secure their regular and prompt supply. No quartermaster's stores were permitted to be sent to the armies except over my signature. The funds were generally deposited to the credit of Bvt. Lieut. Col. William T. Howell, on duty in my office as disbursing officer, on my requisition, and distributed by him to division and brigade quartermasters, on their estimates duly approved by the various commanders and countersigned by me. My printed orders and circulars in the hands of my subordinates prescribed the manner in which they should perform their duties on all points where the regulations and general orders were silent.

An extensive repair depot was established near City Point and placed in charge of Bvt. Lieut. Col. E. J. Strang, who received all serviceable animals and means of transportation from the Washington depot, and made the issues to the armies, and who received from the armies unserviceable stock, wagons, ambulances, &c., and shipped back all that could not be repaired in his shops. He employed a force of about 1,800 carpenters, wheelwrights, blacksmiths, saddlers, corral hands, teamsters, laborers, and guards. During the year ending June 30, 1865, he had repaired 3,653 army wagons and 2,414 ambulances. He had shod 19,618 horses and 31,628 mules. He received 27,116 serviceable horses and 10,893 mules, 436 wagons and 36 ambulances. He received from the troops 16,344 unserviceable horses, 9,684 mules, 1,392 wagons, and 400 ambulances. He received also by the surrender of Lee's army 400 horses, 1,300 mules, 101 wagons, and 90 ambulances. He issued to the troops 31,386 horses, 18,891 mules, 1,536 wagons, and 370 ambulances. He sent back for recuperation and repair 13,575 horses, 4,313 mules, 743 wagons, and 36 ambulances, besides a great amount of harness and other property. I mention these items simply to convey an idea of the duties to be performed at depots. This was only one branch.

As soon as we occupied City Point General McCallum, the able officer in charge of U. S. Military Railroads, had a strong construction corps on the spot prepared to rebuild the railroad up to our lines near Petersburg; and afterward, as fast as the army gained ground to the southeast, a temporary extension was laid close to our forces, until finally it extended to Hatcher's Run, a distance of about nineteen miles. Along this road were stations, as described in my last report on the Orange and Alexandria Railroad, where sidings and platforms were made for the prompt distribution of supplies to the different commands. This road saved much wear and tear of the wagon trains, and enabled the lieutenant-general to concentrate troops rapidly at any desirable point. After the surrender of Lee, this road—the new portion—was dismantled and the material placed in depot, to be disposed of in proper time.

The great field hospital at City Point has been described in other reports. It was a very perfect one for the purpose. The medical officers in charge exercised great taste and judgment in its management. There was a somewhat similar field hospital for the Army of the James at Point of Rocks, on the Appomattox. The medical department of each army had its own wharves, store-houses, transports, and hospitals, under the control of its medical officers. The ordnance and subsistence departments had special wharves and store-houses; so also had General Abbot, who had charge of siege guns and material for the entire line—all constructed by the Quartermaster's Department.

Colonel Strang and the other depot officers showed great energy, assiduity, and good judgment in the management of these heavy duties.

On the first of the fiscal year the organization of the quartermaster's department in the "Armies operating against Richmond" was complete, and never for a moment has it failed during the year to meet the orders and expectations of the lieutenant-general and the principal commanders in the field, so far as I have had opportunity of being informed.

It is undeniable that the officers of the Quartermaster's Department, both in the field and at our depots, have been charged with most important and responsible duties during the rebellion. Had they failed at any time we had no general who could have moved an army. I submit that more consideration is due to a department upon which so much is devolved, and higher grades should be created in order that the chief officers may have a rank that corresponds more nearly with that held by those who fight the troops. It is a noticeable fact that no quartermaster who has served as such during the war has risen by substantial promotion above the old grade. And still there are quartermasters who have done the Army and Republic as great service as any brigadier-general, and, with very few exceptions, any major-general. Officers of the department who are old, too infirm, inert, or otherwise disqualified to take their tours of hard work in the field and on frontier stations should at least be retired, in order that the active and business quartermasters who have borne the brunt of the service during the war may have the rank due the positions they have occupied.

I beg to suggest you will deem it expedient to recommend an increase of the Quartermaster's Department in your annual report to the Honorable Secretary of War—such an increase as will meet the wants of a peace establishment. There have been 400 or 500 volunteer quartermasters appointed during the war. According to the statutes the last of these will go out of service in one year after the termination of the war, which is not yet, however, proclaimed at an end. The increase which I would suggest, and which would be satisfactory, in my opinion, to the principal officers of the department, and would be sufficiently large for the Army as it will probably stand in a year's time, is as follows:

One Quartermaster-General U. S. Army, rank of major-general.

Three division quartermaster-generals, rank of brigadier-general.
Three assistant quartermaster-generals, rank of colonel.
Four deputy quartermaster-generals, rank of lieutenant-colonel.
Twelve quartermasters, rank of major.
Forty-eight assistant quartermasters, rank of captain.

This would only add one major-general, two brigadier-generals, and one major to the present establishment. I suggest three brigadier-generals as "division quartermaster-generals" for the three grand divisions, to wit, the Atlantic Division, Mississippi Division, and Pacific Division. The list of majors will be an increasing one under the law that promotes assistant quartermasters for fourteen consecutive years' service. Such promotions will, of course, create vacancies in the list of captains.

On the 1st of July, 1864, there were on hand in the Armies operating against Richmond means of land transportation as follows: 41,329 horses, 23,961 mules, 4,440 army wagons, 57 two-horse light wagons, and 915 ambulances.

At the beginning of the last campaign my returns show on hand as follows: 24,192 horses, 23,356 mules, 4,071 army wagons, 144 two-horse light wagons, and 907 ambulances.

After the close of the final campaign—say on May 1, 1865—the means of transportation were as follows: 33,948 horses, 25,093 mules, 4,207 army wagons, 140 two-horse light wagons, and 820 ambulances.

This property was used as prescribed in the orders of the lieutenant-general, a copy of which accompanied my last report, and most of it came to Washington with the troops last May and June, and was turned into the depot, as the troops were discharged, for final disposition under your orders. This transportation was in most excellent condition, and rendered services of vital importance on the last grand campaign from Petersburg and Richmond to Appomattox Court-House.

There were many partial movements of the armies from July 1, 1864, to the opening of the last campaign, but they did not render many new dispositions necessary in our department as to the transportation.

On the 30th of July the "battle of the Mine" was fought. On the 9th of August, near noon, there occurred a fearful explosion in the midst of the City Point depot, killing and wounding some 250 employés and soldiers, throwing down over 600 feet in length of warehouses, and tearing up some 180 linear feet of the wharf. It was found that a barge laden with ordnance stores had been blown up. Immense quantities of shot and shell were thrown into the air, and much of it fell in the encampment of the lieutenant-general, wounding, however, only one—Colonel Babcock, of his staff. The lieutenant-general himself seems proof against the accidents of flood and field. It was assumed at the time that the explosion was the result of carelessness on the part of some one in or near the barge, but the developments made in the trial of the assassins of the late President would show that it was the dastardly work of that infernal rebel "torpedo bureau" in Richmond. The damages of the depot were soon repaired.

August 18 to 20 the Weldon road was seized and thereafter held. An attempt was also made on our right at Deep Bottom. September 30 the Fifth and Ninth Corps, of the Army of the Potomac, were engaged at Poplar Grove Church, and the Army of the James captured Fort Harrison and one line of works. October 24 [27] and 25 [28] the

Army of the Potomac was engaged at Hatcher's Run. December 5 [7] the Fifth Corps, supported by the Ninth, made a march toward Weldon. On such occasions the moving columns were generally directed in orders to be provided with a small stated allowance of subsistence, forage, and ammunition wagons and ambulances. The main trains remained parked in safe and convenient positions near the outer defenses of the City Point depot, but always loaded and fully prepared to move forward whenever and wherever needed. It was the rule after having passed the James in June, 1864, that each corps should generally be followed by its own trains.

On the evening of the 23d of January, 1865, it was known that the rebels were apparently preparing to make a raid down the James, with their fleet of iron-clads and wooden boats, for the purpose of destroying our depots on the river, particularly that great one at City Point, where supplies had been accumulated and stored to meet the wants of the armies in case the James River and Northern ports should be closed by ice. The weather was already very inclement, and the Potomac and Delaware were then, or shortly afterward, rendered entirely unnavigable by ice. Early on the 24th the rebel fleet approached our obstructions and one of the iron-clads passed them, but the one following got foul upon them. Our batteries made obstinate resistance and blew up one of the smaller gun-boats. Our men even were led with great effort to the bank of the river and poured volleys of musketry into the ram that had passed the obstructions. The navy at that point was not prepared at the moment for any effective resistance. Had the rebels persisted at that time they could, had they succeeded, have inflicted upon us incalculable losses, the result of which no one can pretend now to estimate; but most fortunately for us they abandoned the raid and retired to their former position. Two or three days later it was impossible for these boats to make a descent. The navy was thoroughly prepared, and I had sent, by order of the lieutenant-general, my aide-de-camp, Bvt. Capt. J. W. French, Eighth Infantry, up the river with vessels laden with coal, who sunk two on the night of the 25th to fill up the gap made in the obstructions. He performed the service under the enemy's guns with great gallantry.

Our lines were extended to Hatcher's Run on the 7th of February. The enemy attacked and carried Fort Stedman, within the lines of the Ninth Corps, on the morning of the 25th of March, but were shortly driven out with a loss of some 4,500 killed, wounded, and prisoners. Meantime the lieutenant-general was preparing to strike the decisive blow of the whole war. The sick were sent to the rear. The different staff departments were ordered to be in readiness with all necessary supplies for the expected march. The arrangements made by me were similar to those described in my reports of other great battles. The trains were laden with ten days' subsistence and forage and sixty rounds per man of ammunition. The troops were fully supplied with clothing, and were required to carry five days' subsistence and forty rounds of ammunition on their persons. The trains were to remain in park, as usual, until the result of the attack should be known.

The movement commenced by the left on the 29th of March. On the evening of April 1 Sheridan overthrew the enemy at Five Forks and gave us possession of the South Side road. On the next night and morning the Sixth Corps, under General Wright, carried the enemy's works in its front. The enemy was driven from his works around

Petersburg and Richmond and fled toward the Danville road. He was pursued with such vigor that our forces reached Burkeville Junction in advance of him, and obliged him to attempt some other road. At Amelia Court-House he lost many of his wagons and troops. Our cavalry hung on his rear and destroyed a great amount of his transportation. The rebel army became utterly demoralized, beaten, dispirited, and was surrendered entire to the lieutenant-general at Appomattox Court-House on the memorable 9th of April.

Immediately after the surrender I inspected the rebel trains and saw they were in a horrible condition. I gave orders for the supply of forage to the animals, and that the transportation should be sent in to the City Point depot. Permission had been given that all private mules and horses might be taken away by their owners. I was not greatly surprised to learn afterward that the greater portion of all the animals, particularly all the good ones, were taken away on this pretext. It was very natural to expect it, and I am told the same was observed after the surrender of other rebel armies.

There finally reached the City Point depot from General Lee's army only 400 horses, 1,300 mules, 101 wagons, and 90 ambulances.

Doubtless many animals, wagons, and ambulances were loaned to Confederate officers to enable them to reach certain points, where they probably turned them over.

Having made all the necessary dispositions, the lieutenant-general left on the 10th to return to City Point. On the 3d I had directed the superintendent of the railroad to repair it at once as far as Burkeville Junction, a distance of fifty-four miles. The gauge had to be reduced to four feet eight and a half inches from Petersburg. When the lieutenant-general and staff reached Burkeville, at noon on the 11th, a special train was in waiting for us, and we arrived at City Point that same night. Supplies were forwarded and the sick and wounded were taken in at once over this road. Subsequently the road was worked by the Government to Danville and Lynchburg.

It is proper to record that I personally accompanied the lieutenant-general and staff on all the campaigns of the year past, and was present in all the principal engagements and battles.

I remained on duty at City Point, directing the reduction of employés, the discharge of transports, and the diminution of expenses generally in the Quartermaster's Department, until the 8th of May, when I received a telegraphic order from the lieutenant-general to report in person to him in Washington. I reported accordingly on the 10th, and since that date have held myself directly subject to his orders from day to day. I established an office for the settlement of outstanding accounts of the armies lately operating against Richmond, and continued it until yesterday, when Colonel Howell, who was my disbursing officer, was ordered to report to you. The office is no longer necessary for that purpose.

The Treasury Department is now engaged in the settlement of my accounts, which have not been entirely settled since 1856. I request the privilege of attending to this duty before I am again assigned to any permanent station outside of this city. It is important to me and to the Government that my accounts shall be closed. I am not responsible now, according to my returns, for any public funds or property, so a better opportunity can never be presented for the settlement. I have stated to you that in addition I will cheerfully attend to any duty in this city, such as service on boards, to which you may wish to have me assigned.

My money accounts for the fiscal year are correctly stated below as follows:

On hand July 1, 1864:	
Received from officers during the year	$12,000
Treasury Department	300,000
Total	312,000
Expended during the year:	
Transferred to other officers during the year	312,000

The officers who have served under me will furnish you the information called for by paragraphs 2, 3, 5, 6, 7, 8, 9, and 11 of your order. My duties have been chiefly administrative.

As all the data for a "statistical report" should be in your office, and as such a report of the operations of the Quartermaster's Department during the war would be of great interest and value, I would respectfully suggest that two or more competent officers be charged with the duty of compiling it. My observations during the past year have only confirmed me in the opinions expressed in previous reports relative to the outfit of our troops and our means of land transportation.

Bvt. Brig. Gen. R. N. Batchelder succeeded me as chief quartermaster of the Army of the Potomac, and continued on that duty until the disbandment of that army. He merited the very high commendations awarded him by all his superiors. He, like myself, has served continuously in the field during the war.

Col. Charles E. Fuller was acting chief quartermaster of the Army of the James on our arrival at James River. Subsequently, and at different dates, Col. J. B. Howard and Bvt. Brig. Gen. George S. Dodge were chief quartermasters of that army, and gave me cordial support. I am very thankful to all the quartermasters who served under me for the uniformly cheerful co-operation extended to me. I have mentioned them more particularly in a special letter asking for brevets, &c.

I beg to repeat my obligations to you and General Rucker and the officers of the Quartermaster's Department in Washington for the support and attention given me in the transaction of my official business during the fiscal year.

With high respect, I am your most obedient servant,

RUFUS INGALLS,

Bvt. Maj. Gen. of Vols., Chief Q. M. Armies before Richmond.

No. 87.*

No. 88.

CHIEF QUARTERMASTER'S OFFICE,
Washington Depot, August 31, 1865.

Maj. Gen. M. C. MEIGS,
Quartermaster-General U. S. Army:

GENERAL: Pursuant to General Orders, No. 39, current series, Quartermaster-General's Office, of July 1, 1865, I have the honor to submit my annual report for the fiscal year ending June 30, 1865.

My annual report of the duties performed at this depot for the fiscal year ending June 30, 1864, in accordance with General Orders,

* For report of Bvt. Maj. Gen. J. L. Donaldson, chief quartermaster Department of the Cumberland, dated June 30, 1865 (here omitted), see Series I, Vol. LII, Part I, p. 680.

No. 29, Quartermaster-General's Office, July 6, 1864, was sent by messenger September 6, 1864.

For the purpose of expediting business and keeping the various operations at this depot distinct from each other, the organization of the several branches, as given below, has been continued during the year. They are as follows:

I. Army-wagon transportation, repair shops, &c., under the personal charge of Bvt. Col. Charles H. Tompkins, quartermaster.

II. Ocean and river transportation, payments of freight, &c., under the supervision of Capt. Edward S. Allen, assistant quartermaster.

III. Chartering and payment of chartered vessels, in charge of Capt. John R. Jennings, assistant quartermaster, succeeded by Capt. James G. Payne, assistant quartermaster.

IV. Contracts for victualing U. S. chartered transports, steam-boat and ship supplies, transportation by canal, &c., under the care of Capt. Henry B. Lacey, assistant quartermaster.

V. Railroad transportation, express, &c., under the charge of Capt. Benjamin Burton, assistant quartermaster.

VI. Transportation of ordnance and ordnance stores at U. S. Arsenal, in care of Capt. Curtis S. Barrett, assistant quartermaster.

VII. Purchase and issue of quartermaster's supplies, interment of deceased soldiers, with the manufacture of coffins, headboards, stoves, tinware, desks, &c.; care of cemeteries at Soldiers' Home, Arlington, Fort Stevens, &c., under the supervision of Capt. James M. Moore, assistant quartermaster.

VIII. Receiving and issuing forage, in charge of Capt. Edward S. Allen, assistant quartermaster, succeeded by Capt. Samuel B. Lauffer, assistant quartermaster.

IX. In charge of Soldiers' Rest, providing meals and quarters for soldiers in transitu, &c., Bvt. Maj. Erskine M. Camp, assistant quartermaster.

X. In charge of construction and repairs, hiring quarters, grounds, hospitals, offices, wharves, and payment of various employés, Capt Elisha E. Camp, assistant quartermaster, succeeded by Capt. John H Crowell, assistant quartermaster.

XI. Receiving and issuing clothing, camp and garrison equipage, &c., under the direction of Military Store-keeper Daniel G. Thomas.

XII. The branch depot of Alexandria, Va., has been under the supervision of Bvt. Lieut. Col. James G. C. Lee, assistant quartermaster.

XIII. The following-named officers, in addition, have also been on duty at this depot and Alexandria during the year, or for short periods of it:

(1) Capt. Calvin Baker, assistant quartermaster; (2) Capt. R. S. Lacey, assistant quartermaster; (3) Capt. John V. Furey, assistant quartermaster; (4) Capt. Thomas G. Whytal, assistant quartermaster; (5) Capt. S. R. Hamill, assistant quartermaster; (6) Capt. W. W. Van Ness [assistant quartermaster]; (7) Lieut. E. R. Graves, Third West Virginia Cavalry; (8) Capt. S. W. Hoskins, assistant quartermaster; (9) Capt. B. O. Carr, assistant quartermaster; (10) Capt. Isaac N. Buck, assistant quartermaster, and (11) Capt. James Gilliss, assistant quartermaster, still remaining.

Defense of Washington.—At the commencement of this fiscal year a command of rebel troops invaded Maryland, burned Chambersburg, Pa., and threatened Baltimore. After the battle of Monocacy, in which a portion of the Sixth Army Corps, just arrived, were engaged, they advanced upon Washington. All available troops were ordered to meet them, guards in the city were withdrawn and their places supplied in part by the quartermaster employés, who were armed for that purpose.

On the 11th of July, 2,500 of these employés were sent to occupy the rifle-pits in the vicinity of Fort Slocum, where they remained until their services were no longer required. This was made the subject of a special report sent you on the 3d of August, 1864, to which you are respectfully referred for particulars.

The timely arrival of portions of the Sixth and Nineteenth Army Corps assured the safety of the city, and the rebels were driven back, but not without some loss.

Battle Cemetery.—By your directions a cemetery, to contain the bodies of those who fell in defense of the Nation's capital, was laid out near Fort Stevens, on the spot consecrated by their blood.

Repairs to canal.—The Chesapeake and Ohio Canal being necessary for the easy and rapid supply of the troops in pursuit of the discomfited rebels, a construction force was sent to repair the locks, &c., injured or destroyed by the rebel forces.

Stores issued and forwarded.—The Sixth and Nineteenth Army Corps had their land transportation renewed and placed in effective condition before leaving, and the canal was used as a means of forwarding supplies of grain and stores. At the same time, requisitions for artillery and ambulance horses and mules, to supply the wants of the Armies operating against Richmond, were promptly filled and forwarded to City Point by water, and large numbers of vessels were in use forwarding forage and supplies to the same place, while grain, forage, and stores were forwarded by canal to Harper's Ferry and the mouth of the Monocacy.

Teamsters.—The number of teamsters at the depot being greatly reduced by fitting out the Sixth and Nineteenth Army Corps, I was obliged not only to advertise, but to send to Philadelphia and other portions of Pennsylvania to supply the want, as the services of contrabands could not be obtained in the Department of Washington.

Unclaimed clothing dyed for irregular issue.—The warehouses being filled with accumulations of unclaimed clothing, camp and garrison equipage, &c., and the room required for other stores, Captain Moore was ordered to turn it in to the military store-keeper, and to take receipts for the same; portions of which were afterward washed and dyed for issue to contrabands and prisoners of war during the approaching winter.

Employés sent to Manassas to fell timber.—In addition to the daily duties of the mechanics at the several repair shops in fitting up wagons and ambulances that had become unserviceable, constructing buildings, &c., they, with laborers and other employés, were engaged for about two weeks in felling timber for a distance of a mile on each side of the Orange and Alexandria Railroad, in the neighborhood of Manassas, in order to break up the lurking-places of guerrillas, under the direction of Brig. Gen. D. C. McCallum, superintendent of Military Railroads.

Horses turned over to Cavalry Bureau.—Early in September, the Cavalry Bureau having taken the entire charge of all horses, the artillery horses then in depot were turned over to it, and were afterward, with necessary cavalry horses, issued from Giesborough depot.

Hospitals, quarters, &c., erected.—A large force of carpenters was employed by Captain Camp, assistant quartermaster, and after he was relieved, to take charge of the depot at City Point, by Captain Crowell, assistant quartermaster, in making additions and repairs to the various hospitals in and around the city, to render them comfortable for the winter, building quarters for regiments of Veteran Reserve Corps stationed in the city, and guards at the several hospitals, of which reports and drawings, with their cost, were forwarded to you each month. For details you are respectfully referred to the annual report on this subject sent you by Capt. John H. Crowell, assistant quartermaster; but the amount of building, repairs, &c., during the first four months of this year, conducted by Capt. E. E. Camp, assistant quartermaster, is, of course, not included therein.

Precautions against incendiaries.—Information having been received of an organization to burn the Northern cities, the quartermaster employés, now regularly organized and drilled by company and battalion, were ordered on duty at night and the number of watchmen increased. By my direction an officer of the depot was detailed each night to perform duty as officer of the day, visiting each shop, warehouse, and corral, from Georgetown to the Eastern Branch, including the Sixth Street Wharf and Kendall Green, which occupied their time from 10 o'clock at night till daylight, to see that the guards and watchmen were on the alert; which duty they performed during a portion of the month of December, and until these guards were relieved by enlisted men of the Veteran Reserve Corps.

This vigilance prevented any attempt to destroy the large amount of stores necessarily kept on hand.

To give a prompt alarm in case of fire, alarm-boxes were put up at different points to connect with the city telegraph lines put in operation in February; fire-plugs were also erected at several of the repair shops and warehouses.

Troops to City Point.—Early in December the Sixth and General Cox's division of the Eighth Army Corps [*sic*] were refitted in mules, wagons, and stores, and shipped to City Point.

Danger from ice.—Apprehending inconvenience and delay to water transportation by the formation of ice in the river during the winter, I applied for and received two ice-boats, and ordered all the Government transports to be plated with suitable iron above and below the water-line, to prevent being cut through by the ice.

Troops forwarded.—During the months of December and January the water transportation branch, besides the routine duty of forwarding quartermaster's supplies, beef-cattle, commissary stores, and ordnance to City Point, was fully occupied in sending forward Hayes' division, Crook's command, and the Provisional Brigade, West Virginia troops, from the Shenandoah Valley, and General Schofield's command from Tennessee.

Hay barges frozen in.—My apprehensions in regard to ice proved well founded. Forage barges passing through the canal from Philadelphia to the Chesapeake Bay were frozen in, and the supply of hay on hand was soon exhausted by the increased number of animals belonging to the above-mentioned troops.

In want of hay.—Capt. H. B. Lacey, assistant quartermaster, was dispatched the latter part of January with tug-boats to extricate these barges, but without success. I was obliged, in consequence, to send trains of wagons into the country to bring what hay could be purchased from the farmers, by which means a supply sufficient for part of a ration was kept up. These purchases were continued throughout the month of March.

Ice blockade.—The cold weather still continuing, I was obliged to order the mail-boats, which had during the year kept up a daily line of communication between this city and City Point, to land at Annapolis, and the mails and passengers were transported to and from that point by rail. This continued, with an intermission of about four days, from the 26th of January to the 21st of February, inclusive, being twenty-three days of ice blockade, which had not occurred before during the war.

General Schofield's army shipped.—It was during this period that the army of General Schofield arrived. The first shipment of the Second Division, Twenty-third Army Corps, animals and baggage, was made from Alexandria; but the ice having again formed, a brigade of 2,000 men, together with General Meagher's division, numbering 5,000 men, were forwarded by rail to Annapolis, and from thence by sea-going steamers. The rest of this command, after being refitted, embarked at Alexandria for North Carolina.

Coal exhausted.—At the commencement of winter I had laid in a store of 15,000 tons of stove coal for issue to hospitals, officers, &c., considering it sufficient for winter use, but early in the spring, this amount being exhausted, I was obliged to have a further supply sent daily by rail from Baltimore, amounting in the aggregate to about 5,000 tons.

Forage barges released.—The weather having moderated and ice in the river fast disappearing, Captain Lacey was again ordered on the 20th of February to Chesapeake City to release the forage barges frozen in the canal, which arrived here during the month of March.

Vessels for prisoners of war.—During the last week of February large shipments of cattle and stores, including the wagon transportation of General Schofield's army, were being sent to the front, when this depot was again called upon to furnish transportation for prisoners of war from Fort Delaware to City Point. Shipments of stores were also regularly made to supply the wants of the Army of the Shenandoah.

Organized employés on duty.—On the 4th of March, owing to the great influx of persons into the city, some of whom might be contemplating mischief, the quartermaster employés, by request of Major-General Halleck, Chief of Staff, were kept on duty day and night at their several armories, and the quartermaster's steam fire brigade at their engine houses, in readiness for any calls that might be made upon them.

Guards increased.—The guards at the warehouses and shops were doubled and so continued for about a week, and every precaution was taken to insure the preservation and security of the Government property.

Supplies for General Sherman.—General Sherman's army having reached North Carolina, a force of carpenters was sent forward to Morehead City to erect warehouses for the reception of stores to be sent for the supply of the troops in that vicinity. Such light-draft steamers as could be obtained, with a number of barges, were loaded with supplies and forwarded by the Albemarle and Chesapeake Canal.

Fires.—On the 1st of April the fire at headquarters Department of Washington occurred, which consumed the temporary buildings erected for its use. Here, as well as at the fire of the Smithsonian Institution, the quartermaster's steam fire brigade did good service and prevented these fires being more destructive, especially as no very effective assistance could be rendered by the common hand engines of the city corporation then in use.

Fall of Richmond.—The grand combinations of the lieutenant-general culminated early in April in the fall of Richmond, the capitulation of the armies of Generals Lee and Johnston, and the subsequent collapse of the rebellion. Large numbers of prisoners were taken, and every available vessel was drawn from this depot to transport them from City Point to Point Lookout, &c.

Precautions against fire.—During the first week in April, when the loyal States were electrified by these successes, and illuminations were so frequent, unusual care and watchfulness were exercised to prevent any disasters from fire. Water-buckets were placed in every building and filled ready for use, and watchmen were doubled. I am happy to be able to state that owing to this vigilance no disaster occurred.

Assassination of the President.—The 14th of April will ever be memorable on account of the dastardly attempt to assassinate the chief officers of the Government, which, in the case of the lamented President, proved too successful. The perpetrator of this infamous act having escaped from the city, it was supposed he would endeavor to find his way through Virginia to the more southern States. Tug-boats, with a few armed men on each, were ordered to patrol the waters of the Potomac and Patuxent, with instructions to examine all vessels and boats, with a view to the arrest of the criminal, and were continued on this duty until after his capture and death. Cavalry were also forwarded by water to Chapel Point, Md., and a daily line of steamers carrying mails and stores was put in operation during their stay.

His funeral.—This depot also took an active part in the preparations made for the President's funeral, and two battalions of its armed and drilled employés formed part of the mournful cortege that followed his remains to the Capitol.

Grand review.—On the 23d and 24th of May the review of the grand armies of the United States, assembled in the vicinity, took place, for which preparations had been made by the mechanics at this depot in erecting sheltered seats for the occupancy of the President, Cabinet officers, members of the diplomatic corps, &c., on both sides of Pennsylvania avenue opposite the Executive Mansion. Ambulances were also hitched up and held in readiness to remove any of the troops who might be overcome by the heat upon this march.

Troops to be mustered out and sent home.—The War Department having ordered the muster out of service and return to their several homes of a large number of these troops, the railroad from this city was tasked to its utmost to provide them transportation; and, besides its ordinary traffic, in two months, from the 29th of May, safely removed about 200,000 officers and men, with 12,000 horses and 4,000,000 pounds of baggage. For details of this movement and all transportation by rail I respectfully refer you to the annual report of Capt. Benjamin Burton, assistant quartermaster, the officer in charge of that branch of the depot.

Transportation to refugees.—Transportation has also been furnished by rail and boat to indigent refugees and others to various points in the Southern States upon the orders of General O. O. Howard, in charge of the Freedmen's Bureau.

Army transportation turned in.—Large numbers of mules and wagons, composing the transportation of the Armies operating against Richmond, and General Sherman's army, being turned in, it was thought best to send the mules to graze, not only to improve their condition, but to save expense, and to prevent disease from having so large a number congregated together.

Grazing camps.—Grazing camps were accordingly established at various points in Maryland and Virginia, contiguous to the city, from which the best results were obtained.

Trains to Louisville.—One thousand six-mule teams complete, with 2,000 extra mules, making 8,000 in all, were also, by order of the lieutenant-general, started from this point for Louisville, Ky., in four divisions, under the charge of Captains Whetsel, Winslow, Wilson, and Mead, of the Quartermaster's Department.

Auction sales.—The accumulation of such a large amount of wagons of various patterns, harness, and animals, which were no longer necessary for army purposes, selections of the best were made by your order. Sales at auction of the remainder were commenced and continued through the month of June. For details of these sales, and all other matters connected with the land transportation branch of the depot, I most respectfully refer you to the annual report, to be made to you direct, by Bvt. Col. Charles H. Tompkins, quartermaster, the officer in charge.

Officers commended.—I take great pleasure in bringing to your notice the ability and energy displayed by the several officers stationed at this depot in the discharge of duties which at times were peculiarly arduous and embarrassing, and for which three of them have been rewarded by brevet rank.

Capt. E. S. Allen, assistant quartermaster.—In this connection I cannot help asking your attention to my communication of May 5, recommending Capt. Edward S. Allen, assistant quartermaster, in charge of water transportation, and whose duties have been so ably and satisfactorily performed, for brevet, which I think he so richly merits.

As these officers will report to you direct the operations of their respective branches during the fiscal year, I respectfully refer you to those reports for details.

Conduct of quartermaster's employés.—I also desire to express my satisfaction at the willingness and unanimity that have characterized the conduct of the several employés, and the heartiness with which they entered upon the performance of duties not properly belonging to them as mechanics and laborers, in perfecting themselves in drill, and in going out under military organization to perform necessary labor that could not be supplied from any other source.

Shipments.—Besides the constant duty of supplying stores to the large armies before Richmond, and to the troops while in West Virginia and the Shenandoah Valley, transportation has been furnished troops and stores to New Berne, Wilmington, Hilton Head, and Savannah.

Assistance rendered.—Assistance of a more general character has been rendered when necessary during the year, of which I only mention the following: One hundred cords of wood and twenty-five tons of coal were loaned in the depth of winter, from the supply on hand at Alexandria, to the city corporation of that place, when it could not otherwise be obtained, and by the timely receipt of which a large amount of suffering to the poor was prevented. Five hundred barrels of flour were transported from Georgetown for the American Union Commission, destined for the poor of Petersburg and Richmond, and barracks at the Virginia end of the Long Bridge were set apart for the shelter of refugees from the Southern States whom the fortunes of war had thrown into the city.

Favors by the Military Railroad Department.—I am indebted to the Military Railroad Department for many favors, in furnishing pump logs, laying railroad track, and enlarging and placing in the most excellent order the wharves at the foot of Sixth street.

Business of the depot.—The business of the depot has been very large during the year, as will be seen by reference to the detailed reports, and has been conducted with a view to the greatest efficiency, combined with the greatest economy.

No defalcation.—I am happy to be able to state that although the large sum $8,500,000 has been disbursed, yet no instance of peculation or defalcation has occurred.

The officers' accounts have been sent in to the department with regularity and promptness, and the numberless reports asked for, voluminous correspondence required, has been conducted with dispatch.

I append a statement of moneys received and disbursed during the year, which is the only form required of me by your Order No. 39.

Very respectfully, your obedient servant,

D. H. RUCKER,

Bvt. Maj. Gen. and Chief Quartermaster Depot, Washington, D. C.

Annual cash statement for the fiscal year ending June 30, 1865.

RECEIPTS.

Amount on hand July 1, 1864			$1,785,745.36
Amount received from officers		$947.11	
Amount received from United States, certificates	$1,847,542.00		
Amount received from United States, cash	5,934,652,48		
		7,782,194.48	
Sales of clothing to officers	23,258.09		
Sales of condemned clothing, camp and garrison equipage	38,043.34		
		61,301.43	
From treasurer of Smithsonian Institution		1,974.25	
Correction of errors taken up		19.80	
			7,846,437.07
Total receipts in the year			9,632,182.43

DISBURSEMENTS.

As per Abstract B	$2,884,820.55
As per Abstract Bb	5,936,537.64
Internal-revenue tax	627.34
Balance of errors taken up	79.80
Total amount of disbursements	8,822,065.33
Balance on hand	810,117.10
	9,632,182.43

The balance on hand is deposited in the First National Bank, Washington, D. C.

D. H. RUCKER,

Brevet Major-General and Quartermaster.

No. 89.*

* For report of Bvt. Brig. Gen. L. C. Easton, dated August 18, 1865 (here omitted), see Series I, Vol. LII, Part I, p. 696.

No. 90.

HEADQUARTERS MILITARY DIVISION OF THE MISSISSIPPI,
Morehead City, N. C., March 16, 1865.

Maj. Gen. M. C. MEIGS,
Quartermaster-General U. S. Army, Washington, D. C.:

GENERAL: In obedience to instructions contained in your letter of the 26th of December, 1864, I have the honor to make the following report:

From the 14th to the 25th of October last found me at Chattanooga, Tenn., hurrying and giving all the assistance in my power to the repair of the road from Chattanooga to Atlanta, which had been destroyed by General Hood's army. On the 26th I joined General Sherman at Gaylesville, a small town about thirty miles west of Rome, Ga., where I received his orders, and proceeded the next day to Atlanta, Ga., by his direction, to superintend the removal of all stores, citizens, sick, &c., from that place to Chattanooga. On entering upon this duty I found the accumulation of supplies and the number of sick, wounded, and negroes surprisingly large for the short time we had occupied the place. The removal of the whole, except some property not worth transportation, was accomplished by the 12th of November, 1864, and the army of General Sherman commenced its march from Atlanta to Savannah, Ga., on the 15th of November, 1864.

The army consisted of four corps of infantry and one cavalry division, as follows, viz:

	Men.	Horses.	Mules.	Wagons.	Ambulances.
Fourteenth Corps	15,680	1,408	4,436	571	112
Fifteenth Corps	18,000	2,164	5,726	666	146
Seventeenth Corps	11,000	2,156	3,107	385	77
Twentieth Corps	14,000	1,740	4,341	598	105
Cavalry corps	5,000	7,000	1,800	300	....
Total	63,680	14,468	19,410	2,520	440

The following was ordered as the allowance of transportation for baggage, &c., on the march.

One wagon to each regiment; two wagons to each brigade headquarters; three wagons to each division headquarters; five wagons to each corps headquarters; one wagon to each battery (there was one battery to each division).

The balance of the transportation was directed to be distributed as follows, viz:

Three wagons to each division for hospital purposes; one wagon to every 100 men, including artillery for ammunition, and the remainder, 1,476 wagons, was used in transporting forage and subsistence, &c.

The army started from Atlanta with four days' grain.

The subsistence transported for the whole army was as follows, viz:

Hard-bread, 20 days' rations; salt meat, 5 days' rations; sugar and coffee, 30 days' rations; soap, rice, candles, 5 days' rations; salt, 80 days' rations.

The quantity of salt taken proved unnecessary, as we found it in great abundance in the country passed through.

The army started from Atlanta with 5,476 head of beef-cattle in addition to the above.

The first grain received was at King's Bridge, on the Ogeechee River. It arrived there and was issued on the 18th of December, so the animals of the army subsisted on the country twenty-nine days (we started with four days' grain), which makes at least 11,145,792 pounds of grain and 15,177,344 pounds of fodder and hay taken from the country and consumed by the army on the march. This is a low estimate of the forage taken from the country, as beef-cattle were fed on the whole route as much as they would eat, and the number of horses, mules, and beef-cattle varied from day to day, all increasing in numbers. I inclose you a statement of beef-cattle captured, &c., marked B.

After General Hood cut the Chattanooga and Atlanta Railroad the animals of the army suffered for want of forage, and a large number of them became very much reduced in flesh and were quite weak when the army commenced its march from Atlanta. This accounts for the large number of animals that gave out and were shot on the road. The character of the mules captured was superior, a small sized or inferior one being seldom met with.

On the arrival of the army in front of Savannah the condition of its animals was far better than it was at the commencement of its march. Those animals that had strength sufficient at the start improved daily, and those that failed and gave out were replaced by a better class of mules than we found in the trains at starting.

There is no way of arriving at the quantity of subsistence taken from the country, but the whole army fared sumptuously and the animals were never better fed. During the whole march and until we took a position before Savannah both men and animals had all they could desire in the way of food.

The army marched by corps and on roads as near parallel to each other as could be found. Each corps had its pontoon train and each division its pioneer force, and with these organizations streams were crossed, roads repaired, and sometimes made, without retarding the movements of the troops.

The management of trains differed somewhat in each corps, but I think the best arrangement was where the train of the corps followed immediately after its troops, with a strong rear guard, in the following order:

First. Corps headquarters baggage wagons.

Second. Division headquarters baggage wagons.

Third. Brigade headquarters baggage wagons.

Fourth. Regimental headquarters baggage wagons.

Fifth. Empty wagons, to be loaded with forage and other supplies taken from the country, with the proper details for loading them.

Sixth. Ammunition train.

Seventh. Ambulance train.

Eighth. General supply train.

As the empty wagons reached farm-houses and other points where supplies could be obtained a sufficient number were turned out of the road to take all at the designated point, and so on through the day until the empty wagons were loaded, making it a rule to take the first supplies come to, and to leave none on the road until all the wagons were loaded. The empty wagons could be loaded by the time the rear of the general supply train came up to them, and they would fall into their proper places in the rear of their division trains, if in time, or in the rear of the general supply train, without retarding the march. This arrangement worked well, and is probably as good as any that could be made for procuring supplies. As a general thing the wagons were required to go but a short distance from the line of march to obtain supplies, there being sufficient near by.

Hogs, turkeys, geese, ducks, and chickens were killed and brought to the road by foraging parties sent out at the head of each column, and loaded into wagons as they came up. The captured beef-cattle and sheep were driven along in their proper places and killed as required. Sweet potatoes of the finest kind were found in great abundance immediately on the road; also turnips, which were generally of an inferior quality.

The portable forge is almost entirely done away with in General Sherman's army. Nearly all the officers prefer carrying a small-sized bellows, using any ordinary box filled with dirt as a fire-box. The bellows is swung between two stakes, usually cut from the woods or taken from some fence, driven into the ground, with a piece nailed across the top to suspend the bellows handle. The box (usually a bread box) is placed at its proper height on four forks or stakes driven into the ground, with pieces laid from one to the other to set the box on. They transport simply the bellows, anvil, and tools, making use of any empty box or barrel for a fire-box. Nearly all the iron-work on the march from Atlanta to Savannah was done with forges of this description. Officers prefer this arrangement to the portable forge, because it does not get out of order and gives a better heat. Since writing this I have received a circular describing Capt. John H. Dickerson's portable forge, which is, I presume, got up from this idea. In the absence of portable forges I would suggest the plan for a forge now used in General Sherman's army, which answers every purpose.

There is one little thing which has been practiced by experienced officers for many years, which would be a great economy in both wagon sheets and wagon bows if officers generally could be made to adopt it; that is, to put their side boards ten or twelve inches wide on all wagons. Wagons are loaded far above their sides; heavy articles are frequently put on top, and over rough roads jar against a bow, snapping it off, or coming between the bows, burst out the sheet. The side boards running the whole length of the wagon and pressing against all the bows prevents this difficulty, and also prevents the loading from coming against a wet sheet. A thin light board of this kind adds very little to the weight of the wagon, and is a great protection to wagon bows and sheets.

For campaigning I would much prefer a wagon made with standards to the bolster and over the hind axle, so that the body can be readily lifted off and removed from the running-gear; this will be a great economy in wagon-beds, as a great many of them are ruined on a march in hauling heavy timber for bridges, poles for corduroy, &c., to say nothing of the convenience of loading, particularly long timber, and making short turns in the woods to get the wagon into position to load. Another advantage is, that on a rainy day the wagon body can be set on the ground, and the loading kept in it as dry as if it were on its wheels.

In camps and, in fact, about garrisons, where wood is obtained from the forest, and where officers do not take the trouble to make wood-racks, a great many wagon-beds are crushed out and ruined by loading firewood on them. With standards wood could be cut long and loaded between them.

These are small things, but should the suggestions be followed I think they would prove a convenience and economy in the end.

Immediately on the receipt of your letter of the 26th December last, directing me to call on the chief quartermasters of General Sherman's army for reports of the operations of the Quartermaster's Department on the campaign from Atlanta to Savannah, I called on the chief quartermasters of the two wings and of the different corps for reports. I have not as yet been able to get reports from either Colonel Conklin, chief quartermaster of the Right Wing, Lieut. Col. G. L. Fort or Lieut. Col. E. M. Joel, chief quartermasters of the Fifteenth and Seventeenth Army Corps.* My report would have been forwarded sooner had I not waited to get reports from these officers. I have finally concluded to make it without them. I will forward these reports as soon as received.

I inclose you a statement of captured and abandoned animals, marked A. I inclose also the reports of Maj. G. E. Dunbar, chief quartermaster of the Cavalry corps; Capt. J. E. Remington, chief quartermaster (acting) of the Fourteenth Army Corps, and of Capt. H. M. Whittelsey, acting chief quartermaster of the Twentieth Army Corps.

I am, general, your obedient servant,

L. C. EASTON,

Brevet Brigadier-General, Chief Quartermaster.

A.—*Statement of the number of animals captured, abandoned, died, killed, &c., by the army under Maj. Gen. W. T. Sherman, on the march from Atlanta to Savannah, from November 15 to December 20, 1864.*

Command.	Captured.			Abandoned, died, &c.		
	Horses.	Mules.	Total.	Horses.	Mules.	Total.
Headquarters Military Division of the Mississippi	3	25	28	4	11	15
Fourteenth Army Corps	545	1,402	1,947	310	447	757
Seventeenth Army Corps	562	1,064	1,626	(a)	(a)	(a)
Fifteenth Army Corps	506	641	1,147	50	193	243
Twentieth Army Corps	410	1,020	1,430	402	524	926
Cavalry command	1,414	773	2,187	2,343	408	2,751
First Michigan Engineers	10	5	15	7	20	27
Total	3,450	4,930	8,380	3,116	1,603	4,719

a No report.

L. C. EASTON,

Brevet Brigadier-General and Chief Quartermaster.

B.—*Statement of cattle on hand at Atlanta, captured en route to Savannah, slaughtered, and remaining on hand when army arrived at Savannah, Ga.*

Command.	On hand.	Captured.	Total.	Slaughtered.	Remaining.
Twentieth Army Corps	429	2,204	2,633	889	1,744
Fourteenth Army Corps	2,047	590	2,637	20	2,617
Fifteenth Army Corps } Seventeenth Army Corps }	1,000	10,500	11,500	9,000	2,500
Total	3,476	13,294	16,770	9,909	6,861

NOTE.—In addition to this there were about 2,000 in droves not connected with the troops.

A. BECKWITH,

Chief Commissary of Subsistence, Colonel and Aide-de-Camp.

* For Fort's report (subsequently received), see No. 93, p. 404.

No. 91.

OFFICE CHIEF QUARTERMASTER, TWENTIETH ARMY CORPS,
Savannah, Ga., January 20, 1865.

Bvt. Brig. Gen. L. C. EASTON,
Chief Quartermaster Military Division of the Mississippi:

GENERAL: In compliance with the requirements of the letter of the Quartermaster-General of the 26th ultimo, I respectfully submit the following memoirs upon the march of the trains and upon the operations of the quartermaster's department of this corps since the army left Atlanta, including all operations up to the occupation of Savannah.

The tabular statements herewith inclosed are copies of a report made by me to the general commanding this corps, and embrace the following statements:

First. Of the amount of forage taken from the country in foraging expeditions sent out under my direction, by which the animals of the army were fed when supplies were cut off by the enemy's destruction of our railroad communications.

Second. Of the number of animals captured, lost, abandoned, and killed, and of the amount of forage taken from the country on the march.

Third. Of the movements of the trains of this corps, the time of breaking and going into camp, showing the distance made each day, the place of encampment, the state of the weather, the condition of the roads, and remarks referring to the operations of the troops, so far as they came under my observation.

The means of transportation of this corps on the 31st of October consisted of 794 army wagons and 110 two-horse ambulances. This number was reduced by turning in a large number of vehicles. We began the march with 598 army wagons and 105 ambulances. Of these we did not lose one.

The animals had while in Atlanta been kept at constant labor in transporting to Rough and Ready the baggage of persons going south when ordered to leave the city, and in work upon the fortifications thrown up by our own troops while holding that place. They had suffered, too, greatly for the want of forage before the foraging expeditions were sent out. Hence, on the march we lost or had to abandon a large number of animals, but were able to more than replace them with stock taken from the country. This was greatly superior to any I had ever seen in Government service. We entered Savannah with animals on an average 100 per cent. better than those we started with; we brought to Savannah few empty wagons; we had on hand every pound of artillery ammunition and almost every pound of small-arm ammunition. No large amount of subsistence stores, except hard-bread, was taken from the train, whilst, on the other hand, a large amount of property of various kinds was added to the loadings.

The troops lived luxuriously and the animals were generously fed. The composition of the column with which we moved was admirable. With a pontoon train, a corps of engineers, and the infantry in part unincumbered and in part distributed along the trains, no impediments delayed us long. We could corduroy many miles of road, rebuild or construct bridges, and bring our wagons through almost bottomless swamps and over almost impracticable roads.

I cannot suggest any defects in organization, personal or material, of the department as shown by the results of this campaign; on the contrary, everything seemed to prove the ability, foresight, and skill of the generals commanding and of the chiefs of the several staff departments. I am at a loss, too, within the limited space allowed me to set forth the manifold incidents of the march, which was full of interest and information. The experience of commanding officers and of officers of every department was greatly enlarged. That experience will hereafter enable the one with wisdom and the other with competent knowledge to conduct campaigns which will add luster to our arms and greatly promote the interests of our Government with a small loss of life and little expenditure of means.

All of which is respectfully submitted.

Your obedient servant,

HENRY M. WHITTELSEY,

Capt. and Actg. Chief Quartermaster Twentieth Army Corps.

Report of foraging expeditions sent out by the Twentieth Army Corps, Army of the Cumberland, from Atlanta, Ga., October, 1864.

Date.	Command.	Army wagons.	Ambulances.	2-horse wagons.	Carts.	Buggies.	Corn.	Fodder.	Subsistence supplies.
1864.							*Pounds.*	*Pounds.*	
Oct. 13	Brigadier-General Geary, Second Division, Capt. G. L. Parker, assistant quartermaster.	420	....	....	....	....	352,800	28,200	Cattle, sheep, hogs.
20	Colonel Robinson, Third Brigade, First Division, Capt. E. P. Graves, assistant quartermaster.	671	33	8	10	11	551,488	30,000	Poultry, lard, butter.
24	Colonel Dustin, Second Brigade, Third Division, Capt. M. Summers, assistant quartermaster.	825	51	(*a*)	(*a*)	(*a*)	607,380	50,000	Meal, honey, sirup, &c.
29	Brigadier-General Geary, Second Division, Capt. G. L. Parker, assistant quartermaster.	652	....	....	....	....	420,800	30,000	
	Total	....	....	....	....	....	1,932,468	138,200	

a Vehicles of all classes.

The trains of the following commands were supplied with forage obtained on these expeditions: Fourth Corps, Fourteenth Corps, Fifteenth Corps, Seventeenth Corps, and Twentieth Corps, headquarters Department of the Cumberland; medical supply, Department of the Cumberland; Cavalry division; Signal Corps, Department of the Cumberland; ordnance, Department of the Cumberland, batteries; Missouri Engineers, Michigan Engineers, post and detachments.

The following is the number of animals fed:

	Horses.	Mules.
Twentieth Corps	1,631	3,962
Other commands	405	3,564
Total	2,036	7,526

Report of animals and forage captured, of animals lost, killed, and abandoned by Twentieth Army Corps, Left Wing, Army of Georgia, on the march from Atlanta to Savannah, Ga., from November 15 to December 21, 1864.

Command.	Animals captured.		Animals lost, killed, and abandoned.		Forage taken from country.			Subsistence.
	Horses.	Mules.	Horses.	Mules.	Corn.	Corn fodder.	Rice fodder.	
					Pounds.	Pounds.	Pounds.	
Headquarters Left Wing and Twentieth Army Corps—corps supply and artillery trains, Capt. J. A. Schoeninger, acting assistant quartermaster.	185	217	246	155	150,000	210,000	95,000	Cattle, sheep, hogs.
Ambulance Corps, Capt. J. F. Rowe, acting assistant quartermaster.	9	45	32	17	47,764	....	17,694	Poultry, &c.
First Division, Capt. G. B. Cadwalader, assistant quartermaster.	20	174	10	10	382,602	469,119	100,000	
Second Division, Capt. G. L. Parker, assistant quartermaster.	84	267	32	32	299,421	262,500	88,000	
Third Division, Capt. H. A. Lacey, assistant quartermaster.	112	317	82	82	348,197	150,000	250,000	
Total	410	1,020	402	524	1,227,984	1,091,619	550,694	

Report of movements of trains Twentieth Army Corps, Left Wing, Army of Georgia, on the march from Atlanta to Savannah, Ga., November 15 to December 31, 1864.

HEADQUARTERS TWENTIETH ARMY CORPS,
OFFICE CHIEF QUARTERMASTER,
Savannah, Ga., January 19, 1865.

Tuesday, November 15.—Left camp 9 a. m.; arrived at Stone Mountain 5 p. m.; distance, 16 miles; roads good; weather fine. Left Atlanta; the public buildings destroyed and part of the city on fire.

Wednesday, November 16.—Left camp 9.30 a. m.; arrived at McGuire's farm 4.30 p. m.; distance, 8 miles; roads good; weather fine.

Thursday, November 17.—Left camp 7.30 a. m.; arrived at near Cornish Creek 6.30 p. m.; distance, 15 miles; roads good; weather fine.

Friday, November 18.—Left camp 7.30 a. m.; arrived at Jones' farm 7.30 p. m.; distance, 16 miles; roads good; weather, rained in the night. Destroying Georgia Railroad—burned depots, tanks, &c., and destroyed track and wood at Social Circle and Rutledge.

Saturday, November 19.—Left camp 7 a. m.; arrived at Brock's farm, beyond Madison, 1 p. m.; distance, 7 miles; roads good; weather rainy. Second Division sent to burn bridge across Oconee River.

Sunday, November 20.—Left camp 8 a. m.; arrived toward Eatonton 4.30 p. m.; distance, 12 miles; roads good; weather cloudy—rained at 5 p. m.

Monday, November 21.—Left camp 7 a. m.; arrived 5 miles beyond Eatonton 12 m.; distance, 13 miles; roads very muddy—bad; weather very rainy. Hard frost this night.

Tuesday, November 22.—Left camp 7.30 a. m.; arrived at Milledgeville 5 p. m.; distance, 15 miles; roads fair; weather very cold, but clear.

Wednesday, November 23.—In camp all day; weather very cold, but clear. Burnt arsenal and penitentiary; destroyed arms and munitions of war.

Thursday, November 24.—Left camp 8 a. m.; arrived near Bluff Creek 4 p. m.; distance, 13 miles; roads fine; weather fine—cold. Built bridge over Buffalo Creek.

Friday, November 25.—Left camp 8 a. m.; arrived at Buffalo Creek 4.30 p. m.; distance, 8 miles; roads fine; weather fine—warmer. Skirmish with the enemy this evening.

Saturday, November 26.—Left camp 7 a. m.; arrived at Sandersville 10 a. m.; by odometer, distance, 8 miles; roads good; weather fine—warm. Skirmishing on entering Sandersville. Fourteenth Corps train precedes ours.

Sunday, November 27.—Left camp 9 a. m.; arrived at Davisborough 6.30 p. m.; distance, 15.27 miles; roads good; weather fine—warm. Burnt the court-house and jail at Sandersville before marching.

Monday, November 28.—Left camp 7.30 a. m.; arrived at Ogeechee River 12 m.; distance, 9.23 miles; roads swampy; weather fine—warm. First and Second Divisions sent to destroy the railroad from Davisborough to the river; we found the bridge across Ogeechee burnt—rebuilt it.

Tuesday, November 29.—Left camp 12 m.; arrived beyond Louisville 5 p. m.; distance, 6.13 miles; roads good, except through the swamps, which we corduroyed; weather fine—warm. Crossed on pontoons, passing through Louisville.

Wednesday, November 30.—Weather fine—warm; roads good, except through the swamps, which we corduroyed. First and Second Division troops rejoin command.

Thursday, December 1.—Left camp 9 a. m.; arrived at Baker's Creek, near Birdsville, 5.15 p. m.; distance, 13.17 miles; roads good, except through the swamps, which we corduroyed; weather fine—warm. Michigan Engineers built bridges across creeks.

Friday, December 2.—Left camp 7.30 a. m.; arrived at Buck Head Church 4.15 p. m.; distance, 10.89 miles; roads good, except through the swamps, which we corduroyed; weather cloudy. Passed the Millen (prison) stockade on our left.

Saturday, December 3.—Left camp 8 a. m.; arrived at Horse Creek 5.15 p. m.; distance, 15.52 miles; roads good, except swamps; weather fine. Some of our troops destroyed a mill half a mile on left of road, burning the sluice gate and flooding the road, delaying the trains 12 hours.

Sunday, December 4.—Left camp 7 a. m.; arrived at pine woods 5 p. m.; distance, 14.73 miles; roads good, except swamps; weather fine. Train of cavalry division (211 wagons) ordered to move with us.

Monday, December 5.—Left camp 4 p. m.; arrived near Little Ogeechee River 6 p. m.; distance, 2.81 miles; roads good, except swamps; weather fine. Roads barricaded by fallen timbers.

Tuesday, December 6.—Left camp 6 a. m.; arrived at Cowpen Creek 4.30 p. m.; distance, 16.26 miles; roads good, except swamps; weather, rained in night. Crossed Turkey Creek. Collected captured horses and mules here to remount cavalry who had lost animals in late action at Waynesborough.

Wednesday, December 7.—Left camp 8.30 a. m.; arrived at Ebenezer Creek, near Springfield, 4 p. m.; distance, 9.68 miles; roads swampy; weather fine.

Thursday, December 8.—Left camp 9 a. m.; arrived at Springfield 12 m.; distance, 0.93 mile; roads swampy; weather fine.

Thursday, December 8.—Left camp 3 p. m.; arrived at Saint Augustine's Creek 7 p. m.; distance, 5.55 miles; roads swampy; weather fine. Not much forage or subsistence stores found in the country passed over in the last two days—it is all rice fields and swamps.

Friday, December 9.—Left camp 9.30 a. m.; arrived near Monteith 5.45 p.m.; distance, 14.15 miles; roads good—turnpike; weather cloudy. Found forts in front and the roads barricaded; attacked the forts—rebels evacuated.

Saturday, December 10.—Left camp 10 a. m.; arrived 5 miles from Savannah 4.30 p. m.; distance, 10.53 miles; roads good—turnpike; weather cloudy. Captured General Harrison, commandant at forts, yesterday.

Sunday, December 11.—Weather fine until the 21st. First day's siege of Savannah.

Monday, December 12.—Winegar's battery captured the Confederate steamer Resolute with 7 officers and 16 men.

Tuesday, December 13.—Steamer Resolute turned over to me; manned her and commenced repairs. Fort McAllister captured. Running the rice mills in the neighborhood.

Wednesday, December 14.—

Thursday, December 15.—Sent 150 wagons to King's Bridge for supplies.

Friday, December 16.—

Saturday, December 17.—Received our first mail.

Sunday, December 18.—

Monday, December 19.—

Tuesday, December 20.—Savannah evacuated.

Wednesday, December 21.—Left camp 12.30 p. m.; arrived 2.30; distance, 5.50 miles; moved into the city.

Twenty-five marching days, averaging 11.25 miles per day, 281.55.

HENRY M. WHITTELSEY,

Captain, Acting Chief Quartermaster Twentieth Army Corps.

No. 92.

OFFICE CHIEF QUARTERMASTER, CAVALRY COMMAND,

Savannah, Ga., January 19, 1865.

Bvt. Maj. Gen. M. C. MEIGS,

Quartermaster-General U. S. Army, Washington, D. C.:

GENERAL: In accordance with instructions received from your office this date, I have the honor to submit the following report of the marches of the cavalry trains and operations of the quartermaster's department from November 15, 1864, up to the time of reaching position before Savannah, December 10, 1864:

Left Atlanta on the morning of the 15th of November, marching toward McDonough. Had a good road, with the exception of one bad hill, until we got within about seven miles of McDonough, when we had a bad creek to cross; here the road in wet weather must be very soft and bad. Passed through McDonough on the 17th. We had good roads from this on until we reached Ocmulgee Mills, on the Ocmulgee River, November 19. On the south side of Ocmulgee River there is a very long, steep hill. It had been raining, and the mud was very deep and heavy on the steepest part of the hill. Before my train arrived there nearly every wagon stalled. There was a large pioneer corps at the hill, but they only helped push when the wagons stalled. I took a small number of negro pioneers I had and shoveled all the mud off to the side of the road. This left the road very slippery, as the soil was clayey. I then had the road picked up into the dry earth and made rough, and the trains went up the hill without any difficulty. I would here remark that I had organized a pioneer corps of fifty negroes, with picks, spades, and axes, and all through the march I found their services invaluable. Indeed, without their services it would have been impossible for me to have got my train along. I think every division train should have a pioneer corps along with it on all marches, and then that quartermasters should see that any bad places in the road are repaired before a wagon is stalled or broken down in them; this is often not the case. My experience is that "one minute's work in time" repairing roads "saves more than nine."

The road from Ocmulgee to Milledgeville is very low and soil clayey. In dry weather roads are very good; but when I moved over them it was raining and the roads were terrible, the wagons often going in up to the beds in mud. At least one-half of the roads would have to be corduroyed in order to pass heavy trains in wet weather. Arrived at Milledgeville November 24.

The road from Milledgeville to Sandersville I found very good until we got near Sandersville, where we had Buffalo Swamp and Buffalo Creek to pass. This was a bad swamp and had to be corduroyed for about half a mile. The road was good from Sandersville to the Ogeechee River and soil sandy. Reached Ogeechee River at night, 28th of November. Enemy attacked rear of my train, but were repulsed. On the south side of the Ogeechee River there is a very bad swamp, and between two and three miles of it had to be corduroyed. The marsh was so soft it required a force constantly at work on it, as the timber all sank down into the ground.

Crossed Big Buck Head Creek at Big Buck Head Church. Here was an admirable place, especially on the south side, for a force to prevent an enemy's crossing. December 3 passed to the east of Millen; roads very low and swampy. In wet weather they must be almost impassable. December 4, on the road from Millen to Springfield, had to cross one very bad swamp, where it was necessary to build a corduroy road for half a mile. From this time until we reached Springfield we had a constant succession of swamps. About ten miles northeast of Springfield there is a swamp five miles wide, and in order to make it available for military operations in wet weather it would be necessary to corduroy the whole five miles. I saw more than 100 wagons stalled in this swamp and a number broken down. The pioneer corps of the army had gone on ahead before the roads were bad, consequently there were but very few men to repair the road.

The regular pioneers usually go in advance of the army and repair some of the worst places. By the time half of the trains have passed over the roads in this marshy country, places that were at first apparently good have become very bad; and as the pioneers are out of reach, the quartermaster has to rely upon his own resources, and I would urge this as another reason why each division quartermaster should be required to have a pioneer corps and then repair the roads where he sees that they need repairing.

I left Springfield on the 8th of December and arrived within six miles of Savannah on the night of 10th instant. Roads mostly very good, but had two or three swamps to pass through. I would respectfully suggest that improvements might be made in running trains. Instead of moving large trains, say 200 wagons, as an entire train, and on good roads hurrying the rear wagons up to "keep closed up," and jamming up together at bad places and waiting, I would divide the 200 wagons into sections of not more than fifty wagons in each, then place the slowest walking teams I had at the head of each section and move the head of each section as slow as I possibly could, allowing for bad places and the little stops that always will occur through the train. This will keep the last team of each section on a fast walk, and will allow the gaps that must occur to be between sections instead of between wagons. This will give the wagon-masters a chance to attend better to the teams under their charge. The sections are bound to come together at every bad place, and by this means will move much more steadily and avoid all hurry and trotting of teams. Owing to the scarcity of forage and the impracticability of hitching the mules away from the wagons, the mules very often eat the wagon tongues and end gates so as to spoil them. The iron to protect them cannot always be procured in the field, and I would suggest that all contractors be required to nail strips of iron along the tops of wagon tongues and end gates to prevent the mules from eating them. I think it would be economy to manufacture jockey sticks out of half-inch round iron instead of wood, as so many of them are broken.

I have made these few suggestions (as per invitation), because I think if acted upon they would benefit the service; and hoping they may not be amiss,

I am, general, very respectfully, your obedient servant,

G. E. DUNBAR,

Maj. and Chief Quartermaster Cav. Command, Army of Georgia.

No. 93.

OFFICE CHIEF QUARTERMASTER, FIFTEENTH ARMY CORPS,
In the Field, South Carolina, January 26, 1865.

Maj. Gen. M. C. MEIGS,
Quartermaster-General:

(Through Brig. Gen. L. C. Easton, chief quartermaster.)

GENERAL: I have the honor to respectfully report, in compliance with the order of the Quartermaster-General, dated at Savannah, Ga., December 26, 1864, that on the 15th day of November last the Fifteenth Army Corps left Atlanta, Ga., with about 850 six-mule teams and 150 two-horse and two-mule ambulances, divided among the four divisions of the corps, which amounted to about forty teams to the thousand troops for duty, not counting non-effective or civil employés. About 225 of these wagons were loaded with ammunition, each carrying 2,500 pounds net ammunition, which was not diminished much until we commenced the siege of Savannah.

About 500 wagons were loaded with commissary stores, forty-eight boxes of hard bread each, and other stores were more heavily loaded.

The remainder of the trains were loaded with hospital stores, pioneer tools and materials, a small quantity of camp and garrison equipage, and officers' private baggage. Eight wagons were loaded with shoes and socks.

Each wagon and ambulance, in addition, on the start, carried five days' forage of grain and three rounds of shoes for its team. Before this forage was expended plenty was found in the country, and until wagons were emptied by issue forage was gathered and brought in by mounted "bummers."

When we set out our mules were in bad condition, having been starved around Atlanta for want of forage, but soon recruited on the march by good care. Fresh mules were gathered to replace the broken down from persons whose names are unknown, and when we arrived at Savannah our trains were very fine.

An active lieutenant and regimental quartermaster was detailed to assist the division quartermaster in the movement of his trains, and usually remained in the rear with a small detachment of negro pioneers and good, fresh mules, ready harnessed, to help forward any wagon in distress. Miles of corduroy were built almost every day by organized pioneers, without which the trains could not have been moved.

The pontoon train belonging to the Army of the Tennessee was badly appointed and utterly without organization, and therefore caused much trouble and delay. The trains of the Fifteenth Corps were often called upon to go back a day and night's march and haul it up, and finally had to take one-half of it to haul all the time. Why it was in such condition is unknown to me. Had it not been for this matter the march would have been made by our trains with ease, and the mules improved every day until we entered Savannah; after which they were soon much reduced for want of forage, having nothing but a very little rice for a considerable time.

I have the honor to be, general, very respectfully, your most obedient servant,

G. L. FORT,

Lieut. Col. and Chief Quartermaster Fifteenth Army Corps.

No. 94.

OFFICE CHIEF QUARTERMASTER, FIFTEENTH ARMY CORPS,
Louisville, Ky., July 1, 1865.

Maj. Gen. M. C. MEIGS,
Quartermaster-General U. S. Army, Washington, D. C.:

GENERAL: I have the honor to respectfully report that at the close of my last annual report, June 30, 1864, I was on duty at Memphis, Tenn., in charge of river transportation and what appertained thereto, by the assignment of Brig. Gen. Robert Allen, chief quartermaster, and reporting to Capt. A. R. Eddy, assistant quartermaster, in charge of the depot, and so continued on duty until September 1. Having been, by direction of the President, assigned to duty as chief quartermaster of the Fifteenth Army Corps, with the rank of lieutenant-colonel from July 21, 1864, was therefore relieved from duty at Memphis, and after transferring the public property in my charge, on the 15th day of September, 1864, left Memphis to join the corps, and proceeded via Cairo, Ill., Louisville, Ky., and Nashville, Tenn., and arrived at Atlanta, Ga., September 25, and reported to Maj. Gen. P. J. Osterhaus, then commanding the corps, and on the 28th of September was announced as chief quartermaster, and immediately entered upon duty. The corps consisted of four divisions.

October 4, 1864.—The corps, with the other armies under the command of General Sherman, started in pursuit of the rebel army under the command of the rebel General Hood.

The mules of the corps were poor and miserable, and we had no forage. Hood was not overtaken, and General Sherman returned with his army to Atlanta, Ga., early in November, and fitted out as well as possible and loaded the trains with supplies, and on the 15th day of November, 1864, severed all communications with the north and set out on a campaign which, after continued skirmishing, hard marching, and a battle at Griswoldville, the assault of Fort McAllister, and the siege of Savannah, terminated in the capture of that city on the 21st day of December. We foraged upon the country and recruited our animals on the campaign, but there being no forage to be had in Savannah, they soon became considerably reduced.

January 8, 1865.—Maj. Gen. John A. Logan returned and resumed command of the corps, and a new campaign was begun through South Carolina.

The corps proceeded to Beaufort, S. C., partly by small ocean steamers and partly by water. It rained in torrents almost every day and the whole country was flooded.

January 28.—The corps began to move from Beaufort; passed Pocotaligo, and then floundered on through the mud and water to Columbia, the capital of the State of South Carolina, which was captured, occupied, and burned on the 17th day of February, having had continued fighting and skirmishing from Savannah.

February 21.—We again resumed our march, and thousands of refugees—white, black, and mixed—followed. The roads were worse. We had to corduroy and bridge miles of swamp every day. Captured Cheraw, S. C., Fayetteville, N. C., and on the 20th and 21st days of March had a battle at and near Bentonville, N. C., and entered Goldsborough, N. C., March 24, where we received supplies.

April 10.—We again set out on another campaign. The roads were very bad. We reached, captured, and entered Raleigh, the capital of North Carolina, April 13, and here we rested until the rebel General Johnston surrendered his army to General Sherman, when we made ready to march homeward.

April 29.—We set out lightly loaded for Washington City, and of course having no opposition, reached Alexandria, Va., via Petersburg and Richmond, May 19, 1865.

Major-General Logan having been assigned to the command of the Army of the Tennessee, Major-General Hazen assumed command of the Fifteenth Army Corps May 22 [23].

May 24.—The corps was reviewed in Washington City, and immediately after commenced embarkation by the Baltimore and Ohio Railroad via Parkersburg, and by the Ohio River in transports, to Louisville, Ky., where the corps went into camp, and now awaits orders.

No public property for which I was accountable has been lost, destroyed, or captured during the year, and all forage gathered and all property captured during the year by the corps has been taken up and accounted for by the division quartermasters.

2. Reference is respectfully made to a statement made in accordance with Form A, to be filed herewith.

3. Reference is respectfully had to a statement made in accordance with Form B, to be filed herewith.

4. Reference is respectfully made to a statement of public moneys, to be filed herewith.

5. Reference is respectfully made to a statement of the amount of transportation furnished during the year, to be filed herewith.

6. I have the honor to respectfully state that I have performed no duties during the year that could not be reported under this head.

7. Reference is respectfully made to a statement made in accordance with Form C, to be filed herewith.

I have the honor to be, very respectfully, your most obedient servant,

G. L. FORT,

Lieut. Col. and Chief Quartermaster Fifteenth Army Corps.

*Statement of quartermaster's property for the fiscal year ending June 30, 1865.**

Statement of public moneys for the fiscal year ending 30th day of June, 1865.

On hand July 1, 1864	$18,552.43
Received from officers during the year	79,302.59
Received from sale of property and other sources during the year	1,135.00
Total received during the year	98,990.02
Expended during the year	23,579.65
Transferred to officers during the year	75,410.37
Total expended and transferred	98,990.02

Statement made in accordance with paragraph 5, section 5, of General Orders, No. 29, Quartermaster-General's Office, series of 1864.

No amounts were paid by me for railroad or other land transportation during the year ending the 30th of June, 1865.

No amounts were paid by me for transportation on rivers or lakes, or for transportation by sail or steam vessels on the ocean, during this year.

The steamers chartered and employed by me on the rivers, as per my roll No. 2, were all paid on voucher, Form No. 22.

Vessels seized and used, the rate of hire of which were not agreed upon, were given vouchers, stating the period of service, but not the rate of pay. This was left to be fixed by Col. L. B. Parsons, chief quartermaster Western river transportation.

The money received by these vessels for private freight and passengers carried by them was indorsed on their vouchers, to be deducted by Colonel Parsons upon settlement.

Estimated amount of transportation furnished for—	Tons.
Subsistence stores	1,876
Ordnance stores	660
Quartermaster's stores	9,108
Medical stores	176
Total	11,820
Number of troops	44,000

Statement of vessels chartered or employed during the fiscal year ending the 30th day of June, 1865.†

* Omitted; but see pp. 648, 649, of Executive Document No. 1, referred to in foot-note (*), p. 249.

† Omitted; but see p. 651 of Executive Document No. 1, referred to in foot-note (*), p. 249.

No. 95.

HEADQUARTERS FOURTEENTH ARMY CORPS,
OFFICE CHIEF QUARTERMASTER,
Louisville, Ky., July 1, 1865.

In accordance with General Orders, No. 29, Quartermaster-General's Office, dated Washington, D. C., July 6, 1864, I submit herewith my annual report for the fiscal year ending the 30th day of June, 1865.

My report as assistant quartermaster, U. S. Volunteers, on duty as such with the Second Division, Fourteenth Army Corps, for fiscal year ending the 30th day of June, 1864, was forwarded from in front of Atlanta, Ga., during the month of July last. Concerning my services previously to the present report I have the honor to refer the department to that report, merely stating here that on the 1st day of July, 1864, I was still on duty, by order of the chief quartermaster of the Department of the Cumberland, as assistant quartermaster, Second Division, Fourteenth Army Corps.

July 1, 1864.—The Second Division, Fourteenth Army Corps, was still lying in front of Kenesaw Mountain, where it remained until the falling back of General Joe Johnston.

July 3.—Started at daylight with the train across Pine Mountain, toward Marietta, Ga., this place having been during the night evacuated by the rebel forces. Owing to the great number of transportation on the road leading from Big Shanty to Marietta, on the right of Kenesaw Mountain, was unable to proceed farther than to the neighborhood of Marietta; went in camp about one mile from Military Institute; water and grazing good; weather warm.

July 4.—Started at daylight; passed by Military Institute; took county cross-roads to the right of Marietta and Chattahoochee Railroad bridge road; camped near a good large spring, about seven miles from Marietta; weather very warm; distance of day's march, eight miles.

July 5.—In camp.

July 6.—Started at daylight on the road leading toward Vining's Station; camped about equal distance from the Chattahoochee River and Vining's Station, to the right of wagon road from Marietta to Chattahoochee bridge; distance of day's march, nine miles; weather very warm.

July 6 to July 17.—In camp; supplies drawn from depot at Marietta; refitted Second Division, Fourteenth Army Corps, with the required estimates of clothing, &c.

July 18.—Started at 2.30 a. m., Vining's Station; camped half a mile beyond Vining's Station, near Chattahoochee River; distance of day's march, four miles; weather very warm.

July 19 to July 23.—In camp repairing transportation.

July 24.—Crossed Chattahoochee River with train; camped four miles from Atlanta, about one mile from railroad.

July 25 to August 3.—In camp; weather very warm; drawing forage from Vining's Station.

August 4.—Directed by Col. A. J. Mackay to receive and issue the full estimates of clothing, camp and garrison equipage, and quartermaster's stores to the Fourteenth Army Corps.

August 5 to August 8.—Very busy issuing; supplies having been sent without invoices, and having been unloaded at Vining's Station without having been notified, causes me to take double care in invoicing as well as issuing same.

August 9 to 19, inclusive.—In camp; was ordered to report, by direction of General Thomas, commanding the department, to commanding officer Fourteenth Army Corps, in the capacity as acting chief quartermaster Fourteenth Army Corps.

August 20.—Troops moving in the morning, but return to old camp at night; weather very fine.

August 21 to August 24.—In camp, transferring transportation to Lieut. A. L. Coe, acting assistant quartermaster, Second Division, Fourteenth Army Corps.

August 25.—Started at 7 a. m.; moved eight miles to the right; weather fine.

August 26.—Started at 12.30 p. m. toward the right; heavy rain, making road very bad; camped at 6.30 p. m.; distance of march, six and a half miles.

August 27.—Moved at daylight in southwest direction; distance of march, one mile.

August 28.—Started at daylight; progress very slow; camped at night at Red Oak Station; weather cloudy.

August 29.—In camp.

August 30.—Moved nearly direct south course to-day; march during day, seven miles.

August 31.—Moved three miles; heavy skirmishing and shelling.

September 1.—Train in camp near Jonesborough; troops heavily engaged.

September 1 to 6, inclusive.—In camp near Jonesborough.

September 7.—Started at daylight for Atlanta.

September 8.—Arrive with train at Atlanta.

September 9 to October 3.—In camp at Atlanta.

CAMPAIGN AFTER HOOD.

October 3, 1864.—Left Atlanta, Ga., on the return after Hood. The Second Division, Fourteenth Army Corps, having been ordered to the rear by the railroad on the 29th of September, I was directed by General J. C. Davis, commanding the corps, to order the trains of that division to remain at Atlanta, Ga.; camped at the railroad bridge across the Chattahoochee; distance of day's march, eight miles.

October 4.—Started at 8.30 a. m.; camped at old camp, eight miles from Marietta, but having been in camp about three hours received marching orders; left again at 4 p. m. on a road leading toward Mount Zion Church; went in camp at 9 p. m.; distance of day's march, nine miles; rained slight showers during the day.

October 5.—Started at daylight on a road leading toward Acworth; weather clear, but very warm; camped one mile from Acworth; good water and grazing.

October 6 to 9.—In camp.

October 10.—Started at daylight to Allatoona Pass, five miles from Acworth; arrived there at 9 a. m.; camped at Allatoona Pass till 8 p. m.; received orders to push forward to Etowah River that night; camped on bank of Etowah; arrived at 2 a. m.

October 12.—Left camp at 7 a. m.; passed through Cartersville, Cass Station; camped at Kingston, Ga.; weather very warm; distance of day's march, sixteen miles; succeeded in drawing grain at Kingston, Ga., for use of corps.

October 13.—Left camp with corps train on upper river road; road very swampy; must be impassable in rainy weather; corduroyed fully two miles of road; camped on Rome and Resaca dirt road, five miles from Rome; country rich; succeeded in getting forage from the country for the first time since leaving Atlanta, Ga.; distance of day's march, thirteen miles.

October 14.—Left camp on Rome and Resaca road; the transportation of the army being all on the road, makes it slow progress; distance of day's march, nine miles; forage plenty; road hilly, and plenty of water.

October 15.—Left camp at daylight; passed through Calhoun Station and Resaca Station; camped two and a half miles from Resaca, on Dalton dirt road; distance of day's march, fourteen and a half miles.

October 16.—Left camp at 2.30 p. m. for Resaca; ordered to make Snake Creek Gap; transportation being all on the Snake Creek Gap road, had to lay over till 7 p. m.; camped near Snake Creek Gap; arrived in camp at 10 p. m.; distance of day's march, seven miles.

October 17.—Passed through Snake Creek Gap, having left camp at 5 a. m.; camped at Ship's Gap; distance of day's travel, fifteen miles; day warm; forage scarce.

October 18.—Left Ship's Gap, on Summerville road; weather clear; distance of day's march, twelve miles.

October 19.—Started at daylight; made ten miles; camped near Chattooga River; weather clear; crossed Chattooga River after dark.

October 20.—Started at 10 a. m.; passed through Summerville, Ga.; town deserted; camped near Tacoosa Creek, bottom land, near Gaylesville, Ala.; distance of day's march, fourteen miles; forage plenty.

October 20 to 29.—In camp; directed train of First Division and Third Division, Fourteenth Army Corps, to report at Rome, Ga., after rations for command, with orders to remain at that point until further orders.

October 30.—Started at 4 a. m. for Rome, Ga., on Rome and Gaylesville road; weather fair; distance of day's march, twenty-six miles; road good.

October 31.—In camp at Rome, Ga.

November 1.—Started at 11.30 a. m.; camped on main road from Rome to Kingston, Ga., eight miles from Rome, near good water; day very fine.

November 2.—Started at daylight for Kingston, Ga.; camped at Kingston, Ga.; weather fine; distance of day's march, five miles.

November 3 to 8.—In camp at Kingston, Ga.

November 8.—Left camp at daylight; passed through Cassville; camped at Cartersville; distance of day's march, sixteen miles; weather cloudy.

November 8 to 12.—In camp at Cartersville, preparing for march toward the sea.

November 13.—Left Cartersville; destroyed bridge across Etowah River; cut loose from communication; passed through Allatoona, six miles; Acworth, five miles; camped at Big Shanty, five miles; distance of day's march, sixteen miles; railroad destroyed effectually.

November 14.—Left camp at daylight; seven miles to Marietta, twelve miles from the Chattahoochee River; camped on the south side of Chattahoochee River; distance of day's march, nineteen miles.

November 15.—Left camp at daylight; arrived with corps train at Atlanta, Ga., about noon, having made with the trains of the Fourteenth Army Corps (Second Division, Fourteenth Army Corps, excepted) 245 miles since the 3d day of October, 1864. Immediately on the arrival at Atlanta I directed the quartermasters of the Fourteenth Army Corps to draw the estimates of clothing and forage required, I having forwarded a special messenger from Kingston, Ga., to Lieut. A. L. Coe, acting assistant quartermaster, Second Division, Fourteenth Army Corps, with the estimates and orders for Lieut. A. L. Coe to draw the same and have everything ready on our arrival at Atlanta. The issues were made with such dispatch that twenty-four hours after our arrival the clothing had been issued to the troops, and all wagons were loaded with the necessary supply for a forward march.

CAMPAIGN THROUGH GEORGIA.

November 16.—Left Atlanta, Ga., at 11.30 a. m.; camped near Atlanta and Augusta Railroad, seventeen miles from Atlanta; weather fair; road leading to the right of Stone Mountain.

November 17.—Started at daylight, road leading through Lithonia Station and Conyers; day fine; forage getting plenty; distance of day's march, fifteen miles; camped near Yellow River.

November 18.—Started at daylight; passed through Covington; day very fine; forage plenty and country well watered; soil sandy; distance of day's march, fifteen miles.

November 19.—Started at daylight; passed through Newborn, or Sandtown, having left the road parallel with the railroad about 9 a. m.; camped four miles from Shady Dale; distance of day's march, seventeen miles; weather cloudy, with occasional slight rain-storms; country rich.

November 20.—Started at daylight; passed through Shady Dale; camped near Eatonton factory, and about fifty bales of cotton destroyed; factory employed about sixty hands in the manufacture of cotton cloth, good water power; country rich; distance of day's march, fourteen miles.

November 21.—Started at daylight; shortly rained very hard all day; country hilly; hills yellow clay mixed with sand, which by the passage of army trains cut up very fast; crossed several creeks at good fords; camped at night at Clopton's Mills; 9 p. m., very high wind, turning exceedingly cold; 4 a. m. of 22d, a light crust of ice on standing water; distance of march, eleven miles.

November 22.—Started at daylight; weather very cold, with high wind; marched eight miles; camped about 2 p. m. at General Cobb's plantation; trains well closed up.

November 23.—Started at daylight; arrived at Milledgeville, the capital of Georgia, about noon; weather fine; forage and water plenty; roads sandy; distance of march, ten miles.

November 24.—Started at noon; crossed Oconee River on bridge; country hilly; soil sandy; forage getting scarcer; camped eight miles from Milledgeville, on Sandersville road; weather fine.

November 25.—Started at daylight; country hilly; have to go some distance off the road to procure sufficient forage for animals; distance of day's march, twelve miles.

November 26.—Started at daylight; slight skirmishing ahead; trains are traveling very compact, with heavy flankers on both sides; weather fine; camped at Sandersville; distance of day's march, six miles; forage plenty and near the main road.

November 27.—Started at daylight, but troops being on the same road, do not get fairly off before noon; weather fine; arrive in camp near Central Railroad after dark; distance of day's march, eight miles.

November 28.—Started at daylight; passed through Davisborough Station; burned station-house, several cotton gins, and effectually destroyed the railroad; crossed Ogeechee River and Rocky Comfort on pontoons; about two miles of very bad swamp; corduroyed through the swamp; arrive with a portion of the corps train at Louisville, Ga.; balance remains on the south side of the Ogeechee River, with orders to push forward at break of day; distance of day's march, fourteen miles.

November 29.—In camp at Louisville; trains all arrive in camp.

November 30.—In camp; weather fine; forage plenty.

December 1.—Left Louisville at daylight on Waynesborough road; day very fine; soil sandy; distance of march, ten miles.

December 2.—Started at daylight; country getting more swampy; saw the first rice field on the campaign; weather fine; distance of march, twelve miles.

December 3.—Started at daylight for Sampson's Station; crossed Buck Head Creek and Rocky Creek, near junction of same, on two boats (pontoons) each; bridges had been destroyed the night previously by some rebel cavalry, said to belong to Wheeler's command; cross three swamps; road seems to be leading around every man's plantation; distance of day's march, eleven miles; camped at Lumpkin's Station at 9 p. m.; slight shower; forage plenty.

December 4.—Started at 9 a. m.; passed Habersham Church; marched thirteen miles on Jacksonborough road, mostly through pine timber.

December 5.—Started at daylight; leave Jacksonborough on our left, and take the old U. S. river mail road; camp at Buck Creek Post-Office; soil sandy; mostly through pine timber, and all low places swampy; have to forage some distance off the road; distance of day's march, sixteen miles.

December 6.—Started at daylight; road passed through swamp immediately after leaving camp on U. S. river mail road, two miles and a half from Savannah River; distance of day's march, twenty-one miles. Scouting and foraging parties find a good many valuable animals hid in the swamps; natives are astonished at the Yankees finding everything; begin to think it is useless to hide from our foragers; quartermasters of the corps are directed to load their trains as heavily as possible with forage and commissary supplies, and, if possible, to forage liberally for that purpose.

December 7.—Marched at daylight; found roads blockaded at four different places and very swampy; camped twenty-seven miles from Savannah, Ga., near Ebenezer Creek; distance of day's march, twelve miles; rained very hard all forenoon.

December 8.—Started at 1 p. m.; crossed two miles of swamp, then Ebenezer Creek; camped near Ebenezer Church; distance of day's march, three miles; twenty-four miles from Savannah, Ga.; rebel gun-boat trying to shell the train, but does no damage.

December 9.—Started at daylight, through very bad swamp; cross two creeks on pontoons; camped four miles from Charleston and Savannah Railroad bridge across the Savannah; distance of march, nine miles, mostly swampy; distance from Savannah, fifteen miles; weather cloudy.

December 10.—Started at daylight; distance of march, four miles; camped near Charleston and Savannah Railroad, eleven miles from Savannah, Ga.; passed a rebel fort pierced for six guns.

December 11.—Started at 11 a. m.; left river road near seven-mile post from Savannah, Ga., for Middle Ground road; camped in a swamp between river road and middle county road; distance of day's march, five miles.

December 12.—Marched at daylight; crossed Central Railroad; camped on Middle Ground road, near Station No. 1, on Central Railroad; traveled three miles and a half; forage from the country reduced to rice and rice straw.

December 13 to December 16.—In camp.

December 17.—Communications fairly open; received to-day the first mail from the North.

December 18 to December 21, inclusive.—In camp, drawing a small amount of forage from King's Bridge, on the Ogeechee River.

December 22.—Entered Savannah; distance from camp, six miles; established headquarters.

December 23 to December 31, inclusive.—At Savannah, Ga.

During my stay at Savannah, Ga., I had the honor of forwarding, as directed by the chief quartermaster Military Division of the Mississippi, Bvt. Brig. Gen. L. C. Easton, my official report of the campaign from Atlanta to Savannah, Ga. To make this report complete, however, in itself, I take the liberty to recapitulate the gross gain of the quartermaster's department of the corps, and most respectfully refer for loss and gain of the different commands of the Fourteenth Army Corps to consolidated report No. 4, herewith annexed. I would most respectfully also draw the attention of the department to the fact that the amount fed to animals during the campaign is by far less than the actual amount consumed. A good many animals during the campaign were picked up by soldiers not connected with regular authorized foraging parties. A good many of these being of a very inferior quality were turned out as soon as the officers commanding the foraging squads got hold of them, and in consequence no account taken of them. In figuring the approximate amount of forage fed I have taken the average number of animals as reported to this office, and allowed to each only the authorized ration.

Total gain in horses during campaign from Atlanta to Savannah, Ga., 232; total gain in mules during campaign from Atlanta to Savannah, Ga., 955; total gain in jacks during campaign from Atlanta to Savannah, Ga., 5; total gain in ponies during campaign from Atlanta to Savannah, Ga., 5; total amount of grain captured during the same time, 1,420,000 pounds; total amount of grain fodder captured during same time, 1,025,000 pounds.

CAMPAIGN THROUGH THE CAROLINAS.

Having been engaged as previously reported from the entrance of the Fourteenth Army Corps in Savannah, Ga., in refitting the corps, clothing for the same being very necessary, as well as rest both for animals and men, headquarters of the Fourteenth Army Corps left Savannah, Ga., on the 25th day of January, 1865, the troops as well as the trains having started several days before, but on account of heavy and constant rains they were for the first time during a year's campaign mud bound. The rain, however, having ceased, headquarters of the corps left Savannah about 11.30 a. m. January 25, 1865, on Middle Ground road, weather being very windy. Camped at night near Eden Church; distance of day's march, twenty miles.

January 26, 1865.—Started at 7.30 a. m. on Springfield road, being most of the distance through swamps; were under the necessity of corduroying constantly; camped at dark in the midst of a swamp three miles from Springfield; distance of day's march, ten miles.

January 27.—Marched at daylight; one mile of very bad swamp before reaching Springfield; leaving Springfield, took Sister's Ferry road; forded Turkey Creek in the immediate neighborhood of Springfield; crossed Ebenezer Creek a few miles on on two pontoons; directly after crossing the last-mentioned creek, a swamp extending about 100 yards, which delayed the passage of the trains for several hours, then timber, with high sandy soil; camped in timber five miles from Springfield; distance of day's march, eight miles.

January 28.—Started at daylight; the road, until striking the old U. S. river mail road, good, then swampy; camped at Sister's Ferry; distance of day's march, five miles.

January 28 to February 4.—In camp at Sister's Ferry, Ga., waiting for Savannah River to recede, it being impossible to get a footing on the South Carolina shore.

February 5.—Crossed Savannah River at Sister's Ferry on pontoon bridge; kept on the north side of the Savannah to Sister's Ferry, S. C., distance about two miles, which was on our arrival on January 28 under water, and in consequence, to enable army trains to proceed, had to be corduroyed.

February 6 and 7.—Receiving supplies, clothing as well as commissaries, at Sister's Ferry, S. C.; supplies and outfits now pretty complete with exception of stockings, of which there is great want in this corps.

February 8.—Trains of the Fourteenth Army Corps on road for Brighton, S. C.; took Hudson Ferry road, which avoids Big Santee Swamp, with exception of an arm of one mile and a half; corduroyed this distance; afterward struck causeway, and road fair; distance of march, seven miles.

February 9.—Marched at daylight on Barnwell Court-House road; road good, and forage, contrary to expectation, is getting plenty; day very fine; roads hilly; soil sandy.

February 10.—Marched at daylight; still on Barnwell Court-House road; saw first white flag at Mrs. Doctor Irwin's, widow lady, claiming protection; camped near Salkehatchie Mills road, on the Savannah Iron Ridge; very good; forage plenty; distance of day's march, twenty-eight miles.

February 11.—Crossed Salkehatchie; bad swamp for three-quarters of a mile; passed through Barnwell Court-House; camped three miles of Barnwell Court-House on Williston road; distance of day's march, six miles.

February 12.—Marched at daylight; passed with train through Williston, on Charleston and Savannah Railroad; camped on south branch of Edisto River; distance of day's march, sixteen miles; weather fine; roads sandy and good.

February 13.—Crossed Edisto on bridge; then one mile and a half of bad swamp; had to corduroy the whole distance; camped on edge of swamp, in large corn-field.

February 14.—Left camp at 9 a. m., on Columbia road, Upper Edisto River; camped on north bank of the same; weather very cold and sleety; distance of day's march, sixteen miles; forage getting very scarce; pine lumber all the way.

February 15.—Marched at daylight; after a few miles, when in the neighborhood of eighteen miles from Columbia, S. C., took Lexington road; road very sandy; country barren; forage scarce for one day's supply, although parties are scouring the country for miles on either side of the road; natives claim from five to ten bushels of corn to the acre; camp in pine timber on Red Bank Creek; distance of day's march, sixteen miles.

February 16.—Started at daylight; passed through Lexington, S. C., at noon; camped on Twelve-Mile Creek; distance, nine miles; weather clear; forage scarce, but water plenty.

February 17.—Started at daylight; crossed the Saluda River on seventeen pontoons; took Columbia and Florence road; camped four miles from Spring Hill road; distance of day's march, fifteen miles; forage to-day plenty; over 3,000 bushels of corn burned by some stragglers against orders.

February 18.—Marched at daylight; camped one mile from Broad River; distance traveled, five miles; road had to be corduroyed for two miles; weather clear and fine.

February 19.—Crossed Broad River on pontoon bridge; camped three miles from Broad River, on Alston road; road for half a mile after leaving the river very bad, swampy, then good.

February 20.—Marched at daylight; camped near Alston and Winnsborough Cross-Roads; road good; soil, red clay; forage plenty; weather fine; distance of march, five miles.

February 21.—Marched at daylight; crossed Little River on bridge; left Winnsborough road and took Chester Court-House road; crossed Jackson's Creek, near Lebanon Church; camped two miles and a half from Adger's Station, on South Carolina and Charlotte Railroad; country rich; weather fine; distance of day's march, ten miles.

February 22.—Marched at daylight; passed through Adger's Station and White Oak Station, on South Carolina and Charlotte Railroad; leave the railroad at the latter point and take the Wateree dirt road; camp near Wateree Church; distance of march, eleven miles; weather fine, but toward evening signs of clouding up; got in camp at 2 p. m.

February 23.—Marched at daylight; crossed Wateree Creek on log bridge; commences to rain; camp near Rocky Mount, on Catawba River; distance of day's march, twelve miles.

February 24.—Started at 11 a. m.; rains in torrents; crossed Catawba River with First Division, Fourteenth Army Corps; banks on both sides very high; soil, red clay; have to corduroy and pull up all teams by run; it requires thirty-two pontoons to bridge the river; river rising very fast.

February 25.—Raining very hard; have to quit passing trains; bridge is broken, and several boats swept away; forage in Catawba Bottom plenty.

February 26.—Still raining; bridge not yet passable; large force at work on it.

February 27.—Still raining; repairing bridge, but current so swift and strong that it is impossible to pass the train; fixing anchors of wood by cutting down large oak trees and tying, by means of fifth-chains, large rocks in the point of the crotch made by the two principal branches of it.

February 28.—Bridge is safe to-day; crossed transportation of the corps on the north side; still raining; mud bottomless; nothing but corduroy of the strongest and heaviest kind will uphold the trains.

March 1.—Started at daylight; roads bottomless; soil, red clay; corduroying all day; on country byroad toward Taxahaw, S. C.; distance of day's march, seventeen miles; still raining.

March 2.—Started at daylight; road still red clay and bottomless; camped at Taxahaw, S. C.; high winds in the evening and appearance of clearing up; forage plenty.

March 3.—Started at daylight; after four miles of red clay soil, which still is next to impassable, strike sandy soil; take the Lancaster and Chesterfield road, twenty miles from Lancaster; leave Lancaster and Chesterfield road nine miles from Chesterfield; take Harley's Ferry road; camped three miles from the cross-roads; the last three miles of red clay soil, requiring corduroy; distance of day's march, twenty-three miles.

March 4.—Started at daylight; after four miles of red clay soil, strike sandy road; distance of day's march, sixteen miles; rained in showers during the day, in the evening clearing up; camped near Sandsborough Ferry, on Pedee River.

March 5 and 6.—In camp.

March 7.—Crossed the Pedee River on pontoon bridge of forty-two pontoons; marched fifteen miles on Fayetteville road; soil, after crossing Pedee River, sandy; forage plenty.

March 8.—Marched at daylight; crossed Lumber River on a bridge—bridge about fifty yards in length; camped near thirty-four-mile post, on Fayetteville road; distance of day's march, twenty miles.

March 9.—Started at daylight; camped at nineteen-mile post from Fayetteville; raining all day; distance of march, fifteen miles; have to corduroy large portions of the road.

March 10.—Marched at daylight; camped at nine-mile post from Fayetteville; distance of day's march, ten miles; still have to corduroy large portions of the road.

March 11.—Marched at daylight; captured Fayetteville, N. C.; distance of day's march, nine miles; established corps headquarters in Government building, near the old U. S. arsenal.

March 12 and 13.—In camp at Fayetteville, drawing commissary supplies and a few pairs of boots and bootees for this corps.

March 14.—Crossed Cape Fear River on seventeen pontoon-boats; camped one mile and a half from the river; weather fine, evening, clouding up.

March 15.—In camp; 12 m. received orders to proceed with train on Raleigh road; road leads through a swamp, and being an old worn-out corduroy, so much the worse; a heavy thunder-storm; distance of day's march, six miles and a half.

March 16.—Wait for trains of corps to close up; 1 p. m. proceed on Raleigh road to the intersection of Goldsborough road; road very bad; have to corduroy continually; distance of day's march, five miles; forage scarce.

March 17.—Started at daylight, with the trains of the corps, on Goldsborough road; road through, as the citizens informed me, is a continual swamp till within the immediate neighborhood of Goldsborough; have to corduroy every inch of two days' road; distance of march, five miles; forage scarce.

March 18.—Started at daylight; nothing but swamp; slow work to get ahead; crossed Black River on a log bridge; distance of day's march, five miles; forage scarce.

March 20.—Started at 1 p. m.; still swamp; corduroyed constantly; distance of day's march, five miles; weather fine.

March 21.—Started at 9 a. m.; crossed South Fork of Falling Creek; road very bad; commenced raining about noon; distance of day's march, five miles.

March 22.—Commenced moving train across North Fork of Falling Creek at 2 a. m.; crossed the creek on a log bridge; two miles after crossing creek strike upland, with sandy soil; camped at cross-roads of Cox's Bridge and Everettsville and Goldsborough and Dead Fields, about three-quarters of a mile from Neuse River, and about five miles from Goldsborough, N. C.; distance of day's march, fifteen miles; weather fine; forage plenty.

March 23.—In camp; ordered trains of the corps to Kinston for supplies; weather fine.

March 24.—Left camp; crossed Neuse River on eight pontoons; established headquarters at Goldsborough, N. C. The capture of Goldsborough, N. C., being the close of the campaign from Savannah, Ga., it will not be amiss at this place to give the gains of the quartermaster's department of the Fourteenth Army Corps during that time. Taking into consideration the long marches through swamps, compelling often that the transportation should be harnessed the largest portion of night and day to enable it to keep up with the troops, has naturally been the cause that the percentage of animals abandoned, killed, and died is larger than on the previous campaign from Atlanta to Savannah, Ga.; the same remarks will apply to the feeding of forage as have been enumerated at length on the close of my report of the Atlanta and Savannah (Ga.) campaign.

For particulars of the captures, &c., of animals during the campaign through the Carolinas, I have the honor to refer to consolidated statement, marked No. 5, herewith annexed. I will only enumerate at this time totals, namely: Total number of horses gained from Savannah to Goldsborough, N. C., 361; number of mules, 806. Total amount of grain captured from Savannah to Goldsborough, N. C., 2,867,820 pounds; total amount of hay, 4,055 pounds. Total amount of fodder captured from Savannah to Goldsborough, N. C., 2,730,460 pounds.

March 25 to April 9, inclusive.—Stationed at Goldsborough, N. C., engaged in completely fitting out the command. How necessary this was it will only need to be mentioned that this corps drew a complete suit for every enlisted man in the command, a good many of the men having really no shoes, stockings, &c., on their arrival at Goldsborough, N. C. I would most respectfully draw the attention of the department to the utter uselessness of sewed boots and bootees for troops on the march. From an experience of four years in the quartermaster's department in the field, I do not hesitate to say and give it as my firm opinion, and have no doubt that the same is shared by every quartermaster in the Western army, that the same, where troops are on the march and cannot draw new ones every two weeks, are worthless; and so well is this understood by every one in this army that it is an impossibility to issue any sewed shoes when any peg shoes can be procured.

April 10.—Having completely fitted out, the trains were ordered to start at daylight on the Smithfield road about two miles from Goldsborough; crossed Little River on a bridge; then road for about six miles good; thence strike swamp, which, it having commenced raining during the forenoon, was soon impassable, and had to fall back on corduroying; camped at night on the crossing of the Smithfield dirt road with the Raleigh and Goldsborough Railroad; distance of day's march, eleven miles.

April 11.—Started at daylight on road through swamps all day; crossed Moccasin Swamp and Creek; distance of day's march, ten miles; corduroyed the whole distance; camped three miles from Smithfield; weather cloudy; forage scarce—hardly any.

April 12.—Started at daylight on road to Smithfield; three miles swamp, and exceedingly hard to corduroy it; arrived at Smithfield with the head of the corps train about 10 a. m.; received the glorious news of Lee's surrender; mass train at Smithfield for the purpose of closing up, the roads being in so bad a condition as to make it nearly impossible to run it in close order. 2 p. m.—Crossed the Neuse River on eight pontoons; take Raleigh road, which is hard and in good condition; camp near Clayton's Station; distance of day's march, fifteen miles.

April 13.—Started at daylight; passed through Clayton's Station; enter Raleigh, N. C., capital of the State, about noon; distance of day's march, fifteen miles; road hilly; red clay; weather cloudy; captured several car-loads of corn and salt; corn slightly damaged by fire.

April 14.—Left Raleigh at 10 a. m. on Hillsborough road, leaving it about seven miles from town, for Jones' Cross-Roads; camped at Jones' Cross-Roads; distance of day's march, fifteen miles; weather sultry and clouding up; roads good; road after leaving railroad in timber.

April 15.—Started at daylight; rain pouring down, making roads impassable; took road to Holly Springs; had to corduroy every foot of the road; distance of day's march, five miles.

April 16.—Started at daylight on Aven's Ferry road; camped with corps trains six miles from Cape Fear River; troops have possession of both banks of the river; roads fair; weather fine; distance of march, six miles; forage plenty.

April 17 to April 19, inclusive.—In camp; foraging on the country.

April 20.—Marched back to Holly Springs; distance, six miles; weather fine.

April 21 and 22.—In camp.

April 23.—General J. C. Davis ordered myself with office to Raleigh to attend to the wants of the quartermaster's department of corps; distance, fifteen miles; road hilly; weather fine.

April 23 to April 27.—In camp; received orders to prepare for homeward march; Johnston's surrender.

April 28 and 29.—Loading trains for homeward march.

April 30.—Leave Raleigh, N. C., on Hillsborough road, to Morrisville Station, then turn to the right for Fish Dam, N. C.; camped on south bank of Winn River; weather fine; roads good; must, however, after a few days' rain, require a good deal of corduroying before passing trains over them; distance of day's march, twenty-nine miles.

May 1.—Marched at daylight; crossed Neuse River—fordable; crossed Tar River on upper ford of Oxford road—fordable, but rocky; camped at Oxford, N. C.; weather fair; distance of day's march, twenty-two miles.

May 2.—Marched at daylight on Boydton (Va.) road; passed through Williamsborough; camped on Roanoke River, at Taylor's Ferry; distance of march, twenty-eight miles; roads good; weather fair; have to wait for pontoon section of Twentieth Corps to come up; river too wide for one section of the pontoon train of the Left Wing.

May 3.—By pontoon train delayed seven hours; crossed Roanoke River at 12 m.; camp at Boydton, Va.; distance of day's march, seven miles; weather fine; road good; thirty-three pontoons required to bridge Roanoke River.

May 4.—March at daylight on Lewiston road; weather cloudy; road red clay; camp at Lewiston, or Lunenburg Court-House; distance of march, twenty-seven miles.

May 5.—Camp broken up, and leave at 5 a. m.; cross south branch of Nottoway Creek at the falls; also north branch of Nottoway Creek—the last has very high banks; pass through Nottoway Court-House at 12 m., having made twenty miles in the forenoon; camp thirteen miles from Nottoway Court-House; distance of day's march, thirty-three miles; weather very warm.

May 6.—Start from camp at 4.30 a. m.; cross Black and White Creek; cross the Appomattox at * * * bridge on nine pontoon boats; camp near Swift Creek, fourteen miles from Richmond; distance of day's march, thirty miles.

May 7.—March at 4.30 a. m.; arrive at Manchester at 9 a. m.; distance of day's march, fourteen miles, having made the trip from Raleigh, N. C., including a delay of seven hours at Taylor's Ferry, N. C., on account of laying pontoon-boats, in seven days and four hours; distance, as traveled by Fourteenth Army Corps, 190 miles, or an average of twenty-seven miles per day.

May 8, 9, and 10.—In camp at Manchester, Va., preparing for march to Alexandria, Va.

May 11.—Start at daylight; cross James River; pass through Richmond, trains going out on the Mechanicsville pike; cross Chickahominy Creek; camp at Hanover Court-House; distance of day's march, eighteen miles; weather sultry, with appearance of thunder-storm. 9 p. m.—Heavy storm; rain falls in torrents.

May 12.—Marched at 7 a. m.; crossed Pamunkey Creek at Page's [Littlepage's] Bridge; pontoons to be relaid every hour; creek rising very rapidly; cross Aquia Creek and Richmond railroad at Chesterfield Station; camp near Mount Carmel Church; distance of day's march, seventeen miles; road hilly; weather fine.

May 13.—Start at 6.30 a. m. on road for Raccoon Ford; pass through Chilesburg and New Market Post-Office; camp at Three-Cornered Handkerchief; distance of march, seventeen miles.

May 14.—Started at 4.30 a. m.; passed Steward's Tavern; camped north side of Rapidan, at Raccoon Ford; weather fine; splendid grazing; distance of march, thirty-three miles.

May 15.—Ordered, with office, forward; leave Raccoon Ford at 4.30 a. m.; pass through Stevensburg, Brandy; cross Rappahannock at Beverly Ford; camp three miles from Warrenton, Va.; distance of day's march, twenty-five miles; country very fertile.

May 16.—Start at 5.30 a. m.; pass through Warrenton, New Baltimore, Buckland, and Gainesville; camp one mile from Centerville, on Fairfax Court-House road; distance of day's march, twenty-five miles.

May 17.—Start at 5.30 a. m.; camp with trains at Fairfax Court-House; report from thence by railroad to General L. C. Easton, chief quartermaster Fourteenth Army Corps.

May 18.—Started with trains for Alexandria; established head-quarters two miles from Alexandria; raining all day.

May 19 to 23.—In camp, refitting men with necessary clothing and camp equipage.

May 24.—Grand review of Sherman's army at Washington City.

May 25.—Cross Potomac River and camp two miles from Washington.

May 26 to June 14.—In camp.

June 15 to June 19.—On board of cars and transported via Baltimore and Ohio Railroad to Parkersburg, Va.; from thence to Louisville by boat.

June 20 to June 30, inclusive.—At camp on Bardstown pike, two miles from Louisville, Ky.

On the arrival of the Fourteenth Army Corps the trains of the same were divided as follows: Each regiment had one wagon; brigade headquarters, three; division headquarters, four teams, and corps headquarters, five teams. The balance of transportation was organized into supply, ammunition, and hospital trains. Each regimental, brigade, and division headquarters team had to carry, besides the baggage, at least five days' rations of forage for the animals of their respective command. The supply and ammunition trains of the corps were in charge of the division quartermaster, and each supply train of a division divided into sections of from twenty-five to thirty teams, in charge of a commissioned officer detailed and held responsible for the taking care of and running of the train. These officers, having two wagon-masters to each section of their trains, were therefore at all times shortly acquainted with any hindrance, of whatever kind it might be, as well at the head as at the rear of their train, and could therefore, under all circumstances, keep their trains closed up—in my opinion one of the most desirable principles in running a train when there is a large amount of transportation on the same road.

I would most respectfully call the attention of the Quartermaster's Department, as far as my opinion and the opinion of all the quartermasters of this corps is concerned, to the utter uselessness of portable forges for active campaigns. Having been on a constant campaign from Chattanooga, in May, 1864, to Washington City, in June, 1865, constantly compelled to use every spare minute for the purpose of repairing transportation and shoeing animals, frequently after a long day's march and after night, has proven that bellows will do better if properly fixed up, are quicker got ready, and suitable as well for repairing a wagon wheel or shoeing an animal. The following description of a blacksmith shop, as attached to wing section of the Second Division, Fourteenth Army Corps, train, as well as most others, will give a slight idea of what, in my opinion, I have found to work with the utmost quickness and dispatch: Fix a wagon bed on a two-horse wagon (ours were all captured) long enough at the rear so as to rest a small-sized blacksmith's bellows, with the nozzle to the rear, the round part resting on the hind axle and the nozzle extending outside of the bed; then fix a small and light frame-work above the bellows, which, when the shop is in operation, supports the lever. A wooden box, two feet square and ten inches deep, filled when in operation with earth, constitutes the forge, it being transported empty on the march. The front part of the wagon is used for transporting one set of blacksmith's tools, one set of wheelwright's tools, horse and mule shoes, &c., and a small quantity of coal. The wagon to be covered and drawn by two or four mules; the latter, on a long campaign, the best. Two blacksmiths and one wagon-maker will be found plenty to keep constantly in good order a section of from twenty-five to thirty teams.

I am, general, very respectfully, your obedient servant,

J. E. REMINGTON,

Lieut. Col. and Chief Quartermaster Fourteenth Army Corps.

*Statement of quartermaster's property for the fiscal year ending June 30, 1865.**

*Statement of clothing and camp and garrison equipage for the fiscal year ending June 30, 1865.**

---

* Omitted.

Statement of public money for the fiscal year ending June 30, 1865.

On hand June 30, 1864		$47.87
Received from officers during the year		48,266.00
Received from sales of property during the year		79.91
Total		48,393.78
Transferred to officers during the year		1,720.00
Expended during the year	$16,557.65	
Paid for purchases during the year	11,378.20	
		27,935.85
Remaining on hand June 30, 1865		18,737.93
Total		48,393.78

J. E. REMINGTON,
Lieutenant-Colonel and Chief Quartermaster Fourteenth Army Corps.

Report of animals captured, abandoned, died, and killed by the quartermaster's department of the Fourteenth Army Corps during the campaign from Savannah, Ga., to Goldsborough, N. C.

Command.	Horses.			Mules.		
	Captured.	Abandoned.	Died and killed.	Captured.	Abandoned.	Died and killed.
Headquarters and Artillery Brigade	79	146	......	121	52	......
First Division	167	51	11	421	143	35
Second Division	287	98	1	493	189	1
Third Division	189	41	13	350	113	46
Total	722	336	25	1,385	497	82
Total gain	361	......	......	806	......	......

J. E. REMINGTON,
Lieutenant-Colonel and Chief Quartermaster Fourteenth Army Corps.

Report of animals captured, abandoned, died, and killed by the quartermaster's department of the Fourteenth Army Corps during the campaign from Atlanta to Savannah, Ga.

Command.	Horses.			Mules.			Jacks.			Ponies.		
	Captured.	Abandoned.	Killed and died.	Captured.	Abandoned.	Killed and died.	Captured.	Abandoned.	Killed and died.	Captured.	Abandoned.	Killed and died.
Headquarters	16	12	......	40	15	......	......	......	......	......	......	......
First Division	116	15	3	204	91	4	......	......	......	......	......	......
Second Division	209	45	6	604	172	10	6	1	......	......	......	......
Third Division	161	104	......	436	84	8	......	......	......	1	......	......
Artillery Brigade	40	57	32	118	62	1	......	......	......	2	......	......
Total	542	269	41	1,402	424	23	6	1	......	3	......	......
Total gain	232	......	......	955	......	......	5	......	......	3	......	......

J. E. REMINGTON,
Lieutenant-Colonel and Chief Quartermaster Fourteenth Army Corps.

Report of animals captured, abandoned, died, killed, and lost by the Fourteenth Army Corps during its campaign through Georgia.

Command.	Horses.					Mules.					Jacks.			Jennies.			Ponies.	
	Captured.	Abandoned.	Died and killed.	Lost.	Total gained.	Captured.	Abandoned.	Died and killed.	Lost.	Total gained.	Captured.	Abandoned.	Total gained.	Captured.	Abandoned.	Total gained.	Captured.	Total gained.
Headquarters	16	12	....	....	4	40	15	....	....	25	....	....	....	....	....	....	....	....
First Division	116	51	3	....	62	204	91	4	....	109	....	....	....	....	....	....	....	....
Second Division	209	43	6	2	158	604	159	10	13	422	6	1	5	1	1	....	....	....
Third Division	161	103	....	1	....	436	84	8	....	344	....	....	....	....	....	....	2	1
Artillery Brigade	40	57	32	....	8	118	62	1	....	55	....	....	....	....	....	....	2	2
Total	542	266	41	3	232	1,402	411	23	13	955	6	1	5	1	1	...	4	3

REMARKS.—Deficiency in horses of Artillery Brigade deducted from gain in horses of Third Division, Fourteenth Army Corps.

Respectfully submitted.

J. E. REMINGTON,
Captain and Acting Chief Quartermaster Fourteenth Army Corps.

SAVANNAH, GA., *January 19, 1865.*

No. 96.

HEADQUARTERS MILITARY DIVISION OF THE MISSISSIPPI,
Saint Louis, Mo., July 24, 1865.

Maj. Gen. M. C. MEIGS,
Quartermaster-General U. S. Army, Washington, D. C.:

GENERAL: In accordance with your verbal instructions given at Washington City the 27th of June last, I have the honor to inclose herewith a report of the operations of your department at Savannah and in North Carolina while supplying General Sherman's army last winter and spring.* The delay which has occurred in rendering this report has been unavoidable on my part, and has been caused by the difficulty of procuring the statements of property issued from the officers who had it in charge. Several of them were on leave of absence, away from their papers, and three are out of service.

Very respectfully, your obedient servant,

L. C. EASTON,
Brevet Brigadier-General, Chief Quartermaster.

[Inclosure.]

HDQRS. MILITARY DIVISION OF THE MISSOURI,
OFFICE CHIEF DEPOT COMMISSARY,
Saint Louis, Mo., July 20, 1865.

Brig. Gen. L. C. EASTON,
Chief Quartermaster Mil. Div. of the Miss., Saint Louis, Mo.:

GENERAL: In obedience to your request I have the honor to report that the Quartermaster's Department transported for the Subsistence

*See Series I, Vol. LIII, p. 44.

Department for the combined armies under General Sherman the following subsistence stores, viz:

Meats:		
Mess pork	pounds	3,302,000
Bacon	do	1,473,271
Salt beef	do	2,810,400
Fresh beef	do	2,266,500
Total	do	9,852,171
Breadstuffs:		
Hard bread	pounds	17,997,450
Flour	do	4,758,600
Corn-meal	do	92,000
Total	do	22,848,050
Vegetables:		
Beans	pounds	706,181
Peas	do	6,900
Rice	do	115,312
Hominy	do	100,159
Potatoes	do	90,820
Mixed vegetables	do	153,720
Total	do	1,173,092
Coffee	pounds	1,652,678
Tea	do	16,705½
Sugar	do	2,734,503
Soap	do	392,168
Salt	do	667,899
Pepper	do	20,205
Candles	do	107,857
Whisky	gallons	46,414
Vinegar	do	74,248
Molasses	do	12,459½
Miscellaneous: Hospital stores, &c	pounds	266,750

These stores were sent from the various Northern cities of Boston, New York, Alexandria, Fortress Monroe, and Norfolk, and were delivered at the ports of King's Bridge, Savannah, Hilton Head, and Morehead City during the months of December, 1864, January, February, March, April, and May, 1865.

I am, sir, very respectfully, your obedient servant,

LOGAN H. ROOTS,
Captain and Commissary of Subsistence, U. S. Volunteers.

*List of vessels and their cargoes sent from Savannah and Hilton Head to Cape Fear River and Morehead City.**

No. 97.

Report of the movements of the train of the Twentieth Army Corps, on the march from Savannah, Ga., to Goldsborough, N. C., January, February, and March, 1865.

HEADQUARTERS TWENTIETH ARMY CORPS,
OFFICE CHIEF QUARTERMASTER,
Near Goldsborough, N. C., March 31, 1865.

Friday, January 27.—Left camp 9.30 a. m.; arrived at Monteith 3 p. m.; distance, 11.50 miles; weather fine, frosty; roads heavy. Last Tuesday week, January 17, the First and Third Divisions, three

* Omitted.

batteries, corps headquarters, and regimental, brigade, and division headquarters trains left Savannah on the new campaign, crossing the islands into South Carolina; to-day the balance of the corps (Second Division troops and corps train) marched from Savannah on west side of river toward Sister's Ferry. General Barnum's brigade takes charge of train.

Saturday, January 28.—Left camp 7.30 a. m.; arrived in pine woods 6.30 p. m.; distance, 14.41 miles; weather fine, but very cold; roads heavy and swampy. Passed through good works, forts, &c., that had been built to oppose our progress to Savannah.

Sunday, January 29.—Left camp 7 a. m.; arrived at Mallett's farm, two miles and a half from Sister's Ferry, 2 p. m.; distance, 11.61 miles; weather fine, cold; roads pretty good. Passed through Springfield—nothing but chimneys standing. Came up with Fourteenth Corps, which left Savannah one day before we did. Ordered to send teams to Sister's Ferry for forage.

Monday, January 30, to Thursday, February 2.—In camp; weather fine, warm, and rainy. Cavalry passing. Wednesday, February 1, our men across the river engaged in corduroying the road, occasionally finding torpedoes.

Friday, February 3.—Left camp 6.30 p. m.; arrived at Sister's Ferry 9 p. m.; distance, 4.28 miles; weather warm and rainy; roads good. Received marching orders at 6.30 p. m.; started immediately for the ferry. Camped for the night on the bank of the river.

Saturday, February 4.—Left camp at 2.45 p. m.; arrived across the river into South Carolina 5 p. m.; distance, 2.80 miles; weather very warm and bright; roads swampy—corduroyed. Crossed pontoons to-day; it was quite an animated scene; some regiments, on touching the South Carolina shore, flung their colors to the breeze and struck up patriotic airs with their bands. Gun-boat Pontiac lying at upper landing. Piles of hard bread and forage on the shore.

Sunday, February 5.—Left camp at 6.30 a. m.; arrived at crossroads near Steep Bottom 6 p. m.; distance, 12.38 miles; weather warm, fine; roads, swamp in forenoon, good in afternoon. Crossed a swamp to-day, four or five miles long, where there was little or no timber; every inch of it had to be corduroyed. Passed through Robertsville; all of it burnt, as were all the houses along the road. Men beginning to find forage in abundance.

Monday, February 6.—Left camp 9.30 a. m.; arrived near Beach Branch 6.30 p. m.; distance, 16.47 miles; weather cloudy—rain in the afternoon; roads pretty good. Buried two men belonging to the First Division who had been killed by the rebel cavalry—murdered, it is supposed. Food of all kinds now being brought in in profusion. More property is destroyed in this State on our march than was destroyed in Georgia. Passed through Lawtonville—nothing but chimneys standing.

Tuesday, February 7.—Left camp 8.30 a. m.; arrived at Duck Branch 6 p. m.; distance, 6.71 miles; weather, rain all day and night; roads very muddy; teams constantly getting stalled. Crossed Duck Branch (Coosawhatchie Swamp), a running stream from eighteen inches to four feet deep, and about 400 yards wide; part of the train had to stay on the other (south) side till morning.

Wednesday, February 8.—Left camp 7.15 a. m.; arrived at Buford's Bridge 5 p. m.; distance, 13.41 miles; weather fine, cold, and dry; roads good, out of the swamps. Crossed Big Swamp and Big Salkehatchie River—a terrible place to cross. Found on the east side of the river extensive rebel works, timber felled, &c. Forts pierced for four guns, commanding the road through the swamp and across the river, showed their intentions, had they found time to get their cannon into position.

Thursday, *February 9*.—Left camp 7 a. m.; arrived at Blackville 5 p. m.; distance, 19.32 miles; weather cloudy and cold; roads good. Rejoined our command here.

Friday, *February 10*.—In camp; weather fine and cold. Resting in camp. First and Third Division troops destroying Charleston and Augusta Railroad. Two brigades of Second Division sent forward to Duncan's Bridge, South Edisto River.

Saturday, *February 11*.—Left camp 7.30 a. m.; arrived at Duncan's Bridge, north side of South Branch of Edisto River, 11.30 p. m.; distance, 9.49 miles; weather fine and warm; roads good. This is a rich country. Forage and subsistence found in immense quantities to-day. Arrived at the river at 10 a. m., and waited till 10 p. m. before we could cross the train. The former bridge having been burnt by the enemy we had to construct one, together with one mile and a half of corduroy, containing six small bridges. General Geary found some of Hood's old troops confronting him, who had erected works on north side of river. Cavalry trains, 211 wagons, and Michigan Engineers, 31 wagons, joined our corps train to-day.

Sunday, *February 12*.—Left camp 8 a. m.; arrived at Jeffcoat's Bridge, North Fork of the Edisto, 4 p. m.; distance, 13 miles; weather beautiful; roads good. Arrived at the river at 4 p. m. and found the enemy on the other side prepared to dispute our passage. First cannon firing (on our march) to-day; it was from the rebels. We lost a few men in building the bridge, and several foragers were captured to-day.

Monday, *February 13*.—Left camp 1.30 p. m.; arrived at Jones' Cross-Roads 3 p. m.; distance, 5.93 miles; weather beautiful; roads good. Cavalry train divided up among the divisions to-day, 65 wagons being assigned to First Division, 66 to Second Division, and 100 to Third Division. Crossed the river this morning; the Second Division troops skirmished across, losing a few men.

Tuesday, *February 14*.—Left camp 8 a. m.; arrived at Columbia Cross-Roads 11.30 a. m.; distance, 7 miles; weather cloudy—rain and sleet all night; everything covered with ice in the morning; roads good. Traveled on good roads this morning, and camped at noon. Escort six miles in front cut off from advance; Capt. Benjamin Reynolds, acting assistant inspector-general, Third Brigade, First Division, captured, with his orderly, at the head of the column.

Wednesday, *February 15*.—Left camp at 8.15 a. m.; arrived near Lexington Court-House 3.15 p. m.; distance, 11.33 miles; weather misty—rained during the night. Skirmished with the enemy's cavalry all day. Crossed over sand hills of considerable height. Second Division lost a few men.

Thursday, *February 16*.—Left camp 8 a. m.; arrived near Columbia and Congaree Rivers 1 p. m.; distance, 7.67 miles; weather fine; roads good. Against orders to forage on flank to-day. Pontoon train (from Fourteenth Corps) joined us.

Friday, *February 17*.—Left camp 9 a. m.; arrived at Saluda River 7 p. m.; distance, 6 miles; weather fine; roads good. Arrived at river at 12 m., and waited until the Fourteenth Corps and cavalry had crossed. First and Second Division train crossing all night.

Saturday, February 18.—Left camp 9.30 a. m.; arrived near Oakville 4.30 p. m.; distance, 9.42 miles; weather fine; roads good. We finished crossing river to-day. One division of pontoon train ordered to march with us. Fifteenth Corps occupy Columbia; we understand they found a great deal of war material, and nearly burnt the whole town.

Sunday, February 19.—Left camp 11 a. m.; arrived at Freshly's Ferry 2.30 p. m.; distance, 5.94 miles; weather fine; roads heavy. Disposed of all wall-tents, nothing but flies being used at all headquarters. Fourteenth Corps at Broad River first, and crossing ahead of us, arrived within a mile of river and waited until morning to cross.

Monday, February 20.—Left camp 8.15 a. m.; arrived at Owens' farm 5 p. m.; distance, 12.21 miles; weather fine; roads good. General Jackson with one division crossed river and picketed all roads. General Ward sends one brigade to picket all roads and approaches to bridge till all is crossed, and then one battery protects pontoniers in taking it up. Found on Owens' farm 2,000 bushels of corn and 40 tons of hay. Crossed Little River to-day.

Tuesday, February 21.—Left camp at 8.30 a. m.; arrived at Beaver Dam Creek, near Winnsborough, 5 p. m.; distance, 11.20 miles; weather fine and pleasant; roads good but hilly. Arrived in Winnsborough at 11 a. m., and found the town already in possession of foragers (bummers) of the Fourteenth and Twentieth Corps, who had plundered it and burned part of it, all of whom, who were caught, were placed under arrest. The Fourteenth Corps arrived at town simultaneously with ourselves. We marched through and camped on the side about four miles.

Wednesday, February 22.—Left camp at 8 a. m.; arrived at Rocky Mount Post-Office 5.30 p. m.; distance, 17.17 miles; weather cloudy; roads bad and hilly. General Sherman joined the corps to-day. Camped half a mile from Wateree River. One of our men belonging to corps supply train found the bodies of two of our soldiers lying in the woods murdered.

Thursday, February 23.—Left camp 9 a. m.; arrived at Colonel Ballard's farm at 1 p. m.; distance, 5.30 miles; weather cloudy, rain during night; roads hilly. Commenced crossing Catawba River at 6 a. m. Obtaining a great many mules and horses now.

Friday, February 24.—Left camp 8.30 a. m.; arrived at Hilliard's plantation 11 a. m.; distance, 2.87 miles; weather, raining hard all day; roads very bad; 11 a. m. met Seventeenth Corps on a road intersecting ours, causing us to camp. Corduroying every foot we came to-day.

Saturday, February 25.—In camp all day; weather showery. Third Division corduroying road ahead.

Sunday, February 26.—Left camp 8 a. m.; arrived at Hanging Rock Post-Office 2.30 p. m.; distance, 10.12 miles; weather fine; roads corduroyed. Marching since noon toward Camden.

Monday, February 27.—Left camp 10.15 a. m.; arrived at Hanging Rock Creek 11.30 a. m.; distance, 2.36 miles; weather fine; roads very bad—hilly. Crossed Hanging Rock Creek and ascended a steep, rocky, muddy hill; going into camp on north side of creek.

Tuesday, February 28.—Left camp 8 a. m.; arrived at Horton's Store 2.30 p. m.; distance, 10 miles; weather, raining; roads very bad. Wagons constantly getting stalled. Captured a perambulating bank from Camden in three wagons.

Wednesday, March 1.—Left camp at 8 a. m.; arrived near Lynch's Creek 2.15 p. m.; distance, 9.22 miles; weather cloudy; roads good.

Eighty-second Illinois was sent eleven miles last night to protect Miller's Bridge, which they did, running the mill alongside of it all night, making flour and meal. We crossed the bridge at noon.

Thursday, March 2.—Left camp at 6.30 a. m.; arrived at Chesterfield Court-House 5.30 p. m.; distance, 20.80 miles; weather misty; roads bad. Troops and head of the train marched hard all day through mud, crossing deep, rough-bottomed creeks, and taking no rest whatever. Skirmishing with the enemy commenced about two miles from town, and lasted into and through the village—two batteries in position shelling the fleeing rebels. Only corps headquarters train got into Chesterfield, the balance of the train being seven to ten miles back, where they camped for the night.

Friday, March 3.—In camp all day; weather fine but cloudy. The balance of the train got up to-day all right. The First Division having been sent to Thompson's Creek to save the bridge, their train was ordered to join them some three miles off.

Saturday, March 4.—Left camp 7.30 a. m.; arrived near Sneedsborough, N. C., two miles from Big Pedee River, 3.30 p. m.; distance, 10.47 miles; weather, rain in morning; roads horribly muddy. There seemed to be in some places no bottoms to the roads—all quicksand. Arriving at the plank road to Cheraw at 2 o'clock and finding the Fourteenth Corps passing, we went into camp, giving them the right of road. Part of our trains to-day were in South Carolina and part in North Carolina. Obtained ten loads of lumber from mill on Thompson's Creek for pontoon purposes.

Sunday, March 5.—In camp all day; weather very fine. General Williams asked permission to march to Cheraw and cross the Pedee there.

Monday, March 6.—Left camp 8.45 a. m.; arrived at north side of Big Pedee 6.45 p. m.; distance, 14.01 miles; weather fine; roads, plank road to Cheraw—half mile—bad road across river. Marched on plank road to Cheraw. At 10 a. m. heard a tremendous explosion; found on arrival at Cheraw that it was caused by powder and fixed ammunition set on fire by Fifteenth Corps soldiers, causing the death of eight persons and wounding many. All the business portion of the town burnt. The Fifteenth Corps had about finished crossing the pontoons on our arrival (2 p. m.). We commenced crossing at 4 o'clock, and were crossing all night.

Tuesday, March 7.—Left camp 8 a. m.; arrived at Station 103, Wilmington and Raleigh Railroad, 5.30 p. m.; distance, 14.50 miles; weather beautiful; roads very good. Passed by 2,000 barrels of rosin on fire—a magnificent sight.

Wednesday, March 8.—Left camp 8 a. m.; arrived near Lumber River 5.30 p. m.; distance, 14.66 miles; weather, rained hard all day; roads bad, nearly all corduroyed; Third Brigade, First Division, sent four miles ahead to hold bridge across Lumber River. We met Fourteenth Corps at forks of road traveling same way as ourselves; gave them the plank road and cut our way two miles through the woods, gaining a wretched dirt road. The rain poured in torrents all day, making the road impassable for rear column without corduroying.

Thursday, March 9.—Left camp 6.45 a. m.; arrived at Buffalo Creek 9.30 p. m.; distance, 8.65 miles; weather, raining hard all day and night; roads, corduroyed the whole distance. Crossed bridge over Lumber River; also six or seven creeks badly swollen by recent rains. Pontoon train joined us. Second and Third Division train had to encamp on side of Lumber River, being unable to cross till morning.

Friday, March 10.—Left camp 10.30 a. m.; arrived near Rockfish Creek 7 p. m.; distance, 13.20 miles; weather cloudy; roads corduroyed. Forage and subsistence abundant to-day. For the last week it has been very scarce, partly because all the army has been together, and partly because this is a wretched poor country. Received General Slocum's order restricting troops from taking anything but forage, &c., and commanding them to destroy no property in North Carolina.

Saturday, March 11.—Left camp 8 a. m.; arrived near Little Rockfish Creek 5 p. m.; distance, 8.10 miles; weather fine; roads corduroyed. First and Third Division troops push ahead; Second Division and one battery protect train. We struck plank road this evening and camped alongside of it, corralling in a very small compass.

Sunday, March 12.—Left camp 6.30 a. m.; arrived at Fayetteville 2 p. m.; distance, 12.23 miles; weather fine—frost at night; roads, plank. Found Fourteenth Corps in possession. The two bridges that spanned Cape Fear River had been burned by the enemy; two pontoon bridges laid. Sent mail North from here; a U. S. steamer arriving about the same time the rebels went out and our troops came in. We are promised some supplies.

Monday, March 13.—Left camp 3.30 p. m.; arrived four miles beyond Fayetteville, on east side Cape Fear River, 7 p. m.; distance, 5.19 miles; weather beautiful; roads good. General Sherman reviewed Twentieth Corps, marching company front through Fayetteville. The rebels in strength ahead of us on the road. Quartermasters ordered to send wagons to river for supplies; also all transportation that can be spared to send refugees, discharged soldiers, and negroes to Wilmington; fifty men from each corps and the discharged men acting as guard; Colonel Balloch, chief commissary of subsistence Twentieth Army Corps, furnishing our contingent with sufficient rations. One hundred sick sent to Fayetteville and shipped to Wilmington.

Tuesday, March 14.—In camp; weather fine. Two (First and Third) divisions unincumbered save with ammunition wagons, and three batteries were ahead, &c. General Geary and Sloan's battery guard train. Same order extends through the army. Train is ordered to move toward Troublefield's Store.

Wednesday, March 15.—Left camp 11.30 a. m.; arrived near South River 7.30 p. m.; distance, 11.15 miles; weather, thunder-storm; roads corduroyed. Most of the train stuck in the mud all night.

Thursday, March 16.—Left camp 9.30 a. m.; arrived at Jackson's farm 5.30 p. m.; distance, 7.29 miles; weather showery; roads corduroyed. The Michigan Engineers who were sent ahead to build a bridge across South River during the night were unable to do so until morning on account of the enemy. The bridge being completed by 10 a. m., we commenced crossing; the enemy threatening our flanks and front, one battery was placed in position and proper disposition made of the troops to cover the trains. On getting to our camping place we found the Fifteenth Corps troops on right of road, lines formed, skirmishers out, batteries in position, everything indicating the presence of the enemy. Our two divisions had a hard fight, driving the rebels, capturing three pieces of cannon and a number of prisoners.

Friday, March 17.—In camp; weather delightful. Sent twenty-four empty wagons to the front for wounded. The train sent to Cape Fear River arrived to-day with supplies—some hard bread, coffee, sugar, boots, and shoes.

Saturday, March 18.—Left camp 6.30 a. m.; arrived near Rainer's Mill 8 p. m.; distance, 8.56 miles; weather fine; roads corduroyed. The plan adopted to-day of repairing the roads was new, and it was good. Not a wagon was allowed to proceed until the road was made good. The consequence was, when they commenced drawing into camp they were all closed up, and kept continually coming in.

Sunday, March 19.—Left camp 6.15 a. m.; arrived at Canaan Church 6 p. m.; distance, 10.50 miles; weather fine; roads corduroyed. Left Wing had a severe fight to-day, the enemy suddenly falling on the Fourteenth Corps, driving it and making some captures from them. The Twentieth came to their relief. Corralled in small compass to-night, and extra precautions taken to guard train.

Monday, March 20.—Left camp 4 p. m.; arrived near Falling Creek 8 p. m.; distance, 4.30 miles; weather fine; roads corduroyed. General Geary started at 2 a. m. with First and Third Brigades for the front, Captain Sloan's battery following. All ammunition and ordnance wagons and empty wagons for wounded sent to front—135 wagons. At 6 a. m. ordered to move train to an adjoining field, park close; run the wagons in twenty deep, close up—ten feet between rows—getting in 600 or 700 wagons in twenty acres space by 11 a. m., and by 1 p. m. a good and efficient breast-work inclosed the trains. As soon as we were all properly cared for orders came to pull out and march toward Goldsborough. Commissary wagons sent to front with supplies.

Tuesday, March 21.—Left camp 6.30 a. m.; arrived at Grantham's Store 3.30 p. m.; distance, 5 miles; weather, rained hard all afternoon; roads corduroyed half way. At 12 m. came upon the Twenty-fourth and Twenty-fifth Corps* marching on a road intersecting ours; managed to fall in on same road, going on it a mile and a half and camping. From 2 until 7 p. m. a furious engagement going on on our left; incessant cannonading and tremendous volleys of musketry could be distinctly heard, supposed to be Fifteenth Corps engaged. Received 200 wagon and ambulance loads of wounded to-night. Ordered to dispatch all the intrenching tools and pioneers to the front. Ordered to march to-morrow six miles to the junction of the Everettsville and Goldsborough road with the Dead Fields and Goldsborough road, and there establish a depot for supplies to be drawn from Kinston. Colonel Mindil, of Second Brigade, Second Division, to command post.

Wednesday, March 22.—Left camp 6.15 a. m.; arrived at Murphy's plantation 1.30 p. m.; distance, 10 miles; weather delightful; roads good. The country around here surpasses anything we have yet seen in North Carolina for food and forage.

Thursday, March 23.—In camp; weather fine, but tremendous winds. Organizing permanent quarters.

Friday, March 24.—In camp. Received orders to move; cannot, our wagons being sent to Kinston for supplies and to the front. Sent for 125 wagons from corps headquarters. The hospital left here to-day, crossing the upper pontoon bridge at 3 p. m. after attempting to get over all day. Seventeenth Corps slaughtering mules by hundreds on the banks of Neuse River. Wagons arrived from corps at 8 p. m. Ordered to load up and concentrate Fourteenth, Twentieth, Fifteenth, and Seventeenth Corps trains here now; intrenched in small space; four brigades and some artillery protect them in case of

---

*Reference is to the Provisional Corps, commanded by Maj. Gen. Alfred H. Terry and consisting of troops detached from the corps named.

an attack, which is not at all improbable, as everything on the road to-day has been threatened by Butler's cavalry. In the middle of the night the brigade belonging to the Seventeenth Corps was withdrawn and sent to guard its train on way from Kinston with supplies.

Saturday, March 25.—Left camp 8 a. m.; arrived three miles from Goldsborough on Wilmington and Weldon Railroad 11 a. m.; distance, 8.37 miles; weather fine—windy; roads excellent. Had a fine march and joined our corps. Encamped in pine woods at 11 a. m., bringing with us (the result of two days' foraging around Murphy's plantation) over 100 loads of corn, most of which is husked and part shelled and in bags.

Total miles traveled, 456.10.

RECAPITULATION.

We have marched 456.10 miles through innumerable and seemingly impassable swamps; crossed twelve rivers, among them the Savannah, Saluda, Broad, Catawba, Great Pedee, Lumber, and Neuse, large streams, requiring pontoon bridges; constructed bridges (sometimes in face of the enemy) over the smaller streams; crossed innumerable creeks, many of them from their size meriting the name of river; corduroyed at least three-fifths of all the roads we have traveled; marching early and late, wet and dry, over swamps, sometimes in sight and sometimes sunk in the mud nearly out of sight, we averaged ten and one-third miles per day for marching days from Savannah, Ga., to Goldsborough, N. C. In all the way we have lost no property by capture and only four wagons and five ambulances by breaking, which could not be repaired on the march.

We have taken from the country: Horses, 858; mules, 1,252; corn, 2,588,902 pounds; hay, 10,500 pounds; fodder, 2,219,001 pounds.

HENRY M. WHITTELSEY,
Captain, Acting Chief Quartermaster Twentieth Army Corps.

No. 98.

OFFICE CHIEF QUARTERMASTER, DEPT. OF THE TENN.,
Nashville, Tenn., August 31, 1865.

Bvt. Maj. Gen. M. C. MEIGS,
Quartermaster-General U. S. Army, Washington, D. C.:

GENERAL: In compliance with General Orders, No. 39, from your office, dated July 1, 1865, requiring officers on duty in the Quartermaster's Department to render an annual report for the fiscal year ending June 30, 1865, I have the honor to report as follows, viz:

From the 1st of July, 1864, to the 7th day of August, same year, I was continuously on duty as chief quartermaster of the Fourteenth Corps and was present with that command during the memorable battles of Resaca, Kingston, Kenesaw, Chattahoochee River, and during a portion of the siege of Atlanta.

On the morning of the 8th of August, being within three miles of the latter-named place, I was relieved of the chief quartermastership of that corps and ordered to report in person to the major-general commanding the Department of the Cumberland for duty as chief quartermaster of the Army of the Cumberland in the field. (General Orders, headquarters, August 8, 1864.)

On the same date I reported and assumed charge as directed.

I remained with the general headquarters during the remainder of the siege of Atlanta and entered that city with it, remaining there until the 31st of October, when I proceeded with the rest of the members of the staff to Chattanooga.

Nothing worthy of note came under my notice while in Atlanta. My principal duty there consisted of providing forage and the necessary details wherewith to obtain it for the entire army.

The troops had already been well supplied with clothing and camp and garrison equipage. There was no dearth of subsistence. Forage had to be obtained from the country, owing to the crossing of the rebel General Hood over the Chattahoochee River and the consequent severance of railroad connection with Chattanooga, the depot of supplies.

There had been no accumulation (beyond ten days) of forage at Atlanta. The railroad had already been taxed to the utmost to supply the army on its onward march from day to day, and with this ten days' supply the break lasted from the 1st to the 26th day of October.

While in Chattanooga the battles of Franklin and Nashville took place. Unable to reach my command, and the necessity of a chief quartermaster's presence with the army being apparent, Lieut. Col. W. G. Le Duc, chief quartermaster Twentieth Corps, was appointed by the major-general acting chief quartermaster in my absence.

I remained in Chattanooga, assuming general charge of the depot and assisting in providing for the wants of Maj. Gen. R. S. Granger in his attack on Decatur, procuring transportation, &c.

On the 5th day of January I received a telegram from Major-General Thomas directing me to repair to Nashville and report to him for further service in the field. I immediately did so, arriving in Nashville on the following 7th.

On the next day but one I proceeded with headquarters to Eastport, Miss., arriving there on the 16th.

At this place my duties consisted of supplying the army with everything it wanted in the shape of clothing, camp and garrison equipage, and forage, and the furnishing of water transportation for the Twenty-third Corps to Louisville, and the Sixteenth Army Corps (General A. J. Smith's command), including Seventh Division, Cavalry Corps, Military Division of the Mississippi, and Artillery Brigade, consisted of four divisions. The aggregate strength in commissioned officers and enlisted men was 17,314; in horses and mules, 6,709; in wagons and ambulances, 484. The embarkation began on the 5th of February and ended on the evening of the 8th. The command was supplied with ten days' rations of forage and fifteen of subsistence. In every other respect it was also well supplied. About forty boats, some of them the finest in service on the Western waters, were employed in transporting this army to New Orleans.

It was while here that the overflow of the Tennessee River, unequaled by any of former years, took place. I may state that I was on duty with the troops in the field near this river during the period of the great (although not to be compared with this) flood in the spring of 1862, by which a large amount of public property was lost. Apprehending a similar flood this spring, I immediately on arriving at Eastport took steps to prevent the accumulation and exposure of public property at this extremely unprotected point. The troops and a quantity of stores had preceded me about ten days. I also proceeded at once to inspect and correct the manifest want of system and proper care of public property then existing. With the view of having the valuable stores afloat, so as to enable us to remove them quickly and with economy in the event of its becoming necessary by reason of high water, and to relieve several steamers under charter detained at the landing with stores on board, and under orders from the major-general commanding to make use of the steamers that come freighted to Eastport to transport General Schofield's corps from Clifton to the Ohio River, I ordered on the next day, by direction of General Thomas, the large wharf-boat, known as the Crescent City, to be towed up from Paducah to Eastport. The wharf-boat arrived on the 27th following, and was immediately assigned for the storage of clothing, camp and garrison equipage, and quartermaster's, medical, and subsistence stores. The stores that were lying exposed on the river bank were at first put on board; afterward those from the steamers.

Previous to my arrival at Eastport large quantities of stores not needed for the army had been received, while those actually required had not come to hand.

Notwithstanding my efforts from time to time to prevent it, large quantities of grain and other quartermaster's stores, in advance of what was required for the supply of the troops and what had been asked for by me, kept coming to hand; hence an undue accumulation of grain at a depot subject at any time to an overflow, and where, besides, there were no means of protecting it against the heavy rains prevalent at that season of the year.

On the 24th of February, before the river had begun to excite apprehensions for the safety of the public property that was, for want of storage room, left on the river bank, I directed Capt. W. A. Warren, assistant quartermaster, to apply to Col. R. R. Stewart, commanding Fifth Division of Cavalry, Military Division of the Mississippi, and post, for a detail of men to report immediately and be worked in conjunction with 300 of Captain Warren's laborers in loading the stores day and night on the boats and barges detained at the landing for that purpose. The detail reported tardily and worked as soldiers badly disciplined usually work.

Soon the river commenced rising, but slowly. I now made requisition on other officers for a further detail of 500 men, and the day following for another 500. With these details I proceeded to transport all the stores on the bank at Chickasaw, distant about two miles from Eastport, and the only near landing accessible and above high-water mark. On account of the backwater the stores could not be taken to the high hills in the rear of Eastport. Finding that my present strength of detail was insufficient to accomplish my purpose, I applied to Brevet Major-General Wilson, commanding Cavalry Corps, Military Division of the Mississippi, whose headquarters was twelve miles distant at Gravelly Springs, for an additional 1,000 men, and stated in my application the apprehension I felt for the safety of forage, unless prompt and energetic measures were taken to remove it ere the river rose to too great a height. I have no knowledge of that application being acted upon. Every effort was made by myself and the officers on duty in the Quartermaster's Department under me at Eastport to save all the property in jeopardy. We had ample time to have removed every sack of grain and other articles of property (that afterward became lost), and would have done so, I am assured, had the details of soldiers asked for reported promptly and worked industriously.

The department is greatly indebted to the foresight of Major-General Thomas in directing me to order up the wharf-boat Crescent City. Without it and its ample means of storage the loss of property would have been immense. The grain in best condition was removed to Chickasaw first; the worst was left to be handled last, and was lost.

After the river had risen to such a height as to submerge the grain all attempts to remove it were abandoned. Even if we had not done so, and had succeeded in getting all or part of it away, it would have been useless for any purpose whatever.

A large portion of the corn received before my arrival and during my stay at Eastport was more or less damaged ere it left the depots on the Ohio River. I am of the opinion that it had been gathered and sacked before maturity. The sacking, too, had been improperly done.

The following statement of property lost to the Government by this unparalleled overflow may be relied on as nearly correct:

Twenty thousand sacks of grain, 12 unserviceable wagons, 10 unserviceable and serviceable ambulances, 75 worn-out wagon beds, a few old tents previously occupied by hired men of the Quartermaster's Department. Its estimated money value is $100,000.

One hundred and forty-eight of the wagons that had been ten feet under water were recovered during my stay at the landing and shipped to Nashville. Many of the wagons and ambulances reported above as lost lodged in trees and driftwood, and could not at the time be got at. I have no doubt, however, but that subsequently upon the subsiding of the waters many of them were recovered.

At one time, about the 28th of February, the waters reached the unprecedented height of thirty (I think) feet above low-water mark.

On the 17th of March I applied to Brevet Major-General Wilson, commanding the troops, for the convention of a board of survey to determine the exact amount of public property lost and damaged by the freshet and to fix the responsibility. Up to the time of my departure the board had not convened.

Although all the officers serving under me exerted themselves manfully to save the public property, one of them, Lieut. Delos Allen, One hundred and nineteenth Illinois Volunteers and acting assistant quartermaster, is deserving of special notice. This young officer displayed the most untiring zeal and industry in this respect. He not only exposed himself day and night to the heavy rains that continued for days, deluging the surrounding country, but oftentimes waded up to his middle in the water, compelling his men at the same time to follow him.

Feeling that my services as chief quartermaster of the army were no longer needed at Eastport, I left that place on the 19th following, and proceeded to report to the major-general commanding at Nashville, arriving there on the 22d.

On the 2d of April, by verbal order of the major-general, I went to Knoxville, Tenn., and while there performed my duties as chief quartermaster of the army then in active service in that section of East Tennessee, and also assumed charge of the depot at Knoxville and the more advanced one of Greeneville. Nothing worthy of note occurred while on this duty, further than I made it my special duty to see to the well-providing of the army with all its necessary wants.

Active operations ending in this quarter, I returned to Nashville on the 30th of the same month. The Fourth Army Corps, which had been lying in the vicinity of Nashville for some time, now refitted and paid off, was ordered to Johnsonville, Tenn., to embark for New

Orleans. I at once proceeded to Johnsonville to superintend the embarkation of the troops.

The corps took up its line of march for Johnsonville, by railroad, on the 15th of June. The means of transportation was limited to eight wagons and teams to every 1,000 men; altogether, the number of animals was 1,300 belonging to the command. Its brigade of artillery and wagon trains marched to the point of embarkation by land. The embarkation of the troops having been completed by the evening of the 18th, on the following day I returned to my station.

The organization of the Army of the Cumberland ceasing to exist, I was relieved of my duties with it by Special Orders, No. 2, headquarters Military Division of the Tennessee, June 25, 1865, and directed to report to Bvt. Maj. Gen. J. L. Donaldson, chief quartermaster of the division, for further orders. This officer then directed me to report for duty to Maj. Gen. George Stoneman, commanding Department of Tennessee. I immediately assumed charge as chief quartermaster of that department.

Not being accountable for public property, with the exception of, at one time, some few articles of office furniture and clothing, camp and garrison equipage, I have none to report as lost, destroyed, or captured by the enemy while under my direction. For the same reason no property captured by our army has fallen into my hands. I may except some cotton, altogether about 585 bales, which, being taken possession of from time to time by Major-General Wilson's forces on their march to Macon, Ga., &c., and shipped to me at Nashville, Tenn., was immediately (as each lot arrived) turned over to the proper officer of the U. S. Treasury Department. I set down $95,000 as its estimated value. The cotton in question has been duly accounted for on my property returns.

*Statement of quartermaster's property for the fiscal year ending June 30, 1865.**

*Statement of clothing, camp and garrison equipage for the fiscal year ending June 30, 1865.**

Statement of public moneys.

On hand July 1, 1864	$6,318.85
Received from officers during the year	296,395.07
Total	302,713.92
Expended during the year	4,968.08
Transferred to other officers during the year	243,512.61
Remaining on hand June 30, 1865	54,233.23
Total	302,713.92

The balance on hand is deposited as follows:

Assistant treasurer, New York City	52,402.46
U. S. depository, Louisville, Ky	158.64
In my hands	1,672.13
Total	54,233.23

*Omitted; but see pp. 687, 688, of Executive Document No. 1, referred to in foot-note (*), p. 249.

Statement of property captured from the enemy, received by Col. A. J. Mackay, assistant quartermaster, and its estimated value, during the fiscal year ending June 30, 1865.

Five hundred and eighty-five bales of cotton (estimated value $95,000) captured by Major-General Wilson's forces on their march southward, and shipped to me for disposition.

I am, general, very respectfully, your obedient servant,

A. J. MACKAY,
Colonel and Chief Quartermaster Department of Tennessee.

No. 99.*

Statement of public moneys received, transferred, &c., by Col. M. C. Garber, chief quartermaster Military Division of the Mississippi, in the field, during the fiscal year ending June 30, 1865.

On hand July 1, 1864	$635.35
Received from officers during the year	143,159.85
Received from the Treasury Department	44,391.00
Total	188,186.20
Expended during the year	10,436.24
Transferred to other officers during the year	162,708.84
Remaining on hand June 30, 1865	15,041.12
Total	188,186.20

The balance is in drafts and U. S. Treasury notes, and is deposited in the First National Bank at Madison, Ind.

I certify that the above statement is correct.

M. C. GARBER,
Colonel and Assistant Quartermaster.

No. 100.

ASSISTANT QUARTERMASTER-GENERAL'S OFFICE,
Cincinnati, Ohio, July 18, 1865.

General M. C. MEIGS,
Quartermaster-General U. S. Army, Washington, D. C.:

GENERAL: In compliance with General Orders, No. 39, from your office, of July 1, 1865, I have the honor to report that from the 1st of July, 1864, to June 30, 1865, I have been on duty as assistant quartermaster-general, with my headquarters in Cincinnati, Ohio. I have not personally had charge of any clothing, or other public property, the chartering or building of steam-boats, construction of railways, or transportation of troops or supplies. A statement of the public moneys received and transferred during the year is herewith. The annual report called for by your General Orders, No. 29, July 6, 1864, was mailed on the 20th of August last.

Very respectfully, your obedient servant,

THOMAS SWORDS,
Assistant Quartermaster-General.

---

* For report of Col. M. C. Garber, dated July 10, 1865 (here omitted), see Series I, Vol. LIII, p. 49.

Statement of public moneys received and transferred during the year.

On hand July 1, 1864	$50,459.07
Received from officers during the year	274.70
Received from the Treasury Department during the year	17,433,340.00
Total	17,484,073.77
Transferred to other officers during the year	17,402,501.95
Remaining on hand June 30, 1865	81,571.82
Total	17,484,073.77
Balance on hand deposited:	
Louisville U. S. depository	50,000.00
Cincinnati U. S. depository	29,179.92
New York City, assistant treasurer	2,391.90
Total	81,571.82

A true copy.

JOHN V. FUREY,
Captain and Assistant Quartermaster.

No. 101.

ASSISTANT QUARTERMASTER-GENERAL'S OFFICE,
Philadelphia, July 28, 1865.

Maj. Gen. M. C. MEIGS,
Quartermaster-General U. S. Army, Washington, D. C.:

GENERAL: I have the honor to inclose herewith a statement of public money received, expended, transferred, &c., at Philadelphia, on account of clothing and equipage of the Army, by me during the months of July and August, two months of the fiscal year ending June 30, 1865, in compliance with General Orders, No. 39, Quartermaster-General's Office, Washington, D. C., July 1, 1865, with a note of my duties since 27th of August, 1864.

I am, general, very respectfully, your obedient servant,

G. H. CROSMAN,
Assistant Quartermaster-General, U. S. Army.

Statement of public money received, expended, transferred, &c., at Philadelphia, Pa., on account of clothing and equipage of the Army, by Col. George H. Crosman, assistant quartermaster-general, U. S. Army, during the months of July and August, two months of the fiscal year ending June 30, 1865, in compliance with General Orders, No. 39, Quartermaster-General's Office, Washington, D. C., July 1, 1865.

DR.		CR.	
Amount on hand June 30, 1864	$305,385.10	Amount expended during two months of the year 1864.	$5,707,564.62
Amount received from officers during two months of the year 1864.	4.74	Amount transferred to other officers during the same period.	566,713.93
Amount received from the Treasury Department during the same period.	5,948,972.00		
Amount received from sales of property and other sources during the same period.	19,916.71		
	6,274,278.55		6,274,278.55

G. H. CROSMAN,
Assistant Quartermaster-General, U. S. Army.

PHILADELPHIA, *July 27, 1865.*

NOTE.—Since my temporary relief by Colonel Perry, on the 27th of August, 1864, I have been engaged, under the previous instructions of the Quartermaster-General, in preparing matter for the publication of a manual for the Quartermaster's Department, and also in the settlement of my accounts with the Treasury.

G. H. C.

No. 102.

OFFICE OF ARMY CLOTHING AND EQUIPAGE,
New York, July 15, 1865.

Maj. Gen. M. C. MEIGS,
Quartermaster-General U. S. Army, Washington, D. C.:

GENERAL: In compliance with General Orders, No. 39, from your office, I have the honor to report that during the fiscal year ending June 30, 1865, I was on duty in this city, in charge of the depot of army clothing and equipage, providing supplies for the Army.

I respectfully submit herewith a statement of public moneys which have come into my hands during the past year.

The duties performed by me do not make it necessary to render the other statements described in the order referred to. My assistant, Captain Darrow, will render a statement of funds and a statement of the quartermaster's property which he has been accountable for. Capt. R. M. Potter will send a statement of clothing and equipage which has passed through his hands.

My last report, for the year ending June 30, 1864, was forwarded to you on the 25th of August, 1864.

I am, general, most respectfully, your obedient servant,

D. H. VINTON,
Colonel and Deputy Quartermaster-General.

Statement of public moneys on account of the Quartermaster's Department which have come into the possession of Col. D. H. Vinton, deputy quartermaster-general, U. S. Army, at New York City, during the year ending June 30, 1865.

On hand July 1, 1864	$785,013.69
Received from Treasury Department during the year	33,845,007.25
Received from sales of property and other sources during the year	7,490.17
Total	34,637,511.11
Expended during the year	2,226,629.76
Transferred to other officers during the year	32,410,881.35
Total	34,637,511.11

D. H. VINTON,
Colonel and Deputy Quartermaster-General.

OFFICE OF ARMY CLOTHING AND EQUIPAGE,
New York City, July, 1865.

No. 103.

DEPUTY QUARTERMASTER-GENERAL'S OFFICE,
San Francisco, Cal., August 16, 1865.

Maj. Gen. M. C. MEIGS,
Quartermaster-General U. S. Army, Washington, D. C.:

GENERAL: In obedience to General Orders, No. 39, July 1, 1865, from the Quartermaster-General's Office, I have the honor to inclose a report of my money transactions for the year ending June 30, 1865.

My last annual report was forwarded October 1, 1864. My duties during the past year have been confined to this immediate station. The constant supervision of some forty-five posts, widely extended over an area of 1,500 by 600 miles, has left me no time for visiting any of the outposts in the department. Transportation of army supplies up and down the coast, up the Columbia, Colorado, and other navigable rivers, upon or near which we have military posts, is furnished promptly by the different lines of steamers and sail vessels, including our own excellent brig General Jesup. It is but necessary to say that the water transportation has been chiefly under the supervision of Major Kirkham, quartermaster, to indicate that it has been promptly and efficiently performed, and with a constant reference to all practicable economy. Our land transportation has been performed in part with our own six-mule teams and army wagons, in small part (as in the mountainous portions of the Humboldt district) by pack-mule trains, and upon the longer and principal routes by contract. Forage supplies in Arizona and Nevada during the past year have been very limited and the price very high. In most other portions of the late Department of the Pacific they have been abundant and much more reasonable in price. At the present period forage of all kinds, except on the extreme frontiers, is 100 per cent. lower than I ever before knew it to be in the Department of the Pacific. We are sufficiently provided with all necessary quartermaster's stores. Excepting in some few articles, our supply of clothing is ample to meet our wants until the receipt of our annual supply from the East in October. The exceptions can be purchased here on very favorable terms. I have been greatly aided and the Government greatly benefited by the receipt of funds upon back estimates up to the 28th of February last, inclusive, by which many old claims were paid off, the credit of the Government better sustained, and purchases made on better terms for cash. Owing to the very considerable appreciation of "legal tenders," I have been able to pay all claims three months ahead of my received estimates, and have been able to omit my estimate for funds for the month of August, instant. (See my letter of July 10, 1865.) In consideration of the prospect of active service among the Indians in parts of Nevada and Idaho, but especially in Arizona, I respectfully suggest the expediency of forwarding the amount of my estimates for March and April at an early date.

Respectfully submitted.

Your obedient servant,

E. B. BABBITT,
Colonel and Chief Quartermaster.

Statement of public funds received and expended on account of the Quartermaster's Department during the fiscal year ending June 30, 1865, by Col. E. B. Babbitt, chief quartermaster Department of the Pacific, San Francisco, Cal., made in compliance with General Orders, No. 39, Quartermaster-General's Office, Washington, July 1, 1865.

Received from officers during the year	$24,331.00
Received from the Treasury Department during the year	6,340,024.00
Total	6,364,355.00
Expended during the year	10,714.26
Transferred to officers during the year	5,467,022.20
Remaining on hand June 30, 1865	886,618.54
Total	6,364,355.00

The balance on hand is deposited as follows:

In the hands of assistant treasurer of the United States, San Francisco, Cal.	871,648.76
In hands of assistant treasurer of the United States, New York	14,703.12
In my hands	266.66
Total	886,618.54

E. B. BABBITT,
Colonel and Chief Quartermaster.

CHIEF QUARTERMASTER'S OFFICE,
San Francisco, Cal., August 15, 1865.

No. 104.

QUARTERMASTER'S OFFICE,
New York, September 22, 1865.

Maj. Gen. M. C. MEIGS,
Quartermaster-General U. S. Army, Washington, D. C.:

GENERAL: In compliance with General Orders, No. 39, current series, from your office, I have the honor to transmit herewith the following statements, viz:

Statement of public moneys received and transferred by me, Capts. F. J. Crilly, C. H. Peck (resigned), and W. H. Bailhache (resigned), while stationed at New York.

Statement of quartermaster's property purchased, transferred, &c., by Capts. F. J. Crilly, C. H. Peck (resigned), W. H. Bailhache (resigned), and A. S. Kimball.

Statement of amount paid on account of rail, river, stage, and wagon transportation by Capts. F. J. Crilly, C. H. Peck (resigned), W. H. Bailhache (resigned), and W. W. Van Ness.

Statement of amount paid on account of ocean and lake transportation by Capts. F. J. Crilly, C. H. Peck (resigned), W. H. Bailhache (resigned), and W. W. Van Ness.

Statement of stores transported under my direction.

Of Forms B, E, and F, I have no statements to make.

I am, general, very respectfully, your obedient servant,

STEWART VAN VLIET,
Brevet Brigadier-General and Quartermaster, U. S. Army.

Statement of public moneys received and transferred by Bvt. Brig. Gen. Stewart Van Vliet, quartermaster, U. S. Army, in the fiscal year ending June 30, 1865.

On hand July 1, 1864	$476.10
Received from officers during the year	6,651.96
Received from Treasury Department during the year	20,271,193.78
Received from sales of property and other sources	75,581.19
Total	20,353,903.03
Expended during the year	4,752.27
Transferred to officers during the year	20,165,410.33
Remaining on hand June 30, 1865	183,740.43
Total	20,353,903.03
The balance on hand was deposited as follows:	
In sub-treasury, New York City	164,774.20
In office safe	132.86
In First National Bank, Philadelphia	18,833.37

STEWART VAN VLIET,
Brevet Brigadier-General and Quartermaster, U. S. Army.

QUARTERMASTER'S OFFICE,
New York, September 22, 1865.

Statement of public moneys received, transferred, and expended by Capt. F. J. Crilly, assistant quartermaster, during the months of July, August, September, and part of October, 1864, while at New York City, under the direction of Bvt. Brig. Gen. Stewart Van Vliet, chief quartermaster Department of the East.

On hand July 1, 1864	$3,359.20
Received from officers	4,269,303.74
Received from sales of property and other sources	6 337.66
Total	4,279,000.60

Expended	$4,276,648.55
Transferred to officers	2,352.05
Total	4,279,000.60

STEWART VAN VLIET,
Brevet Brigadier-General and Quartermaster.

QUARTERMASTER'S OFFICE,
New York, September 22, 1865.

Statement of public moneys received, expended, transferred, &c., by Capt. Charles H. Peck, assistant quartermaster, U. S. Volunteers (since resigned), during the months of July, August, September, October, November, and December, 1864, and part of January, 1865, while on duty at New York City, under the direction of Bvt. Brig. Gen. Stewart Van Vliet, chief quartermaster Department of the East.

On hand July 1, 1864	$3,576.80
Received from officers	252,256.29
Received from sales of property and other sources	103.50
Total	255,936.59
Expended	248,362.52
Transferred to officers	7,574.07
Total	255,936.59

STEWART VAN VLIET,
Brevet Brigadier-General and Quartermaster, U. S. Army.

QUARTERMASTER'S OFFICE,
New York, September 22, 1865.

Statement of public moneys received, expended, and transferred by Capt. William H. Bailhache, assistant quartermaster, U. S. Volunteers (since resigned), during the months of November and December, 1864, and January, February, March, and April, 1865, while on duty at New York City, under the direction of Bvt. Brig. Gen. Stewart Van Vliet, chief quartermaster Department of the East.

On hand July 1, 1864	$0.00
Received from officers	5,890,187.36
Received from sales of property and other sources	855.42
Total	5,891,042.78
Expended	5,667,558.13
Transferred to officers	223,484.65
Total	5,891,042.78

STEWART VAN VLIET,
Brevet Brigadier-General and Quartermaster, U. S. Army.

QUARTERMASTER'S OFFICE,
New York, September 22, 1865.

A.—*Report of quartermaster's stores purchased, transferred, sold, &c., by Capts. F. J. Crilly, C. H. Peck (resigned), William H. Bailhache (resigned), and A. S. Kimball, assistant quartermasters, at New York City, under the direction of Bvt. Brig. Gen. Stewart Van Vliet, chief quartermaster Department of the East, in the fiscal year ending June 30, 1865.**

*Omitted; but see pp. 707–742, of Executive Document No. 1, referred to in foot-note (*), p. 249.

C.—*Statement of amount paid on account of rail, river, stage, and wagon transportation by Capts. F. J. Crilly, Charles H. Peck (resigned), W. H. Bailhache (resigned), and W. W. Van Ness, assistant quartermasters, at New York, under the direction of Bvt. Brig. Gen. Stewart Van Vliet, chief quartermaster Department of the East, during the fiscal year ending June 30, 1865.*

	Transportation.				
	Railroads.	Steam-boats, barges, &c.	Stages.	Wagons, &c.	Total.
Passengers:					
Officers and men	$785, 423. 37	$130, 579. 12	$1, 052. 26	$3, 599. 93	$920, 654. 68
Prisoners of war and other rebels	43, 228. 08	3. 50	80. 00	20. 00	43, 331. 58
Civilians	25, 934. 25	390. 58	13. 90	103. 50	26, 442. 23
Total	854, 585. 70	130, 973. 20	1, 146. 16	3, 723. 43	990, 428. 49
Freight	59, 921. 91	192, 289. 65	80. 00	158, 809. 77	411, 101. 33
Total	914, 507. 61	323, 262. 85	1, 226. 16	162, 533. 20	1, 401, 529. 82
Expenditures	1, 064. 00	3, 815. 67	....	274. 70	5, 154. 37
Grand total	915, 571. 61	327, 078. 52	1, 226. 16	162, 807. 90	1, 406, 684. 19

STEWART VAN VLIET,
Brevet Brigadier-General, &c.

CC.—*Statement of amount paid on account of ocean and lake transportation by Capts. F. J. Crilly, Charles H. Peck (resigned), W. H. Bailhache (resigned), and W. W. Van Ness, assistant quartermasters, at New York City, under the direction of Bvt. Brig. Gen. Stewart Van Vliet, chief quartermaster Department of the East, during the fiscal year ending June 30, 1865.*

Passengers:		
Officers and men	$50, 288. 04	
Civilians	586. 02	
Total		$50, 874. 06
Freight		755, 880. 26
Total		806, 754. 32
Expenditures		2, 228, 097. 60
Grand total		3, 034, 851. 92

STEWART VAN VLIET,
Brevet Brigadier-General, &c.

D.—*Statement of all stores transported by Bvt. Brig. Gen. Stewart Van Vliet, quartermaster, U. S. Army, at New York City, during the fiscal year ending June 30, 1865.*

ANIMALS.

Kind of transportation.	Horses.	Mules.	Cattle.	Sheep.	Total.
Railroads	22, 470	100	....	....	22, 570
Steam-boats, barges, &c	74	....	6, 628	2, 147	8, 849
Total not owned by Government	22, 544	100	6, 628	2, 147	31, 419
Steam-boats, barges, &c., owned by Government	....	....	327	653	980
Grand total	22, 544	100	6, 955	2, 800	32, 399

D.—*Statement of all stores transported by Bvt. Brig. Gen. Stewart Van Vliet, quartermaster, U. S. Army, at New York City, during the fiscal year ending June 30, 1865*—Continued.

STORES.

Kind of transportation.	Commissary of subsistence.	Quartermaster.	Ordnance.	Medical.	Miscellaneous.	Total.
	Tons.	*Tons.*	*Tons.*	*Tons.*	*Tons.*	*Tons.*
Railroads	74, 306	30, 319	29, 816	9, 307	319	144, 067
Steam-boats, barges, &c	150, 819	68, 314	36, 309	11, 809	10, 816	278, 067
Total not owned by Government	225, 125	98, 633	66, 125	21, 116	11, 135	422, 134
Steam-boats, barges, &c., owned by Government	17, 840	6, 840	29, 314	3, 203	2, 014	59, 211
Grand total	242, 965	105, 473	95, 439	24, 319	13, 149	481, 345

STEWART VAN VLIET,
Brevet Brigadier-General and Quartermaster.

No. 105.

WASHINGTON, D. C., *July 27, 1865.*

Bvt. Maj. Gen. M. C. MEIGS,
Quartermaster-General U. S. Army, Washington, D. C.:

GENERAL: At your request I furnish you with the following data, obtained in my recent trip from Santa Fé, N. Mex., to Fort Leavenworth, Kans.:

There are two old and well-established routes from Fort Union (the main depot of supplies for the troops in New Mexico) to Fort Leavenworth, viz, the Raton and the Cimarron routes. The former passes over the Raton Mountain, crossing the Purgatory and Timpas Rivers and the Arkansas River at Bent's Old Fort; then down that stream, passing Fort Lyon, Colo. Ter., forty miles below; thence ninety miles to Choteau's Island, where it unites with a branch of the Cimarron route, called Aubrey's Cut-off; thence down the river eighty miles to where the Cimarron route crosses the Arkansas River. The two routes unite at this point, known as the Cimarron Crossing, and form one route to Fort Leavenworth. The grass on the Raton route is generally good and abundant, but the distance is 100 miles farther than by the Cimarron, and the road is much worse. Fort Lyon, on the Raton route, is a collection of stone buildings erected in 1860–'61 by six companies of the then First U. S. Cavalry, under the late General Sedgwick, then lieutenant-colonel of that regiment. Nothing of any consequence has been done to the buildings since he left them. They are incomplete, but habitable, and are, or were as I passed, occupied, I believe, by three small companies of Colorado Volunteers. The animals, both horses and mules, of this command were not in very good order, which was attributed to the want of grain, of which they had been without entirely for several months until a few days before I passed, when a large supply was received from Fort Leavenworth. The grain for this post should come from the settlements on the Arkansas River, which commence some sixty-five miles above the post, and from those on the Huerfano and Purgatory Rivers, tributaries of the Arkansas from the south, and from which it could be hauled at certainly less expense than from Fort Leavenworth. The crops through the section above referred to I examined closely, and they promise an abundant harvest. Hay can be had in any quantity within from three to ten miles of the post, and should not cost over $15 or $20 per ton delivered and stacked. The quartermaster's and commissary stores are in some buildings known as Bent's New Fort, about one mile below, on the river. It would, I think, be better if the post were completed and the stores provided with storage there.

The Cimarron route branches off from the Raton at or near Fort Union in a northeasterly direction, crosses the Ocate Creek, Red River, McNeiss', Whetstone, and Rabbit Ear Creeks, Cimarron River where the Aubrey Cut-off branches in a northern direction, Sand Creek, and a sand desert of fifty or sixty miles to the Arkansas River, which it crosses, uniting with the Raton route. The grass on the Cimarron route is as good as on the other, but the fuel and water not so plentiful; yet there is enough for passing trains. During very dry seasons the water is quite scarce, and some of it, especially at the Cimarron River, is brackish. It is the route, however, generally traveled by merchants' trains, and now that rebel raids from Arkansas and Texas are not to be feared, should be the route traveled by the Government contractors, as it is nearly if not quite 100 miles shorter than the Raton route, and the contract is so much per 100 pounds per 100 miles. The only encampment of troops on this route is at Cedar Bluffs, a point near what is known as Upper Cimarron Spring, about 140 miles from Fort Union, or nearly half way between that post and the Cimarron Crossing, which is just 300 miles. This encampment consists of three companies of volunteers under Col. Christopher Carson, and is supplied from Fort Union. The command will return to Fort Union in November. A permanent camp or post should be established on this route at or near the present one of Colonel Carson's, where fuel and water can be procured in sufficient quantities. Three companies, one of cavalry and two of infantry, would suffice for the garrison.

From the Cimarron Crossing, where the two routes unite, the road passes down the river about thirty miles to Fort Dodge. This post consists of a few huts made of poles set endwise in the ground and covered with dirt and tents, inclosed by a ditch and a dirt embankment, and garrisoned, I believe, by five companies of volunteers under a Major Armstrong. A few days before I passed two Indians drove off almost all the public animals from this post. These had hardly gotten the stock away before a large number of their people, estimated variously at from 500 to 5,000, showed themselves on the surrounding hills.

The grain for Fort Dodge is hauled from Forts Riley and Leavenworth. Hay is abundant in the river bottom near the post and should not cost over $20 per ton, delivered and stacked. Fuel and building material, like that used in making the huts that they now have, can, I was informed by the post quartermaster, be obtained in sufficient quantities within fifteen miles of the post on either side of the river.

From Fort Lyon to Fort Dodge, a distance of about 200 miles, there are no troops. I am of the opinion that a four-company post, two of cavalry and two of infantry, should be established about half way between these two posts, and that if the troops were active it would protect the travel more from the Indians than anything else that could be done.

The road passes down the river from Fort Dodge for some eight or ten miles, there divides—one part, of 100 miles in length, following the river, with plenty of water; the other passing over the ridge, without water in dry seasons, cutting off some thirty miles and uniting with the river route at Fort Larned, on Pawnee Fork. Fuel on these two roads is scarce, and trains are almost entirely dependent for it on the dried excrement of buffalo and the cattle of trains, familiarly known as "buffalo chips." The grass is good.

Fort Larned is a post of four companies, some sixty-five miles by the ridge road and 100 miles by the river road, below Fort Dodge. It was built in 1858, 1859, and 1860, of logs set endwise in the ground and roofed with earth. It is on the Pawnee Fork, but too far from the road, is surrounded by an abundance of fuel, water, and good grazing. Hay can be cut within a few miles of the post at a cost, I should think, of about $20 per ton, delivered. It is a proper place for a military post and should be the depot of supplies for any troops acting against Indians on that line. The grain for this post comes from Forts Riley and Leavenworth. It can and should come from the country around Council Grove and Fort Riley, and thus save at least transporting it 100 miles.

At Fort Larned the road again divides, one part, a new route, by way of Fort Riley, Kans. There are troops on this route at Fort Ellsworth, where the road crosses the Smoky Hill Fork of the Kansas River, at Fort Riley and at Topeka. The other route (the old Santa Fé trail) continues down the Arkansas River some fifty miles, crosses Walnut, Cow, and Little Arkansas Creeks, to Council Grove, at all of which points are troops; thence via Burlingame and Lawrence to Fort Leavenworth, Kans.

For any further information with regard to distance, &c., I would respectfully refer you to the accompanying journal of my last trip across the plains.*

Very respectfully, your obedient servant,

J. C. McFERRAN,
Major and Quartermaster.

WASHINGTON, D. C., *July 26, 1865.*

Bvt. Maj. Gen. M. C. MEIGS,
Quartermaster-General U. S. Army, Washington, D. C.:

GENERAL: In obedience to your verbal instructions of yesterday, and without other data than such as my memory furnishes, I proceed to give you a synopsis of my services as chief quartermaster Department of New Mexico from the 1st of October, 1862, to the present time.

On the 1st of October, 1862, I relieved Bvt. Lieut. Col. James L. Donaldson, quartermaster, U. S. Army, as chief quartermaster of the department. Colonel Donaldson transferred to me a list of the estimated indebtedness of the quartermaster's department which had accrued under him as chief quartermaster of the Department of New Mexico, amounting to over $425,000. I afterward found the indebtedness to be about $100,000 more. The credit of the department was very low and certified vouchers selling at a ruinous discount. Almost all the supplies at Albuquerque, a subsistence depot, and at Santa Fé, the headquarters of the department, had been destroyed by the officers in charge of them to prevent their falling into the hands of the

*Omitted; but see pp. 746–748, of Executive Document No. 1, referred to in foot-note (*), p. 249.

enemy; Fort Fauntleroy was abandoned, and many of the stores at that point were also destroyed, which, with the abandonment of Forts Fillmore and Stanton and consequent losses of Government property, left the troops in New Mexico with very limited supplies. All this occurred before I became chief quartermaster and had been but partially remedied. By great exertions, assisted by Capt. H. M. Enos, assistant quartermaster, and all my other assistants, and sustained by yourself and the department commander, most of the outstanding debts were paid off, the credit of the Quartermaster's Department restored, and the troops comfortably supplied.

Immediately after I became chief quartermaster a force of six or more companies was put into the field against the Apache tribe of Indians, in and around Fort Stanton, and kept actively engaged almost all winter. These troops were well supplied, and the campaign resulted in the surrender of over 400 out of some 600 or 700, of which the tribe consisted, and in placing them on a reservation near Fort Sumner, 120 miles east of Fort Stanton. The transportation of these Indians to their new home was a duty that devolved upon and was promptly performed by the Quartermaster's Department. During the continuance of the campaign the new posts of Forts Sumner and Wingate, the latter to replace Fort Fauntleroy in the country occupied by the Navajo Indians, had to be located and commenced; the quarters at Fort Stanton and Santa Fé, which had been recklessly burned, had to be repaired; the corrals and stabling at Santa Fé, which were insufficient and miserable, had to be rebuilt almost entirely. It also became necessary to erect suitable buildings at or near Fort Union (which the Texan invasion demonstrated as the proper point for the main supply depot) to quarter the garrison and properly secure the supplies for the entire department—of the subsistence and quartermaster's departments and of clothing and equipage. This work was promptly commenced, and much of it has been completed; the remainder is rapidly approaching completion.

Three other posts—Fort Whipple, in Arizona Territory, near Prescott, the seat of government of that Territory, and over 350 miles west from Albuquerque, N. Mex.; Fort Cummings, sixty miles west of the Mesilla Valley, on the old Butterfield route to California from Little Rock, Ark.; and Fort Bascom, N. Mex., on Red River, about 110 miles southeast of Fort Union—were located, commenced, and are far advanced toward completion.

In the summer of 1863 a large force was organized and put into the field against the Navajo tribe of Indians, the hereditary despoilers of the people of New Mexico for over 200 years, who number in men, women, and childen at least 10,000 or 11,000 souls. Capt. A. B. Carey, Thirteenth U. S. Infantry, one of the best officers in our or any other service, consented, at my request, to act as chief quartermaster of the expedition. Under his able administration the troops were amply supplied with every facility to carry on the campaign, even through an unprecedented hard winter; and it resulted in the surrender and transfer of over 9,000 of the tribe to a reservation over 400 miles from their hereditary homes. This was made by and at the expense of the Quartermaster's Department, with mule and ox wagons, over a desert almost destitute of forage and but little water, except at a few points. The Quartermaster's Department was required and did furnish blankets, cooking utensils, much of the subsistence, &c., for this large number of people. The grain furnished for their subsistence by the Quartermaster's Department was afterward paid for at cost by the

Subsistence Department. After their location on the reservation they were furnished by the Quartermaster's Department with farming implements, animals, &c., to assist them in opening farms.

Other large and small commands were put into the field against the Comanche, Kiowa, and other hostile tribes, and all well equipped and supplied with all that pertains to the Quartermaster's Department, and necessary for their efficiency.

Owing to the demand caused by the necessity of feeding corn and wheat to captured Indians on the reservation, the price of those articles increased very much, and it became necessary to reduce the grain rations to animals to six and seven pounds each per day. This resulted in the loss of a number of horses and mules, and the reduction in the efficiency of all public animals, but not to that extent as to interfere materially with the business of the department, most of the freighting from the main depot to the various posts being done under contract.

In addition to the posts mentioned above as having been located and undergoing repairs or being built, there are two others which were located this summer and are under construction at this time, viz: Fort McRae, about forty miles south of Fort Craig, N. Mex., six miles off the line from Santa Fé to El Paso, and on what is known as the "Jornada del Muerto," or dead man's journey, a desert in a bend of the Rio Grande, almost destitute, for eighty miles, of water; and Fort Selden, at the other end of the "Jornada," where the road comes down to the river. Each of these posts is for quartering two companies, one of cavalry and one of infantry, and they are very important.

The grain for the various posts has usually been purchased in open market at prices approved by the chief quartermaster, and until the last two or three years in sufficient quantities from the producers and merchants to answer all demands. For the last three years the drought and insects have destroyed so much grain that corn has had to be sent out from Fort Leavenworth, Kans. These causes, and the unprecedented rise in the Rio Grande, which has ruined almost all the crops on its banks, have this year reduced the amount raised in New Mexico to less than was ever known before.

Hay for the use of the animals is obtained in the vicinity of the posts, and by contract, at an average cost of about $45 per ton of 2,240 pounds. Some years the crop is short, but usually sufficient can be had to last the winters.

The Department of New Mexico embraced, for most of the time that I was chief quartermaster, the entire Territories of New Mexico and Arizona and a part of Northwestern Texas.

The sources of supplies for troops in the department were Saint Louis, Mo., Fort Leavenworth, Kans., and other points east of those.

From Fort Leavenworth the transportation of these supplies is by ox and mule wagons through the Indian country, a distance of 750 miles to the main depot for the department at Fort Union, N. Mex. There they are received and stored, and from thence distributed as required, by wagon transportation, to the various posts and commands. Their distribution as well as transportation from Fort Leavenworth to the depot (Fort Union) is done by contract, awarded to the lowest responsible bidder, after due public notice; that from Fort Leavenworth to Fort Union being given out by the depot quartermaster at Fort Leavenworth, and that from Fort Union to the various posts by the chief quartermaster Department of New Mexico. This course I consider the best for the United States.

The headquarters of the department are at Santa Fé, the capital of the Territory, and comprising about 6,500 souls, mostly Mexicans. The city, like all other towns in New Mexico, is built of sun-dried bricks, or adobes, twenty inches long, ten inches wide, and four inches thick, some larger and some smaller. The houses constructed of these bricks are cool in summer and warm in winter, are generally one story high, and present at a distance the appearance of a collection of brickkilns.

The above is as full a report as I can make without access to my papers, and for further details I would respectfully refer you to my previous annual report, now in your office.

I think that the quartermaster's department in New Mexico has been as efficient and has met with fewer losses and fewer dishonest agents than in any part of the United States from the 1st of October, 1862, to the present time, and deducting the indebtedness of my predecessor when I relieved him, and the cost of repairs to public buildings, &c., made necessary by damage, abandonment, &c., before I became chief quartermaster, I challenge a comparison of my expenditures with those of any previous year's, confident of its being favorable. I know it will be if the difference between gold and Treasury notes and the increased price of everything consequent upon the war is taken into consideration.

Very respectfully, your obedient servant,

J. C. McFERRAN,
Major and Quartermaster.

No. 106.

DEPOT QUARTERMASTER'S OFFICE,
Cincinnati, Ohio, September 5, 1865.

Bvt. Maj. Gen. M. C. MEIGS,
Quartermaster-General U. S. Army, Washington, D. C.:

GENERAL: In compliance with General Orders, No. 39, current series, from your office, I have the honor to submit this my annual report for the fiscal year ending June 30, 1865. My last annual report was forwarded on October 1, 1864.

This report embraces the following-named papers, which are herewith, viz:

Statement of public moneys for which I have been responsible during the year, marked No. 1.

Form A, statement of quartermaster's property for which I have been responsible during the year, marked No. 2.

Abstract of contracts for clothing and equipage made by me during the year, marked No. 3.

Statements according to Forms B, C, CC, D, E, F, and G are not forwarded, because not required from the nature of my duties during the year.

From June 30, 1864, until September 16, of that year, I had immediate charge of the clothing and equipage branch of the department at this depot. On the latter date I was relieved by Col. W. W. McKim, Quartermaster's Department, having tendered my resignation as captain and assistant quartermaster, U. S. Army, some time previously.

By Special Orders, No. 75, Adjutant-General's Office, February 15, 1865, I was assigned as chief quartermaster of this depot with the rank of colonel, Quartermaster's Department, and ordered to relieve Col. W. W. McKim, Quartermaster's Department, then in charge of this depot, which I did on February 22, 1865, under which order I still continue to serve. As the clothing and equipage branch constitutes the main portion of the business of the depot, such remarks and information as I can furnish in relation thereto will be submitted in connection with the annual report called for by you in letter of August 1, 1865, which report is being prepared as speedily as possible.

Very respectfully, your obedient servant,

C. W. MOULTON,
Colonel and Depot Quartermaster.

No. 1.—*A statement of public moneys for which Col. C. W. Moulton, depot quartermaster at Cincinnati, Ohio, has been responsible during the fiscal year ending June 30, 1865.*

Received from officers during the year	$10,429,618.89
Received from Treasury Department during the year	23,457,996.90
Received from sales of property during the year	16,285.11
Total	33,903,900.90
Expended during the year	18,252,552.18
Transferred to officers during the year	13,034,772.31
Remaining on hand June 30, 1865	2,616,576.41
Total	33,903,900.90
Balance on hand June 30, 1865, deposited as follows:	
Certificate of indebtedness	2,357,848.94
First National Bank, Philadelphia	231,838.15
First National Bank, Cincinnati	12,322.45
Assistant Treasurer United States, New York	14,038.35
Cash in office safe	528.52
	2,616,576.41

C. W. MOULTON,
Colonel and Depot Quartermaster.

A.

No. 2.—*Statement of quartermaster's property for which Col. C. W. Moulton, depot quartermaster at Cincinnati, Ohio, has been responsible during the fiscal year ending June 30, 1865.**

*Abstract of contracts for clothing and equipage made by Col. C. W. Moulton, depot quartermaster at the Cincinnati depot, for the fiscal year ending June 30, 1865.**

No. 107.

CHIEF QUARTERMASTER'S OFFICE,
Saint Louis, Mo., September 19, 1865.

Maj. Gen. M. C. MEIGS,
Quartermaster-General U. S. Army, Washington, D. C.:

GENERAL: In compliance with General Orders, No. 39, Quartermaster-General's Office, Washington, July 1, 1865, I have the honor to call your attention to my last annual report, forwarded to your office September 20, 1864, and to report as follows:

During the fiscal year ending June 30, 1865, I was stationed on duty at Saint Louis, Mo., as chief quartermaster of the Department

*Omitted; but see pp. 752–754, of Executive Document No. 1, referred to in foot-note (*), p. 249.

of the Missouri and of the Saint Louis depot. As chief quartermaster of the depot I have superintended the procurement and issue of all kinds of quartermaster's supplies required, not only for troops serving in the Department of the Missouri, but for those operating in remote sections of country, and having for their bases the depots of Cairo, Memphis, Nashville, Devall's Bluff, Little Rock, Fort Smith, Fort Leavenworth, &c., which have, to a greater or less extent, been supplied from the depot under my control.

From and previous to the commencement of the period for which the report is required until the 30th of November, 1864, I had, in addition to my other duties, personal charge of the procurement and issue of mules and artillery horses, wagons, ambulances, harness, &c., at this depot. On that date (November 30), by your order, the public animals were transferred to Capt. Ingham Coryell, assistant quartermaster, and the affairs pertaining to the First Division of the Quartermaster's Department here became a separate establishment, under the control of Captain Coryell, orders affecting the same proceeding direct to him from Washington.

Soon after I transferred the wagons, ambulances, harness, &c., to Capt. J. L. Woods, assistant quartermaster, who still, under my direction, has charge of that species of property.

In the month of October, 1864, the prosecution of the campaign in this State against the rebel General Price rendered it necessary that the divisions of Generals A. J. Smith and Joseph A. Mower (which had been suddenly brought into this department to meet the pressing emergency then existing) should be newly outfitted and equipped at this depot for the work before them. This was done promptly, without an hour's unnecessary delay, and the troops went forward in good time to the points where they were needed.

The several expeditions against the Indians, organized and conducted by General Sully during the period under consideration, were equipped and supplied from here.

The material required for constructing the new posts established in the Indian country were drawn from this depot.

During the fiscal year I received and disbursed more than fifty millions of dollars of public funds, as shown by the inclosed statement, involving an immense amount of labor and responsibility in the payment of vouchers issued at this depot, in the Departments of the Missouri and Arkansas, and at the several military posts on the Mississippi River as far down as Natchez, Miss., and in supplying with funds for the payment of their employés the officers serving within the scope of country above defined.

I have the honor to transmit herewith the statements required, as follows: (1) Statement of quartermaster's property, Form A; (2) statement of public moneys; (3) statement of amount paid for rail, river, stage, and wagon (other than Government wagon) transportation, Form C.

The other paragraphs and forms required do not come under the scope of my duties.

I am, general, very respectfully, your obedient servant,

WILLIAM MYERS,
Brevet Brigadier-General and Chief Quartermaster.

A.—*Statement of quartermaster's property for the fiscal year ending June 30, 1865.**

---

*Omitted; but see pp. 756-774, of Executive Document No. 1, referred to in foot-note (*), p. 249.

Statement of public moneys, in accordance with Section V, fourth clause, of General Orders, No. 39, dated Quartermaster-General's Office, Washington, D. C., July 1, 1865, of William Myers, brevet brigadier-general and chief quartermaster at Saint Louis, Mo.

On hand July 1, 1864	$55,727.19
Received from officers during the year	1,491,650.48
Received from Treasury Department during the year	52,711,654.57
Received from sales of property and other sources during the year	35,000.66
Total	54,294,032.90
Expended during the year	42,576,348.50
Transferred to other officers during the year	7,295,626.85
Remaining on hand June 30, 1865	4,422,057.55
Total	54,294,032.90

The balance on hand is deposited as follows:

In the First National Bank of Philadelphia	264,123.83
With the assistant treasurer of the United States in New York	1,078,768.00
With the assistant treasurer of the United States in Saint Louis	992,763.16
With the Treasurer of the United States in Washington	2,080,158.22
In an iron safe in my office	1,106.89
Due the United States Government	5,137.45
On hand July 1, 1864: Proceeds of sales of captured and contraband property, and property received from unknown sources	20,919.72
Remaining on hand June 30, 1865	20,919.72

The balance on hand is deposited with the assistant treasurer of the United States in Saint Louis, Mo.

I certify that the above statement is correct.

WILLIAM MYERS,
Brevet Brigadier-General and Chief Quartermaster.

Statement of amount paid on account of rail, river, stage, and wagon transportation by William Myers, brevet brigadier-general and chief quartermaster at Saint Louis, Mo., during the fiscal year ending June 30, 1865.

Kind of transportation.	Passengers.	Freight.	Total.	Expenditures	Grand total.
Railroads	$1,163,843.44	$828,938.81	$1,992,782.25	$267,936.79	$2,260,719.04
Steam-boats, barges, &c	852,454.52	4,353,266.96	5,205,721.48	5,205,254.76	10,410,976.24
Stages	4,143.03		4,143.03		4,143.03
Wagons, &c	18.00	20,932.28	20,950.28	244,216.21	265,166.49
Total	2,020,458.99	5,203,138.05	7,223,597.04	5,717,407.76	12,941,004.80

But one set of sub-vouchers was received with these accounts, which was forwarded to the Third Auditor of the Treasury Department, Washington, D. C., with the accounts. It is therefore impracticable for me to subdivide the passengers, as required in above form.

I certify that the above statement is correct.

WILLIAM MYERS,
Brevet Brigadier-General and Chief Quartermaster.

No. 108.

CHIEF QUARTERMASTER'S OFFICE,
Philadelphia Depot, September 28, 1865.

Bvt. Maj. Gen. M. C. MEIGS,
Quartermaster-General U. S. Army, Washington, D. C.:

GENERAL: In obedience to General Orders, No. 39, Quartermaster-General's Office, current series, I have the honor to inclose herewith my annual report for the fiscal year ending June 30, 1865.

My annual report for the fiscal year ending June 30, 1864, was mailed from Cincinnati, Ohio, November 10, 1864.

I was relieved at Boston, Mass., as assistant quartermaster, by order of the Secretary of War, and turned over the funds and duties to my successor September 1, 1864, and on the 8th idem proceeded, in accordance with said order, via Washington, D. C., to Cincinnati, Ohio, at which place I was assigned to duty as chief quartermaster of the principal depot, with the rank of colonel in the Quartermaster's Department.

By verbal permission of the Secretary of War I went from Washington to Cincinnati via Philadelphia for the purpose of conferring with Col. A. J. Perry, Quartermaster's Department, chief of the division of clothing and equipage, Quartermaster-General's Office, and at that time temporarily in charge of the Philadelphia depot.

I arrived at Cincinnati on the evening of September 15, 1864, and assumed charge of the depot the following day, relieving Col. Thomas Swords, assistant quartermaster-general, U. S. Army.

In compliance with Special Orders, No. 75, Adjutant-General's Office, February 15, 1865, I turned over the duties, &c., devolving upon me as chief quartermaster at Cincinnati, Ohio, to Col. C. W. Moulton on the 23d of February, 1865, and repaired to this city, where I was ordered to relieve Col. Herman Biggs, Quartermaster's Department, in charge of the principal depot.

I arrived at Philadelphia the 26th of February, 1865, and entered upon my duties as chief quartermaster the following day.

I respectfully submit herewith the following statements, called for by General Orders, No. 39:

Statement A.—Quartermaster's property.

Statement B.—Clothing and camp and garrison equipage.

Statement C.—Amount paid on account of rail, river, stage, &c., transportation.

Statement CC.—Amount paid on account of ocean and lake transportation.

Statement D.—Troops and stores transported.

Statement DD.—Troops and stores transported by ocean and lake.

Statement G.—Vessels owned, chartered, &c.

NOTE.—The foregoing statements relate to the business at Boston, Mass., and embrace the two months, from June 1, 1864, to August 31, 1864, while I was on duty at that station.

Statement B.—Clothing and camp and garrison equipage.

Statement BB.—Material.

NOTE.—These two statements relate to the clothing and equipage business at Cincinnati, Ohio, which was my especial care, in addition to my duties as chief quartermaster of the depot, and cover the period during which I was in charge at that station.

Statement A.—Quartermaster's property.

Statement B.—Clothing and camp and garrison equipage.

Statement BB.—Material.

NOTE.—These three statements relate to the clothing and equipage transactions at Philadelphia from the date I took charge of the Philadelphia depot to the 30th of June, 1865.

A statement of public invoices, showing the amount on hand July 1, 1864, and the amount received, expended, transferred, &c., during the fiscal year ending June 30, 1865, is also inclosed.

No property called for by Statements E and F, page 7, General Orders, No. 39, came under my control during the year.

The particular attention of the Quartermaster-General is called to the importance of substituting fire-proof storage accommodations at the Schuylkill Arsenal for the wooden structures now used.

There are about twenty-five wooden sheds and buildings scattered throughout the yard within the walls, and forty-two sheds in the rows adjoining the walls on the south side.

The clothing and equipage on hand has cost the Quartermaster's Department not less than $20,000,000, and is in continual peril from fire.

Locomotives pass along the entire line of the wall on the northerly side many times each day and night.

I have had the storage of goods rearranged, and endeavored to place the more valuable property in the brick buildings, but they are inadequate, and have been for many years, for this purpose. It is therefore necessary to keep large quantities of valuable property in wooden sheds having gravel and tar roofing.

The fire apparatus is kept in good order, and great care is taken to guard against incendiary or accidental fires. Notwithstanding these precautions the risk is imminent and causes constant anxiety.

I respectfully recommend that the irregular clothing and material on hand at the arsenal be sold or removed as soon as practicable, as it has been kept loose, and unless sold or properly packed for shipment or permanent storage, soon will be likely to engender moths, from which damage will ensue to other property.

The importance of proper and uniform standards of clothing and equipage was alluded to in a special report of clothing and equipage transactions transmitted to the Quartermaster-General the 11th instant.

It having been reported to the Quartermaster-General that the specifications for dark-blue cloth and sky-blue kersey recommended from this office in March, 1864, were an imposition, and believing that it is impracticable to conform to them, and impossible to obtain sufficient material of that strength to equip a large army, I respectfully refer to my suggestions upon that subject, and beg to add that whenever the question is to be considered it should not be determined what standard to adopt upon limited and local information, nor until after thorough investigation and careful inquiry of the manufacturers and practical men throughout the country.

The depots at Cincinnati and Philadelphia were reorganized by me to conform to the act of Congress of July 4, 1864, and the duties were distributed among the officers serving with me, in accordance with that law.

I respectfully commend to the consideration of the Quartermaster-General the several officers of the Quartermaster's Department who have served under my orders at Cincinnati and at this depot, for the energetic and faithful manner in which they have discharged the duties assigned them.

The business with which I have been intrusted during the period covered by this report has completely occupied my time and thoughts, and I have endeavored to do my duty to the best of my ability.

I am, general, very respectfully, your obedient servant,

WM. W. McKIM,

Colonel and Chief Quartermaster Philadelphia Depot.

Statement of public moneys received, transferred, &c., by Col. William W. McKim, U. S. Army, Quartermaster's Department, at Boston, Mass., and the Cincinnati and Philadelphia depots, for the fiscal year ending June 30, 1865.

On hand July 1, 1864	$13,698.43
Received from officers during the year	2,328,322.68
Received from Treasury Department during the year	22,643,289.00
Received from sales of property, &c., during the year	878.05
Total	24,986,188.16
Expended during the year	195,163.25
Transferred to other officers during the year	24,791,024.91
Total	24,986,188.16

WILLIAM W. McKIM,
Colonel, Quartermaster's Department, U. S. Army.

A.—*Statement of quartermaster's stores from the 27th day of February, 1865, to the 30th day of June, 1865, inclusive, at Philadelphia depot.**

A.—*Statement of quartermaster's property for the fiscal year ending June 30, 1865, at Boston, Mass.**

B.—*Statement of clothing, camp and garrison equipage, from September 16, 1864, to February 23, 1865, at the Cincinnati depot.**

BB.—*Statement of materials from February 27, 1865, to June 30, 1865, inclusive, at the Philadelphia depot.**

BB.—*Statement showing the receipts and issues of material from September 16, 1864, to February 23, 1865, at the Cincinnati depot.**

B.—*Statement of clothing, camp and garrison equipage, from February 27, 1865, to June 30, 1865, at the Philadelphia depot.**

B.—*Statement of clothing, camp and garrison equipage, for the months of July and August, 1864, at Boston, Mass.**

C.—*Statement of amount paid at Boston, Mass., on account of rail, river, stage, and wagon transportation, by Capt. W. W. McKim, assistant quartermaster, U. S. Army, during the fiscal year ending June 30, 1865.*

PASSENGERS.

Railroads:	
Officers and men	$28,291
Civilians	2,934
Stages: Officers and men	13
Total	31,238

I certify that this statement is correct.

WILLIAM W. McKIM,
Captain and Assistant Quartermaster, U. S. Army.

CC.—*Statement of amount paid at Boston, Mass., on account of ocean and lake transportation by Capt. W. W. McKim, assistant quartermaster, U. S. Army, during the fiscal year ending June 30, 1865.*

Officers and men	$26,723
Freight	78,198
Expenditures	1,985
Total	106,906

I certify that the above statement is correct.

WILLIAM W. McKIM,
Captain and Assistant Quartermaster, U. S. Army.

---

*Omitted; but see pp. 779–805, of Executive Document No. 1, referred to in foot-note (*), p. 249.

D.—*Statement of all troops and stores transported by Capt. W. W. McKim, assistant quartermaster, U. S. Army, Boston, Mass., for the fiscal year ending June 30, 1865.*

Kind of transportation.	Passengers.					Stores.					
	Officers and men under orders.	Soldiers on furlough East to be charged.	Prisoners of war.	Civilians.	Total.	Commissary of subsistence.	Quartermaster's.	Ordnance.	Medical.	Miscellaneous.	Total.
						Tons.	*Tons.*	*Tons.*	*Tons.*	*Tons.*	*Tons.*
Railroads	17, 354	912	....	11	18, 277	458	135	1, 329	10	......	1, 932
Wagons						699	204	1, 451	13	......	2, 367
Total not owned by the Government.	17, 354	912	....	11	18, 277	1, 157	339	2, 780	23	......	4, 299

WILLIAM W. McKIM,
Captain and Assistant Quartermaster, U. S. Army.

DD.—*Statement of troops and stores transported at Boston, Mass., by Capt. W. W. McKim, assistant quartermaster, U. S. Army, for the fiscal year ending June 30, 1865.*

Kind of transportation.	Passengers: Officers and men under orders.	Stores.					
		Commissary of subsistence.	Quartermaster's.	Ordnance.	Medical.	Miscellaneous.	Total.
		Tons.	*Tons.*	*Tons.*	*Tons.*	*Tons.*	*Tons.*
Ocean and lake, not owned by Government	2, 960	956	....	796	....	269	2, 021
Ocean and lake, owned by Government	....	249	68	26	2	....	345
Grand total	2, 960	1, 205	68	822	2	269	2, 366

WILLIAM W. McKIM,
Captain and Assistant Quartermaster, U. S. Army.

*Statement of vessels owned by the Government, chartered, impressed, or employed by Capt. W. W. McKim, assistant quartermaster, U. S. Army, Boston, Mass., during the fiscal year ending June 30, 1865.**

No. 109.

HDQRS. MILITARY DIVISION OF THE ATLANTIC,
OFFICE CHIEF QUARTERMASTER,
Philadelphia, Pa., September 21, 1865.

Maj. Gen. M. C. MEIGS,
Quartermaster-General U. S. Army, Washington, D. C.:

GENERAL: I have the honor to transmit herewith a report of my transactions as chief quartermaster Army of the Potomac for the fiscal year ending June 30, 1865.†

Very respectfully, your obedient servant,

R. N. BATCHELDER,
Captain and Asst. Quartermaster, Brevet Colonel, U. S. Army.

* Omitted; but see p. 808, of Executive Document No. 1, referred to in foot-note (*) p. 249.

† See Series I, Vol. LI, Part I, p. 256.

No. 110.

QUARTERMASTER-GENERAL'S OFFICE,
Washington, D. C., September 12, 1865.

Bvt. Maj. Gen. M. C. MEIGS,
Quartermaster-General U. S. Army, Washington, D. C.:

GENERAL: Herewith I have the honor to transmit my annual report for the fiscal year ending June 30, 1865.

Very respectfully, your obedient servant,

JOHN B. HOWARD,
Brevet Colonel and Assistant Quartermaster.

QUARTERMASTER-GENERAL'S OFFICE,
Washington, D. C., August 1, 1865.

Bvt. Maj. Gen. M. C. MEIGS,
Quartermaster-General U. S. Army, Washington, D. C.:

GENERAL: In compliance with your General Orders, No. 39, of July 1, 1865, calling for an annual report for the fiscal year ending June 30, 1865, I have the honor to submit the following:

My last annual report was forwarded, in accordance with your General Orders, No. 29, of July 6, 1864, on the 26th of September, 1864.

July 1, 1864, I was acting as chief quartermaster of the Cavalry Corps, Army of the Potomac, by virtue of General Orders, No. 151, War Department, dated March 23, 1864, and Special Orders, No. 77, headquarters Army of the Potomac, March 26, 1864.

July 1, 1864, the transportation of the corps was in camp at Old Court-House, near Petersburg, Va., awaiting the return of the command, which had moved to the left of the Army of the Potomac for the relief of the Third Division of the corps, which had met with a severe repulse from the rebels in attempting to destroy the Weldon railroad.

July 2, in camp at the above-mentioned place, the transportation actively employed in conveying supplies of subsistence and forage to the front.

July 3, command returned, when the transportation of the corps was moved to Jordan's Point, on the James River, where a depot was established for receiving and issuing supplies to the command, which, after many hard marches and severe fights, required rest and recuperation.

July 4, 5, 6, 7, 8, 9, and 10, quartermaster's department engaged in shipping dismounted troops and unserviceable horses to Washington, D. C., and drawing clothing and supplies for the command.

July 11, on my application, I was relieved, by Special Orders, No. 54, headquarters Armies of the United States, as acting chief quarmaster Cavalry Corps and ordered to report to Maj. Gen. W. F. Smith, commanding Eighteenth Army Corps, for duty as chief quartermaster of that corps.

July 14, reported, in accordance with orders, to the commanding general Eighteenth Army Corps, entering on duty as chief quartermaster of the corps. My first business was to inspect the transportation and supplies, and ascertain the general condition of my department. The transportation of a portion of the corps was found in a wretched condition; animals poor, harness out of repair, and a large number of wagons unfit for service; small wagon parks were scattered over a large tract of country, and left almost exclusively under control of non-commissioned officers and citizen wagon-masters.

These wagons I directed to be immediately assembled and parked by divisions, and officers of the department directed to remain in close proximity to the trains. In the corps, acting quartermasters were found performing most of the duties pertaining to the regularly appointed officers of the department, and when found incompetent were relieved as rapidly as efficient officers could be obtained to fill their places. A portion of the troops were indifferently supplied with clothing, especially the Third (colored) Division; this deficiency arose from inefficiency on the part of the acting quartermaster of the division, and not from want of supplies at the main depot at City Point. When the proper system of obtaining and distributing supplies to the troops was fully understood no difficulty was found in supplying their wants.

During the time the Eighteenth Corps lay in front of Petersburg the transportation was parked within a short distance of the rear of the troops. The position was selected from necessity and not from choice, the location of trains being such that they were under fire of the rebel batteries; however, but small loss of life or destruction of transportation occurred.

For the purpose of receiving and issuing supplies to the Eighteenth Army Corps a depot had been established at the terminus of the military railroad leading from City Point. At this depot a number of officers had been stationed to conduct the business of the depot. I found that a large quantity of stores and a number of unserviceable horses had been allowed to accumulate at this place, and that there was also a large force of employés in attendance for whom there was not sufficient work. To remedy these evils I deemed it best to break up the depot, turn in all unserviceable property, discharge or transfer employés, and relieve the officers, assigning them to active and useful service.

July 27, by Special Orders, No. 204, headquarters Department of Virginia and North Carolina, I was assigned to duty as chief quartermaster Army of the James. This army consisted of the Tenth, Eighteenth, and a portion of the Nineteenth Corps, one division of cavalry, and a large engineer and medical department.

The position occupied by the Army of the James was to the right of the Army of the Potomac, the right resting on the James River, extending to the Appomattox, the line crossing the latter stream; the left holding position directly in front of Petersburg, and connecting with the right of the Ninth Corps of the Army of the Potomac.

The depots for the supply of the Army of the James were established at Smith's Station, on the line of the City Point Railroad; at Jones' and Sherman's Landings, on the James River, and Broadway and Point of Rocks Landing, on the Appomattox, with the principal depot at Bermuda Hundred. By order of the chief quartermaster of Armies operating against Richmond, City Point had been declared the main depot for the armies. In view of this, two of the depots of the Army of the James were at once broken up, and the others reduced in size, but retained merely to supply the current requirements of the troops. During this time operations were in progress on Dutch Gap Canal, an extensive work that required the employment of a large amount of material and labor. So far as the Quartermaster's Department was concerned, no embarrassment or delay retarded operations.

August 27, General Ord being in temporary command of the department, at my request I was relieved as acting chief quartermaster Army of the James, and directed to report to the commanding officer of the Eighteenth Army Corps.

On the 29th of September the command of Major-General Ord advanced across the James River at Chaffin's Bluff, carrying a strong line of fortifications, taking sixteen guns and many prisoners, effecting a lodgment in rebel fortifications, six miles from Richmond.

October 1 I received a special order from the War Department relieving me temporarily from duty as chief quartermaster Eighteenth Corps, and directing me to report at Saint Louis, Mo., as a member of a board for examination of officers of the Quartermaster's Department for the district comprising the Departments of the Missouri, Kansas, Northern, and Northwest.

In compliance with the order of the War Department I reported October 10 at Saint Louis to the president of the board of examiners.

October 13 the Board met pursuant to order, but owing to the disturbed condition of affairs in Missouri adjourned to meet at Cincinnati, Ohio.

Board met pursuant to adjournment and proceeded with the examination of officers of the Northern Department, adjourning on the 5th of December to assemble at Milwaukee for the purpose of examining officers of the Quartermaster's Department on duty in the Department of the Northwest. Having completed their duties in this department, on the 23d of January, 1865, the Board adjourned to meet at Saint Louis to continue the examination of officers of the Quartermaster's Department stationed in the Departments of the Missouri and Kansas.

The Board met at Saint Louis pursuant to adjournment, and proceeded with the examination of the officers of the Quartermaster's Department.

February 27, 1865, I received a telegraph order from Lieutenant-General Grant relieving me from duty as a member of the board of examiners, and ordering me to report in person to Major-General Ord, commanding the Army of the James, for duty in the field. I reported, in compliance with the order from Lieutenant-General Grant, March 7 to General Ord, and was immediately assigned to duty as chief quartermaster of that army.

Immediately after entering on my duties as chief quartermaster of the army I proceeded as rapidly as possible to place my department in a good condition for the opening campaign, the officers in the department co-operating most cordially with me in my efforts. All unserviceable wagons, harness, mules, cavalry and artillery horses, &c., were condemned and turned into depot. All surplus stores, public or private, were sent to the rear. The troops were supplied with the necessary clothing required for an active campaign, and the transportation of the army was reorganized to correspond precisely with the standard prescribed in orders.

On the 28th of March the Armies operating against Richmond moved, the Army of the James being fully supplied and equipped in every particular, so far as concerns the Quartermaster's Department. The movement of the trains of the Army of the James was similar to the plan adopted in the Army of the Potomac.

March 29, 30, 31, and April 1, transportation in camp at Humphreys Station, drawing additional supplies and awaiting the action of the combined armies.

April 2, transportation in camp at Patrick Station.

April 3, broke camp at 7 a. m., the transportation following in the rear of the army, which was advancing rapidly in pursuit of the retreating rebels.

On the receipt of the news of the capture of Richmond by the general commanding the Army of the James, I was directed to proceed to that city and establish a depot for the supply of the army. I immediately placed the transportation in charge of Lieut. Col. A. B. Lawrence, chief quartermaster of the Twenty-fourth Army Corps, and proceeded to Richmond in compliance with orders. On the route instructions were given to the officers of the Quartermaster's Department in charge of the depots at Bermuda Hundred, Point of Rocks, Broadway Landing, Jones' Landing, Deep Bottom, and Varina Landing to at once break up their respective depots and transfer all the stores to the main depot I proposed establishing at Richmond.

April 4, arrived in Richmond and proceeded at once to establish depots, collect abandoned and captured property, and procure data that would be of future service to the Government. From this date until the final breaking up of the Army of the James I remained on duty in the city of Richmond, transacting the various administrative duties pertaining to the Quartermaster's Department in and around Richmond.

On the 19th of June, by order of the Secretary of War, I was directed to report at Washington for duty in the office of the Quartermaster-General. On the 22d of June I was assigned to duty in the Sixth Division, Quartermaster-General's Office, and immediately entered upon the duties pertaining to that division.

I would respectfully state that with one exception I have been present at all battles fought by the Army of the James from the 1st of July, 1864, to the date of the entire defeat and surrender of Lee's rebel army.

In conclusion, I would state that at the time of the entry of our troops into Richmond a portion of the city was in ruins. Through the burnt district the streets were impassable, being blocked up by the smoking ruins, and the thoroughfares of the city filled with accumulations of ashes, garbage, and rubbish. The gas and water works had ceased operations. The railroads and canal lines leading from the city could not continue running, their works having been destroyed. The various coal mines and manufactories in the vicinity of Richmond had suspended operations. The wharves were old, rotten, and almost entirely useless. In fact, every branch of industry was at a stand-still, and the city was crowded with thousands of idle and destitute. It is difficult at this time to comprehend the embarrassment of the Quartermaster's Department in such a state of affairs, when naturally the department was looked to to bring order out of this confused state of things. It was therefore deemed just and equitable to place at work, for the benefit of the United States, these bands of wandering freedmen, who were enjoying their newly acquired liberty and subsisting at the expense of the Government. Orders were given to have warehouses fitted up for the purpose of accommodating those who were placed at work for the benefit of the Government. In the course of a few days more than a thousand men were engaged in gangs of twenty-five each, under competent foremen, and placed at work removing and clearing away the ruins of the burnt district, unloading vessels, repairing wharves, collecting captured and abandoned property in the city, and storing it in warehouses. Numbers were sent into the country for the purpose of procuring and bringing into the city a large quantity of abandoned cord wood. Others were detailed with the Medical, Commissary, Ordnance, and Engineer Departments.

Considerations of economy and the embarrassing difficulty attending the care and protection of the non-producing element among the liberated slaves led me to recommend the course adopted with reference to the freedmen. It was folly to suppose that the former owners of the unemployed negroes had any feeling that would lead them to care for their former servants. Great suffering would have resulted to the freedmen had not the Government extended to them support and protection.

I do not propose to offer any suggestions with regard to improvements in the personnel or administration of the Quartermaster's Department. In my opinion the organization of the department is as near perfect as it is possible to become. I base this opinion and declaration on the well-known satisfaction that has been given by the Quartermaster's Department in the grand operations of the last four years.

I cannot conceive of a case of failure on the part of the department if the orders that have been promulgated from the office of the Quartermaster-General are honestly and understandingly obeyed.

Herewith inclosed I have the honor to transmit Statements A and B and statement of public funds, as called for in General Orders, No. 39, being the only statements coming under the scope of my duties during the past fiscal year.

Respectfully submitted.

JOHN B. HOWARD,
Brevet Colonel and Assistant Quartermaster.

Statement of public moneys received and disbursed by Col. John B. Howard, assistant quartermaster, during the fiscal year ending June 30, 1865.

On hand July 1, 1864	$318.16
Received from officers during the year	176,511.10
Total	176,829.26
Expended during the year	3,021.44
Transferred to other officers during the year	173,807.82
Total	176,829.26

JOHN B. HOWARD,
Brevet Colonel and Assistant Quartermaster.

No. 111.

ASSISTANT QUARTERMASTER'S OFFICE,
New Orleans, La., September 22, 1865.

Bvt. Maj. Gen. M. C. MEIGS,
Quartermaster-General U. S. Army, Washington, D. C.:

GENERAL: I have the honor to transmit herewith my annual report for the year ending June 30, 1865, in compliance with General Orders, No. 39, Quartermaster-General's Office, dated July 1, 1865.

Owing to the breaking up of the depot and changes of station consequent thereon, I have been unable to forward the report at an earlier date.

I am, sir, very respectfully, your obedient servant,

E. J. STRANG,
Brevet Lieutenant-Colonel and Assistant Quartermaster.

ASSISTANT QUARTERMASTER'S OFFICE,
New Orleans, La., September 22, 1865.

Bvt. Maj. Gen. M. C. MEIGS,
Quartermaster-General U. S. Army, Washington, D. C.:

GENERAL: In compliance with General Orders, No. 39, from your office, dated July 1, 1865, I have the honor to submit herewith my annual report for the year ending June 30, 1865.

My last annual report was mailed on the 15th of September, 1864, and at the date of its close I was in charge of the depot of repairs and wagon transportation for the Army of the Potomac, located at City Point, Va. By Special Orders, No. 78, headquarters Armies of the United States, dated August 23, 1864, I was directed to report to Brig. Gen. Rufus Ingalls, chief quartermaster Armies operating against Richmond, and my duties increased by the addition of the Army of the James, for which, with the Army of the Potomac, I furnished the means of transportation, as well as the repairs of wagons, ambulances, &c.

My duties during the year have consisted in the receipt and issue of animals, wagons, harness, &c.; the general repairs of all means of transportation, including shipping; furnishing transportation for all extra work, such as hauling guns, ammunition, &c.; for siege artillery, railroad ties and material for construction corps, lumber, logs for stockades, fuel, &c., for the depot field hospitals; medical, subsistence, ordnance, and quartermaster's stores, to different points of the army; policing purposes at the hospitals and depot, and all details where troops or temporary commands were without the necessary transportation; also the construction and repairs of the public buildings, wharves, stables, &c., at the depot. No moves of the depot were made during the year, notwithstanding at times the greater part of the employés were doing service at other points.

My force of employés at the beginning of the year numbered as follows, viz:

Wheelwrights	115
Carpenters	18
Laborers	291
Blacksmiths	89
Saddlers	23
Teamsters	381
Clerks, superintendents, wagon-masters, &c	70
Total	987

Together with 273 six-mule teams, 69 four horse and mule teams, 20 two-horse teams, 31 two-horse ambulance teams; the number of animals in the corrals for receiving and issuing purposes, 351; making a total of 575 horses and 1,792 mules, or 2,367 animals.

It was found that this force of mechanical labor and the number of teams were totally inadequate to meet the requirements of the service. I was accordingly directed by General Ingalls to increase my force and extend the operations of my depot until I could meet and supply every want promptly. For this purpose I caused advertisements to be inserted in some of the authorized newspapers of the Northern towns for mechanics and teamsters, and sent agents to secure the men, and also went myself, by order of General Grant, for the same purpose. My force now increased rapidly, until there was employed at the depot under my control the following number, viz:

Wheelwrights	119
Carpenters	78
Laborers	771
Blacksmiths	115
Saddlers	31
Teamsters	431
Clerks, superintendents, wagon-masters, &c	75
Total	1,620

The number of animals, &c., varied according to the exigencies of the service, the average number on hand amounting to 2,095 head. The handling and care of this branch of my department required a large force of employés.

Immediately after arriving at City Point I erected shops, such as had always been used in the field, viz, a portable frame covered with canvas (paulins). My force increasing, it was found necessary to enlarge these shops to the following dimensions: Two wheelwright shops, 190 by 25 feet; two blacksmith shops, 190 by 25 feet; two saddler shops, 60 by 22 feet; one carpenter shop, 80 by 22 feet. As a measure of economy I caused these shops to be covered with boards in place of canvas, and stockades built of logs, also covered with boards, as quarters for the employés (winter was approaching) in place of tents.

My carpenters were employed during the year in constructing and repairing wharves, store-houses, stables, stockades at the hospitals for the accommodation of patients, and barracks for the colored employés of the quartermaster's and subsistence departments, consisting of six buildings, each 100 feet long by 25 feet wide and two stories high; also a chapel 25 by 50 feet.

Your attention is respectfully invited to the supplementary statement, marked G, herewith submitted. It will be perceived that the daily issues of animals to officers averaged 181 head, the number of animals daily shod in the blacksmith shops 140, and the number of wagons and ambulances repaired daily 17. As far as possible, where wagons came to my shop for repairs, I caused "brakes" to be put on them; these brakes were not invoiced to officers, but were considered "repairs," the materials for which I expended.

In the month of March I sent seventy-five blacksmiths, with forges, tools, &c., to White House, on the Pamunkey River, to shoe the animals of General Sheridan's command, returning from the raid around Richmond, and also in the latter part of April sent the same number of blacksmiths to Nottoway Court-House and Petersburg for the same purpose.

In connection with my remarks here, I may add that it is my opinion that the transportation of an army operating in the field can be kept in better repair and at less expense by having a general depot for repairs than by keeping a force of mechanics attached to the different commands.

Many articles were fabricated during the year, the most important of which were the following, viz: Twelve spring wagons, 21,000 pounds horse and mule shoes, 4 sets of ambulance harness, 151 wagon bodies, 1,200 water buckets, 82 office chairs.

In the latter part of February I was ordered to relieve Capt. E. E. Camp, assistant quartermaster, at City Point, of all stores appertaining to means of transportation, such as horse and mule shoes, nails, hardware of all kinds, except tools, sets of harness and parts of harness, wagons, &c. For the care and security of these stores I erected a temporary store-house on the wharf assigned to my depot.

On the 1st of March, in pursuance of orders from General Ingalls, I relieved Capt. J. E. Jones, assistant quartermaster, and assumed charge of the depot field hospitals, in addition to my other duties. I placed a superintendent with a clerk in charge to attend to the current business and visited the hospitals daily.

After the dispersion of the rebel army I was ordered by General Ingalls to establish a corral at Burkeville, for the purpose of receiving surrendered property. I went personally to that place and established the corral and placed a superintendent in charge. The following number of animals and property was received from officers of our army, but not invoiced, viz: Four hundred horses, 1,300 mules, 101 wagons, and 90 ambulances. The animals I sent to Jordan's or Light-house Point, on the James River, a few miles below City Point, where I caused them to be grazed daily. They were in a wretched state from want of food when they came into my possession, but subsequently many of them were issued to our forces in excellent condition.

By virtue of an order from the Secretary of War, 1,500 animals were turned over to various officers for distribution to the poor and freedmen of the Richmond and Petersburg districts.

On the 1st of May, in compliance with instructions received from General Ingalls, I commenced to reduce the proportions of the depot by discharging the bulk of my employés; and by directions of the Quartermaster-General, through General Ingalls, I sold at public auction at Petersburg, Richmond, and City Point, 1,746 horses, 993 mules, 67 wagons, and 89 ambulances, unserviceable property, at prices averaging $25.40, $34.13, $9.02, and $23.05, respectively. The residue of my property, consisting in part of 1,028 horses, 2,074 mules, 573 wagons, 38 ambulances, and 3,340 sets of harness, I transferred to Capt. A. T. Dunton, assistant quartermaster at City Point, and Bvt. Col. C. H. Tompkins, assistant quartermaster at Washington, D. C.

In pursuance of Special Orders, No. 272, War Department, Adjutant-General's Office, dated June 2, 1865, I proceeded to New York, N. Y., and reported on the 12th of June to Brig. Gen. S. Van Vliet, chief quartermaster of the Department of the East, for assignment to duty, and was by that officer temporarily placed in charge of repairs of Government vessels during the absence of Capt. J. R. Jennings, assistant quartermaster, which duty I was performing at the closing of this report.

The following is a statement of the public funds received and disbursed by me during the period embraced in this report:

On hand July 1, 1864	$59,779.75
Received from officers during the year	594,028.50
Received from sales of property and other sources during the year	83,878.95
Total	737,687.20
Expended during the year	643,806.06
Transferred to other officers during the year	71,000.00
Remaining on hand June 30, 1865	22,881.14
Total	737,687.20

The balance on hand is deposited as follows:

Ninth National Bank, New York City	$11,040.59
Bank of the Metropolis, Washington, D. C	28.78
Treasury United States, Washington, D. C	39.69
In my possession	11,772.08
Total	22,881.14

The accompanying statements, marked respectively A and B, are all that are required from the nature of my duties during the past year and in compliance with the general order requiring this report.

I have the honor to be, very respectfully, your obedient servant,

E. J. STRANG,

Brevet Lieutenant-Colonel and Assistant Quartermaster.

A.—*Report of quartermaster's stores received, issued, and remaining on hand during the year ending on the 30th day of June, 1865, by Bvt. Lieut. Col. E. J. Strang, assistant quartermaster, U. S. Volunteers.**

B.—*Yearly report of clothing, camp and garrison equipage, received, issued, manufactured, captured, sold, &c., during the year ending June 30, 1865.**

SUPPLEMENTARY STATEMENT.

G.—*Report of labor performed and public animals shod in Government shops; unserviceable property received from rebel armies; animals recruited; animals, wagons, and ambulances sold at public auction; animals, wagons, and ambulances received and issued at depot of repairs, armies lately operating against Richmond, Va., under direction of Bvt. Lieut. Col. E. J. Strang, assistant quartermaster, U. S. Volunteers, in the field, during the year ending on the 30th of June, 1865.**

No. 112.

DEPOT QUARTERMASTER'S OFFICE,
Fort Leavenworth, Kans., September 22, 1865.

Bvt. Maj. Gen. M. C. MEIGS,
Quartermaster-General U. S. Army:

GENERAL: I have the honor to transmit herewith my annual report for the fiscal year ending June 30, 1865, accompanied by a narrative report, as required by General Orders, No. 39, Quartermaster-General's Office, of July, 1865.

Very respectfully, your obedient servant,

J. A. POTTER,

Colonel and Quartermaster.

DEPOT QUARTERMASTER'S OFFICE,
Fort Leavenworth, Kans., September 15, 1865.

Bvt. Maj. Gen. M. C. MEIGS,
Quartermaster-General U. S. Army:

GENERAL: I have the honor to present herewith my annual report for the year ending on the 30th day of June, 1865. Since the date of my last annual report, mailed to the department on the 30th day of September, 1864, and up to the time of being relieved at Chicago, Ill., my duties there were mostly of a supervising character, retaining in my hands the disbursements of transportation by rail, &c. The officers at said depot, acting under my directions, were as follows: Capt. J. M. Bradshaw, assistant quartermaster, purchase of horses,

*Omitted; but see pp. 823-846, of Executive Document No. 1, referred to in foot-note (*), p. 249.

mules, &c.; Capt. Charles Goodman, assistant quartermaster, in charge of Camp Douglas, Camp Fry, and disbursements appertaining thereto; Capt. L. W. Shepherd, assistant quartermaster, miscellaneous business; Capt. I. C. Barbour, assistant quartermaster, transportation on passes.

The annual reports of these officers will show the amounts and extent of their operations, and would have been sent with this, but as I was relieved early in January, 1865, and ordered to Fort Leavenworth, Kans., they have not been sent to me. I assumed the duties of this depot, Fort Leavenworth, February 1, 1865, relieving Capt. Henry C. Hodges, assistant quartermaster, U. S. Army, and on the 10th of February was directed by Special Orders, No. 41, headquarters Department of the Missouri, to assume the duties of chief quartermaster of the district of country embraced in the late Department of Kansas. These duties and those of depot quartermaster I have continued to discharge up to the present time.

GENERAL REMARKS.

Upon my arrival here I found a state of affairs existing of which I had no previous conception. Major-General Curtis was in command, with Capt. M. H. Insley as chief quartermaster of the department, who was also the depot quartermaster at Fort Scott. For some reason all the certified accounts of the department were being paid by Captain Hodges, the depot quartermaster, instead of the chief quartermaster, to whom such payments properly belonged. Stories of immense frauds were rife, and it was with the utmost care that any fixed data could be found to determine the status of a large number of vouchers afloat and settle upon the mode and manner of payment. Great complaints had been made that certain parties and districts had been deprived of their fair proportion of the funds sent out for the purpose of settling the indebtedness. I adopted the rule of paying a certain percentage to all claimants, until each specified amount furnished was exhausted. This plan seemed to work equal justice to all the parties interested, and soon, by the timely remittances from Washington, the greater part of this floating indebtedness was liquidated. Many of these vouchers were informal and issued by officers temporarily placed on duty as acting assistant quartermasters, and a just and fair discrimination has been exercised, to the best of my ability, to pay none but legitimate expenditures. The disbursements have been large, as will be seen by the statements.

The matter of transportation has been a subject of much study on my part, as all the supplies for the vast region of country from Utah, on the northern route, and Santa Fé, on the southern route, with all intermediate posts, have to be supplied from this depot.

From all the information I have been able to collect, from observation and other sources, I am compelled to say that I think the system of contracting freight is erroneous; that the delays, damages, &c., arising from the careless mode of shipment and want of proper care will be in a great measure avoided by using nothing but Government trains. It is not a sufficient compensation to the Government that the contractor is obliged to pay for the articles lost or damaged in transit, for it often happens that the articles most needed for immediate service are wanting. In scarcely any instance have any articles been missing from our own trains. Time, also being an important element in the shipment of supplies, is saved by the greater rapidity of the Government trains. The contractors are only bound to get all the stores through by a certain date in the fall. No contract should be made unless it has an ample though fixed time for the delivery, dating from the day of shipment. The large accumulation of stock at this depot, teams and wagons, will enable us to send forward, at all times, stores as they may be needed. From the above and many other reasons not necessary now to relate, I am decidedly in favor of the Government doing its own transportation, except in special cases. At such times the depot quartermaster can always hire trains at special rates, not exceeding the present contract rates.

From present appearances the great point of departure for trains another season will be Fort Riley, or that vicinity. The Union Pacific Railroad will be completed to that point, I am assured, by May next. It will be much cheaper for the department to pay transportation direct to Fort Riley, and send across from that point to Kearny, than to ship from Leavenworth. If good progress is made in the railroad from Omaha west, that will be the route for all goods destined for the northern line of posts, via Julesburg and Halleck, while the goods for Denver, Salt Lake, and Santa Fé should go via Riley; those destined for Denver and Utah via the Butterfield route, and those for Santa Fé by the old Santa Fé trail.

The depot of Fort Leavenworth will always be of great importance as the base of distribution for the supplies for all Western posts. From time to time extensive warehouses have been erected, which, although now crowded to their utmost capacity by the large overstock on hand, and the accumulation from the breaking up of other posts, will, under all ordinary circumstances, be sufficient for the department. At present we are obliged to put up temporary sheds for the extra store-room needed.

Water-works have been ordered for the supply of the post and depot, and will be erected during the winter.

A large amount of timber on that part of the Government reserve east of the Missouri River will be made available for use as soon as the steam mills now ordered are put into operation. The improved farms have yielded well this year, and will be a source of profit to the department.

I cannot too strongly urge upon the department the necessity for watching with the utmost care and preventing by timely remonstrance all attempts on the part of scheming politicians to get the reserved lands into market for the purpose of speculation. No one not perfectly well acquainted can estimate its value. I need not extend this report, as the merits and extent of operations at Fort Leavenworth are too well known to need comment.

Respectfully submitted.

J. A. POTTER,
Colonel and Quartermaster.

Statement of moneys received, expended, transferred, and remaining on hand for the fiscal year ending on the 30th day of June, 1865, by Col. Joseph A. Potter, quartermaster at Chicago, Ill., and Fort Leavenworth, Kans.

On hand July 1, 1864	$281,032.42
Received from officers during the year	35,364.80
Received from the Treasury Department during the year	8,638,432.67
Received from the sales of property and other sources during the year	113,479.88
Total	9,068,309.77

Expended during the year	$4,940,375.16
Transferred to officers during the year	1,117,295.02
Remaining on hand June 30, 1865	3,010,639.59
Total	9,068,309.77

The balance on hand is deposited as follows:

At Washington, with Treasurer of United States	585,227.08
At New York, with assistant treasurer of United States	2,199,152.52
At Philadelphia, with First National Bank	50,295.92
At Chicago, Ill., with deputy depositary of United States	6,445.59
At Leavenworth City, with First National Bank	16,212.50
Treasury notes in vaults	153,305.98
Balance	3,010,639.59

Certified that the foregoing statement is correct.

J. A. POTTER,
Colonel and Quartermaster.

No. 113.

OFFICE ASSISTANT QUARTERMASTER,
Winchester, Va., August 15, 1865.

Maj. Gen. M. C. MEIGS,
Quartermaster-General U. S. Army, Washington, D. C.:

GENERAL: In compliance with General Orders, No. 39, Quartermaster-General's Office, dated July 1, 1865, I have the honor to submit the following personal narrative of my services since July 1, 1864, accompanied by statements required therein:

On the 1st of July, 1864, I was on duty at City Point, Va., assisting Capt. P. P. Pitkin, assistant quartermaster and depot quartermaster at that point. On the 11th day of July I was assigned to duty as chief quartermaster Cavalry Corps, Army of the Potomac, by command of Lieutenant-General Grant; entered immediately on duty as ordered; shipped the First and Third Divisions, Cavalry Corps, on board transports for Washington, D. C., and was soon after ordered by General Sheridan, commanding, to join him at Harper's Ferry, Va. The order being approved by Lieutenant-General Grant, I immediately proceeded to comply therewith. On my arrival at Harper's Ferry I found General Sheridan's headquarters at Winchester, Va. I proceeded to Winchester and reported to General Sheridan, when I was directed to report in person to General Torbert, chief of cavalry, as chief quartermaster of the cavalry, Middle Military Division; served in that capacity until the death of Colonel Tolles, chief quartermaster Middle Military Division, which position I retained until the division was dissolved. During my service as chief quartermaster of the cavalry the battles of the Opequon, of Winchester, and Fisher's Hill were successfully fought, the cavalry taking a conspicuous part in all these engagements. No transportation or other public property of importance fell into the hands of the enemy. During my service as chief quartermaster of the Middle Military Division my attention was particularly attracted to the Army of the Shenandoah, numbering from 50,000 to 60,000 men. In consequence of the Winchester and Potomac River Railroad having been entirely destroyed previously, this large number of men, with some 26,000 animals, had to be supplied by teams from Martinsburg, W. Va.

It will be seen that it was no small task to properly arrange the running of these large trains so that the army might not at any time be in need of subsistence, forage, or clothing. The large number of cavalry rendered the supply of forage a difficult task, when it is taken into consideration that the army was in no position to be supplied by means of water transports.

The Baltimore and Ohio Railroad was our only dependence, and great credit is due to the officers of the road for the manner in which supplies were forwarded, and for the promptness in complying with any demands of the commanding general relative to the movements of troops and supplies. It is also becoming in me to mention the efficiency of the chief quartermaster's department, West Virginia, in supplying the army with forage. I am also indebted to Capt. James T. Wray, assistant quartermaster, then depot quartermaster at Martinsburg, for the interest manifested by him in the success of the army in the field, and for the manner in which the quartermaster's department at Martinsburg was conducted by him. His duties were arduous, but were discharged with ability and to my entire satisfaction.

Late in the month of November, 1864, the U. S. Military Railroad Department succeeded in completing the railroad from Harper's Ferry to Stephenson's Station, a point about five miles from Winchester, that being deemed by General Sheridan the most practicable point for the terminus of the road.

Field repair shops were here established under the immediate direction of Capt. James T. Wray, assistant quartermaster, who had been ordered here from Martinsburg. These shops were calculated to keep thoroughly in repair all wagons and ambulances in the army, and to keep the animals well shod, so that in the spring, an active campaign being contemplated, on close inspection the transportation was found to be in as good condition as any in the field, and fit for any emergency.

It affords me great pleasure to testify to the untiring energy displayed by Mr. O. H. Dorrance, the efficient superintendent of the road, and I can safely say that no effort was left unmade by him to answer promptly the requirements of the army to be supplied by the road.

This road being completed, the necessity of running large trains from Martinsburg to points in the field (sometimes 100 miles distant) was obviated, and the transportation of the army was permitted to recuperate. After the successful series of battles in the fall of 1864 in the Shenandoah Valley, the veteran and distinguished Sixth Corps was again sent to the Army of the Potomac. This movement was conducted with celerity and reflects great credit on the Military Railroad and Baltimore and Ohio Railroad companies. The trains belonging to the corps, which were in splendid condition, were sent via Frederick City, Md., to Washington, D. C. The Provisional Division of the army was then transferred to the Army of the James. No discredit can be attached to any one for the manner in which this movement was conducted. Later in the winter one division of the late Nineteenth Army Corps was shipped en route for Savannah, Ga., which movement was conducted with ability. That portion of the Army of West Virginia not including the cavalry was ordered along the Baltimore and Ohio Railroad in West Virginia. The army to which my immediate attention was attracted was now composed only of the cavalry—three divisions, numbering about 20,000 men and animals; one division of infantry, about 10,000 men, and six batteries of artillery. The great cavalry expedition under the command of Major-General Sheridan was now fitted out and on the 27th day of February started for the Army of the Potomac. All are conversant with the success which attended this expedition. The supply train of this command was sent to Washington. Soon after this expedition started, Major-General Hancock being in command, four regiments of his First Army

Corps were sent to this army. They were followed by troops from Ohio and Indiana, one-year's volunteers, numbering some 15,000. The fall of Richmond and the surrender of the different armies of the rebellion having followed the united efforts of our commanding general, the anxiety for the success of our armies soon abated, and soon the mustering out of the troops comprising the army commenced. Every effort has been put forth since that time to curtail the expenses, and on the 30th of June, 1865, the Army of the Shenandoah numbered only 15,000 men, for the most part made up of infantry from the Western States, five regiments of cavalry, and five batteries of artillery.

I have been closely identified with this army since July, 1864, and it affords me great pleasure to say that I know of no officer of the Quartermaster's Department in this army but that has rendered me every assistance in the discharge of my duties.

Having discharged my duties to the satisfaction of the commanding general (as will be seen by General Sherman's [Sheridan's] letter), I sincerely trust that the same will meet with the approval of the department.

I am, general, very respectfully, your most obedient servant,

HENRY PAGE,
Lieutenant-Colonel and Quartermaster, U. S. Volunteers.

Statement of public moneys for the fiscal year ending June 30, 1865, by Lieut. Col. Henry Page, quartermaster, U. S. Volunteers.

On hand July 1, 1864	$1,304.61
Received from officers during the year	52,207.40
Received from Treasury Department	254,700.00
Received from sales of property and other sources	276.85
Total	308,488.86
Expended during the year	19,104.86
Transferred to other officers during the year	267,287.88
Remaining on hand June 30, 1865	22,096.12
Total	308,488.86
The balance on hand is deposited as follows:	
In U. S. Treasury, Washington, D. C	2,652.97
In National Bank of Metropolis	19,220.00
In iron safe in my office	223.15
Total	22,096.12

HENRY PAGE,
Lieutenant-Colonel and Quartermaster, U. S. Volunteers.

No. 114.

MILITARY DIVISION OF THE TENNESSEE,
QUARTERMASTER'S OFFICE, U. S. MILITARY RAILROADS,
Nashville, Tenn., October 18, 1865.

Maj. Gen. M. C. MEIGS,
Quartermaster-General U. S. Army, Washington, D. C.:

GENERAL: I have the honor to transmit herewith my annual report for the fiscal year ending June 30, 1865.

Very respectfully, your obedient servant,

F. J. CRILLY,
Captain and A. Q. M., U. S. Army, Chief Quartermaster U. S. Mil. Railroads, Military Division of the Tennessee.

Recapitulation of papers inclosed.

1. Personal report.
2. Statement of quartermaster's property.
3. Statement of clothing and camp and garrison equipage.
4. Statement of public moneys.
5. Statement of amount paid for transportation by rail, river, and wagon.
6. Statement of amount paid for transportation by ocean and lake.
7. Copy of a communication addressed by myself to Bvt. Maj. Gen. J. L. Donaldson, chief quartermaster Military Division of the Tennessee, relative to expense of running military railroads in this division for the month of July, 1865.
8. Copy of an order received from Bvt. Brig. Gen. D. C. McCallum, director and general manager U. S. Military Railroads, to furnish full statistics of the operations of this department.
9. Statement of amounts of monthly pay-rolls of the U. S. Military Railroads, Military Division of the Mississippi, from November 1, 1863, to January 31, 1864, inclusive, under the direction of J. B. Anderson, general manager.
10. Statement of amount of vouchers audited for material furnished U. S. Military Railroads, Division of the Mississippi, from November 1, 1863, to February 7, 1864, inclusive, under the direction of J. B. Anderson, general manager.
11. Amount of vouchers audited from February 8, 1864, to June 30, 1865, inclusive, under the direction of Bvt. Brig. Gen. D. C. McCallum, director and general manager U. S. Military Railroads.
12. Report of men hired by J. B. Anderson, general manager U. S. Military Railroads, Division of the Mississippi, from November 1, 1863, to January 31, 1864, inclusive.
13. Report of men hired by Bvt. Brig. Gen. D. C. McCallum, director and general manager U. S. Military Railroads, from February 1, 1864, to June 30, 1865, inclusive.
14. Statement of amounts of monthly pay-rolls of U. S. Military Railroads, Division of the Tennessee, audited in 1864 and 1865.
15. Earnings of the U. S. Military Railroads, Division of the Mississippi, from November 1, 1863, to December 31, 1864, inclusive.

MILITARY DIVISION OF THE TENNESSEE,
QUARTERMASTER'S OFFICE, U. S. MILITARY RAILROADS,
Nashville, Tenn., August 22, 1865.

Maj. Gen. M. C. MEIGS,
Quartermaster-General U. S. Army, Washington, D. C.:

GENERAL: I have the honor to report, in accordance with General Orders, No. 39, Quartermaster-General's Office, dated Washington, D. C., July 1, 1865, as follows:

During the fiscal year ending June 30, 1865, I was on duty in New York City until October 31, as purchasing and disbursing quartermaster. On being relieved from duty there I was directed by orders from the Adjutant-General's Office to report to the commanding general and chief quartermaster Military Division of the Mississippi for assignment. I proceeded as far as Calhoun, Ga., to report to General Sherman, who had just started on his march to Savannah. Communication being cut off, I reported to Major-General Thomas, commanding in General Sherman's absence. On the 10th of December I was directed to relieve Col. J. C. Crane and Capt. A. R. Eddy of all duties connected with the U. S. military railroads in the Military Division of the Mississippi, which duties I have performed to the present time, station being Nashville, Tenn.

I forward herewith a statement, Form A, of all the articles of quartermaster's property which have come into my possession during the year while on duty with the military railroads. The report of property purchased, &c., in New York City will be forwarded by General S. Van Vliet, who will make an annual statement of all the quartermaster's property for the New York depot.

I also forward Form B, containing statement of all articles of camp and garrison equipage received by me.

My statement of public money is also appended, together with the amount paid for transportation by rail, river, stage, and wagon other than Government wagons. A statement of the amount paid for transportation by ocean and lake, Form CC, is appended. The nature of my duties not requiring me to furnish transportation of any kind, I therefore make no report for Form D.

My statement, as per Form S, of chartered vessels, &c., will be included in the annual report of General S. Van Vliet, who will report all the vessels chartered at New York City.

The other reports called for I am, in consequence of the nature of my duties, unable to make. I attach a copy of order from General D. C. McCallum, directing that a report be made of the operations of the quartermaster's department of the U. S. Military Railroads from the commencement of the war.

I have the honor to state that there were no records left in this office by my predecessor, or any data from which I could furnish anything reliable.

The accompanying statements are obtained from the auditor of military railroads, and contain all the information it is possible for me to furnish.

I presume the annual report of Col. J. C. Crane will furnish the statements of the disbursements for the first half of the fiscal year.

It may not be out of place here to state what are the duties of the quartermaster on duty with military railroads. The organization consists of one chief quartermaster, stationed at Nashville, with one assistant quartermaster; one assistant quartermaster stationed at Chattanooga, Tenn., and one assistant quartermaster stationed at Memphis. Capt. S. R. Hamill, assistant quartermaster, is stationed at Nashville, and is responsible for all the property on the Nashville and Chattanooga, Nashville and Northwestern, Nashville and Decatur, and on the Memphis and Charleston Railroad from Decatur to Stevenson, Ala.; total number of miles, 429. He has also charge of the general supply store at Nashville, and of the lumber yard, property, saw-mills, and means of transportation of the quartermaster's department.

The rolls of the road above mentioned are made out and certified to by the general superintendent of military railroads, and after being audited and approved by the general manager or chief engineer, in accordance with orders of the War Department, are paid by the chief quartermaster at Nashville.

Capt. W. R. Hopkins, assistant quartermaster, is stationed at Chattanooga, Tenn., and is responsible for all the property on the Chattanooga and Knoxville, Chattanooga and Atlanta, and East Tennessee and Virginia Railroads; total number of miles, 378. Chattanooga being so remote from the auditor's office, and it being impossible for the general manager to visit there monthly, the rolls are made out and certified to by Captain Hopkins; otherwise no vouchers could be issued to discharged employés unless the general manager or chief superintendent was present.

Capt. John Parks, assistant quartermaster, is stationed at Memphis, Tenn., and is responsible for all property on the Memphis and Charleston and Mobile and Ohio Railroads, so far as operated in that part of the State, and for the property on the Memphis and Little Rock Railroad. The rolls for employés of these roads are made out and paid by the quartermaster, for the same reason as at Chattanooga. The consolidated rolls, Form No. 2, at both places are, however, sent to Nashville for audit and approval of the general manager.

Stores are purchased and supplied by the quartermaster on requisition of the general superintendent and chief engineer of the roads.

The question of property responsibility has always been the most difficult matter to arrange owing to the peculiar organization of the military railroad service. In this military division it is organized under the direction of a general superintendent, who has charge of everything relative to transportation and repairs, and a chief engineer in charge of construction. Each was independent of the other, and the quartermaster independent of both, except so far as filling requisitions for supplies and paying the employés.

The mingling of civil and military officials, without any precedent or regulation to govern anomalous cases that constantly arise, would naturally produce collisions of authority, unless all parties worked with the proper spirit and yielded questions of rank and precedence to the more important one of emergencies of service. Fortunately this was the case except in one instance, when the bad temper of one official produced so much bad feeling and annoyance that his resignation was promptly accepted by the general manager. It will be seen, therefore, that the property, although on the returns of the quartermasters, is all in the hands of the officers of the railroad service, who are no ways responsible to him. During the period that Mr. E. L. Wentz was superintendent he completely ignored the authority of the quartermaster, and prohibited any reports being made of the loss or destruction of property. The consequence was that the officer responsible, Capt. G. H. Clemens, assistant quartermaster, on being ordered to be relieved, could not find a tithe of the property his papers called for, and was so involved that a board of survey is now in session, convened by order of Major-General Thomas, to investigate the cause of his large deficiency and fix the responsibility.

A system of reports is now instituted by which the quartermaster is kept advised of the condition of property, and affidavits are furnished for all lost or destroyed, which I believe will effect a more prompt rendition of returns than could be previously obtained.

Owing to the nature of the service, in an enemy's country, but few accurate statistics could be kept of the number of troops or the amount of freight transported. Whole corps and even armies have been frequently transported back and forth in the same week from one end of the military division to the other, on cars of every description, almost in presence of the enemy, so that it was impossible to keep any record of it.

I was directed by Bvt. Maj. Gen. J. L. Donaldson, chief quartermaster Military Division of the Tennessee, to prepare an estimate of the expenses of the road for the month of July, compared with the receipts and the amounts chargeable on account of general transportation, a copy of which is appended. I have examined this report since and believe it to be very nearly correct.

Since writing the foregoing report all the roads operated by the United States, with the exception of the Memphis and Little Rock Railroad, have been turned over to their respective companies on the following dates, viz:

East Tennessee and Virginia Railroad, August 28, 1865; East Tennessee and Georgia Railroad, August 28, 1865; Rogersville and Jefferson Railroad, August 28, 1865; Memphis and Charleston Railroad (from Stevenson to Decatur), September 1, 1865; Memphis and Charleston Railroad (from Memphis to Corinth), September 12, 1865; Nashville and Decatur Railroad line, September 15, 1865; Nashville and Chattanooga Railroad, September 15, 1865; Edgefield and Kentucky Railroad, September 23, 1865; Louisville, Clarksville and Memphis Railroad, ———, 1865; Nashville and Northwestern Railroad, September 1, 1865; Western and Atlantic Railroad, September 25, 1865; Mobile and Ohio Railroad, August 25, 1865.

The roads are now being operated by the companies, the rolling-stock being sold to them by the United States on credit.

It will probably take until the 1st of January next for the different quartermasters in charge of property to close up the business and render the necessary returns.

Very respectfully, your obedient servant,

F. J. CRILLY,
Captain and Assistant Quartermaster, U. S. Army,
Actg. Chief Q. M. U. S. Mil. R. R., Mil. Div. of the Tennessee.

*Statement of quartermaster's property for the fiscal year ending June 30, 1865, by Capt. F. J. Crilly, assistant quartermaster, U. S. Army.**

*Statement of clothing, camp and garrison equipage, for the fiscal year ending June 30, 1865, by Capt. F. J. Crilly, assistant quartermaster.**

Statement of balance remaining on hand July 1, 1864, and of amount received, disbursed, and remaining on hand during the fiscal year ending June 30, 1865, by Capt. F. J. Crilly, assistant quartermaster, U. S. Army.

Balance on hand July 1, 1864	$3,359.20
Received from officers during the year	11,042,952.09
Received from Treasury Department during the year	4,205,500.00
Received from the sales of property and other sources during the year	315,997.08
Total	15,567,808.37
Expended during the year	12,051,163.05
Transferred to other officers during the year	2,330,207.65
Balance on hand June 30, 1865	1,186,437.67
Total	15,567,808.37

The balance on hand ($1,186,437.67) is deposited as follows:

On deposit with First National Bank, Cincinnati, Ohio	500,000.00
On deposit in the U. S. depository, Cincinnati, Ohio	901.55
On deposit in the U. S. depository, Louisville, Ky	690.20
On deposit with assistant treasurer, New York City	7,084.50
On deposit with Treasurer of the United States, payable in certificates of indebtedness	622,860.58
Cash in safe	54,900.84

I certify that the above statement is correct.

F. J. CRILLY,
Captain and Assistant Quartermaster, U. S. Army.

*Omitted; but see pp. 856–873, of Executive Document No. 1, referred to in foot-note (*), p. 249.

C.—*Statement of amount paid on account of rail, river, stage, and wagon transportation, by Capt. F. J. Crilly, assistant quartermaster, during the fiscal year ending June 30, 1865.*

	Transportation.			
	Railroads.	Steam-boats, &c.	Stages, wagons, &c.	Total.
Passengers:				
Officers and men	$177,011.93	$45,456.19	$7,520.00	$229,988.12
Prisoners of war and other rebels			6.00	6.00
Civilians	14.00	4.03		18.03
Total	177,025.93	45,460.22	7,526.00	230,012.15
Freight	24,379.25	73,645.40	32,001.47	130,026.12
Total	201,405.18	119,105.62	39,527.47	360,038.27
Expenditures *a*	7,732,349.87	647.34		7,732,997.21
Grand total	7,933,755.05	119,752.96	39,527.47	8,093,035.48

a The amount reported in column of expenditures exhibits total amount expended by Captain Crilly for the support of railroads operated by the United States in the Military Division of the Tennessee.

I certify that the above statement is correct.

F. J. CRILLY,
Captain and Assistant Quartermaster, U. S. Army.

CC.—*Statement of amount paid on account of ocean and lake transportation, by Capt. F. J. Crilly, assistant quartermaster, during the fiscal year ending June 30, 1865.*

Passengers: Officers and men	$1,145.00
Freight	70,334.61
Total	71,479.61
Expenditures	652,167.86
	723,647.47
	2,387,752.48
Grand total	3,111,399.95

I certify that the above statement is correct.

F. J. CRILLY,
Captain and Assistant Quartermaster, U. S. Army.

MILITARY DIVISION OF THE TENNESSEE,
QUARTERMASTER'S OFFICE, U. S. MILITARY RAILROADS,
Nashville, Tenn., August 7, 1865.

General J. L. DONALDSON,
Chief Quartermaster Military Division of the Tennessee:

GENERAL: In accordance with the instructions of your letter of the 2d instant relative to expense of running military railroads in this division for the month of July, and the amount that would have to be paid to the companies if the roads were run by private parties, I have to report as follows:

EXPENDITURES.

Expense in July for pay of employés	$670,000.00
Cost of wood expended in month of July	80,000.00
Cost of stores expended in repairs during month of July	100,000.00
Total	850,000.00

RECEIPTS.

Received as earnings of the road, from passengers and freight	$140,563.76
Value of product of rolling-mill at Chattanooga, the expense of which is included on the pay-roll, being 693 tons, at $90 per ton	62,370.70
There were transported free over military railroads in this division during the month of July, at the expense of the United States, 35,640 troops and refugees 498,198,046 miles, at 0.0205 cents per mile	102,130.59
Transported during the same time 40,035,900 pounds of Government stores, which, if paid for at Government rates, would have amounted to	75,954.29
Difference between cost of roads as run by the United States and the amount that would have been paid if run by private corporations	468,980.66
Total	850,000.00

Owing to the limited time allowed for making up of this statement it was impossible to obtain full reports of freight and passengers transported, the number given being taken from reports already in. The actual number will greatly exceed this.

The amount collected for private freight and passengers is steadily increasing, as will be seen from the following table of amounts received for the different months of this year:

January	$7,500.00
February	19,320.00
March	23,740.00
April	26,499.64
May	54,121 00
June	83,635.00
July	140,563.76

The receipts for the present month will reach $250,000, and can be increased to any amount that the United States will give facilities for. The month of July exhibits large items of expense for the reason that the reduction of the working force necessary for a state of war had to be done gradually, in order to gather in the tools and public property of all kinds in their possession. These reductions are still taking place at the rate of about 125 per day.

A large number of expensive employés are also profitably employed in the repair of the rolling-stock, so that it may be in complete order to sell. The benefit of this will be very large and cannot be estimated. A large number of additional men are also engaged in watching and taking care of this rolling-stock, which has now become largely surplus. If sales were made of this to reduce the amount down to the actual necessities of the service, both public and private, it would reduce expenses immensely.

The roads run by the United States at Memphis are not included in any of the foregoing reports, as the amount received for freight and passengers there is sufficient to pay the running expenses.

The expense per month for the future will depend upon the length of time that may elapse before some disposition is made of the rolling-stock, and also upon the diminution of the number of free passes now given to refugees and destitute persons returning to their homes.

My estimate of funds for the present month calls for a half million of dollars, which, with the amount received as earnings of the road, will fully cover the expenses.

Very respectfully, your obedient servant,

F. J. CRILLY,

Captain and Assistant Quartermaster, U. S. Army,

Chief Q. M. U. S. Mil. R. R., Mil. Div. of the Tennessee.

WAR DEPARTMENT,
OFFICE MILITARY DIRECTOR AND SUPT. RAILROADS U. S.,
Washington, D. C., August 14, 1865.

Capt. F. J. CRILLY,
Actg. Chief Q. M. Military Railroads, Nashville, Tenn.:

CAPTAIN: I inclose herewith one copy of General Orders, No. 39, Quartermaster-General's Office, dated July 5, 1865, calling for an annual report from officers of the Quartermaster's Department.

This order is sent you with instructions to furnish full statistics of the operations of your department. The statistics should show all expenditures incurred by you in the construction and maintenance of U. S. military railroads, stating as far as possible what the expenditure was for; also the receipts derived from transportation of freight and passengers, so far as they pertain to your department.

It is desired that your report may be rendered as early as practicable, and, as the war is at a close, that it should embrace, in addition to the operations of the past year, a general review and summary for the entire period of the war.

A copy of your report should be sent to this office, in addition to the one sent to the Quartermaster-General.

Very respectfully, your obedient servant,

D. C. McCALLUM,
Brevet Brigadier-General, &c.
Per H. K. COOPER,
In Charge.

Statements of amounts of monthly pay-rolls of U. S. Military Railroads, Division of the Mississippi, from November 1, 1863, to January 31, 1864, inclusive, under the direction of J. B. Anderson, general manager.

1863, November rolls	$47,131.06
1863, December rolls	68,594.20
1864, January	104,621.33
Total	219,346 59

The above statement is correct.

JOHN TRENBATH, *Auditor.*

Statements of amounts of vouchers audited for material furnished U. S. Military Railroads, Division of the Mississippi, from November 1, 1863, to February 7, 1864, inclusive, under the direction of J. B. Anderson, general manager.

Stationery and printing	$4,717.57
Repairs of road	32,433.13
Engines, original cost of	571,805.41
Cars, original cost of	184,471.92
Train supplies	2,828.16
Fuel	33,338.20
Repairs of buildings	2,215.09
Water supply	6,539.20
Bridges	3,808.30
Expense of telegraph	1,515.87
Office expenses	1,442.59
Tennessee and Alabama Railroad	21.74
Expense of engineer's department	347.75
Quartermaster's department	29.50
Postage	15.00
Station expenses	34.65
New buildings	3,557.39
Iron rails	240.50
Material for shops	52,725.71
Total	902,087.68

The above statement is correct.

JOHN TRENBATH, *Auditor.*

*Amounts of vouchers audited from February 8, 1864, to June 30, 1865, inclusive, under the direction of D. C. McCallum, director and general manager of the Military Railroads of the United States.**

Report of men hired by J. B. Anderson, general manager of U. S. Military Railroads, Division of the Mississippi, from November 1, 1863, to January 31, 1864, inclusive.†

Report of men hired by D. C. McCallum, director and general manager U. S. Military Railroads, from February 1, 1864, to June 30, 1865, inclusive.†

Statement of amounts of monthly pay-rolls of the U. S. Military Railroads, Division of the Mississippi and of the Tennessee, audited in 1864 and 1865.†

Earnings of the U. S. Military Railroads, Military Division of the Mississippi, from November 1, 1863, to December 31, 1864.†

No. 115.

OFFICE OF GUN-BOAT FLOTILLA,
Saint Louis, Mo., September 14, 1863.

Brig. Gen. M. C. MEIGS,
Quartermaster-General U. S. Army, Washington, D. C.:

GENERAL: In accordance with General Orders, No. 13, I have to report as follows:

I received my appointment as captain and assistant quartermaster on the 28th of September, 1861, and was ordered to report for duty to Capt. A. H. Foote, U. S. Navy, commanding gun-boat flotilla on the Western waters.

The flotilla was under the command of naval officers and subject to naval rules, while at the same time its whole organization was a part of the Army and its expenditures paid from that department.

I being the only representative of the Army with the flotilla, all requirements for the service were made through me, and I performed the various duties of naval paymaster, store-keeper, and commissary, beyond the general duties of an army quartermaster. In addition, I was required to audit the accounts of each acting assistant paymaster of the gun-boats, involving an examination into their expenditures for a year—a duty which under other circumstances would belong to the Fourth Auditor.

By act of Congress of July 16, 1862, the Western Gun-boat Flotilla was transferred from the War to the Navy Department, but the final transfer was not made until September 30, 1862, and I was not relieved from duty until the 1st of December following, since which time I have been constantly engaged in settling the accounts of the flotilla and making the necessary reports required by the War Department.

Before leaving I transferred a large amount of property to the naval authorities, estimated in the aggregate to be $1,869,574 in value, comprising gun-boats, tugs, transports, and captured steamers and their equipments, clothing, provisions, small-stores, coal barges, naval wharf-boat, and general quartermaster's stores.

---

* Details omitted. The total amount was $10,847,506.40.

† Omitted; but see pp. 878–880, of Executive Document No. 1, referred to in foot-note (*), p. 249.

The total amount received from the U. S. Treasury and other officers in money was $2,920,147.24; add to this estimated value of stores, &c., received from other officers, $226,385; in all, $3,146,532.24.

There were captured at different times from the enemy 5 gun-boats, 15 transport steamers, and 5 wrecks, which, including other property, amounts to $450,000, estimated value. There has been paid in the aggregate for transportation of ordnance and quartermaster's stores, as follows: Express companies, $25,325; railroad companies, $25,381; river, $10,187; and for mileage of officers, $3,161; in all, $64,054.

While under the Army the flotilla, commencing with three small, improvised, wooden gun-boats, hardly able to keep the river open between Saint Louis and Columbus, Ky., increased to ten iron-clads, eleven wooden gun-boats, two large ammunition steamers, thirteen tugs, a hospital boat with everything requisite for the sick and wounded, and a fleet of fifteen chartered and captured transports. There was also attached to the flotilla a floating blacksmith shop and a distributing commissary steamer. Large depots of coal were kept at convenient places on the rivers, and at Cairo, Ill., a new large and superior wharf-boat was purchased, which answered as a general depot for most of the requirements of the flotilla, including offices for the transaction of business.

While every assistance possible was extended by other branches of the Government to the flotilla, yet the officers necessarily were thrown upon their own resources, and a navy had to be formed from new materials, far from what was generally considered its proper element. Officers, sailors, and gun-boats had to be made to suit the exigencies of the times. How well all this was performed history will tell, and the flotilla under the Army will have had a most important bearing upon the final result of the rebellion.

I would refer to the reduction of Forts Henry and Donelson, the evacuation of Columbus, Ky., Island No. 10, Fort Pillow, and the destruction of the rebel fleet off Memphis; in addition, the important part taken by the flotilla in the sanguinary fight at Belmont and the great battle of Shiloh. League after league of the great Mississippi was opened to commerce, until the name of a gun-boat became a terror to the rebels.

For a more detailed account in relation to the above, I would refer you to the accompanying papers, comprising a "Tabular list of gun-boats, transport steamers, and wrecks, captured from the enemy," "Names, tonnage, and earnings of the steam-boats chartered and employed," and "Statement of cash received and disbursed, on what account, together with balance remaining on hand June 30, 1863."

All of which is respectfully submitted.

Very respectfully, your obedient servant,

GEO. D. WISE,

Captain and Assistant Quartermaster, with Gun-boat Flotilla.

Tabular list of gun-boats, transports, steamers, wrecks, &c., captured from the enemy by the gun-boat flotilla, Western waters.

Names.	Gun-boats.	Steamers.	Wrecks.	Where captured.	Estimated value.	Remarks.
General Bragg	1	....	....	Memphis	$50,000	Transferred to the Navy Department.
Sumter	1	....	....	....do	50,000	Do.
Little Rebel	1	....	....	....do	20,000	Do.
General Price	1	....	....	....do	10,000	Do.
Eastport	1	....	....	Savannah, Tenn	20,000	Do.
H. R. W. Hill	....	1	....	Memphis	8,000	Transferred to the Army (commissary boat at Cairo).
Alfred Robb	....	1	....	Tennessee River	8,000	Transferred to the Navy Department.
Kentucky	....	1	....	Island No. 10	5,000	Returned to owners.
De Soto	....	1	....	....do	30,000	Transferred to the Navy Department.
Admiral	....	1	....	....do	10,000	Taken immediate possession of by the Army.
Mars	....	1	....	....do	5,000	Do.
Sovereign	....	1	....	....do	10,000	Transferred to the Navy Department.
Victoria	....	1	....	....do	15,000	Do.
New National	....	1	....	Memphis	30,000	Do.
Catahoula	....	1	....	....do	10,000	Taken immediate possession of by the Army.
Clara Dolson	....	1	....	White River	60,000	Transferred to the Navy Department.
Red Rover	....	1	....	Island No. 10	30,000	Do.
Mohawk	....	....	1	....do	500	Rebel gun-boat. Sunk at Island No. 10.
Grampus	....	....	1	....do	5,000	Rebel transport. Sunk at Island No. 10.
John Simonds	....	....	1	....do	6,000	Do.
Yazoo	....	....	1	....do	8,000	Do.
Prince	....	....	1	....do	15,000	Do.
Winchester	....	....	....	....do	5,000	Do.
Sallie Wood	....	1	....	Tennessee River	6,000	Recaptured and destroyed by the enemy.
General Pillow	....	1	....	Fort Pillow	1,000	Transferred to the Navy Department.
Fair Play	....	1	....	White River	8,000	Do.
Total	....	....	....	....	425,500	

Statement showing amount of cash received, on what account disbursed, and balance remaining on hand June 30, 1863, by Capt. George D. Wise, assistant quartermaster, U. S. Volunteers, Western Gun-boat Flotilla.

	Amount.		Amount.
Paid for general purchases	$592,713.39	Received from other officers	$15,800.00
Paid for purchases on account of clothing, &c.	128,224.38	Received from Treasurer of the United States in money.	2,560,577.24
Paid for purchases on account of subsistence.	30,952.36	Received from Treasurer of the United States in certificates of indebtedness.	343,770.00
Paid for general expenditures	1,473,442.07		
Transferred to officers for disbursement.	402,103.79		
On hand June 30, 1863, with Treasurer of the United States on certificate of indebtedness.	36,303.34		
On hand June 30, 1863, in money, in treasury at Saint Louis.	256,407.91		
	2,920,147.24		2,920,147.24

The above payments include the greater part of the cost of the first seven iron-clad gun-boats, together with the iron-clad gun-boat Benton; also general purchases; purchases of clothing, &c.; commissary stores; the payment of chartered transports; of officers and men employed on captured and other Government steamers and tugs; mechanics and laborers employed at naval depot at Cairo, Ill.; together with the total amount transferred to the acting paymasters of the several gun-boats for pay of officers and men of the gun-boat flotilla.

GEO. D. WISE,
Captain and Assistant Quartermaster.

*Names, tonnage, and earnings of steam-boats chartered and employed by Capt. George D. Wise, assistant quartermaster, U. S. Army, for the gun-boat flotilla on the Western waters.**

No. 116.

CHIEF QUARTERMASTER'S OFFICE,
DEPARTMENT OF NORTH CAROLINA,
Wilmington, March 11, 1865.

Capt. ANDREW AINSWORTH,
Captain of the Port:

CAPTAIN: In compliance with orders received from Major-General Terry, commanding at Wilmington, you will take the tug Davidson and such men and machines as you require and, as soon as the guard reports, you will proceed up the Cape Fear River as far as possible with safety to the tug and men, ascertaining as nearly as possible the amount of obstructions in the river, clearing the river of such obstructions, communicating with General Sherman's scouts, if possible. Seventy-five men will be detailed as guard, with arms and three days' rations, with sufficient officers to command them.

You can send out scouts on the banks of the river at such places as may be necessary to protect the boat.

If necessary, I will send the Christopher, to return with such information as you may obtain from the scouts, contrabands, and all persons that can give you information of service to the commanding general.

You will be cautious in your movements, and go as far as possible.

Respectfully, &c.,

GEO. S. DODGE,
Brevet Brigadier-General and Chief Quartermaster.

FORTRESS MONROE, VA., *October 29, 1865.*

Col. WILLIAM L. JAMES,
Chief Quartermaster Department of Virginia:

SIR: I have the honor to submit the following report in regard to opening communication with General Sherman, made at your request:

On the 11th of March, 1865, I received orders from Brig. Gen. George S. Dodge (a copy of which I inclose†). I also received verbal orders to procure a launch from the Navy Department; also two swivel guns and the necessary ammunition; also a construction party to accompany me to clear obstructions.

I also made arrangements to have a torpedo ready to blow up the rebel steamer Chickamauga if I found her lying across the channel so as to obstruct the passage of the river. We received orders from Major-General Terry to proceed punctually at 2.30 p. m., which order was promptly obeyed. We were informed that the U. S. steamer Eolus, Commander Young commanding, would immediately follow.

Nothing worthy of note occurred until some sixteen miles from Wilmington, N. C. (the highest point attained by the naval vessels). After passing that point large numbers of colored men, women, and children flocked to the banks of the river and appeared wild with delight at our appearance, and wished to come on board, and followed us along the banks of the river for miles, offering us fish, &c.; but we

---

*Omitted; but see p. 883, of Executive Document No. 1, referred to in foot-note (*), p. 249.

†Next, *ante*.

did not deem it policy to receive them on board, not knowing what might transpire as we advanced.

After proceeding some miles farther we found a plantation on fire, on which place there were large lots of cotton and naval stores being consumed by the devouring element. The only persons to be seen were a few colored people, and a white man and a colored boy in a boat endeavoring to escape through the swamp, whom we arrested and took on board. It by this time having become dark, and seeing no signs of the U. S. steamer Eolus, we determined to push forward with all dispatch possible.

On arriving at the point where the Chickamauga was sunk, we found her lying on the left bank of the river with ample room to pass.

Some few miles above this point was a chain stretched across the river, which we were fortunate enough to pass safely over; and it is our belief that the said chain was let down by the negroes in the vicinity. Above this place many trees had been felled so as to throw them across the stream, but the tide had fortunately swept them clear of the channel.

Proceeding, we came to a point called Indian Mills, where we found a battery covering the chain. It had been reported that said battery was garrisoned by Confederate troops. After consultation with Captain Reifle (commanding a detachment of the Thirteenth Indiana Regiment composed of sharpshooters) we came to the conclusion if fired upon to land the troops and endeavor to take the battery by an assault; but as we were not molested we proceeded on our way.

Nothing further of interest occurred until we arrived in the city of Elizabethtown, where we perceived large fires upon the banks of the river. On our arriving off the town we found it in a general conflagration; also boats in the river completely enveloped in flames as well. The heat from the flames was intense, and the dense clouds of smoke made it almost an impossibility to proceed; but still we pushed forward and managed to get safely through.

Proceeding some ten miles farther, we met a mass of burning timber floating down the river, which our colored pilots informed us were portions of the bridge which crossed the river at Fayetteville. By the skill of said pilots we evaded the burning mass with the loss of one boat which was towing astern.

After proceeding some few miles farther, bodies of cavalry were seen along the right bank of the river, which immediately galloped away. From this point the banks of the river were strongly picketed.

Previous orders had been given to extinguish all lights and for all to retain silence on board. A white mist occasionally enveloped the boat, our only marks then to steer by being the branches of the trees along the banks.

On arriving about twelve miles below Fayetteville the Confederates opened fire upon us, which was promptly returned by the troops on board, as well as from the guns on board the launch under the command of Mr. Pool, in charge of the obstruction party. Fortunately no one was hurt on board, although a number of shots struck the pilot-house. This fire was kept up at intervals for several miles.

At 6 a. m. we arrived at our destination. On our arrival we found the place occupied by the troops of General Sherman's command, and sharp skirmishing with the enemy across the river. We proceeded immediately to General Sherman's headquarters and reported March 12 at 7 a. m. The general was much pleased to see us and congratulated us upon our safe arrival.

We received orders from him to remain at Fayetteville until dusk of the evening, as he wished to send down a bearer of dispatches; also mails and passengers. At the time appointed we immediately started for Wilmington, N. C.

After leaving Fayetteville, and proceeding some miles on our way, we met the U. S. steamer Eolus, with whom we held communication, and then proceeded on our way, arriving at Wilmington at daybreak March 13, 1865.

I am, sir, very respectfully, your obedient servant,

ANDREW AINSWORTH,
Captain of the Port, Quartermaster's Department.

No. 117.

HEADQUARTERS DEPARTMENT OF WASHINGTON,
OFFICE CHIEF QUARTERMASTER,
Washington, D. C., September 9, 1865.

Bvt. Maj. Gen. M. C. MEIGS,
Quartermaster-General U. S. Army:

GENERAL: In compliance with General Orders, No. 39, of July 1, from your office, I have the honor to submit the following report of the duties performed by me, together with statement of my money and property responsibility during the fiscal year ending June 30, 1865:

An annual report for the year ending June 30, 1864, was transmitted by me to your office about September 15 last.

On the 1st day of July, 1864, I reported to Brig. Gen. Francis C. Barlow, commanding the First Division, Second Army Corps, and at once entered upon the discharge of the duties of quartermaster of the division, which at that time was in the immediate front of Petersburg, the right of the division resting near the Jerusalem plank road and joined on the left by the Second Division of the corps. No movements of the troops or trains transpired excepting change of the latter from point to point, to improve the parking ground, until July 27, at which date the Second Corps was withdrawn from its position and moved to the north side of the James River, crossing the Appomattox and James Rivers by pontoon bridges, accompanied by a part of the general supply train.

While the corps remained at Deep Bottom it engaged in several skirmishes with the enemy, but without serious loss, and returned with trains to former position on the 3d of August.

Another movement of the corps to the north side of the James River was commenced on the 13th of the same month, the troops embarking in steamers at City Point and landing at Deep Bottom on the night of the 14th, while the ammunition and about one-half of the supply trains were sent under cover of the darkness across the Appomattox and James Rivers by pontoon bridges, and halted on the south side of the latter river, opposite Deep Bottom, the remainder of the corps train moving into park near City Point.

A number of unimportant engagements with the enemy again occurred during the stay of the corps, which, with transportation, recrossed the James and Appomattox Rivers by pontoon bridges on the night of the 22d and resumed its former position, the park of the corps train being established near Birney's Station, on the military railroad.

On the 23d a movement against the enemy's right was made by the First and Second Divisions of the corps, the troops marching out the Jerusalem plank road.

Heavy rain-storms having occurred prior to and during this movement, the roads were made almost impassable for wagons, and rations for the men and forage for officers' horses had to be transported by pack-mules—a slow and troublesome method, but accomplished successfully.

On the 24th the two divisions pushed on to Reams' Station (taking with them the ambulance and part of ammunition trains), on the Weldon and Petersburg Railroad, driving the pickets of the enemy before them, and having effectually destroyed the railroad for a number of miles north to the point held by the Fifth Corps, proceeded to strengthen their position at the station by erecting earth-works, &c., and continued the destruction south toward Stony Creek.

On the 25th the enemy in large force attacked the command and a serious battle ensued, attended with severe loss of men on both sides, and resulting in the withdrawal during the night of the troops of the Second Corps from the railroad. The transportation was brought back in safety. Troops went into camp on the 26th, with the remainder of corps, on the Jerusalem plank road near Petersburg, the trains being parked in the vicinity.

During the interim from this date until the latter part of October the First Division of the Second Corps remained in about the same relative position before Petersburg.

On September 23 a raiding party of the enemy moved around the left flank of the army and succeeded in capturing and carrying off a large number of cattle belonging to the subsistence department, and for a few days serious apprehension was felt as to the safety of the trains, which were accordingly moved at the time nearer to the troops, but subsequently changed from time to time as the condition of the parking ground or the supply of water demanded.

Preparation having been made for some days previous, on the morning of October 25 a general movement of the troops to the left commenced, the trains of the army, excepting ambulances and ammunition wagons, being moved for safety inside of the intrenchments at City Point. The defense of the main works in front of Petersburg, from the plank road to the Appomattox River, was intrusted to the First Division, Second Army Corps.

While the trains remained at City Point the teamsters and other employés of the quartermaster's department were armed and held in readiness for any sudden attack that might be made on the base of supplies.

The operations of the army on the left comprised a series of engagements with the enemy tending toward and materially assisting the accomplishment of the plan of our great military chieftain of grasping the communications of the rebels.

On the 28th the troops of the army engaged in this movement returned to their former positions and the trains joined them.

On the 28th a telegram from the Adjutant-General's Office, War Department, was received by me directing that I should at once repair to this city and report to the commanding general Department of Washington and assume the duties to which I had been assigned on the 24th of that month.

On the morning of the 30th I transferred my property to the officer appointed to relieve me, and leaving City Point, arrived in this city on the 31st. On the following day I reported to General Augur and was assigned as chief quartermaster Department of Washington, in which capacity I was acting at the close of the fiscal year ending June 30, 1865.

Upon assuming the duties of my position the subject of greatest importance to be considered at the time, and demanding immediate attention, was that of providing the supply of wood for the inclement season then commenced. The available quantity on hand was inadequate for the wants, and the arrangements already made in part contemplated the supply by river; but knowing the uncertainty attending water transportation during the winter, and realizing the absolute necessity of obtaining a regular supply through a reliable channel, I at once took steps to provide for the same by cutting along the railroads in Virginia. The cutting was confined as far as possible to the lands of disloyal persons, but landmarks being almost entirely obliterated in that part of Virginia, in some instances wood was taken from the lands of loyal people. An account was kept at this office (as nearly accurate as possible without survey of land) of all wood taken, so as to facilitate a settlement when ownership and loyalty should be established.

The work of cutting being rapidly and steadily pushed forward, insured an abundant stock for issue. From 350 to 400 cords were daily brought by railroad to Alexandria, Va., and this city, thereby affording an ample allowance for the troops and hospitals in both cities, as well as for the garrisons in the forts comprised in the Second, Third, and Fourth Brigades of De Russy's division, south of the Potomac. The supply for the garrisons of the forts in Hardin's division, north of the Potomac, the commands at Great Falls, Poolesville, Chapel Point, and other detached posts, and also for prison camp and general hospital at Point Lookout, was provided by purchase in the vicinities at reasonable prices.

Under instructions from your office I furnished up to the close of the fiscal year to Capt. J. G. C. Lee, assistant quartermaster at Alexandria, Va., 15,616 cords; to Capt. J. M. Moore, assistant quartermaster, 4,005 cords; and also sold to Capt. J. M. Brown, by order of the Secretary of War, 923 cords for issue to destitute colored people in this city.

During the month of January the Twenty-third Army Corps arrived at this point and remained about four weeks. Quarters were provided for as many of the men as possible at the new Freedmen's Hospital, at the barracks at Camp Relief and Camp Stoneman, and elsewhere, but the bulk of the command was encamped on the grounds near Camp Stoneman, the tents for the purpose being drawn by me from the depot and returned when the troops moved.

This corps during its stay, the First Corps (General Hancock's), while in this vicinity, the Army of the Potomac, and the army of General Sherman, when concentrated here, were all amply provided with wood by me, and together consumed about 10,000 cords.

It is estimated that a larger quantity of wood was on hand in my possession at the close of the fiscal year than will be required in this department for a number of months, the same having been provided mostly by the operations of the last winter and early spring, with a view to the quantities needed in coming winter, based on the requirements of the past; but the work of transporting to Alexandria and this city was in rapid progress, the wood being properly piled and protected at these points, and ready for any purpose designated.

During the past winter necessary repairs and some additions were made to the barracks at the forts throughout the chain of fortifications, but the same were as limited as the health and comfort of the troops would allow.

Temporary sheds and stables for protection of animals were erected about the 1st of December on the line of the First Separate Brigade, embracing the fortified points from Fairfax Station to Prospect Hill, while the troops of the command constructed log and stockade quarters, which were covered with lumber.

By the direction of the Secretary of War, through Major-General Augur, the erection of a building for detailed clerks and messengers belonging to Department of Washington on duty in this city was commenced about the 20th of February and completed April 15.

This structure is situated on the corner of Twenty-second and I streets, contains accommodations for 200 men, and it was considered would pay for its cost in about one year by the saving to the Government of the commutation of fuel, quarters, and rations heretofore allowed to that class of men.

On the night of April 1 the frame structure used as public offices pertaining to headquarters Department of Washington, adjoining the brick building corner of Fifteen-and-a-half street and Pennsylvania avenue, was entirely consumed by fire, including part of the furniture.

By direction of the major-general commanding, another building to replace the one destroyed, and intended for the same purpose, was commenced about April 10 and finished May 20 without expense to the Quartermaster's Department, the cost of material and labor in its construction being paid from the fund in the possession of the provost-marshal-general Defenses North of the Potomac.

It having been determined by the proper authorities to retain only a portion of the forts and batteries in this vicinity, the work of removing the guns and other material belonging to the Engineer Department from the works designated to be abandoned was begun about the 29th day of June.

The order from the War Department (paragraph 5, Special Orders, No. 315, War Department, Adjutant-General's Office, June 17) directed that—

> The ground occupied by the defenses to be abandoned will be restored to the proprietors of loyal character, endeavors being first made to liquidate all claims for occupation and damage of every kind by transferring to them the right and title to the buildings and fixtures of timber on the bombproofs, magazines, and stockades erected thereon. In the event that such an arrangement is not made to liquidate the claims in full, the buildings will be torn down and material transported to and used for construction of permanent defenses elsewhere, or sold, as may be found most advantageous.
>
> A sufficient guard will be meantime kept to protect the property from fire and injury.

The preliminary examination and investigation necessary to understandingly carry out such instructions was delegated to me by the major-general commanding, and the preparation to complete data as to the ownership of the property, loyalty of claimants, and damages sustained by the use of their property in such manner was in course of completion June 30, the barracks and buildings at the abandoned posts being meanwhile placed under protection of proper guard.

During the winter and spring temporary repairs were made to the Aqueduct and Long Bridges, rendered necessary by the frequent passage over the same by Government teams.

The furnishing of transportation by rail and river does not rest in this office, but the necessary orders have been issued upon the depot officers for transportation from and to various points during the year for upward of 80,000 men and officers, comprising regiments, detachments, and individual cases; also for 2,522 horses, 276 refugees, 5,680 rebel deserters, 603 paroled prisoners, and 1,437 released prisoners.

The land transportation (wagons and teams) in my possession has consisted of from 500 to 600 teams, mostly of mules, which have been used in hauling from woodlands to the shipping points on the railroads and river, and also in delivering supplies to the various forts and posts.

The animals used have generally been of good condition, although many of the mules received during the winter and early spring were too young and feeble to properly bear the hard labor necessary in hauling from the woods and over the rough and miry roads; but when the armies had concentrated at this point, and turned over to the depot their wagons and teams, a much better class of animals was substituted in their stead, and the close of the fiscal year found this department in possession of transportation animals hardened by service, trained in use, healthy, and fully able to perform the required labor.

I offer no suggestions as to improvements in the pattern of the army wagons and harness, as I consider the class now in use to be simple in arrangement, durable for service, and well adapted for field purposes.

The supply of hay furnished by the depot at times during the winter being limited on account of the closing of the river, it became absolutely necessary for the sustenance of the animals of the cavalry commands on the Upper and Lower Potomac and First Separate Brigade in Virginia, as well as for transportation animals in my possession engaged on woodlands, to purchase (and in some cases make seizures of) hay in the vicinities. By such means a sufficient (but not full) ration was obtained and paid for at prices ranging from $20 to $32 per ton.

The clothing and camp and garrison equipage drawn from the depot has uniformly been of good quality and manufacture, and has been furnished in quantities and of a variety amply sufficient for the health and comfort of the troops.

The disbursements made by me during the fiscal year have been of a miscellaneous nature, including the purchase of fuel, forage, and stationery, payment of court-martial expenses, postage, mileage to officers, commutation of fuel and quarters, extra-duty pay to enlisted men, rentals, hire of employés, apprehension of deserters, &c., which responsibility, together with the property charge and the administrative duty required, has marked this office as one of an almost multifarious character.

The following statement exhibits the amount of moneys on hand July 1, 1864, received and disbursed during the year, and remaining on hand June 30, 1865, and annexed will be found statements (A and B) of quartermaster's property, clothing and camp and garrison equipage for the fiscal year, and also statement (E) of property captured by the enemy.

Other of the statements specified in your General Orders, No. 39, are not required in my report.

To the Quartermaster-General of the Army and his assistants my warmest thanks are tendered for the valuable instruction and advice imparted.

I am, general, very respectfully, your obedient servant,

M. I. LUDINGTON,

Colonel and Chief Quartermaster Dept. of Washington.

Statement of public moneys received and disbursed during the fiscal year ending June 30, 1865, by Col. M. I. Ludington, chief quartermaster Department of Washington.

On hand July 1, 1864	$17.38
Received from officers during the year	13,485.53
Received from Treasury Department during the year	1,136,800.00
Received from sales of property and other sources during the year	14,301.55
Total	1,164,604.46
Expended during the year	916,426.71
Transferred to other officers during the year	231,221.98
Remaining on hand June 30, 1865	16,955.77
Total	1,164,604.46
This balance is deposited as follows:	
In U. S. Treasury, Washington, D. C	13,354.42
In National Bank of Metropolis, Washington, D. C	3,601.35
	16,955.77

I certify that the above statement is correct.

M. I. LUDINGTON,
Colonel and Chief Quartermaster Department of Washington.

WAR DEPT., PROVOST-MARSHAL-GENERAL'S BUREAU,
Washington, D. C., November 8, 1865.

Hon. EDWIN M. STANTON,
Secretary of War:

SIR: I have the honor to submit my annual report of the operations of the Bureau of the Provost-Marshal-General of the United States for the year ending November 1, 1865.

On the 1st of November, 1864, the date to which my last annual report was brought up, the business of recruiting and the draft under the call of July 18, 1864, was in progress.

The number called for was	500,000
Reduced by credits on former calls	265,673
To be obtained	234,327

Number of voluntary enlistments under that call:		
Volunteers—		
White	146,392	
Colored	15,961	
Regulars	6,339	
Seamen	17,606	
Marine Corps	1,874	
Total		188,172
Number of drafted men and substitutes obtained under that call:		
Number held to personal service	26,205	
Number of substitutes for drafted men	28,502	
Number of substitutes for enrolled men	29,584	
Total		84,291
Whole number obtained under the July call		272,463

On the 19th of December, 1864, a call was made for 300,000 men.

Number of voluntary enlistments under this call:		
Volunteers—		
White	130,620	
Colored	10,055	
Regulars	6,958	
Seamen	9,106	
Marine Corps	319	
Total		157,058
Number of drafted men and substitutes under that call:		
Number held to personal service	12,566	
Number of substitutes for drafted men	12,014	
Number of substitutes for enrolled men	12,997	
Total		37,577
Whole number raised under December call		194,635

The suspension of active military operations occurred while the business of the draft under this call was in progress, and orders were issued on the 13th of April, 1865, to discontinue the business of recruiting and drafting, and on the next day all drafted men who had not been forwarded to general rendezvous were ordered to be discharged, and soon after all who had not been forwarded to the field were discharged by order from the Adjutant-General.

The aggregate quotas charged against the several States under all calls made by the President of the United States from the 15th day of April, 1861, up to the 14th day of April, 1865, at which time drafting and recruiting ceased by order of the Secretary of War, was 2,759,049, the terms of service varying from three months to three years, as shown in detail by the books of the Provost-Marshal-General's Office.* The aggregate number of men credited on the several calls and put into service of the United States in the Army, Navy, and Marine Corps during the above period was 2,656,553, leaving a deficiency on all calls when the war closed of 102,496, which would have been obtained in full, in fact in excess, if recruiting and drafting had not been discontinued.* This number does not embrace the "emergency men" put into service during the summer of 1863 by the States of New York, New Jersey, Pennsylvania, nor those furnished by the States of Ohio, Indiana, and Illinois during the Morgan raid, amounting in all to over 120,000 men, who served periods of about two or three weeks.

In estimating the number of troops called into service, it has been the rule of the department to take into account the whole number of men mustered, without regard to the fact that the same persons may have been previously discharged after having been accepted and credited on previous calls.

Under the different calls volunteers have been accepted for various terms of service, viz, three, six, and nine months, and one, two, and three years, respectively; and a large number of persons who had served under one call have subsequently enlisted under another. Thus, a portion of those who enlisted under the call in April, 1861, for 75,000 three-months' men, again enlisted under succeeding calls in July following for three years; others re-entered the service for nine months, or for one or two years, and at the expiration of these periods again re-enlisted for three years, and the entire veteran volunteer force consisted of those who, having served two years, re-enlisted for three years.

*But see a later official compilation, Vol. IV, this series, p. 1269.

It will be observed, therefore, that a large portion of the number counted in filling calls has been furnished, first, by the re-enlistment of those in service, and second, by those who have re-entered the service after discharge from a former enlistment under which they had been credited; that is, the different calls were filled by crediting each accepted enlistment, instead of limiting the credit to the actual number of persons who entered the service anew; and hence to determine the number of men actually entering the service for the first time under the different calls, the number credited should be reduced in the same ratio that the enlistments of the same person have been repeated. The extent of this reduction cannot be calculated at this time, or even estimated with sufficient accuracy to be useful.

It follows, therefore, that, on account of a necessary repetition of credits incident to enlistments, the tax upon the military basis of the country has been less than would appear by considering simply the number of men embraced in the different calls for troops or the number of credits allowed upon these calls.

COMMUTATION MONEY.

The amount of commutation money received from November 1, 1864, to November 1, 1865, was:

On account of draft and substitute fund	$317,130.00
On account of sick and wounded soldiers (from non-combatants, under section 17 of the act of February 24, 1864)	340,987.53
Total	658,117.53
Total amount of draft and substitute fund received under the act approved March 3, 1863	25,902,029.25
Total amount expended	16,387,135.80
Balance remaining in Treasury to credit of this fund	9,514,893.45

There are just claims still outstanding which have to be met from this fund.

VETERAN RESERVE CORPS.

The regiments of the Veteran Reserve Corps have been performing the same duty during the past year as those specified in my last annual report, viz: Performing garrison duty in Washington and its defensive works; at the various depots for recruits and drafted men; at the provost-marshals' rendezvous; escorting recruits to the field, and more recently performing garrison duty at the several rendezvous for muster out of the volunteer forces.

Since the termination of active operations no transfers have been made to this corps, nor have any officers been appointed.

DESERTERS.

The number of deserters arrested since my last annual report is 18,120, nearly all of whom were arrested prior to April 30. The discharge of the deputy provost-marshals and special officers, the stoppage of payment of rewards, and the reduction of the Army have occasioned the reduction of this branch of the business of this office.

DISBURSEMENTS ON ACCOUNT OF VOLUNTEER RECRUITING SERVICE.

The amount expended from the appropriation for collecting, drilling, and organizing volunteers from November 1, 1864, to November 1, 1865, was $1,422,281.73.

The balance of this appropriation remaining in the Treasury is $12,163,386.09, and about half a million dollars still in the hands of the disbursing officers, which is needed to pay outstanding accounts and expenses incurred in mustering out the volunteer forces of the United States.

The amount expended from the appropriation for pay of bounty was $6,648,302.53. The balance of this appropriation remaining in the Treasury is $11,145,392.24. None of this fund remains in the hands of disbursing officers. The several amounts left in their possession when recruiting for the volunteer forces was discontinued has been covered into the U. S. Treasury.

DISBURSEMENTS ON ACCOUNT OF ENROLLMENT AND DRAFT AND APPREHENSION OF DESERTERS.

The amount disbursed on account of enrollment and draft from November 1, 1864, to November 1, 1865, was $3,175,744.06.

The balance of this "draft and substitute fund" remaining in the Treasury is $9,514,893.45, and about $250,000 in the hands of disbursing officers, which is needed to pay outstanding accounts and current expenses of the Bureau.

Amount disbursed by officers of this Bureau from appropriation for "incidental expenses of Quartermaster-General's Department," for apprehension of deserters, $12,158.58.

RETRENCHMENT OF EXPENDITURES.

At the date of my last annual report the number of officers and employés of this Bureau was 4,716, at a cost per month of $311,868.60. The number now on duty and in the employ of the Bureau is 383, at a cost per month of $35,030.32.

As fast as the exigencies of the service permitted I have reduced the force employed. The surgeons and commissioners of boards of enrollment in all the districts, 370 in number, have been discharged. The different districts have been consolidated, and but 33 provost-marshals are now in service, all of whom will be discharged as soon as their services can be dispensed with.

ESTIMATES.

No appropriation of money will be required for the support of this Bureau during the next fiscal year.

I have in course of preparation a full report of the operations of this Bureau, which will contain much statistical and other valuable information, and which I beg leave to submit when completed.

I have the honor to be, sir, very respectfully, your obedient servant,

JAMES B. FRY,
Provost-Marshal-General.

WASHINGTON, *November 10, 1865.*

Hon. W. H. SEWARD,
Secretary of State:

In compliance with your request I have the honor to state that the aggregate strength of the Army is at present 182,784 men, and that, including Louisiana, 81,256 of these men are west of the Mississippi River.

In case of emergency 50,000 additional men could be made disposable east of the Mississippi.

U. S. GRANT,
Lieutenant-General.

WAR DEPARTMENT, BUREAU OF MILITARY JUSTICE,
November 13, 1865.

Hon. E. M. STANTON,
Secretary of War:

SIR: In compliance with your directions I have the honor to submit as follows in regard to the business transacted by this Bureau since March, 1865, the date of my last official report.*

The operations of the Bureau during this period—of about seven and two-thirds months—are briefly presented by the following summary:

1. Number of records of general courts-martial and military commissions received, reviewed, and filed, 16,591.

2. Number of special reports made as to the regularity of proceedings, the pardon of military offenders, the remission or commutation of sentences, and upon the numerous miscellaneous subjects and questions referred for the opinion of this office, including, also, letters of instruction upon military law and practice to judge-advocates, reviewing officers, and others, 6,123.

By comparing these details with those presented in March last it will be perceived that the number of records reviewed is slightly, and that of the special reports very much greater, in proportion to the period of time embraced, than that specified in my last official communication upon the subject, and that the business of the Bureau, especially as an advisory branch of the War Department, has not yet been diminished or sensibly affected by the altered condition of public affairs.

The Digest of Opinions of the Judge-Advocate-General, issued by the Bureau in January last, has, as it is inferred from the commendatory judgment expressed to me by department and other commanders, and the fact that it has come into extensive use throughout the Army, proved of considerable advantage to the service in contributing to establish a uniformity of decision and action in the administration of military justice; and it is proposed, with your approval, to prepare during the coming winter an enlarged edition of the same, containing, in connection with those already published, a selection of the official opinions communicated by me during the past year. The present edition of the work has, indeed, because of the constant demand for copies, been very nearly exhausted.

I have to express my satisfaction with the ability and efficiency with which the officers, as well as the clerks, connected with the office have performed their several duties; and to add that, while the close of the rebellion will doubtless gradually induce a considerable falling off in the business of the Bureau, it is conceived, as this business will probably not be materially diminished for a twelve-month, that the present organization of this branch of the public service may well be continued by Congress.

---

*See Vol. IV, this series, p. 1216.

In concluding this report of the business of this Bureau, it is thought proper to advert to two cases of unusual public importance, which were prepared under its supervision, and tried by military commission, since the last session of Congress—that of the assassins of President Lincoln and their accomplices, and that of Wirz, the keeper of the rebel prison at Andersonville, Ga.

The first of these cases was brought to trial in May last before a court convened by the President, and composed of two major-generals, one brevet major-general, three brigadier-generals, one brevet brigadier-general, a brevet colonel, and a lieutenant-colonel. The Government was represented by the Judge-Advocate-General of the Army, assisted by an experienced military judge-advocate, and by a distinguished lawyer, who had also lately acted for the United States in the conduct of a most important prosecution by court-martial. The accused were defended by counsel of their own selection, seven in number. The trial occupied fifty-three days—between 300 and 400 witnesses, in all, having been examined—and was concluded by seven able and elaborate arguments of counsel, the final reply thereto and argument of Hon. John A. Bingham, on the part of the United States, being annexed hereto as part of this report.* The formal brief review of the case by this Bureau is also appended.*

The inevitable result of this trial had been generally anticipated throughout the country, and has now become matter of history. The most deeply guilty of the conspirators were sentenced to be hung, and their sentence was summarily executed by order of the President. Of the others, three were condemned to imprisonment for life, and one to an imprisonment for six years, at hard labor; and these are now undergoing confinement at the military prison at the Dry Tortugas, Fla.

A full and complete record of the testimony and of the proceedings of the Commission has been prepared under the supervision of an officer of the Government, and will presently be given to the public.† To this publication reference must be had for the details of the evidence upon this momentous state trial.

The case of Wirz was conducted before a commission also constituted by the President, and composed of one major-general, three brevet major-generals, two brigadier-generals, one brevet brigadier-general, one brevet colonel, and one lieutenant-colonel; the prisoner being represented by two counsel of his choice. The victims of the accused had been so numerous that the mass of testimony was nearly as great as that adduced upon the former trial, and the period of time occupied by the investigation even longer. The number of witnesses examined was 148. Of these a considerable proportion had been connected with the rebel military service. Besides the evidence from these sources, much important testimony obtained from the archives of the rebel Government—including the records of the prison at Andersonville—was also laid before the Commission. The capital sentence in the case was forthwith approved by the President, and this criminal has recently paid such penalty as the law could impose for his repeated murders and other atrocious violations of the laws of civilized warfare.

As it would be impossible to present, in the limits of a brief official report, even an abstract of the evidence upon this trial, a copy is

---

*Here omitted; but see House Executive Document No. 1, Thirty-ninth Congress, first session, pp. 1006–1060. Also see foot-note, Series II, Vol. VIII, p. 700.

†Published by Moore, Wilstach & Baldwin, Cincinnati, 1865, under the title "The Assassination of President Lincoln and the Trial of the Conspirators."

herewith submitted of the address of Col. N. P. Chipman, judge-advocate, which, while containing a lucid discussion of the questions of law involved, exhibits also a most faithful summary of the testimony, much of which, indeed, is set forth in the very language of the witnesses. A copy of the formal review of the proceedings, addressed by this Bureau to the President on the 31st ultimo, is also annexed.* It is submitted whether a publication of the record of this case (similar to that undertaken by private enterprise in the instance of the trial of the assassins), or of an abridgment of the same, prepared by some proper person, may not well be authorized by Congress, not only that a permanent memorial of the testimony and proceedings may be preserved, but also that the facts of such testimony may be made accessible to every student of the rebellion.†

A peculiar characteristic of these state trials, and that which must invest them with a deep historical importance, is the fact that, while the accused were in each case adjudged to have been guilty of the crimes with which they were charged, the complicity in those crimes of chiefs of the rebellion was declared by the court in their findings, and upon testimony which is deemed to have fully warranted the conclusions reached. In each case the proof justified the conviction that the prisoners before the court were not merely personally criminals, but conspirators; that they were the hirelings and accomplices of the cabal of traitors of whom Davis was the acknowledged chief, and that these traitors were in fact, as well as in law, equally with the accused, responsible for the detestable deeds which were adduced in evidence. The assassination of the President was portrayed by the testimony as an inspiration of the rebellion, authorized from the seat of government, and executed through its paid agents, whose plan of action was first matured within the territory of a neighboring friendly power.

It is proper to remark that events and testimony disclosed subsequent to this trial have added a powerful support to the conclusions arrived at by the court in reference to the complicity of rebel leaders in the assassination of the President.

The barbarities of Wirz, which resulted in the sacrifice of the lives of at least 10,000 of our helpless prisoners in his hands, were also clearly shown to have been but the revolting features of a system, doubtless devised at Richmond, for the destruction by starvation and fatal cruelties of all the Federal prisoners of war who should come into the enemy's hands. As there is no baseness too infamous to be incompatible with treason, so, for the execution of the details of this inhuman scheme, fit agents were readily found wearing the rebel uniform, and to these were committed the care and custody of Union prisoners. The administration of Wirz, however, though atrocious in the extreme, was but a striking example of the general system of treatment by the enemy of prisoners of war. Of the enforcement of this system throughout the South, at Richmond, Belle Isle, Salisbury, N. C.; Florence, S. C.; Macon and Millen, Ga.; Tuscaloosa, Ala., and at many other localities, the cruelties of Andersonville, as is made to appear by testimony on file in this Bureau, were but a forcible illustration. For the result—for the almost countless deaths and lasting injuries by wounds, by starvation, by inhuman punishments, by the

* See Series II, Vol. VIII, p. 775.

† See Executive Document No. 23, House of Representatives, Fortieth Congress, second session.

maiming and laceration by dogs, by every brutality and by every neglect—the chiefs of the rebel confederacy, the instigators and leaders of the rebellion, should be held responsible; and for these they will be held responsible by the judgment of history and by the abhorrence of the civilized world.

It is to be added that in this case, also, the complicity of the rebel Executive in the crimes of the accused was declared by the court in its findings.

This report cannot well be closed without its bearing testimony to the worth and efficiency of military commissions as judicial tribunals in time of war, as illustrated by these two trials.

These commissions, originating in the necessities of the rebellion, had been proved by the experience of three years indispensable for the punishment of public crimes in regions where other courts had ceased to exist, and in cases of which the local criminal courts could not legally take cognizance, or which, by reason of intrinsic defects of machinery, they were incompetent to pass upon. These tribunals had long been a most powerful and efficacious instrumentality in the hands of the Executive for the bringing to justice of a large class of malefactors in the service or interest of the rebellion, who otherwise would have altogether escaped punishment; and it had indeed become apparent that without their agency the rebellion could hardly, in some quarters, have been suppressed. So conspicuous had the importance of these commissions and the necessity for their continuance become that the highest civil courts of the country had recognized them as a part of the military judicial system of the Government, and Congress by repeated legislation had confirmed their authority and indeed extended their jurisdiction.

But it was not until the two cases under consideration came on to be tried by the military commission that its highest excellence was exhibited. It was not merely in that it was unincumbered by the technicalities and inevitable embarrassments attending the administration of justice before civil tribunals, or in the fact that it could so readily avail itself of the military power of the Government for the execution of its processes and the enforcement of its orders, that its efficacy (though in these directions most conspicuous) was chiefly illustrated. It was rather in the extended reach which it could give to its investigation, and in the wide scope which it could cover by testimony, that its practical and pre-eminent use and service were displayed. It was by means of this freedom of view and inquiry that the element of conspiracy, which gave to these cases so startling a significance, was enabled to be traced and exposed, and that the fact that the infamous crimes which appeared in proof were fruits borne by the rebellion and authorized by its head was published to the community and to the world. By no other species of tribunal and by no other known mode of judicial inquiry could this result have been so successfully attained; and it may truly be said that without the aid and agency of the military commission one of the most important chapters in the annals of the rebellion would have been lost to history, and the most complete and reliable disclosure of its inner and real life, alike treacherous and barbaric, would have failed to be developed.

It is due not only to the late President, who, as Commander-in-Chief, unhesitatingly employed this tribunal in the suppression of crimes connected with the rebellion, but to the heads of the military departments and other commanders, who so resolutely and effectively availed themselves of its simple but potent machinery; to the National Legislatures, which, recognizing its continuance as indispensable during the war, have confirmed and increased its jurisdiction; and to the intelligence and good sense of the people at large, who, disregarding the shallow and disloyal clamors raised against it, have appreciated its service to the country, that this brief testimony to its value as an arm of the military administration, evidenced alike by the fairness of its judgments and by its enlightened and vigorous action, should be publicly and formally borne by this Bureau.

J. HOLT,
Judge-Advocate-General.

WAR DEPARTMENT,
Washington City, November 22, 1865.

MR. PRESIDENT:

The military appropriations by the last Congress amounted to the sum of $516,240,131.70. The military estimates for the next fiscal year, after careful revision, amount to $33,814,461.83. The national military force on May 1, 1865, numbered 1,000,516 men.* It is proposed to reduce the military establishment to 50,000 troops, and over 800,000 have already been mustered out of service. What has occasioned this reduction of force and expenditure in the War Department it is the purpose of this report to explain.

At the commencement of the last session of Congress much had been accomplished toward suppressing the rebellion and restoring Federal authority over the insurgent States. But the rebels still held Richmond as the capital of their so-called Confederate Government, and the semblance of State government existed in Virginia, North Carolina, South Carolina, Georgia, Alabama, Florida, Mississippi, and Texas, while a strong military force occupied a considerable portion of Arkansas and Louisiana. Their principal army, under its favorite commander, General Lee, defended with undaunted front impregnable positions around Petersburg and Richmond. Another army, under General Hood, was moving north, with purpose to invade Tennessee and Kentucky. West of the Mississippi a large force, under General Kirby Smith, threatened Arkansas, Kansas, and Missouri. The chief sea-ports of the rebel States—Wilmington, Charleston, Savannah, and Mobile—were strongly garrisoned and fortified, and our blockading squadrons were unable to prevent trade and supplies reaching the enemy. Pirate steamers, built in foreign ports for rebel cruisers, armed, manned, equipped, and supplied by foreign capital, roamed the high seas, burning our ships and destroying our commerce. Marauders, hired by the rebel Government and harbored on our northern frontier, were setting on foot piratical expeditions against our commerce on the lakes, planning to burn and plunder our towns and cities, and were plotting murder against the President and Vice-President of the United States, in hopes of overthrowing our Government by anarchy. Faith in their final success and hope of open recognition by foreign governments still animated leading traitors.

But now the approaching session of Congress will find the authority of the Federal Government effectually and peacefully exercised over

---

*But see a later official compilation, Vol. IV, this series, p. 1283, showing an aggregate of 1,052,038.

the whole territory of the United States. All the armies heretofore arrayed against the National Government have laid down their arms and surrendered as prisoners of war. Every hostile banner has been hauled down; the so-called Confederate Government is overthrown; its President is a prisoner in close custody, awaiting trial; while its Vice-President and three of its chief executive officers have been recently enlarged from prison by your clemency. All the ordinances, laws, and organizations created or existing under or by virtue of the so-called Confederate Government have been swept away, and by your sanction the people of the insurgent States have organized, or are busily engaged in organizing, State governments in subordination to the Federal authority. In harmony with this new condition of affairs the military force of the Federal Government has been reduced, large armies disbanded, and nearly a million of brave men, lately soldiers in arms, paid and honorably mustered out of service, have gone from camps, garrisons, and posts to their homes, and most of them are engaged already in the peaceful pursuits of civil life.

Among the causes which under Divine Providence have brought about these wonderful results, successful military operations stand first in order. A clear comprehension of these operations requires a brief glance at the military position just before the spring campaigns of 1864.

Notwithstanding the successful campaigns on the Mississippi in 1863, by the reduction of Vicksburg and Port Hudson, severed in twain the rebel territory and restored to us the navigation and commerce of the Mississippi, while the victory at Gettysburg drove back the rebel invaders from the Northern States, yet the military strength of the rebels continued formidable. The Army of Virginia, under General Lee, recovered from its disaster at Gettysburg, occupied its former lines in Virginia, protecting the rebel capital, and holding inactive and in check the Army of the Potomac. Another large army, under General Bragg, re-enforced by Longstreet's corps, threatened the reconquest of Tennessee. After the disastrous battle of Chickamauga our Army of the Cumberland, shut up and surrounded at Chattanooga, unable to move by reason of the inclemency of the weather and impassable roads, was in extreme jeopardy.

At this discouraging juncture a change of military organization was made. The Departments of the Ohio, the Tennessee, and the Cumberland were united in one military division, called the Division of the Mississippi, under Major-General Grant. Command of the Army of the Cumberland was given to Maj. Gen. George H. Thomas, relieving General Rosecrans. A winter campaign was immediately directed against Bragg's army. The battles of Wauhatchie, Lookout Mountain, Missionary Ridge, and Chattanooga opened our communications and routed Bragg's army with heavy loss. The movement of Longstreet's corps against Knoxville to recover East Tennessee also proved a disastrous failure to the rebels, who were driven off and forced back to the mountains.

In the month of February, 1864, General Sherman's movement with a large force from Vicksburg into the interior of the State of Alabama [Mississippi] as far as Meridian, inflicted heavy loss upon the enemy by the destruction of railroads and supplies, the capture of prisoners, and the escape of negroes and refugees. This operation demonstrated the capacity of an invading army to penetrate the rebel States and support itself on the country, and was the forerunner of the great movements in Georgia.

The arrangements for the spring campaigns of 1864 were made, on the part of the Government, to put forth its strength. In all the bureaus of the War Department supplies were provided on a scale of great magnitude to meet any exigency that could be foreseen. The estimates were based upon an army organization of 1,000,000 of men. The States were called upon to strengthen the armies by volunteers; new drafts were ordered and put in execution throughout all the loyal States; vast supplies of arms, ammunition, clothing, subsistence, medical stores, and forage were provided and distributed in depots to meet the wants of the troops wherever they might operate; horses, mules, wagons, railroad iron, locomotives and cars, bridge timber, telegraph cable and wire, and every material for transportation and communication of great armies under all conditions were supplied. Congress with unstinting hand voted large appropriations for recruiting, paying, and supplying the troops. The office of lieutenant-general, to command all the armies, was created by law. Ulysses S. Grant was appointed to the rank by the President, and assumed command as lieutenant-general on the 17th day of March, 1864, from which time the operations of all the armies were under his direction.

The national forces engaged in the spring campaign of 1864 were organized as armies or distributed in military departments as follows:

The Army of the Potomac, commanded by Major-General Meade, whose headquarters were on the north side of the Rapidan. This army was confronted by the rebel Army of Northern Virginia, stationed on the south side of the Rapidan, under General Robert E. Lee.

The Ninth Corps, under Major-General Burnside, was, at the opening of the campaign, a distinct organization, but on the 24th day of May, 1864, it was incorporated into the Army of the Potomac.

The Army of the James was commanded by Major-General Butler, whose headquarters were at Fortress Monroe.

The headquarters of the Army of the Shenandoah, commanded by Major-General Sigel, were at Winchester.

Three armies were united under Maj. Gen. William T. Sherman, viz, the Army of the Cumberland, Major-General Thomas commanding; the Army of the Tennessee, Major-General McPherson commanding, and the Army of the Ohio, Major-General Schofield commanding. General Sherman's headquarters were at Chattanooga. The effective strength of these three armies was nearly 100,000 men and 254 guns, to wit:

	Infantry.	Artillery.	Cavalry.	Total.	Number of guns.
Army of the Cumberland, Major-General Thomas commanding.	54,568	2,377	3,828	60,773	130
Army of the Tennessee, Major-General McPherson commanding.	22,437	1,104	624	24,165	96
Army of the Ohio, Major-General Schofield commanding..	11,183	679	1,697	13,559	28
Grand aggregate	....	....	....	98,497	254

About these figures were maintained during the campaign, the number of men joining from furlough and hospitals compensating for the loss in battle and from sickness.

In the Department of Kentucky there was likewise a large active force, under command of Major-General Burbridge, and also in East

Tennessee, under Major-General Stoneman. Adequate forces were reserved in the Department of Washington, under Major-General Augur, to protect the capital and the immense depots of military supplies at Washington and Alexandria, and also in the Middle Military Department, under Maj. Gen. Lewis Wallace, to cover Baltimore and the important lines of supply and communication in that department. Besides the armies operating actively in the field, troops were assigned to garrison exposed and important strategic points, to guard hospitals, recruiting stations, prison camps, supply depots, railroad lines, and to defend border States and the northern frontier from rebel raids.

In the Department of the South a force was operating against Charleston and in Florida, under General Gillmore.

West of the Mississippi the forces were under the respective departmental commanders. In the Department of the Gulf, embracing Louisiana and Texas, Major-General Banks had his headquarters at New Orleans. The Department of Arkansas was in command of Major-General Steele. Major-General Curtis commanded the troops assigned for the Department of Kansas and the Indian Territory. The troops in the Department of the Missouri were under command of Major-General Rosecrans. The defense of the Northwestern States and Territories against Indians, expeditions to check incursions and reduce hostile tribes, and to protect the overland route to California employed a considerable force under Major-General Pope in the Northwest Department, General Carleton in New Mexico and Arizona, and General Connor in the Indian Territory. The States and Territories on the Pacific Coast required but a small force, under Major-General McDowell.

The headquarters of the lieutenant-general commanding all the armies were with the Army of the Potomac in the field.

Official reports show that on the 1st of May, 1864, the aggregate national military force of all arms, officers and men, was 970,710, to wit:

Available force present for duty*	662,345
On detached service in the different military departments	109,348
In field hospitals or unfit for duty	41,266
In general hospitals or on sick-leave at home	75,978
Absent on furlough or as prisoners of war	66,290
Absent without leave	15,483
Grand aggregate	970,710

The aggregate available force present for duty May 1, 1864, was distributed in the different commands as follows:

Department of Washington	42,124
Army of the Potomac	120,384
Department of Virginia and North Carolina	59,130
Department of the South	18,169
Department of the Gulf	61,865
Department of Arkansas	23,666
Department of the Tennessee	74,170
Department of the Missouri	15,775
Department of the Northwest	5,296
Department of Kansas	4,798
Headquarters Military Division of the Mississippi	476
Department of the Cumberland	119,948
Department of the Ohio	35,416
Northern Department	9,546

*But see explanatory foot-note, p. 136.

Department of West Virginia	30,782
Department of the East	2,828
Department of the Susquehanna	2,970
Middle Department	5,627
Ninth Army Corps	20,780
Department of New Mexico	3,454
Department of the Pacific	5,141
Total	*662,345

Active military operations west of the Mississippi commenced in the month of March, 1864. The principal rebel forces beyond the Mississippi were concentrated under General Kirby Smith at Shreveport, on the Red River. Against this force an expedition was undertaken by Major-General Banks, with a large army from New Orleans, to be co-operated with by troops from the Department of Arkansas, under General Steele, and from the Division of the Mississippi, under General A. J. Smith, and also a large naval force under Admiral Porter. General Banks with his forces reached Alexandria about the 20th of March. Advancing thence toward Shreveport, a series of disasters commenced that ended in the failure of the expedition with heavy loss of men and material. The cause of this failure is still a subject of discussion, not material to the present report. Although by this mishap the enemy was enabled to occupy the attention of a large force designed and that might have been employed in other fields, he was himself kept in check and hindered from taking part in the great campaigns east of the Mississippi.

The campaigns in Virginia opened on the 4th day of May. By simultaneous movements the Army of the Potomac crossed the Rapidan, and City Point, on the south side of the James, was seized and occupied by General Butler. The crossing of the Rapidan was effected without resistance from the enemy. The movement against City Point took him by surprise. The Army of the Potomac was directed at Lee's army, while the city of Richmond was the objective point of the Army of the James.

Minute details of the subsequent campaigns are given in the accompanying reports of the lieutenant-general and other distinguished commanders, so that nothing more than a cursory view of the main results is here required.†

The antagonist armies of Meade and Lee met in conflict near Mine Run on the 5th day of May. Forty-three days of desperate fighting or marching by day and night forced back the rebel army from the Rapidan to their intrenchments around Richmond and carried the Army of the Potomac to the south side of the James River. The

* But see explanatory foot-note, p. 136.

† For these reports (here omitted) see Series I, as follows: Grant's of July 22, 1865, Vol. XXXVI, Part I, p. 12; Meade's of April 30, 1865, Vol. XLVI, Part I, p. 601; Sheridan's of May 16, 1865, *ibid.*, p. 1101; Sherman's of September 15, 1864, Vol. XXXVIII, Part I, p. 61; Sherman's of January 1, 1865, Vol. XXXIX, Part I, p. 580, and Vol. XLIV, p. 7; Sherman's of April 4, 1865, Vol. XLVII, Part I, p. 17; Schofield's of April 3, 1865, *ibid.*, p. 909; Barry's of March 31, 1865, *ibid.*, p. 177; Sherman's of May 9, 1865, *ibid.*, p. 29; Sheridan's of July 16, 1865, Vol. XLVI, Part I, p. 474; Thomas' of January 20, 1865, Vol. XXXIX, Part I, p. 584, and Vol. XLV, Part I, p. 32; Thomas' of June 1, 1865, Vol. XLIX, Part I, p. 342; Butler's of January 3, 1865, Vol. XLII, Part I, p. 966; Terry's of January 25, 1865, Vol. XLVI, Part I, p. 394; Comstock's of January 27, 1865, *ibid.*, p. 406; Ames' of January 16, 1865, *ibid.*, p. 415; Rosecrans' of December 7, 1864, Vol. XLI, Part I, p. 307; Banks' of April 6, 1865, Vol. XXXIV, Part I, p. 194. For report of D. H. Strother, of the operations of the army under General Hunter in West Virginia, see p. 1253 of House Executive Document No. 1, Thirty-ninth Congress, first session.

strength of the enemy's force when the campaign opened, or the extent of his loss, is not known to this Department. Any inequality of numbers between Lee's army and the Army of the Potomac was fully compensated by the advantage of position. Resolute purpose and desperate valor were exhibited on both sides. In the battles of the Wilderness, Spotsylvania Court-House, Jericho Ford, Haw's Shop, and Cold Harbor many brave soldiers and gallant officers perished. Among them were Brigadier-General Wadsworth, Brigadier-General Hays, and Major-General Sedgwick. Lieutenant-General Grant in his report observes:

> The battles of the Wilderness, Spotsylvania, North Anna, and Cold Harbor, bloody and terrible as they were on our side, were even more damaging to the enemy, and so crippled him as to make him wary ever after of taking the offensive. His losses in men were probably not so great, owing to the fact that we were, save in the Wilderness, almost invariably the attacking party, and when he did attack it was in the open field.

Although expectations of destroying Lee's army, and the speedy capture of Richmond and Petersburg, were disappointed, and the enemy had found refuge behind impregnable fortifications, the campaign was still prosecuted with determined purpose toward the same object. While the rebel army was sheltered in his intrenchments the national forces were busy at work outside, strengthening and advancing their position, breaking the communications of the enemy, cutting off and destroying his supplies, narrowing his limits, harassing him by raids, and occupying his attention to prevent detachments or re-enforcements being sent to operate elsewhere.

Active operations were also going on in the Valley of the Shenandoah. On the 1st of May an expedition, under Generals Crook and Averell, was sent out by General Sigel, which reached Wytheville and accomplished the destruction of much rebel property. General Sigel advanced on the 8th day of May with his force from Winchester to New Market, where, met by the enemy under General Breckinridge, he was defeated and fell back to Cedar Creek. General Hunter was then placed in command of the department. He marched with a strong force toward Staunton, and in a brilliant engagement at Piedmont defeated the enemy with severe loss. Advancing to Staunton, he was joined there by Crook and Averell and moved against Lynchburg. Re-enforcements from the enemy having arrived before him, General Hunter retired by way of the Kanawha. Meanwhile, in order to repair the losses of the Army of the Potomac, the chief part of the force designed to guard the Middle Department and the Department of Washington was called forward to the front. Taking advantage of this state of affairs, in the absence of General Hunter's command, the enemy made a large detachment from their army at Richmond, which, under General Early, moved down the Shenandoah Valley, threatening Baltimore and Washington. Their advance was checked at Monocacy, where a severe engagement was fought by our troops under General Wallace, re-enforced by a part of the Sixth Corps under General Ricketts. After this battle the enemy continued to advance until they reached the intrenchments around Washington. Here they were met by troops from the Army of the Potomac, consisting of the Sixth Corps, under General Wright, a part of the Eighth Corps, under General Gillmore, and a part of the Nineteenth Corps, just arrived from New Orleans, under General Emory. By these troops the enemy were driven back from Washington and retreated hastily to Virginia, pursued by our forces under General Wright.

On the 7th day of August, 1864, General Sheridan was placed in command of the military division comprising the Department of Washington, the Department of West Virginia, the Department of the Susquehanna, and the Middle Department. In two great battles—at the crossing of the Opequon on the 19th of September, and at Fisher's Hill on the 22d of September—the rebel army under Early was routed and driven from the Valley with immense loss of prisoners, artillery, and stores. A desperate effort was made by the enemy to recover their position. Early was strongly re-enforced, and on the morning of the 19th of October, in the absence of General Sheridan, his lines were surprised, his position turned, and his forces driven back in confusion. At the moment when a great disaster was impending Sheridan appeared upon the field, the battle was restored, and a brilliant victory achieved. The routed forces of the enemy were pursued to Mount Jackson, where he arrived without an organized regiment of his army. All his artillery and thousands of prisoners fell into Sheridan's hands. These successes closed military operations in the Shenandoah Valley, and a rebel force appeared there no more during the war.

Maj. Gen. William T. Sherman began the brilliant series of his campaigns early in May. The first objective point was Atlanta. To reach that city his armies must pass from the northern limit to the center of the great State of Georgia, forcing their way through mountain defiles and across great rivers, overcoming or turning formidable intrenched positions defended by a strong, well-appointed veteran army, commanded by an alert, cautious, and skillful general. The campaign opened on the 6th day of May, and on the 2d day of September the national forces entered Atlanta. This achievement is thus described in General Sherman's Field Orders, No. 68:

On the 1st of May our armies were lying in garrison, seemingly quiet, from Knoxville to Huntsville, and our enemy lay behind his rocky-faced barrier at Dalton, proud, defiant, and exulting. He had had time since Christmas to recover from his discomfiture on the Mission Ridge, with his ranks filled, and a new commander-in-chief, and second to none in the Confederacy in reputation for skill, sagacity, and extreme popularity. All at once our armies assumed life and action and appeared before Dalton. Threatening Rocky Face, we threw ourselves upon Resaca, and the rebel army only escaped by the rapidity of its retreat, aided by the numerous roads, with which he was familiar, and which were strange to us. Again he took post in Allatoona, but we gave him no rest, and by our circuit toward Dallas and subsequent movement to Acworth, we gained the Allatoona Pass. Then followed the eventful battles about Kenesaw, and the escape of the enemy across the Chattahoochee River.

The crossing of the Chattahoochee and breaking of the Augusta road was most handsomely executed by us, and will be studied as an example in the art of war. At this stage of our game our enemies became dissatisfied with their old and skillful commander, and selected one more bold and rash. New tactics were adopted. Hood first boldly and rapidly, on the 20th of July, fell on our right at Peach Tree Creek and lost. Again, on the 22d, he struck our extreme left, and was severely punished; and finally, again on the 28th, he repeated the attempt on our right, and that time must have become satisfied, for since that date he has remained on the defensive. We slowly and gradually drew our lines about Atlanta, feeling for the railroad which supplied the rebel army and made Atlanta a place of importance.

We must concede to our enemy that he met these efforts patiently and skillfully, but at last he made the mistake we had waited for so long, and sent his cavalry to our rear, far beyond the reach of recall. Instantly our cavalry was on his only remaining road, and we followed quickly with our principal army, and Atlanta fell into our possession as the fruit of well-concerted measures, backed by a brave and confident army.

For military reasons, stated in the report of the lieutenant-general,* it was determined that Atlanta should be destroyed and Sherman's armies push forward to Savannah or some other point on the Atlantic Coast.

Shortly before the fall of Atlanta, General Johnston had been superseded in command of the rebel army by General Hood, who, adopting a different system from that pursued by his cautious predecessor, boldly assumed the offensive, with a view to force General Sherman from Georgia by cutting off his communications and invading Tennessee and Kentucky. Pursuant to this plan, Hood, by a rapid march, gained and broke up at Big Shanty the railroad that supplied Sherman's army, advanced to Dalton, and thence moved toward Tennessee. Hood was followed from Atlanta by General Sherman far enough north to cover his own purpose and assure him against Hood's interrupting the contemplated march to the sea-coast. Sherman turned back suddenly to Atlanta. That city and all the railroads leading to it were destroyed, and on the 15th of November the march commenced for Savannah. Advancing in three columns, and living upon the country, the capital of the State and other large towns were occupied without resistance. General Sherman's command on the 10th of December "closed in on the enemy's works which covered Savannah." Fort McAllister was gallantly carried by assault on the same day.† The city of Savannah, strongly fortified and garrisoned by a large force under General Hardee, was summoned, but surrender was refused. Preparations for assault were made, and in the night of the 20th of December Hardee evacuated the city, and with a large part of his garrison escaped under cover of darkness. The U. S. troops entered the city early in the morning of the 21st of December. Immense quantities of arms, ammunition, ordnance, and military stores were captured, and the cotton that fell into our hands amounted in value to many millions of dollars.

While General Sherman's army was marching south from Atlanta to the sea-coast the rebel army under Hood, strongly re-enforced, was moving north, threatening Tennessee. The task of encountering this formidable foe and defending the border States from invasion was intrusted to Maj. Gen. George H. Thomas, who was ably assisted by his second in command, Major-General Schofield. In his report General Thomas says:

I found myself confronted by the army which, under General J. E. Johnston, had so skillfully resisted the advance of the whole active army of the Military Division of the Mississippi from Dalton to the Chattahoochee, re-enforced by a well-equipped and enthusiastic cavalry command of over 12,000 men, led by one of the boldest and most successful cavalry commanders in the rebel army. My information from all sources confirmed the reported strength stated of Hood's army to be from 40,000 to 45,000 infantry and from 12,000 to 15,000 cavalry. My effective force at this time consisted of the Fourth Corps, about 12,000, under Maj. Gen. D. S. Stanley; the Twenty-third Corps, about 10,000, under Major-General Schofield; Hatch's division of cavalry, about 4,000; Croxton's brigade, 2,500; and Capron's brigade, of about 1,200. The balance of my force was distributed along the railroad and posted at Murfreesborough, Stevenson, Bridgeport, Huntsville, Decatur, and Chattanooga, to keep open our communications and hold the posts above named if attacked until they could be re-enforced, as up to this time it was impossible to determine which course Hood would take—advance on Nashville or turn toward Huntsville. Under these circumstances it was manifestly best to act on the defensive until sufficiently re-enforced to justify taking the offensive. On the 12th of November communication with General Sherman was severed, the last dispatch from him leaving Cartersville, Ga., at 2.25 p. m. on that

---

* See Series I, Vol. XXXVIII, Part I, p. 1.

† McAllister fell December 13, 1864.

date. He had started on his great expedition from Atlanta to the sea-board, leaving me to guard Tennessee or to pursue the enemy if he followed the commanding general's column. It was therefore with considerable anxiety that we watched the force at Florence to discover what course they would pursue with regard to General Sherman's movements, determining thereby whether the troops under my command, numbering less than half those under Hood, were to act on the defensive in Tennessee or take the offensive in Alabama.

When the possibility of Hood following Sherman was over, General Thomas took measures to act on the defensive. Re-enforcements of new regiments were hurried forward to him by the Governors of the Western States. All troops fit for any military duty were collected and sent forward from the hospitals, absentees on leave were called in, the employés in the quartermaster's department were armed and organized for duty in the intrenchments, and two divisions of veteran infantry, under command of General A. J. Smith, that had been serving on the Red River and afterward in Missouri, were pushed forward to General Thomas. By these means his forces were speedily swelled, when concentrated, to an army nearly as large as that of the enemy. The public property and garrisons were drawn in from exposed positions and points not required to be held, the fortifications of Nashville were strengthened, and every preparation was made for a struggle of no ordinary magnitude. Hood advanced to Columbia, where his attempt to cross Duck Creek was checked for a while by General Schofield, who repulsed the enemy many times with heavy loss. Schofield's main force in front of Columbia was withdrawn on the night of the 29th of November and a position taken at Franklin on the morning of the 30th. Here took place one of the most fierce and bloody battles of the war. "The enemy," says General Thomas in his report, "followed closely after General Schofield's rear guard in the retreat to Franklin, and upon coming up with the main force, formed rapidly and advanced to assault our works, repeating attack after attack during the entire afternoon, and as late as 10 p. m. his efforts to break our lines were continued. General Schofield's position was excellently chosen, with both flanks resting on the river, and his men firmly held their ground against an overwhelming enemy, who was repulsed in every assault along the whole line. Our loss, as given by General Schofield in his report,* transmitted herewith (and to which I respectfully refer), is 189 killed, 1,033 wounded, and 1,104 missing, making an aggregate of 2,326. We captured and sent to Nashville 702 prisoners, including 1 general officer and 33 stand of colors. Maj. Gen. D. S. Stanley, commanding Fourth Corps, was severely wounded at Franklin while engaged in rallying a portion of his command which had been temporarily overpowered by an overwhelming attack of the enemy. At the time of the battle the enemy's loss was known to be severe, and was estimated at 5,000. The exact figures were only obtained, however, on the reoccupation of Franklin by our forces, after the battles of December 15 and 16 at Brentwood Hills, near Nashville, and are given as follows: Buried upon the field, 1,750; disabled and placed in hospital at Franklin, 3,800, which, with the 702 prisoners already reported, makes an aggregate loss of 6,252, among whom were 6 general officers killed, 6 wounded, and 1 captured. The important results of this signal victory cannot be too highly appreciated, for it not only seriously checked the enemy's advance, and gave General Schofield time to remove his troops and all his property to Nashville, but it also caused deep depression among the men of Hood's army, making them doubly cautious in their subsequent movements."

---

*See Series I, Vol. XLV, Part I, p. 339.

On the night after the battle of Franklin General Schofield, by the direction of General Thomas, fell back to Nashville, in front of which city, on the heights, a line of battle was formed by noon of the 1st of December. Hood's army appeared before Nashville on the 2d of December. The intense severity of the weather prevented operations for several days. Both armies were icebound for a week previous to the 14th of December, when the weather moderated, and General Thomas, having completed his preparations, issued orders for battle the ensuing day. At an early hour on the morning of the 15th of December General Thomas moved against Hood's army. The battle was furiously contested until nightfall.

The total result was the capture of 16 pieces of artillery and 1,200 prisoners, besides several hundred stand of small-arms and about forty wagons. The enemy had been forced back at all points with heavy loss, and our casualties were unusually light. The behavior of the troops was unsurpassed for steadiness and alacrity in every movement, and the original plan of battle, with but few alterations, was strictly adhered to. The whole command bivouacked in line of battle during the night on the ground occupied at dark, while preparations were made to renew the battle at an early hour on the morrow.

The battle was renewed on the 16th at 6 o'clock in the morning. A 3 o'clock in the afternoon the enemy's strong position on Overton's Hill was assaulted by the Fourth Corps.

Immediately following the effort of the Fourth Corps, Generals Smith's and Schofield's commands moved against the enemy's works in their respective fronts, carrying all before them, irreparably breaking his lines in a dozen places, and capturing all his artillery and thousands of prisoners, among the latter four general officers. Our loss was remarkably small, scarcely mentionable. All of the enemy that did escape were pursued over the tops of Brentwood and Harpeth Hills. General Wilson's cavalry, dismounted, attacked the enemy simultaneously with Schofield and Smith, striking him in reverse, and, gaining firm possession of Granny White pike, cut off his retreat by that route. Wood's and Steedman's troops, hearing the shouts of victory coming from the right, rushed impetuously forward, renewing the assault on Overton's Hill, and, although meeting a very heavy fire, the onset was irresistible, artillery and innumerable prisoners falling into our hands. The enemy, hopelessly broken, fled in confusion through the Brentwood Pass, the Fourth Corps in a close pursuit, which was continued for several miles, when darkness closed the scene and the troops rested from their labors. * * * During the two days' operations there were 4,462 prisoners captured, including 287 officers of all grades from that of major-general, 53 pieces of artillery, and thousands of small-arms. The enemy abandoned on the field all of his dead and wounded.

At the battle of Nashville Hood's army, which at one time was considered the best drilled and most formidable rebel force set on foot during the war, disappeared as an army organization. Commanded successively by Bragg, Johnston, and Hood, many bloody fields proved the courage of the soldiers and the skill of its commanders. The shattered fragments of this army were pursued from Nashville to the Tennessee River by the main forces of General Thomas, and were followed and harassed for 200 miles by detached commands. In his report General Thomas remarks:

To Colonel Palmer and his command is accorded the credit of giving Hood's army the last blow of the campaign, at a distance of over 200 miles from where we first struck the enemy on the 15th of December, near Nashville.

What troops escaped from the pursuit were afterward united with other fragments of rebel forces under General Johnston, and finally laid down their arms to General Sherman at Raleigh.

While the events that have been mentioned were transpiring in the main armies, other military operations of less magnitude, but contributing to the general result by harassing and weakening the enemy, were in progress. A large rebel force under John Morgan invaded Kentucky and was defeated by General Burbridge in a severe engagement at Cynthiana on the 12th day of June. John Morgan was surprised and killed, and his staff captured by General Gillem on the 4th day of September, 1864. In the month of November a rebel expedition under Breckinridge, Duke, and Vaughn was repulsed by General Ammen and driven from East Tennessee. An expedition under General Stoneman and General Burbridge penetrated to Saltville, in Southwestern Virginia, destroyed the works at that place, broke up the railroads, and inflicted great destruction upon the enemy's supplies and communications.

After the withdrawal of our troops from the Red River a large rebel force advanced under Sterling Price into Kansas, and penetrated thence into the Department of the Missouri; but they were at length driven back with heavy loss.

Other military operations of greater or less magnitude occurred during the year, some attended with disaster, some with brilliant success. Of the former class were Kilpatrick's raid against Richmond; the capture of Plymouth and its garrison at the commencement of the year by the rebels under Hoke; the defeat of the expedition from Memphis under General Sturgis; the capture of Fort Pillow by Chalmers and Forrest, and Stoneman's expedition to Andersonville. On the other hand, the raids of Grierson from Memphis in December, of Stoneman and Burbridge into Virginia, of Wilson into Alabama, inflicted sore distress upon the enemy, and brought the rebels to a solemn sense of the sufferings caused to themselves by the war they had undertaken against their Government.

At the commencement of the year 1865 all hearts were more anxious than ever to bring the war to a speedy close. Every preparation to that end was made by the Department and by the military commanders in the field. Adequate appropriations were voted and new popular loans authorized by Congress. Further measures for recruiting the Army, prompted by experience, were enacted. A new draft for half a million of men was put into prompt execution. The State executives renewed their labors in calling for volunteers. The people responded to the demands of the occasion, and rapid recruitment began in all the States, and was at its height when Richmond fell. Troops were at that time being raised, organized, armed, and equipped as fast as they could be conveniently transported to the field. To the coming campaigns through the Carolinas and in Virginia all eyes looked for a speedy and decisive result that should end the war. The military position is thus stated by the lieutenant-general:

> In March, 1865, General Canby was moving an adequate force against Mobile and the army defending it under General Dick Taylor; Thomas was pushing out two large and well-appointed cavalry expeditions—one from Middle Tennessee, under Brevet Major-General Wilson, against the enemy's vital points in Alabama; the other from East Tennessee, under Major-General Stoneman, toward Lynchburg—and assembling the remainder of his available forces preparatory to offensive operations from East Tennessee; General Sheridan's cavalry was at White House; the Armies of the Potomac and James were confronting the enemy under Lee in his defenses of Richmond and Petersburg; General Sherman, with his armies re-enforced by that of General Schofield, was at Goldsborough; General Pope was making preparations for a spring campaign against the enemy under Kirby Smith and Price west of the Mississippi, and General Hancock was concentrating a force in the vicinity of Winchester, Va., to guard against invasion, or to operate offensively, as might prove necessary.

Official reports show that on the 1st of March, 1865, the aggregate national military force of all arms, officers and men, was 965,591, to wit:

Available force present for duty*	602,598
On detached service in the different military departments	132,538
In field hospitals or unfit for duty	35,628
In general hospitals or on sick-leave at home	143,419
Absent on furlough or as prisoners of war	31,695
Absent without leave	19,683
Grand aggregate	965,591

This force was augmented on the 1st of May, 1865, by enlistments to the number of 1,000,516 of all arms, officers and men.†

The aggregate available force present for duty on the 1st of March was distributed in the different commands as follows:

Army of the Potomac	103,273
Headquarters Military Division of the Mississippi	17
Department of the Cumberland	62,626
Department of the Tennessee	45,649
Left Wing, Army of Georgia	31,644
Cavalry Corps, Military Division of the Mississippi	27,410
Headquarters Military Division of West Mississippi	24
Reserve brigades, Military Division of West Mississippi	13,748
Department of the Gulf	35,625
Department of Arkansas	24,509
Department of Mississippi	24,151
Sixteenth Army Corps	14,395
Headquarters Military Division of the Missouri	12
Department of the Missouri	18,557
Department of the Northwest	4,731
Headquarters Middle Military Division	841
Cavalry forces, Middle Military Division	12,980
Nineteenth Army Corps	6,612
Middle Department	2,089
Department of Washington	26,056
Department of West Virginia	15,517
Department of Pennsylvania	820
Department of the East	7,462
Department of Virginia	45,986
Department of North Carolina	34,945
Department of the South	11,510
Department of Kentucky	10,655
Northern Department	11,229
Department of the Pacific	7,024
Department of New Mexico	2,501
Grand total	602,598

The active operations of 1865 began with the reduction of Fort Fisher by a combined expedition of land and naval forces. The port of Wilmington, N. C., during the whole war had been a principal point of foreign trade with the rebels. The advantage of its position defied the most rigorous blockade, and after the fall of Savannah it was the only gate through which foreign supplies could pass to the rebels. The strong works and garrison of Fort Fisher, at the mouth of Cape Fear River, were the main defense of Wilmington. On the 13th of December a force of about 6,500 men under Major-General Butler started from Fortress Monroe to operate in conjunction with a naval force under Admiral Porter against Fort Fisher. General Butler effected a landing on the 25th of December, but re-embarked on the 27th and returned with his troops to Fortress Monroe. The

* But see explanatory foot-note, p. 137.

† But see a later official compilation for April 30, 1865, Vol. IV, this series, p. 1283.

lieutenant-general ordered the enterprise to be renewed by General Terry, who, on the 2d of January, was placed in command of the same troops, with a re-enforcement that made the whole number about 8,000. On the morning of the 13th of January the troops were disembarked, under cover of a heavy effective fire from the fleet. An assault was made in the afternoon of the 15th of January, and, after desperate hand-to-hand fighting for several hours, the works were carried, the enemy driven out, and about midnight the whole garrision, with its commander, General Whiting, surrendered. The fall of Fort Fisher carried with it the other defenses of Cape Fear River. Fort Caswell and the works on Smith's Island fell into our hands on the 16th and 17th, Fort Anderson on the 19th, and, General Schofield advancing, the enemy were driven from Wilmington on the 21st of February.

Early in the month of January Major-General Sherman, having refitted his army, entered upon his campaign from Savannah through the States of South Carolina and North Carolina, the incidents of which are detailed in his accompanying report.* Its result is thus stated in his Special Field Orders, No. 76:

> Waiting at Savannah only long enough to fill our wagons, we again began a march, which, for peril, labor, and results, will compare with any ever made by an organized army. The floods of the Savannah, the swamps of the Combahee and Edisto, the "high hills" and rocks of the Santee, the flat quagmires of the Pedee and Cape Fear Rivers, were all passed in midwinter, with its floods and rains, in the face of an accumulating enemy; and, after the battles of Averasborough and Bentonville, we once more came out of the wilderness to meet our friends at Goldsborough. Even then we paused only long enough to get new clothing, to reload our wagons, and again pushed on to Raleigh and beyond, until we met our enemy suing for peace instead of war, and offering to submit to the injured laws of his and our country.

The operations in General Canby's military division also exercised an important influence at this juncture. After the disaster upon the Red River a change of the military organization west of the Mississippi was made to meet the emergency. The Departments of Arkansas and the Gulf, including Louisiana and Texas, were united in one military division—West Mississippi, under command of Major-General Canby. His efforts were directed to the organization and concentration of the forces and material within his division, and in measures to prevent the rebel troops west of the Mississippi from re-enforcing the armies operating east of that river. In the month of July [August] Fort Gaines, Fort Powell, and Fort Morgan, constituting important defenses of Mobile Bay, were reduced by a combined movement of land forces under General Gordon Granger, detached by General Canby and co-operating with a naval force under Admiral Farragut. Early in the spring of 1865 a large force under Generals A. J. Smith, Gordon Granger, and F. Steele was directed against the city of Mobile. The enemy were driven out of Spanish Fort by bombardment, Fort Blakely was taken by assault, and the city of Mobile was evacuated by the enemy on the 12th of April. The brilliance of these achievements has been overshadowed by the grander scale of operations in other quarters, but their skill and success are worthy of high admiration. After the fall of Savannah, Charleston, and Wilmington the enemy had placed his last hopes on retaining a foothold in the cotton States at Mobile. It was strongly fortified and garrisoned, and orders were issued to hold it at every hazard.

---

*See Series I, Vol. XLVII, Part I, p. 17.

In the latter part of February General Sheridan, under direction of the lieutenant-general, moved from Winchester to Staunton, which place he captured on the 2d of March, taking prisoners, artillery, and military stores. He thence moved on Charlottesville and destroyed the Richmond and Lynchburg Railroad and the bridges across the Rivanna River. Dividing his forces, one column moved to New Market and destroyed the James River Canal; the other column pushed toward Lynchburg, destroying the railroad to Amherst Court-House. These columns, reuniting, moved to the White House, on the Pamunkey, effecting great destruction of the canal on their route, and thence put themselves in communication with the forces around Richmond.

The month of March, 1865, opened the great campaign against Richmond and the army that had so long defended the rebel capital.

Instructions were given by the lieutenant-general on the 24th of March for a general movement of the national forces around Richmond. It commenced on the morning of the 29th of March. Ten days' marching and fighting finished the campaign. Richmond, Petersburg, the Army of Virginia and its commander were captured. Jefferson Davis and his so-called Confederate Government were fugitives or prisoners of war. Davis fled from Richmond on the afternoon of Sunday, the 2d day of April. The national forces occupied Petersburg and entered Richmond Monday morning. Lee's army was pursued until it reached Appomattox Court-House, where on Sunday, the 9th day of April, it laid down its arms on the terms prescribed by General Grant.

From this period the history of the war is but an enumeration of successive surrenders by rebel commanders. On the 26th day of April General Johnston surrendered his command to Major-General Sherman at Raleigh, N. C. General Howell Cobb, with 1,200 militia and five generals, surrendered to General Wilson at Macon, Ga., on the 20th of April. General Dick Taylor, on the 14th [4th] of May, surrendered all the remaining rebel forces east of the Mississippi to General Canby. On the 11th [10th] of May Jefferson Davis, disguised and in flight, was captured at Irwinville, Ga. On the 26th of May General Kirby Smith surrendered his entire command west of the Mississippi to Major-General Canby. With this surrender the organized rebel force disappeared from the territory of the United States. The flag of the United States was lowered at Fort Sumter on the 14th of April, 1861, by Major Anderson, who, long besieged by overwhelming rebel forces, was compelled, with his small garrison, to evacuate the works. On the anniversary of that day, four years later, the rebel forces having been driven from Charleston, the national banner was planted again upon Fort Sumter, under the orders of the President by the hands of General Anderson, with appropriate military and naval ceremonies, and a commemorative address delivered by the Rev. Henry Ward Beecher.

Their victorious campaigns ended, the Armies of the Tennessee and the Cumberland and the Army of the Potomac marched through Richmond to the Federal capital, where they were reviewed by the President and the distinguished commanders under whom they had so long and so gallantly served in the field. After this national ceremony they and their fellow-soldiers in other commands were paid, and, as rapidly as the condition of affairs would admit, were released from the military service of the country; and, returning to their homes in the several States, they were welcomed with the thanks and rejoicings of a grateful people.

One other event may properly be noticed in this report as a part of the military history of the rebellion. While our armies, by their gallantry and courage and the skill of their commanders, were overcoming all resistance in the field to the national authority, a swift and sudden blow was aimed at the national existence and at the life of the Commander-in-Chief of the Army and Navy, which, for atrocity in its circumstances, the cruel art that designed it, and the peril to which it exposed the Government, is unsurpassed in the history of nations. Shortly before the Richmond campaign opened President Lincoln went to the headquarters of Lieutenant-General Grant at City Point, where he remained until the capture of Petersburg and Richmond. After their occupation by our forces he visited those cities, and returned to Washington on the evening of Sunday, the 9th day of April. The dispatch of the lieutenant-general announcing General Lee's surrender was communicated to him about 11 o'clock Sunday night. From that time until he was assassinated his attention was earnestly directed to the restoration of peace and the reorganization of civil government in the insurgent States. In a public address to an assemblage that met at the Executive Mansion on the evening of Wednesday, the 12th of April, to congratulate him on the success of our arms, his views and some of his measures were explained. On the night of the following Friday the President was shot by an assassin, and expired at about 7 o'clock on the morning of Saturday, the 15th of April. This assassination appeared to be part of a deliberate, comprehensive conspiracy to assassinate the President, Vice-President, Secretary of State, lieutenant-general, and other officers of the Government, with a view to its disorganization. About the same hour of the President's murder an effort was made to assassinate the Secretary of State, who was then confined to his bed by serious injuries accidentally received a few days before. He and other members of his family were dangerously wounded. Some of the parties engaged in this conspiracy were tried, convicted, and executed; others are still under sentence of imprisonment for life. The details are given in the report of the Judge-Advocate-General.* The designs upon the Vice-President and the lieutenant-general failed; and upon the death of the President the Vice-President was sworn into office and assumed the duties of President of the United States. These events were promptly communicated to the armies by general orders, and from thenceforth until the present time the Government has been administered by Andrew Johnson as Chief Executive and Commander-in-Chief of the Army and Navy.

The destruction of the rebel military power opened the way to re-establish civil government in the insurgent States. From that period the functions of the military department became simply co-operative with other branches of the Federal Government.

Nashville, Tenn., was the first capital of an insurgent State in which the Federal authority was re-established. The rebel army was driven out on the 23d day of February, 1862, and that city occupied by the Union forces. On the 3d day of March, 1862, Andrew Johnson, then Senator in Congress from the State of Tennessee—the only Senator from an insurgent State who retained his seat in Congress—was appointed Military Governor of the State of Tennessee. He accepted the appointment, and promptly entered upon his duties, and continued to exercise them until his resignation on the 3d day of March, 1865. In all the vicissitudes of the war his administration was

---

*See p. 490.

directed to the establishment and maintenance of the Constitution and laws of the United States within and over the State of Tennessee. Without entering upon details it is sufficient to remark that extension of civil authority kept pace with the reduction of the rebel power. The Federal courts were opened and justice administered. Under his direction, against many discouragements and much opposition, great advance was made toward the full re-establishment of civil authority and the restoration of the State to its practical relations to the Federal Government. He issued a proclamation on the 6th of January, 1864, for the election of township and county officers, justices of the peace, constables, trustees, sheriffs, clerks, registers, and tax collectors. In the month of May a convention was held at Knoxville, East Tenn., to devise measures for restoring civil government in the State. In the month of August another convention was called to meet at Nashville on the 5th of September to reorganize the State. A full convention being prevented by the condition of military affairs, this body recommended that another convention, "elected by the loyal people," should assemble at an early day to revise the State constitution. The Governor issued a proclamation on the 7th of September announcing that he should proceed to appoint officers and establish tribunals "in all the counties and districts of the State whenever the people gave evidence of loyalty and a desire for civil government, and a willingness to sustain the officers and tribunals." A convention was called to meet on the 9th of January, 1865, at Nashville, to revise the State constitution. This convention met, amendments to the State constitution were adopted, slavery was abolished, and provision made for submitting the amendments to the people and for holding elections. The amendments were ratified by popular vote. A Governor, Legislature, and members of Congress were subsequently (on the 4th of March) elected by the people. The Legislature assembled on the first Monday of April; the abolition of slavery was enacted, Senators to Congress elected, and a State government was fully organized, and has since continued in action. This system of reorganization having been found practicable by actual experience, it was adopted by the President, with such modifications as he deemed proper, for all the insurgent States, and is now in course of execution.

The disposition exhibited after the surrender of their armies in all the insurgent States to submit to the national authority dispensed with the necessity of keeping large armies on foot, and indicated the degree to which the war power might be reduced. So much only of the national military force has been kept in each State as is needed to keep the peace, protect the public property, and enforce the laws.

It was apparent that by the surrender of General Lee and his army the military power on which alone the rebellion rested was irretrievably broken, no doubt being entertained that Lee's surrender would be followed by that of Johnston, and perhaps all other commanders of the insurgent forces. The attention of the Department was immediately directed to the following objects, and on the 13th of April, four days after Lee's surrender, public notice was given that orders would be speedily issued to carry them into effect, viz:

First. To stop all drafting and recruiting in the loyal States.

Second. To curtail purchases of arms, ammunition, quartermaster and commissary supplies, and reduce the expenses of the military establishment in the several branches.

Third. To reduce the number of general and staff officers to the actual necessities of the service.

Fourth. To remove all military restrictions upon trade and commerce, so far as might be consistent with the public safety.

These measures have been carried into effect from time to time, as the exigencies of the service would admit. It will be seen from the report of the Adjutant-General that troops to the number of 800,963 have already been mustered, paid off, and disbanded. Further reduction is contemplated. Upon the discharge of troops the services of a great number of staff, field, and general officers were no longer required. Of these some have resigned, and others were honorably mustered out. No doubt in many instances it has been painful for gallant and accomplished officers to leave that service to which they have been accustomed, and where they have won honorable distinction. But it is to the credit of the volunteer service that they have recognized the obligation of the Government to reduce the military establishment with the occasion that called it into existence, and that their own wishes or interest have not been importunately urged against the necessities of the service.

The disposition of the Veteran Reserve Corps presented some considerations of peculiar nature. It was the inclination of the Department to retain it in service until the meeting of Congress. But inquiry showed that a very small per cent. of enlisted men were content to remain in service. All who desired have therefore been discharged, and supernumerary officers mustered out.

Recruiting to fill the regular regiments has continued. Several thousand applications for commissions in the regular service are on file. These commissions, hitherto, have been conferred only by promotion from the ranks. But to secure the requisite number of competent officers a board has been appointed to examine applicants and determine their relative merit. From the list selected by the Board, and in the order of merit, appointments are to be made. Two years' actual service in the war is indispensable for appointment.

The establishment of a well organized militia system is one of the most important subjects that will demand the attention of Congress. This subject has already received careful consideration, and it is believed that after conference with the appropriate committees a practical system may be agreed upon.

Measures for the establishment of homes, and some provision for the aid and relief of wounded and disabled soldiers, is also a subject that will commend itself strongly to every patriotic heart. Whether this duty, which the country owes to patriots who have suffered in the national defense can best be performed by the National Government or administered by the respective State authorities, and whether relief can best be afforded by an increase of pension, or by establishing homes, are points on which opinions differ, and which can only be settled by the wisdom of Congress.

The Board of Visitors to the Military Academy at West Point, in June last, made an elaborate report, which is herewith submitted.* They recommend a reorganization, and a number of measures which, in their opinion, will enhance the benefits of that national institution. To these the attention of Congress is respectfully invited, with the recommendation that the number of cadets be increased, as recommended, and that the superintendence of the institution be no longer confined to the Engineer Bureau. It is believed that the Military Academy is at present well conducted, and that their responsible

*Omitted.

duties are efficiently performed by the officers, professors, and instructors charged with the instruction.

The war appropriations at the last session of Congress, as has been stated, amounted to the sum of $516,240,131.70. The estimates for the next fiscal year, commencing June 30, 1866, are $33,814,461.83.

These estimates are based upon a standing force of 50,000 men, so organized as to admit of an increase, without additional organizations, to 82,600 troops of all arms.

This estimate has been made after conference and careful consideration, and is believed to be adequate for any national exigency, if the country should be blessed with peace. The reduction of the national military force in its rapidity and numbers is without example, and if there be any alarm in the public mind because this reduction is made while grave questions at home and abroad are unsettled, a brief consideration of the subject will show that there is no cause for apprehension.

The force to be retained is small compared with that which was organized to subdue the rebellion. But the only reasons demanding greater force are: First, renewal of the insurrection; second, a foreign war. For either or both emergencies the national resources remain ample. The chief demands for war, as shown by our experience, are: First, troops; second, arms and ammunition; third, clothing; fourth, transportation; and fifth, subsistence supplies.

The troops disbanded were chiefly volunteers, who went to the field to uphold the system of free government established by their fathers and which they mean to bequeath to their children. Their toils and sufferings, their marches, battles, and victories have not diminished the value of that government to them; so that any new rebellion would encounter equal or greater force for its reduction; and none can ever spring up with such advantages at the start or be conducted with superior means, ability, or prospect of success. A foreign war would intensify the national feeling, and thousands, once misled, would rejoice to atone their error by rallying to the national flag. The question of time in which armies could be raised to quell insurrection or repel invasion is therefore the only question relating to troops. Our experience on this point is significant. When Lee's army surrendered thousands of recruits were pouring in, and men were discharged from recruiting stations and rendezvous in every State. On several occasions, when troops were promptly needed to avert impending disaster, vigorous exertion brought them into the field from remote States with incredible speed. Official reports show that after the disasters on the Peninsula, in 1862, over 80,000 troops were enlisted, organized, armed, equipped, and sent into the field in less than a month. Sixty thousand troops have repeatedly gone to the field within four weeks. And 90,000 infantry were sent to the armies from the five States of Ohio, Indiana, Illinois, Iowa, and Wisconsin within twenty days.

When the rebellion commenced the Nation was a stranger to war. Officers had little experience, privates had none. But the present generation of men in this country are now veteran soldiers. For the battle, the march, or the siege, they are already trained. They are as much at home in the tented field as in the farm-house, the manufactory, or the shop. No time is required to train them; and the speed of the railroad and telegraph determines the time required to raise an army in the United States.

Second. As to arms and ammunition. The disbanded armies were allowed to take home their arms at a nominal price. Rust is not likely to gather on the musket or saber borne through the campaigns of 1864 and 1865. The Government retains in its arsenals more than a million of the best quality of arms and equipments. The artillery on hand tasks the Department for its means of storage. The manufacture of ammunition requires materials for which we have in some degree relied upon other countries, because they could be had cheaper. For this reason, and to guard against any mischance, three years' stock of material for ammunition has always been kept in store, and the supply on hand is ample for any war that can be waged against us by any nation.

Third. Clothing, transportation, and subsistence. After selling or distributing among freedmen and refugees all damaged or irregular clothing, the stock of clothing and material in the quartermaster's depots is sufficient for any armies that may be called into service. The water transports and rolling-stock, mules, wagons, and horses held by the Government were adequate to the movement and supply of larger forces, in less time, than had heretofore been known in war. The Government has disposed or is disposing of this transportation, but it remains in this country, and can answer any exigency.

Army subsistence is derived from the country in which military operations are carried on or supplied from other markets. During the war this most vital branch of the service never failed. It answers to the demand, and is ever ready to meet the national call.

It is plain, therefore, that the abundance of our means for war enables the Government of the United States to reduce the standing force to a lower degree than any other nation. Unless war be actually raging, the military force can be brought within very narrow limits. However sudden the exigency calling for an exhibition of military power, it can be promptly met. With our education, habits, and experience, the Nation, while in the midst of peace, is prepared for war.

The present military organization comprehends nineteen departments, embraced in five military divisions, as follows:

1. The Department of the East, Maj. Gen. Joseph Hooker to command, to embrace the New England States, New York, and New Jersey. Headquarters at New York City.

2. The Middle Department, Maj. Gen. W. S. Hancock to command, to embrace the States of West Virginia, Maryland (excepting the counties of Montgomery, that part of Anne Arundel lying south of the Annapolis and Elk Ridge Railroad, and excluding the city of Annapolis, Prince George's, Calvert, Charles, and Saint Mary's), the county of Loudoun, and the Shenandoah Valley as far south as and including Rockingham County, in Virginia, the States of Delaware and Pennsylvania. Headquarters at Baltimore.

3. The Department of Washington, Maj. Gen. C. C. Augur to command, to embrace the District of Columbia, the counties of Montgomery, that part of Anne Arundel lying south of the Annapolis and Elk Ridge Railroad, and including the city of Annapolis, Prince George's, Calvert, Charles, and Saint Mary's, in Maryland, and Alexandria and Fairfax Counties, in Virginia. Headquarters at Washington.

4. The Department of the Ohio, Maj. Gen. E. O. C. Ord to command, to embrace the States of Ohio, Indiana, Illinois, Wisconsin, and Michigan. Headquarters at Detroit.

5. The Department of the Tennessee, Maj. Gen. George Stoneman to command, to embrace the State of Tennessee. Headquarters at Knoxville.

6. The Department of Kentucky, Maj. Gen. John M. Palmer to command, to embrace the State of Kentucky and Jeffersonville and New Albany, in Indiana. Headquarters at Louisville.

7. The Department of the Missouri, Maj. Gen. John Pope to command, to embrace the States of Minnesota, Iowa, Missouri, and Kansas, and the Territories of Colorado, Utah, Nebraska, Dakota, New Mexico, and Montana. Headquarters at Saint Louis.

8. The Department of Virginia, Maj. Gen. Alfred H. Terry to command, to embrace the State of Virginia, excepting Alexandria, Fairfax, and Loudoun Counties and the Shenandoah Valley as far south as and including Rockingham County. Headquarters at Richmond.

9. The Department of North Carolina, Maj. Gen. J. M. Schofield to command, to embrace the State of North Carolina. Headquarters at Raleigh.

10. The Department of South Carolina, Maj. Gen. Daniel Sickles to command, to embrace the State of South Carolina. Headquarters at Charleston.

11. The Department of Georgia, Maj. Gen. James B. Steedman to command, to embrace the State of Georgia. Headquarters at Augusta.

12. The Department of Florida, Maj. Gen. John G. Foster to command, to embrace the State of Florida. Headquarters at Tallahassee.

13. The Department of Mississippi, Maj. Gen. Thomas J. Wood to command, to embrace the State of Mississippi. Headquarters at Vicksburg.

14. The Department of Alabama, Maj. Gen. C. R. Woods to command, to embrace the State of Alabama. Headquarters at Mobile.

15. The Department of Louisiana, Maj. Gen. E. R. S. Canby to command, to embrace the State of Louisiana. Headquarters at New Orleans.

16. The Department of Texas, Maj. Gen. H. G. Wright to command, to embrace the State of Texas. Headquarters at Galveston.

17. The Department of Arkansas, Maj. Gen. J. J. Reynolds to command, to embrace the State of Arkansas and the Indian Territory. Headquarters at Little Rock.

18. The Department of the Columbia, Maj. Gen. F. Steele to command, to embrace the State of Oregon and the Territories of Washington and Idaho. Headquarters at Fort Vancouver.

19. The Department of California, Maj. Gen. Irvin McDowell to command, to embrace the States of California and Nevada, and Territories of New Mexico and Arizona. Headquarters at San Francisco.

1. The Military Division of the Atlantic, Maj. Gen. George G. Meade to command, to embrace the Department of the East, Middle Department, Department of Virginia, Department of North Carolina, and Department of South Carolina. Headquarters at Philadelphia.

2. The Military Division of the Mississippi, Maj. Gen. W. T. Sherman to command, to embrace the Department of the Ohio, Department of the Missouri, and Department of Arkansas. Headquarters at Saint Louis.

3. The Military Division of the Gulf, Maj. Gen. P. H. Sheridan to command, to embrace the Department of Louisiana, Department of Texas, and Department of Florida. Headquarters at New Orleans.

4. The Military Division of the Tennessee, Maj. Gen. G. H. Thomas to command, to embrace the Department of the Tennessee, Department of Kentucky, Department of Georgia, Department of Mississippi, and Department of Alabama. Headquarters at Nashville.

5. The Military Division of the Pacific, Maj. Gen. H. W. Halleck to command, to embrace the Department of the Columbia and Department of California. Headquarters at San Francisco.

Indian hostilities upon the plains and the overland routes to the Pacific Coast have given much annoyance, required the employment of many troops, and occasioned great expense to the military department. Several Indian councils have been held during the past season and large military expeditions sent out against hostile tribes and bands. What has been accomplished by treaty or by fighting will doubtless be exhibited in the official reports of the Indian campaigns, which have not yet reached the Department.

Disbanding the troops reduces at once the amount to be expended in some items of appropriation, but in others requires larger immediate expenditures. Upon their discharge the soldiers became entitled to all the installments of bounty which would have fallen due at later periods, and in many cases exceeding a year's pay. The transportation of large armies from the field in Southern States to their remote homes in the West, or in Eastern and Northern States, made extraordinary drafts on the Quartermaster's Department beyond what would be required for armies marching or encamped. The vast amount of live-stock on hand requires forage until sales can be made. These are effected with the utmost diligence; but still this large item of expenditure continues through a large part of the fiscal year. The financial effects, therefore, of the reduction of the Army and retrenchment of expenditures can only operate to any great extent on the next fiscal year.

To accomplish the great object of promptly reducing the military expenditures, the following general order was made by the Secretary of War on the 28th of April.*

The administrative details of the Department during the great military operations that have been mentioned, and what has been done toward a reduction to a peace establishment, will appear in the reports of the respective chiefs of bureaus.

ADJUTANT-GENERAL'S REPORT.

From the report of the Adjutant-General it will be seen that the recruiting service of the Regular Army is progressing favorably, the number of recruits enlisted for all arms from October 31, 1864, to October 1, 1865, having been 19,555. The regiments comprising it have been distributed to stations, and their ranks are rapidly filling up, thus enabling the Department to relieve regiments of volunteer troops. The present authorized strength of the regular regiments is 1,570 officers and 41,819 enlisted men. This estimate is made on the basis of 42 privates to a company, the number now allowed by law at all except frontier posts.

It is recommended in the report that the maximum standard be fixed at 100 enlisted men to a company.

The Adjutant-General recommends that provisions be made by law for enlisting 100 boys, not under twelve years of age, as musicians, as was done before the laws of 1864 and 1865 prohibited the enlistment of minors under the age of sixteen years; that the laws by which one-half of their pay, during the period of absence, is lost by officers absent with leave for more than thirty days in one year, except from wounds or sickness, be repealed, and that an act be passed providing

* See General Orders, No. 77, Vol. IV, this series, p. 1280.

for the enlistment of meritorious disabled soldiers as superintendents of the National Cemeteries, numbering about forty, each to receive the pay and allowance of an ordnance sergeant.

Eight volumes of reports of battles, with maps and indexes, prepared under the resolution of Congress of May 19, 1864, have been completed and sent to the Government Printing Office. The publication of the greater part of the remaining reports is only deferred until the receipt of others not yet rendered, and which are required to preserve the chronological order observed in the preparation of the volumes already completed. The register of volunteer officers called for by resolution of June 30, 1864, and embracing some 200,000 names, will be completed by the time Congress assembles.

The aggregate of volunteers, drafted men, and substitutes ordered to the field between the 1st of November, 1864, and 30th of April, 1865, was 202,117. The number of volunteers, drafted men, and militia mustered out and discharged within the same period was 61,000. In disbanding the forces no longer required after the cessation of hostilities, the same machinery of mustering officers and depots has been used as in recruiting. Regiments have been sent home as fast as they could be transported and paid, the officers being held responsible for the good behavior of the men. Instances have been rare of any disorders. Much credit is due to mustering officers, paymasters, and railroad companies, through whose efforts troops, numbering in the aggregate 800,963 men, have been transported, mustered out, and paid.

On the 28th of April, 1865, it was ordered that returns be made of the volunteer forces in the field, with a view to their immediate reduction, and in connection with this order regulations were prepared and promulgated for their muster out and discharge. In executing this work promptness and a proper protection of the interests of the Government and the troops were held in view; and among other measures necessary to its completion rendezvous were established in the field as well as in most of the States. At the field rendezvous all surplus property was taken possession of by the staff officers of the respective supply departments, and the muster-out rolls and other discharge papers prepared under the direction of corps commissaries of musters and their assistants. Corps and department commanders were instructed to see that the work was pushed with energy, using for that end the division and brigade commanders, with their respective staff officers to superintend it. As soon as a regiment or other organization had its muster-out papers prepared, it was placed en route to its State for payment and final discharge. At the State rendezvous was located the chief mustering officer of the State, or one or more of his assistants, with paymasters, quartermasters, commissaries of subsistence, and ordnance officers, whose duties were with the payment and final discharge of the troops, their care while awaiting the same, the reception of the public property turned in by them, and their transportation to their homes after discharge.

By the foregoing arrangements the entire force of commissaries and assistant commissaries of musters for troops in the field have been made available for the work, in connection with the chief and other State mustering officers. The most experienced mustering officers and those most familiar with the regimental records were secured, the records from which the mustering-out data were to be obtained were readily accessible, and the loss of records (so common through the neglect of regimental officers) whilst the regiments were en route from the field to their States was avoided. Regimental officers have been held to a rigid accountability in preparing the records, and the interests of the enlisted men thus protected. Order and discipline have been maintained whilst troops were en route to the States and after arrival therein. Troops have been comfortably cared for up to the moment they were paid off and ready to start for their homes. Dissatisfaction among them has been obviated and causes for complaint removed, and all public property has been easily secured and readily accounted for.

The arrangements for the care of discharged troops being completed, orders to muster out and discharge the forces from service were issued as follows:

April 29.—All recruits, drafted men, substitutes, and volunteers remaining at the several State depots.

May 4 [3].—All patients in hospitals, except veteran volunteers and veterans of the First Army Corps (Hancock's).

May 8.—All troops of the cavalry arm whose terms of service would expire prior to October 1.

May 9.—All officers and enlisted men whose terms would expire prior to May 31, inclusive.

May 17.—All organizations of white troops in the Army of the Potomac whose terms of service would expire prior to September 30, inclusive.

May 18.—All organizations of white troops in Major-General Sherman's command whose terms of service would expire prior to September 30, inclusive.

May 29.—All light artillery in the Army of the Potomac, Ninth Army Corps, Army of Georgia, and Army of the Tennessee.

May 29.—All organizations of white troops whose terms of service would expire prior to September 30, inclusive, in armies and departments, except Departments of the East, New Mexico, Pacific, and Northern.

June 2.—All surplus light artillery; that only absolutely required by the necessities of the service in the respective armies and departments to be retained.

June 5.—All dismounted cavalry, all infantry in the Northern Department and Department of the East, and all cavalry in the Department of the East.

June 16.—All troops in the Department of the Pacific whose terms of service would expire prior to October 1.

June 17.—All enlisted men of the Veteran Reserve Corps who would have been entitled to their discharge had they remained with their regiments.

June 28.—Eighteen thousand veterans (infantry) of the Army of the Potomac, 15,000 of the Army of the Tennessee (then consisting of the remaining regiments of the Army of Georgia and Army of the Tennessee), and 7,000 of the Middle Military Division.

June 30.—All surplus troops, except in the Department of the Gulf, Army of the Tennessee, Provisional Corps Army of the Potomac, and First Army Corps. Strength of commands for all arms to be reduced to the minimum necessary to meet the requirements of the service.

July 1.—All remaining veteran regiments of the Army of the Tennessee and Provisional Corps Army of the Potomac (that corps was the remnant of the Army of the Potomac).

July 6.—The remainder of the Army of the Tennessee.

July 7.—The remainder of the Provisional Corps Army of the Potomac.

July 21.—All cavalry in the Department of Virginia except two regiments, all in the Department of North Carolina except one regiment, and all in the Middle Department except one regiment.

August 1.—All white troops, infantry, cavalry, and artillery, in the Department of Texas, which, in the judgment of Major-General Sheridan, could be dispensed with.

August 3.—The same order was extended to the Department of Louisiana.

August 14.—Additional infantry and heavy artillery (white) in military departments as follows: Virginia, 5,000; North Carolina, 8,000; Washington, 8,000; Mississippi, 2,000; Kentucky, 5,000; Middle, 6,000.

August 21.—Three thousand additional white troops in the Department of Arkansas.

September 8.—All surplus troops in the Department of Washington, so as to reduce that command to 6,000 officers and men of all arms.

September 8.—All organizations of colored troops which were enlisted in Northern States.

October 9.—All the remaining forces (white) of the cavalry arm east of the Mississippi.

October 9.—All troops on the Pacific Coast, as many as possible immediately; the remainder on the arrival of the last battalion of the Fourteenth U. S. Infantry.

October 10.—All troops in New Mexico; one regiment immediately, the remainder on the arrival of certain regular troops.

In addition to the foregoing, and from time to time as the services of the troops could be dispensed with, sixty-eight regiments, seven companies, and six battalions were ordered mustered out.

The rapidity with which the work has been executed will be apparent from the fact that to August 7 640,806 troops had been mustered out; August 22, 719,338; September 14, 741,107; October 15, 785,205; November 15, 800,963.

The command of Major-General Sherman (Army of the Tennessee and Army of Georgia) and the Army of the Potomac were first to complete their musters out entirely. Regiments commenced leaving General Sherman's command, then numbering, present and absent, 116,183 officers and men, from the rendezvous near Washington on the 29th of May, and on the 1st of August the last one of the regiments mustered out left Louisville, Ky., to which point the command (after the musters out therefrom were partly completed) was transferred, and the armies composing it merged into one, called the Army of the Tennessee. The work of mustering out the troops was not continuous, it having been interrupted and delayed by the transfer of the two armies from this city to Louisville and their subsequent consolidation.

Regiments commenced leaving the Army of the Potomac (when numbering, including Ninth Corps, 162,851 officers and men, present and absent) from the rendezvous near this city on the 29th of May, and about six weeks thereafter (July 19) the last regiment started for home. During the interval the work, like that from General Sherman's command, was not continuous, it being interrupted and delayed by the movement of the Sixth Corps from Danville, Va., to Washington, and the consolidation, by orders of June 28, of the remaining portion of the army into a provisional corps, numbering, present and absent, 22,699 officers and men.

Thus, for the two commands in question, and between the 29th of May and the 1st of August (two months), 279,034 officers and men, present and absent, were mustered out and placed en route to their homes. Including other armies and departments, the number was increased by August 7 (two months and seven days) to 640,806 officers and men.

From the foregoing it will be seen that the mass of the forces discharged were mustered out by September 14, or within two and a half months from the time the movements of troops homeward commenced. The average per month during that time is 296,442.

By reference to the report of the officer in charge of the Bureau for the Organization of Colored Troops, it will be seen that the increase in the number of these troops since his last annual report is 49,509, of which 4,244 were recruited in the States in rebellion and credited to the loyal States under the provisions of the act of July 4, 1864. The whole number of colored men enlisted into the service of the United States during the rebellion was 178,975. The largest number in service was on the 15th of July, 1865, viz, 123,156. The loss during the war from all causes except muster out was 68,178. There have been 33,234 colored troops mustered out. The number remaining in service after existing orders for muster out shall have been executed will be 85,024. The number of applicants for commissions in colored troops amounted to 9,019, of which 3,790 were examined. Of this number 1,472 were rejected and 2,318 received appointments. The number of soldiers discharged from regiments, &c., of white troops to accept appointments in organizations of colored troops was 1,767. It is ascertained from the reports of inspecting officers that the morale of the organization is good.

PROVOST-MARSHAL-GENERAL.

On the 1st day of November, 1864, the date to which the last annual report of the Provost-Marshal-General was brought up, the business of recruiting and the draft under the call of July 18, 1864, was in progress:

The number called for was		500,000
Reduced by credits on former calls		265,673
To be obtained		234,327
Voluntary enlistments under that call:		
Volunteers—		
White	146,392	
Colored	15,961	
Regulars	6,339	
Seamen	17,606	
Marine Corps	1,874	
Total		188,172
Drafted men and substitutes obtained under that call:		
Number held to personal service	26,205	
Number of substitutes for drafted men	28,502	
Total	54,707	
Number of substitutes for enrolled men	29,584	
Total		84,291
Whole number obtained under the July call		272,463

On the 19th of December, 1864, a call was made for 300,000 men.

Voluntary enlistments under this call:		
Volunteers—		
White	130,620	
Colored	10,055	
Regulars	6,958	
Seamen	9,106	
Marine Corps	319	
Total		157,058
Drafted men and substitutes under that call:		
Number held to personal service	12,566	
Number of substitutes for drafted men	12,014	
Total	24,580	
Number of substitues for enrolled men	12,997	
Total		37,577
Whole number raised under December call		194,635

The suspension of active military operations occurred while the business of the draft under this call was in progress, and orders were issued on the 13th of April, 1865, to discontinue the business of recruiting and drafting, and on the next day all drafted men who had not been forwarded to general rendezvous were ordered to be discharged, and soon after all who had not been forwarded to the field were discharged by orders through the Adjutant-General.

Aggregate quotas charged against the several States, under all calls made by the President of the United States, from the 15th day of April, 1861, to the 14th day of April, 1865, at which time drafting and recruiting ceased	2,759,049
(The terms of service varying from three months to three years, as shown in detail by the books of the Provost-Marshal-General's Office.)	
Aggregate number of men credited on the several calls, and put into service of the United States in the Army, Navy, and Marine Corps, during the above period	2,656,553
Leaving a deficiency on all calls when the war closed of	102,496

Which would have been obtained in full if recruiting and drafting had not been discontinued.*

This number does not embrace the "emergency men" put into service during the summer of 1863 by the States of New York, New Jersey, and Pennsylvania, nor those furnished by the States of Ohio, Indiana, and Illinois during the "Morgan raid," amounting in all to over 120,000 men, who served periods of about two or three weeks.

In estimating the number of troops called into service, it has been the rule of the department to take into account the whole number of men mustered, without regard to the fact that the same persons may have been previously discharged after having been accepted and credited on previous calls.

Under the different calls volunteers have been accepted for various terms of service, viz, three, six, and nine months, and one, two, and three years, respectively; and a large number of persons who had served under one call have subsequently enlisted under another. Thus, a portion of those who enlisted under the call in April, 1861, for 75,000 three-months' men, again enlisted under the succeeding call in July following for three years; others re-entered

* In connection with foregoing statement, see revised table, Vol. IV, this series, p. 1269.

the service for nine months, or for one or two years, and at the expiration of these periods again re-enlisted for three years, and the entire "veteran volunteer" force consisted of those who, having served two years, re-enlisted for three years more.

It will be observed, therefore, that a large portion of the number counted in filling calls has been furnished, first, by the re-enlistment of those in service, and second, by those who have re-entered the service after a discharge from a former enlistment under which they had been credited; that is, the different calls were filled by crediting each accepted enlistment, instead of limiting the credit to the actual number of persons who entered the service anew; and hence to determine the number of men actually entering the service for the first time under the different calls, the number credited should be reduced in the same ratio that the enlistments of the same persons have been repeated. The extent of this reduction cannot be calculated at this time, or even estimated with sufficient accuracy to be useful.

It follows, therefore, that, on account of a necessary repetition of credits incident to enlistments, the tax upon the military basis of the country has been less than would appear by considering simply the number of men embraced in the different calls for troops or the number of credits allowed upon these calls.

The amount of commutation money received from November 1, 1864, to November 1, 1865, was:

On account of draft and substitute fund	$317,130.00
On account of sick and wounded soldiers (from non-combatants, under section 17 of the act of February 24, 1864)	340,987.53
Total	658,117.53
Total amount of "draft and substitute fund" received under the act approved March 3, 1863	25,902,029.25
Total amount expended	16,387,135.80
Balance remaining in Treasury to credit of this fund	9,514,893.45

There are just claims still outstanding which have to be met from this fund.

The regiments of the Veteran Reserve Corps have been performing garrison duty in Washington and its defensive works; at the various depots for recruits and drafted men; at the provost-marshals' rendezvous; escorting recruits to the field, and more recently performing garrison duty at the several rendezvous for muster out of the volunteer forces.

Since the termination of active operations no transfers have been made to this corps, nor have any officers been appointed.

The amount expended from the appropriation for "collecting, drilling, and organizing volunteers" from November 1, 1864, to November 1, 1865, was $1,422,281.73.

The balance of this appropriation remaining in the Treasury is $12,163,386.09, and about $500,000 is still in the hands of the disbursing officers, which is needed to pay outstanding accounts and expenses incurred in mustering out the volunteer forces of the United States.

As fast as the exigencies of the service permitted the force employed has been reduced. The surgeons and commissioners of boards of enrollment in all the districts, 370 in number, have been discharged. The different districts have been consolidated, and but thirty-three provost-marshals are now in service, all of whom will be discharged as soon as their services can be dispensed with.

No appropriation of money will be required for the support of this Bureau during the next fiscal year.

The full report of the operations of the Provost-Marshal-General's Bureau will contain much statistical and other valuable information, which will be submitted when completed.

PAYMASTER-GENERAL.

The Paymaster-General reports that during the fiscal year ending June 30, 1865, $7,839,225.47 were paid to the Regular Army, while $300,738,635.95 were paid to volunteers, and that the total disbursements since June 30, 1864, to the date of his report, amount in the aggregate to $524,054,946.37. Payments amounting to $270,000,000 have been made to about 800,000 mustered-out troops. The highest number of additional paymasters in service during the fiscal year was 447; the number now in service is 210. All the troops retained in service have been paid to June 30, 1865, and many organizations to August 31, 1865, and to all discharged troops in full to date of discharge.

The anticipated payments of bounties to soldiers, and three months' additional pay to officers mustered out, that has fallen due by reason of muster out, amount to $91,750,000.

The whole sum disbursed by the Pay Department since the commencement of the war, viz, from July 1, 1861, to July 1, 1865, amounts to $1,029,239,000.

The total losses and defalcations during the same period, if nothing should be recovered, amount to the sum of $541,000, and it is believed that not less than half of this amount will be recovered. The total expenses of disbursement, including all pay and allowances, commutation of quarters, fuel, and traveling expenses, for four years and four months, amount to $6,429,600.

Thus it is seen that the costs of disbursement to armies in the field, and amid all the hazards of unexampled war, and including all losses and expenses, are less than three-fourths of 1 per cent.

COMMISSARY-GENERAL OF SUBSISTENCE.

The subsistence stores required during the year for distribution to the armies in the field have, as during the earlier years of the war, been purchased in the principal markets of the Northern States. The facilities and cost of transportation to the various points where they were required for issue, the relative prices of the different markets, and a due regard to the general commercial interests of the country, have governed the Subsistence Department in apportioning those purchases among the several market centers of the country. As New Orleans is gradually resuming a healthy commercial condition, a considerable portion of the supplies required for distribution from that point can be obtained in that market. Although the present general condition of the Southern States is not such as to afford a large amount of supplies, still subsistence officers are able in some parts of those States to enter into contracts for the partial supply of the troops serving therein.

The principal purchasing officers have exhibited much ability in the performance of their duties and great fidelity to the interests of the country. The principal commissaries immediately responsible for the subsistence of the several armies in the field have discharged the important and often difficult duties of receiving, protecting, and distributing the supplies forwarded to them with commendable efficiency and success. They have also, by great energy, been able to a considerable extent to subsist the troops upon the resources of the country in which the armies were operating, or through which they were passing. It is believed that during the entire war no campaign, contemplated movement, or expedition has failed on account of the inability of the Subsistence Department to meet its proper requirements, and that the troops, wherever stationed or operating, have, with rare exceptions, been supplied with rations in good and wholesome condition.

The muster out of a large part of the Army, consequent upon the sudden close of active military operations, unavoidably left on hand in some of the depots an excessive supply of subsistence stores. These have been sent to other points where they were required. Surplus and damaged stores will be disposed of by sale. A sufficient quantity of hard bread and other articles have been kept from earlier sale with the view of meeting in an economical manner the wants of those people, white and colored, who by the events of the war have been reduced to a suffering condition.

Under orders of June 29, 1865, the whisky ration was discontinued, and the sale of the supply on hand has already taken place at many points, and will soon be completed.

During the past year, as in previous years of the war, a very considerable income has been derived from the sale of the hides, tallow, and other parts of beef-cattle not issuable as beef to the troops.

Prisoners of war held at thirty-two forts, prison barracks, camps, and hospitals have been well subsisted, having received a sufficient portion and variety of the ration to insure health, leaving in the hands of the several issuing commissaries as "savings" that portion of the ration not deemed necessary for persons living in entire idleness. The pecuniary value of these "savings" has constituted a prison fund, available under the instructions of the Commissary-General of Prisoners, for the purchase of articles necessary for the prison barracks and hospitals, and for meeting other necessary expenses of the prisons. There has been transferred to the Subsistence Department a "savings" credit of the amount of $1,507,359.01, and there remains yet to be transferred an amount not less than $337,766.98, making a total amount of $1,845,125.99.

Under section 3 of the act of July 4, 1864, 1,470 claims have been submitted, of which 50 have been approved for payment, and 413 disallowed; 650 are awaiting explanation, and 357 remain to be examined.

It is proposed to ascertain and exhibit, in a tabular form, the total quantity of each article of subsistence stores purchased for the use of the Army during each year of the war, from 1861 to 1865, inclusive. Such a statement, it is believed, would prove an interesting addition to the commercial statistics of the country.

The officers of the Subsistence Department, regular and volunteer, have, with but few exceptions, discharged their duties with fidelity and success.

SURGEON-GENERAL.

The Surgeon-General reports that the receipts from all sources and available for the expenses of the Medical Department during the fiscal year ending June 30, 1865, were $20,489,680.47. Disbursements during the year, $19,328,499.23, leaving a balance in the Treasury on June 30 of $1,161,181.24.

The ample provision for sick and wounded existing at the date of the last annual report was increased during the ensuing months until a maximum of 204 general hospitals, with a capacity of 136,894 beds, was reached.

Upon the termination of active military movements, immediate measures were taken to reduce the expenses of the Medical Department. Of the 201 general hospitals open on January 1, 1865, 171 have been discontinued. Three of the sea-going hospital transports have been discharged; the fourth is now constantly engaged in transfer of sick and wounded from Southern ports to the general hospitals in New York Harbor. All of the river hospital boats have been turned over to the Quartermaster's Department, and but a single hospital train is retained in the Southwest. The vast amount of medicines and hospital supplies made surplus by the reduction of the Army has been carefully collected at prominent points and is being disposed of at public auction, most of the articles bringing their full value, and in some instances their cost price.

Two hundred and fourteen surgeons and assistant surgeons of volunteers have been mustered out, and of the 265 hospital chaplains appointed during the war twenty-nine only are still in commission.

The returns of sick and wounded show that of white troops 1,057,423 cases have been treated in general hospitals alone from 1861 to July 1, 1865, of which the rate of mortality was 8 per cent. In nearly all sections of the country the health of the troops has been fully equal to that of preceding years, though military movements of unprecedented magnitude have been pushed to successful termination, without regard to seasons. An epidemic of yellow fever prevailed at New Berne, N. C., in the fall of 1864, and the released or exchanged prisoners arriving at Wilmington, N. C., from rebel prisons suffered from an epidemic of typhoid fever. With these exceptions no serious epidemics have appeared, and it is interesting to note that quarantine regulations, strictly enforced by military authority, have proven during the occupation of Southern sea-ports and cities by our troops to be an absolute protection against the importation of contagious or infectious diseases. In view of the apprehensions entertained in regard to the Asiatic cholera, now devastating the shores of the Mediterranean, this becomes a significant fact.

In addition to the alphabetical registers of dead, not yet fully completed, the records of the Medical Department contain 30,000 special reports of the more important forms of surgical injuries, of diseases, and operations. These reports, with statistical data, and a pathological collection numbering 7,630 specimens, furnish a mass of valuable information, which is being rapidly arranged and tabulated, as a medical and surgical history of the war, for the publication of the first volume of which an appropriation will be asked.

In this connection and as illustrating more in detail the importance of this work, the Army Medical Museum assumes the highest value. By its array of indisputable facts, supported and enriched by full reports, it supplies instruction otherwise unattainable, and preserves for future application the dearly bought experience of four years of war. Apart from its great usefulness, it is also an honorable record of the skill and services of those medical officers whose contributions constitute its value, and whose incentive to these self-imposed labors has been the desire to elevate their profession. A small appropriation has been asked to continue and extend this collection.

For recommendation of measures tending to the greater efficiency of the Medical Department, reference is made to the special report from the Surgeon-General's Office, which will be submitted to the appropriate Congressional committees.

QUARTERMASTER-GENERAL

The report of the Quartermaster-General contains a statement of the operations and expenditures of the department under his control during the fiscal year ending 30th of June, 1865. The principal movement of troops by the Quartermaster's Department during that time are described. They have been made promptly and with few accidents, and are striking illustrations of the improvements in the art of war which have been developed during the late contest.

The Twenty-third Army Corps, after fighting at Nashville, in the midst of ice and snow in December, 1864, was, on the conclusion of the campaign in the West, transferred from the valley of the Tennessee to the banks of the Potomac, moving by river and rail down the Tennessee, up the Ohio, across the snow-covered Alleghanies, a distance of 1,400 miles, and in the short space of eleven days was encamped on the banks of the Potomac, then blocked up with the ice of a most severe winter. Vessels were collected to meet this corps, the obstacles interposed by the ice were overcome, and early in February the troops composing it were fighting before Wilmington, on the coast of North Carolina.

The transfer of the Eleventh and Twelfth Corps, under General Hooker, in 1863, from the Potomac to the Tennessee, is the only parallel to this movement. That was an almost unexampled operation at the time. General Hooker's command contained 23,000 men, and was accompanied by its artillery and trains, baggage and animals, and accomplished the distance from the Rapidan, in Virginia, to Stevenson, in Alabama, a distance of 1,192 miles, in seven days, crossing the Ohio River twice. The Twenty-third Army Corps moved 15,000 strong.

Other important operations are described, among which are the supply of the army of Lieutenant-General Grant before Richmond; of the army of General Sherman at Atlanta, preparatory to his march to Savannah; of the same army at the depots on the Atlantic, on his communicating with the coast, first at Savannah and afterward at Goldsborough, at both of which places depots were established, and his army re-enforced and equipped with everything necessary to make successful campaigns.

The transfer of the Twenty-fifth Army Corps, 25,000 strong, in the month of May, from the James to the coast of Texas, is fully described, and the extent and cost of the fleet used in this movement are set forth in full.

Transportation was promptly supplied from all parts of the South to their homes in the North for the immense army which has been disbanded, and the organization of the department which has made it possible to meet these demands so promptly is believed to have been at least as perfect as that of any other nation.

The report gives tables of the quantities of the principal military supplies, clothing, forage, fuel, horses, mules, and wagons which have been purchased, transported, and used during the fiscal year. It contains full statements of the vessels which have been in the service during that time upon the Western rivers and upon the ocean and bays. Many of them have now been discharged from service or advertised for sale, orders for the reduction of the transport fleet having been given as soon as hostilities ceased.

The return of the armies from the South, the transportation of the discharged soldiers to their homes, the transfer of troops to Texas, the return of refugees expelled from the South by General Sherman, and of rebel prisoners released at the termination of the war, have, however, taxed the resources of the Quartermaster's Department heavily during the last spring and summer.

The transport service has been most satisfactorily performed. Upon the ocean a fleet of over 700 vessels has been constantly employed, with the reported loss by storm, by collision, and by fire, of only three; one steamship was destroyed in each of these modes.

The repair of the railroads from Chattanooga to Atlanta by the military railroad branch of the Quartermaster's Department, under the charge of Bvt. Brig. Gen. D. C. McCallum, was referred to in the last annual report. Upon the advance of General Sherman from Atlanta he destroyed the railroad in his rear, blew up all the railroad buildings at Atlanta, sent back his surplus stores and all the railroad machinery which had to that time supplied his army. The stores and the railroad stock were safely withdrawn to Nashville, and after the dispersion of the army of Hood, which had broken the railroad in Georgia and Tennessee in its advance, the Railroad Construction Corps again took the field and reopened railroad communication with Chattanooga, Atlanta, and Decatur. After the fall of Macon and Augusta it became necessary, in order to supply the army of Major-General Wilson, to open railroad communication between Augusta and Atlanta and Macon. This was successfully accomplished.

A division of the Construction Corps, fully organized, under the command of Colonel Wright, with tools and equipments, was transferred, in December and January, from the Tennessee to Savannah, by way of Baltimore. As General Sherman did not repair the railroads of Georgia and South Carolina, but marched northward, lightly equipped, living upon the supplies in his wagon trains, and by foraging upon the enemy, this division of the Construction Corps was transferred to Beaufort, N. C., and after its fall to Wilmington, where it repaired and restocked the railroads from those ports to Goldsborough and to Raleigh. General Sherman's army was thus quickly provisioned, reclad, reshod, and equipped for a march to the James.

The surrender of the rebel armies and pacification of the Southern States have enabled the Quartermaster's Department to return to their former possessors most of the railroads which have been in military possession during the war. The department, in transferring them to their boards of directors—reorganized upon a loyal footing—delivers up the roads and bridges in whatever condition they may be at the time of the transfer.

The great accumulation of railroad engines and cars upon the Western military railroads is being disposed of to the railroads of the Southwest, which have suffered severely from the operations of both armies during the war. Under the orders of the Executive this stock is being delivered to the companies, who are to pay for it within two years, at a valuation fixed by a board of officers and experts assembled by the Government.

The reconstruction of these roads and their successful operation are of great importance, not only to the districts in which they are located, but to the general commerce and prosperity of the country; and the liberal policy pursued toward them will react favorably upon the revenue and credit of the Nation.

The agreement made early in the war with the railroad companies of the loyal States, fixing reduced rates of military transportation, remains in force, and has been extended to the railroads in the Southern States since the termination of hostilities.

Full reports are given of the quantities of clothing, camp and garrison equipage furnished to our armies during the past year, and also during the war. The tables accompanying the Quartermaster-General's report give information on these points, which shows in a favorable light the manufacturing power of the country.

The vast supplies of forage required for the armies have been promptly furnished and transported to the depots. While moving through the Southern country the armies found ample quantities, and it was only when lying still in camp that they had any difficulty in supplying themselves.

During the year over 29,000,000 bushels of grain and 400,000 tons of hay have been provided by the depots of the Quartermaster's Department; 336,000 cords of wood and 832,000 tons of coal have also been supplied by the depots. Troops in the field have supplied themselves with fuel from the forests in which they have operated. The depots of the Quartermaster's Department have, during the war, furnished the Army with 23,000,000 bushels of corn, 78,000,000 bushels of oats, 93,000 bushels of barley, 1,500,000 tons of hay, 20,000 tons of straw, 550,000 cords of wood, and 1,600,000 tons of coal, all of which have been purchased, measured, transported, issued, and accounted for by its officers and agents. At the depot of Washington alone there have been issued during the year 4,500,000 bushels of corn, 29,000,000 bushels of oats, 490,000 tons of hay, 210,000 cords of wood, and 392,000 tons of coal.

The supply of horses and mules for the Army has been regular and sufficient. There were purchased during the fiscal year 141,632 cavalry horses; from September 1, 1864, to 30th of June, 1865, 20,714 artillery horses; and from 1st of July, 1864, to 30th of June, 1865, 58,818 mules. Prices of horses varied during the year from $144 to $185; of mules, from $170 to $195.

The reduction of the Army has enabled the Quartermaster's Department to dispense with large numbers of horses and mules, and to the 17th of October the sales of animals are estimated to have produced $7,000,000.

The teams and animals of the armies have, as during previous fiscal years, averaged about one wagon to twenty-four men in the field, and one horse or mule to every two men.

The burial records of the Quartermaster's Department, which do not include the names of those who fell in battle and were buried immediately on the field by their comrades, show the interment in cemeteries of 116,148 persons, of whom 98,827 were loyal, 12,596 disloyal, and of whom 95,803 were whites and 20,345 colored persons

The military cemeteries at Washington, Alexandria, Arlington, and Chattanooga have been carefully tended and decorated.

An officer, with material and men to mark the graves of our brethren who fell victims to rebel barbarity at Andersonville, was dispatched from Washington as soon as the country was opened to us, and reports that he has inclosed the cemetery and marked the graves of 12,912 soldiers buried therein. Of these the captured records of the prison hospital enabled him to identify 12,461, and their names were recorded upon headboards, painted white, and planted at the head of their graves. On 451 graves he was compelled to put the sad inscription, "Unknown U. S. soldier." The list of these names is in course of publication. The names of those who have been interred in the military cemeteries of the District of Columbia and at Arlington have already been published and distributed to State authorities and public institutions, as well as to newspapers which publish official advertisements, so as to be made accessible to their friends.

The military organization of the operatives and agents of the Quartermaster's Department, referred to in the last annual report, was kept up until the close of the war. It did good service in the fortifications at the attack on Washington in July, at the attack on Johnsonville in the fall, and bore a part in the battle of Nashville on the 15th and 16th of December, 1864, which gave the final blow to the rebellion in the West. Upon the cessation of hostilities this organization was disbanded, its arms restored to the arsenal, and most of its members have returned to peaceful pursuits.

The employment of colored men in the Quartermaster's Department, in connection with the trains of the Army, as laborers at depots, and as pioneers of the troops of the Western army continued to the close of the war. In all these positions they have done good service and materially contributed to the final victory which confirmed their freedom.

The great cost of transportation of supplies across the Western plains and mountains to the depots and posts of the wilderness, and for the supply of troops operating against the Indians, is reported, and the Quartermaster-General calls attention to the importance, in this view, of the vigorous prosecution of the work of the railroads to connect the Mississippi Valley with the Pacific Coast, as a military precaution and a measure of economy, deserving the fostering care of the Government.

Retrenchment in the Quartermaster-General's Bureau.—The Quartermaster-General reports that immediately on the termination of active hostilities, under orders from the Secretary of War he took measures to reduce expenditures; to discharge operatives and agents; to discharge chartered transports, and to sell those belonging to the United States not needed to bring home troops for muster out; to reduce the number of horses in reserve at the depot; to stop the purchase of horses and mules, and to sell those belonging to the troops disbanded; to cease making contracts and purchases of clothing and equipment; to stop the repair and construction of military railroads; to return all such railroads to their former owners, and to sell or dispose of the rolling-stock and other material used thereon.

He reports sales of 128,840 horses and mules, for which the sum of $7,500,000 was received.

Of 5,355 persons employed in the Cavalry Bureau, three-fourths have been discharged. Those still employed are engaged in receiving, caring for, and selling the animals turned in by the armies.

The purchase and manufacture of clothing, which during the past fiscal year had caused an expenditure of between $8,000,000 and $9,000,000 per month, has ceased entirely, and, by compromise with merchants, contracts for clothing and equipment, amounting to $4,000,000, have been canceled.

Twenty-five hundred buildings, vacated, have been ordered for sale.

The sales of buildings, wagons, harness, tools, iron, and other like material have realized thus far $1,000,000.

Over 1,700 miles of military railroad, operated for the department by 23,700 workmen and agents, at a monthly cost of $1,500,000, have been restored to their former owners, and the number of persons employed in completing the accounts, in taking care of and disposing of the railroad property not yet sold or transferred, has been reduced to less than 500, the rest having been discharged.

The rolling-mill at Chattanooga, its product, and the scrap iron there collected have been sold—the mill for $175,000; the rolled iron for $200,000, and the old iron for about $100,000.

Eighty-three engines and 1,009 cars have been sold for $1,500,000. Over 200 locomotives and 2,000 cars have been sold at appraised values, on credit, to the Southern railroads.

Of 588 steam-boats and other boats employed on the Western rivers all but eleven have been put out of commission. The sales of many of those owned by the United States have been effected. These sales are not yet concluded. They will produce about $1,100,000.

Of the transport fleet upon the ocean on the 1st of January last, 460 steamers and vessels of all kinds have been discharged or laid up for sale, and many of them have already been sold. The fleet has been reduced over 100,000 tons, and vessels are daily arriving at home ports to be discharged or sold. The monthly expenses of the transport fleet have been reduced $1,814,130.

A million of dollars has been received from the sales of vessels belonging to the department, which will be increased by future sales.

In all, 83,887 persons employed on wages had been discharged from the service of the Quartermaster's Department at the end of September, 1865, reducing its expenses per month $4,086,093.

The sales of property of all kinds reported and recorded on the books of the Quartermaster-General's Office from the 20th of April to the 8th of November, 1865, amount to $13,357,345.

The cost of forage issued to the armies during the month of March last is estimated at $3,294,000. In the month of September it is estimated at $1,134,000, a reduction in monthly expenditure of $2,160,000. The armies on the eastern coast have been supplied with forage purchased before the end of May last. No considerable purchases have been made in the East since that time. Purchases of forage since May have been confined to the supply of the troops in Georgia and upon the Gulf coast in Texas, and upon the Western plains.

The consumption of coal in the month of March last was 90,685 tons, costing $748,151. In September it had been reduced to 25,592 tons, costing $204,736, a reduction of monthly expenditure of $543,415.

CHIEF ENGINEER.

The report of the Chief Engineer of the Army gives the operations of the department under his charge and the duties of the officers of the Corps of Engineers. This corps consisted, on June 30, 1865, of eighty-five officers, the Military Academy, and five companies of engineer troops. Every member of the corps has been on duty uninterruptedly during the year. At the date of the report twelve officers, being generals in command of troops, were on detached service, and others were on staff duty, or detailed for service under the orders of the Light-House Board and the Department of the Interior, the remainder being on duty at the Military Academy, on sea-coast defenses, survey of the lakes, with the engineer battalion, and as assistants to the Chief Engineer. The particular services rendered by these officers are recited in the narratives and other statements accompanying the report, and comprise the professional duties of the engineer, together with those of the various arms of the service to which the officers have been assigned. In general, every army and military expedition has had assigned to it officers of this corps. Their reports give the plans of attack and defense, as well as the outlines of the marches by the armies to which they were attached, and together constitute a comprehensive statement of the last year's operations of the armies.

The sea-coast defenses have progressed in proportion to the available means and the number of officers who could be assigned to this branch of duty. The efforts of the Engineer Department have been principally directed to constructions for mounting the guns of large caliber now essential in consequence of corresponding armaments in iron floating batteries. The permanent forts on the Gulf, since their repossession by the Government, have been repaired and put in a defensive condition. The available means of the department will suffice to accomplish all that is required at these works and at those of the southern Atlantic coast until plans are matured for modifications adapting them to the existing sea-coast armaments.

The Military Academy has continued to furnish a limited number of graduates for the subordinate grades of the Army, a number, however, which has not for years past sufficed to fill the vacancies in the line and staff occasioned by the casualties of the service. The Chief Engineer, in view of this fact, recommends an increase of the number of cadets, and in order to economize in the expenses of the institution, proposes a mode of selecting candidates from nominees for each vacancy that will, he thinks, with more certainty insure proficiency in studies and the military art by those aspiring to enter the service.

The survey of the Northern lakes has progressed during the year as heretofore. The repairs and preservation of the harbors on the lakes and on the Atlantic have been prosecuted to the full extent of the resources of the department in officers and available funds. Success in this branch of engineering is attended with greater difficulties than are met in most others in which science and skill are called upon to promote the interests of the country. Heretofore the plans of improvements adopted have been directed to secure immediate results, and the source of the evil having been left to exercise its influence, has rendered constant repetitions of labor and expenditures necessary. The Chief Engineer is now calling upon the officers charged with works of this character for plans to arrest the cause of constant obstructions to commerce, and it is hoped that measures may be devised by which these improvements may be made to endure for a longer period, if not to become permanent in their nature.

The expenditures of the Engineer Department during the year amounted to $5,479,420.23.

ORDNANCE BUREAU.

The fiscal resources of the Ordnance Bureau for the past year amounted to $45,783,656.10, and the expenditures to $43,112,531.27, leaving a balance of $2,671,124.83 to the credit of disbursing officers, in the Government depositories, on June 30, 1865.

The estimates for the next year are for objects not confined to a state of war, but for such as are required to keep up a proper state of preparation, and to reserve the large and valuable munitions of war now on hand. On the termination of the war measures were promptly taken to reduce the procurement of supplies and to provide storage for the munitions returned to the arsenals from the armies and captured from the enemy. Commodious fireproof workshops are being erected at Allegheny, Watervliet, and Frankford Arsenals, and it is contemplated to erect similar shops at Washington Arsenal, for which there is an appropriation. These shops can be advantageously used for storage when their entire capacity for manufacturing purposes is not needed.

From the evident importance of arming the permanent fortifications as fast as they are built, the construction of cannon and carriages for this purpose, so far as existing appropriations warrant, has not been intermitted. It is contemplated to increase the capacity of manufacturing sea-coast carriages in proportion to the readiness of the forts to receive them, and to discontinue the fabrication of wooden carriages for field and siege guns in favor of iron carriages, which experiments have shown are preferable for that service. Cast-iron smooth-bore cannon, of large caliber, as now made, are found to be entirely reliable; but not so the heavy rifled cannon, as heretofore made and tried. The failures on trial of the wrought-iron guns made by Mr. Horatio Ames indicate that these guns cannot be relied upon, and that no more of them ought to be made for this department. Two experimental cast-iron 8-inch rifle guns have been made of the model and weight supposed to render them reliable for service. They are now undergoing extreme proof to test them thoroughly.

The manufacture of arms at the National Armory was reduced at the conclusion of hostilities as rapidly as could be done with economy, and at present no new muskets are being made there. With a view to change the model of small-arms from muzzle-loaders to breech-loaders, extensive experiments have been made; but they have not yet resulted in the selection of a model of such decided excellence as to render its adoption for the service advisable. It is hoped that such a model may soon be found. A plan for altering the musket of the present pattern into efficient breech-loaders has been devised, and 5,000 of them are being so altered for issue to troops for practical test. There are nearly 1,000,000 good Springfield muskets on hand, and upward of 500,000 foreign and captured muskets. The latter will be sold whenever suitable prices can be obtained for them, and also other ordnance stores of a perishable nature which are in excess of the wants of the service.

The necessity of providing a suitable depository for gunpowder, with proper magazines for its storage and preservation, which was stated in the last annual report, is again mentioned, and the requisite legislation is urged.

A partial provision for this object, as far as respects a supply for the Mississippi Valley, has been made on the military reserve at Jefferson Barracks.

The Government has not yet acquired a title to the property on Rock Island, taken possession of under the act of July 19, 1864. It is important that this be done with as little delay as practicable. The importance of having full possession and control of Rock Island, including the adjacent islands, and the right of way is stated in the report of the Chief of Ordnance, and additional legislation therefor, if necessary, is recommended.

Several of the Southern arsenals have been reoccupied, and it is intended to reoccupy them all, except that at Fayetteville, N. C., which has been destroyed. The necessary measures have been taken for the preservation of the powder mill at Augusta, and the laboratory and unfinished armory at Macon, Ga., which have been captured.

The number of permanent U. S. arsenals and armories is twenty-eight. The command and supervision of these, together with the inspection services required at the arsenals, the foundries, the powder mills, and other private establishments engaged in work for the Government, furnish constant employment for the whole number of ordnance officers (sixty-four) now authorized by law. The proper discharge of these essential duties requires that that number should be continued as part of the military peace establishment of the country.

The armies in the field have been amply and well supplied with arms and other ordnance stores, and the fortifications have had their armaments kept in order and strengthened and increased by additional guns of heavy caliber and great efficiency.

THE SIGNAL CORPS.

On the 1st of November, 1864, the Signal Corps numbered 168 officers and 1,350 enlisted men, distributed in detachments among the armies in the field and military departments. All that portion of the Signal Corps on duty east of the Mississippi River has been mustered out of service, the act of Congress under which the corps was organized having limited its organization to the duration of the rebellion. There now remain nine officers and thirty-seven enlisted men in the Military Division of the Mississippi and fifteen officers and ninety-nine enlisted men in the Military Division of the Gulf. These detachments are operating with the troops on the plains in Texas and along the southwestern boundary.

The expenditures from appropriations for the Signal service amounted to $8,537.06 during the year ending September 30, 1865. The balance unexpended amounts to $248,062.

MILITARY TELEGRAPH.

The telegraph has continued to be a most efficient and important instrument in military operations. Its officers have shown the same devotion and fidelity which have signalized their efforts during former years. There have been constructed during the year 3,246 miles of military telegraph; 8,323 miles have been in operation during the year, and at its termination 6,228 miles were still in use. The expenditure upon the military telegraph during the fiscal year was $1,360,000; since the beginning of the war, $2,655,500. There have been constructed and operated in all during the war about 15,000 miles of military telegraph. Control has been assumed of the telegraphs of the late rebellious districts as fast as they fell into our hands, and arrangements are now made by which the lines are kept in repair by the stockholders, the United States being at the expense only of purely military lines and stations.

MILITARY PRISONERS AND PRISONERS OF WAR.

The report of the commissioner of exchanges exhibits the exchange transactions during the war, with statistical tables and other information respecting the condition and treatment of prisoners on each side.*

*See Hitchcock to Stanton, Series II, Vol. VIII, p. 799.

Frequent inspections of military prisons have been made from time to time, and all military prisoners have been released except such as were under sentence or awaiting trial for murder, arson, or other grave offenses. Clemency has been extended as liberally as was deemed compatible with public security. All persons imprisoned for offenses against the draft laws have been released, and all deserters from the volunteer service. Since the surrender of Lee's army the danger to the national safety from combinations and conspiracies to aid the rebellion or resist the laws in the States not declared to be insurgent has passed away. It is therefore recommended that the proclamation suspending the writ of habeas corpus in those States be revoked.

The Commissary-General of Prisoners reports that between the 1st of January and the 20th of October there were in our custody 98,802 prisoners of war. Of these 1,955 enlisted into the U. S. service, 63,442 were released after the cessation of hostilities, and 33,127 were delivered in exchange. Besides these, 174,223 prisoners surrendered in the different rebel armies and were released on parole, viz:

Army of Northern Virginia, commanded by General R. E. Lee	27,805
Army of Tennessee and others, commanded by General J. E. Johnston	31,243
General Jeff. Thompson's army of Missouri	7,978
Miscellaneous paroles, Department of Virginia	9,072
Paroled at Cumberland, Md., and other stations	9,377
Paroled by General McCook in Alabama and Florida	6,428
Army of the Department of Alabama, Lieut. Gen. R. Taylor	42,293
Army of the Trans-Mississippi Department, General E. K. Smith	17,686
Paroled in the Department of Washington	3,390
Paroled in Virginia, Tennessee, Georgia, Alabama, Louisiana, and Texas	13,922
Surrendered at Nashville and Chattanooga, Tenn	5,029
Total	174,223

JUDGE-ADVOCATE-GENERAL.

In the Bureau of Military Justice since March 2, 1865, there have been received, reviewed, and filed 16,591 records of general courts-martial and military commissions, and 6,123 special reports have been made as to the regularity of proceedings, the pardon of military offenders, the remission or commutation of sentences, and upon the numerous miscellaneous subjects and questions referred for the opinion of the Bureau, including also letters of instruction upon military law and practice to judge-advocates, reviewing officers, &c. By comparing these details with those presented in March last it will be perceived that the business of this Bureau, especially as an advisory branch of the War Department, has not yet been diminished or sensibly affected by the altered condition of public affairs.

The Digest of Opinions of the Judge-Advocate-General, issued by the Bureau in January last, having come into extensive use throughout the Army, has proved of considerable advantage to the service in contributing to establish a uniformity of decision and action in the administration of military justice. As the present edition of the work has been very nearly exhausted, it is proposed to prepare during the coming winter an enlarged edition, containing in connection with those already published a selection of the official opinions communicated by the Judge-Advocate-General during the present year.

The chief of the Bureau expresses his satisfaction with the ability and efficiency with which the officers and clerks connected with it have performed their several duties, and, in view of the fact that the business of this branch of the public service will probably not be materially diminished for the next twelve months, is of the opinion that its present organization may well be continued by Congress.

FREEDMEN'S BUREAU.

By an act of the last session of Congress a new bureau in the War Department was created, called the Bureau of Freedmen, Refugees, and Abandoned Lands. Its object was to supply the immediate necessities of those whose condition was changed by hostilities and were either escaping or escaped from slavery to obtain freedom, or were driven from their homes by the pressure of war or the despotism of the rebellion. Its aid was designed for the needy of both races, white and black, and to administer as well aid from the Government and from charitable individuals and associations. No appropriation was made to carry this act into effect, but the condition of the people in the insurgent States required prompt relief. The act of Congress authorized the assignment of military officers to duty in the Bureau, and under this provision it was organized. Major-General Howard was assigned to duty as commissioner. Other officers selected by him were assigned for agents and assistants, and an organized system of relief has gone into operation. The report of the commissioner, which has not yet been furnished to the Department, will show the operation of the Freedmen's Bureau during a period of several months and afford some means to judge what regulations are required. It is plain that some such organization is wanted in the insurgent States to relieve promptly great and pressing need arising from the war, and social disorganization resulting from the war. Proper provision for the colored population, whose condition has been changed by direct act of the Federal Government to serve its own purposes in the conflict, is a solemn duty. More or less resistance to the performance of this duty is to be expected while any rebellious or hostile spirit remains, but the obligation to perform it cannot be evaded or thrust aside with national honor or safety. A numerous class of white persons who, without fault in themselves, are suffering want occasioned by the ravages of war have also a just claim for relief. But while discharging these obligations to needy destitute white persons and the freed colored people the utmost care must be observed to guard against establishing a national system of pauperism that might foster a horde of idle officials or dishonest agents, and engender vice, sloth, and improvidence among a large class of persons. To avoid this evil and insure strict supervision it is urgently recommended, first, that all appropriations of money for the Freedmen's Bureau be made in specific terms distinct from any other purpose; second, that the number of agents and employés and their compensation be fixed by law; third, that the duties and powers of the Bureau in respect to persons and property be defined by law.

By the heads of the respective bureaus of the War Department and their staffs the Government has been served with a zeal and fidelity not surpassed by their brethren in the field. To them the honors and distinction of an admiring public have not been opened, but in their respective vocations they have toiled with a devotion, ability, and success for which they are entitled to national gratitude.

Besides the signal success vouchsafed to our arms, other causes contributed to overthrow the rebellion. Among the chief of these may be reckoned:

1. The steadfast adherence of the President to the measure of eman-

cipating the slaves in the rebel States. Slavery was avowed by the leaders of the rebellion to be its corner stone. By that system millions of people, constituting nearly the whole working population of the South, were employed in producing supplies on the plantation, in the workshops and manufactories, and wherever labor was required, thus enabling the white population to fill the rebel armies. The hopes of freedom, kindled by the emancipation proclamation, paralyzed the industrial power of the rebellion. Slaves seized their chances to escape; discontent and distrust were engendered; the hopes of the slave and the fears of the master, stimulated by the success of the Federal arms, shook each day more and more the fabric built on human slavery.

2. The resolute purpose of Congress to maintain the Federal Union at all hazards, manifested by its legislation, was an efficient cause of our success. Ample supplies appropriated for the Army and Navy, revenue laws for supplying the Treasury, careful revision and amendment of the laws for recruiting the Army and enforcing the draft, gave practical direction to the patriotic purpose of the people to maintain a national existence that should afford protection and respect by means of the Federal Union.

3. Patriotic measures adopted by the Governors of loyal States, and the efficient aid they rendered the War Department in filling up the ranks of the Army and furnishing succor and relief to the sick and wounded, largely contributed to the national preservation. Of these measures one of the most important was the aid tendered by the Governors of Ohio, Indiana, Illinois, Iowa, Wisconsin, and Michigan in the opening of the campaign of 1864.

On the 21st day of April, 1864, Governors Brough, Morton, Yates, Stone, and Lewis made an offer to the President to the following effect:

That these States should furnish for the approaching campaign infantry troops—30,000 from Ohio, 20,000 from Indiana, the same number from Illinois, 10,000 from Iowa, and 5,000 from Wisconsin; the term of service to be 100 days; the whole number to be furnished within twenty days; the troops to be armed, equipped, and transported as other troops, but no bounty to be paid, nor any credit on any draft, and the pending draft to go on until the State quota was filled.

After full consideration and conference with the lieutenant-general this offer was accepted by President Lincoln. The State of Ohio organized within four weeks and placed in the field 35,646 officers and men, being 5,646 troops more than the stipulated quota. Other States, less able to meet the contingency, contributed with alacrity all that could be raised.

Although experience had shown that troops raised for a short term were more expensive and of less value than those raised for a longer period, these troops did important service in the campaign. They supplied garrisons and held posts for which experienced troops would have been required, and these were relieved so as to join the armies in the field. In several instances the three-months' troops, at their own entreaty, were sent to the front, and displayed their gallantry in the hardest battles of the campaign.

4. The result of the Presidential election of 1864 exerted an important influence upon the war. Intercepted letters and dispatches between the rebel leaders showed that their hopes of success rested greatly upon the Presidential election. If the Union party prevailed the prosecution of the war until the national authority should be

restored appeared inevitable and the rebel cause desperate. Even on the battle-field the influence of the election was felt. The overwhelming voice of the people at the Presidential election encouraged the heroic daring of our own troops and dismayed those who were fighting in a hopeless cause.

5. The faith of the people in the national success, as manifested by their support of the Government credit, also contributed much to the auspicious result. While thousands upon thousands of brave men filled the ranks of the Army, millions of money were required for the Treasury. These were furnished by the people, who advanced their money on Government securities and freely staked their fortunes for the national defense.

Looking to the causes that have accomplished the national deliverance, there seems no room henceforth to doubt the stability of the Federal Union. These causes are permanent, and must always have an active existence. The majesty of national power has been exhibited in the courage and faith of our citizens, and the ignominy of rebellion is witnessed by the hopeless end of the great rebellion.

EDWIN M. STANTON,
Secretary of War.

GENERAL ORDERS, No. 165. } WAR DEPT., ADJT. GENERAL'S OFFICE, *Washington, November 24, 1865.*

ORDER TO RELIEVE SURPLUS OFFICERS OF THE VETERAN RESERVE CORPS.

Immediately on receipt of this order all officers of the Veteran Reserve Corps whose services can be dispensed with will be relieved and ordered to proceed to their respective places of residence, and from there report by letter to the Adjutant-General of the Army for orders.

The names of all officers so relieved will be reported by the several commanders under whose orders they now are to the Adjutant-General of the Army.

By command of Lieutenant-General Grant:

E. D. TOWNSEND,
Assistant Adjutant-General.

U. S. MILITARY RAILROADS, OFFICE OF CHIEF ENGINEER,
Washington, D. C., November 30, 1865.

General D. C. MCCALLUM,
Director and Gen. Man. Mil. Railroads United States,
Washington, D. C.:

GENERAL: In compliance with your order I have the honor to make the following report of operations in the Construction Department, U. S. Military Railroads:

In my reports of November 1, 1864, and May 20, 1865, the narrative of operations in the Military Division of the Mississippi was carried up to January 1, 1865, the date of my departure from Nashville to join General Sherman at Savannah, and of those in the Department of North Carolina up to May 20, 1865. During my absence Mr. E. L.

Wentz took charge of my department in the West as acting chief engineer until February 10, when he was relieved by your order, and Mr. L. H. Eicholtz, division engineer, appointed acting chief engineer, who continued to act in that capacity until my return. As stated in my last report, all the railroads damaged by General Hood in his invasion of Tennessee had been repaired and were in running order on the 28th of December, except the Nashville and Decatur line. And although the work was pushed forward with the greatest energy on both ends of this line, the large amount of bridging to rebuild delayed its completion until the 12th of February. The following statement shows the amount of damage done to the tracks and bridges on the railroads in Tennessee and Alabama during this invasion. Many buildings were burned and other damage done of which I have not a complete record:

Name of road.	Track destroyed.	Bridges destroyed.
	Miles.	*Feet.*
Nashville and Chattanooga	$7\frac{3}{4}$	809
Nashville and Decatur	6	7,055
Stevenson and Decatur	$\frac{1}{2}$	500
Nashville and Northwestern	1	2,300
Total	$15\frac{1}{4}$	*a*10,663

a Two miles and 103 feet.

About this time a force was sent to Knoxville to repair the East Tennessee and Virginia Railroad, but had scarcely commenced work at Strawberry Plains when, by General Thomas' order, they were withdrawn. A Howe truss wagon-road bridge 350 feet long was built by a portion of the Construction Corps at the turnpike crossing over Duck River at Columbia. On the 25th of February this country was visited by a great freshet, which destroyed or injured to a greater or less extent all the bridges on the Nashville, Decatur and Stevenson line, all on the Nashville and Northwestern, five on the Chattanooga and Atlanta, and two on the Nashville and Clarksville lines. This damage was repaired with the usual rapidity, but was scarcely completed when another freshet on the 3d of March occurred, destroying nearly all this work and doing some additional damage. Again the construction force was distributed on the various lines, and the most important one, the Nashville and Chattanooga line, was put in running order in one week's time. The repairs to all these lines were completed on the 28th of March. In consequence of the destruction of the Red River bridge by this freshet, the Nashville and Clarksville line was abandoned beyond Springfield. On the 12th of March General Thomas ordered the East Tennessee and Virginia Railroad opened from Strawberry Plains to Bull's Gap and "put in condition to sustain as heavy a traffic as was done on the Chattanooga and Atlanta line during the summer of 1864." A large force was at once sent to this work, and commenced operations at Strawberry Plains on the 14th of the month, and reached New Market on the 18th, and Bull's Gap on the 25th. Orders were then received to continue the work and open the road to Carter's Station, twenty miles from Bristol. This point was reached on the 29th of April. Owing to the fact that at the time this road was destroyed or damaged the rails were burned and bent in the track, the repairing was necessarily slow and difficult. And here I will take occasion to remark, as the result of four years' experience in repairing railroads damaged during this war, that the most effectual plan of retarding rapid reconstruction of track is not to tear it up, as has so frequently been done by our own forces as well as by the enemy, but to place fence rails, boards, or any combustible material on the track at intervals and fire it, so as to heat the iron and burn off the ends of the cross-ties. The expansion of the rails by heat when spiked down in line bends them into such shapes that they cannot be straightened and used again, and they, together with the damaged ties, have all to be taken up, the road bed cleared before new ties can be laid down, thus imposing upon the construction force a large amount of labor which is saved to them when the plan of taking up the track is adopted.

The following is a summary of the work done on the East Tennessee and Virginia Railroad:

Eighty-seven miles of track surfaced and repaired; 12½ miles of track laid; 4,424 feet (linear) bridges built; 20,000 cross-ties cut and used; 57,000 feet (linear) timber hewn and used in bridges; 8 water-tanks built. A large amount of work was done in and around Chattanooga. The rolling-mill, with all necessary buildings belonging thereto, was completed, and a track with sidings laid, connecting it with the Nashville and Chattanooga Railroad. Additions were made to the machine-shops in the yard, and a number of new offices and buildings for quarters have been erected. About 5,000 feet of main pipe, six inches diameter, was laid to supply the shops and locomotives with water from the works on Cameron Hill, erected by Colonel Merrill's engineer regiment. These works furnished an abundance of water for about two or three weeks, and then, owing to some defect in their construction, they had to be stopped, and were not again in operation during the time we were in possession of the railroads centering at Chattanooga. Accompanying this report is a map* of Chattanooga, drawn by Mr. John F. Burgin, division engineer, upon which is laid down all the tracks and buildings erected by the Construction Corps at that place. I also transmit with the report a list of the buildings, the dimensions of each, amounting in all to 124, and the total amount of lumber consumed in their construction.† Total number of buildings erected, 124; amount of lumber consumed in their erection, 3,000,000 feet B. M.; number of shingles consumed in their erection, 1,283,000. One of the most important buildings which we erected at Chattanooga is the rolling-mill. Under date of July 31 Mr. Eicholtz furnished you a statement of its cost, amounting to $290,329.51. This sum includes the cost of labor and of materials manufactured by the Construction Corps. The machinery and transportation of same amounted to $120,000, and in my opinion this is all that the mill did actually cost the Government, for the labor expended on it was done from time to time, when the corps was not required for the more important work of rebuilding and maintaining the various lines of railway in the military division. We had to keep a force on hand sufficiently large for every emergency, for any line in use might be seriously damaged at any moment, and additional lines were continually being opened up as the general commanding required them; but there were times when the whole force was not required for this kind of work, and then, and only then, were they employed on the rolling-mill. The mill went into operation about the last of March, and had manufactured up to July 31 2,136 tons; 421 tons issued, 1,715 tons remaining on hand July 31, 1865. The mill has not

*Not found

†Omitted.

been worked to its full capacity. Mr. T. W. Yardley, the efficient superintendent, estimates that it is capable of turning out fifty tons per day. As it is, the mill has more than paid for itself; but had the war continued until this time, and our railroad operations in the Southwest been carried on on the same extensive scale that they had been for the last year, it would have been invaluable.

The large amount of damaged rails on the lines centering at Chattanooga would have furnished an abundance of material for the mill, which could have supplied all the rails required, thus saving the first cost and transportation of new iron, with the additional advantage of having it on the spot where it was wanted. On the 6th of May orders were received from your office to reduce the Construction Corps "to the lowest possible limit." It was at once reduced to 1,200 men, but a further reduction was arrested by General Thomas' order to rebuild the Chattanooga and Atlanta Railroad. This work was commenced on the 10th of May and completed through to Atlanta on the 4th of July. The road had been badly damaged by General Sherman's army before they started for Savannah. The three important bridges over the Oostenaula, the Etowah, and the Chattahoochee Rivers, besides many others of less importance, were all burned; many miles of track were torn up and the rails and ties burned and rendered unfit for relaying; culverts under high embankments were blown up; buildings and water-tanks burned, and, in fact, it was a complete destruction of the railroad from the Etowah to Atlanta. But between the Etowah and Resaca the damage done was not so great, being confined to the destruction of all the bridges and water stations and about one or two miles of track. Between Resaca and Dalton the track had been taken up by the Construction Corps, as stated in my report of May 20. At Marietta our force was met by a force working under the orders of General Winslow, who, by order of Major-General Wilson, had patched up the track from Atlanta to that place and built the bridges over the Chattahoochee River and at the big embankment near Vining's. As much of this work had been done by unskilled laborers who had no chairs and an insufficiency of spikes, it became necessary for our force to relay a good deal of the track. Below is a tabular statement of the work done on this line:

By whom constructed.	Track surfaced and repaired.	Track laid.	Bridging.	Cross-ties.	Timber.	Water-tanks built.
	Miles.	*Miles.*	*Linear ft.*		*Linear ft.*	
Construction Corps	36	49½	2,428	42,500	13,200	6
General Wilson's men	......	17	1,125	37,500	1,800	2
Total	36	66½	3,553	80,000	15,000	8

The cost of General Wilson's work, in addition to the labor of troops, as per settlement of General Winslow with Grant & Co., and approved by General Wilson, is as follows: Seven hundred and twenty-five feet bridging over Chattahoochee River, at $11 per foot, $7,965; amount due for track laying as per check-roll, $7,167; amount for work done at culvert near Vining's, $528; total, $15,670.

For the amount of work done this bill is quite reasonable and should be paid. At Atlanta the Construction Corps laid about three miles of sidings, and built a large freight platform 400 by 30 feet, with a roof over part of it. Upon the completion of the road to

Atlanta and after putting the track in thorough condition a fourth reduction of the corps was made. On the 15th of August it numbered but 200 men, and by the 1st of October it was entirely disbanded. I have retained a few engineers and clerks, whose assistance is necessary in making up the final reports and closing up the Construction Department, U. S. Military Railroads. The following table shows the number of men employed and the amount of the pay-rolls for each month since my report of November 1, 1864:

Month.	Number of men.	Amount of pay-rolls.
1864.		
November	3,428	$231,281.30
December	3,254	242,376.58
1865.		
January	2,589	194,809.27
February	2,883	146,698.18
March	2,759	197,449.44
April	2,703	192,784.81
May	2,447	146,176.01
June	1,587	117,866.91
July	1,141	76,361.00
August	495	20,970.18
September	361	6,637.02
Total	23,647	1,573,410.70
Monthly average	2,149	143,037.33

Exhibit B, accompanying this report, is a tabular statement of the amount of lumber and shingles cut each month at the saw-mills operated by the Construction Corps.* They were five in number, and were located at Loudon, Lenoir, Calhoun, Chickamauga, and Chattanooga.

The total amount of lumber cut was	Feet, B. M.	5,628,456
Issued to transportation department	do	547,448
Issued to other parties	do	147,114
Turned over to Captain Hopkins	do	450,483
		1,145,045
Consumed by Construction Corps	do	4,483,411
Total	do	5,628,456
The total amount of shingles cut was		1,547,355
Issued to transportation department		151,350
Issued to other parties		58,100
Turned over to Captain Hopkins		221,800
Consumed by Construction Corps		1,116,105
Total		1,547,355

Before closing this part of my report I must bear full testimony to the successful management of the affairs in this department during my absence by L. H. Eicholtz, esq., acting chief engineer, and for the minor details of operations I respectfully refer you to his reports, copies of which are on file in your office.

NORTH CAROLINA.

As a full report of operations in this department was made to you on the 20th of May last, it will only be necessary for me to add to it

* Omitted.

for the purposes of this report a brief statement of what was done from that date up to the 1st of July, and to make some slight alterations in it which I find necessary. The lines from Morehead City to Raleigh and from Wilmington to Goldsborough remained in possession of the Government and continued to be operated by our department. The reduction of the force on these roads was gradually continued and expenses reduced in every way possible. Whenever practicable colored laborers (who could be obtained for $15 to $20 per month) were substituted for the more expensive white labor, which in the first place we were compelled to bring from the North, and all men were now employed by the month instead of by the day, as had been necessary during the war, and the allowance of extra time was ordered to be discontinued. On the 6th of July I was relieved of the charge of the Department of North Carolina, but it was not until the 17th that my successor was prepared to take hold of the roads. When transferred to him the roadway was in fine condition, the bridges, water stations, and all other structures in complete order; a large supply of wood, lumber, cross-ties, saw logs, &c., on hand; the rolling-stock in good repair, and, in short, everything in such shape that the roads could be operated with but small comparative outlay for some months to come. At the time I was relieved the following list of supplies were reported on hand in his department by the timber inspector: Seven thousand six hundred and fifty-five cords wood, 11,400 cross-ties, 2,826 piles, 689 pieces hewn timber, 6,500 linear feet saw logs. From the date of my last report until relieved the following amount of materials of the kind named were used in the maintenance of my department:

Kind of material.		Morehead City and Raleigh line.	Wilmington and Goldsborough line.	Total.
Iron rails	tons	103	39	142
Chairs	number	....	200	200
Spikes	kegs	200	48	248
Cross-ties	number	13,500	1,753	15,253
Hewn timber	linear feet	3,200	2,600	5,800
Sawed lumber	feet, B. M.	7,160	3,000	10,160
Nails and spikes	kegs	24	20	44

The following table shows the movement of loaded cars over both roads from the 1st of May to the 17th of July, 1865:

FORWARDED.

From—	To—	Number.
Morehead City	The front	1,427
Do	New Berne	225
New Berne	The front	325
Do	Morehead City	361
Wilmington	Goldsborough	547
Total		2,880

RECEIVED.

At—	From—	Number.
Morehead City	The front	271
Do	New Berne	361
New Berne	The front	556
Do	Morehead City	225
Wilmington	Goldsborough	122
Total		1,535

RECAPITULATION.

Loaded cars received—	
At the front	1,747
At New Berne	1,006
At Morehead City	993
At Goldsborough	547
At Wilmington	122
Total	4,415

The following is a statement of the number, description, condition, and initials of all cars and engines belonging to the Government or in use on the military railroads in North Carolina:

Number.	Description.	Condition.	Initials.
3	Passenger-cars	Running order	U. S. M. R. R.
3	.....do	.....do	W. and W. R. R.
3	.....do	.....do	R. and G. R. R.
3	.....do	.....do	N. C. R. R.
2	.....do	.....do	A. and N. C. R. R.
1	Second-class car	Bad order	N. C. R. R.
1	Baggage-car	Running order	A. and N. C. R. R.
1	.....do	Bad order	W. and W. R. R.
1	Mail car	Running order	A. and N. C. R. R.
1	.....do	Bad order	N. C. R. R.
16	Box-cars	Running order	U. S M. R. R.
3	.....do	Bad order	Do.
10	.....do	.....do	R. and G. R. R.
3	.....do	Running order	Do.
8	.....do	Bad order	W. and W. R. R.
3	.....do	.....do	Petersburg R. R.
2	.....do	.....do	S. and R. R. R.
6	.....do	.....do	N. C. R. R.
2	.....do	Running order	Do.
2	.....do	Bad order	M. C. R. R.
1	.....do	.....do	Vir. Cent. R. R.
1	.....do	.....do	Petersburg and Weldon R. R.
31	Rack-cars	Running order	U. S. M. R. R.
138	Flat-cars	.....do	Do.
1	.....do	Bad order	Do.
4	.....do	.....do	S. and R. R. R.
3	.....do	.....do	C. S. A.
3	.....do	.....do	W. and W. R. R.
11	.....do	.....do	R. and G. R. R.
1	.....do	.....do	Petersburg R. R
3	.....do	.....do	N. C. R. R.

Total number of cars, 271.

RECAPITULATION.

Passenger-cars	15
Mail-cars	2
Baggage-cars	2
Box-cars	57
Rack-cars	31
Flat-cars	164
Total	271

Initials.	Name.	Builder.	Condition.	Remarks.
U. S. M. R. R...	Blue Bird	Baldwin	Needs repairs	
	Union	....do	Good order	
	Vulcan	....do	....do	
	Governor Nye	Norris	Needs repairs	
	Reindeer	....do	Being repaired	
	Secretary	Taunton Locomotive Works	Good order	
	Grape Shot	....do	....do	
	Chief	....do	....do	
	Scout	Jersey City Locomotive Works.	Needs repairs	
	Commodore	Smith & Jackson	Good order	
	Lion	....do	....do	
	Colonel Webster	Manchester Locomotive Works.	Needs repairs	
	Ancient	Norris	Being repaired	
R. & G. R. R ...	Halifax	....do	Needs repairs	Captured.
	Raleigh	....do	....do	Do.
W. & W. R. R..	Wilmington	Manchester Locomotive Works.	Being repaired	Do.
	Perseverance	Baldwin	Good order	Do.
	Goldsborough	Manchester Locomotive Works.	Needs repairs	Do.
	Orange	....do	Being repair	Do.
	General Schofield *a*	Baldwin	Good order	Do.
	President	Norris	Being repaired	Do.
	Lamb *a*	....do	Good order	Do.
	Job Terry	Hinkley	Bad order	Do.
	Stonewall	Norris	....do	Do.
	Brunswick	....do	....do	Do.
	North Carolina	Baldwin	....do	Do.
	Tornado	Anderson	....do	Do.
	(No name)	Manchester Locomotive Works.	....do	Do.

Total number of engines, 28.

a Rebuilt at Wilmington shop by U. S. Military Railroads.

The total cost of labor is shown in the following statement. Although we did not arrive in North Carolina until the 5th of February, still I have included the January rolls in this statement because we left Nashville about the 1st of January, and the time consumed in reaching our destination is, I think, properly chargeable to this department:

Month.	Department.				Total.	Number of men.
	Construction and maintenance.	Machine.	Transportation.	Quartermaster's.		
January	$92,083.01	$4,799.69	$5,023.00		$101,905.70	1,344
February	128,377.69	8,568.86	5,972.55	$1,835.00	144,754.10	2,145
March	191,131.11	17,336.07	15,116.98	2,199.00	225,783.16	2,839
April	176,433.86	27,697.21	14,582.48	2,272.83	220,986.38	3,328
May	95,740.87	14,440.92	31,683.37	2,232.50	144,097.66	3,387
June	50,144.68	15,796.20	26,152.55	2,059.52	94,152.75	1,437
Total					931,679.75	14,480
Average					155,279.95	2,413

I have the honor to be, very respectfully, your obedient servant,

W. W. WRIGHT,

Chief Engineer U. S. Military Railroads.

WAR DEPT., PROVOST-MARSHAL-GENERAL'S OFFICE,
VETERAN RESERVE CORPS BUREAU,
Washington, D. C., November 30, 1865.

Brig. Gen. JAMES B. FRY,
Provost-Marshal-General:

GENERAL: I have the honor to submit the following report of the operations of this Bureau from its organization up to September 30, 1865. In preparing it the principle has been kept in view that a history of the Bureau, conceived with regard to its most important relations, becomes a history of that branch of the Army of which it has been the official center.

Whether the Veteran Reserve Corps has been of service to the country, what has been the method of its organization, what were the errors, and what the merits of that method are the main points that I have attempted to elucidate.

NECESSITY OF THE CORPS.

The Invalid Corps, subsequently styled the Veteran Reserve Corps, sprang from a national necessity. So severe was the draft of the war on the able-bodied manhood of the American people that an intelligent economy of the public forces demanded that some portion of the vast number of men who are unfit for field service should be utilized for military purposes.

To conscript or enlist infirm citizens would have been cruelty and folly, except under the extremest pressure of necessity. But to keep in service experienced soldiers who were simply disabled for the march; to relieve with them more than their own number of able-bodied men, who could thus be sent from the rear to the front; to provide the Government with a reliable military police, urgently needed in a time of raids, riots, and treasonable, or at least injudicious murmurings; to constitute a garrison force admirable for its unity of organization and purpose, and all without the expense of recruiting or the severity of conscription, was a labor of mercy and wisdom.

INTRODUCTORY MEASURES.

The first step in the direction of this result was taken within a year of the commencement of the war. On the 7th of April, 1862, the War Department authorized the chief medical officer in each city to employ as nurses, cooks, and hospital attendants any convalescent wounded or feeble men who could perform such duties, instead of giving them a discharge. In this, however, there was no germ of organization, but rather the contrary; the invalids thus occupied were useful indeed, but they ceased to be soldiers in fact and in spirit; and in too many instances they continued to be mere hangers-on of hospitals long after they were able to resume the musket. Not until nearly a year later did the War Department institute a measure which distinctly pointed to the idea of an Invalid or Veteran Reserve Corps. In General Orders, No. 69, Adjutant-General's Office, March 20, 1863, it was directed that the feeble and wounded men in hospitals who were unfit for field duty, but still not entirely disabled, should be organized into detachments under the charge of officers acting as military commanders. From these invalid detachments were detailed provost, hospital, and other guards, clerks, nurses, cooks, and other extra-duty men. For the first time in the war strictly military authority and system were directed to the utilization of disabled soldiers. Accordingly the invalid detachments were serviceable in their limited sphere of action. They were, however, temporary in their nature, the men were mustered and paid on their detachment rolls, but were not dropped from the rolls of their original companies; and on becoming fit for the field they were returned to their colors.

As before, the hospitals continued to discharge thousands of soldiers whose disabilities merely unfitted them for the march and bivouac, while leaving them entirely competent to act as garrison troops and provost-police. That branch of the Army which should call into military use the large class of semi-healthy men was yet to be devised.

AUTHORIZATION OF AN INVALID CORPS.

The final step in this progress, the result of severe martial experience and urgent national need, was taken at the suggestion of the Provost-Marshal-General and, with the prompt and cordial approval of the Secretary of War, on the 28th of April, 1863, was issued General Order 105, Adjutant-General's Office, opening with the sentence: "The organization of an Invalid Corps is hereby authorized." The order proceeds to direct that it shall consist of companies, and, if thereafter thought best, of battalions, and then follow stringent provisions intended to keep it within its proper limits and render it a Corps of Honor. Three sources of supply are indicated—first, men in the field who had been disabled by wounds or by disease contracted in the line of duty; second, men absent from their colors in hospitals or convalescent camps, or otherwise under the control of medical officers; third, men who had been discharged for injuries received through honorable service. Officers as well as soldiers might be collected from these three classes, and from these alone.

The fact of partial disability must be established in all cases by medical certificates, granted only after personal examination. Meritorious character in regard to intelligence, industry, sobriety, and attention to duty must be vouched for by military superiors.

In the case of officers who had left the service, applications to enter the corps must be made through the acting assistant provost-marshal-general of the State in which the candidate resided, fortified by medical certificates of partial disability incurred in service, by evidence of honorable discharge, and by recommendations from former regimental, brigade, and division commanders. To insure rapid recruitment commandants of regiments throughout the Army were directed to make out rolls of their men and officers who were unfitted for field service and forward them, certified by their own names and those of the examining surgeons, to the Provost-Marshal-General, while medical inspectors, surgeons in charge of hospitals, military commanders, and all others having power to grant discharges were forbidden to release from service any man under their control who might be suitable for the Invalid Corps. Finally, the Provost-Marshal-General was charged with the execution of the order, and the troops organized according to its provisions were placed under his command.

First official year.

ESTABLISHMENT AND NATURE OF THIS BUREAU.

Col. Richard H. Rush, of the Sixth Pennsylvania Cavalry, subsequently colonel of the First Regiment Veteran Reserve Corps, was the first officer assigned to duty by the Provost-Marshal-General as chief of this Bureau. Appointed May 23, 1863, he held the position until November 9 of the same year. From his accession until his official report, dated October 31, 1863, is the first of the three divisions of time into which this history naturally divides itself. It is hardly necessary to explain that toward the Provost-Marshal-General the chief of the Bureau has always stood in the relation of an adjutant toward his commanding officer, deriving from him all his authority and issuing orders only in his name. He has presided over the multifarious minor details of the organization of the corps, but only as an assistant or adjutant. He has issued special orders and occasionally letters of instruction, but always by direction of the Provost-Marshal-General. General instructions and directions have usually been promulgated over the personal signature of the Provost-Marshal-General under the title of circulars. General orders, strictly so named, have in all cases proceeded from the Adjutant-General of the Army, although usually, if not always, suggested by the Provost-Marshal-General. Nevertheless, the labors and responsibilities of the position of chief of the Bureau were sufficient to occupy closely a man of activity and intelligence. Colonel Rush commenced operations with four clerks, but by the end of six months this force had increased to four commissioned officers and six clerks, and the duty performed was so far from light that it demanded night work on an average of five nights in a week. A large proportion of this drudgery arose from the fact that at first all the descriptive lists and other papers relating to the transferred men passed through the office. At a later period this burdensome centralization was remedied.

RECRUITING.

Every proper means was used to fill up the corps as rapidly as possible. In a circular issued May 22, 1863, the Provost-Marshal-General called the attention of officers who had been honorably discharged for wounds and disabilities to the nature of the organization. He directed that the acting assistant provost-marshal-general of each State should at once open a recruiting station for the corps; that he should attach to it a camp of rendezvous provided with the necessary quarters and subsistence for recruits, and that he should send in estimates of the stores needed for a fixed number of companies. One hundred and sixty-one companies were allotted to the loyal States and the District of Columbia in a ratio graduated according to population and other probabilities of enlistment. They were to be organized, uniformed, equipped, and armed at the camp of rendezvous.

In his capacity of superintendent of recruiting the acting assistant provost-marshal-general of the State was held responsible that the depots should be kept supplied with material for this purpose. A discharged soldier wishing to enlist went before an enrollment board, and, if judged a proper subject for the corps, received a certificate to that effect. On this document any district provost-marshal would furnish him transportation to the nearest superintendent of recruiting, who, after satisfying himself that the applicant was of meritorious character, enlisted him.

In case of rejection he was entitled to a ticket of transportation to his home. For a time commandants of companies were empowered to muster in desirable men who presented themselves with proper certificates from an enrollment board. Discharged soldiers of over forty-five years of age, whether they had left the service during the war or previous to it, might be accepted. Enlistments were for three years unless sooner discharged; neither officers nor soldiers might be allowed bounty or premium; they were to be paid like U. S. infantry, except the bounty for re-enlistment.

The Board of Enrollment decided whether the recruits were suitable for the First, or Second, or Third Battalions. Those who were able to bear a musket and do garrison duty were recommended for the First, those who had lost an arm or hand, or who were otherwise so severely injured as to be fit only for hospital guards and attendants, for the Second, while the severest and most hopeless cases of disability were assigned to the Third. In Circular No. 18, June 6, 1863, the Provost-Marshal-General indicated his desire that the first class should equal in number the other two combined. In fact, there never was a Third Battalion; the individuals assigned to it were put in the companies of the Second by General Orders, No. 212, Adjutant-General's Office, July 9, 1863; and the number of men in the corps bearing muskets has always doubled that of those fit merely for hospital and clerical duty. During a period of about a year, indeed, the proportion was 21,000 to 7,000.

Commanders of camps and of recruiting stations were of two classes. They might be permanently disabled officers who had been appointed to commissions in the corps by the Secretary of War, or they might be invalid officers of volunteer regiments in the field, temporarily assigned to this duty. These last were permitted to transfer their services to the corps on proper proof of physical disability, good military history, and meritorious character, and they were to be considered mustered in and were to draw pay from the date of acceptance of appointment or commission. Each commander of a recruiting station sent monthly reports to the superintendent and tri-monthly ones to the Provost-Marshal-General. In August, 1863, this system was discontinued; the recruiting parties were ordered to report to the superintendents of the several States in which they were stationed, and they were assigned by them to companies already formed or forming in the camp of rendezvous. Henceforward the recruiting of the corps was managed by the ordinary machinery of the Provost-Marshal-General's Bureau, except that each superintendent was allowed two invalid officers to aid him in this extra labor. The enlisted men of the companies were subsisted in the usual manner of recruits in the U. S. Army. If possible, rations were drawn from the nearest issuing commissary; otherwise the acting assistant commissary purchased supplies. It was ordered that every independent command of the Invalid Corps should have one officer detailed as acting assistant commissary of subsistence and acting assistant quartermaster. Requisitions were to be approved by the senior officer of the post. All the costs of recruiting, together with the legal miscellaneous expenses of the camps, such as stationery, office furniture, &c., were to be paid on the usual vouchers by the disbursing officer of the Provost-Marshal-General's Bureau. While recruiting a company bore a temporary designation, as, for instance, "First Company, First Battalion, organized at Convalescent Camp, Alexandria, Va.," but after the muster and descriptive rolls had reached Washington a permanent number was assigned to the organization and no other thenceforward used.

TRANSFERS FROM THE FIELD.

The accession of men from the field was regulated with equal care. Commandants of regiments and batteries who had made out rolls of men and officers suitable for the Invalid Corps were directed to forward them each to his own corps commander. It was his duty to transmit them, with his remarks, to the Provost-Marshal-General; then to issue orders transferring the enrolled individuals from their present organizations to the Invalid Corps; lastly, to send them to a rendezvous indicated by the Adjutant-General in the department where his command was then serving. He might forward their arms and equipments with them, or not, at his option. A subsequent order directed that the rolls above mentioned, as well as those furnished by chiefs of hospitals, should state the nature of the transferred man's disability, and whether he was fitted for the First or Second Battalion.

It was soon found that unsuitable officers were sometimes nominated for the organization by corps commanders. Naturally and justly anxious to keep every worthy man in field service, they were apt to decide that any one would do for an invalid corps who had incurred the necessary amount of physical disability, no matter what might be his character as a man or his history as a soldier. It seemed to be considered a proper receptacle for persons who were useless or noxious at the front, but whose offenses were still not flagrant enough to warrant dismissal from the service. In most instances this was probably not so much the error of the chiefs of corps as of other subordinate officers, especially the heads of regiments.

It was decided by the War Department to rescind so much of General Orders, No. 173, as authorized corps commanders to transfer commissions to the Invalid Corps, and to direct that every one desiring a position in it should make written application therefor to the Provost-Marshal-General. His request must be backed by a surgeon's certificate of partial disability, by recommendations from at least three former commanders of rank, and by his full military history. Officers already transferred, but who had not yet received their appointments from the Secretary of War, were to make similar applications.

TRANSFERS FROM HOSPITALS.

The largest accessions were derived, as was natural, from the hospitals. On the 11th of June, 1863, the invalid detachments heretofore mentioned were dissolved and their members, whether commissioned or enlisted, turned over to the corps, provided they possessed the proper moral and physical qualifications. In all general hospitals or convalescent camps rolls of transfer were made out after each regular muster. Not only the wounded and the disabled by disease, but men of over forty-five and under eighteen were held to be proper subjects of action. Unquestionably the most efficient single means of bringing men into the corps was the organization of examining boards to visit hospitals and decide upon the disposition of the patients. The inspections were conducted in accordance with the provisions of General Orders, No. 130, Adjutant-General's Office, May 15, 1863. It contains two lists of physical infirmities, the first disqualifying men for active service, but not for the Invalid Corps; the second disqualifying for the Invalid Corps and qualifying for a discharge. A revised list was published by the same authority in General Orders, No. 212, dated July 9, 1863. Five boards were constituted, headed, respectively, by Surg. R. H. Coolidge, medical inspector, U. S. Army; Col. A. G. Brackett, Ninth Regiment Illinois Cavalry; Capt. J. C. Peterson, Fifteenth Regiment U. S. Infantry; Capt. M. Cogswell, Eighth U. S. Infantry, and Surg. G. L. Sutton, U. S. Volunteers. The following tabular statement will give an idea of the amount and kind of labor performed by these details:

	Transferred to Invalid Corps.	Returned to regiments.	Returned to hospitals.	Recommended for discharge.	Total examined.
Surgeon Coolidge's board	3,366	2,458	1,754	149	7,727
Captain Peterson's board	2,783	1,805	129	324	5,041

Non-commissioned officers and soldiers were transferred with the same rank which they held in their original organizations. They might be mustered out and re-enlisted in the corps, if they chose, but their new term would be for three years unless sooner discharged. Officers who entered from field organizations were to send in their resignations dated the day previous to the acceptance of the new commissions. Transfers from one battalion to another were made on the 1st of every month, after a rigid examination by a surgeon and the senior officer of the post or hospital. Soldiers of the First Battalion who proved unfit for it were shifted to the Second. Those of the Second who became entirely disabled might be discharged, except in cases of good men, injured in the service, who desired to remain. These could be retained and assigned to clerical or other light duty. If they were mustered out for disability and at their own request, it must be so stated on their final papers. The former company and regiment and the State from which the man originally enlisted, as well as the order of transfer to the corps, were also to be noted on all certificates of discharge.

A considerable number of Invalid Corps officers were soon on duty in the hospitals, relieving convalescents who were sufficiently recovered to go to the front. Their position was that of military assistants or military commanders. They were subordinate to the surgeon in charge, and aided him in his administrative and executive duties. The senior attended to the police and discipline of the establishment; was responsible for the clothing, arms, equipments, and descriptive lists of men received; noted on the descriptive rolls all payments and issues of clothing made at the hospital; supervised the muster and pay rolls, the accounts of the patients, the property inventories of deceased men, the reports of deaths and discharges; recorded the deaths and interments and saw that the graves had proper headboards; in the absence of the chaplain kept the chaplain's register.

DISCIPLINE AND ORGANIZATION.

How should discipline be established with promptness and uniformity in an organization needed for immediate use and drawn from every arm of the service? Various directions to this end were issued in orders, circulars, and letters. Each company was to be made up, if possible, of men from different States; it was to be kept intact, as far as its duties would allow, and detachments from it were to be relieved as often as once a week; regular parades and frequent short drills were to be had, both in the camps of rendezvous and at stations; commanding officers were to hold their subordinates to a strict accountability; incorrigibly bad men were to be dishonorably discharged. On the 1st of each month the company commandant was to forward to the Bureau a list of all deaths, desertions, and discharges, with names, rank, former company, regiment, and State. On arriving at a new station he was to report also to the Bureau the strength of his command, the names of men missing on the way, where lost, and whether probably stragglers or deserters.

The formation established for the companies was that of the U. S. infantry, but the maximum was not demanded, and they were usually ordered to stations on attaining a minimum.

On the 5th of September, 1863, the Provost-Marshal-General was authorized by the Adjutant-General to organize the companies into regiments, and on the 26th of the month following he was permitted to appoint colonels and lieutenant-colonels, with commissions dating from September 5, 1863.

UNIFORM.

One of the first steps of the War Department with regard to the corps had been to devise a special uniform for it. For enlisted men it consisted of a dark-blue forage cap and sky-blue trousers, according to the present regulation, and of a sky-blue kersey jacket, trimmed with dark blue and cut long in the waist, like that of the U. S. cavalry. Officers were directed to wear a sky-blue frock coat, with collar, cuffs, and shoulder-strap grounds of dark blue velvet, and sky-blue trousers, with a double stripe of dark blue down the outer seam, the stripes half an inch wide and three-quarters of an inch apart.

The uniform was becoming, but has never been popular. The men did not like to be distinguished from their comrades of the active service by a peculiar costume; they wanted to keep the dark-blue blouse and dress coat in which they had learned their profession and received their honorable disabilities. This feeling was aggravated by the inevitable jealousy between field and garrison regiments, which ripened into something like bitterness between the soldiers of the Invalid Corps and the ranks in which they had so lately marched and fought.

In the case of the officers, the light blue was so far from agreeable to the eye and soiled so easily that they were eventually allowed and then directed to resume the dark-blue frock coat, although retaining the other insignia of their branch of the service.

RESULTS.

Such is the substance of the orders, circulars, and letters of instruction issued with regard to the Invalid Corps during the first six months of its existence. On the 31st of October, 1863 [November 6, 1863*], Colonel Rush submitted a report exhibiting the following results:

The corps contained sixteen regiments, each constituted of six companies of the First and four companies of the Second Battalion. The force was officered by 16 colonels, 16 lieutenant-colonels, 8 majors, 166

---

* See Vol. III, this series, p. 999.

captains, 169 first lieutenants, and 116 second lieutenants, making a total of 491 officers.

The numerical changes during the period are embodied in the following tabular statements:

Number of companies organized monthly.

Month.	First Battalion.	Second Battalion.	Total.
June	16	6	22
July	23	8	31
August	41	30	71
September	18	22	40
October	22	17	39
Total	120	83	203

Return of the corps up to October 31, 1863.

ENLISTED MEN.

Gains:		
Transferred from other organizations	16,448	
Recruited	1,431	
		17,879
Losses:		
Discharged for disability	87	
Discharged by expiration of service	1	
Discharged by order of the General-in-Chief	1	
Discharged dishonorably	26	
		115
Total remaining		17,764

OFFICERS.

Appointed		501
Appointments declined	3	
Appointments revoked	2	
Resigned	2	
Dismissed the service	3	
		10
Total remaining		491
Aggregate officers and men		18,255

Second official year.

On the 9th of November, 1863, Col. M. N. Wisewell, of the Sixth Regiment Veteran Reserve Corps, was assigned to take charge of the Bureau.

EXAMINATION OF OFFICERS.

One of the earliest objects of attention during this official year was the purification of the corps from officers of inferior character and ability. Three days before the accession of Colonel Wisewell a notification had been issued by the Provost-Marshal-General to the effect that the examinations of officers would commence as soon after January 1, 1864, as practicable, and that they would be tested as to their knowledge of regulations and tactics and their general fitness for their present positions and for promotion. The first board of this nature was convened in Washington January 12, 1864, by order of the Adjutant-General, who directed that it should be governed by such instructions as might be prescribed for it by the Provost-Marshal-General. It consisted of seven colonels, a lieutenant-colonel, a surgeon, and a first lieutenant who officiated as recorder. As it soon became evident that one board could not do all the labor of this kind which was required, the Adjutant-General authorized (February 13, 1864) the Provost-Marshal-General to convene others at such times and places as he might designate. Under this order the system continued to work until it was no longer needed. Records of the examinations of all the officers who were then in the corps and of all who have entered it since are preserved in the Bureau. The heads according to which they were tested are as follows: Field service, disability, recommendations, capacity for a commission, general education, intelligence, industry, knowledge of tactics, regulations, Articles of War, discipline and service, record of sobriety, and of attention to duty. Of those who already held appointments in the organization only one-twenty-fourth were thrown out as unsuitable for their positions.

RECRUITING.

On the 31st of December, 1863, the Provost-Marshal-General stopped recruiting for the Second Battalion for the reason that a sufficient number of men were added to it by transfer from the field regiments and the hospitals. In February, 1864, it was decided that men enlisted for the First Battalion should be credited to the quota of their State, township, &c. As the increase of the corps barely balanced the large diminution by discharge, it was ordered that men might be accepted who had served two years in the Army or marines, without regard to disability. Like other recruits, they were to have neither bounty nor premium, and they were only to be received on condition that they were not subject to draft.

TRANSFERS.

Officers discharging men from hospitals or field service because of physical disability were directed, in case the individual was not meritorious, to indorse on the discharge that he was unsuited for the Invalid Corps. So much of General Orders, No. 105, 1863, as forbade the discharge of men fit for the corps was revoked as regarded soldiers who had less than six months to serve. Disabled substitutes and drafted men might be transferred, as well as volunteers. By a circular from the Adjutant-General's Office, January 18, 1864, all invalids who had been mustered on transfer rolls by surgeons in charge of hospitals and all soldiers of the Second Battalion considered well enough for the First Battalion were sent to the Invalid Corps rendezvous nearest the hospital, there to be inspected by an examining board, which had power to confirm the transfer, assign the men to either battalion, return them to the field, or discharge them from the service. It is to be observed that soldiers of the Regular Army were never properly transferred to the corps, and that where this occurred the action was revoked and the individuals sent to the hospitals of their respective regiments.

The corps was influenced by the veteran volunteer movement and a considerable number of the transferred men re-enlisted. It was decided that these cases should count on the quotas of States, &c., as in other branches of the Army, but that they should not be allowed the premium and bounties for future service which were granted to re-enlisted members of field organizations. In other words, the veteran volunteer in the corps only received the $100 due for his original term and such local bounty as he might be paid by the State, county, or township to which he was credited.

ORDINARY OFFICIAL BUSINESS.

Few changes were made during this period in the method of transacting the ordinary official business of the organization. In January, 1864, it was ordered that commandants of companies should no longer forward their monthly returns direct to the headquarters of the corps and of the Army. They were to send them to their proper regimental commanders, who were to transmit consolidated returns to the Provost-Marshal-General and to the superintendent of recruiting in the State where the regiment was stationed. Unattached companies continued to act in this matter as regiments.

CHANGE OF DESIGNATION OF THE CORPS.

One of the most important events in the history of the corps during the year was a change in its designation. General Orders, No. 111, Adjutant-General's Office, March 18, 1864, directed that the name of Invalid Corps should be dropped for that of Veteran Reserve Corps. There were two reasons for this action, one deduced from sentiment and the other from utility. The bitter prejudice of field troops against a garrison organization had found scope in a multitude of sarcasms and jeers which made the title of Invalid Corps a burden. Men frequently begged to be sent back to their old regiments in the field rather than remain in garrison at the price of being called invalids. The second cause for the change was the necessity of enlarging the limits of recruitment. About this period such numbers were discharged through expiration of term of service that the losses very nearly equaled the accessions, and, indeed, during a part of 1864 greatly exceeded them.

A Veteran Reserve Corps might accept classes of men which an Invalid Corps could not. Circular 65, Adjutant-General's Office, 1864, heretofore mentioned as allowing enlistments among discharged soldiers not subject to draft, without reference to disabilities, must be considered as a sequence of this change of title. Notwithstanding the absurdity of the prejudice against the word invalid, the new nomenclature was no doubt a benefit, inasmuch as it removed, at least in part, an obstacle to that esprit de corps which is so essential to the well-being and efficiency of a military organization.

SERVICES—GUARD DUTY.

No statistics of the ordinary duty performed by the corps during this official year have been collected, except the fact that 21,345 recruits, deserters, &c., were guarded by the Tenth Regiment, with a loss of only thirty-five. At this distance of time it would be difficult to obtain data for an accurate or even approximative report on the subject.

It is known, however, that the services rendered by the Veteran Reserves were very arduous, and it is believed that more duty would not have been demanded of a similar number of able-bodied soldiers.

They furnished guards for the rebel prison camps at Rock Island and Chicago, Ill.; Indianapolis, Ind.; Johnson's Island, Ohio; Elmira, N. Y.; Point Lookout, Md.; for the recruiting depots and camps of distribution at Portland, Concord, Boston, New Haven, New York City, Trenton, Pittsburg, Fort Snelling, and Alexandria; they supplied provost-marshals of districts with details to enforce the draft; they conducted the conscripts to rendezvous; they escorted large numbers of substitutes, recruits, and rebel prisoners to and from the front; guarded the railroad between Baltimore and Washington, and performed the patrol and guard duty of the capital; manned a portion of the defenses of Washington during the raid of Early, and for four months before and after guarded many general hospitals, and supplied them with ward-masters, nurses, and clerks; furnished clerks, also, to various military departments and superintendents of recruiting.

SERVICES—FIELD DUTY.

The field service of the corps has, of course, been slight; but when called on for this species of duty it has performed it with as much alacrity and steadiness as other troops; it has shown that it could behave in battle as became a corps of veterans. During the raid of Early upon the rear of Washington a large portion of the threatened front was held by the First, Sixth, Seventh, Ninth, Fourteenth, Nineteenth, and Twenty-fourth Regiments. Of these only the Sixth and Ninth came into collision with the enemy. The Sixth had two slight skirmishes in front of Fort De Russy, with a loss of one officer and four men wounded. The Ninth was brought into action at Fort Stevens, after the rebels had pushed their picket-line to within a short distance of the fortification and disabled a number of the gunners. The regiment charged, drove the enemy some distance, and maintained a sharp skirmish until night, losing 5 killed and 7 severely wounded. While the danger to the capital continued the Veteran Reserves endured the same field exposures as the other troops, and with at least equal cheerfulness.

As the proof of this zeal, and also of the fact that invalid soldiers can for a short time perform severe duty, it is worth while to note the fact that the Sixth Regiment made a day's march of twenty-three miles from one threatened point to another, with only one straggler, and that one excused by the surgeon. Major-General McCook, who commanded the defenses, complimented the Veteran Reserves in his official report as follows:

> To Colonel Gile and the officers and men of the First Brigade, Veteran Reserve Corps, I am largely indebted for the success of my efforts in keeping the enemy from our line until the arrival of the Sixth Corps.

The history of the Eighteenth Regiment Veteran Reserve Corps, during the summer of 1864, is an interesting and even pathetic exhibition of what invalid soldiers can and will do if necessary. It was composed of six Second Battalion companies; that is to say, of men who had been declared unfit not only for field service but for garrison duty; of men so far crippled and enfeebled that the inspecting surgeons had judged them unable to carry a weightier weapon than the sword.

They had, however, been armed with muskets and used as guards to forward soldiers to the Army. They were unfit to march, but they could go by rail or boat, and they could fire on deserters. When

Colonel Johnson took command he found some of his men unable to bear a musket on the right shoulder and some on the left; there were men who could not wear the cartridge-box belt, and men who could not wear the waist belt; some had been excused from the cartridge-box, and had their cartridges in their pockets; one could carry twenty rounds, another ten, and another five. These variations were not dictated by the caprice of the soldiers, but by the judgment of surgeons.

The six companies were assigned to Colonel Johnson on the 7th of May. Four days afterward he received an order to embark at 6 on the following morning for Belle Plain, Va., then a depot of stores and prisoners in the rear of the Army of the Potomac. The regiment numbered 10 officers and 514 men present for duty, and 10 men present sick. The first five days at Belle Plain were passed in a continual rain, without tents, without rubber blankets, without medical stores, without even a surgeon. Until May 24 the regiment guarded the rebel prisoners at the post and escorted detachments of them northward, transmitting in this manner 2,996, with a loss of two escaped and one killed in the attempt. As General Grant advanced toward Petersburg it became necessary to move the base of supplies southward, and on the 23d of May a medical examination was made of the Eighteenth to decide what men could go to Port Royal, a distance of about twenty-five miles by land. The surgeons reported that of the 474 present 166 could march without knapsacks, and that the rest were not able to march at all. The officers all refused to be examined, or represented themselves as fit for the field. While the mass of the regiment, 308 men, were put on a transport and sent by water to their destination, Colonel Johnson with his select band, still miserably provided for active service, set out as a part of the marching column. The first field night of this forlorn hope of invalids was passed in a furious storm of rain and hail, without tents or other cover, the men wrapping themselves in their wet blankets and finding what shelter they could in the corners of rail-fences.

Next morning Colonel Johnson requested that his command might be left to make its own way and take care of itself in its own time.

It could not advance, he said, above a mile an hour; if attacked by guerrillas it could not run away and it would fight; it did not fear any force which was not superior in numbers; its greatest enemy was rapidity of movement. All that day he and his officers coaxed the men on; ordered, pleaded, persuaded, reasoned with the poor fellows who dropped by the roadside; halted those who could walk, to enable those who could only limp to catch up; marched fifteen minutes at a time and then rested ten; accomplished in thirteen hours only twelve miles. On the morning after the conclusion of the journey but 42 of the 166 were able to fall in for roll-call. Then the surgeon who had been assigned to the regiment was ordered to Washington. Colonel Johnson himself attended to the sick; that is, he administered to the lighter cases such medicine as he understood and had; but the graver maladies, the old wounds which had reopened, the limbs which were warped by injuries or helpless with rheumatism, were necessarily neglected. At Port Royal the regiment, now reunited, received its shelter tents. After four days' duty as provost guard it proceeded by transport to White House Landing, on the Pamunkey, where it remained until the 21st of June. Here is the list of duties performed at White House Landing by these six companies of men who had been declared unfit for any purpose but that of the hospital. Guard over rebel prisoners, both at the post and during transportation

North; guard over quartermaster's stores, commissary stores, Sanitary Commission stores, ambulances, and ordnance; guard over the hospitals and the men employed on the railroad; conveyance of the wounded on board the hospital boats.

Every officer and every man was put on duty every day according to the utmost measure of his physical ability. Those who could not walk a beat were posted on the shipping at the landing; those who could not stand, and must sit, on the vessels in the stream. During the stay at White House detachments of the regiment convoyed North by transport 1,500 rebel prisoners without losing one. On the 20th of June it took part in the successful defense of the post against Hampton's raid. Several of the men had been discharged and were on transports about to sail for the North; they returned to the camp, borrowed arms and accouterments, and begged to go into line of battle with their old comrades. Twice during the engagement an aide rode up to Colonel Johnson with the question, "Will your invalids stand?"

"Tell the general," was the answer, "that my men are cripples, and they can't run."

On the 12th of June a medical board examined the regiment and reported that in consequence of wounds or disease contracted in the service four-fifths of it were entirely unfitted for both field and fatigue duty, and recommended that it should be sent to some post where the duties would be light and where the men could obtain diet suitable to their debilitated condition. In consequence of this report the regiment was ordered back to Washington, where it arrived on the 25th of June. Such was the physical exhaustion, notwithstanding several days' rest on the boat, that out of 474 officers and men only five officers and 200 men were able to attempt the two-mile march between Sixth Street Wharf and Cliffburne Barracks, and sixty of this number fell in the streets. The next morning there were 112 officers and men on the sick-list out of an aggregate of 474.

During July, August, and September the regiment guarded the railroad between Washington and Annapolis Junction. The distance being sixteen miles and the number of men for duty only about 400, many of the picket posts (a corporal and three men each) could not be relieved during the entire three months. At Beltsville the line was attacked by a considerable force of Early's cavalry. Sergeant Porter collected twenty men from the posts under his command, formed them in the edge of a wood, and fired six rounds before he was driven from his position. Six of his feeblest men were captured during the retreat, but it was reported by citizens that seven or eight of the cavalry were killed or wounded. While on the railroad the regiment arrested nearly 400 stragglers, one-half of whom proved to be deserters making their way North. During September Companies A and C guarded in Forrest Hall Prison, Georgetown, D. C., 1,140 prisoners, without an instance of escape. In October Companies A, B, C, and D guarded 660 prisoners in Carroll and Old Capitol Prisons. The entire number of prisoners held in confinement by this incomplete regiment of desperately disabled men, during a period of less than six months, was 6,296, of whom only two escaped. What is remarkable in these services is not so much their amount (although that is highly creditable) as the fact that they were performed by soldiers who had been adjudged fit only for hospital duty. It is for this reason that the history of the Eighteenth has been told at greater length than that of any of its comrade regiments. I desire also to call notice to the fact that if this mass of duty had not been accomplished by invalids it would have occupied at least an equal number of able-bodied men, who would thus have been withdrawn from the lines of battle, and in those days it was not easy to obtain all the able-bodied men that were needed for fighting purposes alone.

CHANGES IN ORGANIZATION.

The primary organization of the regiments was a union of six First Battalion with four Second Battalion companies. This arrangement worked imperfectly; the First Battalion men were on garrison duty, and the Second Battalion men scattered through hospitals, reporting to surgeons. The diversity of service and command rendered unity of discipline impossible. During March, April, and May of this official year the regiments were reorganized in such a manner as to consist entirely of First Battalion companies, while the companies of the Second Battalion reassumed their former numbers and returned to their original status as detached organizations.

Numerical changes.

Enlisted men November 1, 1863:			
First Battalion			10,540
Second Battalion			7,224
Total			17,764
GAIN.			
Men transferred to the corps in general orders Adjutant-General's Office since November 1, 1863		18,958	
Transferred by special orders Adjutant-General's Office		4	
Transferred by order of corps commanders		507	
Enlisted in the corps since November 1, 1863		3,416	
Re-enlisted in First Battalion companies since November 1, 1863		2,097	
Re-enlisted in Second Battalion companies since November 1, 1863		461	
Total gain			25,443
			43,207
LOSS.			
Discharged since November 1, 1863:			
By reason of expiration of term—			
First Battalion	3,929		
Second Battalion	2,836		
		6,765	
For disability—			
First Battalian	1,102		
Second Battalion	1,474		
		2,576	
For disability under Circular No. 65—			
First Battalion	62		
Second Battalion	326		
		388	
For purpose of re-enlisting—			
First Battalion	2,097		
Second Battalion	461		
		2,588	
To accept appointments as commissioned officers		49	
To enlist as hospital stewards		20	
Under orders from Adjutant General's Office		63	
For other causes		137	
Total discharged		12,556	
Men of the Regular Army retransferred to their former companies and regiments		29	
Volunteers retransferred to their former companies and regiments, having become fit for active service		377	
To be tried as deserters		71	
Not proper subjects for the corps		567	
Deserted:			
First Battalion	627		
Second Battalion	340		
		967	
Died:			
First Battalion	400		
Second Battalion	266		
		666	
Total loss			15,233
Total number of enlisted men on October 1, 1864			27,974

Number of companies November 1, 1863:		
First Battalion	120	
Second Battalion	83	
	203	
Organized since that date:		
First Battalion	116	
Second Battalion	76	
	192	
Number of companies October 1, 1864:		
First Battalion	236	
Second Battalion	159	
Total		395
The number of officers of the corps on October 31, 1863 was		491
Number appointed since that date		411
		902
Number of officers who have left the service since October 31, 1863:		
Resigned—		
Colonels	3	
Lieutenant-colonels	5	
Majors	2	
Captains	45	
First lieutenants	23	
Second lieutenants	16	
	94	
Honorably discharged—		
Captain	1	
Declined to accept—		
Lieutenant-colonel	1	
Major	1	
First lieutenants	3	
Second lieutenant	1	
	6	
Appointments revoked—		
Captains	5	
First lieutenants	4	
Second lieutenants	2	
	11	
Dismissed—		
Captains	8	
First lieutenants	3	
Second lieutenants	9	
	20	
Deceased—		
Captains	4	
First lieutenant	1	
Second lieutenant	1	
	6	
Total—		
Colonels	3	
Lieutenant-colonels	6	
Majors	3	
Captains	63	
First lieutenants	34	
Second lieutenants	29	
		138
Number of officers October 1, 1864		764
Number of men October 1, 1864		27,974
Aggregate		28,738

Third official year.

The character of this period has been determined to a great extent by three important measures involving the decentralization of official business, the assignment of the Second Battalion to the Surgeon-General, and the discharge from service of the transferred men of the corps.

DECENTRALIZATION OF OFFICIAL BUSINESS.

Up to the close of 1864 all descriptive lists and accounts of pay and clothing of transferred men had been demanded of former company commandants from this Bureau, and had been transmitted by it to the commandants of the companies to which the several men were assigned.

Bearing in mind that over 50,000 men have passed from the active Army into the Veteran Reserve Corps, it is easy to perceive what an immense amount of labor was thus centralized. The system was in accordance with the business customs of armies, but it resulted in an accumulation of clerical work which could be dispersed with advantage. In a circular letter, dated January 2, 1865, Provost-Marshal-General's Office, it was enjoined that thereafter officers of the Veteran Reserve Corps should apply directly to the former company commanders of transferred men for their descriptive lists, supporting each request with a copy of the order of transfer. The diminution in one month of the personal force of the branch from seven commissioned officers and forty-eight clerks to two officers and thirty-one clerks is almost entirely attributable to this change. The office had been crowded in two buildings; it now found sufficient room in one. At least $20,000 have been saved to the Government during the year by this measure. Exteriorly it has worked well. Nearly all the company commandants have been energetic in demanding the descriptive lists of their transferred men, and in case of failure to complete their descriptive rolls they have been promptly reminded of their remissness by the Bureau.

A subsequent circular letter, dated February 10, 1865, Provost-Marshal-General's Office, directed that in case any soldier of the corps died, deserted, or was discharged his company commander should forward a notification of the fact to the adjutant-general of the State from which he originally enlisted.

This labor also had been hitherto performed in the Bureau and had formed no inconsiderable portion of its clerical duty. The object of the measure was of course not only to complete the man's history at the military headquarters of the State, but to check fraudulent or erroneous claims for local bounty, family aid, &c.

In the same economical connection should be mentioned the discontinuance of the invalid-roll system (General Orders, No. 76, Adjutant-General's Office, 1865) and the transfer of disabled men to the corps on the simple recommendation of examining boards. The invalid roll was made out by an officer commanding troops or by a surgeon in charge of a general hospital. It gave the soldier's military history, clothing and pay accounts, moral character, and nature of disability; it needed the indorsements of brigade, division, and corps commanders. Amid the pressure of field operations and the multitude of wounded and sick in the hospitals, it was a document slow in preparation and in transit, and in many instances a long time elapsed between the injury to the man and such official completion of his case as placed him in the ranks of the Veteran Reserve Corps.

Under the new system the examining boards visited the general hospitals once in two months, inspected all patients who were specified as permanently disabled by the surgeon in charge, and made out lists of recommendations for the First or Second Battalion, according to the severity of the injuries. The descriptive lists and clothing and pay accounts were demanded subsequently by the commandants of the respective companies to which the invalids were assigned. Months of the soldier's time were saved thus, and the soldier's time was the Government's money.

TRANSFER OF THE SECOND BATTALION TO THE SURGEON-GENERAL.

The men and officers of the Second Battalion have from the first been used almost entirely for hospital duty. In the early part of this official year an order was issued (General Orders, No. 306, Adjutant-General's Office, December 27, 1864) to the effect that companies or detachments of the battalion, with or without officers, according to the pleasure of the Surgeon-General, might be detached for guards, attendants, nurses, &c., at general hospitals, and that such companies should be mustered by the surgeon in charge, and should not be relieved except by order of the Secretary of War.

Finally it was judged expedient that the department which needed and employed this organization should have entire control of it.

An order was issued (General Orders, No. 43, Adjutant-General's Office, March 21, 1865) that all Second Battalion companies should be under the command of the Surgeon-General, to be assigned to duty at his discretion, and that their returns and rolls should henceforth be transmitted through him to the Adjutant-General of the Army. At this point, therefore, ceases the responsibility of the Bureau for the Second Battalion of the Veteran Reserve Corps.

DISCHARGE OF THE TRANSFERRED MEN.

The third notable event of this official year was General Orders, No. 116 (June 17, 1865), of the Adjutant-General's Office. The war had concluded with the destruction of the rebellion, and the vast volunteer army was being mustered out as rapidly as prudence would permit. What should be done with the men of the Veteran Reserve Corps? The War Department decided that, while those who had enlisted or re-enlisted in it were bound to serve as long as needed by the Government, the transferred men could allege strong claims to be mustered out with their former comrades. They had volunteered with them; they had taken the same oath, with the same purpose; they had shared as long as strength lasted their dangers and labors; why should they not share in their release? It was ordered that all transferred men who had not re-enlisted in the corps might claim their discharge from the date of the muster out of their original regiments. This order has swept the organization of 12,353 men and will eventually remove between 1,200 and 1,300 more.

RESULTS OF EXPERIENCE IN ORGANIZATION.

General Orders, No. 76, Adjutant-General's Office, April 27, 1865, is important as being the result of the official experience of two years and a half in the organization of an invalid corps. It is unquestionable, it is entirely natural, and yet is it eminently praiseworthy that its provisions are more simple, practicable, and efficient than those of many of the preceding orders relating to the same subject? In the opening of the rebellion, when a million of soldiers were forced suddenly upon the Bureau of the War Department, mistakes and shortcomings were inevitable. Amidst the gigantic novelty of the situation it was necessary to use old systems of official business until new ones of a larger grasp and quicker action could be drawn from the almost overwhelming experience of the present. It must be remembered that over 60,000 men have entered the Veteran Reserve Corps, and that at one time it was twice as large as was the entire U. S. Army at the commencement of the war. It is believed that the improvements in its management have corresponded with the general advance in other branches of the War Department.

A single amendment to General Order 76 is suggested. Even under its provisions the period which elapsed between the inspection of the invalid and his actual arrival in the corps was too great, and it occasionally happened that he died, deserted, or otherwise disappeared from the hospital before the order transferring him to the organization was issued.

Would it not have been well to give the examining board authority to order the man at once to the nearest camp of rendezvous, there to await the action of the Adjutant-General? The Veteran Reserve Corps officers attached to hospitals might have taken charge of the detachments. By this plan the movement of transfer would have been expedited, the blanks which now exist in the records with regard to the fate of certain men would have been fewer, and it is not believed that the errors of selection would have been much more numerous.

SERVICES.

The services performed by the Veteran Reserve Corps have been so varied in nature that it is impossible to state them in a compendious exhibit. Where one regiment has escorted thousands of prisoners, convalescents, recruits, and conscripts, whose numbers can be given with accuracy, another has simply guarded important posts and vast stores of public property, thus performing duty which cannot be expressed statistically. After examining the voluminous reports of the regiments for the year, I find it impossible to present their information intelligibly otherwise than by detached summaries.

These epitomes will be brief; they will indeed be little more than the barest memoranda, necessarily unjust to certain organizations, but this error cannot be avoided without a fullness of detail which would render the report too voluminous. It should be observed that the services of the Second Battalion are not stated here for the reason that its records are not under the control of the Bureau.

First Regiment.—At Elmira, N. Y., performing patrol duty and guarding hospitals, store-houses, and camp of rebel prisoners. Up to the close of the war the prisoners constantly in camp averaged between 10,000 and 12,000; frequent attempts to escape and one prisoner recorded as escaped; duty of guarding them very severe. Squads of convalescents, recruits, conscripts, &c., generally 80 or 100 strong, escorted to the front or to other posts; no record of a single escape. Many volunteer troops disbanded at this station; at one time 15,000 present; various disturbances resulted; order restored by this regiment. Two companies on duty at Rochester, N. Y., repressing disorders committed by disbanding regiments.

Second Regiment.—Headquarters at Detroit, Mich., detached companies at various points throughout the North; patrol, escort, and ordinary guard duty. From headquarters the following men have been conducted to the front: Recruits, 1,026; substitutes, 202; conscripts, 140; convalescents, 805; stragglers, 201; deserters, 242; paroled prisoners, 242; total, 2,858; escapes, 16. Similar service performed by the detached companies, but no numerical records forwarded to this Bureau.

Third Regiment.—During part of the year has been stationed at Washington, performing the ordinary duties of the garrison of Washington, of course in conjunction with other troops. While at the Soldiers' Rest an immense number of troops, from 300 to 5,000 per day, passed through to the front. At Alexandria, Va., an average of 600 per day forwarded. At Eastern Branch corral many thousands of Government cattle guarded without loss. Regiment on duty at seventy-five points and in six States at one time. The detachment at New Haven escorted 2,280 men to the front, and (aided by other troops) guarded 6,000 men during the process of organization; duty for six months averaged eight hours per day for each man. One detachment, assisted by a company of the Pennsylvania Bucktails, took charge of the One hundred and ninety-third Regiment New York Volunteers, at that time 200 strong, over 400 having deserted; in about two months the regiment was sent off with 1,022 men. At Burlington, Vt., a violent outbreak in a volunteer brigade was quelled by seventy men of the Third, two of the rioters being shot, some ironed, and many arrested. Duty of regiment severe; for weeks together on guard every other day; men known to fall asleep with exhaustion while walking their beats. Discipline excellent, notwithstanding that 608 men were received and 863 discharged, &c., during the year.

Fourth Regiment.—Principally at Rock Island Barracks and Camp Butler, Ill., guarding rebel prisoners, escorting exchanged men to the front, and performing ordinary guard duty of camps and public stores. Prisoners escorted to different points for exchange, 3,825; escapes, 2.

Fifth Regiment.—Duty in the West. Headquarters at Indianapolis, Ind. Has guarded Government property and the rebel prisoners at Camp Morton, the latter averaging 4,000 present. Prisoners frequently planned outbreaks; several shot in the attempt to escape. Service severe; men on guard duty every other day; at one time patrol added to the ordinary guard; a battery of mountain howitzers manned by the regiment; officers and men sleeping on their arms for two weeks. Four companies aided in breaking up the Chicago plot. Frequent details to arrest disloyal men and conduct soldiers to the front. During February, March, and April 2,000 prisoners escorted to City Point for exchange. The regiment complimented for its services in a letter written by the adjutant-general of the State.

Sixth Regiment.—Nine companies guarded rebel prisoners on Johnson's Island at the opening of the official year. Forty-five per cent. of the men present for duty on guard every day. Daily average of prisoners, 2,761; number escorted to other posts, 1,144; total of these last escaped, 3. Company H patrolled disaffected counties for six months, enforcing the draft. Its operations were by night and involved much marching and exposure. It arrested over 100 deserters. Eight companies were stationed for a time at Cincinnati, guarding public property; 45 per cent. of the men present constantly on guard.

Seventh Regiment.—Has performed continuous service as a part of the garrison of Washington. At one time guarded twenty-five posts in the city. One-third of the men and officers almost constantly on duty.

Eighth Regiment.—From November 1, 1864, to June 15, 1865, guarded rebel prisoners at Camp Douglas, Chicago. Daily number of prisoners varied from 9,000 to 11,800; number escaped, 8. Between

1,000 and 2,000 prisoners forwarded for exchange. Recruits forwarded, 1,954; stragglers and deserters, 308; bounty jumpers, 10; substitutes, 4; convalescents, 5; political prisoners, 10; total, 2,291; escapes, 6. Over 100 bushwhackers from Southern Illinois, who had come to Chicago to aid the projected rising of the prisoners, were captured by this regiment and other troops of the Veteran Reserve Corps.

Ninth Regiment.—Duty as part of the garrison of Washington. During considerable periods men detailed every other day. In March an average of 350 men on guard out of a total of 889. April, duty still more severe; most of the small posts permanent; not men enough to relieve them. Regiment also shared in the patrol duty of the city, and up to April escorted men to the front. Number of arrests by the patrols of the garrison, 1,670 officers and 10,020 men; forwarded by the regiment, rebel prisoners, 300; state and military prisoners, 270; convalescents, 1,300; no escapes reported.

Tenth Regiment.—Duties in Washington, similar to those of the Ninth. The list of posts and routes on which this regiment has done guard duty covers nearly seven foolscap pages. One hundred and sixty-five details were furnished to escort soldiers or rebel prisoners; but it is impossible to state the number so forwarded; some squads were 500 or 600 strong.

Eleventh Regiment.—Commenced the official year in charge of rebel prisoners at Point Lookout, Md. Duties severe; men on guard every other day, and sometimes oftener; in shelter tents during part of the winter; weather unusually cold. Every day the regiment guarded hundreds of prisoners who were kept at work on the wharves and fortifications. Three companies guarded the shores of the Potomac and its light-houses, a portion of the men being used as mounted scouts and patrols; this detachment captured 50 blockade-running boats, 50 smugglers, 2 officers, and 1 man of Mosby's command and a large number of Federal deserters. The garrison of Point Lookout at one time numbered only 650 men to guard 22,000 rebel prisoners. Between 18,000 and 20,000 prisoners were escorted to other posts by detachments of this regiment. Since the breaking up of the prison camp the Eleventh has performed guard and patrol duty at Washington and various other points in the Eastern States.

Twelfth Regiment.—Commenced the year at Alexandria, Va.; guarded Government property and patrolled the streets; protected the railroad from guerrillas. One company guarded the military prison at Alexandria, with a monthly average of 400 bounty jumpers, &c., or a total of 2,900, with but three escapes. The other nine companies have been stationed chiefly in Washington; have guarded the military prison, Government store-houses, &c.; men on duty nearly every other day. The regiment has shared with other regiments of the corps the responsible service of guarding the assassins of President Lincoln.

Thirteenth Regiment.—Guard duty at various posts in New England; forwarded by detachment at headquarters (Gallupe's Island, Boston, Mass.), recruits, 7,819; conscripts, 2,106; convalescents, 926; prisoners, 21; total, 10,882; escapes, 145. Of the 12,024 men at the camp or rendezvous between November 1, 1864, and June 1, 1865, only three escaped; losses in transportation generally owing to circumstances beyond the control of the guards. This service very severe; men constantly on duty for many days and nights consecutively; large bribes offered by bounty jumpers and refused. Twenty-seven volunteer organizations, numbering 7,920 men, mustered out at this post. At Beach Street Barracks 18,721 men have passed through and been rationed under the supervision of Companies B and C. At Readville, Mass., 3,468 volunteers have been mustered out under supervision of Company B. From Camp Gilmore Companies F and H have forwarded to the field 1,009 recruits, 817 substitutes, 2 conscripts, and 48 deserters, being a total of 1,876, with 31 escapes. In addition a patrol of sixty men per day; ordinary guard duty every other day, frequently for several days in succession. From November 1, 1864, to June 11, 1865, Company D was the only force on duty at the State draft rendezvous, guarding an unknown but very large number of recruits, substitutes, &c. The officers of the regiment have been occupied as closely as the men; they have performed their company duties and special duties at the same time; also a great deal of important detached service.

Fourteenth Regiment.—One company (K) has been stationed during the year on the Government farms, Camp Wadsworth, Va. The remainder of the regiment has done duty at Camp Distribution, at Alexandria, Va., and in Washington, D. C., as garrison. Daily number of recruits, conscripts, convalescents, and deserters at Camp Distribution waiting escort to the front varied from 2,000 to 10,000. Duty very severe, the camp being large, the posts numerous, the winter uncommonly cold, and many of the men suffering from recent wounds. Sentinels frequently relieved from post and sent to hospital by order of the surgeon. In Alexandria and Washington the regiment has guarded or aided in guarding Government corrals, large depots of public stores, Washington Street Prison (500 rebel prisoners), Old Capitol and Carroll Prisons, and the Arsenal while used as a place of confinement for the assassins of President Lincoln.

In addition to their ordinary duties, the officers have performed a vast amount of special duty and detached service, thirteen being detailed at one time. They have made sixty-seven trips in charge of convalescents, recruits, conscripts, and deserters, escorting a total of 14,793, with a total loss of 325. When it is considered that this service covered in all a period of 317 days, and that thousands of the men guarded were professional bounty jumpers or similarly desperate characters, this loss will not appear surprising.

Fifteenth Regiment.—Commenced the official year at Camp Douglas, Chicago, in conjunction with Eighth Regiment Veteran Reserve Corps and Twenty-fourth Ohio Battery. Guarded Government property and patrolled Chicago; guarded and escorted stragglers, conscripts, substitutes, and rebel prisoners. Up to the close of the war the prisoners constantly on hand averaged from 9,000 to 13,000. Only thirteen escaped from camp and none during the transportation. The regiment aided in escorting 1,000 deserters and stragglers and between 2,000 and 3,000 substitutes and conscripts, of whom only six escaped while under charge of officers of the Fifteenth. Strength of garrison varied between 500 and 700. Men on guard every third day or every other day. The regiment aided in preventing the outbreak of the Chicago conspiracy. Officers constantly and closely employed, frequently on two or three lines of duty at once.

Sixteenth Regiment.—This regiment, generally under command of Major Gaebel, carried on a campaign of several months in the mountains of Pennsylvania, where deputy provost-marshals and enrolling officers had been killed and wounded by disloyal persons engaged in resisting the draft. Treasonable organizations 500 or 600 strong were broken up. The expeditions were made through a wooded and mountainous country in winter, amid snow and ice, chiefly by night, and many of the men were badly frost-bitten. Hundreds of deserters and recusants were arrested; some were killed in skirmishes; one man of the regiment killed. The Sixteenth also forwarded deserters, recruits, conscripts, &c., to posts and camps of distribution. The number of persons thus arrested and guarded during the year is as follows: Deserters from regiments in the field captured and forwarded, 2,810, of whom 27 escaped; convalescents forwarded, 3,447, with 46 escapes; deserters from the draft captured and forwarded, 3,743, with 26 escapes; volunteers forwarded, 5,700. Total guarded, 15,637; total escapes, 99; number escorted up to July 1, 1865, averaged daily 150; number escorted during the remainder of the year averaged daily 63.

The following facts are interesting as exhibiting the amount of duty occasionally performed by officers of the corps. Col. Charles M. Prevost, of this regiment, has commanded draft rendezvous, Springfield, Ill., since November 19, 1864; has superintended the forwarding of about 25,000 men to the front, and the discharge and final payments of sixty-three regiments and seven batteries, and has still thirty-four regiments to muster out. Lieut. Col. Stephen Moore has been on several important details of special duty while commanding provisional brigade and draft rendezvous at Elmira, N. Y. Second Lieut. George R. Buffum tried in six months, as judge-advocate, 151 cases, covering 5,503 cap pages, and returned 41 cases to department headquarters, principally in consequence of the muster out of all the witnesses, which fact was not verified without a large correspondence.

Seventeenth Regiment.—On duty during the year at Indianapolis, Ind., patrolling the city, guarding U. S. arsenal, State arsenal, and Government store-houses, and conducting men to the front. Forwarded 1,300 conscripts, 1,335 deserters, 3,400 recruits, 3,062 stragglers, 1,040 convalescents; total, 10,137; escapes, 56. Nineteen of the escaped men were lost by one officer, who was court-martialed by the commandant of the regiment, but permitted to send in his resignation. General duty very severe; men sometimes on guard for sixty hours. During one period of eight days the average detail for guard was one-half the regiment. Officers generally on double duty.

Eighteenth Regiment.—On duty as part of the garrison of Washington. In conjunction with other troops of the garrison, it has guarded 664 military and state prisoners in Carroll Prison, and 1,005 in Old Capitol Prison. Unaided, it has escorted 2,163 stragglers, 1,506 deserters, 4,668 recruits, 23,319 convalescents; total guarded and forwarded, 33,775; total escapes reported, 4.

Nineteenth Regiment.—Duty at Elmira, N. Y., and other points in the State, guarding public property and military prisoners, and forwarding men to the front or to camps of distribution. No statistical report.

Twentieth Regiment.—Commenced the year at Point Lookout, Md., guarding the rebel prisoners there in conjunction with the Eleventh Regiment Veteran Reserve Corps and the Fifth Massachusetts Colored Cavalry. Eighty men as mounted patrols, 40 as artillerymen in a battery, 140 as provost guard, 43 on other detached service as clerks, orderlies, &c; only 321 present with the regiment. Men on duty every other day; frequently detailed the very morning they were relieved; many detachments to escort exchanged prisoners. The sick list ran as high as fifty-two in consequence of the constant duty and the exposure to winter weather. Average number of prisoners present about 16,000; no escapes reported from guards furnished by the regiment. Since the close of the war the Twentieth has been divided among various posts, performing everywhere as much duty as is ever demanded of able-bodied men.

Twenty-first Regiment.—Has performed duty at Trenton, Philadelphia, Pittsburg, Baltimore, Washington, Albany, and Indianapolis, in detachments of one or more companies, guarding camps of rendezvous, public property, rebel prisoners, and escorting soldiers of various classes to the front. It has had in charge 2,511 stragglers and deserters, 3,684 drafted men and substitutes, 32,122 recruits, and 6,000 rebel prisoners, being a total of 44,317 men, with 341 escapes. At camps guarded by this regiment volunteers to the number of 461 officers and 12,880 men have been mustered out of service.

Twenty-second Regiment.—On duty by detachments, chiefly in Indiana, but also in Illinois, Ohio, Wisconsin, Connecticut, and Maryland, guarding camps of rendezvous, military prisons, public stores, and escorting rebel prisoners, recruits for the Union armies, &c. Conscripts forwarded, 15,000; recruits, 13,575; deserters, 1,019; with a total loss of 28. Rebel prisoners guarded, 23,003; none reported escaped. Deserters from the draft and persons engaged in resisting it arrested in Indiana and Illinois. One squad killed a rebel recruiting officer, wounded 1 of his men, and captured 16, with a large amount of stolen goods, counterfeit money, and arms.

Twenty-third Regiment.—Duty in Wisconsin, Minnesota, Missouri, Kentucky, and Iowa. Company A has escorted over 500 men for the Army, losing so far as known but 5. Company B has escorted 500 rebel prisoners and over 3,000 recruits, deserters, &c., with no escapes to report. The train from Louisville to Lebanon repeatedly attacked by guerrillas; was successfully defeated by a detachment of this company. The company defeated one band of bushwhackers, killing its leader, Captain Mitchell, wounding several of his followers, and capturing 10 horses, with a loss to the company of 2 men wounded. Twenty-three men of the company routed a band of 48 guerrillas, killing and wounding 23 men and capturing 26 horses. The Indian prisoners at Davenport, Iowa, 500 in number, were guarded by Company G. The other companies have performed their full share of labor in the ordinary duties of the corps.

Twenty-fourth Regiment.—In Washington as a part of the garrison of Washington, performing its full share of duties. No statistical report.

From the foregoing incomplete report of the services of the First Battalion during a single year an inference may be drawn as to the services of the entire corps during the entire period of its existence. It should be considered that the latter six months of the year in question have been a period of peace, no troops being forwarded to the front and few prisoners remaining on hand to be guarded, while the numerical strength of the organization has diminished from 28,738 to less than 8,000. It is believed that an equal number of able-bodied volunteers could not have performed the garrison, provost, and hospital duties of the Army more thoroughly than they have been performed by this body of invalids. In economy, both of men and money, the advantage of the Veteran Reserve Corps to the country has been enormous and obvious. To employ an invalid at $13 a month, with rations and clothing, obtaining from him the service of a healthy man, is certainly better than to pension him at $8 a month, receiving no return whatever, and hiring an able-bodied man to fill his place at the cost of pay, rations, clothing, and enormous bounties. It must be remembered that the veterans who were enlisted or re-enlisted into the corps received no Government bounties whatever.

Numerical changes—third official year.

Aggregate of corps October 1, 1864		27,974
Gain of Second Battalion from October 1, 1864, to October 1, 1865	6,668	
Enlisted men—		
Transferred	9,120	
Re-enlisted	935	
Recruited	428	
Returned from desertion	35	
		17,186
		45,160

LOSSES.

Net loss of unassigned detachment	1,228	
Second Battalion loss up to assignment to Surgeon-General	8,198	
Enlisted men discharged—		
By expiration of term	3,478	
For disability	2,363	
By Circular 65, Adjutant-General's Office, 1864	198	
By General Orders, No. 116, Adjutant-General's Office, 1865	12,353	
For purpose of re-enlisting	403	
For other causes	1,490	
Number enlisted men deserted	984	
Number enlisted men died	351	
Second Battalion turned over to the Surgeon-General	8,687	
		39,733
Number enlisted remaining October 1, 1865		5,427

Numerical changes in the Veteran Reserve Corps from its organization to September 30, 1865.

Enlisted men—		
Transferred	45,037	
Enlisted	5,275	
Re-enlisted—		
First Battalion	3,032	
Second Battalion	461	
Returned from desertion	35	
Second Battalion gain from October 1, 1864, to October 1, 1865	6,668	
		60,508

LOSSES.

Second Battalion loss from October 1, 1864, up to assignment to Surgeon-General	8,198
Enlisted men discharged—	
For disability—	
First Battalion	3,555
Second Battalion	1,474
Expiration of term—	
First Battalion	7,048
Second Battalion	2,836
Dishonorably	26
By Circular 65, Adjutant-General's Office, 1864—	
First Battalion	260
Second Battalion	326
By General Orders, No, 116, Adjutant-General's Office, 1865	12,353
To re-enlist—	
First Battalion	2,500
Second Battalion	461
To enlist as hospital stewards	20
For promotion	49
By orders Adjutant-General's Office	64
For other causes	1,624

Men of the Regular Army retransferred	29	
Men of the volunteer force—		
Retransferred as fit for field duty	377	
Retransferred to be tried for desertion	71	
Not proper subjects for the corps	567	
Enlisted men deserted—		
First Battalion	611	
Second Battalion	340	
Enlisted men died—		
First Battalion	751	
Second Battalion	266	
Net loss of Second Battalion from October 1, 1864, to October 1, 1865	1,228	
Second Battalion turned over to Surgeon-General	8,687	
		55,081
Enlisted men remaining in corps October 1, 1865		5,427

Numerical changes in officers of the Veteran Reserve Corps since its organization.

Officers appointed	1,036	
Restored from dismissal	1	
Retransferred from Surgeon-General	59	
		1,096

LOSSES.

Declined to accept appointments	15	
Appointments revoked	29	
Resigned	181	
Dismissed the service	37	
Honorably discharged	15	
Deceased	15	
Cashiered	4	
Mustered out	4	
Acceptance withdrawn	1	
Dropped from rolls	1	
Turned over to the Surgeon-General	136	
		438
Total officers, October 1, 1865 (First Battalion)		658

PERSONAL CHANGES IN THE OFFICE.

At the commencement of the official year, November 1, 1864, the personal force of the office consisted of six officers and fifty-two clerks. In consequence of the economical measures heretofore mentioned, and of the diminution in the numbers of the corps, this force has decreased until it now amounts to one officer and nine clerks.

Col. M. N. Wisewell, Veteran Reserve Corps, was relieved from duty as chief of the Bureau on the 20th of December, 1864. Capt. James McMillan, of the Second Regiment U. S. Infantry, subsequently appointed brevet major, replaced him, and held the position until October 2, 1865, since which the undersigned has been in charge.

I have the honor to be, very respectfully, your obedient servant,

J. W. DE FOREST,

Capt., Veteran Reserve Corps, and Actg. Asst. Adjutant-General.

CIRCULAR No. 53. } WAR DEPT., ADJUTANT-GENERAL'S OFFICE, *Washington, December 1, 1865.*

I. Enlisted men of the Veteran Reserve Corps within the respective military departments who have, under General Orders, No. 155, current series, from this office, elected to remain in service will be consolidated, under the orders of the respective department commanders, into as many companies of the maximum strength as the number will permit, and complete muster and descriptive rolls thereof forwarded to this office with a view to their numerical designation as "Independent companies, Veteran Reserve Corps." To enable the consolidation to be made, chief mustering officers of States will report the enlisted men who may be serving under their control to the department commander.

II. Whenever regimental and company organizations of the Veteran Reserve Corps are broken up by the operation of General Orders, Nos. 155 and 165, current series, from this office, regimental and company commanders will look to the prompt completion of existing records, and cause the same to be forwarded to this office. Further returns and records will not be thereafter required, and their rendition will be discontinued accordingly.

Regimental and company funds will be transferred to the nearest officer of the Subsistence Department, and returns thereof rendered as required by the Army Regulations.

E. D. TOWNSEND,
Assistant Adjutant-General.

WASHINGTON, *December 4, 1865.*

FELLOW-CITIZENS OF THE SENATE AND HOUSE OF REPRESENTATIVES:

To express gratitude to God, in the name of the people, for the preservation of the United States is my first duty in addressing you. Our thoughts next revert to the death of the late President by an act of parricidal treason. The grief of the nation is still fresh; it finds some solace in the consideration that he lived to enjoy the highest proof of its confidence, by entering on the renewed term of the Chief Magistracy to which he had been elected; that he brought the civil war substantially to a close; that his loss was deplored in all parts of the Union; and that foreign nations have rendered justice to his memory. His removal cast upon me a heavier weight of cares than ever devolved upon any one of his predecessors. To fulfill my trust I need the support and confidence of all who are associated with me in the various departments of the Government, and the support and confidence of the people. There is but one way in which I can hope to gain their necessary aid: It is, to state with frankness, the principles which guide my conduct, and their application to the present state of affairs, well aware that the efficiency of my labors will in a great measure depend on your and their undivided approbation.

The Union of the United States of America was intended by its authors to last as long as the States themselves shall last. "The Union shall be perpetual," are the words of the Confederation. "To form a more perfect Union," by an ordinance of the people of the United States, is the declared purpose of the Constitution. The hand of Divine Providence was never more plainly visible in the affairs of men than in the framing and the adopting of that instrument. It is, beyond comparison, the greatest event in American history; and, indeed, is it not of all events in modern times the most pregnant with consequences for every people of the earth? The members of the convention which prepared it brought to their work the experience of the Confederation, of their several States, and of other republican governments, old and new; but they needed and they obtained a wisdom superior to experience. And when, for its validity, it required the approval of a people that occupied a large part of a continent and acted separately in many distinct conventions, what is more wonderful than that after earnest contention and long discussion all feelings and all opinions were ultimately drawn in one way to its support? The Constitution to which life was thus imparted contains within itself ample resources for its own preservation. It has power to enforce the laws, punish treason, and insure domestic tranquillity. In case of the usurpation of the government of a State by one man, or an oligarchy, it becomes a duty of the United States to make good the guaranty to that State of a republican form of government, and so to maintain the homogeneousness of all. Does the lapse of time reveal defects? A simple mode of amendment is provided in the Constitution itself, so that its conditions can always be made to conform to the requirements of advancing civilization. No room is allowed even for the thought of a possibility of its coming to an end. And these powers of self-preservation have always been asserted in their complete integrity by every patriotic Chief Magistrate—by Jefferson and Jackson, not less than by Washington and Madison. The parting advice of the Father of his Country, while yet President, to the people of the United States, was that "the free Constitution, which was the work of their hands, might be sacredly maintained;" and the inaugural words of President Jefferson held up "the preservation of the General Government in its constitutional vigor as the sheet anchor of our peace at home and safety abroad." The Constitution is the work of "the people of the United States," and it should be as indestructible as the people.

It is not strange that the framers of the Constitution, which had no model in the past, should not have fully comprehended the excellence of their own work. Fresh from a struggle against arbitrary power, many patriots suffered from harassing fears of an absorption of the State governments by the General Government, and many from a dread that the States would break away from their orbits. But the very greatness of our country should allay the apprehension of encroachments by the General Government. The subjects that come unquestionably within its jurisdiction are so numerous that it must ever naturally refuse to be embarrassed by questions that lie beyond it. Were it otherwise the Executive would sink beneath the burden, the channels of justice would be choked, legislation would be obstructed by excess, so that there is a greater temptation to exercise some of the functions of the General Government through the States than to trespass on their rightful sphere. "The absolute acquiescence in the decisions of the majority" was at the beginning of the century enforced by Jefferson "as the vital principle of republics," and the events of the last four years have established, we will hope forever, that there lies no appeal to force.

The maintenance of the Union brings with it "the support of the State governments in all their rights;" but it is not one of the rights of any State government to renounce its own place in the Union or to nullify the laws of the Union. The largest liberty is to be maintained in the discussion of the acts of the Federal Government; but there is no appeal from its laws, except to the various branches of that Government itself, or to the people, who grant to the members of the legislative and of the executive departments no tenure but a limited one, and in that manner always retain the powers of redress.

"The sovereignty of the State" is the language of the Confederacy and not the language of the Constitution. The latter contains the emphatic words:

The Constitution and the laws of the United States which shall be made in pursuance thereof, and all treaties made or which shall be made under the authority of the United States, shall be the supreme law of the land, and the judges in every State shall be bound thereby, anything in the constitution or laws of any State to the contrary notwithstanding.

Certainly the Government of the United States is a limited government, and so is every State government a limited government. With us this idea of limitation spreads through every form of administration, general, State, and municipal, and rests on the great distinguishing principle of the recognition of the rights of man. The ancient republics absorbed the individual in the State, prescribed his religion, and controlled his activity. The American system rests on the assertion of the equal right of every man to life, liberty, and the pursuit of happiness; to freedom of conscience; to the culture and exercise of all his faculties. As a consequence, the State government is limited as to the General Government in the interest of union, as to the individual citizen in the interest of freedom.

States, with proper limitations of power, are essential to the existence of the Constitution of the United States. At the very commencement, when we assumed a place among the powers of the earth, the Declaration of Independence was adopted by States; so also were the Articles of Confederation; and when "the people of the United States" ordained and established the Constitution it was the assent of the States, one by one, which gave it vitality. In the event, too, of any amendment to the Constitution, the proposition of Congress needs the confirmation of States. Without States one great branch of the legislative government would be wanting. And if we look beyond the letter of the Constitution to the character of our country, its capacity for comprehending within its jurisdiction a vast continental empire is due to the system of States. The best security for the perpetual existence of the States is the "supreme authority" of the Constitution of the United States. The perpetuity of the Constitution brings with it the perpetuity of the States. Their mutual relation makes us what we are, and in our political system their connection is indissoluble. The whole cannot exist without the parts, nor the parts without the whole. So long as the Constitution of the United States endures the States will endure. The destruction of the one is the destruction of the other. The preservation of the one is the preservation of the other.

I have thus explained my views of the mutual relations of the Constitution and the States because they unfold the principles on which I have sought to solve the momentous questions and overcome the appalling difficulties that met me at the very commencement of my administration. It has been my steadfast object to escape from the sway of momentary passions, and to derive a healing policy from the fundamental and unchanging principles of the Constitution.

I found the States suffering from the effects of a civil war. Resistance to the General Government appeared to have exhausted itself. The United States had recovered possession of their forts and arsenals, and their armies were in the occupation of every State which had attempted to secede. Whether the territory within the limits of those States should be held as conquered territory, under military authority emanating from the President as the head of the Army, was the first question that presented itself for decision.

Now, military governments, established for an indefinite period, would have offered no security for the early suppression of discontent, would have divided the people into the vanquishers and the vanquished, and would have envenomed hatred rather than have restored affection. Once established, no precise limit to their continuance was conceivable. They would have occasioned an incalculable and exhausting expense. Peaceful emigration to and from that portion of the country is one of the best means that can be thought of for the restoration of harmony, and that emigration would have been prevented; for what emigrant from abroad—what industrious citizen at home—would place himself willingly under military rule? The chief persons who would have followed in the train of the army would have been dependents on the General Government, or men who expected profit from the miseries of their erring fellow-citizens. The powers of patronage and rule which would have been exercised, under the President, over a vast, and populous, and naturally wealthy region, are greater than, unless under extreme necessity, I should be willing to intrust to any one man; they are such as, for myself, I could never, unless on occasions of great emergency, consent to exercise. The willful use of such powers, if continued through a period of years, would have endangered the purity of the general administration and the liberties of the States which remained loyal.

Besides, the policy of military rule over a conquered territory would have implied that the States whose inhabitants may have taken part in the rebellion had, by the act of those inhabitants, ceased to exist. But the true theory is that all pretended acts of secession were, from the beginning, null and void. The States cannot commit treason, nor screen the individual citizens who may have committed treason, any more than they can make valid treaties or engage in lawful commerce with any foreign power. The States attempting to secede placed themselves in a condition where their vitality was impaired, but not extinguished—their functions suspended, but not destroyed.

But if any State neglects or refuses to perform its offices, there is the more need that the General Government should maintain all its authority, and, as soon as practicable, resume the exercise of all its functions. On this principle I have acted, and have gradually and quietly, and by almost imperceptible steps, sought to restore the rightful energy of the General Government and of the States. To that end provisional Governors have been appointed for the States, conventions called, Governors elected, Legislatures assembled, and Senators and Representatives chosen to the Congress of the United States. At the same time the courts of the United States, as far as could be done, have been reopened, so that the laws of the United States may be enforced through their agency. The blockade has been removed and the custom-houses re-established in ports of entry, so that the revenue of the United States may be collected. The Post-Office Department renews its ceaseless activity, and the General Government is thereby enabled to communicate promptly with its officers and agents. The courts bring security to persons and property; the opening of the ports invite the restoration of industry and commerce;

the post-office renews the facilities of social intercourse and of business. And is it not happy for us all that the restoration of each one of these functions of the General Government brings with it a blessing to the States over which they are extended? Is it not a sure promise of harmony and renewed attachment to the Union that, after all that has happened, the return of the General Government is known only as a beneficence?

I know very well that this policy is attended with some risk; that for its success it requires at least the acquiescence of the States which it concerns; that it implies an invitation to those States, by renewing their allegiance to the United States, to resume their functions as States of the Union. But it is a risk that must be taken; in the choice of difficulties it is the smallest risk; and to diminish, and, if possible, to remove all danger, I have felt it incumbent on me to assert one other power of the General Government—the power of pardon. As no State can throw a defense over the crime of treason, the power of pardon is exclusively vested in the Executive government of the United States. In exercising that power I have taken every precaution to connect it with the clearest recognition of the binding force of the laws of the United States, and an unqualified acknowledgment of the great social change of condition in regard to slavery which has grown out of the war.

The next step which I have taken to restore the constitutional relations of the States has been an invitation to them to participate in the high office of amending the Constitution. Every patriot must wish for a general amnesty at the earliest epoch consistent with public safety. For this great end there is need of a concurrence of all opinions and the spirit of mutual conciliation. All parties in the late terrible conflict must work together in harmony. It is not too much to ask, in the name of the whole people, that on the one side the plan of restoration shall proceed in conformity with a willingness to cast the disorders of the past into oblivion; and that, on the other, the evidence of sincerity in the future maintenance of the Union shall be put beyond any doubt by the ratification of the proposed amendment to the Constitution, which provides for the abolition of slavery forever within the limits of our country. So long as the adoption of this amendment is delayed, so long will doubt and jealousy and uncertainty prevail. This is the measure which will efface the sad memory of the past; this is the measure which will most certainly call population and capital and security to those parts of the Union that need them most. Indeed, it is not too much to ask of the States which are now resuming their places in the family of the Union to give this pledge of perpetual loyalty and peace. Until it is done, the past, however much we may desire it, will not be forgotten. The adoption of the amendment reunites us beyond all power of disruption. It heals the wound that is still imperfectly closed; it removes slavery, the element which has so long perplexed and divided the country; it makes of us once more a united people, renewed and strengthened, bound more than ever to mutual affection and support.

The amendment to the Constitution being adopted, it would remain for the States whose powers have been so long in abeyance to resume their places in the two branches of the National Legislature, and thereby complete the work of restoration. Here it is for you, fellow-citizens of the Senate, and for you, fellow-citizens of the House of Representatives, to judge, each of you for yourselves, of the elections, returns, and qualifications of your own members.

The full assertion of the powers of the General Government requires the holding of circuit courts of the United States within the districts where their authority has been interrupted. In the present posture of our public affairs strong objections have been urged to holding those courts in any of the States where the rebellion has existed; and it was ascertained by inquiry that the circuit court of the United States would not be held within the district of Virginia during the autumn or early winter, nor until Congress should have "an opportunity to consider and act on the whole subject." To your deliberations the restoration of this branch of the civil authority of the United States is, therefore, necessarily referred, with the hope that early provision will be made for the resumption of all its functions. It is manifest that treason, most flagrant in character, has been committed. Persons who are charged with its commission should have fair and impartial trials in the highest civil tribunals of the country, in order that the Constitution and the laws may be fully vindicated; the truth clearly established and affirmed that treason is a crime; that traitors should be punished and the offense made infamous; and, at the same time, that the question may be judicially settled, finally and forever, that no State, of its own will, has the right to renounce its place in the Union.

The relations of the General Government toward the 4,000,000 of inhabitants whom the war has called into freedom have engaged my most serious consideration. On the propriety of attempting to make the freedmen electors by the proclamation of the Executive I took for my counsel the Constitution itself, the interpretations of that instrument by its authors and their contemporaries, and recent legislation by Congress. When at the first movement toward independence the Congress of the United States instructed the several States to institute governments of their own, they left each State to decide for itself the conditions for the enjoyment of the elective franchise. During the period of the Confederacy there continued to exist a very great diversity in the qualifications of electors in the several States; and even within a State a distinction of qualifications prevailed with regard to the officers who were to be chosen. The Constitution of the United States recognizes these diversities when it enjoins that, in the choice of members of the House of Representatives of the United States, "the electors in each State shall have the qualifications requisite for electors of the most numerous branch of the State Legislature." After the formation of the Constitution it remained, as before, the uniform usage for each State to enlarge the body of its electors according to its own judgment; and under this system one State after another has proceeded to increase the number of its electors until now universal suffrage, or something very near it, is the general rule. So fixed was this reservation of power in the habits of the people, and so unquestioned has been the interpretation of the Constitution, that during the civil war the late President never harbored the purpose—certainly never avowed the purpose—of disregarding it; and in the acts of Congress during that period nothing can be found which during the continuance of hostilities, much less after their close, would have sanctioned any departure by the Executive from a policy which has so uniformly obtained. Moreover, a concession of the elective franchise to the freedmen, by act of the President of the United States, must have been extended to all colored men, wherever found, and so must have established a change of suffrage in the Northern, Middle, and Western States, not less than in the Southern and Southwestern. Such an act would have created a new class of voters, and would have been an assumption of power by the President which nothing in the Constitution or laws of the United States would have warranted.

On the other hand, every danger of conflict is avoided when the settlement of the question is referred to the several States. They can, each for itself, decide on the measure, and whether it is to be adopted at once and absolutely, or introduced gradually and with conditions. In my judgment, the freedmen, if they show patience and manly virtues, will sooner obtain a participation in the elective franchise through the States than through the General Government, even if it had power to intervene. When the tumult of emotions that have been raised by the suddenness of the social change shall have subsided it may prove that they will receive the kindest usage from some of those on whom they have heretofore most closely depended.

But while I have no doubt that now, after the close of the war, it is not competent for the General Government to extend the elective franchise in the several States, it is equally clear that good faith requires the security of the freedmen in their liberty and their property, their right to labor, and their right to claim the just return of their labor. I cannot too strongly urge a dispassionate treatment of this subject, which should be carefully kept aloof from all party strife. We must equally avoid hasty assumptions of any natural impossibility for the two races to live side by side in a state of mutual benefit and good will. The experiment involves us in no inconsistency; let us, then, go on and make that experiment in good faith, and not be too easily disheartened. The country is in need of labor, and the freedmen are in need of employment, culture, and protection. While their right of voluntary migration and expatriation is not to be questioned, I would not advise their forced removal and colonization. Let us rather encourage them to honorable and useful industry, where it may be beneficial to themselves and to the country, and instead of hasty anticipations of the certainty of failure, let there be nothing wanting to the fair trial of the experiment. The change in their condition is the substitution of labor by contract for the status of slavery. The freedman cannot fairly be accused of unwillingness to work so long as a doubt remains about his freedom of choice in his pursuits and the certainty of his recovering his stipulated wages. In this the interests of the employer and the employed coincide. The employer desires in his workmen spirit and alacrity, and these can be permanently secured in no other way. And if the one ought to be able to enforce the contract so ought the other. The public interest will be best promoted if the several States will provide adequate protection and remedies for the freedmen. Until this is in some way accomplished there is no chance for the advantageous use of their labor, and the blame of ill success will not rest on them.

I know that sincere philanthropy is earnest for the immediate realization of its remotest aims; but time is always an element in reform. It is one of the greatest acts on record to have brought 4,000,000 of people into freedom. The career of free industry must be fairly opened to them, and then their future prosperity and condition must, after all, rest mainly on themselves. If they fail, and so perish away, let us be careful that the failure shall not be attributable to any denial of justice. In all that relates to the destiny of the freedmen we need not be too anxious to read the future;

many incidents which, from a speculative point of view, might raise alarm will quietly settle themselves. Now that slavery is at an end, or near its end, the greatness of its evil in the point of view of public economy becomes more and more apparent. Slavery was essentially a monopoly of labor, and as such locked the States where it prevailed against the incoming of free industry. Where labor was the property of the capitalist the white man was excluded from employment, or had but the second best chance of finding it, and the foreign emigrant turned away from the region where his condition would be so precarious. With the destruction of the monopoly free labor will hasten from all parts of the civilized world to assist in developing various and immeasurable resources which have hitherto lain dormant. The eight or nine States nearest the Gulf of Mexico have a soil of exuberant fertility, a climate friendly to long life, and can sustain a denser population than is found as yet in any part of our country. And the future influx of population to them will be mainly from the North or from the most cultivated nations in Europe. From the sufferings that have attended them during our late struggle let us look away to the future, which is sure to be laden for them with greater prosperity than has ever before been known. The removal of the monopoly of slave labor is a pledge that those regions will be peopled by a numerous and enterprising population, which will vie with any in the Union in compactness, inventive genius, wealth, and industry.

Our Government springs from and was made for the people—not the people for the Government. To them it owes allegiance; from them it must derive its courage, strength, and wisdom. But while the Government is thus bound to defer to the people, from whom it derives its existence, it should, from the very consideration of its origin, be strong in its power of resistance to the establishment of inequalities. Monopolies, perpetuities, and class legislation are contrary to the genius of free government, and ought not to be allowed. Here there is no room for favored classes or monopolies; the principle of our Government is that of equal laws and freedom of industry. Wherever monopoly attains a foothold it is sure to be a source of danger, discord, and trouble. We shall but fulfill our duties as legislators by according "equal and exact justice to all men," special privileges to none. The Government is subordinate to the people; but, as the agent and representative of the people, it must be held superior to monopolies, which, in themselves, ought never to be granted, and which, where they exist, must be subordinate and yield to the Government.

The Constitution confers on Congress the right to regulate commerce among the several States. It is of the first necessity, for the maintenance of the Union, that that commerce should be free and unobstructed. No State can be justified in any device to tax the transit of travel and commerce between States. The position of many States is such that if they were allowed to take advantage of it for purposes of local revenue the commerce between States might be injuriously burdened, or even virtually prohibited. It is best while the country is still young, and while the tendency to dangerous monopolies of this kind is still feeble, to use the power of Congress so as to prevent any selfish impediment to the free circulation of men and merchandise. A tax on travel and merchandise in their transit constitutes one of the worst forms of monopoly, and the evil is increased if coupled with a denial of the choice of route. When the vast extent of our country is considered it is plain that every obstacle to the free circulation of commerce between the States ought to be sternly guarded against by appropriate legislation within the limits of the Constitution.

The report of the Secretary of the Interior explains the condition of the public lands, the transactions of the Patent Office and the Pension Bureau, the management of our Indian affairs, the progress made in the construction of the Pacific Railroad, and furnishes information in reference to matters of local interest in the District of Columbia. It also presents evidence of the successful operation of the homestead act, under the provisions of which 1,160,533 acres of the public lands were entered during the last fiscal year—more than one-fourth of the whole number of acres sold or otherwise disposed of during that period. It is estimated that the receipts derived from this source are sufficient to cover the expenses incident to the survey and disposal of the lands entered under this act, and that payments in cash to the extent of from 40 or 50 per cent. will be made by settlers, who may thus at any time acquire title before the expiration of the period at which it would otherwise vest. The homestead policy was established only after long and earnest resistance. Experience proves its wisdom. The lands in the hands of industrious settlers, whose labor creates wealth and contributes to the public resources, are worth more to the United States than if they had been reserved as a solitude for future purchasers.

The lamentable events of the last four years and the sacrifices made by the gallant men of our Army and Navy have swelled the records of the Pension Bureau to an unprecedented extent. On the 30th day of June last the total number of pensioners was 85,986, requiring for their annual pay, exclusive of expenses, the sum of $8,023,445. The number of applications that have been allowed since that date will require a large increase of this amount for the next fiscal year. The means for the payment of the stipends due under existing laws to our disabled soldiers and sailors, and to the families of such as have perished in the service of the country, will no doubt be cheerfully and promptly granted. A grateful people will not hesitate to sanction any measures having for their object the relief of soldiers mutilated and families made fatherless in the efforts to preserve our national existence.

The report of the Postmaster-General presents an encouraging exhibit of the operations of the Post-Office Department during the year. The revenues of the past year, from the loyal States alone, exceeded the maximum annual receipts from all the States previous to the rebellion in the sum of $6,038,091; and the annual average increase of revenue during the last four years, compared with the revenues of the four years immediately preceding the rebellion, was $3,533,845. The revenues of the last fiscal year amounted to $14,556,158 and the expenditures to $13,694,728, leaving a surplus of receipts over expenditures of $861,430. Progress has been made in restoring the postal service in the Southern States. The views presented by the Postmaster-General against the policy of granting subsidies to ocean mail steamship lines upon established routes, and in favor of continuing the present system, which limits the compensation for ocean service to the postage earnings, are recommended to the careful consideration of Congress.

It appears from the report of the Secretary of the Navy that while at the commencement of the present year there were in commission

530 vessels of all classes and descriptions, armed with 3,000 guns and manned by 51,000 men, the number of vessels at present in commission is 117, with 830 guns and 12,128 men. By this prompt reduction of the naval forces the expenses of the Government have been largely diminished, and a number of vessels, purchased for naval purposes from the merchant marine, have been returned to the peaceful pursuits of commerce. Since the suppression of active hostilities our foreign squadrons have been re-established, and consist of vessels much more efficient than those employed on similar service previous to the rebellion. The suggestion for the enlargement of the navy-yards, and especially for the establishment of one in fresh water, for iron-clad vessels, is deserving of consideration, as is also the recommendation for a different location and more ample grounds for the Naval Academy.

In the report of the Secretary of War a general summary is given of the military campaigns of 1864 and 1865, ending in the suppression of armed resistance to the national authority in the insurgent States. The operations of the general administrative bureaus of the War Department during the past year are detailed, and an estimate made of the appropriations that will be required for military purposes in the fiscal year commencing the 1st day of July, 1866. The national military force on the 1st day of May, 1865, numbered 1,000,516 men.* It is proposed to reduce the military establishment to a peace footing, comprehending 50,000 troops of all arms, organized so as to admit of an enlargement by filling up the ranks to 82,600, if the circumstances of the country should require an augmentation of the Army. The volunteer force has already been reduced by the discharge from service of over 800,000 troops, and the Department is proceeding rapidly in the work of further reduction. The war estimates are reduced from $516,240,131 to $33,814,461, which amount, in the opinion of the Department, is adequate for a peace establishment. The measures of retrenchment in each bureau and branch of the service exhibit a diligent economy worthy of commendation. Reference is also made in the report to the necessity of providing for a uniform militia system, and to the propriety of making suitable provision for wounded and disabled officers and soldiers.

* * * * * * *

ANDREW JOHNSON.

CIRCULAR No. 54. | WAR DEPT., ADJUTANT-GENERAL'S OFFICE, *Washington, December 19, 1865.*

VOLUNTEERS (WHITE AND COLORED), INFANTRY, CAVALRY, AND ARTILLERY, IN VARIOUS MILITARY DEPARTMENTS—SERVICES NO LONGER REQUIRED—ORDERED MUSTERED OUT OF SERVICE, UNDER SPECIAL INSTRUCTIONS, OF DATES SET OPPOSITE THE ORGANIZATIONS, RESPECTIVELY:

I. White troops.

Connecticut.—Eighth Infantry, November 24, 1865; Eleventh Infantry, November 24, 1865.

---

*But see Vol. IV, this series, p. 1283, for statement showing an aggregate of 1,052,038.

Illinois.—Thirty-ninth Infantry, November 24, 1865.

Indiana.—One hundred and thirtieth Infantry, November 24, 1865.

New Hampshire.—Second Infantry, November 24, 1865.

New York.—Forty-first Infantry, November 24, 1865; Fifty-fourth Infantry, November 27, 1865; One hundred and third Infantry, November 24, 1865.

Ohio.—Sixty-seventh Infantry, November 24, 1865.

Pennsylvania.—Forty-seventh Infantry, November 27, 1865; One hundred and eighty-eighth Infantry, November 24, 1865.

Vermont.—Ninth Infantry, November 24, 1865.

Virginia.—First Infantry (Loyal East Virginia, Company A), November 24, 1865.

II. Colored troops.

United States.—Second Light Artillery (Batteries F and I), December 11, 1865; Second Light Artillery (Batteries C and D), December 13, 1865; Fourteenth Heavy Artillery, November 24, 1865; Third Cavalry, December 11, 1865; Eleventh Infantry, December 11, 1865; Twelfth Infantry, December 11, 1865; Thirteenth Infantry, December 11, 1865; Twenty-first Infantry, December 13, 1865; Thirtieth Infantry, November 24, 1865; Thirty-third Infantry, December 13, 1865; Thirty-ninth Infantry, November 24, 1865; Forty-seventh Infantry, December 13, 1865; Forty-eighth Infantry, December 13, 1865; Fifty-fifth Infantry, December 13, 1865; Sixty-first Infantry, December 12, 1865; Sixty-third Infantry, December 16, 1865; Seventy-sixth Infantry, December 13, 1865; Seventy-eighth Infantry, December 13, 1865; Ninety-second Infantry, December 13, 1865; One hundredth Infantry, December 2, 1865; One hundred and fourth Infantry, December 2, 1865; One hundred and thirty-sixth Infantry, December 13, 1865; One hundred and thirty-seventh Infantry, December 13, 1865; One hundred and thirty-eighth Infantry, December 13, 1865.

MEMORANDA.—*December 11, 1865.*—Major-General Thomas, commanding Military Division of the Tennessee, was ordered to reduce the aggregate force of white troops in the Departments of Georgia, Alabama, and Mississippi to 7,000 men, regulars included.

E. D. TOWNSEND,
Assistant Adjutant-General.

WAR DEPARTMENT, ADJUTANT-GENERAL'S OFFICE,
Washington, December 21, 1865.

Hon. HENRY T. BLOW, M. C.,
Washington, D. C.:

SIR: Referring to your interview of this date with Acting Assistant Secretary of War, and in connection with letters to you from His Excellency the Governor and Adjutant-General of Missouri, relative to the muster out of the remaining organizations of Missouri Volunteers, I have the honor to inform you that the exigencies of the service have demanded the retention of the said troops in service for a longer period than was anticipated. In October last it was expected that all would have been mustered out by the 1st instant. No means have been spared to hasten the discharges as rapidly as the services of the troops could be dispensed with, and those yet in service will be discharged at the earliest date practicable. The public interest, however, will not permit an order for the discharge of all at the same time.

At this time it is believed that the Twelfth and Thirteenth Regiments of Cavalry (on the plains) and the Fifteenth Regiment of Infantry (in Texas) cannot be relieved.

The attention of Major-General Thomas, commanding Military Division of the Tennessee, has been invited to your request relative to the Eleventh, Twenty-first, and Forty-ninth Regiments of Infantry, now serving in the Department of Alabama.

On the 11th instant General Thomas was ordered to reduce the aggregate force of white troops in the Departments of Alabama, Mississippi, and Georgia to 7,000 men, and it is very likely that the musters out of the Eleventh, Twenty-first, and Forty-ninth Regiments will fall under that order.

I have the honor to remain, very respectfully, your obedient servant,

THOMAS M. VINCENT,
Assistant Adjutant-General.

CIRCULAR No. 55. — WAR DEPT., ADJUTANT-GENERAL'S OFFICE,
Washington, December 22, 1865.

REGULATIONS AND INSTRUCTIONS RELATIVE TO MUSTERS OUT OF OFFICERS AND MEN OF THE FIRST ARMY CORPS.

I. Muster out of enlisted men.

TELEGRAM.] WAR DEPARTMENT, ADJUTANT-GENERAL'S OFFICE,
Washington, December 9, 1865.

Maj. Gen. W. S. HANCOCK,
Commanding Middle Department, Baltimore, Md.:

Until further orders the men of the First Army Corps will be mustered out as their terms of service expire, which is determined by the muster-in roll, and furnished discharges in the usual manner by the commissary of musters.

SAMUEL BRECK,
Assistant Adjutant-General.

II. Transportation of enlisted men.

TELEGRAM.] WAR DEPARTMENT, ADJUTANT-GENERAL'S OFFICE,
Washington, December 14, 1865.

Maj. Gen. W. S. HANCOCK, U. S. Volunteers,
Commanding First Army Corps, Baltimore, Md.:

Members of the First Army Corps, on being discharged on account of expiration of term, will not receive transportation allowances from the Pay Department, but will be furnished with transportation in kind by the Quartermaster's Department to the station of the district provost-marshal who furnished transportation to Washington, or a designated State rendezvous, under the regulations promulgated in Circular No. 86, series of 1864, from this office.

In all cases quartermasters furnishing transportation will note the fact on the discharge papers of the soldier.

By order of the Secretary of War:

THOMAS M. VINCENT,
Assistant Adjutant-General.

WAR DEPARTMENT, ADJUTANT-GENERAL'S OFFICE,
Washington, December 16, 1865.

Maj. Gen. W. S. HANCOCK,
Commanding First Army Corps, Baltimore, Md.:

GENERAL: Referring to the telegraphic instructions from this office of the 14th instant, relative to transportation of men of the First Corps after their muster out of service, I am directed to inform you that the evidence as to the "station of the district provost-marshal" will be the certificate of the company commander, countersigned by the mustering officer charged with the musters out.

The said certificate, when presented to the quartermaster furnishing transportation, will determine the point to which the soldier is entitled to be transported.

I have the honor to remain, very respectfully, your obedient servant,

THOMAS M. VINCENT,
Assistant Adjutant-General.

III. Muster out of commissioned officers.

WAR DEPARTMENT, ADJUTANT-GENERAL'S OFFICE,
Washington, December 21, 1865.

Maj. Gen. W. S. HANCOCK, U. S. Volunteers,
Commanding First Army Corps, Baltimore, Md.:

GENERAL: Referring to your letter of the 19th instant, relative to surplus officers of the First Army Corps, I have the honor to inform you that when the discharges from any one regiment shall have reduced it below the minimum it will be deprived of its colonel and one assistant surgeon. Each company when reduced below the minimum will be deprived of the second lieutenant.

In reaching the reduced standard as herein fixed the musters out of the officers will be made by the proper mustering officer immediately upon the reduced condition of the command being reached. In addition to the usual muster-out rolls, please report by letter to this office the names of the officers mustered out.

When the discharges cause the strength of regiments and companies to fall much below the minimum, you are authorized to exercise your discretion in ordering the muster out of additional officers. Officers not absolutely necessary to the reduced command should not be retained.

It is proper to add that for the present it is not intended to consolidate the reduced companies of any one regiment so as to form complete ones. It is desired that you will present that question for consideration when, in your opinion, the proper time for consolidation shall have arrived, holding in view the length of individual enlistments.

I am, general, very respectfully, your obedient servant,

THOMAS M. VINCENT,
Assistant Adjutant-General.

E. D. TOWNSEND,
Assistant Adjutant-General.

GENERAL ORDERS, No. 175. } WAR DEPT., ADJT. GENERAL'S OFFICE,
Washington, December 28, 1865.

(*December 1, 1865.—Revoking the suspension of the privilege of the writ of habeas corpus in the States and Territories of the United States, except in certain States and Territories named.*)

BY THE PRESIDENT OF THE UNITED STATES:

A PROCLAMATION.

Whereas, by the proclamation of the President of the United States of the fifteenth day of September, one thousand eight hundred and sixty-three, the privilege of the writ of habeas corpus was, in certain cases therein set forth, suspended throughout the United States;

And whereas, the reasons for that suspension may be regarded as having ceased in some of the States and Territories:

Now, therefore, be it known that I, Andrew Johnson, President of the United States, do hereby proclaim and declare that the suspension aforesaid and all other proclamations and orders suspending the privilege of the writ of habeas corpus in the States and Territories of the United States are revoked and annulled, excepting as to the States of Virginia, Kentucky, Tennessee, North Carolina, South Carolina, Georgia, Florida, Alabama, Mississippi, Louisiana, Arkansas, and Texas, the District of Columbia, and the Territories of New Mexico and Arizona.

In witness whereof I have hereunto set my hand and caused the seal of the United States to be affixed.

Done at the city of Washington this first day of December, in the year of our Lord one thousand eight hundred and sixty-five, and of the Independence of the United States of America the ninetieth.

[L. S.] ANDREW JOHNSON.

By the President:

WILLIAM H. SEWARD,
Secretary of State.

By order of the Secretary of War:

E. D. TOWNSEND,
Assistant Adjutant-General.

Principal officials of the War Department and its bureaus during the year 1865.

[Compiled from official records.]

SECRETARY OF WAR.

Edwin M. Stanton.

ASSISTANT SECRETARY OF WAR.

Charles A. Dana, to July 31, 1865.

ADJUTANT-GENERAL.

Brig. Gen. Lorenzo Thomas.*

JUDGE-ADVOCATE-GENERAL.

Brig. Gen. Joseph Holt.

INSPECTOR-GENERAL.

Col. Randolph B. Marcy (senior).

QUARTERMASTER-GENERAL.

Brig. Gen. Montgomery C. Meigs.

COMMISSARY-GENERAL OF SUBSISTENCE.

Brig. Gen. Amos B. Eaton.

SURGEON-GENERAL.

Brig. Gen. Joseph K. Barnes.

PAYMASTER-GENERAL.

Col. Benjamin W. Brice.

CHIEF OF ENGINEERS.

Brig. Gen. Richard Delafield.

CHIEF OF ORDNANCE.

Brig. Gen. Alexander B. Dyer.

PROVOST-MARSHAL-GENERAL.

Brig. Gen. James B. Fry.

OFFICE DIRECTOR AND GENERAL MANAGER
MILITARY RAILROADS UNITED STATES,
Washington, February 8, 1866.

Hon. EDWIN M. STANTON,
Secretary of War, Washington, D. C.:

SIR: I have the honor to submit the following report of operations of the U. S. Military Railroads for the year ending June 30, 1865. These operations we conducted in six different fields, as follows:

I. Virginia.
II. Military Division of the Mississippi.
III. Georgia.
IV. North Carolina.
V. Missouri.
VI. Arkansas.

I.—VIRGINIA.

On the 1st day of July, 1864, the military railroad lines in operation in Virginia were as follows:

Name of line.	Terminal stations. From—	To—	Length.
			Miles.
Alexandria and Washington	Alexandria	Washington	7
Alexandria, Loudoun and Hampshire	....do	Falls Church	10
Orange and Alexandria	....do	Springfield	8
Norfolk and Petersburg	Norfolk	Suffolk	23
Seaboard and Roanoke	Portsmouth	....do	17
City Point and Petersburg	City Point	Near Petersburg	8
Winchester and Potomac	Harper's Ferry	Halltown	6
Total			79

*On detached service; Col. Edward D. Townsend in charge of the office.

During the entire year the Alexandria and Washington line was in constant and uninterrupted use, except for three days, from February 18 to 21, 1865, when it was stopped by the falling of a span of Long Bridge with U. S. military railroad locomotive Charles Minot upon it.

The bridge generally, and the draw span particularly, being unsafe, a track was laid on the 20th and 21st of February over the new railroad bridge erected across the Potomac by the Alexandria and Washington Railroad Company, which has since remained in constant use.

The Alexandria, Loudoun and Hampshire Railroad was used to supply the Convalescent Camp three miles from Alexandria and the garrisons of some of the forts south of the Potomac; also to partially supply the quartermaster's department of Washington with fuel.

The Orange and Alexandria Railroad was opened from Springfield to Rappahannock River, fifty miles from Alexandria, between September 28 and October 2, but at once abandoned to Manassas Junction. It was operated to that point in connection with the Manassas Gap Railroad until November 10, when it was abandoned beyond Fairfax, sixteen miles from Alexandria, for the remainder of the year. On the 27th day of June, 1865, the road was turned over to the Board of Public Works of Virginia.

The Manassas Gap Railroad was opened from Manassas Junction to Piedmont, thirty-four miles, between October 3 and 11, 1864, with the design of continuing it to Front Royal, seventeen miles farther, to supply General Sheridan's army operating in the Valley of Virginia; but the line was so infested with guerrillas, and was so imperfectly guarded, it was found difficult, if not impossible, to operate it, and was therefore abandoned. The iron was taken up between October 27 and November 10 from Piedmont to Manassas Junction, and carried to Alexandria, from whence it was taken to the Winchester and Potomac Railroad and used for relaying the track of that line.

The Norfolk and Petersburg and Seaboard and Roanoke lines were run continually to Suffolk, twenty-three miles from Norfolk, during the year, for local military purposes.

During the fall and winter of 1864 eighteen miles of new railroad were built as an extension from the City Point and Petersburg line, passing around to the south and southwest of the city of Petersburg.

Upon the surrender of Petersburg and Richmond, early in April, 1865, the Petersburg and Richmond Railroad was opened to the south bank of James River, opposite Richmond. The destruction of the railroad bridge across that river by the retiring rebels prevented running trains into the city. Upon the surrender of General Lee the Petersburg and Lynchburg Railroad was opened to Burkeville, and shortly after the surrender of the last rebel army under General J. E. Johnston, the Richmond and Danville Railroad was opened through to Danville, 140 miles.

The gauge of the Petersburg and Lynchburg Railroad was originally five feet, but not having rolling-stock of that gauge on hand, the gauge was changed to four feet eight and one-half inches, and the line completed by the Construction Corps from Petersburg to Burkeville, fifty-two miles, between April 3 and 11—eight days.

The Winchester and Potomac Railroad was opened from Harper's Ferry to Halltown, six miles, between August 14 and 19, and thence to Stephenson's, twenty-two miles more, from November 2 to 24, 1864, and was continually used thereafter to supply the army operating in the Valley of Virginia. The entire track and sidings were relaid and new bridges built.

At the close of the year, June 30, 1865, the railroads in use, or that had been operated within the year in Virginia, were as follows:

Name of line.	Terminal stations.		Length.
	From—	To—	
			Miles.
Alexandria and Washington	Alexandria	Washington	7
Alexandria, Loudoun and Hampshire	....do	Vienna	15
Orange and Alexandria	....do	Rappahannock	50
Manassas Gap	Manassas	Piedmont	34
Norfolk and Petersburg	Norfolk	Suffolk	23
Seaboard and Roanoke	Portsmouth	....do	17
City Point and Army, and branches	Pitkin, &c	Humphreys, &c	18
South Side	City Point	Burkeville	62
Richmond and Danville	Manchester	Danville	140
Richmond and Petersburg	Petersburg	Manchester	22
Clover Hill Branch	Clover Hill	Coal Mines	18
Winchester and Potomac	Harper's Ferry	Stephenson's	28
Total			434

The following table exhibits the number of persons employed upon the military railroads of Virginia each month during the year and the amount paid for their services:

Month.	Number of men.	Amount paid.
July	2,512	$143,297.59
August	2,103	136,753.76
September	2,369	148,703.46
October	2,479	167,042.97
November	3,412	173,646.68
December	3,241	173,839.84
January	3,152	178,670.50
February	3,327	187,811.78
March	3,926	204,576.62
April	4,542	251,353.88
May	3,674	214,549.50
June	1,983	127,181.53
Total	36,720	2,107,428.11
Monthly average	3,060	175,619.00

II.—MILITARY DIVISION OF THE MISSISSIPPI.

The following table exhibits the lines in operation within this division on the 1st day of July, 1864:

Name of line.	Terminal stations.		Length.
	From—	To—	
			Miles.
Nashville and Chattanooga	Nashville	Chattanooga	151
Nashville, Decatur and Stevenson	....do	Stevenson	200
Nashville and Northwestern	....do	Tennessee River	78
Chattanooga and Knoxville	Chattanooga	Knoxville	112
Chattanooga and Atlanta	....do	Big Shanty	107
Cleveland and Dalton	Cleveland	Dalton	27
Rome Branch	Kingston	Rome	17
Memphis and Charleston	Memphis	Grand Junction	52
Louisville City	River Landing	Louisville and Nashville Railroad depot.	2
Total			746

Nashville and Chattanooga Railroad, 151 miles.

This was the great military thoroughfare over which passed all supplies for the armies in the Atlanta campaign, over which re-enforcements were sent to General Sherman, and by which the largest number of sick and wounded were sent to the rear. When it first passed under control of this department it was in a very dilapidated condition, and its appointments were utterly inadequate for the business required to be done on it. For several months trains returning from the front were sent around by Stevenson and Decatur to Nashville, eighty-seven miles farther, on account of the impossibility of passing them by the Nashville and Chattanooga line.

About 115 miles of main track and sidings were relaid with new iron, cross-ties, and ballast, and forty-five new water-tanks erected. Long sidings were laid, capable of holding five to eight heavy freight trains, at intervals not more than eight miles apart, and telegraph stations established at most of them. At Nashville some ten miles of sidings were laid to facilitate handling trains and to store engines and cars when accumulated there. At Chattanooga about the same length of sidings was laid.

About September 1, 1864, the rebel General Wheeler destroyed seven miles of track between Nashville and Murfreesborough, and in December Hood destroyed 7¾ miles of track and 530 feet of bridges between the same stations.

Excepting in these two instances this road suffered very little from the rebels during the year.

Chattanooga and Atlanta Railroad, 136 miles.

Next in importance as a military line was the railroad from Chattanooga to Atlanta. It was opened through in August, 1864, immediately after the evacuation of Atlanta by the rebel army. Extensive repairs were required to the twenty-nine miles of road from Big Shanty to Atlanta. The most important work was the Chattahoochee bridge, 780 feet long and 90 feet high, which was completed by the Construction Corps in four days and a half.

While occupied as a military road this was more infested with guerrillas than any other line during the war.

Early in October General Hood made his great raid in rear of General Sherman's army and destroyed in all 35½ miles of track and 455 lineal feet of bridges. In thirteen days after he left trains were run over the entire road from Chattanooga to Atlanta. Twenty-five miles of the track and 230 feet of bridges in one stretch between Tunnel Hill and Resaca were reconstructed in eight days and a half.

When General Sherman left on his march to Savannah in November this road was abandoned between Atlanta and Dalton, 100 miles; the track between Atlanta and Etowah River, forty-six miles, was torn up and destroyed, while between Resaca and Dalton, sixteen miles, the rails were taken up and carried to Chattanooga.

By order of Major-General Thomas the road was reconstructed from Dalton to Atlanta between May 10 and July 4, 1865. Sixty-six miles of track were laid, 36 miles repaired, and 3,553 lineal feet of bridging rebuilt.

Chattanooga and Knoxville Railroad, 112 miles.

This road was operated with great regularity through the year, excepting a part of August and through September, 1864, when General Wheeler tore up and destroyed twenty-five miles of the track. It was reopened October 1 and not afterward molested by the enemy.

Knoxville and Bristol line, 110 miles, to Carter's Station.

By order of General Thomas repairs were commenced near Knoxville March 14, and completed to Carter's Station April 23, 1865. Twelve miles of track were rebuilt, 94 miles repaired, and 4,400 lineal feet of bridges constructed.

Nashville, Decatur and Stevenson line, 200 miles.

This line was used successfully with no more excitement than occasional guerrilla raids and attacks until August, 1864, when Generals Forrest and Wheeler tore up twenty-nine miles and a half of track and burned several bridges. The track was at once repaired between Nashville and Pulaski, but between Pulaski and Athens, Ala., the bridges were not rebuilt nor was the road used until the following February.

During Hood's Nashville campaign in November and December all the bridges then standing were destroyed between Nashville and Decatur, on the Tennessee River—some by one army, some by the other. The work of reconstruction commenced December 19, three days after the battle of Nashville, and was completed February 10, 1865. In that time 6 miles of track were relaid and 7,055 lineal feet of trestle bridges rebuilt, consuming 1,045,675 feet (B. M.) timber.

Near the close of February and again in March most of these bridges were swept away by extraordinary floods, and were rebuilt—some of them twice or three times—and at last replaced by permanent truss bridges.

Nashville and Northwestern line, 78 miles.

This line while being operated was greatly annoyed by guerrillas until November 30, when it was abandoned. On the 5th of November General Forrest burnt the buildings at Tennessee River, but did no further damage at the time. During Hood's occupation of the country near Nashville, from November 30 to December 16, all the bridges were destroyed. Repairs were commenced January 2 and completed February 13; 2,200 lineal feet of bridging were rebuilt. In February, March, and April most of these bridges were swept away by floods, some of them three times. In each case they were promptly repaired, and in the spring of 1865 were replaced by permanent truss bridges.

Nashville and Clarksville line, 62 miles.

In August, 1864, by order of General Sherman, this road was repaired and opened in order to furnish another railroad communication with navigable water for supplying the Nashville depot. Important bridges were destroyed by floods at various times and rebuilt, until in April, 1865, it was abandoned, excepting the twenty-eight miles nearest Nashville.

Memphis and Charleston and Mississippi Central line.

In West Tennessee and North Mississippi the railroad was opened and abandoned during the year as follows:

Operated to Grand Junction, 52 miles, from Memphis, July 1, 1864.
Opened to Holly Springs, Miss., 75 miles, August 2, 1864.
Opened to Tallahatchie River, 100 miles, August 6, 1864.
Abandoned back to Grand Junction August 18, 1864.
Reopened to Tallahatchie River August 23, 1864.
Abandoned again to Grand Junction August 24, 1864.
Abandoned to White's Station, 10 miles, September 6, 1864.
Abandoned to Memphis October 15, 1864.
Opened to Collierville, 24 miles, December 20, 1864.
Abandoned January 1, 1865.
Reopened to Germantown, 15 miles, February 28, 1865.
Abandoned March 4, 1865.
Reopened to Collierville, 24 miles, March 24, 1865.
Reopened to La Fayette, 32 miles, April 2, 1865.
Reopened to Moscow, 39 miles, May 13, 1865.
Reopened to La Grange, 49 miles, May 14, 1865.
Reopened to Grand Junction, 52 miles, May 20, 1865.
Opened to Pocahontas, 75 miles, June 30, 1865.

Each time the road was abandoned it was badly damaged; bridges, trestles, and cattle guards were burned and several miles of track torn up.

Mobile and Ohio line, 26 miles.

That portion of the Mobile and Ohio Railroad between Columbus, Ky., and Union City, Tenn., twenty-six miles, was reopened May 15, 1865, having been abandoned after Forrest's raid in May, 1864, and not afterward used.

Summary of distances operated during the year ending June 30, 1865.

Name of line.	Terminal stations.		Length.
	From—	To—	Miles.
Nashville and Chattanooga	Nashville	Chattanooga	151
Nashville, Decatur and Stevenson	do	Stevenson	200
Nashville and Northwestern	do	Johnsonville	78
Nashville and Clarksville	do	Clarksville	62
Shelbyville Branch	Wartrace	Shelbyville	9
Chattanooga and Knoxville	Chattanooga	Knoxville	112
Cleveland and Dalton	Cleveland	Dalton	27
Knoxville and Bristol	Knoxville	Carter's Station	110
Rogersville and Jefferson	Bull's Gap	Near Rogersville	12
Chattanooga and Atlanta	Chattanooga	Atlanta	136
Rome Branch	Kingston	Rome	17
Atlanta and Macon	Atlanta	Rough and Ready	11
Memphis and Charleston	Memphis	Pocahontas	75
Mississippi Central	Grand Junction	Tallahatchie River.	48
Mobile and Ohio	Columbus, Ky	Crockett, Tenn	35
Louisville City	River Landing	Louisville and Nashville Railroad Depot.	2
Total			1,085

At Nashville, the headquarters of military railroads in the division, extensive arrangements were made to repair locomotives and cars, and do such other indispensable work as could not with safety be trusted to other hands or sent to other places. Owing to the crowded state of the city it was necessary to erect quarters for the employés collected there, numbering several thousand, and to provide hospital accommodations for them. The table on page 17 [593] contains list of the buildings erected for these purposes.

Large provision was made also at Chattanooga for similar objects. The general aim was to make Nashville and Chattanooga the points at which all operations should center, where necessary supplies of all kinds could be procured, repairs of all kinds made, and in case of destruction to the communications between the two places, operations could be conducted with equal facility from either in any direction.

Where buildings and machinery would probably remain permanent in the event of peace, they were well constructed, in order that they might be sold to advantage; where they would only be used during the war, they were built as cheaply as possible.

The transportation performed during the year it is impossible to state with any accuracy. Supplies were forwarded to the front, or wherever the armies were operating or troops stationed, upon the requisition of proper officers, and the quantities thus forwarded can be approximately stated. It was the duty of this department to do the transportation only; the cars were loaded and unloaded by employés of the quartermaster's or other staff department to which their contents belonged.

Of the great number of troops, of sick and wounded, of contrabands, refugees, prisoners, and released rebels, it is impossible to form an estimate at all approaching correctness. Whole corps, and even armies, were sometimes moved hundreds of miles in cases of emergency, and in immediate presence of the enemy, upon the verbal order of the general-in-chief, and no note taken of numbers of men, horses, artillery, or other loading. The design and aim was to make the railroad a transportation machine to aid in working out the combinations of the commander of the military division, and it was held at all times in readiness for that single object.

No record was kept of the contrabands, refugees, and rebel deserters that poured back in a steady, continuous stream from the front during the period of active operations. General Sherman ordered all sent to the rear who could not feed themselves, and they were placed upon the first train going in that direction by post commanders and turned adrift on reaching Nashville.

No less than 1,000 per day must have thus traveled for a time, and it is certainly within bounds to estimate the whole movement, exclusive of troops, sick and wounded, and persons traveling with official transportation, at 150,000 persons during the year.

Among the great movements may be mentioned that of the Fourth Corps from Dalton, Ga., to Athens, Ala.; of the Army of the Ohio from Dalton to Pulaski, Tenn.; of the Fourth Corps from Athens to Carter's Station, 352 miles, and from Carter's Station to Nashville, 373 miles. The latter movement employed 1,498 cars.

Two and sometimes three hospital trains were kept running continually from the extreme front through to Louisville, Ky., the cars and motive power being furnished by this department for the entire distance.

The following table shows the quantity of transportation sent from Nashville upon requisitions of the quartermaster's department only:

Month.	Number of cars used.				Tons of stores.	Number of troops.
	Stores.	Troops.	Empty.	Total.		
July	3,208	300	....	3,508	25,664	18,000
August	3,166	325	282	3,773	25,328	19,100
September	2,698	144	1,081	3,923	21,584	10,297
October	3,698	563	1,699	5,960	29,584	31,150
November	1,671	1,249	1,307	4,227	13,368	65,450
December	360	137	783	1,280	2,280	6,850
January	2,420	346	479	3,245	19,360	17,300
February	2,415	399	854	3,668	19,320	19,950
March	2,169	588	195	2,952	17,352	24,400
April	2,639	330	738	3,707	21,112	16,500
May	1,935	406	1,020	3,361	15,480	20,300
June	2,677	886	244	3,807	21,416	34,419
Total	29,056	5,673	8,682	43,411	232,448	283,716
Monthly average	2,421⅓	472¾	723½	3,617 7/12	19,337⅓	23,643

The following table exhibits the total movement of cars at Nashville Station during the year, excluding those used for local railroad purposes:

Month.	Forwarded.	Received.	Total.
July	4,618	4,493	9,111
August	4,781	4,744	9,525
September	4,384	4,058	8,442
October	6,225	6,031	12,256
November	4,764	5,569	10,333
December	1,754	1,622	3,376
January	4,571	4,271	8,842
February	4,710	4,718	9,428
March	3,990	4,379	8,339
April	5,110	5,331	10,441
May	4,113	4,584	8,697
June	4,437	4,793	9,230
Total	53,457	54,563	108,020
Monthly average	4,454	4,546	9,001

The foregoing figures will perhaps give some idea of the magnitude of movements through this military division.

As an item to show the peculiar hazard attending military railroad operations, it may be stated that during the last six months of the fiscal year the wrecking train picked up and carried to Nashville sixteen wrecked engines and 294 car-loads of car-wheels, axles, bridge-irons, &c. Most of the wrecks were caused by guerrillas and rebel raids.

The cost of doing the work and the number of men employed is shown in the following statement:

Month.	Number of persons.	Amount of pay-rolls.	Paid for materials, supplies, &c.	Total.
July	11,184	$605,580.15	$920,324.43	$1,525,904.58
August	12,445	695,839.20	887,477.97	1,583,317.17
September	14,693	784,223.15	635,442.72	1,419,665.87
October	15,282	906,693.15	731,227.39	1,637,920.54
November	14,621	874,184.15	478,318.37	1,352,502.52
December	11,924	577,143.70	43,404.05	620,547.75
January	12,596	806,138.86	557,470.53	1,363,609.39
February	13,101	805,723.05	694,930.32	1,500,653.37
March	13,427	881,527.74	908,077.73	1,789,605.47
April	13,673	947,479.52	706,746.52	1,654,226.04
May	13,047	828,151.85	465,806.62	1,293,958.47
June	10,523	643,053.69	431,863.40	1,074,917.09
Total	156,516	9,355,738.21	7,461,090.05	16,816,828.26
Monthly average	13,043	779,644.85	621,757.50	1,401,402.35

III.—GEORGIA.

In December a portion of the Construction Corps of the Military Division of the Mississippi, with some transportation men, were ordered from Tennessee to Savannah, Ga., to operate such roads as General Sherman should require.

Before this force reached Savannah General Sherman's army had left on his march to North Carolina, and the construction force was turned back from Hilton Head about the 1st of February and sent to New Berne, N. C.

Eleven miles of the Savannah and Gulf Railroad were operated for local military purposes and to supply the citizens of Savannah with fuel; and the tracks and buildings of the Georgia Central Railroad lying within the city of Savannah were also used.

By an order of the department commander all the railroad property was turned over to the original owners about the 20th day of June, 1865.

IV.—NORTH CAROLINA.

The railroad from Morehead City to Batchelder's Creek, forty-four miles long, was operated by the depot quartermaster at New Berne until the 1st of February, 1865, but no reports were made to this office. By order of Lieutenant-General Grant a force was detailed January 25, 1865, from the Virginia Construction Corps to rebuild the track, but a few days after they reached the ground a detachment arrived of the Construction Corps from the Military Division of the Mississippi.

This detachment had been ordered from Tennessee to Savannah in anticipation of their services being required on the Georgia and South Carolina coast, but on reaching Hilton Head they were ordered to Morehead City, and landed in North Carolina February 5.

As the Union army advanced from the coast the railroad was repaired, and trains ran to Goldsborough on the 25th of March, the day after General Sherman's army arrived. Repairs were at once commenced on the road between Goldsborough and Wilmington, ninety-five miles, to provide another line of supplies, and trains commenced running April 4.

On the 10th of April movements toward the interior were resumed, and the railroad opened to Raleigh, forty-eight miles from Goldsborough, April 19. Eight miles of torn-up track were relaid in this distance.

Various repairs were made to other railroads in North Carolina, but shortly after the surrender of General Johnston's army the Construction Corps was disbanded and the transportation force reduced to its minimum.

The total length of railroads opened and used in this department was as follows:

Name of line.	Terminal stations.		Length.
	From—	To—	
			Miles.
Atlantic and North Carolina	Morehead City	Goldsborough	85
Wilmington and Weldon	Wilmington	do	95
North Carolina	Goldsborough	Hillsborough	88
Raleigh and Gaston	Raleigh	Cedar Creek	25
Total			293

In rebuilding and repairing the above lines 33 miles of track were relaid, and 2,991 lineal feet of bridges built, consuming 779,510 feet (B. M.) timber.

At Morehead City the Construction Corps built a wharf covering an area of 53,682 square feet, consuming 700,000 feet (B. M.) timber, and costing $32,086.

The following table shows the number of persons employed each month in this department and the amount paid for their services:

Month.	Number of persons.	Amount paid.
1865.		
February	2,145	$144,754.10
March	2,839	225,783.16
April	3,328	220,986.38
May	3,387	144,097.66
June	1,437	94,152.75
Total	13,136	829,774.05
Monthly average	2,625	165,954.81

V.—MISSOURI.

In October, 1864, orders were received to have the bridges rebuilt which had been destroyed by the rebels on the main line of the Pacific Railroad of Missouri and its Southwestern Branch.

This work required the construction of 1,680 lineal feet of truss bridges, which, with the cost of replacing trestles carried away by floods and other incidental expenses, amounted to $170,564.65.

VI.—ARKANSAS.

The only line used in this department for military purposes was a portion of the Memphis and Little Rock Railroad between Devall's Bluff, on White River, and Little Rock, forty-nine miles long.

It did not come under control of this office until May 1, 1865. At that time it was in exceedingly very bad order, and required large expenditures to make it capable of doing the work required of it.

Table, page 18 [593], exhibits the business and expenditures during the two months of May and June, 1865, together with such information as could be obtained of previous earnings and expenses before coming under my charge, extending back to September 1, 1864.

The total number of miles operated within the year was as follows:

	Miles.
In Virginia	434
In Military Division of the Mississippi	1,079
In North Carolina	293
In Arkansas	49
Total	1,855

The rolling-stock provided at the beginning of the year was believed ample for the wants of the service, but when the army of General Sherman was at Atlanta its full capacity had been reached, allowing a reasonable margin for casualties occasioned by accident or design. In October, 1864, information was given that Sherman's army would march on Augusta, Ga., and depend upon the railroad for supplies. It was impracticable to accomplish it over the increased length of line with the rolling-stock then on hand, and to be ready for any service or contingency thirty-two additional locomotives of five-feet gauge were ordered from the manufacturers.

The transfer of the Army of the Mississippi to Savannah rendered these engines unnecessary in the Southwest, but their completion was hastened, to be prepared to open lines on the Atlantic Coast should the movement of the armies render it desirable. With the termination of hostilities no occasion remained for their use in any department, and they were sold at public auction.

Of the engines contracted for prior to July 1, 1864, sixty-six of five-feet gauge were placed upon the Nashville Railroad between July 1 and December 31, 1864.

One thousand four hundred and forty-four freight-cars were delivered upon the same roads during the fiscal year.

Twenty cars were added to the equipment at Memphis.

Two locomotives and thirty cars of five and a half-feet gauge were built and sent to the Memphis and Little Rock Railroad in Arkansas.

On all the military railroads was employed the following rolling-stock, including that captured from the enemy and rendered serviceable by repairing or rebuilding:

Division or State.	Locomotives.		Cars.	
Virginia		52		631
Military Division of the Mississippi:				
Nashville	216		2,838	
Memphis	21		200	
Columbus	2		37	
		239		3,075
North Carolina		29		262
Arkansas		10		98
Total		330		4,066

The foregoing statement includes only the locomotives and cars employed in active service, and does not embrace those built in the fall and winter of 1864, which were never placed upon the military railroads owing to the close of the war, but were subsequently sold at the points where manufactured, or at places where they had been stored to await events.

Thirty-five locomotives and 492 freight-cars of five-feet gauge were thus provided for North Carolina and the Military Division of the Mississippi.

Fifty cars of four feet eight and a half inch-gauge were also provided for Virginia and North Carolina.

In the Western States ten platform-cars of four feet eight and a half inch-gauge were purchased and used on the railroad north of the Ohio River to transport freight-cars of five-feet gauge from the manufacturers' works to Louisville, one of which was destroyed by a collision on being thrown from the track.

Summary of cars provided but not placed in active use.

Five-feet gauge cars	492
Four feet eight and a half inch-gauge cars for Virginia and North Carolina	50
Four feet eight and a half inch-gauge cars for car transportation	10
Total	552

The railroad service during the past year has formed an important element in the several campaigns, but more especially was this the case in supplying the Southwestern army under General Sherman over the distance of 365 miles from its base of supplies on the Tennessee River to Atlanta, through an enemy's country.

This line, from the very fact of its great length, was imperfectly guarded, as troops could not be spared from the front for that purpose; this rendered the railroad service one of great risk and hazard, and at times it was only by the force of military authority that men could be held to duty. The Government was peculiarly fortunate in having in its service civilian officers of great nerve, honesty, and capability, to whom the whole country owes a debt of gratitude.

Among them I take the liberty of naming A. Anderson, chief superintendent and engineer; W. W. Wright, chief engineer Military Division of the Mississippi; J. J. Moore, general superintendent and chief engineer railroads in Virginia; W. J. Stevens, general superintendent U. S. Military Railroads, Division of the Mississippi; L. H. Eicholtz, acting chief engineer, Military Division of the Mississippi, during the absence of W. W. Wright in North Carolina; A. F. Goodhue, engineer and superintendent military railroads West Tennessee and Arkansas. Also the following commissioned officers: Capt. F. J. Crilly, assistant quartermaster, Nashville, Tenn., and Bvt. Col. H. L. Robinson, assistant quartermaster, Washington, D. C.

There never was an order issued to either of these gentlemen by the commanding generals or myself that was not promptly and energetically carried out, regardless of personal comfort or safety, and it was this kind of spirit infused into subordinates that enabled us to accomplish unprecedented results.

In conclusion, I trust I may be pardoned for stating that without the most perfect organization and operation of the construction and transportation departments, added to the loyalty, devotion, and ability of these gentlemen, to whom the principal active operations were intrusted, the campaign of Sherman, at least for the time, would have proved, instead of a triumphant success, a signal failure. The question resolved itself simply into one of supplies, as it was evident his army had the power to overcome the enemy if the necessary materials could be forwarded to the front, and not otherwise.

Very respectfully, your obedient servant,

D. C. McCALLUM,

Brevet Brigadier-General, Director and General Manager Military Railroads United States.

List of buildings erected at Nashville, Tenn., for U. S. Military Railroad purposes.

Kind of building.	Number.	Length.	Width.	Height.
		Feet.	*Feet.*	
Machine-shop	1	195	88	2 stories.
Do	1	80	65	Do.
Pattern shop	1	100	48	Do.
Blacksmith and boiler shop	1	450	62	1 story.
Roundhouse	1	*a* 85	.....	
Carpenter shop	1	200	40	Do.
Tin shop	1	65	40	Do.
Copper shop	1	60	27	Do.
Store-house	1	175	36	Do.
Do	1	150	35	Do.
Hospital buildings	8	705	201	Do.
Assistant quartermaster's office	1	72	40	2 stories.
Office for auditor	1	56	20	Do.
Office for master machinist	1	90	25	3 stories.
Office for master carpenter	1	38	18	1 story.
Printing office	1	45	36	2 stories.
Mess-houses *b*	77	.....	.....	1 story.
Car shop *c*	1	202	77	23 feet.
Machine and blacksmith shop *c*	1	126	47	Do.
Machine-shop	1	55	35	17 feet.
Boiler room	1	35	18	8 feet.
Paint shop *c*	1	112	47	23 feet.
Brick dry house	1	40	15	17 feet.
Coal house	1	35	20	8 feet.
Iron store-house	1	20	14	16 feet.
Oil-house, waste, &c	1	40	18	18 feet.
Coke and sand house	1	50	20	1 story.

a Feet diameter with twenty-seven stalls. *b* Fitted with bunks, tables, &c. *c* Skylights.

DEPARTMENT OF ARKANSAS.

Statement of the business of the Memphis and Little Rock line of U. S. Military Railroads from September 1, 1864, to June 30, 1865.

Month.	Earnings.				Hire of employés.	Freight carried.		
	Passengers.	Freight.	News agency.	Total.		Government.	Private.	Total.
1864.						*Pounds.*	*Pounds.*	*Pounds.*
September	$1,133.55	$1,023.21	....	$2,156.76	$9,721.05	....	....	....
October	2,010.00	3,600.10	....	5,610.10	15,815.72	....	....	....
November	1,687.25	3,306.52	....	4,993.77	23,044.24	....	....	....
December	1,879.00	3,956.16	....	5,835.16	24,971.36	....	....	....
1865.								
January	1,672.00	6,251.13	....	7,923.13	23,827.15	....	....	....
February	1,719.00	2,001.68	....	3,720.68	24,108.19	....	....	....
March	1,872.00	2,760.72	....	4,632.72	24,696.74	....	....	....
April	2,577.50	1,874.28	....	4,451.78	21,736.51	....	....	....
May	6,147.75	2,430.03	$166.66	8,744.44	*a*31,253.63	5,531,808	296,713	5,828,521
June	8,103.25	4,408.70	166.66	12,678.61	*a*36,735.78	8,155,622	842,685	8,998,307
Total	28,801.30	31,612.53	333.32	60,747.15	235,910.37	13,687,430	1,139,398	14,826,828

a Expenditures.

OFFICE CHIEF ENGINEER AND GEN. SUPT.
MILITARY RAILROADS OF VIRGINIA,
Alexandria, Va., March 1, 1866.

Brig. Gen. D. C. MCCALLUM,
Director and General Manager
Military Railroads United States, Washington, D. C.:

GENERAL: I have the honor to submit a report of operations in the U. S. Military Railroad service, Department of Virginia, from July 1, 1865, to February 28, 1866. During that time the following roads have been operated in this department:

Washington and Alexandria; Alexandria, Loudoun and Hampshire; South Side; Richmond and Petersburg and Clover Hill Branch; Richmond and Danville; Winchester and Potomac.

Accompanying this report you will find sundry tabular statements as follows:

Table No. 1.—Gives a statement of the number of railroads with their length and number of miles in use July 1, 1865, and date of transfer.

Table No. 2.—Shows number of persons employed each month from July 1, 1865, to February 28, 1866.

Table No. 3.—Shows distribution of labor and material from July 1, 1865, to February 28, 1866.

Table No. 4.—Shows amount of material received and used from July 1, 1865, to February 28, 1866.

Table No. 5.—Shows amount of receipts for passage and freight from July 1, 1865, to February 28, 1866.

Table No. 6.—Gives estimated value of property on military railroads of Virginia, February 28, 1866.

Table No. 7.—Gives statement of material delivered to railroad companies for which they have given bonds.

Table No. 8.—Gives statement of engines and cars leased to railroad companies from July 1, 1865, to February 28, 1866.

Table No. 9.—Gives number of passengers and troops carried from July 1, 1865, to February 28, 1866.

The short time these roads were in operation and the small amount of business done from July 1, 1865, to date of transfer to the original companies will make but a meager narrative report. I will, however, proceed to give a statement of operations on each road separately, and will commence with the

ALEXANDRIA AND WASHINGTON RAILROAD.

An average of three passenger trains each way continued to run over the road in addition to a large number of freight trains run for the movement of troops en route home, and hauling wood for use of Quartermaster's Department. August 3 the following order was received from you:

> You will turn over the Washington, Georgetown and Alexandria Railroad to that company in accordance with letter of instructions from Quartermaster-General's Office, dated August 2, 1865; and also one dated May 19, 1865, copies of which are herewith inclosed. Mr. Joseph B. Stewart, secretary of said railroad company, is authorized to receive the same.

Agreeably to instructions I notified Mr. Stewart and he assumed control of the railroad August 8, thus closing my connection with this road. By your order the new Long Bridge was taken possession of February 19, 1865, track laid on it, and trains commenced running

February 21. The old bridge was abandoned as a railroad bridge, but we continued to keep it in repair and work the draws for the passage of boats and travel.

November 14, 1865, I received orders from you to turn it over to the Interior Department, and the transfer was made November 15. The necessary tools, &c., for working the draws were turned over with it.

ALEXANDRIA, LOUDOUN AND HAMPSHIRE RAILROAD.

This road was but little used further than running one regular train daily each way for the accommodation of troops at Vienna and Convalescent Camp (three miles and a half from Alexandria), and hauling an occasional train of wood for use of quartermaster's department. July 14 the following order was received from you.

You will turn over the Loudoun and Hampshire Railroad to Mr. Lewis McKenzie, agent of the Board of Public Works of the State of Virginia, who is duly authorized to receive and receipt for the same. No claim upon this road nor any rights of property which the United States may have acquired therein during the course of the war will be compromised, nor will any questions respecting the same be considered as affected by this turning over the road.

Mr. McKenzie not being ready to receive the road at the date above mentioned, we continued to run it and your instructions were not carried into effect until August 8, 1865, at which time it was turned over.

SOUTH SIDE RAILROAD.

The short time this road was run since date of last report will cause me to make but a mere mention of operations. We continued to run the road (from City Point to Burkeville, sixty-two miles), transporting troops en route North from North Carolina, until July 24, 1865. At this date the road was turned over to the company. The whole force, with the exception of some sixteen men left to take care of property, were brought to Alexandria and discharged, and all the property removed from City Point to Alexandria, with the exception of railroad iron, lumber, wood, and cross-ties. The railroad iron was sold at public auction October 11, under the direction of General Robinson, assistant quartermaster, and during the month of December the balance of material was invoiced by him to Captain Barnes, assistant quartermaster, the officer in charge at City Point. After weighing and measuring all material and seeing that it was properly received by the parties who purchased it, our force left for Alexandria and were discharged January 1, 1866.

RICHMOND AND PETERSBURG RAILROAD AND CLOVER HILL BRANCH.

This road not being of any further importance as a military railroad, on account of the troops of General Sherman's army leaving the post at Manchester (opposite Richmond), where they received supplies prior to their march overland to Alexandria and Washington, and application having been made by Governor Peirpoint to have the road transferred to the company, by your order it was turned over July 3, 1865, and all material, &c., removed to City Point.

RICHMOND AND DANVILLE RAILROAD.

We continued to run this as a military railroad until July 4, 1865, at which time it was surrendered to the company. It was used mainly for furnishing supplies and transporting Sixth Army Corps between Danville and Manchester (140 miles) and transporting troops arriving at Danville from North Carolina for the North by way of Burkeville and City Point. All the rolling-stock used by us on this road was captured. The locomotive engines were eighteen in number and were turned over to the company with the road. All movable property belonging to the Government was sent to City Point. Twenty-four new locomotive engines and about 274 new cars (all five-feet gauge) were stored at Manchester. A force of men were kept in charge of this rolling-stock until sold by General Robinson, assistant quartermaster, October 3, 1865.

WINCHESTER AND POTOMAC RAILROAD.

During the months of July and August this road was kept busy furnishing supplies and transporting troops belonging to General Hancock's corps. By September 1 most of these troops were sent to other points or mustered out and nothing was done on the road, with the exception of running two regular passenger trains daily each way with mails, an occasional car-load of freight, and Adams Express business. But few passengers were carried, on account of the terminus of the road being at Stephenson's (four miles from Winchester), most of the travel going by stage to Martinsburg. This continued until the transfer of the road. December 15 I was directed by you to turn over the road to the company, and notified that the company would be admitted to the privileges of the Executive order of October 14, 1865. An inventory was taken of all Government property and a fair valuation placed on it. It was then tendered that company, but they declined purchasing it, they having arranged with the Baltimore and Ohio Company to operate the road for them. The transfer of the road was made January 20, 1866. All rolling-stock, material, &c., were brought to Alexandria, with exception of lumber and wood. This was invoiced to Major Flagg, post quartermaster at Harper's Ferry, by General Robinson, assistant quartermaster. The forces on this road were brought to Alexandria and discharged January 26, 1866.

The large quantity of rolling-stock and other material collected at Alexandria from the different roads, and the large supply of new material in the store-house, caused us to keep a large force to protect and put it in good condition for sale. The first sale took place October 17, 18, and 19, when all the engines and cars then stored at Alexandria were sold at prices in most cases far in advance of cost. Another sale of store-house material took place December 12, 13, and 14, and again January 10, 11, and 12, leaving but a small amount on hand except the rolling-stock and material brought from Winchester and Potomac road, which has been advertised to be sold April 10, 1866. Tracks at Point Lookout and Dodge's Wharf, Georgetown, were taken up, together with portions of the track at Annapolis and Fortress Monroe, and the iron brought to Alexandria and sold. Please see tabular statements for further information. This sums up the report of my operations in the Department of Virginia from July 1, 1865, to February 28, 1866.

Respectfully submitted.

J. J. MOORE,

Chief Engineer and Gen. Supt. Mil. Railroads of Virginia.

[Table No. 1.]

Schedule of military railroads operated in the Department of Virginia from July 1, 1865, to February 28, 1866.

Road.	From—	To—	Length.	Transferred to company.
			Miles.	
Washington and Alexandria	Washington	Alexandria	$7\frac{1}{2}$	August 8, 1865.
Alexandria, Loudoun and Hampshire	Alexandria	Vienna	15	Do.
South Side	City Point	Burkeville	62	July 24, 1865.
Richmond and Petersburg	Manchester	Petersburg	21	July 3, 1865.
Clover Hill Branch		Clover Hill	18	Do.
Richmond and Danville	Manchester	Danville	140	July 4, 1865.
Winchester and Potomac	Harper's Ferry	Stephenson's	28	January 20, 1866.

[Table No. 2.]

*Number of persons employed each month from July 1, 1865, to February 28, 1866.**

[Table No. 3.]

Distribution of labor and material from July 1, 1865, to February 28, 1866.

Account.	Labor.	Material.	Total.
Alexandria railroads	$82, 878. 52	$25, 513. 20	$108, 391. 72
City Point railroads	22, 589. 00		22, 589. 00
Norfolk railroads	230. 00		230. 00
Winchester and Potomac Railroad	30, 226. 49	1, 786. 30	32, 012. 79
Virginia railroads	26, 551. 06	81, 925. 79	108, 476. 85
Total	162, 475. 07	109, 225. 29	271, 700. 36

[Table No. 4.]

Amount of material received and used from July 1, 1865, to February 28, 1866.

Month.	On hand.	Received.	Used.	On hand.
July	$687, 267. 40	$8, 547. 89	$10, 191. 63	
August			161, 779. 80	
September			88, 291. 85	
October			3, 541. 64	
November		62. 86	4, 233. 18	
December			7, 648. 85	
January				
February				$420, 191. 20
Total	687, 267. 40	8, 610. 75	275, 686. 95	420, 191. 20

[Table No. 5.]

Receipts for passage and freight from July 1, 1865, to February 28, 1866.

	July.	August.	September.	October.	November.	December.	January.	Total.
Passage	$8, 651. 94	$3, 158. 40	$2, 647. 25	$2, 112. 60	$1, 762. 20	$1, 635. 05	$827. 55	$20, 794. 99
Freight	3, 589. 30	1, 467. 08	531. 75	893. 60	588. 52	285. 95	305. 25	7, 661. 45
Total	12, 241. 24	4, 625. 48	3, 179. 00	3, 006. 20	2, 350. 72	1, 921. 00	1, 132. 80	28, 456. 44

*Detailed statement (here omitted) shows an average total of $417\frac{5}{8}$ persons employed during the period represented, including chief engineers and general superintendents, superintendents, engineers, clerks, printers, agents and dispatchers, draughtsmen, supervisors, store-keepers, timber inspectors, conductors, brakemen, enginemen, firemen, wipers, commissary department, carpenters, car department, machinists and helpers, blacksmiths and helpers, boiler makers and helpers, copper and tin smiths, messengers, stationary engineers, teamsters, painters, laborers, watchmen, and photographers. The highest number employed (in July, 1865) was 1,360, and the lowest number (in January, 1866) was 75.

[Table No. 6.]

Estimated value of property on military railroads of Virginia February 28, 1866.

Locomotive engines	$32,000
Box freight-cars	13,650
Flat-cars	2,000
Stock-cars	1,300
Passenger-cars	3,400
President's car	8,000
Hand-cars	300
Stationary engine	800
Pumping engines	2,400
Iron and steel	500
Office furniture	600
Printing department	1,542
Buildings	10,000
Store-house report	29,372
Total	105,864

[Table No. 7.]

Material delivered to railroad companies, for which they have given bond.

Date.	Railroad.	Amount.
July 12, 1865	Orange and Alexandria	$90,395.74
July 19, 1865	Richmond, Fredericksburg and Potomac	7,449.27
August 15, 1865	Petersburg and Weldon	65,000.00
August 17, 1865	Virginia Central	70,000.00
November 1, 1865	Wilmington and Weldon	40,000.00
December 11, 1865	Western North Carolina	6,062.17
Do	Alexandria, Loudoun and Hampshire	62,592.96
January 5, 1866	Manassas Gap	4,623.51
		346,123.65

[Table No. 8.]

Statement of engines and cars leased to railroad companies from July 1, 1865, to February 28, 1866.

Railroad.	Date.	Engines.		Passenger-cars.		Freight-cars.		Grand total.
		Rate per day.	Total.	Rate per day.	Total.	Rate per day.	Total.	
Orange and Alexandria	July	$20.00	$760.00	$3.50	$108.50	$2.00	$1,842.00	$2,710.50
	August	20.00	2,500.00	3.50	227.50	2.00	3,826.00	6,553.50
	September	20.00	3,060.00	3.50	402.50	2.00	6,088.00	9,550.50
	October	20.00	2,040.00	3.50	238.00	2.00	4,502.00	6,780.00
	November					2.00	964.00	964.00
Norfolk and Petersburg	September	20.00	60.00			2.00	18.00	78.00
Virginia Central	August	20.00	1,120.00			2.00	1,120.00	2,240.00
	September	20.00	2,400.00			2.00	2,400.00	4,800.00
	October	20.00	1,200.00			2.00	1,200.00	2,400.00
Seaboard and Roanoke	August	20.00	30.00	2.00	1.00			31.00
	September	20.00	40.00	2.00	40.00	2.00	44.00	124.00
	October	20.00	40.00			2.00	8.00	48.00
Richmond and Petersburg.	July	20.00	560.00					560.00
	August	20.00	1,200.00	3.50	94.50			1,294.50
	September	20.00	1,200.00			3.50	105.00	1,305.00
South Side	July	20.00	480.00	3.50	112.00	2.00	682.00	1,274.00
	August	20.00	360.00	3.50	84.00	2.00	484.00	928.00
	September					2.00	720.00	720.00
Alexandria, Washington and Georgetown.	February	20.00	160.00					160.00

RECAPITULATION.

Orange and Alexandria	$26,558.50
Norfolk and Petersburg	78.00
Virginia Central	9,440.00
Seaboard and Roanoke	203.00
Richmond and Petersburg	3,159.50
South Side	2,922.00
Alexandria, Washington and Georgetown	160.00
Total	42,521.00

[Table No. 9.]

Number of passengers and troops carried from July 1, 1865, to February 28, 1866.

Alexandria railroads	12,590
Winchester and Potomac Railroad	41,200
Richmond and Danville Railroad	2,405
South Side Railroad	18,840
Richmond and Petersburg Railroad	1,308
Total	76,343

WAR DEPT., PROVOST-MARSHAL-GENERAL'S BUREAU,
Washington, D. C., March 17, 1866.

Hon. E. M. STANTON,
Secretary of War:

SIR: The act of Congress creating the office of Provost-Marshal-General was approved March 3, 1863. I was appointed to it March 17, 1863.

Within a few weeks from that date the net-work of organization adopted under the law was extended over the loyal States and the counties and towns of the same, and the principal duties of the Bureau, to wit, the arrest of deserters, the enrollment of the national forces for draft, and the enlistment of volunteers, had been commenced.

When the Bureau was put in operation the strength of the Army was deemed inadequate for offensive operations. Nearly 400,000 recruits were required to bring the regiments and companies then in service up to the legal and necessary standard. Disaster had been succeeded by inactivity, and the safety of the country depended on speedy and continued re-enforcement of the Army. The insufficiency of the system of recruitment previously pursued had been demonstrated, and the Army was diminishing by the ordinary casualties of war, but more rapidly by the expiration of the terms for which the troops had engaged to serve. To meet the emergency a new system of recruitment was inaugurated. The General Government, through this Bureau, assumed direct control of the business which had heretofore been transacted mainly by the State governments. The provost-marshals of the several Congressional districts, aided by a commissioner and surgeon in each, were made recruiting officers. Springing directly from the people, and at the same time exercising the authority and representing the necessities and wishes of the Government, they reached the masses and were able, without abating the requirements of the conscription, to promote volunteering and to examine, enlist, muster, clothe, and forward recruits as fast as they could be obtained. The quotas of districts and sub-districts were made known, each locality was advised of the number it was required to furnish, and that, in the event of failure, the draft would follow.

This system (though administered under difficulties and discouragements further alluded to in the accompanying report) met the wants of the service; recruits were rapidly obtained by voluntary enlistment or draft, and such strict regard was paid to their physical fitness, before accepting them, as to greatly reduce the enormous loss on account of discharges for physical disability, which had prevailed during the first two years of the war.

The following is a condensed summary of the results of the operations of this Bureau from its organization to the close of the war:

1. By means of a full and exact enrollment of all persons liable to conscription under the law of March 3, and its amendments, a complete exhibit of the military resources of the loyal States in men was made, showing an aggregate number of 2,254,063 men, not including 1,000,516 soldiers * actually under arms when hostilities ceased.

2. One million one hundred and twenty thousand six hundred and twenty-one *a* men were raised at an average cost (on account of recruitment exclusive of bounties) of $9.84 per man; while the cost of recruiting the 1,356,593 raised prior to the organization of the Bureau was $34.01 per man. A saving of over 70 cents on the dollar in the cost of raising troops was thus effected under this Bureau, notwithstanding the increase in the price of subsistence, transportation, rents, &c., during the last two years of the war.

3. Seventy-six thousand five hundred and twenty-six deserters were arrested and returned to the Army.

The vigilance and energy of the officers of the Bureau in this branch of business put an effectual check to the widespread evil of desertion, which at one time impaired so seriously the numerical strength and efficiency of the Army.

4. The quotas of men furnished by the various parts of the country were equalized, and a proportionate share of military service secured from each, thus removing the very serious inequality of recruitment which had arisen during the first two years of the war, and which, when the Bureau was organized, had become an almost insuperable obstacle to further progress in raising troops.

5. Records were completed showing minutely the physical condition of 1,014,776 of the men examined, and tables of great scientific and professional value have been compiled from these data. *b*

6. The casualties in the entire military force of the Nation during the war of the rebellion, as shown by the official muster-rolls and monthly returns, have been compiled, showing, among other items, 5,221 commissioned officers and 90,868 enlisted men killed in action, or died of wounds while in service; 2,321 commissioned officers and 182,329 enlisted men who died from disease or accident, making an aggregate of 280,739 officers and men of the Army who lost their lives in service. *c*

---

a This number does not embrace the naval credits allowed under the eighth section of the act of July 4, 1864, nor credits for drafted men who paid commutation, the recruits for the Regular Army, nor the credits allowed by the Adjutant-General subsequent to May 25, 1863, for men raised prior to that date.

b The results of the earlier examination of recruits by the medical officers of the Bureau were not obtained in detail.

c These figures have been carefully compiled from the complete official file of muster-rolls and monthly returns, but yet entire accuracy is not claimed for them, as errors and omissions to some extent, doubtless, prevailed in the rolls and returns.† Deaths (from wounds or disease contracted in service) which occurred after the men left the Army are not included in these figures.

---

* But see consolidated abstract for April 30, 1865, Vol. IV, this series, p. 1283.

† A compilation made in 1885, with greatly increased data at command, resulted in the augmentation of the number of deaths, from all causes, to 359,528. See foot-note (†), pp. 664, 665.

7. The system of recruitment established by the Bureau under the laws of Congress, if permanently adopted (with such improvements as experience may suggest) will be capable of maintaining the numerical strength and improving the character of the Army in time of peace, or of promptly and economically rendering available the national forces to any required extent in time of war.

8. Through the instrumentality of the Bureau there was disseminated throughout the loyal States a knowledge of the routine of business in the various bureaus of the War Department, which was essential to intelligent and effective co-operation in the recruitment, through popular effort, of the armies of the Republic.

The extension of the Bureau over the country brought together the Government and the people by closer ties, nurtured that mutual confidence and reliance through which the civil war was conducted to a successful termination, and developed a consciousness of national strength which will promote future peace and prosperity.

9. The results, under the act for enrollment and draft, were attained without cost to the Government; the Bureau never asked or required an appropriation of money for these purposes. Twenty-six million three hundred and sixty-six thousand three hundred and sixteen dollars and seventy-eight cents were raised by its own operations in conformity to law. Out of this sum all of the expenses of enrollment and draft and additional ones called for by special laws were met. A balance of no less than $9,390,105.64 remains (January 1, 1866) to the credit of the Bureau in the Treasury of the United States.

The foundations of the success of the Bureau which I have controlled, under your orders and supervision, have been—

1. The hearty co-operation of the civil officers of the different States, sustained by the devoted loyalty and earnestness of the masses of the people.

2. The judicious legislation of Congress.

3. The just, faithful, intelligent, industrious, and unflinching performance of duty on the part of the subordinate officers of the Bureau.

I deem it my duty, as it is my pleasure, to refer by name to the last-mentioned public servants, whose merits would not otherwise be as fully known as they deserve.

The officers immediately associated with me in the conduct of the business and to whom I am particularly indebted are the following:

Col. George D. Ruggles, aide-de-camp, assistant adjutant-general, and brevet brigadier-general, who served as principal assistant to the Provost-Marshal-General from the organization of the Bureau to August 16, 1864.

Col. N. L. Jeffries, Veteran Reserve Corps, and brevet brigadier-general, U. S. Volunteers, who has served as principal assistant to the Provost-Marshal-General from August 17, 1864, to the present time.

Maj. Chauncey McKeever, assistant adjutant-general and brevet brigadier-general, U. S. Army, who served in charge of Deserters' Branch from April 18, 1863, until August 26, 1863, and in charge of Mustering and Disbursing Branch from August 26, 1863, until the present time.

Capt. W. R. Pease, Seventh U. S. Infantry, who served in charge of Deserters' Branch from August 28, 1863, until April 30, 1864.

Maj. Henry E. Maynadier, Twelfth U. S. Infantry, who served in charge of the Enrollment Branch from May 19, 1863, until May 20, 1864.

Maj. Theodore A. Dodge, Veteran Reserve Corps, and brevet colonel, U. S. Volunteers, who served in charge of the Enrollment Branch from May 20, 1864, until December 5, 1864, and in charge of the Deserters' Branch from December 5, 1864, until the present time.

Maj. George E. Scott, Veteran Reserve Corps, who served in charge of the Deserters' Branch from May 2, 1864, until December 5, 1864, and in charge of the Enrollment Branch from December 5, 1864, until the present time.

Maj. S. F. Chalfin, assistant adjutant-general and brevet colonel, U. S. Army, who served as chief of the Disbursing Branch of this Bureau from March 23, 1863, until April 7, 1864.

Maj. George W. Burton, assistant adjutant-general of volunteers, who served as chief of the Disbursing Branch of this Bureau from April 7, 1864, until March 8, 1865.

Bvt. Maj. H. R. Rathbone, captain, Twelfth U. S. Infantry, and assistant adjutant-general of volunteers, who has served as chief of the Disbursing Branch of this Bureau from March 8, 1865, until the present time.

Col. Richard H. Rush, Sixth Pennsylvania Cavalry, who served in charge of the Veteran Reserve Corps Branch from May 23, 1863, until November 9, 1863.

Col. M. N. Wisewell, Veteran Reserve Corps, who served in charge of the Veteran Reserve Corps Branch from November 9, 1863, until December 20, 1864.

Bvt. Maj. James McMillan, captain, Second U. S. Infantry, who served in charge of the Veteran Reserve Corps Branch from December 20, 1864, until October 2, 1865.

Capt. J. W. De Forest, Veteran Reserve Corps, who has served in charge of the Veteran Reserve Corps Branch from October 2, 1865, until the present time.

Bvt. Lieut. Col. J. H. Baxter, surgeon, U. S. Volunteers, who has served as chief medical officer of the Bureau from January 11, 1864, until the present time.

The officers detailed as assistant provost-marshals-general in the several States deserve, as a class, honorable mention. Their names are borne on the register, entitled Document 33, appended to this report.

I ask special attention to the faithful and efficient manner in which the district provost-marshals, commissioners, and surgeons, as a class, have performed the duties devolving upon them from the commencement of their term of office to the close of the war.

In general these officers were appointed each upon the recommendation of the representative of his district in Congress. Mostly without military experience, they undertook the discharge of duties not only arduous in themselves, but rendered additionally so by the fact that they were without precedent, as no like service had hitherto been required of officers of the Government.

In order to perform the duties defined by the enrollment act and the regulations of this Bureau and others specially assigned to them, they were obliged to acquaint themselves with the business of the Adjutant-General's Office, the Quartermaster's, Commissary, and Ordnance Departments, in the details of clothing, subsisting, arming, and equipping of conscripts and recruits, and forwarding them to the Army.

Moreover, there was no district in which the Board of Enrollment was free from the annoyance of evil-disposed persons hostile to the Government, who were ever ready and willing to embarrass its operations by stimulating resistance to the draft or discouraging enlistments.

In some places, where this element seemed likely for a time to predominate, the firmness and energy of these officers enforced the law and convinced the seditious that resistance was futile.

But the healthy influence exercised by them was not confined to combating and disarming the enemies of the Government in their districts. It was also manifested in the great moral force exerted by them and their subordinates throughout the country in maintaining the national cause and aiding in the formation and dissemination of a proper public sentiment regarding the recruitment of the loyal Army and the prosecution of the struggle for the integrity of the Union.

The conscription was not presented as a popular measure, but as one of stern necessity, and it was not to be expected that the officers whose business it was to enforce it could escape the odium cast upon it by its opposers.

It was difficult to convince the drafted man, whose family depended on his labor for support, and who was unable to provide a substitute or pay commutation, that the law which forced him to enter the service was intended for his benefit, or that the Board of Enrollment had not done him injustice in refusing to exempt him.

The opponents of the measure were prompt to render pretended sympathy and encourage opposition by misrepresenting facts, magnifying cases of real hardship, or creating imaginary grievances where real ones were wanting.

The action of civil courts was invoked and the officers subjected to harassing litigation, and in many instances fines were imposed upon them for acts done in their official capacity, pursuant to the orders of superior and competent authority.

It gives me great pleasure to bear testimony to the satisfactory manner in which the duty has been discharged, notwithstanding the above-mentioned obstacles.

I am confident that there is no class of public servants to whom the country is more indebted for valuable services rendered than to the district provost-marshals and their associates (comprising the boards of enrollment), by whose efforts the Army of the Union which suppressed the rebellion was mainly recruited.

I have deemed it proper to allude to this subject, because it has been considered by the War Department that upon these officers brevet rank for meritorious services could not properly be bestowed. Their names appear in the register, Appendix, Document 34.

The exigencies of the service rendered it impracticable to state the operations of the Bureau in detail in the annual reports heretofore submitted.

With the return of peace, it is deemed appropriate and important that the statistical and other information of professional and historical value acquired by the Bureau should be preserved in permanent form, and with a view to this I submit the subjoined report.

In conclusion, I beg leave to remark that while I am aware that no bureau can claim special credit for faithful performance of duty, still it may be properly said that, in accomplishing the results before enumerated, this Bureau has the merit of having acted under extraordinary circumstances and difficulties, such as the vastness of the powers conferred on it, the peculiar character of the laws governing it, and, above all, the novelty in our country of the measure of conscription; and yet, without neglecting or evading any public duty, the rights of citizens have been duly considered and personal liberty always respected, excepting in such measures as were necessary for the levying of troops and arrest of deserters, in execution of acts of Congress, and in these only invaded to the extent required to provide for the public safety, so far as it depended on this branch of the service.

I am, sir, very respectfully, your obedient servant,

JAMES B. FRY,
Provost-Marshal-General.

The subjects embraced in the accompanying report are subdivided as follows:

Part I.—Strength and position of the U. S. Army at the commencement of the rebellion, with an account of the measures adopted for its increase during the year 1861; the recruitment of the Army during the year 1862, with a reference to the laws under which it was conducted.

Part II.—The necessity for a change in the method of raising troops; passage of the act for enrolling and drafting the national forces, its objects, and the organization and operations of the Bureau of the Provost-Marshal-General under it during the year 1863.

Part III.—Operations of the Bureau of the Provost-Marshal-General during the year 1864, with an explanation of the method of assigning quotas, and an account of the re-enlistment and reorganization as veteran volunteers of the armies in the field during the winter of 1863–'64.

Part IV.—Recruitment of men of African descent, and the enlistment of men in rebel States for the credit of loyal States.

Part V.—Naval enlistments and credits, with an explanation of the discrepancies which arose between the number of men called for and the number actually obtained.

Part VI.—Statement of the casualties in the entire military force of the United States from the beginning of the war to the close of hostilities in April, 1865.

Part VII.—The subject of bounty discussed, with tabular statements showing the bounties paid during the rebellion by the United States and by the different States and districts.

Part VIII.—Desertion.

Part IX.—Medical examination of recruits, &c., with statistical tables deduced therefrom.

Part X.—The Veteran Reserve Corps.

Part XI.—Disbursements, accounts, &c., including an account of the commutation fund arising from the payment of money by drafted men to secure exemption, as authorized by law.

Part XII.—Appendix, containing subordinate reports, various laws, regulations, statistical tables, &c.

REPORT.

PART I.

CONDITION OF THE ARMY OF THE UNITED STATES AT THE OUTBREAK OF AND DURING THE REBELLION PREVIOUS TO THE ORGANIZATION OF THE PROVOST-MARSHAL-GENERAL'S BUREAU.

No fact was more patent in the early stages of the rebellion than the inadequacy of the force at the command of the Government for the suppression of the insurrection and vindication of the Federal authority throughout the country. On the 1st of January, 1861, the Army of the United States was composed as follows: *a*

	Present.	Absent.	Present and absent.
Commissioned officers	727	371	1,098
Enlisted men	13,930	1,374	15,304
Total*	14,657	1,745	16,402

This force was scattered over the territory of the United States from the Atlantic and Gulf of Mexico to the Pacific Ocean. Between January 1, 1861, and January 1, 1862, it was, in addition to ordinary casualties, reduced by the resignation and desertion of 313 commissioned officers who joined the rebellion. Notwithstanding the influence brought to bear upon the rank and file of the Army, they were not materially affected by desertion during the same time. But few, if any, enlisted men turned against the Government.

The leaders of the rebellion commenced as early as December, 1860, to prepare the Southern States for armed resistance to the Government. With the spread of the secession movement from State to State, the military ardor of the Southern people became more and more aroused, and organizations, under State auspices, sprang up everywhere, and before the loyal Northern States actually began their preparations for the defense of the Government the South had a force larger than the Army of the United States ready for the conflict. No addition was made to the force at the disposal of the Government until April 9, 1861, when under the authority of the twenty-fourth section of the act of March 3, 1803, *b* a call was made by the President, through an order of the Secretary of War, *c* upon the District of Columbia for ten companies for muster into the service of the United States. Other calls were made upon the District during the same month, but troops were not obtained under them without embarrassment and difficulty and some conciliation on the part of the Government. The first companies called out could not be mustered, because a large number of the men declined to be sworn into service. In one company with 100 men on its rolls, all except the officers, one sergeant, one corporal, one musician, and ten privates refused to parade for muster. Disloyalty was probably the motive of some. Others alleged their willingness to serve in defense of the District of Columbia, but declined to muster without a guaranty that they should not be required to serve beyond its limits. It was finally stipulated, as a condition of muster, that they were "to serve within the District and not go without it." Thirty-eight companies of the District militia were finally mustered into the United States service for three months, thirty-five under the conditions specified above and three without conditions. It is proper to state that these troops, in whole or part, did subsequently serve out of the District without opposition or protest.

a For details, see Appendix, Doc. 1, Table 1.
b See Appendix, Doc. 35.
c See Appendix, Doc. 32.

* But see revised table, Vol. I, this series, p. 22.

The call of April 15, 1861, for 75,000 militia for three months.

On the 12th of April, 1861, Fort Sumter was attacked by the rebels, and on the 15th of that month the first decided step was taken toward offensive efforts on the part of the Government against the rebellion. On that day the proclamation calling for 75,000 militia, to aid in suppressing the revolutionary combinations of certain States and to cause the laws to be duly executed, was issued.[a]

The call was made under the twenty-fourth section of the act approved March 3, 1803, heretofore referred to.[b] No recruits were raised for this force after the original muster into service of the different organizations composing it. Before these troops could be fully organized and brought properly into service their enlistments began to expire. Their only active experience was in the brief campaign terminating in the first battle of Bull Run. It went to demonstrate most strikingly the inefficiency of militia called into service for short periods.

Call of May 3, 1861, for forty regiments of volunteers for three years, and for eight regiments of regulars and 18,000 seamen.

On the 3d of May, 1861, the President issued a proclamation calling into service, in addition to the 75,000 militia called for by his proclamation of April 15, 1861, thirty-nine regiments of volunteer infantry and one of cavalry, amounting to 42,034 men, for the period of three years, unless sooner discharged, increasing the Regular Army by eight regiments, amounting to 22,714 officers and men, and directing the enlistment of 18,000 seamen.[a] No quotas were assigned to States under this call. The patriotism of the loyal people was aroused to the highest pitch, and an intensely warlike spirit was kindled all over the North. A universal desire to enter the service of the Government was manifested, and more offers of men were made than could be accepted. The call for volunteers was more than filled, seventy-one regiments of volunteer infantry, one regiment of volunteer heavy artillery, and ten batteries of volunteer light artillery having been accepted and mustered into the service before the 1st of July.[c] This call was legalized during the extra session of Congress by the third section of the act approved August 6, 1861, and by section 1 of the act approved July 29, 1861.[d] But few men were obtained for the regular force called for. The regiment of cavalry and regiment of artillery and one regiment of infantry were completed after considerable delay. The remaining regiments of infantry, though partially formed, were not fully organized during the war for want of recruits.

The first battle of Bull Run was fought on the 21st of July, 1861. Great as this calamity seemed to the national cause, Congress was equal to the emergency. Instead of losing heart it gathered new courage and, under the impulse of the disaster, it redoubled its efforts for the suppression of the rebellion. Profiting by the experience of the past as to the inefficiency of troops enlisted for short terms of service, it passed on the 22d, 25th, and 31st of July a succession of acts[c] authorizing the President to accept the services of volunteers,

---

a See Appendix, Doc. 36.
b For quotas and number of troops furnished under this call, see Appendix, Doc. 6, Table 3.
c They are embraced in the figures in Tables 2 and 3, Doc. 6, Appendix.
d See Appendix, Doc. 35.

either as cavalry, infantry, or artillery, in such numbers, not exceeding 1,000,000, as he might deem necessary for the purpose of repelling invasion and suppressing insurrection, and directing that the volunteers thus accepted should serve for not exceeding three years nor less than six months.

These acts of Congress were published in general orders from the Adjutant-General's Office. The people responded so readily and enthusiastically to the appeals of Congress and the Executive that no formal call was issued. Regiments and companies were immediately offered in large numbers by States and individuals, and, as circumstances seemed to demand, requisitions were made on the Governors. Individuals received special authority to raise military organizations (termed independent acceptances), in some instances, without reference to the State authorities. The necessity for system and equality in the apportionment of the demands of the Government for troops upon the several States was not recognized at this early period of the war. This neglect subsequently bore its legitimate fruit in the confusion and inequality of apportionment attending later calls, when military service was no longer popularly regarded as a privilege, but exacted as a duty. Some States, during this period, raised and offered troops which were declined, but which, if accepted, would have made up no more than their fair share of the total taken from all the States. It sometimes happened that troops thus rejected went from their own State into other States, and were there accepted and credited. When it became necessary in 1862 to make further calls, the credits to States for men furnished under these acts were made up in the manner shown in another part of this report. Under that adjustment the States from which they had been declined were on this account declared to be deficient, and were called upon to make good a deficiency which they had not been permitted to avoid. Claims and complaints arising from these causes, which doubtless were in many instances well founded, though not well authenticated, were brought forward subsequently and much embarrassed the business of this Bureau.

The system of independent acceptances was terminated by orders from the Secretary of War, dated February 21, 1862.

The Border States, it will be remembered, suffered greatly from civil commotion in the summer and fall of 1861. Their lawful authorities found themselves unable to keep down the disloyal spirit and suppress the armed outbreaks within their jurisdiction without the assistance of the Federal Government. Appeals were made by the Governors of Missouri and Maryland for authority to raise militia forces for service within the limits of these States to aid in establishing and maintaining law and order. The authority being obtained, the Governor of Missouri raised one regiment of infantry of 770 men, two batteries of artillery of 171 men, and fourteen regiments of cavalry of 10,083 men, which force was to serve during the war and co-operate with the troops in the service of the United States in repelling invasion and suppressing rebellion in said State.

Similar authority empowered the Governor of Maryland to raise a force of 4,500 men for service within the limits of that State. The raising of these troops for State service at the expense of the United States was subsequently approved by the act of Congress of February 13, 1862,[a] which limited, however, the number authorized for the State of Missouri to 10,000, those in excess being mustered out. The same act provided, however, that no volunteers or militia from any

[a] See Appendix, Doc. 35.

State or Territory should be mustered into the service of the United States on any terms or conditions confining their services to the limits of said State or Territory or their vicinities.

Under the authority of the acts of Congress referred to in the foregoing, a force of 637,126 men was in service in the spring of 1862.*a* The popular impression was then that this immense number would be sufficient for overthrowing the military power of the rebellion, and putting down all armed resistance to the Federal Government. Subsequent events proved it erroneous, but Congress and the people deemed it necessary to check the enormous current expenditures by discontinuing the enlistment of men for the Army. The popular demand was yielded to, and on the 3d of April the volunteer recruiting service was closed by general order from the War Department.*b*

Under this order recruitment for the Army was immediately stopped, the property at the rendezvous sold, and the offices closed throughout the country.

Owing to the unexpected and unfavorable turn of the fortunes of war in the following months, and the consequent depletion of the armies in the field, the recruiting service was resumed by general orders of June 6, 1862.*c*

The recruiting business had been so effectually closed under the general order of April 3 that the resumption of it was attended by about the same difficulties that were encountered when it was first undertaken. Before they had been fairly overcome the disastrous result of the campaign in the Peninsula exercised its discouraging effects and interfered with the progress of recruitment.

Call of July 2, 1862, for 300,000 men for three years' service.

The numerical losses the Army had experienced prior to July 1, 1862,*d* rendered large additions to it absolutely necessary. This public need was recognized with their usual foresight by the Governors of Maine, New Hampshire, Vermont, Connecticut, New York, New Jersey, Pennsylvania, Maryland, Virginia, Michigan, Tennessee, Missouri, Indiana, Ohio, Minnesota, Illinois, and Wisconsin, who with the president of the Military Board of Kentucky, on the 28th of June, 1862,*b* requested the President of the United States at once to call upon the several States for such number of men as might be required to fill up the military organizations in the field, and increase the Army to such force as might be necessary to garrison and hold all the numerous cities and military positions that had been captured, and to finish the work of crushing the rebellion. The President, in his response of the date of July 1, 1862,*e* announced that he had decided to call into the service an additional force of 300,000 men.

At the time this call was made the war had been in progress a little more than one year. The attempt to take Richmond had resulted in failure. The desire to enter the service, prompted by the first ebullition of military ardor, had subsided, and was replaced by the popular demand that the different States should furnish proportional numbers of men for the Army. No such distribution had been previously made, and in order that this call might be fairly apportioned it was

---

a See Appendix Doc. 1, for strength of the entire military force of the United States at certain dates in 1861, 1862, 1863, 1864, and 1865.

b See Appendix Doc. 16.

c See Appendix, Doc. 17.

d See Appendix, Doc. 1, giving strength of the Army at various dates.

e See Appendix, Doc. 18.

necessary to establish with each State an account showing what it had furnished and what it ought to have furnished up to the date of this call, and make the assignment of the new call in conformity thereto.

To ascertain the amount of service which either one of the States should have rendered if it had borne its just share, or, in other words, what part of the aggregate service, furnished up to this period by all the States, was justly due from each State, it became necessary to compare the population of each State with the aggregate population of all the States from which troops were required. It was obvious that each State should contribute in proportion to the number of its inhabitants. This was required by the statute of July 22, 1861,*a* chapter 9, section 1, for the apportionment of volunteers among the several States, and there was at that time no better basis to act upon.

The number of men (and periods of their service) furnished by all the States prior to the call of July, 1862, was ascertained from the records of the Adjutant-General's Office, and the account of each State determined as follows:

The proportion of troops which should have been furnished by any State was to the number furnished from all the States as the number of inhabitants of that State was to the aggregate number of inhabitants of all the States. The solution of this formula gave for each State the number of troops which it should have furnished in order to make up its equal and just share of the service rendered by all the States prior to the call of July 2, 1862. If the number of troops actually furnished by any State, as shown by the records of the Adjutant-General's Office, fell short of this required proportion, that deficit was charged; if the number exceeded, it was credited to the State in question.*b*

Draft of August 4, 1862, for 300,000 militia for nine months' service.

The great depletion of the old regiments by the campaigns of 1862 induced special efforts during the summer and fall of that year to secure recruits for them. It was, however, perceived early in August that these efforts would not meet with success, and that the call of July 2, where filled at all, would be filled mainly by new organizations. These the Governors of States authorized partly from a misapprehension of the real needs of the service, and partly from a more or less well-founded belief that, without the stimulus of commissions in new regiments, individual efforts, heretofore so successful in raising men, would not be made by influential parties in different localities. In view of this failure and the pressing want of troops, a draft for 300,000 militia, to serve for a term of nine months, was ordered by the President on the 4th of August, 1862.*c* The order directed that if any State failed to furnish its quota of men under the preceding call for volunteers, the deficiency should be made up by a special draft from the militia by the 15th of August. It also announced that steps would be taken for the promotion of officers for meritorious services, for preventing the appointment of incompetent persons as offi-

a See Appendix, Doc. 35.

b For results of this calculation and statement of troops raised under this call, see Appendix, Doc. 6, Table 3.

c See Appendix, Doc. 19.

cers in the volunteer and regular forces, and for ridding the service of the unworthy ones already commissioned.[a]

This order was the first step taken by the Government toward carrying out the maxim upon which the security of republican governments mainly depends, viz, that every citizen owes his country military service. To its adoption, and the subsequent rigorous resort to conscription, the salvation of the Union is due, more than to any other cause.

The draft under this order commenced on the 3d of September, 1862, and was conducted by the State authorities. Of the 300,000 men called for about 87,000 were credited as having been drafted into the service under the call. This number was much reduced by desertion before the men could be got out of their respective States, and but a small portion of them actually joined the ranks of the Army.

This draft constituted the last demand of the General Government for men previous to the inauguration of the system of conscription in the following spring. It will appear evident that a just execution of a conscription law in the future by an equitable apportionment of quotas depended, to a great extent, on correctness in the distribution of the last call by the State authorities, and the accuracy with which the records were kept and preserved for reference. Upon subsequent examination it was found that the quotas assigned by the War Department to States had not generally been distributed by the State and local authorities in proportion to the men previously furnished by the different districts or towns, and that the accounts of men furnished by the minor localities were neither complete nor correct. This fact afterward occasioned serious difficulty when the new conscription law was put into operation, and caused unjust complaints against the Provost-Marshal-General's Bureau for omissions before its creation, for which no branch of the General Government was responsible. It is a matter of record that under the volunteer system prevailing in the early part of the war different localities contributed men very unequally, owing to varying degrees of patriotism and various other causes. When the Government required further levies, and ordered the draft of August 4 to obtain them, the quotas were assigned on the basis of population, and it was proper, therefore, in apportioning them, that the men already contributed should be taken into consideration. The War Department kept the record of the number of men furnished by each State, and allotted quotas to States according to the number previously furnished. The adjustment of quotas within the State was committed to the State authorities by order of the War Department,[b] with the direction that they be apportioned by the Governors among the several counties, and, when practicable, among the subdivisions of counties, so that allowance should be made to the counties and subdivisions for volunteers previously furnished.

The rule prescribed at this time by the Secretary of War[b] of apportioning the number of men to be raised among the different localities, so that the whole number called for should be obtained, and each place required to furnish its share after due allowance was made for what it had previously furnished, is the same subsequently observed by this Bureau. Unfortunately, it was not generally applied to the State draft of 1862, as required by the orders of

---

a For quotas assigned and troops raised under this call, see Appendix, Doc. 6 (table of all troops called for and furnished).

b See Appendix, Doc. 20, Art. 1.

the War Department. I endeavored, soon after the creation of my office, to obtain a statement, showing the account of each sub-district, from the officers who had charge of the records, but without success. The difficulties arising from the radical change effected by the enrollment act in the mode of raising troops, through the transfer of the labor and responsibility connected therewith from the State to the U. S. authorities, were increased by the absence of this information.

PART II.

Public recognition of the necessity of a general conscription.

During the latter part of 1862 the necessity for a radical change in the method of raising troops in order to prosecute the war to a successful issue became more and more apparent. The demand for re-enforcements from the various armies in the field steadily and largely exceeded the current supply of men. The old agencies for filling the ranks proved more and more ineffective. It was evident that the efforts of the Government for the suppression of the rebellion would fail without resort to the unpopular, but nevertheless truly republican, measure of conscription. The national authorities, no less than the purest and wisest minds in Congress,[a] and intelligent and patriotic citizens throughout the country, perceived that, besides a more reliable, regular, and abundant supply of men, other substantial benefits would be derived from the adoption and enforcement of the principle that every citizen, not incapacitated by physical or mental disability, owes military service to the country in the hour of extremity. It would effectually do away with the unjust and burdensome disproportion in the number of men furnished by different States and localities.

But it was not easy to convince the public mind at once of the justice and wisdom of conscription. It was a novelty, contrary to the traditional military policy of the Nation. The people had become more accustomed to the enjoyment of privileges than to the fulfillment of duties under the General Government, and hence beheld the prospect of compulsory service in the Army with an unreasonable dread. Among the laboring classes especially it produced great uneasiness. Fortunately, the loyal political leaders and press early realized the urgency of conscription, and by judicious agitation gradually reconciled the public to it. When the enrollment act was introduced in Congress in the following winter the patriotic people of the North were willing to see it become a law.

The passage of the enrollment act.

After a protracted, searching, and animated discussion, extending through nearly the whole of the short session of the Thirty-seventh Congress, the enrollment act was passed, and become a law on the 3d of March, 1863.[b] It was the first law enacted by Congress by which the Government of the United States appealed directly to the Nation to create large armies without the intervention of the authorities of the several States.

The main objects of the law were, in general terms: First, to enroll and hold liable to military duty all citizens capable of bearing arms not exempted therefrom by its provisions; second, to call forth the

---

[a] See Appendix, Doc. 30.

[b] See Appendix, Doc. 35.

national forces by draft when required; third, to arrest deserters and return them to their proper commands.

The public safety would have been risked by longer delay in the enactment of this law. A general apathy prevailed throughout the country on the subject of volunteering. Recruiting had subsided, while desertion had greatly increased and had grown into a formidable and widespread evil. The result of the important military operations during the first months of 1863 had been unfavorable and exercised a depressing effect on the public mind. The battle of Stone's River left the Army of the Cumberland crippled upon the field and forced it to inactivity for months in an intrenched camp. Our advance on Vicksburg by way of Haynes' Bluff had been repulsed with serious loss. A knowledge of the extent of the disaster at Fredericksburg had reached and dispirited the loyal people. The first attack on Fort Sumter by the navy had failed. The short but bloody and disastrous campaign of Chancellorsville was made, and the Army of the Potomac once more confined to the defensive. The rebel army was stronger in numbers than at any other period of the war. And last, not least, a powerful party in the North, encouraged by these events, opposed the raising of the new levies and especially the enforcement of the new conscription law.

At this inauspicious stage of affairs this Bureau was brought into existence.

The duties required of it under the enrollment act were of vast extent. The means for securing the ends proposed were inadequately provided. No appropriation of money was made for its support. The only officers authorized under the law were Provost-Marshal-General with the rank of colonel and a provost-marshal for each Congressional district with the rank of captain. For the purposes of enrollment and draft a board was created in each district, consisting of the provost-marshal, a civilian, and a surgeon. This board had power to appoint persons to make the enrollment. No other means were designated by the original act to carry out its designs.

Organization of the Bureau of the Provost-Marshal-General.

On the 17th of March, 1863, I was assigned to duty as Provost-Marshal-General by order of the Secretary of War,*a* in pursuance of section 5 of the enrollment act.*b*

The raising of troops by draft was alone assigned by law to this Bureau. But on the 1st of May, 1863, an order was issued *c* giving it the superintendence of the entire volunteer recruiting service. The connection between these two modes of raising troops was so close that in order to insure harmony and success in their management it was necessary that both should be under the same bureau.

On the 28th of April, 1863, the Bureau was charged by general orders *d* framed by the chief of the Bureau with the organization of an Invalid Corps (later called Veteran Reserve Corps). The troops of the corps were to be under its control.

The business of the Bureau having become regulated in a general way, my own office was organized into seven several branches, viz:

First branch—general and miscellaneous business.—This embraced all that did not belong to other branches designated below. Two officers were put on duty in it. The first was, in fact, principal

a See Appendix, Doc. 21.
b See Appendix, Doc. 35.
c See Appendix, Doc. 22.
d See Appendix, Doc. 23.

assistant and second in command to myself in the Bureau. The second acted in the capacity of an assistant adjutant-general.

Second branch—enrollment, draft, &c.—One officer only was on duty in this branch, but it received the special attention of the chief of the Bureau and principal assistant.

Third branch—deserters, their arrest, return, descriptive lists, &c.—One officer.

Fourth branch—medical affairs, statistics, &c.—One officer with occasional assistants for inspections, &c.

Fifth branch—the Invalid or Veteran Reserve Corps.—But one officer was permanently in this branch, but during the organization of the corps there were others from time to time as circumstances required.

Sixth branch—disbursements, accounts, &c., under the enrollment act.—One officer in charge, with four assistants, who paid by checks the accounts of the provost-marshals.

Seventh branch—disbursements, accounts, &c., under the appropriation for collecting, organizing, and drilling volunteers.—But one officer was on duty in this branch.

An adequate number of clerks was employed in each branch.

Acting assistant provost-marshals-general.

The law created no office intermediate between that of Provost-Marshal-General and provost-marshals of districts. In organizing the Bureau it was found to be indispensable to have an officer in each State to superintend the operations of the district provost-marshals and other subordinates of the Bureau and conduct the intercourse necessary with the State authorities. The exigencies of the public service limited as a general rule the selection of officers to fill these important positions to those incapable of active duty, but notwithstanding this, excellent men for the purpose were secured from the regular and volunteer forces. They were assigned to their posts in April, 1863, under special instructions from this office and were designated acting assistant provost-marshals-general and superintendents volunteer recruiting service for their respective States. They established their offices and organized them for business upon the same general plan as that adopted for this office, but on a scale modified to suit their more limited duties. As an illustration of the organization and management of these offices, a report from Bvt. Brig. Gen. James Oakes, acting assistant provost-marshal-general for Illinois, is appended. *a*

Selection of boards of enrollment and preparation of regulations.

The field being wholly new, unexplored, and untried, the selection of suitable persons to compose the boards of enrollment was a matter of difficulty and embarrassment. In some districts there were applicants who had no recommendations, and in others persons were recommended who had expressed no willingness to accept the positions. Before proper appointments could be made it was necessary to get reliable information upon which to act. This necessarily consumed some time, and after the information was obtained and appointments made, delay was encountered in their acceptance, and some of the appointees declined altogether, rendering new selections necessary. The provost-marshals were first selected and their headquarters designated. They were assigned to duty with the view of commencing the arrest of

---

a See Appendix, Doc. 11.

deserters at the earliest practicable moment. The commissioners and surgeons were next appointed, and by making every possible exertion most of the boards of enrollment were fully organized early in May, 1863. The time consumed in making a careful selection of officers caused no delay in accomplishing the objects of the law. This period was industriously devoted to the preparation of a code of regulations,[a] without which the boards, if sooner organized, could have made no useful progress in their principal duties.

Devising the blank forms, which were indispensable to secure uniformity and efficiency in the novel and complicated business to be conducted by the Bureau, formed an important feature in the preparation of the regulations. A copy of these regulations, the same in their general features as originally adopted, but modified in details to meet changes in the law and the experience of the Bureau, is appended to this report. Although prepared in advance, for the execution of a measure entirely new and experimental, they have been found to provide well for the requirements of the service; and if it shall ever become necessary hereafter to resume the business of the Bureau, it is thought that they will, with the other information accompanying this report, render it comparatively an easy task to revive what was not originated without great labor and difficulty. These regulations, and the orders subsequently issued, were perhaps more exacting as to the performance of the duties required, and in the observance of forms and details, than would have been necessary in a bureau composed of experienced commissioned officers, and charged only with duties of a purely military character. The appointees were generally taken from civil life. They knew that their appointments had been made mainly through local and political influence; they were distant from headquarters, and with great powers, not clearly defined in or limited by law; they were, owing to the disturbed state of the country and the party divisions of the time, exposed to the temptations of undue and dangerous exercise of authority. In order that there should be no misunderstanding as to their duty and responsibility to the United States, and that they might be strengthened to bear up against local pressure and interest, a rigid obedience was required to rules and orders which exacted a systematic performance of duty, and which, by means of frequent reports and returns, made in compliance with them, kept the chief of the Bureau informed, in minute detail, of the management of each office. Decided advantages to the General Government resulted from this wholesome rigor. There are not many instances on record in which officers of this Bureau stepped out of their proper sphere of duty, or attempted to subordinate the public to local or private interests, and but few, if any, in which such attempts have not been defeated. The views expressed above as to the repressive influence of the strict regulations adopted are not intended to cast any reflection on the intentions, or depreciate the merits, of the officers of the Bureau, whose integrity and devotion I have already expressly acknowledged.

Organization of boards of enrollment.

For the performance of the duties required of them by law, and the regulations of the Bureau, the Board of Enrollment in each Congressional district was organized as follows, viz:

Three regular clerks were appointed. One of these, in addition to his other duties, acted as recorder of the Board. As the wants of the

---

[a] See Appendix, Doc. 37.

service increased, temporary clerks were engaged from time to time, and paid for the time actually employed. The business of the office was subdivided and apportioned among the clerks, to correspond with the division of duties in the superior offices.

Deputy provost-marshals were allowed in each district, the number varying according to circumstances. At times they were limited to two, but when the occasion required, as many as one for each county in a district were authorized.

Special agents for the detection and arrest of deserters and the performance of miscellaneous duties were authorized. The number of special agents employed also varied, but seldom exceeded five to a district. The average number was three to a district.

Enrolling officers were employed at the rate of one for each sub-district (generally consisting of a town, township, or ward). These officers were only retained long enough to make the enrollment, and were occasionally re-employed temporarily for its correction when necessary. Their compensation was at the rate of $3 per diem when actually employed.

No board or provost-marshal was permitted to appoint a clerk, deputy, or special agent without first obtaining authority to do so from this office, giving the name of the person to be employed, rate of compensation proposed, and filing the oath of allegiance required by law.

To illustrate in detail the management of these district officers, the report of Capt. Henry C. Naill, provost-marshal of the Fourth District of Maryland, is appended to this report.[a]

The enrollment.

Steps were taken as early as practicable after the organization of the Bureau to put in force sections 3, 4, 8, 9, and 10 of the enrollment act, approved March 3, 1863.[b] The boards of enrollment were organized early in May, 1863, and at once subdivided their districts for the purpose of enrollment. Towns, townships, and wards were generally adopted as the most convenient subdivisions. But one enrolling officer was employed for each sub-district, as the law allowed no more. They were sworn to execute faithfully, and without partiality or favor, the duties of their office, which were defined in special instructions; and all precautions practicable at the time were taken against the employment of incompetent or dishonest persons.

Some of the districts consisted of forty counties, and some were 120 by 200 miles in extent, while others in large cities presented obstacles as formidable as geographical extent to a speedy and correct enrollment.

To subdivide, and find for each subdivision a person competent and willing to make the enrollment, took time, and was attended with difficulty, especially in the sub-districts, where there were large numbers of people opposed to the Government and the war, and hostile to this particular measure.

The enrollment was commenced about the 25th of May, 1863, and pushed forward with all possible dispatch. It was to form a complete register of that portion of the national forces not in the service. It was to give the names of all men liable to be called on for military duty, by lot or draft, and to furnish the basis for determining the proportion of troops to be furnished by the different parts of the

---

[a] See Appendix, Doc. 12.

[b] See Appendix, Docs. 6 and 35.

country. It was to provide the means for establishing between the Government and each locality an account of military service, in which a charge was to be made of all that was due, and credit given for all that should be paid. Under it every citizen legally liable, who was called upon for his proportion of military duty, was certain that it would be duly credited to him. Nothing could be more satisfactory to all who were willing to do their share in defense of their country.

As the law made the enrollment the basis for distributing among the different States and districts their respective quotas under the calls of the Government for troops, justice required that it should be as nearly perfect as the nature of things permitted it to be made. The correctness or incorrectness of the method adopted for computing quotas, and the arithmetical calculations by which they were ascertained, though sometimes complicated, are susceptible of prompt and conclusive demonstration to all reasonable minds.

No well-founded differences or disputes between the Government and the localities called upon, in regard to quotas of troops to be furnished, can arise from any other cause than imperfections, real or alleged, in the enrollment. The features of the law, and the circumstances under which its execution was to be commenced, were such that in the first enrollment perfection could not be attained, and owing to this fact, and the pressing necessity for an enrollment to establish a basis upon which the re-enforcement of the armies could begin, nothing more was practicable than to effect an enumeration, which, though it might contain errors, would be made under the same rules alike in all parts of the country, and which could be subsequently revised and corrected. Sections 1, 2, and 14 of the act of March 3, 1863, are as follows:

Be it enacted by the Senate and House of Representatives of the United States of America in Congress assembled, That all able-bodied male citizens of the United States, and persons of foreign birth who shall have declared on oath their intention to become citizens under and in pursuance of the laws thereof, between the ages of twenty and forty-five years, except as hereinafter excepted, are hereby declared to constitute the national forces, and shall be liable to perform military duty in the service of the United States when called out by the President for that purpose.

SEC. 2. *And be it further enacted*, That the following persons be, and they are hereby, excepted and exempt from the provisions of this act, and shall not be liable to military duty under the same, to wit: Such as are rejected as physically or mentally unfit for the service; also, first, the Vice-President of the United States, the judges of the various courts of the United States, the heads of the various Executive Departments of the Government, and the Governors of the several States. Second, the only son liable to military duty of a widow dependent upon his labor for support. Third, the only son of aged or infirm parent or parents dependent upon his labor for support. Fourth, where there are two or more sons of aged or infirm parents subject to draft, the father, or, if he be dead, the mother, may elect which son shall be exempt. Fifth, the only brother of children not twelve years old, having neither father nor mother, dependent upon his labor for support. Sixth, the father of motherless children under twelve years of age dependent upon his labor for support. Seventh, where there are a father and sons in the same family and household, and two of them are in the military service of the United States as non-commissioned officers, musicians, or privates, the residue of such family and household, not exceeding two, shall be exempt. And no persons but such as are herein excepted shall be exempt: *Provided, however*, That no person who has been convicted of any felony shall be enrolled or permitted to serve in said forces.

SEC. 14. *And be it further enacted*, That all drafted persons shall, on arriving at the rendezvous, be carefully inspected by the surgeon of the Board, who shall truly report to the Board the physical condition of each one; and all persons drafted and claiming exemption from military duty on account of disability, or any other cause, shall present their claims to be exempted to the Board, whose decision shall be final.

It will be seen from these sections that the law governing the enrollment was ambiguous. Under some provisions of it only the enrollment of those citizens seemed to be required between the specified ages who were not excepted from the operation of the act. Under others it seemed to be its purport that a full enumeration should be effected by the enrolling officers, and that the exceptions and exemptions should be made by the Board of Enrollment after the draft. Section 12 provided that 50 per cent. more than were required should be drawn to fill the places of those who might be exempted by the Board, thus sustaining the view that the Board of Enrollment after the draft, and not the enrolling officer, should decide questions of exemption arising under the law.

Whatever might be the ultimate and formal interpretation of the law in this respect, the paramount duty of the Bureau was to complete an enrollment at the earliest practicable date, make it as nearly correct as possible, and under it commence the urgently needed re-enforcement of the armies. The enrollment could be made without injustice to any one, as those who were granted the special favor of exception and exemption from the operations of the act could receive the privilege to which they were entitled after being drafted. To have undertaken so to make the enrollment as not to include those who were excused from military service by special enactment would have been to defeat the purpose of the act, in an attempt as a first duty to secure to a privileged class the immunities extended to them before they were ascertained to be due. Supposing all enrolling officers to have been honest and capable, the difficulties and delays they would have met in attempting to decide in advance all cases of exemption which would be presented by persons of the numerous class excepted by the act would have prevented the completion of the enrollment in time to be of use during the war. To this should be added the opposition to be encountered in making an enrollment of any kind, and the fact that the enrollers had, necessarily, to be selected in haste, were but temporarily employed, without power to summon witnesses, and exposed by their irresponsibility and the absence of supervision to the temptation of bribery and favoritism. All this made it clear that the best interests of the Government required that the enrolling officers should not be invested with the power of deciding the questions of exemptions arising under the act. In order, therefore, to get an enrollment for immediate use which, as stated, would be as fair to one place as to another, and which could subsequently be corrected in all places alike, I directed the boards of enrollment to instruct their enrolling officers to enroll all male citizens of the United States, and persons of foreign birth who had declared on oath their intention to become citizens, under and in pursuance of the laws thereof, between the ages of twenty and forty-five years, and not permit the omission from the enrollment lists of the names of persons who might claim to belong to the classes excepted by the law, and to reserve the question of their exemption for consideration after the draft.

The following extract from a report made by Captain Erhardt, the provost-marshal of the Fourth District, New York City, the enrollment of which was made the subject of special complaint, illustrates the method of making the enrollment and the pains taken to avoid errors. The mode of operation was not identically the same in all the districts, but varied only according to the circumstances existing in different districts and the character of the officers and employés engaged in the work. Captain Erhardt says:

I have the honor to state that there have been enrolled in my district—

Of first class	54,372
Of second class	23,405
Making a total of names enrolled	77,777

From these were taken those who actually lived in this district, and those alone were borne upon the consolidated lists sent to the Provost-Marshal-General, viz:

Of the first class	30,844
Of the second class	11,148
A total of	41,992

With this exception, that those who were not known to live in any other district, by their own refusal to give their residence, doing business in this, were presumed to live in this, and were sent on the consolidated lists accordingly. These names were in the proportion of perhaps 1 to 50, so that perhaps 800 may be on the consolidated lists so subject to draft here who may show, in case of their being drafted, that they reside in another district and are not liable. This list, with the deductions of those who reside here, would leave 35,785 enrolled here not borne upon the consolidated lists of this district.

The enrollment of this district was made by an enrolling officer for each election district, who reported at the headquarters of the district each day with the filled sheets, which were then given in, and an account kept of the amount of sheets (filled) each enrolling officer brought in. The enrollment was completed on the 29th day of June, and the number of names returned to this office amounted to 54,372 of class one, and 23,405 of class two; total number, 77,777.

The consolidation was made by first making an alphabetical list of each ward. The names were carefully revised, and the residence of every person within the ages named in the act, residing in this district, marked by the ward of this district in which he resided. They were then transferred to another copy, care being taken to gather all who resided in the ward, copying from other wards. On the completion of that copy the lists were again revised for the purpose of ascertaining duplicates in this manner: By taking the first name of each letter and going through all the rest of the letter, to ascertain that that name was down but once; then taking the second name, and again going through those remaining, until the whole had undergone a careful and actual scrutiny; and in the same manner with class two. This was the work of many days and nights, yet it resulted in a correct list. When a doubt arose as to whether the party under search was a duplicate, an enrolling officer was sent to the residence of such a party to ascertain whether such name was a duplicate or not.

Upon the completion of that copy another copy was made, and all errors stricken from and transfers made, should any be found in it. After a careful revision of that copy the final copy was made for the department, and from that the cards prepared for the draft, and carefully compared with the list, and verified by actual count.

Numerous and weighty obstacles were encountered in making this enrollment. The large floating population of the country, and the disposition and right of our people to go from place to place without let or hindrance, rendered it exceedingly difficult to perfect it. Most of the embarrassments resulted, however, from the opposition encountered in almost every house, if not to the act itself, at least to its application to the particular persons whose names were sought for enrollment. The law made it the duty of this Bureau to take, but did not make it the duty of anyone to give, the names of those liable to draft. Every imaginable artifice was adopted to deceive and defeat the enrolling officers. Open violence was sometimes met with. Several enrollers lost their lives.[a] Some were crippled. The property of others was destroyed to intimidate them and prevent the enrollment. In certain mining regions organized bodies of men openly

[a] See table of casualties, Doc. 38.

opposed the enrollment, rendering it necessary that the U. S. authorities should send troops to overcome their opposition. There were secret societies, newspapers, and politicians who fostered and encouraged this widespread opposition.

Under these serious drawbacks the first enrollment was made. It was no more imperfect than had been expected, and the first draft (as explained hereafter in this report) was, according to it, conducted in such a manner as to neutralize to a great extent (if not entirely) the irregularities and hardships that might have resulted from the errors it contained.

An enrollment having been made as the first and indispensable requisite to the execution of the law, and the determination and ability of the Government to carry out the measure to the fullest extent required for the re-enforcement of the armies having been established by the enforcement of the first draft in July, 1863, the subject of revising and perfecting the enrollment with a view to future drafts was taken up as soon as the boards of enrollment could get time for it, to wit, in November, 1863. On the 17th of that month Circular No. 101 was issued.*a* It referred, first, to the complaints made relative to errors in the enrollment of the national forces by the omission of persons whose names should have been enrolled, and by the addition of names of persons who, by reason of alienage and for other causes, ought not to have been enrolled; and as it was desirable that the department should have such information as might be necessary in order to do full justice to all parties, it directed that the Board of Enrollment of each district should have printed lists of the names and residences of all persons enrolled in each sub-district prepared and exposed to public view in at least five places in each sub-district, and in as many more as the Board might deem necessary. It further required that public notice should be given by advertisement upon the list of names and in the newspapers, inviting corrections, &c., and that the boards of enrollment should use all diligence in collecting the necessary information and making the requisite notes to perfect the enrollment lists.

As a draft was then pending (to commence in the following January), the time for making corrections was limited to the 20th of December. This was to give the officers time to attend to other business preliminary to draft. When it was necessary, however, and could be properly done, the time for correction was extended by special authority.

Notwithstanding the opportunity thus afforded, the appeals made to the people, and the efforts of the officers of the Bureau, the corrections, though extensive, were not so thorough as had been hoped.

The people generally at that time did not seem to appreciate their interests in perfecting the lists, and gave but little aid in the work, perhaps in the hope and belief that every call was the last which would be necessary. The officers of the Bureau were more faithful in perfecting the lists, but they prosecuted their labors under some of the discouragements met in making the first enrollment.

Assertions and arguments as to the inaccuracy of the enrollment, which had not been presented to the boards of enrollment when corrections could have been made by the opportunity stated above, were subsequently urged upon the Bureau as reasons for delaying drafts. They took a variety of forms. Some of them, raising questions of

---

a See Appendix, Doc. 24, Art. 3.

legality, were laid before the Solicitor of the War Department in April, 1864, and were noticed by him as follows:*

As soon as the pressure of business permitted, the correction of the enrollment was resumed under orders dated June 25, 1864, which were slightly modified and republished on the 15th of November, 1864, in the following terms: †

At the time these instructions were issued the draft of 1863, under the original enrollment, had been completed, and the draft which began May 1, 1864, for deficiencies in all calls prior to and including that of March 14, 1864, was nearly closed. These drafts had begun to make it apparent to the people that it was certainly for the interest of each town, ward, &c., to have correct lists, to the end, first, that each locality might be called upon for no more than a fair share of all the troops to be raised, and, secondly, that all who were properly liable should be so recorded, in order not to increase unduly the chances to be drafted of those whose names were already on the lists. But beside this, when the fairness of this method of raising troops became properly understood, and the necessity for its adoption was generally acknowledged among the people, the opposition which had interfered with former efforts subsided and gradually disappeared. In many instances it was even replaced by activity and zeal on the part of committees and individuals in pointing out errors and furnishing data for corrections. Hence the lists were rapidly corrected, and when the business of the Bureau was practically stopped in April, 1865, the enrollment was as nearly correct as it can well be made under existing laws.

Between July 1, 1864, and April 30, 1865, 461,073 names were added to the enrollment lists, and 1,231,439 names stricken off.

The enrollment shows the national forces not called out to have consisted of 2,245,063 men on the 30th day of April, 1865. This does not include the 1,000,516 men in the field on the 30th day of April, 1865.‡

Careful estimates and calculations, based upon the best data to be obtained, lead to the conclusion that notwithstanding the losses during the war, there were more men in the loyal States properly subject to the call of the Government for military service at the close of the rebellion than at its beginning. Moreover, in estimating the military strength of the Government when hostilites ceased, the fact should be borne in mind that the troops, colored and white, raised in States in rebellion and the sources from which more such could have been supplied, are not considered, no enrollment of the national forces having been made in those States.

Remarks on the subject of enrollment and the proper basis for an equitable distribution of the burden of military service.

The original act required the enrollment to be composed of two classes: The first, comprising all persons subject to do military duty between the ages of twenty and thirty-five years and all unmarried persons subject to military duty above the age of thirty-five and under the age of forty-five; the second class, comprising all other persons

*See Whiting to Fry, April 11, 1864, Vol. IV, this series, p. 224.

†See Circular No. 39, Provost-Marshal-General's Office, November 15, 1864, Vol. IV, this series, p. 935.

‡But see consolidated abstract, Vol. IV, this series, p. 1283, showing an aggregate of 1,052,038.

subject to military duty; that is, all married persons between thirty-five and forty-five who fulfilled the required conditions. The law provided that the second class should not be called out in any district until the first class was exhausted. This classification increased and complicated the duties of the Bureau, and had the effect of making those belonging to the second class indifferent to the operations of the law and the filling of quotas by volunteers, they being practically exempt from draft. The amendment passed February 24, 1864,[a] abolishing the classification and consolidating all into one and the same class, resulted therefore in benefit to the service.

Considering all the circumstances attending the subject of enrollment in this country, I think, while it is the best basis for raising troops that could be found, there is no degree of efficiency and integrity on the part of those intrusted with the administration of the present law that can secure a perfect enrollment or one as nearly perfect as it should be for an equal distribution of the burden of military service in a great and protracted war. If the late war had continued so long as to render more calls for troops necessary the correctness of this statement would have become apparent. In anticipation of such a necessity, previous to the meeting of the last Congress, amendments as follows were prepared by me, but were not adopted:

Be it enacted by the Senate and House of Representatives of the United States of America in Congress assembled, That it shall be the duty of each male resident of the United States, over eighteen years of age, within thirty days from such date as may be announced by the Secretary of War, to have his name enrolled on the enrollment list of the sub-district in which he resides, unless, upon application to the Board of Enrollment of the district, it shall appear that such person is not liable to enrollment under the acts approved March three, eighteen hundred and sixty-three, for enrolling and calling out the national forces, and as amended by the act approved February twenty-four, eighteen hundred and sixty-four, in which case he shall be furnished with a certificate of his non-liability to enrollment, signed by the members of the Board of Enrollment, setting forth therein the reasons why he is exempt from the performance of military duty; and any person liable to enrollment who shall hereafter change his place of residence shall notify the provost-marshal of the district of his removal, and shall, within thirty days, file with the Board of Enrollment of the district to which he has removed his certificate of enrollment in the sub-district where he last resided, whereupon such Board of Enrollment shall proceed to enroll him and furnish him with a certificate of his enrollment. And every male resident over eighteen years of age shall, within thirty days after becoming liable to enrollment, either on account of arriving at proper age, declaring an intention to become a citizen of the United States, or other cause, apply to the provost-marshal of the district in which he resides and procure his proper enrollment.

SEC. 2. *And be it further enacted*, That any person who shall refuse or neglect to comply with the provisions of the foregoing section, or who shall cause, procure, or shall willfully attempt to procure an incorrect or improper enrollment of himself or any other person, either by misstating his or their name, age, occupation, or residence, or by committing any act with intent to secure a false enrollment of himself, or any other person, such person so offending, on being convicted thereof by a military commission, shall pay a fine of not less than two hundred nor more than one thousand dollars, and be enlisted and mustered into service as a soldier, to serve for the period for which the draft is made, if on examination he be found fit for service; if unfit, then he shall be imprisoned not to exceed one year nor less than three months. One-half of the fine herein prescribed to be paid to the informer and the other to the credit of the draft and substitute fund.

SEC 3. *And be it further enacted*, That any person who shall procure himself to be enrolled as of a sub-district other than his true residence shall not, in the event of his being drafted, be exempt on the ground of non-residence, but if found fit for duty shall be held to personal service, and credited on the quota of the sub-district in which he resides; nor will the fact that he is erroneously enrolled exempt him from enrollment and draft in the sub-district of his residence.

---

[a] See Appendix, Doc. 35.

SEC. 4. *And be it further enacted*, That all questions of non-liability to enrollment and draft, on account of unsuitableness of age or non-residence, shall be determined prior to draft, and boards of enrollment will not hereafter grant exemptions to drafted men on the ground of non-residence or being under or over age.

It was not proposed, in case these amendments had been adopted, to abandon the system pursued under the present law, but to retain so much of the old system as might be necessary to the full success of the new.

The total expenses arising under the enrollment act would be reduced at least two-thirds by the method suggested above.

When once in operation it would be more satisfactory to the people, as the main source of hardship under the present system is not in taking by lot those properly subject to military duty, but in the necessity imposed on the Bureau of drafting and dealing with those who are not fit for nor liable to duty. Under the plan proposed all this class would, at their leisure before the draft, secure certificates which would prevent their being disturbed.

It has been stated that the population was taken as the basis in settling the accounts of the different States for troops raised prior to the passage of the enrollment act in March, 1863. The apportionments so made resulted in inequality in the distribution of the calls for troops in consequence of the great disparity among the different States in the proportion of males fit for military duty included in their respective populations. It has been contended by some persons, even since the enrollment was made, and especially by a board which convened in New York City in 1864, that population is the only safe and proper basis for distributing the Government's demands for volunteers. This view is based on the theory that a call for troops is a money-tax upon the States and communities, that men can only be obtained by means of large bounties, and that States and communities acting upon this theory compel, by a direct tax, each man to contribute his share of money, thus throwing the burden upon property as directly as if Congress laid a direct tax for the same purpose, and hence, that representative population is the constitutional basis for an equitable apportionment of quotas. The public interest would be seriously injured by the adoption of this theory. It is unsound and cannot be relied on to meet the necessities of a great war. Its practical application would demoralize the military spirit of the people and exhaust the finances of the country. The true principles are embodied in the enrollment acts, namely, that the country must look to its citizens for its safety and honor; that when engaged in war, military service may be rightfully required of every male citizen of proper age and suitable physical and mental condition; that the number of men to be taken at any one time from a community, whether they go voluntarily or by draft, shall be in proportion to the number of men liable to military duty in that community, and not to the number of its residents, including men, women, and children. Some statistical information on this subject may be found in the following table:

Table showing the population by sexes, and the preponderance of either sex in certain States according to the Census of 1860, and the total number enrolled April 30, 1865, with the ratio of enrollment to male and total population.

States.	Males.	Females.	Excess of males over females.	Excess of females over males.	Total population.	Number enrolled April 30, 1865.	Ratio of enrollment to male population.	Ratio of enrollment to total population.
Maine	317,189	311,090	6,099	....	628,279	46,121	14.53	7.34
New Hampshire	159,816	166,257	....	6,441	326,073	26,302	16.45	8.07
Vermont	158,786	156,312	2,474	....	315,098	23,326	14.69	7.40
Massachusetts	596,713	634,353	....	37,640	1,231,066	105,650	17.70	8.58
Rhode Island	84,133	90,487	....	6,354	174,620	16,256	19.32	9.30
Connecticut	225,994	234,153	....	8,159	460,147	40,708	18.00	8.84
New York	1,933,532	1,947,203	....	13,671	3,880,735	431,462	22.31	11.11
New Jersey	336,045	336,972	....	927	673,017	70,055	20.84	10.40
Pennsylvania	1,454,319	1,451,796	2,523	....	2,906,115	263,436	18.11	9.06
Delaware	55,829	54,639	190	....	110,468	7,011	12.55	6.34
Maryland	296,585	313,275	....	16,690	609,860	55,802	18.81	9.15
Dist. of Columbia	35,499	39,581	....	4,082	75,080	10,725	30.21	14.28
Ohio	1,190,162	1,149,349	41,813	....	2,339,511	205,867	17.29	8.79
Indiana	699,260	651,168	48,092	....	1,350,428	153,238	21.91	11.34
Illinois	900,761	809,190	91,751	....	1,709,951	274,409	30.46	16.04
Kentucky	479,312	450,889	28,423	....	930,201	104,082	21.71	11.18
Missouri	564,841	502,240	62,601	....	1,067,081	133,501	23.63	12.51
Michigan	393,486	353,112	40,374	....	746,598	75,248	19.12	10.07
Wisconsin	407,459	368,432	39,027	....	775,891	54,737	13.43	7.05
Iowa	354,593	320,420	34,173	....	675,013	82,803	23.35	12.26
Minnesota	91,930	77,824	14,106	....	169,754	18,556	20.18	10.81
Kansas	59,178	48,026	11,152	....	107,204	23,022	38.90	21.47
Total	10,795,422	10,466,768	422,618	93,964	21,262,190	2,222,317	*a*20.61	*a*10.51

a Average ratio per cent.

It will be seen from this table and Table 3, Document 6, of Appendix, that some of the Western States, with quotas under the calls of 1861 and 1862 (assigned on the basis of population) nearly the same as some of the Eastern States, furnished all required, and yet had a much larger proportion of men liable to military duty left than Eastern States which did not fill the quotas assigned under those calls, and were, in consequence, charged with a deficiency on subsequent calls. In some instances, therefore, where a deficiency existed it may be attributed somewhat to excessive quotas in 1861 and 1862, assigned on the basis of population, and the excess of troops furnished by some States may, on the same principle, be due in a measure to their surplus of men.

The States showing the larger ratios of enrollment to male population are—

First. Those to which the more recent immigration has been most considerable, meaning immigration both from foreign countries and that resulting from the movement from the Atlantic States westward. Under this head Indiana, Illinois, Missouri, Iowa, Minnesota, and Kansas are examples.

Second. Those States having large cities, to which all able-bodied men resort for employment, especially those near the depots of foreign immigration, in which males from abroad remain upon landing, or to which they most readily find their way, such as New York, New Jersey, Pennsylvania, and Maryland. The State of New York is the most striking instance of the above, containing, as it does, the chief depot of foreign immigration, and, as well, a metropolitan district with a population of more than a million of people, to which men are attracted with a view of finding ready employment in the various pursuits incident to large cities. The States showing the smallest percentage of enrollment with reference to male population are those most strictly rural, such as Maine, 14½ per cent., New Hampshire, 16½ per cent., Vermont, 14½ per cent., and Delaware, 12½ per cent. These are at the same time States affected but slightly by foreign immigration on the one hand, and from which, on the other, young men are attracted by the more expansive fields of the West. The District of Columbia exhibits a large ratio of enrollment to male population, 30¼ per cent., which is accounted for by the fact that large numbers of enrolled men have been brought to the District by the civil and semi-military employment incident to the Government business within and the military operations around it.

By reference to the ratio of enrollment of the entire population in each State it will be noticed that the ratios obtain in nearly the same proportion as when compared with the male population only. In the States of Maine, Vermont, New York, New Jersey, Pennsylvania, and Delaware, the population of the sexes being nearly equal, their relative proportions are about the same.

The proportion in Kansas and Illinois is noticeable, and is accounted for by the large excess of males over females. The same is true in a modified degree of the States of Ohio, Indiana, Kentucky, Michigan, Wisconsin, Iowa, and Minnesota, while in the States of New Hampshire, Massachusetts, Rhode Island, and Connecticut, the relative proportion is smaller for the inverse reason.

A glance at the table will show the solid column presented by the Western States under the head of "Excess of males over females," and the corresponding increase in the ratio of enrollment.

Draft of 1863, being the first made under the enrollment act.

It was required that troops should be produced by means of the act at the earliest possible date. To accomplish this the draft had to be commenced in each district as soon as it could be enrolled.

But as the enrollment was completed in some districts many months before it was in others, it was not possible to determine what proportion of any given number the district first enrolled should furnish. It was therefore decided not to call for a fixed number, but to make a draft in each and every district as soon as it was enrolled for one-fifth of its enrolled men of the first class, thus drafting from each district the same proportion of men found by the enrollment to be in it. The draft being made in this manner, an order as follows was issued:

> Whenever any drafted man shall show to the Board of Enrollment of the district in which he may have been enrolled that he was improperly enrolled, having been, when enrolled, an alien, a non-resident of the district, not of proper age, or in the service on the 3d of March, 1863, he shall be discharged by the Board, and his place in the quota shall not be filled from the 50 per cent. drawn in addition to the quota to supply vacancies created by exemptions arising under the second section of the enrollment act.

It was claimed in some localities, especially in New York, that the quota required was too great, because, as was alleged, the enrollment included aliens, non-residents, &c., and was thus excessively large. That cause of complaint was essentially removed by the above order, in connection with the plan of taking as the quota for the draft one-fifth of the enrollment of each district.

No proclamation was issued for this draft. Serious opposition to the enforcement of the law, it was thought, would be less likely to arise if the draft was quietly and successfully made in the districts where it was first undertaken. As soon, therefore, as a district was enrolled its quota was ascertained, and the President made an order in the following form for drafting therein:

EXECUTIVE MANSION,
Washington, D. C., ——, *1863*.

I, Abraham Lincoln, President of the United States of America and Commander-in-Chief of the Army and Navy thereof, having taken into consideration the number of volunteers and militia furnished by and from the several States, including the State of ——, and the period of service of said volunteers and militia since the commencement of the present rebellion, in order to equalize the numbers among the districts of the said States, and having considered and allowed for the number already furnished as aforesaid, and the time of their services aforesaid, do hereby assign —— as the first proportional part of the quota of troops to be furnished by the —— district of the State of ——, under this the first call made by me on the State of ——, under the act approved March 3, 1863, entitled "An act for enrolling and calling out the national forces, and for other purposes," and, in pursuance of the act aforesaid, I order that a draft be made in the said —— district of the State of —— for the number of men herein assigned to said district, and 50 per cent. in addition.

In witness whereof I have hereunto set my hand and caused the seal of the United States to be affixed. Done at the city of Washington this —— day of ——, in the year of our Lord one thousand eight hundred and sixty-three, and of the Independence of the United States the eighty-eighth.

This order, with the special instructions necessary in the case, was communicated by me to the provost-marshal of the district, and the State authorities were informed as to the action to be taken, and their co-operation solicited. The first drawings took place in the State of Rhode Island. They commenced on the 7th of July, 1863, and were made there, and soon after in the other New England districts, without difficulty.

On the 11th of July the drawing commenced in the city of New York. On the 13th the business was broken up by a mob, composed mainly of foreigners. The headquarters of two of the provost-marshals were burned and the public property was destroyed, excepting the records, which were, fortunately, removed to a place of safety.

The disturbance in New York City was followed by resistance to the draft in Boston and Troy. The riots in these cities, however, were but feeble responses to the great effort made in New York to defeat the execution of the enrollment act. Quiet was promptly restored in Boston by the local authorities. Though interrupted for the moment, the draft was not abandoned. On the 17th of July the following order was issued.*

A large body of troops having been withdrawn from the field and sent to New York to enforce the law and maintain order, the draft was resumed on the 19th of August, and was carried through without further resistance.

---

*See Circular No. 48, Provost-Marshal-General's Office, Vol. III, this series, p. 524.

The results in detail of this draft are shown in Table 5, Document 6, of Appendix.

The number of names drawn was		292,441
Failed to report	39,417	
Discharged (quota of sub-district being full)	447	
Discharged per order	13	
		39,877
Number examined		252,564
Number exempted		164,394
Number found liable to duty		88,170
Held to personal service		9,880
Furnished substitutes		26,002
Paid commutation		52,288
		88,170

The examination of the drafted men was conducted with great faithfulness and fairness, and yet out of 252,564 men examined under this draft, but 9,880 failed to secure exemption from personal service under some one of the special provisions of the law, as set forth in sections 2 and 13 of the enrollment act approved March 3, 1863.[a]

Of all held to service, only 26,002 furnished substitutes; so that after drafting 292,441 men, but 35,882 soldiers were obtained. The proportion of exemptions on account of mental and physical infirmities under this draft was not unduly large. The following facts appear from tables herewith:[a]

Rates rejected per 1,000 on account of mental and physical infirmities.

United States in 1863	316.91
France:	
From 1831 to 1843	324.04
In 1859	317.00
Great Britain:	
From 1832 to 1851	318.59
In 1862	401.00
Belgium from 1851 to 1855	320.06

In accordance with section 13 of the act, the Secretary of War, on the 30th of June, 1863, announced that the amount to be paid by any person who might be drafted, in order to secure exemption from service, was $300.

Fifty-two thousand two hundred and eighty-eight of those examined under this draft and found liable and fit to perform military duty secured exemption by paying $300 each.

A fund of $15,686,400 thus accrued under this draft, and, being appropriated by section 13 for the procuration of substitutes, it was used as hereinafter explained under the head of "Call of October 17, 1863."

The large proportion of exemptions defeated, in a measure, the object of the law, and a modification reducing the causes of exemption was urgently demanded by the public exigencies of that period. The necessity for a change having been demonstrated by actual test and practical experience, the more rigid features subsequently introduced as amendments to the law were accepted by the people generally, and added nothing to the difficulties encountered in carrying out the measure.

---

[a] See Appendix, Doc. 8.

This draft, though not directly fruitful in producing men, served the essential purpose of substituting the reality for the semblance of conscription, and of establishing the power and determination of the Government to proceed in the re-enforcement of its armies. When it was resorted to volunteering had stopped, and would not have been again started without the spur of the draft. Having applied it and increased the bounties to the largest practicable limit, a call for volunteers was made on the 17th of October, 1863, *a* and the 5th of January following was fixed as the day for commencing a second draft in all localities that had not furnished their quota of volunteers by that time.

Indefiniteness in certain parts of the law caused misunderstanding and embarrassment in effecting the draft. The most marked instances of this were the following: First, an order was issued from this office on the 12th of July, 1863, in the following terms, to wit:

Any drafted person paying $300, under section 13 of the enrollment act, is thereby exempt from further liability under that draft, but not from any subsequent draft. Any drafted person furnishing an acceptable substitute is exempt from military service for the period for which said substitute is mustered into the service.

The intention and effect of this order was to encourage the presentation of men instead of money. It was in accordance with the law, as interpreted by the Solicitor of the War Department in the following opinion:

It has been claimed that persons paying $300 are discharged from further liability, not only under that draft but under all other drafts which may be ordered during the time for which they were originally drafted. This supposed exemption has been asserted through misapprehension of the language and meaning of the statute.

The liability of certain citizens of the United States to do military duty is declared in the first section of the act, viz: "All able-bodied citizens, &c., between the ages of twenty and forty-five (except, &c.) are hereby declared to constitute the national forces, and shall be liable to perform military duty in the service of the United States when called out by the President for that purpose." Provisions are made for enrolling said forces; and "All persons thus enrolled shall be subject, for two years after the 1st day of July succeeding the enrollment, to be called into the military service of the United States, and to continue in service during the present rebellion, not, however, exceeding three years." These quotations show that the liability of enrolled men to be called into the military service exists, and is derived from the declaratory clauses of the statute, and is fixed and made personal by the enrollment, even if no draft be made or if no persons are actually called into the service. Liability is not destroyed if no service is required or rendered, as a debt is not discharged while payment is not called for or received.

Whenever the President determines to call out a portion of the national forces the Board of Enrollment must make a draft, or selection by lot; the persons drafted are required to be notified of the draft by a special notice, "requiring them to appear at a designated rendezvous and report for duty."

The duty or liability imposed upon the citizen by the drafts, as stated in the statute, is to appear and report for duty, the liability to serve as a soldier having been imposed upon him, not by the draft, but by the declaratory sections of the act above cited; and when he is discharged from liability under that draft, either by furnishing a substitute, or by paying the commutation money, or by being sent home as a supernumerary in accordance with section 16, he is simply released from his obligation to "report for duty" under the notice which has been served on him. In other words, whether a drafted man is discharged as an exempt, or released from his obligation to "report for duty" by paying his money or furnishing his substitute, or discharged because "the required number shall have been obtained," in all these cases he is discharged from further liability under that draft, and that only. But no discharge takes away his liability to be deemed part of the "military forces," nor his liability to be continued as "enrolled," nor his liability to do military duty under any succeeding draft.

---

a See Appendix, Doc. 36.

If a person was in the service on the 3d of March, 1863, or has served out the period of the first draft, he still belongs to the "national forces," and is liable to any future draft.

As the draft, notice, and service thereof add to the enrolled man no new liability, except that of "reporting for duty" and of being treated as a deserter in case of "failure to appear and report," it follows that release from "further liability under a draft" does not take away liability to do military duty, but only liability to be punished for failure to appear and report after due service of notice. The thirteenth section provides two modes of obtaining discharge from that liability, viz: First, by tendering an acceptable substitute on or before the day fixed for the appearance of the drafted man to take his place in the draft; or, second, the payment of a sum, to be fixed by the Secretary of War, for the procuration of such substitute, and thereupon such person so furnishing a substitute or paying the money shall be discharged from any further "liability under that draft;" and any person "failing to report" after due service of notice as herein described, without furnishing a substitute or paying the required sum therefor, shall be deemed a deserter, &c.

This language also strengthens the conclusion that the liability under that draft means liability to "report for duty," a failure to perform that duty subjecting the offender to be treated as a deserter.

If the statute had made no other provision than that found in section 13, there might have been some force in the suggestion that persons who pay the money were placed upon the same footing as those who furnish the substitute, and there would be some plausibility in the suggestion that as the money paid for commutation is "for the procuration of a substitute," the party paying it should be placed on an equality of exemption with him who has actually furnished such substitute. But if this suggestion were correct it would be immaterial, because the exemption provided in the thirteenth section for those who pay money or furnish substitutes is limited in terms to liability under that draft, and not extended to exemption from any succeeding draft, nor to exemption from "military duty."

All question as to the extent of exemption is removed by reference to the seventeenth section, which provides that "any person enrolled and drafted according to the provisions of this act, who shall furnish an acceptable substitute, shall thereupon receive from the Board of Enrollment a certificate of discharge from such draft," which (certificate) shall exempt him from military duty during the time for which he was drafted, &c.

This section provides not that the person who furnishes a substitute shall be free from further liability under that draft, but that he shall be free from all military duty for a given time, and therefore by law free from all subsequent drafts for the period for which he was originally drafted. This exemption is wholly different from that provided in section 13, and is in addition thereto. An exemption from all liability to do military duty for a limited period is quite different from an exemption from a requisition "to appear and report" at a given time and place.

Statutes must be so constructed that all clauses thereof should be operative, and all parts of the law should be taken into consideration in determining the meaning of any particular provision thereof.

The object of the law was to raise men and not to collect money. It was obviously to give those who procured substitutes a decided advantage over those who should pay the money, because the money is not what was wanted, and it might not be sufficient to enable Government to obtain substitutes. If it were sufficient, the burden of getting substitutes is placed upon the Government. Congress may well have thought it just to give less advantages to those who avoided their duty of serving the country in time of war by paying a small sum of money than to those who performed it by taking the field in person or by substitutes.

The construction of this statute is made still more plain by considering the peculiar language of the seventeenth section. This section provides that the Board of Enrollment shall give "a certificate of discharge from the draft" to him who furnishes an acceptable substitute, and that "that certificate" shall exempt him from military duty during the time for which he was drafted. It is not the payment of money nor the furnishing a substitute that exempts the drafted man from "military service;" it is "the certificate of the Board of Enrollment" which has that effect. That certificate cannot lawfully be given to the man who pays money; it must be given to him whose substitute is accepted.

To say that one who has only paid money is entitled to a "certificate" is to insert a new provision in the act. To say that he is entitled to the same exemption as one who has the "certificate" is to deprive section 17 of that act of its force and effect. The provision for exemption in section 17 is important only because it gives to those who furnish substitutes an exemption not given them by the thirteenth section, which had already secured them a discharge from further liability under that draft.

Hence the conclusion seems undeniable that the seventeenth section must be ignored as of no effect upon the question of exemption, or else it must add something to section 13, the thirteenth section having secured a discharge from further liability under that draft to those who either pay the money or produce the substitute. Section 17 follows up the subject by authorizing the issue by the Board of a certificate to those who find substitutes, which certificate shall discharge them from all liability under all drafts to do any military duty for a given time, to be stated therein; while the person who pays money and is discharged from further liability "under that draft" is released from his duty to enter the service at that time; but, not being released from his enrollment, is liable to any subsequent draft if such draft should be made.

WILLIAM WHITING,
Solicitor of the War Department.

I executed the law thus expounded by the Solicitor until November 1, 1863, when the subject, still being regarded as one in doubt, was brought to the immediate notice of the President, who examined it and ordered as follows:

The State receives the same credit for a man who has paid commutation as if the drafted citizen had gone in person or furnished a substitute; and, in like manner, towns which have raised the money to pay for their quotas receive the same credit as if actual substitutes had been furnished. It is ordered that every citizen who has paid the $300 commutation shall receive the same credit therefor as if he had furnished a substitute, and is exonerated from military service for the time for which he was drafted, to wit, for three years.

When the law was amended on the 24th of February, 1864,*a* the doubt was removed by a proviso that "if any drafted person shall hereafter pay money for the procuration of a substitute under the provisions of the act to which this is an amendment, such payment of money shall operate only to relieve such person from draft in filling that quota, and his name shall be retained on the roll in filling future quotas," &c.

Writs of habeas corpus.—During this draft the practice of serving writs of habeas corpus on the officers of the Bureau became so prevalent as to interfere seriously with the progress of the business. The rule of the Bureau in regard to such writs issued by U. S. courts was to obey the writs and abide by the judgment of the court. In the cases of like writs issued by State courts the course pursued was in accordance with the following opinion of the Solicitor of the War Department.*

The courts, in many cases, still claiming jurisdiction, regarded the officer making the return as guilty of contempt. This condition of things imposed upon the officers of the Bureau difficult and embarrassing labors, and materially impeded the successful performance of their duties.

A further obstacle was met in civil courts assuming jurisdiction in cases of claims for exemption from military duty. Section 14 of the enrollment act says:

* * * All persons drafted and claiming exemption from military duty on account of disability, or any other cause, shall present their claims to be exempted to the Board, whose decision shall be final.

The statute thus made the Board of Enrollment the special and only tribunal before which claims for exemption could be tried, wisely

a See act in Appendix, Doc. 35.

* For opinion, see Circular No. 36, Provost-Marshal-General's Office, July 1, 1863, Vol. III, this series, p. 460.

prescribing that the decision of the Board should be final. But, notwithstanding this, certain judges assumed jurisdiction in cases of claims for exemption, both before and after the boards had given final decision on them, as required by the statute. According to the opinion of these judges there was practically no finality in the examination of drafted men unless they were all exempted by the boards. In one instance, during the daily examination of men, a judge ordered the records of the Board of Enrollment to be delivered to him in court. The order was not obeyed inasmuch as obedience to it would have been a violation of the law, and might have delayed for an indefinite period the business of the Board in that district.

In Pennsylvania an attempt was made to obstruct the draft by means of a bill in chancery; and an injunction was granted by a majority of the supreme court of that State, which, however, was not obeyed.

The action of the civil courts in the foregoing particulars threatened for a time, in several districts, to defeat, or at least to suspend, the business of raising troops and of arresting deserters, and either to throw the officers of this Bureau into custody, or keep them so constantly before the courts as to prevent their attendance upon the duties for which they were appointed, and thus to defeat the raising of an army according to the law. These difficulties were subsequently terminated by the proclamation of the President, dated September 15, as follows:*

In accordance with the above proclamation I issued Circular No. 85.*a* It directed that if a writ of habeas corpus should, in violation of the aforesaid proclamation, be sued out and served upon any officer in the military service of the United States, commanding him to produce before any court or judge any person in his custody by authority of the President of the United States, belonging to any one of the classes specified in the President's proclamation, it should be the duty of such officer to make known by his certificate, under oath, to whomsoever may issue or serve such writ of habeas corpus, that the person named in said writ "is detained by him as a prisoner under authority of the President of the United States."

Such return having been made, if any person serving, or attempting to serve, such writ, either by the command of any court or judge, or otherwise, and with or without process of law, should attempt to arrest the officer making such return and holding in custody such person, the said officer was thereby commanded to refuse submission and obedience to such arrest, and if there should be any attempt to take such person from the custody of such officer, or arrest such officer, he should resist such attempt, calling to his aid any force that might be necessary to maintain the authority of the United States and render such resistance effectual.

The time when drafted men might pay commutation or present substitutes.

Section 13 of the original enrollment act is as follows:

SEC. 13. *And be it further enacted*, That any person drafted and notified to appear as aforesaid may, on or before the day fixed for his appearance, furnish an acceptable substitute to take his place in the draft; or he may pay to such person as the Secretary of War may authorize to receive it such sum, not exceeding three hundred dollars, as the Secretary may determine, for the procuration of

a See Appendix, Doc. 24, Art. 2.

* See Vol. III, this series, p. 817.

such substitute, which sum shall be fixed at a uniform rate by a general order made at the time of ordering a draft for any State or Territory; and thereupon such person so furnishing the substitute, or paying the money, shall be discharged from further liability under that draft. And any person failing to report after due service of notice, as herein prescribed, without furnishing a substitute, or paying the required sum therefor, shall be deemed a deserter, and shall be arrested by the provost-marshal and sent to the nearest military post for trial by court-martial, unless, upon proper showing that he is not liable to do military duty, the Board of Enrollment shall relieve him from the draft.

I understood it to be the meaning and intention of the law to limit the privilege of putting in a substitute, or paying money, to the period prior to the time fixed for the drafted man's actual appearance, and that during this period he should determine which of the three things he would do—furnish a substitute, pay the commutation money, or appear in person for duty. According to my construction, the privilege of doing either of the first two was to terminate by law with "the day fixed for his appearance." On or before that day he was to pay commutation money or present for duty a substitute or himself.

He could do either of the first two things without being troubled to appear at all. Whichever offer he made the Government was required to accept. If he presented himself, and upon examination was found suitable for military duty, I did not consider it in the meaning of the law or the interests of the service that the case should be reopened, and that one of the two special privileges expiring by law with the day fixed for his appearance should be renewed. To allow this would reduce the number of conscripts, delay the procuring of men, and add to the labors and complications of the Bureau. The draft was resorted to only as a stern necessity, after other means of recruiting had failed. The object was to re-enforce its armies. That object could not properly be sacrificed or subordinated to the preferences or prejudices of the parties unpleasantly affected by the draft. It was urged that being an obnoxious measure it should be administered with gentleness and generosity. The principle thus asserted was not disputed in this Bureau. On the contrary, it was made to apply to all of our people—those in front of the enemy as well as those at home. But all tenderness (not required by law) to those who stayed at home and waited to be drafted—all consideration for them which would delay the execution of the draft and reduce the number of conscripts furnished by it—was clearly harshness and cruelty to the men who had gone forth voluntarily, and whose safety as well as that of the country depended on prompt re-enforcements.

The law did not permit the drafted men to provide substitutes or pay commutation after the day fixed for their appearance. It was not practicable on the day fixed for their appearance both to complete their examination and go through the operation of receiving their money or substitutes. I therefore directed that they must decide before their examination and abide by the choice. The following are official opinions rendered by the Judge-Advocate-General on the subject:

In the case of a drafted man who fails to furnish a substitute, or pay commutation, on or before the day fixed for his appearance.

OPINION.

Under the thirteenth section of the enrollment act, it is clear that a party drafted and wishing to furnish a substitute or pay the commutation must do so "on or before the day fixed for his appearance." The privilege expires with that day. If he fails to report himself, and is arrested as a deserter, he has still the right to go before the Board of Enrollment and prove that "he is not liable to do military duty;" but if, on hearing his claim to exemption, he is held to be liable, he cannot escape personal service. He is also, under such circumstances, subject to be proceeded against as a deserter.

J. HOLT,
Judge-Advocate-General.

* * * * * * *

The right to furnish a substitute or pay the commutation is derived wholly from the enrollment act. That act gives the right only on or before the day fixed for the party's appearance. It does not exist afterward, simply because the law does not give it.

* * * * * * *

J. HOLT,
Judge-Advocate-General.

On the 18th of July, 1863, the following circular was issued permitting men to pay commutation or provide substitutes after they had been examined and found liable to duty, with the result that, instead of doing either, many availed themselves of the opportunity to abscond.*

The substitution of colored for white men under the draft of July, 1863.

This draft was made in order to fill up the ranks of the depleted regiments in the field, especially those in the Army of the Potomac. During its progress every variety of artifice was put in practice, especially by those opposed to the war, not only to escape service, but to do so at the least possible cost, without regard to the interests of the Government. One method was to take advantage of the ignorance and necessities of negroes and buy them up at a cheap rate as substitutes for drafted white men. So far as this practice was permitted to prevail the purpose of this draft, filling up the ranks of the old regiments (which were composed of white troops), was defeated The traffic was carried on among those negroes already freed, and did not benefit those held in bondage, nor was it designed to do so by the persons engaged in it. In view of these facts, and of the further fact that the Government could not at that time put negroes to good use as soldiers, the laws in reference to the status of negroes were examined to see whether they required that a negro should be taken as a substitute for a white man under the draft then in progress.

The legislation affecting the status and rights of this class of persons had been gradual and was incomplete. The result of it was before the Bureau in the following opinion of the Solicitor of the War Department:

In regard to the employment of persons of African descent in the military service, their pay, and emoluments.

By the eleventh section of the act of July 17, 1862, entitled "An act to define the pay and emoluments," &c., the President was authorized to employ as many persons of African descent as he should deem necessary and proper for the suppression of this rebellion, and to organize and use them in such manner as he judged for public welfare. No provision was specially made for their compensation in that act.

By the fifteenth section of the act of July 17, entitled "An act to amend the act calling forth the militia," &c., it is provided that each person enrolled under that act (authorizing the raising of 100,000 volunteers for nine months), who should enlist in the infantry under the provisions of section 3 of that act, should be entitled to receive his first month's pay and $25 bounty upon the mustering of his company or regiment into the service of the United States. (See section 3.)

* See Circular No. 51, Provost-Marshal-General's Office, July 18, 1863, Vol. III, this series, p. 535.

2. All persons enrolled under that act are entitled to receive (by section 15) the pay and rations now allowed by law to soldiers, according to their respective grades: *Provided*, That persons of African descent who should be employed under the law should receive $10 per month and one ration each per day, of which $3 might be paid in clothing. By the act of March 3, 1863, cooks of African descent are entitled to receive for their full compensation $10 per month and one ration each per day, $3 of which monthly pay may be in clothing.

It seems, therefore, that in accordance with the foregoing acts persons of African descent received into the service of the United States as volunteers under said act are entitled to receive as pay $10 per month and one ration daily, of which monthly pay $3 per month may be in clothing.

WILLIAM WHITING,
Solicitor of the War Department.

APRIL 25, 1863.

Congress made a distinction, especially in the matter of bounty, between white and colored troops, and continued it up to July, 1864, as shown in this report, under the head of "Colored men and their relation to the military service." It does not appear whether this resulted only from the general principles governing supply and demand, or from a supposed difference in the value as soldiers of these two classes of persons.

The Solicitor, when consulted on the particular point of accepting negroes as substitutes for white men, under the draft then being made, was of opinion that it would not be in accordance with the meaning and intention of the laws in force at the time to do so. In compliance with special instructions from the President, an order was issued on the 20th of July, 1863, *a* directing that men of African descent should only be accepted as substitutes for each other.

Exemption of clergymen and persons of conscientious scruples, &c.

Under the law as it stood at the time this draft was made, no exemptions were allowed on account of religious creeds or conscientious scruples against bearing arms. The amendments approved February 24, 1864, however, granted exemptions to persons of this class, under certain strict limitations. The action of the Bureau in this matter is shown in the following report, in answer to a resolution of the House of Representatives.*

Under the original act embarrassment frequently arose in the attempt to secure, as required by law, military service under the draft from ministers of the gospel, but more especially from members of the society of "Friends, or Quakers." The experience of the Bureau, in this respect, was substantially the same as that of the Government during the ante-Revolutionary period, with the same class of persons. *b*

The call of October 17, 1863.

As heretofore stated, the draft discussed in the foregoing produced by its direct operation but 35,882 men, of whom 26,002 were substitutes. This number was far below the re-enforcements required by the armies, which had been greatly depleted by the campaigns of the summer. Their commanders being very urgent in their demands for additional men, a plan was devised under the law to procure them with the fund accumulated by the payment of exemption money under this draft. Fifty-two thousand two hundred and eighty-eight of the drafted men examined, found liable and fit to perform military

a See Appendix, Doc. 24, Art. 1. *b* See Appendix, Doc. 31.

* See Fry to Stanton, February 7, 1865, Vol. IV, this series, p. 1154.

duty, had secured exemption by paying $300 each, making a total of $15,686,400, which the law required should be used in procuring substitutes. The method of employing this money for this purpose was such as to provide men at the earliest practicable day.

The object being, as under the draft, to procure recruits (substitutes) for the ranks of the organizations then in the field, detailed instructions were issued as soon as the business connected with the draft permitted in any district for the payment of various bounties, rewards, and premiums.

In addition to these inducements the spur of an impending draft, made effective by the remembrance of its enforcement during the past summer, was deemed necessary to stimulate recruiting. Accordingly, on the 17th of October the President issued a proclamation, as follows:*

The 5th of January was fixed as the day of draft in order to give Congress time to amend the enrollment act. The plan referred to above had essentially but two objects: First, to offer a large bounty to the man presenting himself as a recruit, this bounty being divided into installments and distributed through the period of his enlistment; second, to secure the services of active and reliable men as recruiting agents, who, liberally remunerated by the premium allowed for each man they presented, would devote themselves wholly to the business, be under the control of the Government, and held responsible for their behavior.

A dread of the draft on the part of some, and a commendable pride in having their localities escape compulsory service on the part of others, resulted in defeating these two main objects. To fill their respective quotas and avoid the draft, towns, counties, and States offered bounties and premiums so greatly in excess of those offered by the Government as to make the latter of inappreciable effect, especially as the local bounties were generally paid in full at the time of enlistment.

In the anxiety of towns and States to fill quotas useful regulations and wholesome restraints upon fraud and abuse were, in some instances, pronounced by the public to be unnecessary and vexatious obstacles to success in recruiting, and were consequently defeated or disregarded.

Such was the case in relation to the rule requiring that recruiting agents should be limited in number and under the control of and responsible to the Government, and should have the monopoly of the business. It was urged upon the Bureau that the interest of the people in raising men was destroyed or restrained by a rule which permitted only certain authorized agents to receive premiums for presenting recruits and prevented the people at large from doing so. As the amount of local bounties and premiums (or "hand money," as it was termed) increased, and the pecuniary inducements to volunteering offered by the Government became more insignificant in comparison with those provided by the States and subordinate localities, and as the impending and dreaded draft could only be avoided by the action of the people in procuring volunteers, it seemed best to conform to the popular demand and remove the restriction as to recruiting agents.

The opportunities for fraud and gain in connection with the increase of local bounties grew rapidly, and with the business open

*See General Orders, No. 340, Adjutant-General's Office, October 19, 1863, Vol. III, this series, p. 892.

to the bad as well as the good very soon produced the class of men known as bounty and substitute brokers. The net-work with which they covered the country was so well contrived and so skillfully managed that it was difficult for recruits or substitutes to get into the service without passing through their hands. The result of abandoning the first plan of the Bureau—that of selecting and controlling the recruiting agents and limiting their number—was to throw the business into the hands of the brokers, who were generally bad and dishonest men, instead of having it conducted by men of good character, who could be held responsible for their acts.

The wrongs to individuals and the injury to the recruiting service and the cause of the country, resulting from the operations of these substitute and bounty brokers and from the large local bounties, are hereinafter discussed. They are of such character and extent as to prove the necessity under similar circumstances, if they should arise hereafter, of an entire suppression of substitute brokerage as practiced during the late war.

The draft under this call, which was to have taken place on January 5, 1864, did not commence at that time, in consequence of the progress made in procuring volunteers, and of the fact that the law for drafting remained unamended. The amendments were not made until February 24, 1864. An account, however, of all troops furnished by the different localities under this call, and of all obtained by the draft preceding it, was kept in the manner shown hereafter, in order that proper credit could be given in any draft which should subsequently be made.

PART III.

The calls of February 1 and March 14, 1864.

On the 30th of January, 1864, I reported to you as follows:

WAR DEPARTMENT, PROVOST-MARSHAL-GENERAL'S OFFICE,
Washington, D. C., January 30, 1864.

Hon. EDWIN M. STANTON,
Secretary of War:

SIR: I have the honor to recommend that the total quota of the entire first draft under the enrollment act be fixed at 500,000, and that it be now apportioned among the different localities in accordance with opinion of Hon. William Whiting, Solicitor of the War Department, as contained in Circular No. 3, of January 7, 1864, from this office,[a] and that the apportionment be immediately communicated to all concerned. I would further recommend that the 10th of March next be fixed as the time for commencing the draft for all quotas in all localities where they are not furnished by the 1st of March.

You will observe that as the President's call for men dated October 17, 1863, was for 300,000, the foregoing proposition to make the total quota for draft 500,000 is virtually making an additional call for 200,000 men, less the number obtained by the late draft. I think it is best to make such an additional call, and to make it at this time.

* * * * * * *

I am, sir, very respectfully, your obedient servant,

JAMES B. FRY,
Provost-Marshal-General.

Approved.

E. M. STANTON.

On the 1st of February, 1864, the President issued an order for draft as follows:*

The report above shows the manner in which the quotas and credits were arranged. The credits allowed on and applied in reduction of

[a] See Appendix, Doc. 26, [Art. 1].

*See General Orders, No. 35, Adjutant-General's Office, February 1, 1864, Vol. IV, this series, p. 59.

this call for 500,000 troops embraced all those arising from the tentative draft commenced in July, 1863, and all those under the call of October 17, 1863. This call of February 1 was in fact only for 200,000 men, less the number obtained directly by the draft.

To take advantage of the time during which Congress had provided that large bounties should be paid for volunteers, and to meet an anticipated reduction in the number of men to be obtained for the Army under the preceding call, on account of the law requiring that men going into the Navy should be credited, a call for 200,000 more men was made, as shown below, and the draft (fixed for the 10th of March) was postponed to allow volunteering under the new call.

The original act of March 3, 1863, was amended February 24, 1864. The first section of the amendment provided that the President of the United States should be authorized, whenever he should deem it necessary during the present war, to call for such number of men for the military service of the United States as the public exigencies might require.

Under the provisions of this act the President, on the 14th of March, issued a proclamation *a* in which a call was made and a draft ordered for 200,000 men for the military service (Army, Navy, and Marine Corps) of the United States to supply the force required to be drafted for the Navy, and to provide an adequate reserve force for all contingencies. It designated the 15th of April, 1864, as the time up to which the quotas assigned to the different wards, towns, townships, &c., might be filled by voluntary enlistments, and directed that a draft should be commenced as soon after that date as practicable in each ward of a city, town, &c., which had not then filled its quota. It directed that the Government bounties then paid should continue until April 1, 1864, and that on and after that date $100 bounty only should be paid as provided by the act approved July 22, 1861.

The draft commenced as required by the foregoing order, and was completed without serious difficulty or opposition.

The results of these calls, viz, the draft of 1863 and the call of February 1, 1864, for 500,000 men, including the 300,000 called for October 17, 1863, and that of March 14, 1864, for 200,000 additional, are given in table herewith. *b* They may be recapitulated as follows:

Number called for		700,000
Reduced by reduction in quotas after their distribution among the States	45,274	
Reduced by reduction in credits on account of excess over all quotas previously assigned	162,901	
Reduced by reduction in credits on account of drafted men who paid commutation	84,733	
Total reduction		292,908
Leaving the number to be obtained		407,092

The whole number of voluntary enlistments under these calls was 489,462, viz:

Volunteers:		
White	325,366	
Colored	11,378	
Veteran volunteers	136,507	
Regulars	7,776	
Seamen	7,697	
Marines	738	
Total voluntary enlistments		489,462

a See Appendix, Doc. 36.

b See Appendix, Doc. 6, Tables 6, 7, and 8.

The whole number of drafted men and substitutes obtained was 48,209, viz:

Number held to personal service	13,296	
Number of substitutes for drafted men	34,913	
		48,209
Whole number obtained under these calls*		537,671

Leaving a surplus of 130,579, which was carried forward to call of July 18, 1864.

Call of July 18, 1864.

On the 18th of July, 1864, a call *a* was made for 500,000 men for one, two, or three years' service, with the proviso that said call should be reduced by all credits which might be established under section 8 of the act approved July 4, 1864, on account of persons who have entered the naval service during the rebellion, and for men furnished to the military service in excess of calls previously made, and by reductions on account of corrections made in the enrollment after quotas were assigned.

The results of this call may be recapitulated as follows:

The number called for was		500,000
Reduced by—		
Excess credits on former calls	130,579	
Corrections of enrollment	22,675	
Naval credits, act of July 4, 1864	64,882	
Veterans not before allowed	11,869	
Credits allowed by adjustment	35,290	
Paid commutation (section 17, act of February 24, 1864)	378	
Total reductions		265,673
Total number to be obtained		234,327

The whole number of voluntary enlistments under that call was 188,172, viz:

Volunteers:		
White	146,392	
Colored	15,961	
Regulars	6,339	
Seamen	17,606	
Marine Corps	1,874	
Total voluntary enlistments		188,172
The total number of drafted men and substitutes obtained under that call was 54,707, viz:		
Number held to personal service	26,205	
Number of substitutes for drafted men	28,502	
	54,707	
Number of substitutes before draft for enrolled men	29,584	
Total		84,291
Whole number obtained under the July call †		272,463

During the time devoted to filling the call of July 18, 1864, and the following call of December 19, 1864, the treatment by the rebels of

a See Appendix, Doc. 36, and Doc. 6, Table 9.

* But see Vol. IV, this series, p. 1266, for revised statement of the total number of men furnished under these calls.

† But see Vol. IV, this series, p. 1267, for revised statement of the total number of men furnished under this call.

our troops who fell into their hands became generally known throughout the country. There was probably nothing in all the operations of the rebel armies or authorities which acted so unfavorably upon our recruitment as the inhumanity with which the insurgents treated the prisoners of war held by them. Men who would cheerfully enlist in the cause of the Union and take all the chances of civilized warfare, were not so willing to expose themselves to the protracted torture that awaited them if, by the fortunes of war, they fell into the hands of the enemy. If it was purposed by the cruelty shown to the victims of Andersonville and like places of torture to discourage the recruitment of the Union armies, this object was to a certain extent accomplished.

Action in certain contingencies under the call of July 18, 1864.

The thirteenth section of the enrollment act provides that * * * "any person failing to report after due service of notice as herein prescribed, without furnishing a substitute or paying the required sum therefor, shall be deemed a deserter, and shall be arrested by the provost-marshal and sent to the nearest military post for trial by court-martial, unless upon proper showing that he is not liable to do military duty, the Board of Enrollment shall relieve him from the draft."

Under this section it was claimed that when the quota of a district had once been drawn, no additional draft could be made for the deficiency occasioned by the failure of the drafted men to report. It was urged that men drawn in the draft were, in law and in fact, in the military service, and that it was the duty of the Government to arrest delinquents and not to require new men to make good the deficiency occasioned by the failure of drafted men to report.

To this I replied that the act of March 3, 1863, declared that all able-bodied male citizens of proper age, with the exceptions enumerated in the act, were liable to be called upon to perform military duty, and that by drafting a man the Government acquires a jurisdiction and control over him to the same extent as if he had voluntarily enlisted in the service. If he deserts, or if, on examination by the Board of Enrollment, he is rejected, he is not one of the "required number obtained" in the language and meaning of the statute. Like the enlisted recruit, the drafted man is liable to be held to service; but if, on examination, the one is exempted by the Board of Enrollment, or the other rejected by the mustering officer, no credit could be given for either, because they are not "obtained" in the meaning of the law.

The object of the draft is not to fill quotas; it is to raise troops, and it should be executed with that view; and as every able-bodied citizen of the proper age is subject to be called under arms, no drafted man has just cause of complaint because he is required to render his share of military service. The fact that the "required number" has already been drawn is no reason why others should not be drawn, if necessary, to obtain the number required for duty. If the required number is not "obtained" because some have been exempted and others failed to report and eluded arrest, or being arrested are found unfit for service, the object of the law would be defeated if the draft did not proceed until the required number is obtained.

When a man is drafted in lieu of one who has failed to report, he is not "required" to fill a deficiency on account of the failure of the first party to report, because it has not been ascertained that the drafted man who has failed to report would be accepted, and until accepted he would not be counted on the quota, and therefore not being counted, his failure to report creates no deficiency, but leaves the matter in the same condition, so far as credit is concerned, as if he had not been drafted. As well might a drafted man claim to be discharged because an enlisted recruit who has been rejected by a mustering officer is not credited upon the quota.

The principle here announced is in exact accordance with the legal opinion [a] of the Judge-Advocate-General of the Army, given September 10, 1863. Were a different rule to be adopted, it would occasion manifest injustice to those States in which former drafts have been made and the quotas filled by men actually put in service, in addition to those who were drafted and failed to report. Not only that, but by a different ruling all those who have been drafted to fill the places of men who failed to report would be illegally held to service and ought to be discharged.

By the amendatory enrollment act of February 24, 1864, it is provided that the required number and 100 per cent. in addition shall be drawn. Now, if it were granted that all drawn are in fact (as well as in law) in the military service, and if none of those drawn should report, not only would the quota be filled without the Government getting a man, but the locality would have an excess equivalent to the quota assigned and could not be expected to furnish men on future calls.

Call of December 19, 1864.

On the 19th day of December, 1864, a call [b] was made for 300,000 men to serve for one, two, or three years.

Under this call the whole number of voluntary enlistments was 157,058, viz:

Volunteers:	
White	130,620
Colored	10,055
Regulars	6,958
Seamen	9,106
Marine Corps	319
Total voluntary enlistments	157,058

The whole number of drafted men and substitutes for drafted men was 24,580, viz:

Number held to personal service	12,566	
Number of substitutes for drafted men	12,014	
Total	24,580	
Number of substitutes for enrolled men	12,997	
Total drafted men and substitutes		37,577
Whole number raised under December call*		194,635

As the suspension of active military operations occurred while the business of the draft under this call was in progress, orders were issued on the 13th of April, 1865, to discontinue the business of recruiting and drafting; and on the next day all drafted men who

[a] See Appendix, Doc. 29. [b] See Appendix, Doc. 36.

*But see Vol. IV, this series, p. 1268, for revised statement of the total number of men furnished under this call.

had not been forwarded to general rendezvous were ordered to be discharged, and soon after all who had not been forwarded to the field were discharged by orders through the Adjutant-General.

Quotas and troops furnished under all calls.

The aggregate quotas charged against the several States under all calls made by the President of the United States from the 15th day of April, 1861, to the 14th day of April, 1865, at which time drafting and recruiting ceased, was 2,759,049,* the terms of service varying from three months to three years, as shown in detail in Appendix, Document 6, Tables 2 and 3.

The aggregate number of men credited on the several calls and put into service of the United States in the Army, Navy, and Marine Corps during the above period was 2,690,401,* leaving a deficiency on all calls when the war closed of 68,648, which would have been obtained in full if recruiting and drafting had not been discontinued.

This number does not embrace the "emergency men" called into active service for short periods, amounting in all to over 72,000, and hereinafter specially noted.

Assignment of quotas December 19, 1864.

Prior to the act of July 4, 1864,*a* the period of military service was fixed at three years for drafted men and volunteers. This act, however, probably with a view to relieve the hardships of the conscription, provided that the draft should be made for one year, and volunteers be accepted for one, two, and three years' service. Shortly after, to wit, July 18, 1864, a call *b* was made under it for 500,000 men for one, two, and three years. Under the law each sub-district had the right to furnish men for one or all of these periods, and it could not be determined in advance what class of recruits or what proportion of each class would be furnished. As the three-years' period embraced both the others, and as all existing excesses and deficiencies consisted of three-years' men, I deemed it best to retain that period as a basis for calculating the number of men required, reserving the question of the value of the amount of service furnished until it could be properly determined, after ascertaining what number of each class had been put in by each locality, when excess of service could be credited and deficiency could be charged, as heretofore. The superiority of three-years' men over one-year men in service was undisputed, and was recognized by Congress, triple bounty being paid for that period as an inducement for men to enlist for it. In accordance with the act of March, 1863, *a* requiring that in making up the credits the term of service should be considered, as well as the number of men furnished, I announced that credit would be given on future calls for the amount of service furnished under this call—that is to say, the aggregate years of service which the sub-district furnished would be regarded as the value of the quota raised, whether composed of one, two, or three years' men, or of portions of all classes. This admitted of counting each man as a unit in filling this call, the three-years' basis being retained, and the deficiency or excess in amount of service furnished being reserved for consideration

a See Appendix, Doc. 35. *b* See Appendix, Doc. 36.

* But see revised statement, Vol. IV, this series, p. 1269.

when quotas under a subsequent call were to be apportioned, as provided by the act last referred to. This view of the subject was presented to the Solicitor of the War Department immediately after the passage of the act of July 4, who, upon examination of the several acts of Congress bearing upon the subject, fully sustained it, as will appear by his opinion, dated August 1, 1864.[a]

The call of July 18,[b] 1864, contained a proviso directing that "this call shall be reduced by all credits which may be established under section 8 of the aforesaid act, on account of persons who have entered the naval service during the present rebellion, and by credits for men furnished to the military service in excess of calls heretofore made."

Under this provision the call was reduced from 500,000 to less than 300,000, rendering necessary an additional call, which was issued by the President on the 19th day of December, 1864,[b] for 300,000 men.

It was known that in addition to the ordinary losses incident to active operations the Army during the year 1865 would be greatly reduced by the expiration of the term of enlistment of a large number of troops, embracing all the three-years' men of 1862 who had not re-enlisted in veteran organizations, the two-years' men of 1863, and the one-year men of 1864. To meet this reduction and maintain the effective strength of the Army the last call was made for actual men, and embraced no margin for reduction on account of credits for troops previously raised, as explained in a letter to the Governor of Vermont, from which the following is an extract:

> The pending call is not for 300,000 men subject to fair credits, but it is for 300,000 remaining after all fair credits have been deducted; and it is impossible to concede what Vermont asks without coming out short of the 300,000 men, or making other localities pay for the partiality shown her.
>
> * * * * * * *
>
> Yours, truly,
>
> A. LINCOLN.

It was not intended, however, to deprive any district or town of its proper credit for men furnished under previous calls, nor to release any district or locality from furnishing its quota under that call in addition to its deficiency existing under former calls. The object was to raise 300,000 men in such manner that the excess or deficiency on previous calls in every sub-district would be taken into account, either to diminish or to increase the share of the 300,000 which the sub-district would be required to furnish. No other proper method of distribution could have been adopted to carry out the orders of the President, produce 300,000 men under the call, and do justice to all sections of the country.

As many districts and towns were in excess—that is, had furnished more than their quotas under former calls—it was evident that they would have less than a pro rata share to furnish under this call, while those districts and towns that were deficient under former calls would be called upon for more than a pro rata share under this.

The exact amount of excess or deficiency depended upon the amount of service furnished under previous calls. In determining this I considered not only the number of men raised, but the period for which they engaged to serve as required by law.[c]

---

[a] See Appendix, Doc. 27, Art. 1.
[b] See Appendix, Doc. 36.
[c] Act March 3, 1863, section 12.

In computing the quotas under the December call the correct principle adopted by the Secretary of War in ordering the quotas under the preceding calls was followed. In accordance with the opinion of the Solicitor of the Department the same basis—three years—was retained, and all men entering the service were counted as units in filling the December call. The excess or deficiency in amount of service furnished, resulting from the longer or shorter periods for which the men filling the call were enlisted, was reserved for consideration at the next call.

In order to ascertain the amount of service furnished prior to the December call I followed the rule heretofore observed of multiplying the number of men previously raised by the number of years for which they were enlisted, regarding the term of enlistment as the period of service.

It was impossible to follow the individual fortune or history of each soldier to determine whether or not he had actually served the whole period of his enlistment, or to make any estimate which would work so fairly as the rule adopted. But six months had as yet elapsed since the troops under the July call had been raised, and the precise length of time any of these would actually serve could not be determined in advance. It was known, however, that as a rule soldiers serve out their term of enlistment unless they are killed in action, die, or are discharged for disability, in all of which cases their term of enlistment expires as well as their term of service. Deserters do not go out of service, but are required to make good the time lost by desertion. Therefore I adhered to the rule which I had always observed, and which had been adopted by the Adjutant-General prior to the organization of this Bureau, and treated the "term of enlistment" and the "term of service" as identical, so far as related to the question of credit for troops raised.[a]

Having multiplied the number of men raised by the number of years for which they enlisted or were drafted, the product was the number of years of service furnished.

Thus, where a given sub-district had put in service ten three-years' men, fifteen two-years' men, and twenty one-year men it had furnished in all just eighty years of service, viz:

$$
\begin{aligned}
10 \times 3 &= 30 \\
15 \times 2 &= 30 \\
20 \times 1 &= 20 \\
\text{Total} \ldots &\ \overline{80}
\end{aligned}
$$

Having ascertained the amount of service furnished under former calls, the difference between that amount and the amount required under former calls was the deficiency or excess.

Thus, if the number required from a sub-district under former calls was 100, and the amount furnished was 80, that sub-district would be deficient twenty years of service, which, in order to do justice to other sub-districts, it would be required to make up.

On the other hand, if the amount furnished by the sub-district was 120, it would then have an excess of twenty years' service, to be applied to its credit.

The amount of excess and deficiency was readily obtained, but it consisted of years, while the quotas to be apportioned were to consist of men for one, two, and three years' service, to be accepted for

[a] See Appendix, Doc. 27, Art. 2.

whichever of these terms the different localities saw fit to present them. Instead of being a simple proposition requiring but little calculation to solve, it was an intricate problem attended with much labor and perplexity.

In the first place, the call was for one, two, and three years' men. It could not be required of a locality to furnish any particular number of each class, or any one of the periods in exclusion of the others. But while it was the privilege of each locality to select the class, or the number of each class of troops to be raised, it was my duty to determine the value of the quota furnished (which depended upon the periods of service as well as the number of men) in order to keep the accounts of the different districts, and see that each supplied its proper share.

As the call was for a fixed number of men, with the privilege to them of enlisting for one, two, and three years, it was proper that each man accepted, whether for one or another of these periods, should count as one in filling the call; but in ascertaining subsequently the amount of service furnished by the locality each man would be rated according to the period of his enlistment. It was therefore necessary to adopt a method of calculation that would accomplish this object and at the same time take into account the years of service in which the district was deficient or in excess under former calls.

In order to do this I retained three years as the basis of calculation. This has been the rule under all calls, and as remarked by the Solicitor of the War Department in his opinion heretofore referred to, "it is not material what unit is taken as the basis of equalization if that unit is uniformly the same. It is on the assumption that the mode of calculation heretofore adopted will be continued by the Provost-Marshal-General that the present call has been based."

Taking three years as the basis, the amount of service required was the product obtained by multiplying the number of men called for by 3, making 900,000 years of service required under this call. This amount the President demanded in addition to all previously furnished, and it was to be distributed to all the districts and sub-districts in proportion to the number enrolled in each, and taking into account the excess and deficiency under former calls. The aggregate of the excess of all the districts was added to the amount required in the same manner as if the call had been originally that much greater, and had been filled or partially filled in such districts as had furnished excess, and to which extent these districts were now entitled to credit, leaving still to be provided the 900,000 years of service.

Having thus added the aggregate excess to the call, the sum was apportioned to the several districts according to their enrollment, and then from the share of each district thus found I deducted the full amount of the excess which the district had actually furnished; the remainder was the number of years of service required from each district under this call, increased by the deficiency or diminished by the excess it had under former calls.

It will be observed that while the whole of the excess was added to the call in the first instance it was afterward subtracted by deducting from the quota of each locality its own excess, the sum of which excesses forms the total excess added, leaving the aggregate amount required just 900,000 years of service.

The following extract from the report of an interview between the President and a committee appointed by the Legislature of Rhode Island shows President Lincoln's views on the subject, and gives in his language a clear illustration of the principle acted upon:

The President at this point interrupted the committee to say that complaints from several States had already been made to the same effect, and in one instance the subject had been so earnestly pressed to his attention that he had personally taken the pains to examine for himself the formula which the Provost-Marshal-General had adopted for the calculation and distribution of the quotas for the different States, and had arrived at the conclusion that it was impossible for any candid mind to doubt or question its entire fairness.

In order that your committee might be fully possessed of his opinion upon this subject the President read the following paper, the original of which had been forwarded to His Excellency the Governor of the State of Vermont.*

The committee give the following interesting account of further remarks on the same subject by the President and officers of the War Department.

The President further stated that although the plan that had been adopted by the Provost-Marshal-General for the assignment of the respective quotas met his entire approval, and appeared to him to be the only one by which exact justice could be secured, in view of the fact that the aggregate of the credits due to all the States exceeded very considerably the number of men called for, and that men, and not an adjustment of balances, was the object of the call, he had, for the purpose of satisfying the minds of all parties, designated a board of officers to examine into the system and report their conclusions.

Having obtained the number of years of service required from each locality, I divided that number by 3, to find the number of men. This gave the quota in men of the districts under the call.

The method followed was this, in substance: The call, 300,000, was multiplied by 3, making 900,000 as the number of years of service required; this product, after being apportioned to the different districts, was divided by 3, which gave the quotas of the districts, amounting in the aggregate to 300,000 men.

It is hardly necessary to add that multiplying the number called for by 3, and afterward dividing the product by the same number, neither increases nor diminishes the number called for; nor does the fact that three years was assumed as the basis of calculation increase the number of men called for, or in any manner affect the amount of service required.

The same rule was applied to all the districts and sub-districts without exception, and whenever the quota of one district was apparently greater than that of another containing an equal number of enrolled men, the difference resulted from the fact that the latter was deficient, or the former in excess, in amount of service under previous calls.

The deficiency or excess might have been occasioned by a greater or less number of men, or by the inequality of the periods of service of the same number of men. Whatever cause produced the one or the other, it was simple justice and manifest law to equalize the quotas and require from each locality its full share and no more under all the calls.

The difference between this call and former calls was this: Hitherto the calls were intended to be reduced by all existing surplus, as in the case of the July call already adverted to, while this (December) call was intended to produce 300,000 in addition to all surplus or excess.

To illustrate: Suppose the entire amount of surplus in the United States to have been 600,000 years of service, or its equivalent, 200,000

* See Lincoln to Smith, February 8, 1865, Vol. IV, this series, p. 1157.

men, a call designed to produce 300,000 men, allowing surplus to be credited on the call, would necessarily have been for 500,000 men.

Instead, therefore, of making the call for 500,000, the sum of the surplus and the number to be raised, the surplus was excluded, and the actual number of men required was called for, thus making the deduction for excess before issuing the call, instead of after, as had been done formerly.

The latter rule fixed with certainty the number of men to be obtained, while the former embraced a margin covering all surplus, and necessarily increased the number called for.

A call for 500,000, which was only intended to raise 300,000 new men, would not only produce the same effect at home and abroad as a call designed to put 500,000 men in service, but would mislead commanders in the field, who had no reason to suppose that the whole number called for would not be furnished.

It was the custom of the people to compute the number of men raised by adding together the different calls, thus showing a much greater number than had actually been furnished. It is scarcely necessary to allude to the constant efforts of the enemies of the Government to discourage enlistments for the Union Army, and to inspire the hopes of the rebel Government and people by magnifying the cost at which we had thus far prosecuted the war.

According to the formula adopted the proper quotas were arrived at, and though much of its workings seemed to the people inexplicable, its final results were correct and just. In subsequent calls, if there had been occasion therefor, this appearance of oppression and injustice, together with the seeming mystery in the operations of the formula, would have vanished, and in course of time we should have had a system of conscription whose symmetrical details and efficiency would have been satisfactory to all.

I have deemed it proper to treat this branch of the subject somewhat in detail because it has been made the object of criticism and animadversion by the press, and by parties affected by the rule which required deficient districts to make good their deficiency. The discussion of the rule adopted, and the experience had under it, confirm the fact that not only was the rule the right one, but that it was the only one which could have been properly used.

Before leaving this subject it may not be out of place to refer to the judicious guidance derived by this Bureau from the official advice of the Solicitor of the War Department. The military statutes regulating the action of the Provost-Marshal-General have been numerous, complicated, and sometimes apparently conflicting. To carry them into execution many orders had to be issued, and from time to time modified or entirely withdrawn. Some of these orders may have seemed arbitrary or illegal; but whenever a doubt was expressed in regard to the legality of the action of this Bureau the questions of law were submitted to the Solicitor. His opinions were in some instances printed and promulgated with or as a part of my orders. It is remarkable that not a single instance occurred in which the correctness of any of these opinions was disputed, so far as is known to this Bureau. In every case the legal opinion answered all objections to the order. It was enough to satisfy the people that the position taken was in accordance with the law. This silenced all further complaints and opposition. When it is remembered that the questions thus decided affected the personal rights and duties of many thousands of citizens, no better proof can be offered of the high moral character of the people than their general willingness to fulfill a public duty as soon as they recognized the legality of its exaction.

Special calls in 1862, 1863, and 1864—call of June 15, 1863.

In the early summer of 1863 the principal rebel army assumed the offensive and entered upon an invasion of the North. In view of this threatening emergency the President issued a call for 100,000 men,[a] to serve for six months, of which the State of Maryland was to furnish 10,000, the State of Pennsylvania 50,000, the State of Ohio 30,000, the State of West Virginia 10,000. These troops were to be mustered in as infantry, artillery, and cavalry, in proportions fixed by the War Department. The States called upon were to be respectively credited, under the enrollment act, for the militia services rendered under this call.

Sixteen thousand three hundred and sixty-one men were mustered into service under this call.[b]

Special force for service in Kentucky.

Under the act approved February 7, 1863,[c] "authorizing the raising of a volunteer force for the better defense of Kentucky," said force not to exceed 20,000 men, rank and file, to serve for the period of twelve months, there were raised eight regiments of infantry, 7,383; one regiment of cavalry, 1,157; two batteries of artillery, 240; re-enlisted for three years.

Troops called out in 1862 and 1863, for periods of three months or less.

A call was made on the 25th of May, 1862, by the President, upon the States of Pennsylvania and New York, for three-months' militia, in consequence of an incursion into Maryland and Pennsylvania threatened by the enemy, after a successful attack upon our forces at Winchester in the Shenandoah Valley.

This call was responded to, but previous to the muster in of the troops offered by Pennsylvania the emergency which seemed to demand their immediate service passed away, and on the 27th of the same month the call was countermanded and revoked by the Governor. The State of New York, however, had furnished 8,588 men, who were mustered into service for three months.

In September, 1862, 25,000 of the State militia were called out, by proclamation of the Governor of Pennsylvania, dated September 11, 1862, and by authority of the President's letter of the same date, for service within the State to repel invasion. These troops were not mustered into service, but were recognized and paid by the United States. They were discharged and forwarded to their homes September 24, having been in service two weeks.

In June, 1862, the State of Illinois furnished for special service, in response to a call from the War Department, five regiments, amounting in the aggregate to 4,696 men, who were mustered into the U. S. service for three months.

In the month of June, 1862, the State of Indiana furnished two regiments, which were raised, organized, and mustered into service

---

[a] See Appendix, Doc. 36.
[b] For details, see Appendix, Doc. 6, Table 3.
[c] See Appendix, Doc. 35.

for three months, under special orders, to guard the rebel prisoners in "Camp Morton," captured at Fort Donelson. An emergency demanding their services in the interior of Kentucky, the larger part of them were ordered there in August, and remained until the expiration of their term of service.

On the 21st of June, 1862, Indiana furnished for special service in Kentucky one regiment for thirty days, consisting of 771 officers and men, who were raised, equipped, mustered in, and sent forward in forty-eight hours. The Seventy-eighth Regiment (sixty-days' volunteers) was organized for same service as above, and sent forward in August, 1862. Strength, 621 officers and men.

In June, 1863, New York and Pennsylvania were called upon by the President for troops to meet the emergency created by the rebel invasion which culminated in the battle of Gettysburg. Under this call 13,971 militia were sent forward by New York between June 15 and July 3, 1863, to aid in repelling the invasion, who served about thirty days.

Pennsylvania furnished 25,042 militia, who were mustered into State service, but paid by the United States, and in addition, 7,062 militia, who were mustered into the U. S. service.

These troops were discharged during the latter part of August and first part of September.

The foregoing enumeration of men called out for short periods only embraces those mustered into the U. S. service, with the exception of those from Pennsylvania, who were by special agreement mustered into State service only, though taken up and paid by the United States. Besides these, some of the States called their militia to arms to meet emergencies directly affecting them; but as these troops were not mustered into the service or pay of the United States, they are not further alluded to in this report.

Instances of the rapidity with which troops were raised by particular localities.

The following cases are cited as instances of the rapidity with which troops were furnished by different localities in times of emergency:

Under the call of July 2, 1862, for 300,000 three-years' men, and of August 4, 1862, for 300,000 nine-months' men, the quota of the State of Illinois, under each call, was 24,148 [26,148], or an aggregate of 52,296.

The promptness with which these calls were responded to by this State is without parallel in the history of the war.

The adjutant-general of the State, in his report dated January 1, 1863, says:

The order of the Secretary of War, making the call upon the State, assumed that a draft would be necessary; and in anticipating that the States would not be able to contribute their quotas of the call in July for three-years' service, announced that if any State should not furnish its quota of the three-years' volunteers, the deficiency would be made up by a special draft from the militia.

On the evening of the 9th of August, 1862, the Adjutant-General of the Army decided, on fixing the quota of volunteers, not to regard those in the field before the call.

To raise 52,296 volunteers (with perhaps the exception of 1,000 who had enlisted between July 7 and August 5) but thirteen days were allowed. In the event of a failure, a draft would be made for the deficiency. The floating population of the State who would enlist had done so. These new volunteers must come, if come at all, from the farmers and mechanics of the State. Farmers were in the midst of their harvest; and it is no exaggeration to say that, animated by a common purpose and firmly resolved on rescuing the Government, over 50,000 of them left their harvests ungathered, their tools on the benches, the plow in the furrows, and before eleven days expired the demands of the country were met and both quotas filled.

When the historian shall write the records of these eventful days in August, 1862, no prouder record can be erected to the honor and memory of a free people than a plain, full narrative of actual realities.

The records of this office corroborate the foregoing statement, and show that 58,689 men were put into service by the State of Illinois under these two calls.

Under the call for 100-days' troops in April, 1864, preparatory to the opening campaigns of that year, the Governor of Ohio offered 30,000 men for active service "for 100 days, unless sooner discharged."

He ordered his troops to rendezvous in the most eligible places in their respective counties on the 2d day of May, and to report by telegraph at 4 o'clock of the same day the number present for duty.

Reports were received the same day at 7.30 o'clock that 38,000 men were in camp, and clamorous to be sent forward. Then came the labor of consolidation, organization, muster, and equipment. By the 16th of May the regiments were ready to be forwarded.

Between the 5th and 16th of May, a period of twelve days, forty-one regiments and one battalion of seven companies, in all 36,254 men, were consolidated, organized, mustered, clothed, armed, equipped, and presented for transportation to the field.

On the 24th of May, twenty-two days from the time this Ohio force rendezvoused, all the regiments had left the State for active service.

The greatest number of three-years' men put into service in any one month under the call of October 17, 1863, was in the month of February, 1864, viz, 69,533.

The greatest number of three-years' men raised in any one month under the call of July 18, 1864, was in the month of September following, when 115,000 men were put into service.

In the month of February, 1865, pending the draft under the call of December 19, 1864, 69,000 men were put into service for one, two, and three years, of which the States of Ohio, Indiana, Illinois, and Wisconsin furnished 41,012, viz:

Ohio	10,984
Indiana	11,317
Illinois	13,696
Wisconsin	5,015
Total	41,012

or 60 per cent. of the entire number raised by all the States.

During the months of February and March, 1865, 136,000 men were put into service, of which the above-named States furnished 66,934, viz:

Ohio	18,783
Indiana	17,993
Illinois	22,016
Wisconsin	8,142
Total	66,934

or 49 per cent. of the entire number raised by all the States during these two months.

It is proper to remark that no troops were required from Connecticut, Iowa, and Kansas under the call of December 19, 1864, for the reason that they had a large excess of credits in advance of the call, while the quotas which would ordinarily have been assigned to the States of New Hampshire, Vermont, Massachusetts, and Rhode Island were reduced by reason of a proportionate excess of credits over former calls.

Hundred-days' troops called for in 1864.

During the winter of 1863–'64 the army in the field was strengthened by new recruits, and was reorganized, as just shown under the head of "Veteran Volunteer Force," over 136,000 of the men in service having re-enlisted for a new period of three years.

As the season for active operations approached, further re-enforcements were deemed necessary, mainly to relieve from garrison and defensive duty experienced troops, in order that they might take active part in the great campaign which opened in the East with the battle of the Wilderness and in the West with the advance on Atlanta.

An offer[a] was therefore accepted by the President on the 23d of April, 1864, from the Governors of Ohio, Indiana, Illinois, Iowa, and Wisconsin to furnish an aggregate of 85,000 infantry to serve for one hundred days, the whole to be furnished within twenty days from the date of notice of their being required. The results of this recruitment in the different States are given in table in Appendix.[b] The State of Ohio was particularly successful in this effort. Between the 1st and 24th of May, 1864 (inclusive), a period of twenty-four days, forty-two regiments raised under this call left the State, fully armed and equipped.

In the month of July, 1864, special calls, not embraced in that just named, were made upon the States of New York and Pennsylvania for 4,000 men for the term of one hundred days.

In addition to the above, the States of New Hampshire, New Jersey, Maryland, and Kansas offered to furnish stated numbers of one-hundred-days' troops, and authority was given by the War Department to raise them.

The extent to which men were furnished under these calls and offers is shown in Appendix, Document 6, Table 4.

Representative recruits.

The commutation feature of the enrollment law was repealed by the act approved July 4, 1864. In anticipation of its passage and the consequent rise in the price of substitutes it was determined to make an effort to procure some recruits without a formal call. At this time the call of July 18, 1864, had not been made, and the business of filling the call of March 14, 1864, was nearly completed. The draft had borne heavily in many places upon those liable to it, and the sympathy of that large class not liable to conscription, but possessed of ample means, seemed to be aroused in their behalf. An appeal was therefore made to their patriotism and generosity in the following order.

CIRCULAR No. 25. } WAR DEPARTMENT, PROVOST-MARSHAL-GENERAL'S OFFICE,
Washington, D. C., June 26, 1864.

Persons not required by law to perform military duty have expressed a desire to be personally represented in the Army. In addition to the contributions they have made in the way of bounties they propose to procure recruits at their own expense and present them for enlistment in the service.

Their patriotism is worthy of commendation and encouragement. Provost-marshals, and all others acting under this Bureau, are ordered to furnish all the facilities in their power to enlist and muster promptly the acceptable representative recruits presented in accordance with the design herein set forth.

---

[a] See Appendix, Doc. 18, Art. 2.
[b] See Appendix, Doc. 6, Table 3.

The name of the person whom each recruit thus represents will be noted on the enlistment and descriptive rolls of the recruit and will be carried forward from those papers to the other official records which form his military history.

Certificates of this personal representation in the service will be forwarded from this office and issued by provost-marshals.*

JAMES B. FRY,
Provost-Marshal-General.

The "certificate" was prepared on parchment paper, bearing the arms of the United States engraved. The circular order above given was printed on the face of the certificate, which also bore the following:

To all who shall see these presents, greeting:

Whereas, ——, of ——, in the State of ——, a citizen of the United States, not being required by law to perform any military service, has voluntarily and at his own expense furnished ——, of ——, in the State of ——, as a representative recruit to serve in his stead in the military forces of the Union, he is, in accordance with the foregoing order, entitled to this official acknowledgment of his disinterested patriotism and public spirit.

JAMES B. FRY,
Brigadier-General and Provost-Marshal-General.

By the Provost-Marshal-General:

—— ——,
Captain and Provost-Marshal, —— *District of* ——.

This appeal, though carefully distributed throughout the United States and very generally commended, was not attended with material success. Only 1,292 representative recruits were put in service.† The lamented late President, Abraham Lincoln, was one of the first to answer this appeal and put a personal representative into the ranks. The names of all persons (including several ladies) by whom representative recruits were furnished are given in the Appendix, Document 39.

The re-enlistment and reorganization in 1863 and 1864 of regiments then in service (termed, after reorganization, "veteran volunteers").

The loss by expiration of enlistment of entire regiments and companies, after they had seen service enough to become valuable soldiers, proved a serious drawback to military operations during the first two years of the war. Soon after the organization of this Bureau its attention was directed to the discovery and application of a remedy for this evil. An examination in the summer of 1863 showed that, of the 956 volunteer regiments, 7 independent battalions, 61 independent companies, and 158 volunteer batteries, then in service, the terms of 455 regiments, 3 battalions, 38 independent companies, and 81 batteries would expire prior to December 31, 1864, leaving the Army to consist at that date of 501 regiments, 4 independent battalions, 23 independent companies, and 77 batteries, and such new men in addition as could be raised in the meantime.

The importance of retaining in the field as many as possible of these experienced organizations was evident.

To effect this a scheme was prepared and submitted by me for the re-enlistment of three-years' men still in service having less than one year longer to serve, and of men enlisted for nine months or less who had less than three months to serve.

---

* Some verbal differences exist between this copy and the circular as printed in Vol. IV, this series, p. 453, which see.

† Subsequently increased to 1,296. See foot-note (*), p. 932.

The inducements held out were:

First. A furlough of at least thirty days to both officers and men of the organizations re-enlisting for three years. Where a large proportion re-enlisted the regiment was sent home in a body at Government expense, and during its stay reorganized and recruited its ranks.

Second. A bounty of $400, anticipated from the commutation fund and payable in installments, was authorized for every soldier re-enlisting under this plan. His accounts arising from his first enlistment were closed up and payment of dues made. The second enlistment was to take effect at its date, and thus shorten the first enlistment by so much as had not yet expired. It was stipulated that, if the Government did not require these troops for the full period of three years, they should, nevertheless, when honorably mustered out on that account, be entitled to the whole amount of bounty remaining unpaid. The rank of the officers was made continuous from the date of their original muster into service.

Third. The force thus reorganized was termed "veteran volunteers," and, as an honorable distinction, "service chevrons" were authorized for it by the War Department.

This plan was not carried into effect until late in the fall of 1863, when the great campaigns of that year had closed, and the troops, resting from their labors and looking forward to a season of comparative inactivity, were most anxious to visit their homes. That privilege was guaranteed to them by your general order of November 21, 1863,[a] and eminent success in their reorganization promptly followed.

By this expedient over 136,000 tried soldiers, whose services would otherwise have been lost, were secured, and capable and experienced officers continued in command. The exact value of the services rendered by any particular part of the military forces may not be ascertained, but it may safely be asserted that the veterans thus reorganized and retained performed, in the closely contested campaigns subsequent to their re-enlistment, a part essential to the final success which attended our arms. In his official report of 1864 the Secretary of War says in relation to this subject, "I know of no operation connected with the recruitment of the Army which has resulted in more advantage to the service than the one referred to."

The patriotic determination of these troops who had taken a prominent part in the war to continue it until brought to a satisfactory close was the foundation of the success which attended this enterprise. Its advantages were not only those resulting from the actual military force thus retained. It produced a favorable effect on the recruiting service generally, and was as encouraging to the friends of the Government as discouraging to the insurgents.

Explanation of difference between men called for and men raised.

In estimating the number of troops called into service it has been the rule of the department to take into account the whole number of men mustered, without regard to the fact that the same persons may have been previously discharged after having been accepted and credited on previous calls.

Under the different calls volunteers have been accepted for various terms of service, viz, three, six, and nine months, and one, two, and three years, respectively, and a large number of persons who had served under one call have subsequently enlisted under another.

---

[a] See Appendix, Doc. 25, Art. 2.

Thus a portion of those who enlisted under the call in April, 1861, for 75,000 three-months' men again enlisted under the call in July following for three years; others re-entered the service for nine months, or for one or two years, and at the expiration of these periods again re-enlisted for three years; and the entire "veteran volunteer" force consisted of those who, having served two years, re-enlisted for three years more.

It will be observed, therefore, that a large portion of the number counted in filling calls has been furnished, first, by the re-enlistment of those in service, and, second, by those who have re-entered the service after a discharge from a former enlistment under which they had been credited; that is, in filling the different calls each accepted enlistement was credited, instead of limiting the credit to the actual number of persons who entered the service anew; and hence, to determine the number of men actually entering the service for the first time under the different calls, the number credited should be reduced in the same ratio that the enlistments of the same persons have been repeated. The extent of this reduction cannot be calculated at this time, or even estimated with sufficient accuracy to be useful.

It follows, therefore, that, on account of a necessary repetition of credits incident to enlistments, the tax upon the military basis of the country has been less than would appear by considering simply the number of men embraced in the different calls for troops, or the number of credits allowed upon these calls.

But the necessary repetition of credits, incident to repeated enlistments properly made of the same men, is not the only cause of discrepancy between the number of men called for and the actual drain upon the population of the country resulting from the successive calls. While it was true that the success attained in the recruitment of the armies resulted mainly from the patriotism of the people, and was greatly advanced by the labors of many zealous citizens and efficient committees, it is a fact that there were places in which the military service demanded by patriotism was entirely or in part evaded, and that at enormous cost in local taxes.

During the last two years of the war, but more especially under the last two calls for troops, the desire to escape the draft was so great in some localities that the necessity of providing suitable re-enforcements for the armies was subordinated to the simple object of filling quotas. Through the fraud and deceit of persons engaged in this nominal re-enforcement of the Army, substitutes and recruits, morally, mentally, and physically unfit for the service, were credited, and then had to be discharged without performing any duty, thus contributing to the necessity for new calls.

The forgery of enlistment papers was resorted to, and the preparation of papers for fictitious credits, of a character less criminal, though as injurious to the Army, by depriving it of recruits, was practiced with success in many places.

Committees of citizens, selected and instructed to "fill the quota" of their respective localities, conscientiously anxious, perhaps, to satisfy their fellow-citizens and relieve them from the draft, apparently lost sight of the wants of the service, and devoted themselves to securing credits to the exclusion of enlisting men. This is illustrated by the official report of the committee which was selected by the people of the city and county of New York to represent and act for them in this matter, and which continued in operation for two years. In discussing their proceedings under the call of July 18, 1864, for troops then needed to strengthen the armies in the field, they say (p. 231):

We obtained what few men we could by enlistments, but lent our best efforts to filling our quota by other means. * * * Prior to July the subject of crediting men enlisted into the Navy since the rebellion and up to February 24, 1864, had been broached in Congress. Your committee saw in this a means to fill the quota under the present call (July 18, 1864). Having been advised that Congress was likely in some way to authorize these credits, your committee determined to be forehanded, and, in anticipation of the passage of the law allowing such credits, they commenced the labor of accumulating the necessary evidence on which to base the claim for New York County, should such a law pass.

* * * * * * *

It was deemed important to keep this matter quiet until we were fully prepared to make our claim, backed up with the necessary documentary evidence, not only because we desired to prevent efforts on the part of other localities to rob us of our rights, but for the reason that we wished all doubtful points as to the construction of the law to be settled on the application of some locality other than New York, whose claim on this behalf could not be so large, but the principle of settlement in which case would of necessity equally apply to us. In view of the very unfair manner in which we believed we had been treated in an application for a revision of the enrollment, we feared that New York had little to expect of the Government officials in the way of aid in filling our quota, &c.

Again, the labors of certain parties to procure recruits for Hancock's corps are depreciated by this committee when compared with its method of filling quotas. The committee says:

As we were trying only to fill our quota, and they cared nothing for the quota, but only for the Second Army Corps, it is by no means singular that the county reaped little benefit from their operations.

It was thus that this committee put itself on record as having been engaged in filling quotas when the Army waited for recruits.

As New York City and County made frequent complaints to you of unfair treatment on the part of this office, I beg, in justice to this Bureau, to introduce two other extracts from the official report of this committee.

The committee claimed, under the call of July 18, 1864, over 26,000 credits, prepared as shown above, for naval enlistments said to have been made prior to February 24, 1864. Through the action of a commission appointed to investigate the matter, 19,477 credits were allowed and went in reduction of the number of men expected and needed from the county of New York. About 6,000 of the 26,000 naval credits claimed were assigned by the commission to Brooklyn. In commenting on this the committee says:

In all the injustice of which New York had to complain in the matter of the last call and the enrollment, in no respect has so great an outrage been committed upon us as was by this commission when * * * they allowed Brooklyn to step in and carry off 6,000 men (credits) "belonging to us."

This being the greatest cause New York had for complaint, it is submitted that the others must have been slight indeed. They probably arose from the action of the Bureau, correctly attributed to it by the committee in the following extract, made as a complaint, though in reality a compliment:

It did really seem as if the Provost-Marshal-General's department was determined that, with every change of law, they would establish the rule which would draw the largest number of men, &c.

Under the calls of July 18, 1864, and December 19, 1864, the true quotas of New York County, determined as the quotas of other places, were 42,152, viz:

Quota under call of July 18, 1864, 21,133. Of this number the county furnished by enlistments but	2,585
And by draft	843
Making a total of only	3,428

The balance being made up by naval credits reported by commission.

Quota under call of December 19, 1864, 21,019. On account of complaints made, the President reduced this to 15,762. Of this number the county furnished by enlistments	4,229
And by draft	790
Making a total of	5,019

A very large proportion of the enlistments were "bounty jumpers," of no value, but rather a positive injury to the service.

PART IV.

Colored men and their relation to the military service, as established by laws and orders during the late war, and their recruitment as soldiers.

At the commencement of the rebellion, April 15, 1861, the Army was composed exclusively of white troops. The regulations of the Army governing the recruiting service (par. 1299) provided that "any free white male person above the age of eighteen," &c., "might be enlisted." Negro slavery existed in fifteen States of the Union, and fugitive slaves escaping from one State to another were delivered up on claim of their owners.

The first legislation by Congress directly affecting colored persons was the act approved March 13, 1862.[a] It prohibited all officers or persons in the military or naval service of the United States from employing any of the forces under their respective commands for the purpose of returning fugitives from service or labor who escaped from any persons to whom such service or labor was claimed to be due, and provided that any officer found guilty by a court-martial of violating this article should be dismissed from the service.

This was followed by an act,[a] approved July 17, 1862, the twelfth section of which authorized the President to receive into the service of the United States, for the purpose of constructing intrenchments, or performing camp duty, or any other labor, or any military or naval service for which they were found competent, persons of African descent, and provided that such persons should be enrolled and organized, under such regulations, not inconsistent with the Constitution and laws, as the President might prescribe.

The thirteenth section of this act directs—

> That when any man or boy of African descent, who by the laws of any State shall owe service or labor to any person who during the present rebellion has levied war, or has borne arms against the United States, or adhered to their enemies by giving them aid and comfort, shall render any such service as is provided for in this act, he, his mother, and his wife and children, shall forever thereafter be free, any law, usage, or custom whatsoever to the contrary notwithstanding: *Provided*, That the mother, wife, and children of such man or boy of African descent shall not be made free by the operation of this act, except where such mother, wife, or children owe service or labor to some person who during the

[a] See Appendix, Doc. 35.

present rebellion has borne arms against the United States, or adhered to their enemies by giving them aid and comfort.

The fourteenth section provides that "the expenses incurred to carry this act into effect shall be paid out of the general appropriation for the Army and volunteers."

The fifteenth section directs that—

All persons who have been or who shall be hereafter enrolled in the service of the United States under this act shall receive the pay and rations now allowed by law to soldiers, according to their respective grades: *Provided*, That persons of African descent, who under this law shall be employed, shall receive ten dollars per month and one ration, three dollars of which monthly pay may be in clothing.

The amount of pay allowed to infantry soldiers (white) at the passage of this act was $13 per month, and an allowance in clothing of $3.50 per month, and one ration each.

The act entitled "An act to suppress insurrection, to punish treason and rebellion, to seize and confiscate the property of rebels, and for other purposes," approved July 17, 1862,[a] provides that whoever shall commit treason "shall suffer death" and all his slaves be "declared free."

Section 9 provides—

That all slaves of persons who shall hereafter be engaged in rebellion against the Government of the United States, or who shall in any way give aid or comfort thereto, escaping from such persons and taking refuge within the lines of the Army; and all slaves captured from such persons or deserted by them and coming under the control of the Government of the United States, and all slaves of such persons found on [or] being within any place occupied by rebel forces and afterward occupied by the forces of the United States shall be deemed captives of war, and shall be forever free of their servitude, and not again held as slaves.

Section 10 provides—

That no slave escaping into any State, Territory, or the District of Columbia, from any other State, shall be delivered up, or in any way impeded or hindered of his liberty, except for crime, or some offense against the laws, unless the person claiming said fugitive shall first make oath that the person to whom the labor or service of such fugitive is alleged to be due is his lawful owner, and has not borne arms against the United States in the present rebellion, nor in any way given aid and comfort thereto; and no person engaged in the military or naval service of the United States shall, under any pretense whatever, assume to decide on the validity of the claim of any person to the service or labor of any other person, or surrender up any such person to the claimant, on pain of being dismissed from the service.

Section 11 declares—

That the President of the United States is authorized to employ as many persons of African descent as he may deem necessary and proper for the suppression of this rebellion, and for this purpose he may organize and use them in such manner as he may judge best for the public welfare.

And by the latter section the authority of the President to receive into the service persons of African descent is extended, giving him authority to employ as many of this class of persons as he might deem necessary for the suppression of the rebellion.

The pay of this class of persons, as fixed by the twelfth section of the preceding act, was not changed.

Section 12 declares—

That the President of the United States is hereby authorized to make provision for the transportation, colonization, and settlement, in some tropical country beyond the limits of the United States, of such persons of the African race, made free by the provisions of this act, as may be willing to emigrate, having first obtained the consent of the government of said country to their protection and settlement within the same, with all the rights and privileges of freemen.

---

[a] See Appendix, Doc. 35.

Under the authority conferred by the two preceding acts of Congress the President, on the 22d day of July, issued the following order:

First. Ordered, "That military commanders within the States of Virginia, South Carolina, Georgia, Florida, Alabama, Mississippi, Louisiana, Texas, and Arkansas, in an orderly manner, seize and use any property, real or personal, which may be necessary or convenient for their several commands as supplies, or for other military purposes; and that while property may be destroyed for proper military objects, none shall be destroyed in wantonness or malice."

Second. "That military and naval commanders shall employ as laborers, within and from said States, so many persons of African descent as can be advantageously used for military and naval purposes, giving them reasonable wages for their labor."

Third. "That as to both property and persons of African descent, accounts shall be kept sufficiently accurate and in detail to show quantities and amounts, and from whom both property and such persons shall have come, as a basis upon which compensation can be made in proper cases; and the several departments of this government shall attend to and perform their appropriate parts toward the execution of these orders."

On the 22d day of September, 1862, the President issued a proclamation *a* announcing:

First. "That it was his purpose, upon the next meeting of Congress, to again recommend the adoption of a practical measure tendering pecuniary aid to the free acceptance or rejection of all slave States, so called, the people whereof may not then be in rebellion against the United States, and which States may then have voluntarily adopted, or thereafter may voluntarily adopt, immediate or gradual abolishment of slavery within their respective limits."

Second. "That the effort to colonize persons of African descent, with their consent, upon this continent or elsewhere, with the previously obtained consent of the governments existing there, should be continued."

Third. "That on the first day of January following all persons held as slaves within any State or designated part of a State, the people whereof shall then be in rebellion against the United States, should be then, thenceforward, and forever free; and the Executive government of the United States, including the military and naval authority thereof, will recognize and maintain the freedom of such persons, and will do no act or acts to repress such persons, or any of them, in any efforts they may make for their actual freedom."

Fourth. "That the Executive would, on the first day of January aforesaid, by proclamation designate the States and parts of States, if any, in which the people thereof, respectively, should then be in rebellion against the United States; and the fact that any State, or the people thereof, should on that day be, in good faith, represented in the Congress of the United States by members chosen thereto at elections wherein a majority of the qualified voters of such State should have participated, should, in the absence of strong countervailing testimony, be deemed conclusive evidence that such State and the people thereof were not then in rebellion against the United States."

On the 1st day of January, 1863, the immortal decree of emancipation *a* proclaimed freedom to the blacks of all the States declared in rebellion, with the exception of certain parishes in Louisiana.

---

a See Appendix, Doc. 36.

By an act approved March 3, 1863, it is provided as follows: *a*

That cooks shall be detailed, in turn, from the privates of each company of troops in the service of the United States, at the rate of one cook for each company numbering less than thirty men, and two cooks for each company numbering over thirty men, who shall serve ten days each.

That the President of the United States be, and he is hereby, authorized to cause to be enlisted, for each cook, two under-cooks of African descent, who shall receive for their full compensation ten dollars per month and one ration per day, three dollars of said monthly pay being in clothing.

On the 30th of July, 1863, the President ordered as follows:*

The act of February 24, 1864,*a* amendatory of the enrollment act, section 24, provided—

That all able-bodied male colored persons between the ages of twenty and forty-five years, resident in the United States, shall be enrolled according to the provisions of this act, and of the act to which this is an amendment, and form part of the national forces; and when a slave of a loyal master shall be drafted and mustered into the service of the United States, his master shall have a certificate thereof, and thereupon such slave shall be free; and the bounty of one hundred dollars, now payable by law for each drafted man, shall be paid to the person to whom such drafted person was owing service or labor at the time of his muster into the service of the United States. The Secretary of War shall appoint a commission in each of the slave States represented in Congress, charged to award each loyal person to whom a colored volunteer may owe service a just compensation, not exceeding three hundred dollars, for each such colored volunteer, payable out of the fund derived from commutations, and every such colored volunteer on being mustered into service shall be free. And in all cases where men of color have been heretofore enlisted, or have volunteered in the military service of the United States, all the provisions of this act, so far as the payment of bounty and compensation are provided, shall be equally applicable as to those who may be hereafter recruited. But men of color, drafted or enlisted, or who may volunteer into the military service, while they shall be credited on the quotas of the several States, or subdivisions of States, wherein they are respectively drafted, enlisted, or shall volunteer, shall not be assigned as State troops, but shall be mustered into regiments or companies as United States colored troops.

It will be observed that the able-bodied male colored persons were thenceforward to form part of the national forces. But it was provided, in the case of a slave being drafted, that the $100 bounty then allowed to drafted men should be paid to his master; and where a slave entered the service as a volunteer, instead of receiving the bounty which was allowed to other recruits, the master was entitled to receive a compensation from the Government, not to exceed $300. It was further provided that men of color drafted or enlisted should "be credited upon the quotas of the several States or subdivisions of States."

A fair construction of this statute authorizes the payment of $100 bounty to free colored men who might be drafted; and in lieu of bounty to the slave it gave him his freedom, while his master, if loyal, received a compensation for the loss of his services.

Up to this time and until the passage of the act entitled "An act making appropriations for the support of the Army for the year ending the thirtieth day of June, eighteen hundred and sixty-five, and for other purposes," approved June 15, 1864,*a* there was no law providing for the payment of bounty to colored volunteers, either free or slave, and the pay of colored troops still remained at $10 per month, as fixed by the act of July 17, 1862.

The act just cited provides—

That all persons of color who have been or may be mustered into the military service of the United States shall receive the same uniform, clothing, arms, equip-

a See Appendix, Doc. 35.

*Embodied in General Orders, No. 252, Adjutant-General's Office, July 31, 1863, Series II, Vol. VI, p. 163.

ments, camp equipage, rations, medical and hospital attendance, pay and emoluments, other than bounty, as other soldiers of the regular or volunteer forces of the United States of like arm of the service, from and after the first day of January, eighteen hundred and sixty-four; and that every person of color who shall hereafter be mustered into the service shall receive such sums in bounty as the President shall order in the different States and parts of the United States, not exceeding one hundred dollars.

This section placed colored troops on an equal footing with white troops in all respects touching pay and allowances, but withheld the bounty as hitherto, except in such amount as the President might order, not to exceed $100.

The third section provided—

That all persons enlisted and mustered into service as volunteers under the call, dated October seventeen, eighteen hundred and sixty-three, for three hundred thousand volunteers, who were at the time of enlistment actually enrolled and subject to draft in the State in which they volunteered, shall receive from the United States the same amount of bounty without regard to color.

This section was practically inoperative for the reason that but few colored persons were enrolled, drafted, or credited on the call of October 17, 1863. The law directing the enrollment of colored men was not passed until February 24, 1864, and the colored men raised by draft or voluntary enlistment prior to this date were credited to the call of February 1, 1864 (which was being filled when the law directing the enrollment and draft of colored men was passed), and to the subsequent calls.

The fourth section provided—

That all persons of color who were free on the nineteenth day of April, eighteen hundred and sixty-one, and who have been enlisted and mustered into the military service of the United States, shall, from the time of their enlistment, be entitled to receive the pay, bounty, and clothing allowed to such persons by the laws existing at the time of their enlistment. And the Attorney-General of the United States is hereby authorized to determine any question of law arising under this provision. And if the Attorney-General aforesaid shall determine that any of such enlisted persons are entitled to receive any pay, bounty, or clothing, in addition to what they have already received, the Secretary of War shall make all necessary regulations.

In conformity with this section the Secretary of War ordered as follows:*

An act approved July 4, 1864,[a] provided—

That the President of the United States may, at his discretion, at any time hereafter, call for any number of men as volunteers, for the respective terms of one, two, and three years, for military service; and any such volunteer, or, in case of draft, as hereinafter provided, any substitute, shall be credited to the town, township, ward of a city, precinct, or election district, or of a county not so subdivided, toward the quota of which he may have volunteered or engaged as a substitute; and every volunteer who is accepted and mustered into the service for a term of one year, unless sooner discharged, shall receive and be paid by the United States a bounty of one hundred dollars; and if for a term of two years, unless sooner discharged, a bounty of two hundred dollars; and if for a term of three years, unless sooner discharged, a bounty of three hundred dollars, one-third of which bounty shall be paid to the soldier at the time of his being mustered into the service, one-third at the expiration of one-half of his term of service, and one-third at the expiration of his term of service. And in case of his death while in service, the residue of his bounty unpaid shall be paid to his widow, if he shall have left a widow; if not, to his children; or if there be none, to his mother, if she be a widow.

---

a See Appendix, Doc. 35.

---

*See Circular No. 60, Adjutant-General's Office, August 1, 1864, Vol. IV, this series, p. 564.

This section authorized the payment of like bounty to all persons enlisting, omitting the distinction hitherto observed in regard to colored troops, and was evidently intended to allow the same amount to both classes, and bounties were paid accordingly.

Section 3 provides "That it shall be lawful for the Executive of any of the States to send recruiting agents into any of the States declared to be in rebellion, except the States of Arkansas, Tennessee, and Louisiana, to recruit volunteers under any call under the provisions of this act, who shall be credited to the State and to the respective subdivisions thereof, which may procure the enlistment," but was repealed by the act of March 3, 1865.*a*

Section 14 of an act*a* approved July 4, 1864, provided—

That the widows and children of colored soldiers who have been, or who may be hereafter, killed, or who have died or may hereafter die of wounds received in battle, or who have died or may hereafter die of disease contracted in the military service of the United States, and in the line of duty, shall be entitled to receive the pensions now provided by law, without other proof of marriage than that the parties had habitually recognized each other as man and wife, and lived together as such for a definite period next preceding the soldier's enlistment, not less than two years, to be shown by the affidavits of credible witnesses: *Provided, however*, That such widow and children are free persons: *Provided further*, That if such parties resided in any State in which their marriage may have been legally solemnized the usual evidence shall be required.

Section 5 of an act approved March 3, 1865,*a* provided—

That all persons of color who were enlisted and mustered into the military service of the United States in South Carolina, by and under the direction of Major-General Hunter and Brigadier-General Saxton, in pursuance of the authority from the Secretary of War, dated August twenty-fifth, eighteen hundred and sixty-two, "that the persons so received into service, and their officers, to be entitled to and receive the same pay and rations as are allowed by law to other volunteers in the service"—and in every case where it shall be made to appear to the satisfaction of the Secretary of War that any regiment of colored troops has been mustered into the service of the United States, under any assurance by the President or the Secretary of War, that the non-commissioned officers and privates of such regiment should be paid the same as other troops of the same arm of the service—shall, from the date of their enlistment, receive the same pay and allowances as are allowed by law to other volunteers in the military service; and the Secretary of War shall make all necessary regulations to cause payment to be made in accordance herewith.

Section 22 provided—

That the third section of the act entitled "An act [further] to regulate and provide for the enrolling and calling out the national forces, and for other purposes," approved July fourth, eighteen hundred and sixty-four, be, and the same is hereby, repealed.

The foregoing embraces the entire legislation and the most important Executive orders touching the relation of colored men to the military service.

The classes of colored persons who received bounty under the foregoing laws and the amounts respectively paid to them are shown by the following order of the Paymaster-General, viz:

PAYMASTER-GENERAL'S OFFICE,
Washington, D. C., May 26, 1865.

BOUNTIES TO COLORED TROOPS.

1. All persons of color who have been enlisted and mustered into the service of the United States, and are mustered on the rolls as "free on or before April 19, 1861," are entitled to bounty as follows, viz:

If enlisted prior to October 24, 1863, $100.

---

a See Appendix, Doc. 35.

If enlisted in an old organization after October 24, 1863, and prior to April 1, 1864, $300.

If enlisted in a new organization after December 24, 1863, and prior to April 1, 1864, $300.

If enlisted between April 1, 1864, and July 17, 1864, inclusive, $100.

2. All persons of color enlisted and mustered into service under the President's call for 300,000 volunteers, dated October 17, 1863, who were at the time of enlistment enrolled and subject to draft in the State where enlisted, are entitled to bounty as follows, viz:

Enlisted in any organization of colored troops between October 17 and October 24, 1863, $100.

Enlisted in an old organization after October 24, 1863, and prior to April 1, 1864, $300.

Enlisted in a new organization after December 24, 1863, and prior to April 1, 1864, $300.

Remark to be entered on the muster-roll: "Enrolled and subject to draft in the ——— enrollment district of the State of ——— at time of enlistment."

3. All enlistments of colored men after July 18, 1864, for one, two, or three years, entitle them to bounty of $100, $200, and $300, respectively.

4. Colored soldiers who have been, or hereafter shall be, discharged by reason of wounds received in battle, on skirmish or picket, or in action, or in the line of duty, and who are otherwise entitled under existing laws to bounty, are entitled to receive the same bounty as if they had served out the full term of enlistment.

5. All persons of color drafted under the act of March 3, 1863, and prior to September 5, 1864, and their substitutes, are entitled to a bounty of $100, provided they serve two full years. They have also the same pay and allowance as white soldiers.

6. Under section 2, act of June 15, 1864, no bounty was ordered by the President for persons of color who should enlist between that date and July 19, 1864, unless free April 19, 1861.

7. For colored persons, when discharged, the final papers should contain the same data for bounty as was required to elucidate their claims upon the muster-rolls. Paymasters, when they can consistently do so, should aid in conveying information on this point to all interested.

B. W. BRICE,
Paymaster-General.

The following brief outline of the recruitment of colored persons is taken mainly from the reports and records of the Bureau for Colored Troops, and is inserted here in connection with the foregoing recapitulation of the laws and orders on the subject.

The acceptance of colored men as soldiers in the service of the United States began in Louisiana by the muster in, on the 27th of September, 1862, of the First Louisiana Native Guards, subsequently designated Seventy-third Regiment U. S. Colored Troops.

Four other regiments were raised in that military department and mustered in prior to March 7, 1863, two of them before the 1st of January, 1863.

The efforts made in the early summer of 1862 to raise colored troops in South Carolina did not result in the muster of an organization until January 31, 1863, when the First South Carolina Volunteers, subsequently designated Thirty-third U. S. Colored Troops, was mustered into the service as soldiers. Three other regiments were mustered in in that department prior to July 1, 1863.

In April, 1863, a regiment was completed in Kansas, called the First Kansas Volunteers, subsequently designated Seventy-ninth U. S. Colored Troops. Another regiment then in process of organization was some time after completed.

Early in the spring of 1863 the organization of colored troops was commenced in the Mississippi Valley under the personal supervision of the Adjutant-General of the Army. His first regiment was mustered into service on the 1st of May, 1863, as the First Arkansas Volunteers of African Descent, afterward designated Forty-sixth

Regiment U. S. Colored Troops. Five other regiments raised in like manner were mustered in prior to June 30, 1863.

The Fifty-fourth and Fifty-fifth Regiments of Massachusetts Volunteers were colored troops. They were organized in Massachusetts, and were mustered into service between March 30 and June 22, 1863. They were organized, officered, &c., by the State authorities, like other regiments of volunteers, and so continued until mustered out.

The foregoing colored troops were raised prior to the commencement of the operations of the Bureau for Colored Troops, which was created by General Orders, No. 143,*a* dated May 22, 1863.

Under the immediate supervision of that Bureau, a regiment designated the First U. S. Colored Troops was mustered into service in the District of Columbia on the 30th of June, 1863, and simultaneously with this a regiment was mustered in in North Carolina.

At this period, June, 1863, the recruitment of colored troops was going on all over the country, and so continued until stopped by orders on April 29, 1865, in consequence of no more troops being required.

With the exception of the two Massachusetts regiments above mentioned, the military organizations composed of colored men were mustered directly into the service of the United States, and were organized and officered by officers acting under the authority of the United States, and not of any particular State.

Since March 27, 1865, all appointments of officers for these troops have been made exclusively by the War Department, and after an examination by a board of officers. Prior to that time the Adjutant-General of the Army, in the Mississippi Valley, made appointments, in the name of the Secretary of War, to the regiments which he organized; and department commanders made, subject to the approval of the President, provisional appointments to the regiments organized by them.

The recruitment of men of color by draft and substitution was exclusively under the control of this Bureau, but their recruitment as volunteers was mainly under the Bureau for Colored Troops, especially established for that purpose. To present together the entire results of these operations, which, however, were produced in the main by the action of the Bureau for Colored Troops, the following extract is made from the report of the chief of that Bureau:

On the 15th of July, 1865, the date on which the last organization of colored troops was mustered in, there were—

In the service of the United States 120 regiments of infantry, numbering in the aggregate	98,938
Twelve regiments of heavy artillery	15,662
Ten companies of light artillery	1,311
Seven regiments of cavalry	7,245
Grand aggregate	123,156

The foregoing is the largest number of colored troops in service at any one time during the war.

The entire number of troops commissioned and enlisted in this branch of the service during the war is 186,017.*b*

a See Appendix, Doc. 25, Art. 1.

b See Appendix, Doc. 8, for the opinions of surgeons of boards of enrollment as to the physical fitness of colored men for military service.

The States in which this force was recruited or drafted are as follows, viz:

State	Number	State	Number
Maine	104	Louisiana	24,052
New Hampshire	125	Arkansas	5,526
Vermont	120	Tennessee	20,133
Rhode Island	1,837	Kentucky	23,703
Massachusetts	3,966	Michigan	1,387
Connecticut	1,764	Ohio	5,092
New York	4,125	Indiana	1,537
New Jersey	1,185	Illinois	1,811
Pennsylvania	8,612	Missouri	8,344
Delaware	954	Minnesota	104
Maryland	8,718	Iowa	440
District of Columbia	3,269	Wisconsin	165
Virginia	5,723	Kansas	2,080
North Carolina	5,035	Texas	47
West Virginia	196	Colorado Territory	95
South Carolina	5,462	At large	733
Georgia	3,486	Not accounted for	5,083
Florida	1,044	Officers	7,122
Alabama	4,969		
Mississippi	17,869	Total *	186,017

Recruiting of men in States in rebellion to be credited to loyal States.

(Under section 3 of the act approved July 4, 1864.)

The law authorizing recruiting in the rebel States was published on the 6th of July, 1864; on the 9th regulations to carry it into effect were issued. Every facility which the War Department could control was afforded to make the law effective for raising troops. The results were as follows:

Total number of recruiting agents appointed by Governors of loyal States to recruit in rebel States	1,045
Total number of recruits credited through these agents	5,052

These recruits are embraced in the preceding enumeration of volunteers mustered into service. They were credited to the States by whose agents they were obtained.

The authority granted under this act was repealed by section 22, act of March 3, 1865, and on the 8th of March *a* a circular was issued from this office announcing the fact for the information and guidance of all concerned.

No material advantage to the service resulted from this undertaking. All, or nearly all, of the recruits to be had in the rebel States were being obtained through the proper military officers and agents of the War Department. Without increasing the number of men enlisted, the law enabled States in the North to lay claim to credits for the men enlisted in the South, and thus reduce their quota for draft. To obtain these credits local bounties were lavishly provided. They were unnecessary, and did not have the effect of increasing the number of recruits obtained, but in many instances enriched bounty brokers and corrupted military officers.

a See Appendix, Doc. 26, Art. 2.

*But see Foster's report (October 20, 1865), giving an aggregate of 186,097, p. 138.

PART V.

Enlistments for the naval service and Marine Corps.

On the 3d of May, 1861, the President issued a call, in which he directed the enlistment of 18,000 seamen.

Section 8 of the act approved July 4, 1864, required that all persons in the naval service of the United States who entered said service during the present rebellion, and who were not credited to the quota of any town, district, ward, or State, by reason of their being in said service and not enrolled prior to February 24, 1864, should be enrolled and credited to the quota of the town, ward, district, or State in which they respectively resided, upon satisfactory proof of their residence made to the Secretary of State.

In carrying into effect this law of Congress the Secretary of War decided that men enlisted in the Navy should be credited to the State in which they enlisted, unless it was proved that they properly belonged elsewhere; and for the purpose of determining what credits the several States were entitled to, under the law given above, the Secretary of War appointed commissioners, consisting of the Governor of the State and an officer of the Army. The aggregate of credits allowed by the commissioners for enlistments in the Navy from April 15, 1861, to February 24, 1864, was 67,334. The distribution among the different States appears in a table presented on the following page.

Section 9 of the act approved February 24, 1864, and section 3 of the act approved July 1, 1864, required that credits should be given for enlistments into the Naval service or Marine Corps, in the same manner as for enlistments in the Army.

Under these acts credits were allowed as follows, viz:

For men enlisted into the naval service between February 24, 1864, and June 30, 1865	35,073
For men enlisted into the Marine Corps between February 24, 1864, and June 30, 1865	2,536
Total	37,609

On the 24th of February, 1864, a joint resolution was passed by Congress, entitled "A resolution relative to the transfer of persons in the military service to the naval service." This resolution provided—

First. "That the Provost-Marshal-General be, and he is hereby, directed to enlist such persons as may desire to enter the naval service of the United States," &c.; and

Second. "That the President of the United States may direct the transfer of persons in the military service to the naval service," &c.

In accordance with the first branch of this resolution, a circular was issued from this office directing provost-marshals, in addition to their other duties, to recruit for the naval service and Marine Corps, and establishing rules for this purpose.

This resolution was repealed by act approved June 3, 1864, and instructions were issued accordingly.

From this date enlistments were made and credits given as required by section 9 of the act approved February 24, 1864, and section 3 of the act approved July 1, 1864, nothing further being required of this Bureau than to credit on the quotas assigned for draft the enlistments reported by the Navy Department as having been made by it for that branch of the service. The fact that the recruitment for the two branches of the service was conducted according to entirely different rules and forms, and that in the matter of credits to be allowed on the draft for naval enlistments there was a divided responsibility between the War and Navy Departments, contributed materially to the frauds and abuses in filling quotas from which the service suffered, especially during the last year of the war.

Number of naval enlistments allowed by commissioners under section 8, act approved July 4, 1864.

Maine	3,097	Delaware	79
New Hampshire	371	Maryland	2,217
Vermont	103	West Virginia	------
Massachusetts	16,834	District of Columbia	558
Rhode Island	------	Kentucky	5
Connecticut	1,804	Ohio	1,076
New York (southern division)	26,090	Indiana	71
New York (northern division)	737	Illinois	1,171
New York (western division)	1,600	Missouri	134
New Jersey	1,858		
Pennsylvania (eastern division)	7,613	Total *	67,334
Pennsylvania (western division)	1,916		

PART VI.

Casualties in the military forces.†

As this Bureau was required to supply recruits to fill the gaps caused by casualties in the Army, and to increase from time to time its numerical strength, I have deemed it proper to ascertain the causes of loss to which the Army has been subjected, and the extent to which each cause has prevailed.

The casualties which occurred to the military forces of the Nation from the outbreak to the suppression of the rebellion have therefore

*For total number of sailors and marines furnished during the war, see Vol. IV, this series, p. 1270.

†Since the date of this report the acquisition of muster-rolls, muster-cut rolls, returns, and other official papers affording evidence of death, discharge, and desertion not accessible to the Provost-Marshal-General, together with amendments of personal records, have materially changed the statements and inferences herein given. Up to the present time no compilation has been made by the War Department which enables it to publish an accurate statement of these casualties. The latest compilation of the number of deaths, made in 1885, gives the following result, viz:

Regular Army.

	Officers.	Men.	Total.
Killed in action	85	1,262	1,347
Of wounds received in action	59	877	936
Of disease	107	2,985	3,092
Accidental (except drowned)	1	103	104
Drowned	4	89	93
Murdered	1	15	16
Killed after capture	......	1	1
Suicide	2	25	27
Executed by U. S. military authorities	......	6	6
Sunstroke	......	7	7
Other known causes	1	62	63
Causes not stated	......	106	106
Aggregate	260	5,538	5,798

been compiled from the official muster-rolls and returns into Tables I, II, and III, herewith presented.*a*

It is to be especially observed that these tables have been drawn entirely from a careful examination of the regular monthly returns and muster and pay rolls of the Army. The rolls, made up by the company commanders on blanks furnished by the Adjutant-General's Office, and according to directions printed on the blanks themselves, are the forms on which the members of the companies are paid, the record on which the military history of each man is required to be stated, and one of the principal authorities to which the War Department refers for official information concerning the final disposition of every soldier. As the penalties against false musters and returns are exceedingly severe, applying not only to the company commander, but also to the mustering officer, and as all means within the limits of Army discipline are used by superior officers to insure correct knowledge of the condition of the troops under their command, the muster and pay rolls are usually a trustworthy, as they are an official, source of information concerning Army statistics.

It is, however, certain that all the casualties which have occurred do not appear on the rolls, just as it is equally certain that they are not all to be found in any one set of records. The accompanying statistics are presented as derived from this source alone, and as containing only such percentage of error as may have crept into a system of record which was intended to be perfect, and which was unquestionably brought to a high standard at least as early in the war as any other.

One of the advantages which may be fairly expected from the publication of these tables is, that attention will thereby be drawn to such imperfections as exist in the rolls, and that this will lead to their correction by a comparison with other sources of official information.

Volunteer Army.

	Officers.	Men.	Total.
Killed in action	4,057	61,654	65,711
Of wounds received in action	2,164	39,912	42,076
Of disease	2,688	218,806	221,494
Accidental (except drowned)	141	3,869	4,010
Drowned	102	4,749	4,851
Murdered	36	468	504
Killed after capture	14	89	103
Suicide	24	340	364
Executed by U. S. military authorities		261	261
Executed by enemy	4	60	64
Sunstroke	5	301	306
Other known causes	61	1,910	1,971
Causes not stated	28	11,987	12,015
Aggregate	9,324	344,406	353,730
Grand aggregate regulars and volunteers	9,584	349,944	359,528

The foregoing figures, however, are only approximative and should not be accepted as conclusive. Revision of the death records is still in progress. In addition to the officers of the Regular Army reported on page 664, there were 27 killed in action, 14 died of wounds received in action, 8 died of disease, and 1 drowned, a total of 50, who, at the time of death, held commissions in the Volunteer Army, with which they are counted. These added to the Regular Army would make a total loss therein of 310 officers and 5,538 men.

a See pages 78–83 [671] of Report.

The tables exhibit the number of casualties, and also the ratio per thousand to the total of men in service, under the following heads: 1. States and groups of States. 2. Regulars, volunteers, and colored troops. 3. Armies and arms of service. The ratios have been calculated by proportioning the total casualties to the total number of men credited, and each item of casualty to the corresponding figure of total credit.

Highly interesting and valuable facts are deducible from these tables. Final deductions cannot, however, be drawn until additional and collateral information is obtained. For example, the comparative zeal and efficiency of the troops of the different arms and States cannot be inferred from the ratio of casualties in action, without considering in addition the more or less perilous character of the service demanded of each of them. Again, at respective periods, the proportion of deaths from disease should be considered in connection with the relative salubrity of the regions in which the troops from different sections of the country served, the exact nature of the service, whether field, camp, or garrison, and their supply, equipment, and discipline. Certain conclusions, however, can already be correctly drawn from this statistical exhibit, and these it will not be premature to state.

*Comparative mortality of officers and enlisted men.**

From a careful compilation of the rolls, and without including deaths after muster out, which resulted from military service previously rendered, it appears that 280,739 men and officers have lost their lives in the Army. Of this number 5,221 commissioned officers and 90,886 enlisted men have been killed in action or died of wounds, while 2,321 commissioned officers and 182,329 enlisted men have died of disease or, in some few cases, from accident.

It will be observed that of killed in battle and died of wounds, there is one officer to every eighteen enlisted men, showing somewhat greater mortality on the part of the officers, who, supposing the organizations to be full, constitute about a twenty-fifth part of the forces.

On the other hand, only one officer to ninety men has died of disease. This remarkable disproportion, so greatly to the advantage of the commissioned class, is owing to several causes. Officers are better sheltered than men; and their food is generally better in quality and more varied in kind, so that they suffer less from diseases of the digestive organs. They are not so much crowded together in tents and quarters, and are therefore less subject to contagious and epidemic maladies. They have superior advantages in regard to personal cleanliness. As prisoners of war, too, they were generally treated more leniently, and so furnished fewer names to the mortality lists of Andersonville, Salisbury, and other similar dens of death. Another favoring circumstance, and by no means the least potential, was the superior morale, the hopefulness and elasticity of spirit, which is given to a man by investing him with a commission and its accompanying authority, responsibility, and chances of advancement.

It is worthy of note that in the colored troops the disproportion between commissioned officers and enlisted men under these heads is still more remarkable. In killed or died of wounds the officers lost one in about forty-two, while the men lost but about one in sixty-six. But under the head of deaths by disease the officers show a loss of only one in seventy-seven, while that of the men rises to the enor-

---

* But see foot-note (†), pp. 664, 665.

mous proportion of nearly one in seven, which is by far the highest mortality from this cause exhibited in the records of the Army. The general proportion of deaths from disease among white troops is less than one in seventeen.

*Deaths in action and from wounds.**

The proportion per thousand which each loyal State and group of States furnished to the item of mortality appears in the following table:

Maine	44.37	Michigan	44.82
New Hampshire	47.27	Wisconsin	42.01
Vermont	58.22	Minnesota	25.33
Massachusetts	47.76	Iowa	45.44
Rhode Island	22.34	Kansas	61.01
Connecticut	35.48	California	12.34
New York	35.68	West Virginia	37.90
New Jersey	25.21	Kentucky	25.10
Pennsylvania	31.75	Missouri	21.74
Delaware	25.63	New England States	44.76
Maryland	17.04	Middle States	31.79
District of Columbia	3.62	Loyal States (general ratio)	35.10
Ohio	36.55	Border States	25.32
Indiana	30.01	Western States	36.81
Illinois	34.80	Colored troops	16.11

It is observable that in general the battle mortality ranges highest in the northern tier of States, whether Eastern or Western. The high ratio of New England under this head, 44.76, is correlative with the ratios of Iowa, 45.44, of Michigan, 44.82, and of Wisconsin, 42.01. Even New York, notwithstanding the enormous number of bounty jumpers who swelled its credit without going to increase its field mortality, exhibits the proportion of 35.68 killed or died of wounds, which is slightly above the general ratio of the loyal States. On the other hand, the ratio of the Border States is but 25.32, which is 9.78 below the general ratio and 19.44 below that of New England; and as a rule the ratio of the southern tier of loyal States is either below the general ratio or not far removed from it.

As an explanation of the superior battle mortality of the extreme northern section of the country I suggest the fact that, this region being far removed from the seat of war, it was not necessary for any portion of the troops raised in it to remain at home on garrison duty, and they were therefore kept almost constantly at the front. Hence also, at least in part, the high ratio of this section under other heads of casualty resulting in an especial manner from field service, such as deaths by disease and discharges for disability.

A remarkable exception to the rule above noted is Kansas, which was a frontier State during nearly the whole contest, and which, nevertheless, shows the highest battle mortality of the table. But the population of Kansas is a peculiarly pugnacious one, rendered such by its origin and history. The same singularly martial disposition which induced above half the able-bodied men of the State to enter the Army without bounty, may be supposed to have increased their exposure to the casualties of battle after they were in the service.

*Deaths by disease.**

The variations of figures to be considered in connection with this subject resulted in part from the varied nature of the service required

* But see foot-note (†), pp. 664, 665.

of troops drawn from different localities. For instance, an undue proportion of New England troops was used in the unhealthy Departments of the South and Gulf; and to this circumstance we may attribute in a measure the fact that 70.45 per thousand of the men credited to the Eastern States died of disease. The men of the West were poured into the feverish valleys of the Mississippi and its southern tributaries; and this aided, no doubt, to swell their mortality by disease to the proportion of 71.55 per thousand. The Border State contingents, serving mainly in the same localities, lost from this cause 66.76 per thousand. All the above ratios are higher than the general one of the loyal States, which is but 59.22. On the other hand, the Middle States, whose men fought to a large extent in the Army of the Potomac, suffered under this head to the amount of only 37.88 per thousand, which is 33.67 below the ratio of the Western States and 21.34 below the general ratio. Virginia was a healthier field of service than the bottoms of the Tennessee or the lowlands of Louisiana and South Carolina; and it seems certain, moreover, that the Army of the Potomac was the best provided of all our large armies.

Again, it is to be noted that those States which show large mortality on the battle-field likewise show large mortality by disease. Generally, a battle is but the culmination of preceding physical exertions and hardships, such as severe marching, want of rest, exposure, hunger, &c., all of which are causes and conditions of sickness. Moreover, where there are many deaths in battle, there must be a proportionate number of wounded; and men enfeebled by gunshot injuries naturally sink all the easier under subsequent maladies and hardships.

*Discharges for disability.**

This branch of the subject is in a measure correlative with the inferences under the foregoing heads. Wherever the table shows a large ratio of deaths by disease and deaths by battle it usually exhibits a similar proportion of discharges for disability. In New England it is 97.07 per thousand; in the Western States, 91.50: in the Border States, 65.99; in the Middle States, only 58.53.

*Desertions.**

It appears beyond dispute that the crime of desertion is especially characteristic of troops from large cities and of the districts which they supply with recruits. The ratio per thousand of desertions to credits throughout the loyal States is 62.51. In the State of New York it rises to 89.06, and in the small States near New York City it is still higher. In New Jersey it is 107.00; in Connecticut, 117.23; in New Hampshire, 112.22. Yet the general ratio of New England is but 74.24, the ratio of Massachusetts being 66.68, that of Vermont 51.75, and that of Maine 43.90. In the West, where large cities are rare, the average ratio sinks to 45.51.

It is probable that a more minute examination of the statistics of the Army than has yet been made would reveal the fact that desertion is a crime of foreign rather than native birth, and that but a small proportion of the men who forsook their colors were Americans. It is a notorious circumstance that the great mass of the professional bounty jumpers were Europeans. In general, the manufacturing

*But see foot-note (†), p. 664.

States, as, for instance, Massachusetts, Connecticut, Rhode Island, New York, and New Jersey, rank high in the column of desertion; and this result is to be attributed not only to the fact that such States are dotted with towns and cities, but to the secondary fact that these towns and cities are crowded with foreigners. The respectable and industrious part of this population did, indeed, produce a mass of faithful troops; but with these were mixed a vast number of adventurers, unworthy of any country, who had no affection for the Republic, and who only enlisted for money.

In general, those States which gave the highest local bounties are marked by the largest proportion of deserters. The bounty was meant to be an inducement to enlistment; it became, in fact, an inducement to desertion and fraudulent re-enlistment.

It is a singular and at first sight a puzzling fact that two extreme Western States, Kansas and California, are distinguished, respectively, by the high ratios in desertion of 117.54 and 101.86. But it must be remembered that more than half the male population of Kansas entered the service, and that consequently its contingent contained an unusually large percentage of men whose presence was necessary to the subsistence and protection of their families. In further explanation of this fact something may be attributed to a lax state of discipline natural in border regiments serving for the most part in a somewhat irregular defense of their own frontiers. As for California, it is to be observed that a portion of the contingent of that State consisted of men levied in the large cities of the East or of adventurers from all quarters of the globe collected in the cosmopolitan thoroughfares of San Francisco.

*Casualties of colored troops.**

In the casualties among the colored troops the most striking circumstance is the enormous proportion of deaths by disease. The ratio is no less than 141.39 per thousand, while the highest ratio on the volunteer list is 114.02 (Iowa), and the general volunteer ratio is 59.22. This disparity is the more remarkable because the colored troops were not so severely exposed during the war to the hardships of field service proper, as is evident from the fact that their battle mortality is but 16.11 per thousand, while that of the volunteers is 35.10. The ratio of deaths by disease among the colored troops compares still more unfavorably with that of the regulars, which is but 42.27 per thousand. It seems to indicate that the negro, in the condition in which the war found him, was less able than the white to endure the exposures and annoyances of military service. It may be assumed that where one man dies of disease at least five others are seriously sick, so that a large proportion of the colored troops must have been constantly upon the sick-list. The cause of this difference of stamina in the two races is worthy of more space than can here be given to it. It is merely suggested that it is moral rather than physical; that the greater susceptibility of the colored man to disease arose from lack of heart, hope, and mental activity, and that a higher moral and intellectual culture would diminish the defect. This view is supported by the opinions of surgeons of boards of enrollment on the abstract question of the physical fitness of the colored men examined by them. (See Appendix, Doc. No. 8.)

---

* But see foot-note (†), pp. 664, 665.

It is singular at first sight that in discharges for disability the ratio of the colored troops is less than half that of the volunteers, the former being 37.92 per thousand and the latter 75.99. A smaller proportion of the negroes than of the whites were wounded; but this fact alone will not, it is believed, explain the whole difference. It will prove, probably, that the colored soldiers rarely applied for discharge on the ground of disability, and, secondly, that their diseases were usually of an acute and mortal rather than of a chronic and merely enfeebling nature.

In desertion the loss is 67.00 per thousand, which is slightly above the general volunteer ratio of 62.51.

*Casualties of Regular Army.**

The most fruitful source of casualties in the Regular Army is desertion; it reaches the high ratio of 244.25 per thousand, while in the volunteers it is but 62.51. The inference is irresistible that the men who enlisted in the regular service were far inferior in character to the troops furnished by the States; and it will probably be found on examination that they were more commonly levied in the large cities and embrace a far larger proportion of foreigners. The regular service did not secure that noble class of native-born soldiers which local pride and State patriotism poured into the volunteer organizations.

In discharges for disability the regulars and volunteers do not greatly vary, the former showing a loss of 75.99 per thousand, and the latter 78.81. The slight difference here is fully accounted for by the fact that the battle mortality of the volunteers (35.10) is somewhat higher than that of the regulars (30.55).

Under the head of deaths by disease the influence of superior discipline in securing cleanliness and other conditions of health is apparent. The loss of the regulars is only 42.27, while that of the volunteers is 59.22.

In honorable discharges both regulars and colored troops contrast advantageously with the volunteers. Here the regulars lose 17.88 per thousand, the colored troops 15.08, and the volunteers 67.24. Honorable discharge indicates influence of friends, of members of Congress, &c., exerted to obtain the release of a man from service who is physically able to remain in it.

Explanation of section 3, Table III.

The proportional analysis of the table of casualties by services and arms of service, marked section 3, shows the ratios which each service—regular, volunteer, and colored troops—and each arm of service—cavalry, artillery, and infantry—furnished to each thousand of casualties, and also to each thousand of every species of casualty. In examining this table, each column must be considered by itself, inasmuch as each is based on a different element of the total of casualties. For instance, under the head of "killed or died of wounds," the divisor used is the total "killed and died of wounds" of the entire Army, while under the head of "died of disease" the divisor used is the total "died of disease" of the entire Army.

Thus the first column simply exhibits the fact that of every thousand men killed in battle and died of wounds 21 were regulars, 948 (nearly) were volunteers, and 31 were colored; also the fact that of

*But see foot-note (†), pp. 664, 665.

the same thousand 123 (nearly) were cavalry, 32 were artillery, and 845 (nearly) were infantry.

The proportions which the cavalry, artillery, and infantry of the three services separately furnished to this same battle mortality of one thousand are also exhibited.

The ratios, comparing the three services—regulars, volunteers, and colored troops—with each other, are not only interesting, but become important when viewed in connection with the fact that the ratios per thousand of men furnished to the Army by the three services were: Regulars, 25.29; volunteers, 904.13; colored troops, 70.58. Thus it appears that to every thousand of men killed in battle or died of wounds, the volunteers contributed forty-three more than their proportionate number, the regulars four less, and the colored troops thirty-nine less.

It should be stated, however, that the proportion of men furnished is based partly, so far as the regular and volunteer services are concerned, on estimates, it being impossible as yet to give the numbers with perfect accuracy.

In this connection I take occasion to repeat that none of these tables and none of the inferences derived from them are advanced as absolutely exhaustive or incontrovertible, and that I simply offer them for consideration as being derived from the most complete data yet compiled on the subject, and as in the main correct. I am confident that they will be found of great value when they shall be used as comparative data in constructing and correcting other similar tables which may be prepared by other bureaus.

TABLE I.

*Statement of casualties in the volunteer and regular armies of the United States, and the colored troops, divided by States and independent organizations, from the commencement of the rebellion up to August 1, 1865.**

TABLE II.

*Recapitulation of casualties in the regular and volunteer armies and colored troops.**

TABLE III.

SECTION 1.—*Proportional analysis of the table of casualties by States; ratio, 1,000.**

SECTION 2.—*Proportional analysis of table of casualties.**

SECTION 3.—*Proportional analysis of table of casualties by armies and arms of service.**

PART VII.

Bounty.

Prior to March 3, 1863, *a* the Government was dependent upon voluntary enlistments for the recruitment of its armies. It was soon judged necessary by Congress to stimulate recruiting by offering to recruits inducements intended to compare favorably with the price of ordinary labor and at the same time provide means for the support of the family

a See Appendix, Doc. 35.

* These tables (here omitted) are published in House Executive Document No. 1, Thirty-ninth Congress, first session, Vol. IV, pp. 78-83. See also foot-note (†), pp. 664, 665.

or others dependent on the labor of the recruit. With this object bounties were allowed from time to time by the United States as follows: *a*

From commencement of war to July 18, 1864, by the act of July 22, 1861, a bounty of $100 was allowed to all volunteers who served a period of two years or during the war, $25 of which was paid upon muster in under the act of June 21, 1862, and the remainder at expiration of service.

From June 25, 1863, to April 1, 1864, in accordance with General Orders, No. 191, of June 25, and No. 305, of September 11, 1863, a bounty of $400 was paid to all veterans enlisting and re-enlisting for three years or the war, in installments, as follows:

Upon being mustered into service	$25
At the first regular pay-day, or two months after muster in	50
At the first regular pay-day after six months' service	50
At the first regular pay-day after the end of the first year's service	50
At the first regular pay-day after eighteen months' service	50
At the first regular pay-day after two years' service	50
At the first regular pay-day after two and a half years' service	50
At the expiration of three years' service, if honorably discharged	75

General Orders, No. 324, of September 28, 1863, increased the payment on muster in to $60, and reduced the last payment to $40.

From October 24, 1863, to April 1, 1864, in accordance with circular of October 24, 1863, from this office, a bounty of $300 was paid to all new recruits enlisting for three years in old organizations, in installments, as follows:

Upon being mustered into service	$60
At first regular pay-day, or two months after muster in	40
At first regular pay-day after six months' service	40
At first regular pay-day after the end of the first year's service	40
At first regular pay-day after eighteen months' service	40
At first regular pay-day after two years' service	40
At the expiration of three years' service, if honorably discharged	40

From December 24, 1863, to April 1, 1864, in accordance with telegram from the Adjutant-General's Office, dated December 24, 1863, a bounty of $300 was paid to new recruits enlisting for three years in any three-years' organization in service or in process of completion. Authorized by the acts of January 13 and March 3, 1864.

This bounty was paid in installments, in the same manner as prescribed in circular of October 24, 1863, from this office, for the payment of bounty to new recruits enlisting in old organizations.

From July 19, 1864, to end of war, authorized by the act of July 4, 1864, bounty was paid as follows:

To recruits enlisting for one year	$100
To recruits enlisting for two years	200
To recruits enlisting for three years	300

This bounty was paid in installments, as follows:

One-third of the bounty at the time of muster in, one-third at the expiration of one-half of term of service, and the remaining one-third at the expiration of term of service.

From November 28, 1864, to the end of the war, in accordance with General Orders, No. 287, of November 28, 1864, a special bounty of $300 from the draft and substitute fund was paid to men enlisting in the First Army Corps upon being mustered into service.

This bounty was in addition to that authorized by the act of July 4, 1864.

---

a See Doc. 6, table of bounties.

In addition to the foregoing, the following bounties were authorized, but were only paid in exceptional cases:

The act of July 17, 1862, authorized the payment of $25 bounty to men enlisting for nine months under that act upon muster in. The same act authorized the payment of $50 to men enlisting for twelve months under that act, one-half to be paid the recruit upon joining his regiment, and the other half at the expiration of service.

The act of March 3, 1863, authorized the payment of a bounty of $50, one-half to be paid upon re-enlistment, and the balance at the expiration of the term of service, to such of the volunteers and militia then in the service of the United States as should re-enlist for one year.

Under the operation of the enrollment law, localities which had recruited the least number had, in addition to their proportion of future quotas, to make good their former deficiencies, and it became necessary for them to adopt some plan that would stimulate recruiting to that extent, or submit to the enforcement of the draft.

The law[a] regulating Government bounty provided "that every volunteer accepted and mustered into the service for a term of one year, unless sooner discharged," should "receive and be paid by the United States a bounty of $100; and if for a term of two years, unless sooner discharged, a bounty of $200; and if for a term of three years, unless sooner discharged, a bounty of $300; one-third of which bounty" was to be "paid to the soldier at the time of his being mustered into the service, one-third at the expiration of one-half of his term of service, and one-third at the expiration of his term of service. And in case of his death while in service, the residue of his bounty unpaid" was to be "paid to his widow, if he shall have left a widow; if not, to his children; or if there be none, to his mother, if she be a widow."

A recruit enlisting for one year receives the one-third of $100 on being mustered in, another third in six months, and the remainder at the expiration of his term of service.

If we compare this with the exorbitant bounties paid in advance by local authorities as hereafter explained, its comparative insignificance will readily demonstrate how little the Government bounty effected in raising volunteers.

It should be remarked that while the Government always paid bounty by installments, the local authorities almost uniformly paid in advance, the tendency of the former system being to obtain men and keep them, of the latter, mainly to obtain men to fill the quotas. Experience had taught that men would more readily enlist for a moderate bounty paid in advance than for a much greater one payable in installments.

Under the pressure of the draft the local authorities did not stop to consider the encouragement large cash bounties offered to desertion. They saw that bounty paid in hand would secure recruits, and they relied upon the Government to arrest deserters, forgetting that for the sake of exorbitant bounty one man might enlist and desert a dozen different times, or as often as opportunity occurred, and the more money he received the greater the facility for desertion. If, on the other hand, the inducement to desert was removed by paying the bounty in installments, the inducement to enlist was also diminished, because, to be attractive, bounty must be paid in advance; but if paid in advance, then the objections above stated will attach.

---

[a] See Appendix, Doc. 35.

This inaugurated the local bounty system. The localities mentioned began with offering a moderate amount, which proved sufficient at first to attract the attention of recruits, who felt themselves at liberty to select their place of enlistment. With the development of this system this amount was rapidly increased, owing to the fact that the several localities became competitors, and that success depended upon the amount offered. The amount was the more readily increased in consequence of the general impression that every call was the last. Persons proposing to enter the service would seek the largest bounty, and the locality that paid the highest price secured the most recruits. This increase continued until, at the end of the war, in some localities, the bounty, Government, State, and local, had reached $1,500 per man. How much it would have increased if additional troops had been called for it is difficult to say, but enough was developed to demonstrate the ruinous effects of the system upon the country and its resources.

After conscription became necessary, the quota of each district was based upon its enrollment. The enrolled men constituted the material with which its quota was to be filled. Any influence calculated to raise recruits in one district for the benefit of another, that is, to attract them from the one to the other, was unjust to the Government and to the district from which the men were taken. Where District No. 1, for instance, could induce the men of District No. 2 to enlist to its own credit, it to that extent deprived District No. 2 of the means of filling the quota for which it was liable, and as No. 1 could not be required to furnish more than its quota, the Government lost all that No. 2 was unable to furnish.

In many of the districts exorbitant bounties were paid, while neighboring districts were unable to pay, perhaps, one-half as much, and the enrolled men of the latter were induced to enlist to the credit of the former, which, by this means, would escape the draft. The latter, with no material left with which to fill its quota, except that which the country could least afford to spare—the actual producers—men fixed to the soil—was compelled to abide the issue of the draft.

This injustice became so flagrant that the attention of Congress was directed to the subject, and an effort was made to prevent the evil by a law requiring all volunteers to be credited to their places of actual residence.

The attempt to carry out this provision was only partially successful. Where recruits or substitutes were presented as rapidly as the interest of the service required them, it was difficult to prove that they were not residents of the locality to which they claimed to belong and desired to be credited. If collateral proof was required to support their claim, it was readily afforded by the adroit management of recruiting agents or substitute brokers. Besides, men who were induced to enlist for the sake of bounty were generally those who sacrificed but little in changing their actual residence a day or two previous to enlistment, thus defeating, by a literal compliance, the spirit of the law.

Under these circumstances the business of recruiting assumed a mercenary character.

The enormous profits which the system yielded to those engaged in it soon developed a class of persons known as "substitute brokers," who sprang up in various towns and cities, and who soon, to a great extent, monopolized the business of presenting volunteers and substitutes.

The object of these parties being to enrich themselves, it mattered little to them whether the men they furnished were fit for service, already deserters from the Army, or persons known as professional "bounty jumpers"—that is, men who made enlisting and deserting a vocation. Again, the anxiety of the citizens to have their respective quotas promptly filled induced submission to the evil, or at least for the time being prevented proper effort for its detection and prevention. By this system profligate and corrupt men amassed fortunes from the money raised for the purpose of paying local bounties to soldiers, and thus diverted it to the benefit of those who were least of all entitled to receive it. While enriching themselves they, on the one hand, appropriated the money which heavy taxation had produced, and on the other they furnished, in many instances, men whose only object was to obtain a Government and local bounty, and then desert or seek to be discharged. It is scarcely necessary to allude to the effect upon a regiment when the places of even a few of its slain veterans were filled with such material. Veterans who had enlisted early in the rebellion, without expectation of bounty, had good cause to murmur when late in the war unworthy recruits came among them rich with bounty for one year's enlistment.

After the call of December 19, 1864, General L. C. Baker, then special agent of the War Department, was at my request ordered to investigate, under my direction, frauds in the recruiting service. These abuses could not be thoroughly probed if his operations were limited to that branch of business pertaining to my Bureau (draft and volunteer recruitment), and his operations, therefore, reached the naval recruiting service, which was controlled by the Navy Department, and the recruiting service of the Regular Army, which was controlled by the Adjutant-General. The character and extent of the frauds and abuses in each of these branches of the general recruiting service appear, so far as they were developed by this investigation, in General Baker's official report. General Baker is entitled to special credit for the zeal and ability with which he conducted the investigation.

A plan of recruitment, based upon the bounty system, will necessarily be more expensive than any other, and, as a rule, produce soldiers of an inferior class; and although bounty is unquestionably calculated to stimulate recruiting, it does not always accomplish that object at the proper time. For when it is visible, as it was during the late war, that in the anxiety to obtain recruits the bounties offered constantly increased, the men who intend to enlist at one time or another are induced to hold back, with the hope, at a later day, of receiving a higher compensation and having to serve for a shorter period.

In time of peace a sufficient number of recruits to meet the requirements of the service can usually be procured without the aid of bounty, and in time of war the country can least afford the cost, besides needing the service of better men than those who enter the Army simply for mercenary motives.

I beg leave to submit that for the purpose of maintaining or increasing the Army the law of Congress, as embodied in the act known as the enrollment act and its amendments, with the single additional amendment hereinbefore mentioned, is ample in itself for any emergency which the country has witnessed or is likely to meet in the future, without resorting to any system of bounties by the Government or local authorities. It has seemed the more necessary to present these views and facts, because it is absolutely essential that they be properly weighed and considered when a war begins, and before a system of bounties is inaugurated, for once involved in the system it is extremely difficult, if not impossible, to escape from it, or even restrict the rapid growth of its evils.

PART VIII.

Desertion.

There can be no cause so just or so beloved that war in its behalf will not be attended by desertion among its defenders. The extent of the evil is governed by circumstances, but is always directly affected by the relative leniency or severity with which the crime is treated. Our experience in this regard during the late war has been costly and extensive, and is worthy of special note.

Prior to the commencement of the war in April, 1861, the Army Regulations authorized a reward of $30 for the arrest and delivery of a deserter to an officer of the Army. It was then and is still the duty of every officer to arrest deserters, but the duty did not belong specially to any class of officers and the arrests made were generally by the police of cities for the reward offered. During the spring and summer of 1861 large bodies of volunteer troops were called into service, and desertion became frequent. Looking back by the light of experience, it would seem that this fact should have induced an increase of the reward offered or the adoption of other measures to check the evil; but, on the contrary, few arrests were made, the severity of punishment was not increased, and an order was issued from the Adjutant-General's Office on the 7th of September, 1861, reducing the reward from $30 to $5, the latter amount to cover all the expenses of apprehension and delivery. This proved prohibitory to action, and the economy practiced was found in the end to have been expensive. The evil grew, and on the 7th of April, 1862, by General Orders, No. 36, from the Adjutant-General's Office, the duty of collecting stragglers and deserters was especially assigned to the military commanders of cities, but both their authority and means were so limited that little improvement resulted, notwithstanding that in June and July, 1862, general orders were published requiring and commanding all absentees to return under severe penalties, and calling upon the civil as well as the military authorities to contribute their services to this end.

On the 24th of September, 1862, a general order was issued appointing Simeon Draper, esq., Provost-Marshal-General, and authorizing various assistants, with a view to checking the evil from which the service was then seriously suffering. I have no data from which to determine the extent of this effort or its true results, but it is certain that the abuse was not removed.

Sections 5, 6, 7, 24, and 26 of enrollment act[a] approved March 3, 1863, laid the foundation of a system for correcting the evil of desertion. It was made the duty of a provost-marshal-general in Washington to ascertain and communicate to a provost-marshal appointed in each Congressional district such facts connected with the desertion of the different men of that class as would be likely to facilitate their arrest, and the law required the provost-marshals to seek out, arrest, and return deserters. Any person procuring or enticing a soldier to desert, or harboring, concealing, giving employment to, or aiding in carrying him away was made liable to imprisonment and fine.

---

[a] See Appendix, Doc. 35.

Section 21 of the act approved March 3, 1865, provided that, in addition to the other lawful penalties for the crime of desertion, all deserters who did not return within sixty days should be deemed to have relinquished their right of citizenship and their right to become citizens, and were disqualified from holding office under the United States. The same penalties were prescribed for all who might subsequently desert either from actual military service or to escape the draft.

The Articles of War prescribe the death penalty for the convicted deserter in time of war. The law on the subject is therefore sufficient.

The business in my office relating to deserters has formed a distinct branch, as heretofore shown in statement of the organization of the office. It received the earliest attention of the Bureau, and was continually looked after with special care. The report of the officer lately in immediate charge of it is in Appendix, Document 7.

On the 16th of July, 1863, the reward for apprehending a deserter was increased to $10, and in September, 1863, it was further increased to $30, at which it remained until March 11, 1865, when an order was issued by the Secretary of War discontinuing all rewards for the arrest of deserters; this order having, however, been since modified so as to allow the reward of $30 for the arrest of deserters from the Regular Army.

As required by orders, the various commanders of troops made to this office, from time to time, reports of the desertions from their commands. From these documents, which, however, are not entirely complete, it appears that 268,530 desertions have taken place since the war commenced in 1861. But it must be borne in mind that many of those embraced in this return were not deserters in fact, but men who, without the knowledge of their officers, became unavoidably absent from various causes—sickness, injuries, accidents, intentionally or unintentionally overstaying their furloughs, &c.—and, being reported to this office as deserters, went to swell the aggregate, notwithstanding that their absence was afterward satisfactorily accounted for. This aggregate is further increased by the fact that the same men deserted and were reported more than once.

In the war just closed there was too much marching and fighting to permit regimental and company commanders to make full and accurate returns, covering all points; but from the best data furnished, it is thought that the aggregate of desertions, 268,530, should be reduced 25 per cent. on the above account, leaving the actual desertions 201,397. This includes drafted men who deserted after being examined and held to service, but does not include the drafted men who failed to report in response to the draft.

It will be observed from the table[a] that of those reported as deserters, 92,095, or nearly two-fifths of all reported, deserted prior to April 1, 1863, when the duty of their arrest was assumed by this Bureau. It is not known how many deserters were arrested between the beginning of the war and April 1, 1863. Since that date 75,909 have been arrested through the instrumentality of this Bureau, making an average of about 3,000 per month. Thus nearly two-thirds as many deserters have been arrested by this Bureau and returned to the service as have deserted since the Bureau was established. When it is remembered that some of these criminals joined the enemy and more went to foreign parts, it is fair to conclude that no large proportion remained with impunity within our jurisdiction. It is known,

---

[a] See Appendix, Doc. 7.

however, that many have returned, since, with the close of the war, danger of arrest and punishment passed away.

Special causes operating to produce desertion in the U. S. Army during the late rebellion.

In the late war of rebellion there seem to have been some special causes operating to produce desertion, which it is well to mention in detail:

First. For the first two years of the war the Government had to depend on the services, voluntarily presented, of men who, with abundant patriotism, had no knowledge of military law and obligation and no conception of discipline; men who had always freely acted according to their own ideas and wishes, restrained by no other legal requirements than those of the civil law governing a free people. It is not strange that among such men many should have absented themselves, in the beginning of the war, from ignorance as to their duties and obligations and become technically deserters, but without really deserting the flag or abandoning the cause. It is a well-ascertained fact that numbers who deserted the commands to which they belonged in the early part of the war subsequently joined other branches of the service without the inducements of bounty and proved to be good and faithful soldiers. The mode of organizing troops was fruitful of evil in this regard. The men elected their officers generally without knowledge as to the requirements of the places to be filled or the fitness of the persons chosen. The majority ruled in the election, and issues not connected with the military service often governed it. A dissatisfied and often highly intelligent minority was frequently the result, and desertion, both before and after sufficient trial to prove the fitness or the unfitness of the officers, occurred, and was regarded by the parties resorting to it more as a refusal on their part to ratify a contract than as the commission of a grave crime. The remedy for this was only to be found in abandoning the system of electing officers, and adopting that of having them appointed by those competent to judge of their qualifications for the duty required.

Second. The large bounties paid to recruits both encouraged and facilitated desertion, as explained in the chapter on bounties.

Third. The want of adequate means for the arrest of deserters in the early part of the war, and the consequent impunity with which they returned to and remained at their homes, and the failure to administer prompt and adequate punishment for the worst phases of the crime, when occasion offered, contributed more, perhaps, than anything else to the evil of desertion.

The evils of desertion do not need enumeration. There was one, however, which may be mentioned as particularly observable during the war, viz, the discouragement to volunteering that resulted from the exaggerations indulged in by deserters as to the harsh treatment they had met with, and the false stories they spread abroad of the cruelty and unnecessary hardships to which the men were subjected by their officers.

Lives sacrificed, battles lost, and war prolonged, in consequence of the depletion of the ranks of the armies by desertion, were the natural fruits of the want of rigor in dealing with this evil in the early stages of the war. Undue mercy to deserters was in reality harsh cruelty to those who remained true to their flag.

PART IX.

Medical examination and statistics.

For the proper instruction of surgeons of boards of enrollment, and establishment of a uniform understanding of the prescribed medical regulations, it became necessary to organize a branch to which all medical questions should be referred. For this purpose the medical branch of this Bureau was organized January 11, 1864.

Forms for medical record books of the examination of recruits, substitutes, drafted and enrolled men, were at once prepared and forwarded to the surgeons of the several boards of enrollment, with circular letters containing full information as to the appropriate construction of the several sections of paragraph 85 of the Revised Regulations of the Bureau, which defines the diseases and infirmities that disqualify men for military service.

Medical officers were detailed as inspectors of boards of enrollment and instructed in reference to their duties. During the operations of the draft these officers made frequent tours of inspection and contributed largely to the establishment of a uniform system of medical examination.

Monthly medical reports, containing the date of examination, name, age, occupation, residence, nativity, height, color of eyes, hair, and complexion, chest measurement, married or single, white or colored, physique, and results of examination, were required from surgeons of boards of enrollment, and examined and tabulated by the medical branch of the Bureau.

By means of these records a complete history of the medical examination of 1,014,776 men has been preserved. It afforded the means of examining into complaints as to improper action in holding to service or enlisting men physically unfit, with an intelligent understanding of the facts in the case, and insured a radical discovery and exposure of attempts at fraudulent enlistment.

The medical statistics which the Bureau has thus been able to collect, a portion of which accompanies this report,[a] are greater in extent, and believed to contain in a minute and available form more valuable information, than this or perhaps any other country has hitherto possessed.

PART X.

The Veteran Reserve Corps.

As heretofore stated, the laws for enrolling and drafting the national forces and arresting deserters, under which this Bureau was instituted, were adopted solely from the necessity of strengthening the armies in the field to an extent sufficient to insure success against the enemy. To realize this purpose in the fullest measure it was desirable to avoid any weakening of the force then in the field by employing a portion of it in enforcing these laws. The first steps toward

[a] See Appendix, Doc. 8.*

* Here omitted; but see Executive Document No. 1, House of Representatives, Thirty-ninth Congress, first session, Vol. IV, pp. 258–699. Attention is also directed to a later official compilation, entitled "Statistics, Medical and Anthropological, of the Provost-Marshal-General's Bureau," by Col. J. H. Baxter, chief medical purveyor, U. S. Army, and published by authority of Congress in 1875.

organizing this Bureau, however, showed the indispensability of a military force of some kind for the efficient execution of the various provisions of the enrollment act.

A plan was therefore submitted by my letter of April 17, 1863, by which it was proposed, first, to retain the military services for garrison, hospital, and provost duty of that class of deserving officers and men who, from wounds received in action or disease contracted in the service, were unfit for further duty in the field, and who would otherwise be discharged, but were still able to perform light duty; second, to bring back for like purpose those who had previously been discharged on similar grounds, were unfit for active service, and not liable to draft.

The necessity for the action taken on this plan was not limited to the wants of this Bureau. The drain caused by the war on the able-bodied men of the country had been so severe that an intelligent economy of the public strength demanded that some portion of the vast numbers of soldiers unfit for field service should be utilized for military purposes. To enlist or conscript disabled men, except under the extremest pressure of necessity, would have been cruelty and folly; but to keep in service experienced soldiers, who were simply disabled for the march; to relieve with them at least an equal number of able-bodied men, who could thus be sent to the front; to provide the Government with a reliable military police force, urgently needed in time of raids, riots, and the like, and to constitute a garrison force with unity of organization and purpose, and of high military esprit, and all this without the expense of recruitment or the severity of conscription, seemed to be a most desirable object. That the object was attained to an extent not at first even hoped for, the history of the Veteran Reserve Corps fully attests.

It is proper to state that prior to the organization of the corps the practice of discharging partially disabled soldiers had been somewhat limited, and that some of the invalids were required to perform light duties. Being, however, retained on the rolls of their respective companies, they weakened the Army, for, though absent in person, their places could not be filled by recruits, as they formed part of the authorized strength of the organizations to which they belonged.

The plan of organization for the Invalid or Veteran Reserve Corps was announced in General Orders, No. 105, dated April 28, 1863.[a] The Provost-Marshal General was charged with the execution of the order, and the troops raised under it were placed under his control. Stringent measures were adopted with a view to admitting only such disabled officers of good habits as were well indorsed for good conduct in the field, and possessed of the industry, education, and intelligence necessary to make efficient officers and form an honorable as well as useful corps.

Competent boards were instituted to examine the officers applying for admission, the question of disability being determined by medical men in the service of the Government. No applicant was examined for appointment until he had filed in this office satisfactory recommendations from his superiors in the field as to good character and behavior in active service.

There were three sources from which the material for the formation of the corps could be drawn: (1) Men still in the field who had been disabled by wounds or by disease contracted in the line of duty; (2) men absent from their colors in hospitals or convalescent camps, or

---

[a] See Appendix, Doc. 23.

otherwise under the control of medical officers; (3) men who had been honorably discharged on account of wounds or other disability resulting from military service. Officers as well as soldiers were received from these three classes, and from these alone.

The material thus obtained was at first organized into companies and battalions of infantry. The companies were composed of men from various States, and often from all the different arms of the service, thus adding to the ordinary difficulties of organization, discipline, and instruction. These were, however, rapidly overcome through the industry, zeal, and ability with which the instructions of the Bureau were carried out by the officers of the corps, who were selected with great care and regard both to gallantry and fitness.

Before the end of June, 1863 (prior to the commencement of the first draft), sixteen companies of the First Battalion and six of the Second Battalion were in readiness for duty. The number rapidly increased until the returns of October 31, 1863, showed the corps to consist of 491 officers and 17,764 enlisted men.

The First Battalion companies were composed of men capable of carrying muskets and performing garrison duty. The Second Battalion companies were composed of men of an inferior degree of physical ability, but who were fit for hospital duty, as guards, clerks, attendants, &c. They were armed with swords and pistols.

On the 5th of September, 1863, the organization of regiments was authorized. Each regiment was made to comprise six companies of the First Battalion and four of the Second, the design being that each regiment thus constituted should be able to furnish proper details at any point where it might be stationed for garrison and hospital duty. After trial it was found best to have the regiments composed only of First Battalion companies, and their organization was modified accordingly. The second battalion companies were retained as separate organizations, and were finally, March 21, 1865, turned over to the Medical Department of the Army, for which they had always been mainly intended.

On the 1st of October, 1864, the corps consisted of 764 commissioned officers and 28,738 enlisted men, organized into 24 complete infantry regiments of the First Battalion and 153 unassigned companies of the Second Battalion.

On the 31st of May, 1865, the corps consisted of 762 commissioned officers and 29,852 enlisted men.

As soon as it was ascertained, in April, 1865, that the rebellion was overcome, the appointment of officers and the enlistment and transfer of men to the corps were discontinued. The orders of the War Department for the reduction of the vast Volunteer Army were made so far applicable to the Veteran Reserve Corps as to allow the discharge of all who desired it. This resulted in reducing the corps by the 31st of December, 1865, to 644 commissioned officers and less than 1,000 enlisted men. The men were consolidated into independent companies and officered, and the remainder of the officers not on special service were ordered to their homes to await instructions. Two hundred and ninety-five of the officers are on duty in the Freedmen's Bureau.

On the 13th of December, 1865, a resolution passed the House of Representatives requesting the Secretary of War to suspend action as to mustering out the officers of the corps until the subject could be considered by Congress.

Over 60,000 men entered the Veteran Reserve Corps, and at one time it was twice as large as was the entire Regular Army at the commencement of the war. The discipline and instruction acquired by the corps were highly creditable. Its services were always valuable, but were too varied to be briefly enumerated, inasmuch as, where one regiment escorted thousands of prisoners, convalescents, recruits, and conscripts, whose numbers can be given with accuracy, another simply defended and held important military lines and positions, aided in the enrollment and draft, or guarded vast depots of public property, thus performing duty which, from its nature, is not capable of exact definition. During its entire existence the corps was in the performance of duties which would otherwise have been necessarily performed by as great a number of able-bodied troops detached from the armies in the field. Its career has been one of usefulness as well as of honor; it has accomplished all that could have been hoped of it, and more. Men who could no longer endure a full day's march, but who could still garrison important positions, hold lines of defense, and otherwise promote the public interests, have held its commissions and filled its ranks. Of every 100 of its officers, 82 were disabled by gunshot wounds, 13 by disease, 5 by accidental injuries, and all in the service of their country in her time of need. Tried on their entrance to the corps by the requisites of good character, meritorious military history, and invalidism contracted in the execution of soldierly duty, the officers and men have performed their varied and responsible labors with zeal, integrity, ability, and educated intelligence. To the justice and magnanimity of the Nation, in the claims they may present for further military service or other suitable employment, I recommend the many officers and men of the corps who have so far suffered for their country that they can no longer put forth their full strength for their own support.

PART XI.

Commutation money.[a]

The thirteenth section of the original enrollment act, March 3, 1863,[b] provided that a drafted man might secure exemption from service under the draft by paying to such person as the Secretary of War might designate to receive it such sum, not exceeding $300, as the Secretary might determine.

In June, 1863,[c] preparatory to the first draft, the Secretary of War fixed $300 as the sum to be paid, and designated the Provost-Marshal-General as the person to receive it. It was collected in accordance with the following plan:

By direction of the Secretary of War and the Secretary of the Treasury, the collector of internal revenue in each district was required to collect the commutation money from drafted men who desired to pay it for the purpose of securing the exemption authorized by law. Receipts given to the drafted men by the collector for the money so paid were presented by the drafted man to the Board of Enrollment, who gave him in return a certificate of exemption, according to form subscribed by the Bureau.

The Board of Enrollment was required to make to this office weekly abstracts of exemptions, and to accompany the same with the receipts for the commutation, in consideration of which the men named in the abstract had been exempted.

The receipts thus obtained through the Board of Enrollment

---

[a] For details as to this fund, see Appendix, Doc. 9.
[b] See Appendix, Doc. 35, Art. 4.
[c] See Appendix, Doc. 24.

acquainted the Bureau with the exact liability on this account of the different collectors.

The collectors were required, by the orders of the Secretary of War, to deposit these funds to the credit of Col. James B. Fry, Provost-Marshal-General, in the designated U. S. depositories, according to the rules governing them as collectors of internal revenue, and to forward to this office weekly summary statements of commutation moneys received and deposited, accompanying the same by a copy of the certificate of deposit and an abstract, showing the names of the drafted men who paid the money, the date and amount of payment, with such remarks as were pertinent.

These returns were compared with those received from the boards of enrollment, and it thus appeared whether or not the collectors had deposited all the money received by them.

Deeming it proper to make myself accountable to the Treasury Department for this money, the same as if I had receipted to that Department for it, I forwarded to the Treasury weekly returns of the funds, showing the collectors through whom it had been received, the U. S. depositories in which it was placed, and the amount disbursed and remaining on hand.

The sum of $15,665,475.95 was received and deposited to my credit[a] prior to February 23, 1864. The accounts relating to the receipt and disbursement of this sum have been examined and finally approved by the Comptroller of the Treasury.

On that date a joint resolution of Congress was approved, requiring that the money which had been paid by drafted persons under the enrollment acts, or which might thereafter be paid under any act for like purposes, should be paid into the Treasury of the United States, and drawn out on requisitions like other public moneys, and should be used for the expenses of the draft and for the procuration of substitutes, for which purposes this resolution especially appropriated it. Subsequent to the announcement of this resolution the money was collected by the same process as theretofore, but it was deposited to the credit of the Treasurer of the United States.

The whole amount of commutation money received was:

From Maine	$610,200.00
New Hampshire	208,500.00
Vermont	593,400.00
Massachusetts	1,610,400.00
Rhode Island	141,300.00
Connecticut	457,200.00
New York	5,485,799.25
New Jersey	1,265,700.00
Pennsylvania	8,634,300.00
Delaware	416,100.00
Maryland	1,131,900.00
District of Columbia	96,900.00
Kentucky	997,530.00
Ohio	1,978,087.53
Missouri	
Illinois	15,900.00
Indiana	235,500.00
Michigan	614,700.00
Wisconsin	1,533,600.00
Iowa	22,500.00
Minnesota	316,800.00
Total	26,366,316.78

[a] For full statements of accounts of this fund and their settlement by the Treasury Department, see Appendix, Doc. 9.

This sum was collected by the Bureau at an expense of less than seven-tenths of one per cent., and without the loss of a dollar through neglect, accident, fraud, or otherwise.

It has been disposed of as follows:

Disbursed on account of enrollment and draft, procuration of substitutes, &c., $16,976,211.14. (For details, see Appendix, Document 9.)

Balance to the credit of the Bureau in the Treasury of the United States, January 1, 1866, $9,390,105.64.

There are yet outstanding accounts to be paid from this fund.

The act of February 24, 1864, required that a just compensation be allowed from this fund to each loyal person to whom a colored volunteer owed service at the time he entered the Army. The amount necessary for this purpose is not known.

Disbursements, accounts, &c.

The appropriations for the regular supply departments of the Army—Subsistence, Quartermaster's Department, &c.—being properly applicable only to the support of soldiers after they have been fully received into the military service, could not be used to defray the expenses of this Bureau for raising troops.

The small annual appropriation for the recruitment of the Regular Army was only sufficient to meet the demands upon it for that purpose. In August, 1861, an appropriation of $20,000,000 was made by Congress for "collecting, drilling, and organizing volunteers." Further appropriations for this purpose were subsequently made, as shown hereafter.

The enrollment act was passed March 3, 1863, without an appropriation of money for its support.

The small sums found to be immediately necessary in putting the Bureau into operation were obtained by temporary transfer from the contingent fund of the War Department.

In May, 1863, the volunteer recruiting service, including the control of the fund for "collecting, drilling, and organizing volunteers," and the appropriation for "pay of bounty" (made July 5, 1862), and by subsequent acts, was transferred to this Bureau.

Under the first draft, which commenced July 7, 1863, the commutation money paid by drafted men to secure exemption began to accumulate, and soon became available for the expenses of enrollment and draft and the procuration of substitutes.

The funds, therefore, which have been under the control of the Bureau are the following:

1. The fund for collecting, drilling, and organizing volunteers:	
Appropriation for fiscal year ending—	
June 30, 1862	$20,000,000.00
June 30, 1863	5,000,000.00
June 30, 1864	10,700,000.00
June 30, 1865	5,000,000.00
Total	40,700,000.00

2. The fund for pay of advance bounty:	
Appropriation for fiscal year ending—	
June 30, 1863	7,500,000.00
June 30, 1864	5,000,000.00
Amount appropriated December 23, 1863, to supply deficiencies in former appropriations	20,000,000.00
Appropriation for fiscal year ending June 30, 1865	5,000,000.00
Total	37,500,000.00

3. The fund for enrollment and draft and procuration of substitutes:

Received from payment by drafted men of commutation money—	
Up to October 31, 1863	10,518,000.00
From November 1, 1863, to October 31, 1864	15,188,399.25
From November 1, 1864, to December 31, 1865	659,917.53
Total	26,366,316.78

By section 17 of the act approved February 24, 1864,[a] members of religious denominations who fulfilled the conditions prescribed in the act secured exemption from service under the draft by paying $300 each.

This money was collected in the manner heretofore explained for collecting commutation money, but as required by law it was deposited in the Treasury for the benefit of sick and wounded soldiers, and in order that it might be applied to that purpose it was placed subject to the requisitions of the Medical Department of the Army.

The total amount of this fund collected and deposited by this Bureau was $463,987.53.

The disbursements from these funds have been as follows:

From the fund for collecting, drilling, and organizing volunteers:	
Disbursed during the fiscal year ending September 30, 1862 (prior to the organization of this Bureau)	$13,779,897.27
Disbursed during the months of October, November, and December, 1862, and January, February, March, and April, 1863 (prior to the organization of this Bureau)	6,732,802.40
Total disbursed prior to the organization of this Bureau	20,512,699.67
Disbursed during the months of May, June, July, August, and September, 1863 (subsequent to the organization of this Bureau)	1,086,891.00
Disbursed during the fiscal year ending September 30, 1864 (subsequent to the organization of this Bureau)	4,164,741.51
Disbursed during the fiscal year ending September 30, 1865 (subsequent to the organization of this Bureau)	1,422,281.73
Disbursed during the months of October, November, and December, 1865 (subsequent to the organization of this Bureau)	231,278.00
Total disbursed subsequent to the organization of this Bureau	6,905,192.24
Fund for pay of advance bounty:	
Disbursed during the fiscal year ending—	
June 30, 1863	2,175,975.00
June 30, 1864	18,000,897.00
June 30, 1865	6,176,696.43
Total bounty fund disbursed by this Bureau	26,353,568.43

This Bureau paid only the first installment of bounty due the recruit at date of muster into service. The remaining installments were paid by the Pay Department as they became due.

The fund (arising from commutations) for enrollment and draft and procuration of substitutes:

Disbursed during the years 1863, 1864, and to December 31, 1865	$16,976,211.14
Total disbursements from the fund for enrollment and draft and procuration of substitutes	16,976,211.14
Total amount of funds which have been subject to control of the Bureau on all accounts	$104,566,316.78
Total disbursements on all accounts	70,747,641.49
Total unexpended balance of all funds	33,818,645.29

[a] See Appendix, Doc. 35.

The disbursements from the first two named appropriations, to wit, "Collecting, organizing, and drilling volunteers," and "Pay of advance bounty," were made by officers of the Regular Army, assigned especially to that duty, and stationed at convenient points in the different States. They were supplied with funds by requisitions on the Treasury, and made their returns to that Department in a manner similar to that of disbursing officers in the regular supply departments of the Army, acting under the direction of the Adjutant-General until May 1, 1863, and of the Provost-Marshal-General from that date to the present time.

In organizing the Bureau of the Provost-Marshal-General it was of course foreseen that the business would require in every district the expenditure of money for a great variety of purposes. There were many strong reasons why the accounts should, if possible, be paid without putting money into the hands of the provost-marshals as disbursing officers. Accordingly, a plan differing from that pursued by other bureaus was adopted. Provost-marshals were instructed as to what indebtedness they could properly incur, and were furnished with the forms of vouchers and returns to be used. They were directed, after preparing and certifying the vouchers, to send them for payment to the Provost-Marshal-General at Washington. With a view to their prompt settlement, a special branch was established in this office, consisting, besides the necessary clerks, &c., of one officer in charge and four assistants, as disbursing officers, each in charge of a division. The accounts of the Bureau were distributed for examination and payment as fast as received among these four divisions, as follows:

First Division, payment of employés; Second Division, payment of employés; Third Division, payment of travel pay to drafted men, postage, telegrams, advertising, subsistence and lodging of employés not in military service, and expenses of arrest of deserters; Fourth Division, payment of expenses in purchase of public property and of rents and transportation.

The officers in charge of these four disbursing divisions were furnished with funds by requisition on the Treasury. They kept deposits in the various U. S. depositories throughout the region of country in which they had to make payments. As soon as the accounts received from provost-marshals were examined and found to be correct the disbursing officers paid them by checks on the most convenient depository, drawn in favor of the party entitled to the money. (For details see Appendix, Document 9.)

This system had various advantages, among which may be mentioned the following, viz:

1. No accounts were paid until the Provost-Marshal-General (who was required by law to audit them) was satisfied that they were correct. An immense saving of money unquestionably resulted from this. As the accounts had to be examined in Washington and pronounced correct and just according to the rules of this Bureau and the Treasury Department before they could be paid, the officers and parties interested were thereby stimulated to promptness and accuracy in their preparation.

2. The Treasury Department had to keep accounts with only four officers instead of nearly 200, as would have been the case if provost-marshals had been made disbursing officers. Uniformity in the payments was secured and the chances for loss were greatly diminished by using a few instead of many disbursing officers, and having them in Washington under the immediate supervision of the Bureau, and requiring that their time be given exclusively to this business.

3. By relieving the provost-marshals of the responsibility of disbursing public money, not only was the Government saved from loss that would necessarily have resulted from their inexperience, but these officers escaped complications which would probably have embarrassed them for years in their settlements with the Treasury.

4. Under the plan pursued the persons to be employed, the leases to be made, &c., had to receive the approval of the Bureau before payments were made, and thus unnecessary and improper contracts for services and property were prevented.

APPENDIX.*

PART XII.

DOCUMENT No. 1.

Strength of the Army at various dates.

TABLE No. 1.—*Strength of U. S. Army January 1, 1861.*†

TABLE No. 2.—*Strength of the Army at various dates, compiled by the Adjutant-General of the Army, after a thorough revision of his records.*‡

DOCUMENT No. 2.

Recruitment of European armies.§

DOCUMENT No. 3.

Recruitment of the British army.§

DOCUMENT No. 4.

Recruitment of the French army.§

DOCUMENT No. 5.

The organization of the rebel armies.

Although it was found impossible to obtain sufficiently comprehensive data from which to prepare a complete history of the creation and recruitment of the forces that confronted our own armies for four years, all the laws and general regulations issued by the rebel authorities relative to this subject, and some general information connected therewith, have been collated and are submitted.*a*

a The following statements in regard to the organization of the rebel armies are based upon data obtained mainly from the "Archive Bureau of the War Department." The data are authentic, and the facts and figures herein given afford means for interesting and valuable deductions.

* For such of the documents embraced in this Appendix and which are not, under their respective heads, indicated as being elsewhere printed in this publication (and are here omitted), see Executive Document No. 1, House of Representatives, Thirty-ninth Congress, first session, Vol. IV. See also explanatory foot-note (*) p. 679.

† Omitted, but see Vol. I, this series, p. 22.

‡ Omitted, but see later revised statements in Vol. I, pp. 301, 775; Vol. II, pp. 185, 957; Vol. III, pp. 179, 460, 1198; Vol. IV, pp. 465, 1034, 1283, all of this series.

§ Omitted; see explanatory foot-note (*), p. 679.

THE COMMAND OF THE REBEL ARMIES.

By the second section of the constitution adopted by the rebel Congress at Montgomery, Ala., the President of the Confederacy was Commander-in-Chief of the militia of the several States when called into the actual service of the Confederate States. In his military capacity as Commander-in-Chief he was authorized by section 4 of the act approved August 21, 1861, to appoint for his personal staff two aides-de-camp, with the rank, pay, and allowance of colonel of cavalry. By act of April 2, 1862, the number authorized was increased to six.

Prior to March, 1862, the President does not seem to have shared with or delegated to any of his subordinates the duties of General-in-Chief of his armies.

On the 13th of that month, however, an order was published assigning "General Robert E. Lee to duty at the seat of Government," and he was charged, "under the direction of the President, with the conduct of the military operations in the armies of the Confederacy." On the 25th of the same month an act was passed providing specially a staff for a general assigned as above.

On the 24th of February, 1864, an order, as follows, was published, viz:

GENERAL ORDERS, No. 23.]

General Braxton Bragg is assigned to duty at the seat of the Government, and, under the direction of the President, is charged with the conduct of military operations in the armies of the Confederacy.

This superseded General Lee.

On the 6th of February, 1865, an order and a law, as follows, were published, which continued in force until the downfall of the Confederacy:

GENERAL ORDERS, No. 3. } ADJUTANT AND INSPECTOR GENERAL'S OFFICE, *Richmond, February 6, 1865.*

I. The following act of Congress is published for the information of the Army:

"AN ACT to provide for the appointment of a General-in-Chief of the armies of the Confederate States.

"SECTION 1. The Congress of the Confederate States of America do enact that there shall be appointed by the President, by and with the advice and consent of the Senate, an officer who shall be known and designated as 'General-in-Chief,' who shall be ranking officer of the Army, and as such shall have command of the military forces of the Confederate States.

"SEC. 2. That the act providing a staff for the general who may be assigned to duty at the seat of Government is hereby repealed, and that the General-in-Chief who may be appointed under the provisions of this act shall have a staff not less than that now allowed a general in the field, to be assigned by the President, or to be appointed by him, by and with the advice and consent of the Senate.

"Approved January 23, 1865."

II. General Robert E. Lee having been duly appointed General-in-Chief of the armies of the Confederate States will assume the duties thereof, and will be obeyed and respected accordingly.

III. General Orders, No. 23, of 1864, is hereby revoked.

By order:

S. COOPER,
Adjutant and Inspector General.

PREPARATIONS FOR WAR MADE BY THE SECEDING STATES PRIOR TO THE ORGANIZATION OF THE CONFEDERACY.

The different States that undertook to rebel against the authority of the Federal Government commenced to call out and equip troops for the field, under their militia laws, before the organization of the

Provisional Confederate Government, as it was termed, on the 8th of February, 1861. The extent to which this preparation was carried is indicated by the statements in the following letters relating to Virginia and South Carolina:

HEADQUARTERS STATE OF SOUTH CAROLINA,
March 6, 1861.

Maj. Gen. M. L. BONHAM,
Commanding Volunteer Forces of South Carolina:

GENERAL: The number of companies organized and received under the act of General Assembly of December 17, 1860, is 104—in the aggregate amounting to 8,835 rank and file, constituting ten regiments of ten companies each. The force is divided into four brigades, constituting one division.

Respectfully,
S. R. GIST,
Adjutant and Inspector General of South Carolina.

HEADQUARTERS, *Richmond, June 15, 1861.*

His Excellency JOHN LETCHER,
Governor of Virginia:

SIR: Agreeably to your request, I submit the statement of the military and naval preparations for the defense of Virginia from the period of her separation from the United States Government to the date of transfer of the military operations of the State to the Confederate Government. Arrangements were first made for the establishment of batteries, to prevent the ascent of an enemy by hostile vessels. As soon as an examination was made for the selection of sites their construction was begun, and their armament and defense committed to the Virginia navy.

Preparations were also begun for receiving into the service of the State volunteer companies, and for organizing, arming, and equipping them. Mustering officers were appointed, rendezvous established, and provision made for their subsistence and shelter. The primary estimate of the number of troops of all arms required, based upon the points to be defended, amounted to 51,000 men. The estimated quota of each portion of the State has been furnished except from the western section. Arrangements were made for calling out volunteers from the western section at the same time and in the same manner as from the eastern section, but as yet it has been feebly responded to.

Complete returns from the troops in the field have not, and from the nature of things cannot, for some time, be received; but from the best source of information within our reach the number of Virginia troops is about 35,000. This amount probably falls below the real number, for, referring to the report of the colonel of ordnance, it will be seen that he has issued 2,054 rifles and carbines and 41,604 muskets, in addition to pistols and sabers to the cavalry. Thirteen thousand arms have also been issued from Lexington, and several thousand from the arsenal at Richmond have been issued to troops from other States; but many of the Virginia companies, supposed to be about 5,000 men, were armed and equipped when received into the service of the State. Should the number of unarmed companies from other States not differ materially from the number of armed companies from this State, the number of Virginia troops in the field may be assumed to be about 40,000. When it is remembered that this body of men were called from a State of profound peace to one of unexpected war, you will have reason to commend the alacrity with which they left their homes and families and prepared themselves for the defense of the State.

The assembling the men, however, was not the most difficult operation. Provision for their instruction, subsistence, equipment, clothing, shelter, and transportation in the field required more time and labor. Ammunition of every kind had to be manufactured; carriages of the guns for river, land, and field service had to be made, with the necessary implements, caissons, batteries, wagons, &c.

	Guns.
One hundred and fifteen guns for field service have thus been provided, from which twenty-eight batteries of four guns each have been furnished, with the requisite horses, harness, &c	115
For the defense of James River, two batteries and two steamers have been provided, mounting altogether forty guns, ranging in caliber from 32-pounders to 8 and 9 inch columbiads. Arrangements are also in process for mounting sixty guns of different weights on the defenses around Richmond, and a naval battery of six 12-pound howitzers is in process of organization	40

	Guns.
On York River three batteries have been constructed, mounting thirty guns of calibers similar to the guns of James River	30
Sites for batteries on the Potomac have also been selected, and arrangements were in process for their construction, but the entire command of that river being in the possession of the United States Government, and larger forces required for their security than could be devoted to that purpose, the batteries at Aquia Creek have only been prepared. Twelve guns are in position there	12
On the Rappahannock River a four-gun battery of 32-pounders and 8-inch columbiads has been erected	4
Six batteries have been erected on the Elizabeth River to guard the approaches to Norfolk and the navy-yard. They mount eighty-five guns, 32-pounders and 8 and 9 inch columbiads	85
To prevent the ascent of the Nansemond River, and the occupation of the railroad from Norfolk to Richmond, three batteries have been constructed on that river, which will mount nineteen guns	19
The frigate United States has been prepared for a school-ship, with a deck battery of nineteen guns, 32-pounders and 9-inch columbiads, for harbor defense	19
Total	324

The frigate Merrimac has been raised and is in the dry dock, and arrangements are made for raising the Germantown and Plymouth.

In addition to the batteries described, other works have been constructed for the land defense, exceeding in many instances the works on the batteries themselves. An extensive line of field-works has been erected for the security of Norfolk on the sides toward the bay. Redoubts for the same purpose have been constructed at Jamestown Island, Gloucester Point, Yorktown, and across the neck of land below Williamsburg.

I have confined myself to a general narrative of operations, and for the details refer you to the reports of the several chiefs of staff.

Very respectfully, &c.,

R. E. LEE,
General, Commanding.

Thus as early as the months of December, 1860, and January and February, 1861, the seceding States put themselves in readiness to answer promptly the first call for troops made upon them by the so-called Provisional Confederate Government. When organized, February 8, 1861, that Government found an army awaiting its call.

THE FIRST ACTION OF THE CONFEDERATE GOVERNMENT IN RAISING AN ARMY.

On the 28th of February, 1861, an act was approved "to raise provisional forces for the Confederate States of America, and for other purposes." It provided:

That to enable the Government of the Confederate States to maintain its jurisdiction over all questions of peace and war, and to provide for the public defense, the President be, and he is hereby, authorized and directed to assume control of all military operations in every State, having reference to or connection with questions between said States, or any of them, and powers foreign to them.

That the President is hereby authorized to receive from the several States the arms and munitions of war which have been acquired from the United States, and which are in the forts, arsenals, and navy-yards of the said States, and all other arms and munitions which they may desire to turn over and make chargeable to this Government.

That the President be authorized to receive into the service of this Government such forces now in the service of said States as may be tendered, or who may volunteer, by consent of their State, in such number as he may require, for any time not less than twelve months, unless sooner discharged.

That such forces may be received, with their officers, by companies, battalions, or regiments, and when so received shall form a part of the Provisional Army of the Confederate States, according to the terms of their enlistment; and the President shall appoint, by and with the advice and consent of Congress, such general officer or officers for said forces as may be necessary for the service.

That said forces, when received into the service of this Government, shall have the same pay and allowance as may be provided by law for volunteers entering the service, or for the Army of the Confederate States, and shall be subject to the same rules and government.

Approved February 28, 1861.

The arms, &c., referred to in section 2 of the above act as acquired from the United States, and the requirement in section 3 that the troops should not be accepted for a less period than twelve months, were important features in the organization of the first rebel armies.

Action was commenced under this law as early as March 9, 1861, as shown by the following letter:

CONFEDERATE STATES OF AMERICA, WAR DEPARTMENT,
Montgomery, March 9, 1861.

His Excellency A. B. MOORE,
Montgomery, Ala.:

SIR: Under the act of Congress "to raise provisional forces for the Confederate States," a copy of which I had the honor to inclose to you a few days ago, this Government now needs for immediate service, at Charleston, 3,000 troops; Fort Pulaski, 1,000 troops; Fort Morgan, 1,000 troops; Pensacola, 5,000 troops; Mississippi River, below New Orleans, 700 troops; Texas, 1,000 troops.

I therefore request that Alabama shall furnish for Fort Morgan 1,000 and for Pensacola 1,000 infantry, the troops to be sent forward to these points with as little delay as possible, and on their arrival they will be mustered into the service of the Confederate States.

If you can supply this requisition immediately without the publication of your order, it would be better to do so, as it is advisable, as far as practicable, to keep our movements concealed from the Government of the United States.

I have the honor to be, very respectfully, your obedient servant,

L. P. WALKER,
Secretary of War.

A similar letter was addressed to the Governor of each of the following States, calling for troops to serve at the points named below:

Mississippi to furnish for Pensacola 1,500 infantry; Florida to furnish for Pensacola 500 infantry; Georgia to furnish for Pensacola 1,000 infantry, and for Fort Pulaski 1,000 infantry; Louisiana to furnish for Pensacola 1,000 infantry, and for the Mississippi River, below New Orleans, designed to garrison Forts Jackson and Saint Philip, 700 infantry.

On the 6th of March, 1861, "An act to provide for the public defense" was approved, authorizing the President to employ the militia, military, and naval forces of the Confederate States of America, and to ask for and accept the services of any number of volunteers, not exceeding 100,000, &c.

Additional calls for troops, dated April 8 and April 16, 1861, were made under this act, as shown by the following letters:

CONFEDERATE STATES OF AMERICA, WAR DEPARTMENT,
Montgomery, April 8, 1861.

His Excellency F. W. PICKENS,
Charleston, S. C.:

SIR: The discontinuance by the United States of negotiations with the commissioners representing this Government, of which doubtless you have before this been made aware, leaves no doubt as to the policy we should pursue. A large force will probably, and if at all, almost immediately, be needed to resist the coercive measures of the Washington Administration.

To meet this condition of affairs this Department, acting with reference to the power vested in the Executive by the act of the Congress entitled "An act to provide for the public defense," suggests to Your Excellency the necessity of calling at once for 3,000 volunteers, to be drilled, equipped, and held in instant readiness to meet any requisition from this Department.

These troops will, of course, not be receiving pay until they shall be mustered into service, but the emergency is so pressing that Your Excellency will fully appreciate the great importance of thorough preparation, especially in regard to instant capacity to move. A similar request has been addressed to the Executive of each of the Confederate States. Asking an early reply to the suggestions above made,

I am, very respectfully, your obedient servant,

L. P. WALKER.

A similar letter was addressed to the Governor of each of the following States, calling for the number of volunteer troops appended:

Florida, 1,500; Georgia, 3,000; Louisiana, 3,000; Texas, 3,000; Alabama, 3,000; Mississippi, 3,000.

CONFEDERATE STATES OF AMERICA, WAR DEPARTMENT,
Montgomery, April 16, 1861.

His Excellency the GOVERNOR OF FLORIDA,
Tallahassee, Fla.:

In addition to the 1,500 troops for which I had the honor, under date of the 8th instant, to make a conditional call upon the State of Florida, I now beg leave to request Your Excellency to hold in readiness for instant movement 2,000 volunteer troops, armed and equipped, or as nearly so as practicable, and subject in all respects to requisitions from this Department as the troops called for in my letter of the 8th instant. This call is precisely similar, except as to number, and in addition to that of the 1,500.

The importance of holding the entire force now and previously called for in absolute readiness Your Excellency will fully appreciate, in view of the hostile purpose of the Washington Government, as indicated in the recent proclamation of the President of the United States, which has just reached this Department, and which, in the opinion of this Government, makes this additional call necessary.

Very respectfully, your obedient servant,

L. P. WALKER.

A similar letter was addressed to the Governor of each of the following States, calling for additional volunteer troops, as follows:

Georgia, 5,000; Louisiana, 5,000; Mississippi, 5,000; South Carolina, 5,000; Texas, 5,000; Alabama, 5,000.

So far as appears by the foregoing letters, the Confederate Government had called into its military service 36,900 men before the attack on Fort Sumter, April 12, 1861, and on the 16th of April, immediately after the surrender of that post, this number was increased by 32,000.

Besides the militia and volunteers placed at the disposal of the rebel leaders by the foregoing acts of their Congress, an act was approved on the 6th day of March establishing the Regular Army of the Confederate States of America, which was to be composed of one corps of engineers, one corps of artillery, six regiments of infantry, one regiment of cavalry, and the staff departments already established by law. Subsequent acts authorized a zouave regiment and light artillery. The rules governing the recruitment of this force were taken verbatim from the Regulations for the Army of the United States, edition of 1857. To what extent this Regular Army was recruited does not appear.

On the 8th of May, 1861, an act to raise additional forces to serve during the war was approved, empowering the President, in addition to the volunteer force already authorized, to accept the services of volunteers who might offer themselves without regard to the place of enlistment, either as cavalry, mounted riflemen, artillery, or infantry, in such proportion of these several arms as he might deem expedient, to serve for and during the war unless sooner discharged, and to accept the volunteers so offering in companies, to be organized by him into squadrons, battalions, or regiments, and to appoint all field and staff officers, except the company officers, who were to be elected by the men composing the company; and if accepted, the officers so elected should be commissioned by the President.

The act of February 28 gave to the President authority only to receive into his service such forces then in the service of the States as might be tendered, or as might volunteer by consent of their States. The next act, of March 6, removed these two restrictions and authorized the President to employ the militia, military, and naval forces of the Confederate States of America, and to ask for and accept the services of any number of volunteers not exceeding 100,000, &c. The act of May 6 removed the limitation as to numbers and gave to the President the power to appoint the field and staff officers for the organizations accepted under it. By the act of May 11 the President was relieved of the delay of a formal call, was authorized to prescribe the term of service for which the volunteers offering under the act should be accepted, and was empowered to commission all officers entitled to commissions.

By the act approved May 11, 1861, the President was authorized to receive into service such companies, battalions, or regiments, either mounted or on foot, as might tender themselves, and he might require, without the delay of a formal call upon the respective States, to serve for such time as he prescribed, and "to commission all officers entitled to commissions of such volunteer forces as may be received under the provisions of this act," &c.

These acts and the subsequent legislation on recruitment, to be found in full in Appendix to this report, give evidence of the immediate decline of the regard for State rights after the organization of the Confederacy, and establish the fact that the rebel leaders recognized the necessity of cogent military legislation sooner than the loyal people.

Prior to December 11, 1861, there was no law to enlist men in the Provisional Army of the Confederate States for a longer period than twelve months. On that date an act was approved providing for converting the troops then in service into three-years' troops, and the enlistment for that period of all troops thereafter. A bounty of $50 was allowed by this act to all soldiers enlisting or re-enlisting in accordance with it.

For the purpose of filling up with three-years' recruits the companies then in service, the rebel authorities sent recruiting parties from the different regiments and companies to the neighborhoods where their commands were raised to procure volunteers. These efforts do not seem to have met with success. On the 23d of January, 1862, and on the 29th of January, 1862, acts were approved, the first of which required regular contingents of troops from the different States, while the second indicated that State drafts were necessary to obtain them.

With the exception of an act approved April 21, 1862, to organize bands of "partisan rangers," no important legislation was had for recruiting the rebel armies by volunteers subsequent to that last referred to.

CONSCRIPTION RESORTED TO BY THE REBELS.

On the 16th of April, 1862, an act of the rebel Congress was approved to "further provide for the public defense," the preamble to which recites "the exigencies of the country and the absolute necessity of keeping in the service our gallant Army, and of placing in the field a large additional force to meet the advancing columns of the enemy invading our soil." This act established conscription. It authorized the President "to call and place in the military service, for three years, unless the war shall have sooner ended, all white men who are residents of the Confederate States, between the ages of eighteen and thirty-five years at the time the call or calls may be made, who are not legally exempt from military service;" and it further required that "all of the persons aforesaid who are now in the armies of the Confederacy, and whose term of service will expire before the end of the war, shall be continued in service for three years from the date of their original enlistment," &c. The ninth section of this act provided, "That persons not liable for military duty may be received as substitutes for those who are, under such regulations as may be prescribed by the Secretary of War."

The method of enrolling and collecting the military force under this act was prescribed in orders from time to time. It was strict from the beginning, and became more summary under subsequent acts as the war progressed. The earlier orders did not require or authorize the enrollment of the persons entitled to exemption by law, but trial seems to have proved the inexpediency of this mode of procedure, and subsequent orders required enrollment of all, and left the question of exemption to be considered only after enrollment.

EXEMPTIONS.

No exemptions were allowed in the act above referred to. On the 21st of April, 1862, however, an act was passed exempting various classes of persons. This was subsequently repealed by act of October 11, 1862, which greatly enlarged the list of exempts, permitting, among other things, the exemption of one man as agent or overseer on a plantation of twenty negroes, and an additional man for every twenty negroes on two or more plantations within five miles of each other, &c. In addition to the enumerated exemptions "the President" was authorized to exempt such as he thought proper, on the ground of justice, equity, or necessity.

On the 1st of May a further extension of the privileges of exemption was made to owners of plantations, but was coupled with the condition that for every person so exempted and during the period of such exemption the owners should pay into the Treasury $500 per annum.

On the 17th of February, 1864, all laws granting exemptions were repealed and a new list was enacted which reduced the number of exempted classes, but introduced the system of "details," as it was termed, by granting power to the "Secretary of War, under the direction of the President, to exempt or detail such other persons as he may be satisfied ought to be exempted on account of public necessity," &c. Exemption was granted by this act to one man on each plantation having over fifteen able-bodied field hands between sixteen and fifty years of age, on condition that the exempt should, within twelve months, under a security and penalty to be fixed by the Secretary of War, deliver to the Government 200 pounds of meat for each slave on the plantation between the specified ages.

Camps of instruction were established in the different States for the persons enrolled for military service and placed under the command of officers specially appointed for that purpose. The enrolled men were first required to assemble at a designated place in their respective counties, parishes, &c., where they were subjected to a mental and physical examination by surgeons detailed by "the President" for that duty. If found fit for military duty they were sent to the camps of instruction.

On the 27th of September, 1862, this conscription act was amended by an act authorizing "the President" to call out "white men who are residents of the Confederate States, between the ages of thirty-five and forty-five," &c., thus making the limit of age eighteen and forty-five years.

Notwithstanding the sweeping rigor of the conscription created by these laws, its results do not seem to have been satisfactory to the rebel leader of the Army of Northern Virginia, as appears from the following letter:

HEADQUARTERS ARMY OF NORTHERN VIRGINIA,
February 11, 1863.

Hon. JAMES A. SEDDON,
Secretary of War:

SIR: I think it very important to increase the strength of all our armies to the maximum by the opening of the next campaign. Details of officers and men have been sent from all the brigades of this army to collect deserters and absentees. By the return of last month, forwarded to the Department to-day, you will perceive that our strength is not much increased by the arrival of conscripts. Only 421 are reported to have joined by enlistment, and 287 to have returned from desertion, making an aggregate of 708, whereas our loss by death, discharges, and desertions amounts to 1,878. Now is the time to gather all our strength and to prepare for the struggle which must take place in the next three months. I beg you to use every means in your power to fill up our ranks.

I have the honor to be, with great respect, your obedient servant,

R. E. LEE,
General.

On the 28th of December, 1863, an act was approved prohibiting substitution.

On the 5th of January, 1864, an act was approved canceling the exemptions previously granted to persons liable to duty who had furnished substitutes.

On the 17th of February, 1864, an act was approved declaring "that from and after the passage of this act all white men residents of the Confederate States between the ages of seventeen and fifty shall be in the military service of the Confederate States for the war."

NO DRAFTING UNDER REBEL CONSCRIPTION.

It will be observed that under the mode of conscription adopted by the rebels no drafting was necessary. All were declared by the law to be in the military service and were required to enroll themselves accordingly (excepting those entitled to exemption), and the duties of the Conscript Bureau were therefore greatly simplified. Nevertheless, great difficulties were still encountered, as shown by the following report of the chief of the rebel Bureau of Conscription, which also gives interesting information as to the state of the military resources of the rebels at the time the report was made:

REPORT.

BUREAU OF CONSCRIPTION,
Richmond, April 30, 1864.

Hon. JAMES A. SEDDON,
Secretary of War:

SIR: I have the honor to submit my report concerning the operations of the conscription service from the 1st of January to the 1st of April, 1864. This report indicates but a very meager portion of the work which has been performed. The results are the scanty gleanings from an almost unlimited and nearly exhausted field of labor, every inch of which has to be searched, analyzed, and classified in every relation to the great problem of recruiting and maintaining the armies.

No attribute which pertains to society or civil economy but has been subjected to the scrutiny and action of this Bureau and its agencies. With the incompetent means under its control all has been done which could be effected by zeal and diligence. The results indicate this grave consideration for the Government, that fresh material for the armies can no longer be estimated as an element of future calculation for their increase, and that necessity demands the invention of devices for keeping in the ranks the men now borne on the rolls. The stern revocation of all details, an appeal to the patriotism of the States claiming large numbers of able-bodied men, and the accretions by age, are now almost the only unexhausted sources of supply. For conscription from the general population, the functions of this Bureau may cease with the termination of the year 1864.

Papers A, B, C, and D are the reports of the officers of this Bureau relative to matters with which they are respectively charged and exhibiting statements and views which I deem worthy of your consideration.

Papers E, F, G, H, I, J, K, L, M, and N, hereto attached, exhibit the various operations of the conscript service in the diverse functions allotted to it. From these, however, are excluded an immense mass of work which it is not deemed necessary to report, because it is of a character not demanding record in this Bureau. The returns furnished are unavoidably incomplete, and I respectfully refer to the latter portion of this report for the explanation.

Papers O and P will exhibit very valuable reports from Colonel Blake, the register of this Bureau, in regard to the military capabilities of Georgia and Virginia. Within a few days I expect to receive from the same intelligent and zealous officer similar reports on North Carolina, South Carolina, and Alabama.

Paper Q is a list of the enrolling officers whose commissions have been vacated. The case is fully stated below. These various exhibits show that much good work has been done, although the numbers recorded in this Bureau do not manifest a large increase to the Army. A rigid and universal inspection, not only of company rolls, but personal and also pay rolls, will prove that more men have been received into the service irregularly since the 1st of January than have gone through the conscription authorities.

The results of conscription since the 1st of January have not been equal to the anticipations of the country, and, perhaps, not quite up to the calculations of this Bureau.

I. The act of Congress entitled "An act to put an end to the exemption from military service of those who have heretofore furnished substitutes," approved January 5, 1864, has not furnished the number of men which it was supposed would be brought into the service by that law. It has been found that a number of persons having substitutes come within the classes exempted by the act of February 17, 1864, and other large numbers belong to those classes who are the subjects of detail for the industrial productions. Wealthy farmers, enterprising manufacturers, and mechanics were the persons chiefly furnishing substitutes. Besides these many patriotic persons of feeble health, but within the conditions of the regulations, sent in substitutes, and on being enrolled have been detailed for service out of the field. The Bureau, under your instructions, has been very cautious in allowing such details. I regret to state that there seems to have been a general effort to keep principals of substitutes out of the Army.

It is proper to add that the calculation of enrolling officers is, that a larger number of this class have gone into the Army without reporting to the enrolling officers than have been passed by them through the camps. The result of the law, therefore, has been better than is exhibited by the records of this Bureau.

II. It has been found exceedingly difficult to interpret the "Act to organize forces to serve during the war," so as to adapt its provisions to just administration under the agencies provided for conscription. The purpose of the law seems to be that while all men are made liable to military service the productive industry must be maintained as necessary to the public defense. Under the classes of exemption there are but a limited number engaged in production. Of persons "owning fifteen able-bodied hands" a very small minority produce more than they consume, rarely having a surplus of grain or meat to sell, and a large majority of such persons between the ages of seventeen and fifty are already in the service. The surplus producers, those on whom the country and the Army must depend for supplies, are the classes having much less than "fifteen hands," and down to single laborers on farms. As numerous as this class is, it has already been drained of men to a point which requires great caution in making further abstractions. My opinion is that the agriculture of the country cannot safely spare more than a very small additional draft. I am not sure that the public defense would not be strengthened instead of weakened by adding to the labor thus employed.

III. In manufactures and mechanical arts the like necessity seemed to exist. Perhaps no civilized country was ever so barren of manufactures and mechanical arts as the States of the Confederacy at the beginning of the war; and certainly no country since the blockade was established has needed them more. No one article of clothing or mechanical production was supplied within these States, so that, under the blockade, it has become an absolute necessity, even for the meager supply now existing, that every manufacturer and mechanic should be kept to his art. As the stock which existed at the beginning of the war approaches absolute exhaustion this necessity of course increases. Prudence requires great caution in further diminishing this class. The Army and the people must be fed and clothed, and the munitions of war must be furnished, and the persons engaged in these purposes are already too few for the ends. It is in the class of non-producers that the enrolling officer must chiefly look for his recruits to the Army, and it is in determining who these non-producers are that the conscript authorities are engaged in hourly contest with every authority, every prejudice, every interest, and every fear which exists in the Confederacy. Governors and judges demand some local convenience; others, pecuniary or other interests, and the needs of every occupation are magnified into public necessities. Towns and cities demand able-bodied men for police; banks and brokers, for clerks; charitable institutions, for wardens; public functionaries, for subalterns, and all on the plea that such are necessary for the public good. There is one universal effort to keep men from the field. Since I took charge of this Bureau no authority, association, or individual has offered one man to the military service. Against all this the conscription authorities are daily contending. The results evince that the officers have been doing their duty.

IV. I regret that I am compelled to report that in no department of Government has the law been rigidly complied with in the matter of details. The plea of public necessity has been so strenuously urged and so distinctly proved that continuations have been allowed beyond the contemplation of law. I respectfully recommend that as soon as the reserves are organized the law be rigidly enforced.

V. The functions of conscription are now narrowed down to a system of delicate gleaning from the population of the country, involving the most laborious, patient, cautious, and intelligent investigation into the relations of every man to the public defense. There are but few left whose appropriate duties in those relations have not been defined, and it thence becomes the province of the conscription agents to weigh and determine whether those relations may not be disturbed for the purpose of sending more men into the field and distributing them for the general service.

The efficiency of the Bureau in these investigations has been seriously impaired by the failure to retain in office about seventy officers, selected by you for their peculiar fitness for and accurate training in those duties.

These officers (paper Q) were selected by you with great care and accurate discrimination and appointed or assigned to enrolling service. With few exceptions, all other officers in that service were assigned by accident or by reason of unfitness for other duties; and from this cause, when I came to the Bureau, I found the service confused and languid, and the administration of the conscript laws necessarily unsatisfactory. Chiefly by the zealous and intelligent aid of these seventy officers thus selected, the system was organized and the administration became fruitful, not only in men for the field, but in managing the external police of the armies, and also in furnishing a large amount of information on which to base the military policy of the country. These officers were the chiefs who controlled, informed, and energized the ungenial agencies filtered into the conscript from the debris of the general service. They were the practiced and trained soldiers and judges on whom I relied to sustain me in my hard duty of wringing from the wasted population the scanty remnant of men, and at the same time to preserve, as far as our military need would permit, the enfeebled productive energies of the country. These officers have been discharged by the operation of a law which does not provide adequate compensation to the public service.

In the States of Virginia, North Carolina, and South Carolina these officers were the principal agents of conscription, and in these States conscription has been eminently successful. In Georgia, Alabama, Mississippi, and Florida the officers were altogether casual, and from these States came all the complaints of the evils and failures of conscription.

The Invalid Corps bill has furnished no substitutes for these officers, and I have no authority to ask or receive officers from any other source except such as may be sent by the casualties of the field, or on declarations of incompetence. I cannot too strongly express my dismay at the almost certain prospect of the utter failure of the conscription service during the coming vital campaign if it is made dependent on the accidental officers who are fitfully and irregularly assigned to its duties. On the 1st day of April no branch of the public service was working with more order and efficiency than that under the control of this Bureau. All obstacles and impediments—and they were of the gravest character—were yielding to the intelligence, the indomitable zeal and devotion of the officers. On the 1st day of May over a large portion of the Confederacy the service will be paralyzed. Leaving out the plea of harsh and cruel dealing with these officers, a large majority of whom are disabled by wounds and disease, and have resigned higher to take inferior commissions, I regard this statement I have made as sufficient warrant for me to suggest a recommendation that Congress make some provision for reinstating these officers in the enrolling service with their proper commissions.

VI. Another grave interruption has come, of the occasional but too frequent assignment of officers commanding in the field, to the duty of conscription and recruiting in particular localities. In every instance this has unduly disturbed the production of the country—has violated legal rights—has failed to send men into the field—and has been unjust to the general service. In no instance has an officer commanding in the field, charged with local conscription, sent a conscript out of his department. The assumption by local authorities to determine liability to service has uniformly been detrimental, keeping unnecessarily many from the field and impeding and delaying the conscript officers in sending others.

VII. In my report of December 5, 1863, I estimated that nearly one-third more men went into the field directly under the compulsion of the law than passed through the camps of instruction. My belief is that the proportion has been increased since the passage of the acts of 5th of January and 17th of February—that is, that the conscript rolls and assignments will not exhibit one-half the number of men who have gone into the service since the 5th of January. Proper returns to the Adjutant and Inspector General's Office should make an accurate exhibit of these accretions. General orders have been inoperative to prevent this mode of direct volunteering; and requisitions for the men by enrolling officers and this Bureau have been unheeded. The abuse exists in every military department. Your attention is respectfully and earnestly invited to this matter, and a rigid inspection of company rolls is recommended.

VIII. The applications for details in the various departments of the Government and in other pursuits have increased and are daily increasing. The allegation of public necessity is generally set forth, and it is very difficult for this Bureau to determine. I have endeavored to limit such details as rigidly as possible, but have not succeeded to the extent which it appears to me the public service demands. My opinion is that all proper labor, except of mechanical experts and agriculturists, can, by due effort, be furnished from the exempt classes, the Reserves, the Light-duty Conscripts, and the Invalid Corps, and that there is no absolute necessity, at this time, for one detail in ten of the able-bodied men between eighteen and forty-five. I believe stern adherence to a rule embracing this conclusion would not diminish the vigor of the productive industry to any appreciable extent.

The exceptions are very rare which involve a permanent necessity of departing from the provisions of sections 8 and 9 of the act of February 17, 1864. At present there is not one department of the Government or one enterprise in the country which is not clamoring for such departure. The various bureaus of Government ask over 12,000 able-bodied men. The railroads ask at least one brigade beyond the allowance of exempts. The express companies demand nearly a regiment, and State authorities fully 10,000. Wherever a contract is made with the Government in which a large profit is provided, the Government is immediately called upon to do the work for which it pays. Thus a railroad, an express, telegraph, or manufacturing company contracts with the Government and lays its profits; it then asks the Government to detail from the Army or abstain from the military use of all the labor necessary to fulfill the contract. The evil is an enormous one. The authority of this Bureau is not competent to the remedy.

IX. In many localities it has been found expedient, indeed necessary, to suspend wholly or partially the operations of conscription. This has been done in localities between the lines of our armies and those of the enemy—so far as the reserve classes are concerned—for the obvious reason of preventing those classes from becoming prisoners of war, and it has been extended to all classes within the enemy's lines from the impossibility of the enrolling officers operating. In the First Congressional District of North Carolina the whole matter has been turned over to the Governor of that State, the men to be used for State defense.

X. Frequent complaints are made of the inefficiency and corruption of the enrolling officers. Such complaints are made against the generals in the field and all the departments of the Government. In the case of enrolling officers they are sometimes well founded, and active efforts are made to remedy the evils. In general, however, these complaints are the results of ignorance, or the baffled endeavor to escape the service, or of malice, because the duty of the officers of conscription requires them to exempt certain persons for sufficient legal reasons. I can congratulate you on the assurance that the chief officers in the enrolling service discharge their duties with as much zeal, intelligence, and efficiency as any officers in the Government. There may be defects in the administration of the conscript laws and dereliction among the officers, but I have no hesitation in asserting that the country and the Government has just reason to be satisfied both with the system and the officers. As to the officers of this Bureau immediately under my eye, I have, without undue assumption, great pride in testifying to their zeal, their apt intelligence, their untiring industry and absorbing devotion in the public service.

In view of the important and delicate service you have confided to my administration, I cannot refrain from the expression of my grateful acknowledgment to you and to the eminent public servant who acts as your assistant for the patient and courteous consideration you have given to all my applications, and for the enlightened, judicious, and prompt instructions by which you have authorized and enabled me to execute your orders. Of the nature, the extent, the intricacy, and the delicacy of the duties to be performed by the conscription authorities, you have, and what is extremely rare in the country, a full and clear comprehension, and in their performance you have generously permitted me to avail myself habitually of your direct and minute counsels.

JOHN S. PRESTON,
Colonel and Superintendent.

The results of the operations of the Recruiting or Conscript Bureau of the rebels, between April, 1862, when it was created, and February, 1865, are given in detail in the following report:

HOUSE OF REPRESENTATIVES,
February 23, 1865.

Laid on the table and ordered to be printed.
By the Chair—

MESSAGE OF THE PRESIDENT.

RICHMOND, VA., *February 21, 1865.*

The HOUSE OF REPRESENTATIVES:

In response to your resolution of the 30th ultimo I herewith transmit for your information a communication from the Secretary of War relative to the accessions to the Army from each State since April 16, 1862; to the number of persons liable to conscription who have been exempted or detailed, and to the number of those between the ages of eighteen and forty-five, and not unfitted for active service in the field, who are employed in the several States in the manner indicated in your inquiry.

JEFFERSON DAVIS.

COMMUNICATION FROM THE SECRETARY OF WAR.

CONFEDERATE STATES OF AMERICA, WAR DEPARTMENT,
Richmond, Va., February 20, 1865.

The PRESIDENT OF THE CONFEDERATE STATES:

SIR: I have received the following resolution of the House of Representatives, adopted on the 30th ultimo, and referred by Your Excellency to this Department for attention:

"*Resolved*, That the President be respectfully requested to communicate to this House: First, the number of soldiers from each State added to the military service by enrollment, volunteering, or otherwise since the enactment of the act of April 16, 1862, commonly known as the 'conscript act;' second, the number of those within the conscript age exempt or detailed, discriminating as to the classes of each in each State; third, the number of those within the ages of eighteen and forty-five years not disabled or unfit for active service in the field who are employed in the respective States in executing the law of conscription, or in connection with post commissaries and post quartermasters, or otherwise, in derogation of existing laws."

In response I have the honor to transmit herewith a report from the superintendent of conscription containing the information called for by the House.

Very respectfully, your obedient servant,

JOHN C. BRECKINRIDGE,
Secretary of War.

REPORT OF THE SUPERINTENDENT OF BUREAU OF CONSCRIPTION.

CONFEDERATE STATES OF AMERICA,
WAR DEPARTMENT, BUREAU OF CONSCRIPTION,
Richmond, Va., February —, 1865.

Hon. J. C. BRECKINRIDGE,
Secretary of War:

SIR: I have the honor to invite your attention to the papers herewith inclosed, respectively marked A, B, C, D, E, F, G, H, I, K, and L, in response to a call for information of the 30th ultimo by the House of Representatives of the Confederate States, by the following resolution, which was referred by you to this Bureau, with instructions to furnish the information required.*

The paper marked A shows the number of persons enrolled and assigned to the Army since the passage of the act of Congress approved April 16, 1862.

B gives an approximate estimate of the number who have volunteered since the passage of said act. These persons, for the most part, regarded it as disgraceful to be conscribed, and went directly to the Army, avoiding enrollment and assignment from the camp of instruction. There is, therefore, no record of them at the camps and no means of making an estimate. Though called "volunteers," their joining the service was compulsory, and should be accredited to the energy exhibited in the enforcement of conscription. This estimate is regarded as much too small.

C exhibits the number of persons ascertained by the Medical Board to be incapable of performing service in the field, who have been assigned under the eighth section of the act of Congress approved February 17, 1864, to the various branches of service for which they were recommended by said Board.

D exhibits the number of persons exempted of the several classes of exempts enumerated in the said act of Congress.

E exhibits the number of agricultural details.

F exhibits the number of details allowed for reasons of public necessity.

G exhibits the number of details allowed the several bureaus and departments of service upon the certificates of the chiefs or heads thereof that the persons applied for were indispensable to the public service, exclusive of the details of contractors, artisans, mechanics, &c., for Government service.

H exhibits the details of contractors with the Government to furnish supplies; also allowed upon certificates of heads of departments that the persons applied for were indispensable.

I exhibits the number of details of artisans, mechanics, &c. These are also allowed upon certificates of the chiefs or heads of departments that the persons applied for are experts, skilled, and indispensable to the public service, in conformity with General Orders, No. 77, Adjutant and Inspector General's Office, of 1864.

K exhibits the number of deserters returned to the Army by the agencies of conscription. This statement is not called for by the resolution, but it is deemed important for the information of Congress.

L is a recapitulation of the several statements furnished.

The records of the Bureau do not show that any persons between the ages of eighteen and forty-five years, capable of service in the field, are employed in the business of conscription except officers whose commands have been consolidated, and have, therefore, no appropriate service in the field, and the drill-masters assigned to the business of conscription. Conscripts employed as enrolling officers are taken from the list of those unfit for field service.

This Bureau has no means of showing the number of persons between eighteen and forty-five years of age, capable of field service, who are in the employment of post quartermasters or post commissaries. It is not informed, and it is not usually stated, where the commissaries or quartermasters applying for details are stationed. The details under existing orders can only be granted upon the certificate of the Quartermaster and Commissary Generals that the persons applied for are experts and indispensable to the public service, and the place or post of employment is not regarded as an element of the necessity which demands the detail. Hence the Bureau institutes no inquiry upon the point.

In order to render the report as accurate as the imperfect agencies allowed to the enrolling service will admit, it has been delayed till the present time to obtain the latest information from the commandants of the various States, furnished by their monthly consolidated returns.

I am, sir, very respectfully, your obedient servant,

JNO. S. PRESTON,
Brigadier-General and Superintendent.

---

*Resolution (here omitted) embodied in next, *ante*.

A.—*Number of conscripts enrolled and assigned to the Army from camps of instruction since the act of Congress, April 16, 1862.*

Virginia	13,933
North Carolina	21,348
South Carolina	9,120
Georgia	8,993
Alabama, exclusive of the operations of General Pillow	14,875
Mississippi, exclusive of the operations of General Pillow	8,061
Florida, suspended and under General Cobb till January, 1863	362
East Louisiana, from September report, commenced in August, 1864	81
East Tennessee	5,220
Total	81,993

B.—*Approximate estimate of men who have joined the Army since April, 1862, without passing through camps of instruction.*

Virginia	15,000
North Carolina	8,000
South Carolina	6,800
Georgia	26,400
Alabama	10,060
Mississippi	3,032
Florida	2,000
East Louisiana	500
East Tennessee	500
Total	72,292

This is merely an approximate estimate, and the exact number can only be obtained from the Adjutant and Inspector General's Office. This number is regarded as being too small.

C.—*Assignments under section 8 of the act of Congress of February 17, 1864.*

	Virginia.	North Carolina.	South Carolina.	Georgia.	Alabama.	Mississippi.	Florida.	East Tennessee.	East Louisiana.	Total.
Conscription service	696	66	308	137	144	164	42	11	40	1,60[illegible]
Quartermaster's Department	725	334	168	159	271	208	16	20	......	1,90[illegible]
Commissary Department	154	38	94	65	100	254	10	18	......	73[illegible]
Ordnance Department	56	16	18	75	46	12	1	......	......	22[illegible]
Engineer Department	9	7	9	7	9	......	......	......	......	4[illegible]
Navy Department	6	1	10	3	6	......	......	......	......	2[illegible]
Post-Office Department	25	......	4	......	......	1	......	19	......	4[illegible]
Medical Department	578	52	64	290	67	31	......	1	......	1,08[illegible]
Treasury Department	74	2	14	......	......	1	6	......	......	9[illegible]
Niter and Mining Department	8	43	3	......	6	1	......	1	......	6[illegible]
Provost guard	109	46	103	163	86	126	......	......	......	63[illegible]
Post guard	44	20	222	8	......	17	7	......	......	318
Camp guard	2	7	73	53	189	......	11	19	......	354
Hospital guard	33	73	......	......	40	50	2	......	......	198
Bridge guard	......	......	......	2	......	......	......	......	......	2
Similar guard	271	11	38	2	82	......	......	......	......	404
Total	2,790	716	1,128	964	1,046	865	95	89	40	7,733

D.—*Exemptions.*

State.	Age.	Physical disability.	Confederate officers.	State officers.	Ministers of religion.	Superintendents and physicians of deaf, dumb, and blind.	Editors.	Newspaper employés.	Superintendent, State public printer, and employés.	Apothecaries.	Physicians.	Presidents and teachers of schools and colleges.	Superintendents, physicians, and nurses in public hospitals.	Overseers and agriculturists.	Railroad officers and employés.	Mail contractors.	Drivers of post coaches and hacks.	Non-combatants.	Foreigners.	By order of War Department.	Miscellaneous.	Total.
Virginia	18 and 45	6, 242	30	1, 894	373		31	183		106	643	242		448	1, 108	136	68	99	24	3	926	12, 556
	17 and 18	117						1						3								121
	45 and 50	386			103			2		7	113	22		102		2	4	8	1		15	762
	Total	6, 745	30	1, 894	476		31	186		113	756	264		553	1, 108	138	72	107	25	3	941	13, 439
North Carolina	18 and 45	(*a*)	43		334	4	17	87		27	320	164		219	889	97	43	289	141	46		
	17 and 18							3		2					28		2	31				
	45 and 50		26		66	1	4	9		2	54	9		27	50	3	2	22	26	3		
	Total	7, 885	69	5, 589	400	5	21	99		31	374	173		246	967	100	47	342	167	49		16, 564
South Carolina	18 and 45	1, 726	21	140	266		11	59		48	350	168	731	812	41	9	1					4, 383
	17 and 18	107						7					5	17	1							138
	45 and 50	700	4	167	66		3	4		5	92	28	127	117	5	1						1, 318
	Total	2, 533	25	307	332		14	70		53	442	196	863	946	47	10	1					5, 839
Georgia	18 and 45	2, 463	50	(*b*)	378	15	12	124		43	487	195		1, 214	853	106	20		12			
	17 and 18	106						5						10	18							
	45 and 50	331	15		71	3		7		3	105	17		346	131		2					
	Total	2, 900	65	8, 229	449	18	12	136		46	592	212		1, 570	1, 002	106	22		12			15, 346
Alabama	18 and 45	2, 665	10	762	537		27	119	3	68	593	307		874	770	41	14		126	8		6, 922
	17 and 18	195		2				8		1				6	73		1		1	2		289
	45 and 50	1, 073	11	571	189		6	28		12	203	45		567	247	7	5		40	3		3, 007
	Total	3, 933	21	1, 333	726		33	155	3	81	796	352		1, 447	1, 090	48	20		167	13		10, 218

Mississippi	18 and 45	1,402	2	91	210	1	6	11		36	343	119		465	258	15			1	1	1	2,962
	17 and 18	65						1						4	22							92
	45 and 50	552	3	138	42	1		2		3	60	15		192	36	10						1,054
	Total	2,019	5	229	252	2	6	14		39	403	134		661	316	25			1	1	1	4,108
Florida	18 and 45	183	5	99	13		3	6		5	23	3		124	135	8	1		1			609
	17 and 18	6						2		1					1							10
	45 and 50	48	1	21	7					1	4	2		29	16							129
	Total	237	6	120	20		3	8		7	27	5		153	152	8	1		1			748
East Tennessee	18 and 45	270	6	38	44		2	4		2	38	13			62	2		66				547
	17 and 18																					
	45 and 50	21		2											3							26
	Total	291	6	40	44		2	4		2	38	13			65	2		66				573
East Louisiana	18 and 45																					
	17 and 18																					
	45 and 50																					
	Total	55	24	46	15	15	1				20	4		41					3	10		219
	Grand total																					67,054

a The special report of the commandant failed to discriminate the ages of State officers and those found physically disabled.
b The report of commandant failed to discriminate the ages of exempts as State officers.

E.—*Agricultural details.*

State.	Age.	Over 15 hands.	Between 10 and 15.	Between 5 and 10.	Less than 5.	Miscellaneous.	Total.
Virginia	18 and 45	3	10	53	81	....	147
	17 and 18	....	1	....	9	....	10
	45 and 50	3	29	215	201	....	448
	Total	6	40	268	291	....	605
North Carolina	18 and 45	....	7	40	102	....	149
	17 and 18	....	....	....	3	....	3
	45 and 50	....	1	8	68	....	77
	Total	....	8	48	173	....	229
South Carolina	18 and 45	12	14	16	8	5	55
	17 and 18	....	1	1	5	....	7
	45 and 50	17	22	99	68	28	234
	Total	29	37	116	81	33	296
Georgia	18 and 45	312	157	218	93	56	836
	17 and 18	7	3	1	10	10	31
	45 and 50	99	105	224	155	59	642
	Total	418	265	443	258	125	1,509
Alabama	18 and 45	3	6	14	14	....	37
	17 and 18	....	....	....	....	....	....
	45 and 50	1	....	....	....	....	1
	Total	4	6	14	14	....	38
Mississippi	18 and 45	....	3	3	9	....	15
	17 and 18	....	....	....	....	....	....
	45 and 50	....	....	....	5	....	5
	Total	....	3	3	14	....	20
Florida	18 and 45	....	....	2	....	....	2
	17 and 18	....	....	....	....	....	....
	45 and 50	5	2	7	2	....	16
	Total	5	2	9	2	....	18
East Tennessee	18 and 45	....	1	1	....	....	2
	Total	....	1	1	....	....	2
	Grand total	....	....	....	....	....	2,717

NOTE.—Since General Orders, No. 77, Adjutant and Inspector General's Office, only men found for "light duty" have been detailed as agriculturists.

F.—*Details on account of public necessity.*

State.	Age.	Railroad companies.	Telegraph companies.	Navigation companies.	Cotton and wool factories.	Paper mills.	Iron manufactories.	Foundries.	Printing establishments.	Fire department.	Police department.	Gas works.	Salt manufactories.	Shoemakers.	Tanners.	Blacksmiths.	Millers and mill engineers.	Millwrights.	Ferrymen.	Wheelwrights.	Wagon makers.	Indigent circumstances.	Express company.	Equity, justice, and necessity.	Miscellaneous.	Total.
Virginia	18 and 45	68	93	45	...	...	4	2	5	...	22	3	30	1	5	3	4	1	...	...	...	3	27	2	47	365
	17 and 18	...	...	...	2	...	8	2	...	...	...	...	3	2	7	1	19	1	...	...	...	90	...	2	4	141
	45 and 50	11	...	12	30	...	5	37	4	16	5	...	8	126	59	97	123	24	3	61	21	634	...	51	138	1,465
	Total	79	93	57	32	...	17	41	9	16	27	3	41	129	71	101	146	26	3	61	21	727	27	55	189	1,971
North Carolina	18 and 45	88	14	1	3	...	...	...	...	...	...	...	...	32	10	18	22	2	...	...	5	17	1	...	22	235
	17 and 18	11	...	...	...	...	...	...	...	...	...	...	...	...	...	...	...	...	...	...	...	1	...	66	...	78
	45 and 50	26	...	...	...	...	...	...	...	...	...	...	5	11	4	18	23	1	...	...	3	6	...	8	19	124
	Total	125	14	1	3	...	...	...	...	...	...	...	5	43	14	36	45	3	...	...	8	24	1	74	41	437
South Carolina	18 and 45	120	1	3	144	1	11	...	1	...	15	...	1	27	7	19	24	2	...	3	6	19	11	17	19	451
	17 and 18	21	...	...	34	...	...	...	...	...	5	...	...	...	...	...	...	...	...	...	...	6	...	22	2	90
	45 and 50	31	12	...	26	...	1	...	1	...	17	...	11	22	8	30	50	5	...	7	6	78	2	177	31	515
	Total	172	13	3	204	1	12	...	2	...	37	...	12	49	15	49	74	7	...	10	12	103	13	216	52	1,056
Georgia	18 and 45	319	3	14	277	15	18	22	10	...	42	...	27	74	47	94	108	12	2	20	11	89	46	45	67	1,426
	17 and 18	28	...	...	18	...	...	2	...	...	...	...	...	2	...	...	1	...	...	...	...	2	...	5	1	62
	45 and 50	56	1	...	28	3	1	5	3	...	15	...	2	44	17	50	38	8	4	17	12	164	7	149	39	660
	Total	463	4	14	323	18	19	29	13	...	57	...	29	120	64	144	147	20	6	37	23	255	53	203	107	2,148
Alabama	18 and 45	3	...	12	...	...	...	...	1	1	...	1	4	5	5	6	14	4	...	2	2	4	...	...	14	78
	17 and 18	...	...	...	...	...	...	...	...	...	...	...	...	...	...	...	...	...	...	...	...	...	...	...	...	...
	45 and 50	...	...	1	...	...	...	...	...	...	...	...	...	...	...	1	2	...	...	...	1	...	...	...	3	8
	Total	3	...	13	...	...	...	...	1	1	...	1	4	5	5	7	16	4	...	2	3	4	...	...	17	86

F.—*Details on account of public necessity*—Continued.

State.	Age.	Railroad companies.	Telegraph companies.	Navigation companies.	Cotton and wool factories.	Paper mills.	Iron manufactories.	Foundries.	Printing establishments.	Fire department.	Police department.	Gas works.	Salt manufactories.	Shoemakers.	Tanners.	Blacksmiths.	Millers and mill engineers.	Millwrights.	Ferrymen.	Wheelwrights.	Wagon makers.	Indigent circumstances.	Express company.	Equity, justice, and necessity.	Miscellaneous.	Total.
Mississippi	18 and 45													10	6	8	7			3				2	2	38
	17 and 18																									
	45 and 50													2		1	3			1					2	9
	Total													12	6	9	10			4				2	4	47
Florida	18 and 45	6											14	2		4	1					1				28
	17 and 18																									
	45 and 50	1											1	2		7	4					8				23
	Total	7											15	4		11	5					9				51
East Tennessee	18 and 45												7													7
	17 and 18																									
	45 and 50																									
	Total												7													7
	Grand total																									5, 803

NOTE 1.—Nearly all of these men between eighteen and forty-five have been found unfit for duty in the field.
NOTE 2.—No report received from Louisiana since September, 1864.

G.—*Details for Government service, bureaus and departments (not including contractors or artisans, mechanics, &c.).*

State.	Class.	Conscription Department.	Quartermaster's Department.	Commissary Department.	Ordnance Department.	Engineer Department.	Navy Department.	Post-Office Department.	Medical Department.	Treasury Department.	Niter and Mining Bureau.	Miscellaneous.	Total.
Virginia	18 and 45	3	125	55	141	43	6	35	18	86	1,128	....	1,640
	17 and 18	14	5	1	12	....	....	1	....	....	8	....	41
	45 and 50	197	255	88	53	....	6	4	14	80	58	....	760
	Total	214	385	144	206	43	12	40	32	166	1,194	....	2,421
South Carolina	18 and 45	148	44	36	7	15	33	3	5	36	....	....	327
	17 and 18	....	....	1	....	....	....	....	....	4	....	....	5
	45 and 50	160	24	22	1	....	7	2	....	9	....	1	226
	Total	308	68	59	8	15	40	5	5	49	....	1	558
Georgia	18 and 45	193	194	161	61	21	44	13	43	27	19	11	795
	17 and 18	....	2	2	6	1	1	....	2	....	2	....	16
	45 and 50	49	68	39	15	9	6	4	7	5	2	1	205
	Total	242	264	202	82	31	51	17	52	32	23	12	1,016
Alabama	18 and 45	....	4	....	2	....	....	....	15	10	175	....	206
	17 and 18	....	....	....	....	....	....	....	....	....	3	....	3
	45 and 50	....	1	....	....	....	....	....	2	....	6	....	9
	Total	....	5	....	2	....	....	....	17	10	184	....	218
Mississippi	18 and 45	....	1	1	....	....	....	....	....	....	....	....	2
	17 and 18	....	....	....	....	....	....	....	....	....	....	....	....
	45 and 50	....	....	....	....	....	....	....	1	....	....	....	1
	Total	....	1	1	....	....	....	....	1	....	....	....	3
Florida	18 and 45	5	7	208	....	....	....	....	....	....	....	....	220
	17 and 18	....	....	....	....	....	....	....	....	....	....	....	....
	45 and 50	48	3	4	....	....	....	....	....	....	....	....	55
	Total	53	10	212	....	....	....	....	....	....	....	....	275
East Tennessee	18 and 45	....	15	....	....	....	....	....	....	1	86	....	102
	17 and 18	....	....	1	....	....	....	....	....	....	....	....	1
	45 and 50	18	1	....	....	....	....	....	....	....	....	....	19
	Total	18	16	1	....	....	....	....	....	1	86	....	121
	Grand total	....	....	....	....	....	....	....	....	....	....	....	4,612

NOTE.—Those in the conscription service have been found fit only for light duty. Details granted on certificates of heads of departments that the persons are indispensable, in conformity to General Orders, Nos. 77 and 82, Adjutant and Inspector General's Office, 1864.

H.—*Details of contractors to furnish supplies.*

State.	Class.	Quartermaster's Department.	Commissary Department.	Ordnance Department.	Engineer Department.	Navy Department.	Post-Office Department.	Medical Department.	Treasury Department.	Niter and Mining Bureau.	State quartermaster's department.	Total.
Virginia	18 and 45	41	8	81		19		4	1	67		221
	17 and 18											
	45 and 50	9						2		20		31
	Total	50	8	81		19		6	1	87		252
North Carolina	18 and 45	9	2	4			4			33	27	79
	17 and 18											
	45 and 50						2			12		14
	Total	9	2	4			6			45	27	93
South Carolina	18 and 45	20	4	10					1	28		63
	17 and 18											
	45 and 50	2		2				1		5		10
	Total	22	4	12				1	1	33		73
Georgia	18 and 45	59	22	90	26	3	6	7		2		215
	17 and 18			3		1						4
	45 and 50	6	4	7	3			1				21
	Total	65	26	100	29	4	6	8		2		240
Alabama	18 and 45	16	1	5				2		17		41
	17 and 18											
	45 and 50	1						1		1		3
	Total	17	1	5				3		18		44
East Tennessee	18 and 45									14		14
	17 and 18											
	45 and 50									1		1
	Total									15		15
	Grand total											717

NOTE.—Detailed on certificates of heads of departments that these persons are skilled and indispensable, in conformity with General Orders, Nos. 77 and 82, Adjutant and Inspector General's Office, 1864.

I.—*Government details of artisans, mechanics, &c.*

State.	Class.	Quartermaster's Department.	Contractors with Quartermaster's Department.	Commissary Department.	Contractors with Commissary Department.	Ordnance Department.	Contractors with Ordnance Department.	Engineer Department.	Navy Department.	Contractors with Navy Department.	Post-Office Department.	Contractors with Post-Office Department.	Medical Department.	Contractors with Medical Department.	Treasury Department.	Contractors with Treasury Department.	Niter and Mining Bureau.	Contractors with Niter and Mining Bureau.	State quartermaster's department.	Total.
Virginia	18 and 45	461	39	5	35	874	726	82	398	9			1				26	625		3,281
	17 and 18	9				5												14		28
	45 and 50	35	1	10	2	29	1	12	46				1				9	29		175
	Total	505	40	15	37	908	727	94	444	9			2				35	668		3,484
North Carolina	18 and 45	154		26		454	134	14	100	3	13		20		2		399	271	191	1,781
	17 and 18	3															4	6	1	14
	45 and 50	39		2		3			8								12	26		90
	Total	196		28		457	134	14	108	3	13		20		2		415	303	192	1,885
South Carolina	18 and 45	4	59	1	1	15	74	2	1					16		37	7			217
	17 and 18		4			1	3									1	1			10
	45 and 50	8	12			11	3							2		4	4			44
	Total	12	75	1	1	27	80	2	1					18		42	12			271
Georgia	18 and 45	101	85	17	7	49	27		2	29	6	1	3	8				184		519
	17 and 18	5	3			2				1								2		13
	45 and 50	23	8	2		2				1				1				12		49
	Total	129	96	19	7	53	27		2	31	6	1	3	9				198		581
Alabama	18 and 45	3	45			61	1	21	6								333	48		518
	17 and 18		3														9	4		16
	45 and 50		15				1	2									14	4		36
	Total	3	63			61	2	23	6								356	56		570

I.—*Government details of artisans, mechanics, &c.*—Continued.

State.	Class.	Quartermaster's Department.	Contractors with Quartermaster's Department.	Commissary Department.	Contractors with Commissary Department.	Ordnance Department.	Contractors with Ordnance Department.	Engineer Department.	Navy Department.	Contractors with Navy Department.	Post-Office Department.	Contractors with Post-Office Department.	Medical Department.	Contractors with Medical Department.	Treasury Department.	Contractors with Treasury Department.	Niter and Mining Bureau.	Contractors with Niter and Mining Bureau.	State quartermaster's department.	Total.
East Tennessee	18 and 45	1	5		1													155		162
	17 and 18																	1		1
	45 and 50																	6		6
	Total	1	5		1													162		169
	Grand total																			6,960

NOTE.—Detailed on certificates of heads of departments that "these persons are skilled experts and indispensable," in conformity with General Orders, Nos. 77 and 82, Adjutant and Inspector General's Office, 1864.

K.—*Deserters returned to the Army.*

Virginia	8,596
North Carolina	8,832
South Carolina, since September, 1862	2,514
Georgia	5,173
Alabama, since February, 1864	5,055
Mississippi, since February, 1864	2,031
Florida	220
East Louisiana, since August, 1864	75
East Tennessee, since November, 1863	560
Total	*21,056

L.—*Recapitulation.*

Number of conscripts assigned to the Army from camps of instruction	81,993
Deserters returned to the Army	*21,056
Assignments under section 8 of the act of February 17, 1864	7,733
Approximate estimate of men who have joined the Army without passing through camps of instruction	76,206
Total number of exempts	66,586
Agricultural details	2,717
Details on account of public necessity	5,803
Government details—bureaus and departments—not including artisans and mechanics	4,612
Detail of contractors to furnish supplies	717
Details of artisans and mechanics	6,960

REBEL LEGISLATION RELATIVE TO THE EMPLOYMENT OF NEGROES FOR MILITARY PURPOSES.

On the 17th of February, 1864, the first action was taken by the rebel Congress for employing colored men for military purposes by the passage of the act "to increase the efficiency of the Army by the employment of free negroes and slaves in certain capacities."

By this act the free negro men in the Confederacy between the ages of eighteen and fifty were "held liable to perform such duties with the Army, or in connection with the military defenses of the country in the way of work upon fortifications, or in Government works for the production or preparation of material of war, or in military hospitals, as the Secretary of War or the commanding general of the Trans-Mississippi Department may from time to time prescribe; and while engaged in the performance of such duties shall receive rations and clothing, and compensation at the rate of $11 a month, under such rules as the said Secretary may establish," &c. Authority to employ for like purposes slaves to the number of 20,000 was granted by the same act, the wages of this class being paid to the owners of the slaves, and their impressment being authorized if they were not offered in sufficient numbers.

"An act to increase the military forces of the Confederate States," approved March 30, 1865, authorized the employment of negroes as soldiers. It recited—

That if, under the previous sections of this act, the President shall not be able to raise a sufficient number of troops to prosecute the war successfully and maintain the sovereignty of the States and the independence of the Confederate States, then he is hereby authorized to call on each State, whenever he thinks it expedient, for her quota of 300,000 troops, in addition to those subject to military

*So in copy, but the factors (if correctly stated) make the sum of 33,056.

service under existing laws, or so many thereof as the President may deem necessary for the purposes herein mentioned; to be raised from such of the population, irrespective of color, in each State, as the proper authorities thereof may determine.

The surrender of the rebel armies and the overthrow of the so-called Confederate Government in April, 1865, followed so close upon this legislation that no negro soldiers were recruited under it.

In connection with this legislation the following order is of interest:

GENERAL ORDERS, No. 60. } WAR DEPT., ADJT. AND INSP. GENERAL'S OFFICE, *Richmond, August 21, 1862.*

I. Whereas, Major-General Hunter, recently in command of the enemy's forces on the coast of South Carolina, and Brigadier-General Phelps, a military commander of the enemy in the State of Louisiana, have organized and armed negro slaves for military service against their masters, citizens of this Confederacy; and whereas, the Government of the United States has refused to answer an inquiry whether said conduct of its officers meets its sanction, and has thus left to this Government no other means of repressing said crimes and outrages than the adoption of such measures of retaliation as shall serve to prevent their repetition:

Ordered, That Major-General Hunter and Brigadier-General Phelps be no longer held and treated as public enemies of the Confederate States, but as outlaws, and that in the event of the capture of either of them, or that of any other commissioned officer employed in drilling, organizing, or instructing slaves with a view to their armed service in this war, he shall not be regarded as a prisoner of war, but held in close confinement for execution as a felon, at such time and place as the President shall order.

By order:

S. COOPER,
Adjutant and Inspector General.

*Partial statement of casualties in the rebel armies from April, 1861, to March, 1865, compiled from incomplete returns in possession of the Government (Archive Bureau).**

DOCUMENT No. 6.

Historical report—Enrollment Branch, Provost-Marshal-General's Bureau.

WAR DEPT., PROVOST-MARSHAL-GENERAL'S BUREAU,
Washington, D. C., March 17, 1866.

Bvt. Maj. Gen. JAMES B. FRY,
Provost-Marshal-General United States:

GENERAL: In obedience to your instructions I have the honor to submit this as a history of the business and operations of the Enrollment Branch of the Provost-Marshal-General's Bureau from its organization to date.

I am, general, very respectfully, your obedient servant,

GEO. E. SCOTT,
Major, Veteran Reserve Corps.

ORGANIZATION, OFFICERS, ETC.

This branch was organized about the 1st day of June, 1863, and Capt. Henry E. Maynadier, U. S. Army, placed in charge, with a small force of clerks.

---

*Omitted; see explanatory foot-note (*), p. 687. It is published on p. 141 of the Executive Document therein referred to.

To this branch was assigned the duty of superintending the operations of boards of enrollment in making the enrollment of their districts, and in keeping accounts with such districts of all volunteers recruited and credited. In case of a draft the quotas were worked out in this office and transmitted to the acting assistant provost-marshals-general of State or division, to be by them in turn transmitted to their provost-marshals. Also to keep all reports relating to the enrollment and draft, so that information could at any time be obtained of the number of men charged to a State or district, and the offsetting credit for men raised.

On the 20th of May, 1864, Capt. (now Maj.) T. A. Dodge, Veteran Reserve Corps, took charge of this branch, relieving Captain Maynadier, and continued in charge until December 5, 1864, when a transfer was made by assigning Major Dodge to the Deserters' Branch, and Capt. (now Maj.) George E. Scott, Veteran Reserve Corps, to the charge of the Enrollment Branch Provost-Marshal-General's Bureau.

ENROLLMENT.

At the time this branch went into operation boards of enrollment had been very generally appointed and commenced operations.

The first duty of the boards was to appoint deputy provost-marshals and to make an enrollment of their districts. In order to do this they first subdivided their districts, generally making a township or each ward of a city a sub-district. At first, in some instances, where the towns or wards were small, two or more were included in one sub-district, but experience soon dictated that each town and ward should be a distinct locality upon their record, and changes were gradually made accordingly.

As soon as this subdivision was made enrolling officers were appointed, one for each sub-district, and the enrollment was at once commenced. Each enrolling officer was furnished with a full set of instructions, printed sheets, and a portfolio, and directed to make the enrollment. The sheets contained columns for the residence, name, age, occupation, color, and previous military service (if any) of the person enrolled.

This enrollment was at first divided into two classes. The first class comprised all those between the ages of twenty and thirty-five years, and all unmarried men between the ages of thirty-five and forty-five years. The second class comprised all other persons subject to do military duty. By the provisions of the act of March 3, 1863, the first class was to be entirely exhausted before the second class could be called upon. From the tenor of the act it was found necessary to create a third class, comprising those who were in the military service at the date of its passage. Enrolling officers were required to enroll all persons between the prescribed ages, and were allowed no latitude whatever, it being reserved for the boards of enrollment to determine who of the enrolled men should be exempt when properly brought before them. Where possible these officers were required to hand in the names enrolled to the boards at the end of each day, not less than one sheet (twenty names) being considered a day's work. If at a distance from the headquarters of the Board they handed the sheets to the deputies, who forwarded them at least as often as twice a week. The deputies in all cases exercised a supervision over the enrolling officers. The work of consolidation was commenced as soon as the sheets began to arrive in the office by entering the names alphabetically upon the sheets ruled and printed for the purpose. Each of the three classes was consolidated separately, and, upon completion, a fair copy was made and transmitted to the Provost-Marshal-General.

Much difficulty was experienced in obtaining the services of reliable men to make the enrollment, this duty in some parts of the country being dangerous to life from the disaffection of the inhabitants. The "conscription act," as it was very generally called, was regarded by the disloyal portion of the people as arbitrary and inhuman, and their passions and feelings were worked upon by the disloyal "press" to such an extent that violence was frequently offered to the enrolling officer. In some instances these officers were attacked and badly beaten, the sheets destroyed, and the work before done neutralized. Some of these officers were murdered, and others could do nothing unless protected by a strong military force. Many men, on the approach of an enrolling officer, left their homes, and their wives, mothers, or children gave false names, or grossly misrepresented the age of the person to be enrolled.

Every effort was made to obtain a correct list of all liable to do military duty by the examination of the State enrollment sheets of 1862; poll lists and assessors' lists were examined and compared with the lists taken by the enrolling officer; and in mining districts, where the greatest difficulties were encountered, the enrollment was sometimes necessarily made entirely from the pay-rolls of the mines.

In the face of all these difficulties it is not to be wondered at that the original enrollment was very defective. The first draft developed the fact that in some localities it was excessive; in others it appeared that but few, if any, men capable of or liable to do military duty were drawn.

As these facts were developed measures were taken to have the enrollment corrected, and on the 17th of November, 1863, Circular No. 101 was issued by the Provost-Marshal-General to boards of enrollment, directing that lists of those heretofore enrolled be printed and publicly posted throughout the district, and all persons were invited to assist in their correction. A list of the causes for which names could be stricken from the lists was appended, and persons were invited to see that those not enrolled in their neighborhood, though liable, had their names entered on the lists. In case of alienage, non-residence, unsuitableness of age, &c., boards were to require the same evidence before striking a name off the list which would be required to exempt the person if drafted. In case of physical disability a personal examination by the surgeon of the board was required.

These instructions resulted in striking from the lists a large number of names, though but few were added.

Section 6, amendment to enrollment act, dated February 24, 1864, provided for the enrollment of all persons liable to draft whose names had been omitted by the enrolling officers; all persons who shall arrive at the age of twenty years before the draft; all persons discharged from the military or naval service of the United States who had not been in such service two years during the present war, and all persons who had been exempted under the provisions of the second section of the act to which this is an amendment, who were not exempted by the provisions of this act, and directing the release of all persons who, between the time of the enrollment and draft, shall have arrived at the age of forty-five years.

Section 11 of the same act provided for the consolidation of the classes as provided by section 3, act of March 3, 1863, and which was accordingly done.

By Circular No. 8, Provost-Marshal-General's Office, March 1, 1864, the enrollment of all colored persons (slaves) held liable to military duty was ordered, and provost-marshals were directed to furnish the persons to whom the said persons owed service a list of all so enrolled, specifying name, age, and date of enrollment. This circular applied only to the then slave States of South Carolina, Maryland, Kentucky, and Missouri, and the instructions were immediately carried out.

June 25, 1864, Circular No. 24, Provost-Marshal-General's Office, was issued, calling the attention of boards of enrollment to the first section of the act above quoted, and to Circular No. 101, series of 1863, making the commissioner directly responsible for the correctness of the enrollment, and informing the boards that the duty of revision was continuous. Civil officers, clergymen, and prominent citizens were invited to assist the officers of this Bureau, and the importance of having a correct list of all liable to do military duty, and none others, was particularly impressed upon them.

It was not until about this time that the people became awakened to the importance of this duty to themselves and the Government, and in many localities the proper spirit began to be manifested. Boards of enrollment of widely extended and thinly populated districts were requested and directed to hold sessions at remote points to revise the enrollment sheets of those sections. Civil officers interested themselves to have the names of deserving persons stricken off and others added to the lists, and gradually the enrollment was brought to a point as near perfection as it can well be made in a population so largely "floating" as is that of the United States.

Boards of enrollment were appointed in the State of California and the Territories, and instructed to make an enrollment in accordance with the provisions of the enrollment act, and these instructions were carried out so far as practicable, but the difficulty of obtaining reliable enrolling officers at the rate of compensation offered, the great extent of country covered by the said State and Territories, the constant changing of the population, and the resistance offered in the mining districts, all combined to render the labor performed void and without effect.

The enrollment upon which quotas under the various calls were based is as follows:

Draft of July, 1863, for 20 per cent. of persons enrolled in Class I.

Quotas under call of March 14, 1864, based on 3,112,279.

Quotas under call of July 18, 1864, based on 3,024,429.

Quotas under call of December 19, 1864, based on 2,485,475.

The enrollment as reported to this Bureau April 30, 1865, the date upon which all corrections ceased, is 2,254,063. There can be no doubt that the latter figures showed the true military strength of the United States liable to draft at that date, as both boards of enrollment and civil officers had for months been laboring in every conceivable manner to have the lists corrected. Between December 31, 1864, and April 30, 1865, 189,124 men had been credited on the call of December 19, 1864, and that number deducted from the enrollment. Add that number to the number enrolled April 30, 1865, and we have 2,443,187, showing a difference of only 43,288 between those figures and the enrollment upon which quotas under the call of December 19, 1864, were based. I am satisfied these quotas were equitably distributed, so far as the enrollment affected them.

Before closing this report I shall offer a few suggestions on the subject of enrollment, based upon experience and the remarks contained in the reports of provost-marshals.

DRAFTING.

Four drafts have been made under the direction of this Bureau.

First. Commencing about the 1st of July, 1863, for one-fifth of the persons enrolled in the first class; made under the provisions of the act of March 3, 1863, entitled "An act for enrolling and calling out the national forces, and for other purposes."

Second. Commencing about the 15th of April, 1864, for deficiencies under calls for 700,000 volunteers; made under provisions of the act of March 3, 1863, and amendment thereto, approved February 24, 1864.

Third. Commencing about 19th of September, 1864, for deficiencies under call of July 18, 1864, for 500,000 volunteers; made under provisions of act of March 3, 1863, and amendments thereto, approved February 24 and July 4, 1864.

Fourth. Commencing about February 20, 1865, for deficiencies under call of December 19, 1864, for 300,000 volunteers; made under provisions of act of March 3, 1863, and amendments thereto, approved February 24 and July 4, 1864, and March 3, 1865.

MODE OF DRAFTING, &C.

The general rule observed in drafting has been as follows: Immediately upon the completion of the enrollment of a district the name of each person enrolled was written on a card, together with the number of the sub-district in which enrolled and his number on the enrollment sheet. These cards were uniform in size and color, and when all the names had been written the cards were compared with the names on the sheets, and if found correct were carefully filed away in envelopes, by sub-districts, until the draft was ordered.

Upon receipt of orders to draft a wheel or box was prepared, according to instructions contained in the Regulations of the Provost-Marshal-General's Bureau. Public notice was given through the newspapers and other sources of information. Civil officers and prominent individuals were invited to attend and witness the proceedings. On the day before the draft took place the cards were taken out of the packages and again compared with the enrollment sheets, and all necessary corrections made to correspond with the changes in the enrollment. The draft was made as publicly as possible. When all was prepared the name of the first sub-district to be drawn was called and two representatives from that locality were invited to test the correctness of the cards with the enrollment sheets. The cards were placed in the wheel (or box) and well shaken up; a blindfolded man then placed his hand in the wheel and drew therefrom a single card, passed it to the commissioner of the Board, who, in a loud tone, read out the name and locality written thereon, and then passed it to a clerk, who entered the name and residence (sub-district) upon a previously prepared sheet, numbered the name and card 1, and then passed the card to another clerk, who filled out the notice of draft and filed the card away. So on until the required number were drawn. The remaining cards were then taken out of the wheel, counted, and the representatives of the sub-district requested to sign an acknowledgment that the draft had been conducted in a fair and impartial manner. The next sub-district was then drawn, and so on until the number required from the district, with the per cent. allowed by law, was drafted.

Upon the completion of the drawing the notices were served upon those drafted with all possible dispatch. From 75 to 125 men were required to report each day, commencing upon the third day after draft.

When a drafted man reported he was required to show his "notice," and if possible be identified by others from the same sub-district. He was then asked if he claimed exemption, and if so, upon what grounds. If for physical disability he was turned over to the surgeon of the Board for examination; if for alienage, unsuitableness of age, &c., his claim was heard by the whole Board. If he desired to furnish a substitute or to pay commutation money he was allowed five days in which to carry out his intentions. In some instances bonds were required of the drafted man before the furlough was granted. Substitutes were accepted after a rigid examination by the surgeon to discover physical defects, and the commissioner to discover the "moral status" of the person presented.

When a drafted man was "held to service" he was at once prepared for the rendezvous by being put in uniform and furnished with one knapsack, haversack, canteen, and blanket; also with a knife, fork, spoon, and tin cup and plate, and sent to securely guarded quarters until such time as he should be sent away.

Substitutes, if accepted, were at once uniformed and never furloughed.

When a squad of convenient size was collected, duplicate extracts of their names, &c., were made from the muster and descriptive rolls of drafted men and substitutes, and the squad forwarded under guard to the rendezvous, where one copy of the roll of the squad was left with the commandant and the other receipted and returned to the provost-marshal.

The above formula, required by the Regulations, was observed in the districts under the first draft, and has not been changed under any of the subsequent drafts.

Draft of July, 1863.—This draft was ordered about July 1 in all the districts of the loyal States where the enrollment had been completed on that date, and as it was completed in other districts they also were ordered to draft.

As the enrollment was reported to the Bureau in numbers, quotas were assigned, being for about 20 per cent. of those enrolled in the first class. In drafting, 50 per cent. was added to the number required to allow for exemptions. Drafted men electing to commute or furnish substitutes were at first required to pay the money to the receiver, or present the substitute to the Board on or before the day fixed for their examination, as seemed to be required by the terms of the law; but the rule was subsequently changed so as to allow them to be examined, and if held to service they could then commute or furnish substitute. Under the first ruling of this Bureau many persons paid commutation money who subsequently, on examination, were exempted. The amounts so paid have been refunded.

The order for this draft was the signal for violent disturbance in many portions of the loyal States, and much blood was shed before these disturbances were quieted. In some portions of the country, particularly in the city of New York, certain districts in Pennsylvania, Indiana, and Illinois, the draft was conducted under the protection of troops sent there to overawe the lawless, and in other districts the draft was deferred until troops could be furnished to protect the officers.

This draft was not completed until late in the year and produced but few men for the service. Its practical operations, however, were of much value in pointing out the defects of the act under which it was made, the provisions of which were strictly complied with.

A large number of persons were exempted under this draft by the payment of "commutation money," many localities entirely clearing themselves by raising money and advancing it to the persons drafted. This appeared to be the favorite method adopted by disloyal sections to prevent the re-enforcement of the armies in the field with men.

Draft under call of March 14, 1864.—The second draft was commenced about the 15th day of April, 1864, and was for deficiencies under the calls of the President of October 17, 1863, for 300,000 volunteers for three years' service; February 1, 1864, for 200,000 men (in addition to the call of October 17, 1863) for three years' service, and March 14, 1864, for 200,000 men to supply the wants of the Navy and to provide for contingencies, or, the calls being added together, for 700,000 men for three years' service.

The product of the draft of 1863 was credited upon the call of October 17, 1863 (no call having been made for any specified number when that draft was ordered), and all volunteers recruited under the call were credited up to the day of draft. This latter proviso stimulated recruiting to a wonderful extent, and many sub-districts having the fear of draft before them entirely filled their quotas before the day of draft. To this fact more than any other must be attributed the small number of men produced by draft under these calls.

At this time there appears to have been a conflict of opinion as to whether the amendment of February 24, 1864, authorized the drawing of 50 per cent. in addition to the number required from the districts, and in some districts in Pennsylvania and Kentucky this per cent. was drawn; but upon the opinion of Solicitor Whiting being obtained that the said amendment did not authorize the drawing of more than the number required, those so drawn in the per cent. were discharged.

But few, if any, disturbances of the peace occurred during the progress of this draft, the people having learned to look upon the draft as a military necessity. The abolition of many of the objectionable features of the original act by the amendment of February 24, 1864, also tended to produce this result.

Over 30,000 persons paid commutation money during the progress of this draft, though the number was considerably below the previous draft, "substitution" having the preference.

This draft was very generally wound up by the 1st of July, and the enrollment having been revised, a further call was made by the President as follows:

Draft under call of July 18, 1864.—This call was made under the provisions of the amendment to enrollment act, approved July 4,

1864; was for 500,000 volunteers for one, two, or three years' service, and fifty days was to be allowed in which to fill quotas by volunteering before the draft took place.

The quotas under this call were to be reduced by all naval enlistments occurring from the commencement of the war up to February 24, 1864, and men furnished in excess of all previous calls.

Quotas were immediately assigned from this office, and the draft ordered to commence upon the 5th of September following. Commissioners were appointed to decide upon the claims of the several States for the naval recruits mentioned above, and when they reported the proper "naval credits" and excesses on previous calls were allowed each State and district in reduction of the quotas previously assigned.

Drafting commenced September 19, 1864, in all districts which had not filled their quotas. One hundred per cent. additional was drawn to allow for exemptions under the provisions of the amendment under which this call was made, and in accordance with the provisions of the same act, only those persons belonging to religious denominations mentioned in section 17, act of February 24, 1864, were allowed to procure exemption by the payment of commutation money.

Provost-marshals were required to ascertain and report the period of service of each man credited upon this call, and an "account of terms of service" was established and kept with each sub-district and district.

Operations under this draft had been very generally wound up by the 19th of December, 1864, when another call was made by the President for 300,000 volunteers.

Draft under call of December 19, 1864.—This call was also for volunteers for one, two, or three years' service; fifty days to be allowed in which to fill quotas by volunteering before draft took place, in accordance with the act of July 4, 1864.

In assigning quotas under this call the requirements of the last clause of section 12, act of March 3, 1863, were carried out. All surpluses on calls prior to July 18, 1864, were considered as representing three-years' men. These, together with the terms of service of all men enlisted and credited upon the July call, were reduced to a one-year basis; the call of July 18, 1864, was deducted therefrom and the remainder considered as representing the surplus in years of service, furnished by the loyal States over all calls. To this surplus was added the call of December 19, 1864, multiplied by 3 (to reduce it to a one-year basis), and the product was called the "gross quota" of the United States. Then as the enrollment of the United States was to its "gross quota," so was the enrollment of any State to its "gross quota." From the gross quota of any State was deducted its surplus after satisfying the call of July 18, 1864, and the remainder divided by 3 to reduce it to the number of men to be furnished by the said State as its ratio of the 300,000 men called for. The same principle was followed in regard to districts. The net quotas of States and districts were worked out in this office and sent to the acting assistant provost-marshals-general of States and divisions upon a printed formula in which the principle was explained.

The "people" did not understand this principle. All previous quotas had been assigned by the simple rule of proportion, and the process could be readily understood by the meanest intellect. This new principle, rendered necessary by the very terms of the law, filled them with wonder and dismay, and almost every district in the loyal

States sent forward a committee to inquire into its workings and to see if they had had full credit for all surpluses in "years of service," which they seemed to consider as equivalent to so many men. For weeks this branch was kept busy both day and night explaining to committees the *modus operandi* by which results were arrived at, and I believe that with one exception every individual and committee left the department satisfied that the quota of his or their district was equitable.

Immediately upon the assignment of quotas under this call the work of recruiting was commenced and prosecuted rapidly in every part of the country. Provost-marshals were required to report the number of men recruited each day and all interested were given to understand that so long as boards of enrollment were kept busy mustering in recruits the draft in their district would be delayed. Drafting, however, generally commenced between the 20th day of February and the 15th day of March, 1865, though the deficiencies in most districts were but small and the men were reporting in large numbers when the final successes of our armies in the field prompted the order of April 14 [13], 1865, to "suspend recruiting and drafting."

The same day an order was issued by telegraph to "discharge all drafted men not forwarded to rendezvous," and all operations under this draft were ordered to be closed on the 30th of the same month.

This Bureau has continued to allow credits upon this call for all enlistments not reported in time to be contained in report for April, 1865, and for enlistments of regulars and colored troops up to June 30, 1865.

The following table will show the number of men obtained by draft, and the number who paid commutation money, under each call:

Calls.	Men furnished.	Paid commutation.
Draft of July, 1863	35,882	52,288
Draft under calls of February and March, 1864	12,303	32,678
Draft under call of July 18, 1864	84,291	1,298
Draft under call of December 19, 1864	36,173	460
Total	168,649	86,724

The column "men furnished" includes substitutes for enrolled men.

DUTIES OF THE OFFICE, REPORTS, RETURNS, ETC.

Up to the date of the organization of this branch of the Provost-Marshal-General's Bureau accounts had been kept with States only of volunteers called for and recruited, in the office of the Adjutant-General of the United States. Quotas had been assigned, based upon the male population of the loyal States as shown by the census of 1860, and credits allowed the States from reports of mustering officers.

Immediately upon the organization of this branch accounts were opened with each district of the loyal States; they were charged with all quotas assigned from the Adjutant-General's Office, and credited with all troops furnished as shown by the records of that office.

From organization of the Provost-Marshal-General's Bureau up to July 1, 1864, quotas on which draft was to be made were assigned by this office, and as mustering officers reported credits to the Adjutant-General they were transmitted to this office and allowed to the proper localities by reporting the same to the acting assistant provost-marshal-general of the proper State or division.

On this date, July 1, 1864, the whole system of keeping accounts was changed. Mustering officers were required to report tri-monthly and monthly the enlistments and musters made by them during these periods to the acting assistant provost-marshal-general of the State or division to which the recruit was to be credited. The monthly report was accompanied by the proper muster and descriptive roll of the men borne in numbers on the said monthly report, and the acting assistant provost-marshal-general, in his capacity as superintendent of recruiting service, issued the order to credit to the proper provost-marshal. At the end of each month a "return of credits to districts" was made to this office, showing the number and class of credits to each district during the month; also showing the quota assigned and the surplus or deficiency of the district at that date. From these returns the information necessary for the records of this office was extracted.

Provost-marshals were required to keep accounts with each sub-district in their districts, charging them with quotas, and crediting them with all men raised to their credit by enlistment or draft. They made a return monthly to this office, showing the exact standing of each sub-district on the last day of the month.

After a draft was completed provost-marshals were required to forward a muster-roll of all men drawn in the draft. During the progress of a draft they forwarded a "weekly abstract of exemptions," showing for what cause each man was exempted. At the expiration of the time for drafted men to report a "final report of the draft" was rendered, showing the number drawn, the number exempted for each cause, and the number who failed to report. Also a muster and descriptive roll of "drafted men held," and a "statement of substitutes accepted and enlisted" during the progress of the draft.

The necessary information was extracted from these reports, and they were then filed away for future reference. Various other temporary reports have been received as the exigencies of the service required.

This branch is also the repository of the enrollment sheets of the loyal States, consisting of the original enrollment made in May and June, 1863 (bound in book form); corrections to the same made from November 17, 1863, to January 5, 1864; a revision of the same made during the months of May and June, 1864, and monthly corrections made from July 1, 1864, to April 30, 1865. These sheets make an enormous bulk, weighing several tons. Owing to a want of space they are merely tied up and marked with the name of the State, number of the district, date of corrections, and whether stricken from or added to, and then filed away by States. A report of corrections to the enrollment is made by each provost-marshal monthly, showing the number enrolled in each sub-district at date of last report, the number added to or stricken from each during the month, and the number enrolled at the date of the report. From these reports is extracted the figures upon which quotas are based. Tri-monthly reports of business and general transactions have always been rendered by provost-marshals. These reports are in the form of a letter, and often contain valuable information and suggestions.

A full set of record books is kept by the branch, consisting of "letters received," "letters sent," "indorsements and memoranda," "quotas and credits by States," and "quotas and credits by districts."

An average of about 500 communications have been received monthly, fully nine-tenths of which require to be answered by letter or indorsement. Those not returned with indorsement are neatly filed away.

Communications to this branch relate principally to questions of enrollment, disputed credits, requests for certificates of credit to obtain local bounty, and applications for return of commutation money, each involving much time and labor in their proper investigation.

Applications for return of commutation money receive the most rigid scrutiny, and require a close examination of the papers presented in connection with orders and circulars, and a careful consideration of the circumstances attending each case. In all cases before a claim is decided upon a report and opinion of the Board of Enrollment of the district in which the claim originated is required.

The following will show the number of applications heretofore received by this branch and the disposition made of them.

Whole number of applications received, 757; number approved and ordered to be paid, 311; number disapproved and filed, 297; number now on hand, 149.

The general result as to the number of men obtained for the Army and Navy by this Bureau since its organization may be summed up as follows:

Product of the drafts (men)	168,649
Number who paid commutation money for the procuration of substitutes, under act March 3, 1863	85,457
Number who paid commutation money under section 17, act of February 24, 1864 (conscientiously opposed to bearing arms)	1,267
Volunteer recruits (Army and Navy, and Regulars)	1,076,558
Total	1,331,931

In connection herewith I have the honor to submit a statement of the number of men called for by the President of the United States, and the number furnished by each State, Territory, and the District of Columbia, from April 15, 1861, to April 30, 1865; also a table containing the results as shown by the final reports of the draft under calls of July, 1863, March 14, 1864 (which includes calls of October 17, 1863, and February 1, 1864), July 18, 1864, and December 19, 1864.

I will here conclude the report of the branch under my charge and respectfully submit the following general remarks:

Several suggestions present themselves in relation to enrollment, recruiting, substitution, bounties, &c., among which the following are offered as worthy of attention:

Enrollment.—In a population so largely floating as is that of the United States much trouble will always exist in securing an accurate enrollment; and in order to do so as far as practicable it is recommended that enrolling officers be appointed only after a careful examination into their capacity and integrity, and that all persons between the prescribed ages be compelled, by such laws as may hereafter be enacted, to appear before the enrolling officer of their subdistrict or Board of Enrollment of the district and enroll themselves, giving age, residence, and occupation, or be exempted if not liable to do military duty; and all those who voluntarily fail to report should be subject to such penalties and liabilities as Congress may prescribe, and men arriving at the designated age for liability for military duty should, with those passing beyond and once enrolled, be compelled to report the fact to such officer connected with the Board of Enrollment of the district as may be designated for the locality in which they reside. In like manner let it be made the duty of all persons liable to do military duty coming into a district for the purpose of acquiring a residence, or removing from a district with intention to reside elsewhere, to report as aforesaid to the proper officer for enrollment; and it should be made the duty of each district provost-marshal to furnish the provost-marshal of the district from which such new resident had removed with a certificate that he had been duly enrolled, and until such certificate is received let it be unlawful to strike the name of such person from the list. It should be made the duty of the local authorities to furnish the boards of enrollment within whose district they exercise jurisdiction with a monthly or quarterly report of the death of such persons as were liable to the performance of military duty in order that the rolls may be kept continuously correct.

Enrolling officers, assuming them to be men of fidelity and integrity, might safely be instructed not to enroll persons manifestly and permanently disabled, as, from "total blindness," "loss of right eye," "deafness," "loss of a limb or limbs," "permanent lameness," &c.; the particular disabilities which he might act upon could be enumerated after the manner of the list of "disqualifying diseases" now enumerated in the Regulations, or he might be instructed to report the names of such persons upon separate rolls, stating the disability in full for the action of the proper authority. Duty and interest would be combined to secure a reasonably correct enrollment; and by the enactment of a statute making it obligatory upon every male person in the United States who had reached the age rendering him liable to military duty to report himself for registry (or enrollment), as above, and making the neglect to do so a penal offense, punishable, for instance, with disfranchisement until the law was complied with, and in case the names of such persons failing to report for registry should be communicated to the Board through other sources, requiring them if drafted and accepted to serve personally, the desired end might be attained.

The foregoing should apply to all aliens, to persons having conscientious scruples against bearing arms, and to all classes and description of persons, without distinction, whose ages are within the prescribed limits.

The interests of the General Government demand that the enrollment should be kept well up. The migratory character of the population of this country, especially in the Western States, and the anticipated changes in the population of and migration to the Southern States, renders this necessary if it is expected to arrive at the true or even approximate military strength of the Union.

The enrollment and corrections thereto up to April 30, 1865, is as near perfect as possible, under the present system, in the States not engaged in the late rebellion; but, as whatever legislation is taken on the subject of enrollment hereafter must embrace all the States and Territories, it would, in my opinion, be as well to start with a new general enrollment as a basis upon which continuous corrections could be made from time to time and in the manner above contemplated.

The enrollment law was at first considered by a large majority of the people as arbitrary and unjust, and all those concerned in its execution were regarded with prejudice and distrust. This law with its various amendments is now recognized as necessary, liberal, and humane, and full confidence is expressed in the integrity and impartiality of those who were appointed to administer it.

The laws governing the Provost-Marshal-General's Bureau are well adapted to its workings, and the amendments adopted have been suggested by experience and have proved practically beneficial.

Substitution.—By act of Congress (sections 4 and 5, act of February 24, 1864) any person enrolled may furnish at any time previous to a draft an acceptable substitute who is not liable to draft, nor at the time in the military or naval service of the United States, and such person so furnishing a substitute shall be exempt from draft during the time for which such substitute shall have been accepted; and any person drafted into the military service of the United States may, before the time fixed for his appearance for duty at the draft rendezvous, furnish an acceptable substitute who may or may not be liable to draft. If liable to draft, the name of the principal shall be again placed on the roll, and shall be liable to draft on future calls, but not until the present enrollment shall be exhausted; if the substitute is not liable to draft, the principal shall be exempt during the time for which such substitute is not liable to draft. In either case the exemption shall not exceed the term for which such person shall have been drafted.

Section 16, act of March 3, 1865, provides that persons who were drafted for one year and who furnished substitutes for three years should be exempt from military duty during the time for which such substitutes were not liable to draft, not exceeding the time for which such substitutes were mustered into service, anything in the act of February 24, 1864, to the contrary notwithstanding.

The system of substitution is, within itself, very simple, and is doubtless the most practical and equitable way of avoiding personal service by those who, from inclination, business interests, or other causes, were unwilling to give personal response to the calls of the Government. The services rendered by a large number of substitutes have been valuable, while in some instances the reverse of this is true, owing in part to the disreputable character of the substitutes themselves and to the bad influences brought to bear upon them by an unprincipled class of men usually termed "substitute brokers," who tempted and instructed them in the arts of desertion and "bounty jumping."

To guard against the enlistment of this class of men boards of enrollment should be required to conform strictly to the requirements of paragraph 7, Circular No. 33, Provost-Marshal-General's Office, series of 1863, which reads as follows:

> All persons who may be drafted and who desire to present substitutes shall give notice in writing to the Board of Enrollment that on such a day they will present a substitute, giving his name, residence, age, and state whether he is an alien or citizen.

The principal should be required personally to present his substitute, who should undergo a rigid examination with a view to his moral as well as physical qualifications, and if accepted the principal should pay the sum agreed upon between them to the mustering officer, who in turn should deposit it in the U. S. Treasury, to be paid to the substitute as hereinafter recommended.

Substitute brokers should not be allowed access to the office of the provost-marshal during the examination of the substitute unless accompanied by the principal, nor be permitted to see the substitute after enlistment.

With few exceptions these brokers are the most reckless and disreputable class of men to be found in the country, and were they allowed free access to the recruits or substitutes after enlistment they would entice and aid them to desert by the use of every artifice a fertile imagination could invent.

Bounties.—It is respectfully recommended that instead of paying large local bounties "in hand" to recruits or substitutes, it be paid into the Treasury of the United States, and that provisions be made for its payment by installments extending through the term of service for which the man enlists, and that the amount retained and unpaid should be forfeited to the United States in the event of desertion, and thus avoiding the inducements to desert for the purpose of jumping other bounties, to those who enlist merely for bounty with a determination to escape on the first opportunity.

While Government bounties only were paid the men enlisted were of a good class and could be relied upon, but as soon as large local bounties were offered and paid in advance a set of desperate characters presented themselves who would enlist and "jump" bounties as often as opportunities presented. A man now in the Albany Penitentiary undergoing an imprisonment of four years confessed to having "jumped the bounty" thirty-two times.

General Orders, No. 305, Adjutant-General's Office, series of 1864, goes far toward preventing desertion up to the time that the recruit arrives at his regiment and receives his first payment. With the first payment he receives the bounty (retained until the recruit arrives at his regiment, and paid at the time he receives his first payment, as required by the terms of the order), and with this usually large amount of money at his disposal, if of the class alluded to, he deserts immediately.

Reporting and distributing credits.—Under existing orders monthly reports of commissaries of musters and muster-in rolls are forwarded to the acting assistant provost-marshal-general of the State or division to which the musters are to be credited, and he (the acting assistant provost-marshal-general), after taking the necessary data for credit, is required to transfer the reports and rolls to the adjutant-general of the State.

Credits are given from the reports, verified from the muster-in rolls.

It has frequently happened that the roll arrived before the report, or vice versa. As a general rule the roll seldom accompanies the report. To remedy this objection it is respectfully recommended that, if practicable, the commissaries of musters should be required to forward the rolls and reports together; otherwise there is no way of verification, as the credits are distributed as soon as reports are received by the acting assistant provost-marshal-general.

As the reports and accompanying rolls are both transferred to the adjutant-general of the State, there is nothing left in the office of the acting assistant provost-marshal-general to support his accounts in the matter of distribution of credits, or for reference to settle questions concerning disputed credits.

The muster-in rolls contain all the information required by the State authorities, and it is recommended that in case it is impracticable for the commissary of musters to forward the report and rolls together, the report be retained by the acting assistant provost-marshal-general for his voucher, and that discretion be given him to allow credits from the rolls in case they arrive before the corresponding reports are received, and that mustering officers be instructed to indorse upon their reports the name, place of credit, period of service, organization for which mustered, and date of muster of each man borne in numbers upon the report. This appears to me to be the only method by which correctness in crediting men can be attained, as, should errors be discovered in the numbers or names borne upon the report, it can be immediately referred to the proper officer for correction.

This method would require more time in making up the report, but the loss of time would be amply compensated by the facility with which discrepancies could be discovered and remedied. Credits could be satisfactorily distributed from the reports or rolls, whichever came first to hand, and all questions of credits, bounties, &c., adjusted from them, names and locations being borne upon each. Numbers alone afford no clue in an investigation.

Proposed amendment to section 23, act of March 3, 1865.—The following is respectfully suggested as an additional provision to section 23, act of March 3, 1865: That when a call shall have been made, and the quota of a sub-district assigned under such call, the percentage of the number required to the number enrolled in said sub-district be determined, say one in six, eight, or ten, as the case may be, and that such number of men from the same sub-district, associating themselves together and furnishing an acceptable substitute, enrolled and liable to draft, or otherwise, be discharged from further liability under such call, and their names be kept out of the "draft wheel" should a draft take place.

Proposed amendment to section 14, act of March 3, 1865.—It is also recommended that section 14, act of March 3, 1865, be so far modified as to allow persons to volunteer from a sub-district after it shall have filled its quota under any call, and be credited to any locality within the district that they may select. By this action the call would be more promptly filled, and no injustice done the sub-district where the recruit resided, as, before a quota would be assigned under a succeeding call the enrollment of the sub-district would be corrected and reduced by reason of the above-mentioned class of recruits being in the service, and quotas would be assigned in accordance with such correction.

Draft.—It is not believed that any improvement can be made in the method of conducting the draft as prescribed in the Revised Regulations for the Government of the Provost-Marshal-General's Bureau, and fully set forth in my report proper, under the head of "Drafting."

Experience teaches that the several calls made by the Government since January 1, 1863, would not have been filled without resort to the draft, and that the most effective mode of recruiting was by an announcement of a call for troops, and the assignment of quotas to the respective sub-districts, followed by a notice that unless the quota was filled by volunteering within a fixed time a draft would be made.

The fifty days' grace allowed by law to fill quotas by volunteering has in no instance proved sufficient. The fear of the draft has, within the past two years, been the moving incentive in filling up the Army and Navy with volunteers and substitutes for enrolled men, as they are offered more freely because of the pressure of the draft in abeyance. As soon as a call is satisfied, all efforts to recruit for the credit of localities invariably cease, although convinced that another call must soon follow until renewed under the stimulus of another call and the certainty of another draft.

In the opinion of the most loyal and intelligent men throughout the country, the establishment of the Provost-Marshal-General's Bureau as the connecting link between the Government and the people, placing the entire military resources of the country immediately in the hands and at the disposal of the General Government, has proved a most wise and effective measure for the suppression of the rebellion and in the preservation of the Government against the machinations of open enemies as well as the wiles and intrigues of secret foes; the condition of the country being such at the time of its inauguration that it would have been impossible without this measure to have furnished men in available numbers to meet the pressing emergency forced upon us.

The historian who would trace accomplished results to their true and genuine causes must assign to the law constituting this Bureau a most important place among the agencies by which the great work of restoring the national authority has been so happily accomplished. The true turning point of the war was reached when the first "draft wheel" began to revolve, under the provisions of the act of March 3, 1863. The general effect of this law throughout the country has been highly favorable to loyalty. No one department has brought its operations so directly and closely home to the people, or has given such a feeling of security, such a confidence in and such assurance of the power of the Government to preserve itself, conquer its enemies, and protect all its citizens. Next to the success of its arms, the ability of the Government to bring men into the field at its call, and the manner in which it has been done by this Bureau in the execution of the "enrollment act," in spite of innumerable and apparently insuperable difficulties, has best demonstrated that power.

By the continuance of this Bureau the National Government would not again become dependent upon the will and caprice of the various State Governors, some of whom might, as in times past, be disposed to cripple and break down rather than aid the national authorities.

In the services of a single officer in each district might be secured the enumeration of the inhabitants, the enrollment of such as are subject to do military duty, and the recruitment of the Army; and if Congress should continue or establish an office in each Congressional district throughout the country, combining in it the duty of collecting and collating statistics for the Census, Pension, and other bureaus, the interests of the whole country would be advanced, and Government would have machinery in operation that could always be depended on, either for collecting valuable statistics in time of peace or recruiting its armies in time of war, and would be able to know and to use its whole military strength at any moment.

It is impossible to review the history of the Provost-Marshal-General's Bureau without being impressed with the extent and importance of its operations, and the skill and labor required to establish the system throughout the land, and conduct it from nothing to its present position of power and success, whereby the authority and influence of the Government is felt in every ward and township throughout the loyal States. Established in the darkest hour of the struggle, the outgrowth of a stern and vital need, it has seen the darkness disappear and the Nation saved, and once more on the high road to prosperity and power. How great has been its influence in bringing about this result cannot yet be rightly determined. We can estimate in words and figures the material force which it has brought to bear upon the struggle, but how much influence it has exerted in bringing into action the latent patriotism of the people, and to strengthen their determination to fight the fight through to victory, cannot yet be calculated nor resolved by statistics.

Too much credit cannot be claimed for the officers acting as assistants to the Provost-Marshal-General for the various States and divisions, and the district provost-marshals, who undertook their very difficult and arduous duties amidst dangers, opposition, and almost total want of sympathy on the part of the people, and yet by their firmness, prudence, and constant labor were enabled to overcome all opposition, and contributed largely toward establishing the Bureau in the confidence of the people.

Boards of enrollment, with rare exceptions, were composed of men of high character, respectability, and worth. By their unceasing attention to their duties they have proved their earnest devotion to the work assigned them. Having no precedent established by which to be governed—the field being entirely new—the result of their two years' labor establishes the practicability of the system under which they were ordered to work.

As the people became better informed of the perplexing and responsible nature of the duties pertaining to the position of the Provost-Marshal-General, they have been convinced of the integrity and fairness of his administration; and it is but just to add that his subordinate officers, without exception, testify to his fair and decided management in instituting and organizing a new system, under new laws, and the complete development of this system to its present practical working perfection. They have been granted every facility necessary for a faithful execution of their duties, and while the Provost-Marshal-General has exacted diligence and efficiency, he has maintained toward them the highest official courtesy and forbearance, rendering the service under him agreeable and satisfactory. Under extraordinary trials he has borne himself with patience, courage, and nerve; the world can never know or understand the many difficulties that surrounded the chief of this Bureau, or how successfully they have been met and overcome by him and his subordinates.

In conclusion I will add that the details of this branch (enrollment) of the Bureau have been complicated and laborious, and the discharge of the various duties pertaining to it has required industry and intelligence.

The chief clerk, Alva L. Morris, and assistants have rendered valuable aid in the prompt dispatch of business, and in the accurate compilation of the records of this office, now in progress of completion. This work is unremitting and has been done with fidelity.

Respectfully submitted.

GEO. E. SCOTT,
Major, Veteran Reserve Corps.

TABLE NO. 1.—*Statement showing the enrollment of each district in the loyal States on the 30th day of April, 1865, the date upon which corrections ceased.**

RECAPITULATION.

State	Enrollment	State	Enrollment
Maine	46,121	Kentucky	104,082
New Hampshire	26,302	Missouri	133,501
Vermont	23,326	Ohio	205,867
Massachusetts	105,650	Indiana	153,238
Rhode Island	16,256	Illinois	274,409
Connecticut	40,708	Iowa	82,803
New York	431,462	Michigan	75,248
New Jersey	70,055	Wisconsin	54,737
Pennsylvania	263,436	Minnesota	18,556
Delaware	7,011	Kansas	23,022
Maryland	55,802		
District of Columbia	10,725	Aggregate	2,254,063
West Virginia	31,746		

TABLE NO. 2.—*Chronological statement of the number of men called for by the President of the United States, the periods of service, total quotas assigned, and total number of men obtained under each call, from April 15, 1861, to December 19, 1864.*†

TABLE NO. 3.—*Statement of the number of men called for by the President of the United States and the number furnished by each State and Territory and the District of Columbia from April 15, 1861, to June 30, 1865.*†

*Detailed statement omitted in view of the recapitulation following.

†Omitted; but see later compilations, showing final adjustment of quotas and credits, Vol. IV, this series, pp. 1264–1269.

TABLE NO. 4.—*Statement of troops mustered into the service of the United States for a less period than six months (including all three-months' men) not heretofore credited on any quota, since the commencement of the rebellion, but which would have been proper credit upon a subsequent call, in accordance with provisions of section 15, act of March 3, 1865.**

States	Periods of service.			Total number of men.	Number of years of service.	Equivalent in 3-years' men.
	3 months.	100 days.	4 months.			
Maine	771			771	193	64
New Hampshire	932	167		1,099	279	93
Vermont	782			782	195	65
Massachusetts	4,983	6,809	121	11,913	3,157	1,052
Rhode Island	3,147			3,147	787	262
Connecticut	2,402			2,402	600	200
New York	16,922	5,640		22,562	5,775	1,925
New Jersey	3,123	769		3,892	992	331
Pennsylvania	20,175	7,675		27,850	7,147	2,382
Maryland		1,297		1,297	355	118
West Virginia	900			900	225	75
District of Columbia	4,720			4,720	1,180	393
Ohio	12,357	36,254		48,611	13,022	4,341
Indiana	6,409	7,197		13,606	3,574	1,191
Illinois	9,516	11,328		20,844	5,483	1,828
Michigan	781			781	195	65
Wisconsin	817	2,134		2,951	784	261
Minnesota	930			930	232	77
Iowa	915	3,901		4,816	1,298	433
Missouri	10,591			10,591	2,648	883
Kansas	650	441		1,091	283	94
Total	101,823	83,612	121	185,556	48,404	16,133

TABLE NO. 5.—*Final reports of the draft of July, 1863.*†

TABLE NO. 6.—*Recapitulation, draft of July, 1863.*

States.	Number drawn.	Failed to report.	Discharged, quota full.	Discharged, per order.	Total.	Number examined.	Held to service.			
							Personally held.	Furnished substitutes.	Paid commutation money.	Total accepted.
Maine	16,089	1,729			1,729	14,360	842	1,749	1,986	4,577
New Hampshire	8,002	329	6		335	7,667	181	2,240	571	2,992
Vermont	7,074	335			335	6,739	409	631	1,885	2,925
Massachusetts	32,077	2,880	1	5	2,886	29,191	807	2,322	3,703	6,832
Rhode Island	4,321	249	4		253	4,068	117	679	463	1,259
Connecticut	11,539	938	1		939	10,600	181	2,238	1,513	3,932
New York	95,795	15,772	40	8	15,820	79,975	2,300	6,998	15,912	25,210
Pennsylvania	82,314	11,173	303		11,476	70,838	3,472	6,953	17,672	28,097
Delaware	2,454	275			275	2,179	207	227	435	869
Maryland	5,619	836			836	4,783	109	368	1,106	1,583
District of Columbia	5,798	1,170			1,170	4,628	349	701	318	1,368
Michigan	6,424	1,032	28		1,060	5,364	280	651	1,644	2,575
Wisconsin	14,935	2,697	64		2,761	12,174	627	245	5,080	5,952
Total	292,441	39,415	447	13	39,875	252,566	9,881	26,002	52,288	88,171

*These credits (as finally adjusted) are embraced in the abstract printed in Vol. IV, this series, pp. 1264–1269.

†Omitted in view of the recapitulation following in Table No. 6.

TABLE NO. 6.—*Recapitulation, draft of July, 1863*—Continued.

States.	Exempted for the following causes:											
	Physical disability.	Only son of a widow, &c.	Only son of aged parents.	Elected under fourth clause.	Only brother of children under 12.	Father of motherless children.	Two brothers in service.	Convicted of felony.	In service March 3, 1863.	Aliens.	Over 45 years of age.	Over 35 years and married.
Maine	6,035	395	582	524	8	197	99	3	353	327	43	527
New Hampshire	2,537	226	370	344	3	117	27	4	94	225	14	177
Vermont	2,199	125	259	98	2	74	47	5	83	357	30	220
Massachusetts	12,547	876	614	363	13	364	138	35	505	3,367	228	1,010
Rhode Island	1,334	146	79	123	3	33	32	4	228	361	23	145
Connecticut	3,199	384	245	158	8	141	84	6	135	1,261	78	478
New York	25,701	2,724	2,269	705	55	935	609	47	1,221	8,348	1,064	5,611
Pennsylvania	20,230	2,029	1,541	1,107	29	923	617	31	2,421	4,796	664	4,203
Delaware	697	100	37	15	3	27	20		60	110	2	116
Maryland	1,126	278	72	35	10	74	14	6	250	583	105	326
District of Columbia	1,124	269	62	8	4	91	6	15	145	489	98	347
Michigan	1,617	83	122	17	1	80	34	4	69	339	42	117
Wisconsin	2,785	264	459	79	15	135	100	2	159	847	102	754
Total	81,131	7,899	6,711	3,576	154	3,191	1,827	162	5,723	21,410	2,493	14,031

States.	Exempted for the following causes:												
	Under 20 years of age.	Non-residents.	Paroled prisoner.	Under size.	Dead.	Drafted twice.	Enlisted in the Navy.	Not identified.	Substitutes in service Mar. 3, 1863.	Not notified.	Drunkard.	Mental disability.	Discharged, volunteers in lieu of.
Maine	99	447			33	22		17		25		29	
New Hampshire	54	253			30	15				1		71	
Vermont	85	193			5	6							
Massachusetts	225	1,017		27	62	6	6					35	
Rhode Island	63	235											
Connecticut	160	320				5			3		1		
New York	2,038	2,515		43	43	46		12		44		64	119
Pennsylvania	1,413	1,410			90	11	1		712			29	
Delaware	80	43											
Maryland	165	16			29				12			13	
District of Columbia	189	413											
Michigan	48	57			2				5			10	
Wisconsin	177	228	1		15	15		1	3			6	
Total	4,796	7,147	1	70	309	126	7	30	735	70	1	257	119

TABLE NO. 6.—*Recapitulation, draft of July, 1863*—Continued.

States.	Exempted for the following causes:												
	Promoted.	Furnished substitutes before draft.	Quakers furloughed.	Enrolled twice.	Illegally drafted.	Absent at sea.	Paroled by rebels.	Deducted by order of acting assistant provost-marshal-general.	Rebel deserters.	Discharged on writ of habeas corpus.	Discharged, order Secretary of War.	Illegal notification.	In service when drafted.
Maine	2		6		2		7		1				
New Hampshire			2		3						1		21
Vermont													
Massachusetts													16
Rhode Island													
Connecticut	1								1				
New York		1		63		1		118	3				126
Pennsylvania	1		1	5					3	3	1	10	348
Delaware													
Maryland											6		
District of Columbia													
Michigan													
Wisconsin				4							1		6
Total	4	1	9	72	5	1	7	118	8	3	9	10	517

States.	Exempted for the following causes:												
	Enlisted after draft.	Other causes.	Unaccounted for.	In six months' service.	Discharged, order of Provost-Marshal-General.	Slaves.	Erroneous enrollment.	Discharged, order of acting assistant provost-marshal-general.	Enlisted previous to draft.	Discharged, credits allowed.	Deserters.	Dropped from list.	Total exemptions.
Maine													9,783
New Hampshire		66			19		1						4,675
Vermont									23		3		3,814
Massachusetts		849							56				22,359
Rhode Island													2,809
Connecticut													6,668
New York							213		27				54,765
Pennsylvania	7	9	11	39			46						42,741
Delaware													1,310
Maryland						16	64						3,200
District of Columbia													3,260
Michigan	2							4	3	126	1	6	2,789
Wisconsin							1		63				6,222
Total	9	924	11	39	19	16	325	4	172	126	4	6	164,395

RECAPITULATION, JULY, 1863.

Whole number drawn		292,441
Failed to report	39,415	
Discharged, quota full	447	
Discharged per order	13	
		39,875
Number examined		252,566
Total number exempted		164,395
		88,171
Held to personal service	9,881	
Furnished substitutes	26,002	
Paid commutation	52,288	
		88,171

TABLE No. 7.—*Final reports of the draft of March 14, 1864.**

TABLE No. 8.—*Recapitulation, draft under call of March 14, 1864.*

States.	Number drawn.	Failed to report.	Discharged, quota full.	Discharged per order.	Total.	Number examined.	Held to service.			
							Personally held.	Furnished substitutes.	Paid commutation money.	Total accepted.
New Hampshire	1,573	132	32	....	164	1,409	24	596	121	741
Vermont	347	47	1	54	102	245	12	27	89	128
Massachusetts	9,505	2,287	44	....	2,331	7,174	105	743	1,615	2,463
New York	11,713	2,655	196	1	2,852	8,861	153	2,003	2,267	4,423
New Jersey	13,520	2,552	107	....	2,659	10,861	380	2,438	4,170	6,988
Pennsylvania	29,334	7,859	442	....	8,301	21,033	676	608	10,046	11,330
Delaware	2,081	389	......	....	389	1,692	90	16	951	1,057
Maryland	11,498	3,812	6	....	3,818	7,680	484	843	2,538	3,865
Kentucky	9,186	2,672	4	1	2,677	6,509	421	531	3,241	4,193
Ohio	18,648	3,163	301	13	3,477	15,171	596	943	6,290	7,829
Michigan	2,037	746	67	....	813	1,224	112	92	323	527
Minnesota	4,004	879	27	....	906	3,098	363	71	1,027	1,461
Total	113,446	27,193	1,227	69	28,489	84,957	3,416	8,911	32,678	45,005

States.	Exempted for the following causes:									
	Physical disability.	Mental disability.	Aliens.	Over 45 years of age.	Under 20 years of age.	Non-residents.	In service when drafted.	Discharged, order of acting assistant provost-marshal-general.	In service March 3, 1863.	Dead.
New Hampshire	423	16	15	54	1	12	17	118	2	10
Vermont	94	....	2	5	......	5	3		4	1
Massachusetts	2,008	1	1,023	394	10	177	49	......	......	24
New York	2,388	3	632	824	96	209	87	......	16	22
New Jersey	2,079	....	592	690	42	244	196	......	......	......
Pennsylvania	5,096	6	1,223	955	464	547	402	......	......	66
Delaware	369	....	84	......	96	......	42	......	......	......
Maryland	2,150	6	462	675	154	87	131	......	......	32
Kentucky	1,392	12	242	307	96	45	102	......	......	32
Ohio	3,909	2	637	695	85	373	961	......	30	60
Michigan	515	....	95	27	4	26	11	......	3	5
Minnesota	1,050	6	118	213	18	85	123	......	......	24
Total	21,473	52	5,125	4,839	1,066	1,810	2,124	118	55	276

*Omitted in view of the recapitulation following in Table No. 8.

TABLE NO. 8.—*Recapitulation, draft under call of March 14, 1864*—Continued.

States.	Exempted for the following causes:												
	Convicted of felony.	Enlisted previous to draft.	Discharged, volunteers accepted in lieu of.	Erroneous enrollment.	Furnished substitutes before draft.	Enlisted in Navy.	Two years in service.	Dropped from list.	By Circular 28.	Illegally drafted.	Not notified.	Suspended by board.	All other causes.
New Hampshire													
Vermont	1	2											
Massachusetts			534	93	11	3	11	203	1	61	12	30	66
New York				30			34	88					
New Jersey							30						
Pennsylvania			612	15	17		16					105	115
Delaware				44									
Maryland				112			4						
Kentucky				7		9	4				44		
Ohio		19	42		1		20			5			
Michigan		6			1						4		
Minnesota													
Total	1	27	1,188	301	30	12	119	291	1	66	60	135	181

States.	Exempted for the following causes:											
	Paid commutation previously.	Indian.	Enrolled twice.	Drafted twice.	Unaccounted for.	Discharged by order of President.	Illegal notification.	Rebel deserters.	Skilled mechanic.	Exempted in previous draft.	In one hundred days' service.	Total exemptions.
New Hampshire												668
Vermont												117
Massachusetts												4,711
New York	3	1	5									4,438
New Jersey												3,873
Pennsylvania	19		5	4	24	1	11					9,703
Delaware												635
Maryland								1	1			3,815
Kentucky								10		14		2,316
Ohio				3							500	7,342
Michigan												697
Minnesota												1,637
Total	22	1	10	7	24	1	11	11	1	14	500	39,952

RECAPITULATION, MARCH 14, 1864.

Whole number drawn		113,446
Failed to report	27,193	
Discharged, quota full	1,227	
Discharged, per order	69	
		28,489
Number examined		84,957
Total number exempted		39,952
		45,005
Held to personal service	3,416	
Furnished substitutes	8,911	
Paid commutation	32,678	
		45,005

TABLE NO. 9.—*Final reports of draft under call of July 18, 1864.**

*Omitted in view of the recapitulation following in Table No. 10.

TABLE NO. 10.—*Recapitulation, draft under call of July 18, 1864.*

States.	Number drawn.	Failed to report.	Discharged, quota full.	Discharged per order.	Total.	Number examined.	Held to service.			
							Personally held.	Furnished substitutes.	Paid commutation money.	Total accepted.
Maine	7, 795	1, 676	1, 978	1	3, 655	4, 140	815	881	11	1, 707
New Hampshire	901	2	669	......	671	230	3	117	......	120
Vermont	214	29	24	......	53	161	10	8	......	18
Connecticut	492	76	168	......	244	248	21	89	2	112
New York	10, 227	3, 432	3, 364	......	6, 796	3, 431	47	1, 708	5	1, 760
New Jersey	5, 423	996	1, 399	......	2, 395	3, 028	134	1, 324	11	1, 469
Pennsylvania	29, 228	8, 351	3, 723	5	12, 079	17, 149	2, 392	2, 560	171	5, 123
Delaware	2, 980	490	13	......	503	2, 477	82	740	......	822
Maryland	7, 090	2, 639	402	......	3, 041	4, 049	625	902	31	1, 558
District of Columbia	4, 370	2, 044	......	......	2, 044	2, 326	329	418	19	766
West Virginia	1, 426	662	322	132	1, 116	310	33	55	......	88
Kentucky	16, 805	6, 831	190	658	7, 679	9, 126	1, 439	1, 981	24	3, 444
Missouri	16, 945	8, 369	444	......	8, 813	8, 132	1, 031	1, 608	......	2, 639
Ohio	27, 598	5, 527	4, 378	9	9, 914	17, 684	3, 285	3, 129	176	6, 590
Indiana	33, 968	5, 387	3, 660	......	9, 047	24, 921	6, 841	4, 654	690	12, 185
Illinois	26, 213	8, 087	1, 268	......	9, 355	16, 858	3, 196	5, 067	49	8, 312
Michigan	7, 370	1, 801	1, 748	......	3, 549	3, 821	822	662	23	1, 507
Iowa	7, 548	702	1, 273	1	1, 976	5, 572	1, 862	1, 197	67	3, 126
Wisconsin	20, 804	7, 901	967	1	8, 869	11, 933	2, 875	1, 269	16	4, 160
Minnesota	4, 521	1, 157	426	......	1, 583	2, 938	363	133	3	499
Total	231, 918	66, 159	26, 416	807	93, 382	138, 536	26, 205	28, 502	1, 298	56, 005

States.	Exempted for the following causes:													
	Physical disability.	Mental disability.	Furnished substitutes before draft.	In service when drafted.	Not notified.	Aliens.	Drafted twice.	Over 45 years of age.	Under 20 years of age.	Dead.	Non-residents.	Paid commutation previously.	Two years in service.	Illegally drafted.
Maine	1, 993	15	7	76	2	72	3	131	21	8	88	1	3	5
New Hampshire	64	....	....	5	....	8	....	16	1	1	14	......	1	....
Vermont	25	....	....	......	....	5	....	......	......	....	2	......	....	....
Connecticut	88	1	....	3	....	18	....	17	2	....	5	2	....	....
New York	1, 024	6	4	51	....	220	....	212	43	3	54	19	8	....
New Jersey	632	17	3	115	....	259	1	198	31	....	33	142	11	....
Pennsylvania	4, 642	49	187	1, 370	7	728	6	1, 008	213	85	617	1, 026	28	....
Delaware	673	7	....	503	....	13	....	148	38	65	......	107	4	....
Maryland	1, 492	4	....	44	....	195	....	385	81	17	112	72	12	....
District of Columbia	440	....	....	56	....	295	....	262	80	16	223	......	46	....
West Virginia	107	5	....	12	....	5	....	16	19	4	14	2	1	....
Kentucky	2, 557	34	109	578	481	246	7	613	101	60	162	235	....	....
Missouri	2, 811	6	17	202	....	1, 118	62	880	96	73	194	......	10	....
Ohio	4, 905	43	115	1, 108	....	632	5	813	156	97	944	314	22	....
Indiana	7, 501	92	49	495	....	173	....	699	103	27	614	......	10	4
Illinois	5, 487	35	1	251	....	1, 082	....	794	168	12	571	......	23	....
Michigan	1, 244	7	12	248	....	157	....	91	25	14	96	20	3	....
Iowa	1, 687	17	2	45	....	262	....	183	38	20	183	2	3	....
Wisconsin	4, 239	26	50	585	....	842	....	1, 143	134	59	607	12	4	....
Minnesota	978	11	....	406	....	125	....	273	12	19	211	157	1	....
Total	42, 589	375	556	6, 153	490	6, 455	84	7, 882	1, 362	580	4, 744	2, 111	190	9

TABLE No. 10.—*Recapitulation, draft under call of July 18, 1864*—Continued.

States	Exempted for the following causes:													
	Enlisted in Navy.	Enrolled men furnished substitutes.	Volunteers, in lieu of.	Indians.	Erroneous enrollment.	Rebel deserters.	Convicted of felony.	Deserters.	Discharged, order of Secretary of War.	Skilled mechanic.	Discharged, order of Provost-Marshal-General.	Circular 31.	Circular 28.	In charge of military commission.
Maine	8													
New Hampshire														
Vermont		4	107											
Connecticut														
New York				1	24	1	1							
New Jersey			111					6						
Pennsylvania			1,873		145	8	1		12					
Delaware					97									
Maryland	3				35	6			7	5	3	9	9	
District of Columbia						14			10	102				
West Virginia						12								5
Kentucky					11	173			1					
Missouri						21			1	2				
Ohio			1,538		144	22	1							
Indiana			2,790		113	41			5					
Illinois						45	3		2					
Michigan			374		5									
Iowa						2	1		1					
Wisconsin			1	3		3			1					
Minnesota			246											
Total	11	4	7,040	4	574	348	7	6	40	109	3	9	9	5

States.	Exempted for the following causes:													
	Discharged, order of acting assistant provost-marshal-general.	In rebel service.	Illegal notification.	Discharged, order of the President.	All other causes.	Exempted previously.	Refugees.	Enlisted after draft.	Enlisted before draft.	Enrolled twice.	Suspended by board.	Paroled prisoner.	Discharged, credits allowed.	Total exemptions.
Maine														2,433
New Hampshire														110
Vermont														143
Connecticut														136
New York														1,671
New Jersey														1,559
Pennsylvania	3		11	2						5				12,026
Delaware														1,655
Maryland														2,491
District of Columbia							16							1,560
West Virginia	20													222
Kentucky		38	18	1	239	18								5,682
Missouri														5,493
Ohio					233		2							11,094
Indiana	1							15	4					12,736
Illinois										2			70	8,546
Michigan			1		17									2,314
Iowa														2,446
Wisconsin										63	2	1		7,775
Minnesota														2,439
Total	24	38	30	3	489	18	18	15	4	70	2	1	70	82,531

RECAPITULATION.

Whole number drawn 231,918
Failed to report 66,159
Discharged, quota full 26,416
Discharged, per order 807
93,382

Number examined 138,536
Total number exempted 82,531
56,005

Held to personal service 26,205
Furnished substitutes 28,502
Paid commutation 1,298
56,005

TABLE NO. 11.—*Final reports of the draft under call of December 19, 1864.**

TABLE NO. 12.—*Recapitulation, draft under call of December 19, 1864.*

States.	Number drawn.	Failed to report.	Discharged, quota full.	Discharged, per order.	Total.	Number examined.	Held to service.			
							Personally held.	Furnished substitutes.	Paid commutation money.	Total accepted.
Maine	3,440	355	607	1,044	2,006	1,434	334	309	10	653
New Hampshire	330	1	293	....	294	36	2	9	......	11
Vermont	108	18	52	4	74	34	6	6	......	12
New York	33,753	9,886	3,716	9,673	23,275	10,478	710	2,623	13	3,346
New Jersey	13,382	2,657	2,247	3,542	8,446	4,936	437	1,692	15	2,144
Pennsylvania	37,997	3,926	5,852	16,904	26,682	11,315	2,075	2,515	282	4,872
Delaware	1,120	289	2	48	339	781	46	165	......	211
Maryland	5,112	1,920	7	1,126	3,053	2,059	208	343	3	554
District of Columbia	4,170	2,740	....	....	2,740	1,430	290	294	1	585
West Virginia	1,754	352	50	632	1,034	720	209	164	......	373
Kentucky	3,430	....	....	3,330	3,330	100		10	......	10
Missouri	4,574	1,075	....	3,181	4,256	318	......	30	......	30
Ohio	4,154	678	847	504	2,029	2,125	360	437	13	810
Indiana	7,190	848	1,027	1,195	3,070	4,120	756	528	94	1,378
Illinois	5,872	1,432	1,850	896	4,178	1,694	342	337	6	685
Michigan	6,291	715	1,209	2,064	3,988	2,303	595	360	18	973
Wisconsin	2,656	1,144	206	243	1,593	1,063	220	107	1	328
Minnesota	2,271	22	41	1,642	1,705	566	136	55	2	193
Kansas	1,420	419	5	380	804	616	119	208	2	329
Total	139,024	28,477	18,011	46,408	92,896	46,128	6,845	10,192	460	17,497

* Omitted in view of the recapitulation following in Table No. 12.

TABLE NO. 12.—*Recapitulation, draft under call of December 19, 1864*—Cont'd.

States.	Exempted for the following causes:												
	Physical disability.	Mental disability.	In service when drafted.	Aliens.	Over 45 years of age.	Under 20 years of age.	Non-residents.	Paid commutation in 1863 and 1864.	Two years in service.	Erroneous enrollment.	Dead.	Volunteers accepted in lieu of.	Furnished substitutes before draft.
Maine	696	11	22	7	24	6	14	1	....	....	....	....	....
New Hampshire	22	....	....	....	....	....	1	....	....	1	1	....	....
Vermont	6	....	....	....	1	....	....	....	....	....	....	15	....
New York	2,934	30	123	1,335	1,444	126	182	58	127	36	20	355	89
New Jersey	1,385	17	102	674	349	54	46	124	36	....	....	....	4
Pennsylvania	3,572	62	221	476	872	114	351	188	58	23	34	120	153
Delaware	365	4	12	12	48	19	....	70	1	37	2	....	....
Maryland	716	3	58	203	232	31	59	45	28	24	13	7	....
District of Columbia	280	....	28	134	147	30	71	....	20	53	3	....	....
West Virginia	189	6	17	14	45	16	20	....	....	....	2	....	....
Kentucky	37	....	1	11	16	3	4	1	....	....	1	....	1
Missouri	177	1	16	25	38	2	19	....	3	....	5	....	1
Ohio	418	7	82	77	110	22	63	7	....	20	5	491	3
Indiana	1,002	6	209	10	96	22	96	15	1	32	8	832	11
Illinois	727	5	35	32	90	18	77	....	3	....	7	6	....
Michigan	884	6	8	57	62	12	53	7	3	....	3	186	1
Wisconsin	438	2	54	89	83	17	22	....	2	....	....	10	11
Minnesota	180	2	60	17	32	7	15	....	....	41	1	....	....
Kansas	182	2	1	2	54	5	34	....	3	....	....	....	....
Total	14,210	164	1,049	3,175	3,743	504	1,127	516	285	267	105	2,022	274

States.	Exempted for the following causes:												
	Rebel deserters.	Furnished substitutes in 1863.	Drafted twice.	Deserters.	By order of President of United States.	Enrolled twice.	Exempted in draft of March 14, 1864.	Enlisted in Navy.	All other causes.	Promoted.	Deducted by order of General Fry.	Discharged, order of Secretary of War.	Exempted previous to draft.
Maine	....	....	....	....	....	....	....	....	....	....	....	....	....
New Hampshire	....	....	....	....	....	....	....	....	....	....	....	....	....
Vermont	....	....	....	....	....	....	....	....	....	....	....	....	....
New York	6	15	27	2	1	1	1	4	209	1	6	....	....
New Jersey	1	....	....	....	....	....	....	....	....	....	....	....	....
Pennsylvania	17	....	1	....	5	15	....	67	7	....	53	5	1
Delaware	....	....	....	....	....	....	....	....	....	....	....	....	....
Maryland	23	....	....	....	....	....	....	....	....	....	....	....	....
District of Columbia	14	....	....	....	....	....	....	....	....	....	....	54	....
West Virginia	37	....	....	....	....	....	....	....	....	....	....	....	....
Kentucky	3	....	....	....	....	....	....	....	....	....	....	....	11
Missouri	1	....	....	....	....	....	....	....	....	....	....	....	....
Ohio	5	....	....	....	....	3	....	....	....	....	....	2	....
Indiana	14	....	....	....	....	....	....	....	....	....	....	....	....
Illinois	8	....	....	....	....	1	....	....	....	....	....	....	....
Michigan	....	....	....	....	....	....	....	....	20	....	....	....	....
Wisconsin	....	....	....	....	....	....	....	....	7	....	....	....	....
Minnesota	....	....	....	....	....	....	....	....	....	....	....	....	....
Kansas	2	....	....	....	....	....	....	....	....	....	....	....	....
Total	131	15	28	2	6	20	1	71	243	1	59	61	12

TABLE NO. 12.—*Recapitulation, draft under call of December 19, 1864*—Cont'd.

States.	Exempted for the following causes:													
	Suspended by Board.	Illegal notification.	Enlisted after draft.	Convicted of felony.	Skilled mechanic.	Section 23.	Circular 31.	Circular 28.	Convicted by a military commission.	Refugees.	Illegally drafted.	Not notified.	Discharged, credit allowed.	Total exemptions.
Maine														781
New Hampshire														25
Vermont														22
New York														7,132
New Jersey														2,792
Pennsylvania	19	3	5	1										6,443
Delaware														570
Maryland				2	11	45	1	4						1,505
District of Columbia									2	9				845
West Virginia										1				347
Kentucky						1								90
Missouri														288
Ohio														1,315
Indiana			48	2		23					3	312		2,742
Illinois														1,009
Michigan			1			12					1		14	1,330
Wisconsin														735
Minnesota						18								373
Kansas				1						1				287
Total	19	3	54	6	11	99	1	4	2	11	4	312	14	28,631

RECAPITULATION.

Whole number drawn		139,024
Failed to report	28,477	
Discharged, quota full	18,011	
Discharged, per order	46,408	
		92,896
Number examined		46,128
Total number exempted		28,631
		17,497
Held to personal service	6,845	
Furnished substitutes	10,192	
Paid commutation	460	
		17,497

TABLE NO. 13.—*Estimate of the number of men to whom U. S. bounty has been paid, the amount paid each man, and the total amount paid, from May 3, 1861, to the end of the war.**

*Omitted; see explanatory foot-note (*), p. 687.

TABLE NO. 14.—*Table of bounties, other than U. S.*

States and districts.	Calls of 1863.			Call of March 14, 1864.			Call of July 18, 1864.	
	Average bounty paid.	Average cost per man.	Aggregate bounty paid.	Average bounty paid.	Average cost per man.	Aggregate bounty paid.	Average bounty paid.	Average cost per man.
MAINE.								
First District	$299.08			$199.35			$345.14	
Second District	284.93						303.34	
Third District				268.33			356.23	
Fourth District	298.00						488.00	
Fifth District	105.30			100.23			248.19	
Total								
NEW HAMPSHIRE.[a]								
First District		$417.00	$1,045,918.00		$395.00	$373,182.00		$693.00
Second District		445.00	967,574.00		349.00	276,024.00		766.00
Third District		401.00	807,623.00		485.00	344,823.00		797.00
Total								
VERMONT.								
First District				241.11	274.67	502,105.00	610.41	702.66
Second District				312.02	282.18	757,599.00	665.85	704.88
Third District				145.32	160.75	404,570.28	543.50	720.20
Total								
MASSACHUSETTS.								
First District	300.00	117.22		150.00	171.62		150.00	
Second District	63.06			158.58	192.44		203.00	
Third District				40.00	6.37		225.00	
Fourth District				40.00	101.84		225.00	
Fifth District				8.00	8.05		197.00	
Sixth District	127.00			148.00	135.00		231.00	
Seventh District	330.00	58.53		262.50	110.61		433.50	
Eighth District	71.22	57.52		119.79	116.69		224.98	197.53
Ninth District	300 00	300.00		206.98	206.98		304.59	304.59
Tenth District	402.74	74.12		492.91	183.33		433.44	228.18
Total								
Grand total								
RHODE ISLAND.								
First District								
Second District								
Total								
CONNECTICUT.								
First District			561,495.51		[b] 259.87	546,332.17		[c] 391.07
Second District								158.38
Third District								438.50
Fourth District								207.35
Total								
NEW YORK.								
Southern Division.								
First District	276.53	300.00	63,050.00	324.89	350.00	806,399.57	593.39	593.39
Second District	300.00		106,500.00	300.00	284.32	678,000.00	294.72	275.00
Third District	300.00		128,100.00	300.00	248.82	1,240,500.00	296.23	275.00

a Includes calls of October, 1863, and February 1, 1864.
b Average cost, including calls of 1863 and February, 1864.

bounty, paid from the beginning to the end of the late war.

Call of July 18, 1864.	Call of December 19, 1864.			Grand aggregate bounty paid.	Remarks.
Aggregate bounty paid.	Average bounty paid.	Average cost per man.	Aggregate bounty paid.		
	$377.64			$2,532,388.69	The acting assistant provost-marshal of Maine reports his statement incomplete from his inability to obtain information from many towns.
	367.51			1,444,346.28	
	399.62			2,084,366.00	
	493.00			642,137.00	
	419.03			1,134,406.00	
				7,837,643.97	
$1,630,074.00		$646.00	$441,901.00	3,491,075.00	Average under call of 1863, $421; under Mar. 14, 1864, $406; under July 18, 1864, $745; under Dec. 19, 1864, $639. Average cost per man under all calls, $557.59.
1,363,575.00		627.00	438,334.00	3,045,508.00	
1,310,310.00		643.00	636,974.00	3,099,730.00	
				9,636,313.00	
485,893.00	606.05	590.50	423,026.00	1,411,024.00	Under call of Mar. 14, 1864, are included calls of Oct.. 1863, and Feb., 1864.
985,463.00	553.21	526.74	401,634.00	2,144,696.00	
385,887.81	475.51	462.27	182,596.79	973,054.88	
				4,528,774.88	
		199.28		872,638.23	The average cost per man is as correct as the information can be obtained.
	146.46	126.54		1,479,799.04	
	175.00	164.91		1,200,908.31	
	175.00	149.98		1,209,593.67	
	171.00	175.34		1,070,349.00	
	196.00	204.00		1,461,967.87	
	150.00	195.89		1,293,505.29	
	233.20	203.86		1,119,904.00	
	209.93	209.93		1,276,616.00	
	414.75	238.13		1,214,144.00	
				12,199,425.41	
				10,766,124.95	Aggregate additional bounties paid by the State which cannot be specified by districts.
				22,965,550.36	
				330,792.28	In this State the amounts cannot be divided under the different calls. This aggregate is taken from the report of the adjutant-general of the State.
				489,976.32	
				820,768.60	
1,031,332.17				2,139,100.31	Acting assistant provost-marshal-general reports that this is all the information he can obtain.
				1,124,806.74	
				2,229,839.10	
				1,393,808.12	
				6,887,554.27	
1,501,889.01	746.18	746.18	611,869.87	2,983,208.45	Average bounty paid, call of 1863, $297.65; Mar. 14, 1864, $322.48; July 18, 1864, $339.32; Dec. 19, 1864, $452.59.
188,350.00	362.39	363.98	496,475.00	1,469,325.00	
326,150.00	318.83	313.99	446,800.00	2,141,550.00	

c Average cost, including all calls of 1863 and 1864.

TABLE NO. 14.—*Table of bounties, other*

States and districts.	Calls of 1863.			Call of March 14, 1864.			Call of July 18, 1864.	
	Average bounty paid.	Average cost per man.	Aggregate bounty paid.	Average bounty paid.	Average cost per man.	Aggregate bounty paid.	Average bounty paid.	Average cost per man.
NEW YORK—continued.								
Fourth District	$300.00	$300.00	$26,700.00	$300.00	$300.00	$52,500.00	$230.77	$230.77
Fifth District	300.00	300.00	149,700.00	300.00	300.00	216,000.00	269.30	269.30
Sixth District	300.00	300.00 (308.32)	109,800.00	300.00	300.00 (243.93)	144,600.00	269.38	269.38 (16.33)
Seventh District	300.00	300.00	95,100.00	300.00	300.00	130,200.00	272.72	272.72
Eighth District	300.00	300.00	113,100.00	300.00	300.00	117,000.00	275.86	287.55
Ninth District	300.00	300.00	64,200.00	300.00	300.00	116,100.00	290.90	290.90
Tenth District	300.00		304,800.00	500.00	483.00	1,306,500.00	600.00	478.00
Total								
Northern Division.								
Eleventh District					300.00	516,600.00		550.00
Twelfth District			342,016.46		*a*312.50 140.18	513,593.74		699.29
Thirteenth District			46,668.62		*a*306.55 321.62	737,525.00		693.95
Fourteenth District			344,635.64		*a*300.00 153.58	*b* 23,220.00 465,955.00		850.17
Fifteenth District								
Sixteenth District		175.41	84,277.44		*a*344.96 300.00	384,843.11		728.09
Seventeenth District					285.54	449,702.00		742.00
Eighteenth District					*a*285.06 766.97	1,175,927.00		575.39
Nineteenth District		43.25	13,200.00		487.34	546,786.04		817.77
Twentieth District		150.00	189,300.00		*a*300.00 300.00	1,197,300.00		1,000.00
Total								
Western Division.								
Twenty-first District	50.00		146,250.00	300.00		537,300.00	1,060.00	
Twenty-second District.	50.00		182,900.00	350.00		803,300.00	430.00	
Twenty-third District	50.00		105,050.00	300.00		748,500.00	932.47	
Twenty-fourth District			177,114.11			705,765.86		
Twenty-fifth District				300.00		900,000.00	950.00	
Twenty-sixth District	122.72		792,400.00	375.00		1,495,925.00	925.00	
Twenty-seventh District.				228.60		927,658.00	551.46	
Twenty-eighth District			244,957.28			525,000.00		
Twenty-ninth District	37.50		103,050.00	311.50		408,460.00	600.00	
Thirtieth District	74.42		230,000.00	225.50		544,000.00	266.32	
Thirty-first District				300.00		680,700.00	700.00	
Total								
NEW JERSEY.								
First District		300.00			*a*425.00 525.00			600.00
Second District					232.66			425.27
Third District					363.29			568.06
Fourth District					314.08			505.74
Fifth District					372.14			598.87
Total								
PENNSYLVANIA.								
Eastern Division.								
First District					254.48	733,682.04		395.04
Second District					250.00	889,500.00		391.83
Third District		69.20	9,550.00		254.59	935,638.00		405.89
Fourth District					258.53	988,089.16		418.91
Fifth District		122.00	366.00		316.59	724,813.50		470.75
Sixth District		300.00	171,000.00		310.85	985,395.00		517.73

a Call of February 1. *b* Hand money.

than U. S. bounty, &c.—Continued.

Call of July 18, 1864.	Call of December 19, 1864.				
Aggregate bounty paid.	Average bounty paid.	Average cost per man.	Aggregate bounty paid.	Grand aggregate bounty paid.	Remarks.
$3,000.00	$403.97	$403.97	$61,000.00	$143,200.00	Figures within the brace show only amounts paid to recruits put into service through district provost-marshals. Figures in () are taken from report of O. Blunt, esq., and include average and aggregate expenditures for bounties for the county of New York (Fourth to Ninth Districts, inclusive).
27,200.00	419.87	419.87	190,200.00	583,100.00	
26,400.00	424.94	424.94 (472.76)	184,000.00	464,800.00 (10,594,391.68)	
12,000.00	419.85	419.85	169,200.00	406,500.00	
32,000.00	361.76	354.59	61,50^.00	323,600.00	
16,000.00	368.18	368.18	64,800.00	261,100.00	
1,516,800.00	700.00	477.00	1,011,500.00	4,139,600.00	
....	....	....	....	23,510,375.13	
757,445.00	....	497.00	258,000.00	1,532,045.00	This statement is as correct as was possible to obtain.
1,705,558.84	....	563.93	779,990.56	3,341,159.60	
2,059,025.00	....	639.46	700,800.00	3,544,018.62	
b 38,375.00 2,591,312.81	....	569.62	*b* 80,500.00 893,162.00	142,095.00 4,295,065.45	
....	....	....	....	....	
978,565.73	....	617.25	280,852.50	1,728,538.78	
1,104,096.00	....	506.70	317,706.00	1,871,504.00	
1,488,558.00	....	618.40	*c* 81,450.00 832,993.00	81,450.00 3,497,478.00	
1,784,078.76	....	668.42	702,411.84	3,046,476.64	
1,964,000.00	....	550.00	728,200.00	4,078,800.00	
....	....	....	....	27,158,631.09	
1,502,900.00	670.00	....	769,112.00	2,955,562.00	
998,000.00	500.00	....	719,600.00	2,703,800.00	
1,911,575.00	574.13	....	740,635.00	3,505,760.00	
2,227,514.20	....	....	886,198.76	3,996,592.93	
2,281,900.00	700.00	....	679,000.00	3,860,900.00	
1,811,150.00	700.00	....	728,000.00	4,455,575.00	
1,713,386.00	571.75	....	643,218.00	3,284,262.00	
2,464,160.72	....	....	690,362.00	3,924,480.00	
1,263,189.00	550.00	....	464,941.00	2,239,640.00	
800,000.00	396.31	....	600,000.00	2,374,000.00	
1,415,400.00	650.00	....	563,550.00	2,659,650.00	
....	....	....	....	35,960,221.93	
....	....	625.00	....	....	All the information which could be obtained from the authorities by this Bureau. The total or grand aggregate is an estimate of the comptroller of the treasury of the State.
....	....	629.82	....	....	
....	....	508.64	....	....	
....	....	643.85	....	....	
....	....	724.42	....	....	
....	....	....	....	23,868,966.62	
				749,795.44	Amount paid by the city of Philadelphia through citizens and veteran bounty committees, &c.
207,000.00	....	427.31	364,393.00	1,305,075.04	
772,300.00	....	409.13	479,500.00	2,141,300.00	
427,405.00	....	413.91	461,518.00	1,814,311.00	
452,008.80	....	475.76	855,894.63	2,295,992.59	
560,200.71	....	504.30	603,651.44	1,889,031.65	
1,097,593.00	....	551.67	883,226.12	3,137,214.12	

c Paid by State.

TABLE NO. 14.—*Table of bounties, other*

States and districts.	Calls of 1863.			Call of March 14, 1864.			Call of July 18, 1864.	
	Average bounty paid.	Average cost per man.	Aggregate bounty paid.	Average bounty paid.	Average cost per man.	Aggregate bounty paid.	Average bounty paid.	Average cost per man.
PENNSYLVANIA—cont'd.								
Seventh District			*a* $54,240.00		$300.00	$1,067,100.00		$234.22
Eighth District		$95.61	76,108.00		266.43	807,559.00		239.6[illegible]
Ninth District			103,028.00		255.99	492,281.00		461.36
Tenth District		50.00	60,250.00		301.32	781,320.00		427.43
Eleventh District	*b* $61.10	166.62	*c* 143,402.80		311.34	608,042.16		440.68
Twelfth District					304.26	327,384.00		452.71
Total								
Western Division.								
Thirteenth District				$250.00	130.00		$475.00	240.00
Fourteenth District				250.00	250.00		440.00	440.00
Fifteenth District				250.00	200.00		450.00	450.00
Sixteenth District				100.00	100.00		500.00	500.00
Seventeenth District				217.00	125.00		362.00	260.00
Eighteenth District				265.00	265.00		425.00	425.00
Nineteenth District				300.00	300.00		500.00	500.00
Twentieth District				250.00	250.00		150.00	150.00
Twenty-first District				150.00	200.00		475.00	500.00
Twenty-second District				194.00	214.94		447.00	251.95
Twenty-third District				200.00	205.00		500.00	505.00
Twenty-fourth District				275.00	300.00		450.00	475.00
Total								
DELAWARE.								
Delaware					71.26	245,715.68		381.01
MARYLAND.								
First District								
Second District					337.57	843,932.50		454.10
Third District					571.21	1,428,017.50		578.63
Fourth District					164.82	412,056.00		154.73
Fifth District					9.99	29,990.00		39.53
Total								
DISTRICT OF COLUMBIA.								
District of Columbia								
WEST VIRGINIA.								
First District	138.00			226.00			304.00	
Second District	134.00			175.00			318.00	
Third District	30.00			88.00			105.00	
Total								
KENTUCKY.								
First District								
Second District								
Third District								
Fourth District								
Fifth District								
Sixth District								157.04
Seventh District								2.49
Eighth District								
Ninth District								35.86
Total								

a Call of 1862, bounty paid to 124th Pennsylvania Volunteers.

b Calls prior to 1865.

than U. S. bounty, &c.—Continued.

Call of July 18, 1864.	Call of December 19, 1864.				
Aggregate bounty paid.	Average bounty paid.	Average cost per man.	Aggregate bounty paid.	Grand aggregate bounty paid.	Remarks.
$491,150.00		$530.34	$513,900.00	$2,126,390.00	
1,129,374.00		366.18	749,582.00	2,762,623.00	
825,837.00		516.18	843,443.00	2,264,589.00	
897,603.00		495.68	671,158.00	2,410,331.00	
620,044.00		472.96	588,363.00	1,959,851.96	
529,215.00		487.63	287,211.00	1,143,810.00	
				26,000,314.96	
	$525.00	520.00		364,700.00	Acting assistant provost-marshal-general reports this statement as near correct as can be obtained.
	535.00	535.00		2,112,922.00	
	500.00	500.00		2,200,000.00	
	500.00	500.00		1,148,258.00	
	400.00	530.00		927,839.96	
	475.00	475.00		1,221,730.00	
	600.00	600.00		1,439,995.00	
	700.00	500.00		935,100.00	
	525.00	550.00		1,210,350.00	
	512.00	536.57		2,266,877.00	
	550.00	555.00		2,220,500.00	
	625.00	650.00		1,106,400.00	
				17,154,671.96	
774,708.01		282.66	116,175.37	1,136,599.06	All the information which can be obtained. The grand aggregate is nearly correct, but the aggregates under the different calls cannot be exactly divided.
				369,000.00	All the information which can be obtained. The grand aggregate is nearly correct, but the aggregates under the different calls cannot be exactly divided.
552,645.00		362.43	359,900.00	1,756,477.50	
887,055.00		227.76	290,400.00	2,605,472.50	
143,287.00		570.02	845,912.00	1,401,255.00	
29,990.00		129.19	78,807.00	139,787.00	
				6,271,992.00	
	75.00			134,010.00	Major Lodor reports, on information obtained from Mayor Wallach, only bounties paid was $75 per man (no call stated). City still disbursing.
	461.00			586,856.00	This information includes only a portion of the State. The acting assistant provost-marshal-general thinks it will be impossible to obtain any further information.
	389.00			214,576.00	
	290.00			63,305.00	
				864,737.00	
					This statement is correct and shows all local bounties paid in the State.
		4.90	3,400.00	3,400.00	
		36.96	15,300.00	15,300.00	
		177.77	232,350.00	232,350.00	
289,890.00		134.91	95,920.00	385,810.00	
6,800.00		.89	1,017.00	7,817.00	
32,600.00		33.78	15,300.00	47,900.00	
				692,577.00	

c Includes amount paid prior to 1863.

TABLE NO. 14.—*Table of bounties, other*

States and districts.	Calls of 1863.			Call of March 14, 1864.			Call of July 18, 1864.	
	Average bounty paid.	Average cost per man.	Aggregate bounty paid.	Average bounty paid.	Average cost per man.	Aggregate bounty paid.	Average bounty paid.	Average cost per man.
OHIO.								
First District	$50.00	$36.71	$19,350.00	$89.00	$40.61	$168,425.00	$325.00	$194.77
Second District	50.00	44.61	19,050.00	100.00	43.50	177,700.00	350.00	238.42
Third District				80.00	80.00	267,590.00	90.00	90.00
Fourth District	200.00	200.00	65,400.00	400.00	400.00	283,600.00	400.00	400.00
Fifth District				150.00	150.00	201,400.00	500.00	500.00
Sixth District				100.00	100.00	119,900.00	250.00	250.00
Seventh District	100.00	100.00	7,900.00	100.00	100.00	114,400.00	395.00	395.00
Eighth District		100.00		100.00	100.00	76,900.00	500.00	500.00
Ninth District	120.00	120.00	70.920.00	154.00	154.00	224,014.00	445.00	445.00
Tenth District				50.00	50.00	190,400.00	400.00	400.00
Eleventh District				100.00	100.00	219,800.00	125.00	125.00
Twelfth District	85.00		44,625.00	125.61	140.00	181,068.00	349.29	324.32
Thirteenth District	100.00		39,400.00	137.00	70.00	190,450.00	278.00	121.00
Fourteenth District	125.00	125.00	130,750.00	150.00	150.00	261,500.00	300.00	300.00
Fifteenth District				100.00	100.00	92,400.00	300.00	300.00
Sixteenth District	173.00		80,321.00	173.61	115.00	350,140.00	379.55	183.00
Seventeenth District	160.00		26,720.00	160.00	92.00	185,980.00	450.00	247.00
Eighteenth District	100.00	100.00	84,200.00	150.00	150.00	198,500.00	400.00	400.00
Nineteenth District				200.00	200.00	528,800.00	350.00	350.00
Total								
INDIANA.								
First District			259,587.45			29,900.00	235.00	235.00
Second District							87.50	87.50
Third District				296.40	296.40	10,375.00	281.92	281.92
Fourth District				221.20	221.20	12,272.00	276.48	276.48
Fifth District			309,359.45	121.72	121.72	46,673.10	318.65	318.65
Sixth District							320.00	320.00
Seventh District							444.10	444.10
Eighth District							121.40	121.40
Ninth District				163.66	163.66	14,520.00	252.00	252.00
Tenth District								
Eleventh District				181.00	181.00	32,300.00	282.75	282.75
Total								
ILLINOIS.								
First District				110.64	50.00	445,214.40	477.33	250.00
Second District				118.30	40.00	309,600.00	579.65	275.00
Third District	106.20		75,825.00	98.07	25.00	175,750.00	504.00	250.00
Fourth District				25.00		725.00	330.51	250.00
Fifth District							739.11	300.00
Sixth District	100.00		34,300.00	125.00	45.00	16,625.00	400.00	275.00
Seventh District				275.00	10.00	550.00	1,055.95	270.00
Eighth District							350.00	225.00
Ninth District							25.07	200.00
Tenth District							362.50	250.00
Eleventh District								
Twelfth District				300.00		8,100.00	470.00	175.00
Thirteenth District							274.20	125.00
Total								
MICHIGAN.								
First District	100.00	70.26		*a*150.00 150.00	*a*159.69 165.76		300.00	345.14
Second District	162.00	56.84		*a*136.00 155.00	*a*181.71 191.02		325.00	359.61
Third District	150.00	70.07		*a*200.00 250.00	*a*205.16 282.57		300.00	392.19
Fourth District	204.00	49.11		*a*204.00 190.00	*a*154.06 131.31		275.00	300.07
Fifth District	154.00	55.26		*a*170.00 186.00	*a*242.67 233.15		300.00	386.44
Sixth District	150.00	40.39		*a*175 00 190.00	*a*160.48 175.92		287.00	206.98
Total								

a Call of February 1, 1864.

than U. S. bounty, &c.—Continued.

Call of July 18, 1864.	Call of December 19, 1864.				
Aggregate bounty paid.	Average bounty paid.	Average cost per man.	Aggregate bounty paid.	Grand aggregate bounty paid.	Remarks.
$573,975.00	$330.00	$231.22	$243,430.00	$1,005,180.00	
581,850.00	375.00	351.09	473,500.00	1,252,100.00	
374,925.00	425.00	425.00	639,575.00	1,282,090.00	
226,400.00	400.00	400.00	308,000.00	883,400.00	
763,000.00	442.00	442.00	512,648.00	1,477,048.00	
617,000.00	510.00	510.00	641,190.00	1,378,090.00	
228,394.00	437.00	437.00	272,345.00	623,039.00	
231,400.00	510.00	510.00	238,160.00	546,460.00	
651,605.00	545.00	545.00	926,212.00	1,872,751.00	
447,600.00	350.00	350.00	397,800.00	1,035,800.00	
436,975.00	300.00	300.00	306,900.00	963,675.00	
695,137.00	474.25	466.60	638,551.00	1,559,381.00	
331,000.00	500.00	500.00	525,000.00	1,085,850.00	
440,100.00	500.00	500.00	478,000.00	1,310,350.00	
263,550.00	475.00	500.00	583,250.00	939.200.00	
630,168.00	515.12	504.00	685,175.00	1,745,804.00	
745,050.00	500.00	500.00	495.750.00	1,453,500.00	
647,900.00	450.00	450.00	476,150.00	1,406,750.00	
625,105.00	450.00	450.00	583,000.00	1,736,905.00	
....	....	....	....	23,557,373.00	
....	345.75	345.75	525,235.40	814,722.85	This statement is believed to be close approximation.
700.00	299.54	299.54	31,150.00	31,850.00	
354,928.32	334.10	334.10	514,203.32	879,506.64	
292,301.00	338.50	338.50	416,879.00	721,452.00	
144,225.72	362.25	362.25	145,902.05	646,160.32	
899,450.00	372.40	372.40	562,299.21	1,461,749.21	
393,470.00	446.10	446.10	810,060.00	1,203,530.00	
125,000.00	439.25	439.25	1,075,000.00	1,200,000.00	
204,330.00	405.25	405.25	385,318.00	604,168.00	
590,000.00	411.00	411.00	996,915.00	1,619,215.00	
....	....	....	....	9,182,354.02	
876,386.25	527.27	400.00	1,860,735.64	3,182,336.29	In this table the average cost per man is only an approximation, as correct as it could be given.
642,480.00	609.03	450.00	1,125,520.00	2,077,600.00	
627,484.63	600.47	450.00	1,576,801.38	2,395,861.01	
58,500.00	362.62	320.00	911,998.00	971,223.00	
572,905.00	508.55	400.00	1,770,769.00	2,343,674.00	
456,000.00	500.00	400.00	543,500.00	1,050,425.00	
183,735.00	845.38	500.00	1,088,002.00	1,272,287.00	
344,750.00	350.00	300.00	766,850.00	1,111,600.00	
8,400.00	374.09	280.00	413,200.00	421,600.00	
29,700.00	386.27	200.00	586,749.00	616,499.00	
....	321.05	200.00	292,800.00	292,800.00	
881,250.00	400.00	350.00	496,000.00	1,385,350.00	
34,550.00	300.00	200.00	140,400.00	174,950.00	
....	....	....	....	17,296,205.30	
....	375.00	506.06	....	1,610,809.00	
....	328.00	440.22	....	1,493,006.00	
....	375.00	505.65	....	1,845,950.00	
....	400.00	354.15	....	1,480,172.00	
....	370.00	386.66	....	1,582,518.00	
....	385.00	304.05	....	1,652,400.00	
....	....	....	....	9,664,855.00	

TABLE NO. 14.—*Table of bounties, other*

States and districts.	Calls of 1863.			Call of March 14, 1864.			Call of July 18, 1864.	
	Average bounty paid.	Average cost per man.	Aggregate bounty paid.	Average bounty paid.	Average cost per man.	Aggregate bounty paid.	Average bounty paid.	Average cost per man.
WISCONSIN.								
First District			*a*$107, 535. 44				*b*$217.54	
Second District			*c*292, 845. 00			$76, 556. 00		
Third District			*c*120, 238. 63			338, 629. 23		
Fourth District	$180. 60		*c*233, 257. 00					
Fifth District	100. 00			$100. 00			300. 00	
Sixth District	125. 00			250. 00			300. 00	
Total								
IOWA.								
First District					$21. 55	31, 974. 00		$39. 68
Second District			87, 136. 00		32. 06	26, 160. 20		260. 72
Third District			218, 635. 00		131. 55	41, 418. 00		446. 79
Fourth District					64. 37	123, 046. 00		117. 03
Fifth District			3, 000. 00		73. 53	66, 807. 00		58. 17
Sixth District		$171. 26	*a*130, 223. 00		179. 91	52, 700. 00		474. 28
Total								
MINNESOTA.								
First District	200. 00	200. 00		300. 00	300. 00		300. 00	300. 00
Second District		100. 00		100. 00			275. 00	275. 00
Total								
MISSOURI.								
First District				138. 93	75. 95	67, 725. 00		191. 12
Second District								
Third District								50. 00
Fourth District								
Fifth District								100. 00
Sixth District								92. 44
Seventh District				100. 00	100. 00	18, 100. 00		124. 31
Eighth District								
Ninth District								101. 39
Total								
KANSAS.								
Northern District								
Southern District								
Total								

a Includes bounties paid in 1861, 1862, and 1863.

b See July, 1864.

than U. S. bounty, &c.—Continued.

Call of July 18, 1864.	Call of December 19, 1864.				
Aggregate bounty paid.	Average bounty paid.	Average cost per man.	Aggregate bounty paid.	Grand aggregate bounty paid.	Remarks.
$494,914.23	$304.52		$314,874.64	$917,324.31	
321,786.00			481,347.00	255,545.50	Amount paid by tax and private subscriptions for all calls.
				1,172,534.00	
358,752.29			440,347.23	697,871.00	Amount which cannot be stated under separate calls.
				1,257,967.38	
	625.63		*d* 1,224,892.00	95,965.00	Paid substitutes.
				1,458,149.00	
	300.00				
	325.00				
				5,855,356.19	Impossible to obtain further information.
2,540.00		$104.41	19,920.00	54,534.00	
46,929.50		319.79	64,278.50	224,504.20	
403,760.00				663,813.00	
80,517.00		162.33	14,285.00	217,848.00	
6,050.00		120.18	13,583.00	89,440.00	
77,089.00		876.76	105,020.00	365,032.00	
				1,615,171.20	
	300.00	300.00		1,037,462.00	
	275.00	275.00		963,002.00	
				2,000,464.00	
408,926.60		67.23		476,651.60	Acting assistant provost-marshal-general reports that this is the best information he can give.
			1,142.95	1,142.95	
2,000.00				2,000.00	
17,700.00		88.86	3,910.00	21,610.00	
34,480.00		300.00	35,400.00	69,880.00	
149,800.00		222.56	147,785.00	315,685.00	
83,954.00			93,200.00	177,154.00	
100,375.00		201.45	117,650.00	218,025.00	
				1,282,148.55	
	203.86	170.00	53,207.00	53,207.00	No bounties paid in State, except under call of Dec. 19, 1864.
	200.00	37.83	4,200.00	4,200.00	
				57,405.00	

c Includes prior calls. *d* Includes all calls for the year 1864.

DOCUMENT NO. 7.

Report of "Deserters' Branch."

PROVOST-MARSHAL-GENERAL'S OFFICE,
Washington, D. C., December 31, 1865.

Brig. Gen. JAMES B. FRY,
Provost-Marshal-General, Washington, D. C.:

GENERAL: I have the honor to submit my report of the proceedings of the "Deserters' Branch" of your Bureau since its organization in the spring of 1863, and have prefixed a few pages about the arrest of deserters before its establishment.

The "paper work" of arresting deserters (to which this branch has been confined) has not been liable to many changes, and I have had but few improvements to suggest, considering that, as now constituted, the branch is in an effective condition. I have given a sketch of its working, which will suffice to reorganize it if needful, and which forms an index to its records.

Until September, 1861, arrests of deserters were made in conformity with section 152, Army Regulations, which offered $30 reward for the apprehension and delivery of a deserter to an officer of the Army at the most convenient post or recruiting station; and at that time General Orders, No. 73, substituted a reward of $5 instead of $30. This sum included all expenses, and but few deserters were arrested—these chiefly by citizens.

In April, 1862, General Orders, No. 36, Adjutant-General's Office, laid the duty of "collecting stragglers" and deserters on the military commanders of cities, nothing being ordered with regard to country districts. This was the first organized attempt to arrest and punish the many deserters from our volunteer forces then at large.

In June, General Order 61 called attention to the great number of officers absent on leave, and notified all such that they would be considered "absent without leave" unless found at their posts within fifteen days from the date of the order, or excused by the Adjutant-General on proper certificate of disability. Those still unfit for duty, but able to travel, were to report at Annapolis, or Camp Chase, Ohio, for examination and medical treatment, or discharge.

General Order 65 forbade commanding officers of companies or regiments to give "furloughs on any pretext whatever," as such furloughs would not relieve a soldier from the charge of desertion and the consequent penalty; and called upon military commanders to publish in some newspaper a notice requiring all soldiers in the vicinity, not on treatment in a U. S. hospital, to report without delay, on penalty of being considered deserters.

General Order 72 revoked all furloughs granted to paroled prisoners and ordered them to report without delay to certain specified rendezvous or be considered deserters and dealt with accordingly, and directed all commanding, mustering, and recruiting officers, and requested Governors of States, to make known the order as far as possible.

In July, General Order 78 called attention to the full medical facilities afforded to all soldiers in U. S. hospitals, and said that "the unauthorized removal of soldiers from under the control of the U. S. authorities by any agents whatever subjects them to loss of pay and other penalties of desertion."

General Order 92 called upon all officers and soldiers absent without proper authority to return to duty before August 11, and prescribed a muster of each regiment and corps on the 18th of August, all absentees from the same to be considered deserters; and further said:

The U. S. marshals in the respective districts, the mayor and chief of police in any town or city, the sheriff of the respective counties in each State, all postmasters and justices of the peace, are authorized to act as special provost-marshals to arrest any officer or private soldier fit for duty who may be found absent from his command without just cause, and convey him to the nearest military post or depot. The transportation, reasonable expenses of this duty, and $5 will be paid for each officer and soldier so arrested and delivered.

By General Orders, No. 140 (September 24), there was instituted a corps of provost-marshals, to be controlled by a provost-marshal-general, whose duty was to arrest deserters, spies, &c. To perform this they were to call upon any available military force at hand, or to employ the assistance of citizens, constables, sheriffs, or police officers. Col. S. Draper was made Provost-Marshal-General under this order. There are no available records to show how many deserters were arrested by this organization, but they were undoubtedly few.

The above shows the difficulties encountered, and the ineffectual remedies adopted before the establishment of your Bureau. With an army as large as ours, it has been found cheaper to have a regular system of provost-marshals throughout the country, by whose means at least two-thirds of the deserters have been returned to duty and their comrades deterred from following their example.

On the 3d of March, 1863, the first enrollment act became law. It provided, *inter alia*, for the appointment of a provost-marshal for every Congressional district, and a provost-marshal-general, who should furnish them with the name and residence of all deserters from the Army and Navy when reported to him by their commanding officers, and made it the duty of provost-marshals to arrest all such.

Under section 26 of this act the President, on the 10th of March, issued a proclamation pardoning all deserters who should voluntarily report before April 1. The number who returned is not on record.

On the 24th of March, 1863, General Orders, No. 72, required commanders of regiments, independent battalions, companies, and batteries, surgeons in charge of hospitals or detachments, and all persons in the military service controlling detached parties, to report on the last day of every month to the Provost-Marshal-General the names of all men of their command who had deserted during the previous month, or who had not been already reported. This report was to be made in the form of a descriptive list, setting forth, also, their place of residence, and such available information as might lead to their arrest.

On the establishment of your Bureau, Maj. Chauncey McKeever was ordered to receive the reports called for by the above order and attend to all official correspondence relating to deserters. This branch was thus organized April 8, 1863, with a force of eight clerks.

The reports of deserters began to come in early in April. At first the originals were forwarded to the acting assistant provost-marshals-general of the States to which the regiments of the deserters belonged. But it was found after a few weeks' experience that this system was inadequate, and about the beginning of May the clerical force of the branch was increased, and a copy of the descriptive list of each deserter was sent to the provost-marshal of the district in which the deserter was supposed to reside, the original reports being kept on file. This system has since that time been adhered to.

Considerable difficulty was experienced in procuring the reports from commanding officers, and many had to be notified time and time again before the reports were obtained. Even at this date, despite numerous notifications, some reports are missing, and, as the delinquent regiments have mostly been mustered out, the record of deserters can never be entirely completed.

It was constantly found necessary to urge the provost-marshals to energy in arresting deserters by means of circulars and letters. Until the reward was increased to $30, however, few arrests were made. The reward was a powerful stimulus to exertion on the part of both citizens and special officers, many of which latter elected to relinquish their monthly pay and take the reward instead.

The manner in which the payment of the reward of $5 and expenses incurred was made was intricate. The vouchers necessary to secure the payment of the reward from a disbursing quartermaster were a certificate from a provost-marshal, or officer commanding a military post, that a deserter (identified in the certificate by name, company, and regiment) had been received by them, and that the person apprehending the same (whose name and description were also given) was entitled to the proper reward. Expenses incurred were given in detail, specifying to whom paid and for what the expense was necessary. Examining and testing the correctness of the expenses incurred was too complicated a system to work well.

Considerable trouble was experienced in the beginning of 1863 in the issue by State courts of writs of habeas corpus in the case of deserters arrested, provost-marshals in many instances giving the deserters up to the civil authorities, whereby they often escaped punishment. To obviate this difficulty, Solicitor Whiting gave an opinion on the legality of the writ in such cases, which was made public in Circular 36 from this office. It instructs provost-marshals to make due answer to the writ whenever issued, apprising the State court from which it issued that the prisoner was under custody of the United States, whereupon they could proceed no further. If an attempt were made by the State court to control the provost-marshal, he was authorized to resist by force. The language of Chief Justice Taney was quoted in support of this authorization. The answer of the provost-marshal to the writ was to specify that he was provost-marshal, appointed by the President, under authority of an act of Congress; that the prisoner was a deserter, held nnder the act, and that his production in court would be in violation of his (the provost-marshal's) duties. To this any other material facts were to be added which he might consider necessary. Since the issue of this circular no further cases have occurred.

By General Orders, No. 222, Adjutant-General's Office, July 16, 1863, the reward of $5 was increased to $10—a decided improvement.

Enrolled and drafted men have frequently sought to evade service by changing residence and absconding, believing that they could not be arrested; and accordingly, in Circular 47 (July 17), the opinion of Mr. Whiting was issued, to the effect that "there is no way or manner in which a person once enrolled can escape his public duties, and, when drafted, the rights of the United States against him are secured, and it is only by performance of his duty to the country that he will escape liability to be treated as a criminal." A notification of draft left at his last place of residence was held to be enough to convict him of desertion unless he answered it in person or by payment of commutation. Many of these men hereupon reported voluntarily, and more were arrested and held to service.

Many cases of deserters being furnished as substitutes having occurred, Circular 64 (August 16) made principals furnishing such still liable to service, unless a second and acceptable substitute was put in his place.

It was decided by the General-in-Chief (and promulgated in letter from Adjutant-General's Office, August 28, 1863) that men arrested as deserters from regiments mustered out of service should be examined, and, if found to be such, should be assigned to some regiment of the same State to serve out all the time lost by desertion. This has been since the invariable practice.

Circular 82 ordered that drafted men failing to report, and arrested, would he held to service, unless disability were clearly proved to the Board of Enrollment, in which case they would be discharged.

Finally, in September, 1863, General Orders, No 325, Adjutant-General's Office, increased the reward for arresting deserters to $30, which was to include all expenses. This increase of reward made both more uniformity and less trouble in the payment for arrests of deserters, and also considerably increased the number of arrests. Some persons were arrested who proved upon strict examination (as ordered by Circular 94, from this office) not to be deserters. These were, of course, at once discharged, and no reward was paid. In other cases rewards were paid and afterward returned to the disbursing officer when the arrest was proved wrongful. No rewards were allowed for the arrest of drafted men failing to report, unless they were held to service.

Some minors who have deserted have been screened from punishment by issue of writ of habeas corpus. In the case of Leroy Whitman (March 16, 1864) it was adjudged that he was guilty of desertion, though he had enlisted as a minor, because with the knowledge and without the objection of his father. Since then no such writs have been issued. At the time the act approved February 13, 1862, repealing all laws authorizing the discharge of minors, though promulgated, did not seem to have been generally understood.

To facilitate arrests, post commanders and surgeons in charge of U. S. hospitals were instructed (Circular 46, Adjutant-General's Office, June 21, 1864) to report desertions as soon as ascertained to the nearest provost-marshal.

By Circular 85, Adjutant-General's Office, November 28, 1864, it was decided that deserters who had returned under the President's proclamation of March 10, 1863, must make good the time lost by desertion, in addition to their unexpired term of service, although relieved from punishment.

By an order consequent upon an opinion of Mr. Whiting, of January 5, 1865, it was decided that all persons gaining exemption by fraud were liable to be proceeded against as deserters. This was to remedy an extensive evil, all manner of frauds being attempted in order to evade service. In the case which especially called forth this opinion a drafted man gave his brother $300 to pay his commutation, who, instead of doing so, presented himself as the principal, and was exempted on the ground of "physical disability." This is but one of the many instances of sharp practice.

By enrollment act approved March 3, 1865, all principals aiding their substitutes to desert were made a second time liable to service.

Under the same act all deserters failing to report under the President's proclamation authorized thereby were disfranchised. No steps have yet been taken to carry out this provision.

The following officers have been in charge of this branch:

Maj. Chauncey McKeever, assistant adjutant-general, from April 8, 1863, to October 1, 1863.

Capt. W. R. Pease, Seventh Infantry, from October 1, 1863, to November 23, 1863.

Capt. Henry Stone, assistant adjutant-general of volunteers, from November 23, 1863, to February 9, 1864.

Capt. W. R. Pease, Seventh Infantry, February 9, 1864, to May 2, 1864.

Capt. George E. Scott, Veteran Reserve Corps, from May 2, 1864.

On the 5th of December I relieved the last named, since which date I have been in charge.

It has not been found advisable since May, 1863, materially to change the manner of informing provost-marshals of the descriptions and whereabouts of deserters. The commanding officer of a regiment reports to this office the deserters during a certain month on a blank, which gives descriptive list, residence, supposed whereabouts, and any other facts which may tend to identify them. This report is received, and a copy of the description of every deserter thereon is forwarded to the provost-marshal where he is probably to be found, and the report filed away. When there are several places which he would probably frequent, descriptive lists are sent to the several provost-marshals. This work (as desertions have averaged 5,000 or 6,000 a month) is necessarily large, and it has been sometimes necessary to employ from twenty to thirty clerks at copying. It has also been inculcated upon provost-marshals and acting assistant provost-marshals-general diligently to interchange descriptive lists of deserters when they are known or supposed to be in another district or State. Every possible care has been taken to keep provost-marshals advised of the whereabouts of deserters; and it is believed that the arrests, which are nearly two-thirds of the desertions, show that the work has been well done.

The clerks have mostly been detailed men, generally from the Veteran Reserve Corps.

Experience has proved that the best method of arresting deserters is to offer $30 reward, to include all incidental expenses. Fewer deserters are arrested when the reward is smaller, and the necessary expenses incident to their arrest, which are paid in addition to the smaller reward, generally swell the whole amount to more than $30, not to mention the additional labor necessitated in examining vouchers, &c.

In the payment of rewards provost-marshals were instructed to examine each case to ascertain whether the deserter was culpable, or the victim of misapprehension of duty. Frequent cases have occurred of soldiers being arrested by having overstayed their sick-leaves through ignorance of what steps to take to protect themselves, in most of which no rewards were paid. The prompt payment for arrests, more than any other circumstance, tends to make them frequent; and in some districts, where few arrests have been made, it has been owing to the time taken to get the reward paid (often from three to six months), the nearest disbursing quartermaster being hundreds of miles distant from the provost-marshal's headquarters.

The President's proclamation of March 10 [11], 1865, did not meet with the response anticipated. It was extensively published everywhere, and constant attention was called to its provisions through the public press by editorials and otherwise; still, only 1,755 availed themselves of it. At the expiration of the sixty days allowed for the voluntary return of deserters orders were issued to recommence their arrest; but as almost all deputies and special agents had before that time been discharged and the reward discontinued, but few arrests have since been made.

The large bounties given to volunteers have undoubtedly been an inducement to many to desert for the purpose of re-enlisting; but a still greater inducement has been the leniency with which the most culpable deserters have been treated. Had the extreme penalty attached to desertion been invariably carried into execution, bounty-jumping and desertion would not have reached such gigantic proportions. The time elapsing, too, between arrest and trial give the reckless and often skillful deserter opportunity to escape. In the case of desperate and well-known offenders, a speedy trial and short shrift would have exerted a salutary influence.

It is curious how the stories circulated by deserters gain credence. To palliate their crime they tell tales of hardships endured by them, and of barbarities practiced upon them by their officers; and, though generally false in every respect, these stories are retailed through the country by themselves and friends, exaggerated in every possible way, and believed by many. Being tied up by the thumbs, though not a severe punishment, sounds to those who suppose it means "hung up by the thumbs" like a most barbarous proceeding. These stories would seem, from the reports of provost-marshals, to have been among the most serious obstacles to recruiting.

Of the deserters regained, about 42 per cent. have been arrested by special officers, 33 per cent. by citizens, and 25 per cent. have voluntarily surrendered themselves, including those under the President's proclamations.

The work of this branch needed at the season of hardest labor (December, 1864), besides about fifteen copyists, a clerk for superintendent of the roll-room; one for examining and preparing reports from regiments' copyists and keeping the list of work done by them; one for briefing the reports; one having charge of the files of reports; one having charge of the book in which the regimental reports and number of desertions therein reported are entered, and one to keep the "deserters-arrested" book, in which a summary of the monthly return of the provost-marshals is entered; besides which the current business required a chief clerk and two or three clerks to keep the letter book, "letters-received" books, and indorsement book.

This force seems to have been necessary to do the work of this branch at a time when desertions reported averaged about 6,000 a month, and deserters arrested 4,000.

It is thought that no better suggestions can be made as to the mode of carrying on the bureau of deserters (if it should ever again be established), than to sketch the modus operandi which has been adopted, after two years' experience, as the best calculated to secure the prompt arrest of deserters.

Monthly returns are made by the "commandants of regiments, battalions not included in regiments, independent companies or batteries and detachments, surgeons in charge of hospitals and detachments, and all persons in the military service commanding or controlling commissioned officers or enlisted men on special or detached service," of the names of all deserters from their respective commands who have deserted since their last report. The first report is called the "Organization report," and is to give the desertions from the organization of the command till the day of rendering it, usually the end of any specified month. (Our organization reports were dated March 31, 1863.) This report must "be made in the form of a descriptive list, setting forth in the case of each deserter, his name, rank, regiment or company, description, place of birth, residence, occupation, place of enlistment, date of last payment, account of bounty due, date and place of desertion, and the place where he can probably be found, with such remarks as may be pertinent in the matter, or may aid in the arrest and punishment of the offender." They will be made in triplicate, one copy to be forwarded direct to the Provost-Marshal-General, with "deserters" indorsed under "official business" on the envelope, and one through the usual channels to the Adjutant-General, who remits them to the Provost-Marshal-General. In the case of surgeons, the duplicate will be sent through the Surgeon-General. The triplicate should be retained.

It has been found convenient to cause the men returned from desertion to be entered on this report under a separate heading.

It is very difficult to obtain these reports, notifications to those who should render them being generally ineffectual. In case repeated orders are disregarded, a request to the Adjutant-General to stop the pay of the delinquent officers until all returns are made is usually successful in causing the reports to be sent.

When received these reports are first uniformly folded and the date of receipt marked on the lower edge, and then briefed, giving merely regiment, number of desertions, and number returned from desertion; and then the numbers in the brief are entered in a book kept for the purpose, where each command from which returns are due is allotted a separate space. This enables the number of reports and deserters for any given month to be ascertained at a glance. The reports are then "districted," *i. e.*, a note is made in a marginal column of the report giving the district in which each deserter is likely to be found. A special clerk must be employed on this work, as a directory is continually needed to ascertain in what district any place specified in the column "where probably to be found" is situated. A copy of the descriptive list of the man is then made out and forwarded to the provost-marshal of that district, and a consolidated copy of all descriptive lists sent to provost-marshals of a State or division to the acting assistant provost-marshal-general of that State or division. Finally, the regimental return is filed away (each command having a separate pigeonhole), systematically arranged by States and regiments, so that easy reference can be made to them.

Reports are sent tri-monthly by provost-marshals of the number of deserters arrested by them and the disposition made of them; and accompanying the third tri-monthly report is a monthly report giving the names, rank, company, regiment, date of arrest and by whom arrested, expenses incurred, reward paid, date of disposal, and how disposed of. With this return is sent a receipt for each man turned over to the military and other authorities on a "descriptive list of deserters." The name of each deserter is recorded alphabetically in the "deserters-arrested" book, and then the reports are filed away by districts, so that the name of any man being given, the history of his arrest can at once be found, or the arrest by any provost-marshal at any date can be at once ascertained.

There are nineteen volumes of deserters arrested. In 1864 they were kept by States alphabetically, which was not as good for reference.

There are five volumes of records of the number of deserters reported.

Two volumes contain the record of the number of descriptive lists sent from this office to provost-marshals, and in one volume is entered date of receipt of the return of deserters arrested.

Letters of transmittal received with reports, and letters acknowledging receipt of descriptive lists sent to provost-marshals, are filed separately.

It has been suggested that on every man's descriptive list at enlistment there be entered such marks as he may have about him, to facilitate his identification in case he should desert. Such marks as many men have tattooed on their forearms and hands, birthmarks, scars, &c., might be noted under "remarks" on every enlistment paper.

The miscellaneous business pertaining to the arrest of deserters (answering communications about exceptional cases, &c.) is conducted in strict accordance with the Adjutant-General's pamphlet of instructions.

The blank department has been under the control of the officer in charge of the "Deserters' Branch," and it may be well to give a sketch of its business.

As soon as the blanks are received from the Public Printer they are carefully counted, and a colored strip of paper inserted to mark every hundred, so that the number on hand can at any time be ascertained at a glance. They are then piled up and a record made of the exact number in an appropriate volume.

Provost-marshals make quarterly requisitions for the estimated number of blanks needed during the ensuing quarter, and such other requisitions from time to time as may prove necessary. These requisitions go through the acting assistant provost-marshals-general and are approved by them. They are filled as soon as received and then briefed and filed. An invoice is sent by mail at the same time with the blanks and a receipt from the provost-marshal to sign and return, which is then briefed and entered in the letters-received book and filed.

Attached to this report will be found two tabular statements, one of "deserters reported," from May, 1861, to December 31, 1865, and the other of "deserters arrested," from May, 1863, to December 31, 1865. They are both as correct as the records of the Bureau can make them.

Since the organization of this Bureau the desertions reported have been 278,644. This number is much too large. Many of those reported as deserters are not so in reality, but are men who became unavoidably absent from their commands by falling sick on the march, being injured in action without the knowledge of their officers, and reported "missing" and subsequently "deserted," and by intentionally or unintentionally overstaying their furloughs, &c. Most of this class afterward voluntarily reported, but having been placed in the "return of deserters" have swelled the aggregate.

It will be observed that 91,088 (or nearly two-fifths of those reported as deserters) deserted prior to the organization of this Bureau. It is not known how many of these were apprehended prior to that time.

The aggregate of arrests is 77,181, an average of about 2,412 a month. Allowing 25 per cent. (which is a small estimate) for deserters reported who are not deserters in reality, it appears that the number of arrests made by the employés of this Bureau is nearly two-thirds of the number of desertions during the same period.

In 1863 the monthly desertions averaged 4,647; in 1864 they averaged 7,333; in 1865 they averaged 4,368.

The deserters of 1864 include all drafted men who have been assigned to regiments and deserted en route to the field, and some who, being held to the draft, have deserted before reaching general rendezvous. This accounts for the increase of desertions during that year.

I am, general, very respectfully, your obedient servant,

T. A. DODGE,
Major, Veteran Reserve Corps, and Bvt. Col. of Vols.

TABLE NO. 1.—*Statement of deserters reported by regimental and other commanders to the Provost-Marshal-General's Bureau from their organization to December 31, 1865.**

TABLE NO. 2.—*Statement of the number of deserters arrested in the several States and Territories, including the District of Columbia, from May 1, 1863, to December 31, 1865.*†

DOCUMENT NO. 8.

Report of Medical Branch.

WAR DEPT., PROVOST-MARSHAL-GENERAL'S BUREAU,
Washington, D. C., March 17, 1866.

Bvt. Maj. Gen. JAMES B. FRY,
Provost-Marshal-General:

GENERAL: In compliance with your order dated September 2, 1865, I have the honor to submit for your information the following historical report of the operations of the Medical Branch of your Bureau from its organization to the present date, and a preliminary report of the medical statistics on file therein.

I have the honor to be, general, very respectfully, your obedient servant,

J. H. BAXTER,
Surgeon and Brevet Colonel, U. S. Volunteers,
Chief Medical Officer Provost-Marshal-General's Bureau.

HISTORICAL REPORT OF THE MEDICAL BRANCH PROVOST-MARSHAL-GENERAL'S BUREAU.

Section 6 of the act approved March 3, 1863, for enrolling and calling out the national forces, and for other purposes, made it the duty of the Provost-Marshal-General, with the approval of the Secretary of War, to institute rules and regulations for the government of his subordinates, and to require stated reports of all proceedings on their part. In pursuance of the above, surgeons of boards of enrollment were called upon to furnish reports of the results of their examination of men for the Army, and in order to establish uniformity among them it was deemed necessary that a commissioned medical officer should be detailed for service under the Provost-Marshal-General, whose duty it should be to advise and direct surgeons of boards of enrollment in the performance of their duties, and who should have the custody of all reports and returns from them, for the purpose of their proper preservation and discussion.

---

* Detailed statement (here omitted) shows an aggregate of 278,644.
† Detailed statement (here omitted) shows an aggregate of 77,181.

The organization of a medical branch of your Bureau had not been completed prior to the date of your order assigning me to duty as chief medical officer, a copy of which is as follows, viz:

WAR DEPARTMENT, PROVOST-MARSHAL-GENERAL'S BUREAU,
Washington, D. C., January 11, 1864.

Surg. J. H. Baxter, U. S. Volunteers, having reported for duty in accordance with Special Orders, No. 5, Adjutant-General's Office, War Department, 1864, is hereby assigned to duty as chief medical officer.

JAMES B. FRY,
Provost-Marshal-General.

Upon the receipt of the above order, which created the Medical Branch of this Bureau, I immediately opened an office in quarters assigned for that purpose.

Under the previous able administration of Lieut. Col. R. H. Coolidge, medical inspector, U. S. Army, all medical matters pertaining to your Bureau had been conducted with rare skill and executive ability.

A list of diseases and disabilities, for the government of surgeons of boards of enrollment, had been prepared by a medical board, of which Medical Inspector Coolidge was president, and medical questions in regard to the formation of the Invalid Corps had received his assiduous care and attention. I take this occasion to express my personal and official obligations to this experienced and patriotic officer (whose recent death has deprived the medical corps of one of its most zealous and accomplished members) for his valuable counsel so freely tendered me in the establishment of this branch of your Bureau.

By personal inspection of many boards of enrollment and by correspondence I acquainted myself with the difficulties under which surgeons of boards labored, and by circular letters and forms for medical record books and reports, issued from this branch, a uniformity of action was established which resulted not only to the good of the Bureau, but rendered less onerous and more correct the performance of the duties devolving upon the surgeons of boards of enrollment.

The record books are similar to those prescribed in the pamphlet issued by the Adjutant-General entitled "Instructions for Officers of the Adjutant-General's Department, and Others of Kindred Duties;" *i. e.*, "letters received," "letters sent," and "indorsement and memoranda;" and the method adopted in keeping said books has not differed in any material point from that laid down in the work referred to, which is so universally followed that I do not deem it necessary to detail it in this report. The medical reports accumulated so rapidly and were of such size that it was thought necessary to open a separate book in which to record their receipt. This book is entitled "Record of Medical Reports Received."

Immediately upon the receipt of the mail from the office of "general and miscellaneous business" it was opened and examined by the chief clerk of this branch, and all letters pertaining to this office or involving medical questions, with the exception of letters of transmittal of the regular "medical reports," properly indorsed and entered in the book of "letters received;" after which those letters requiring the attention and action of the chief medical officer were submitted to him and disposed of according to his direction.

The "medical reports" were first entered in the "record of medical reports received," submitted to the chief medical officer or to one of the medical officers on duty in the branch, by whom they were examined as to the medical points involved, after which they were sent to the "examining room," where they passed through a thorough examination by a corps of competent clerks, and if no errors were detected after this second examination, they were placed in wrappers and filed by States and districts to be tabulated in future.

If, however, the surgeon making the report had not complied strictly with instructions previously issued, the report was returned to him through the acting assistant provost-marshal-general of his State, with indorsement enumerating the errors, and with directions to either forward a new report or the original carefully revised and corrected.

The stated medical reports are of two kinds, viz: "Monthly medical reports" and "Reports of the medical statistics of drafts" (Form 58); the former received monthly, and the latter at the close of each draft from each Congressional district.

The "monthly medical reports" were made by the surgeons of boards of enrollment upon blanks furnished from this office, being copied from the "medical record books" kept by the surgeons. These reports contained a complete and minute record of the physical examination of all recruits, substitutes, drafted and enrolled men during each month. The following data, given in the case of each man examined, will show more clearly the value of these reports, viz:

Date of examination, number ditto, name, age, height, complexion, color of eyes and hair, nativity, residence, occupation, measurements of chest, white or colored, married or single, physique, and result of examination, stating also the disease or disability for which the man was rejected or exempted.

"Reports of medical statistics of drafts" were rendered at the close of each draft, and were also made upon blanks furnished from this office (Form 58). Each of these reports comprised a series of four tables.

The first table exhibited the number of drafted men of each occupation physically examined, the number exempted for each distinct disease or disability alphabetically arranged, the number appearing before the Board, also the number of each occupation exempted under each section of paragraph 85, Revised Regulations Provost-Marshal-General's Bureau.

The second table exhibited the total number of drafted men exempted under each section of the above-mentioned paragraph and the ratio exempted under each section per 1,000 examined.

The third table by nativities embraced the vital statistics of all men examined under the draft for which the report was rendered, and the fourth table being a consolidation of the third.

The whole number of clerks employed or detailed for duty in this branch from its organization to the present date is forty-two; greatest number employed at any one time, seventeen; average number employed per month, eight.

A large proportion of the clerical force of this branch have been soldiers detailed from the Veteran Reserve Corps. A large majority of the citizen clerks had served in the Union Army or Navy previous to their appointment. Out of sixteen clerks on duty in this branch at present date, twelve have served in the Army or Navy and have rendered a total of forty-two years and seven months' service, making an average of three years and six months, or an average of two years and eight months for the whole force.

By a reference to Schedule A, a list of all commissioned medical officers who have been on duty in this branch since its organization may be found; dates when each officer was detailed and relieved, to what duty assigned, &c.

VIEWS IN REFERENCE TO THE LIST OF DISEASES AND INFIRMITIES FOR THE EXEMPTION OF DRAFTED MEN AND CHANGES RECOMMENDED.

The several sections of paragraph 85, in which are enumerated the diseases and disabilities for which drafted men should be exempted, have proved, as a general rule, acceptable, and but few cases have presented themselves deserving exemption which could not be classified under its requirements.

Of course no precise enumeration of all the particular diseases or disabilities which could disqualify drafted men for military service was possible, but paragraph 85 was given as a general guide, yet directing, as far as practicable, the judgment of examining surgeons. By rendering as definite as possible the list of disqualifying mental and physical disabilities, much trouble and annoyance were saved to surgeons of boards and promptness of decision facilitated. Moreover, the drafted man seemed better satisfied if it was possible to point out to him that the surgeon, in his decision not to exempt him from service, simply obeyed the instructions received from higher sources.

Experience has proved some few alterations necessary, and I respectfully submit the following changes which present themselves to my mind as desirable and worthy your consideration. For the purpose of making these changes the more readily comprehended, I write out in full the section as, in my opinion, it should read after all amendments:

PARAGRAPH 85.

SECTION 1. No change.

SEC. 2. No change.

SEC. 3. Epilepsy. For this disability *the statement of the drafted man is insufficient*, and the fact *must* be established by the duly attested affidavit of a physician in good standing who has attended him *in* the disease within six months immediately preceding his examination by the Board, or in default of such evidence, the affidavits of at least three respectable citizens who have seen him in a convulsion within six months, and have personal knowledge of his being subject to repeated attacks.

SEC. 4. Paralysis, general or of one limb, or chorea; their existence to be adequately determined. Decided atrophy or hypertrophy of a limb.

SEC. 5. No change.

SEC. 6. No change.

SEC. 7. No change.

SEC. 8. No change.

SEC. 9. No change.

SEC. 10. No change.

SEC. 11. Chronic rheumatism, involving change of structure or distortion.

SEC. 12. Total loss of sight of either eye; cataract of either eye; loss of crystalline lens of either eye.

SEC. 13. Partial loss of sight of both eyes, vision being so greatly impaired as to leave no doubt of the man's inability to perform military duty. Serious permanent diseases of the eye or eyelids, so manifestly affecting the use of the eyes as to leave no doubt of the man's incapacity for military service. Near-sightedness does not exempt, unless excessive and confirmed.

SEC. 14. Loss of nose; deformity of nose so great as seriously to impede respiration; ozena with caries.

SEC. 15. Decided deafness, dependent on organic change, or proved by other satisfactory evidence, so decided as to leave no doubt of the man's unfitness for military service. Chronic purulent otorrhœa.

SEC. 16. Incurable diseases or deformities of either jaw, which greatly impede mastication or speech—anchylosis of jaw; caries of the bones of the face, if in progress; cleft palate (bony); extensive loss of substance of the cheeks, or salivary fistula.

SEC. 17. No change.

SEC. 18. Loss of tongue, or diseases thereof sufficient to interfere seriously with the use of that organ.

SEC. 19. No change.

SEC. 20. Loss of a sufficient number of teeth to interfere seriously with mastication.

SEC. 21. Tumors or wounds of the neck, impeding respiration or deglutition. Torticollis, if of long standing and well marked.

SEC. 22. Deformity of the chest, curvature of the spine, or caries of the spine, ribs, or sternum, sufficient to prevent the carrying of arms or military equipments.

SEC. 23. Hernia, except small umbilical.

SEC. 24. Artificial anus, stricture of the rectum, prolapsus ani, fistula in ano, if extensive or complicated.

SEC. 25. Old and ulcerated internal or external hemorrhoids, if in degree sufficient to leave no doubt of the man's unfitness for military service.

SEC. 26. Loss of penis; epispadia or hypospadia.

SEC. 27. Chronic organic stricture of the urethra, which seriously impedes the passage of urine, or which is complicated with disease of the bladder, urinary fistula. Recent or spasmodic stricture of the urethra does not exempt.

SEC. 28. Incontinence of urine, stone in the bladder, or gravel, ascertained beyond doubt, absolutely disqualifies.

SEC. 29. Confirmed or malignant sarcocele; hydrocele, if complicated with organic disease of testicle. Varicocele is not disqualifying unless excessive and severe.

SEC. 30. No change.

SEC. 31. No change.

SEC. 32. No change.

SEC. 33. Loss of right thumb. Loss of third phalanx of all the fingers of either hand. Loss of index and middle finger of same hand. Permanent extension or contraction of two fingers of either hand. All the fingers adherent.

SEC. 34. Permanent defects or deformities of the feet, such as will necessarily prevent marching.

SEC. 35. No change.

SEC. 36. No change.

I respectfully recommend that paragraph 87 should be amended to read as follows:

The surgeon of the Board of Enrollment will keep three medical record books, in which he will record the following results of his examinations of all men he may inspect—

First. Of drafted men. Date of examination, number, name, where drafted (town or county), age, nativity, occupation, height, weight, color of eyes, hair, and complexion, chest measurements at inspiration and expiration, married or single, white or colored, and result of examination. He will also record under head of remarks, if exempted, the disease or disability for which exemption was granted; if not exempted, the disease or disability for which exemption was claimed.

Second. Of enrolled men the same, except "where enrolled" (town and county) in place of "where drafted." If stricken from the enrollment lists, state under head of remarks the particular disease or disability for which the enrolled man was found unfit. If not stricken therefrom, the disease or disability for which he claimed unfitness.

Third. Of recruits and substitutes. Date of examination, number, name, age, nativity, occupation, height, weight, color of eyes, hair, and complexion, chest measurements at inspiration and expiration, married or single, white or colored, recruit or substitute, and result of examination. Under remarks, if rejected, state the reason why; if accepted, record some mark or scar which may be on his person by which he may hereafter be identified.

The surgeon of the Board of Enrollment will also forward a monthly medical report of the drafted and enrolled men and recruits and substitutes he has examined. This report will be a copy of the medical record books above enumerated, and will be forwarded in duplicate the 1st day of each month; one copy direct, and one copy through the acting assistant provost-marshal-general.

Immediately on the completion of a draft in any district the surgeon of the Board of Enrollment will compile and forward to this office the statistics of the causes of exemption on account of physical or mental disability from such draft in his district (Form 58). This report will be accompanied by a detailed statement of such other facts as may be of scientific importance to the medical profession. This report will also be forwarded in duplicate, one copy direct, and one copy through the acting assistant provost-marshal-general. In the keeping of his records and preparation of reports the surgeon of the Board will be entitled to a clerk whenever the services of one may be necessary.

MEDICAL EXAMINATION OF MEN FOR MILITARY SERVICE AND FRAUDS TO BE GUARDED AGAINST.

The medical examinations of men for the military service were made in a large, well-lighted room, where they could be exercised briskly, and with the windows so arranged that the light fell equally upon every portion of it.

Upon entering the room the recruit, substitute, or drafted man was directed to divest himself of all his clothing. This was usually done in the presence of the surgeon, for this reason, that he was not then expecting to be noticed, and should he feel disposed to conceal any existing defects, as stiff joints, &c., he would in this way be thrown off his guard, and the attempted fraud at once detected without further examination.

He was first questioned in regard to his name, age, nativity, occupation, his general health and that of his family, whether any hereditary taints existed, and if he had ever suffered from any disease or accident, and if so, what; thus endeavoring to obtain all the information possible concerning him and at the same time enable the surgeon to judge of his mental as well as his physical qualifications.

He was then placed under a stationary measuring rod, directed to stand erect while his height was accurately noted, and a graduated tape was passed around the chest over the inferior angles of the scapula and directly over the nipple, and the measurement taken both at inspiration and expiration. After this the color of the eyes, hair, and the complexion were noted, and a general inspection of the whole body was now made, noticing the muscular development and general appearance, at the same time looking carefully for any tumors, ulcers, varicose veins or chronic swellings of the extremities, or any defect that could disqualify him for the service.

The head was then examined for any depressions or irregularities that might exist; the eyes, eyelids, ears, nose, teeth, palate, and fauces carefully noticed.

The chest was then inspected; respiration and the action of the heart observed, and anything that could be discovered by inspection, auscultation, or percussion noted.

He was next directed to stand erect, place his heels together, and raise his hands vertically above his head, the backs together, and was told to cough and make other expulsive movements, while the abdomen, inguinal rings, and scrotum were examined for hernia; the penis was then examined for epispadia, hypospadia, and venereal disease; the groin for glandular enlargements, and the testicles for atrophy, induration, or other diseases.

He was then directed to bend over, the fingers touching the floor, the legs straight and widely distended, and separating the nates, the fissure, for hemorrhoids, fistula, prolapsus, or any disease of the anus, was carefully inspected; and while in this position firm pressure was made on different portions of the spine to discover any disease or tenderness, if such existed.

Next he was directed to extend his arms straight from the body and then bring them together on the same level, behind and in front, pronate and supinate them rapidly, strike out from the shoulder, flex the arm upon the shoulder, and the forearm upon the arm, and open and close the fingers rapidly. In this way almost any defect of the upper extremities were discovered.

He was then told to walk rapidly, and then to run around the room several times, hop first on one foot and then on the other, with his heels together to raise himself upon his toes, then flex and extend the thigh, leg, and ankle, kick first with one foot and then the other, and make several leaps in the air. While thus excited he was again examined for chest diseases and also for hernia.

The eyesight was next tested by placing him at one end of the room while the surgeon stood at the other, and asking him the number or color of objects displayed to each eye separately. The hearing was also tested at the same time by modulating the tones of the voice while conversing with him, and covering one ear while endeavoring to discover any defects that might exist in the other.

The remaining portion of the record was then made out, result of examination recorded, and in case of rejection the disease or infirmity for which he was found unfit for military service written out in full.

In case of recruits and substitutes, when accepted, some mark or scar which was on their body was recorded for the purpose of future identification.

The number of men that can be examined per day with accuracy depends not only upon the character of the men examined, but whether or not they are drafted men, as much more time must be devoted to them in answering all their questions and listening to and deciding upon their claims for exemption than in the examination of recruits or substitutes. Forty, however, is a fair average, of all classes, of the number of men that can be examined per day with accuracy.

Various modes were adopted for the detection of frauds practiced by recruits and substitutes to enter, and by drafted and enrolled men to escape the service.

The volunteer and the drafted man are governed by very different motives in presenting themselves for examination; for while the former tries to conceal every physical defect, the latter is equally anxious to magnify every slight ailment. If the volunteer resorts to false teeth, hair-dye, and falsehoods to conceal his age, bandages for varicose veins, and the application of ice for hernia, the drafted man also feigns deafness, blindness, liver and kidney complaints, or any other disease that will avail him in his extremity.

When deafness is feigned, the following method was found useful for detecting it: The man was seated directly in front of the surgeon and close to him; a watch was then placed against one of his ears and he was asked in a loud tone "if he could hear it;" to which he usually answered in the affirmative. The watch was then withdrawn a few inches, and the question repeated in a low tone several times, gradually withdrawing the watch and sinking the voice until it was scarcely more than a whisper; while his attention was fixed upon the watch he did not notice how far the surgeon had moved from him, or in what tone he was speaking.

The would-be blind man was detected by telling him that he must accompany the surgeon to a place prepared to test the eyesight; and taking him up and down stairs, over logs, boxes, and impediments of all kinds, and if he avoided all these his blindness was not considered sufficient to unfit him for the military service.

Cardiac disease is often feigned, and men frequently present themselves for examination after having undergone violent physical exercise; in such cases they should be allowed to wait and sit quietly for at least half an hour, and then by careful examination the attempted fraud can usually be detected at once.

The frauds against which the examining surgeon has to guard, it will be seen, are as various as the characters of the men examined, and no rules can be given to govern in such cases; but to guard successfully against these frauds, aside from professional skill, he should be conversant with the frailties and idiosyncrasies of human nature and be able to turn his knowledge to account, for he must rely to a great extent upon his own judgment.

SURGEONS OF BOARDS OF ENROLLMENT, WITH RECOMMENDATIONS AS TO THEIR FUTURE APPOINTMENT AND STATUS.

Medical, like all other talent, should not be expected without proper compensation; and, although this Bureau obtained it, it is nevertheless true that the great majority of the late surgeons of boards continued in the position from a patriotic desire to serve their country, or a personal feeling of pride (that, having commenced, they would continue to end), fearing, perhaps, that in the case of resignation their enemies would ascribe it to the fact that they were obliged to do so for faults committed in the performance of their duties.

Many surgeons of boards received the appointment unsought, having been recommended by their respective members of Congress on account of their high standing in community. They were men of ability and honesty, and, indeed, in their recommendations of physicians for the position of surgeons of boards of enrollment, members of Congress seem to have selected, as a rule, only those who, on account of attainments, experience, and honesty, they considered best fitted for the position.

The position of the surgeon on boards of enrollment has been one of much responsibility.

Maligned by those whom he failed to consider entitled to exemption, and accused of exempting those not disabled, he has been placed between two dilemmas. If he exempted too great a proportion he was liable to censure from his official superiors. If the number of exempted men was small, the community accused him of forcing cripples and men at the point of death into the Army. Should he reject a large per cent. of substitutes or recruits, the district, being anxious to fill the quota and thus escape the draft, accused him of being hypercritical in his examinations, and said that he rejected able-bodied men.

On the other hand, he was liable not only to official censure in case he accepted disabled substitutes and recruits, but his pay was liable to be stopped, and all expenses attending the enlistment of the disabled man deducted therefrom.

His position being then one by no means enviable, it is a matter of no little surprise that the services of medical gentlemen of such ability in their profession were secured or retained.

I would recommend, instead of the present method of appointing surgeons of boards of enrollment, that they be supplied by detail of those medical officers in the service who, by experience and talent, are evidently fitted for the position. I would also suggest that they have, while serving on boards of enrollment, the rank, pay, and emoluments of surgeons in the Army.

Should this be found impracticable, I would recommend that surgeons of boards of enrollment be appointed and commissioned as such only after due and careful examination as to their ability to perform the duties pertaining to the position, and that they have the rank, pay, and emoluments of surgeons in the Army.

It is also important that they be stationed in other States and districts than those in which they reside, and that their stations be changed at least once in six months, or after the completion of each draft.

This would obviate the great difficulty with which surgeons of boards of enrollment have had to contend, viz, the pressure of sectional feelings, and their being stationed where a proper discharge of duties would not interfere with their future professional prospects or their individual feelings.

There also should be detailed upon the staff of each acting assistant provost-marshal-general a commissioned medical officer of experience and ability to act as medical inspector, and, under the direction of such acting assistant provost-marshal-general, to have supervision of all medical matters pertaining to boards of enrollment in the State or division to which he may be assigned.

Such medical officer should examine and forward all medical reports of surgeons of boards, and report at least monthly the result of his labors. He should be guided in his decisions by the regulations of this Bureau, and by such other instructions as might be sent him by order of the Provost-Marshal-General.

The detail of such an officer would obviate many of the difficulties which have been encountered in the past experience of this Bureau.

MEDICAL BOARDS OF RE-EXAMINATION AND RENDEZVOUS CAMPS.

I am convinced that no little injustice has been done surgeons of boards of enrollment by medical boards of re-examination at rendezvous camps. Surgeons of boards of enrollment, for instance, decided not to exempt drafted men with whom they were personally acquainted, and knew that there existed no physical or mental disability sufficient to entitle them to exemption. Yet, upon the arrival of these men at rendezvous camps, their representations of physical unfitness appeared so well founded that the boards of re-examination, although perfect strangers to the applicants, have recommended the men for discharge and reported the surgeon of the Board as negligent in the discharge of his duty.

This has also been the case with recruits and substitutes who received large bounties, and on their arrival at rendezvous camps feigned or produced such disabilities as to secure their discharge.

This has been a subject of much complaint from surgeons of boards, who have produced evidence in particular cases of this kind to prove their complaints well grounded. Circular No. 15, Adjutant-General's Office, 1865, corrects this difficulty, but, unfortunately, it was issued but a few days before all drafting and recruiting were stopped.

It will, however, be a matter of great importance to the interest of the service, should any future recruitment of the Army become necessary by draft or through boards of enrollment, that the requirements of this circular be strictly observed and carried into effect, viz.*

IMPORTANCE AND EXTENT OF RECORDS ON FILE IN THIS BRANCH.

The final reports of surgeons of boards of enrollment give the medical results of the examination of 605,045 drafted men who were examined during the progress of the several drafts, exhibiting the distinct diseases for which these men were found unfit for military service.

A grand total of the drafted men examined and exempted is as follows:

Drafted men examined	605,045
Drafted men exempted for physical or mental disability	155,730
Ratio exempted per 1,000 examined	257.38

There are also, in addition to the above records on file in this branch of your Bureau, monthly medical reports, giving the minute medical examination, including name, age, nativity, occupation, height, chest measurement at inspiration and expiration, complexion, color of eyes and hair, white or colored, married or single, physique, and result of examination of 508,735 recruits, substitutes, drafted and enrolled men, and the reports of boards of examination showing the disabilities for which enlisted men were recommended for transfer to the Veteran Reserve Corps.

In addition to the statistical records already enumerated, able and valuable reports have been received from surgeons of boards of enrollment, giving, as the result of their experience, information upon the following subjects:

First. Experience in the examination of men for military service and number examined.

*See Circular No. 15, Adjutant-General's Office, April 7, 1865, Vol. IV, this series, p. 1259.

Second. General geographical description of Congressional district, with prevalent diseases and causes conducive thereto; character of its inhabitants, their modes of life, and occupations.

Third. Reasons why any particular diseases or disabilities have disqualified a greater ratio per 1,000 from military service.

Fourth. Views in reference to the list of disqualifying diseases and disabilities, as given in the Revised Regulations Provost-Marshal-General's Bureau, and what changes recommended.

Fifth. Statement in minute detail of method of examining men for military service.

Sixth. The number of men that can be physically examined per day with accuracy.

Seventh. Frauds most to be guarded against, which are practiced by drafted and enrolled men to escape, and by substitutes and recruits to enter the service, and other obstacles contended with in the discharge of duties, with suggestions as to the best method of avoiding or overcoming these difficulties in future.

Eighth. What nationality presents the greatest physical aptitude for military service.

Ninth. Experience as to the physical qualifications of the colored race for military service.

Tenth. Views as to the operation of the enrollment law as it now exists, with recommendations and suggestions thereto.

These reports cover 2,000 pages in manuscript, and have evidently been carefully prepared, and the important information and useful suggestions contained therein are of great interest and value, not only to the medical profession of our own, but to that of other nations.

From all this data much important medico-scientific information can be deduced, not only in reference to the natives of this country, but of many others.

More than fifty different nativities are included among these records of the examination of men for the Army.

Of the most important questions which can be discussed I would mention the following:

First. The physical condition of each State or Congressional district of the United States.

Second. The prevalence of certain diseases and causes conducive thereto in any section of the United States.

Third. Influence of geographical situation on disease, as climate, hydrological condition, geological formation.

Fourth. Influence of occupation on disease.

Fifth. Influence of age on disease.

Sixth. Influence of height on disease.

Seventh. Influence of temperament.

Eighth. Influence of marriage on disease.

Ninth. What nationality presents the greatest physical aptitude for military service.

Tenth. Physical qualifications of the colored race for military service.

Eleventh. Frauds practiced by drafted and enrolled men to escape, and by recruits and substitutes to enter military service, and the best method of detecting, avoiding, or overcoming these difficulties in future.

Twelfth. Height of the inhabitants of each Congressional district in the United States; the average height in each State and in the United

States; also the same information in regard to each of the different nativities.

Thirteenth. The chest measurement of the inhabitants of each Congressional district in the United States; the average in each State and in the United States; also the same information in reference to each of the different nativities.

Fourteenth. Comparison between mental and physical diseases.

Fifteenth. Practical experiences and suggestions.

Sixteenth. Medical statistics of the Veteran Reserve Corps.

It will be observed that the tables presented with this report relate only to the prevalence of certain diseases in each Congressional district of the United States, in each State, and in the United States; the number of drafted men, recruits, and substitutes examined, and number exempted, together with ratio exempted per 1,000 examined; the more minute discussion of the subject being impossible for want of time.

Of the importance of the information to be derived from the records on file in this branch of your Bureau I need not speak in extenso.

The medical records of foreign countries relate only to the natives of those particular countries, and do not equal in extent or minuteness those on file in this branch.

The medical reports of recruiting the armies of Great Britain treat almost exclusively of Englishmen, Irishmen, and Scotchmen, from whom those armies are recruited.

Reports of conscription in France and Belgium relate to the natives of those countries alone.

Our own country containing numerous representatives of all other nations, presents the rare opportunity of comparing the physical conditions and aptitude for military service of nearly every nation in the world, for among the recruits and substitutes nearly all nations were represented.

The medico-military history of this country may properly be divided into three divisions:

First. The physical aptitude of the entire Nation for military service, and the character and degree of frequency of disqualifying diseases among its inhabitants of military ages.

Second. The disqualifying causes which render unfit for military service that comparatively small portion of the Nation who have entered the Army.

Third. The records of that still smaller portion who, having been disabled in military service, have been discharged therefrom.

In the Medical Branch of your Bureau are filed medical records relating to the physical aptitude of this Nation for military service.

The important and highly interesting medical records, showing in what way the soldier has been disabled, are on file in the Surgeon-General's Office, and when published will doubtless present to the world highly scientific medical results never before equaled in reference to the hygiene of armies.

The Pension Bureau contains the records of those who, having been discharged from service on account of wounds or diseases, return to civil life.

The important question relating to the physical aptitude of the colored race for military service can be discussed, as also the question as to whether the colored race are more subject to any particular diseases than the white race.

From the result of all these data and experience thus gained, fixed rules can be deduced for the government of future recruiting. For example, the relation of weight to height; the relation of chest circumference to height and weight; the relation of height, chest measurement, and weight to age.

The health statistics of this Nation can now from these records be to a very great extent made known, and medical questions of great importance in reference to the beneficial effect of different sections of the United States on disease, or the effect of occupation thereon, be ascertained and made public.

PREFACE TO TABLES.

In presenting the following tables I have the honor to call your attention to the fact that they are submitted without comment. The period of time which has elapsed since the organization of this branch of your Bureau has scarcely permitted the completion of tabular views of the prevalence of disease. In order to carry out the original plan it would require another year at least in which to finish the report. All of those questions which have been referred to, in speaking of the extent and value of the records on file here, remain untouched, or have been made the subjects of such incomplete investigation as will preclude the opinions that may have been formed from admission into this report.

It is scarcely necessary, now that the attention of the world has been so generally directed to the subject of vital statistics, to insist upon the importance of data more comprehensive and extensive than any other government has as yet collected.

It is beyond dispute that these tables exhibit a more complete view of the physical condition of this Nation than has been heretofore compiled; and it is not unreasonable to expect that when they shall have been more completely discussed they will be found to throw light upon the causes of many of the more common diseases to which mankind are subject.

The only condition under which any researches of this nature can aspire to a true scientific value is that in which the investigator, proceeding from the observation of phenomena, arrives finally at the laws regulating their manifestation. Whether this could be done in the case of these records has not been tried by the test of experience. It would not be premature, however, to declare that the accompanying data afford an opportunity never surpassed for the determination of the truth of some of the most important principles which the science of health has ascertained. This is the case, because, both on account of their magnitude and the variety of the conditions they embrace, they afford the opportunity of comparison with the varied but less extensive tables of European statisticians.

In the future elaboration of the records on file in this branch it may be expected that the results which will be deduced will be ascertained and compared with each other.

That a series of tabular illustrations of the various conditions of race, age, height, complexion, occupation, geographical position, &c., will be presented and an explanation of them attempted, and that in the future these labors will enable the Government of the United States to publish a work more complete in its character than has yet been issued by any foreign power.

Among the questions that have been already referred to as possibly capable of solution through a more complete study of the records of this office, there are some which have not as yet attracted the attention of statistical writers. Of these, "what nationality presents the greatest aptitude for the military service" is the first.

In alluding to it in this preliminary report all subsequent remarks are based solely upon the opinions expressed by the surgeons of boards of enrollment to whom the question was proposed. It is needless, then, to say that the following criticisms are not presented as demonstrable truths.

For the most part these officers have given it as the result of their experience that the physical, moral, and intellectual characteristics of the American gave him the precedence over other nations in respect to his fitness for war. A smaller proportion have recorded their opinion in favor of the Germans. Still fewer decide for the Irish; one or two for the English and Scotch.

It is believed that, from its nature, this point is one which it will be exceedingly difficult, if not impossible, to determine definitely.

For this opinion several reasons may be assigned. Among these it might be urged that the data upon which a decision must be founded embrace not the nations (whatever they may be) with which the comparison is made, but that portion residing in this country—not, perhaps, the best specimens of the race—and men who certainly have experienced or are in the transition state of those multifarious modifying influences known under the generic term of acclimation.

It has been frequently asserted (and not without foundation in history for the remark) that *ceteris paribus*, all first-class nations excel their enemies upon their own soil. However this may be, it would afford a ground for the opinions expressed by the great majority of the surgeons that, because of his physique *élan*, and intelligence, the American was the best type of the soldier on this continent.

The last subject to which I shall refer in these concluding remarks is embraced in the question concerning the "physical qualifications of the colored race for military service."

In reference to this question, which, in order that it may be properly decided, involves a comparison between the two most widely different types of mankind, viz, the Caucasian and the negro, a few prefatory remarks can alone be presented. The materials which would enable us to discuss this subject more fully exist, but, as was before said, no time has been permitted for their elaboration.

A sufficiently careful investigation, however, of the vital statistics relating to negro substitutes and recruits has already been made to enable me to say that when they shall have been tabulated the conclusions at which ethnologists have arrived in regard to the typical physical characteristics of the race will be found to be borne out in all important particulars. Excluding all hypotheses concerning the origin and permanence of type, and solely basing these criticisms upon the data which we possess, it may also be proper to say that, according to the information we have been able to obtain, it may be doubted whether the moral idiosyncracies which anatomists have founded upon their peculiarities of structure can be shown to exist to so great a degree as most anthropologists have supposed.

That the organization of the negro differs from that of any other of the great races of men no one, perhaps, will be hardy enough to dispute; but that this difference and those anatomical peculiarities that form the contrast between this and other types involve an unfitness for the service, does not appear to be the case. A study of the opinions expressed by 115 surgeons engaged in the examination of both black and white recruits and substitutes goes to substantiate an idea which is common among ethnological authorities, viz, that no race is equally adapted to all circumstances of life; that mankind obey the same general laws that govern the distribution of floræ and faunæ upon the earth, and that the isotherms between which are limited the health and development of the negro do not comprehend less space upon its surface than those within which the others are confined.

It may be confidently affirmed that the statistics of this office which refer principally to physico-geographical influences and to the effects of the intermixture of blood upon the negro, when taken in connection with those parts of the Surgeon-General's forthcoming report in which he is regarded as amenable to the vicissitudes of war, will form a more complete and reliable physical history of this race than exists at this time.

It would not be in accordance with the plan of this report to enter upon a discussion of the comparative aptitude for military service exhibited by the two types of mankind of which I have been speaking, without the accompanying tables as evidence of the data upon which my opinions were based.

It appears, however, that, of the surgeons of boards of enrollment, five have given their opinion that the negro recruits and substitutes examined by them were physically a better class of men than the whites; nineteen that they were equal; two that they were inferior. A favorable opinion as to their fitness for the army is expressed by seventeen; a doubtful one, because of insufficient data on which to ground the decision, by forty-three; an unfavorable opinion by nine, and by twenty a statement of not having come to any conclusion upon the subject.

The question of the prevalence of disease among the negro inhabitants of different sections of the country is one upon which at present no specific opinion can be expressed. As in the case of the white race, it may be shown hereafter that their maladies conform to those general principles which have been heretofore established. The discussion of the physical characteristics of the negro, as involving the propriety of his use in war, only belongs to this department. It is difficult and, in the present state of science, most uncertain to erect upon any general characteristics of organization anything but the most general rules concerning the effect of that structure upon the moral and intellectual nature. It may be said, however, that there are not more instances of disqualifying causes of this nature among the negroes, in proportion to the number examined, than are to be found in the records of exemption among the white race.

A résumé of the points upon which the completed results of the statistics of this Bureau may be expected to bear will comprehend the physical history of all recruits and substitutes of this race, viz, the height, age, weight, capacity of chest, health, &c. In the form of tables the comparison of equal numbers of both races will be made, exhibiting the resemblance or contrast between the two and their approach toward the ascertained standard of physical perfection; the effect of climatic causes upon the race, as evinced by the prevalence of disqualifying diseases in different localities; also the results of the intermixture of the races, as shown by the comparative healthfulness of the pure negro and the mulatto, as well as the most common infirmities to which both are subject; the moral status of the races, as far as disqualifying conditions are shown to result from infractions of the prevailing laws of propriety and temperance, &c.

The foregoing comprehend, perhaps, all the points which belong to the province of the statistician and physician to determine, but it is plain how much will be accomplished for the physical history of mankind when these results shall have been made known with those already referred to in the archives of the Surgeon-General's Office.

The historical and political significance of such a work addresses itself to the reason without the necessity of an explanation. But, in conclusion, it might not be inappropriate to say that, whatever the exigencies of the state may be, there are laws of the natural world which heretofore and in all conceivable conditions have and must supersede the legislation of mankind.

To utilize and control successfully any animal it is indispensable to know the vital and physical necessities of his being; not less so in the government of men.

The physical history of a race illuminates not only the past but the future, and is alike indispensable to those whose profession it is to superintend the phenomena of the body or the mind. No rational expectation can be entertained that the accidents of legislation can be eliminated until the knowledge of those laws which inevitably sway the destinies of the world are known, and no hope exists that the history of races can have other than an empirical value unless the causes which produce their idiosyncracies can be ascertained.

It is not only in these departments that accuracy is to be expected to attend the completion of the physical history of humanity. It is alike applicable to the efforts of hygienic science to preserve the health of the world and to the physician who combats the diseases of individuals. There lies hidden within this domain the nature of those occult physiological forces that preside over the growth, maturity, and decay of nations.

ENUMERATION OF TABLES.

I respectfully submit the following statistical tables, illustrative of the mental and physical disabilities occurring under the first, second, third, and fourth drafts made under the enrollment act, showing the number of drafted men exempted and ratio per 1,000 of those exempted to the number examined by the several boards of enrollment, and comparing these statistics with those of foreign countries.

Tables are also given showing the number of recruits and substitutes examined, the number rejected by surgeons of boards of enrollment, and the ratio rejected per 1,000 examined during the months of September, October, November, and December, 1864, and January, February, March, and April, 1865; in addition to which tables giving the average height and chest measurements at expiration and inspiration are annexed.

These statistical tables are 158 in number, and are divided as follows.*

Tables Nos. 1, 2, 3, 4, 5, 6 relate to the medical statistics of the first draft, under call of July, 1863, viz:

Table No. 1, showing, by Congressional districts of each State, the distinct diseases and disabilities, alphabetically arranged, for which drafted men were found unfit for military service; also the total number examined, total number exempted, and the ratio exempted per 1,000 examined in each district, under the draft of 1863 (being the first draft under the enrollment act).

*All tables here omitted; see explanatory foot-note (*), p. 679.

Table No. 2, showing, by States, the distinct diseases and disabilities, alphabetically arranged, for which drafted men were found unfit for military service; also the total number examined, total number exempted, and the ratio exempted per 1,000 examined in each State, under the draft of 1863 (being the first draft made under the enrollment act).

Table No. 3, showing, by Congressional districts of each State, the distinct diseases and disabilities, classified, for which drafted men were found unfit for military service; also the total number exempted in each district, total number examined, and the ratio exempted per 1,000 examined in the United States, under the draft of 1863 (being the first draft made under the enrollment act).

Table No. 4, showing, by States, the distinct diseases and disabilities, classified, for which drafted men were found unfit for military service; also the total number exempted in each State, total number examined, and ratio exempted per 1,000 examined in the United States, under the draft of 1863 (being the first draft made under the enrollment act).

Table No. 5, showing the total number examined, the total number exempted, and the ratio exempted per 1,000 examined for each distinct disease or disability, alphabetically arranged, in the United States; also the total number examined, the total number exempted, and the ratio exempted per 1,000 examined for each disease or disability, alphabetically arranged, in each State, under the draft of 1863 (being the first draft under the enrollment act).

Table No. 6, showing the total number examined, the total number exempted, and the ratio exempted per 1,000 examined for each class of diseases and disabilities in the United States; also the total number examined, the total number exempted, and the ratio exempted per 1,000 examined for each class of diseases and disabilities in each State, under the draft of 1863 (being the first draft made under the enrollment act).

Tables Nos. 7, 8, 9, 10, 11, 12 contain the medical statistics of the second draft, made for deficiencies arising under call of March 14, 1864, being the second draft under the enrollment act, as follows:

Table No. 7, showing, by Congressional districts of each State, the distinct diseases and disabilities, alphabetically arranged, for which drafted men were found unfit for military service; also the total number examined, the total number exempted, and the ratio exempted per 1,000 examined in each district, under the draft made under the call of March 14, 1864 (being the second draft under the enrollment act).

Table No. 8, showing, by States, the distinct diseases and disabilities, alphabetically arranged, for which drafted men are found unfit for military service; also the total number examined, the total number exempted, and the ratio exempted per 1,000 examined in each State, under the draft made under the call of March 14, 1864 (being the second draft made under the enrollment act).

Table No. 9, showing, by Congressional districts of each State, the distinct diseases and disabilities, classified, for which drafted men were found unfit for military service; also the total number exempted in each district, the total number examined, and the ratio exempted per 1,000 examined in the United States, under the draft made under the call of March 14, 1864 (being the second draft made under the enrollment act).

Table No. 10, showing, by States, the distinct diseases and disabilities, classified, for which drafted men were found unfit for military service; also the total number exempted in each State, the total number examined, and the ratio exempted per 1,000 examined in the United States, under the draft made under the call of March 14, 1864 (being the second draft made under the enrollment act).

Table No. 11, showing the total number examined, the total number exempted, and the ratio exempted per 1,000 examined for each distinct disease and disability, alphabetically arranged, in the United States; also the total number examined, the total number exempted, and the ratio exempted per 1,000 examined for each disease or disability, alphabetically arranged, in each State, under the draft made under the call of March 14, 1864 (being the second draft made under the enrollment act).

Table No. 12, showing the total number examined, the total number exempted, and the ratio exempted per 1,000 examined for each class of diseases and disabilities in the United States; also the total number examined, the total number exempted, and the ratio exempted per 1,000 examined for each class of diseases and disabilities in each State, under the draft made under the call of March 14, 1864 (being the second draft made under the enrollment act).

Tables Nos. 13, 14, 15, 16, 17, and 18 present the medical statistics of the third draft, made under call of July 18, 1864, and contain the following data:

Table No. 13, showing, by Congressional districts of each State, the distinct diseases and disabilities, alphabetically arranged, for which drafted men were found unfit for military service; also the total number examined, the total number exempted, and the ratio exempted per 1,000 examined in each district, under the draft made under the call of July 18, 1864 (being the third draft made under the enrollment act).

Table No. 14, showing, by States, the distinct diseases and disabilities, alphabetically arranged, for which drafted men were found unfit for military service; also the total number examined, the total number exempted, and the ratio exempted per 1,000 examined in each State, under the draft made under the call of July 18, 1864 (being the third draft made under the enrollment act).

Table No. 15, showing, by Congressional districts of each State, the distinct diseases and disabilities, classified, for which drafted men were found unfit for military service; also the total number exempted in each district, the total number examined, and the ratio exempted per 1,000 examined in the United States, under the draft made under the call of July 18, 1864 (being the third draft made under the enrollment act).

Table No. 16, showing, by States, the distinct diseases and disabilities, classified, for which drafted men were found unfit for military service; also the total number exempted in each State, the total number examined, and the ratio exempted per 1,000 examined in the United States, under the draft made under the call of July 18, 1864 (being the third draft made under the enrollment act).

Table No. 17, showing the total number examined, the total number exempted, and the ratio exempted per 1,000 examined for each distinct disease or disability, alphabetically arranged, in the United States; also the total number examined, the total number exempted, and the ratio exempted per 1,000 examined for each disease or disability, alphabetically arranged, in each State, under the draft made under the call of July 18, 1864 (being the third draft made under the enrollment act).

Table No. 18, showing the total number examined, the total number exempted, and the ratio exempted per 1,000 examined for each class of diseases and disabilities in the United States; also the total number examined, the total number exempted, and the ratio exempted per 1,000 examined for each class of diseases and disabilities in each State, under the draft made under the call of July 18, 1864 (being the third draft made under the enrollment act).

Tables Nos. 19, 20, 21, 22, 23, and 24 relate to the fourth draft made under the call of December 19, 1864, and give the following information:

Table No. 19, showing, by Congressional districts of each State, the distinct diseases and disabilities, alphabetically arranged, for which drafted men were found unfit for military service; also the total number examined, the total number exempted, and the ratio exempted per 1,000 examined in each district, under the draft made under the call of December 19, 1864 (being the fourth draft made under the enrollment act).

Table No. 20, showing, by States, the distinct diseases and disabilities, alphabetically arranged, for which drafted men were found unfit for military service; also the total number examined, the total number exempted, and the ratio exempted per 1,000 examined in each State, under the draft made under the call of December 19, 1864 (being the fourth draft made under the enrollment act).

Table No. 21, showing, by Congressional districts of each State, the distinct diseases and disabilities, classified, for which drafted men were found unfit for military service; also the total number exempted in each district, the total number examined, and the ratio exempted per 1,000 examined in the United States, under the draft made under the call of December 19, 1864 (being the fourth draft made under the enrollment act).

Table No. 22, showing, by States, the distinct diseases and disabilities, classified, for which drafted men were found unfit for military service; also the total number exempted in each State, the total number examined, and the ratio exempted per 1,000 examined in the United States, under the draft made under the call of December 19, 1864 (being the fourth draft made under the enrollment act).

Table No. 23, showing the total number exempted, the total number examined, and the ratio exempted per 1,000 examined for each distinct disease and disability, alphabetically arranged, in the United States; also the total number exempted, the total number examined, and the ratio exempted per 1,000 examined for each distinct disease and disability, alphabetically arranged, in each State, under the draft made under the call of December 19, 1864 (being the fourth draft made under the enrollment act).

Table No. 24, showing the total number exempted, the total number examined, and the ratio exempted per 1,000 examined for each class of diseases and disabilities in the United States; also the total number exempted, the total number examined, and the ratio exempted per 1,000 examined in each State, under the draft made under the call of December 19, 1864 (being the fourth draft made under the enrollment act).

In Tables Nos. 25, 26, 27, and 28 will be found the consolidated medical results of all the drafts made under the enrollment act, and from these tables may be learned the following statistical information:

Table No. 25, showing, by States, the distinct diseases and disabilities, alphabetically arranged, for which drafted men were found unfit for military service; also the total number examined, the total number exempted, and the ratio exempted per 1,000 examined in each State, under all the drafts made under the enrollment act.

Table No. 26, showing, by States, the distinct diseases and disabilities, classified, for which drafted men were found unfit for military service; also the total number exempted in each State, the total number examined, and the ratio exempted per 1,000 examined in the United States, under all the drafts made under the enrollment act.

Table No. 27, showing the total number exempted, the total number examined, and the ratio exempted per 1,000 examined for each distinct disease and disability, alphabetically arranged, in the United States; also the total number exempted, the total number examined, and the ratio exempted per 1,000 examined for each disease and disability in each State, under all the drafts made under the enrollment act.

Table No. 28, showing the total number exempted, the total number examined, and the ratio exempted per 1,000 examined for each class of diseases and disabilities in the United States; also the total number exempted, the total number examined, and the ratio exempted per 1,000 examined in each State, under all the drafts made under the enrollment act.

The tables from No. 29 to No. 140, inclusive, exhibit by angular lines the prevalence of diseases and disabilities for which drafted men were exempted under all drafts, and are given for the purpose of facilitating the study of Table No. 27, and render unnecessary a minute examination and comparison with each other of the ratios indicating the prevalence of diseases in each State and the United States.

Tables Nos. 141, 142, 143, 144, and 145 show the number of recruits examined and rejected for physical or mental disabilities in the following manner:

Table No. 141, showing, by Congressional districts of each State, the distinct diseases and disabilities, alphabetically arranged, for which recruits were found unfit for service; also the total number examined, total number rejected, and the ratio rejected per 1,000 examined in each district, for the months of September, October, November, and December, 1864, and January, February, March, and April, 1865.

Table No. 142, showing, by States, the distinct diseases and disabilities, alphabetically arranged, for which recruits were found unfit for service; also the total number examined, the total number rejected, and the ratio rejected per 1,000 examined in each State, for the months of September, October, November, and December, 1864, and January, February, March, and April, 1865.

Table No. 143, showing, by Congressional districts of each State, the distinct diseases and disabilities, classified, for which recruits were found unfit for service; also the total number rejected in each district, total number examined, and the ratio rejected per 1,000 examined in the United States, for the months of September, October, November, and December, 1864, and January, February, March, and April, 1865.

Table No. 144, showing, by States, the distinct diseases and disabilities, classified, for which recruits were found unfit for service; also the total number rejected in each State, total number examined, and ratio rejected per 1,000 examined in the United States, for the months of September, October, November, and December, 1864, and January, February, March, and April, 1865.

Table No. 145, showing the total number of recruits examined, the total number rejected, and the ratio rejected per 1,000 examined for each distinct disease or disability, alphabetically arranged, in the United States; also the total number examined, the total number rejected, and the ratio rejected per 1,000 examined for each disease or disability, alphabetically arranged, in each State, for the months of September, October, November, and December, 1864, and January, February, March, and April, 1865.

In the same manner as in the case of recruits, Tables Nos. 146, 147, 148, 149, and 150 illustrate the medical results of the examination of substitutes.

Table No. 146, showing, by Congressional districts of each State, the distinct diseases and disabilities, alphabetically arranged, for which substitutes were found unfit for service; also the total number examined, total number rejected, and the ratio rejected per 1,000 examined in each district, for the months of September, October, November, and December, 1864, and January, February, March, and April, 1865.

Table No. 147, showing, by States, the distinct diseases and disabilities, alphabetically arranged, for which substitutes were found unfit for service; also the total number examined, total number rejected, and the ratio rejected per 1,000 examined in each State, for the months of September, October, November, and December, 1864, and January, February, March, and April, 1865.

Table No. 148, showing, by Congressional districts of each State, the distinct diseases and disabilities, classified, for which substitutes were found unfit for service; also the total number rejected in each district, total number examined, and the ratio rejected per 1,000 examined in the United States, for the months of September, October, November, and December, 1864, and January, February, March, and April, 1865.

Table No. 149, showing, by States, the distinct diseases and disabilities, classified, for which substitutes were found unfit for service; also the total number rejected in each State, total number examined, and ratio rejected per 1,000 examined in the United States, for the months of September, October, November, and December, 1864, and January, February, March, and April, 1865.

Table No. 150, showing the total number of substitutes examined, the total number rejected, and the ratio rejected per 1,000 examined for each distinct disease or disability, alphabetically arranged, in the United States; also the total number examined, the total number rejected, and the ratio rejected per 1,000 examined for each disease or disability, alphabetically arranged, in each State, for the months of September, October, November, and December, 1864, and January, February, March, and April, 1865.

Tables Nos. 151, 152, 153, 154, and 155 have been compiled from the latest statistical records that could be obtained of Great Britain, France, and Belgium, and are given for the purpose of comparison with like statistics of the United States.

Table No. 151, showing the causes of rejection of the recruits found unfit for service at the headquarters of each of the recruiting districts in Great Britain, in the ten years from April 1, 1842, to March 31, 1852.

Table No. 152, showing the number of young men exempted from military service on account of physical unfitness in France in each year from 1831 to 1843, inclusive, and specifying the various causes of exemption. (Compiled from the "Comptes Rendus au Roi sur le Recrutement de l'Armée.")

Table No. 153, showing the number of enrolled militia and different causes of exemption during the period of five years from 1851 to 1855 in each of the provinces of Belgium. (Document "Statistiques publiés par le Ministre de l'Intèrieur:" Bruxelles, 1857.)

Table No. 154, showing the number of recruits examined, the number rejected for physical and mental disability, and the ratio rejected per 1,000 examined in Great Britain, for each year from 1832 to 1851, and from 1860 to 1862, inclusive; also giving the total examinations, total rejections for physical and mental disability, and the ratio per 1,000 rejected.

Table No. 155, showing the number of young men examined, number exempted for physical and mental disability, and the ratio per 1,000 exempted in France in each year from 1831 to 1843, inclusive. (Compiled from the "Comptes Rendus au Roi sur le Recrutement de l'Armée.")

Table No. 156, showing the ratios of exemptions or rejections from military service for mental and physical infirmities in the United States, France, Great Britain, and Belgium.

Table No. 157, showing, by nationalities, the average height and chest measurements at expiration and inspiration of 340,179 drafted men, recruits, and substitutes examined by the several boards of enrollment of the United States for military service.

Table No. 158, showing, by States, the average height and chest measurements at expiration and inspiration of 233,806 drafted men, recruits, and substitutes, natives of the United States, examined for military service.

In preparing the statistical tables of height and chest measurement it is to be regretted that sufficient time was not permitted in which to compile them in the more preferable and scientific manner which is now adopted by statisticians, viz, the number examined of each nationality of each particular height or chest measurement. It is, however, believed that they will be of interest and practical value in the form in which they are presented.

In conclusion, I have the honor to state that some discrepancy will be observed in the results of the number examined and exempted, given in the tables herewith submitted, and those submitted by the Enrollment Branch of your Bureau. It does not, however, materially affect the ratio of exemptions, and arises from the fact that, in a few cases, later returns have been received by the Enrollment Branch than those on file in this office.

In a few districts the reports are not incorporated in the tables presented on account of being imperfect.

The ratio exempted for physical or mental disability per 1,000 examined in the fourth draft may seem disproportionately small when compared with the results of the other drafts. In the fourth draft many men who reported to boards of enrollment were discharged by the order discontinuing recruiting and drafting, and although they are counted in the total examined by the Board, yet numbers who would probably have been exempted for physical disabilities were not examined by the surgeon, such examination being unnecessary, as the drafted men were discharged by the order above cited.

It is respectfully submitted that the valuable and interesting information contained in the reports and records on file in this branch of your Bureau should not be lost, and that it would be not only of interest, but scientific importance, that minute results deduced therefrom should be made public.

I have the honor to be, general, very respectfully, your obedient servant,

J. H. BAXTER,
Surgeon and Bvt. Col., U. S. Vols., and
Chief Medical Officer Provost-Marshal-General's Bureau.

SCHEDULE A.—*List of officers who have been on duty under the Medical Branch of the Provost-Marshal-General's Bureau since its organization.*

No.	Name.	Rank.	Under whose authority.	Date of assignment to duty.	Date of order relieving from duty.
1	Baxter, J. H. (brevet colonel)	Surgeon, U. S. Volunteers.	Secretary of War	Jan. 11, 1864	
2	McKibbin, D. J	do	do	Feb. 10, 1864	June 2, 1865
3	Stewart, W. D	do	do	Aug. 8, 1864	Dec. 21, 1864
4	Moses, Israel *a*	do	do	Aug. 8, 1864	
5	Cantwell, J. Y	do	do	Sept. 20, 1864	May 22, 1865
6	Fisher, J. C	do	do	Sept. 14, 1864	Oct. 28, 1864
7	Mursick, George A. *a*	Assistant surgeon, volunteers.	do	Sept. 20, 1864	
8	McDermott, W. J. *b*	do	do	Dec. 9, 1864	Oct. 20, 1865
9	Delany, Alfred *a*	do	do	Mar. 18, 1865	
10	Radcliffe, S. J. *a*	do	do	Mar. 28, 1865	
11	Stanton, J. O. *b*	Surgeon, First Army Corps.	do	Mar. 8, 1865	Oct. 21, 1865
12	Rizer, M	do	do	Mar. 13, 1865	Sept. 2, 1865
13	Stevens, Joseph	do	do	Mar. 16, 1865	Mar. 24, 1865
14	Reynolds, F	do	do	Mar. 24, 1865	Mar. 24, 1865
15	McDowell, A. W	do	do	Mar. 25, 1865	June 16, 1865
16	Merritt, David *c*	do	do		Mar. 31, 1865
17	Greely, G. P	do	do	April 3, 1865	June 16, 1865
18	Harris, E. B. *b*	do	do	April 3, 1865	Oct. 13, 1865
19	Wonsetler, G. *c*	do	do		April 7, 1864
20	McMillen, G. W	do	do	April 14, 1865	April 22, 1865
21	Mulford, W. C	Assistant surgeon, First Army Corps.	do	Mar. 10, 1865	June 16, 1865
22	Miller, G. W	do	do	Mar. 16, 1865	Mar. 24, 1865
23	Trautman, C. T	do	do	Mar. 16, 1865	Mar. 24, 1865
24	Cummings, G. W	do	do	Mar. 22, 1865	Mar. 31, 1865
25	Paine, R. E	do	do	Mar. 29, 1865	Mar. 31, 1865

a These officers were on duty for short periods with boards appointed for the examination of enlisted men for transfer to the Veteran Reserve Corps, but no copies of the special orders relieving them have ever been furnished this office.
b Mustered out of service. *c* Reported for duty, but not assigned.

DOCUMENT No. 9.

Report of the Disbursing Branch of Provost-Marshal-General's Bureau.

WAR DEPARTMENT,
PROVOST-MARSHAL-GENERAL'S OFFICE,
Washington, D. C., January 1, 1866.

Bvt. Maj. Gen. JAMES B. FRY,
Provost-Marshal-General United States:

GENERAL: In obedience to your instructions I have the honor to submit the following report of the operations of the Disbursing Branch of this Bureau:

In conformity with the act approved March 3, 1863, creating a Provost-Marshal-General's Bureau, and making it the duty of the Provost-Marshal-General "to audit all accounts connected with the service under his direction," a disbursing branch was organized, and a chief officer placed in charge, with four assistant disbursing officers, whose duties were the examination and payment of all accounts pertaining to the Bureau.

Funds were deposited at principal points throughout the country with the several assistant treasurers and designated depositaries, and held subject to the order and for the payment of checks drawn by the disbursing officers above mentioned.

This course was deemed safer, more expeditious and economical, and was adopted instead of the more expensive mode of appointing disbursing officers at numerous points, or intrusting public moneys in the hands of provost-marshals, who, however trustworthy, were from their inexperience thought to be unfitted for such responsible and intricate duties, and whose time, moreover, would doubtless be fully occupied with the other duties of their office.

A geographical division of labor, each division paying all classes of accounts incurred in its section, was the course pursued until July 1, 1864, when the system was entirely and advantageously changed.

Since that date the salaries of all employés have been paid by the First and Second Divisions, the former paying the districts of the Eastern and the latter those of the Western States. The payments of all other accounts have been divided between the Third and Fourth Divisions as follows:

Third Division: Travel pay of discharged drafted men, postage, telegrams, advertising, subsistence, and lodging, and expenses incurred in the arrest or pursuit of deserters.

Fourth Division: Purchases of public property of this Bureau, rent, and transportation; the latter class of accounts being very large and involving more labor than those first mentioned.

Since April, 1865, reductions have been made both in the divisions and the clerical force employed therein, as rapidly as the public interests would admit; and at this date but one of the four divisions remains for the payment of outstanding claims.

A statement (No. 1) giving the names, date of assignment, &c., of all officers detailed for duty in this branch will be found annexed to this report.

The internal arrangement of this branch is similar in most respects, as far as regards the hours and division of labor, classification of clerical force, amount of compensation, &c., to that of the other military bureaus.

The largest number of clerks on duty at any one time was during the month of January, 1865, when there were seventy-one employed.

The number as shown by the report for October, 1865, was thirty, and a careful computation shows an average of fifty-four per month for the entire period of the operations of this branch.

In order to form some idea of the duties discharged by this clerical force, the following statement is submitted, which, when it is considered that every letter and account received has been subjected to a careful examination and to all the checks that secure complete action, it will be seen that the force employed was as limited as the circumstances would possibly admit.

Of letters received, indorsements made, letters sent, and accounts examined and paid from May, 1863, to January, 1866, there were—

Letters received	69,267
Letters sent	20,659
Indorsements made	20,929
Accounts examined and paid	105,398
Checks drawn	155,127

EMPLOYÉS.

All appointments of employés for duty in the offices of provost-marshals and acting assistant provost-marshals-general have been made by this branch since the date of its organization, with the exception of those for California, Nevada, and Oregon, and Washington Territory, which on account of their remoteness have been made by the acting assistant provost-marshals-general of the States and Territory referred to.

The course pursued, and which has proved entirely satisfactory, has been to require provost-marshals to submit the name of the employé, the necessity for the employment, and whether permanent or temporary, and in the latter instance the probable duration of the same; and in the case of regular clerks to submit also a specimen of their handwriting. The approval or disapproval of the acting assistant provost-marshal-general has been required in every instance, and though not accepted as final, it has proved of material assistance in deciding upon the merits of or necessity for the appointment. The several employés of provost-marshals are designated and known as clerks, deputy provost-marshals, special agents, assistant surgeons, enrolling and notifying officers, civil guards, and janitors.

The duties of deputy provost-marshals and special agents are similar in character, viz, the pursuit and arrest of deserters. The former, however, are held to be more permanent and reliable officers, frequently assisting the provost-marshals in other duties, such as the correction of enrollment lists, instructing enrolling officers when remote from headquarters, &c., whilst the latter are confined to the one line of duty, and their employment often of a temporary character, many of them accepting the authorized reward for the arrest of deserters in lieu of a stated compensation.

The duties of the other employés are sufficiently indicated by their several designations, and are fully set forth in the regulations of the Bureau.

The average number employed in each district has been about three clerks, five temporary clerks, four deputies, three special agents, one assistant surgeon, and one janitor.

To include the members of boards of enrollment, civil guards, enrolling officers, and persons whose services were only occasionally required, would show during active operations an average estimate of twenty-five persons to each district.

Although every effort has been made to keep the number of employés within the limits prescribed by regulations, circular, &c., yet experience has conclusively shown that while a general average might be maintained, no positive standard could be adopted without manifest injury to the interests of the service; for what would more than suffice for the proper performance of the duties of one district, would, from local and other causes, be wholly inadequate in another.

On the 31st day of October, 1864, the total number of officers and employés of the Provost-Marshal-General's Bureau was 4,716, at a cost per month of $311,868.40.

About the latter part of April a diminution was commenced, and by the 31st day of October, 1865, the force was reduced to 383, at a cost per month of $35,050.32.

On the 31st day of December last all provost-marshals and their clerks were discharged, and all expenses connected with the enrollment and draft fund closed except the payment of outstanding claims.

Appointments under this Bureau have been to a great extent filled by discharged soldiers—they being always preferred when found capable of performing the duties.

Appendix No. 2 will show the number and classification of all persons employed in the offices of provost-marshals and acting assistant provost-marshals-general throughout the States on the 31st day of October, 1864 and 1865.*

PAYMENTS.

The principal business of this branch, with its divisions and subdivisions as heretofore described, may be divided into two classes—payments of employés and payments of all other accounts. All persons employed by provost-marshals and acting assistant provost-marshals-general, with the exception of commissioned officers and enlisted men, are paid monthly on receipt rolls, or on vouchers in cases where it has been found impracticable to bear their names on the receipt roll for the month in which the services were rendered. The rates of pay allowed the several grades of employés of this Bureau are as follows:

Clerks	per month	$75.00 to	$150.00
Deputy provost-marshals	do		100.00
Special agents	do	65.00	100.00
Assistant surgeons	do		100.00
Janitors	do		40.00
Clerks, temporary	per day	2.00	3.00
Enrolling officers	do		3.00
Civilian guards	do	1.50	2.50

In consequence of the very high rates of all kinds of labor, cost of living, &c., in the States and Territories on the Pacific Coast, and in order to maintain some degree of uniformity with the same class of expenditures in the Eastern and Western States, instructions were given in August, 1864, to pay all employés in gold at the rates above mentioned.

The total amount disbursed by this branch from date of organization to January 1, 1866, was, on account of enrollment and draft		$8,067,437.27
Incidental expenses Quartermaster's Department		119,204.89
Total		8,186,642.16
Of this amount there was paid—		
For services	$6,205,994.73	
For rent	210,680.97	
For transportation	508,942.93	
For purchase of public property	144,733.22	
For incidental expenses Quartermaster's Department	119,204.89	
For advertising	159,466.85	
For stationery and printing	308,025.31	
For miscellaneous accounts	529,593.26	
		8,186,642.16

The amount paid for services as above set forth does not include the pay of provost-marshals, commissioners, and surgeons, who were paid by the Pay Department of the Army to the extent of about $1,740,000.

For amounts received and disbursed by each disbursing officer of this branch, see Appendix No. 3.†

*Statement (here omitted) shows 3,243 on October 31, 1864, and 306 on October 31, 1865. "On December 31, 1865, all these employés were discharged with the exception of a limited number of clerks transferred to the offices of the several acting assistant provost-marshals-general."

†Omitted. The total amount disbursed was $8,186,642.16, as shown above.

The system of making all payments in one office has been found, after an experience of three years, to possess decided advantages over that of making payments through the medium of disbursing officers stationed at different points throughout the country. Some of the advantages which the practical administration of the system has shown may be enumerated as follows:

First. It secures greater expedition, for the reason that a large proportion of the claims are for contingent expenditures, and which it would be necessary to refer to the Bureau for approval before paying, and so incurring unnecessary delay.

Second. It is more economical, it being well understood that the reduction of any of the forms of labor to a specialty secures not only superior results, but the greatest possible saving.

Third. It is more equitable to the parties in interest, for by the consolidation of all payments in one office all precedents and other evidence upon which to base a decision are within immediate reach, to the full extent of its financial operations, thus securing uniformity and correctness of action.

COMMUTATION MONEY.

Section 13 of the act for enrolling and calling out the national forces, and for other purposes, approved March 3, 1863, provided that "any person drafted and notified to appear * * * may pay to such person as the Secretary of War may authorize to receive it, a sum for the procuration of a substitute, not exceeding three hundred dollars," and this maximum sum was accordingly fixed as the amount of commutation money to be paid by a drafted man to secure exemption from military service.

In order to avoid the large expense of making special appointments of persons to receive this money, the collectors of internal revenue were directed, in addition to their other duties, to act as "receivers of commutation money," subject to such instructions as might be prescribed by the Provost-Marshal-General.

The whole amount of commutation money received up to January 1, 1866, was $26,366,616.78.

The whole expense of collecting these twenty-six millions of commutation money was the comparatively trifling sum of $176,758.37, or less than seven-tenths of 1 per cent. This includes all incidental expenses and the percentage paid receivers on the sums received, the latter being graduated as follows:

On the first $10,000, 2½ per cent.; on the next $15,000, 2 per cent.; on the second $25,000, 1 per cent.; on the third $25,000 one-fourth of 1 per cent.; on all sums above $100,000, one-eighth of 1 per cent.

By the last clause of section 2, act approved July 4, 1864, the payment of commutation money, except by "non-combatants," was abolished, each able-bodied drafted man being required to serve in person or furnish an acceptable substitute.

The persons known as "non-combatants," and further described in section 10 of the act first mentioned, were exempted on payment of $300, which money, amounting in the aggregate to $463,987.53, was deposited to the credit of the fund for "sick and wounded soldiers."

There is no commutation money remaining in the hands of receivers, all such funds having been deposited in the U. S. Treasury, and the accounts closed.

Receivers have, with but few exceptions, promptly deposited with the assistant treasurers and designated depositaries the sums received by them, and have rendered statements of the same with commendable accuracy.

REMARKS.

The leasing of premises required for the use of provost-marshals has from several causes involved considerable labor and correspondence. The difficulties arising from it have, however, in some measure, been obviated by the adoption of a form of lease, the terms of which are thought just and equitable, and so far simplified as to be readily comprehended, and by requiring all provost-marshals to show the necessity for agreements made by them, the specific purpose for which the premises are to be used, and whether temporarily or otherwise. All expensive dwellings, excessive rates, and vague or indefinitely worded leases have invariably been disapproved.

Any discrepancy or informality appearing in accounts has been made a matter of immediate investigation, no incorrect voucher being filed away to await the action of the claimant.

A large number of disallowed claims have been transmitted for reconsideration and adjustment, and in cases where additional and satisfactory evidence of the validity of the claim has been adduced payment has been allowed.

During the early part of last year accounts of several of the disbursing officers of this Bureau were referred, by the Second and Third Auditors U. S. Treasury, for "official examination;" but, in consequence of the pressure of current business of the office, this examination was not commenced until quite recently, but is now rapidly progressing, and is likely to be completed at an early period. These accounts, as well as those lately received, are rigidly scrutinized, in order that it may be ascertained that the regulations, circulars, &c., have been properly complied with.

The Bureau (so far as pertains to the enrollment and draft) may properly be termed self-sustaining, for the reason that not a single dollar has been appropriated by Congress for its support, or for the liquidation of any part of the large expenditures that have been incurred thereby during the entire period of its operations.

The $26,366,616.78 commutation money received from drafted men for the procurement of substitutes has probably been as profitably and successfully employed as any similar amount obtained by contribution or legislative enactment.

Not only have the expenses incident to the employment of a vast corps of clerks, deputies, special agents, enrolling officers, and the miscellaneous expenditures pertaining to the whole machinery of the draft been defrayed from this fund, but it has placed 168,649 drafted men in the Army, besides enlisting, through the instrumentality of its provost-marshals, over 1,000,000 of volunteers and substitutes.

The value of these results and of the great saving to the Government will be more clearly understood when it is considered that the money received from the 87,874 men who paid commutation money was ostensibly for the procuration of a similar number to fill their places; whereas this Bureau has not only placed twelve times that number in the Army, and defrayed the entire expenditure of the draft, as before stated, but has now remaining to its credit (or the credit of the fund) several millions of dollars—more than sufficient to cover the whole amount expended by the Pay Department for pay of provost-marshals, commissioners, surgeons, and officers detailed for duty in the Bureau.

It may, therefore, be claimed that every man placed in the Army by this Bureau, over and above the 87,874 above mentioned, were placed there without expense to the Government and furthermore, that the draft itself did not cost the Nation a single dollar.

Attention is respectfully invited to the "historical report" of this branch, recently submitted, in which will be found a detailed exhibit of its affairs, together with many items of exclusively bureau interest which are of necessity omitted in so brief a statement as this.

I would not do justice to my own feelings if I were to conclude this report without acknowledging my great indebtedness to the officers and employés of this branch for their cordial and zealous assistance, or if I were to omit to bear testimony to the faithful and efficient manner in which they have invariably performed their arduous and responsible duties.

Very respectfully, your obedient servant,

H. R. RATHBONE,

Capt., Twelfth Infty., and Bvt. Maj., U. S. Army, and Maj. and A. A. G. of Vols., in Charge Disbursing Branch.

No. 1.—*List of officers who have served in the Disbursing Branch from date of organization (May 1, 1863) to present time.*

No.	Name and rank.	Regiment.	To what duty assigned.	When detailed.	When relieved.	Remarks.
1	Capt. S. F. Chalfin	Fifth Artillery	Chief of Disbursing Branch	Mar. 23, 1863	Apr. 7, 1864	Assistant adjutant-general, U. S. Army, from June 25, 1863. Relieved by Captain Burton.
2	Capt. G. W. Burton	Commissary of Subsistence, volunteers.	do	Oct. 23, 1863.—Special Order 475, paragraph 13.	Mar. 8, 1865	Appointed major and assistant adjutant-general, volunteers. Relieved by Brevet-Major Rathbone.
3	Capt. H. R. Rathbone	Twelfth Infantry	do	Dec. 19, 1864		Appointed major and assistant adjutant-general, volunteers.
1	Capt. H. C. Wood	Eleventh Infantry	Disbursing officer, Fourth Division.	Apr. 29, 1863.—Special Order 194, paragraph 20.	July 29, 1864	Relieved by Captain Lodor.
2	Capt. James Curtis	Fifteenth Infantry	Disbursing officer, First Division	May 5, 1863.—Special Order 203, paragraph 16.	Aug. 31, 1863	Relieved by Captain McMillan.
3	Capt. F. H. Barroll	Second Infantry	Disbursing officer, Second Division.	May 6, 1863.—Special Order 204, paragraph 3.	July 1, 1865	Relieved by Captain Dana.
4	Capt. H. B. Hendershott	Second Artillery	Disbursing officer, Third Division	May 13, 1863.—Special Order 214, paragraph 15.	Mar. 30, 1864	Do.
5	Capt. S. B. Lawrence	Sixteenth Infantry	Assistant to chief of Disbursing Branch.	Aug. 15, 1863.—Special Order 354, paragraph 21.	Oct. 30, 1864	Transferred to General Fry's office.
6	Capt. James McMillan	Second Infantry	Disbursing officer, First Division	Aug. 20, 1863.—Special Order 371, paragraph 7.	Dec. 19, 1864	Relieved by Captain Rathbone.
7	Capt. H. Keteltas	Fifteenth Infantry	Disbursing officer, Miscellaneous Accounts.	Mar. 26, 1864.—Special Order 128, paragraph 48.	Apr. 1, 1865	Relieved by Captain Smedberg.
8	Capt. S. Dana	Seventeenth Infantry.	Disbursing officer, Third Division	Apr. 9, 1864.—Special Order 143, paragraph 48.		In charge of consolidated divisions.
9	Capt. R. Lodor	Fourth Artillery	Disbursing officer, Second Division.	June 21, 1864.—Special Order 215, paragraph 39.	Dec. 9, 1865	Relieved by Captain Dana.
10	Capt. W. R. Smedberg	Fourteenth Infantry	Disbursing officer, Miscellaneous Accounts.	Feb. 11, 1865.—Special Order 68, paragraph 21.	Aug. 16, 1865	Relieved by Captain Lodor.
11	Capt. J. McL. Hildt	Third Infantry	Disbursing officer, First Division	Mar. 16, 1865.—Special Order 128, paragraph 11.	Aug. 17, 1865	Do.

COMMUTATION.

The amounts of commutation money received by receivers thereof (collectors of internal revenue) under the act of March 3, 1863, and deposited by them with the U. S. Treasurer, assistant treasurers, and designated depositaries, &c., to your credit, as Provost-Marshal-General, from July 18, 1863, the date of the first transaction, to February 23, 1864, the date at which the final balance remaining in your hands was turned over to the Treasurer of the United States in compliance with the joint resolution aforesaid, are as follows.*

Recapitulation of commutation money by States.

State.	Deposited to the credit of—			Total.
	Provost-Marshal-General.	Treasurer United States, Nov. 1, 1864.	Treasurer United States, Dec. 31, 1865.	
Maine	$582, 300. 00	$16, 800. 00	$11, 100. 00	$610, 200. 00
New Hampshire	171, 300. 00	37, 200. 00	....	208, 500. 00
Vermont	561, 600. 00	31, 200. 00	600. 00	593, 400. 00
Massachusetts	1, 051, 800. 00	546, 000. 00	12, 600. 00	1, 610, 400. 00
Rhode Island	138, 300. 00	1, 500. 00	1, 500. 00	141, 300. 00
Connecticut	450, 300. 00	6, 000. 00	1, 200. 00	457, 500. 00
New York	4, 714, 500. 00	753, 299. 25	18, 000. 00	5, 485, 799. 25
New Jersey	....	1, 169, 700. 00	96, 000. 00	1, 265, 700. 00
Pennsylvania	5, 290, 800. 00	3, 201, 300. 00	142, 200. 00	8, 634, 300. 00
Delaware	128, 700. 00	287, 100. 00	300. 00	416, 100. 00
Maryland	284, 100. 00	819, 300. 00	28, 500. 00	1, 131, 900. 00
District of Columbia	95, 400. 00	900. 00	600. 00	96, 900. 00
Kentucky	....	942, 300. 00	55, 230. 00	997, 530. 00
Ohio	....	1, 935, 300. 00	42, 787. 53	1, 978, 087. 53
Minnesota	....	307, 800. 00	9, 000. 00	316, 800. 00
Illinois	....	8, 100. 00	7, 800. 00	15, 900. 00
Indiana	....	48, 600. 00	186, 900. 00	235, 500. 00
Michigan	495, 600. 00	101, 700. 00	17, 400. 00	614, 700. 00
Wisconsin	1, 499, 100. 00	28, 500. 00	6, 000. 00	1, 533, 600. 00
Iowa	....	....	22, 500. 00	22, 500. 00
Total	15, 463, 800. 00	10, 242, 599. 25	660, 217. 53	26, 366, 616. 78

Total commutation money received		$26, 366, 616. 78
Add donations and amount left by deserters, &c		1, 675. 95
Total received		26, 368, 292. 73
Deduct—		
Deposited for sick and wounded soldiers	$463, 987. 53	
Disbursed on account of enrollment and draft	4, 370, 708. 15	
Disbursed on account of premiums and bounties	11, 898, 079. 52	
In hands of officers	111, 042. 19	
Returned by disbursing officers to Treasury	73, 323. 00	
Unaccounted for *a*	35, 928. 89	
		16, 953, 069. 28
Balance available in Treasury, as shown by books of this Bureau		9, 415, 223. 45
Deduct settlements by Second Auditor		135, 860. 00
		9, 279, 363. 45
In hands of officers		111, 042. 19
Total available January 1, 1866		9, 390, 405. 64

a NOTE.—Two hundred and seventy dollars deposited by Capt. J. McL. Hildt to the credit of the Treasurer of the United States (III T, 66) has not been included in the above amount, although the certificates are on file in this office, for the reason that the amount should be credited to appropriation for "pay of volunteers," as appears from information on file in disbursing branch.

Disbursements by officers of the Provost-Marshal-General's Bureau from its organization to December 31, 1865 (being itemized from July 1, 1864, to December 31, 1865, inclusive).†

* Details omitted; see general summary in report of Provost-Marshal-General under the heads "Commutation Money" and "Disbursements, Accounts, etc.," pp. 682, 684, and the recapitulation following.

† Details omitted in view of the recapitulation following.

RECAPITULATION.

State, &c.	Service.	Rent.	Transportation.	Public property.	Incidental expenses of Quartermaster's Department.	Printing.	Stationery.	Postage.	Subsistence.	Miscellaneous.	Total.
Maine	$100, 712. 36	$3, 264. 64	$48, 600. 99	$4, 190. 93	$159. 56	$5, 574. 87	$4, 464. 67	$3, 182. 79	$11. 24	$2, 629. 89	$172, 791. 94
New Hampshire	35, 633. 00	1, 670. 45	11, 955. 47	1, 349. 70	298. 47	1, 213. 67	1, 657. 93	877. 04		811. 68	55, 467. 41
Vermont	33, 311. 96	1, 004. 99	12, 592. 47	910. 38	310. 79	929. 22	1, 322. 91	1, 478. 08	13. 50	2, 258. 69	54, 132. 99
Massachusetts	139, 013. 90	9, 400. 37	17, 747. 65	1, 411. 99	759. 35	5, 959. 08	4, 214. 93	2, 982. 76		3, 790. 73	185, 280. 76
Rhode Island	24, 604. 59	1, 304. 58	468. 42	649. 84		297. 74	495. 73	107. 76		428. 59	28, 357. 25
Connecticut	43, 486. 98	3, 719. 90	1, 438. 24	1, 309. 17	464. 34	1, 211. 06	2, 196. 67	524. 63	140. 00	1, 295. 03	55, 786. 02
New York	527, 586. 77	34, 983. 24	57, 610. 64	12, 606. 61	5, 555. 26	14, 159. 54	17, 360. 47	14, 400. 03	1, 872. 81	13, 502. 17	699, 637. 54
New Jersey	100, 122. 97	4, 621. 81	4, 507. 27	1, 827. 71	464. 44	1, 216. 10	3, 209. 26	1, 415. 75		3, 084. 61	120, 469. 92
Pennsylvania	449, 507. 13	16, 542. 44	60, 071. 58	7, 539. 15	5, 782. 48	14, 838. 09	13, 541. 78	13, 343. 13	23. 58	22, 546. 86	603, 736. 22
Delaware	25, 172. 95	425. 00	4, 829. 71	1, 640. 04	9. 60	112. 70	433. 90	252. 28		572. 84	33, 449. 02
Maryland	86, 367. 19	4, 722. 00	2, 693. 07	2, 817. 36	353. 30	2, 053. 60	3, 068. 21	1, 497. 17		2, 978. 15	106, 550. 05
Provost-Marshal-General's Bureau	226, 674. 35	8, 251. 00	1, 035. 64	7, 867. 21		3, 299. 19	18, 421. 27	38, 440. 86		10, 630. 89	314, 620. 41
District of Columbia	39, 078. 01	110. 00	62. 60	1, 397. 99	142. 50	1, 039. 08	1, 906. 05	225. 51		1, 782. 93	45, 744. 67
West Virginia	34, 562. 41	901. 96	3, 373. 02	1, 058. 90	224. 40	320. 50	2, 157. 53	1, 110. 44		338. 10	44, 047. 26
Kentucky	169, 265. 35	4, 342. 47	1, 159. 60	2, 024. 83	548. 67	2, 293. 22	3, 569. 84	1, 844. 66		3, 789. 17	188, 837. 81
Missouri	103, 039. 83	2, 799. 53	3, 922. 10	857. 22	363. 34	2, 088. 92	2, 975. 32	1, 069. 51		529. 64	117, 645. 41
Ohio	292, 431. 24	9, 922. 37	41, 982. 04	1, 874. 04	2, 499. 93	6, 655. 75	10, 723. 83	7, 726. 95	39. 79	15, 207. 48	389, 063. 42
Indiana	184, 128. 29	5, 078. 62	15, 682. 25	11, 330. 66	720. 27	3, 054. 26	7, 594. 56	4, 512. 49		4, 668. 53	236, 769. 93
Illinois	279, 155. 39	8, 534. 58	16, 053. 53	5, 191. 63	875. 76	3, 897. 92	9, 504. 17	7, 913. 96	15. 62	5, 457. 12	336, 599. 68
Michigan	119, 670. 41	2, 750. 25	27, 386. 93	958. 42	534. 20	3, 761. 34	2, 689. 96	2, 658. 78	139. 12	3, 423. 32	163, 972. 73
Wisconsin	131, 799. 87	2, 776. 43	34, 350. 46	3, 357. 84	457. 62	5, 747. 85	4, 029. 58	1, 919. 33	23. 69	3, 450. 63	187, 913. 30
Iowa	97, 386. 31	2, 843. 31	20, 333. 23	1, 118. 73	1, 404. 87	1, 241. 74	2, 309. 09	1, 458. 28	36. 72	1, 970. 51	130, 102. 79
Kansas	22, 010. 57	1, 126. 11	500. 71	239. 93	199. 60	238. 30	623. 95	448. 04		381. 45	25, 768. 66
Nebraska Territory	4, 851. 25	210. 00	556. 87	46. 00	147. 55	31. 50	38. 55	82. 02		128. 20	6, 091. 94
Colorado Territory	4, 407. 01	175. 00	428. 43			49. 50	77. 30	76. 65		162. 30	5, 376. 19
Dakota Territory	3, 285. 58	78. 00	43. 30	92. 00		32. 25	62. 71	34. 80		40. 60	3, 669. 24
Minnesota	68, 161. 90	2, 481. 04	25, 167. 00	541. 04	417. 26	2, 385. 61	2, 216. 88	1, 143. 07		3, 679. 61	106, 193. 41
California and Nevada					261. 22	28. 00	40. 50			47, 796. 59	48, 126. 31
Oregon and Washington Territory										33, 233. 09	33, 233. 09
Total	3, 345, 427. 57	134, 040. 09	414, 553. 22	74, 209. 32	22, 954. 78	83, 730. 60	120, 907. 55	110, 726. 77	2, 316. 07	190, 569. 40	4, 499, 435. 37

The expenditures of the Bureau prior to July 1, 1864, cannot conveniently be itemized in accordance with the above form, and are consequently omitted in detail in this table. They amounted in the aggregate to $3, 687, 206. 79
Which being added to the amount expended from July 1, 1864, to December 31, 1865 (as per table), viz 4, 499, 435. 37

Shows a total expenditure from May 1, 1863, to December 31, 1865, of 8, 186, 642. 16

DOCUMENT NO. 10.

Historical report of the disbursements in the Volunteer Recruiting Branch, Provost-Marshal-General's Bureau.

WAR DEPT., PROVOST-MARSHAL-GENERAL'S OFFICE,
Washington, D. C., February 1, 1866.

Bvt. Maj. Gen. JAMES B. FRY,
Provost-Marshal-General:

GENERAL: I have the honor to submit a historical report of the operations of this branch of your Bureau from its organization to January 1, 1866:

ORGANIZATION OF OFFICE.

The first appropriation for collecting, drilling, and organizing volunteers was made by Congress August 5, 1861, the disbursement of which was placed under the control and direction of the Adjutant-General of the Army, but the records do not show that any separate branch was established for the purpose of managing the disbursement of this fund until May, 1862, and the records of the office did not get fairly under way until the middle of June, 1862.

Lieut. Col. W. A. Nichols, assistant adjutant-general, was placed in charge at the opening of the office, and remained so until May 1, 1863—the date upon which the recruitment of the volunteer forces was placed under your control—when he was relieved by Maj. O. D. Greene, assistant adjutant-general.

Major Greene was relieved by me August 26, 1863, since which time I have remained in charge of the office.

RECORDS.

At the opening of the office the record books prescribed by the regulations of the Adjutant-General's Department were established, but as the business of the office increased it became necessary from time to time to introduce other books of record, which will be described in their proper places hereafter, in connection with the subject-matter to which they appertain.

APPROPRIATION FOR COLLECTING, DRILLING, AND ORGANIZING VOLUNTEERS.

The total amount appropriated by Congress for collecting, drilling, and organizing volunteers is as follows:

For fiscal year ended June 30—		
1862		$20,000,000.00
1863		5,000,000.00
1864		10,700,000.00
1865		5,000,000.00
Total amount appropriated		40,700,000.00
Total amount expended to January 1, 1866	$27,427,126.62	
Total amount in hands of disbursing officers January 1, 1866	1,164,188.00	
Total amount drawn from the Treasury January 1, 1866		28,591,314.62
Remaining in the U. S. Treasury January 1, 1866		12,108,685.38
Total amount of expenditure for fiscal year ended September 30—		
1862		$13,779,897.27
1863		7,819,693.40
1864		4,164,741.51
1865		1,422,281.73

General Orders, No. 58, of August 15, 1861, from the Adjutant-General's Office, appoint the officers of the Regular Army on mustering duty throughout the United States disbursing officers of the funds appropriated by Congress for collecting, drilling, and organizing volunteers, and charge them with the payment of all proper claims duly authenticated and certified by the various recruiting volunteer officers. This order also directs disbursements to be made in the manner prescribed for the recruiting service of the Regular Army.

General Orders, No. 70, of September 3, 1861, from the Adjutant-General's Office, announce what this appropriation is intended for, and define and prescribe the accounts and expenses which shall be paid from it.

In accordance with these orders requisitions for funds were made by the officers charged with disbursements, and for the purpose of keeping a correct record of all requisitions drawn upon the Secretary of War from the fund, a book, known as "Register of Requisitions, Volunteer Service," was opened, headed as follows:

No.	Rank.	Names of officers for whom funds are required.	Regiments.	Stations.	Date of requisitions.	Amount.	Remarks.

It was found necessary to open an account with each officer to whose credit funds had been placed. For this purpose a book, known as "Volunteer Disbursing Service, Monthly Statements," was opened, headed as follows:

Date.	Amount on hand last month.	Amount received.	Amount expended and accounted for.	Amount on hand.	Remarks.

EXAMINATION OF CLAIMS PRIOR TO MAY 1, 1863.

Disbursing officers continued until December, 1862, to pay accounts of recruiting officers and others, in accordance with General Orders, No. 70, of 1861; but owing to their inexperience in this line of duty many claims were paid which had been made up and presented by unprincipled parties for the purpose of defrauding the United States. In order to put a stop to this nefarious business, and to protect the Government against such frauds, it was found necessary to issue General Orders, No. 198, of December 3, 1862, from the Adjutant-General's Office. This order prohibited disbursing officers from paying any accounts for expenses incurred in collecting, drilling, and organizing volunteers prior to July 1, 1862, unless such account had been audited and ordered paid by the War Department.

In consequence of this order numerous claims of this class were referred to this office by disbursing officers, which greatly increased the business of the office. Brig. Gen. W. Scott Ketchum was designated by the Secretary of War to audit this class of accounts, under special instructions from him. The manner of procedure in examining them is as follows: When an account is received at this office it is entered in the book of "Letters Received," the amount of the account, the company and regiment for which the expense was incurred, and the nature of the service rendered, or the expense incurred, is stated. The account then passes into the hands of the examining clerk, who gives it a critical and thorough examination, comparing all dates, &c., given therein with the muster-rolls and other records of the Adjutant-General's Office which are likely to throw any light upon the case. When subsistence, lodgings, and transportation of recruits are charged, and the names of the recruits are given, reference is made to the muster-in rolls to see if said recruits have been mustered into the U. S. service, and the dates of enlistment and muster-in are compared with the dates given in the accounts, so that any expense incurred for a recruit prior to enlistment, or subsequent to muster into the U. S. service, may be deducted or disallowed. When the signature of the officer certifying to the account looks suspicious, or forgery is suspected, it is compared with the same officer's signature on any muster-roll or other official paper on file in the Adjutant-General's Office. Where the regulations have not been complied with in every particular, such fact is noted. The result of the examination is briefly stated, and with the account is submitted to General Ketchum for official action. When the account has been acted upon, indorsed by that officer and returned to this office, it is copied in the "Indorsement Book," and when the account is ordered paid it is referred to the proper disbursing officer for payment. Where exceptions are taken to the account it is referred to the disbursing officer nearest the residence of claimant, with instructions to furnish him or his attorney, as the case may be, with a copy of the indorsement of the War Department, in order to give him (claimant) an opportunity to perfect his claim and establish its justness.

Where a claim has been found fraudulent and rejected it is referred to Bvt. Col. L. C. Turner, judge-advocate, U. S. Army, in order that the rejection may be confirmed, or, in case there be good grounds for prosecuting the parties presenting the same, under the act of Congress approved March 2, 1863, to prevent and punish frauds upon the Government of the United States, that proceedings may be instituted against them by the U. S. attorney for that district. Should the claim be returned to this office by Colonel Turner as rightly rejected, it is filed and not reconsidered or returned to claimant without special instructions from the Secretary of War.

All claims for expenses incurred in connection with the recruiting service prior to May 1, 1863, are audited by General Ketchum.

DRAFT ACCOUNTS, 1862.

The Secretary of War having ordered that certain expenses incurred in enrolling and drafting 300,000 militia for nine months' service, under the order of the President of the United States of August 4, 1862, be paid from this appropriation, all accounts for expenses incurred under this call are examined in this office, under the regulations of the Army and General Orders, No. 99, of August 9; No. 121, of August 29, and No. 201, of December 8, 1862, from the Adjutant-General's Office, and submitted to the War Department. When acted upon and returned they are disposed of in the same manner as accounts of recruiting officers, heretofore described.

Separate books were opened to keep the record of this class of accounts, but they were found impracticable, unnecessary, and they were abandoned. The book of "Letters Received," "Indorsement Book," and "Letter Book" give a full history of such accounts.

The number of claims of recruiting officers and others for expenses incurred in recruiting volunteers prior to May 1, 1863, examined in this office and acted upon by the War Department, to January 1, 1866, is 4,402. Of this number 745 were rejected and referred to Bvt. Col. L. C. Turner, judge-advocate, U. S. Army.

The draft accounts of the following States have also been examined in this office: Maine, New Hampshire, Vermont, Massachusetts, New York, New Jersey, Pennsylvania, Maryland, Delaware, Indiana, Illinois, Wisconsin, Minnesota, Michigan, Iowa.

These accounts were forwarded by the Governors of the respective States to the Adjutant-General of the Army, in compliance with General Orders, No. 201, of December 8, 1862, from the Adjutant-General's Office. In order to give some idea of the amount of labor expended on them, it may be well to state that some of them consisted of over 6,000 vouchers, and that each voucher received a separate examination.

EXAMINATION OF CLAIMS SUBSEQUENT TO MAY 1, 1863.

The recruitment of the volunteer forces of the United States having been placed under your control May 1, 1863, all claims of recruiting officers and others for expenses incurred in recruiting subsequent to that date are examined and acted upon in this office.

The examination of these claims is conducted in the same manner and under the same general rules and regulations as those for expenses incurred prior to May 1, 1863, to November 13, 1863, when the regulations were somewhat modified by General Orders, No. 366, of November 13, 1863, from the Adjutant-General's Office, and subsequently by General Orders, No. 131, of March 31, 1864, from the same office, which last order rescinded General Orders, No. 75, of 1862. The number of claims of recruiting officers and others for expenses incurred in connection with the recruiting service subsequent to May 1, 1863, examined and acted upon in this office to January 1, 1866, is 4,603; of this number 674 have been rejected or disallowed.

Large numbers of claims for expenses incurred, both prior and subsequent to May 1, 1863, still continue to be presented.

PREMIUMS.

General Orders, No. 74, of July 7, 1862, from the Adjutant-General's Office, authorized the following premiums to be paid from the fund for collecting, drilling, and organizing volunteers, viz: For volunteer recruits for old regiments, $3; for new regiments, $2; to be paid either to the person bringing the recruit or to the recruit in person, in case he presents himself, as soon as the recruit had been inspected by the surgeon and mustered in.

The payment of a premium of $4 to recruits for old regiments was authorized by letter from the Adjutant-General's Office July 26, 1862, for the purpose of rapidly filling up old volunteer regiments.

These premiums were, as a general rule, paid by the disbursing officers; but when not paid by them General Orders, No. 90, of April 7, 1863, direct that the premium shall be entered on the muster-in roll, and so continued upon every subsequent muster and pay roll until the soldier is paid by a paymaster.

Premiums continued to be paid in accordance with the foregoing orders and instructions until June 4, 1863, when General Orders, No. 163, of that date, from the Adjutant-General's Office were issued, which limited the premium to volunteer recruits to $2. In accordance with the last-mentioned order this premium was paid until January 11, 1864, when General Orders, No. 16, were issued, annulling all orders previously issued authorizing the payment of this premium.

This order, however, was not intended to apply to colored recruits, and a premium of $2 was continued to be paid to them until July 19, 1864, when Circular No. 27 from this office was issued prohibiting the payment of all premiums for the presentation of recruits.

Circular of October 24, 1863, from this office, authorized the payment of premiums for the presentation of accepted recruits from draft and substitute fund, as follows:

For the presentation of an accepted "veteran" recruit, $25; for the presentation of an accepted recruit, not "veteran," $15.

These premiums were paid in accordance with the above-mentioned circular until March 1, 1864, when they were reduced as follows: (See telegram of February 29, 1864, from this office.)

For the presentation of an accepted "veteran" recruit, $15; for the presentation of an accepted recruit, not "veteran," $10.

These premiums were paid until July 19, 1864, the date of Circular No. 27, of that year, from this office, which prohibited the payment of all premiums.

DISBURSEMENTS FROM APPROPRIATION FOR COLLECTING, DRILLING, AND ORGANIZING VOLUNTEERS.

Under the act of Congress approved January 31, 1823, disbursing officers were required to render their accounts quarter-yearly to the proper accounting officers of the Treasury, and in compliance with this act accounts were so rendered until the passage of the act of Congress approved July 17, 1862, which required disbursing officers to render their accounts monthly to the proper accounting officers of the Treasury.

As the officers disbursing this fund were acting under the direct instructions of this office so far as related to the disbursement of this fund, it was considered expedient as well as necessary that their accounts should first receive an administrative examination in this office before action was taken on them in the office of the Second Auditor, and for this purpose they are sent to this office as soon as received at the Treasury.

EXAMINATION OF DISBURSING OFFICERS' ACCOUNTS.

The mode adopted for the examination of disbursing officers' accounts under the appropriation for collecting, drilling, and organizing volunteers is as follows:

As soon as the account is received at this office it is entered in a book kept for that purpose and headed as follows:

Names of disbursing officers.	Rank.	Regiment.	When received and acknowledged.	Month or quarter.

The account is then placed on file until its proper turn for examination shall have arrived, when it is delivered to the examining clerk. Each voucher is then carefully examined under the orders and regulations in force at the time the expenditure was made; and where any expenditure was made not in accordance with regulations, such fact is noted and placed upon the list of exceptions taken to the account.

In order to ascertain the precise amount paid out on account of the different items chargeable to this fund, an analysis of each account is made by the examining clerk. In order to keep a correct record of this, and also to show exactly how each officer's account stands for each month, a book, known as "Volunteer Service Expenditure," is kept, headed as follows:*

So that a correct record might be kept of each account, from the time it is received at this office until it is sent to the Second Auditor, it was found necessary to open a book known as "Record of Accounts of Disbursing Officers, Volunteer Service," headed as follows:*

The property return of each disbursing officer, accounting for all property received and expended during the month, is also examined at the same time and then filed with the account.

When the exceptions taken to the account are completed and copied into the Exception Book, they are filed with the account, officially acknowledged, and the account is then referred to the Second Auditor of the Treasury for final settlement.

A copy of the exceptions taken is also sent to the disbursing officer, and in case he makes explanations to the exceptions, they are forwarded to the Second Auditor of the Treasury.

The number of monthly and quarterly accounts received at this office pertaining to this appropriation to January 1, 1866, is		2,535
Number examined to May 1, 1863	144	
Number examined from May 1, 1863, to January 1, 1866	1,801	
Total number examined and sent to Treasury to January 1, 1866		1,945
Total number remaining in office January 1, 1866		590

APPROPRIATION FOR PAY OF BOUNTY.

The total amount appropriated by Congress for the pay of advance bounty to volunteers since the commencement of the war is as follows:

Fiscal year ending June 30, 1863	$7,500,000.00
Fiscal year ending June 30, 1864	5,000,000.00
Amount appropriated December 23, 1863, to supply deficiencies in previous appropriations	20,000,000.00
Fiscal year ending June 30, 1865	5,000,000.00
Total amount appropriated	37,500,000.00
Balance remaining in Treasury January 1, 1866	11,296,018.82
Total amount expended	26,203,981.18

All funds belonging to this appropriation in the hands of disbursing officers July 1, 1865, when the payment of bounties ceased, were promptly covered into the U. S. Treasury, as directed by you.

In order to keep a correct record of all requisitions drawn upon the Secretary of War from this appropriation a book, known as "Register of Requisitions for Bounties," was opened, headed as follows:*

It was also found necessary to open an account with each officer

*Forms omitted.

disbursing this fund, and for that purpose a book was opened, known as "Monthly Statement—Pay of Bounty to Regulars and Volunteers on Enlistment," headed as follows:*

The act of Congress approved June 21, 1862, promulgated in General Orders, No. 74, of July 7, 1862, from the Adjutant-General's Office, authorized the payment of $25 of the $100 bounty authorized by act of July 22, 1861, to volunteer recruits on enlistment and muster in.

This advance bounty was paid by the disbursing officer as soon as the recruit, if for an old regiment, was inspected and mustered into the U. S. service; and if for a new regiment, as soon as the company to which he belonged was organized and mustered in.

When this advance bounty was not paid at the time the recruit was mustered in it was entered on the muster-in roll and so continued upon every subsequent muster and pay roll until the soldier was paid by a paymaster, as provided by General Orders, No. 90, of April 7, 1863, from the Adjutant-General's Office.

All volunteers who enlisted under the call of the President of July 18, 1864, were entitled to bounty as follows, under the act of July 4, 1864:

Recruits enlisting for one year	$100.00
Recruits enlisting for two years	200.00
Recruits enlisting for three years	300.00

The first installment of this bounty was paid by disbursing officers to recruits on muster in as follows:

To recruits enlisting for one year	$33.33
To recruits enlisting for two years	66.66
To recruits enlisting for three years	100.00

This advance bounty was paid in the same manner and under the same regulations as the $25 advance bounty previously discussed.

DISBURSING OFFICERS' ACCOUNTS UNDER APPROPRIATION FOR PAY OF BOUNTY.

These accounts, like those under appropriation for collecting, drilling, and organizing volunteers, are sent to this office for administrative examination as soon as received at the office of the Second Auditor. They are taken up in their regular turn, examined under the orders and regulations in force at the time the expenditures were made, and disposed of in the same manner as accounts under appropriation for collecting, drilling, and organizing volunteers.

For the purpose of keeping a correct record of the analyses of disbursing officers' accounts under the appropriation for pay of bounty, a book, known as "Volunteer Service Expenditures," is kept, headed as follows:*

Another book is kept for the purpose of keeping a correct record of these accounts from the time they are received at this office until they are sent to the Treasury, known as "Record Book of Accounts of Disbursing Officers, Volunteer Service," and headed as follows:*

The number of monthly and quarterly accounts of disbursing officers pertaining to the appropriation for pay of bounty received at this office to January 1, 1866		1,875
Number examined to May 1, 1863	5	
Number examined between May 1, 1863, and January 1, 1866	1,411	
Total number examined and sent to Treasury to January 1, 1866		1,416
Remaining in office		459

* Forms omitted.

DRAFT AND SUBSTITUTE FUND.

Statement of the condition of the draft and substitute fund December 31, 1865.

Amount drawn from the Treasury in favor of mustering and disbursing officers		$14,424,345.00
Amount disbursed to December 31, 1865	$10,042,304.48	
Amount transferred to officers not accounting to this office	4,269,435.00	
Amount unaccounted for by disbursing officers *a*	35,929.00	
Amount covered into the U. S. Treasury by disbursing officers	73,323.00	
Amount in hands of mustering and disbursing officers December 31, 1865	3,353.52	
		14,424,345.00

DISBURSEMENTS FROM DRAFT AND SUBSTITUTE FUND.

Bounties paid from this fund.—Circular of November 4, 1863, from this office, directs the payment of $35, a part of the $60 advance bounty authorized by General Orders, No. 324, of September 28, 1863, from the Adjutant-General's Office, and circular of October 24, 1863, from this office, from this fund. Letters from the War Department, dated November 29, 1863, to Maj. Gen. B. F. Butler, and of December 22, 1863, to Maj. Gen. Q. A. Gillmore, authorized the payment of a bounty not to exceed $10 per man for colored recruits. This bounty was also paid from this fund.

General Orders, No. 287, of November 28, 1864, from the Adjutant-General's Office, authorized the payment of a special bounty of $300 to men enlisting in the First Army Corps (General Hancock's), and direct that said bounty shall be paid from this fund.

Premiums paid from draft and substitute fund.—Circular of October 24, 1863, from this office, authorized the payment of premiums for the presentation of accepted recruits from this fund, as follows:

For the presentation of an accepted "veteran" recruit	$25
For the presentation of an accepted recruit not "veteran"	15

These premiums were paid in accordance with the above-mentioned circular until March 1, 1864, when they were reduced as follows: (See telegram of February 29, 1864, from this office.)

For the presentation of an accepted "veteran" recruit	$15
For the presentation of an accepted recruit not "veteran"	10

These premiums were paid until July 19, 1864, the date of Circular No. 27, of that year, from this office, which prohibited the payment of all premiums.

That a correct record might be kept of all moneys of this fund placed in the hands of disbursing officers, a book was opened for that purpose, headed as follows:*

DISBURSING OFFICERS' ACCOUNTS UNDER DRAFT AND SUBSTITUTE FUND.

Accounts of disbursing officers under this fund are received, examined under the orders and regulations governing them at the time the expenditures were made, and disposed of in the same manner

a One of these officers has been dismissed the service, another is deceased, and the accounts of the third are now undergoing investigation.

* Form omitted.

as disbursing officers' accounts under appropriations for "collecting, drilling, and organizing volunteers," and "pay of bounty."

The number of disbursing officers' monthly accounts, appertaining to this fund, received at this office to January 1, 1866, is	830
Number examined and sent to Treasury to January 1, 1866	539
Remaining in office	291

CLERKS AND EMPLOYÉS OF DISBURSING OFFICERS.

The selection of clerks and other employés necessary to the transaction of public business in the offices of mustering and disbursing officers has been left entirely to the discretion of such officers, but the number and the salary have in all cases been fixed by this office.

As a general rule, the payment of a greater salary than $100 per month to clerks has not been authorized, and where this has been exceeded it was only to chief clerks.

The greatest number of officers on mustering and disbursing duty at any time was 195, and the number on that duty February 1, 1866, was 40.

BOUNTIES PAID BY THE UNITED STATES DURING THE WAR.

The act of Congress approved July 22, 1861, authorized the payment of $100 bounty to volunteers. This was the only bounty paid by the United States to June 25, 1863, the date of General Orders, No. 191, from the Adjutant-General's Office, which authorized the payment of a bounty of $400 to all veterans re-enlisting for three years or the war, to be paid by installments as directed in said order.

This bounty ($400) continued to be paid to all veterans re-enlisting, in accordance with General Orders, No. 191, of June 25, No. 305, of September 11, and No. 324, of September 28, 1863, until April 1, 1864.

Circular letter of October 24, 1863, from this office, authorized the payment of a bounty of $300 to new recruits enlisting in old organizations, to be paid by installments as directed in said circular. This bounty was paid in accordance with the conditions of the above-mentioned circular until April 1, 1864.

An order from the Adjutant-General's Office, dated December 24, 1863, authorized the payment of the $300 bounty to new recruits enlisting in any three-years' organization in service or in process of formation. This bounty continued to be paid in accordance with this order until April 1, 1864.

The only bounty paid by the United States between March 31, 1864, and July 19, 1864, was the $100 authorized by the act of July 22, 1861.

Circular No. 27, of July 19, 1864, from this office, authorized the payment of bounties as follows, in accordance with the act approved July 4, 1864:

To recruits enlisting for one year	$100
To recruits enlisting for two years	200
To recruits enlisting for three years	300

A special bounty of $300 was paid from the draft and substitute fund to men enlisting in the First Army Corps, in addition to the bounty authorized by Circular No. 27, of July 19, 1864, from this office, in accordance with General Orders, No. 287, of November 28, 1864, from the Adjutant-General's Office.

With this exception, the bounty authorized by Circular No. 27, of July 19, 1864, from this office, was the only bounty paid by the United

States from the date of said circular to the end of the war. Drafted men and substitutes for drafted men were paid the $100 bounty until the passage of the act of Congress approved July 4, 1864, when it was decided that all authority for the payment of bounty to drafted men and substitutes had been rescinded by that act.

Letters from the War Department, dated November 29, 1863, to Maj. Gen. B. F. Butler, and of December 22, 1863, to Maj. Gen. Q. A. Gillmore, authorized the payment of a bounty not to exceed $10 per man for colored recruits. This bounty was also paid from this fund.

General Orders, No. 115, of June 15, 1865, from the Adjutant-General's Office, fixed July 1, 1865, as the date upon which the United States should cease to pay bounty to recruits for the military service.

Tabular statement showing the bounties paid by the United States during the war.

By what authority paid.	To whom paid.	Between what dates paid.	Amount.
Act of July 22, 1861	All volunteers	From commencement of war to July 18, 1864.	$100
General Orders 191, of June 25, 1863, Adjutant-General's Office.	Veterans	From June 25, 1863, to April 1, 1864.	*a* 400
Circular, October 24, 1863, Provost-Marshal-General's Office.	New recruits enlisting in old organizations.	From October 24, 1863, to April 1, 1864.	300
Telegram, December 24, 1863, from Adjutant-General's Office.	New recruits enlisting in any three-years' organization authorized by the War Department.	From December 24, 1863, to April 1, 1864.	300
Act approved July 4, 1864, and Circular No. 27, of 1864, from Provost-Marshal-General's Office.	Volunteers enlisting for one year.	From July 19, 1864, to July 1, 1865.	100
	Volunteers enlisting for two years.	do	200
	Volunteers enlisting for three years.	do	300
General Orders 287, Adjutant-General's Office, November 28, 1864.	Men enlisting in First Army Corps.	From November 28, 1864, to July 1, 1865.	*b* 300
Letters of War Department, November 29, 1863, and December 22, 1863, to Generals Butler and Gillmore.	Colored recruits		10

a Veteran *b* Special.

SECOND AUDITOR'S AND PAYMASTER-GENERAL'S CASES.

Numerous letters of inquiry as to the payment of advance bounty to certain soldiers are sent to this office by the Second Auditor of the Treasury and the Paymaster-General of the Army.

Each inquiry is examined and reported upon separately and consumes much time and labor.

These reports are based upon information obtained from the muster-in rolls on file in the Adjutant-General's Office, and from the bounty accounts of mustering and disbursing officers on file in this office. In many cases all the rolls of a regiment have to be examined to find the name of the man about whom inquiry is made; and where there was more than one officer disbursing in the State at the time the man was mustered in, each one of these officer's bounty accounts has to be examined to ascertain whether the man was paid or not.

To give some idea of the amount of labor expended on these reports I will state that the number reported on and returned to the Second Auditor and Paymaster-General from January, 1864, to January 1, 1866, is 6,268. These inquiries are increasing daily in number.

CONTRACTS.

For the purpose of keeping a record of all contracts approved for subsisting and lodging recruits, rent of recruiting offices, &c., a book known as "Contracts, Collecting, Drilling, and Organizing Volunteers," was opened, headed as follows:*

The number of contracts approved in this office to January 1, 1866, is 1,241, as follows:

Number approved to May 1, 1863	43
Number approved between May 1, 1863, and January 1, 1866	1,198
Total number approved	1,241

One copy of each contract is filed in this office, and another copy is sent to the Second Comptroller of the Treasury.

REPORTS.

The reports required from mustering and disbursing officers are as follows:

First. Weekly report of all public funds on hand pertaining to the appropriations for collecting, drilling, and organizing volunteers, pay of bounty, and draft and substitute fund; for the purpose of condensing and keeping a record of these reports, a book, known as "Book of Weekly Reports," is kept, headed as follows:*

Second. A monthly report of "persons and articles hired and employed." This report gives the name of each employé, the salary paid, the date and source of the approval. It also gives a list of all articles hired, with the rate of hire, and the source and authority for hiring. These reports are filed in the office.

CLERKS AND EMPLOYÉS.

Continual changes have taken place in the clerical force of this office from its organization to the present time. Only six clerks were employed in the beginning, but as the business of the office increased the force was increased, and on the 1st of May, 1863, there were eighteen clerks employed. The greatest number employed at any time was forty-five, and the number borne on the register of the office at the present time is twenty-three; two of these are not on duty in this office—one being in the bureau of rebel archives, and one in General Ketchum's office.

Until very lately the majority of the clerks employed in this office were enlisted men detailed from the general service and Veteran Reserve Corps.

The clerks now employed in this office are classified as follows:

One of class four, $1,800 per annum; one of class three, $1,600 per annum; one of class two, $1,400 per annum; seventeen of class one, $1,200 per annum; one enlisted man, sergeant, general service; two enlisted men, privates, Veteran Reserve Corps. The other employés now engaged in this office are: One messenger, private, general service; one janitor, $60 per month; one fireman and laborer, $50 per month.

To give an idea of the amount of labor performed by the clerical force of this office from its opening to the 1st of January, 1866, the following figures are submitted:

* Form omitted.

Total number of monthly and quarterly accounts examined to May 1, 1863	149
Total number of monthly and quarterly accounts examined from May 1, 1863, to January 1, 1866	3,751
	3,900
Total number of claims of recruiting officers and others connected with the recruiting service examined to May 1, 1863	651
Total number of claims of recruiting officers, &c., examined from May 1, 1863, to January 1, 1866	8,354
	9,005
Total number of Second Auditor's and Paymaster-General's cases	6,268
Total number of contracts approved prior to May 1, 1863	43
Total number of contracts approved from May 1, 1863, to January 1, 1866	1,198
	1,241
Total number of letters sent prior to May 1, 1863	3,213
Total number of letters sent from May 1, 1863, to January 1, 1866	7,025
	10,238
Total number of letters received prior to May 1, 1863	4,416
Total number of letters received from May 1, 1863, to January 1, 1866	18,553
	22,969
Total number of indorsements prior to May 1, 1863	1,932
Total number of indorsements from May 1, 1863, to January 1, 1866	18,749
	20,681
Total number of telegrams received to May 1, 1863	111
Total number of telegrams received from May 1, 1863, to January 1, 1866	354
	465
Total number of telegrams sent to May 1, 1863	140
Total number of telegrams sent from May 1, 1863, to January 1, 1866	470
	610

GENERAL REMARKS.

In the early part of the war the recruitment of volunteers was almost entirely under the control of the Governors of States, and so continued until this branch of the service was placed under your control, when superintendents of volunteer recruiting service were appointed for each State. The great disadvantage to the Government, and the unnecessary expenses incurred in the recruitment of volunteers, under the system then in force, became every day more and more obvious, and steps were at once taken to correct this evil and place the whole matter under the exclusive control of the officers of the General Government.

With this view the recruitment of volunteers for old organizations was first placed under the control of the superintendents of volunteer recruiting service in each State, and in the latter part of March, 1864, the recruitment of all volunteers, both for new and old organizations, was placed under their charge. The advantages arising from this change can be seen upon an examination of the records of this office.

Under the new system all recruiting officers were required to report to the superintendent of volunteer recruiting service, to be by him assigned to duty; they were not allowed to incur any expense without his authority, and no accounts were to be paid unless approved by him. The necessity for recruiting officers to pay for expenses incurred by them in the subsisting, lodging, and transportation of recruits was entirely obviated, and had they all followed the regulations governing the recruiting service and the special instructions given them there would have been no claims for reimbursements since March, 1864.

While the recruitment of volunteers was under the control of the State authorities it was exceedingly easy for dishonest parties to make out and present fraudulent claims, and it is believed that many accounts of this kind were paid by disbursing officers. This became so apparent that General Orders, No. 198, of December 3, 1862, were issued, prohibiting disbursiug officers from paying any accounts for recruiting expenses incurred prior to July 1, 1862, until they had been audited and ordered to be paid by the War Department.

Under the present system but few, if any, fraudulent claims have been paid.

The total amount expended from the fund for collecting, drilling, and organizing volunteers, for the recruitment of volunteers from August 5, 1861—the date of first appropriation—to April 30, 1863, was *a*	$16,512,699.67
Amount expended by the several States in raising volunteers in 1861 and 1862 and for which claims for reimbursement have been presented to the Third Auditor	29,631,185.99
Total amount expended for the raising of volunteers from the commencement of the war to April 30, 1863	46,143,885.66
Total number of men put into the service during the same time	1,356,593
Average cost per man	$34.01
The total amount expended from the fund for collecting, drilling, and organizing volunteers for the recruitment of volunteers from May 1, 1863, to January 1, 1866, was	6,905,192.24
Amount expended in recruitment of volunteers and enrollment and draft from draft and substitute fund from June 1, 1863, to January 1, 1866, was	4,122,522.97
Total amount expended in the recruitment of volunteers and enrollment and draft from May 1, 1863, to January 1, 1866	11,027,715.21
Total number of men put into service by draft and volunteering during the same time	1,120,621
Average cost per man	$9.84

In arriving at the foregoing statement no consideration has been taken of the amount paid by disbursing officers since May 1, 1863, for recruiting expenses incurred prior to that date, as it is believed that that amount is certainly as great, most probably greater, than the amount now due for recruiting expenses incurred since May 1, 1863, but not yet paid.

It will be seen by this statement that, although the premium on gold and cost of subsistence, lodgings, rent of offices, stationery, &c., was much higher in 1864–'65 than in 1861–'62, yet the expense of putting each man into the service was nearly four times greater during the first two years of the war than it was during the last two years.

I have the honor to be, general, very respectfully, your obedient servant,

CHAUNCEY McKEEVER,
Brevet Brigadier-General and Assistant Adjutant-General.

---

a The actual amount expended during this time was $20,512,699.67, but of this amount $4,000,000 was used for paying bounties by order of the Secretary of War.

DOCUMENT No. 11.

Historical report of the operations of the Office of Acting Assistant-Provost-Marshal-General, Illinois.

OFFICE ACTG. ASST. PROV. MAR. GEN., ILLINOIS,
Springfield, August 9, 1865.

Brig. Gen. JAMES B. FRY,
Provost-Marshal-General, Washington, D. C.:

GENERAL: In compliance with the request contained in your communication of April 27, 1865, I have the honor to submit the following historical report of the operations of this office since it commenced business, with such remarks and suggestions as my experience and observation may seem to warrant.

Your letter directing me to require similar historical reports from the several district provost-marshals in my jurisdiction was received May 5, 1865, and the necessary instructions were immediately issued. My own report has been delayed partly on account of the tardy return of the district reports, the reception of which was necessary to the completeness of my own. The last remaining district reports (Fifth and Tenth Districts) are only just received. The delay has been further caused by the necessity of temporarily transferring a portion of the clerical force of this department to that of the chief mustering and disbursing office, in order to meet the great pressure caused by the return of large numbers of detachments and regiments to Camp Butler for payment and final discharge, and also by the onerous duties connected with the muster out, &c., of batteries of artillery sent to the State for that purpose, men discharged from hospitals, paroled prisoners, &c. This demand upon my clerical force still continues, and is not likely to be diminished for some weeks to come.

It will be my aim to conform this report as closely as possible to the objects specified in your letter requiring it, and to keep steadily in view the great object of the Government in calling for these final statements, namely, that it may hereafter have the full benefit of the experience of your Bureau during the war.

Accordingly, I shall not dwell upon points of minor or casual interest, but endeavor to explain fully the organization and practical workings of the different business departments of these headquarters, giving special prominence to such features as are more difficult and intricate in their nature, a knowledge of which would be of particular value should operations ever be resumed.

In order that the body of the report may proceed continuously to the close, all tabular statements, consecutively arranged and numbered, will be found in the form of an appendix, to which reference will be made as occasion requires.

OFFICE ROOMS.

In obedience to orders, I took post in this city as acting assistant provost-marshal-general for the State of Illinois and established my office April 27, 1863. As you are aware, the field was to me wholly new and untried, and I was obliged to feel my way along as circumstances required, perfecting myself in the requirements of my new position as rapidly as possible, and adapting means to ends with such skill and judgment as I could command.

The Bureau of the Provost-Marshal-General had just been established, and its practical operation, as well as its adaptation to meet the great national exigency which called it into being, had yet to be tested. The gigantic proportions which the war had assumed, the recent reverses to the Federal arms, and the enormous expansion of the military policy of the Government, together with the hitherto untried expedient of raising men by conscription, had, at the time I assumed the duties of my office here, conspired to create a state of feverish excitement and apprehension in the public mind, all of which added to the embarrassments already referred to.

Two small rooms, not very accessible or commodious, sufficed for a few months for the comparatively limited requirements of the office; but by the close of the summer of 1863 the rapidly expanding business of the position made it necessary to secure larger quarters, and I accordingly rented a small frame building, consisting of four rooms with ample grounds attached, and much more eligibly situated than the place at first occupied. I had scarcely become established in my new quarters when the inauguration of the vigorous system of recruiting adopted in September, 1863, of which I was made superintendent for Illinois, required a still further increase of office accommodations, which was for the time being supplied by an additional building containing seven rooms, conveniently situated immediately opposite the one just referred to. These two buildings answered the purpose until the spring of 1864, when the continued and rapid increase of the business of the office demanded a still further enlargement of office facilities, and resulted in the transfer of my headquarters to the building which I now occupy, being a large brick structure containing fifteen rooms, with ample grounds, and most eligibly and pleasantly situated. While referring to this subject I would add that my experience in the use of office rooms and facilities, through all the gradations from the poorest up to the best, is decidedly in favor of the last, even on the score of economy to the Government, the increased amount and improved quality of the work that can be done in an office possessing all necessary conveniences more than counterbalancing the additional expense.

CLERKS.

For about a month after opening the office I managed to transact the business with the assistance of but one clerk, and during the next three months I had but two; after which, the great expansion of the work of the office already referred to required a corresponding increase in my clerical force. The largest number of clerks on duty at any one time in my office, as acting assistant provost-marshal-general of Illinois, was ten. For a full tabular view of the several clerks on duty in this department, with the dates of their several contracts, dates of approval, and discharge or resignation, rates of compensation, and the duties to which each was assigned, see Schedule No. 1, in the Appendix to this report.

The Provost-Marshal-General is aware of how much depends upon the ability and fidelity of the necessary clerical force in the effective conduct of any business, but especially in the discharge of duties requiring such promptitude and accuracy as those connected with the subordinate departments of his Bureau. In this respect I cannot but consider myself as having been peculiarly fortunate, and refer with especial pleasure to the devotion and faithfulness, and to the spirit of cheerful and hearty co-operation, which have always characterized the clerks in my employ. They have never hesitated to work beyond hours, and without regard to hours, including nights and even Sundays, whenever requested to do so by me, and oftentimes without my solicitation, when the known exigencies of their several departments of the public business seemed to them to require it; while their capabilities and adaptation to the duties of their several desks have been such as to leave me nothing to desire.

OFFICERS.

From the opening of my office till June 4, 1863, I was without the assistance of any commissioned officer. June 4, 1863, First Lieut. James W. Davidson, Forty-ninth Ohio Volunteer Infantry, under Special Orders, No. 221, Adjutant-General's Office, dated May 18, 1863, reported to me for duty, and remained till August 8, 1863, when he was relieved. This officer proved capable and efficient, and rendered valuable service, especially in connection with the Veteran Reserve Corps, then known as the Invalid Corps. Other officers were assigned to me from time to time as the demands of the service required. The whole number of officers reporting to me for duty in this department from the organization of the office to the present time is sixteen, varying in rank from major to second lieutenant. For list of these officers, including name and rank, arm and regiment, date of reporting, authority, date of relief, and the particular duties which each had in charge, see Schedule No. 2, Appendix.

While I am permitted to say of these officers, in general terms, that they have acquitted themselves well, it is proper to refer with especial commendation to Maj. Addison S. Norton, additional aide-de-camp; Capt. John A. Haddock, Twelfth Regiment Veteran Reserve Corps; First Lieut. James W. Davidson, Forty-ninth Ohio Infantry; First Lieut. Charles E. Hay, Third U. S. Cavalry; First Lieut. John F. Cleghorn, Twenth-second Regiment Veteran Reserve Corps; First Lieut. B. F. Hawkes, Seventeenth Regiment Veteran Reserve Corps; First Lieut. and Bvt. Maj. Harry C. Egbert, Twelfth U. S. Infantry, and Second Lieut. Simeon G. Butts, Twelfth Regiment Veteran Reserve Corps, to whose ability and steady faithfulness I am much indebted for the successful management of the respective branches of business to which they were severally assigned, as well as for their valuable aid in the prosecution of the general business of the office.

BUSINESS DEPARTMENTS.

As soon as the nature and scope of my duties were sufficiently developed to admit of it I commenced to systematize and classify the several branches of the public business connected with the office. The subdivision was at first necessarily but partial, and the boundaries of each department not very clearly defined or strictly adhered to. But as the work progressed, and the assistance of a corps of trained clerks rendered it practicable, the work of classification was gradually perfected. The smoothness, promptitude, and efficiency of the operations of the office have been commensurate with the completeness of the divisions of labor and the distinctness of the lines of demarcation defining them. It is believed that the different departments and desks among which the work was finally distributed, and which have been in operation since the removal of the office to the present building, are as complete and as well adapted to the prompt and thorough transaction of the public business as the nature of the case and the clerical force and number of officers at my disposal will admit. The present arrangement is as follows:

1. General and miscellaneous business.
2. Accounts.
3. Deserters.
4. Enrollment quotas and credits.
5. Returns and reports.
6. Veteran Reserve Corps.
7. Medical branch.

A brief account of the mode of conducting each of these departments, and of the character and extent of the business committed to each, is hereto subjoined:

1. *General and miscellaneous business.*—At the opening of the office this department was the only one, and, of course, comprehended all the business. As the work became systematized, and separate departments were organized, the general or unclassified business of the office naturally fell to this branch. Its relation to the whole work was of a very intimate and important character, and the duties devolving on the chief clerk in charge of it were onerous and responsible, requiring much discrimination and good judgment. In the distribution of the mail matter received at the office, all such miscellaneous correspondence and documents as did not properly fall within the province of any other desk was sent, by the officer in charge of mails received, to the chief clerk of the general department, and by him examined and disposed of as each case required. Such papers as demanded my personal attention were placed by themselves and sent to my room, others to the co-ordinate clerks of the department, with the necessary memorandum indicating the tenor of the replies to be made, or other proper disposition thereof, while such as seemed to require a more careful investigation and guarded answer received the attention of the chief clerk himself. Most of the general correspondence with the office of the Provost-Marshal-General, special reports, &c., were also in charge of that clerk, who was expected to keep himself familiar with the general progress of the business of this branch of the office in all its relations, and to be prepared to furnish such information and data as I might from time to time require, and to refer promptly to any letters or other records of the office that I might wish to consult.

A reference to the amount of labor performed in this department may not be out of place. In the month of July, 1864, there were sent from this desk 710 letters and 215 indorsements, amounting to 925 documents, or an average of over 34 for each working day. The number of papers received was about the same, making an aggregate of over 1,800 communications and other papers, or nearly 70 for each working day, which were canvassed and properly disposed of at this desk alone. The record of business at this desk for the month of January, 1865, which may be taken as about an average month in the amount of labor required, shows that 308 letters were received, and 228 letters and 443 indorsements were sent from this department, the indorsements covering 266 pages, medium, making a total of 671 communications acted on in that month, or about 25 per day. If to the above estimate 14 circulars are added, of which an average of 14 copies each were made, it gives an aggregate of 867, or more than 32 per day for the working days in that month.

The aggregate number of letters sent from this desk in 1864 was 5,520, and of indorsements sent in the same period 1,510, making a total of 7,030. The number of letters received at this desk in 1864 was 7,154, making a grand total of 14,184 communications and papers which passed under notice and received proper attention in this branch alone during that year. This estimate does not include a vast number of mere letters of transmittal, which, while they required but little thought, necessarily consumed, in the aggregate, much time. The letters sent required no less than 460 quires of letter paper.

The foregoing statements are not made because of any intrinsic importance which they are supposed to possess, but to convey some idea of the magnitude of the work required to be done, and to indicate the necessity which has constrained me from time to time to ask your approval of my employment of additional clerks.

The chief clerk of this branch was also charged with the preparation of such general circulars to the district provost-marshals in my jurisdiction as were required to carry out the orders of the Provost-Marshal-General, or to meet the various circumstances arising in the progress of the work in this State. These circulars were numbered consecutively for each year, for convenience of reference. A copy was made for each provost-marshal, and a manuscript copy retained for file, in addition to the copy taken in the impression book, making at least fourteen manuscript copies of each circular, the average length of each of which has not been less than three letter pages. The number of these circulars for the year 1863 was 81; for 1864, 265; for 1865, to the present time, 80; making a total of 426 different circulars, containing 1,278 pages, or 17,892 pages for the fourteen copies which were made of each circular. This total should, in fact, be largly increased to include the additional copies which were often made for other parties, such as mustering and disbursing officers, recruiting officers, &c.; and the whole should be considered in connection with my previous statement of the amount of labor necessarily performed in this branch.

It has been my aim not only to convey your instructions, when received, to my subordinates through the medium of the general circulars above described, but also to anticipate, as far as possible, through the same medium, such exigencies or difficulties as could plainly be foreseen; thereby preventing misunderstandings at district headquarters, avoiding the necessity of correspondence on their part, and preparing them to meet each emergency as it arose. I cannot too highly commend the practical utility of such a system of circular instructions.

As already intimated in speaking of the business which fell within the province of this department, many of the questions to be decided were not only entirely new to myself, but some of them were of so difficult and intricate a character as to require great care and laborious examination before any action could be safely taken.

This department was in charge of Mr. Newton Bateman from May 12, 1863, to January 9, 1865, when he resigned to assume the duties of the office of superintendent of public instruction for this State, to which office he was elected in November, 1864. To Mr. Bateman's superior business ability, zeal, and diligence I am deeply indebted. I ever found him an invaluable assistant in all the varied duties he was called upon to discharge while in the office. Upon the resignation of Mr. Bateman, Bvt. Maj. Harry C. Egbert, first lieutenant, Twelfth U. S. Infantry, was placed in charge of the department, the duties of which, although at first comparatively new to him, he discharged with great ability, promptitude, and fidelity, and to my entire satisfaction until April 29, 1865, when he was relieved from duty; since which time, the business of that character having greatly decreased, the department has been in charge of a clerk in this office.

The books of this department are as follows:

Letters received, in which is entered an abstract, or in case of an important letter, the entire communication, each letter being numbered, and, when recorded, note being made of the volume in which the record is made.

Indorsement book, which is kept in accordance with the regulations prescribing the same.

Impression books, which, for the sake of convenience, are of three kinds—one for letters to the Provost-Marshal-General, another for district provost-marshals, and the third for miscellaneous letters.

Book of telegrams received, in which are copied verbatim all telegrams received at this office.

Book of telegrams sent, in which all telegrams sent from this office are copied accurately and fully.

(Each of the above-named books has an index, generally in separate form, that being found in practice the most convenient way of keeping the same.)

Book of appointments, in which have been recorded all appointments made in this office and in each of the offices of the district provost-marshals, giving date of appointment, rate of compensation, date of approval, and date of discharge.

2. *Department of accounts.*—The department of accounts was made a distinct subdivision of this office July 14, 1864, and to it were assigned such papers and records pertaining to accounts and contracts as could be separated from other records; but as the records in the early history of the office were so limited, compared with what the greatly increased business of the department has since caused them to become, much of the information concerning these branches of business must be sought in the general records of the office, at least for the first twelve months of my service as acting assistant provost-marshal-general for Illinois.

The duty of auditing or examining such accounts as passed through the office was, upon the establishment of this department, assigned to its chief clerk and his assistants, and, in addition to the accounts of the Provost-Marshal-General's Department, all accounts to be approved by me as superintendent of volunteer recruiting service for Illinois have been audited in this department.

The record books used in this department are such as are required by a circular from the Bureau of Accounts under the appropriation for "collecting, drilling, and organizing volunteers," Provost-Marshal-General's Office, dated September 24, 1863, including record book of claims, book of letters received, and indorsement book. These books have been kept as nearly in accordance with the published directions of the Adjutant-General of the Army as we have been able to understand them, and are believed to have been very accurately and neatly kept. Besides these the letter impression book, in which are taken copies of all letters sent, and a record of checks received, have been in use; the latter showing the date and number of the check; by whom and in whose favor drawn; where payable; on what account; and a reference to the folio where the account is recorded, and the date of delivery to the claimant, and his signature acknowledging the receipt of the same.

A record of employés, embracing all persons employed by me, as well as by the district provost-marshals in this State, was made in a book sent from the office of the Provost-Marshal-General for that purpose, and is a very complete history in most cases of the employés in the several districts. Nearly or quite three months' time was occupied in perfecting this record.

Attention is respectfully invited to Schedules 3, 4, and 5, Appendix, which give in concise and tabulated form some information of interest compiled from the records of this department.

Schedule 3 shows the number of claims placed on record in this department and the amount of the same; also the amount to which I have given my approval.

Schedule 4 shows the different items of expense attendant upon the conduct of this office, exclusive of pay of officers, with the amount of each.

Schedule 5 is a very suggestive exhibit of the amount of service alleged to have been performed in taking and revising the enrollment of the State, given by months and by districts and reduced to years and days.

3. *Department of deserters.*—From the opening of my office to August 13, 1863, the business connected with deserters was a part of the general transactions of the office and conducted as such by the clerk in charge. The rapid increase, however, of this branch of the business and the urgency of my instructions from Washington in relation to it rendered it necessary to constitute it a separate department, which was done on the above date, and the same was placed in charge of First Lieut. Charles E. Hay, Third U. S. Cavalry, with one assistant, who continued to manage the affairs of the desk with marked efficiency until February 29, 1864, when, Lieutenant Hay having been assigned to duty in the office of superintendent of volunteer recruiting service, the desk of deserters was turned over to Mr. John C. Reynolds, one of my earliest and best clerks, who conducted its affairs with great assiduity and energy until November 18, 1864, when the department was assigned to First Lieut. B. F. Hawkes, Seventeenth Regiment Veteran Reserve Corps, in whose charge it remained until he was relieved from duty and ordered to his regiment, when the desk was again returned to the efficient and successful management of Mr. Reynolds.

The aggregate number of descriptive lists of deserters from Illinois organizations received at this office from that of the Provost-Marshal-General is 13,357; from other sources some 620 lists have been received, making a total of 13,977 lists.

Of each of these lists twenty copies have been made in this office, as follows:

One copy to each provost-marshal of Illinois	13
One copy to the acting assistant provost-marshals-general of the States of Missouri, Iowa, Minnesota, Michigan, and Indiana	6
One consolidated copy	1
Total	20

Making the enormous number of 279,540 lists which have been transcribed, mailed, and deposited in this office.

Of the 13,977 deserters reported to this office, 5,805, or over 40 per cent., have been arrested, as shown by Schedule No. 6, Appendix.

It is proper to observe that arrests for the year 1863 did not commence in most districts until June 10 of that year, although the time embraced in the schedule for 1863 dates from May 18. The table includes arrests for the year 1865 only up to May 31. For the first twenty days of June, 1865, six arrests have been made, being two in the Third District, and one each in the First, Fourth, Sixth, and Thirteenth Districts.

The data from which Schedule No. 6 is compiled have been taken from the duplicate tri-monthly reports of provost-marshals, on file in this office. The clerical force employed in copying the lists has, with one exception, consisted of members of the Veteran Reserve Corps.

When the many obstacles hereinafter referred to are considered, it is submitted that the percentage of arrests actually made is not discreditable to the energy and skill of the officers and others who have had the business in charge, the results being the return to the Army in the space of two years of about six full regiments of men, or an average of 242 per month for the whole time.

4. *Department of quotas and credits.*—The department of quotas and credits was organized August 1, 1864. To it has been assigned the recording of the enrollments; the calculations of quotas; the reception, record, and disposal of all papers sent to the acting assistant provost-marshal-general of Illinois, under Circular 52, Adjutant-General's Office, series of 1864; the recording of quotas and credits; the periodical and special reports of the same, both to the Provost-Marshal-General and to the provost-marshals; the accounts with the sub-districts for men due and furnished, and all correspondence relating to the matters under its charge. It has required from one to six clerks, and on extra occasions has drawn in to its assistance all available force in the joint offices under my control. Its average has been three clerks.

Books of department of quotas and credits.—The books kept are the usual books of correspondence, namely, letters received, indorsement and impression book of letters sent, besides those peculiar to this department, which are next described.

I. Enrollments A and B are records of the enrollment and its revisions. The former shows in tabular form by districts and sub-districts the original enrollment by classes; then the first revision, ordered November 17, 1863, showing number dropped and added, and net result; then the second revision, ordered May 5, 1864, showing number added and dropped and net result. The latter book records the monthly revisions in the same way, as shown by the printed heading, thus:

Monthly revisions.

Congressional district.			January, 1865.				February, 1865.		
Sub-district.	Designation of sub-district.	County.	Prior.	Added.	Dropped.	Remaining.	Added.	Dropped.	Remaining.

II. Credits L is a record of the reports or other vouchers upon which credits are authorized to be given by regulations and instructions. Such papers are recorded in this book in such a way as to arrange the credits of any one report in the regular order of districts and sub-districts, as known in this office, and at the same time to show the class of each credit, and the term of service for which the men credited are mustered in. This is the original book record of the credits, from which all others are made up and with which they must accord.

The reports, after entry in book L, are filed away by months, all relating to the credits of any one month being so indorsed, and filed together.

A sample of book L will be found in the Appendix, marked Schedule No. 7.

III. From credits L entries are made into the books in which accounts are kept directly with sub-districts, a page being allowed for each of the 1,476 sub-districts, and the set of books making four volumes this year. A sample page is given. (See Appendix, Schedule No. 8.)

The first column refers to the book of entry of the items contained in the lines. As the account of each sub-district is reported at the close of each month to the provost-marshal of the district, the column of "periodical reports" shows what number of credits were reported in any given month, while the columns headed "due" and "over" show the balance on the account from time to time. The column headed "equivalent in one-year men" shows how many years' service go to the credit of the sub-district, as the other columns show the men, their classes, and terms of service. These books are credits E and F, for 1864; credits G, H, I, K, for 1865.

IV. From the columns of "periodical reports" in these books entries are carried to another book in which the sub-districts are grouped by counties, and in which the monthly credits are entered in successive columns, so as to show the credits of the sub-districts of a county consolidated. This book (credits D) merely collects in closer form the results of the accounts with the sub-districts.

V. There is also made up from the books of accounts with sub-districts a book of monthly statements of credits, which consolidates all the credits of a month by districts and counties, and also by classes and terms of service. This is credits M, a sample of which will be found in Appendix, marked Schedule No. 9.

Another book belonging to the series has been begun, but never yet completed, owing to the constant demands of the current work of the department of quotas and credits. It is book N, consisting of historical and tabular statements of the assignment of quotas and credits in 1864 and 1865.

Sub-districts.—The original division of the districts into sub-districts for purposes of enrollment and draft was left to the provost-marshals. Every county is organized for school purposes into Congressional townships of six miles square. Some have a further organization into what are called towns, the limits of which are not always coincident with those of the townships, but often include two or more whole townships, and still more frequently embrace parts of townships, the boundaries of the towns being wholly arbitrary. In many other counties, particularly in the southern part of the State, the only division besides the townships is into election precincts, the boundaries of which are also arbitrary and variable. The different views of the provost-marshals led to various methods of division and enrollment. In the Ninth, Tenth, and Thirteenth Districts only were the townships and precincts at once made the units of the division; and these remained unchanged except that some cities were afterward divided into sub-districts by the wards. In the Twelfth and part of the Eleventh the sub-districts were made of the townships of the United States land survey, singly or in groups. In other districts two or more towns were grouped together. The First and Second Districts changed to the system by single towns upon the second revision of the enrollment, under orders dated May 5, 1864; and upon permission of the War Department I attempted to make a uniform system of division by the smallest civil units of territory, in preparation for the draft under the call of December 19, 1864. To effect this an entirely new enrollment was made in the Twelfth District. It was not effected in four counties of the Eleventh District because of the resignation of the provost-marshal just after instructions for the change were given. Before the change could be completed under the new officer the new quotas were to be assigned without delay.

The best division in this State is that attempted by me as above said, with some modifications. Some of the smaller cities prefer not to be divided or to be set off from the townships in which they are situated. In all cases where the local organizations are such that the people and authorities desire no division into wards or parts, I would ascertain and respect their wishes. In some cases it happens that a town or village lies upon the very line of division between two townships, in consequence of which any division of credits by volunteering from the town is arbitrary, and it is better for the two townships to go together. In the Sixth District two such unions were made during the pendency of the last draft. In fine, I regard the last system adopted as the best for convenience in this office, for convenience in enrollment, for proper distribution of credits, and for stimulating the local authorities to activity in filling quotas.

Schedule 10, Appendix, shows the number of sub-districts at various times, as practically in use.

Quotas and credits.—So far as this office is concerned, the first dealing with quotas and credits followed upon the call of July 18, 1864, for 500,000 men. A settlement between the War Department and the State of Illinois was first had in the early part of August, 1864, in consequence of which it was arranged that the standing of districts and sub-districts in Illinois should be ascertained and declared here, with the use of the records in the office of the adjutant-general of Illinois.

From his records were obtained the statements of quotas of 1861 and 1862, calculated to counties only. The quotas of February and March, 1864, under the call for 700,000 men, and the quotas on the call of July 18, 1864, were calculated in this office, and the county quotas of the tables of the adjutant-general's office, Illinois, were carried out to sub-districts in proportion to the enrollment. The quotas under the call of December 19, 1864, were calculated in this office in the manner directed by the Provost-Marshal-General. In no case has the calculation of quotas or the keeping of accounts of credits been referred to the provost-marshals. It would have been necessary to furnish them all the data for the calculations, and it was deemed much better for accuracy, and even for economy, to have the work done at this central office, and by a few clerks, rather than to burden the district offices with work for which each would need extra clerks, and which would not then be done with approximate uniformity and correctness. Besides, in practice it was found most equitable to calculate directly from the State quota to the local quotas, which could be done here only.

This equity appeared most plainly on the last call, when, if the calculation had been made from the State to districts and then to sub-districts, it would have come to pass that sub-districts which had not furnished their due proportion of recruits would have been exempted from all claim, because their neighbors in the same district had done more than their own share; and whatever was gained by such delinquent sub-districts in one part of the State would have fallen as an additional burden upon sub-districts in other parts of the State where martial ardor or patriotic zeal had been more equably manifested.

For the several quotas, aggregated by districts, see Schedule No. 11, Appendix.

While this table of quotas is strictly correct as to the numbers given out as quotas for the several dates named, yet it is practically wrong, owing to the fact that the State of Illinois had really filled up the number claimed of her up to December 31, 1864, and had furnished 1,158 men more. These 1,158 men were not credited to the State on the new quota under the call of December 19, 1864, but were taken into consideration in assigning the quota, thereby decreasing it; so that if the State had gone on to fill exactly the last quota of 32,902, she would have furnished 1,158 men more than the sum total of all quotas assigned. Hence the practical sum of the quotas is 1,158 larger than the result of the table referred to, being 231,420 instead of 230,262.

Distribution of credits.—By the settlement between the War Department and the State of Illinois, in August, 1864, spoken of above, the number to be credited to Illinois up to July 1, 1864, was fixed at 181,178. Of this number, 144,086 were credits prior to October 1, 1863, and for the distribution of them recourse was had to the records of the adjutant-general's office, Illinois, which furnished a distribution of them to counties only. From the same office were obtained records showing the distribution to counties, towns, &c., of 16,186 veterans, 1,120 recruits mustered in the field, 405 regulars, and 21 naval recruits, all enlisted and mustered between October 1, 1863, and July 1, 1864. The rolls of the associate office of chief mustering and disbursing officer for Illinois furnished the evidences for the distribution of the remainder of the total credits allowed.

The particulars of this distribution were fully reported in my letter to the Provost-Marshal-General of September 7, 1864. Briefly, it may be said that all credits were assigned to sub-districts as far as possible from the records, with revision of manifest errors and careful judgment in doubtful cases; that credits inuring to the State at large without assignment of residence were distributed pro rata on the most recent enrollment and added to the credits to the counties at large; that the county credits were again distributed pro rata in like manner to the sub-districts. As stated in the letter of September 7, 1864, only 35,191 were specifically assigned to sub-districts; the remainder, 145,987, were assigned by pro rata calculations.

The credits above named were all for three-years' men.

An interval of one month elapsed between the settlement with Illinois and the beginning of the system of recording and declaring credits initiated by Circular No. 52, Adjutant-General's Office, series of 1864. For that month the credits distributed were 144 recruits reported to me from the War Department, 762 veterans reported by the adjutant-general of Illinois, and 1,035 naval recruits, ascertained by commission, consisting of His Excellency Governor Richard Yates and myself, appointed July 14, 1864, to ascertain the naval credits due to Illinois for enlistments prior to February 24, 1864. These amount to a total of 1,941, which were distributed by the same rules as were used in the greater distribution preceding. These credits were for one, two, and three years—viz, 761, 9, and 1,171, respectively.

From the 1st of August, 1864, when the system of Circular No. 52 began, to December 31, 1864, which closed credits on calls prior to December 19, 1864, credits were distributed for 15,399 men of various classes and terms of service, as shown from time to time in my regular and special reports. Of these, 8,392 were drafted men and substitutes and 7,007 were voluntary enlistments.

Credits since December 31, 1864, to May 31, 1865, have been 27,658, of which 2,053 are for drafted men and substitutes and 25,605 are from voluntary enlistments.

For a tabular statement of the credits of these various periods by districts, see Schedule No. 12, Appendix.

A noticeable fact appears from comparison of the preceding paragraphs. It appears that of the men raised during the last five months of 1864, 54½ per cent. were drafted men or substitutes for drafted or enrolled men, while during the first five months of 1865 the same classes are less than 7½ per cent. of the number raised, though the number of the later period is 80 per cent. larger than that of the former. This great difference arises from the greater popular interest during the latter period, and the organized efforts of counties and towns to fill their quotas by volunteering. Where the civil authorities had not power or inclination to act, citizens' committees in many instances raised money by subscription and paid local bounties. Had the call continued, it would have required but little drafting, which would nowhere have been heavy, to fill the whole quota of the State.

It should be stated also that while I have been limited in the allowance of credits by regulations and laws excluding certain credits until the quotas on the present call should be full, papers have passed through my office showing men enlisted and mustered for whom it is certain no credit had ever been given, and other papers bearing names for which it is probable that credit has not been allowed. The number of these I have not recorded, but they are probably some hundreds, which should be added to the total of credits in the schedule (12), diminishing in equal number the deficit of Illinois at the close of the call. A few credits have come in since May 31, up to which date the tabular statements are made.

Balance of quotas and credits.—It would be expected that the difference between the total quotas and total credits, whether the whole State or separate districts be considered, would be the deficit or surplus, as reported in my monthly return of credits for May 31, 1865, but in no instance is this true. Table 13 (Appendix) compares in columns 1 and 2 the final columns of the tables of quotas and of credits, as given in Schedules 11 and 12, and shows in columns 3 and 4 the apparent deficits and surpluses; then gives in columns 5 and 6 the deficits and surpluses of my return of May 31, and in columns 7 and 8 the discrepancies between the apparent and reported deficits and surpluses. There is also added in columns 9 and 10 the total of deficits and surpluses obtained by adding the footings of accounts with sub-districts, without offsetting one against the other, as is done in obtaining the district balances.

When the discrepancy columns are footed and compared, it will be seen that the difference between them is 1,158 surplus, which is exactly the number spoken of in the remarks concerning the table of quotas (Table 11), as deducted in advance from the quota, instead of being counted against it. Thus the quota under the call of December 19, 1864, might have been 34,060 (32,902 + 1,158) and the 1,158 surplus of the whole State (as its accounts stood on December 31, 1864) might have been allowed to count against the quota, as it is made to count against the sum of the quotas, by including it in the total credits, and taking the difference of the sums. In that case the balance of apparent deficits and surpluses and the balance of reported deficits and surpluses would be the same number, 5,244 (5,567 — 323), which is also the sum of 4,086 (difference between apparent deficits and surpluses) and 1,158 (the difference of discrepancy columns). And as 1,158, the difference of the discrepancy columns, is the surplus of the whole State on December 31, 1864, so the numbers corresponding to the districts in the discrepancy columns, from which this difference of 1,158 is derived, are themselves the balances of deficit and surplus of the several districts, the total result arising from offsetting the surpluses of some districts against the deficits of others. These are, in fact, the district balances of December 31, 1864, which were in turn made up from balancing the surpluses and deficits of sub-districts.

The accounts of quotas and credits in this office are kept, in the first place, with sub-districts, and totals for districts are obtained generally by aggregating the numbers relating to sub-districts. Except in the monthly return of credits, the surpluses of some sub-districts do not offset the deficits of others; hence there may be a large surplus in the district, taken as a whole, while there are still due sundry quotas from sub-districts. This will explain further how the Thirteenth District has still due 557, according to my monthly return of May 31, or 619, according to my account with sub-districts, while the district, as a whole, has a large surplus. The quota on the call of December 19, 1864, having been distributed directly from the State quota to sub-districts, 831 men were demanded from the sub-districts in the Thirteenth District, which had furnished the smallest proportion of men. Since then the district has furnished 274 men, 212 of which have gone to the credit of the delinquent sub-districts, and the other 62 have gone to increase the surplus of sub-districts owing nothing; hence the real deficiency by sub-districts is 619. The deficiency remaining upon subtracting from the quota of the district all men furnished by it since December 31, 1864, is 557; while it appears by the table that if the total credits were allowed to offset the total quotas directly, the district, as a whole, would have a large surplus, viz, 4,410.

The paramount importance and peculiar intricacy and difficulty attaching to the duties of the department of enrollment quotas and credits have seemed to warrant the foregoing minute and extended account of the manner in which the records have been kept. It is believed that they are as correct and reliable as the nature of the case will admit. Great labor and pains have been bestowed upon these records, and it is believed that scarcely an inquiry can be made relative to the transactions of this department touching any district, sub-district, or the State at large to which these records will not furnish a satisfactory answer. The desk since its first separate establishment has been in charge of Dr. Samuel Willard as chief clerk, who has discharged its difficult and responsible duties with great fidelity and distinguished ability.

5. *Returns and reports.*—During the progress of the draft under the call of July 18, 1864, which commenced in September of that year, the difficulty of securing correct reports of the draft, in obedience to the urgent orders of the Provost-Marshal-General, was so great that it was found absolutely necessary to make a specialty of reports and returns, which was accordingly done, and the desk placed in charge of Mr. Thomas R. Bryan, whose whole time was fully employed in the performance of its duties, which he continued to discharge in a very competent and satisfactory manner, until the close of the war so diminished the number of reports and returns as to render it practicable to discontinue the department as a specialty, which was done on the 13th of May, 1865, it being then merged into the general business department and its duties transferred to Mr. John C. Reynolds.

The duties of Mr. Bryan while in charge of this branch will be readily understood from its designation. He was required to make himself perfectly familiar with the forms and instructions issued by the Provost-Marshal-General; to see that the district provost-marshals transmitted their reports punctually; to compare them with the prescribed forms, and return for correction such as were not in accordance therewith; to give proper instructions to such provost-marshals as required them, and to hold himself in readiness at all times to furnish me with such information as I might call for concerning the conditions and operations of his department. The results fully justified my expectations in establishing the desk, greatly facilitating the dispatch of the public business during that period of extreme pressure.

6. *Veteran Reserve Corps.*—On the 13th day of June, 1863, Capt. John A. Haddock, of the Invalid Corps, reported for duty at these headquarters, and immediately took post as general recruiting officer for that corps, and to assist in its organization in Illinois. Captain Haddock entered with great energy and success upon the duties assigned him, enlisting up to the time that he was relieved, February 8, 1864, fifty-four men, besides rendering me valuable assistance in the general business connected with the organization of the corps in this State. He was a most worthy, capable, and efficient officer, of whose services I greatly regretted to be deprived.

In July, 1863, Capt. Wells Sponable and Lieuts. James W. Davidson and Benjamin B. Baker, of the Invalid Corps, reported for duty, and were placed on recruiting service, the net results of which amounted to eleven men.

In August, 1863, all recruiting at detached stations was, by order of the Provost-Marshal-General, discontinued, and thereafter, until April 27, 1864, recruiting for the corps was restricted to the successive recruiting officers at these headquarters, who have obtained in all nine recruits.

July 2, 1864, Capt. E. R. P. Shurly, Eighth Regiment Veteran Reserve Corps, by authority of the Provost-Marshal-General, was placed on general recruiting service for the corps, with post at Chicago, where he remained until the 7th of the following September, and obtained four recruits.

April 27, 1864, district provost-marshals were empowered, by authority from Washington, to enlist men for the Veteran Reserve Corps, but without effect, except in the First and Third Districts, where nineteen recruits were obtained.

The foregoing is a summary of the general recruiting service for the corps up to the present time, showing the enlistment of ninety-seven men.

Under the provisions of the War Department allowing recruits for the First Battalion, Veteran Reserve Corps, to be credited to their place of residence, and under the influence of the large local bounties paid in certain localities, many were induced to enter the corps, and were enlisted by regimental recruiting officers at Camp Douglas and Rock Island. But all such enlistments immediately ceased upon receipt of the order of the Provost-Marshal-General of February 24, 1865, disallowing credits for enlistments in the Veteran Reserve Corps.

It is ascertained from the monthly regimental returns of the superintendents of recruiting service for the Fourth, Eighth, and Fifteenth Regiments Veteran Reserve Corps stationed in this State, that the total enlistments and re-enlistments in said regiments for the year 1864 were 189 men, and for the first four months of 1865 36 men. Four men have also been enlisted for the Eleventh Regiment Veteran Reserve Corps, making a total of 229 men from the regimental recruiting service, which, added to the 97 already reported, makes an aggregate of 326 as the number enlisted and re-enlisted in this State since the organization of the Invalid Corps.

Many causes have conspired to lessen the number of men transferred from hospitals to the Veteran Reserve Corps in this State. The largest proportion of men of Illinois regiments in the military departments bordering on the Mississippi who have been sent to hospital have been absorbed in the immense general hospitals at Memphis and Saint Louis. The same is true of Illinois soldiers in the Departments of the Cumberland and Tennessee, most of them being retained in the extensive hospitals at Nashville and Louisville. From these hospitals great numbers of Illinois soldiers have been transferred to the Veteran Reserve Corps, not entering the State, however, until organized into companies. To the same effect is the fact that the surgeons in charge of the general hospitals at Camp Butler and Mound City have been repeatedly instructed to forward their convalescents to Cincinnati and Saint Louis, for transfer to the Veteran Reserve Corps, thus depriving companies in this State of the men to which they were rightfully entitled. It is but just to state, however, that as soon as the attention of the proper authorities was called to the unfair workings of the system practiced it was discontinued.

The number of men transferred from hospitals in this State to the corps under my supervision and orders amounts to 730, being 169 for the year 1863, 211 in 1864, and 350 in 1865.

Two companies have been organized in this State by authority not emanating from these headquarters, having at the time of organization about ninety men each; and two companies have been organized under my direction belonging to the First and Second Battalions, respectively. The former numbered eighty men, and was originally known as the First Company, First Battalion, Invalid Corps, but afterward received the Bureau designation of the One hundred and sixteenth Company, First Battalion. It was subsequently incorporated into the Twenty-third Regiment Veteran Reserve Corps, as Company E. The Second Battalion company, numbering eighty-eight men, was originally known as the First Company, Second Battalion, subsequently receiving the Bureau designation of the One hundred and seventh Company, Second Battalion, by which it is still known.

Enough men have been enlisted and transferred in this State to constitute a maximum regiment, and but for the fact that large numbers of men have constantly been required to re-enforce companies whose ranks were being reduced by expiration of service and discharged, many more companies would doubtless have been organized.

One hundred and seventy-one applications from former officers and eight from enlisted men for commissions in the Invalid Corps and Veteran Reserve Corps have been forwarded through these headquarters to the Provost-Marshal-General, showing that whatever disinclination has existed on the part of enlisted men to enter the corps, no such backwardness has been displayed by resigned and discharged officers to obtain commissions therein.

While the results of recruiting for the Veteran Reserve Corps, as now detailed, are confessedly small, the causes which have conspired to this end are obvious, among the more potent of which may be mentioned the following:

First. The extraordinary bounties paid by the Government, especially to those who had previously seen service, as an inducement for them to re-enter active service, while all bounties have been withheld for enlistments in the Veteran Reserve Corps.

Second. The high wages for all kinds of manual labor incident to the withdrawal of such vast numbers of men from the agricultural districts of the State to supply the demands of the Army, the wages thus paid far exceeding the compensation received by an enlisted man (without bounty) in the Veteran Reserve Corps.

Third. The causeless and senseless jealousy and dislike manifested toward the corps by soldiers of active regiments in the field, and which have been communicated to many who, having been discharged for disability, would have been proper candidates for the corps.

In view of these difficulties, and others to which I have referred, it is hoped that the results obtained, though far less than were anticipated, will not be considered as discouraging, and that my efforts to carry out the views of the Government in this most laudable department of the public service will not be regarded as lacking in earnestness and energy.

7. *Medical branch.*—This branch was organized April 10, 1865, and Surg. Martin Rizer, First Army Corps, placed in charge. The first duty assigned Surgeon Rizer was the inspection of the medical records and proceedings of the various district boards of the State. Owing to the fact that I had previously had no officer competent to the duties of such inspection and supervision of the medical departments of the district provost-marshals' offices, many irregularities and imperfections were found by Surgeon Rizer to exist in some of said departments. The results of his various inspections have been reported to this office in writing and forwarded to the Provost-Marshal-General.

It is to be regretted that the services of Surgeon Rizer, or some other generally equally competent medical officer, could not have been secured at an earlier period, to take supervision of the medical branch of the bureau. It cannot be doubted that very many remissnesses and irregularities would thereby have been avoided, and the final results of the examination of recruits, drafted men, &c., would have been presented in a much more full and accurate form, thus rendering the experience of this branch of the service far more available to the Government for future use. Surgeon Rizer has done all he could under the circumstances, and has done it well.

ORGANIZATION OF DISTRICT BOARDS OF ENROLLMENT.

It being important that the machinery of the Bureau of the Provost-Marshal-General should be completed and set in operation as soon as possible, instructions were issued from this office, immediately after opening the same, to the various district provost-marshals, to consummate their arrangements and report their organizations at the earliest practicable period. The dates of the respective district organizations, with headquarters, as reported to this office, the same being arranged in the order of time, are as follows:

Sixth District, organized May 18, 1863, headquarters Joliet.

Fifth District, organized May 26, 1863, headquarters Peoria.

Ninth District, organized May 26, 1863, headquarters Mount Sterling.

Third District, organized May 28, 1863, headquarters Dixon.

Fourth District, organized May 28, 1863, headquarters Quincy.

Twelfth District, organized May 28, 1863, headquarters Alton.

Thirteenth District, organized May 28, 1863, headquarters Cairo.

Seventh District, organized May 29, 1863, headquarters Danville.

Eighth District, organized May 29, 1863, headquarters Springfield.

First District, organized June 1, 1863, headquarters Chicago.

Tenth District, organized June 1, 1863, headquarters Carlinville.

Second District, organized June 4, 1863, headquarters Belvidere.

Eleventh District, organized June 9, 1863, headquarters Salem.

The headquarters of the Second District were subsequently removed, by order of the Provost-Marshal-General, to Marengo; those of the Tenth to Jacksonville, and those of the Eleventh to Olney, the change in each case being greatly to the benefit of the service.

The provost-marshals of the First, Second, Sixth, Seventh, Eighth, and Ninth Districts have continued in office as originally appointed down to the present time.

The provost-marshal of the Third District resigned, for special reasons; but was reinstated at his own request in about a week, that brief interval being filled by Mr. Seymour E. Treat, as acting provost-marshal.

In the Fourth District Capt. James Woodruff resigned March 24, 1864, and was succeeded by Capt. Henry Asbury, who resigned March 24, 1865, and was succeeded by Capt. William H. Fisk, the present incumbent.

In the Fifth District Capt. James M. Allan was relieved January 20, 1865, by Maj. A. S. Norton, who served till March 23, 1865, as acting provost-marshal of that district, when Capt. C. C. Mason, who was appointed March 8, 1865, entered upon the duties of the office, and still holds the position.

In the Tenth District Capt. William M. Fry served until January 17, 1865, when, he having resigned, Capt. George W. Hamilton was appointed, who served until May 6, 1865, when his appointment was revoked; and Maj. A. S. Norton was ordered to take post as acting provost-marshal of that district, which position he still holds.

The first provost-marshal of the Eleventh District was Capt. Mortimore O'Kean, who resigned March 7, 1864, and was succeeded by Capt. E. S. Condit, who served until November 25, 1864, when, upon his resignation, the present incumbent, Capt. John C. Scott, was appointed.

Capt. George Abbott was first commissioned as provost-marshal of the Twelfth District, and held the position until December 28, 1864, when he was allowed to resign, and was relieved by Maj. A. S. Norton, who served as acting provost-marshal until January 11, 1865, when Capt. William H. Collins, the present incumbent, assumed the duties of the office.

In the Thirteenth District the commission of Capt. W. C. Carroll, the original appointee, was revoked May 27, 1863, and the present incumbent, Capt. Isaac N. Phillips, was commissioned in his stead.

For a full statement of the original composition of the respective boards of enrollment and all subsequent changes see Schedule No. 14, Appendix.

ENROLLMENT.

In obedience to pressing instructions from Washington, the provost-marshals in my jurisdiction were directed by Circular No. 3, from this office, dated June 5, 1863, to convene their respective boards of enrollment, establish their sub-districts, and to push forward the enrollment with all practicable vigor and dispatch. Information and instructions had been previously issued from this office to some of the provost-marshals, and the enrollment was already in progress in several of the districts, but the above was the earliest date at which any detailed instructions respecting the enrollment were issued from this office to all of the provost-marshals.

The instructions from the Provost-Marshal-General and from this office were carried out by most of my subordinates in letter and spirit, and with great energy and success.

In compliance with Circular No. 101, Provost-Marshal-General's Office, series of 1863, I issued a circular letter of instructions to my provost-marshals under date of November 27, 1863, directing them to proceed at once to the correction of their enrollment lists; and in accordance with my said circular and subsequent instructions the lists were revised in the various districts of the State during the month of December, 1863, and the early part of the year 1864.

In obedience to the orders of the Provost-Marshal-General instructions for a second revision of the enrollment were issued from this office May 6, 1864, in Circular No. 51, series of that year. Your orders for monthly revisions of the enrollment were communicated to the provost-marshals in my jurisdiction, with detailed instructions for the same, in Circular No. 99, from this office, dated July 7, 1864.

For a tabular statement showing the date of the completion of the original enrollment, and of the first and second revisions ordered by me November 27, 1863, and May 6, 1864, see Schedule No. 15, Appendix.

In order to facilitate the keeping up of the enrollment and to lessen the expense to the Government, I applied for and received from the Provost-Marshal-General authority to cause an enumeration to be made throughout the State of all persons between the ages of seventeen and twenty, and forty-two and forty-five years, noting the year, month, and day of birth of each person so enumerated; and full instructions to that effect were issued from this office to all district provost-marshals in Circular No. 67, dated May 27, 1864. The object of said special enrollment, as stated in my communication requesting leave to make the same, was to furnish each board with a record from which all persons arriving at and passing beyond the line of liability to military service could be ascertained in their respective offices, and that the names of the former might be added to the lists, and those of the latter dropped therefrom, by the clerks in the office, thereby greatly diminishing the number of special enrolling officers required to purge and perfect the lists, and lessening the expense in very nearly a corresponding ratio. Such special enumeration was accordingly made, with results, in most cases, corresponding to my anticipations.

Deeming it for the interests of the service, and that it would contribute to economy and promptitude in keeping up the enrollment, I also requested and obtained permission to appoint a superintendent of enrollment for each county, who should seek out and recommend suitable persons for assistant enrolling officers, and exercise a general supervision over the work in their respective counties. Instructions to that effect were issued from this office in Circular No. 66, dated May 23, 1864. The plan worked well and contributed largely to the prompt and economical maintenance of the enrollment.

On the 7th of July, 1864, district provost-marshals were instructed that, in order to carry into effect the provisions of Circular No. 24, Provost-Marshal-General's Office, series of 1864, they would be required to make continuous corrections of the enrollment lists and report the same on the last day of each month, beginning with July. To this end they were directed to complete the preparation of the special lists of persons between the ages of seventeen and twenty, and between forty-two and forty-five, already referred to, and to refer to the said lists when completed, to facilitate their monthly revisions. They were further required to impose upon each deputy and salaried special agent, in addition to his other duties, the constant revision of the enrollment of one county.

Where the number of deputies and special agents were not equal to the number of counties in a district, provost-marshals were directed to appoint an enrolling officer for each of the remaining counties, and, in accordance with the authority above referred to, it was made the duty of these deputies, special agents, and other county enrolling officers to keep up the enrollment in their respective counties. To aid them in this copies of the enrollment lists of his county, with full instructions for the discharge of his duties, were required to be furnished to each officer intrusted with the enrollment of a county. Provost-marshals were required to forward their monthly reports promptly at the end of each month, with duplicate copies of the recapitulation of the same.

I repeatedly enjoined upon my district provost-marshals the strictest practicable economy in the execution of their duties, the most watchful supervision over the conduct of their subordinates and employés, and the prompt discharge of all persons engaged in the enrollment who failed to render to the Government a just equivalent of service for the pay received.

In order to systematize the work and prevent confusion, provost-marshals were required to set apart certain days in each month for hearing and determining claims for exemption from enrollment, for which purpose they were directed to allow a sufficient time, and were authorized to decline the consideration of claims for exemption on any other than the specified days. Adherence to this rule was for a portion of the time absolutely essential in order to enable district boards to transact their necessary current business. Provost-marshals were directed to recommend suitable places for holding examinations, to be approved by the Secretary of War, in accordance with the provisions of section 14, amended enrollment act, February 24, 1864.

In granting exemptions provost-marshals were enjoined to be governed strictly by the instructions of the Provost-Marshal-General, and to use great care to avoid fraud, imposition, and injustice. No exemptions were permitted to be granted except for the causes specified in the circular of the Provost-Marshal-General, viz, permanent physical or mental disability, alienage, non-residence, unsuitableness of age, and two or more years of service in the present war. Persons removed from one sub-district to another, in the same district, were not allowed to be stricken from the rolls of the former sub-district until their names were entered upon the rolls of the latter; and persons removing from a district were not to be stricken from the rolls until the Board should be duly certified that said persons were enrolled in their new place of residence. Provost-marshals were also directed to hold their lists constantly subject to public inspection, as required by the Provost-Marshal-General.

For a more detailed statement of the various methods adopted for taking, revising, and maintaining the enrollments in the respective districts, and the comparative excellence of the several plans pursued, attention is respectfully invited to the reports of the several district provost-marshals, which have already been forwarded.

DRAFT.

It became apparent soon after the call of the President of July 18, 1864, for 500,000 men, that the quota of Illinois under that call could not be filled without a draft, and in compliance with intimations from Washington I had admonished the various boards of enrollment to complete all their preparations and hold themselves in readiness to commence drafting as soon as orders were received from me to that effect, but on no account to begin operations until so notified. I had been myself directed not to begin the draft in any district until so ordered by the Provost-Marshal-General, and discretion was given me to commence drafting, when orders should be received, in such districts of the State as to me might seem most expedient.

At length, September 12, 1864, I received a telegraphic order directing me to begin the draft without delay, and in the exercise of the discretion above mentioned, and for reasons which seemed to me satisfactory, but which need not be here enumerated, I selected the Fourth, Eighth, Tenth, and Twelfth Districts as those in which operations should first be initiated, and I immediately telegraphed the provost-marshals of said districts to begin the draft promptly on the 19th day of September, 1864, following my telegraphic order with a circular letter of instructions dated September 15, 1864.

The districts next ordered to draft were the First, Fifth, Sixth, and Seventh, the provost-marshals of which were directed by Circular No. 172, from this office, dated September 21, 1864, to commence drafting September 26, 1864.

September 23, 1864, instructions were issued to the remaining districts of the State, to wit, the Second, Third, Ninth, Eleventh, and Thirteenth, to commence the draft on the 29th of September, 1864.

The orders of the Provost-Marshal-General and from this office found the several boards of enrollment fully prepared, and the draft began in each case promptly as ordered, and was prosecuted with vigor.

Under the call of December 19, 1864, for 300,000 men, no draft was ordered in the First, Third, Fifth, and Eighth Districts of this State. To the provost-marshals of the remaining districts orders to draft were issued as follows: To Seventh District, March 18, 1865, to commence March 21, 1865; Eleventh and Thirteenth Districts, same date, to commence March 23, 1865; Fourth and Tenth Districts, March 24, 1865, to commence March 28, 1865; Second, Sixth, Ninth, and Twelfth Districts, April 6, 1865, to commence April 12, 1865.

The Second District had drawn but fifty-four men, when, in consequence of the sudden and total overthrow of the rebel armies and the virtual close of the war, orders were received to discontinue recruiting and drafting and to discharge all drafted men not forwarded to rendezvous. The fifty-four men are accordingly reported as discharged. In like manner the men drafted in the Ninth and Twelfth Districts were discharged by order before any had been forwarded to general rendezvous. Orders to arrest the draft were received by the provost-marshal of the Sixth District before he had actually commenced drafting.

For a summary tabulated statement showing the proceeds of the draft under each call in each district, giving separately drafted men held to service and substitutes, see Schedule No. 17 in the Appendix to this report. Said schedule presents the net results of the draft, and of course only includes those drafted men and substitutes who were forwarded to general rendezvous and actually put into service.

A complete consolidated statement, showing in detail the results of the draft in each district and for the whole State, with the number discharged for the various causes authorized by regulations, the number who paid commutation, &c., will also be found in the Appendix hereof, Schedule No. 18.

For a tabulated summary of the statistics of the draft in Illinois in 1864 and 1865, including all supplementary drafts, and showing, by districts, first, total number drawn; second, whole number reporting; third, whole number failing to report; fourth, whole number discharged without examination; fifth, number examined as to physical fitness for service; sixth, whole number examined; seventh, number discharged for physical disability; eighth, number discharged for other causes; ninth, whole number discharged after examination; tenth, number held to service; eleventh, number furnishing substitutes; twelfth, number serving personally, see Schedule No. 19, Appendix.

The column (No. 4) headed "discharged without examination" includes those discharged by reason of the quota of sub-district being full and those discharged under order of the Provost-Marshal-General of April 14, 1865, directing the discharge of all drafted men not then forwarded to general rendezvous.

The average enrollment of the State on which the quotas under calls of July 18 and December 19, 1864, were based was 306,349. The following interesting and suggestive facts and percentages are deduced from the recorded statistics of the draft on file in this office:

Enrollment basis of the State, 306,349; whole number drafted, 32,279, being 10.53 per cent. of enrollment.

Of the number so drafted (32,279)—

	Number.	Per cent.
Reported	22,439	69.25
Failed to report	9,840	30.75
Discharged without examination	3,899	12.07
Examined	18,540	57.12
Discharged on examination	9,595	29.72
Discharged for other causes than physical disability	3,381	10.47
Examined as to physical fitness	15,159	46.65
Discharged for physical disability	6,214	19.25
Held to service upon examination	8,945	27.40
Served personally	3,541	10.66
Furnished substitutes	5,404	16.74

Of those examined (18,540)—

	Number.	Per cent.
Discharged for other causes than physical disability	3,381	18.23
Examined as to physical fitness	15,159	81.77

Of the whole number physically examined (15,159)—

	Number.	Per cent.
Discharged for physical disability	6,214	40.98
Held to service	8,945	59.02

Of the whole number held to service (8,945)—

	Number.	Per cent.
Furnished substitutes	5,404	60.41
Served personally	3,541	39.59

While the order to stop recruiting and drafting was hailed with universal rejoicing, yet, as elsewhere observed, most of the communities in which the quotas were still unfilled had become so thoroughly aroused, and the local appliances to stimulate volunteering were in such vigorous and successful operation, that but little more drafting would anywhere have been necessary to clear the State of her entire obligation under the last call.

PERSONS ARRESTED—NOT DESERTERS.

As was to have been expected, it became necessary from time to time in the prosecution of the work to make arrests of various persons in different parts of the State for violations of the enrollment act and sundry other offenses. Although the number of such arrests has not been large, yet it is deemed proper to the completeness of this report that reference should be made to the subject.

A summary statement, showing the number of such arrests in each district and the grounds upon which the arrests were made, will be found in the Appendix hereof, and attention thereto is respectfully invited. (See Schedule No. 20.)

EXPENSES.

I have constantly endeavored faithfully to carry out the urgent instructions received from Washington from time to time relative to the importance of practicing the most rigid economy consistent with the effective prosecution of the work and the true interests of the service, both at these headquarters and in the offices of the respective provost-marshals of my jurisdiction. The views of the Provost-Marshal-General on this subject have been by me repeatedly and earnestly impressed upon all of my subordinates, who have, I think, as a general rule, faithfully endeavored to conform their expenditures to instructions received, and to contribute by careful circumspection to lighten the burdens of the Government as much as possible. The total expenditures of this office since its organization, exclusive of pay of officers, was referred to while discussing the business department of these headquarters, and will be found in Schedule No. 4 of the Appendix. In order to ascertain the total expenditures in each district, and the grand aggregate for the whole State since the organization of the machinery of the Provost-Marshal-General's Bureau in Illinois, I addressed a special circular to each district provost-marshal, requiring them to transcribe from their records the necessary data and report the same to this office. The results, tabulated by districts, and showing, first, total expenditures; second, cost of transportation; third, net cost; fourth, number of men furnished, including deserters; fifth, cost per man, will be found in the Appendix to this report, Schedule No. 21. The column headed "net cost" is found by deducting the cost of transportation, &c., from "total cost" in each district. The comparative smallness of expenditures in the Fourth District is explained by the fact that the men raised in that district were mostly transported and subsisted by the quartermaster's and commissary departments, so that those items of expense do not appear in the records of the provost-marshal of that district. The cost per man in the different districts varies very widely, varying from $8.97 in the Fourth District to $34.58 in the Thirteenth; or, leaving out the Fourth District for reasons above given, from $11.20 per man in the First District to $34.58 in the Thirteenth District, as aforesaid. Many causes have contributed to these great variations of comparative cost, among which should be mentioned the different degrees of business ability and tact characterizing the respective provost-marshals, but the principal cause is to be found in the widely different circumstances and facilities for the transaction of business in the different portions of the State where the district headquarters are located.

It will be seen from Schedule No. 21 that 52,221 men, including deserters and drafted men, have been raised and put into the military service of the United States from Illinois since the organization of this office (April 27, 1863), at an aggregate cost to the Government of $702,891.37, being an average cost per man for the whole State of $13.46. This estimate, as before remarked, is exclusive of the cost of transportation, &c., including only those items of expenditure connected with the provost-marshals' offices, and appearing upon their records. When all other expenses are taken into the account, including premiums paid for procuring recruits, &c., the average cost per man for the whole State will, of course, be greatly enhanced; but it is hoped that the exhibit, taken upon the basis assumed in the schedule, will not be considered discreditable to the practical economy manifested by the officers of your Bureau in this State.

I have thus briefly traced the organization, progress, and results of the work intrusted to me as acting assistant provost-marshal-general for Illinois. It remains, in compliance with the invitation of your letter of April 27, 1865, to which this report is responsive, to add some general observations suggested by my experience in this field for the past two years, in the hope that they may prove of some value should it, unfortunately, be necessary to resume operations.

GENERAL REMARKS.

1. *Centralization.*—No fact has been more clearly demonstrated by my experience in this work during the past two years than that the interests of the service require a greater concentration of all the more material and responsible elements of the business at the office of the acting assistant provost-marshal-general. All data essential to the correct computation of quotas, credits, &c., should be sent to the central office. Duplicate copies of the original enrollment lists should also be forwarded to this office. In like manner, during the progress of a draft, the names of persons drafted each day, and all other important data, should be transmitted to the central office, instead of only numerical statistics, as heretofore, which afford no means of verification in respect to individuals should misunderstandings arise.

Many cases have occurred in relation to the enrollment and draft which could have been satisfactorily adjusted with far less labor and time had such facilities of verification been at hand; while for lack of them many other questions of much importance to sub-districts and individuals could not be placed in a satisfactory light to the parties interested. As you have already been apprised, I did not at the first deem it expedient to intrust the calculation of quotas and credits, or any part thereof, or of any other important data requiring great circumspection and accuracy, to the district boards of enrollment. All of such calculations have been made in this office, and I am entirely convinced that any other course would have resulted in irretrievable errors and difficulty. The nice and intricate calculations required by instructions can be safely made only by a corps of trained and reliable experts, such as it has been my good fortune to have in my employ in this department.

It is further obvious that the acting assistant provost-marshal-general, being appointed directly by the Government of the United States and amenable for his official acts only to the department at Washington, is not only less liable to be unconsciously warped by the pressure of local influences, or to be affected by the importunities of individuals, than district provost-marshals and their associates, but, moreover, a knowledge of these facts and of the independent and unbiased position of the Government officer strongly predisposes the people to acquiesce in his opinions and abide by his impartial judgments, even in preference to leaving the determination of difficult questions to their own local officers.

Several instances have occurred which strikingly confirm the statement just made. I was importuned to allow the provost-marshal of the Second District, in conjunction with the civil authorities, to readjust the quotas and credits of a certain county in said district, and qualified permission to do so was obtained from the Provost-Marshal-General. But after a few days of ineffectual effort to harmonize the conflicting views and interests of the citizens they acknowledged their inability to effect a satisfactory adjustment and voluntarily referred the whole matter back to me, and from my action in the premises no disposition to appeal was ever manifested. Similar instances corroborative of the opinion here advanced occurred also in the Sixth and several other districts.

The paramount importance of requiring duplicate copies of the original enrollment lists to be transmitted to this office for file, and also full reports of the names of drafted men, will further appear in connection with the matter of credits, hereinafter considered. In no other way, it is believed, can the fraudulent practices which have largely obtained in the matter of credits be effectually prevented.

As related to the idea of a strongly centralized administration of the affairs of your Bureau in each State, I would also earnestly recommend that, in case operations should ever be resumed, the account of the Government should be kept with States only, disregarding all minor subdivisions, as Congressional districts, counties, precincts, &c., and that the calculation of quotas and credits and the management of all the details of the draft for each State be intrusted to the respective acting assistant provost-marshals-general. Your attention has already been frequently called to the discrepancies between the records of your office and mine, arising from the fact that while the Washington basis has been the Congressional district the unit of calculation in this office has of necessity been the sub-district.

Let the Government ascertain the number of men required to be raised and apportion the same among the respective States as quotas, leaving it to the respective acting assistant provost-marshals-general, with such aid as can be obtained from the State and local authorities, to adjust and apportion the State quota among such units of territory as may by law be established as sub-districts, and to execute the draft whenever one may be necessary, and account to the Government for the proceeds, to be applied as credits on the quota of the State. Each State thus becomes debtor to the Government for so many men, and is credited from time to time by volunteers, drafted men, &c., furnished, until the account is balanced. Whenever the books at Washington show that any State is in arrears let requisition be made through the acting assistant provost-marshal-general for the number of men due, and let him, with a full knowledge of all the facts and circumstances of the case, proceed to make the necessary assessment upon the delinquent sub-districts and raise the men by draft or otherwise.

It does seem clear to me that this plan would greatly simplify the work both at the Washington office and in the respective States, while it would avoid many previously existing causes of perplexing discrepancies of record. All that the Government wants is the men, and all that the people of the different States want is a simple, direct, and palpably just and intelligible distribution of the burden. It is manifest that the apportionment of quotas from the State's indebtedness directly to the ultimate sub-district unit, instead of circuitously through the Congressional district, is an immense saving of labor and greatly enhances the probability of accuracy, while it is not seen that a single valid objection can be advanced against so simple a plan of operations; and it is entirely certain that, taking this State as an example, the one end in view—the filling of the prescribed quota—would have been more promptly, smoothly, and effectively accomplished.

I would further recommend in connection with the point under advisement that not only all books and other stationery be furnished by the acting assistant provost-marshal-general to the district boards of enrollment, as is now the case, but also that all necessary circulars, advertisements, and other official printing be executed, as far as possible, under the direct supervision of the acting assistant provost-marshals-general of States, and that a uniform system of keeping all accounts and records be prescribed by your Bureau and enforced through your assistant in each State. The benefits arising from the application of this principle to the matter of books and stationery have been very marked, and have resulted in great economy of expenditure, and there is no doubt that like advantages would follow the application of the same rule to the matters above indicated. With a strict uniformity of records and accounts we should know precisely what information could be furnished at once upon requisition and what could not, and unity, instead of diversity, would characterize all the detailed business transactions of the Bureau.

2. *Enrollment.*—The starting point and basis of the whole system of replenishing the National Army through the agency of the Bureau of the Provost-Marshal-General is the enrollment of the arms-bearing population of the country. Upon its completeness and correctness depends the equity of credits allowed and quotas imposed. If the enrollment is right, all is right; if wrong, all is wrong. To no other subject have I given more attention and thought. It cannot be denied that the enrollments made under existing laws were far from being perfect, and it is equally undeniable, I think, that the errors contained in said enrollments were not due so much to remissness on the part of enrolling officers (some of whom, doubtless, were incompetent and unfaithful) as to grave defects in the laws themselves under which they acted. In fact, it is believed that most of the imperfections can never be avoided under the present system.

It is not intimated that the several enrollment acts were not as carefully matured and as wisely adapted to the end in view as was possible at the time; much less is it intended to challenge the wisdom and necessity of the policy of military conscription or the administrative ability of the Provost-Marshal-General.

The organization of the Bureau was, in my estimation, an absolute necessity of the Government, and contributed to an incalculable extent toward the final overthrow and destruction of the rebellion. Its aid was essential and invaluable not only on account of the vast accessions to the Army secured through its direct agency, but also, indirectly, through the significant revelation which it afforded to our enemies at home and abroad of the ability of the Government to summon to the national defense the whole military strength of the country, and that, too, by the stern ordeal of the draft. And the conduct of the Bureau has, in my judgment, been characterized by great ability, energy, and prudence. The defects of the present laws are, for the most part, such as no forecast could anticipate, and which could only be developed by experience and time.

I am therefore clearly convinced that a radically different policy should be adopted in case the agency of your Bureau should again be called into requisition. Instead of endeavoring to search out and hunt up every person liable to military service through the agency of a vast multitude of petty enrolling officers, upon whose capacity and fidelity it is not possible in all cases to rely, I think the Government should impose its supreme demands directly upon the people themselves, and require them, under the sternest penalties, to report themselves for enrollment. If the Government has a right to the military service of its citizens in times of public peril, rebellion, and war, it has a right to secure such services in the simplest, cheapest, and most direct manner.

The policy advocated is not new; it is as old as the principles and method of Federal, State, and local taxation. It is the duty of tax-payers to call at the office of the collector and discharge their indebtedness, or, in default, to suffer their property to be sold by public auction. The collector does not go to the tax-payer, but the tax-payer comes to the collector, and so I think it should be with a military enrollment.

As soon as the emergency requiring a conscription can be foreseen let the acting assistant provost-marshals-general of States be required, through their respective district provost-marshals and otherwise, to give general and emphatic public notice through the newspapers, circulars, handbills, &c., that a draft is impending, and that all persons between the prescribed ages must appear before the Board of Enrollment of their district and be duly enrolled or exempted for cause, as the case may be, or suffer the consequences. Let the several boards be required to hold meetings for that purpose in a sufficient number of places in each county for the proper and speedy accommodation of all liable to enrollment, and let a sufficient time be allowed for the purpose at each point. Immediately upon the termination of the period assigned for reporting, let public notice be likewise given that the lists will be finally closed within a certain time—say ten days—after which all voluntarily failing to report shall be subject to the penalties and liabilities provided by law. Let it be enacted that any person liable to enrollment, and finally failing or refusing to report to the proper officers for that purpose, shall be heavily fined, or imprisoned, or both, as Congress shall prescribe, and that all such persons so failing to report, but whose names may be communicated through other sources to the Board of Enrollment, shall, if drafted and accepted, be compelled to serve personally. Let the foregoing rule apply to aliens, to persons having conscientious scruples against bearing arms, and to all classes and descriptions of persons, without distinction, whose ages are within the prescribed limits.

In like manner let it be made the duty of all persons coming into a district for the purpose of residence, or removing from a district with intention to reside elsewhere, to report as aforesaid to the proper officers for enrollment, and make it the duty of each district provost-marshal to furnish the provost-marshal of the district from which such new residents have removed with a certificate that they have been duly enrolled; and until such certificate is received let it be unlawful to strike the names of such persons from the lists.

As already remarked, no enrollment should be ordered until it is clearly foreseen that a draft must be made, taking care, however, to allow a sufficient time between enrollment and draft for the thorough and careful perfection of the lists, so that none can plead that opportunity was not afforded them for compliance with the law.

It will be seen that under the operation of such an enrollment act as is here proposed not only is the original enrollment made with incomparably less difficulty, time, and expense, but it becomes thereafter throughout the whole continuance of the war, and without any additional expense whatever, self-revising, so that each State will thereafter be always ready for any new assignment of quotas and any additional drafts. It is also morally certain that an enrollment made under the provisions of such a law would be far more complete and reliable than by the present or any other system; for, beyond all question, just as but a very small percentage of the tax-payers of a community incur the hazard of losing their estates by neglecting to pay their taxes, so a like unimportant portion of the arms-bearing population of any sub-district would voluntarily incur the stern penalties of imprisonment and fine by seeking to evade the requirements of such a military enactment; and not only would the number of delinquents be very small from the nature of the case, but it would be constantly and rapidly reduced by the hearty assistance rendered by all who had themselves complied with the law, every one of whom would be urged by the strongest incentives of personal interest to bring forward such delinquents or report them for punishment.

As already intimated, I am fully convinced that it is not only the indisputable right of the Government in time of war to secure the services of its citizen soldiery in the summary manner here recommended, but that the justice and reasonableness of the exercise of the right would be generally acquiesced in by the people, especially in view of its impartial fairness, simplicity, and economy, and the swift retribution which would by it overtake tories and cowards and skulkers of every name and class. In respect to the superior economy of the proposed measure, a glance at the expense account connected with the enrollment in this State, and I doubt not equally in every other State, is conclusive. By reference to Schedule No. 5 of the Appendix to this report it will be seen that the Government has paid, in the various enrollments and revisions which have been made in this State, for 47,282 days' service, at $3 per day, amounting to $141,840, being about $16 per man for each of the 8,941 men obtained by the draft. And by comparison of the cost of enrollment alone, as above stated, with the grand aggregate of all the expenditures incurred by the district provost-marshals of Illinois, $702,891.37 (see Schedule No. 21), it will be seen that the former amounts to more than 20 per cent. of the latter. In other words, the Government has paid for the single work of making and revising the enrollment lists in this State more than one-fifth of the entire sum required to keep in operation the whole machinery of the bureau from its organization until now. A further comparison of the schedules referred to shows that the enrollment expense averages more for each man obtained by the draft than the grand average per man of the whole 52,221 men sent to the field from this State during my administration.

Not only would the advantages already enumerated inevitably flow from the proposed amendment, but the cumbrous machinery of the district offices would be at once relieved and simplified by the discharge of a vast number of enrolling officers, amounting to over 1,000 in the State, with the laborious and perplexing duties connected with the proper selection, instruction, and supervision of so large a force of employés.

I have not considered it necessary or proper to indicate, in detail, the provisions of such an enrollment act as would secure the foregoing most beneficial results. Such details belong to the Provost-Marshal-General and to Congress, to whose wisdom it is my province to leave them, in full confidence that they would be judiciously and effectively adjusted; but I would earnestly recommend, by the high considerations of national sovereignty in time of war, by the completeness and reliability which should characterize the vital work of a military enrollment; by the pains and penalties which should be meted out to those who would ignominiously shrink from bearing a part in the public defense, and by the necessity of rigid economy of expenditures, that, should operations ever be resumed, the enrollment act should be amended in accordance with the suggestions which I have made.

Should the present mode of enrollment be continued, substantially, I should still have some suggestions to make by which its practical operation could be, I think, materially improved; but my sense of the necessity of a radical change is so strong and my conviction is so clear that the Provost-Marshal-General and Congress would never again rely upon a method of enrollment so unwieldy and inefficient as the present, that I have foreborne to advert to the means by which the working of the existing system might be rendered more satisfactory.

3. *Place of credit.*—I would recommend that existing orders and regulations be so modified as to make the place of actual residence, as shown and verified by the enrollment lists, the only and inflexible rule of credits. To this end let each district provost-marshal furnish the Board of Enrollment of every other district in the State with a duplicate of his enrollment lists, in addition to the copy forwarded to the acting assistant provost-marshal-general, as hereinbefore recommended; or, let acting assistant provost-marshals-general be required to consolidate and publish the enrollment lists of the whole State and furnish each district board of enrollment with a copy. With these records before it each board could at once determine the truth or falsity of every allegation of a recruit or substitute as to his particular place of residence. If the statement of the man should be verified by the enrollment list of the proper sub-district, he should be enlisted and credited accordingly; but if the enrollment list does not sustain said statement, then the desired credit should be refused.

It is believed that such a rule, properly guarded, would effectually prevent the grievous and unanswerable complaints which have come up to this office from sub-districts in the agricultural portions of the State, and from small settlements and villages, that they were robbed and depleted of their arms-bearing population by the wealthy cities and towns under the temptation of enormous bounties, with which they could not possibly compete, being thus compelled to fill quotas based upon an enrollment a large percentage of which, having been credited elsewhere, could not be present to bear their portion in the responsibility of a draft.

Next to the errors of the enrollment, the practical injustice of the rule and manner of credits which has very extensively prevailed in this State, and no less, I presume, in other States, has been the most prolific source of irritation and hard feeling. It is simply impossible to convince the honest people of a sub-district that it is right or just to place them at the mercy of their wealthy neighbors, to be stripped of their young men and left to meet the emergencies of the draft with but a fraction of their rightful resources. It is confidently believed that the only true principle is, first, to obtain a complete and reliable enrollment, and then make each sub-district responsible for its own quota, insuring it credit for every man enlisted from it, making actual residence, as shown and verified by the enrollment lists, the rule and test of the place of credit in every case. It is further believed that the same rule should apply in the case of the enlistment of aliens, minors, persons over age—in a word, in the case of all persons who may for any reason not be liable to enrollment, so far as the question of residence can in such cases be determined, proper evidence of which could easily be prescribed and required.

I am aware that the adjustment of this matter upon a basis that shall be just alike to the public interests of the sub-district and the private interests of the individual is extremely difficult; but the number and enormity of the wrongs which have been committed and endured under existing permissive regulations, or, rather, in spite of the spirit and intent of existing orders, call loudly for a remedy; and I do not see that any other would be more effective and, in the main, just than the one suggested.

4. *Substitute brokers.*—In my judgment the strong hand of the Government should be laid upon the whole heartless crew of substitute brokers, whether as principals or subordinates, and all others who would make merchandise of the necessities and calamities of the country. The whole business is founded upon a supreme and sordid selfishness, and prosecuted with a degree of unprincipled recklessness and profligacy unparalleled in the annals of corruption and fraud. The traffic is too odious to be engaged in by respectable men, or, if such persons do embark in it with honest intentions at first, they soon become so corrupted by the nefarious practices to which competition compels them to resort as to lose all claim to the character of honorable men. The whole thing is demoralizing to those engaged in it, whether as agents or subjects, and a disgrace to the people who connive at it and the Government that tolerates it. It presses into the service, by devices which no vigilance can wholly prevent, great numbers of men wholly unfit for military duty. It disgraces the honest soldier and the service by conferring the dignity of the Federal uniform upon branded felons; upon blotched and bloated libertines and pimps; upon thieves, burglars, and vagabonds; upon the riff-raff of corruption and scoundrelism of every shade and degree of infamy which can be swept into the insatiable clutches of the vampires who fatten

upon the profits of the execrable business. It is the parent and support also of the herd of bounty jumpers who have prowled the country during the last twelve months, scandalously selling themselves again and again to the highest bidder, regardless of their plighted faith and the solemnities of their oaths to the Government.

The enormous gains of the business clothe its agents with a power of bribery against which there is reason to fear that not a few of the commissioned officers of the Government have proved unable to stand. Many well-known facts render this more than a mere surmise. Members of boards of enrollment who were penniless when they received their commissions have retired from the service with a display of means utterly incompatible with the assumption of their honesty, and yet so adroitly has the business been conducted that no clue can be obtained whereby to prove their guilt.

A business that thus interferes with the military operations of the Government, demoralizing and corrupting both people and soldiery, and bringing the force of a tremendous temptation to bear upon the very officers of the Government to swerve them from rectitude—a business that makes bounty jumpers by hundreds, a set of dastards who, to the crime of desertion, add the meanness of constructive theft and robbery—a business that tends to stain the proud name of the soldier of the Republic, and entail, by vilest fraud, an expense of untold thousands. Such a business not only cannot be right, but must be considered as falling within the sphere of the national authority in time of war.

I therefore suggest and recommend that substitute brokerage be suppressed by proper authority, as a military offense, and that all persons found guilty of engaging therein be liable to summary trial and punishment by court-martial or military commission; and that any provost-marshal, commissioner, surgeon, or other officer of the Provost-Marshal-General's Bureau who shall countenance and encourage, or in any manner aid and abet any system of substitute brokerage, or the agents thereof, or who shall receive any bribe from, or have any pecuniary or other connection with, substitute brokers, shall be dishonorably and summarily dismissed the service.

5. *Deserters.*—The number of deserters arrested and returned to the service from Illinois during my administration as acting assistant provost-marshal-general is 5,805, as shown by Schedule No. 6, Appendix. While it is believed that this result will compare favorably with that attained in any other State of like geographical situation and general circumstances, yet I am persuaded that under a different policy the number of arrests would have been very largely increased.

This topic has been so fully presented in several of the historical reports of my district provost-marshals, and the views therein advanced are, in many instances and particulars, so just and practical, that I need here do but little more than advert to and indorse them.

Incalculable evil has resulted from the clemency of the Government toward deserters. By a merciful severity at the commencement of the war the mischief might have been nipped in the bud, and the crime of desertion could never have reached the gigantic proportions which it attained before the close of the conflict. The people were then ardent and enthusiastic in their loyalty, and would have cheerfully and cordially assented to any measures deemed necessary to the strength and integrity of the Army. They had heard of the "Rules and Articles of War," and were fully prepared to see them applied in their sternest rigor to every miscreant who should basely desert the flag. They understood that it was war with which the Government had to deal, and they expected and desired that an earnest and inflexible war policy would be at once inaugurated and carried out, and that deserters from the Army would be remorselessly arrested, tried by court-martial, and, if guilty, be forthwith shot to death with musketry.

This was unquestionably the almost universal attitude of the public mind when hostilities began, and the just expectations of the people should not have been disappointed. Arrest, trial, and execution should have been the short, sharp, and decisive fate of the first deserters. All the people would have said amen, and the crime of desertion, except in rare instances, would have ceased, just as it did in Mexico as soon as the deserters who fought us at Cherubusco were captured and hung. This is human nature, and it will ever remain so. Let the grim but indispensable code of war be enforced by a few examples of death by musketry or hemp, and the lesson will not need to be repeated, while mere paper penalties soon come to be disregarded and despised.

I trust that these remarks will not be considered in the light of an irrelevant homily upon an abstract theory, or as the utterance of mere truisms. I make them as being germane to the main purpose of the department in calling for these final reports, which is to gather up the fruits of our past experience for future use. And I deliberately declare my conviction that the people were ready for the most rigid and, if necessary, the most sanguinary enforcement of the Rules and Articles of War upon all military criminals; and that by a swift visitation of death upon convicted deserters in those early and decisive months of the war the habits of desertion and of contempt for penalties threatened but never executed never could have prevailed to the frightful extent that they now do. The Government was far behind the people in this matter, and so continued until long and certain impunity had thrown such swarms of deserters and desperadoes into every State that it was then too late to avert the calamity. It was impossible to hang or shoot all of them, and so none were shot or hung, and thus the terrible evil went on with steadily increasing rapidity to the end.

I state these things so that if we have another war the Government may start right—put deserters to death, enforce military law, strike hard blows at the outset, tone up the national mind at once to a realization that war is war, and to be sure that such a policy will be indorsed and sustained by the people.

There are other suggestions to be made in respect to deserters, but the one I have already advanced—the non-enforcement of the penalties provided by the military code for the crime of desertion, especially at the beginning—is, beyond all question, the grand fundamental cause of the unparalleled increase of that crime and of the inability of district provost-marshals, with their whole force of special agents and detectives, to rid the country of deserters. They came nearly as fast as, and sometimes faster than, they could be caught and sent back to the field. The supply seemed inexhaustible. The same deserters were arrested, sent to the rendezvous, forwarded to the front, put into the ranks without the pretense of trial or investigation, only to desert and return to the State, to be again arrested and put through the same mockery as before. The same men have been arrested and rearrested for desertion from two to five times. (See reports of Captains James, Eustace, and others.)

Not only should the extreme penalty be meted out to deserters found worthy of it, but far heavier pecuniary losses should attach than are now authorized. The reward allowed for the arrest of deserters has proved in this State entirely inadequate. Coupled, as it is, with the liability that the person arrested will not prove to be a deserter, and with the risk and danger attending capture, a sufficient number of the right kind of men cannot be found to engage in the business—in Illinois, at least—for the reward offered by the Government; and since even that has been withdrawn, no deserters are now arrested.

In my judgment the reward should not be less than $100 for each deserter arrested and restored to the service, the agent to bear all the expenses of every kind connected with the arrest and delivery at general rendezvous. This seems a large bounty, but I am satisfied that it would be in the end more economical even than the inadequate sums heretofore allowed. It would at once place a large and formidable force of detectives in the field, a knowledge of which, in addition to the heavy amount charged against deserters, would operate as a powerful check to desertions, the number of which would rapidly diminish. With such a stimulus I am satisfied that scarcely a deserter would have remained in Illinois after the end of the first year of the war. It is true that higher motives should enlist the services of citizens in such a work, but in point of fact such is not the case, and we must take things as they really are. I would also recommend stringent measures in the case of officers who restore deserters to duty without even the form or pretense of trial, as required by regulations. My attention has been called again and again to instances of that kind, the whole effect of which is discouraging to provost-marshals and demoralizing to the discipline of the Army.

6. *Bounties.*—It has seemed to me that if the Government deems it expedient to offer large bounties as an inducement to volunteer, it would be more prudent not to pay any part or installment of such bounties in advance. The large amount received from the Government by the soldier before he leaves the general rendezvous, added to the local bounty, which is often still larger, constitutes a very strong temptation to desert—too strong in many instances for resistance. I would therefore recommend, should the policy of large bounties be hereafter continued, that no part be paid until after the soldier has served a certain time.

But I am of the opinion that a still better policy would be, in future wars, to dispense with Government bounties altogether as a means of promoting volunteering, and, instead, to increase the regular pay of the soldier to such an extent as would enable him, with prudence and economy, to support his family or dependents while in the Army, relying upon the spirit of the people and such local bounties as particular communities might offer to secure volunteers, and when these resources failed, call in the aid of the draft.

The drain upon the National Treasury to pay such large bounties to such vast numbers of men is prodigious, and if continued would be absolutely ruinous. The amount of bounty necessary to secure a given result at successive stages of a war is, moreover, necessarily greater and greater. A sum that secures volunteers enough to fill one call will prove inadequate for the next call; and so the amount must be increased as the war goes on, until the resources of the Federal Treasury become unequal to tne demand. Nor is this the only evil. Those who respond to the first call of their country and enter the service without any stimulus but patriotism regard with disfavor those who could only be induced to take up arms by the pressure of pecuniary motives, while those who subsequently receive a still larger bounty are disliked in turn by their predecessors, to whom a less amount was paid; and so the effect is not only to engender bitter and jealous feelings among the soldiers, but also to induce those not yet enlisted to wait for still greater offers, and thus defeat the very end in view.

The bad effects above mentioned have been realized in this State to a large extent. The ill-nature produced by the disparity of benefits received by different portions of the regiment has, in many instances, been injurious to the morale of the whole command, while taunts and retorts, criminations and recriminations, have impaired the efficiency of the men by diverting attention from duty to angry disputations. I am convinced that, upon the whole, the evils of large Government bounties are greater than the benefits, and do not doubt that a different policy should obtain in case great armies are again to be called into service.

7. *Term of service—Short enlistments.*—Although not directly called for by the scope of this report, I may be allowed to express my sense of the inexpediency of enlisting men for short periods. In my opinion, all enlistments should have been, from first to last, for three years or the war. The evils of short enlistments are too obvious to require mention. They are not only expensive and vexatious, but involve the hazard of the defeat and miscarriage of the most skillfully planned campaign, or even the loss of a battle, on the very eve of victory. The spectacle described by General McDowell in his report of Bull Run—that of regiments whose time had expired "marching to the rear to the sound of the enemy's cannon"—should never be possible in time of war. It would seem that our experience of the miserable effects of short enlistments in the Mexican war should have been sufficient.

I know that there is no diversity of opinion at the War Department as to the policy of short enlistments, and that the only question there has been in reference to the practicability of filling up the Army with three-years' men. On this point I believe that if "three years or the war" had been the watchword of the Government at the outset, and steadily persisted in, there would have been no serious difficulty in raising the men.

It is known that the patriotism of the country flamed so high in 1861 that tens of thousands of volunteers were rejected after the call was filled, and that thousands who could not get in in their own States sought admission to the Army through the organizations of other States. No questions were asked in those months of ardent feeling about the term of service; they would have gone in for five years or the war if it had been so required. Then was the time to have initiated the rule of long enlistments, which could, in my opinion, have been successfully adhered to throughout the war. I am sure that this opinion is entertained by the great mass of loyal men of this State.

My purpose in commenting upon this subject would not be completed if I failed to notice the jealousy and bad feeling created in the Army by the presence in the same regiment of three-years' men who had enlisted without bounty, and recruits having but six or nine months or a year to serve, for which brief term they had received heavy bounties. In the adjustment, too, of the quota and credit accounts of the respective States the whole business would have been infinitely simplified, and innumerable obscurities and complaints avoided, if one uniform rule of three years' service had been adopted and enforced in all the States.

It would be easy to multiply arguments on the subject, but I will only add that, knowing long enlistments to be the true policy of the Government in time of war, and fully believing that, if begun in time, such policy could be practically carried out, it should by all means be the settled rule of enlistments in the future wars.

8. *Resistance.*—At the time I was ordered to take post in this city, as acting assistant provost-marshal-general of Illinois, no signal success had crowned the national arms, and the public mind was much depressed and in a state of feverish apprehension. Advantage was taken of this discouraging aspect of affairs by the enemies of the Government, and threats of resistance and defiance to the provisions of the enrollment act, then just passed, were freely made in various parts of the State, eliciting much uneasiness on the part of good men. Though not sharing in the fears that were entertained respecting the imminence of an actual outbreak, I deemed it prudent to enjoin upon my subordinates the exercise of great circumspection and forbearance and the careful avoidance of all unnecessary irritation while in the discharge of their duties. The measure about to be inaugurated by the Government was not only new and hitherto untried in this country, but one against which the people had conceived a most violent prejudice, and common sagacity dictated the pursuance of such a course as would allay the excitement and fears of the people and lead them gradually to a more rational view of the nature and necessity of conscription, while the inflexible purpose of the Government to enforce the law regardless of all opposition and menace was at the same time firmly exhibited.

Under instructions in harmony with the foregoing policy the work began and progressed rapidly and satisfactorily in almost every district. The disloyal elements of the State, which were not lacking in numbers or virulence, were awed by the calm strength and quiet determination exhibited by the Government, and shrank from open collision, while the friends of a stern prosecution of the war rapidly discarded their fears and prejudices and ranged themselves firmly on the side of the Government and its officers.

At a very early period after the work commenced an enrolling officer was assaulted and almost killed in the streets of Chicago; but the summary arrest and condign punishment of the miscreant settled the question at once in that city and district, and exerted a wholesome influence upon the disaffected in other portions of the State.

At a later period more serious resistance was made in the Ninth, Tenth, Eleventh, and Thirteenth Districts, in each of which the aid of the military was at different times called to the assistance of the provost-marshals. One county of the Thirteenth District (Williamson) was obliged to be enrolled in the presence and by the aid of a company of cavalry, and a bitter and dangerous spirit was for a time manifested; but the certainty of invoking upon themselves the prompt and irresistible strength of the military arm dissuaded the insurgents from the hazards of actual collision, and the excitement gradually died away.

A military force had also to be sent into Fayette, Clark, Coles, Morgan, Fulton, and some other counties, and a few men were killed and wounded on both sides before the disturbances were quelled. The most serious outbreaks occurred near Manchester, Scott County, Tenth District, and at Charleston, Coles County, Seventh District, to both of which places I was obliged to send a strong force, and many prisoners were taken and variously disposed of, as provided by regulations and laws. In each case the insurgents dispersed upon the appearance of the military. Full reports of my action in those affairs have been forwarded to the office of the Provost-Marshal-General.

The difficulties above mentioned nearly all occurred in connection with the enrollment. The only serious opposition after the draft was connected with the service of notices upon drafted men, and occurred chiefly in Fulton, Clark, and Fayette Counties. But the presence of troops held the leaders in check, and the notices were finally served in every instance.

Although but few actual collisions have occurred in the State, a bitter and dangerous temper has frequently been manifested, and formidable combinations have existed in various localities, with the avowed purpose of armed resistance to the enforcement of the laws; and I am entirely satisfied that the presence in the State of the requisite military force was all that prevented the bloody culmination of their threats in many localities, if not a general and formidable insurrection, especially toward the close of the year 1864.

My experience has demonstrated the comparative uselessness of infantry in dealing with roving bands of deserters, assassins, and desperadoes, such as have infested portions of this State the past two years. These gangs are usually well mounted, familiar with all the woods and swamps and byroads of the country, and can of course successfully elude the infantry and defy their pursuit. I would therefore recommend, should occasion require the resumption of operations under the enrollment act, that a sufficient force of cavalry be placed at the disposal of the acting assistant provost-marshals-general to meet all emergencies likely to arise in connection with the enforcement of the enrollment and draft.

It is not needful to look for the causes of nearly all the opposition which I have encountered in this State. It is due mainly to the (as I think) mistaken clemency of the Government in dealing with deserters, upon which I have elsewhere remarked, and the machinations of a few disloyal political leaders, aided by the treasonable utterances of corrupt and profligate newspapers. The swarms of deserters whom assured impunity brought to the State exerted a most baleful and contaminating influence both in preventing enlistments and also in giving head and venom to the lawless gangs that attempted to resist and defy the authorities.

But the grand cause—the only really guilty and formidable source of the dangers through which Illinois has passed—is to be found in the steady streams of political poison and arrant treason which have been permitted to flow from the wicked, reckless, and debauched newspaper press of the State. But for this the enrollment and draft would have passed off with scarcely a ripple of disturbance. The terrible effect of such daily teachings upon the ignorant and deluded masses can well be imagined. The Government, with all its officers, aims, and purposes, has been maligned, calumniated, aspersed, and defied with a persistent fiendishness and a truculent hatred that would have seemed incredible and impossible. And chief among these instigators of insurrection and treason, the foul and damnable reservoir which supplied the lesser sewers with political filth, falsehood, and treason, has been the Chicago Times—a newspaper which would not have needed to change its course an atom if its place of publication had been Richmond or Charleston instead of Chicago—a sheet which has been bought by tens of thousands by Southern emissaries, with Southern gold, for gratuitous Southern distribution, to keep alive the delusion and spirits of the Southern people, and protract the war—a paper that rebel leaders have ever regarded as their best Northern ally in Illinois, and whose editorials have been read with delight by Davis and his fellow-traitors since the war began. The pestilent influence of that paper in this State has been simply incalculable. I have not the slightest doubt that it is responsible for the shedding of more drops of the patriot blood of Illinois soldiers than there are types in all of its four pages of political slime and scandal. The conspiracy that came so near wrapping Chicago in flames and drenching her streets with blood was fomented and encouraged by the teachings of the Chicago Times. Without that paper there would have been no conspiracy. In my opinion, without desiring in the least to abridge the regulated liberty of the press, it is as much the duty of the Government to suppress such newspapers in time of public danger and war as it is to storm the fortresses, sink the navies, and destroy the armies of the common enemy; and should war again break out I would urge the prompt adoption of that policy. In illustration of the truth of this estimate of the Times, attention is respectfully invited to the special report of Capt. William James, provost-marshal of the First District, a copy of which has been forwarded to the Provost-Marshal-General.

9. *Medical officers.*—I would recommend that in any future organization of the Bureau of the Provost-Marshal-General a competent medical officer be assigned to duty at the headquarters of acting assistant provost-marshals-general of States, to direct and supervise the transactions of surgeons of boards of enrollment, attend to the prompt rendition of correct medical reports, and take the general responsibility of the right conduct of the medical branch of the bureau in their respective States. The importance of such an addition to the corps of permanent officers at these headquarters became evident to me as soon as the draft had developed the imperfect manner in which the medical records of district surgeons had been kept, and my conviction of the utility and necessity of such a chief of the medical branch has been confirmed by the good effects which have followed the arrival and services at this post of Surg. Martin Rizer, who has greatly contributed to the efficiency of this branch since he has been on duty here.

As previously intimated, it is much to be regretted that the policy of attaching a medical officer to the staff of acting assistant provost-marshals-general of States was not adopted at an earlier day, especially in view of the severe loss that will accrue to the Government, and to the cause of medical science, from the very meager and imperfect final medical reports which, I regret to say, have, in most instances, been forwarded from district surgeons, and which it was already too late to remedy, except in part, when Surgeon Rizer reported for duty at these headquarters. Such an opportunity of enlarging the boundaries of medical science and enriching the profession with an almost boundless profusion and variety of curious facts and interesting statistics, as the experience of the last four years has afforded, will hardly occur again in many generations.

A glance through the excellent report of Surg. Moses F. Bassett, of the Fourth District, will show how exceedingly valuable an equally full statement of results and opinions from each of our thirteen districts would have been, while with proper supervision in the past even that report could have been made much richer and better. I would earnestly advise that the results of past experience in the medical branch be still saved to the country, as far as possible, in the form of special reports, &c., to be made by competent officers detailed for that purpose.

10. *Government attorney.*—I would also respectfully recommend to the Provost-Marshal-General the expediency of designating, should operations be resumed, a legal adviser of approved ability and discretion, to take post at the headquarters of the acting assistant provost-marshals-general of States during the progress of drafting, to whom questions involving principles of a purely legal character might be referred for his opinion, counsel, and advice. The expense to the Government would be inconsiderable, as the time during which the services of such a person would be needed would not be long, while the benefits of a prompt and reliable determination of legal questions, in the midst of the hurry and excitement of a draft, would be of the greatest value.

The Provost-Marshal-General is aware that legal points, upon which the military officers of the Government are not supposed to be prepared to give an authoritative opinion, are constantly arising, and during the progress of a draft it is often impossible to submit such points to the Provost-Marshal-General in time to answer the emergency.

11. *Medical examinations.*—It is with deference submitted that the minute description and detailed statement of the disqualifying and nondisqualifying diseases and infirmities, the presence or absence of which is made by regulations the test of the fitness or unfitness of a recruit or drafted man for military duty, should be abolished; and that instead it should simply be provided that all men found upon careful examination to be, in the judgment of the surgeon, mentally and physically capable of active military service, shall be accepted and enlisted, and all not found to be so capable shall be rejected.

In my estimation the minuteness and prolixity of existing instructions relative to medical examinations perplex and embarrass more than they aid the judgment of surgeons. A conscientious surgeon will reject a man of whose actual ability for duty he has no moral doubt, because the regulations seem to him so to require, while a dishonest surgeon will, for a consideration, reject a man under pretense of some technical disability having no existence in fact, but to which his construction of the prescribed rules give color of truth. And, worst of all, under a similar plea of technical necessity a bad or malicious surgeon may send to the field a man more fit for a hospital than for the Army, and thus perpetrate a crime against humanity little better than constructive murder.

I am satisfied that many instances have occurred under each of the three classes above described, especially under the first and second classes, while it has been impossible, as the rules stand, to correct the error in the first case, or to detect and punish the crime in the second and third cases. It would seem plain that competent and honest surgeons do not need such minute specifications, while on the other hand dishonest or incompetent surgeons are as likely to be misled by them as to be assisted, or to willfully misconstrue or abuse them for their own private ends.

The importance of securing professional ability of the highest available order and at least an average degree of integrity for the position of surgeon to boards of enrollment can hardly be overestimated. The opportunities of bribery and fraud enjoyed by those officers in time of draft (and improved by not a few) are innumerable, and of such a character as to defy detection, although the moral evidence of guilt may be most conclusive. I would therefore further recommend that no district surgeons be hereafter commissioned except upon examination and award duly made by a commission of surgeons of approved honor and ability, to be designated and appointed by the Government for that purpose. I have no Utopian expectation that such a change would be a radical cure of the evil, but I am sure that it would greatly lessen it, and throw some additional safeguards about the interests of the Government and of the people.

12. *Railroads and war.*—Most of the railway companies in this State have manifested a praiseworthy disposition not only to carry out their covenants with the Government in good faith relative to the transportation of troops, military stores, and munitions of war, but have also shown a spirit of generous co-operation and patriotism, cheerfully submitting to temporary interruptions of their regular business and to all the annoyances and losses incident to a state of war. I regret that there should have been any exceptions to the above statements, but there have been such exceptions, and of so marked a character as to require a notice in this report. During the most active period of recruiting my provost-marshals on the lines of some of the roads have frequently been unable to induce the companies to halt their trains at the points and hours necessary for the proper accommodation of detachments of recruits that were waiting to be forwarded to general rendezvous, thus adding to the expense of subsisting and lodging, or compelling the shipment of the men at an hour that would bring them to the rendezvous in the night. The same evil has also occurred during the progress of the draft, resulting in the escape and desertion of many drafted men and substitutes.

It is true that in most cases the officers of the roads have promptly repudiated the acts of their subordinates when informed thereof, and directed them to afford all necessary facilities to provost-marshals for the transportation of their men; but great inconvenience and detriment to the service nevertheless occurred during the interval between the reception at this office of the provost-marshal's report of the difficulty and my reference of the matter to the proper railroad authorities. In a few cases no active measures were taken to remedy the evil, and no disposition was manifested to co-operate with the officers of the Government in their efforts to push forward troops to the front.

I have also to report instances of needless and shameless inhumanity on the part of some companies in the character of the accommodations furnished to soldiers. Brave men, including many sick and wounded, have been crowded into common box-cars in the dead of winter, without fires, or fuel, or lights, or any other conveniences that had been enjoyed by the cattle that occupied the cars before them, and in this condition the poor fellows were compelled to make journeys of hundreds of miles. In other instances the same class of cars were used in the hottest weather, and without having been cleansed of the filth left by the cattle, hogs, and other stock. Many deaths have occurred from diseases caused by the cold, suffocation, and stench endured in those trains, while a few were not able to hold out to the end of the route, and were taken out dead.

The Government cannot afford to permit the possibility of such cruel and brutal treatment of good soldiers and brave men to gratify the heartless avarice of corporations which have been enriched by the war. I would therefore recommend that such changes be made in the regulations touching the use of railway lines for military purposes in time of war as shall preclude the possibility of a recurrence of conduct so disgraceful to humanity and so prejudicial to the interests of the service. The remedy should be sharp and summary. In making this suggestion I would not forget the great and signal benefits which the Government has derived during the late war from the use of the railroad lines built up by private enterprise; but it is held that nothing can justify such wanton and heartless abuses.

13. *Exodus from the State—Passes.*—Some effective means should be provided to prevent the exodus from the country of persons liable to enrollment and draft. Many thousands of such persons left this State for the remote Western Territories, California, Oregon, &c., on the eve of the late drafts, leaving their places to be filled by others, and thus adding to the burdens of those who remained at home. I am aware of the popular irritation caused by a general system of passes, but it is not seen in what other way the interests of the service and the rights of those who will not sneak out of the country to avoid their just share of military obligation can be adequately protected. The Provost-Marshal-General is assured that the evil had become in this State one of very serious magnitude, and it is therefore recommended that, should a draft be hereafter necessary, some system of passes should be adopted that would effectually check the wholesale withdrawal of the arms-bearing population from their respective States and localities. Should the suggestions elsewhere made in this report, relative to the manner of future enrollments, be carried into effect the necessary duration of the restraint of the pass system would be greatly lessened and its inconveniences be proportionally diminished.

CONCLUSION.

In closing this report I would refer with a high sense of obligation to the prompt assistance and generous confidence which have ever been extended to me by the Provost-Marshal-General, and to the uniform courtesy and co-operation of the officers of his Bureau, as well as those of the other branches of the War Department with which I have been in official relations. I believe it due to truth to say that the complicated affairs of the Provost-Marshal-General's Department, with its vast theater of operations, its wilderness of details, its gigantic system of agencies and co-operative machinery, and its immense and perilous responsibilities, have been conducted with signal ability. The difficulties which have environed the head of the Bureau in the inauguration and successful prosecution of a military measure of such stupendous magnitude, and one hitherto untried in the history of the Government, can only be appreciated by those who have had some practical acquaintance with the subject.

It is my pleasant duty also to refer to the diligence, patriotic fidelity, and marked ability with which most of the provost-marshals in my jurisdiction have performed their important and perplexing duties. Their responsibilities have often been of a very grave character, calling for the exercise of high qualities of prudence, nerve, and tact. They have usually met every emergency with commendable sagacity and skill, and acquitted themselves in a manner alike honorable to the State of which they are citizens and beneficial to the interests of the Government.

I may particularly mention Capts. William James, of the First District; A. B. Coon, of the Second; John V. Eustace, of the Third; James Woodruff and his successors, of the Fourth; Isaac Keys, of the Eighth; William M. Fry, of the Tenth; John C. Scott, of the Eleventh, and William H. Collins, of the Twelfth, all of whom have shown themselves eminently capable and efficient, and displayed marked administrative and executive abilities as officers.

It is to be hoped that the great lessons of this war will not be lost upon the country. Aside from its glorious termination, the rich experiences and teachings which it has left as a legacy to us and our children are not few or small. It has accustomed our people to the disabilities and hardships incident to a state of war. It has demonstrated to the world the invincible power of citizen soldiery in a just cause, and how soon they may acquire the discipline and steadiness of veterans. It has especially taught us how to raise, arm, equip, muster, organize, drill, and employ great armies. And if these lessons are wisely improved the Nation would embark in another war, whether foreign or domestic, with incomparably greater advantages for its successful prosecution than were possessed at the commencement of the late rebellion.

I am sensible of the imperfections of this report. It has been impossible to speak of many subjects worthy of notice without extending the paper to an unwarrantable length, and equally so to do full justice even to those matters which I have treated of. I have only aimed to advert briefly to such considerations as seemed to be of greatest practical interest, and to have a more important bearing upon the efficiency of the Bureau of the Provost-Marshal-General should operations ever be resumed.

Trusting that it may be regarded as at least partially responsive to the tenor of the letter in obedience to which it has been prepared,

I am, general, very respectfully, your obedient servant,

JAMES OAKES,

Bvt. Brig. Gen., U. S. A., Actg. Asst. Prov. Mar. Gen., Illinois.

*List of schedules.**

1. List of clerks.
2. List of officers.
3. Number and amount of claims recorded.
4. Statement of expenses.
5. Service rendered by enrolling officers.
6. Deserters arrested.
7. Sample of book of credits, L.
8. Sample of book of accounts with sub-districts.
9. Sample of book of credits, M.
10. Table showing number of sub-districts.
11. Table of district quotas.
12. Table of district credits.
13. Comparative view of quotas and credits, deficits, and surpluses.
14. Boards of enrollment.
15. Dates of enrollment and revisions.
16. Result of the several enrollments and revisions.
17. Net proceeds of each draft, by districts.

*All omitted. See explanatory foot-note (*), p. 687.

18. Statement of results of draft.
19. Statistics of the draft.
20. Statement of persons arrested, not deserters.
21. Statement of expenses of districts.

DOCUMENT NO. 12.

Historical report of the operations of the office of the provost-marshal of the Fourth Congressional District of Maryland, from the date of its commencement of business.

OFFICE OF PROVOST-MARSHAL, FOURTH DIST. MARYLAND,
Frederick, August 20, 1865.

Brig. Gen. JAMES B. FRY,
Provost-Marshal-General, Washington, D. C.:

GENERAL: I have the honor, in obedience to instructions from the acting assistant provost-marshal-general for Maryland and Delaware, dated April 29, 1865, directing this office to prepare and submit through that office to the Provost-Marshal-General a complete history of the operations of this office since it commenced business, to submit the following history, to wit:

PROVOST-MARSHAL.

Pursuant to the act of Congress approved March 3, 1863, "for enrolling and calling out the national forces, and for other purposes," James Smith, of Cumberland, Alleghany County, Md., a lawyer by profession, was appointed by the President provost-marshal of the Fourth Congressional District of Maryland, to date from May 16, 1863, with the rank of captain of cavalry.

Capt. James Smith having been suspended by order of the Provost-Marshal-General, Capt. Jonathan W. Barley, Veteran Reserve Corps, inspector at the office of the acting provost-marshal-general of the State, was assigned to duty as acting provost-marshal, by Special Orders, No. 66, dated Office of the Acting Assistant Provost-Marshal-General for Maryland and Delaware, August 20, 1864, and entered upon duty August 22, 1864.

Capt. James Smith having been discharged, Henry Clay Naill, of Sam's Creek, Frederick County, Md., a surveyor by profession, was appointed by the President to succeed him as provost-marshal September 12, 1864, and having duly qualified, pursuant to Special Orders, No. 77, dated Office of the Acting Assistant Provost-Marshal-General for Maryland and Delaware, Baltimore, Md., September 20, 1864, entered upon the discharge of his duties September 21, 1864.

The provost-marshal conducted all of the correspondence of the office, examined all deserters who were apprehended and brought before him, and heard and determined all claims as to property seized in the hands of unauthorized persons and delivered at his headquarters, and directed the general business of the office.

COMMISSIONER OF ENROLLMENT.

John J. Thomas, of Hancock, Washington County, Md., a merchant by occupation, was appointed by the President commissioner of the Board of Enrollment of the Fourth Congressional District of Maryland May 16, 1863, and, having taken the oath of office, entered upon duty May 26, 1863.

The duties of the commissioner were to superintend the enrollment and keep the lists corrected, and prepare all reports appertaining thereto, and also to attend the sessions of the Board of Enrollment.

Recruiting and drafting having been suspended April 14, 1865, and there being no further need of his services, he was honorably discharged the service April 30, 1865.

SURGEON OF THE BOARD OF ENROLLMENT.

Charles J. Baer, M. D., of Middletown, Frederick County, Md., was appointed by the President surgeon of the Board of Enrollment of the Fourth Congressional District of Maryland May 16, 1863, and having qualified, entered upon duty May 24, 1863.

The duties of the surgeon of the Board were to make the medical examinations of drafted men, substitutes, and recruits, to keep a record of the result of the examinations, and report the same to the Provost-Marshal-General, and to attend the sessions of the Board of Enrollment.

Drafting and recruiting having been discontinued, and there being no further need of his services, he was honorably discharged the service June 15, 1865.

ESTABLISHMENT OF HEADQUARTERS.

By direction of the Provost-Marshal-General, the provost-marshal established his headquarters at Frederick City, Md., June 1, 1863.

The provost-marshal found it very difficult to lease a building suitable for the transaction of the business of his office. This was attributable to the fact that property holders were apprehensive that any building occupied by an officer of the Government for Government purposes would, in the event of an invasion of Maryland by the Confederate army, be more liable to be destroyed by the enemy. The provost-marshal succeeded, however, in procuring such accommodations as enabled him to proceed with the business of his office.

The business of the office as it continued greatly increased, and the provost-marshal found the accommodations at his headquarters totally inadequate for the transaction of the public business, and he accordingly procured another building at the earliest day possible, which was fitted up in such apartments as were adapted to the prompt transaction of business, which was found to be advantageous to the service.

It is the opinion of this office that three rooms do not afford sufficient accommodations for the successful transaction of the business of a provost-marshal, and I would respectfully state that the experience of this office convinces me that the duties of the provost-marshal and the Board of Enrollment cannot be satisfactorily performed with less than five rooms; and I would further state that a building with five rooms can be leased with very little additional expense.

The provost-marshal should have a medium-sized room, and it is highly important that the Board of Enrollment should have a large and well-lighted room for the examination of recruits, substitutes, and drafted men. There should be one large room for the clerical force of the office, and a room in which to keep clothing, so assorted that the proper-sized articles may be promptly selected when needed for uniforming men. There should also be a room for the reception and accommodation of the people who are seeking admission to the provost-marshal or the Board of Enrollment. This is found almost indispensable in inclement weather and in the winter season.

NOTICE CONVENING THE BOARD OF ENROLLMENT.

The provost-marshal having established his headquarters, notified the commissioner of enrollment and the surgeon of the Board that the Board of Enrollment would convene for the transaction of business on the 10th day of June, 1863, and hold a session each day thereafter, except Sundays.

BOARD OF ENROLLMENT.

The Board of Enrollment was composed of the provost-marshal, who was president, the commissioner, and the surgeon.

The provost-marshal designated one of his clerks as recorder of the Board of Enrollment.

The Board of Enrollment held a session every day, except Sunday, and usually convened at 9 a. m., and continued in session until all of the business before it was transacted.

When recruiting was active, or a draft in progress, the Board sat without reference to hours. All recruits and drafted men were examined in the presence of the Board.

TERRITORY EMBRACED IN THE FOURTH CONGRESSIONAL DISTRICT OF MARYLAND.

The Fourth Congressional District of Maryland is composed of that portion of Western Maryland embracing Alleghany, Washington, Frederick, and Carroll Counties.

Pursuant to instructions from the acting assistant provost-marshal-general of the State, dated December 21, 1863, the Congressional district was resubdivided by the Board of Enrollment into fifty-nine sub-districts, each election district constituting a sub-district.

APPOINTMENT OF ENROLLING OFFICERS.

The Board of Enrollment having subdivided the Congressional district into sub-districts, one enrolling officer was appointed for each sub-district.

The enrolling officers having received their appointments, subscribed to the oath of office prescribed in Circular 24, Provost-Marshal-General's Bureau, series of 1863, before a justice of the peace of the county in which they resided, to which oath was attached a 5-cent stamp, and the oath in each case forwarded to the Provost-Marshal-General.

The names of the enrolling officers were borne upon the monthly report of persons employed and articles hired; and they were paid at the rate of $3 per day on duplicate vouchers (Form 19), by the Provost-Marshal-General's Bureau, for the time actually employed.

Great difficulty was encountered in procuring the services of men who were competent to make the enrollment correctly, and much delay was occasioned thereby.

ENROLLMENT.

The Board of Enrollment having subdivided the Congressional district into forty sub-districts, and appointed an enrolling officer for each, who had duly qualified, the enrolling officers were furnished with the proper blanks (Forms 35 and 36), and proceeded to enroll all able-bodied male citizens of the United States, and residents of foreign birth who had declared on oath their intention to become citizens, between the age of twenty and forty-five years, as follows:

First class.—The first class embraced all persons between the ages of twenty and thirty-five years, and all unmarried persons above the age of thirty-five and under forty-five years. This class was enrolled on Schedule I, Class I, Form 35.

Second class.—The second class included all married persons between the ages of thirty-five and forty-five years. This class was enrolled on Schedule II, Class II, Form 36.

The number enrolled in Class I	12,659
The number enrolled in Class II	6,451
Total	19,110

The number of men enrolled in Classes I and II who were in the military service of the United States March 3, 1863, was 2,559.

This enrollment was commenced July 20, and completed October 5, 1863.

An additional enrollment was made in March and April, 1864, in pursuance of sections 6 and 24 of the act approved February 24, 1864, amendatory to the act of March 3, 1863.

This enrollment embraced all men whose names had been omitted by the enrolling officers; all persons who had arrived at the age of twenty years before the draft; all aliens who had declared their intention, on oath, to become citizens; all persons discharged from the military or naval service of the United States who had not been in such service two years during the present war, and all persons who had been exempted under the second section of the act approved March 3, 1863, but who were not exempted by the provision of the act approved February 24, 1864; also all colored persons held to service (slaves) who were liable to military duty.

The latter class was enrolled in accordance with instructions contained in Circular No. 8, Provost-Marshal-General's Bureau, series of 1864.

The number of colored persons held to service, enrolled, was 571.

CONSOLIDATION OF THE ENROLLMENT.

The names of all persons enrolled in Classes I and II (Forms 35 and 36) were transferred in alphabetical order from the partial lists to the consolidated lists, except such as were in the military or naval service of the United States March 3, 1863.

Those of Class I were consolidated on Schedule I (Form 37); those in Class II, on Schedule II (Form 38), and those who were in the military service of the United States on the 3d of March, 1863, were borne on the consolidated enrollment lists in a class by themselves:

The number consolidated in Class I	11,400
The number consolidated in Class II	5,151
The number consolidated who were in the service March 3, 1863	2,559
Total	19,110

The consolidated enrollment lists were forwarded to the Provost-Marshal-General as soon as they were completed, and the partial lists were retained by the district provost-marshal.

The names of all persons who were enrolled under the provisions of section 6 of the act approved February 24, 1864, were reported to the Provost-Marshal-General upon sheets of consolidated enrollment lists at the end of each month for the purpose of correcting the lists on file. (See Circular, Nos. 24 and 39, series of 1864.)

The enrollment of colored persons held to service, made pursuant to section 24 of the act approved February 24, 1864, was not consolidated, but a list with a recapitulation of the number enrolled was made for each sub-district and forwarded to the acting assistant provost-marshal-general of the State for transmission to the Provost-Marshal-General.

Copies of these lists were retained by the district provost-marshal.

CARDS BEARING THE NAMES OF ENROLLED MEN.

The consolidation of the enrollment having been completed, the provost-marshal caused the names of each person enrolled to be written on cards of uniform size, shape, and color.

These cards were then assorted by sub-districts, verified by comparison with the enrollment lists, numbered and placed in an envelope marked with the number of the sub-district and the number of cards contained in it and sealed.

After all the sub-districts had been thus prepared the envelopes were put into one, which was sealed up and put away until the day of the draft.

REVISION OF THE ENROLLMENT.

In compliance with Circular No. 101, Provost-Marshal-General's Office, series of 1863, the Board of Enrollment had printed lists of the names of all persons enrolled in Class I posted in five or more places in each sub-district, and gave notice as required by said circular, and proceeded to examine the claims of all persons who applied to be stricken from the enrollment lists on account of alienage, non-residence, unsuitableness of age, and permanent physical disability.

These examinations were continued until December 20, 1863, after which time no cases were to be heard; but as there were many applicants whose claims had not been considered, the time for hearing such cases was extended to January 5, 1864, by direction of the Provost-Marshal-General, and the examinations were accordingly continued until that period.

The number borne on the enrollment lists was considerably reduced by this process; but as my predecessor kept no record of the number examined and the number exempted, except those exempted for manifest permanent physical disability, I am unable to give the result of these examinations.

The number stricken from the lists for manifest permanent physical disability was 322.

Instructions were received in May, 1864, to make further corrections of the enrollment lists by striking therefrom the names of such persons as were not liable to military duty, and adding thereto the names of such as were, who had not been enrolled.

To effect this the commissioner of enrollment and an assistant surgeon of the U. S. Army, detailed by the acting assistant provost-marshal-general of the State, proceeded to Westminster, the county seat of Carroll County, Md., to hear the claims of persons enrolled in said county to be stricken from the enrollment lists; and the provost-marshal and surgeon of the Board heard applications of the other counties of the district at the district headquarters.

The examinations under said instructions were closed June 29, 1864.

The number stricken from the enrollment lists during this period was 1,206.

Circular No. 24, dated War Department, Provost-Marshal-General's Office, Washington, D. C., June 25, 1864, having been received early in the month of July, 1864, inviting the attention of boards of enrollment to section 6 of the act approved February 24, 1864, and calling attention to paragraphs 55, 56, 57, 58, 59, 60, 61, and 62, Revised Regulations for the Bureau of the Provost-Marshal-General, and making the correction of the enrollment lists a continuous duty to which the labors of the Board of Enrollment must be directed, the Board, in compliance with said circular, had copies of the enrollment lists open to the examination of the public, and gave public notice that any person enrolled might appear before the Board and claim to have a name stricken from the list if he could show to the satisfaction of the Board that the person named was not properly enrolled on account of, first, alienage; second, non-residence; third, over age; fourth, permanent physical disability, &c.

Civil officers, clergymen, and all other prominent citizens were invited to give the Board their co-operation in the correction and revision of the enrollment lists.

The Board devoted all the time that could be spared from other less pressing duties to hearing and acting upon claims for exemption.

The draft under the call of July 18, 1864, being in progress, very little was accomplished by this effort to correct the enrollment.

Attention was again called to the necessity of correcting the enrollment lists in every sub-district in the district by Circular No. 39, dated War Department, Provost-Marshal-General's Office, Washington, D. C., November 15, 1864; and while the Board was responsible as a body for the enrollment, the commissioner of the Board was required by this circular to give his particular attention to the correction, revision, and preservation of the lists, and to the preparation of all reports and returns in regard to them, and to promptly forward to the Provost-Marshal-General's Office monthly reports of the corrections made in the enrollment.

Circular No. 39, series of 1864, is a reproduction and revision of Circular No. 24 of the same series.

The importance of correcting the enrollment lists had at that time become apparent to every one, and it was the interest, both of the United States and of the citizens, that all who were liable to military duty should be enrolled, and all who were unfit for duty should be stricken off. A universal interest in this matter prevailed in the district, and immediate steps were taken to perfect the enrollment lists.

By direction of the acting provost-marshal-general of the State, dated November 21, 1864, a copy of the enrollment lists of each sub-district was made and placed in the hands of a committee composed of the most worthy and reliable citizens in each of the several sub-districts, and public notice given in the newspapers published in the several counties comprising the Congressional district, notifying the citizens that a deputy provost-marshal be sent to each county to confer with them as to the most practicable mode of correcting the enrollment lists, and furnish them with full information in the premises.

Alleghany County being remote from the district headquarters, it was deemed advisable to send the assistant surgeon of the Board with the deputy provost-marshal of said county to the several sub-districts thereof, with instructions to examine persons claiming to be stricken from the enrollment on account of physical disability and all other causes, and notice was accordingly given that they would attend at certain places on certain days to examine the claims of all persons applying to be stricken from the enrollment lists.

By this means Alleghany County was thoroughly canvassed.

The deputy provost-marshal of Washington County operated among the committees constituted as aforesaid in said county, and where claims were made on account of physical disability they were referred to the Board of Enrollment for their examination.

The deputy provost-marshal of Carroll County operated in a similar manner in said county, and the Board had immediate supervision of Frederick County, as the district headquarters was in said county.

When the various committees had completed the revision of the enrollment in the several sub-districts they reported their result in writing, under oath duly attested before a justice of the peace, to the Board of Enrollment, and the Board, in the presence of the deputy provost-marshal of the county and the respective committees, carefully examined and decided upon each case reported in the respective sub-districts.

This mode of correcting the enrollment was found to be effective, and if conducted with proper care and scrutiny by the Board of Enrollment I can see no objection to it.

ASSIGNMENT OF QUOTAS.

The following is a tabular statement of the quotas assigned to the Fourth Congressional District of Maryland under the several calls for which drafts were made in said district, viz:

The quota under the call of March 14, 1864, and deficiencies under former calls	1,573
The quota under the call of July 18, 1864	2,069
The quota under the call of December 19, 1864.	1,750

RECONSTRUCTION OF THE QUOTAS.

The quota under the call of July 18, 1864, as originally announced by the acting assistant provost-marshal-general of the State, on the 25th day of July, 1864 (2,069 men), was reduced to 1,843 men by reconstruction of said quota, based upon the corrected enrollment as reported August 31, 1864.

THE MODE OF MAKING THE DRAFT.

The quota under the call for which a draft was to be made having been ascertained and announced, the provost-marshal gave public notice in the newspapers that a draft would be made on a certain day, and notified the Governor of the State, by telegraph and by mail, that a draft would be made, giving the day, the hour, and the place, and requesting him to acknowledge the receipt thereof by telegraph and by mail.

He also invited all prominent military and civil officers on duty in the vicinity, and some of the most prominent citizens, to be present to witness the drawing.

On the day of the draft the Board of Enrollment opened the envelopes containing the packages of tickets of the several sub-districts in the presence of those in attendance, and opened the envelope containing the cards of the first sub-district.

These cards were counted as they were placed in the box, for the purpose of ascertaining whether they agreed with the number written on the envelope.

This having been done, the commissioner announced that the draft for the first sub-district for so many men would commence.

A trusty person was selected by the provost-marshal and blindfolded, and drew from the box a single card, which he handed to the commissioner, who read aloud the name on it.

The clerk immediately entered the name drawn on a list previously prepared, opposite No. 1.

Thus the draft was continued until the required number of names was drawn, when the cards remaining in the box were taken out and counted, so as to verify the whole number originally put in.

Great care was taken to enter the names on the roll exactly in the order in which they were drawn.

The remaining sub-districts were proceeded with in like manner.

DRAFTS UNDER VARIOUS CALLS.

Draft under the call of March 14, 1864.—The quota of the Fourth Congressional District of Maryland, after deducting all credits for enlistments up to May 10, 1864, under the call of March 14, 1864, and deficiencies under former calls, being 1,463 men, the acting assistant provost-marshal-general of the State directed, by a communication dated May 16, 1864, that a draft for that number of men be made on the 19th day of May, 1864.

This number (1,463) was assigned to the several sub-districts in the Congressional district in proportion to the number enrolled therein, allowing all additional credits that may have accrued to the sub-districts entitled to them.

The arrangements having been completed, a draft was made, in compliance with the instructions of the acting assistant provost-marshal-general of the State, May 19, 1864, for 1,362 men, that number being the deficiency remaining to be raised under said call, and the drawing was continued from day to day until the 28th instant, when the whole number had been drawn.

The number obtained from this drawing not being sufficient to fill the quota, a second drawing was made June 23, 24, and 25, 1864, for 632 men.

The number obtained from the 632 men drafted in the second drawing still being insufficient to fill the quota, a third drawing was made July 29 and 30, 1864, and August 5 and 6, 1864, for the remaining deficiency, which was 294 men and 100 per cent. in addition.

The quota was not entirely filled in some of the sub-districts from this draft, but no additional drawing was made.

Draft under the call of July 18, 1864.—The quota under the call of July 18, 1864, was 1,843 men, which number was distributed among the several sub-districts in proportion to the number enrolled in each.

Orders having been received from the acting assistant provost-marshal-general of the State, under date of September 13, 1864, to draft for the deficiency under the call of July 18, 1864, commencing with the deficient sub-districts, where there was the least volunteering, a draft was made September 19, 20, and 21, 1864, for 472 men and 100 per cent. in addition, to fill the quotas in said sub-districts.

Not having obtained a sufficient number of men to fill the quota by said drawing, a second drawing was made December 7 and 16, 1864, for 159 men and 100 per cent. additional.

The number obtained from this drawing still being insufficient to fill the quotas, a third drawing was made January 23, 1865, for forty-one men and 100 per cent. in addition, to fill the quota of the remaining deficient sub-districts.

It having become apparent that sub-district No. 41 (Hauvers) could not fill its quota by recruiting, a draft was also made in said sub-district for five men and 100 per cent. additional.

The quota under this call having been furnished by most of the sub-districts by recruiting and otherwise, no additional drawing was made.

Draft under call of December 19, 1864.—The quota under the call of December 19, 1864, as announced by the acting assistant provost-marshal-general of the State January 25, 1865, was 1,750 men.

This number was assigned to the several sub-districts of the Congressional district in proportion to the number of persons enrolled in each.

Great activity was displayed in recruiting for this call, and the quotas of most of the sub-districts were rapidly filled.

A draft was made, however, on the 5th and 6th of April, 1865, in those of the deficient sub-districts where little or no effort had been made to fill the quotas, for 355 men and 100 per cent. in addition.

While the examination of these men was progressing an order was received from the acting assistant provost-marshal-general of the State, dated April 14, 1865, suspending recruiting and drafting, and all examinations were immediately suspended.

NOTIFICATION OF DRAFTED MEN.

Previous to the day of draft a sufficient number of blank notices were filled up as far as possible.

As soon as the drawing commenced a clerk designated for the purpose inserted the names of the drafted men in the proper place in the notice.

As soon as the drawing was completed the Board of Enrollment determined upon the time for drafted men to report, care being taken to notify persons drafted in such manner that the drafted men would be required to report for examination in squads of manageable size and at successive convenient periods, so as to avoid the confusion incident to too great a number reporting on the same day.

It was found expedient to require 120 men to report each day. Of this number from 50 to 75 would usually report, which was about as many men as could be examined with proper care.

To avoid embarrassment it was necessary to notify those drawn in the quota to report considerably in advance of those drawn in the per centum, in order to allow time to look up the delinquents in the quota, and thereby protect those drawn in the per cent. from being improperly held to service, it being the intention of the Bureau to hold drafted men in the order in which they were drawn.

As soon as the notices for drafted men were prepared and signed they were placed in the hands of the deputy provost-marshals of the respective counties, who were made responsible for their prompt delivery to the proper enrolling officers, and they were also required to see that they were served on the proper parties without delay.

All persons serving notices were required to report the names of the persons notified, the day on which the notices were served, and the place where served, and whether delivered to the party or left at his last place of residence; and if drafted men were absent, where they could probably be found, together with any additional information that might be useful in enforcing the draft.

It was also made the duty of deputies, special agents, detectives, and enrolling officers to see that drafted men reported promptly on the day stated in their notices, and if they failed to do so to arrest them and deliver them to the provost-marshal.

It was also enjoined on all good citizens to aid these officers in the performance of this duty.

THE MANNER OF RECEIVING AND EXAMINING DRAFTED MEN.

When the drafted men reported their names were registered in a book for the purpose in the order in which they presented themselves, and they were received in a private room in squads of three men at a time and stripped, and the first man on the list was admitted to the examining room, where the Board of Enrollment was in session.

The man to be examined was asked his name, age, where he resided, in what sub-district he had been drafted, and whether he made any claim to exemption.

If he made a claim which did not require an examination as to his physical or mental condition, the provost-marshal proceeded to investigate the nature of the claim; and having heard the statement of the claimant, and taken the proof, if any was offered, he submitted the case to the Board for its action.

If it was a case requiring a physical examination, the man was examined by the surgeon in the presence of the other members of the Board, and the result of the examination was reported by the surgeon with his views, and the Board made a decision.

If the man was granted an exemption by the Board, a record of the examination and action of the Board was made and the proper papers furnished to the man.

If held to service, he was asked whether he desired to furnish a substitute; and if so, what extension of time he wished.

If he elected to furnish a substitute and desired an extension of time, he was granted a few days if he was known to be a reliable man, or had reliable men to vouch for him; otherwise he was uniformed and sent to rendezvous, and was allowed to furnish a substitute at any time before being sent from the general rendezvous.

The examination of drafted men was conducted with great care, as the Board of Enrollment was constantly exposed to impositions attempted to be practiced by drafted men who would feign diseases and disqualifications when none existed.

The Board strived, on the other hand, to avoid doing injustice to those who, from inexperience and total ignorance of business, were unable to present their cases with faithfulness to themselves, and who, although they may have had a good claim to exemption, were ignorant of it, and were often disposed from a false delicacy tc waive an examination.

It was the practice of the Board to examine every man and determine for themselves his fitness or unfitness for military duty, thereby avoiding complaints and applications for redress by drafted men who might afterward conceive the impression that if they had been examined they would have been exempted.

It is the opinion of this office that drafted men should not be allowed to waive an examination.

THE MANNER OF DISPOSING OF DRAFTED MEN.

When drafted men were held by the Board and elected to render personal service, their descriptive rolls were made out in triplicate, as required by paragraph 73, Revised Regulations, and they were uniformed and sent under guard to the rendezvous, where they were comfortably quartered, subsisted, and guarded by the commandant of the post until a sufficient number had accumulated to forward a squad to the general rendezvous.

Where they offered substitutes and the substitutes were accepted the record in their cases was completed, and they were furnished with the proper certificate of exemption and released.

THE MANNER OF FORWARDING DRAFTED MEN.

When a sufficient number of drafted men had accumulated at the rendezvous to justify forwarding a squad to the general rendezvous descriptive rolls were made out in duplicate for the party.

A sufficient guard was detailed to take charge of the men and conduct them to general rendezvous and deliver them to the commandant thereof with the rolls, one copy of which was retained by him and the other returned with a receipt for the party as delivered to him on the back.

The returned copy was forwarded to the Provost-Marshal-General's Office at the end of each month. (See paragraph 74, Revised Regulations.)

DETAILS OF THE OPERATION OF SUBSTITUTION.

Enrolled and drafted men were authorized by law to furnish substitutes.

Enrolled men were allowed to furnish prior to draft substitutes not liable to draft nor at the time in the military or naval service of the United States. (See section 4, act approved February 24, 1864.)

Drafted men could, before the time fixed for their appearance for duty at the draft rendezvous, furnish acceptable substitutes under the following rules and regulations, viz:

That if the substitute was not liable to draft the person who furnished him was exempt during the time the substitute was not liable to draft, not exceeding the time for which he was drafted; and if such substitute was liable to draft the name of the person furnishing him was again placed on the rolls and he was liable to draft on future calls, but not until the enrollment was exhausted, and his exemption could not exceed the term for which he was drafted. (See section 5, act approved February 24, 1864.)

When substitutes for enrolled or drafted men were presented to the Board of Enrollment the provost-marshal put the substitute on oath and gave him a careful examination as to whether there was any impediment to his entering the military service, and if no objection was found to exist he was stripped and examined as to his suitableness in every respect for the military service, which was determined by the enrolling Board in the manner prescribed for examining recruits.

If the substitute proved to be acceptable he was then enlisted into the service of the United States, and the Board gave the person who furnished the substitute a certificate of exemption. (See paragraphs 96, 97, 98, and 99, Revised Regulations Provost-Marshal-General's Bureau, and Circular No. 33, series of 1863.)

As soon as the substitute was enlisted the money received by him was counted in his presence, put in an envelope, and sealed up, the amount and the name of the substitute indorsed on the envelope, and the amount also entered in the column of "remarks" on his descriptive roll.

The money was kept by the provost-marshal until the substitute was forwarded to the general rendezvous, when he put it into the hands of the officer in charge of the squad, who delivered the money with the men to the commandant of the general rendezvous and took his receipt for the same.

Section 16 of the act approved March 3, 1865, provided that persons who were drafted for one year and who furnished substitutes for three years were exempt from military duty during the time for which such substitutes were not liable to draft, not exceeding the time for which such substitutes were mustered into the service, anything in the act of February 24, 1864, to the contrary notwithstanding.

Substitutes were forwarded to the general rendezvous in the same manner as drafted men.

RECRUITING ASSOCIATIONS.

Section 23, act approved March 3, 1865, provided that any person or persons enrolled in any sub-district could, after a notice of a draft and before the same had taken place, cause to be mustered into the service of the United States such number of recruits not subject to draft as they deemed expedient, which recruits stood to the credit of the persons thus causing them to be mustered in and were taken as substitutes for such persons or so many of them as were drafted to the extent of the number of such recruits and in the order designated by the principals at the time such recruits were thus, as aforesaid, mustered in.

When the number of recruits furnished by the association exceeded the number of men drafted from such association the excess, though credited to the sub-districts, created no claim for the exemption of any person whomsoever.

Members of these associations who were drafted and secured exemption under the twenty-third section aforesaid were exempt from that draft, but were liable to be drafted on future calls.

Recruits furnished by associations and taken as substitutes for drafted men who were members of the association were credited at the time of muster in to the sub-district to which the association belonged.

The recruits presented by said associations were received, examined, and disposed of as volunteers.

REPRESENTATIVE RECRUITS.

Representative recruits were received and enlisted in accordance with Circular No. 25, Provost-Marshal-General's Office, series of 1864, and were disposed of as substitutes.

VOLUNTEERING—THE MANNER OF PROCURING RECRUITS.

Various means were resorted to when the different calls were announced to encourage recruiting. Large posters, setting forth the inducements offered to enter the service, were displayed throughout the district, and patriotic appeals were made through the columns of the newspapers.

Letters were written to prominent citizens urging them to give the matter their attention.

Deputies and special agents were sent among the people to exhort them to renewed efforts. But the most effective mode of recruiting was the announcement of the call for troops and the assignment of the quotas to the respective sub-districts, followed with a notice that unless the quota was raised by volunteering a draft would be made.

This being done, in most instances draft committees were formed in each of the sub-districts, a local bounty offered, and the business of furnishing substitutes prior to draft and procuring recruits to the credit of the respective sub-districts was pushed forward with spirit and energy for the purpose of filling the quotas of the sub-districts so as to avoid the draft.

The experience of this office shows conclusively that bounties paid in hand at the time the recruit entered the service operated as the greatest stimulant to volunteering. But I would here state that it is all important to the service that men should be restrained from deserting by making bounties payable in installments, one installment payable at the termination of the term of service.

The premium of $25 and $15 paid to any person who would present an acceptable recruit, which was authorized by circular letter dated War Department, Adjutant-General's Office, October 24, 1863, was, in my judgment, a judicious arrangement.

These premiums afforded to persons a fair compensation for services rendered, and energetic men were induced to engage in procuring recruits.

I would respectfully state that in the spring of 1864 recruiting was successfully prosecuted in this district by this means.

It has also been found advantageous to recruiting to send recruiting parties into the district when a draft is pending.

These parties formed a nucleus, and by the co-operation of those who were liable to draft they were enabled to recruit successfully.

THE MANNER OF EXAMINING RECRUITS.

The Board of Enrollment was guided in the examination of recruits by the regulations for the recruiting service.

It was found necessary, however, from circumstances developed by the progress of the war to exercise the greatest amount of caution and throw every safeguard it was possible around this branch of the service in order to prevent improper and fraudulent enlistments.

To this end it was the practice of the Board of Enrollment when the recruit was presented to put him on oath and subject him to a close examination, with the view of learning his history before having him stripped for a medical examination.

If the man proved to be acceptable in all other respects, he was then stripped, and the examining surgeon gave him a most careful medical examination, in the presence of the Board of Enrollment only, in the daytime, in a large and well-lighted room, where he was required to walk about and exercise his limbs briskly. If he was rejected by the surgeon as physically unfit for service, his descriptive list was taken, and any prominent marks on his person were noted, together with any information that might be useful in making up the medical statistics of examinations.

If the man was found to be suitable for the military service, his descriptive list was taken in a book for that purpose, and a full and complete record of his examination was taken by the examining surgeon. The recruit was then sent into an adjoining room for enlistment.

ENLISTING RECRUITS.

The recruit having been accepted, his enlistment papers were made out in triplicate and properly signed, and he was duly enlisted into the service of the United States, in accordance with the recruiting regulations, and his enlistment papers were disposed of as directed by Circular No. 22, Provost-Marshal-General's Office, series of 1864.

A record book was kept of all enlistments into the service of the United States. (See Circular 22, Provost-Marshal-General's Office, series of 1864.)

THE MANNER OF MUSTERING VOLUNTEERS.

The recruits having been examined and duly enlisted, the provost-marshal then explained to them the nature and duties of the service and mustered them into the U. S. service in accordance with the mustering regulations.

Muster and descriptive rolls were made out in quadruplicate and disposed of as required by Circular No. 22, Provost-Marshal-General's Office, series of 1864.

THE MANNER OF PROVIDING FOR VOLUNTEERS.

As soon as volunteers were mustered into the U. S. service they were sent under guard to the rendezvous, where they were quartered in a commodious building and subsisted and guarded by the commandant of the post until a sufficient number had accumulated to forward a detachment to the general rendezvous.

THE MANNER OF FORWARDING VOLUNTEERS.

When a sufficient number of recruits had accumulated to justify forwarding a squad, a muster and descriptive roll was made in duplicate for the detachment and sent with the party to the general rendezvous. One copy was retained by the commandant and the other was receipted by him on the back for the number of men delivered and returned. Volunteers were in all cases forwarded under guard.

Any money received by volunteers at the time they enlisted was counted in their presence and placed in an envelope, and the amount and the name of the recruit indorsed on the envelope.

The amount of money was also entered on the muster and descriptive roll of the man in the column of remarks, and the money was retained by the provost-marshal and sent to the general rendezvous with the man by the officer in charge of the detachment, who turned it over to the commanding officer and took his receipt.

Many of the volunteers who were raised in and credited to this district were mustered into the service by the different assistant commissaries of musters who were at the time on duty within the district.

THE MANNER OF CREDITING VOLUNTEERS.

Volunteers who were not liable to draft were credited to the locality to which they elected to give their credit. Persons who were liable to draft were credited to the locality in which they were enrolled.

The sub-district, town, county, Congressional district, and State to which they were credited were noted in the column of remarks on their muster and descriptive rolls. All credits for volunteers were reported to the acting assistant provost-marshal-general of the State every ten days.

THE MANNER OF ARRESTING DESERTERS.

The importance of securing the arrest of all deserters and stragglers from the Army was so apparent that especial attention was given to this branch of the service.

The deputy provost-marshals of the respective counties and the special agents were required to give this part of their duties careful attention and see that deserters were not permitted to pass through the district without being apprehended.

In order to provide against their escape it was found advisable to authorize a large number of citizens to arrest deserters, whose remuneration was the $30 reward allowed for the apprehension and delivery of deserters.

The persons so authorized operated in various parts of the district, under the supervision of the deputy provost-marshals, who were required to see that all places through which deserters would likely attempt to escape were diligently guarded, and that a sufficient force was on hand to intercept them and insure their apprehension and delivery to the proper officer.

Great care had to be exercised in the selection of persons of courage, integrity, and energy to arrest deserters during the last year of the war, as large bounties were paid to persons entering the Army, and there was constant danger of deserters offering to the persons authorized to arrest them a larger amount than the $30 paid for the arrest of deserters; and it was found prudent and judicious to hold those making arrests to a strict accountability for their conduct.

All persons who were delivered as deserters at this office received a careful and fair examination as to their intention to abandon the service, and when they alleged with any reasonable show of truth that they could prove their innocence, the proper officers were communicated with and the merits of the case ascertained before final action was taken.

When there was a reasonable doubt it was the practice of this office to give the prisoner the benefit thereof and turn him over as a straggler, instead of a deserter, with proper explanatory remarks in the column of remarks on the descriptive list forwarded with him.

Special care has been exercised not to oppress any soldier arrested by extorting from him admissions which would criminate him, by inflicting punishment, or examining him with unreasonable severity.

It was of rare occurrence, however, that soldiers who were arrested as deserters failed, upon examination, to give correct information as to the company and regiment to which they belonged.

I could easily conceive the importance and necessity of announcing the instructions relative to the examination of deserters, contained in the communication dated Provost-Marshal-General's Bureau, January 26, 1865.

It is the opinion of this office that the reward of $30 allowed by General Orders, No. 325, dated War Department, Adjutant-General's Office, Washington, D. C., September 28, 1863, is a fair remuneration to the party making the arrest, and that a less amount would have proved detrimental to the service.

All deserters delivered at this office were turned over, immediately after their examination, to the commandant of the post, with duplicate descriptive rolls, one of which was receipted by him and returned to this office and forwarded, with the monthly report of deserters arrested, to the Provost-Marshal-General.

In every case where a soldier was arrested and brought to this office as a deserter, and found upon examination to be such, duplicate vouchers (Form 21) for the reward of $30 were made out in favor of the person delivering the deserter, and that amount was in each case charged upon the descriptive list forwarded with the deserter.

Since the organization of this office the following number of deserters and stragglers have been apprehended and turned over to the military authorities, viz:

Deserters arrested	978
Stragglers arrested	55
Total	1,033

I am convinced from experience and observation that the prompt arrest of deserters, and their speedy return to their regiments, and the stoppage of the $30 reward against their pay, had the most salutary effect in restraining enlisted men from abandoning the service.

THE MANNER OF KEEPING RECORDS.

Record of deserters arrested.—A book was kept in which the descriptions of all deserters received were entered, with such dates and remarks as were proper to complete, as far as practicable, the histories of the arrests and disposition made of the men.

Stragglers were arrested and disposed of and reported in the same manner as deserters, but with proper explanatory remarks in each case.

No reward was allowed for the arrest of stragglers.

Record of drafted men.—A book was kept in which an exact and complete roll of persons drawn in the draft was entered.

This book was ruled and headed to correspond with the descriptive roll of drafted men. (Form 33.)

The disposition which was made of drafted men was noted in this book in the column of remarks, and as far as practicable their military history completed.

Record of public property seized.—A book ruled with the following headings was kept, in which to record all public property seized in the hands of unauthorized persons, and turned into the Quartermaster's Department by this office, viz:

Number or quantity, articles seized, when, where, from whom, by whom, condition, estimated value, disposition, to whom turned over, when, where, remarks.

Record of the enrollment.—The enrollment was consolidated on consolidated enrollment lists, by sub-districts alphabetically arranged, and bound in volumes of suitable size for convenient reference.

Record of the proceedings of the Board of Enrollment.—A fair record of each day's proceedings of the Board of Enrollment was kept by the recorder of the Board in a book for that purpose.

Record of letters sent.—A letter book was kept in which all letters sent were recorded and numbered in the order of their dates.

This book was kept in accordance with instructions for officers of the Adjutant-General's Department.

Record of letters received.—A book was kept in which a record of all letters received was made, in accordance with the mode adopted by the Adjutant-General's Office.

This book also contained reference to the indorsement book in all cases where a record of indorsements was made in the indorsement book, and was indexed.

Record of indorsements.—A book of indorsements and memoranda was kept, in which all indorsements on communications referred to this office and those made by this office were recorded.

Record of telegrams.—A book was kept in which all telegrams received were recorded and numbered in the order of their dates.

Record of special orders.—A book in which all special orders issued from this office were recorded was kept, in the usual form of preserving such records.

The orders were recorded in the order of their number and date.

MEDICAL RECORDS.

Record of the examination of volunteers.—A book was kept by the surgeon of the Board, in which a full record of the description of all recruits who had been examined by the Board of Enrollment and the result of such examinations were recorded, together with any additional information that might be useful to the Bureau.

Record of the examination of enrolled men.—A book was kept by the surgeon of the Board, in which was recorded the description of the enrolled men who applied to be stricken from the enrollment lists, with the result of the examinations and the decision of the Board in each case.

Record of the examination of drafted men.—A book was kept by the surgeon of the Board, in which the description and result of the examination of drafted men were recorded in each case, care being taken in all cases where the persons examined had been exempted to give the particular section of paragraph 85, Revised Regulations Provost-Marshal-General's Bureau, under which he was exempted.

Record of the examination of substitutes.—A book was kept by the surgeon of the Board, in which the record of the description and result of the examination of all substitutes was made, and if accepted the name of the principals for whom they became substitutes.

Tabular statement of the examination of volunteers, enrolled men, drafted men, and substitutes.

Classes.	Number examined.	Number rejected.	Number accepted.
Volunteers	831	62	769
Enrolled men	2,943	1,829	1,114
Drafted men	2,654	1,042	1,612
Substitutes	704	143	561
Total	7,132	3,076	4,056

For further information on this subject attention is invited to the medical reports of the surgeon of the Board of Enrollment.

MANNER OF KEEPING AND SETTLING ACCOUNTS.

The following mode of keeping and settling accounts has been adopted as best suited to the business of this office:

The accounts having been examined and ascertained to be a proper charge against the United States, they were made out on the proper blank forms furnished by the Provost-Marshal-General's Bureau, in the manner prescribed by the Revised Regulations.

The following form has been adopted by this office for keeping the account of vouchers transmitted to the Provost-Marshal-General's Office for payment, and of checks received in payment thereof.

This form embraces a list of all vouchers forwarded during the month, each month being kept separately:

United States to vouchers, Dr.

Date of voucher.	No. of voucher.	Name of claimant.	Nature of account.	Amount.	When forwarded for payment.

United States by checks, Cr.

Date of voucher.	No. of check.	Name of receiver.	Nature of account.	Amount of check.	Amount of account.	Date of receipt of check.

In addition to the above form the following has been adopted for keeping the accounts of each individual separately, viz:

Name of person.			Dr.	Cr.
Date of receipt of check.	Date of voucher.	Nature of account.	To check.	By voucher.

The receipt of all checks issued by the Provost-Marshal-General's Bureau in payment of accounts transmitted from this office was immediately acknowledged on the proper form and the date of receipt recorded.

The checks were immediately transmitted to the persons in whose favor they were drawn, whose receipt for the same was obtained and filed in this office.

THE MANNER OF KEEPING ACCOUNT OF VOUCHERS ISSUED FOR APPREHENDING DESERTERS.

The following form was adopted to account for vouchers given for the apprehension and delivery of deserters, viz:

Date of voucher.	No. of voucher.	Name of claimant.	Amount.	When delivered.

Vouchers for the reward of $30 for the apprehension and delivery of deserters were given only in case the party arrested was found upon examination to be a deserter.

The vouchers were given to the persons who delivered the deserters to the provost-marshal.

Vouchers were not given to commissioned officers, deputy provost-marshals, special agents, nor salaried officers for the arrest of deserters.

Vouchers for the reward of $30 for the arrest of deserters were paid by the nearest disbursing quartermaster of the United States.

I would respectfully state, in connection with this subject, that the delay which usually attended the payment of vouchers for arresting, securing, and delivering deserters made it very difficult to secure the services of suitable persons for that duty. Those who were engaged in arresting deserters were compelled to dispose of the vouchers at a heavy discount to brokers, in order to obtain means to defray the current expenses incurred in making the arrests and transporting the deserters to the nearest provost-marshal, which was, in many instances, very great.

I would therefore respectfully suggest that the interest of the service, in my judgment, requires that provision should be made for the prompt payment of this class of vouchers, as the duty of arresting deserters is attended with great privation and risk and the reward of $30 greatly reduced by the expenses incurred.

It seems to me that this difficulty could be obviated by having these vouchers paid by a disbursing officer of the Provost-Marshal-General's Bureau instead of the disbursing quartermaster of the United States.

THE MANNER OF REPORTING CREDITS AND DEFICIENCIES.

Credits from all sources and deficiencies remaining were reported every ten days to the acting assistant provost-marshal-general of the State on the following form, to wit:

Sub-district.	Deficiency, by sub-district, in whole Congressional district.	Surplus, by sub-district, in whole Congressional district.	Source of credits.				Total credits during each ten days.	Total deficiency, by sub-district, in the whole Congressional district.	Surplus, by sub-district, in the whole Congressional district.	Number of men who have been sent to general rendezvous for whom receipts have been obtained.				Number of men who have been accepted into the Navy for whom receipts have been obtained.			Total receipted for.
			Substitutes for enrolled men prior to draft.	Drafted men held to service.	Substitutes for drafted men.	Surplus arising from draft under former calls.				Substitutes for enrolled men.	Drafted men held to service.	Substitutes for drafted men.	Surplus arising by draft under former calls.	Substitutes for enrolled men.	Drafted men.	Substitutes for drafted men.	

RETURN OF QUOTAS AND CREDITS.

A return of quotas and credits was made monthly on the blank form furnished for that purpose by the Provost-Marshal-General's Bureau.

This return embraced an exhibit, by sub-districts, of the quotas and deficiencies on the first day of the month for which it was made, the credits arising from all sources during the month, and the deficiency or surplus, as the case might be, at the end of the month.

THE MANNER OF PROVIDING, STORING, ISSUING, AND ACCOUNTING FOR CLOTHING.

A large quantity of clothing was received from the Quartermaster's Department soon after this office was established and receipted for by the provost-marshal.

This clothing was stored in a secure and dry store-room, from which it was taken in small quantities as it was needed for uniforming men.

A small quantity of each variety of clothing was kept on hand at the office of provost-marshal, where it was issued to volunteers, drafted men, and substitutes entering the service.

All persons to whom clothing was issued were required to sign receipt rolls (Form 52, Quartermaster-General's Department) in duplicate.

Returns of clothing were made to the Quartermaster-General's Department at the end of each month, on Form 51, Quartermaster-General's Department, accompanied by the receipt roll of clothing (Form 52, Quartermaster-General's Department) issued to men entering that month, as a voucher.

MONTHLY RETURNS AND REPORTS RENDERED TO THE PROVOST-MARSHAL-GENERAL.

The reports and returns required by paragraph 108, Revised Regulations of the Provost-Marshal-General's Bureau, were rendered by this office to the Provost-Marshal-General at the time and in the manner therein prescribed.

MONTHLY REPORT OF SUBSTITUTES AND RECRUITS WHO DESERTED FROM HEADQUARTERS.

Monthly reports of all substitutes and recruits who deserted from headquarters and en route to general rendezvous were made by this office, in compliance with Circular No. 30, Provost-Marshal-General's Office, series of 1864.

TRANSPORTATION.

Transportation was furnished by railroad companies and stage-coach lines on blank requisitions furnished by the Provost-Marshal-General's Office, properly filled up by this office.

After the requisitions were taken up by the company furnishing the transportation they were returned to this office, where they were examined, and if found to be correct the proper vouchers were made out on the proper blanks in favor of the company furnishing the transportation and given to the claimant for collection.

Transportation was furnished to drafted men on requisitions attached to the bottom of the notice of draft, signed by the provost-marshal.

Vouchers were made out for the transportation furnished on these requisitions in the same manner as those furnished by the Provost-Marshal-General, as above stated.

REPORTS OF DEBITS AND CREDITS.

Tri-monthly and monthly reports of debits and credits were rendered to the acting assistant provost-marshal-general of the State, giving the "credits for voluntary enlistments," "credits for enlistments in the Navy and Marine Corps," "credits by draft," "miscellaneous credits," &c., on blank forms furnished for that purpose.

ASSISTANT SURGEONS.

The duties of the surgeon of the Board of Enrollment having become too onerous, it was deemed necessary by the Provost-Marshal-General to assign to duty with him an assistant surgeon.

The following-named persons have been on duty in that capacity in this office:

Actg. Asst. Surg. H. M. Drach was assigned to duty June 14, 1864.

Actg. Asst. Surg. Robert H. Goldsmith relieved Actg. Asst. Surg. H. M. Drach June 23, 1864.

Actg. Asst. Surg. H. M. Drach relieved Actg. Asst. Surg. Robert H. Goldsmith August 2, 1864, and was relieved ——, 1865, and ordered to report to the medical director Eighth Army Corps, Baltimore, Md.

James Williard, M. D., was appointed assistant surgeon of the Board of Enrollment March 20, 1865, under the thirteenth section of the act of Congress approved February 24, 1864, but never entered upon duty.

A record of substitutes furnished by enrolled men prior to draft was kept in a book prepared for that purpose in the following form, viz:

Name of principal.	Name of substitute.	Army or Navy.	Mustered or enlisted.			Where credited.	Remarks.
			When.	Where.	By whom.		

DEPUTY PROVOST-MARSHALS.

The following-named persons were appointed deputy provost-marshals in the Fourth District of Maryland from time to time, to wit.*

See paragraph 11, Regulations Provost-Marshal-General's Bureau, and paragraph 138, Revised Regulations Provost-Marshal-General's Bureau.

SYSTEM OF SUBSTITUTION.

The system of substitution authorized by the enrollment act of March 3, 1863, and the acts amendatory thereof operated, in my judgment, greatly to the detriment of the service. In intelligence, moral

*Omitted.

character, and indeed in almost every respect, the principals were greatly superior to the substitutes furnished by them for the military service.

Men of character would not enlist as substitutes; hence a very unreliable and worthless class of persons offered as such, and the result was that a large number of very inferior men thus entered the service and either deserted or became a burden to it; and in many instances where they deserted it was for the sole object of re-entering the service with a view to obtain an additional bounty.

Another objection to substitution was the temptation held out by it to persons to engage in the business of furnishing substitutes, and thereby fall into every species of villainy to reap the reward that the business might yield, directing their operations exclusively to their own emolument.

It is a well-established fact that persons have entered the service a number of times within a very brief period and for a large sum each time. In this fraudulent procedure I have no doubt they were often prompted and aided by a class of men known as "substitute brokers."

And it has been equally well established that substitute brokers as a class were unscrupulous men, having an eye exclusively to money-making, and with very few exceptions felt no interest in the good of the service.

That substitute brokers and their runners oppressed the principals and robbed the substitutes as far as they could without detection is equally true.

The runners, as they were denominated, were employed by the substitute brokers to procure substitutes for their agencies, and were the most odious and detestable class of men known to the service.

The system of furnishing substitutes was denounced by the ablest officers of the American Revolution as very injurious to their cause, and I have no doubt it will be discovered to have proved equally so in the recent war.

SPECIAL AGENTS.

The following-named persons were appointed special agents in accordance with paragraph 12 of the Regulations for the Government of the Provost-Marshal-General's Bureau for 1863, and paragraph 138, Revised Regulations Provost-Marshal-General's Bureau, to wit.*

In addition to the above eighty-four men were authorized to arrest deserters, whose compensation was only the reward of $30 allowed for the apprehension and delivery of deserters. These men were authorized with the understanding that they were also to collect public property, &c., in addition to arresting deserters without any additional pay.

STATEMENT OF PUBLIC PROPERTY SEIZED.

The following is a statement of the property belonging to the Government which was gathered up by this office and restored to the proper officers, as required by section 23 of the act of March 3, 1863.*

There were many articles of little or no value recovered, in addition to what is above reported, which it is deemed impracticable to report in this statement.

---

* Omitted.

THE DIFFICULTIES ENCOUNTERED.

The principal difficulties encountered in performing the duties of this office consisted in obtaining suitable quarters for the transaction of the business of the office (which has been treated at length under the head of establishment of headquarters), and in procuring enrolling officers.

The chief difficulty, however, was that of obtaining enrolling officers, but I am unable to discover any more practicable mode of making the enrollment than the one adopted. Surely no one could be more competent to make the enrollment than a person who resides in the locality and is familiar with the names and residences of those to be enrolled; and it only remains with the provost-marshal in making the appointment to select the officer with reference to strict integrity and capacity and urge upon him the importance and necessity of accepting the appointment.

It is my opinion that the enrolling officers should be examined by the provost-marshal as to their fitness before entering upon the duties. This would, in my judgment, have prevented much of the embarrassment which has been the result of incompetency.

MERITS AND DEMERITS OF THE LAWS, REGULATIONS, AND ORDERS GOVERNING THE PROVOST-MARSHAL-GENERAL'S BUREAU.

I have not been able, as far as my experience and observation have gone, to discover any serious defects in existing laws, regulations, and orders governing the Provost-Marshal-General's Bureau. On the contrary, I have been impressed with their practical adaptation to the wants and interests of the service.

The only defect, in my judgment, which I have discovered in the laws which I deem of sufficient importance to mention is the restriction imposed by section 14, act approved March 3, 1865, touching credits to sub-districts, &c. This section reads as follows:

That hereafter all persons mustered into the military or naval service, whether as volunteers, substitutes, representatives, or otherwise, shall be credited to the State, and to the ward, township, precinct, or other enrollment sub-district where such persons belong by actual residence (if such persons have an actual residence within the United States), and where such persons were or shall be enrolled (if liable to enrollment).

* * * * * *

This section, if I give it a correct interpretation, disqualifies persons who have an actual residence in one sub-district, or persons who have been enrolled, from being credited to another under any circumstances. The protection afforded to persons enrolled in one sub-district against the encroachments of the people enrolled in others is, in my judgment, proper until the quota of that sub-district, under the call then pending, has been filled, but after this has been accomplished it is my opinion that all persons residing or who may be enrolled in such sub-district should be allowed to enlist to the credit of any other locality they may elect in the Congressional district.

The reason which prompts me to make this suggestion is that the citizens of most of the sub-districts have heretofore offered local bounties as an inducement to persons to enlist to the credit of their respective sub-districts until the quotas thereof under the pending call have been filled, and the State and the several counties have also offered large bounties to persons who would enlist and be credited as part of the quota under said call.

When the quota of any sub-district has been filled persons enlisting to the credit thereof in excess of the quota receive no bounty from these sources.

The bounties in sub-districts, the quotas of which have been filled, having ceased, persons residing or enrolled therein have no inducement to enlist to the credit thereof, and if they are not permitted to enlist to the credit of localities where the quotas have not been raised, and when bounties are still being offered, they will remain out of the service, and it will thereby suffer.

And if persons enrolled in one sub-district should, after the quota thereof had been filled, enlist to the credit of another, their names would then be stricken from the enrollment list and no injury could be done to the sub-district in which they were enrolled in assigning quotas under future calls.

I have no suggestions to make in regard to the regulations and orders in addition to those already expressed in preceding portions of this report.

RESULTS OF DRAFT UNDER THE DIFFERENT CALLS.

Call of March 14, 1864, and deficiencies under former calls.

Credits:	
By white volunteers	86
By colored volunteers	2
By veterans	69
By seamen	43
By draft	1,245
By substitutes for enrolled men	8
Total	1,453

Call of July 18, 1864.

Credits:	
By surplus under former calls	191
By reconstruction of quotas—by revision of enrollment	226
By naval enlistments	621
By white volunteers	239
By colored volunteers	203
By seamen	81
By marines	27
By regulars	3
By representative recruits	1
By drafted men	120
By substitutes for drafted men	166
By substitutes for enrolled men	169
By veteran volunteers	80
Total	2,127

Call of December 19, 1864.

Credits:	
By white volunteers	906
By colored volunteers	21
By enlistments in the Regular Army	3
By seamen	67
By drafted men held to service	42
By drafted men who paid commutation	24
By substitutes for drafted men	48
By substitutes for enrolled men	373
Total	1,484
Whole number of men credited	5,064

I am, general, very respectfully, your obedient servant,

HENRY C. NAILL,

Captain and Provost-Marshal, Fourth District of Maryland.

Document No. 13.

Final report of the surgeon of the Board of Enrollment of the Twelfth District of Ohio, Circleville, June 15, 1865.

Prov. Mar.'s Office, Twelfth District of Ohio,
Circleville, June 15, 1865.

General: In obedience to instructions I have the honor to submit the following report:

My experience as surgeon of the Board of Enrollment of the Twelfth District of Ohio dates from May 10, 1864.

The first drafting done in this district was commenced on the 12th of May, 1864, to fill a deficiency of 654 men under the call of March 14, 1864.

Since the date of this connection with the department, under the several calls of March, July, and November, 1864, the following number of physical examinations of recruits, substitutes, drafted men, and enrolled men have been made, and the results of which are shown by Tables Nos. 1, 2, 3, 4, 5, 6, 7, and 8.

Table No. 1 shows the total number physically examined, the total number actually appearing before the Board, the total number actually and constructively examined, and the ratio rejected and exempted for all causes, and for physically disability of each class, respectively.

Table No. 2 shows the number of each class and total examined, the number of each class, total number and the ratio rejected and exempted per 1,000 examined under each section of paragraph 85, the number and ratio rejected and exempted for other causes, and total number and ratio rejected and exempted.

Table No. 3 shows the nativity, average measurements of the chest, average heights, and ages of recruits, substitutes, and drafted men examined from July 4, 1864, to April 30, 1865.

Table No. 4 shows the number of recruits and substitutes examined from July 4, 1864, to April 30, 1865; the average measurements of the chest and average heights and ages of those accepted as compared with the rejected; the number, average measurements of the chest, heights, and ages of the natives of Ohio accepted and rejected as compared with the natives of other States and countries, and the average measurements of the chest, heights, and ages of the total number examined.

Table No. 5 shows the total number physically examined, the number exempted for hernia and its classification, and the ratio rejected per 1,000 physically examined of recruits, substitutes, and drafted and enrolled men.

Table No. 6 shows the number of recruits and substitutes, natives of Ohio, of less age than twenty years; the number, twenty and not exceeding forty-five years of age, and the ratio rejected per 1,000 examined of each; the number of drafted men examined of forty and less than forty-five; the number under forty years of age, and the ratio exempted per 1,000 examined of each class.

Table No. 7 shows the colored recruits and substitutes examined from July 4, 1864, to April 30, 1865; the number rejected; causes of rejection and ratio rejected per 1,000 examined.

Table No. 8 shows the number examined, the average measurements of the chest, height, and age of colored Americans and white Americans; colored aliens and white aliens; total number examined, and average measurements of the chest, height, and age.

In the presentation of these observations the classification and order of disability as given in paragraph 85, Revised Regulations Provost-Marshal-General's Bureau, for drafted men, has been adopted for recruits and substitutes. In doing so it is understood to embrace the diseases, but not in that specific degree as applied to drafted men.

The ratio of rejections of substitutes has been much greater than recruits, or the exemptions of drafted men. A large per cent. of this class of applicants for the service has been composed of bounty-jumpers, convicts, alien thieves, deserters, half-starved paupers, broken-down libertines, and drunkards—persons having no principle in themselves or interest in the Government, and who have been spirited from place to place as mere chattels in the hands of speculators and unprincipled brokers; while recruits are mostly from the young and resident class of laboring population, and have to some extent been selected by a partial examination of the recruiting officer previous to enlistment.

The ratio of exemptions of drafted men for physical and mental disability will always appear much greater than the rejections made of recruits if based upon the number physically examined, but much less if made upon the number appearing before the Board, or number constructively examined. The difference in the number actually reporting or constructively examined and the number physically examined is a material one. In all calculations upon the former it is presumed that the disabled drafted man never fails to report for examination; and all others appearing before the Board, furnishing substitutes, evidence of alienage, unsuitableness of age, incorrect enrollment, and other causes, are physically not disqualified for military service; and to base the comparative ratio of physical disqualification upon numbers not physically examined may erroneously show a much less degree of infirmity than really exists, while the latter always exhibits an excess of the correct number.

If the object is to obtain the ratio of disqualification in any given number of enrolled or drafted men, it then becomes necessary to embrace all disqualifying causes in the determination of that number.

In these reported rejections of recruits and substitutes there are included other causes than physical and mental—as want of stature, under age, over age, and bad character; all which are denominated legal and moral causes. Quite a large per cent. of rejected recruits and more than half of all the rejections of substitutes come under this head. Therefore, to place the several classes seemingly upon the same basis, a column of ratios rejected per 1,000 for physical and mental disability of all actually, as well as a column of all actually and constructively, examined is given. But the inequality is not removed, as a large per cent. of drafted men entering into reports as exempted, and consequently examined, include the "100-days' men," those paying commutation under draft prior to the act approved July 4, 1864, and drafted men released by voluntary enlistments, all of whom are examined constructively; and while they greatly diminish the ratio exempted for physical and mental causes by increasing the number examined, fail to add their just proportion of existing physical and mental disability. The number examined, including only recruits, substitutes, and drafted men, amounts to 5,484. Of this number 743 were rejected and exempted for physical and mental disability, showing a ratio of disqualification of 135.4 per 1,000 examined. Separated into classes, the ratios rejected and exempted per 1,000 examined are as follows:

Recruits	128.8
Substitutes	156.8
Drafted men	135.1

This shows a less ratio rejected for physical and mental causes of drafted men than actually exists, and but for the reasons stated would appear greater than that of substitutes. (See Table No. 1.)

The ratio of rejections of recruits and substitutes differs from that of drafted men under the several sections of the paragraph embracing the causes of exemption. The difference is explained by the voluntary and involuntary nature of the presentations of the applicants, and by the ruling applied to the different classes. The decidedly feeble man, the confirmed consumptive, the paralytic, the deaf, and those having ulcers of long standing seldom enlist; while indifference and negligence on the part of this class to be relieved from enrollment places their names in the wheel, and many times their persons before the Board of Enrollment for examination as drafted men.

Under sections 8, 20 and 29, diseases of the skin, loss of teeth, and hydrocele, the ratio rejected of recruits and substitutes is greater than for drafted men.

TABLE NO. 1.—*Showing the number physically examined, the number appearing before the Board, the number actually and constructively examined, the ratio rejected and exempted for all causes, and for physical disability of each class, respectively.**

TABLE NO. 2.—*Showing the number of each class, and the ratio rejected and exempted per 1,000 examined, under each section of paragraph 85, and the number and ratio rejected for other causes, and the total number and ratio rejected and exempted.**

TABLE NO. 3.—*Showing measurements of chest, heights, and ages of recruits, substitutes, and drafted men examined from July 4, 1864, to April 30, 1865, in the Twelfth District of Ohio.**

THE TWELFTH DISTRICT OF OHIO.

The Twelfth District is composed of six counties, Pickaway, Ross, and Pike forming the western, and Fairfield, Hocking, and Perry the eastern portion of the district. The western counties embrace sixty miles in length of the Scioto Valley, the corn-growing Eden of Ohio. The eastern counties are composed of elevated table-land and mountains; the former is well adapted to agriculture, and the latter abound in iron, coal, building stone, oil, whortleberries, hoop poles, and shingles.

The district is divided into eighty-five sub-districts, containing a total population in 1860 of 139,456.

June, 1863, 18,371 names of persons of twenty years of age and under forty-five were enrolled as liable to do military duty; one in seven and five-tenths of the total population.

---

*Omitted.

The principal towns are the county seats, and contain a population as follows:

Circleville City	4,500
Chillicothe	7,600
Waverly	1,000
Lancaster City	4,300
Logan	1,500
New Lexington	800
Total	19,700

Total population of the county towns, 19,700; a little more than one-seventh of the total population of the district.

Health.—The elevated and mountainous nature of the eastern counties renders this portion of the district remarkably exempt from endemic and epidemic forms of disease, while the valley, comprising the western counties, is equally noted for the prevalence of marsh miasmatic fever and the hydra manifestations of this subtle poison. This inexplicable endemic constitution of locality, constantly emanating and administering a poison to the nervous centers and the secreting organs, causes a much larger per cent. of permanent walking invalids than is found in sections exempt from this influence. Typhoid fever, pneumonia, bronchitis, diphtheria, and intermitting fever embrace the principal sporadic and endemic acute diseases incident to this locality. Since the prevalence of diphtheria in the autumn of 1860 no epidemic form of disease has been manifest.

Inhabitants.—Politically, a majority of the district is decidedly, and perhaps not honestly, adverse to the present administration. At one time, organizing and publicly drilling in several sections, they viciously contemplated resistance to law and the enforcement of the draft under the call of July 18, 1864; and looking upon every man in the service of the Government as a public enemy, they made threats of great violence and committed numerous private injuries. This continued until reasons, best known to the property holders enlisted in the hazardous enterprise, induced a change in the conduct of this disaffected class, becoming in sentiment suddenly and greatly improved; and under the stimulating influence of large local bounties and impending draft many of the most infatuated entered the service by voluntary enlistments, and others relieved the district of their molestation and influence by making a change of residence unaccompanied by any change of enrollment.

Socially.—With a fair system of public schools, four chartered institutions of learning, a State farm, and the ideopoietic power of the draft, there still exists a great deficiency of the rudiments of common information and morals.

Many of the elder portion of the present inhabitants are natives of other States—Pennsylvania, North Carolina, South Carolina, and a few of the first families of Virginia. These form the basis and give cast and character to the society, institutions, modes of business, and manner of living.

The interests of the district are principally agricultural, and the inhabitants are industrious and economical. All can, and most do, obtain comfortable homesteads; and some have accumulated wealth and live in the full consciousness of the superior advantages and influence of the American Union. Of the total number enrolled 13,628 are farmers and 4,743 embracing all other occupations.

The aggregate amount of land under cultivatiom is about 600,000 acres. Of this 150,000 is devoted to wheat and 260,000 to Indian corn, and which yields annually over 1,500,000 bushels of wheat and 10,000,000 bushels of corn. Nearly 200,000 acres are seeded with other crops—rye, oats, barley, buckwheat, potatoes, and meadow. Total yield annually, 14,000,000 bushels of grain and 120,000 tons of hay—an income on these of more than $10,500,000.

In addition to the agricultural resources are the mining and manufacturing interests of no small importance. The former is yearly becoming of greater significance. Perry and Hocking Counties, far inferior in agricultural products, are rich in undeveloped mineral resources, and are fast competing in wealth with other seemingly more favored portions of the district.

Excepting the manufacture of whisky, flour, and leather, little else beyond local consumption is produced. The revenue paid on whisky for the fiscal year ending June 30, 1864 (most of which was assessed at 20 cents per gallon), amounted to $558,183.36.

Physical.—The physical development of the inhabitants is commensurate with the demand for labor and the agricultural and mineral resources; and the soldier from this class of yeomanry should, from habits of life, be able to endure great fatigue; and the Government may well accept with pride and satisfaction the men elected to fill the quotas of this district, as they have been furnished from the best physical development produced in this locality. (See Table No. 3.) Although the number examined shows nativities of thirty nine States and countries, a great majority are natives of Ohio, and have enjoyed a country life, not of an easy, indolent, or luxurious character, but one subject to and requiring great physical endurance. In the heat of summer and cold of winter they have been accustomed to active laborious duties.

TABLE No. 4.—*Showing measurements of chest, heights, and ages of recruits and substitutes physically examined from July 4, 1864, to April 30, 1865.**

Of the total number, 2,568 were farmers and farm laborers, and 572 including other occupations; 2,204 natives of Ohio, and 936 including the natives from all other States and countries.

The average physical development of the natives of Ohio is equal to that of all other States and countries collectively, although many were youthful, reducing the average age of those accepted to twenty-three seven-tenths, or five years below the average of those from other States and countries; and the ratio rejected per 1,000 examined is considerably less than other nativities collectively. (Table 4.)

Ratio rejected per 1,000 examined, recruits and substitutes:	
Natives of Ohio	353.1
Other States and countries	480.9
Total number	391.4

The greatest number exempted for physical disability under any one section of paragraph 85, Revised Regulations, or for disability referred to therein (Table No. 2), has been for hernia; and, contrary to the commonly received opinion, more cases of right than left inguinal hernia are met with.

TABLE No. 5.—*Showing the number rejected and exempted for hernia, and physically examined, from May 10, 1864, to April 30, 1865, 6,528.**

Table No. 5 shows the number physically examined, and the relative frequency of the classification, as found in applicants for service, and as cause of exemption of enrolled and drafted men.

*Omitted.

The influence of malaria, causing chronic change of function or structure of the internal organs (section 5), and the youthful exposure to accidents, dislocations, and fractures (section 37) in the rural districts, and which are frequently unattended by medical or surgical skill, leaving the sufferer with an unnecessary permanent deformity and disability, may to some extent account for the large ratios under these two sections.

For causes other than physical and mental disability, the rejections exhibit a still much greater proportion ———. Seventy-seven per 1,000 examined of recruits have been rejected for want of physical development, implying a deficiency of age. And the experience attained in this department tends to confirm that of others made in the field, that the minimum age is too low for recruits, and the maximum at least five years too great for drafted men, to obtain efficient and enduring soldiers. Few boys of eighteen years of age are sufficiently matured to endure fatigue, exposure, and change of living consequent to the soldier, while the age of forty with the laboring man in this climate brings many ills unknown or uncared for below this period. The former is shown in the examinations of those under twenty years of age, and the latter is manifest in the exemptions of drafted men. In the examination of 752 recruits and substitutes under twenty, and natives of Ohio, the ratio rejected per 1,000 examined amounts to 355, while 911 examined of twenty, and not exceeding forty years of age, natives of the same State, shows a ratio rejected of only 183 per 1,000 examined. In the examination of 1,396 drafted men, 138 of the number were forty and under forty-five years of age. The ratio exempted per 1,000 physically examined of those under forty is 284, and those forty and under forty-five amounts to 369, and the greater number of the accepted, or not exempt, bearing evidence of an inferior class. As an established consequence, the greater the ratio rejected of any class, comparatively the more it increases the suspicions of the character and efficiency of those accepted.

TABLE No. 6.—*Showing the number of natives of Ohio of less than twenty years of age, and the number more than twenty years of age, of recruits and substitutes examined from July 4, 1864, to April 30, 1865, and the number of drafted men less than forty, and the number forty and less than forty-five years of age, physically examined, and the ratio rejected and exempted for each class.*

Class.	Number physically examined.	Number rejected and exempted.	Ratio rejected and exempted per 1,000 examined.
Ohio recruits and substitutes:			
Less than 20 years	752	267	355.0
More than 20 years	911	167	183.3
Total	1,663	434	260.9
Drafted men:			
Less than 40 years of age	1,258	358	284.5
More than 40 and less than 45	138	51	369.5
Total	1,396	409	296.5

Paragraph 85 of the Revised Regulations of the Provost-Marshal-General's Bureau, section 3.—Of the numerous claims for exemption under section 3, paragraph 85, Revised Regulations, only two and three-tenths per 1,000 of all examined have been exempted for epilepsy. "The statement of the drafted man being insufficient," the affidavit "of a physician in good standing who has attended him in the disease within the six months immediately preceding his examination" can but seldom be procured. Epileptics do not usually employ a physician in the disease; most certainly so in the country among the poorer class, who soon become accustomed to know they will recover from the attack before medical aid could be obtained. And in many instances, no doubt, injustice is done parties afflicted with this unhappy malady. And I would suggest, as "fits," or epilepsy, could be determined as a matter of fact by duly attested affidavits of two or more respectable witnesses, requiring a description of manner, duration, and character of the same, leaving the medical inspector to determine the nature of the manifestations might work greater justice toward this unfortunate class, without opening wider than now the door for fraudulent practices.

EXAMINATION—"MINUTE DETAIL."

The examination of men for the service is conducted in the following manner and in the order herein stated:

A record is made with pencil in a small book ($4\frac{1}{2}$ by $7\frac{1}{2}$), writing day and date, name of the person to be examined in full; age, nativity, occupation, social relation, complexion, eyes and hair, where credited or where drafted, and if a substitute, the name of the person for whom he is a substitute, the sub-district where drafted or enrolled, with full descriptive list.

The following diagrams will more intelligibly explain the form and manner of making these most useful entries (marked No. 2 and No. 2.)*

Four books of this kind are kept in the examination room, marked upon the back of each the character of the entries, thus: "Recruits examined from February 16, 1865, to ———, 1865."

Books for substitutes, drafted and enrolled men are, in like manner, also marked, and when filled with names, the month and day thereof is written, completing the indorsement upon the back and showing the period of examinations contained in each.

One applicant only is recorded on a single page, and when a sufficient number of entries have been made spectators are required to leave the room; the doors are closed and locked, preventing all egress and ingress, and the men divest themselves of all clothing excepting pants and drawers. The first name recorded in any one of the books is called, and the man is placed with his back to a stationary measure, and the height taken in feet and inches, which is recorded at the right, filling the descriptive list; he is then measured by means of a graduated tape around the chest, at the lower border of the pectoralis major muscle, and the number of inches obtained at the termination of ordinary expiration; he is then requested to take a full, prolonged inspiration, and the measurement is again recorded. These measurements are always placed at the terminus of the name. Having measured in like manner all to be examined, the men divest themselves of the remaining clothing, and the surgeon proceeds in the

*Omitted.

same order of names, by a rehearsal of questions, eliciting answers to the statements contained in the record, with such other interrogatories as may tend to establish a correct opinion of the age, nativity, alienage, intelligence, health, and liability to periodical diseases; and qualifications, legal, mental, and physical, required of recruits, substitutes, and drafted men.

Any marks, scars, or change of conformation is next observed and noted. This being satisfactory, the head, eyes, ears, nose, teeth, and throat are inspected. The cranium is examined by tact; the eyes, eyelids, ears, nose, teeth, palate, and fauces by ocular inspection. The sight is tested by reading, or small objects at proper distances, with the right and then the left eye.

The hearing is tested by conversation. If a recruit or substitute, in a low tone of voice; if a drafted man claiming deafness, in a loud tone, coming down the scale rapidly, at the same time interesting him with answers relating to himself, and which will most always detect attempted imposition.

Any disease or peculiarity of the head, eyes, ears, teeth, or palate is now noted in the book, immediately under the description of the applicant or previous remarks.

The chest and organs contained are next in order of examination. The symmetry, development, and subclavian regions are carefully inspected; the frequency of respiration and the heart's action are observed, and any deviation from a normal standard is noted. The man is now required to walk briskly several times around the room, throwing the heels against the gluteal muscles each step, then to cross the room, first on one foot and then upon the other; to throw the arms erect over the head and to place the back of the hands together in this position; to flex and extend the forearms, hands, thumbs, and fingers; to pronate and supinate the hands, and to extend and flex the toes. He is now again examined with reference to the organs of the chest, and any material change in respiration and circulation from this exercise is noted, also all other causes tending to disability observed.

The abdomen is next in order. The gastric and hypochondriac regions are examined by tact; the finger is introduced into the inguinal space, and the party required to pass the arms over the head, to cough, and stooping, lift at dead weight, &c. Where hernia is claimed but not apparent, or where the state of the abdominal rings creates the least suspicion of this disability, if a recruit or substitute, he is required to lean forward upon his hands, placing his feet widely apart, that hemorrhoids, fissures, or fistula may, if in existence, be discovered. The drafted man can tell his own ills. The result of this is now recorded.

The spine and extremities are examined, and any deformity, scar, or mark is noted; and any disability found minutely described. After this, any remark calculated to identify the party by association is in order. The result of the examination is determined at any stage when a disqualifying cause is found to exist, by writing after a description of disabilty the words "rejected," if a recruit or substitute; and "exempt," if a drafted or enrolled man, completing the examination as represented in Diagram No. 2.

The certificate of examination on triplicate enlistment papers of the recruits accepted is now signed by the surgeon, and the enlistment papers of those not accepted are marked upon the face "rejected."

The records of examination are passed to the clerk of the examination room, who prepares two lists of those accepted or not exempt, giving the sub-district where credited and regiment for muster, if a recruit; if a substiute, the name, and also that of the party for whom he is a substitute, and where enrolled or drafted; and if a drafted man, when and where drafted. (See Lists Nos. 1 and 2.)

List No. 1 is given as a certified requisition for muster to the provost-marshal, who proceeds to muster the recruits and enlist the substitutes upon this evidence of physical fitness.

The drafted men not exempt sign duplicate clothing receipts and separate receipts for the spoon, knife, fork, and plate, and which is required to be witnessed by the surgeon.

The drafted men exempted are furnished with a certificate of exemption (Form 31 or 32), signed by the members of the Board of Enrollment; the substitutes accepted sign their enlistment papers (Form 39) and their clothing receipt.

The names upon the lists are now called, and the men answering stand in file in the order in which the names occur, and those rejected and exempted are discharged from the room. The mustering officer now musters the recruits and enlists the substitutes.

List No. 1.

CIRCLEVILLE, OHIO, *February 13, 1865.*

For muster, enlistment, and service:

No.	Name.	Where credited.	Remarks.
1	Thomas Bowers	Springfield Township and Ross	184th Regiment Ohio Volunteer Infantry.
2	James Williamson	Perry Township and Hocking	179th Regiment Ohio Volunteer Infantry.
3	Joshua F. Whip	Jackson Township and Pickaway	Substitute for John Hammel, enrolled.
4	William Sheran	Wayne Township and Pickaway	Substitute for Thomas Foster, drafted.
5	Daniel D. Hayley	Huntington Township and Ross	Drafted Dec. 21, 1864.
6	James R. Brown	Benton Township and Pike	Drafted Nov. 19, 1864.

List No. 2.

CIRCLEVILLE, OHIO, *February 18, 1865.*

John R. Botkin, accept, subsist, and lodge the following-named men:

Recruit	1	Thomas Bowers	Springfield, Ross, 184th Regiment.
Do	2	James Williamson	Perry, Hocking, 179th Regiment.
Substitute	3	Joshua F. Whip	Jackson, Pickaway, for John Hammel.
Do	4	William Sheran	Wayne, Pickaway, for Thomas Foster.
Drafted	5	Daniel D. Hayley	Huntington, Ross, Dec. 21, 1864.
Do	6	James R. Brown	Benton, Pike, Nov. 19, 1864.

By order: GEORGE W. ROBY,

Captain and Provost-Marshal, Twelfth District of Ohio.

The recruits mustered sign duplicate clothing receipts, which are witnessed in due form; after which the names are again called, and the men, placed two and two, are marched to the clothing room to obtain their new purchase, and from thence to the barracks, where they are by the orderly turned over, with list No. 2, to the person in charge of the premises.

All this portion of the service is necessarily transacted in the examination room, and constitutes a part of the details of the examination. Much time and great care is required to make those primary steps in the record and lists correctly, as they are to be used in making the muster and descriptive rolls, and constitute the basis of the records of the office.

Number examined.—With the limited facilities afforded the surgeon for making those examinations, fifty men is the average number that can be physically examined per day with accuracy. With three rooms instead of one, 120 could be examined in ten hours, if all were present at the proper time.

More time is consumed in the examination of drafted men than either recruits or substitutes; it is so necessarily. To treat them kindly, the surgeon must show every attention, hearing every manner of claim; must look at affidavits and medical certificates, and hear parol testimony, &c., although he remains, if possible, more the same opinion still. The recruit or substitute may be rejected upon hearing an answer to a single question, while a drafted man in justice can make no statement nor answer to any question having the least weight or influence in his case.

At the end of each day the entries made in the memorandum books of recruits, substitutes, and drafted men are transcribed into a book ruled for the purpose in the manner designated by Form A.* From this book or blotter the monthly reports are made and forwarded. The contents are also transcribed into the Medical Record in full. The drafted men are again transcribed into the Medical Record for Drafted Men. The names of enrolled men examined are passed through a separate set of books in like manner, and are transcribed into the Medical Record for Enrolled Men. The footings for each day of each class, in the Medical Record for Recruits, Substitutes, and Drafted Men, is made in red ink below the terminus of the last name for that day in the space "Remarks," and footings of each page in like manner is made at the margin, the one acting as a check upon the other; and at the end of each month the sum of the two footings are arranged in separate tables, and, if free from error, will show like results. These tables are recorded at the page ending the month for the purpose of aiding in obtaining information in future reference.

It being practically inconvenient to keep a medical-record book for recruits and substitutes and one separately for drafted men, I have carried forward in separate columns recruits, substitutes, and drafted men, showing a complete record in one place [of] the business of each day.

As enrolled men are not examined during recruiting and drafting, they appear upon books for that purpose only.

The measurement of the chest will differ materially if made at different points, and in the absence of any positively established rule the measurements have been made around, at, or immediately above the origin of the pectoralis major muscle. Expiration at ordinary and not forced contraction of the chest, and inspiration at full inflation. Many subjects with good lungs will not make that free inspiration their ability would permit, and are indifferent to the request; while boys of eighteen and too youthful to be accepted, having imagined or been informed that success depended upon the size of the chest, will inflate themselves with an elasticity almost equal to Æsop's toad.

---

*Omitted.

If the forced voluntary expulsion of air from the lungs and the free and forced inspiration could be obtained, these measurements would show much nearer than now the true mobility of the chest. But it is not possible in the dispatch of business to obtain full consent by making the subject understand the object, it being to them a species of novelty. Therefore forcible expiration has not been insisted upon, and the inspirations have not in all cases been satisfactorily forced.

FRAUDS.

The frauds most to be guarded against as practiced by enrolled and drafted men, to escape service, are those sustaining claims of insanity, imbecility, general physical disability, and deafness.

These are generally subjects of contract, secured by some enterprising firm engaged in the business, and which usually is composed of an active, venerable, and experienced attorney at law and an elastic country doctor. With these legal qualifications as a firm, the claim of the drafted man is presented with an overwhelming array of affidavits, and which always renders the statements more or less suspicious; and if by counter-testimony the claim is decided untrue as to degree or nature of the disability, it is frequently pressed at general rendezvous to a successful termination, greatly to the detriment and influence of the district Board. Experience has determined that affidavits procured for drafted men by this class of "friends of the Government" are generally unreliable, and should be accepted with great caution and due allowance.

The medical partner of one of these firms presented a drafted man with the oral statement that the party was an "idiot," and had been one for a number of years. He was armed with a bundle of affidavits, his own among the number, fully establishing insanity, with liability to a recurrence. Upon investigation of the case the whole sworn insanity or "idiocy" was founded upon an attack of mania a potu a number of years since. While in this state of phrensy he made an attempt to kill his wife, the after reflection of which reformed him of the habit of intemperance, but could not release him from the draft. Many varieties of analogous illustrations might be given, showing the character of the great mass of evidence in those contract claims of premeditated fraud by parties who no doubt labor for a stipulated compensation.

Some of these claims are so strongly fortified and ingeniously managed by counsel that in the absence of other and more reliable testimony they would be accepted as any other established matter of fact. For this reason it would be much better not to hear those claims at general rendezvous than to decide them merely upon the testimony presented by persons having a pecuniary interest in the success of the same.

By section 21, amended act, approved March 24, 1864, these attempts are made a penal offense, knowing the claims to be false; yet many experts are willing to engage in a business, for a liberal compensation, directly opposed to the spirit of the act.

It would relieve the surgeon (as well as the Board of Enrollment) of this special annoyance if every man presenting the claim of a drafted person, and those writing or obtaining affidavits, or in any other way assisting in the procuration of the release of the drafted person, were required to file in every instance their affidavits that they have not and never expect to receive, and never will receive, directly or indirectly, any compensation for the act or services rendered in the case. And the drafted man should also be required to file a similar affirmation that he has not paid, directly or indirectly, any person or persons money or other valuable consideration; that he has not made any gift or present to any person in consideration of services rendered, or that may be rendered, in his behalf as a drafted man, and that he never will, upon any contingency, or otherwise, so pay, donate, or give anything in consideration thereof.

It is not easy to prove an attorney knows a claim to be false, while perjury might readily be established in the continuation of these fraudulent practices.

The frauds most to be guarded against in recruits and substitutes are of a legal character, as age, alienage, &c. Substitutes, to relieve persons furnishing them for a definite period of time, must be procured from that class of persons not liable to enrollment and draft. And to admit alienage of parties upon their own affirmation, or the same supported by substitute brokers, or others pecuniarily interested, "to the best of their knowledge and belief," has not been satisfactory, and the Board has required official certificates, if recently from another Government, and if residents of the United States, the additional affidavits of two or more freeholders of respectability, embracing the following points: Length of time known the party; his residence and occupation; that he never at any time assumed the rights of a citizen, by voting or other act, and this to be certified by the clerk of the court of the county claiming residence in. This most effectually prevented bounty-jumping, by deterring agents engaged in the business from presenting for examination those unable to sustain a satisfactory record.

Minors are of two classes—those eighteen years of age, who appear sufficiently developed for twenty-one, and those eighteen who are young enough to be classed at fifteen. The former are mostly applicants as substitutes for two years; and many times, to their great surprise, when residents of the district, find their names upon the enrollment lists in time to prevent the crime of perjury.

PHYSICAL APTITUDE.

Physical aptitude for military service must be derived from actual observation. And the information contained in this brief space is in some particulars at variance with the statements of Prof. Robert Barthelow, who claims a decided preference for the white, and prefers the pure negro to any admixture, and offers the reason, that "in the United States the pure African is rarely found," and "few negroes having admixture with white blood are free from scrofula, independently of locality." This statement is not sustained by the examinations made at this office of 296 colored men of all shades, from the black wool to the blue eyes, fair skin, and light hair, embracing natives of twelve States and Canada.

Not more than two of this number were rejected for causes involving a reasonable supposition of a scrofulous diathesis.

Physical examinations also demonstrate the admixture with the white, "while it elevates his intellectual powers and gives symmetry to his form," does not lower his health and efficiency.

Table No. 7, which has been carefully and accurately prepared, shows the causes of rejection, and the ratio rejected per 1,000, of all colored recruits and substitutes physically examined, from July 4,

1864, to April 30, 1865, and which shows the ratio rejected of colored recruits to be a small fraction more than half as great as that of the same class of examinations of white applicants; and while the rejections have been much less, the physical development of those accepted is equal to the white of this nation, and better than that of all other nations collectively.

Colored men are well muscled, have good eyes, good teeth, good lungs, and a digestion seldom a source of torment from coarse food. They are active, are inured to hardships, are not liable to experience ill effects from malaria and the heat of summer sun; they sustain well and recover readily from injury or disease, and will not "freeze," or lose the powers of "reproduction," nor "become extinct" much sooner than the white man. (See Table 8.)

TABLE NO. 7.—*Showing the number and the ratio per 1,000 of colored men rejected.*

TWELFTH DISTRICT OF OHIO.

Colored men examined from July 4, 1864, to April 30, 1865.	Number of recruits examined, 207.		Number of substitutes examined, 89.		Total number examined, 296.	
	Recruits rejected.	Ratio rejected per 1,000 physically examined.	Substitutes rejected.	Ratio rejected per 1,000 physically examined.	Ratio rejected per 1,000 examined for physical disability, colored recruits and substitutes.	Ratio rejected for all causes per 1,000 physically examined, colored recruits and substitutes.
Organic disease, internal organs	1	4.8				
Diseases of the skin	1	4.8				
Chronic rheumatism	1	4.8				
Eyes and eyelids, diseases of	2	9.6				
Chest and spine	1	4.8				
Hernia	4	19.4	9	101.1		
Testicles, diseases of	2	9.6				
Joints, diseases of	3	14.5	2	22.5		
Feet, deformity of	1	4.8				
Varicose veins, lower extremities	1	4.8				
Ulcers, chronic			1	11.3		
Want of physical development	6	29.0	15	168.4		
Legal causes	4	19.3	9	101.1		
Total	27	130.4	36	404.4	101.8	213.7

TABLE No. 8.—*Showing measurements of chest, heights, and ages of recruits and substitutes accepted, as classified into Americans and aliens, white Americans and colored Americans, white aliens and colored aliens, examined from July 4, 1864, to April 30, 1865.*

Class.	Number accepted.	Measurement of chest.						Height.			Age.		
		Average measurement at inspiration.	Average measurement at expiration.	Greatest measurement at inspiration.	Least measurement at inspiration.	Greatest measurement at expiration.	Least measurement at expiration.	Average height of all examined.	Greatest height of any examined.	Least height of any examined.	Average age of all examined.	Greatest age of any examined.	Least age of any examined.
		In.	*In.*	*In.*	*In.*	*In.*	*In.*	*Ft. In.*	*Ft. In.*	*Ft. In.*	*Years*	*Yrs.*	*Yrs.*
Americans	1,616	35.10	33.17	44.0	29.5	42	26	5 7.39	6 4	5 0	24.58	44	16
Aliens or foreign born	139	35.49	33.60	41.0	30.0	39	27	5 6.35	6 6	5 0	27.05	43	18
Total number accepted.	1,755	35.13	33.20	44.0	29.5	42	26	5 7.31	6 6	5 0	24.78	44	16
White Americans	1,383	35.05	33.04	42.5	29.5	41	26	5 7.45	6 4	5 0	24.43	44	16
Colored Americans	233	35.43	33.91	44.0	30.5	42	29	5 7.05	6 4	5 1	25.45	44	18
While aliens or foreign born.	138	35.48	33.59	41.0	30.0	39	27	5 6.32	6 6	5 0	27.09	43	18
Colored aliens or foreign born.	1	36.50	35.00	36.5	36.5	35	35	5 10.00	5 10	5 10	21.00	21	21
Total	1,755	35.13	33.20	44.0	29.5	42	26	5 7.31	6 6	5 0	24.78	44	16

The muscular development of the limbs of those examined has been good. If there is a deficiency of the gastrocnemius peculiar to this race, those having this distinctive mark have failed to appear before the Board.

Their feet are flat, but not of a nature to disqualify them from performing well active infantry service.

This experience touching their physical qualifications and the comparisons that may justly be drawn would tend to establish the conclusion that they present a greater physical aptitude for military service than any other nation, and even greater than the white population of the same nation.

ENROLLMENT LAW.

Several sections of the present enrollment act as amended might be subject to some improvement in their working operation; and no one stands more at fault perhaps than section 21, amended act, February 24, 1864.

This section is intended to prevent or punish the fraud before the Board of Enrollment; and nineteen-twentieths of all violations come under the observation of the surgeon, and who must become informer or chief witness; and a few cases and the attendance upon subpœnas at long distances will satisfy any reasonable person or any other man that few prosecutions or convictions, however prevalent this evil may exist, as it has existed before every board of enrollment in this country, will ever be made.

The experience obtained in prosecutions under this section has been satisfactory upon one point at least—that there should be a provision fully compensating witnesses for the time and expense necessarily incurred in the attendance upon the requisite legal proceedings in these cases.

I am, general, very respectfully, your obedient servant,

N. E. JONES,

Surgeon Board of Enrollment, Twelfth District of Ohio.

Disposition of Documents 14 to 39, accompanying the final report of the Provost-Marshal-General.

[Compiled in the War Records Office.]

No.	Description.	Where published.		
		Series.	Volume.	Page.
14	General Orders, No. 111, Adjutant-General's Office, June 10, 1865	3	5	52
15	General Orders, No. 15, Adjutant-General's Office, May 4, 1861	3	1	151
16	General Orders, No. 33 (par. III), Adjutant-General's Office, April 3, 1862.	3	2	2
17	General Orders, No. 60, Adjutant-General's Office, June 6, 1862	3 2	2 3	109 654
18	Governors of States to the President, June 28, 1862	3	2	180
Art. 1	The President to the Governors, July 1, 1862	3	2	187
18 Art. 2	Governors of Ohio, Indiana, Illinois, Iowa, and Wisconsin to the President, Apr. 21, 1864.	3	4	237
19	President's call for 300,000 militia for nine months	3	2	291
20 Art. 1	General Orders, No. 99, Adjutant-General's Office, Aug. 9, 1862	3	2	333
20 Art. 2	General Orders, No. 121, Adjutant-General's Office, Aug. 29, 1862	3	2	482
21	General Orders, No. 67, Adjutant-General's Office, Mar. 17, 1863	3	3	74
22	General Orders, No. 111 (par. I), Adjutant-General's Office, May 1, 1863	3	3	179
23	General Orders, No. 105, Adjutant-General's Office, Apr. 28, 1863	3	3	170
24 Art. 1	Circular No. 54, Provost-Marshal-General's Office, July 20, 1863	3	3	548
24 Art. 2	Circular No. 85, Provost-Marshal-General's Office, Sept. 17, 1863	3	3	818
24 Art. 3	Circular No. 101, Provost-Marshal-General's Office, Nov. 17, 1863	3	3	1074
24 Art. 4	Circular No. 34, Provost-Marshal-General's Office, June 30, 1863	3	3	427
25 Art. 1	General Orders, No. 143, Adjutant-General's Office, May 22, 1863	3	3	215
25 Art. 2	General Orders, No. 376, Adjutant-General's Office, Nov. 21, 1863	3	3	1084
26 Art. 1	Circular No. 3, Provost-Marshal-General's Office, Jan. 7, 1864	3	4	12
26 Art. 2	Circular No. 5, Provost-Marshal-General's Office, Mar. 8, 1865. (Sections 13-27, act of Mar. 3, 1865.)	3	4	1224
27 Art. 1	Opinion of Solicitor of War Department, Aug. 1, 1864	3	4	562
27 Art. 2	Opinion of Attorney-General, Feb. 9, 1865	3	4	1158
28	Order of Provost-Marshal-General stopping recruiting, Apr. 29, 1865	3	4	1282
29	Opinion of Judge-Advocate-General, Sept. 10, 1863	3	3	784
30	....	......	(*a*)	......
31	....	......	(*a*)	......
32	Cameron's call for ten companies of militia from the District of Columbia.	1	51 i	321
33	....	......	(*a*)	......
34	....	......	(*a*)	......
35	Section 24 of act approved Mar. 3, 1803	......	(*a*)	......
	General Orders, No. 49, Adjutant-General's Office, Aug. 3, 1861. (Act approved July 22, 1861.)	3	1	380
	Act for relief of the Ohio and other volunteers	3	1	403
	Act of July 25, 1861	3	1	383
	General Orders, No. 54, Adjutant-General's Office, Aug. 10, 1861. (Act of July 29, 1861.)	3	1	395
	General Orders, No. 48, Adjutant-General's Office, July 31, 1861	3	1	372
	Act of Aug. 3, 1861. (Public—No. 38)	3	1	396
	Act of Aug. 5, 1861. (Public—No. 52)	3	1	401
	Act of Aug. 6, 1861. (Public—No. 53)	3	1	402
	Act of Aug. 6, 1861. (Public—No. 58)	3	1	402
	General Orders, No. 15, Adjutant-General's Office, Feb. 15, 1862. (Appropriation for completing defenses of Washington.)	3	1	888
	Act of Mar. 13, 1862	3	1	937
	General Orders. No. 31, Adjutant-General's Office, Mar. 27, 1862	3	1	952
	General Orders, No. 43, Adjutant-General's Office, Apr. 19, 1862	3	2	22

a Follows herein.

Disposition of Documents 14 to 39, accompanying the final report of the Provost-Marshal-General—Continued.

No.	Description.	Where published.		
		Series.	Volume.	Page.
35	General Orders, No. 53 (par. I), Adjutant-General's Office, May 16, 1862	3	2	40
	General Orders, No. 55 (par. I), Adjutant-General's Office, May 24, 1862	3	2	67
	Act of July 2, 1862. (Additional medical officers)	3	2	224
	Act of July 2, 1862. (Oath of office, &c.)	3	2	227
	Resolution of July 12, 1862. (Public—No. 42)	3	2	282
	Act of July 17, 1862. (Public—No. 160)	3	2	275
	Joint resolution of July 17, 1862. (Public—No. 54)	3	2	276
	Act of July 17, 1862. (Section 20)	3	2	279
	Act of July 17, 1862. (Public—No. 166)	3	2	280
	Act of July 17, 1862. (Public—No. 167)	3	2	282
	General Orders, No. 3, Adjutant-General's Office, Jan. 3, 1863	3	3	3
	General Orders, No. 7, Adjutant-General's Office, Jan. 7, 1863	3	3	4
	Act of Feb. 7, 1863. (Public—No. 17)	3	3	39
	Act of Feb. 9, 1863. (Public—No. 23)	3	3	43
	Joint resolution of February 16, 1863. (Public—No. 9)	3	3	85
	Act of Mar. 2, 1863. (Public—No. 47)	3	3	88
	Act of Mar. 3, 1863. (Public—No. 57)	3	3	93
	Act of Mar. 3, 1863. (Public—No. 58)	3	3	94
	Act of Mar. 3, 1863. (Public—No. 54)	3	3	88
	General Orders, No. 400, Adjutant-General's Office, Dec. 28, 1863	3	3	1194
	Resolution of Jan. 16, 1864	3	4	38
	Act of Feb. 24, 1864	3	4	128
	General Orders, No. 202, Adjutant-General's Office, May 26, 1864	3	4	409
	General Orders, No. 215, Adjutant-General's Office, June 22, 1864. (Sections 2-5, Act of June 15, 1864.)	3	4	448
	Act of July 1, 1864. (Public—No. 173)	3	4	612
	Act of July 4, 1864. (Public—No. 196)	3	4	472
	General Orders, No. 29, Adjutant-General's Office, Feb. 28, 1865	3	4	1204
	Resolution of Mar. 3, 1865. (Public—No. 25)	3	4	1228
	General Orders, No. 31, Adjutant-General's Office, Mar. 8, 1865)	3	4	1223
	Act of Mar. 3, 1865. (Public—No. 61)	3	4	1226
	Act of Mar. 3, 1865. (Public—No. 63)	3	4	1227
	Act of Mar. 3, 1865. (Public—No. 71)	3	4	1227
36	President's proclamation of Apr. 15, 1861	3	1	67
	President's proclamation of Apr. 19, 1861	3	1	89
	President's proclamation of Apr. 27, 1861	3	1	122
	President's proclamation of May 3, 1861	3	1	145
	President's proclamation of Aug. 12, 1861	3	1	405
	President's proclamation of Aug. 16, 1861	3	1	417
	President's proclamation of Apr. 10, 1862	3	2	14
	President's proclamation of May 10, 1861	3	1	184
	President's proclamation of May 12, 1862	3	2	31
	Trade regulations, May 12, 1862	3	2	32
	President's proclamation of May 19, 1862	3	2	42
	President's proclamation of July 1, 1862	3	2	185
	President's proclamation of July 25, 1862	3	2	274
	President's proclamation of Sept. 22, 1862	3	2	584
	President's proclamation of Sept. 24, 1862	3	2	587
	President's proclamation of Jan. 1, 1863	3	3	2
	President's proclamation of Mar. 10, 1863	3	3	60
	President's proclamation of Mar. 30, 1863	3	3	106
	President's proclamation of Apr. 2, 1863	3	3	111
	President's proclamation of Apr. 20, 1863	3	3	124
	President's proclamation of May 8, 1863	3	3	198
	President's proclamation of June 15, 1863	3	3	360
	General Orders, No. 315, Adjutant-General's Office, Sept. 17, 1863	3	3	817
	President's proclamation of Sept. 15, 1863	3	3	817
	President's proclamation of Sept. 24, 1863	3	3	837
	President's proclamation of Oct. 3, 1863	3	3	859
	President's proclamation of Oct. 17, 1863	3	3	892
	President's proclamation of Dec. 8, 1863	2	6	680
	President's proclamation of Dec. 16, 1863, discontinuing discriminating duties of tonnage, &c., as respects vessels of Nicaragua.*a*	.....	.....	.....
	President's proclamation of Feb. 18, 1864	3	4	126
	President's proclamation of Mar. 26, 1864	2	6	1113
	Order of the President of May 19, 1864, withdrawing consular functions from Charles Hunt, consul for Belgium at Saint Louis, Mo.*a*	.....	.....	.....
	President's proclamation of July 5, 1864	1	39 ii	180
	President's proclamation of July 7, 1864	3	4	475
	President's proclamation of July 8, 1864	3	4	477
	President's proclamation of July 18, 1864	3	4	515
	President's proclamation of Aug. 18, 1864, making Newport, Vt., a port of exportation.*a*	.....	.....	.....
	President's proclamation of Oct. 20, 1864	3	4	788

a Omitted.

Disposition of Documents 14 to 39, accompanying the final report of the Provost-Marshal-General—Continued.

No.	Description.	Where published. Series.	Volume.	Page.
36	President's proclamation of Oct. 31, 1864, admitting Nevada *a*	.....	.....	.....
	President's proclamation of Nov. 19, 1864	3	4	941
	President's proclamation of Dec. 19, 1864	3	4	1002
	President's proclamation of Jan. 10, 1865, making Saint Albans, Vt., a port of exportation. *a*	.....	.....	.....
	General Orders, No. 22, Adjutant-General's Office, Feb. 17, 1865	3	4	1177
	President's proclamation of Mar. 11, 1865	3	4	1229
	President's proclamation of Mar. 17, 1865	3	4	1242
	Rewards for arrest of felons, Apr. 4, 1865 *a*	.....	.....	.....
	President's proclamation of Apr. 11, 1865	3	5	107
	President's proclamation of Apr. 11, 1865	3	5	107
	President's proclamation of Apr. 11, 1865	3	4	1260
	Executive order of Apr. 29, 1865	3	5	105
	President's proclamation of May 2, 1865	1	49 ii	566
	Order rescinding regulations prohibiting exportation of arms, &c., May 3, 1865.	3	5	4
	Executive order of May 9, 1865	3	5	13
	President's proclamation of May 10, 1865	3	5	18
	President's proclamation of May 22, 1865	3	5	105
	President's proclamation of May 29, 1865	3	5	37
	General Orders, No. 107, Adjutant-General's Office, June 2, 1865	3	5	49
	General Orders, No. 110, Adjutant-General's Office, June 7, 1865	3	5	51
	President's proclamation of June 13, 1865	3	5	103
	President's proclamation of June 13, 1865 *b*	3	5	37
	President's proclamation of June 17, 1865 *b*	3	5	37
	President's proclamation of June 17, 1865 *b*	3	5	37
	President's proclamation of June 21, 1865 *b*	3	5	37
	President's proclamation of June 23, 1865	3	5	106
	President's proclamation of June 24, 1865	3	5	104
	President's proclamation of Aug. 29, 1865	3	5	103
	President's proclamation of Oct. 12, 1865	3	5	125
	President's proclamation of Apr. 2, 1866	3	5	1007
37	Revised Regulations, Provost-Marshal-General's Bureau, Sept. 1, 1864 *	3	4	651
38	Casualties in Provost-Marshal-General's Bureau *c*	.....	.....	.....
39	List of persons who put in representative recruits, and names of recruits *c*	.....	.....	.....

a Omitted. *b* Same as May 29, 1865, with necessary changes. *c* Follows herein.

DOCUMENT No. 30.

Necessity for a change in the method of raising troops.

From the results of the draft above discussed and of the call preceding it for 300,000 volunteers, it became apparent that, without further legislation, the armies could not be sufficiently strengthened to prosecute the war successfully and that in the re-enforcements which had been and were being furnished a ruinous inequality was arising among the different States and districts.

The necessity for a change of system in raising troops was recognized by President Lincoln, as shown by a letter from him dated August 4, 1862, to Count A. de Gasparin, from which the following is an extract:

Hence our great Army * * * has dwindled rapidly, bringing the necessity for a new call earlier than was anticipated. We shall easily obtain the new levy, however. Be not alarmed if you shall learn that we shall have resorted to a draft for part of this. It seems strange even to me, but it is true, that the Government is now pressed to this course by a popular demand. Thousands who wish not to personally enter the service are nevertheless anxious to pay and send substitutes,

*As published with the final report of the Provost-Marshal-General, these Regulations differ in some respects from those printed in Vol. IV, this series, p. 651 *et seq.* A comparison with House Executive Document No. 1, Thirty-ninth Congress, first session, Vol. IV, Part II, p. 276 *et seq*, will disclose the differences.

provided they can have assurance that unwilling persons similarly situated will be compelled to do likewise. Besides this, volunteers mostly choose to enter newly formed regiments, while drafted men can be sent to fill the old ones, wherein, man for man, they are quite doubly as valuable.

This subject received the early attention of the Congress which assembled in December, 1862. The following extracts from the remarks of distinguished Senators and Members of the House present correctly and forcibly the importance of the subject:

To fill the thinned ranks of our battalions we must again call upon the people. The immense numbers already summoned to the field, the scarcity and high rewards of labor, press upon all of us the conviction that the ranks of our wasted regiments cannot be filled again by the old system of volunteering. If volunteers will not respond to the call of the country, then we must resort to the involuntary system. (Senator Henry Wilson.)

Volunteers we cannot obtain and everything forbids that we should resort to the temporary expedient of calling out the militia. Such a call would waste the resources and absorb the energies and increase but little the military forces of the country. The needs of the Nation demand that we should rely not upon volunteering, nor upon calling forth the militia, but that we should fill the regiments now in the field, worn and wasted by disease and death, by enrolling and drafting the popoulation of the country under the constitutional authority to raise and support armies. (Senator Henry Wilson.)

I agree with the Senator from Massachusetts that it is necessary to fill up the ranks of our Army, and that it is necessary there should be a conscription bill. (Senator Richardson.)

Now, in regard to this conscription question, I will say, for myself, that I regretted much, when this war was first organized, that the conscription rule did not obtain. I went from the extreme east to the extreme west of the loyal States. I found some districts where some bold leaders brought out all the young men and sent them or led them to the field. In other districts—and they were the most numerous—the people made no movement toward the maintenance of the war; there were whole towns and cities, I may say, where no one volunteered to shoulder a musket and no one offered to lead them into the service. The whole business has been unequal and wrong from the first. The rule of conscription should have been the rule to bring out men of all classes and make it equal throughout the country; and therein the North has failed. (Senator McDougall.)

The necessity for a bill of the character of that under consideration has long existed. I think it would have been far better for the country if it had been enacted at the extra session in July, 1861. For a want of a general enrollment of the forces of the United States and a systematic calling out of those forces, we have experienced all the inconveniences of a volunteer system, with its enormous expense, ill discipline, and irregular efforts, and have depended upon spasmodic efforts of the people, elated or depressed by the varying fortunes of war or the rise or fall of popular favorites in the Army. I believe I hazard nothing in saying that we should have lost fewer men in the field and from disease and been much nearer the end of this destructive war had we earlier availed ourselves of the power conferred by the Constitution and at last proposed to be adopted by this bill. For short and irregular efforts no force can be better than a volunteer army. With brave and skillful officers and a short and active term of service, volunteer troops are highly efficient. But when a war is to last for years, as this will have done, however soon we may see its termination, it must depend for its success upon regular and systematic forces. Thinned regiments must be filled up; otherwise we may have the spectacle of a vast array of troops upon paper, nominally representing an enormous force, while little but the shell of an organization remains. Such filling up is not possible to any degree under the volunteer system, as the Government has had occasion to know in this war, because fresh volunteers prefer to organize into regiments of their own forming, where they have a voice in the creation of their officers, and hence some hopes of immunity from the toils of war, or a blindness to many faults destructive to military discipline. The consequence is that, by means of discharges, sick-leaves, deaths, and the various accidents of war, it will in many cases take four or five regiments, if consolidated, to make one full one. Supernumerary officers are paid out of the public purse for services they are not called upon to perform, and new officers, lacking experience, are in charge of the new and, hence, full regiments, when the older and experienced officers would be more efficient and make more effective use of the new troops if they had the disciplining and leading of them.

These considerations show the inherent weakness of the volunteer system. Our Government is the only power on earth that depends upon volunteer forces to conduct a protracted war. Even the rebels, of the same political traditions with ourselves, severed from this Republic, early in the war discarded the idea of maintaining the war by volunteer forces, and resorted to a draft, thus imitating the European governments, who have brought the art of war to the perfection of a positive science. It has been repeatedly insisted by eminent European military gentlemen that our Government must fail if it relied upon the volunteer force for the protracted effort needed to subdue the flames of this vast civil war. Aside from the enormous cost entailed, absorbing the monetary resources of the Government, they insisted that the necessary discipline could not be had; that however gallant our volunteer soldiery—and none have ever disputed that quality—the highest efficiency of the soldier could only be secured when he was under the complete control of the organizing power, and had learned to know what volunteers can never be taught—that obedience is as necessary a quality as courage.

Perhaps it is too late to learn the lesson of experience and remedy the defects of the present system. It is certainly not too late, unless it is too late to save the Republic.

The practical operation of the volunteer system has been that the earnest lovers of the country among the people, the haters of the rebellion, the noblest and best of our citizens, have left their homes to engage in this war to sustain the Constitution; while the enemies of civil liberty, those who hate the Government and desire its failure in this struggle, have staid at home to embarrass it by discontent and clamor. By this system we have had the loyal States drained of those who could be relied upon in all political contests to sustain the Government; going forth to fight the manly foe in front, the covert foe left behind has opened a fire in the rear. Under the garb of democracy, a name that has been so defiled and prostituted that it has become synonymous with treason and should henceforth be a byword and hissing to the American people, these demagogues in this hall and out of it have traduced the Government, misrepresented the motives of loyal men, gnashed their teeth at measures designed to crush out treason and punish traitors, and, by misrepresenting the objects of the war, led ignorant supporters and constituencies to refrain from enlistments and into an attitude of hostility to the Administration that must cause glee in Jeff. Davis' dominions and in hell itself. Even the measures of taxation necessary to raise the means to pay the soldier his hard-earned pittance have been made the subject of stereotyped harangues, calculated to excite sectional discord and inaugurate the "revolution in the North," which these men have over and over threatened against the Government and by such public proclamation in effect promised to Jeff. Davis and that part of his supporters operating in the rebel States. The system of voluntary enlistments has left these men full scope for their nefarious work, and it would be strange if this bill found favor in their eyes. The operation of the bill would be to cause the burden of this onerous public service to fall evenly upon the country, and require of the semi-loyal that he perform his duty. The business of discouraging enlistments would be done away with. It is a pity that our mistaken system has ever given it scope. The bill goes upon the presumption that every citizen not incapacitated by physical or mental disability owes military service to the country in its hour of extremity, and that it is honorable and praiseworthy to render such service. (Hon. Mr. Sargent.)

In a letter to the Governor of New York, dated August 7, 1863, President Lincoln says:

We cannot match the rebels in recruiting our armies if we waste time to re-experiment with the volunteer system, already deemed by Congress, and palpably, in fact, so far exhausted as to be inadequate.

The replies from the Governors of several of the States to the President's first call for troops, dated April 15, 1861, are further testimony as to the insufficiency of the laws then governing for raising troops and the necessity for legislation of the kind subsequently had. The replies are as follows, viz:

From Governor Letcher, of Virginia:

The militia of Virginia will not be furnished to the powers at Washington for any such use or purpose as they have in view. Your object is to subjugate the Southern States, and a requisition made upon me for such an object—an object, in my judgment, not within the purview of the Constitution or the act of 1795—

will not be complied with. You have chosen to inaugurate civil war, and, having done so, we will meet it in a spirit as determined as the Administration has exhibited toward the South.

From Governor Ellis, of North Carolina:

Your dispatch is received, and, if genuine—which its extraordinary character leads me to doubt—I have to say in reply that I regard the levy of troops made by the Administration for the purpose of subjugating the States of the South as in violation of the Constitution and a usurpation of power. I can be no party to this wicked violation of the laws of the country and to this war upon the liberties of a free people. You can get no troops from North Carolina. I will reply more in detail when your call is received by mail.

From Governor Magoffin, of Kentucky:

Your dispatch is received. In answer I say, emphatically, Kentucky will furnish no troops for the wicked purpose of subduing her sister Southern States.

From Governor Harris, of Tennessee:

Tennessee will not furnish a single man for coercion, but 50,000, if necessary, for the defense of our rights or those of our Southern brethren.

Governor Jackson, of Missouri:

Your requisition is illegal, unconstitutional, revolutionary, inhuman, diabolical, and cannot be complied with.

From Governor Rector, of Arkansas:

None will be furnished. The demand is only adding insult to injury.

It may be interesting to state the fact that, notwithstanding the positive refusals contained in the foregoing replies to furnish troops for the Government service, the people of the States named furnished troops for the U. S. service as follows:*

Virginia (including what is now West Virginia)	31,882
North Carolina	4,358
Kentucky	75,514
Tennessee	29,727
Missouri (in addition to a large number of home guards, Missouri State Militia)	104,834
Arkansas	5,472

Document No. 31.

"On the 9th day of the eighth month, in the year 1757, at night, orders came to the military officers in our county (Burlington) directing them to draft the militia and prepare a number of men to go as soldiers to the relief of the English at Fort William Henry, in New York government. A few days after there was a general review of the militia at Mount Holly, and a number of men chosen and sent off under some officers. Shortly after there came orders to draft three times as many, to hold themselves in readiness to march when fresh orders came; and on the 17th day of the eighth month there was a meeting of the military officers at Mount Holly, who agreed on a draft, and orders were sent to the men so chosen to meet their respective captains at set times and places—those in our township to meet at Mount Holly, amongst whom were a considerable number of our society. My mind being affected herewith, I had fresh opportunity to see and consider the advantage of living in the real substance of religion, where practice doth harmonize with principle. Among the officers are men of understanding, who have some regard to sincerity where they see it; and in the execution of their office, when they have

*But see revised statements, Vol. IV, this series, p. 1269.

men to deal with whom they believe to be upright-hearted, to put them to trouble on account of scruples of conscience is a painful task, and likely to be avoided as much as easily may be. But where men profess to be so meek and heavenly-minded and to have their trust so firmly settled in God that they cannot join in wars, and yet by their spirit and conduct in common life manifest a contrary disposition, their difficulties are great at such a time. Officers, who in great anxiety are endeavoring to get troops to answer the demands of their superiors, seeing men who are insincere pretend a scruple of conscience in hopes of being excused from a dangerous employment, are likely to handle them roughly. In this time of commotion some of our young men left the parts and tarried abroad till it was over; some came and proposed to go as soldiers; others appeared to have a real tender scruple in their mind against joining in wars, and were much humbled under the apprehension of a trial so near. I had conversation with several of these to my satisfaction. At the set time when the captain came to town, some of those last mentioned went and told him, in substance, as follows: That they could not bear arms for conscience sake; nor could they hire any to go in their places, being resigned as to the event of it. At length the captain acquainted them all that they might return home for the present, and required them to provide themselves as soldiers and to be in readiness to march when called upon. This was such a time as I had not seen before, and yet I may say, with thankfulness to the Lord, that I believed this trial was intended for our good, and I was favored with resignation to Him."

DOCUMENT No. 33.

Register of officers detailed as acting assistant provost-marshals-general, under the act approved March 3, 1863.

No.	Name.	Rank.	Post.	When assigned.	When relieved.
1	J. W. T. Gardiner	Major, U. S. Army	Augusta, Me	By S. O. No. 194, A. G. O., Apr. 29, 1863	By S. O. No. 402, A. G. O., Nov. 17, 1864.
2	R. M. Littler	Brevet lieutenant-colonel, volunteers, and major, Veteran Reserve Corps.	do	By S. O. No. 402, A. G. O., Nov. 17, 1864	By S. O. No. 580, A. G. O., Nov. 2, 1865, to take effect conditionally Nov. 1, 1865.
3	Charles Holmes	Captain, U. S. Army	do	By S. O. No. 548, A. G. O., Oct. 16, 1865	By S. O. No. 22, A. G. O., Jan. 17, 1866.
4	Thomas C. J. Bailey	Captain, 17th U. S. Infantry	do	By S. O. No. 81, A. G. O., Feb. 21, 1866.	
5	Oscar A. Mack	Major and aide-de-camp	Concord, N. H	By S. O. No. 264, A. G. O., June 15, 1863	By S. O. No. 497, A. G. O., Nov. 9, 1863.
6	E. W. Hinks	Brigadier-general, U. S. Volunteers.	do	By S. O. No. 497, A. G. O., Nov. 9, 1863	By S. O. No. 125, A. G. O., Mar. 23, 1864.
7	William Silvey	Brevet major and captain, 1st Artillery.	do	By S. O. No. 125, A. G. O., Mar. 23, 1864.	
8	H. B. Hendershott	Captain, 2d U. S. Artillery	Brattleborough, Vt	By S. O. No. 197, A. G. O., May 1, 1863	By S. O. No. 214, A. G. O., May 13, 1863.
9	T. G. Pitcher	Brigadier-general, U. S. Volunteers.	do	By S. O. No. 221, A. G. O., May 18, 1863	By S. O. No. 340, A. G. O., Oct. 10, 1864.
10	William Austine	Brevet colonel and major, U. S. Army.	do	By S. O. No. 340, A. G. O., Oct. 10, 1864.	
11	F. N. Clarke	Major, 5th U. S. Artillery	Boston, Mass	By S. O. No. 185, A. G. O., Apr. 23, 1863	By S. O. No. 21, A. G. O., Jan. 16, 1866.
12	Norman J. Hall	Captain, U. S. Army	do	By letter, dated Jan. 17, 1866.	
13	William Silvey	Captain, 1st U. S. Artillery	Providence, R. I	By S. O. No. 194, A. G. O., Apr. 29, 1863	By S. O. No. 117, A. G. O., Mar. 14, 1864.
14	Wesley Owens	Captain, 5th U. S. Cavalry	do	By S. O. No. 117, A. G. O., Mar. 14, 1864	By S. O. No. 288, A. G. O., Sept. 1, 1864.
15	Horace Neide	Lieutenant-colonel, Veteran Reserve Corps.	do	By S. O. No. 301, A. G. O., Sept. 10, 1864	By letter, Apr. 22, to take effect Apr. 30, 1865.
16	Delavan D. Perkins	Major and additional aide-de-camp, U. S. Army.	Hartford, Conn	By S. O. No. 189, A. G. O., Apr. 25, 1863	By S. O. No. 229, A. G. O., July 7, 1864.
17	F. D. Sewall	Colonel, Veteran Reserve Corps	do	By S. O. No. 229, A. G. O., July 7, 1864	By S. O. No. 39, A. G. O., Jan. 25, 1865.
18	C. C. Gilbert	Major 19th U. S. Infantry	do	By S. O. No. 39, A. G. O., Jan. 25, 1865	By S. O. No. 21, A. G. O., Jan. 16, 1866.
19	W. R. Pease	Major, U. S. Army	do	By letter, Jan. 17, 1866.	
20	F. Townsend	Major 9th U. S. Infantry	Albany, N. Y., Northern Division.	By S. O. No. 185, A. G. O., Apr. 23, 1863	By S. O. No. 16, A. G. O., Jan. 12, 1866, to take effect Feb. 1, 1866.
21	A. S. Diven	Major and assistant adjutant-general, volunteers.	Elmira, N. Y., Western Division.	By S. O. No. 217, A. G. O., May 15, 1863	By S. O. No. 437, A. G. O., Dec. 9, 1864.
22	John A. Haddock	Major, Veteran Reserve Corps	do	By S. O. No. 437, A. G. O., Dec. 9, 1864	By S. O. No. 166, A. G. O., Apr. 10, 1865.
23	Samuel B. Hayman	Major 10th U. S. Infantry	do	By S. O. No. 166, A. G. O., Apr. 10, 1865	By S. O. No. 16, A. G. O., Jan. 12, 1866, to take effect Feb. 1, 1866.
24	Robert Nugent	Colonel 69th New York Volunteers.	New York, N. Y., Southern Division.	By S. O. No. 178, A. G. O., Apr. 18, 1863	By letter, Provost-Marshal-General, Oct. 28, 1863.
25	William Hays	Brigadier-general, U. S. Volunteers.	do	By S. O. No. 480, A. G. O., Oct. 27, 1863	By S. O. No. 49, A. G. O., Jan. 31, 1865.
26	E. W. Hinks	Brigadier-general, U. S. Volunteers.	do	By S. O. No. 49, A. G. O., Jan. 31, 1865	By S. O. No. 98, A. G. O., Feb. 27, 1865.
27	R. I. Dodge	Major 12th U. S. Infantry	do	By S. O. No. 98, A. G. O., Feb. 27, 1865	By S. O. No. 16, A. G. O., Jan. 12, 1866. In charge of the State of New York, with his office at Albany, N. Y., to take effect Feb. 1, 1866.

28	John H. Alexander	Lieutenant-colonel 4th Maryland Volunteers.	Baltimore, Md., for Delaware and Maryland.	By S. O. No. 215, A. G. O., May 14, 1863.	
29	N. L. Jeffries	Major and assistant adjutant-general, volunteers.	do	By S. O. No. 360, A. G. O., Aug. 13, 1863	By S. O. No. 273, A. G. O., Aug. 17, 1864.
30	William H. Browne	Colonel, Veteran Reserve Corps	do	By S. O. No. 273, A. G. O., Aug. 17, 1864.	
31	C. F. Ruff	Lieutenant-colonel 3d U. S. Cavalry.	Harrisburg, Pa., Western Division.	By S. O. No. 194, A. G. O., Apr. 29, 1863	By S. O. No. 233, A. G. O., May 25, 1863.
32	J. V. Bomford	Lieutenant-colonel 16th U. S. Infantry.	do	By S. O. No. 233, A. G. O., May 25, 1863	By S. O. No. 245, A. G. O., July 22, 1864.
33	R. I. Dodge	Captain, 8th U. S. Infantry	do	By S. O. No. 245, A. G. O., July 22, 1864	By S. O. No. 98, A. G. O., Feb. 27, 1865.
34	E. W. Hinks	Brigadier-general, U. S. Volunteers.	do	By S. O. No. 98, A. G. O., Feb. 27, 1865	By S. O. No. 285, A. G. O., June 7, 1865.
35	W. N. Grier	Lieutenant-colonel 1st U. S. Cavalry.	do	By S. O. No. 285, A. G. O., June 7, 1865.	
36	C. C. Gilbert	Captain, 1st U. S. Infantry	Philadelphia, Pa., Eastern Division.	By S. O. No. 373, A. G. O., Aug. 21, 1863	By S. O. No. 39, A. G. O., Jan. 25, 1865.
37	J. Hayden	Major 10th U. S. Infantry	do	By S. O. No. 39, A. G. O., Jan. 25, 1865	By S. O. No. 238, A. G. O., May 18, 1865.
38	William B. Lane	Brevet major and captain, 3d U. S. Cavalry.	do	By S. O. No. 238, A. G. O., May 18, 1865.	
39	R. C. Buchanan	Lieutenant-colonel 4th Infantry	Trenton, N. J	By S. O. No. 194, A. G. O., Apr. 29, 1863	By S. O. No. 389, A. G. O., Nov. 8, 1864.
40	John Ely	Colonel, Veteran Reserve Corps	do	By S. O. No. 387, A. G. O., Nov. 7, 1864	By S. O. No. 21, A. G. O., Jan. 16, 1866.
41	Llewellyn Jones	Major, U. S. Army	do	By letter, dated Jan. 17, 1866.	
42	Joseph Darr, jr	Major, 1st Virginia Cavalry	Wheeling, W. Va	By S. O. No. 194, A. G. O., Apr. 29, 1863	By S. O. No. 234, A. G. O., July 11, 1864.
43	John Ely	Colonel, Veteran Reserve Corps	do	By S. O. No. 234, A. G. O., July 11, 1864	By S. O. No. 387, A. G. O., Nov. 7, 1864.
44	E. P. Hudson	Captain, Veteran Reserve Corps	do	By S. O. No. 387, A. G. O., Nov. 7, 1864	By S. O. No. 21, A. G. O., Jan. 16, 1866.
45	George McGown	Captain, U. S. Army	do	By letter, Jan. 17, 1866.	
46	William H. Sidell	Major 15th U. S. Infantry	Louisville, Ky	By S. O. No. 279, A. G. O., June 24, 1863, to date June 4, 1863.	
47	Edwin A. Parrott	Colonel 1st Ohio Infantry	Columbus, Ohio	By S. O. No. 194, A. G. O., Apr. 29, 1863	By S. O. No. 74, A. G. O., Feb. 15, 1864.
48	J. H. Potter	Colonel 12th New Hampshire Volunteers.	do	By S. O. No. 74, A. G. O., Feb. 15, 1864	By S. O. No. 290, A. G. O., Sept. 2, 1864.
49	James A. Wilcox	Colonel 190th Ohio Volunteers	do	By S. O. No. 290, A. G. O., Sept. 2, 1864.	
50	Bennett H. Hill	Major, 2d U. S. Artillery	Detroit, Mich	By S. O. No. 185, A. G. O., Apr. 23, 1863	By S. O. No. 410, A. G. O., July 31, 1865.
51	John H. Knight	Captain, 18th U. S. Infantry	do	By S. O. No. 410, A. G. O., July 31, 1865.	
52	Conrad Baker	Colonel 1st Indiana Cavalry	Indianapolis, Ind	By S. O. No. 194, A. G. O., Apr. 29, 1863	By S. O. No. 273, A. G. O., Aug. 17, 1864.
53	James G. Jones	Colonel 42d Indiana Infantry	do	By S. O. No. 273, A. G. O., Aug. 17, 1864	By S. O. No. 340, A. G. O., Oct. 10, 1864.
54	T. G. Pitcher	Brigadier-general, U. S. Volunteers.	do	By S. O. No. 340, A. G. O., Oct. 10, 1864.	
55	James Oakes	Lieutenant-colonel 4th U. S. Cavalry.	Springfield, Ill	By S. O. No. 194, A. G. O., Apr. 29, 1863.	
56	E. B. Alexander	Colonel 10th U. S. Infantry	Saint Louis, Mo	By S. O. No. 197, A. G. O., May 1, 1863.	
57	Thomas Duncan	Major, 3d U. S. Cavalry	Davenport, Iowa	By S. O. No. 266, A. G. O., June 16, 1863.	
58	Charles S. Lovell	Lieutenant-colonel 18th U. S. Infantry.	Madison, Wis	By S. O. No. 194, A. G. O., Apr. 29, 1863	By S. O. No. 571, A. G. O., Dec. 24, 1863.*
59	James D. Greene	Colonel 6th U. S. Infantry	do	By S. O. No. 571, A. G. O., Dec. 24, 1863	By S. O. No. 215, A. G. O., June 21, 1864.
60	G. R. Giddings	Lieutenant-colonel 16th U. S. Infantry.	do	By S. O. No. 407, A. G. O., July 29, 1865.	
61	Anderson D. Nelson	Captain, 10th U. S. Infantry	Saint Paul, Minn	By S. O. No. 194, A. G. O., Apr. 29, 1863	By S. O. No. 260, A. G. O., June 12, 1863.
62	T. M. Saunders	Captain, 3d U. S. Artillery	do	By S. O. No. 260, A. G. O., June 12, 1863	Died Jan. 26, 1864.

*Again assigned June 21, 1864; relieved July 29, 1865.

Register of officers detailed as acting assistant provost-marshals-general, under the act approved March 3, 1863—Continued.

No.	Name.	Rank.	Post.	When assigned.	When relieved.
63	John T. Averill	Lieutenant-colonel 6th Minnesota Volunteers.	Saint Paul, Minn	By S. O. No. 57, A. G. O., Feb. 5, 1864	By S. O. No. 445, A. G. O., Aug. 17, 1865.
64	F. P. Cahill	Colonel, Veteran Reserve Corps	do	By S. O. No. 445, A. G. O., Aug. 17, 1865	By S. O. No. 601, A. G. O., Nov. 15, 1865.
65	William H. Rossell	Captain, U. S. Army	do	By S. O. No. 601, A. G. O., Nov. 15, 1865.	
66	Sidney Clarke	Captain and assistant adjutant-general, volunteers.	Leavenworth, Kans., for Kansas, Nebraska, Colorado, and Dakota Territories.	By S. O. No. 239, A. G. O., May 28, 1863	By S. O. No. 73, A. G. O., Feb. 14, 1865.
67	William W. Lowe	Captain, 5th U. S. Cavalry	do	By S. O. No. 73, A. G. O., Feb. 14, 1865.	
68	Pinkney Lugenbeel	Brevet major and captain, 19th Infantry.	Portland, Oreg., for Oregon and Washington Territory.	By S. O. No. 354, A. G. O., Aug. 10, 1863	By S. O. No. 489, A. G. O., Nov. 3, 1863.
69	Thomas C. English	Lieutenant-colonel 1st Washington Territory Volunteers, and captain, 9th U. S. Infantry.	do	By S. O. No. 489, A. G. O., Nov. 3, 1863	By S. O. No. 510, A. G. O., Nov. 17, 1863.
70	N. H. McLean	Major and assistant adjutant-general, U. S. Army.	do	By S. O. No. 510, A. G. O., Nov. 17, 1863	By S. O. No. 222, A. G. O., June 29, 1864.
71	Thom^s C. English	Colonel 1st Washington Territory Volunteers, and Major 5th U. S. Infantry.	do	By S. O. No. 222, A. G. O., June 29, 1864.	
72	George P. Andrews	Captain and brevet major, 3d Artillery.	San Francisco, Cal., for California and Nevada.	By S. O. No. 354, A. G. O., Aug. 10, 1863	By S. O. No. 510, A. G. O., Nov. 17, 1863.
73	John S. Mason	Brigadier-general, U. S. Volunteers.	do	By S. O. No. 510, A. G. O., Nov. 17, 1863	By S. O. No. 117, A. G. O., Mar. 10, 1865.
74	George P. Andrews	Captain and brevet major, 3d Artillery.	do	By S. O. No. 117, A. G. O., Mar. 10, 1865	By S. O. No. 141, A. G. O., Mar. 23, 1865.
75	Hugh B. Fleming	Captain, 9th U. S. Infantry	do	By S. O. No. 141, A. G. O., Mar. 23, 1865	By S. O. No. 21, Military Division of the Pacific, Nov. 6, 1865.
76	Washington Seawell	Colonel, U. S. Army	do	By letter, dated Dec. 5, 1865.	

DOCUMENT No. 34.

Register of the members of the boards of enrollment, appointed under the act approved March 3, 1863.

No.	Name.	Rank.	District.	State.	When appointed.	Remarks.
1	Charles H. Doughty	Provost-marshal	1	Maine	Apr. 24, 1863	Honorably discharged Oct. 31 1865.
2	Edward S. Morris	Commissioner	1	do	Apr. 30, 1863	Appointment canceled Aug. 10, 1864.
3	Samuel C. Adams	do	1	do	Aug. 10, 1864	Honorably discharged May 8, 1865.
4	Theo. H. Jewett	Surgeon	1	do	Apr. 30, 1863	Resigned Jan. 22, 1864.
5	Charles W. Thomas	do	1	do	Jan. 22, 1864	Honorably discharged June 15, 1865.
6	John S. Baker	Provost-marshal	2	do	Apr. 24, 1863	Resigned Aug. 15, 1864.
7	Nahum Morrill	do	2	do	Sept. 27, 1864	Honorably discharged Oct. 31, 1865.
8	Joel Perham, jr	Commissioner	2	do	Apr. 30, 1863	Honorably discharged May 8, 1865.
9	Alex. Burbank	Surgeon	2	do	Apr. 30, 1863	Honorably discharged June 15, 1865.
10	A. P. Davis	Provost-marshal	3	do	Apr. 24, 1863	Honorably discharged Aug. 15, 1865.
11	Henry A. Williams	Commissioner	3	do	Apr. 30, 1863	Resigned Dec. 2, 1864.
12	Joseph T. Woodward	do	3	do	Dec. 12, 1864	Honorably discharged May 8, 1865.
13	Greenlief A. Wilbur	Surgeon	3	do	Apr. 30, 1863	Honorably discharged June 15, 1865.
14	Elijah Low	Provost-marshal	4	do	Apr. 30, 1863	Honorably discharged Oct. 31, 1865.
15	Charles H. Chandler	Commissioner	4	do	Apr. 30, 1863	Resigned Dec. 12, 1864.
16	John E. Godfrey	do	4	do	Jan. 17, 1865	Honorably discharged May 8, 1865.
17	Sumner A. Patten	Surgeon	4	do	Apr. 30, 1863	Honorably discharged June 30, 1865.
18	Andrew D. Bean	Provost-marshal	5	do	Apr. 30, 1863	Appointment revoked Sept. 29, 1864.*
19	William H. Fogler	do	5	do	Nov. 15, 1864	Resigned Jan. 26, 1865.
20	Alvin G. Crocker	Commissioner	5	do	Apr. 30, 1863	Honorably discharged May 8, 1865.
21	Samuel B. Hunter	Surgeon	5	do	Apr. 30, 1863	Resigned Nov. 2, 1864.
22	A. J. Billings	do	5	do	Nov. 15, 1864	Honorably discharged June 15, 1865.
23	John S. Godfrey	Provost-marshal	1	New Hampshire	Apr. 30, 1863	Relieved by special order, Adjutant-General's Office, Dec. 18, 1863.
24	Nathaniel Wiggin	do	1	do	Dec. 29, 1863	Resigned July 23, 1864.
25	Daniel Hall	do	1	do	July 30, 1864	Honorably discharged Oct. 10, 1865.
26	Jeremiah C. Tilton	Commissioner	1	do	Apr. 30, 1863	Honorably discharged May 8, 1865.
27	Jeremiah T. Hall	Surgeon	1	do	Apr. 30, 1863	Honorably discharged June 15, 1865.
28	Anthony Colby	Provost-marshal	2	do	Apr. 30, 1863	Resigned June 16, 1864.
29	Hosea Eaton	do	2	do	July 1, 1864	Honorably discharged Sept. 30, 1865.
30	Henry F. Richmond	Commissioner	2	do	Apr. 30, 1863	Appointment revoked Nov. 21, 1863.
31	Samuel Upton	do	2	do	Nov. 25, 1863	Honorably discharged May 8, 1865.
32	R. B. Carswell	Surgeon	2	do	Apr. 30, 1863	Honorably discharged June 15, 1865.
33	Chester Pike	Provost-marshal	3	do	Apr. 30, 1863	Honorably discharged Oct. 10, 1865.
34	Francis A. Faulkner	Commissioner	3	do	Apr. 30, 1863	Honorably discharged May 8, 1865.
35	Dixi Crosby	Surgeon	3	do	Apr. 30, 1863	Honorably discharged June 15, 1865.
36	Cyrus R. Crane	Provost-marshal	1	Vermont	Apr. 24, 1863	Honorably discharged Oct. 15, 1865.
37	Andrew C. Brown	Commissioner	1	do	Apr. 24, 1863	Honorably discharged May 8, 1865.
38	Benjamin F. Morgan	Surgeon	1	do	Apr. 24, 1863	Honorably discharged June 15, 1865.
39	Gilman Henry	Provost-marshal	2	do	Apr. 24, 1863	Honorably discharged Oct. 15, 1865.

*Again appointed February 2, 1865; honorably discharged October 31, 1865.

Register of the members of the boards of enrollment, appointed under the act approved March 3, 1863—Continued.

No.	Name.	Rank.	District.	State.	When appointed.	Remarks
40	Darwin H. Ranney	Commissioner	2	Vermont	Apr. 24, 1863	Honorably discharged May 8, 1865.
41	Carlton P. Frost	Surgeon	2	do	Apr. 24, 1863	Honorably discharged June 15, 1865.
42	Rolla Gleason	Provost-marshal	3	do	Apr. 24, 1863	Honorably discharged Oct. 15, 1865.
43	Elisha White	Commissioner	3	do	Apr. 24, 1863	Honorably discharged May 8, 1865.
44	John L. Chandler	Surgeon	3	do	Apr. 24, 1863	Honorably discharged June 15, 1865.
45	Albert D. Hatch	Provost-marshal	1	Massachusetts	Apr. 29, 1863	Honorably discharged Oct. 15, 1865.
46	Nathaniel Hinckley	Commissioner	1	do	Apr. 29, 1863	Honorably discharged May 8, 1865.
47	Foster Hooper	Surgeon	1	do	Apr. 29, 1863	Resigned Oct. 26, 1863.
48	Frederick H. Hooper	do	1	do	Nov. 2, 1863	Honorably discharged June 15, 1865.
49	John W. D. Hall	Provost-marshal	2	do	Apr. 29, 1863	Honorably discharged Oct. 15, 1865.
50	Nathaniel Wales	Commissioner	2	do	Apr. 29, 1863	Honorably discharged May 8, 1865.
51	H. B. Hubbard	Surgeon	2	do	Apr. 29, 1863	Honorably discharged June 15, 1865.
52	George A. Shaw	Provost-marshal	3	do	Apr. 29, 1863	Resigned Dec. 31, 1863
53	John W. Le Barnes	do	3	do	Jan. 18, 1864	Resigned Feb. 23, 1865.
54	W. H. McCartney	do	3	do	Feb. 28, 1865	Honorably discharged Dec. 31, 1865.
55	John W. Le Barnes	Commissioner	3	do	Apr. 29, 1863	Promoted provost-marshal Jan. 18, 1864.
56	William W. Titcomb	do	3	do	Jan. 30, 1864	Honorably discharged May 8, 1865.
57	Joseph H. Streeter	Surgeon	3	do	Apr. 29, 1863	Honorably discharged June 15, 1865.
58	William Greene Howe	Provost-marshal	4	do	Apr. 29, 1863	Resigned March 11, 1865.
59	John Phillips	do	4	do	Mar. 15, 1865	Honorably discharged June 15, 1865.
60	Halsey J. Boardman	Commissioner	4	do	Apr. 29, 1863	Honorably discharged May 8, 1865.
61	Henry I. Bowditch	Surgeon	4	do	Apr. 29, 1863	Honorably discharged June 15, 1865.
62	Daniel H. Johnson, jr	Provost-marshal	5	do	Apr. 29, 1863	Honorably discharged Oct. 15, 1865.
63	Henry W. Moulton	Commissioner	5	do	Apr. 29, 1863	Resigned Dec. 20, 1864.
64	James D. Black	do	5	do	Dec. 27, 1864	Honorably discharged May 8, 1865.
65	Daniel Perley	Surgeon	5	do	Apr. 29, 1863	Honorably discharged June 15, 1865.
66	Horatio G. Herrick	Provost-marshal	6	do	Apr. 29, 1863	Honorably discharged Oct. 15, 1865.
67	Phineas E. Davis	Commissioner	6	do	Apr. 29, 1863	Resigned Feb. 15, 1864.
68	Samuel W. Hopkinson	do	6	do	Feb. 25, 1864	Honorably discharged May 8, 1865.
69	John L. Sullivan, jr	Surgeon	6	do	Apr. 29, 1863	Honorably discharged June 15, 1865.
70	Homer A. Cooke	Provost-marshal	7	do	Apr. 29, 1863	Appointment revoked June 15, 1863.
71	S. Benton Thompson	do	7	do	June 15, 1863	Honorably discharged Oct. 15, 1865.
72	Addison Grant Fay	Commissioner	7	do	Apr. 29, 1863	Honorably discharged May 8, 1865.
73	David S. Fogg	Surgeon	7	do	Apr. 29, 1863	Honorably discharged June 15, 1865.
74	Samuel V. Stone	Provost-marshal	8	do	Apr. 29, 1863	Honorably discharged Oct. 15, 1865.
75	Charles H. Deans	Commissioner	8	do	Apr. 29, 1863	Honorably discharged May 8, 1865.
76	Oramel Martin	Surgeon	8	do	Apr. 29, 1863	Honorably discharged June 15, 1865.
77	David H. Merriam	Provost-marshal	9	do	Apr. 29, 1863	Honorably discharged Oct. 15, 1865.
78	Zenas W. Bliss	Commissioner	9	do	Apr. 28, 1863	Resigned Aug. 23, 1864.
79	Samuel J. Storrs	do	9	do	Aug. 26, 1864	Honorably discharged May 8, 1865.
80	E. C. Richardson	Surgeon	9	do	Apr. 29, 1863	Honorably discharged June 15, 1865.
81	James H. Morton	Provost-marshal	10	do	Apr. 29, 1863	Resigned May 20, 1863.
82	Henry M. Morehouse	do	10	do	July 6, 1863	Honorably discharged Dec. 4, 1865.

83	Graham A. Root	Commissioner	10	do	Apr. 29, 1863	Resigned July 5, 1863.
84	James H. Morton	do	10	do	July 6, 1863	Honorably discharged May 8, 1865.
85	Samuel Duncan	Surgeon	10	do	Apr. 29, 1863	Honorably discharged June 15, 1865.
86	William E. Hamlin	Provost-marshal	1	Rhode Island	Apr. 28, 1863	Honorably discharged Apr. 30, 1865.
87	William Y. Potter	Commissioner	1	do	Apr. 28, 1863	Do.
88	Charles G. McKnight	Surgeon	1	do	Apr. 28, 1863	Do.
89	A. B. Chadsey	Provost-marshal	2	do	Apr. 28, 1863	Do
90	James H. Coggeshall	Commissioner	2	do	Apr. 28, 1863	Do.
91	Fenner H. Peckham	Surgeon	2	do	Apr. 28, 1863	Do.
92	Lucius G. Goodrich	Provost-marshal	1	Connecticut	Apr. 30, 1863	Honorably discharged Oct. 5, 1865.
93	George M. Ives	Commissioner	1	do	Apr. 30, 1863	Honorably discharged May 8, 1865.
94	Harry A. Grant	Surgeon	1	do	Apr. 30, 1863	Resigned Feb. 3, 1864.
95	J. S. Curtis	do	1	do	Mar. 1, 1864	Honorably discharged June 15, 1865.
96	Benjamin S. Pardee	Provost-marshal	2	do	Apr. 30, 1863	Resigned Nov. 17, 1863.
97	Richard M. Clarke	do	2	do	Dec. 14, 1863	Honorably discharged Oct. 5, 1865.
98	D. R. Wright	Commissioner	2	do	Apr. 30, 1863	Honorably discharged May 8, 1865.
99	Edwin A. Parke	Surgeon	2	do	Apr. 30, 1863	Honorably discharged June 15, 1865.
100	Isaac H. Bromley	Provost-marshal	3	do	Apr. 30, 1863	Resigned Aug. 2, 1864.
101	Theodore C. Kibbe	do	3	do	Aug. 8, 1864	Honorably discharged Oct. 5, 1865.
102	Samuel Bingham	Commissioner	3	do	Apr. 30, 1863	Honorably discharged May 8, 1865.
103	Robert McCurdy Lord	Surgeon	3	do	Apr. 30, 1863	Honorably discharged June 15, 1865.
104	J. E. Dunham	Provost-marshal	4	do	Apr. 30, 1863	Discharged Sept. 9, 1863.
105	William H. Riley	do	4	do	Sept. 9, 1863	Appointment revoked Jan. 9, 1864.
106	Leverett W. Wessells	do	4	do	Jan. 9, 1864	Honorably discharged Oct. 5, 1865.
107	Jasper P. Brewster	Commissioner	4	do	Apr. 30, 1863	Discharged Sept. 9, 1863.
108	Frederick Ellsworth	do	4	do	Sept. 9, 1863	Appointment revoked Jan. 9, 1864.
109	Edward J. Alvord	do	4	do	Jan. 9, 1864	Honorably discharged May 8, 1865.
110	Samuel T. Salisbury	Surgeon	4	do	Apr. 30, 1863	Dismissed by sentence of general court-martial Nov. 9, 1863.*
111	W. H. Trowbridge	do	4	do	Dec. 22, 1863	Honorably discharged June 15, 1865.
112	Edwin Rose	Provost-marshal	1	New York	Apr. 15, 1863	Died Jan. 12, 1864.
113	James A. Fleury	do	1	do	Jan. 30, 1864	Honorably discharged May 31, 1865.
114	W. S. McCoun	Commissioner	1	do	Apr. 17, 1863	Honorably discharged May 8, 1865.
115	John Ordronaux	Surgeon	1	do	Apr. 17, 1863	Resigned Aug. 4, 1863.
116	George N. Richardson	do	1	do	Aug. 13, 1863	Appointment revoked Sept. 5, 1863.
117	Philemon F. Prior	do	1	do	Sept. 5, 1863	Honorably discharged June 15, 1865.
118	Samuel T. Maddox	Provost-marshal	2	do	Apr. 15, 1863	Resigned June 27, 1864.
119	Samuel W. Waldron	do	2	do	Aug. 9, 1864	Dismissed the service June 5, 1865.
120	Charles W. Cheshire	Commissioner	2	do	Apr. 17, 1863	Dismissed by sentence of general court-martial July 29, 1865.
121	George S. Woodman	Surgeon	2	do	Apr. 17, 1863	Discharged Apr. 28, 1865.
122	Stephen B. Gregory	Provost-marshal	3	do	Apr. 15, 1863	Appointment revoked Apr. 18, 1864.
123	E. B. Fowler	do	3	do	July 6, 1864	Honorably discharged Nov. 30, 1865.
124	Abner M. Beebe	Commissioner	3	do	Apr. 17, 1863	Honorably discharged May 8, 1865.
125	Nelson L. North	Surgeon	3	do	Apr. 17, 1863	Resigned Feb. 10, 1864.
126	G. T. Dougherty	do	3	do	Feb. 22, 1864	Resigned Oct. 5, 1864.
127	S. N. Fisk	do	3	do	Oct. 18, 1864	Honorably discharged June 15, 1865.
128	Joel B. Erhardt	Provost-marshal	4	do	Apr. 15, 1863	Resigned Apr. 26, 1865.
129	Daniel McFarland	Commissioner	4	do	Apr. 17, 1863	Honorably discharged May 22, 1865.

* Revoked Feb. 28, 1866, and was honorably discharged as of date of dismissal.

Register of the members of the boards of enrollment, appointed under the act approved March 3, 1863—Continued.

No.	Name.	Rank.	District.	State.	When appointed.	Remarks.
130	James O'Rorke	Surgeon	4	New York	Apr. 17, 1863	Honorably discharged June 15, 1865.
131	John Duffy	Provost-marshal	5	do	Apr. 15, 1863	Dismissed Dec. 16, 1863.
132	H. P. West	do	5	do	Dec. 31, 1863	Honorably discharged Oct. 5, 1865.
133	H. P. West	Commissioner	5	do	Apr. 17, 1863	Promoted provost-marshal Dec. 31, 1863.
134	David Miller	do	5	do	Jan. 9, 1864	Honorably discharged May 8, 1865.
135	Ernest Krackowizer	Surgeon	5	do	Apr. 17, 1863	Resigned June 1, 1863.
136	Joseph Hilton	do	5	do	June 3, 1863	Honorably discharged June 15, 1865.
137	James W. Farr	Provost-marshal	6	do	Apr. 15, 1863	Appointment revoked Nov. 11, 1863.
138	Theo. B. Bronson	do	6	do	Nov. 11, 1863	Resigned Apr. 25, 1864.
139	Charles R. Coster	do	6	do	May 18, 1864	Resigned Apr. 30, 1865.
140	Charles A. Lamont	Commissioner	6	do	Apr. 17, 1863	Appointment revoked Nov. 11, 1863.
141	Robert Edwards	do	6	do	Nov. 11, 1863	Resigned Dec. 11, 1863.
142	Samuel Glover	do	6	do	Jan. 9, 1864	Honorably discharged May 8, 1865.
143	James W. Powell	Surgeon	6	do	Apr. 17, 1863	Appointment revoked Nov. 11, 1863.
144	Alfred L. Loomis	do	6	do	Nov. 11, 1863	Honorably discharged June 15, 1865.
145	Frederick C. Wagner	Provost-marshal	7	do	Apr. 29, 1863	Honorably discharged Dec. 31, 1865.
146	Boardman Baldwin	Commissioner	7	do	Apr. 17, 1863	Died Oct. 13, 1863.
147	Samuel G. Acton	do	7	do	Oct. 20, 1863	Honorably discharged May 8, 1865.
148	John R. Vankleek	Surgeon	7	do	Apr. 17, 1863	Honorably discharged June 15, 1865.
149	Benjamin F. Manierre	Provost-marshal	8	do	Apr. 15, 1863	Honorably discharged May 31, 1865.
150	Spencer Kirby	Commissioner	8	do	Apr. 17, 1863	Honorably discharged May 8, 1865.
151	George F. Woodward	Surgeon	8	do	Apr. 17, 1863	Resigned May 9, 1864.
152	William C. Roberts	do	8	do	May 9, 1864	Honorably discharged June 15, 1865.
153	Charles E. Jenkins	Provost-marshal	9	do	Apr. 15, 1863	Resigned Dec. 7, 1863.
154	William Dunning	do	9	do	Jan. 2, 1864	Honorably discharged May 31, 1865.
155	John M. Sands	Commissioner	9	do	Apr. 17, 1863	Honorably discharged May 8, 1865.
156	William H. Thomson	Surgeon	9	do	Apr. 17, 1863	Honorably discharged June 15, 1865.
157	Moses G. Leonard	Provost-marshal	10	do	Apr. 15, 1863	Resigned Feb. 16, 1864.
158	William W. Pierson	do	10	do	Feb. 25, 1864	Honorably discharged Oct. 5, 1865.
159	James Ryder	Commissioner	10	do	Apr. 17, 1863	Honorably discharged May 8, 1865.
160	George B. Upham	Surgeon	10	do	Apr. 17, 1863	Resigned Aug. 18, 1864.
161	Lewis F. Pelton	do	10	do	Aug. 27, 1864	Honorably discharged June 15, 1865.
162	Abram L. Nanny	Provost-marshal	11	do	Apr. 15, 1863	Resigned Apr. 19, 1864.
163	James N. Pronk	do	11	do	Apr. 26, 1864	Honorably discharged Oct. 31, 1865.
164	John C. Holley	Commissioner	11	do	Apr. 17, 1863	Appointment revoked Dec. 12, 1864.
165	James L. Stewart	do	11	do	Dec. 12, 1864	Honorably discharged May 8, 1865.
166	John C. Boyd	Surgeon	11	do	Apr. 17, 1863	Honorably discharged June 15, 1865.
167	Isaac Platt	Provost-marshal	12	do	Apr. 15, 1863	Dismissed the service Feb. 13, 1864.
168	William S. Johnston	do	12	do	Feb. 17, 1864	Honorably discharged Oct. 31, 1865.
169	Joseph Wild	Commissioner	12	do	Apr. 17, 1863	Honorably discharged May 8, 1865.
170	William H. Pitcher	Surgeon	12	do	Apr. 17, 1863	Appointment revoked Feb. 13, 1864.
171	A. E. Van Dusen	do	12	do	Apr. 19, 1864	Appointment revoked Oct. 5, 1864.
172	T. C. Payne	do	12	do	Oct. 5, 1864	Honorably discharged June 15, 1865.

173	Joshua Fiero, jr	Provost-marshal	13	do	Apr. 15, 1863	Resigned Dec. 4, 1863.
174	John Lyon	do	13	do	Jan. 2, 1864	Honorably discharged Oct. 31, 1865.
175	George T. Pierce	Commissioner	13	do	Apr. 17, 1863	Honorably discharged May 8, 1865.
176	Abram H. Knapp	Surgeon	13	do	Apr. 17, 1863	Honorably discharged June 15, 1865.
177	John O. Cole	Provost-marshal	14	do	Apr. 15, 1863	Resigned Dec. 22, 1863.
178	S. H. H. Parsons	do	14	do	Jan. 7, 1864	Honorably discharged Dec. 31, 1865.
179	Weidman Dominick	Commissioner	14	do	May 8, 1863	Honorably discharged May 8, 1865.
180	S. Oakley Vanderpool	Surgeon	14	do	Apr. 17, 1863	Honorably discharged June 15, 1865.
181	Charles Hughes	Provost-marshal	15	do	Apr. 15, 1863	Resigned June 20, 1864, and appointed commissioner July 16, 1864.
182	James Forsyth	do	15	do	June 25, 1864	Honorably discharged Dec. 31, 1865.
183	do	Commissioner	15	do	Apr. 17, 1863	Resigned and appointed provost-marshal June 25, 1864.
184	Charles Hughes	do	15	do	July 16, 1864	Honorably discharged May 8, 1865.
185	Charles L. Hubbell	Surgeon	15	do	Apr. 17, 1863	Honorably discharged June 15, 1865.
186	George Clendon, jr	Provost-marshal	16	do	Apr. 15, 1863	Appointment revoked Feb. 13, 1865.
187	Andrew J. Cheretree	do	16	do	Apr. 7, 1865	Honorably discharged Oct. 31, 1865.
188	A. P. Brand	Commissioner	16	do	Apr. 17, 1863	Honorably discharged May 8, 1865.
189	George Page	Surgeon	16	do	Apr. 17, 1863	Resigned Nov. 23, 1863.
190	J. Platt Foote	do	16	do	Dec. 4, 1863	Honorably discharged June 15, 1865.
191	S. C. F. Thorndike	Provost-marshal	17	do	Apr. 15, 1863	Honorably discharged Dec. 31, 1865.
192	Schuyler F. Judd	Commissioner	17	do	May 11, 1863	Appointment revoked Dec. 16, 1863.
193	William Stephenson	do	17	do	Dec. 17, 1863	Honorably discharged May 8, 1865.
194	Henry Hewitt	Surgeon	17	do	Apr. 17, 1863	Resigned Dec. 27, 1864.
195	G. F. Cole	do	17	do	Jan. 5, 1865	Discharged the service Apr. 27, 1865.
196	James P. Butler	Provost-marshal	18	do	Apr. 15, 1863	Honorably discharged Oct. 31, 1865.
197	Bradford T. Simmons	Commissioner	18	do	Apr. 17, 1863	Honorably discharged May 8, 1865.
198	Uriah Potter	Surgeon	18	do	Apr. 17, 1863	Resigned Jan. 30, 1865.
199	Alexander M. Vedder	do	18	do	Feb. 8, 1865	Honorably discharged June 15, 1865.
200	Samuel Gordon	Provost-marshal	19	do	Apr. 15, 1863	Honorably discharged Oct. 31, 1865.
201	George S. Gorham	Commissioner	19	do	Apr. 17, 1863	Honorably discharged May 8, 1865.
202	Solomon F. McFarland	Surgeon	19	do	Apr. 17, 1863	Resigned June 24, 1864.
203	George Douglass	do	19	do	July 15, 1864	Honorably discharged June 15, 1865.
204	Frederick Emerson	Provost-marshal	20	do	Apr. 15, 1863	Honorably discharged Oct. 31, 1865.
205	Arthur Pond	Commissioner	20	do	Apr. 17, 1863	Honorably discharged May 8, 1865.
206	Edward S. Walker	Surgeon	20	do	Apr. 17, 1863	Honorably discharged June 15, 1865.
207	Joseph P. Richardson	Provost-marshal	21	do	Apr. 15, 1863	Dismissed the service Dec. 20, 1864.
208	Peter B. Crandall	do	21	do	Jan. 14, 1865	Discharged May 31, 1865.
209	Ivers Monroe	Commissioner	21	do	Apr. 17, 1863	Honorably discharged May 8, 1865
210	Welcome A. Babcock	Surgeon	21	do	Apr. 17, 1863	Honorably discharged Apr. 28, 186
211	Addison L. Scott	Provost-marshal	22	do	Apr. 15, 1863	Honorably discharged Oct. 15, 1865.
212	Daniel Q. Mitchell	Commissioner	22	do	Apr. 17, 1863	Honorably discharged May 8, 1865.
213	James B. Murdock	Surgeon	22	do	Apr. 17, 1863	Honorably discharged June 15, 1865.
214	Alonzo Wood	Provost-marshal	23	do	Apr. 15, 1863	Appointment canceled Oct. 13, 1863.
215	Anson W. Evans	do	23	do	Nov. 20, 1863	Died July 28, 1864.
216	Webster R. Chamberlin	do	23	do	Aug. 1, 1864	Resigned Mar. 4, 1865.
217	Park Wheeler	do	23	do	Mar. 16, 1865	Honorably discharged Dec. 31, 1865.
218	William Andrews	Commissioner	23	do	Apr. 17, 1863	Honorably discharged May 8, 1865.
219	John H. Knapp	Surgeon	23	do	Apr. 17, 1863	Honorably discharged June 15, 1865.
220	John N. Knapp	Provost-marshal	24	do	Apr. 15, 1863	Appointment revoked Dec. 20, 1864.

Register of the members of the boards of enrollment, appointed under the act approved March 3, 1863—Continued.

No.	Name.	Rank.	District.	State.	When appointed.	Remarks.
221	Benjamin B. Snow	Provost-marshal	24	New York	Dec. 20, 1864	Honorably discharged Oct. 15, 1865.
222	James M. Servis	Commissioner	24	do	May 7, 1863	Honorably discharged May 8, 1865.
223	George W. Davis	Surgeon	24	do	May 7, 1863	Honorably discharged June 15, 1865.
224	William T. Remer	Provost-marshal	25	do	Apr. 15, 1863	Honorably discharged Oct. 15, 1865.
225	Jacob A. Mead	Commissioner	25	do	Apr. 17, 1863	Honorably discharged May 8, 1865.
226	Zara H. Blake	Surgeon	25	do	Apr. 17, 1863	Honorably discharged June 15, 1865.
227	Edward C. Kattell	Provost-marshal	26	do	Apr. 15, 1863	Honorably discharged Oct. 15, 1865.
228	James N. Eldridge	Commissioner	26	do	May 6, 1863	Honorably discharged May 8, 1865.
229	Samuel B. Foster	Surgeon	26	do	Apr. 17, 1863	Honorably discharged June 15, 1865.
230	Marvin J. Green	Provost-marshal	27	do	May 15, 1863	Appointment revoked May 30, 1863.
231	Samuel M. Harmon	do	27	do	May 30, 1863	Resigned July 18, 1864.
232	William W. Hayt	do	27	do	July 23, 1864	Resigned Oct. 6, 1864.
233	John T. Wright	do	27	do	Oct. 5, 1864	Honorably discharged Dec. 31, 1865.
234	William T. Post	Commissioner	27	do	Apr. 17, 1863	Resigned Aug. 8, 1863.
235	James Miles	do	27	do	Aug. 8, 1863	Resigned June 13, 1864.
236	John T. Wright	do	27	do	July 2, 1864	Appointed provost-marshal Oct. 5, 1864.
237	Allen A. Van Arsdale	do	27	do	Oct. 7, 1864	Honorably discharged May 8, 1865.
238	Joshua B. Graves	Surgeon	27	do	Apr. 17, 1863	Dismissed the service Sept. 15, 1863.
239	Hollis S. Chubbuck	do	27	do	Sept. 15, 1863	Honorably discharged June 15, 1865.
240	O. H. Palmer	Provost-marshal	28	do	Apr. 15, 1863	Resigned July 8, 1863.
241	Roswell Hart	do	28	do	June 26, 1863	Resigned Jan. 17, 1865.
242	Isaac F. Quinby	do	28	do	Jan. 21, 1865	Honorably discharged Oct. 15, 1865.
243	S. H. Clark	Commissioner	28	do	Apr. 17, 1863	Honorably discharged May 8, 1865.
244	Azel Backus	Surgeon	28	do	Apr. 17, 1863	Honorably discharged June 15, 1865.
245	Levi F. Bowen	Provost-marshal	29	do	Apr. 15, 1863	Honorably discharged Oct. 15, 1865.
246	Wells Hendershott	Commissioner	29	do	Apr. 17, 1863	Honorably discharged May 8, 1865.
247	Peter P. Murphy	Surgeon	29	do	Apr. 17, 1863	Resigned Dec. 26, 1863.
248	John Root	do	29	do	Dec. 29, 1863	Resigned Jan. 10, 1865.
249	Elias C. Holt	do	29	do	Feb. 13, 1865	Dismissed the service Apr. 22, 1865.
250	Gustavus A. Scroggs	Provost-marshal	30	do	Apr. 15, 1863	Resigned Feb. 10, 1864; reappointed provost-marshal Nov. 25, 1864; honorably discharged Dec. 31, 1865.
251	William F. Rogers	do	30	do	Feb. 16, 1864	Appointment revoked Nov. 19, 1864.
252	do	Commissioner	30	do	Apr. 17, 1863	Appointed provost-marshal Feb. 16, 1864.
253	Orlando Allen	do	30	do	Feb. 19, 1864	Resigned Apr. 18, 1864.
254	Jonathan Austin	do	30	do	Apr. 21, 1864	Resigned Mar. 8, 1865.
255	Warren Granger	do	30	do	Mar. 14, 1865	Honorably discharged May 8, 1865.
256	John S. Trowbridge	Surgeon	30	do	Apr. 17, 1863	Honorably discharged June 15, 1865.
257	George W. Palmer	Provost-marshal	31	do	Apr. 15, 1863	Resigned Dec. 2, 1864.
258	Rodney R. Crowley	do	31	do	Dec. 6, 1864	Honorably discharged Oct. 15, 1865.
259	Charles S. Cary	Commissioner	31	do	Apr. 17, 1863	Resigned Dec. 7, 1864.
260	Enos C. Brooks	do	31	do	Dec. 21, 1864	Honorably discharged May 8, 1865.
261	Horace H. Gliddon	Surgeon	31	do	Apr. 17, 1863	Honorably discharged June 15, 1865.
262	Robert C. Johnson	Provost-marshal	1	New Jersey	May 2, 1863	Appointment revoked Mar. 24, 1864.

263	Alexander Wentz	do	1	do	Apr. 25, 1864	Honorably discharged Nov. 15, 1865.
264	James M. Scovel	Commissioner	1	do	May 2, 1863	Resigned Nov. 27, 1863.
265	Philip J. Gray	do	1	do	Dec. 8, 1863	Honorably discharged Apr. 30, 1865.
266	John R. Stevenson	Surgeon	1	do	May 2, 1863	Honorably discharged June 15, 1865.
267	James B. Coppuck	Provost-marshal	2	do	May 2, 1863	Honorably discharged Nov. 15, 1865.
268	James Wilson	Commissioner	2	do	May 2, 1863	Resigned Sept. 2, 1864.
269	Jacob R. Freese	do	2	do	Sept. 27, 1864	Honorably discharged Apr. 30, 1865.
270	Richard R. Rogers	Surgeon	2	do	May 2, 1863	Honorably discharged June 15, 1865.
271	William M. Shipman	Provost-marshal	3	do	May 2, 1863	Honorably discharged Nov. 15, 1865.
272	Ezra M. Hunt	Commissioner	3	do	May 2, 1863	Honorably discharged Apr. 30, 1865.
273	George B. Chetwood	Surgeon	3	do	May 2, 1863	Resigned June 17, 1863.
274	Robert Wescott	do	3	do	June 24, 1863	Honorably discharged June 15, 1865.
275	James M. Brown	Provost-marshal	4	do	May 2, 1863	Honorably discharged Nov. 15, 1865.
276	Peter S. Decker	Commissioner	4	do	May 2, 1863	Honorably discharged Apr. 30, 1865.
277	William Pierson, jr	Surgeon	4	do	May 2, 1863	Resigned Feb. 9, 1864.
278	Edward T. Whittingham	do	4	do	Feb. 16, 1864	Resigned Sept. 28, 1864.
279	J. S. Stigers	do	4	do	Oct. 17, 1864	Honorably discharged June 15, 1865.
280	Elias N. Miller	Provost-marshal	5	do	May 2, 1863	Resigned June 1, 1864.
281	Henry J. Mills	do	5	do	June 6, 1864	Honorably discharged Nov. 15, 1865.
282	Samuel A. French	Commissioner	5	do	May 2, 1863	Died Jan. 19, 1864.
283	Stephen Quaif	do	5	do	Feb. 13, 1864	Honorably discharged Apr. 30, 1865.
284	Isaac A. Nichols	Surgeon	5	do	May 2, 1863	Resigned Dec. 2, 1863.
285	Jeremiah H. Cross	do	5	do	Dec. 11, 1863	Honorably discharged June 15, 1865.
286	William E. Lehman	Provost-marshal	1	Pennsylvania	Apr. 18, 1863	Do.
287	Charles Murphy	Commissioner	1	do	Apr. 18, 1863	Appointment revoked Dec. 18, 1863.
288	John B. Kenney	do	1	do	Dec. 24, 1863	Honorably discharged May 8, 1865.
289	Nicholas H. Marselis	Surgeon	1	do	Apr. 18, 1863	Appointment revoked Oct. 16, 1863.
290	James S. De Benville	do	1	do	Oct. 20, 1863	Honorably discharged June 15, 1865.
291	Edwin Palmer	Provost-marshal	2	do	Apr. 18, 1863	Do.
292	William M. Bull	Commissioner	2	do	Apr. 18, 1863	Resigned Dec. 27, 1864.
293	Benjamin F. Kern	do	2	do	Dec. 31, 1864	Honorably discharged May 8, 1865.
294	Robert W. Ritchie	Surgeon	2	do	Apr. 18, 1863	Honorably discharged June 15, 1865.
295	Jacob S. Stretch	Provost-marshal	3	do	Apr. 18, 1863	Do.
296	Franklin D. Sterner	Commissioner	3	do	Apr. 18, 1863	Resigned Dec. 20, 1864.
297	William J. Donohugh	do	3	do	Dec. 27, 1864	Honorably discharged May 8, 1865.
298	Alexander C. Hart	Surgeon	3	do	Apr. 18, 1863	Honorably discharged June 15, 1865.
299	Davis M. Lane	Provost-marshal	4	do	Apr. 18, 1863	Honorably discharged Sept. 30, 1865.
300	Charles B. Barrett	Commissioner	4	do	Apr. 18, 1863	Honorably discharged May 8, 1865.
301	J. Ralston Wells	Surgeon	4	do	Apr. 18, 1863	Honorably discharged June 15, 1865.
302	Mahlon Yardley	Provost-marshal	5	do	Apr. 18, 1863	Honorably discharged Dec. 31, 1865.
303	William M. Taylor	Commissioner	5	do	Apr. 18, 1863	Honorably discharged May 8, 1865.
304	E. F. Leake	Surgeon	5	do	Apr. 18, 1863	Resigned Feb. 17, 1865.
305	J. H. Mears	do	5	do	Feb. 21, 1865	Honorably discharged June 15, 1865.
306	John J. Freedley	Provost-marshal	6	do	Apr. 18, 1863	Appointment revoked Apr. 22, 1864.
307	William H. Yerkes	do	6	do	Nov. 17, 1864	Honorably discharged Sept. 30, 1865.
308	Francis J. Weidner	Commissioner	6	do	May 6, 1863	Appointment canceled May 12, 1863.
309	D. H. Washburn	do	6	do	May 18, 1863	Appointment revoked Apr. 22, 1864.
310	D. Morgan Casselberry	do	6	do	May 26, 1864	Appointment revoked Dec. 3, 1864.
311	Reuben Guth	do	6	do	Dec. 3, 1864	Honorably discharged May 8, 1865.
312	William Corsen	Surgeon	6	do	Apr. 18, 1863	Honorably discharged June 15, 1865.

Register of the members of the boards of enrollment, appointed under the act approved March 3, 1863—Continued.

No.	Name.	Rank.	District.	State.	When appointed.	Remarks.
313	Enos L. Christman	Provost-marshal	7	Pennsylvania	Apr. 18, 1863	Honorably discharged Nov. 30, 1865.
314	John C. Price	Commissioner	7	do	Apr. 18, 1863	Honorably discharged May 8, 1865.
315	Reuben H. Smith	Surgeon	7	do	Apr. 18, 1863	Honorably discharged June 15, 1865.
316	Henry S. Kupp	Provost-marshal	8	do	May 15, 1863	Resigned Mar. 10, 1864.
317	Jacob C. Hoff	do	8	do	Mar. 17, 1864	Resigned Oct. 19, 1864.
318	George W. Durrell	do	8	do	Nov. 9, 1864	Honorably discharged Sept. 30, 1865.
319	Jacob C. Hoff	Commissioner	8	do	May 15, 1863	Appointed provost-marshal March 17, 1864.
320	George W. Harrison	do	8	do	Mar. 17, 1864	Honorably discharged May 8, 1865.
321	Peter G. Bertolet	Surgeon	8	do	May 15, 1863	Resigned Nov. 15, 1864.
322	Martin Luther	do	8	do	Nov. 25, 1864	Honorably discharged June 15, 1865.
323	A. W. Bolenius	Provost-marshal	9	do	Apr. 18, 1863	Appointed a line officer in Invalid Corps Feb. 24, 1864.
324	Thaddeus Stevens, jr	do	9	do	Feb. 25, 1864	Honorably discharged Sept. 30, 1865.
325	Eli Overdeer	Commissioner	9	do	Apr. 18, 1863	Honorably discharged May 8, 1865.
326	Patrick Cassidy	Surgeon	9	do	Apr. 18, 1863	Died July 12, 1864.
327	John L. Atlee, jr	do	9	do	July 21, 1864	Honorably discharged June 15, 1865.
328	Charlemagne Tower	Provost-marshal	10	do	Apr. 18, 1863	Resigned Apr. 7, 1864.
329	James W. Bowen	do	10	do	Apr. 11, 1864	Honorably discharged Sept. 30, 1865.
330	John H. Kinports	Commissioner	10	do	Apr. 18, 1863	Resigned Mar. 8, 1864.
331	David Bowman	do	10	do	Mar. 26, 1864	Honorably discharged May 8, 1865.
332	James S. Carpenter	Surgeon	10	do	May 5, 1863	Honorably discharged June 15, 1865.
333	Samuel Yohe	Provost-marshal	11	do	Apr. 18, 1863	Honorably discharged Dec. 31, 1865.
334	Henry C. Wolfe	Commissioner	11	do	May 1, 1863	Resigned Jan. 19, 1865.
335	George H. Miller	do	11	do	Feb. 15, 1865	Honorably discharged May 8, 1865.
336	Charles H. Humphreys	Surgeon	11	do	May 1, 1863	Honorably discharged June 15, 1865.
337	S. Nelson Bradford	Provost-marshal	12	do	May 9, 1863	Resigned Feb. 1, 1865.
338	Myron B. Helme	Commissioner	12	do	May 4, 1863	Honorably discharged May 8, 1865.
339	Horace P. Moody	Surgeon	12	do	May 4, 1863	Honorably discharged June 15, 1865.
340	Charles M. Manville	Provost-marshal	13	do	Apr. 18, 1863	Appointment revoked Mar. 14, 1865.
341	James H. Phinny, jr	Commissioner	13	do	Apr. 18, 1863	Appointment canceled May 20, 1863.
342	Alex. J. Frick	do	13	do	May 21, 1863	Appointment revoked June 1, 1863.
343	Michael C. Grier	do	13	do	June 1, 1863	Honorably discharged May 8, 1865.
344	Wm. S. Baker	Surgeon	13	do	Apr. 18, 1863	Honorably discharged June 15, 1865.
345	John K. Clement	Provost-marshal	14	do	Apr. 18, 1863	Appointment revoked Nov. 15, 1864.
346	William H. Patterson	do	14	do	Dec. 9, 1864	Honorably discharged Dec. 31, 1865.
347	Charles C. Rawn	Commissioner	14	do	Apr. 18, 1863	Appointment revoked Dec. 9, 1864.
348	Charles Hower	do	14	do	Dec. 9, 1864	Honorably discharged May 8, 1865.
349	George Lotz	Surgeon	14	do	Apr. 18, 1863	Appointment revoked June 19, 1863.
350	Samuel T. Charlton	do	14	do	May 14, 1863	Resigned Dec. 7, 1864.
351	P. R. Wagenseller	do	14	do	Dec. 9, 1864	Honorably discharged June 15, 1865.
352	Robert M. Henderson	Provost-marshal	15	do	Apr. 18, 1863	Honorably discharged Nov. 10, 1865.
353	Benjamin McIntire	Commissioner	15	do	Apr. 18, 1863	Resigned Dec. 21, 1864.
354	Alexander B. Anderson	do	15	do	Jan. 25, 1865	Honorably discharged May 8, 1865.
355	William S. Roland	Surgeon	15	do	Apr. 18, 1863	Honorably discharged June 15, 1865.

356	George Eyster	Provost-marshal	16	do	Apr. 18, 1863	Honorably discharged Sept. 30, 1865.
357	John T. McIlhenny	Commissioner	16	do	Apr. 18, 1863	Resigned Feb. 2, 1864.
358	John Culp	do	16	do	Feb. 13, 1864	Honorably discharged May 8, 1865.
359	Raymond S. Seiss	Surgeon	16	do	Apr. 18, 1863	Resigned Mar. 7, 1864.
360	Samuel G. Lane	do	16	do	Mar. 11, 1864	Resigned Aug. 13, 1864.
361	William C. Lane	do	16	do	Aug. 17, 1864	Honorably discharged June 15, 1865.
362	James D. Campbell	Provost-marshal	17	do	Apr. 18, 1863	Dismissed the service Jan. 25, 1864.
363	A. M. Lloyd	do	17	do	Jan. 27, 1864	Honorably discharged Sept. 30, 1865.
364	Mathias S. Harr	Commissioner	17	do	Apr. 18, 1863	Honorably discharged May 8, 1865.
365	Abraham Rothrock	Surgeon	17	do	Apr. 18, 1863	Honorably discharged June 15, 1865.
366	William W. White	Provost-marshal	18	do	Apr. 18, 1863	Dismissed the service Jan. 11, 1864.*
367	William H. Blair	do	18	do	Jan. 11, 1864	Honorably discharged Nov. 30, 1865.
368	Robert Hawley	Commissioner	18	do	Apr. 18, 1863	Honorably discharged May 8, 1865.
369	James H. Dobbins	Surgeon	18	do	Apr. 18, 1863	Resigned Nov. 2, 1863.
370	Thomas F. Duncan	do	18	do	Dec. 16, 1863	Honorably discharged June 15, 1865.
371	Hugh S. Campbell	Provost-marshal	19	do	Apr. 18, 1863	Honorably discharged Sept. 30, 1865.
372	Jerome Powell	Commissioner	19	do	Apr. 18, 1863	Resigned Sept. 8, 1864.
373	Edward Souther	do	19	do	Sept. 14, 1864	Honorably discharged May 8, 1865.
374	John Mechling	Surgeon	19	do	Apr. 18, 1863	Resigned Apr. 11, 1864.
375	Charles M. Matson	do	19	do	Apr. 21, 1864	Honorably discharged June 15, 1865.
376	David V. Derickson	Provost-marshal	20	do	Apr. 18, 1863	Honorably discharged Nov. 10, 1865.
377	Henry Wetter	Commissioner	20	do	Apr. 18, 1863	Honorably discharged May 8, 1865.
378	Salmon S. Bates	Surgeon	20	do	Apr. 18, 1863	Resigned Aug. 22, 1864.
379	Theodore B. Lashells	dc	20	do	Sept. 29, 1864	Honorably discharged June 15, 1865.
380	William B. Coulter	Provost-marshal	21	do	Apr. 18, 1863	Honorably discharged Sept. 30, 1865.
381	Augustus Row	Commissioner	21	do	Apr. 18, 1863	Honorably discharged May 8, 1865.
382	Frederick C. Robinson	Surgeon	21	do	Apr. 18, 1863	Honorably discharged June 15, 1865.
383	James A. Herron	Provost-marshal	22	do	Apr. 18, 1863	Appointment revoked June 5, 1863.
384	James Heron Foster	do	22	do	June 5, 1863	Honorably discharged Dec. 31, 1865.
385	William H. Campbell	Commissioner	22	do	Apr. 18, 1863	Honorably discharged May 8, 1865.
386	Robert B. Simpson	Surgeon	22	do	Apr. 18, 1863	Honorably discharged June 15, 1865.
387	James W. Kirker	Provost-marshal	23	do	Apr. 18, 1863	Honorably discharged Sept. 30, 1865.
388	Josiah Copley	Commissioner	23	do	Apr. 18, 1863	Honorably discharged May 8, 1865.
389	John S. Kuhn	Surgeon	23	do	Apr. 18, 1863	Resigned Aug. 7, 1863.
390	A. Perchment	do	23	do	Aug. 14, 1863	Honorably discharged June 15, 1865.
391	John Cuthbertson	Provost-marshal	24	do	Apr. 18, 1863	Died Sept. 21, 1865.
392	Milo R. Adams	Commissioner	24	do	Apr. 18, 1863	Honorably discharged May 8, 1865.
393	Robert D. Wallace	Surgeon	24	do	Apr. 18, 1863	Resigned Feb. 15, 1865.
394	E. L. King	do	24	do	Apr. 12, 1865	Appointment revoked June 2, 1865.
395	Edwin Wilmer	Provost-marshal	1	Delaware	May 1, 1863	Dismissed by sentence of general court-martial June 15, 1865.
396	Leonard E. Wales	Commissioner	1	do	May 1, 1863	Resigned Sept. 23, 1864.
397	Samuel Biddle	do	1	do	Sept. 30, 1864	Honorably discharged Apr. 30, 1865.
398	Lawrence M. Cahall	Surgeon	1	do	May 1, 1863	Resigned Aug. 31, 1863.
399	Daniel G. Fisher	do	1	do	Aug. 31, 1863	Appointment revoked Apr. 22, 1865.
400	John Frazier, jr	Provost-marshal	1	Maryland	May 16, 1863	Appointment revoked Feb. 15, 1864.
401	William J. Leonard	do	1	do	Feb. 15, 1864	Appointment revoked Sept. 15, 1864.
402	Andrew Stafford	do	1	do	Sept. 15, 1864	Honorably discharged Aug. 10, 1865.
403	David Blockson	Commissioner	1	do	June 1, 1863	Appointment revoked Feb. 15, 1864.
404	Charles R. Mullekin	do	1	do	Feb. 15, 1864	Honorably discharged Apr. 30, 1865.
405	William H. Farrow	Surgeon	1	do	May 16, 1863	Honorably discharged June 15, 1865.

* Dismissal revoked and honorably discharged January 11, 1864.

Register of the members of the boards of enrollment, appointed under the act approved March 3, 1863—Continued.

No.	Name.	Rank.	District.	State.	When appointed.	Remarks.
406	Robert Cathcart	Provost-marshal	2	Maryland	May 16, 1863	Honorably discharged Dec. 31, 1865.
407	L. M. Haverstick	Commissioner	2	do	May 16, 1863	Resigned Aug. 1, 1864.
408	Jonathan J. Chapman	do	2	do	Aug. 6, 1864	Honorably discharged Apr. 30, 1865.
409	J. Robert Ward	Surgeon	2	do	May 16, 1863	Honorably discharged June 15, 1865.
410	Leopold Blumenberg	Provost-marshal	3	do	May 16, 1863	Dismissed the service Jan. 17, 1865.
411	Henry Clayton	do	3	do	Jan. 17, 1865	Honorably discharged May 31, 1865.
412	William Brooks	Commissioner	3	do	May 16, 1863	Honorably discharged Apr. 30, 1865.
413	Thomas F. Murdoch	Surgeon	3	do	May 16, 1863	Honorably discharged June 15, 1865.
414	James Smith	Provost-marshal	4	do	May 16, 1863	Appointment revoked Sept. 12, 1864.
415	Henry Clay Naill	do	4	do	Sept. 12, 1864	Honorably discharged Oct. 31, 1865.
416	John J. Thomas	Commissioner	4	do	May 16, 1863	Honorably discharged Apr. 30, 1865.
417	Charles J. Baer	Surgeon	4	do	May 16, 1863	Honorably discharged June 15, 1865.
418	John C. Holland	Provost-marshal	5	do	May 16, 1363	Temporarily relieved July 27, 1864; reinstated Aug. 30, 1864; honorably discharged Aug. 10, 1865.
419	J. W. Witwright	Commissioner	5	do	May 16, 1863	Honorably discharged Apr. 30, 1865.
420	Robert E. Dorsey	Surgeon	5	do	May 16, 1863	Honorably discharged June 15, 1865.
421	William P. Wainwright	Provost-marshal	1	Dist. of Columbia	June 19, 1863	Resigned June 25, 1863.
422	Henry A. Scheetz	do	1	do	June 26, 1863	Appointment revoked June 2, 1864.
423	Henry A. Scheetz	Commissioner	1	do	May 3, 1863	Appointed provost-marshal June 26, 1863.
424	Francis W. Blackford	do	1	do	July 30, 1863	Dismissed by sentence of general court-martial Jan. 4, 1865.
425	Henry A. Jones	do	1	do	Feb. 6, 1865	Honorably discharged June 15, 1865.
426	John B. Keasbey	Surgeon	1	do	May 30, 1863	Dismissed by sentence of general court-martial Feb. 7, 1865.
427	B. Gesner	do	1	do	Apr. 3, 1865	Honorably discharged June 30, 1865.
428	Benjamin B. Stone	Provost-marshal	1	West Virginia	Sept. 9, 1863	Honorably discharged Oct. 5, 1865.
429	William D. Smith	Commissioner	1	do	Sept. 9, 1863	Resigned Dec. 31, 1864.
430	Charles F. Scott	do	1	do	Mar. 8, 1865	Honorably discharged May 8, 1865.
431	R. W. Hazlett	Surgeon	1	do	Sept. 9, 1863	Honorably discharged June 15, 1865.
432	James Evans	Provost-marshal	2	do	Sept. 9, 1863	Honorably discharged Oct. 5, 1865.
433	Jesse Teter	Commissioner	2	do	Sept. 9, 1863	Honorably discharged May 8, 1865.
434	Samuel D. Kelly	Surgeon	2	do	Sept. 9, 1863	Died June 27, 1864.
435	Thomas Kennedy	do	2	do	July 6, 1864	Honorably discharged June 15, 1865.
436	Joseph C. Wheeler	Provost-marshal	3	do	Sept. 9, 1863	Resigned June 22, 1864.
437	James A. Smith	do	3	do	Aug. 2, 1864	Honorably discharged Oct. 5, 1865.
438	George C. Bowyer	Commissioner	3	do	Sept. 9, 1863	Honorably discharged May 8, 1865.
439	James Putney	Surgeon	3	do	Sept. 9, 1863	Resigned Jan. 9, 1865.
440	S. G. Shaw	do	3	do	Jan. 24, 1865	Honorably discharged June 15, 1865.
441	Charles H. Sargent	Provost-marshal	1	Ohio	Apr. 30, 1863	Appointment canceled May 12, 1863.
442	A. E. Jones	do	1	do	May 19, 1863	Honorably discharged Dec. 18, 1865.
443	John Ferris	Commissioner	1	do	Apr. 30, 1863	Honorably discharged May 8, 1865.
444	David Judkins	Surgeon	1	do	Apr. 30, 1863	Resigned May 25, 1864.
445	W. H. Mussey	do	1	do	June 17, 1864	Resigned Dec. 12, 1864.
446	F. B. Mussey	do	1	do	Jan. 5, 1865	Honorably discharged June 15, 1865.
447	Thomas R. Roberts	Provost-marshal	2	do	Apr. 30, 1863	Resigned Feb. 14, 1865.

448	Samuel H. Dunning	do	2	do	Feb. 21, 1865	Honorably discharged July 10, 1865.
449	William H. McKinney	Commissioner	2	do	Apr. 30, 1863	Appointment revoked September 22, 1863.
450	M. P. Gaddis, jr	do	2	do	Sept. 22, 1863	Honorably discharged May 8, 1865.
451	John A. Murphy	Surgeon	2	do	Apr. 30, 1863	Honorably discharged June 15, 1865.
452	John Mills	Provost-marshal	3	do	Apr. 30, 1863	Honorably discharged Sept. 30, 1865.
453	Montgomery P. Alston	Commissioner	3	do	Apr. 30, 1863	Resigned Oct. 6, 1863; reappointed Oct. 20, 1863; honorably discharged May 8, 1865.
454	W. L. Schenck	Surgeon	3	do	Apr. 30, 1863	Honorably discharged June 15, 1865.
455	Abraham C. Deuel	Provost-marshal	4	do	Apr. 30, 1863	Honorably discharged Sept. 30, 1865.
456	Matthias H. Jones	Commissioner	4	do	May 27, 1863	Resigned Aug. 19, 1864.
457	George D. Burgess	do	4	do	Sept. 15, 1864	Honorably discharged May 8, 1865.
458	E. D. Gilson	Surgeon	4	do	Apr. 30, 1863	Resigned Dec. 2, 1864.
459	Israel Fisher	do	4	do	Dec. 12, 1864	Honorably discharged June 15, 1865.
460	Daniel S. Brown	Provost-marshal	5	do	Apr. 30, 1863	Resigned Feb. 2, 1865.
461	Charles D. Robbins	do	5	do	Feb. 14, 1865	Honorably discharged Sept. 30, 1865.
462	John Walkup	Commissioner	5	do	Apr. 30, 1863	Resigned Feb. 22, 1864.
463	T. E. Cunningham	do	5	do	Feb. 29, 1864	Honorably discharged May 8, 1865.
464	Corban J. Neff	Surgeon	5	do	Apr. 30, 1863	Honorably discharged June 15, 1865.
465	Joseph K. Marlay	Provost-marshal	6	do	Apr. 30, 1863	Honorably discharged Sept. 30, 1865.
466	George B. Gardner	Commissioner	6	do	Apr. 30, 1863	Honorably discharged May 8, 1865.
467	George B. Bailey	Surgeon	6	do	Apr. 30, 1863	Resigned April 1, 1864.
468	David Noble	do	6	do	Apr. 1, 1864	Honorably discharged June 15, 1865.
469	James A. Wilcox	Provost-marshal	7	do	Apr. 30, 1863	Vacated Sept. 2, 1864, and appointed acting assistant provost-marshal-general of Ohio.
470	Benjamin Nesbitt	do	7	do	Sept. 5, 1864	Honorably discharged Dec. 18, 1865.
471	S. S. Henkle	Commissioner	7	do	Apr. 30, 1863	Honorably discharged May 8, 1865.
472	M. Lemen	Surgeon	7	do	Apr. 30, 1863	Honorably discharged June 15, 1865.
473	William Shunk	Provost-marshal	8	do	Apr. 30, 1863	Honorably discharged Sept. 30, 1865.
474	James Cobean	Commissioner	8	do	Apr. 30, 1863	Honorably discharged May 8, 1865.
475	Timothy B. Fisher	Surgeon	8	do	Apr. 30, 1863	Honorably discharged June 15, 1865.
476	John J. Steiner	Provost-marshal	9	do	Apr. 30, 1863	Resigned Mar. 17, 1865.
477	F. A. Wildman	do	9	do	Mar. 27, 1865	Honorably discharged Sept. 30, 1865.
478	Benjamin Turner	Commissioner	9	do	Apr. 30, 1863	Appointment canceled July 13, 1863.
479	Rice Harper	do	9	do	July 2, 1863	Honorably discharged May 8, 1865.
480	M. Skinner	Surgeon	9	do	Apr. 30, 1863	Appointment revoked Feb. 22, 1865.
481	James M. Corey	do	9	do	Mar. 29, 1865	Honorably discharged June 15, 1865.
482	Charles Kent	Provost-marshal	10	do	Apr. 30, 1863	Honorably discharged Dec. 9, 1865.
483	William O. Ensign	Commissioner	10	do	Apr. 30, 1863	Honorably discharged May 8, 1865.
484	Silas Bailey	Surgeon	10	do	Apr. 30, 1863	Resigned Jan. 17, 1865.
485	E. D. Peck	do	10	do	Feb. 2, 1865	Honorably discharged June 15, 1865.
486	Benjamin F. Cory	Provost-marshal	11	do	Apr. 30, 1863	Discharged April 29, 1865.
487	James W. Longbon	Acting provost-marshal.	11	do	Apr. 29, 1865	Honorably discharged Sept. 30, 1865.
488	Isaac Roberts	Commissioner	11	do	Apr. 30, 1863	Resigned Aug. 16, 1864.
489	James W. Longbon	do	11	do	Aug. 25, 1864	Appointed acting provost-marshal Apr. 29, 1865; honorably discharged as such Sept. 30, 1865.
490	David Coleman	Surgeon	11	do	Apr. 30, 1863	Resigned Dec. 15, 1864.
491	Orlando C. Miller	do	11	do	Dec. 28, 1864	Honorably discharged June 15, 1865.
492	George W. Roby	Provost-marshal	12	do	Apr. 30, 1863	Resigned Jan. 10, 1865.
493	William D. Wesson	do	12	do	Feb. 6, 1865	Honorably discharged Dec. 9, 1865.

Register of the members of the boards of enrollment, appointed under the act approved March 3, 1863—**Continued.**

No.	Name.	Rank.	District.	State.	When appointed.	Remarks.
494	Martin Kagay	Commissioner	12	Ohio	Apr. 30, 1863	Honorably discharged May 8, 1865.
495	John W. Lewis	Surgeon	12	do	Apr. 30, 1863	Dismissed the service Apr. 19, 1864.
496	Nelson E. Jones	do	12	do	May 10, 1864	Honorably discharged June 15, 1865.
497	John A. Sinnet	Provost-marshal	13	do	Apr. 30, 1863	Honorably discharged Dec. 9, 1865.
498	Isaac Hadley	Commissioner	13	do	Apr. 30, 1863	Honorably discharged May 8, 1865.
499	Thaddeus A. Reamy	Surgeon	13	do	Apr. 30, 1863	Resigned Dec. 12, 1863.
500	J. J. Hamil	do	13	do	Dec. 17, 1863	Honorably discharged June 15, 1865.
501	James L. Drake	Provost-marshal	14	do	Apr. 30, 1863	Honorably discharged Sept. 30, 1865.
502	John Rounds	Commissioner	14	do	Apr. 30, 1863	Honorably discharged May 8, 1865.
503	James D. Robison	Surgeon	14	do	Apr. 30, 1863	Honorably discharged June 15, 1865.
504	Levi Barber	Provost-marshal	15	do	Apr. 30, 1863	Honorably discharged Sept. 30, 1865.
505	Joseph L. Kissinger	Commissioner	15	do	Apr. 30, 1863	Resigned Aug. 22, 1864.
506	Rodolph de Steigner, jr	do	15	do	Sept. 6, 1864	Honorably discharged May 8, 1865.
507	Charles Robertson	Surgeon	15	do	Apr. 30, 1863	Resigned Mar. 29, 1865.
508	David McCartney	Provost-marshal	16	do	Apr. 30, 1863	Resigned Dec. 10, 1863.
509	A. T. Ready	do	16	do	Dec. 24, 1863	Resigned Oct. 5, 1864.
510	John A. Norris	do	16	do	Oct. 19, 1864	Honorably discharged Sept. 30, 1865.
511	Oliver Keyser	Commissioner	16	do	Apr. 30, 1863	Honorably discharged May 8, 1865.
512	David McClenahan	Surgeon	16	do	Apr. 30, 1863	Honorably discharged June 15, 1865.
513	John F. Oliver	Provost-marshal	17	do	Apr. 30, 1863	Honorably discharged Sept. 30, 1865.
514	S. M. Craine	Commissioner	17	do	Apr. 30, 1863	Appointment revoked July 20, 1863.
515	Joseph Means	do	17	do	July 20, 1863	Resigned Jan. 23, 1865.
516	Johnston Armstrong	do	17	do	Feb. 13, 1865	Honorably discharged May 8, 1865.
517	L. M. Whiting	Surgeon	17	do	Apr. 30, 1863	Honorably discharged June 15, 1865.
518	Frederick A. Nash	Provost-marshal	18	do	Apr. 30, 1863	Honorably discharged May 19, 1865.
519	John Barr	Commissioner	18	do	Apr. 30, 1863	Resigned Mar. 31, 1864.
520	John Kirkpatrick	do	18	do	Apr. 16, 1864	Honorably discharged May 8, 1865.
521	Henry C. Beardslee	Surgeon	18	do	Apr. 30, 1863	Honorably discharged June 15, 1865.
522	Darius Cadwell	Provost-marshal	19	do	Apr. 30, 1863	Honorably discharged Dec. 18, 1865.
523	Charles S. Field	Commissioner	19	do	Apr. 30, 1863	Honorably discharged May 8, 1865.
524	George W. Howe	Surgeon	19	do	Apr. 30, 1863	Honorably discharged June 15, 1865.
525	Blythe Hynes	Provost-marshal	1	Indiana	May 1, 1863	Resigned May 19, 1864. *
526	Cyrus K. Drew	do	1	do	May 25, 1864	Resigned Aug. 1, 1864.
527	James W. Wartman	do	1	do	Aug. 8, 1864	Resigned Sept. 5, 1864.
528	Alvah Johnson	do	1	do	Nov. 22, 1864	Honorably discharged Oct. 31, 1865.
529	Nathaniel Usher	Commissioner	1	do	May 1, 1863	Resigned Aug. 29, 1864.
530	James W. Wartman	do	1	do	Sept. 13, 1864	Honorably discharged May 8, 1865.
531	William G. Ralston	Surgeon	1	do	May 1, 1863	Honorably discharged May 30, 1865.
532	J. B. Meriweather	Provost-marshal	2	do	May 1, 1863	Honorably discharged July 31, 1865.
533	John J. Morrison	Commissioner	2	do	May 1, 1863	Resigned Dec. 1, 1864.
534	Andrew J. Hay	do	2	do	Dec. 14, 1864	Honorably discharged May 8, 1865.
535	William F. Collum	Surgeon	2	do	May 25, 1863	Honorably discharged May 30, 1865.
536	S. Stansifer	Provost-marshal	3	do	May 1, 1863	Resigned Mar. 28, 1865.

537	James B. Mulky	....do	3	....do	Apr. 5, 1865	Honorably discharged Oct. 31, 1865.
538	John R. B. Glasscock	Commissioner	3	....do	May 1, 1863	Honorably discharged May 8, 1865.
539	Albert G. Collier	Surgeon	3	....do	May 1, 1863	Honorably discharged May 30, 1865.
540	John C. McQuiston	Provost-marshal	4	....do	May 1, 1863	Resigned Mar. 2, 1864.
541	Henry B. Hill	....do	4	....do	Mar. 11, 1864	Honorably discharged Oct. 31, 1865.
542	Henry B. Hill	Commissioner	4	....do	May 1, 1863	Appointed provost-marshal Mar. 11, 1864.
543	Robert D. Brown	....do	4	....do	Mar. 15, 1864	Honorably discharged May 8, 1865.
544	Edward P. Bond	Surgeon	4	....do	May 1, 1863	Honorably discharged May 30, 1865.
545	Isaac Kinley	Provost-marshal	5	....do	May 1, 1863	Honorably discharged Aug. 19, 1865.
546	James A. McMeans	Commissioner	5	....do	May 16, 1863	Honorably discharged May 8, 1865.
547	John E. Beverley	Surgeon	5	....do	May 16, 1863	Honorably discharged May 30, 1865.
548	David Braden	Provost-marshal	6	....do	May 1, 1863	Honorably discharged Dec. 31, 1865.
549	William J. Wallace	Commissioner	6	....do	May 1, 1863	Resigned Jan. 19, 1865.
550	Dennis Gregg	....do	6	....do	Jan. 27, 1865	Honorably discharged May 8, 1865.
551	Thomas B. Harvey	Surgeon	6	....do	May 1, 1863	Honorably discharged May 30, 1865.
552	Richard W. Thompson	Provost-marshal	7	....do	May 1, 1863	Resigned Feb. 23, 1865.
553	Daniel A. Conover	....do	7	....do	Feb. 28, 1865	Honorably discharged Oct. 31, 1865.
554	George K. Steele	Commissioner	7	....do	May 1, 1863	Resigned Oct. 9, 1864.
555	Daniel A. Conover	....do	7	....do	Oct. 17, 1864	Appointed provost-marshal Feb. 28, 1865
556	Thomas C. Bailey	....do	7	....do	Feb. 28, 1865	Honorably discharged May 8, 1865.
557	Albert G. Preston	Surgeon	7	....do	May 1, 1863	Honorably discharged May 30, 1865.
558	James Park	Provost-marshal	8	....do	May 1, 1863	Honorably discharged Oct. 31, 1865.
559	William C. Kise	Commissioner	8	....do	May 1, 1863	Appointment canceled Oct. 24, 1863.
560	William S. Lingle	....do	8	....do	Oct. 24, 1863	Appointment revoked Jan. 16, 1864.
561	George Nebeker	....do	8	....do	Jan. 28, 1864	Honorably discharged May 8, 1865.
562	Zachariah B. Gentry	Surgeon	8	....do	May 1, 1863	Resigned Apr. 20, 1865.
563	William Wirt Wallace	Provost-marshal	9	....do	May 1, 1863	Appointment revoked Nov. 21, 1863.
564	K. G. Shryock	....do	9	....do	Nov. 21, 1863	Honorably discharged Oct. 31, 1865.
565	James B. Belford	Commissioner	9	....do	May 1, 1863	Honorably discharged May 8, 1865.
566	Daniel Dayton	Surgeon	9	....do	May 1, 1863	Honorably discharged May 30, 1865.
567	Hiram Iddings	Provost-marshal	10	....do	May 1, 1863	Honorably discharged Oct. 31, 1865.
568	William S. Smith	Commissioner	10	....do	May 18, 1863	Honorably discharged May 8, 1865.
569	Stephen Morris	Surgeon	10	....do	May 1, 1863	Honorably discharged May 30, 1865.
570	Thomas B. McCarty	Provost-marshal	11	....do	May 1, 1863	Resigned May 30, 1863.
571	Calvin Cowgill	....do	11	....do	June 2, 1863	Honorably discharged Oct. 31, 1863.
572	J. G. Stilwell	Commissioner	11	....do	May 1, 1863	Resigned Dec. 6, 1864.
573	John L. Knight	....do	11	....do	Dec. 14, 1864	Honorably discharged May 8, 1865.
574	Constantine Lomax	Surgeon	11	....do	May 1, 1863	Resigned Mar. 21, 1865.
575	William T. Mendenhall	....do	11	....do	Mar. 31, 1865	Honorably discharged May 30, 1865.
576	William James	Provost-marshal	1	[Illinois]	May 7, 1863	Honorably discharged Dec. 31, 1865.
577	Isaac L. Milliken	Commissioner	1	....do	May 20, 1863	Honorably discharged May 5, 1865.
578	Joseph W. Freer	Surgeon	1	....do	May 7, 1863	Honorably discharged May 30, 1865.
579	Amos B. Coon	Provost-marshal	2	....do	May 7, 1863	Honorably discharged Oct. 15, 1865.
580	William D. Barry*	Commissioner	2	....do	May 7, 1863	Honorably discharged May 5, 1865.
581	Aaron Lewis	Surgeon	2	....do	May 7, 1863	Honorably discharged May 30, 1865.
582	John V. Eustace	Provost-marshal	3	....do	May 7, 1863	Resigned Nov. 7, 1864; reappointed Nov. 15, 1864; honorably discharged Oct. 15, 1865.
583	W. A. Youngman	Commissioner	3	....do	May 7, 1863	Honorably discharged May 5, 1865.
584	Chancellor Martin	Surgeon	3	....do	May 7, 1863	Died Mar. 14, 1864.

*Again appointed September 13, 1864; resigned November 9, 1864.

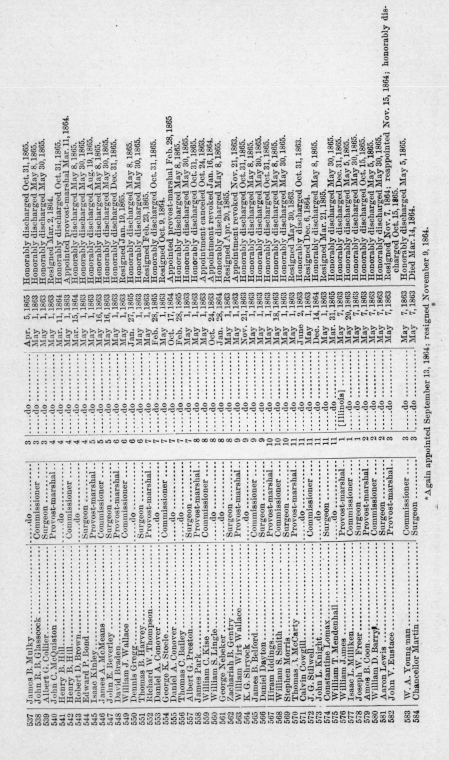

Register of the members of the boards of enrollment, appointed under the act approved March 3, 1863—Continued.

No.	Name.	Rank.	District.	State.	When appointed.	Remarks.
585	Elias S. Potter	Surgeon	3	[Illinois]	Mar. 26, 1864	Honorably discharged May 30, 1865.
586	James Woodruff	Provost-marshal	4	do	May 7, 1863	Resigned Mar. 4, 1864.
587	Henry Asbury	do	4	do	Mar. 17, 1864	Resigned Mar. 24, 1865.
588	William H. Fisk	do	4	do	Apr. 5, 1865	Honorably discharged Oct. 15, 1865.
589	John McKinney, sr	Commissioner	4	do	May 7, 1863	Resigned Mar. 4, 1864.
590	John K. Allen	do	4	do	May 26, 1864	Died Nov. 4, 1864.
591	William H. Hart	do	4	do	Nov. 23, 1864	Honorably discharged May 5, 1865.
592	Charles Coolidge	Surgeon	4	do	May 7, 1863	Resigned Feb. 19, 1865.
593	Moses F. Bassett	do	4	do	Mar. 8, 1865	Honorably discharged May 30, 1865.
594	James M. Allen	Provost-marshal	5	do	May 7, 1863	Appointment revoked Jan. 25, 1865.
595	C. C. Mason	do	5	do	Mar. 8, 1865	Honorably discharged Dec. 31, 1865.
596	Richard A. Yoe	Commissioner	5	do	May 7, 1863	Honorably discharged May 5, 1865.
597	Thomas Hall	Surgeon	5	do	May 7, 1863	Resigned Aug. 28, 1863.
598	Robert Boal	do	5	do	Sept. 30, 1863	Honorably discharged May 30, 1865.
599	Abel Longworth	Provost-marshal	6	do	May 7, 1863	Honorably discharged Oct. 15, 1865.
600	S. Simmons	Commissioner	6	do	May 7, 1863	Honorably discharged May 5, 1865.
601	Robert M. McArthur	Surgeon	6	do	May 7, 1863	Honorably discharged May 30, 1865.
602	William Fithian	Provost-marshal	7	do	May 7, 1363	Honorably discharged Oct. 15, 1865.
603	John S. Wolfe	Commissioner	7	do	May 7, 1863	Appointment revoked June 15, 1863.
604	Samuel Frazier	do	7	do	June 29, 1863	Appointment revoked Feb. 18, 1864.
605	James S. Wright	do	7	do	Mar. 17, 1864	Resigned Dec. 7, 1864.
606	Houston L. Taylor	do	7	do	Jan. 13, 1865	Honorably discharged May 5, 1865.
607	Joseph T. Miller	Surgeon	7	do	June 3, 1863	Resigned Dec. 16, 1864.
608	Winston Somers	do	7	do	Jan. 13, 1865	Honorably discharged May 30, 1865.
609	Isaac Keys	Provost-marshal	8	do	May 7, 1863	Resigned May 10, 1865.
610	Clinton Jones	Commissioner	8	do	May 7, 1863	Appointment canceled May 27, 1863.
611	Burrel T. Jones	do	8	do	May 27, 1863	Resigned Mar. 7, 1864.
612	John W. Smith	do	8	do	Mar. 17, 1864	Resigned Feb. 16, 1865.
613	William S. Curry	do	8	do	Feb. 21, 1865	Honorably discharged May 5, 1865.
614	Z. H. Whitmire	Surgeon	8	do	May 7, 1863	Resigned Dec. 17, 1864.
615	E. R. Babcock	do	8	do	Dec. 29, 1864	Honorably discharged May 30, 1865.
616	Benjamin F. Westlake	Provost-marshal	9	do	May 7, 1863	Honorably discharged Oct. 15, 1865.
617	C. C. Sturtevant	Commissioner	9	do	May 7, 1863	Honorably discharged May 5, 1865.
618	R. M. Worthington	Surgeon	9	do	May 7, 1863	Resigned Feb. 9, 1865.
619	Charles N. Irwin	do	9	do	Feb. 28, 1865	Honorably discharged May 30, 1865.
620	William M. Fry	Provost-marshal	10	do	May 7, 1863	Resigned Dec. 10, 1864, to take effect Jan. 1, 1865.
621	George W. Hamilton	do	10	do	Jan. 17, 1865	Appointment revoked May 6, 1865.
622	Samuel W. Moulton	Commissioner	10	do	May 7, 1863	Resigned Aug. 8, 1863.
623	Benjamin Sammon	do	10	do	Aug. 19, 1863	Honorably discharged May 5, 1865.
624	David Prince	Surgeon	10	do	May 7, 1863	Resigned Aug. 1, 1863.
625	John L. White	do	10	do	Aug. 1, 1863	Resigned Mar. 31, 1864.
626	Nathaniel English	do	10	do	Apr. 16, 1864	Honorably discharged May 30, 1865.
627	Mortimore O'Kean	Provost-marshal	11	do	May 7, 1863	Resigned Feb. 4, 1864.

628	Edward S. Condit	do	11	do	Mar. 15, 1864	Resigned Nov. 9, 1864.
629	John C. Scott	do	11	do	Nov. 25, 1864	Honorably discharged Oct. 15, 1865.
630	W. B. Archer	Commissioner	11	do	May 7, 1863	Honorably discharged May 5, 1865.
631	F. R. Payne	Surgeon	11	do	May 7, 1863	Resigned Oct. 26, 1863.
632	Samuel McClure	do	11	do	Nov. 2, 1863	Resigned Feb. 1, 1865.
633	George W. Haynie	do	11	do	Mar. 9, 1865	Honorably discharged May 30, 1865.
634	George Abbott	Provost-marshal	12	do	May 7, 1863	Resigned Jan. 10, 1865.
635	William H. Collins	do	12	do	Dec. 29, 1864	Honorably discharged Dec. 31, 1865.
636	John E. Detrich	Commissioner	12	do	May 7, 1863	Resigned Nov. 1, 1864.
637	Elihu H. Henry	do	12	do	Nov. 22, 1864	Resigned Apr. 3, 1865.
638	L. M. Phillips	do	12	do	Apr. 11, 1865	Honorably discharged May 5, 1865.
639	John H. Weir	Surgeon	12	do	June 3, 1863	Resigned May 5, 1864.
640	William C. Pierce	do	12	do	May 18, 1864	Appointment revoked Mar. 9, 1865.
641	A. B. McChesney	do	12	do	Mar. 9, 1865	Honorably discharged May 30, 1865.
642	William C. Carroll	Provost-marshal	13	do	May 7, 1863	Appointment revoked May 27, 1863.
643	Isaac N. Phillips	do	13	do	May 27, 1863	Honorably discharged Oct. 15, 1865.
644	A. J. Kuykendall	Commissioner	13	do	May 7, 1863	Resigned July 4, 1864.
645	Benjamin L. Wiley	do	13	do	July 16, 1864	Honorably discharged May 5, 1865.
646	T. H. Burgess	Surgeon	13	do	May 7, 1863	Resigned July 4, 1864.
647	Isaac M. Neely	do	13	do	July 20, 1864	Honorably discharged May 30, 1865.
648	John S. Newberry	Provost-marshal	1	Michigan	Apr. 24, 1863	Resigned Nov. 12, 1863.
649	Mark Flanigan	do	1	do	Nov. 25, 1863	Honorably discharged Oct. 15, 1865.
650	Henry L. Hall	Commissioner	1	do	Apr. 24, 1863	Resigned July 1, 1863.
651	Henry F. Kellogg	do	1	do	July 7, 1863	Honorably discharged May 5, 1865.
652	George Landon	Surgeon	1	do	Apr. 24, 1863	Honorably discharged May 30, 1865.
653	R. C. Denison	Provost-marshal	2	do	Apr. 24, 1863	Honorably discharged Oct. 15, 1865.
654	Orrin T. Welsh	Commissioner	2	do	Apr. 24, 1863	Honorably discharged May 5, 1865.
655	Homer O. Hitchcock	Surgeon	2	do	May 19, 1863	Resigned Feb. 17, 1865.
656	Evan S. Bonnine	do	2	do	Mar. 8, 1865	Honorably discharged May 30, 1865.
657	Robert J. Barry	Provost-marshal	3	do	Apr. 24, 1863	Honorably discharged Oct. 15, 1865.
658	Smith W. Fowler	Commissioner	3	do	Apr. 24, 1863	Honorably discharged May 5, 1865.
659	Hulburt B. Shank	Surgeon	3	do	Apr. 24, 1863	Honorably discharged May 30, 1865.
660	Norman Bailey	Provost-marshal	4	do	Apr. 24, 1863	Honorably discharged Oct. 15, 1865.
661	Noyes L. Avory	Commissioner	4	do	Apr. 24, 1863	Resigned Nov. 4, 1864.
662	Thaddeus Foot	do	4	do	Dec. 3, 1864	Honorably discharged May 5, 1865.
663	Alonzo Platt	Surgeon	4	do	Apr. 24, 1863	Honorably discharged May 30, 1865.
664	Charles M. Walker	Provost-marshal	5	do	Apr. 24, 1863	Appointment revoked Nov. 9, 1863.
665	Willard M. McConnell	do	5	do	Nov. 9, 1863	Honorably discharged Oct. 15, 1865.
666	Thomas Goldsmith	Commissioner	5	do	Apr. 24, 1863	Resigned Aug. 4, 1863.
667	Albert Draper	do	5	do	Aug. 14, 1863	Appointment revoked Nov. 9, 1863.
668	Henry C. Miller	do	5	do	Nov. 9, 1863	Honorably discharged May 5, 1865.
669	Frank B. Galbraith	Surgeon	5	do	Apr. 24, 1863	Appointment revoked Nov. 9, 1863.
670	Isaac Paddock	do	5	do	Nov. 9, 1863	Honorably discharged May 30, 1865.
671	Randolph Strickland	Provost-marshal	6	do	Apr. 24, 1863	Honorably discharged Oct. 15, 1865.
672	Henry Raymond	Commissioner	6	do	Apr. 24, 1863	Honorably discharged May 5, 1865.
673	Elbridge G. Gale	Surgeon	6	do	Apr. 24, 1863	Honorably discharged May 30, 1865.
674	James M. Tillapaugh	Provost-marshal	1	Wisconsin	Apr. 24, 1863	Dismissed the service April 9, 1864.
675	Edwin L. Buttrick	do	1	do	Apr. 19, 1864	Resigned May 4, 1864.
676	Irving M. Bean	do	1	do	May 10, 1864	Honorably discharged Oct. 15, 1865.
677	A. H. Barnes	Commissioner	1	do	Apr. 24, 1863	Appointment revoked Apr. 15, 1864.

Register of the members of the boards of enrollment, appointed under the act approved March 3, 1863—Continued.

No.	Name.	Rank.	District.	State.	When appointed.	Remarks.
678	Charles M. Baker	Commissioner	1	Wisconsin	Apr. 20, 1864	Honorably discharged May 5, 1865.
679	James Diefendorf	Surgeon	1	do	Apr. 24, 1863	Resigned Feb. 9, 1864.
680	M. C. Hoyt	do	1	do	Feb. 19, 1864	Dismissed by sentence of general court-martial Dec. 20, 1864.
681	John B. Douseman	do	1	do	Feb. 24, 1865	Honorably discharged May 30, 1865.
682	S. J. M. Putnam	Provost-marshal	2	do	Apr. 24, 1863	Honorably discharged Oct. 15, 1865.
683	N. S. Greene	Commissioner	2	do	Apr. 24, 1863	Resigned Aug. 24, 1863.
684	L. B. Caswell	do	2	do	Aug. 29, 1863	Honorably discharged May 5, 1865.
685	Charles R. Head	Surgeon	2	do	Apr. 24, 1863	Honorably discharged May 30, 1865.
686	John G. Clark	Provost-marshal	3	do	Apr. 24, 1863	Resigned Mar. 22, 1865.
687	W. L. Lincoln	do	3	do	Apr. 1, 1865	Honorably discharged Oct. 15, 1865.
688	John A. Bingham	Commissioner	3	do	Apr. 24, 1863	Resigned Oct. 12, 1863.
689	James Bintliff	do	3	do	Oct. 13, 1863	Resigned Apr. 1, 1864.
690	Edwin E. Bryant	do	3	do	June 13, 1864	Resigned Mar. 22, 1865.
691	Charles Armstrong	do	3	do	Apr. 1, 1865	Honorably discharged May 5, 1865.
692	John H. Vivian	Surgeon	3	do	Apr. 24, 1863	Resigned Feb. 25, 1865.
693	Darius Mason	do	3	do	Apr. 4, 1865	Honorably discharged May 30, 1865.
694	Elihu L. Phillips	Provost-marshal	4	do	Apr. 24, 1863	Resigned Feb. 27, 1865.
695	Charles S. Hamilton	do	4	do	Mar. 8, 1865	Honorably discharged Oct. 15, 1865.
696	Charles Burchard	Commissioner	4	do	Apr. 24, 1863	Resigned Jan. 17, 1865.
697	Danville L. Townsend	do	4	do	Jan. 31, 1865	Honorably discharged May 5, 1865.
698	Luther H. Cary	Surgeon	4	do	Apr. 24, 1863	Honorably discharged May 30, 1865.
699	Curtis R. Merrill	Provost-marshal	5	do	Apr. 24, 1863	Honorably discharged Oct. 15, 1865.
700	William A. Bugh	Commissioner	5	do	May 21, 1863	Honorably discharged May 5, 1865.
701	Horace O. Crane	Surgeon	5	do	Apr. 24, 1863	Honorably discharged May 30, 1865.
702	Benjamin F. Cooper	Provost-marshal	6	do	Apr. 24, 1863	Honorably discharged Oct. 15, 1865.
703	L. S. Fisher	Commissioner	6	do	Apr. 24, 1863	Honorably discharged May 5, 1865.
704	Dugald D. Cameron	Surgeon	6	do	Apr. 24, 1863	Honorably discharged May 30, 1865.
705	Robert B. Rutledge	Provost-marshal	1	Iowa	Apr. 30, 1863	Honorably discharged Oct. 31, 1865.
706	Johnson Pierson	Commissioner	1	do	Apr. 30, 1863	Honorably discharged May 5, 1865.
707	Joshua M. Shaffer	Surgeon	1	do	Apr. 30, 1863	Honorably discharged May 30, 1865.
708	Philo E. Hall	Provost-marshal	2	do	Apr. 30, 1863	Resigned Feb. 20, 1865.
709	Henry Egbert	do	2	do	Mar. 11, 1865	Honorably discharged Dec. 31, 1865.
710	William F. Davis	Commissioner	2	do	Apr. 30, 1863	Resigned Jan. 7, 1864.
711	L. H. Washburn	do	2	do	Jan. 20, 1864	Resigned Jan. 12, 1865.
712	P. R. Bohn	do	2	do	Jan. 24, 1865	Honorably discharged May 30, 1865.
713	Egbert S. Barrows	Surgeon	2	do	Apr. 30, 1863	Do.
714	Shubael P. Adams	Provost-marshal	3	do	Apr. 30, 1863	Honorably discharged Oct. 31, 1865.
715	D. B. Henderson	Commissioner	3	do	Apr. 30, 1863	Resigned June 10, 1864.*
716	J. H. Powers	do	3	do	July 19, 1864	Resigned Sept. 26, 1864.
717	Edward A. Guilbert	Surgeon	3	do	Apr. 30, 1863	Resigned May 19, 1864.†
718	Allen Phillips	do	3	do	May 30, 1864	Appointment revoked Feb. 13, 1865.
719	James Matthews	Provost-marshal	4	do	Apr. 30, 1863	Honorably discharged Oct. 31, 1865.
720	E. N Gates	Commissioner	4	do	Apr. 30, 1863	Honorably discharged May 5, 1865.

721	Joseph C. Hinsey	Surgeon	4	do	Apr. 30, 1863	Resigned Mar. 14, 1864.
722	N. S. Hamlin	do	4	do	Apr. 2, 1864	Honorably discharged May 30, 1865.
723	Samuel C. Brownell	Provost-marshal	5	do	Apr. 30, 1863	Honorably discharged Oct. 31, 1865.
724	J. N. Cornish	Commissioner	5	do	Apr. 30, 1863	Resigned Dec. 9, 1863.
725	E. S. Hedges	do	5	do	Dec. 15, 1863	Honorably discharged May 5, 1865.
726	John P. Fenley	Surgeon	5	do	Apr. 30, 1863	Honorably discharged May 30, 1865.
727	Warner H. Curtiss	Provost-marshal	6	do	Apr. 30, 1863	Honorably discharged Oct. 31, 1865.
728	Woolsey Welles	Commissioner	6	do	Apr. 30, 1863	Honorably discharged May 5, 1865
729	William R. Smith	Surgeon	6	do	Apr. 30, 1863	Resigned May 6, 1864.
730	Richard Stebbins	do	6	do	Nov. 25, 1864	Honorably discharged May 30, 1865.
731	Charles H. See	Provost-marshal	1	Minnesota	Apr. 24, 1863	Appointment revoked Mar. 1, 1865.
732	Ormango Allen	do	1	do	Mar. 1, 1865	Honorably discharged Sept. 30, 1865.
733	Charles C. Cole	Commissioner	1	do	Apr. 24, 1863	Appointment revoked Mar. 1, 1865.
734	Reuben Reynolds	do	1	do	Mar. 1, 1865	Honorably discharged May 5, 1865.
735	William M. Mayo	Surgeon	1	do	Apr. 24, 1863	Dismissed the service Feb. 21, 1865.
736	E. C. Cross	do	1	do	Mar. 1, 1865	Honorably discharged May 30, 1865.
737	George H. Keith	Provost-marshal	2	do	Apr. 24, 1863	Honorably discharged Sept. 30, 1865.
738	Joseph A. Thacher	Commissioner	2	do	Apr. 24, 1863	Honorably discharged May 5, 1865.
739	Jared D. Wheelock	Surgeon	2	do	Apr. 24, 1863	Resigned Oct. 25, 1864.
740	Jacob H. Stewart	do	2	do	Nov. 2, 1864	Honorably discharged May 30, 1865.
741	Charles D. Colman	Provost-marshal	1	Missouri	June 2, 1863	Dismissed the service, sentence of general court-martial, July 7, 1865.
742	Nathaniel McDonald	Commissioner	1	do	June 2, 1863	Resigned Nov. 10, 1864.
743	Arba N. Crane	do	1	do	Nov. 22, 1864	Appointed acting provost-marshal May 1, 1865; honorably discharged May 30, 1865.
744	Julian Bates	Surgeon	1	do	June 2, 1863	Honorably discharged May 30, 1865.
745	C. C. Manwaring	Provost-marshal	2	do	June 2, 1863	Died May 14, 1864.
746	Henry C. Wright	do	2	do	May 19, 1864	Honorably discharged Dec. 31, 1865.
747	L. D. Morse	Commissioner	2	do	June 2, 1863	Honorably discharged May 5, 1865.
748	William Taussig	Surgeon	2	do	June 2, 1863	Resigned Jan. 20, 1865.
749	Emil Seeman	do	2	do	Jan. 24, 1865	Honorably discharged May 30, 1865.
750	Charles W. Noell	Provost-marshal	3	do	June 2, 1863	Resigned Apr. 7, 1864.
751	Carroll R. Peck	do	3	do	May 7, 1864	Honorably discharged Oct. 15, 1865.
752	James A. Greason	Commissioner	3	do	July 18, 1863	Honorably discharged May 5, 1865.
753	James R. McCormick	Surgeon	3	do	June 2, 1863	Honorably discharged May 30, 1865.
754	William F. Bodenhamer	Provost-marshal	4	do	June 2, 1863	Appointment revoked Mar. 7, 1864.
755	John M. Richardson	do	4	do	Mar. 7, 1864	Resigned Jan. 3, 1865.
756	J. T. Hubbard	do	4	do	Jan. 13, 1865	Honorably discharged Oct. 15, 1865.
757	J. W. D. L. F. Mack	Commissioner	4	do	June 2, 1863	Resigned Nov. 10, 1863.
758	A. M. Julian	do	4	do	Feb. 22, 1864	Appointment revoked Jan. 18, 1865.
759	James L. Robberson	do	4	do	Jan. 17, 1865	Honorably discharged May 5, 1865.
760	Nicholas B. Hocker	Surgeon	4	do	June 2, 1863	Resigned Dec. 31, 1863.
761	E. Ebert	do	4	do	Jan. 14, 1864	Honorably discharged May 30, 1865.
762	Asa C. Marvin	Provost-marshal	5	do	June 2, 1863	Appointment revoked Sept. 26, 1864.
763	Charles M. Ward	do	5	do	Sept. 26, 1864	Honorably discharged Oct. 15, 1865.
764	A. S. O'Bannon	Commissioner	5	do	June 2, 1863	Honorably discharged May 5, 1865.
765	Bernard Bruns	Surgeon	5	do	June 2, 1863	Died Mar. 31, 1864.
766	John R. Veeter	do	5	do	June 16, 1864	Honorably discharged May 30, 1865.
767	Abraham Comingo	Provost-marshal	6	do	June 2, 1863	Appointment revoked Apr. 20, 1865.

* Again appointed October 10, 1864: honorably discharged May 5, 1865.

† Again appointed February 13, 1865; honorably discharged May 30, 1865.

Register of the members of the boards of enrollment, appointed under the act approved March 3, 1863—Continued.

No.	Name.	Rank.	District.	State.	When appointed.	Remarks.
768	R. W. Finley	Commissioner	6	Missouri	June 2, 1863	Appointed acting provost-marshal Apr. 21, 1865; honorably discharged Oct. 15, 1865.
769	Franklin Cooley	Surgeon	6	do	June 2, 1863	Honorably discharged May 30, 1865.
770	William Fowler	Provost-marshal	7	do	June 19, 1863	Resigned Apr. 8, 1865.
771	do	Commissioner	7	do	June 2, 1863	Appointed provost-marshal June 19, 1863.
772	Abram C. Miller	do	7	do	June 19, 1863	Appointed acting provost-marshal Apr. 21, 1865; honorably discharged Oct. 15, 1865.
773	William Bertram	Surgeon	7	do	June 2, 1863	Resigned June 2, 1864.
774	Wesley Jones	do	7	do	June 13, 1864	Honorably discharged May 30, 1865.
775	John F. Benjamin	Provost-marshal	8	do	June 2, 1863	Resigned May 11, 1864.
776	Henry W. Hollingsworth	do	8	do	May 19, 1864	Honorably discharged Dec. 31, 1865.
777	Isaac N. Lewis	Commissioner	8	do	June 2, 1863	Resigned Feb. 15, 1865.
778	Joseph G. Easton	do	8	do	Feb. 21, 1865	Honorably discharged May 5, 1865.
779	Zebulon T. Knight	Surgeon	8	do	June 2, 1863	Honorably discharged May 30, 1865.
780	William F. Switzler	Provost-marshal	9	do	July 6, 1863	Appointment revoked Oct. 4, 1864.
781	Walter L. Lovelace	do	9	do	Oct. 4, 1864	Resigned Dec. 13, 1864.
782	William B. Adams	do	9	do	Dec. 23, 1864	Honorably discharged Oct. 15, 1865.
783	do	Commissioner	9	do	June 2, 1863	Appointed provost-marshal Dec. 23, 1864.
784	Theodore Bruere	do	9	do	Jan. 24, 1865	Honorably discharged May 5, 1865.
785	Stephen S. Reynolds	Surgeon	9	do	June 2, 1863	Resigned Dec. 27, 1864.
786	Charles F. Walden	do	9	do	Jan. 5, 1865	Honorably discharged May 30, 1865.
787	Roland H. Hall	Provost-marshal	1	Kentucky	May 8, 1863	Appointment revoked Sept. 27, 1864.
788	John H. Morgan	do	1	do	Sept. 27, 1864	Honorably discharged Oct. 31, 1865.
789	Albert Bradshaw	Commissioner	1	do	May 8, 1863	Honorably discharged May 5, 1865.
790	William W. Kidd	Surgeon	1	do	May 8, 1863	Died Oct. 25, 1864.
791	John M. Best	do	1	do	Nov. 14, 1864	Honorably discharged June 15, 1865.
792	John R. Grissom	Provost-marshal	2	do	June 2, 1863	Honorably discharged Oct. 31, 1865.
793	N. B. Allen	Commissioner	2	do	May 8, 1863	Honorably discharged May 5, 1865.
794	Augustus Webber	Surgeon	2	do	May 8, 1863	Resigned Sept. 5, 1863.
795	John W. Compton	do	2	do	Sept. 5, 1863	Honorably discharged June 15, 1865.
796	Atwood G. Hobson	Provost-marshal	3	do	July 28, 1863	Honorably discharged Oct. 31, 1865.
797	P. B. Hawkins	Commissioner	3	do	July 27, 1863	Resigned Nov. 12, 1863.*
798	William J. Hobson	do	3	do	Dec. 10, 1863	Resigned Mar. 11, 1864.†
799	J. M. Bailey	Surgeon	3	do	June 23, 1863	Resigned Nov. 12, 1863.
800	Amos Rist	do	3	do	Dec. 10, 1863	Resigned Mar. 11, 1864.
801	Jonathan R. Bailey	do	3	do	Mar. 28, 1864	Honorably discharged June 15, 1865.
802	T. T. Alexander	Provost-marshal	4	do	May 8, 1863	Resigned Dec. 7, 1863.
803	James M. Fidler	do	4	do	Jan. 16, 1864	Honorably discharged Dec. 31, 1865.
804	John B. Cochran	Commissioner	4	do	May 8, 1863	Resigned Mar. 9, 1864.
805	Frederick B. Merrimee	do	4	do	Mar. 31, 1864	Honorably discharged May 5, 1865.
806	Robert B. Winlock	Surgeon	4	do	May 8, 1863	Resigned Apr. 6, 1864.
807	John C. Maxwell	do	4	do	Apr. 16, 1864	Honorably discharged June 15, 1865
808	George W. Womack	Provost-marshal	5	do	May 8, 1863	Honorably discharged Dec. 31, 1865.

809	Will R. Hervey	Commissioner	5	do	May 25, 1863	Resigned Mar. 2, 1865.
810	Alexander Magruder	do	5	do	Mar. 14, 1865	Honorably discharged May 5, 1865.
811	Theo. S. Bell	Surgeon	5	do	May 8, 1863	Resigned Feb. 1, 1865.
812	James Gardner	do	5	do	Feb. 16, 1865	Honorably discharged June 15, 1865.
813	G. W. Berry	Provost marshal	6	do	May 8, 1863	Died June 17, 1864.
814	Edward H. Samuels	do	6	do	July 1, 1864	Resigned Nov. 28, 1864.
815	George W. Hawkins	Commissioner	6	do	May 8, 1863	Resigned Aug. 19, 1864.
816	Robert A. Athey	do	6	do	Aug. 29, 1864	Honorably discharged May 5, 1865.
817	E. P. Buckner	Surgeon	6	do	May 8, 1863	Honorably discharged June 15, 1865.
818	Thomas H. Moore	Provost-marshal	7	do	May 8, 1863	Appointment revoked Mar. 20, 1865.
819	William Goodloe	do	7	do	Mar. 20, 1865	Honorably discharged Dec. 31, 1865.
820	Orlando Brown	Commissioner	7	do	May 27, 1863	Honorably discharged May 5, 1865.
821	Stephen F. Gano	Surgeon	7	do	May 8, 1863	Honorably discharged June 15, 1865.
822	Robert Hays	Provost-marshal	8	do	May 8, 1863	Honorably discharged Oct. 31, 1865.
823	Harmon K. Wilson	Commissioner	8	do	May 8, 1863	Honorably discharged May 5, 1865.
824	James D. Foster	Surgeon	8	do	May 8, 1863	Honorably discharged June 15, 1865.
825	William C. Grier	Provost-marshal	9	do	May 8, 1863	Resigned May 29, 1865.
826	William L. Hurst	Commissioner	9	do	June 2, 1863	Appointment revoked Feb. 13, 1865.
827	F. B. Trussell	do	9	do	Feb. 13, 1865	Honorably discharged May 5, 1865.
828	Joshua Barnes	Surgeon	9	do	June 13, 1863	Resigned Nov. 9, 1863.
829	Alfred Spalding	do	9	do	Nov. 30, 1863	Honorably discharged June 15, 1865.
830	James McCahon	Provost-marshal	1	Kansas	July 7, 1863	Appointment revoked Apr. 5, 1865.
831	Clark J. Hanks	do	1	do	Apr. 5, 1863	Honorably discharged Aug. 21, 1865.
832	Edward Russell	Commissioner	1	do	Apr. 30, 1863	Resigned Aug. 23, 1864.
833	William Tholen	do	1	do	Aug. 30, 1864	Appointment revoked Apr. 5, 1865.
834	Martin R. Dutton	do	1	do	Apr. 5, 1865	Honorably discharged May 5, 1865.
835	Tiffin Sinks	Surgeon	1	do	Apr. 30, 1863	Honorably discharged May 30, 1865.
836	Alexander R. Banks	Provost-marshal	2	do	Apr. 30, 1863	Appointment revoked Oct. 7, 1863.
837	A. J. Shannon	do	2	do	Oct. 7, 1863	Resigned Dec. 29, 1864.
838	Theo. C. Sears	do	2	do	Jan. 13, 1865	Honorably discharged Sept. 30, 1865.
839	F. B. Baker	Commissioner	2	do	Oct. 7, 1863	Honorably discharged May 5, 1865.
840	George J. Tallman	Surgeon	2	do	July 7, 1863	Appointment revoked Apr. 5, 1865.
841	Samuel C. Harrington	do	2	do	Apr. 5, 1865	Honorably discharged May 30, 1865.
842	Oscar F. Davis	Provost-marshal	1	Nebraska Territory.	May 4, 1863	Honorably discharged May 20, 1865.
843	John Wanless	do	1	Colorado Territory.	Apr. 30, 1863	Resigned Mar. 27, 1865.
844	Robert Cleveland	do	1	do	Mar. 27, 1865	Honorably discharged May 20, 1865.
845	William H. Parks	do	1	California	July 31, 1863	Appointment revoked May 12, 1865.
846	Joshua C. Sargent	do	1	do	May 12, 1865	Honorably discharged Oct. 15, 1865.
847	William B. Latham, jr	Commissioner	1	do	July 31, 1863	Honorably discharged Apr. 30, 1865.
848	Lorenzo Hubbard	Surgeon	1	do	July 31, 1863	Do.
849	Robert Robinson	Provost-marshal	2	do	July 31, 1863	Honorably discharged Oct. 15, 1865.
850	Sylvester Tryon	Commissioner	2	do	July 31, 1863	Honorably discharged Apr. 30, 1865.
851	A. B. Nixon	Surgeon	2	do	July 31, 1863	Do.
852	A. Jones Jackson	Provost-marshal	3	do	July 31, 1863	Honorably discharged Oct. 15, 1865.
853	David Dwyer	Commissioner	3	do	July 31, 1863	Resigned Mar. 22, 1864.
854	Edward W. Roberts	do	3	do	Aug. 16, 1864	Honorably discharged Apr. 30, 1865.
855	L. C. Lane	Surgeon	3	do	July 31, 1863	Do.

* Again appointed March 28, 1864; resigned August 22, 1864.

† Again appointed August 27, 1864; honorably discharged May 5, 1865.

Register of the members of the boards of enrollment, appointed under the act approved March 3, 1863—Continued.

No.	Name.	Rank.	District.	State.	When appointed.	Remarks.
856	Julius M. Keeler	Provost-marshal	1	Oregon	May 22, 1863	Honorably discharged June 15, 1865.
857	Joseph M. Drew	Commissioner	1	....do	June 19, 1863	Resigned May 16, 1864.
858	Benjamin F. Whitson	....do	1	....do	June 7, 1864	Honorably discharged Apr. 30, 1865.
859	Wilson Bowlby	Surgeon	1	....do	June 19, 1863	Resigned Apr. 15, 1864.
860	Eugene R. Fiske	....do	1	....do	May 20, 1864	Honorably discharged Apr. 30, 1865.
861	James W. Porter	Provost-marshal	1	Washington Territory.	May 30, 1863	Honorably discharged June 15, 1865.
862	Leander Holmes	Commissioner	1	....do	Nov. 30, 1863	Honorably discharged Apr. 30, 1865.
863	J. B. Cole	Surgeon	1	....do	Mar. 8, 1864	Died Jan. 11, 1865.
864	George P. Waldron	Provost-marshal	1	Dakota Territory.	Apr. 30, 1863	Honorably discharged May 20, 1865.
865	Jacob L. Van Bokkelen	....do	1	Nevada Territory.	Apr. 30, 1863	Honorably discharged June 10, 1865.

Register of officers in military service detailed temporarily as members of boards of enrollment.

No.	Name and rank.	Acting.	District.	State.	When detailed.	Remarks.
1	Capt. Edward T. Sanford, 1st District of Columbia Cavalry	Provost-marshal	2	Maine	Aug. 31, 1864	Relieved Sept. 27, 1864.
2	....do	....do	5	....do	Sept. 28, 1864	Relieved Nov. 15, 1864.
3	Surg. L. A. Edwards, U. S. Army	Surgeon	4	Connecticut	Sept. 9, 1863	Relieved Dec. 15, 1863.
4	Maj. L. C. Bootes, 14th U. S. Infantry	Provost-marshal	2	New York	July 7, 1864	Relieved Aug. 9, 1864.
5	Bvt. Maj. A. Thieman, 12th U. S. Infantry	....do	2	....do	Apr. —, 1865	Relieved May 13, 1865.
6	Maj. L. C. Bootes, 14th U. S. Infantry	....do	3	....do	Apr. 22, 1864	Relieved July 6, 1864.
7	First Lieut. John J. Knox, Veteran Reserve Corps	....do	16	....do	Feb. 21, 1865	Relieved Apr. 7, 1865.
8	Lieut. Col. D C. Poole, Veteran Reserve Corps	....do	21	....do	Dec. 22, 1864	Relieved Jan. 14, 1865.
9	Maj. W. H. H. Beadle, Veteran Reserve Corps	....do	21	....do	Mar. 11, 1865	Relieved Oct. 15, 1865.
10	Surg. J. O. Stanton, First Army Corps	Surgeon	21	....do	Mar. 11, 1865	Relieved May 25, 1865.
11	Maj. Silas Ramsey, aide-de-camp	Provost-marshal	23	....do	Oct. 13, 1863	Relieved Nov. 20, 1863.
12	Capt. A. A. Yates, Veteran Reserve Corps	....do	23	....do	Mar. 10, 1865	Relieved Mar. 16, 1865.
13	Maj. John A. Haddock, Veteran Reserve Corps	....do	30	....do	Nov. 4, 1864	Relieved Nov. 25, 1864.
14	Capt. Charles P. Clark, 99th Pennsylvania Volunteers	....do	3	Pennsylvania	Sept. 18, 1863	Relieved Oct. 10, 1863.
15	Maj. John A. Haddock, Veteran Reserve Corps	....do	6	....do	May 26, 1864	Relieved Nov. 4, 1864.
16	Maj. John Devereux, Veteran Reserve Corps	....do	6	....do	Nov. 4, 1864	Relieved Nov. 17, 1864
17	Lieut. Col. D. C. Poole, Veteran Reserve Corps	....do	12	....do	Feb. 10, 1865	Relieved May 27, 1865
18	Capt. John J. Knox, Veteran Reserve Corps	....do	12	....do	May 27, 1865	Relieved Oct. 15, 1865.

19	Capt. T. E. Douglass, Veteran Reserve Corps	....do	13	....do	Mar. 14, 1865	Relieved Sept. 30, 1865.
20	Lieut. Col. Edward Campbell, 85th Pennsylvania Volunteers	....do	17	....do	Jan. 26, 1864	Relieved Jan. 27, 1864.
21	Lieut. Col. F. A. H. Gaebel, Veteran Reserve Corps	....do	24	....do	Sept. 23, 1865	Relieved Sept. 30, 1865.
22	Capt. M. M. Blunt, 12th U. S. Infantry	....do		Delaware	Apr. 26, 1865	Do.
23	Maj. H. B. Judd, U. S. Army	....do		....do	Sept. 30, 1865	Relieved Dec. 15, 1865.
24	Capt. Jonathan W. Barley, Veteran Reserve Corps	....do	4	Maryland	Aug. 25, 1864	Relieved Sept. 12, 1864.
25	Capt. James O. P. Burnside, Veteran Reserve Corps	....do	5	....do	July 27, 1864	Relieved Aug. 30, 1864.
26	Capt. J. C. Putnam, Veteran Reserve Corps	....do		Dist. of Columbia	June 2, 1864	Relieved Jan. 4, 1865.
27	Lieut. Col. D. C. Poole, Veteran Reserve Corps	....do		....do	June 28, 1864	Relieved Aug. 25, 1864.
28	Maj. J. R. O'Beirne, Veteran Reserve Corps	....do		....do	Jan. 4, 1865	Relieved July 18, 1865.
29	Bvt. Lieut. Col. J. McL. Hildt, 3d U. S. Infantry	....do		....do	aJuly 24, 1865	Relieved Aug. 4, 1865.
30	Capt. R. Lodor, 4th U. S. Artillery	....do		....do	Aug. 4, 1865	Relieved Dec. 11, 1865.
31	Bvt. Maj. Samuel Dana, U. S. Army	....do		....do	Dec. 11, 1865	
32	First Lieut. John J. Knox, Veteran Reserve Corps	Commissioner		....do	Oct. 24, 1864	Relieved Feb. 23, 1865.
33	Maj. Lucius V. Bierce, U. S. Volunteers	Provost-marshal	3	Ohio	Nov. 18, 1864	Relieved Mar. 30, 1865.
34	Capt. W. R. Riddle, Veteran Reserve Corps	....do	18	....do	Feb. 17, 1865	Relieved Feb. 21, 1865.
35	Capt. S. M. Barber, Veteran Reserve Corps	....do	18	....do	Feb. 21, 1865	Relieved Mar. 9, 1865.
36	Capt. A. Collins, Veteran Reserve Corps	....do	18	....do	Mar. 9, 1865	Do.
37	Lieut.Col. Charles E. Brown, 63d Ohio Volunteers	....do	18	....do	Mar. 21, 1865	To be mustered out of service July 14, 1865.
38	Maj. Aquila Wiley, Veteran Reserve Corps	....do	18	....do	July 14, 1865	Relieved Sept. 30, 1865.
39	Maj. A. S. Norton, additional aide-de-camp	....do	5	Illinois	Jan. 26, 1865	Relieved Mar. 8, 1865.
40	....do	....do	10	....do	May 6, 1865	Relieved Oct. 15, 1865.
41	Maj. H. Bartling, 8th Colored Artillery	....do	1	Kentucky	Sept. 23, 1864	Ordered under arrest and relieved Sept. 27, 1864.
42	Capt. William Starling, Veteran Reserve Corps	....do	4	....do	Dec. 28, 1863	Relieved Jan. 16, 1864.
43	Maj. H. A. Mitchell, Veteran Reserve Corps	....do	6	....do	Sept. 20, 1864	Relieved Aug. 11, 1865.

a In charge.

RECAPITULATION.

Resigned	201
Commissions vacated by new appointments	14
Revoked	68
Canceled	9
Died	14
Honorably discharged by reason of services being no longer required	533
Dismissed	18
Relieved by Special Orders, No. 560, Adjutant-General's Office. dated December 18, 1863, and returned to his duty in Quartermaster's Department, in which he was captain	1
Discharged	7
Total	865

DOCUMENT NO. 35.

Laws relative to the raising of troops.

(Section 24 of act approved March 3, 1803.)

SEC. 24. That the President of the United States be authorized and empowered, on an invasion, or insurrection, or probable prospect thereof, to call forth such a number of militia, and from such county, and in such a manner, whether by routine of duty or otherwise, as he may deem proper; and for the accommodation, equipment, and support of the militia so at any time to be called forth, the President of the United States may appoint such quartermasters, commissaries, and other staff as to him shall seem proper, and to fix their pay and allowances, and shall also take such measures for procuring, transporting, and issuing all orders which may be necessary. Orders for the militia to be called forth as aforesaid shall be sent to the commanding officer of the District of Columbia, with a notification of the place or places of rendezvous, who shall immediately take measures for detaching the same, with the necessary number and ranks of officers, by detail and rotation of duty or otherwise, as he may be ordered. Whenever any militia shall be called forth into actual service as aforesaid, they shall be governed by the Articles of War which govern the troops of the United States. And courts-martial shall be held as therein are directed, to be composed of militia officers only, for the trial of any person in the militia; but to the cashiering of any officer, or capital punishment of any person, the approbation of the President of the United States shall be necessary. And when any militia shall be in actual service, they shall be allowed the same pay and rations as are allowed to the militia of the United States. If a sudden invasion shall be made into either county in this District, or in case of an insurrection in either county, the commanding officer of the militia of the District, or of such county, is hereby authorized and required to order out the whole or such part of the militia as he may think necessary, and in such manner as he may think best, for repelling or suppressing such invasion or insurrection; and shall call on the commanding officers of the adjacent counties for such aid as he may think necessary, who shall forthwith and in like manner furnish the same; and in the event of any militia ordered out by a commanding officer of the county, or of the District, as herein authorized, such officer shall immediately notify the same, and the cause thereof, to the commanding officer of the District, or to the President of the United States, as the case may require.

DOCUMENT NO. 38.

Casualties.

Casualties among the employés of the Provost-Marshal-General's Bureau, while in the performance of their legal duties, apprehending deserters, enrolling and drafting the national forces, &c.

Killed	38
Wounded	60
Total	98
Injured in property in addition to the above	12

The above includes only the employés proper of the Bureau, and does not embrace the losses among troops and special forces employed in suppressing riots, and whose reports of casualties have been made through the ordinary military channels.

Document No. 39.

List of persons who put in representative recruits, and names of recruits *

MAINE.

District.	Name of principal.	Name of recruit.	Residence of principal.
First	Francis P. Adams	Michael Ryon	Newfield.
Fifth	Nehemiah Abbott	Thomas May	Belfast.
First	John B. Brown	George Francis	Portland.
Do	Edward P. Burnham	Henry B. King	Saco.
Do	James Baily	Franklin H. Eaton	Portland.
Second	Henry Bonney	S. R. Bearce	Lewiston.
Do	John Butler.	Hercy Day	Do.
Fourth	Samuel A. Barker	Emory C. Dunn	Bangor.
First	George W. Cobb	Hugh Dointy	Westbrook.
Do	Rensselaer Cram	Hartly D. Leonard	Portland.
Do	Cyrus S. Clark	George N. Phelps	Do.
Do	Jesse Dyer	John Danalry	Do.
Second	A. K. P. Dixon	N. W. Farwell	Lewiston.
Fourth	George E. Dale	Loring Merrill	Bangor.
Do	James Dunning	James Mahoney	Do.
Do	do	Richard Firth	Do.
Do	do	James H. Duffy	Do.
Fifth	J. G. Dickerson	Benjamin Sprague	Belfast.
First	Rufus Gibbs	Daniel B. Jackson	Bridgton.
Do	Sewell N. Gross	Thomas Wilson	New Gloucester.
Fifth	William Grindle	William C. Boyd	Penobscot.
First	Miss Maria T. Hersey	Daniel A. Brown	Portland.
Do	Robert Holyoke	Eli St. Julien	Do.
Do	T. C. Hersey	George H. Rand	Do.
Fifth	Paul R. Hazeltine	John Wilkinson	Belfast.
Do	Prescott Hazeltine	John Deller	Do.
Third	Edward Hawes	David Woodbury	Waterville.
First	George E. B. Jackson	John Quinn	Portland.
Fourth	William Jewell	Alvah M. Young	Bangor.
Third	Edward C. Lowe	William J. Sharpe	Waterville.
Fifth	Mark H. Lufkin	Hezekiah Greenlow	Deer Isle.
First	Nathaniel J. Miller	Isaac F. Polly	Portland.
Do	Jacob McClellan	Valentine R. Jackson	Do.
Second	William F. Murray	E. P. Crosby	Phillips.
Third	Charles M. Morse	Andrew H. Porter	Waterville.
Fourth	Elihab W. Metcalf	James A. Durgan	Bangor.
Do	Franklin Muzzy	Franklin L. Perkins	Do.
Third	Joshua Nye	George C. Tracy	Waterville.
Fifth	Salathiel Nickerson	Eugene Manly	Belfast.
First	John C. Proctor	George N. Floyd	Portland.
Do	John P. Perly	Gardiner B. Boynton	Bridgton.
Do	Samuel F. Perly	George N. Furbush	Naples.
Do	do	John McCarty	Do.
Do	E. N. Perry	Hiram Downs	Cape Elizabeth
Second	A. J. Potter	George A. Preble	Bath.
Do	Reuben D. Pratt	Jesse L. Lyford	Lewiston.
Fourth	Joab W. Palmer	Charles Belcher	Bangor.
Fifth	Augustus Perry	Edward Stokes	Belfast.
Do	William O. Poor	A. J. Ross	Do.
First	Hosea J. Robinson	Lewis Rone	Portland.
Second	Charles Richardson	A. D. Lockwood	Lewiston.
Fifth	Andrew J. Ross	Andrew Spearin	Belfast.
First	Samuel E. Spring	Charles Barnard	Portland.
Do	Andrew Spring	David H. Leighton	Do.
Do	Andrew S. Sawyer	Frederick Hardy	Cape Elizabeth.
Fourth	Isaiah Stetson	Thomas E. Wiggin	Bangor.
Do	George Stetson	James A. Strout	Do.
Fifth	Albert Small	Henry Stokes	Belfast.
Do	James E. Stinson	Joseph Driscoll	Deer Isle.
First	William W. Thomas	Stephen Noyes, jr	Portland.
Do	Hananiah Temple	Joseph Wilbur	Saco.
Fifth	J. R. Talbot	James Burgess	East Machias.
First	George W. Woodman	Daniel Hennessy	Portland.
Fourth	Aaron A. Wing	George S. Sullivan	Bangor.
Fifth	Henry Whiting	Calvin J. Sergeant	Ellsworth.
First	Abner Lowell	George Dance	Portland.†
Do	St. John Smith	John Jones	Portland.†

*In connection with this list see remarks of Provost-Marshal-General, under the head of "Representative recruits," p. 649.

†Added since preparation of original list.

List of persons who put in representative recruits, and names of recruits—Cont'd.

NEW HAMPSHIRE.

District.	Name of principal.	Name of recruit.	Residence of principal.
Second	James O. Adams	John Williams	Manchester, ward 6.
First	Robert Bradford	John Scott	Francestown.
Second	Charles H. Brooks	Charles H. Robinson	Peterborough.
Do	Thomas E. Bixby	Charles E. Wells	Francestown.
Do	Robert B. Carswell	John Brown	Weare.
Do	Andrew C. Cochran	Patrick Mullen	Peterborough.
Do	Erastus B. Claggett	Hugh McGuire	Lyndeborough.
Do	Moody Currier	Charles Clarke	Manchester.
Third	Reuel Durkee	William Gilson	Croydon.
Second	Hosea Eaton	George Hutchinson	New Ipswich.
Do	Isaac Elwell	James McKeever	Concord.
Do	Herman Foster	Alonzo M. Flanders	Manchester.
Third	William W. George	Monroe Clough	Canaan.
Second	Eli S. Hunt	George Adams	Peterborough.
Do	Israel Herrick	John Morgan	Lyndeborough.
Third	Solomon E. Jones	George Williams	Washington.
Second	Thomas Little	Frank Clark	Peterborough.
First	Benjamin F. Martin	George B. Jenness	Manchester.
Second	Humphrey Moore	Almond Lord	Milford.
Do	Nancy Moore	William Waugh	Manchester.
Do	A. P. Morrison	William Simpson	Peterborough
Do	N. G. Ordway	James Robinson	Warner.
First	Henry Peyser	Charles Neff	Portsmouth.
Second	Horace Patter	Joseph De Marce	Manchester.
Do	Edward H. Rollins	Edwin F. Dexter	Concord.
Third	Daniel Richardson	John Williams	Lebanon.
Second	Ezekiel A. Straw	Edward B. Leonard	Manchester.
Do	Frederick Smith	Edward F. Brown	Do.
Do	Edward P. Spalding	Edward O'Connor	Lyndeborough.
Do	Albert Smith	Benjamin Moody	Peterborough.
Third	Benjamin Smith	Charles Hill	Lebanon.
Second	George F. Wheeler	Charles H. Littlefield	Peterborough.
Do	Josiah Wheeler	Charles Campbell	Lyndeborough.

VERMONT.

District.	Name of principal.	Name of recruit.	Period of service.
Second	Bethro W. Bartholomew	Asa H. Pepper	1 year.
Do	.....do	Thomas F. S. Thurber	Do.
Third	L. J. Bishop	Richard Roach	3 years.
First	George Chipman	Edward Dougherty	
Do	A. J. Downing	Peter Barrett	
Do	Mrs. Mary H. Dana		
Do	S. P. Giddings	George Gregory	
Do	William T. Hall	Patrick McCann	
Do	L. B. Hurd	Paul Eglin	
Do	Job Lyman	Charles Price	Do.
Do	Horace Loomis	Hollis Tyron	Do.
Second	Hon. Justin S. Morrill	Charles Parmenter	Do.
Do	Chester Pierce	Alfred Tensmeyer	Do.
First	C. K. W. Strong	James T. Maybury	
Do	John H. Squier	Jordan Parker	
Do	Samuel A. Wilkins	Elisha Walker	

MASSACHUSETTS.

District.	Name of principal.	Name of recruit.	Date of enlistment.
First	Samuel Atwell	David Ross	Dec. 21, 1864
Second	Mrs. Eben Adams	William Richardson	Aug. 12, 1864
Do	Dr. E. Alden	Peter Slater	Aug. 20, 1864
Do	Mrs. James H. Anthony	Stephen Barry	Sept. 1, 1864
Do	Mrs. Wyman Abercrombie	Robert Pigotts	Nov. 30, 1864
Fourth	Joseph W. Aborn	Joseph Hutchinson	Aug. 20, 1864
Do	Francis Amory	Lewis Jones	Oct. 15, 1864
Do	.....do	Isom Newton	Oct. 12, 1864
Do	.....do	Robert Johnson	Dec. 2, 1864
Do	.....do	Lawson Madison	Dec. 2, 1864
Do	Robert E. Apthorp	Jesse Wyatt	Jan. 5, 1865

List of persons who put in representative recruits, and names of recruits—Cont'd.

MASSACHUSETTS—Continued.

District.	Name of principal.	Name of recruit.	Date of enlistment.
Fourth	Paul Adams	Richard Flowers	Dec. 27, 1864
Do	Alex. Agassiz	Franklin Griffin	Sept. 5, 1864
Do	E. G. Alden	John McCarpenter	Jan. 30, 1865
Do	H. O. Apthorp	Simon Evans	Feb. 20, 1865
Sixth	Mrs. Elisha Atkins	James Johnson	Sept. 23, 1864
Do	George S. Adams	Emett Boton	Oct. 13, 1865
Do	Daniel Allen	Frank Craskey	Jan. 16, 1865
Do	William E. Allen	Benjamin Folz	Sept. 21, 1864
Seventh	Henry C. Allen	Benjamin Brooks	Oct. 6, 1864
Ninth	Justin W. C. Alles	Edward Robinson	Jan. 16, 1865
Tenth	James T. Ames	Pinckney Jourdan	Sept. 2, 1864
Do	William C. Allen	John Kirk	Nov. 30, 1864
Do	William S. Ames	James Levi	Aug. 12, 1864
Eighth	John H. Aldrich	Shadrach Fraynor	Apr. 6, 1865
First	Charles C. Bearce	Lafayette Clark	Aug. 15, 1864
Do	Henry H. Baker	Robert Jamison	Aug. 12, 1864
Do	Horatio Barrows	John Weaver	Aug. 2, 1864
Second	David H. Bates	Howard White	Jan. 28, 1865
Do	Silas P. Briggs	Dabner Lewis	Oct. 13, 1864
Do	De Witt Clinton Bates	Dennis Riley	Oct. 13, 1864
Do	John Brewster	Frank Robinson	Jan. 19, 1865
Do	Elias S. Beales	Lawrence Turner	Aug. 20, 1864
Do	Z. L. Bicknell	Trimus Wadkins	Aug. 27, 1864
Do	Edmund Baylees	John Keys	Aug. 1, 1864
Do	Mrs. E. L. Baylees	Edward Heekey	Aug. 6, 1864
Third	William L. Bullard	Sandy Simons	Dec. 6, 1864
Do	Charles A. Babcock	Fleming Briggs	Aug. 20, 1864
Do	Thomas J. Bancroft	Edward Taylor	Oct. 12, 1864
Do	Samuel G. Bowdlear	James Steale	Oct. 12, 1864
Do	Mrs. W. J. Bowditch	Andrew Horton	Oct. 12, 1864
Do	John A. Burnham	Henderson Keller	Jan. 11, 1865
Do	Mrs. J. A. Burnham	Richard Stevens	Jan. 11, 1865
Do	Miss Jennie D. Burnham	Clayburn Wilson	Feb. 20, 1865
Do	Miss Maria D. Burnham	George Washington	Feb. 25, 1865
Do	John A. Burnham, jr	George King	Feb. 20, 1865
Fourth	P. A. Bruce	Richard Williams	Oct. 13, 1864
Do	Albert Bowker	John H. Diggs	Dec. 5, 1864
Do	John A. Blanchard	John Hodge	Jan. 12, 1865
Do	Dr. H. I. Bowditch	Gilbert Baldwin	Aug. 20, 1864
Do	Mrs. Olivia Bowditch	Green Warren	Feb. 8, 1865
Do	Miss Olivia Y. Bowditch	Charles Legg	Feb. 8, 1865
Do	Charles Beek	William Crunn	Dec. 29, 1864
Do	N. Boynton	Sancho Bryant	Sept. 5, 1864
Do	Mrs. N. Boynton	John Brown	Sept. 5, 1864
Fifth	Henry Bancroft	Samuel Aye	Sept. 1, 1864
Do	Robert Brookhouse	Robert H. Fort	Sept. 9, 1864
Do	John Bertram	William Roberts	Oct. 21, 1864
Do	Mary A. Bertram	James Helpin	Oct. 29, 1864
Do	Annie P. Bertram	Joseph Anderson	Jan. 19, 1865
Sixth	James Brown	Pleasant Spradley	Jan. 4, 1865
Do	Daniel R. Bickford	Simon Evans	Sept. 23, 1864
Do	George H. Bailey	Alexander Jackson	Sept. 16, 1864
Do	Dexter Bryant	William Parsons	Sept. 21, 1864
Do	H. A. Breed	Robert Morgan	Sept. 20, 1864
Do	N. W. Bridge	Simon Windham	Sept. 23, 1864
Do	William J. Bride	Peter Williams	Sept. 20, 1864
Do	Charles V. Bemis	Elijah Roberts	Jan. 16, 1865
Do	Mrs. Henry W. Bigelow	Martin Davis	Feb. 24, 1865
Do	William Ellery Bright	David Stone	Oct. 14, 1864
Do	Jonathan B. Bright	Henry J. Scarborough	Oct. 21, 1864
Do	Charles Burchard	John E. Simpson	Sept. 21, 1864
Do	William A. Balcom	William Wallace	Aug. 19, 1864
Seventh	Joseph H. Billings	Richard Hurd	Oct. 14, 1864
Do	Lewis Burr	Timothy Dodson	Sept. 30, 1864
Do	John Burr	William H. Smith	Jan. 4, 1865
Do	Jackson Burr	John T. Roberson	Jan. 21, 1865
Do	Isaac G. Braman	Connel Holt	Aug. 9, 1864
Do	Hiram Barker	Robert Savage	Aug. 26, 1864
Do	Daniel Baxter	William Collins	Oct. 13, 1864
Do	George H. Brooks	John Cobb	Oct. 14, 1864
Do	Joseph Breck	Jacob Crocker	Oct. 20, 1864
Do	William D. Bickford	William Dosier	Jan. 11, 1865
Do	S. D. Benjamin	Sydney Paris	Sept. 27, 1864
Do	Mary Benjamin	William Simpson	Dec. 22, 1864
Do	Zenos Brown	Josephus Jones	Jan. 16, 1865
Do	Benjamin Brown	Thomas Smith	Oct. 16, 1864
Eighth	Ira Broad	Alfred Holland	Sept. 27, 1864
Do	George W. Bascom	Charles Walker	Sept. 9, 1864
Do	William B. Boyd	Henry Watts	Oct. 8, 1864

List of persons who put in representative recruits, and names of recruits—Cont'd.

MASSACHUSETTS—Continued.

District.	Name of principal.	Name of recruit.	Date of enlistment.
Eighth	Warren P. Bush	Richard Overton	Oct. 7, 1864
Do	J. C. Bigelow	Henry Evans	Oct. 6, 1864
Do	Daniel W. Batcheldor	William Williams	Jan. 23, 1865
Do	Willard Brown	William Sullivan	Sept. 21, 1864
Ninth	Charles C. Bassett	John Meed	Sept. 29, 1864
Do	Mrs. Hiram Barnes	Franklin Strahan	Oct. 7, 1864
Do	David Billings	John Kennedy	Jan. 16, 1865
Do	Gilbert Bascom	Samuel McLean	Jan. 16, 1865
Do	Elisha Belden	Mingo Jenkens	Sept. 1, 1864
Do	Charles Blackmur	Patrick Bany	Aug. 15, 1864
Tenth	G. T. Barker	Cephas Lancaster	Nov. 30, 1864
Do	John V. Barker	Richard Mansfield	Nov. 23, 1864
Do	Charles T. Barker	Baze North	Nov. 30, 1864
Do	Otis R. Barker	Stephen Pannan	Dec. 24, 1864
Second	John A. Burgess	John Grant	Apr. 6, 1865
Fourth	David H. Blaney	Thomas Grant	Apr. 6, 1865
Eighth	Chandler Batchelder	Paul Blunt	Apr. 6, 1865
Ninth	Joseph D. Billings	William Smith	Apr. 6, 1865
Do	William D. Billings	Jim Brown	Apr. 6, 1865
Tenth	W. S. Bullard	George Wright	Apr. 6, 1865
First	Alexander C. Childs	James Bruce	Oct. 13, 1864
Do	Benj. B. Church	Benjamin Dregs	Aug. 24, 1864
Do	Latham Cross	Samuel Briden	Dec. 3, 1864
Do	Christopher A. Church	George W. Wheeler	Aug. 15, 1864
Do	do	Joseph Allen	Aug. 20, 1864
Do	Cyrus W. Chapman	Richard Bryant	Aug. 21, 1864
Second	William T. Cobb	James Green	Aug. 20, 1864
Do	Edward Capen, jr	Dennis Davis	Jan. 16, 1865
Do	Susan H. Cowan	Burton Cooper	Jan. 9, 1865
Third	E. A. M. Clark	Dennis Evans	Dec. 14, 1864
Do	C. W. Clark	Samuel Brown	Dec. 14, 1864
Do	Samuel D. Crane	Lorenzo Dow	Aug. 20, 1864
Do	Gilman Currier	Henry Bottley	Dec. 15, 1864
Do	Charles G. Currier	John Smith	Dec. 15, 1864
Do	Mrs. Frederick Cabot	Peter Butler	Aug. 26, 1864
Do	Miss M. E. Cabot	Spencer Clark	Aug. 20, 1864
Do	Frederick T. Chase	John Fitzgerald	Oct. 31, 1864
Fourth	Edward F. Chapin	David Chew	Oct. 12, 1864
Do	Horace D. Chapin	Sidney Hunt	Oct. 12, 1864
Do	Herman Chapin	Washington Conor	Dec. 2, 1864
Do	James F. Clark	Henry Murral	Dec. 5, 1864
Do	C. C. Chadwick	Robert Williams	Jan. 13, 1865
Do	Joshua Crane	Timothy A. Holmes	Jan. 21, 1865
Do	Samuel Cabot, M. D	Andy Linn	Aug. 20, 1864
Do	Faulkner Chapman	Stephen Gregory	Sept. 5, 1864
Do	Francis L. Chapman	Ephraim Davis	Oct. 12, 1864
Do	George W. Colburn	Charles Hutchinson	Jan. 20, 1865
Do	Luke Carter	Stephen Turner	Jan. 30, 1865
Do	Franklin K. Cushing	John Cash	Aug. 20, 1864
Do	Josiah P. Cook	Peter McCurley	Jan. 6, 1865
Fifth	Robert Couch	Frederick Meschack	Sept. 9, 1864
Do	James B. Curwen	Hiram Harris	Sept. 6, 1864
Sixth	Francis Coggswell	Peter Boston	Oct. 12, 1864
Do	Frederick L. Church	Isaac Jupiter	Sept. 12, 1864
Do	Dr. George Coggswell	Henry Hogans	Sept. 16, 1864
Do	William C. Childs	Watson Randolph	Jan. 16, 1865
Do	Charles Choate	Alexander Dillingham	Sept. 27, 1864
Seventh	George W. Carnes	Henderson Lucas	Jan. 11, 1865
Do	Patrick Colby	Abraham Smith	Jan. 28, 1865
Do	William R. Champney	John Jackson	Jan. 28, 1865
Do	James H. Coggswell	Napoleon Bonaparte	Feb. 20, 1865
Do	J. V. B. Coburn	John Elsey	Oct. 4, 1864
Do	George W. Coburn	Robert Granton	Sept. 27, 1864
Do	James G. Carney	Daniel Russell	Sept. 16, 1864
Do	George S. Curtis	Alfred Curtis	Oct. 14, 1864
Do	Isaac H. Carey	Benjamin Mitchell	Nov. 21, 1864
Do	Nathaniel H. Carey	William Mitchell	Nov. 16, 1864
Eighth	Gates Chapman, jr	John Jones	Sept. 1, 1864
Do	James P. Clarke	James Wright	Oct. 4, 1864
Ninth	Eli F. Cady	Silas Canfield	Aug. 31, 1864
Tenth	Henry Chickering	Robert Houston	Oct. 16, 1864
Do	George W. Campbell	Eli Royand	Dec. 24, 1864
Do	George Campbell	George Rochester	Dec. 27, 1864
Do	David Campbell	James Jones	Jan. 23, 1865
Do	Edwin Clapp	Henry Jourdan	Jan. 19, 1865
Do	Col. Thaddeus Clapp	Charles Montgomery	Jan. 19, 1865
Do	P. A. Chadbourne	Etheridge Wright	Sept. 28, 1864
Do	Luther Childs	James Gill	
Third	Miss Sarah Cabot	Peter Weeks	Apr. 6, 1865

List of persons who put in representative recruits, and names of recruits—Cont'd.

MASSACHUSETTS—Continued.

District.	Name of principal.	Name of recruit.	Date of enlistment.
Fourth	Harriet J. Colby	Charles Owen	Apr. 6, 1865
Commonwealth	John Collamore	Jim Rivers	Apr. 6, 1865
First	Walter C. Durfee	Benjamin Johnson	Aug. 15, 1864
Do	Daniel E. Damon	Cornelius Henderson	Oct. 21, 1864
Do	Charles Dillingham	Boston Chapman	Aug. 2, 1864
Second	Benjamin F. Dean	Richard Manly	Sept. 12, 1864
Do	Theodore Dean	Simon Jenkins	Oct. 18, 1864
Third	Charles E. Davis, jr	Charles C. Byam	Nov. 26, 1864
Fourth	Charles H. Dow	Lewis Nutterville	Oct. 12, 1864
Do	E. C. Dyer	Houston Holmes	Sept. 5, 1864
Do	Francis Draper	James Mahan	Dec. 21, 1864
Do	Richard H. Dana	John Rollins	Dec. 2, 1864
Do	Miss C. L. Donnison	Jonathan Scarborough	Dec. 21, 1864
Do	Alexander Dickinson	Seneca A. Blake	Nov. 7, 1864
Do	Eben Denton	Solomon T. Bick	Oct. 31, 1864
Do	E. F. Davies	James Mack	Sept. 5, 1864
Do	John Davenport	Lewis Monroe	Dec. 9, 1864
Do	E. S. Dixwell	William J. Pamplin	Jan. 13, 1865
Do	E. M. Dunbar	Joseph Swinton	Jan. 30, 1865
Do	Miss L. A. Dana	Logan Carson	Jan. 18, 1865
Do	Miss E. E. Dana	Tilman Currier	Jan. 18, 1865
Do	Warren Damon	David White	Feb. 20, 1865
Eighth	Ethan Davis	Harrison Selden	Sept. 1, 1864
Do	Paul Daniel	James Hubbard	Oct. 12, 1864
Do	P. W. Dudley	Minton Burnett	Jan. 16, 1865
Tenth	Thomas Durant	Burton Jones	Nov. 30, 1864
Fourth	Dr. John H. Dix	John Smith	Apr. 6, 1865
Do	do	Washington Boss	Apr. 6, 1865
Do	Charles Deane	John Owen	Apr. 6, 1865
Seventh	John Dunkley	John Legree	Apr. 6, 1865
Do	Joseph Dunkley	John Smith	Apr. 6, 1865
Do	J. S. Dudley	John Grant	Apr. 6, 1865
Third	Edward Everett	Adam Whiteman	Aug. 31, 1864
Do	Jonathan Ellis	John Jameson	Aug. 20, 1864
Fourth	John S. Emery	Benjamin Dorth	Dec. 5, 1864
Do	Daniel S. Emery	Benjamin Dunnell	Dec. 2, 1864
Do	William S. Eaton	Robert Barry	Dec. 19, 1864
Do	George B. Emerson	Jesse Fields	Sept. 5, 1864
Fifth	Ezra Eames	James Walker	Sept. 9, 1864
Do	Mrs. Ephraim Emmerton	Scipio Thompson	Oct. 18, 1864
Do	Alvah A. Evans	Jonathan G. Day	Sept. 7, 1864
Sixth	George D. Edmonds	James Wembley	Sept. 16, 1864
Do	Thomas Emmerson	George Washington	Jan. 19, 1865
Do	do	Robert Long	Sept. 16, 1864
Do	Betsey H. Emmerson	Stephen Colman	Jan. 16, 1865
Tenth	William P. Elliott	Frank Williams	Aug. 25, 1864
Do	Joseph Emerson	Henry Mack	Sept. 8, 1864
First	J. D. Flint	Frederick J. Yank	Aug. 11, 1864
Second	E. S. Fellows	Dawsey Pleasant	Nov. 23, 1864
Do	Mrs. Washington M. French	Reuben Sargent	Dec. 24, 1864
Do	George A. Field	George W. Harris	Aug. 31, 1864
Third	Morrill Frost	Edward Cordelius	Aug. 30, 1864
Do	N. L. Frothingham	Jacob S. Hamilton	Aug. 27, 1864
Fourth	Jabez Fisher	William Beck	Oct. 12, 1864
Do	Herbert G. Fisher	Samuel Parky	Dec. 5, 1864
Do	Arthur L. Fisher	George Panky	Dec. 6, 1864
Do	William B. Fisher	Peter Hays	Dec. 2, 1864
Do	A. W. Farrar	Willis Blow	Oct. 23, 1864
Do	E. Farnsworth	Brown Washington	Aug. 29, 1864
Do	D. B. Flint	George Williams	Dec. 14, 1864
Do	Isaac Fay	Perry Nevils	Jan. 30, 1865
Fifth	Charles Fitz	Richard Thomas	Sept. 5, 1864
Sixth	I. V. Fletcher	John Jenkins	Feb. 4, 1865
Do	David Fairbanks	Samuel Harris	Oct. 12, 1864
Do	Jonathan Frost	James Baker	Sept. 16, 1864
Do	Mark Fisk	Benjamin Jordan	Sept. 16, 1864
Do	John Field	William McGuinn	Oct. 17, 1864
Do	Peter Folsom	Alexander Williams	Nov. 16, 1864
Do	George A. Fuller	James Smith	Aug. 19, 1864
Seventh	Richard F. Fuller	William G. Sanborn	Sept. 24, 1864
Eighth	Simeon G. Fisher	Henry Ringold	Nov. 9, 1864
Do	Samuel Fletcher	Lewis Paine	Oct. 7, 1864
Do	Charles Fowler	John L. Troup	Oct. 7, 1864
Ninth	John H. Fairbanks	Alexander Richardson	Sept. 19, 1864
Do	Sidney Fairbanks	Jim Gore	Sept. 21, 1864
Tenth	W. O. Fletcher	Dick Heywood	Aug. 21, 1864
Second	Jonah French	Jim Richardson	Apr. 6, 1865
Sixth	Mrs. F. O. French	Cupid Vanderhaust	Mar. 4, 1865
Seventh	Benjamin Fobes	Burtis Butler	Apr. 6, 1865

List of persons who put in representative recruits, and names of recruits—Cont'd.

MASSACHUSETTS—Continued.

District.	Name of principal.	Name of recruit.	Date of enlistment.
Seventh	Granville Fuller	Sandy Edwards	Apr. 6, 1865
Eighth	Elisha B. Fisk	John Morgan	Apr. 6, 1865
Tenth	Miss Jennie L. Field	Wamey Kennedy	Apr. 6, 1865
Commonwealth	Charles Follen	Paul Blunt	Apr. 6, 1865
Do	do	Paul Bryant	Apr. 6, 1865
First	David R. Green	Frank Butts	Dec. 3, 1864
Second	Samuel Gove	David P. Bowman	Oct. 20, 1864
Do	Reuben Green	Henry Simmons	Aug. 25, 1864
Do	Mrs. John Glover	Charles Thomas	Dec. 27, 1864
Do	Jeremiah Gray	Alexander Lyons	Aug. 30, 1864
Do	Peleg S. Gardner	Joseph Jenkins	Oct. 18, 1864
Third	Henry F. Gardner	Samuel Clarke	Oct. 8, 1864
Do	Miss Matilda Goddard	Alfred Thompson	Oct. 12, 1864
Do	Nathaniel Goddard	Lafayette Bentley	Oct. 12, 1864
Do	Mrs. Louisa M. Goddard	John Beasley	Oct. 12, 1864
Do	Phineas E. Gay	Benjamin Howe	Aug. 26, 1864
Fourth	Charles B. Grinnel	Sandy Mitchel	Aug. 30, 1864
Do	Lydia S. Gale	Columbus McKee	Aug. 20, 1864
Do	B. A. Gould	Benjamin Black	Feb. 20, 1865
Do	Joseph Greely	Richard Freeman	Oct. 22, 1864
Sixth	Joseph H. Gibson	Samuel Johnson	Oct. 13, 1864
Do	Addison Gage	Stephen Douglas	Sept. 16, 1864
Seventh	Joshua G. Gooch	John Grundy	Aug. 19, 1864
Ninth	E. F. Gunn	Stephen Morris	Oct. 3, 1864
Tenth	Emerson Gaylord	Randolph Young	Aug. 25, 1864
Do	Sereno Gaylord	James Brown	Sept. 21, 1864
Do	J. Z. Goodrich	Ebenezer Bateman	Sept. 28, 1864
Do	James R. Gillett	Joshua Johnson	Sept. 5, 1864
Sixth	Smith Gerrish	Closs Jackson	Mar. 4, 1865
Seventh	John Gordon	Napoleon Kinlear	Apr. 6, 1865
Commonwealth	Mrs. Henry Green	Hector Williams	Apr. 6, 1865
First	Nathaniel Hinkley	Samuel W. Brown	Aug. 16, 1864
Do	Maria G. Hoadley	Robert Forrester	Aug. 15, 1864
Do	Jonathan Howland	Albert Jones	Dec. 3, 1864
Do	Mrs. C. G. Hoadley	George Harrison	Dec. 3, 1864
Do	Miss C. E. Hoadley	Ephraim Crocker	Dec. 3, 1864
Do	Mrs. A. T. Hunt	Peter Sagars	Dec. 3, 1864
Second	Nathaniel H. Hunt	Dennis Woods	Jan. 11, 1865
Do	Lewis W. Hobart	Richard Oliver	Jan. 28, 1865
Do	Francis J. Humphrey	Samuel Priest	Aug. 20, 1864
Do	William L. Hathaway	Jacob Jackson	Dec. 21, 1864
Do	Henry C. Harding	William Williams	Aug. 20, 1864
Do	Reuben Hersey	Andrew Jones	Aug. 25, 1864
Do	John E. Howard	William Major	Aug. 8, 1864
Do	Albert Humphrey	Alfred Trent	Aug. 28, 1864
Do	Abner Holbrook	James Blackburn	Nov. 14, 1864
Do	James Humphrey	Franklin Harris	Dec. 29, 1864
Third	Charles Hall	Isaac Mayhorn	Dec. 31, 1864
Do	George Higginson	William H. Furman	Dec. 14, 1864
Do	William S. Houghton	Joseph Wilson	Oct. 12, 1864
Do	Ichabod Howland	William Bolivar	Aug. 26, 1864
Fourth	J. W. Harris	Moses Williams	Oct. 11, 1864
Do	Harriet K. Hunt	Montgomery Price	Aug. 20, 1864
Do	James P. Higginson	Washington Sarsy	Aug. 20, 1864
Do	George O. Hovey	Richmond Alexander	Dec. 2, 1864
Do	Benjamin Humphrey	Thomas Moore	Oct. 11, 1864
Do	Louisa G. Higginson	Benjamin Bigsby	Oct. 17, 1864
Do	Francis Hall	Joshua Knight	Sept. 5, 1864
Do	David B. Hadley	Charles Stowe	Dec. 17, 1864
Do	A. E. Hildreth	Mark Merryweather	Jan. 30, 1865
Do	Estes Howe	John Henry	Jan. 30, 1865
Do	James Winthrop Harris	Taylor Withers	Feb. 22, 1865
Do	U. Tracy Howe	John Williams	Mar. 7, 1865
Do	J. M. Hollingsworth	Joreh B. Loud	Dec. 14, 1864
Sixth	David J. C. Hidden	George Jennings	Jan. 24, 1865
Do	Sylvester S. Hill	Edward Johnson	Sept. 23, 1864
Do	James B. Homer	Reuben Butler	Feb. 4, 1865
Do	George W. Hills	William Gray	July 11, 1864
Do	Edward O. Holmes	Hugo Heyman	July 11, 1864
Do	James Hunnewell	George F. Shaw	Sept. 27, 1864
Seventh	Charles A. Hamblett	Alexander Maxfield	Dec. 21, 1864
Do	George Hamblett	Titus Walley	Feb. 17, 1865
Do	John M. Hollingsworth	Jacob Henderson	Sept. 27, 1864
Eighth	Thomas J. Hall	William Johnson	Oct. 1, 1864
Do	Asa Hapgood	Edwin P. Martin	Nov. 16, 1864
Ninth	Asa Hill	Dennis Caldwell	Sept. 30, 1864
Do	George W. Hubbard	Orange Drake	Oct. 1, 1864
Second	David N. Hollis	Adam Singleton	Apr. 6, 1865
Third	Charles D. Head	E. Davis	Apr. 6, 1865

List of persons who put in representative recruits, and names of recruits—Cont'd.

MASSACHUSETTS—Continued.

District.	Name of principal.	Name of recruit.	Date of enlistment.
Fourth	Samuel Hall, jr	Peter Brown	Apr. 6, 1865
Sixth	Dudley Hall	Dick Wright	Mar. 4, 1865
Fourth	William R. Inman	Samuel C. Gates	Sept. 27, 1864
Do	P. T. Jackson	William Riggs	Aug. 30, 1864
Do	Mrs. Susan M. Jackson	Andy Jennings	Jan. 5, 1865
Do	John Jeffries, jr	Hampton Wade	Jan. 13, 1865
Sixth	William Jenkins	John Whideman	Oct. 9, 1864
Seventh	Cyrus Jones	Jim Walley	Feb. 17, 1865
Fourth	D. B. Kidder	Levi Webb	Oct. 12, 1864
Do	Chester W. Kingsley	David Johnson	Sept. 5, 1864
Sixth	Samuel Knight	Thornton Walker	Sept. 16, 1864
Do	Francis H. Knight	Thornton Alexander	Sept. 16, 1864
Do	William H. Keith	Henry Johnson	Nov. 25, 1864
Do	Rufus Kendrick	Daniel Morton	Mar. 4, 1865
Eighth	William Knowlton	William Sherman	Sept. 28, 1864
Do	William Kendall	William Adams	Jan. 19, 1865
Ninth	Calvin Kelton	Daniel Bruce	Oct. 13, 1864
Tenth	Ensign H. Kellogg	John Mallen	Jan. 23, 1865
Do	Lorenzo A. Kellogg	Reuben Kennedy	Sept. 2, 1864
Second	William F. Lock	John Bell	Feb. 20, 1865
Do	John P. Lovell	John Ward	Aug. 25, 1864
Do	Henry Lord	Augustus Hank	Nov. 25, 1864
Do	Charles D. Lathrop	Charles J. Newcomb	Sept. 17, 1864
Third	Miss Rebecca A. Lowell	Lemon Strickland	Nov. 23, 1864
Do	Miss Anna C. Lowell	James Smiley	Nov. 23, 1864
Do	George Lewis	Michael Cushing	July 15, 1864
Fourth	B. Lincoln	William Gilmore	Aug. 20, 1864
Do	Albert P. Lovejoy	John Brady	Dec. 21, 1864
Do	Charles G. Loring	Harry Jones	Oct. 17, 1864
Do	Charles G. Loring	Daniel Watson	Feb. 15, 1865
Do	....do	George Johnson	Feb. 15, 1865
Do	Miss Isa E. Loring	James Bright	Oct. 23, 1864
Do	F. C. Loring	John A. Payne	Jan. 28, 1865
Do	Mrs. Anna S. Loring	Thomas Gosney	Jan. 17, 1865
Do	Miss Mary G. Loring	William Hazzard	Jan. 29, 1865
Do	John Livermore	Hiram W. Aldrich	Dec. 21, 1864
Do	Caroline H. Livermore	Charles A. Bridge	Dec. 21, 1864
Do	Emma C. Livermore	Orlando L. Doherty	Dec. 21, 1864
Do	Mary C. Livermore	John Green	Dec. 21, 1864
Do	George Livermore	William McBride	Jan. 30, 1865
Do	Elizabeth C. Livermore	Samuel Wilson	Jan. 30, 1865
Do	Charles C. Livermore	Preston Green	Jan. 12, 1865
Do	H. W. Longfellow	Alexander Thackston	Jan. 12, 1865
Do	Israel Livermore	Peter Davis	Mar. 7, 1865
Sixth	Edward Lawrence	Robert Davis	Oct. 13, 1864
Do	George W Little	Dennis Easter	Oct. 13, 1864
Do	George Lawton	George Iglen	Nov. 24, 1864
Seventh	Eliab Lee	Richard Corwin	Mar. 8, 1865
Eighth	James Lovering	Alexander Scott	Dec. 22, 1864
Tenth	W. C. Langdon	John Walker	Oct. 12, 1864
Fourth	John A. Lowell	Henry Griffin	Apr. 6, 1865
Do	Augustus Lowell	Prince Hamilton	Apr. 6, 1865
Do	J. Russell Lowell	Paul Owen	Apr. 6, 1865
Second	Alvah Morrison	Jack Carter	Oct. 12, 1864
Third	Joseph Murdock	Albert Jenkins	Oct. 18, 1864
Do	Richard Moffatt	Ephrain Jenkins	Oct. 4, 1864
Fourth	Issac B. Mills	Charles May	Dec. 9, 1864
Do	George Morey	William Hawley	Dec. 12, 1864
Do	Watson Matthews	Charles Harden	Dec. 21, 1864
Do	Rev. Summer Mason	Samuel Jackson	Dec. 21, 1864
Do	Lorenzo Marett	Spencer Jurnigan	Dec. 21, 1864
Do	Calvin Morse	Cornelius Briggs	Dec. 27, 1864
Do	Nathaniel G. Manson	James Brown	Dec. 27, 1864
Fifth	Dr. William Mack	Jackson Hays	Nov. 14, 1864
Seventh	Francis Monroe	Edmund Bailey	Mar. 8, 1865
Ninth	Garry Munson	Kato Little	Jan. 16, 1865
Do	Clesson Merriman	Lewis L. Fairchilds	Aug. 16, 1864
Tenth	Francis F. McLean	Jacob Sheppard	Sept. 17, 1864
Second	Alvah Morrison, 2d	Elick Scott	Apr. 6, 1865
Do	Bradford Marble	John Wilson	Apr. 6, 1865
Sixth	Frederick May	Quenters Hunt	Mar. 4, 1865
First	Seth Nickerson	David R. Arlett	Oct. 30, 1864
Third	John A. Newell	George A. Moore	Aug. 20, 1864
Fourth	Samuel Neal	Henry G. Marmon	Jan. 16, 1865
Tenth	H. S. Noyes	Gibson Mahaka	Aug. 12, 1864
Fourth	George Nichols	Kipp Mitchell	Apr. 6, 1865
Second	Henry Newton	George Jones	Oct. 10, 1864
Sixth	Miss Lucy Osgood	Anthony Gaines	Oct. 12, 1864
Tenth	Charles M. Owen	Samuel Dudley	Dec. 28, 1864

List of persons who put in representative recruits, and names of recruits—Cont'd.

MASSACHUSETTS—Continued.

District.	Name of principal.	Name of recruit.	Date of enlistment.
Tenth	Mrs. Sarah B. Owen	Joseph Wheeler	Jan. 23, 1865
First	David Parker, 2d	James P. Yates	Oct. 26, 1864
Second	Edward D. Peters	Richard Olmstead	Aug. 8, 1864
Third	R. F. Payne	John Hammond	July 19, 1864
Fourth	Henry A. Pierce	Jacob Thomas	Aug. 20, 1864
Do	John G. Palfrey	Lewis Williams	Aug. 20, 1864
Do	Henry Potter	George Jefferson	Sept. 5, 1864
Do	George C. Piper	Thomas Brown	Dec. 19, 1864
Fifth	Aifred Peabody	Jas. Sanford Myer	Sept. 6, 1864
Do	Edwin R. Peabody	Elmo Bradford	Sept. 6, 1864
Do	Mrs. Jerusha Peabody	Richmond Robinson	Oct. 21, 1864
ixth	Henry A. Paige	Eldrege K. Hewitt	Oct. 22, 1864
Do	Miss Helen Porter	Peyton Richardson	Feb. 24, 1865
Seventh	Jonas O. Peck	Henry Miller	Sept. 25, 1864
Do	Charles W. Pierce	James Monroe	Sept. 27, 1864
Do	Charles F. Pierce	Lewis McPherson	Sept. 28, 1864
Do	John C. Potter	Madison Johnson	Oct. 18, 1864
Eighth	Samuel A. Porter	Benjamin Glover	Sept. 22, 1864
Ninth	Lewis J. Powers	George H. Mason	Aug. 12, 1864
Tenth	Thomas F. Plunkett	Benjamin Price	Jan. 19, 1865
Do	Theo. Pomeroy	Abram Reynolds	Mar. 4, 1865
Do	Robert Pomeroy	Richard Birdswood	Mar. 9, 1865
Do	Capt. Jabez Peck	Lewis Clark	Mar. 4, 1865
Fourth	Theophilus Parsons	Morgan Heard	Apr. 6, 1865
Eighth	Israel Plummer	Jim Burrough	Apr. 6, 1865
Ninth	John Parks	Robert Wigfall	Apr. 6, 1865
Second	Mary Jane Quincy	Michael Wilsford	Aug 12, 1864
Do	Edward E. Rice	Frank Smith	Aug. 20, 1864
Do	Charles Robinson	Amos Young	Dec. 24, 1864
Do	Enoch Robinson	Lewis Wilson	Jan. 19, 1865
Do	Josiah Reed	Thomas Bass	Nov. 14, 1864
Do	Elias Richards	George Foster	Nov. 14, 1864
Third	John Rogers	Bowlin Gilbert	Aug. 20, 1864
Do	William C. Reeves	James Kelly	Nov. 10, 1864
Fourth	Edward S. Rand	Asam Butler	Dec. 10, 1864
Do	H. B. Rogers	Patrick Phillips	Jan. 19, 1865
Do	Mrs. H. B. Rogers	John Smith	Jan. 23, 1865
Do	H. B. Rogers	Leonard F. Dunn	Feb. 28, 1865
Do	Mrs. A. P. Rogers	John L. Tracy	Mar. 16, 1865
Do	William T. Richardson	Richard O'Donnell	Dec. 20, 1864
Do	H. C. Rand	Hampton Higgins	Feb. 20, 1865
Sixth	Daniel Russell	David Jones	Oct. 28, 1864
Do	Jos. C. Robinson	Anderson Minor	Sept. 20, 1864
Do	Miss Emily Ruggles	Matt. Briggs	Dec. 22, 1864
Do	John Roberts	Richard Lynchcomb	Nov. 15, 1864
Do	Royal E. Robbins	James Phillips	Nov. 15, 1864
Do	Mrs. Thomas Richardson	Isaac Cummings	Mar. 4, 1865
Seventh	James Richardson	Absalom Perkins	Mar. 8, 1865
Do	Henry Richardson	Virgil Hedliston	Mar. 8, 1865
Ninth	Mary S. Rogers	George Roy	Oct. 6, 1864
First	George P. Richardson	Hector Cashere	Apr. 6, 1865
Fourth	Z. L. Raymond	Joe Kiddles	Apr. 6, 1865
Tenth	N. F. Roys	Edward Freeman	Apr. 6, 1865
Seventh	John F. Robbins	Henson Dyson *a*	
Second	Rev. R. P. Storrs	John W. Miner	Aug. 25, 1864
Do	Jonathan Slade, 2d	Clem. Spears	Dec. 22, 1864
Do	Farnham H. Smith	Patrick Daniels	Sept. 27, 1864
Do	William L. Slade	George Williams	Mar. 4, 1865
Third	Mrs. Mary L. Shaw	John Scott	Dec. 5, 1864
Do	Miss M. L. Shaw	James Scott	Dec. 5, 1864
Do	Edward A. Strong	William Taylor	Oct. 12, 1864
Do	D. D. Stackpole	George Edwards	Aug. 20, 1864
Fourth	William B. Spooner	Sebon Ring	Aug. 20, 1864
Do	Mrs. William B. Spooner	Frank Williams	Oct. 13, 1864
Do	William F. Shaw	Albert Prince	Oct. 12, 1864
Do	Nathaniel D. Samin	Neil Kenny	Dec. 21, 1864
Do	Martin L. Smith	James A. Stewart	Dec. 20, 1864
Do	Mrs. W. V. Spencer	William Butler	Dec. 22, 1864
Do	John Sargent	John C. Gattis	Jan. 4, 1865
Do	Jared Sparks	Lewis Jackson	Dec. 19, 1864
Do	A. C. Sanborn	Alfred Lewis	Dec. 19, 1864
Fifth	Francis H. Silsbee	Michael Burke	Oct. 26, 1864
Do	Benjamin H. Silsbee	William Graham	Oct. 26, 1864
Sixth	Andrew Sawtelle	Sidney Johnson	Sept. 16, 1864
Do	Daniel Saunders	Dick Stanwood	Oct. 12, 1864
Do	Amos Stone	Henry Jones	Sept. 16, 1864
Do	Redmond St. Croix	Francis Morgan	Mar. 14, 1865

a Enlisted in District of Columbia.

List of persons who put in representative recruits, and names of recruits—Cont'd.

MASSACHUSETTS—Continued.

District.	Name of principal.	Name of recruit.	Date of enlistment.
Sixth	George L. Stearns	Patrick Galliger	Dec. 3, 1864
Do	Mrs. Mary E. Stearns	Daniel Raskins	Dec. 21, 1864
Do	George H. Sweetser	William Beresford	July 20, 1864
Seventh	Elial Shumway	John Hitchings	Sept. 27, 1864
Eighth	William P. Shumway	Thomas Brooks	Sept. 30, 1864
Ninth	C. L. Swan	Josephus Mathews	Sept. 13, 1864
Do	G. A. Smith	William Fitz Hugh	Sept. 30, 1864
Do	Orvin Sage	Oliver Dyer	Sept. 27, 1864
Tenth	De Witt S. Smith	Abram Brown	Oct. 11, 1864
Do	Daniel Stearns	Robert Jenkins	Oct. 17, 1864
Do	Mrs. M. F. Stearns	Titus Micah	Oct. 17, 1864
Do	Henry Stearns	Ned Alston	Oct. 17, 1864
Do	Mrs. M. B. Stearns	Thomas Coleman	Oct. 21, 1864
Do	William Stowe	Bony Knight	Aug. 12, 1864
Do	John B. Stebbins	Andrew Jones	Nov. 14, 1864
Do	Sumner Southworth	Harry Dickson	Jan. 9, 1865
Second	Avery P. Slade	Brown Waley	Apr. 6, 1865
Sixth	Joseph Swan	Abram Mitchell	Mar. 4, 1865
Do	Daniel Swan	Lewis Jenkins	Mar. 4, 1865
Ninth	Jabez Stanton	Jacob Edward, jr	Apr. 6, 1865
Third	Charles Stoddard	William H. Cowder	Jan. 24, 1865
First	Robert Tuckerman	Harvey McGill	Oct. 12, 1864
Do	Henry Tabor	Nathan McCoy	Oct. 12, 1864
Second	James P. Thorndike	William Morris	Aug. 25, 1864
Do	William Sidney Thayer	Robert Smith	Jan. 16, 1865
Do	Edward Turner	Thomas Johnson	Sept. 8, 1864
Do	E. B. Taylor	Thomas Brown	Sept. 6, 1864
Third	John Tappan	Alex. Rowe	Oct. 12, 1864
Do	W. W. Titcomb	William Griffitt	Aug. 26, 1864
Do	Charles Tappan	Andrew Wilson	Oct. 25, 1864
Do	Supply C. Thing	William H. Isaacs	July 14, 1864
Fourth	James F. Tweedy	Wallace Diggs	Dec. 2, 1864
Do	John H. Tweedy, jr	John W. Jackson	Dec. 2, 1864
Do	L. L. Tower	Brown Murphy	Dec. 19, 1864
Sixth	Wm. True Jackson	Cam. Gruggs	Sept. 12, 1864
Do	Edward Taylor	Randall Spradley	Dec. 24, 1864
Do	Rev. John L. Taylor	Henry Jordan	Dec. 27, 1864
Do	Amos Tufts	Tilson Ewing	Oct. 12, 1864
Ninth	Lewis Thorp	William Freeman	Dec. 4, 1864
Do	Walter Thorp	Moses Wilkinson	Feb. 3, 1865
Tenth	Henry Talmage	Mack Williams	Jan. 23, 1865
Sixth	Samuel Train	John Waring	Mar. 4, 1865
Do	Mark Temple	William Harris	Mar. 4, 1865
Second	James H. Upham	William Stokes	Aug. 20, 1864
Seventh	A. O. Varnum	Dick Wright	Apr. 6, 1865
Do	Daniel Varnum	Jim Bailey	Apr. 6, 1865
First	G. B. Weston	William Alexander	Aug. 30, 1864
Do	Mrs. G. B. Weston	Cato Kitchen	Oct. 14, 1864
Do	J. W. Wheelwright	Henry Clay	Sept. 2, 1864
Second	John D. Witcher	John L. Smith	Jan. 19, 1865
Do	William Wilber	Thomas McDonald	Jan. 19, 1865
Do	Cyrus Washburn	Ransom Clarke	Nov. 25, 1864
Do	Daniel Wilber	Simon Garrison	Mar. 4, 1865
Third	William W. Warren	Thomas Trowbridge	Aug. 23, 1864
Do	Warren J. Whitney	George West	Oct. 12, 1864
Do	Henry A. Whitney	Samson Steele	Oct. 12, 1864
Do	Thomas C. Wales	George Washington	Oct. 12, 1864
Do	Mrs. T. C. Wales	Fortune Jenkins	Dec. 15, 1864
Do	Annie Willard	William Alston	Dec. 15, 1864
Do	Henry Wenzell	George Hill	Oct. 13, 1864
Do	Henry B. Wenzell	James Sheridan	Dec. 9, 1864
Fourth	Edward W. Wigglesworth	James Barry	Dec. 10, 1864
Do	George Wigglesworth	Peter Dix	Dec. 20, 1864
Do	Thomas Worcester	Joseph Caswell	Jan. 13, 1865
Do	Morrill Wyman	John H. Henderson	Sept. 5, 1864
Do	John M. S. Williams	Thomas Leonard	Jan. 4, 1865
Do	Mrs. E. M. L. Williams	William P. Fuller	Jan. 4, 1865
Do	Mrs. Emily L. Williams	John J. Richards	Jan. 9, 1865
Do	Miss Caroline Williams	Hugh McVey	Jan. 11, 1865
Do	J. B. Williams	William Kidwell	Jan. 11, 1865
Do	Caled Woods	John McGrath	Jan. 14, 1865
Fifth	Parker Wells	Edwin Ackworth	Sept. 1, 1864
Do	W. D. Wheelwright	William Collins	Oct. 21, 1864
Sixth	Horatio Wellington	Thomas Jefferson	Sept. 23, 1864
Do	Edward Whitney	Stebney Black	Mar. 4, 1865
Do	Luther F. Whitney	Michael Curtin	July 28, 1864
Do	George W. Warren	John F. Wilbur	Aug. 3, 1864
Eighth	Harvey Waters	Henry Green	Nov. 30, 1864
Do	Paul Whitin	William Jackson	Feb. 28, 1865

List of persons who put in representative recruits, and names of recruits—Cont'd.

MASSACHUSETTS—Continued.

District.	Name of principal.	Name of recruit.	Date of enlistment.
Eighth	John C. Whitin	Joseph Jenkins	Feb. 28, 1865
Ninth	David F. Wood	Henry Williams	Feb. 2, 1865
Do	Moses Wood	Alfred Sawyer	Sept. 13, 1864
Do	J. S. Ward	Dempsey Spate	Mar. 8, 1865
Do	Nelson D. White	Lewis Robinson	Oct. 10, 1864
Do	Harvey Wyman	Evans McGee	Jan. 9, 1865
Tenth	Jerome Wells	Edmund Randall	Sept. 1, 1864
Do	Marshal Wilcox	William Green	Oct. 11, 1864
Fourth	N. D. Whitney	Hiram Gadsden	Apr. 6, 1865
Do	Theodore D. Whitney	Charles Cooper	Apr. 6, 1865
Do	George D. Whitney	James Brown	Apr. 6, 1865
Do	Mrs. Carrie F. Whitney	John Brown	Apr. 6, 1865
Do	Thomas Wigglesworth	Samuel Jenkins	Apr. 6, 1865
Do	Miss Ann Wigglesworth	William Cuyler	Apr. 6, 1865
Eighth	Charles P. Whitin	Sam. Rivers	Apr. 6, 1865
Do	Eli Warner	Henry Pringle	Apr. 6, 1865
Tenth	D. R. Williams	Robert Simmons	Apr. 6, 1865
Do	Stephen Walley	Jack Simmons	Apr. 6, 1865
Commonwealth	J. Sullivan Warren	David Robinson	Apr. 6, 1865
Do	Miss Mary Wigglesworth	Jemmy Perry	Apr. 6, 1865
Do	Edward Warren	William Boarn	Apr. 6, 1865
Second	Atherton Wales	Wilson Sheppard	Aug. 20, 1864
Fourth	Joseph E. Worcester	Elias Johnson	Feb. 20, 1865
Sixth	Thomas E. Whitcomb	John Jackson	Nov. 28, 1864

RHODE ISLAND.

District.	Name of principal.	Name of recruit.	Date of enlistment.
Second	Henry Howard	John Holland	Aug. 19, 1864
Do	Mrs. Henry Howard	William H. Chaplin	Aug. 19, 1864

CONNECTICUT.

District.	Name of principal.	Name of recruit.	Date of enlistment.
Third	Miss Elizabeth C. Greene	Charles Hall	Aug. 2, 1864
Do	Miss A. E. Greene	Daniel Huntington	Aug. 5, 1864
First	William H. Hunter	Charles White (one year)	Oct. 7, 1864
Do	William T. Lee	Michael Ahern (three years)	July 27, 1864
Do	Lyman H. Tuttle	James F. King (one year)	Sept. 27, 1864

NEW YORK.

NORTHERN DIVISION.

District.	Name of principal.	Name of recruit.	On call of—
Fourteenth	J. J. Austin	Charles L. Terrill	July 18, 1864
Do	Henry M. Benedict	Nelson Martell	July 18, 1864
Sixteenth	Edwin S. Bogue	J. Frank Wait	July 18, 1864
Eighteenth	Master Walter Butler	William Carroll	July 18, 1864
Nineteenth	Norman Bissell	George D. Barringer	July 18, 1864
Twelfth	Edward C. Cline	Levi Gounder	July 18, 1864
Eighteenth	James M. Cook	Charles M. Price	July 18, 1864
Twentieth	Zenas Eldred	Timothy Guilfoil	July 18, 1864
Sixteenth	Thomas S. Gray	Morgan F. Smith	July 18, 1864
Fourteenth	William Newton	Joseph W. Stevens	July 18, 1864
Do	T. W. Olcott	J. R. Bradstreet	July 18, 1864
Sixteenth	William H. Richardson	Jerome B. Tallman	July 18, 1864
Do	Samuel T. Richards	Marshal L. Brown	July 18, 1864
Twelfth	Charles W. Swift	Theodore Roloff	July 18, 1864
Fourteenth	R. M. Van Sickler	Richard W. Stevens	July 18, 1864
Do	C. P. Williams	John W. Robe	July 18, 1864

List of persons who put in representative recruits, and names of recruits—Cont'd.

NEW YORK—Continued.

SOUTHERN DIVISION.

District.	Name of principal.	Name of recruit.	Date of enlistment.
First	Thomas Barron	John Hart	Sept. 27, 1864
Eighth	William O'Brien	Frederick Sinclair	Sept. 3, 1864
Do	John O'Brien	George Muller	Sept. 8, 1864
Ninth	Henry K. Bull	James N. Drake	July 26, 1864
Tenth	D. J. Blauvelt	Herman Ramalade	Aug. 9, 1864
Do	William F. Bates	John Meyers	Sept. 14, 1864
Do	William R. Brown	Philip Trainor	Sept. 20, 1864
Third	Anthony F. Campbell	Patrick F. Mallin	July 11, 1864
Eighth	George Collins, jr	James Higgins	July 19, 1864
Do	Victor L. Conrad	Eilert Kuch	Aug. 29, 1864
Do	Peter Cooper	Martin Schlotter	Nov. 22, 1864
Do	do	Daniel Reardon	Dec. 5, 1864
Tenth	Hugh N. Camp	John Pennington	Sept. 14, 1864
Third	Sidney Dorlan	William Brown	July 11, 1864
Eighth	Charles Donohue	James J. Turpie	Sept. 7, 1864
Seventh	Charles Easton	Joseph Reich	Nov. 11, 1864
Third	J. W. Frothingham	Gustav Blum	Mar. 10, 1865
Tenth	Charles B. Fosdick	Benjamin Buckbee	June 3, 1864
Do	J. H. Godwin, jr	Samuel G. Hodnett	July 5, 1864
Eighth	Edwin M. Hulburt	Noah Easton (colored)	Aug. 18, 1864
Do	Richard M. Hoe	Frederick W. Foger	Mar. 15, 1865
Ninth	Edgar Ketchum	Jeremiah Murphy	July 25, 1864
Sixth	Cyrus H. Loutrel	Robert Hoffman	July 25, 1864
Tenth	William F. Moller	John Moorhouse	Nov. 14, 1864
First	A. W. Nathans	Peter Stoneman	Sept. 27, 1864
Do	George L. Peck	John Meddillish	Nov. 30, 1864
Eighth	Percy R. Pyne	James P. Varick	Apr. 5, 1865
Tenth	Samuel Purdy	John McMann	Aug. 3, 1864
Ninth	Benjamin F. Raynor	Richard Williams	Mar. 11, 1865
Fourth	John S. Sammis	John Morrow	Nov. 30, 1864
Tenth	H. F. Spaulding	Patrick Shelly	July 9, 1864
Eighth	William L. Taylor	John Entwistle	Mar. 14, 1865
Ninth	Abram Wakeman	John Hodges	July 1, 1864

WESTERN DIVISION.

District.	Name of principal	Name of recruit.	Date of call.
Twenty-fourth	James C. Avery	Patrick Halpin	July 18, 1864
Do	Charles E. Avery	Agiduis Van Ord	July 18, 1864
Do	Martha R. Avery	Lafayette Robinson	July 18, 1864
Do	Mrs. E. H. Avery	Isaac B. Race	July 18, 1864
Twenty-fifth	Stephen H. Ainsworth	Willis Cooper	July 18, 1864
Thirtieth	Allen W. Adams	Benjamin Fields	July 18, 1864
Twenty-fourth	Joseph P. Barber	Joseph Thompson	July 18, 1864
Twenty-sixth	George D. Beers	James W. Vangilder	July 18, 1864
Twenty-seventh	Alvine C. Barney	John Bennitt	July 18, 1864
Thirtieth	Daniel S. Bennett	Robert Griffin	July 18, 1864
Do	Charles V. D. Blackman	William Wilson	July 18, 1864
Thirty-first	David H. Bowles	John A. Hazzard	July 18, 1864
Twenty-fourth	John H. Chedell	John S. Cummings	July 18, 1864
Do	Mrs. John H. Chedell	Jackson Shuman	July 18, 1864
Twenty-fifth	Frank O. Chamberlin	Peter Washington	July 18, 1864
Twenty-ninth	Duncan Cameron	James R. Landers	July 18, 1864
Twenty-fourth	Rufus Dunham, M. D	Charles W. Eastman	July 18, 1864
Do	E. G. Day	William Booth	July 18, 1864
Do	George B. Daniels	Benton H. Benham	July 18, 1864
Twenty-eighth	John H. Denio	William H. Lee	July 18, 1864
Thirtieth	Philip Dorsheimer	John Sims	July 18, 1864
Do	Charles Ensign	Allen Curry	July 18, 1864
Do	Elisha W. Ensign	George Allen	July 18, 1864
Thirty-first	Frederick Eaton	Charles Smith	July 18, 1864
Do	Reuben E. Fenton	Henry B. Taylor	July 18, 1864
Twenty-fifth	George W. Gates	William Uphamer	July 18, 1864
Thirtieth	Solomon S. Guthrie	Alexander Curry	July 18, 1864
Do	Henry D. Garvin	Arthur Benton	July 18, 1864
Twenty-third	Arthur Holmes	James E. McCormick	July 18, 1864
Twenty-fourth	Henry Henion	Cornelius L. Younglove	July 18, 1864
Do	William Hills	George Applegate	July 18, 1864
Do	George Hocknell	Huntington Jay	July 18, 1864
Twenty-sixth	John H. Hawes	Charles Wright	July 18, 1864
Thirty-first	John D. Hillier	Jackson Kelly	July 18, 1864
Twenty-seventh	Thomas A. Johnson	George H. Taylor	July 18, 1864

List of persons who put in representative recruits, and names of recruits—Cont'd.

NEW YORK—Continued.

District.	Name of principal.	Name of recruit.	Date of call.
Twenty-fourth	John E. Leonard	James Richey	July 18, 1864
Do	Miss E. Leonard	John Doyle	July 18, 1864
Do	George W. Leonard	George A. Phillips	July 18, 1864
Twenty-third	De Witt C. McGraw	William W. Douglass	July 18, 1864
Do	Daniel McGraw	John Martin	July 18, 1864
Twenty-fourth	Christopher Morgan	David B. Carrovan	July 18, 1864
Do	Mary E. P. Morgan	James S. Moore	July 18, 1864
Do	Adam Miller	Michael Reachert	July 18, 1864
Do	George W. Mead	Melvin N. Smith	July 18, 1864
Twenty-ninth	Abel Minard	Thomas Anderson	July 18, 1864
Twenty-third	Timothy R Porter	John McDonnell	July 18, 1864
Twenty-fourth	George W. Peck	James Knox	July 18, 1864
Do	George R. Peck	James Bohan	July 18, 1864
Do	Asa S. Parker	Alexander De Witt	July 18, 1864
Twenty-ninth	Hopkins C. Pomeroy	Barney Quinn	July 18, 1864
Thirtieth	William H. Peabody	Louis Bueckner	July 18, 1864
Twenty-fourth	A. R. Reynolds	William L. Braman	July 18, 1864
Thirtieth	Dexter P. Rumsey	Benjamin Corey	July 18, 1864
Twenty-fourth	Shirley R. Snow	George W. Van Alstyne	July 18, 1864
Twenty-sixth	John Southworth	George Hemmingway	July 18, 1864
Do	do	Louren Stone	July 18, 1864
Twenty-eighth	Henry R. Selden	Michael Gill	July 18, 1864
Twenty-ninth	Franklin Spaulding	John Firth	July 18, 1864
Do	Thomas Scovil	George Williams	July 18, 1864
Thirtieth	James G. Stevens	George Anderson	July 18, 1864
Do	William E. Sanders	James Thomas	July 18, 1864
Do	Jacob Schoellpopf	George Washington	July 18, 1864
Thirty-first	Newton Slawson	Johnson D. Ensign	July 18, 1864
Do	Patrick Shafer	Marcus L. Weiser	July 18, 1864
Thirtieth	George Taylor	Giles Billinger	Dec. 19, 1864
Thirty-first	E. C. Topliff	Patrick Whalen	July 18, 1864
Twenty-fourth	Willie B. Woodin	Thomas B. Baird	July 18, 1864
Do	William Wasson	Robert O. Burgess	July 18, 1864
Do	Annette Wasson	George Foster	July 18, 1864
Do	William H. S. Wasson	Jacob Ganthuer	July 18, 1864

NEW JERSEY.

District.	Name of principal.	Name of recruit.	Date of enlistment.
Third	John A. Anderson	Charles Rosenburry	Aug. 3, 1864
Fifth	Joseph Battin	Samuel Tierney	July 18, 1864
Third	Capt. William M. Shipman	John Coyle	Sept. 14, 1864
Fifth	Thomas B. Stewart	Franklin A. Dennis	July 18, 1864
First	William P. Tatem	James Hamilton	Apr. 8, 1865
Second	Mrs. Lydia A. Troth	Henry Marshall	Aug. 29, 1864

PENNSYLVANIA.

EASTERN DIVISION.

District.	Name of principal.	Name of recruit.	Date of enlistment.
Third	Lewis Audenreid	Charles A. Friele	
Do.	do	Edward A. Johnson	
Fourth	Samuel F. Altemus	Alfred Roberts	Sept. 1, 1864
Ninth	Benjamin F. Appold	Leonard Shields	
Fourth	C. B. Barrett	Samuel Black	Aug. 25, 1864
Do	Boadil Brown	Austin L. Vansant	Aug. 29, 1864
Do	N. B. Brown	William Johnson	Aug. 31, 1864
Do	J. R. Blackston	Jacob Ackerman	Aug. 31, 1864
Do	Thomas Bell	Thaddeus K. Sasportas	Sept. 2, 1864
Do	A. B. Burton	William McKinney	Sept. 3, 1864
Do	do	Harry Beck	Sept. 3, 1864
Do	Mrs. C. B. Barrett	Casper Durler	Sept. 5, 1864
Do	Miss Jane L. Barrett	Joseph F. Topper	Sept. 5, 1864
Do	Miss Rebecca S. Barrett	Alonzo Mahan	Sept. 6, 1864
Do	Miss Clara M. G. Barrett	Joseph Grosser	Sept. 8, 1864
Sixth	George Bullock	William Reed	July 30, 1864
Seventh	John M. Broomhall	Elwood H. Gilbert	Aug. 31, 1864
Ninth	Mrs. Isabella Bachman	John Thomas	
Do	Isaac O. Bruner	Samuel Deckert	
Tenth	David P. Brown	Thomas Brannan	July 19, 1864

List of persons who put in representative recruits, and names of recruits—Cont'd.

PENNSYLVANIA—Continued.

District.	Name of principal.	Name of recruit.	Date of enlistment.
Second	Samuel Coffin	William Reasoner	Oct. 8, 1864
Fourth	James B. Craig	Francis Homer	Sept. 1, 1864
Fifth	Mrs. Joseph S. Clark	Thomas Rushton	
Do	Mrs. E. W. Clark	Augustus Blankinhorn	
Do	Master E. W. Clark	Theodore A. Rainor	
Do	Master Clarence M. Clark	Thomas Hickey	
Ninth	Mrs. W. G. Case	Oristus A. Hipple	
Tenth	Henry L. Cake	Francis J. Smith	Sept. 5, 1864
Twelfth	Mrs. Jane Courtney	John McGraw	Oct. 12, 1864
Seventh	Joseph G. Cummins	John J. Wilson (colored)	Mar. 6, 1865
Do	William D. Christman	James Cummings (colored)	Mar. 6, 1865
Ninth	Columbia Bank	Benjamin Pymen	
Fourth	James E. Dingee	William Gilmour	Mar. 10, 1865
Second	James M. Earle	John P. McWilliams	Oct. 8, 1864
Fourth	Thomas S. Ellis	Jacob F. Souder	Aug. 27, 1864
Ninth	Samuel Evans	John M. Lowery	
Do	Mrs. Mary S. Evans	Charles Reuter	
Second	H. G. Freeman, jr	George E. Tyrell	July 28, 1864
Fourth	Lewis G. Filbert	Callaman Fink	Aug. 8, 1864
Do	Samuel Field	Mark Daans	Aug. 27, 1864
Do	John Gibson	George W. Brown	Aug. 13, 1864
Do	....do	Patrick McGraw	Aug. 20, 1864
Ninth	A. S. Green	John Frantz	
Twelfth	Jacob Gould	John Brader	Aug. 31, 1864
Second	C. J. Hoffman	Michael Lynn	Aug. 2, 1864
Do	George Hammersley	Michael Francis	Aug. 16, 1864
Do	Joseph Harrison, jr	George Hamilton	Oct. 13, 1864
Fourth	William Howell	Abraham Anderson	Sept. 1, 1864
Do	Mrs. William Howell	Daniel Brown	Sept. 2, 1864
Do	Zophar C. Howell	Mansfield S. Hamilton	Sept. 3, 1864
Do	Mrs. William S. Hall	James Lawson	Sept. 26, 1864
Fifth	Henry Howe	Herman Dalhous	
Ninth	Mrs. J. G. Hess	William Gross	
Second	John Horner, jr	Wilhelm Hess	Feb. 7, 1865
Fourth	James C. Johnston	James T. Robinson	Sept. 2, 1864
Do	John G. Johnston	Charles Brislin	Sept. 3, 1864
Ninth	John A. Jackson	James White	
Tenth	William Johns	Evan James	Sept. 12, 1864
Second	J. E. Kingsley	Matthew Youn	Oct. 15, 1864
Fourth	George Kern	John Anderson	Aug. 25, 1864
Do	Charles B. Keen	Neil Boyce	Sept. 2, 1864
Do	Mrs. Mary Krupp	Andrew Rose	Sept. 3, 1864
Sixth	Benjamin Kenderdine	Lewis Kelly	Feb. 14, 1865
Second	John T. Lewis	John Atkinson	Oct. 12, 1864
Fourth	Henry C. Lea	John Seif	July 27, 1864
Do	....do	Joseph Coyle	Aug. 25, 1864
Second	Joseph B. Myers	Stephen Conness	Aug. 5, 1864
Do	S. A. Mercer	Joseph Dwyer	Aug. 31, 1864
Fourth	John R. McCurdy	Robert Johnson	July 19, 1864
Do	....do	James F. Mulligan	Sept. 1, 1864
Do	Joseph Manuel	William Waltier	Sept. 1, 1864
Do	James Miller	Dennis McCafferty	Sept. 2, 1864
Do	E. Spencer Miller	Charles W. Mohorter	Sept. 3, 1864
Ninth	Mrs. Rebecca A. Martin	Frederick Stutz	
Second	Henry Maule	Merrill Moready	Feb. 7, 1865
Eighth	G. A. Nicolls	Michael Dolan	Aug. 5, 1864
Do	Mrs. G. A. Nicolls	Philip J. Decker	Aug. 23, 1864
Fourth	Dell Noblitt	Dallas Meyers	Feb. 3, 1865
Second	George W. Paullin	Henry Weill	July 25, 1864
Do	Waterman Palmer	Ernst Degen	July 26, 1864
Do	Thomas H. Powers	James Eagan	Aug. 31, 1864
Fourth	Thomas Potter	James O'Neill	July 28, 1864
Seventh	John C. Price	George Enos (colored)	Mar. 4, 1865
Fourth	Henry E. Rood	Barney Coyle	Aug. 25, 1864
Do	Mrs. John M. Riley	Sylvester B. Cameron	Sept. 9, 1864
Do	Miss Ellen K. Riley	William H. Hibbs	Sept. 9, 1864
Fifth	Samuel W. Roop	James White	
Ninth	Miss Annie E. Rhinehart	William Nixon	
Fourth	James A. Rothermell	William H. Pool	Mar. 7, 1865
Second	William James Sill	Samuel Pennie	Aug. 30, 1864
Do	Solomon Smucker, jr	George C. Stevens	Oct. 4, 1864
Do	Thomas Sparks	John Kennedy	Oct. 14, 1864
Fourth	E. D. Saunders	Charles Hill	Aug. 25, 1864
Do	R. C. Shelmerdine	John Smith	Aug. 27, 1864
Do	R. Q. Shelmerdine	Charles Hauser	Aug. 30, 1864
Do	Caroline Sellers	Cornelius White	Sept. 1, 1864
Ninth	Samuel Shoch	James A. Loney	
Do	Mrs. Edward K. Smith	Samuel Moore	

List of persons who put in representative recruits, and names of recruits—Cont'd.

PENNSYLVANIA—Continued.

District.	Name of principal.	Name of recruit.	Date of enlistment.
Twelfth	Mrs. Jane Scranton	Benjamin Thomas	Oct. 12, 1864
Seventh	R. H. Smith	Abram Enos (colored)	Mar. 4, 1865
Fourth	Henry C. Townsend	Edward S. Tobias	Aug. 26, 1864
Do	John D. Taylor	Ford G. Troup	Sept. 1, 1864
Third	Hugh Wilson	Silas Burton	
Fourth	Jane G. Whilden	Charles Barron	Aug. 18, 1864
Ninth	Rudolph Williams	Frederick Strich	
Do	George Young, jr	George Trump	

WESTERN DIVISION.

District.	Name of principal.	Name of recruit.	Residence of principal.
Twenty-fourth	David Aiken	Thomas C. Best	Washington Borough.
Fourteenth	George Bergner	James E. Barnes	Harrisburg.
Twenty-fourth	Caleb Burwell	George W. Risher	Monongahela Township.
Twenty-third	J. Heron Foster	William T. Black	Provost-marshal Twenty-third District.
Thirteenth	Evenuel Houpt	John Williams	
Fourteenth	William L. Harris	Henry G. Gebhart	East Buffalo Township.
Thirteenth	M. C. Mercur	Levi Ennis	
Twenty-second	Hon. J. K. Moorhead	Michael Nolan	Pittsburg.
Do	do	John Dougherty	Do.
Do	do	John Hayes	Do.
Do	do	William Morton	Do.
Do	do	George Henry	Do.
Twenty-fourth	John Minor	Cyrus Logan	New Brighton.
Thirteenth	Mrs. Rachael A. Paxton	Henry O'Brien	
Nineteenth	Henry Patton	A. Allen Hoover	Curwinsville.
Twenty-third	John Ralston	George W. Brink	
Seventeenth	Hon. John Scott	James Wilson	Huntingdon.
Twentieth	Mrs. Elizabeth M. Tarr	John Ryan	Venango Township.
Thirteenth	Hon. David Wilmot	William S. Briggs	Towanda.

MARYLAND.

District.	Name of principal.	Name of recruit.	Date of enlistment.
Second	Thomas H. Blick	James Dye	Nov. 5, 1864
Do	John W. Cathcart	Charles H. James	Aug. 18, 1864
Fourth	Elias Emmett	Henry Smith	Aug. 8, 1864
Second	Thomas P. Stran	William Jones	Aug. 9, 1864
Third	T. McKendree Teal	Albert Unterkoffer	Sept. 13, 1864
Do	Milton Whitney	Frederick Smith	Aug. 13, 1864
Do	George W. Whistler	Jason Hodnett	Nov. 10, 1864

DISTRICT OF COLUMBIA.

District.	Name of principal.	Name of recruit.	Credited to—
	John G. Adams	John Dangerfield	Third subdistrict.
	Mrs. E. F. Adams	George Gassaway	Do.
	Samuel T. Davis	William Jones	Fourth subdistrict.
	William Gunton	Michael Trotty	Third subdistrict.
	Horatio King*	Charles Taylor	Do.
	Abraham Lincoln	John S. Staples	Do.
	John E. Latham	Robert Tate	First subdistrict.
	Leroy Tuttler	Jacob Bentler	Third subdistrict.

* Added since preparation of original list.

List of persons who put in representative recruits, and names of recruits—Cont'd.

KENTUCKY.

District.	Name of principal.	Name of recruit.	Remarks.
Fifth	William B. Belknap	Green Penneck	
Do	John G. Baxter	Stephen Kelly	
First	John Bolinger	James Harvey (colored)	
Fifth	Michael Ennright	James Haley	
Sixth	James H. Easton	Alfred Watson	
Fifth	T. C. Fisher	Richard Pollard	
Do	Warner G. Herr	Sam. Herr	
Do	Will. R. Hervey	Jerry Bratton	Commissioner of board.
Do	William E. Hughes	Sanford Talbott	
Do	William Kaye	Anderson Huffman	
Second	Jesse H. Lansford	John H. Shannon	
Sixth	R. C. Lovell	Jesse White	
First	G. H. Morrow	Archer Farmer (colored)	
Do	J. A. McNutt	Avants Washington (colored).	
Fifth	Z. M. Sherley	Charles Ashcroft	
Do	Joshua F. Speed	Tilghman (colored)	
Do	E. D. Stamford	Tom Stamford	
Sixth	Bradford Shinkle	Joseph Beverley	
Do	Amos Shinkle	Robert Williams	
Ninth	John Seaton	William Charleston	
Fifth	George W. Womack	Henry Thompson	Provost-marshal.

OHIO.

District.	Name of principal.	Name of recruit.	Remarks.
Second	J. P. Appenzeller	L. Briedenstien	
Do	Jonas Butterfield	John W. Carr	
Sixth	Ruel Besson	James Green (colored)	
Do	Mrs. Ruel Besson	James Bass (colored)	
Tenth	George R. Betts	Joseph B. Warner	
Do	Edward P. Bassett	George N. Buchler	
Do	Silas Bailey	Reuben P. Clark	
Fourteenth	Jabez L. Burrill	Warren D. Chambers	
Eighteenth	Bolivar Botts	John McDaniel	
Do	William Bingham	William P. Hart	
Second	Joseph Crilley	Charles Bright	
Seventh	S. V. R. Carpenter	Nathan W. Moore	
Eleventh	John Campbell	Ampudia Earwood	
Do	George Clark	James I. Jaynes	
Eighteenth	William T. Cushing	Andrew Gauter	
Do	Leonard Case	Jurger Eiling	
Do	Jeremiah Coonrod	William Finger	
Second	James Dalton	Charles Saunders	
Do	John Dorsch	Wallace W. Gonelle	
Fourth	G. Volney Dorsey	Jonathan Townsend	
Fifteenth	Josiah H. Duvall	George W. Allen	
First	Seth Evans	Richard Cue	
Do	Willie Eggleston	John G. Brown	
Do	Miss Julia Eggleston	August Wride	
Second	John W. Ellis	Andrew N. Hays (colored)	
Twelfth	William N. Entrekin	Robert G. Manner	
First	James A. Frazier	Orrin Carey	
Second	Arad Geary	Josiah Raines	
Do	W. M. Gibson	William Brien (colored)	
Do	J. W. Goslin	Joseph Morgan	
Third	David Gebhart	Henry P. Shaffer	
Nineteenth	Albon B. Gardner	David B. Governor (colored)	
First	James E. Hopkins	Stephen Perkins	
Second	J. C. Hanover	James Marshall (colored)	
Do	John P. Haise	John Gansmann	
Do	L. R. Hull	Thomas Delaney	
Fourth	Oben Hayes	James L. Funk	
First	Charles E. Johnson	Joseph Donnelly	
Second	Alfred Joute	Nicholas Rulias	
Do	Thomas Jenkins	John Boone	
Fourteenth	William Jones	Milton Holt	
Seventeenth	Thomas L. Jewett	James T. Devoe	
First	George Keck	James Edwards	
Do	Miss Nellie Keck	John Marston	
Do	Joseph R. Kinney	William Urich	
Tenth	Charles A. King	Frank Gibson	
Do	Joel W. Kelsey	Lafayette Allen	
First	William L. Lockman	Albert Fanning	
Second	T. D. Lincoln	John W. Childers	

List of persons who put in representative recruits, and names of recruits—Cont'd.

OHIO—Continued.

District.	Name of principal.	Name of recruit.	Remarks.
Second	T. D. Lincoln, jr. (10 years)	Andrew Donough	
Do	T. Ledyard Lincoln	John Milam	
Third	P. P. Lowe	David B. Kline	
First	James Mack	David McAllister	
Do	Thomas McLean	John Hamilton	
Do	B. J. McMahon	Abraham Carpenter	
Second	G. Mendellhall	William Girle	
Do	Henry Miller	George Weimar	
Do	E. J. Miller	C. T. Bell	
Do	B. Mackentire	David King (colored)	
Third	Felix M. Marsh	Stephen Overman	
Ninth	Jay O. Moss	Xavier Gutter	
Eighteenth	George W. Merrill	Warren Bradley	
Do	Martin McHugh	John McRobertson	
Do	Charles McNeall	Jean Pagain	
Seventh	Andrew Nicholson	Edwin Peters	
Tenth	John T. Newton	Charles W. Lane	
Eighteenth	Henry Newberry	William Jones	
Tenth	John R. Osborn	John Kinkler	
First	Charles G. Pearce	Joseph A. Anderson	
Second	M. D. Potter	R. L. Logan	
Third	J. H. Pierce	Abner B. Posse	
Tenth	Elijah G. Peckham	James Gander	
Eleventh	John Peebles	John W. Rose	
Eighteenth	James Pannell	Jerry Bruce	
First	Cornelius M. Ray	John Ryan	
Do	Adam N. Riddle	Frank Hetteshimer	
Second	Henry Runk	George Ruger	
Do	William Reese	John Searand	
Seventh	Amor Reese	Milton Gregory	
Ninth	Peter Reinhart	John W. Harker	
Tenth	John Ray	Albert Pexton	
Do	Samuel A. Raymond	Josiah N. Smith	
Do	do	Henry Boyce	
First	Henry Stewart	Throw Welsh	
Do	P. W. Strader	William Smith	
Second	William Summer	J. C. Harvey	
Do	William Shaffer	John M. Henderson	
Do	Charles J. Stedman	N. S. Thoroman	
Do	F. F. Shaw	E. Flanigan	
Do	George F. Stedman	William H. Schrivers	
Third	John R. Shaffer	Milton Arnold	
Seventh	Alfred P. Stone	David C. Gregory	
Ninth	Ebenezer P. Sadler	John Larkin	
Tenth	William H. Smith	James Anderson	
Do	do	James Irving	
Do	Dennison Steele	Bennett Bartlett	
Fourteenth	John Scott, jr	William Wiggins	
Eighteenth	George B. Senter	William Gerard	
Do	Rufus P. Spalding	Joseph Porter	
First	A. D. E. Tweed	Mitchell Furie	
Second	Griffin Taylor	B. Underhill	
Do	Samuel Tappin	Watty Grant (colored)	
Do	E. S. Tice	Jerry Mohanna	
Seventeenth	Benjamin Votaw	Solomon N. Snyder	
First	Charles H. L. Walker	Albert L. Colby	Sept. 1, 1864.*
Do	J. T. Warren	John Tipton	
Do	E. Wassennich	Rupert Schuarunger	
Do	Isaac C. Winans	Charles Schmidt	
Second	James F. Wellington	Frederick Stulz	
Do	Jacob Wirth	Henry H. Maler	
Do	L. Worthington	Harvey McIllvaine	
Do	Charles P. Wilstach	John P. Gardner	
Do	George W. Ward	William Morris	
Eighth	Lewis Wormstead	Lorenzo G. Tipton	
Tenth	R. M. Waite	John Hall	
Fifteenth	John P. Wolfe	Albert Robinson	

* Added since preparation of original list.

List of persons who put in representative recruits, and names of recruits—Cont'd.

INDIANA.

District.	Name of principal.	Name of recruit.	Date of call.
Third	J. D. Buckley	William O. Reynolds	July 18, 1864
Ninth	Mrs. Laura Blowing	James M. Grover	July 18, 1864
Eighth	Samuel Bürford	Julian Buffington	Dec. 19, 1864
Second	Walter B. Creed	Jerry Williams	July 18, 1864
Eighth	Clark Devol	Milton Overton	July 18, 1864
Do	Nelson Fordyce	Frank Wheeler	July 18, 1864
Ninth	Mrs. Lydia George	George W. Woods	July 18, 1864
Eighth	William Gailey	Levi S. Hatch	Dec. 19, 1864
Ninth	John A. Herricks	Jacob Karcher	July 18, 1864
Do	do	George McCreary	July 18, 1864
Do	Mrs. John A. Herricks	Allen Bolin	July 18, 1864
Eighth	Relief Jackson	Jerry Smith	July 18, 1864
Third	H. H. Marley	Samuel Denny	July 18, 1864
Ninth	Mrs. Mary Marble	John R. Pierce	July 18, 1864
Eighth	George Nebeker	Thomas Sailes	July 18, 1864
Ninth	John Reynolds	Henry Fisher	July 18, 1864
Do	do	James Thompson	July 18, 1864
Sixth	Henry Schnull	John Shea	July 18, 1864
Do	James M. Tomlinson	John Russell	July 18, 1864
Third	James G. Wright	William Ragan	July 18, 1864
Eighth	Joseph Yundt	Emanuel Lancaster	July 18, 1864

ILLINOIS.

District.	Name of principal.	Name of recruit.	Date of enlistment.
First	George Armon	John Macoboy	Aug 10, 1864
Second	Mrs. Wright Allen	Benjamin Clark	Sept. 5, 1864
Ninth	Marshall Ayers	James Elwood	Sept. 20, 1864
First	Chauncey T. Bowen	Andrew Long	July 27, 1864
Do	James H. Bowen	James Kelsey	July 27, 1864
Do	George L. Bowen	Charles W. Brent	July 28, 1864
Do	Augustus H. Burley	Thomas Ward	Mar. 1, 1865
Fifth	William Burris	William Thomas	Sept. 8, 1864
Sixth	Jacob Bales	Thomas W. Damner	Mar. 30, 1865
Tenth	John Burrowman	John R. Haster	Oct. 31, 1864
Do	Coonrod Behrens	Josephus Kirk	Oct. 31, 1864
First	Howard Z. Culver	James Smith	July 29, 1864
Do	Charles E. Culver	John Cook	July 29, 1864
Do	Mrs. William H. Carter	Zach. V. Purdy	Mar. 13, 1865
Do	Thomas Church	Henry L. Markham	Mar. 16, 1865
Fourth	Frederick Collins	William C. Dickhut	Feb. 27, 1865
Fifth	Nathaniel B. Curtis	Amos P. Jones	Sept. 1, 1864
Fourth	Gershom B. Dimmock	Alvin S. Black	Feb. 20, 1865
Seventh	Joseph Dale	Henry Dixon	Aug. 26, 1864
Do	Charles M. Dale	William Hilley	Aug. 26, 1864
First	John F. Eberhardt	Columbus M. Pope	Feb. 27, 1865
Do	Alex. N. Fullerton	Wesley Stubbs	Aug. 17, 1864
Do	Mrs. C. B. Farwell	Ferdinand Fox	Sept. 6, 1864
Do	Henry Farnam	James Smedt	Nov. 7, 1864
Do	J. W. Freer	Charles W. Roberts	Feb. 25, 1865
Do	Samuel T. Foss	James Oakes	Feb. 27, 1865
Fourth	Matthew Finlay	William Black	Dec. 19, 1864
Tenth	Jacob Fisher	Alfred M. Walton	Oct. 31, 1864
First	George W. Gage	Daniel Higginbottom	Apr. 8, 1865
Fourth	Elijah Gove	Daniel Cropley	Jan. 5, 1865
Do	Mrs. Elijah Gove	George F. Voeth	Jan. 6, 1865
First	Gilbert Hubbard	Edwin Crane	Aug. 8, 1864
Do	Joseph H. Hurlbut	Frederick B. Bowman	Aug. 19, 1864
Do	Charles M. Howe	John T. Siferd	Sept. 3, 1864
Do	C. C. P. Holden	Alonzo P. Ide	Feb. 15, 1865
Do	L. P. Hilliard	Henry P. Merlett	Feb. 21, 1865
Do	C. N. Holden	Louis Winter	Mar. 10, 1865
Do	Mrs. Sarah J. Holden	Harris Durkee	Mar. 10, 1865
Third	Nathaniel Halderman	Hugh McConnell	Aug. 1, 1864
Sixth	Joseph H. Herd	Huron Warren	Sept. 6, 1864
Do	George V. Huling	George Smith	Nov. 17, 1864
Tenth	Lycurgus Harpool	Daniel Harlan	Oct. 31, 1864
Do	Benjamin F. Hazler	John Browner	Nov. 14, 1864
First	John F. Irwin	John R. Powley	Mar. 1, 1865
Do	Capt. Wm. James, prov. mar.	Daniel Chadd	Mar. 10, 1865
Second	Mrs. Richard Jackson	Christian Luck	Sept. 6, 1864
Seventh	Ephraim Jennings	Daniel A. Radley	Aug. 22, 1864
First	George M. Kimbark	Whitfield N. Alley	Aug. 3, 1864
Do	C. Kann	Gerard Smith	Feb. 16, 1865

List of persons who put in representative recruits, and names of recruits—Cont'd.

ILLINOIS—Continued.

District.	Name of principal.	Name of recruit.	Date of enlistment.
Second	Elisha A. Kirk	Warren P. Sheffield	Sept. 26, 1864
Sixth	Calvin Knowlton	Martin B. Hale	Sept. 5, 1864
Tenth	John N. Kellenberger	Lewis J. Linn	Oct. 31, 1864
First	Mrs. J. T. Lester	Levi Eames	Mar. 11, 1865
Second	Mrs. F. E. Latham	Gilbert Hays	Sept. 6, 1864
Ninth	James C. Leonard	Charles Linthecome	Sept. 5, 1864
First	Mrs. Marian Munger	John McAfee	Aug. 2, 1864
Do	Master Wesley Munger	John Maussner	Aug. 8, 1864
Do	Henry S. McGraw	George W. Crane	Aug. 24, 1864
Do	Hugh Martin	Baylor Taylor	Apr. 8, 1865
Third	Henry A. Mills	Thomas McConnell	Aug. 9, 1864
Fourth	Mrs. Anna McFadden	August Vogel	Feb. 21, 1865
Do	John L. Moore	Thomas Watson	Feb. 27, 1865
Sixth	A. H. Marsh	George Sweet	Sept. 23, 1864
Third	John Nycum	George Kinney	Aug. 9, 1864
First	H. G. Powers	Henry Currier	Mar. 8, 1865
Do	William Pratt	Daniel Gross	Mar. 10, 1865
Second	Mrs. Mary Penfield	Russell T. Page	Sept. 2, 1864
Fourth	William B. Powers	James H. Eastwood	Jan. 5, 1865
Sixth	Edwin Porter	Henry Mayars	Sept. 26, 1864
Do	N. S. Pierce	Alex. M. Friland	Sept. 27, 1864
First	George L. Raymond	Rudolph Zunker	July 29, 1864
Do	B. W. Raymond	James Hart	Aug. 19, 1864
Do	Robert Reid	Joseph Gotthelf	Mar. 6, 1865
Do	Mrs. Rowena P. Reynolds	Fred. Haasman	Apr. 8, 1865
Do	Charles B. Sawyer	Henry Saunders	Sept. 9, 1864
Second	Mrs. Cherrick Shoonmaker	Henry Newmaier	Sept. 6, 1864
Do	Mrs. Ostrom Stone	Frank Schimmelpfenig	Sept. 6, 1864
Fourth	John W. Spencer	Lemuel Lewis	Sept. 9, 1864
Sixth	George S. Stubbins	James Parker	Apr. 14, 1865
Ninth	Mrs. Louisa Spear	Edward Boulter	Feb. 14, 1865
First	Edward J. Tinkham	Frank Foley	Feb. 21, 1865
Second	Wait Talcott	Charles H. Redington	Sept. 1, 1864
Do	Sylvester Talcott	John W. Whipple	Sept. 29, 1864
Third	Jos. L. Tomlinson	Harrison Clay Skeels	Aug. 29, 1864
Fifth	Jane Underhill	Thomas R. Stevens	Sept. 2, 1864
First	Evart Van Buren	Ayers Arnold	Sept. 6, 1864
Do	Jos. Linton Waters	Adam Simpson	Feb. 21, 1865
Second	Mrs. E. B. Wilder	Michael Driver	Sept. 6, 1864
Fourth	Edward Wells	Silas E. Bristol	Feb. 20, 1865
Do	Mrs. Edward Wells	Carl Walstadt	Feb. 20, 1865

MICHIGAN.

District.	Name of principal.	Name of recruit.	Date of muster.
Fourth	Chauncey B. Allyn	James Douglass	Feb. 11, 1865
First	Austin Burt	James Bell	Aug. 23, 1864
Second	Walton J. Barnes	Augustus Thies	Aug. 19, 1864
Do	Israel Bostwick	Stephen Ladon	Sept. 20, 1864
Do	Edwin R. Clark	George Russell	Aug. 6, 1864
Do	J. J. Dennis	Mustered by Captain Barry; unknown.	Aug. —, 1864
Do	George D. Ford	Warren Brown	July 22, 1864
First	Daniel W. Heath	William Roberts	Aug. 22, 1864
Do	Clinton H. Johnson	Chrisler Lamperan	Aug. 18, 1864
Second	John H. Jones	George Brightman	Sept. 9, 1864
Do	William Joseph	Alonzo McLaughlin	Sept. 9, 1864
Do	Edwin O. Lamphere	Philander S. Alden	Aug. 30, 1864
Third	George Luther	Briggs A. Whipple	Sept. 8, 1864
First	E. J. Penniman	Frederick Williams	July 29, 1864
Do	Bradford Smith	George B. Sage	Aug. 15, 1864

List of persons who put in representative recruits, and names of recruits—Cont'd.

WISCONSIN.

District.	Name of principal.	Name of recruit.	Date of call.
First	S. Bryant	George A. Taylor	July 18, 1864
Do	Henry Bunker	Jared Brown	July 18, 1864
Second	Jervis Bemis	Edward Martin	July 18, 1864
Do	S. G. Benedict	Asa R. Green	July 18, 1864
Fourth	Thomas N. Blackstock	Simon Schwalbe	July 18, 1864
Second	Henry J. Cowles	Calvin T. Smith	July 18, 1864
Fifth	William H. Doe	Charles F. Weed	July 18, 1864
Fourth	George End	Carl Fick	July 18, 1864
Second	Alexander Graham	David J. Dann	July 18, 1864
Fourth	George S. Graves	Emery A. Lewis	July 18, 1864
First	Jefferson P. Harlow	Thomas C. Hall	July 18, 1864
Fifth	Henry Hewett	Dennis T. Turkey	July 18, 1864
Sixth	John T. Kingston	John C. Hutchinson	July 18, 1864
Second	John M. May	Nelson F. Randolph	July 18, 1864
Fourth	James H. Mead	Chauncey Forbush	July 18, 1864
Do	C. F. Moore	Ezra G. Van Camp	July 18, 1864
Sixth	E. S. Miner	Patrick Gilbridge	July 18, 1864
Do	Walter D. McIndoe	H. Monroe Orrick	July 18, 1864
First	Daniel Newhall	August Miller	July 18, 1864
Second	R. T. Pember	George M. Gorch	July 18, 1864
First	Daniel G. Rogers	Valentine C. Noblet	July 18, 1864
Sixth	John Rennie	Moska Gazick	July 18, 1864
Second	Eli A. Spencer	Sebastian Hursh	July 18, 1864
Fourth	Milton W. Simmons	Charles O. Bowles	July 18, 1864
First	E. B. Simpson	Richard Maguire	Dec. 19, 1864
Second	Charles J. Taggert	George H. Cox	July 18, 1864
Fourth	J. O. Thayer	John Herman	July 18, 1864
Sixth	Thomas Weston	Samuel Bernard	July 18, 1864

IOWA.

District.	Name of principal.	Name of recruit.	Date of call.
Third	William B. Allison	Myron Booth	July 18, 1864
Sixth	Stephen B. Ayres	Joshua N. Miller	July 18, 1864
First	Justus Clark	Peter Brown	July 18, 1864
Fourth	John B. Coulter	Ansell Mann	July 18, 1864
Third	J. Duncan	John Harrington	July 18, 1864
Second	C. Stewart Ells	Albert Strather	July 18, 1864
First	John G. Foote	Frank Hoskins	July 18, 1864
Second	Daniel Gould	Nathan J. Leamar	July 18, 1864
Do	Nathan P. Hubbard	George W. Moss	July 18, 1864
Fifth	G. Holland	Jesse Baldwin	July 18, 1864
Do	H. M. Hoxie	Levi B. Maulsby	July 18, 1864
Second	Royal L. Mack	Joseph Page	July 18, 1864
Third	John D. Merritt	Danford Weaver	July 18, 1864
Fifth	Peter Myers	Andrew J. Raus	July 18, 1864
Second	Hiram Price	James W. Morrison	July 18, 1864
Do	William A. Remington	Charles W. Hazen	July 18, 1864
Fourth	Lemuel H. Reynolds	George Fleck	Dec. 19, 1864
Second	Robert Smyth	James Countryman	July 18, 1864
Third	P. C. Sampson	John W. Arnold	July 18, 1864

MINNESOTA.

District.	Name of principal.	Name of recruit.	Date of muster.
First	John A. Matthews	Charles Kidney	Mar. 28, 1865
Second	Roger S. Munger	Albert A. Morrell	Aug. 19, 1864
Do	Joel A. Whitney	Rezo Potvene	Aug. 23, 1864

MISSOURI.

District.	Name of principal.	Name of recruit.	Date of muster.
Fourth	Martin C. Hubble	Christopher C. Tribley	Jan. 27, 1865

List of persons who put in representative recruits, and names of recruits—Cont'd.

KANSAS.

Residence of principal.	Name of principal.	Name of recruit.	Date of muster.
Leavenworth	William Clough, jr.	William Rutherford	Jan. 7, 1865
Do	Miss Mary R. Clough	Isom Welch	Mar. 20, 1865
Do	Elcana Hensley	John Price	Jan. 7, 1865
Do	Arthur B. Havens	John Kramperts	Jan. 7, 1865
Kennekuk	Dr. John B. Irvin	Archy Steel	Dec. 14, 1864
Leavenworth	Mrs. Johanna Kuntz	Charles Thompson	Feb. 27, 1865
Do	Daniel W. Wilder	John Sweeney	Dec. 22, 1864
Atchison	Samuel F. Walters	Lorin E. Harris	Jan. 7, 1865

RECAPITULATION.

States.	Number of recruits.	States.	Number of recruits.
Maine	65	Kentucky	21
New Hampshire	33	Ohio	115
Vermont	16	Indiana	21
Massachusetts	586	Illinois	90
Rhode Island	2	Michigan	15
Connecticut	5	Wisconsin	28
New York	119	Iowa	19
New Jersey	6	Minnesota	3
Pennsylvania	125	Missouri	1
Delaware	......	Kansas	8
Maryland	7		
District of Columbia	7	Total number of representative recruits.*	1,292
West Virginia	......		

WAR DEPARTMENT ADJUTANT-GENERAL'S OFFICE,
Washington, March 28, 1866.

Hon. E. M. STANTON,
Secretary of War:

SIR: I have the honor to submit the following summary exhibit in regard to the volunteer troops of the Army of the United States, viz:

SUMMARY.

	White.	Colored.	Aggregate.
In service Jan. 9, 1866 *a*	57,590	65,766	123,356
In service Mar. 10, 1866	27,171	39,814	66,985
Ordered mustered out since Jan. 9	30,419	25,952	56,371
Ordered mustered out since Mar. 10	10,106	9,597	19,703
Total reductions made and ordered since Jan. 9	40,525	35,549	76,074

a This number is that recently communicated to the House of Representatives in answer to a resolution dated January 5, 1866.

The musters out ordered will be mostly completed by May 1 (the work will be well advanced by April 10), and there will then be left in service 17,065 white volunteers and 30,217 colored; total, 47,282. It is proper to add that the Seventeenth Regiment U. S. Infantry has been ordered to Texas, and upon its arrival Major-General Sheridan

*Since the preparation of this statement 4 have been added—2 from Maine, 1 from the District of Columbia, and 1 from Ohio—making a total of 1,296.

has been instructed to muster out all additional white volunteers in that department (there are now in service there 3,681 white, present and absent) that he can spare. This contemplated reduction will be in addition to that referred to in the summary.

I am, sir, very respectfully, your obedient servant,

THOMAS M. VINCENT,
Assistant Adjutant-General.

MOBILE, ALA., *April 4, 1866.*

General JOSEPH HOLT,
Judge-Advocate-General:

The proclamation of the President is unofficially before me.* I have several cases ready and pending against citizens before commissions. Shall I proceed with or suspend them if writs of habeas corpus are issued in cases already tried? Please advise me what course I shall pursue.

C. R. WOODS,
Major-General.

[Indorsement.]

WAR DEPARTMENT, *April 5, 1866.*

In the opinion of this Department the President's proclamation of the 3d [2d] of April does not invalidate proceedings before military tribunals having jurisdiction of the alleged offenses, nor divert or limit the jurisdiction or authority of such tribunals. But it is a declaration of the President's purpose to dispense with such tribunals to the utmost possible extent consistent with the public peace and welfare and rely on the appropriate action of civil authorities. All pending trials may be proceeded in to final adjudication, remitting the sentences to the Judge-Advocate-General for review before execution. All other cases should be transferred to the civil authorities or discharged, except such special cases as in the judgment of the military commander should be submitted to the Executive for special instructions upon the facts, of which a full and clear detail should be made to enable the President to decide the proper action. In respect to writs of habeas corpus, they should be obeyed without resistance by military authority unless otherwise instructed upon special facts to be reported by the military commandant to superior authority in Washington.

EDWIN M. STANTON,
Secretary of War.

OFFICE OF CHIEF ENGINEER, U. S. MILITARY RAILROADS,
Washington, D. C., April 24, 1866.

General D. C. MCCALLUM,
Director and General Manager Military Railroads U. S.:

GENERAL: I have the honor to submit the following final report showing the amount and cost of work done for construction and maintenance of way on the several military railroads in what was the Military Division of the Mississippi, and also on the military railroads in the Department of North Carolina. This report only embraces the operations on these roads subsequent to the time they were placed in

---

*Embodied in General Orders, No. 84, October 4, 1866, p. 1007.

your charge. There are no means at my command of ascertaining the amount of work done or its cost previous to that time.

The railroads included in this report in the Military Division of the Mississippi are the Nashville and Chattanooga, Shelbyville Branch, McMinnville and Manchester, Nashville and Decatur, Mount Pleasant Branch, Memphis and Charleston (Eastern Division), Chattanooga and Knoxville, Cleveland and Dalton Branch, Nashville and Northwestern, Chattanooga and Atlanta, Rome Branch, Atlanta and Macon, Nashville and Clarksville, Knoxville and Bristol, Rogersville Branch, Memphis and Charleston (Western Division), Mississippi Central, Mobile and Ohio, Louisville City; and in the Department of North Carolina the Atlantic and North Carolina, Wilmington and Weldon, North Carolina, Raleigh and Gaston.

The cost of material used and labor performed on buildings is not included in the following statements of cost. All other materials not specified are included in the cost of labor. Having made full reports to you under date of May 20 and November 30, 1865, of all operations on the military railroads in North Carolina while I filled the position of chief engineer and general superintendent, I deem it unnecessary to repeat them here, and have therefore in this report confined myself exclusively to the items of construction and maintenance of way.

On the 19th of December, 1863, I received your order to accompany you "to Chattanooga, Tenn., with such portion of the construction force as could be spared from the front" in Virginia.

One division of the Construction Corps, numbering about 285 men, was taken, and we arrived in the Military Division of the Mississippi on the 1st of January, 1864. At the time of our arrival the Nashville and Chattanooga Railroad (151 miles long, extending from Nashville to Chattanooga) was being operated between Nashville and Bridgeport, and the Tennessee River and Running Water bridges were building. Our construction force was at once put to work between Bridgeport and Chattanooga, the bridge builders to assist in the completion of the Running Water and other bridges, and the track layers to repair the track and relay the portion that had been destroyed. This work was completed and the first train run into Chattanooga on the 14th of January, some three weeks sooner than was deemed possible previous to our taking charge of the work. There was great rejoicing in the army in Chattanooga at the completion of the railroad, and feeling confident that a sufficiency of supplies could now be obtained, the chief commissary of the Department of the Cumberland issued full rations to the whole army on and after that day, the first time this had been done since the occupation of the town. Although this road was now completed, it was not in condition to sustain the heavy traffic that would necessarily be thrown upon it when General Sherman's whole army would have to be supplied over it. The superstructure was old and much worn and had never been of first-class character. The rail used was light and of the U-pattern and laid on longitudinal stringers, which were so much decayed in many places that they would not hold the spikes. Accordingly orders were given to relay the track over the whole road with T-rail in the best manner. For this work, and that to be done on the other lines which were to be opened up, a large additional force was required, and arrangements were at once made for an abundant supply of men. The work of relaying the track was prosecuted steadily until completion, though necessarily at a great disadvantage in consequence of the large number of trains constantly on the road. When turned over to the company the road was in every respect in excellent condition. The following statement embraces the whole construction work done on this line, with the exception of some small pieces of track rebuilt, which had been destroyed by guerrillas, and of which no account was kept.

Track.

	Miles.
Rebuilt in first instance	115
Rebuilt after Wheeler's raid in 1864	7
Rebuilt after Hood's invasion	7¾
Total main track	129¾

Side-tracks.

Location.	Length.	Location.	Length.
	Feet.		*Feet.*
Nashville	38,628	Tunnel	264
Barracks	1,600	Tantalon	1,500
Glen Cliff Station	2,368	Condit	2,000
Antioch	990	Anderson	354
La Vergne	895	Stevenson	1,673
Smyrna	2,260	Bolivar	1,640
Stone's River	1,660	Bridgeport	9,472
Winsted	2,408	Carpenter's	1,037
Christiana	1,500	Alley's Spur	159
Fosterville	775	Whiteside	850
Normandy	929	Hooker	350
Tullahoma	609	Chattanooga	10,072
Estill Springs	1,582		
Decherd	13,732	Total	100,277
Cowan	970		

	Miles.
Main track	129¾
Side track, 100,277 feet, or	19
Total track laid by Government	148¾

Bridges.

No.	Location.	Height.	Length.	Remarks
		Feet.	*Feet.*	
1	Mill Creek, No. 1	16	260	Rebuilt five times.
2	Mill Creek, No. 2	18	250	Rebuilt four times.
3	Mill Creek, No. 3	16	256	Do.
4	Hurricane	....	....	
5	Smyrna	20	120	Rebuilt three times.
6	Stewart's Creek	29	183	Do.
7	Overall's Creek	20	160	Do.
8	Stone's River	22	420	Do.
9	Lytle's Creek	10	135	Do.
10	Murfreesborough	9	140	Not destroyed.
	Do	6	40	
	Do	6	50	
	Creek Branch	7	50	
11	Stone's River (East Fork)	22	270	Rebuilt.
12	Christiana	....	73	Do.
13	Bellbuckle	7	82	Do.
	Bragg's Bridge	9	128	Not destroyed.
14	Wartrace	14	241	Rebuilt.
15	Garrison's Fork	24	178	Rebuilt twice.
16	Duck River	30	350	Do.
17	Poorhouse Creek	13	100	Do.
18	Elk River	60	470	Rebuilt.
19	Cowan Creek	26	160	Do.
20	Crow Creek (South Fork)	17	160	Rebuilt twice.
21	Dry Trestle, No. 1	12	84	Rebuilt.
22	Dry Trestle, No. 2	10	75	Do.
23	Crow Creek, No. 1	15	225	Not destroyed.
24	Crow Creek, No. 2	11	225	Do.
25	Crow Creek, No. 3	19	348	Rebuilt.
26	Crow Creek, No. 4	16	254	Do.
27	Crow Creek, No. 5	11	160	Do.

Bridges—Continued.

No.	Locations.	Height.	Length.	Remarks.
		Feet.	*Feet.*	
28	Crow Creek, No. 6	8	100	Not destroyed.
29	Crow Creek, No. 7	12	155	Rebuilt.
30	Crow Creek, No. 8	18	143	Do.
31	Crow Creek, No. 9	11	234	Not destroyed.
32	Crow Creek, No. 10	21	240	Rebuilt.
33	Crow Creek, No. 11		226	Do.
34	Tennessee River	....	1, 520	
35	Ben's Creek	10	100	
36	Widow's Creek	24	127	Do.
37	Dry Creek, No. 1	22	140	
38	Nickajack	34	200	Rebuilt twice.
39	Dry Creek, No. 2	34	203	Rebuilt.
40	Dry Trestle	16	301	
41	Running Water	120	789	
42	Lookout Creek	36	155	Rebuilt twice.
43	Chattanooga	38	263	Rebuilt.

	Lineal feet.
Total bridging	10, 543
Amount rebuilt	12, 236
Total length of bridging on this line	22, 779
Bridges not destroyed	1, 052
Total built by Government	21, 727
Or 4 miles 607 feet.	

A portion of this bridging was built by contract. The total cost of contract work was $385,216.71.

Water stations.

Where built.	Number of tanks.	Where built.	Number of tanks.
Nashville	5	Murfreesborough	2
Florence	1	Fosterville	2
Christiana	2	Garrison's Fork	2
Bellbuckle	2	Decherd	2
Normandy	3	Tantalon	2
Cowan	2	Stevenson	2
Anderson	4	Chattanooga	2
Poison Hollow	1		
Antioch	1	Total	35

The following tabular statement shows the cost of labor performed on this road for construction and maintenance of way, and the number of men in the Construction Corps employed each month:

Month.	Construction Corps.		Transportation Department.	Total.
	Number of men.	Amount of pay-rolls.	Amount of pay-rolls.	
1864.				
January	887	$31,130.16	....	$31,130.16
February	450	35,183.92	$53,270.73	88,454.65
March	338	26,784.45	51,970.14	78,754.59
April	264	16,324.18	83,233.97	99,558.15
May	144	13,132.81	88,977.16	102,109.97
June	181	12,271.36	99,046.30	111,317.66
July	202	13,856.63	91,534.53	105,391.16
August	157	10,098.73	103,278.39	113,377.12
September	392	7,589.55	112,042.78	119,632.33
October	64	3,891.00	106,443.78	110,334.78
November	56	3,513.78	99,183.54	102.697.32
December	622	21,290.81	114,568.49	135,859.30
1865.				
January	50	2,688.00	110,944.35	113,632.35
February	57	4,389.00	144,909.61	149,298.61
March	97	6,072.50	165,423.61	171,496.11
April	111	7,332.00	154,675.61	162,007.61
May	107	7,748.75	117,329.30	125,078.05
June	63	4,937.75	68,401.58	73,339.33
July	51	2,548.25	61,340.14	63,888.39
August	....	....	67,937.67	67,937.67
September	....	....	21,258.31	21,258.31
Total	4,293	230,783.63	1,915,769.99	2,146,553.62
Monthly average	226	12,146.50	95,788.49	102,216.84

Summary of cost.

	Quantity.	Rate.	Total cost.
Materials:			
Iron rails ..... tons	11,900	$120 per ton	$1,428,000.00
Chairs ..... pounds	595,000	8 cents per pound	47,600.00
Spikes ..... do	892,500	8½ cents per pound	75,862.50
Cross-ties	392,557	50 cents per tie	196,278.50
			1,747,741.00
Labor exclusive of that done on buildings			1,946,553.62
Contract work on bridges			385,216.71
Total			4,079,511.33

The Nashville and Chattanooga Railroad was relinquished as a military road and turned over to the company September 15, 1865.

THE NASHVILLE AND DECATUR RAILROAD

Extends from Nashville to the Memphis and Charleston Railroad at a point near Decatur, Ala., and is 120 miles long. The repairs were completed and the road opened in March, 1864. Much of the work in opening it the first time was done by soldiers, and I have no account of the cost of what they did. General Dodge was in command of the force employed on this work. The following statements show the amount of work done and the cost of that done by the Military Railroad Department:

Track.

	Miles.
Main track rebuilt in first instance	2
Main track rebuilt after Forrest's raid	7½
Main track rebuilt after Wheeler's raids	22
Total main track	31½

Sidings.

Location.	Feet.
Eaton Depot	1,000
Nashville Junction	8,025
Brentwood	300
Franklin	290
Columbia	1,150
Prospect	600
Athens	1,480
Decatur Junction	1,170
	14,015
Add main track rebuilt	163,680
Total	177,695

Or 34 miles 815 feet.

Bridges.

No.	Location.	Height.	Length.	Remarks.	Rebuilt.
		Feet.	*Feet.*		*Feet.*
1	Brown's Creek	12	38	Not destroyed	
2	Little Harpeth	14	74		
3	Spencer's Creek	17	38		
4	Big Harpeth	38	187	Rebuilt twice and partly rebuilt twice	454
5	West Harpeth	13	58		
6	Near Spring Hill	12	53		
7	Spring Creek	15	21		
8	Carter's Creek, No. 1	18	112	Rebuilt twice and partly rebuilt twice	286
9	Carter's Creek, No. 2	21	184	do	470
10	Carter's Creek, No. 3	20	94	do	235
11	Carter's Creek, No. 4	20	94	Rebuilt twice and partly rebuilt once	228
12	Carter's Creek, No. 5	30	235	Rebuilt twice and partly rebuilt twice	587
13	Rutherford's Creek, No. 1.	26	130	Rebuilt three times and partly rebuilt twice.	455
14	Rutherford's Creek, No. 2.	27	265	Rebuilt twice and partly rebuilt three times.	723
15	Rutherford's Creek, No. 3.	30	295	do	811
16	Rutherford's Creek, No. 4.	50	270	Rebuilt twice and partly rebuilt twice	676
17	Duck River	72	627	Rebuilt twice	1,254
18	Lytle's Creek	14	22		
19	Hurricane Creek	14	22		
20	Harris Trestle	29	232		
21	Kalioka Trestle	37	1,130	Rebuilt	1,130
22	Grace's Trestle	42	637	do	637
23	Robinson's Forks	18	126	do	126
24	Richland Creek, No. 1	32	160	Rebuilt twice	320
25	Richland Creek, No. 2	37	180	do	360
26	Richland Creek, No. 3	35	180	do	360
27	Pigeon Roost Creek	12	50	Rebuilt	50
28	Richland Creek No. 4	41	315	Rebuilt twice	630
29	Tunnel Trestle	38	822	Rebuilt	822
30	Elk River	40	625	Rebuilt three times	1,875
31		10	48		
32	Mill Creek	30	330	Rebuilt	330
33	White Sulphur	71	570	do	570
34	Mud Creek	5	62	do	62
35	do	9	102	do	102
36	Athens Creek	10	134	do	134
37	do	11	64	do	64
38	Swan Creek	11	340	do	340
39	do	11	129	do	129
40	Black Creek	6	225	do	225
41	Junction Trestle	16	275	do	275
	Total		9,555		14,720

	Feet.
Total bridging	9,555
Amount rebuilt	14,720
Total built by Government	24,475

Or 4 miles 3,155 feet.

A portion of this bridging was built by contract, the cost of which amounted to $637,768.46.

Water stations.

Where built.	Number of tanks.	Where built.	Number of tanks.
Little Harpeth	1	Carter's Creek	2
West Harpeth	1	Lynnville	2
Lytle's Creek	2	Near Tunnel	1
Pulaski	1	McDonald's	1
Elkmont	2		
Franklin	2	Total	15

The following tabular statement shows the cost of labor on this road for construction and maintenance of way, and the number of men in the Construction Corps employed each month:

Month.	Construction Corps.		Transportation Department.	Total.
	Number of men.	Amount of pay-rolls.	Amount of pay-rolls.	
1864.				
February			$5,641.75	$5,641.75
March			10,631.99	10,631.99
April			15,405.07	15,405.07
May			18,299.10	18,299.10
June			16,209.39	16,209.39
July			18,828.20	18,828.20
August			26,574.16	26,574.16
September			23,357.52	23,357.52
October			27,043.23	27,043.23
November	564	$5,850.71	21,149.85	27,000.56
December	1,208	32,238.82	125,291.87	157,530.69
1865.				
January	1,320	78,187.23	32,058.73	110,245.96
February	601	27,616.95	26,518.82	54,135.77
March	309	19,686.45	29,034.54	48,720.99
April	75	6,891.25	28,243.64	35,134.89
May	150	6,574.50	27,760.82	33,335.32
June			22,506.06	22,506.06
July			17,382.13	17,382.13
August			20,983.98	20,983.98
September			3,869.15	3,869.15
Total	4,227	177,045.91	515,850.00	692,835.91
Monthly average	604	25,290.27	25,762.50	34,641.79

Summary of cost.

	Quantity.	Rate.		Total cost.
Materials:				
Iron rails ... tons	2,732	$120 per ton		$327,840.00
Chairs ... pounds	136,000	8 cents per pound		10,880.00
Spikes ... do	204,000	8½ cents per pound		17,340.00
Cross-ties	120,840	50 cents per tie		60,420.00
				416,480.00
Labor			$692,835.91	
Contract work on bridges			549,326.13	
				1,242,162.04
Total				1,658,642.04

The Nashville and Decatur Railroad was relinquished as a military road and turned over to the company September 15, 1865.

THE MEMPHIS AND CHARLESTON RAILROAD

Extends from Memphis, Tenn., to Stevenson, Ala., and is 271 miles long. The eastern end of this line, from Stevenson to near Decatur, eighty miles long, was repaired and put in running order in March, 1864. The following statements show the amount of work done on it by this department and the cost of same:

Track.

	Feet.
Main track	18,440
Sidings at—	
Decatur Junction	275
Fackler's	700
Stevenson	2,900
Chattanooga	1,800
Total track	24,115
Or 4 miles 2,995 feet.	

Bridges.

Location.	Height.	Length.	Remarks.	Rebuilt.
	Feet.	*Feet.*		*Feet.*
Little Piney	15	109	Rebuilt	109
Big Piney	12	153	....do	153
Big Limestone	10	210	....do	210
Little Limestone	13	72	....do	72
Beaver Dam	22	252	Not destroyed	
Bradford's Creek	26	32	....do	
Indian Creek	17	154	Rebuilt	154
Flint River	25	302	Rebuilt twice	604
Hurricane Creek	12	271	Rebuilt	271
Paint Rock	38	313	Rebuilt twice	626
Mud Creek	14	315	Rebuilt	315
Crow Creek	20	265	....do	265
Total		2,448		2,779

	Feet.
Total bridging	2,448
Deduct amount not destroyed	284
	2,164
Add amount rebuilt	2,779
Total built by Government	4,943

A portion of this bridging was built by contract and cost $88,442.33.

Water stations.

Where built.	Number of tanks.	Where built.	Number of tanks.
Little Piney	1	Brownsborough	1
Huntsville	2	Near Woodville	1
Gurley's	2	Stevenson	4
Scottsborough	1		
Indian Creek	1	Total	13

The following statement shows the cost of labor for construction and maintenance of way:

Month.	Amount of pay-rolls.	Month.	Amount of pay-rolls.
1864.		1865.	
January		January	$16,029.36
February	$2,333.85	February	13,259.40
March	1,834.38	March	14,517.26
April	7,263.68	April	14,121.81
May	9,523.28	May	13,880.40
June	11,184.42	June	11,253.02
July	9,418.08	July	8,691.05
August	13,287.07	August	10,491.98
September	13,178.75	September	7,738.41
October	13,521.60		
November	10,574.97	Total	216,308.18
December	14,205.41	Monthly average	10,815.40

Summary of cost.

	Quantity.	Rate.		Total cost.
Materials:				
Iron rails ... tons	360	$120 per ton		$43,200.00
Chairs ... pounds	18,000	8 cents per pound		1,440.00
Spikes ... do	27,000	8½ cents per pound		2,295.00
Cross-ties	57,500	50 cents per tie		28,750.00
				75,685.00
Labor			$216,308.18	
Contract work on bridges			88,442.33	
				304,750.51
Total				380,435.51

This portion of the Memphis and Charleston Railroad was relinquished as a military road and turned over to the company September 1, 1865.

THE CHATTANOOGA AND KNOXVILLE

Or East Tennessee and Georgia Railroad extends from Chattanooga to Knoxville, 110 miles, with a branch from Cleveland to Dalton twenty-seven miles long. Repairs were commenced on this road in January, 1864, and it was completed to the Tennessee River, at Loudon, on the 13th of February following. The portion of the road north of the Tennessee River had not been injured and was being operated with the rolling-stock captured by the Union forces at Knoxville. A trestle bridge over the Tennessee River was immediately commenced, and the work upon it had progressed so far that it would have been completed on the 14th of March, but on the 25th of February General Schofield, commanding the Department of the Ohio, ordered the work to be stopped, and it was not resumed until March 12. The trestle bridge was completed on the 13th of April, and trains commenced running through between Chattanooga and Knoxville.

Track.

The track of this road had been broken and injured in a number of places, but none of the breaks were of great extent. The longest one was that next to Chattanooga, being about three miles long. The cross-ties, however, over the whole road were very much decayed, and much work was done in replacing them with new ones after trains commenced running. The road was occasionally broken by guerrillas, but never seriously injured until Wheeler's raid in August, 1864, when about twenty-five miles of track were torn up and destroyed.

	Miles.
Main track laid in first instance	5½
After several small raids	1
After Wheeler's raid in 1864	25
On Dalton branch, in first instance	2
After Hood's invasion	1½
Total main track	35

Sidings.

Location.	Length.	Location.	Length.
	Feet.		*Feet.*
Chattanooga	1,155	Sweetwater	220
Stone Quarry	550	Philadelphia	1,450
Tunnel	250	Lenoir's	1,050
Tyner's	787	Saw Mill	420
Ooltewah	445	Erin	850
McDonald's	2,455	Knoxville	4,760
Cleveland	310	West leg of Y	920
Mouse Creek	1,470		
Reagan's	740	Total	17,832

Total length of track laid, 38 miles 1,992 feet.

Bridges.

The only important bridges on this line are those over the Hiwassee and Tennessee Rivers. Both of these were built of trestles in the first place, but afterward replaced with permanent structures. The following are the demensions of these bridges:

	Height.		Total length.	Rebuilt.
	Feet.	*Spans.*	*Feet.*	*Feet.*
Hiwassee	47	3	301	301
Tennessee	85	11	1,700	1,700
Total			2,001	2,001

Total bridging built by Government, 4,002 feet.

The permanent bridges were built by contract and cost $161,990.26.

Water stations.

Where built.	Number of tanks.
Chattanooga	2
Ooltewah	2
Tunnel	1
Riceville	3
Sweetwater	2
Total	10

The following tabular statement shows the cost of labor on this road for construction and maintenance of way, and the number of men in the Construction Corps employed each month:

Month.	Construction Corps.		Transportation Department.	Total.
	Number of men.	Amount of pay-rolls.	Amount of pay-rolls.	
1864.				
February	1,222	$83,437.54	....	$83,437.54
March	919	64,094.18	....	64,094.18
April	1,127	62,224.60	$3,404.86	65,629.46
May	202	4,135.60	6,908.19	11,043.79
June	244	3,995.79	8,537.04	12,532.83
July	....	....	11,677.03	11,677.03
August	....	....	11,321.66	11,321.66
September	724	44,592.24	13,518.25	58,110.49
October	....	....	15,228.04	15,228.04
November	....	....	12,858.42	12,858.42
December	....	....	908.14	908.14
1865.				
January	....	....	17,680.76	17,680.76
February	....	....	20,224.04	20,224.04
March	....	....	27,131.03	27,131.03
April	....	....	30,229.93	30,229.93
May	....	....	26,344.91	26,344.91
June	....	....	15,776.80	15,776.80
July	....	....	13,938.45	13,938.45
August	....	....	8,386.95	8,386.95
Total	4,438	262,479.95	244,074.50	506,554.45
Monthly average	740	43,746.65	14,357.32	26,660.76

Summary of cost.

	Quantity.	Rate.	Total cost.
Materials:			
Iron rails ....tons..	3,080	$120 per ton	$369,600.00
Chairs ....pounds..	152,000	8 cents per pound	12,160.00
Spikes ....do....	228,000	8½ cents per pound	18,240.00
Cross-ties	284,061	50 cents per tie	142,030.50
			542,030.50
Labor			506,554.45
Contract work on bridges			161,990.26
Total			1,210,575.21

The Chattanooga and Knoxville Railroad was relinquished as a military road and turned over to the company August 28, 1865.

THE NASHVILLE AND NORTHWESTERN RAILROAD

Is seventy-eight miles long and extends from Nashville to the Tennessee River at Johnsonville. It was partly built before the war. On the 22d of October, 1863, the Secretary of War ordered this road to be constructed for "military purposes," and placed it in charge of Andrew Johnson, then Military Governor of Tennessee, who was empowered to "employ an engineer and other officers and workmen necessary to complete it without delay." Col. W. P. Innes was acting as engineer at the time the railroads in this military division were taken charge of by the U. S. Military Railroad Department, and had a considerable force of soldiers and civilian laborers employed on the road. But as the work was not progressing to the satisfaction of the general commanding, he relieved Colonel Innes and placed the construction of the road in your charge. This order of General Grant's was given on the 17th of February, 1864, and on the 25th of the same month I received your order directing me to adopt the most energetic means at my command to complete the Nashville and Northwestern Railroad. I at once made an examination of the work to be done and found it to consist of a rather formidable amount of grading, bridging, track laying, and other work incident to the construction of a new railroad, and proceeded to take the necessary steps to complete the work as directed. I appointed Lieut. Col. John Clark engineer of construction, and by General Grant's direction sent North for 2,000 mechanics and laborers in addition to the force then on the road. Some time after we had got fairly under way Governor Johnson, claiming the right under the above-mentioned order of the Secretary of War to appoint an engineer, also selected Colonel Clark, who then filled this double position until the work of construction was so far completed that the track was connected through, an event which took place on the 10th day of May, 1864. Governor Johnson continued to exercise semi-control over the operations on this road until it was formally taken possession of by General Sherman and placed absolutely under the control of the general manager of military railroads, in accordance with the order of the President of the United States dated August 6, 1864. The Transportation Department then took charge of the movements of trains, and the maintenance of way, together with construction work, remained in my department.

On the 20th of August I appointed W. R. Kingsley, esq. (who had been connected with the road as division engineer since April), engineer in charge of construction and maintenance of way. He continued to perform the duties of this position faithfully and satisfactorily until the 1st of April, 1865, when, all construction work being done, the maintenance of way was turned over to the transportation department. The line of this road as originally located crossed the Tennessee River nearly perpendicular to the course of that stream and at an elevation of fifty-two feet above low water and nine feet above high water. The approach to the river was an embankment seventeen feet high above the surface of the ground on the river bank. The object of making this a military railroad being the transportation of army supplies from the Tennessee River to Nashville, it became necessary to construct ample and convenient arrangements for the transfer of freight from steam-boats to cars. Accordingly two large transfer freight-houses were designed and built, one on each side of the railroad, with tracks starting from main line at the bluff and curving right and left until parallel with the buildings and river bank. The freight-house or shed on the north or lower side, 600 feet long by 30 feet wide, was hastily knocked up so as to bring it into immediate use, and the levee in front graded off to the water's edge with a slope of 9 degrees or about 16 feet rise in 100 feet horizontal. The freight-house on south side, 600 feet long and 90 feet wide, was a much more complete building. The floor was two feet and a half above high-water mark and the levee in front graded to a slope of 14 degrees, on which it was designed to lay railroad tracks from low-water mark to floor of freight-house. The plan for transferring freight from steam-boats to cars was to load from the boats onto small cars, which were hauled up the levee to the level of the freight-house floor by a wire rope passing round a pulley or spool, which was dropped into or lifted out of gear with the main shaft by a lever. This main shaft was 500 feet long and passed through the center of the building immediately below the floor or platform and was operated by an engine located in the middle of the building. The freight was then passed directly through the building and loaded into cars on the opposite side. The levee was of sufficient length to allow at least four or five boats to unload at the same time, and the side tracks were so arranged that a whole train of cars could be loaded at once, and as soon as loaded could be moved away and another train run right alongside the house. This plan would undoubtedly have enabled us to handle a large amount of freight with great rapidity and ease, but we had not the opportunity of bringing it to a practical test, for just as everything was about completed Hood's invasion of Tennessee took place and Johnsonville was evacuated by our troops, and during their absence the freight-house was burned, as is supposed, by rebel sympathizers in the neighborhood. However, the engine and all the most valuable parts of the machinery were saved by being taken to Nashville.

All could have been saved if we had had sufficient transportation for it. Although the road was opened through to Johnsonville after Hood's defeat at Nashville, but little work was done in rebuilding the houses and platforms at that point. Grading off the levee involved considerable work; about 30,000 cubic yards of earth had to be moved. It was designed to pave it, or put on a covering of broken stone, but owing to the delay in furnishing gun-boat protection to our boats, which were to bring stone down the river for this purpose, the work was but partially carried out. A row of piles were to have been driven at the edge of the water to protect the levee and prevent its washing away at time of floods, but the pile driver for this purpose never reached Johnsonville. It is but proper for me to state here that the work on the buildings and levee at Johnsonville was much delayed by the confusion and embarrassment caused by the conflict of authority incident to a divided control of the work. In the first place, I was ordered to erect these buildings; then Colonel Donaldson, senior and supervising quartermaster Department of the Cumberland, assumed the charge of them and appointed a quartermaster to superintend their erection. But under his management the work progressed so slowly that finally the quartermaster's department was relieved, and again I was ordered to complete it. Had I been allowed to go on in the first place and carry out my plans, the works would all have been completed and in use three months before the evacuation of the place, instead of being not quite completed at that time. The following is a statement of the work done on this road:

Graduation.

The amount of grading was very considerable, but I am unable to give the number of cubic yards moved, because when we took charge of this road I had no time to measure it, and I had no assistants to do it for me. By the time I procured the requisite assistance much of the work had been done. Thorough cuts of as much as forty and fifty feet in depth and 800 feet in length were taken out and high embankments made. Even where the grading had been done previously much labor was required to dress up the embankments and clean out the cuts.

Superstructure.

The total length of track laid was:

	Miles.
Main line	46½
Sidings	4¼
Total	50¾

Seven different patterns of rails were used in the track; the amount of each kind is given below. With the exception of No. 1 and the U-rail, the iron was purchased by the Government. No. 1 pattern is the fish-joint bar belonging to this road, and the U-rail was taken from the Nashville and Chattanooga Railroad.

Pattern.	Weight per yard.	Amount.
	Pounds.	*Tons.*
No. 1	56¼	1,315.61
No. 2	49⅘	149.70
No. 3	45	382.11
No. 4	45	40.04
No. 5	60	1,096.84
No. 6	56¼	1,469.48
U	48	23.50
Total		4,477.28
Deduct No. 1 pattern		1,315.61
Balance furnished by Government		3,161.67

One hundred and seven thousand cross-ties were used in laying the track. A considerable number was found on the line of this road, but we had to make the greater part.

Bridging.

The following table shows the location, dimensions, and amount of bridges and trestles on this road. Many of these structures had to be rebuilt several times in consequence of being carried away by high water or destroyed by the enemy.

Statement of bridges and trestles on the Nashville and Northwestern Railroad.

Distance from Nashville.	Name.	Number of spans or bents.	Height.	Length.	Remarks.
Miles.			*Feet.*	*Feet.*	
0	Nashville Trestle	170	21–28	2,151	
4.57	Richland Creek, No. 1	2	15	76	Rebuilt once.
5.36	Richland Creek, No. 2	1	9	66	Rebuilt twice.
5.75	Richland Creek, No. 3	1	9	65	Do.
6.53	Branch Richland Creek	2	10	35	
6.72	.....do	1	8	17	
	.....do	1	8	26	
7.52	Over road	1	10	32	
8.91	Trestle over road	6	20	75	Rebuilt five times.
13.39	Harpeth River, No. 1	2	34	87	Do.
13.94	Harpeth River, No. 2	2	36	201.5	Rebuilt four times.
15.31	Harpeth River, No. 3	1	42	180	Do.
17.43	Harpeth River, No. 4	2	38	201.4	Do.
21.21	Harpeth River, No. 5	1	32	236.9	Do.
23.14	Harpeth River, No. 6	12	24	180	
	.....do	2	24	201.8	Rebuilt once.
23.56	Harpeth River, No. 7	10	24–30	180	
	.....do	2	33	203.3	Do.
24.66	Turnbull River	43	12	516	
24.66	.....do	2	27	259	
24.66	.....do	20	20–25	270	
25.37	Trestle	66	20–32	792	
25.66	Sullivan's Branch	3	16	39	Rebuilt twice.
25.66	.....do	1	48	89.7	
25.66	.....do	102	26–46	1,326	
26.44	Trestle	17	36–26	306	
27.18	.....do	21	38–24	262	
40.95	.....do	18	17–28	238	
41.71	.....do	17	14–25	225	
47.53	.....do	75	20–33	1,067	
49.49	.....do	30	19	442	
52	.....do	58	7–13	837	
52.38	.....do	8	10	145	

Statement of bridges and trestles on the Nashville and Northwestern Railroad—Continued.

Distance from Nashville.	Name.	Number of spans or bents.	Height.	Length.	Remarks.
Miles.			*Feet.*	*Feet.*	
53	Trestle	37	13-12	470	
53.44	.....do	2	18	40	
54.19	.....do	62	30-48	910	
55.79	.....do	70	40-72	980	
56.18	.....do	11	30-39	180	
	Branch Trace Creek	1	7	24	
60.05	.....do	2	8	47	
63.56	Trace Creek	2	14	216	Slightly injured and repaired.
64.01		1	10	20	
64.61	Flood Creek	2	3	30	
66.51	.....do	3	4	35	
71.44		22	18	272	
73.08	Trace Creek	1	25	114	Rebuilt four times.
74.44	Trestle	3	15	66	
78	Trestle at Johnsonville	121	12-18	1,525	
	Total			15,956	

Or 3 miles and 114 feet.

Add to this amount rebuilt, 5,366 feet, and we have a total of four miles and 200 feet of bridging and trestle on this road built by the Government. The lumber consumed in these structures amounted to 4,098,509 feet, B. M. A portion of this bridging was built by contract, amounting to $182,789.11.

The following table shows the location of and amount of lumber in the buildings on this road:

For what purpose.	Location.	Lumber.	Shingles.	Remarks.
		Feet, B. M.		
House for trackmen	Nashville	8,000	5,000	
House for switchmen	.....do	1,500		
Tool-house	.....do	3,000	5,000	
House for trackmen	Section 3	7,863	5,000	
Do	Section 6	5,000	5,000	
Telegraph office	Section 18	6,000		Destroyed.
House for trackmen	Section 20	5,728	5,000	
Do	Section 24	15,037		Do.
Telegraph office	.....do	8,500	3,500	Destroyed and rebuilt.
Blacksmith shop	.....do	5,000		
Outbuildings	.....do	800		Do.
House for trackmen	Section 29	10,162		
Telegraph office	Section 32	5,000	3,500	
Do	Section 42	11,000	3,500	Do.
Do	Section 50	11,000	3,500	Do.
House for trainmen	.....do	4,000		Destroyed
House for trackmen	.....do	2,800		Do.
Telegraph office	Section 57	4,800		Do.
Do	Section 66	6,800		Do.
House for trackmen	Section 77	6,800		Do.
House for yardmen	Johnsonville	18,200	4,200	Do.
House for engineers and firemen	.....do	25,200	22,000	Do.
House for station agent	.....do	28,900	21,000	Do.
Outbuildings	.....do	1,000		Do.
Wheelwright shop	.....do	5,570		Do.
Blacksmith shop	.....do	5,000		Do.
Saw-mill	.....do	6,656		Destroyed and rebuilt.
House for carpenters	.....do	11,800		Destroyed.
Depot	.....do	175,000	90,000	Destroyed and rebuilt.
House for railroad purposes	.....do	110,400		
House for track hands	.....do	6,540		
House for mill hands	.....do	20,000		
Upper freight-house	.....do	1,097,600	566,000	Destroyed.
Lower freight-house	.....do	165,000		Destroyed and partly rebuilt.
Total		1,805,656	742,200	

Water Stations.

Fourteen of these were built and located, as shown in the following table, containing in the aggregate 63,700 feet, B. M., of lumber:

Distance from Nashville.	Capacity.	Remarks.
Miles.		
7½	One tank	
16½	.....do	Discontinued.
17½	.....do	Destroyed and rebuilt.
24½	.....do	Destroyed.
27½	.....do	
28	.....do	
45	.....do	
53½	Two tanks	
59¼	One tank	Do.
66¼	.....do	Do.
71¾	.....do	
75¼	.....do	Destroyed and rebuilt.
77½	.....do	Do.
78	Two tanks	Do.

Saw-mill No. 1, at Johnsonville, was run by our department during the months of September, October, and November, 1864, and during that time cut 488,000 feet, B. M., of lumber.

Cost.

Work done by soldiers.—The Twelfth Regiment U. S. Colored Infantry, commanded by Colonel Thompson, commenced work on the 15th of November, 1863, and were relieved April 23, 1864. Average number of men employed during this time, 200.

The Thirteenth Regiment U. S. Colored Infantry, commanded by Col. John A. Hottenstein, commenced work on the 19th of November, 1863, and were relieved May 10, 1864. Average number of men employed, 500.

The First Missouri Engineers, commanded by Col. Henry Flad, commenced work on the 24th of February, 1863, and were relieved August 1, 1864. Average number of men employed, 1,000.

The First Michigan Engineers, commanded by Col. William P. Innes, were employed on the road for some time, but I was unable to get a statement of the number of effective men or the length of time they worked.

All this work done by soldiers, together with all done by civilian laborers up to September 1, 1864, is properly chargeable to construction of new road.

The following tabular statements of cost of labor performed and materials purchased previous to the time the road was placed entirely under the control of the Military Railroad Department have been furnished by Maj. A. W. Wills, assistant quartermaster, from the papers of Capt. F. H. Ruger, assistant quartermaster, who was quartermaster for the road, but is since deceased:

Statement of purchases made by Captain Ruger.

Month.	Amount.	Month.	Amount.
1864.		1864.	
January	$4, 598. 83	June	$15, 853. 84
February	9, 678. 64	July	16, 880. 07
March	27, 351. 46	August	39, 532. 19
April	15, 848. 43		
May	24, 138. 05	Total	153, 881. 51

Statement of amount paid for labor by Captain Ruger.

Month.	Amount.	Month.	Amount.
1863.		1864.	
November	$10, 576. 67	April	$60, 369. 50
December	11, 440. 70	May	57, 789. 61
1864.		June	52, 561. 02
		July	43, 629. 59
January	15, 428. 90	August	54, 214. 45
February	16, 244. 19		
March	35, 849. 54	Total	358, 104. 17

The following statement is furnished by Lieut. Col. O. Cross, deputy quartermaster-general, Pittsburg, Pa.:

Statement of materials purchased by Lieut. Col. O. Cross, deputy quartermaster-general, U. S. Army, for the Nashville and Northwestern Railroad.

6,720,510 pounds iron rails, at $91.50 per ton	$274, 520. 71
143,250 pounds spikes, at 6 cents per pound	8, 595. 00
75,000 pounds spikes, at 7½ cents per pound	5, 625. 00
227,615 pounds chairs, at 6 cents per pound	13, 656. 90
Total	302, 397. 61

The lumber purchased by Colonel Cross is omitted because it was used on buildings.

Statement of pay-rolls on the Nashville and Northwestern Railroad, paid by the U. S. Military Railroad Department.

Month.	Number of men.	Amount of pay-rolls.
1864.		
September	1, 195	$73, 248. 15
October	1, 228	58, 010. 68
November	989	50, 456. 84
December	821	48, 339. 90
1865.		
January	723	44, 474. 99
February	700	38, 176. 65
March	567	39, 231. 13
April	444	31, 704. 94
May	405	20, 194. 23
June	311	11. 813. 95
July	317	12. 105. 85
August	302	12, 423. 25
September	10	545. 00
Total	8, 012	440, 725. 56

Summary of cost.

Materials:		
Purchases made by Captain Ruger		$153,881.51
Iron rails, chairs, and spikes purchased by Lieutenant-Colonel Cross		302,397.61
Spikes other than above, 100,000 pounds, at 8½ cents per pound		8,500.00
Cross-ties, 50,000, at 50 cents per tie		25,000.00
Total		489,779.12
Labor:		
Amount paid by Captain Ruger	$358,104.17	
Amount paid by U. S. Military Railroad Department	440,725.56	
		798,829.73
Contract work on bridges		182,789.11
Total		1,471,397.96

In the above no estimate is made for the value of work done by the soldiers. I have been informed that an amount of iron belonging to this company was used on other military railroads prior to 1864, but have made no deduction for the same, as I have no means of giving full and accurate information of operations previous to that time. The Nashville and Northwestern Railroad was relinquished as a military road and turned over to the company September 1, 1865.

THE CHATTANOOGA AND ATLANTA

Or Western and Atlantic Railroad extends from Chattanooga to Atlanta, 136 miles, with a branch from Kingston to Rome seventeen miles long. The reconstruction and maintenance of this line was in many respects the most difficult and interesting of any military railroad operation during the war. By it the Confederate army under General Johnston made their retreat from Buzzard Roost to Atlanta, and upon its rapid and prompt reconstruction General Sherman's army depended for the supplies necessary for his successful movement on Atlanta. As Johnston fell back from one strong position to another he did such damage to the road as it was supposed would delay or prevent Sherman's pursuit, but in no instance was he successful in this object. However great the damage done, it was so speedily repaired that General Sherman soon ceased to fear any delay from this cause and made his advance movements with perfect confidence that the railroad in his rear would be "all right." Being from the nature of the case entirely ignorant of the obstacles to be encountered at each advance, the construction force had to be prepared for any emergency, either to build a bridge of formidable dimensions or lay miles of track, or perhaps push back to some point on the line and repair damages done by guerrillas or raiding parties. These attacks on the line to the rear were of such frequent occurrence, and often of so serious a character, that to insure speedy repairs it became necessary to station detachments of the Construction Corps at various points along the road, and also collect supplies of construction materials, such as iron rails, chairs, spikes, cross-ties, and bridge timber, at points where they would be comparatively safe and easily obtained when required. These precautionary measures proved of the utmost importance in keeping the road open. The detachments stationed along the line were composed of bridge-builders and track-layers, and had an ample supply of tools for either kind of work. Each detachment was under the command of a competent engineer or supervisor, who had orders to move in either direction, within certain limits, as soon as a break occurred and make the necessary repairs without delay, working day and night when necessary. Under this arrangement small breaks were repaired at once at any point on the line, even when the telegraph wires were cut and special orders could not be communicated to the working parties. When "big breaks" occurred one or more divisions of the Construction Corps were moved as rapidly as possible thereto, either from Chattanooga or "the front." Construction trains loaded with the requisite tools and materials were kept ready at each end of the road to move at a moment's notice.

By order of General Thomas the work of reconstruction commenced on the 1st of March, 1864, and the road to Ringgold and a short distance beyond was completed on the 20th of the same month. The advance movement of the army from Ringgold took place on the 6th of May, and the railroad was completed and trains run to Tunnel Hill early on the morning of the 9th. Fears being entertained by some that the tunnel had been mined by the enemy, a locomotive was run through it to test the matter, but it was found to be all safe. The enemy having fallen back to Resaca, the road was opened up on the 15th to Tilton while the battle was still in progress a few miles beyond that station, and next day the construction trains ran into Resaca with the advance of our army. The railroad bridge over the Oostenaula River was still burning on our arrival here, and the work of rebuilding delayed somewhat in consequence. However, we got fairly started to work next morning, and the bridge was completed and other necessary repairs made to the track, and the trains pushed forward and overtook the army on the morning of the 20th at Kingston. Beyond this point the track was immediately put in order to Cass Station, but not farther, until the army again reached the railroad south of Allatoona Pass. I received General Sherman's order to build the Etowah bridge on the 3d of June at Chattanooga, but owing to the delay in getting the construction trains over the road did not reach the Etowah River until the night of the 5th, and then with only one division of the bridge-builders. The other division ordered to this work did not arrive until twenty-four hours afterward. The bridge was commenced on the morning of the 6th and finished at noon on 11th. There was an abundance of timber prepared on the line of the railroad for this work, but the trains sent to bring it up were detained so long for running orders that we could not wait for it, and a large amount had to be cut near the site of the bridge and dragged by hand to the work. Notwithstanding these delays this bridge, 600 feet long and 67 feet high, was built in five days and a half. As soon as it was completed trains ran to Big Shanty, which was made the depot of supplies until after the capture of Kenesaw Mountain. On the 3d of July I received General Sherman's order to open the railroad to Marietta. The contruction trains were detained some time at Tunnel Hill by a small rebel raid on the road near Buzzard Roost, but reached Big Shanty on the morning of the 5th and commenced work at once. The road was opened on the 6th to Vining's Station, which is only ten miles from Atlanta. We commenced work on the Chattahoochee bridge by order of General Thomas on the 23d of July, but next day received orders to stop the work, which was accordingly done at noon on the 24th. Orders were received on the 2d of August to resume work, which was done at noon on that day, and the bridge was finished and trains passed over it at noon on the 5th and ran within three miles of Atlanta. The Chattahoochee bridge is 780 feet long and 92 feet high, and was built in precisely four days and a half. No night work was done upon it whatever, but the men worked from daylight till dark, with one hour intermission at noon for dinner. A division of the Construction Corps was held at the Chattahoochee until Atlanta was won, and they then completed the railroad into the city on the 3d of September, the day after General Slocum took possession of it.

Track.

By the original location the Atlanta line crossed the Knoxville line twice within a few miles of Chattanooga. Both roads having been destroyed in the vicinity of that place, it was deemed unnecessary to rebuild both entire, and as the Knoxville road was the shorter and better line, it was rebuilt and the Atlanta line was connected with it near the crossing of the Chickamauga Creek, some five miles from Chattanooga, thus shortening the distance to Atlanta about two miles. Two connections were made, the first being merely for temporary use. The track between the junction and Tunnel Hill had been badly damaged and much of it required relaying; besides a number of small breaks at other points, some two miles near Marietta had been taken up and the rails removed. A similar break, but not of such extent, was found near Vining's Station. Guerrillas and raiding parties were more or less successful in destroying portions of track during the whole time we held the road; but the crowning effort of this kind was made in October, 1864, when Hood, getting to the rear of Sherman, threw his whole army on the road, first at Big Shanty and afterward north of Resaca, and destroyed in the aggregate thirty-five and a half miles of track and 455 lineal feet of bridges, killing and capturing a large number of our men. Fortunately, however, the detachments of the Construction Corps which escaped were so distributed that even before Hood had left the road two strong working parties were at work, one on each end of the break at Big Shanty, and this gap of ten miles was closed and the force ready to move to the great break of twenty-five miles in length north of Resaca as soon as the enemy had left it. The destruction by Hood's army of our depots of supplies compelled us to cut nearly all the cross-ties required to relay this track and send to a distance for rails. The cross-ties were cut near the line of the road and many of them carried by hand to the track, as the teams to be furnished for hauling them did not get to the work until it was nearly completed. The rails used on the southern end of the break had to be taken up and brought from the railroads south of Atlanta, and those for the northern end were mostly brought from Nashville, nearly 200 miles distant. Notwithstanding all these disadvantages under which we had to labor, this twenty-five miles of the track was laid and the trains were running over it in seven and a half days from the time the work was commenced. When Sherman cut loose from his railroad line of supply in November, 1864, and commenced his march to the sea, he very effectually destroyed the road between the Etowah and Atlanta, and by his order we took up the track between Resaca and Dalton, sixteen miles, and brought the iron to Chattanooga. In May, 1865, General Thomas ordered the road to be reopened through to Atlanta. It was completed on the 4th of July following.

The following is a statement of track laid:

Main track laid—	Miles.
In opening the road	18¾
After numerous small raids	10
After Hood's great raid	35½
In 1865, by General Thomas' order	66½
Total	130¾

Sidings.

Location.	Length.	Location.	Length.
	Feet.		*Feet.*
Chattanooga	15,940	Acworth	1,900
Chickamauga	1,200	Big Shanty	1,305
Graysville	1,420	Marietta	3,450
Ringgold	2,000	Ruff's	1,040
Dalton	4,550	Vining's	1,540
Steedman	1,360	Chattahoochee	1,250
Tilton	700	Atlanta	15,670
Summit	1,255		
Etowah	300	Total	56,270
Sherman	1,490		

Or 10¾ miles.

	Miles.
Main track	130¾
Sidings	10¾
Total track laid	141½

Bridges.

Name.	Height.	Number of spans.	Length.	Remarks.	Rebuilt.
	Feet.		*Feet.*		*Feet.*
Chickamauga, No. 1	37	2	201	Rebuilt twice	402
Chickamauga, No. 2	16	1	80	....do	160
Chickamauga, No. 3	28	2	221	....do	442
Chickamauga, No. 4	22	2	223	....do	446
Chickamauga, No. 5	16	1	42		
Chickamauga, No. 6	19	1	27		
Chickamauga, No. 7	18	2	256	Rebuilt twice	512
Chickamauga, No. 8	25	2	265	....do	530
Chickamauga, No. 9	18	2	148	....do	296
Chickamauga, No. 10	16	1	136	....do	272
Chickamauga, No. 11	18	1	141		
Chickamauga, No. 12	19	1	124		
Chickamauga, No. 13	12	1	125		
Chickamauga, No. 14	13	1	124		
Buzzard Roost	15	1	87	Rebuilt	87
Old Brewery	15	1	40	....do	40
Tilton	20	1	100	Rebuilt twice	200
Resaca	35	7	842	....do	1,684
Etowah	67	5	598	....do	1,196
Allatoona Creek	18	1	163	....do	326
Near Vining's	35	1	400	Rebuilt	400
Chattahoochee	92	6	780	Rebuilt twice	1,560
Total			5,123		8,553

Total bridging built by Government 13,676 feet, or 2 miles 3,116 feet.

A small portion of this bridging was built by contract amounting to $25,757.63.

Water Stations.

Where built.	Number of tanks.	Where built.	Number of tanks.
Chattanooga	1	Graysville	2
Chickamauga Creek, No. 2	2	Old Brewery	2
Greenwood	2	Resaca	1
Tilton	2	Rogers'	1
Kingston	2	Moon Station	1
Allatoona	1	Atlanta	1
Kenesaw	1		
Tunnel	1	Total	20

The following tabular statement shows the cost of labor performed on this road for construction and maintenance of way and the number of men in the Construction Corps employed each month:

Month.	Construction Corps.		Transportation Department.	Total.
	Number of men.	Amount of pay-rolls.	Amount of pay-rolls.	
1864.				
March	368	$21,974.93	....	$21,974.93
April	458	17,008.75	$4,279.85	21,288.60
May	1,467	91,434.66	7,858.19	99,292.85
June	1,052	52,807.31	12,400.71	65,208.02
July	1,063	67,081.60	17,788.75	34,870.35
August	1,213	50,792.45	18,630.36	69,422.81
September	897	42,516.71	21,180.38	63,697.09
October	2,002	124,588.40	23,902.27	148,490.67
November	1,977	101,578.27	20,182.81	121,761.08
December	....	....	1,447.58	1,447.58
1865.				
January	559	11,960.85	16,282.14	28,242.99
February	106	1,325.00	21,780.46	23,105.46
March	....	....	21,610.49	21,610.49
April	....	....	21,384.34	21,384.34
May	888	44,002.75	28,082.50	72,085.25
June	1,112	85,070.06	29,802.92	114,872.98
July	467	33,353.48	42,272.96	75,826.44
August	364	14,527.60	54,178.22	68,705.82
September	143	3,613.95	23,744.36	27,358.31
Total	14,136	763,936.77	386,809.29	1,150,746.06
Monthly average	642	34,724.40	20,358.38	60,565.58

In the reconstruction of this road in 1865 some work was done on the Atlanta end by order of General Wilson. The cost and description of this work, other than that done by soldiers, was as per settlement of General Winslow and Grant & Co., as follows:

Seven hundred and twenty-five feet bridging over Chattahoochee River, at $11 per lineal foot	$7,965.00
Amount for track laying, as per check-roll	7,167.00
Amount for work done at culvert near Vining's	528.00
Total	15,670.00

Summary of cost.

	Quantity.	Rate.	Total cost.
Materials:			
Iron rails .... tons	9,960	$120 per ton	$1,195,200.00
Chairs .... pounds	566,000	8 cents per pound	45,280.00
Spikes .... do	849,000	8½ cents per pound	72,165.00
Cross-ties	129,000	50 cents per tie	64,500.00
			1,377,145.00
Labor, as per tabular statement			1,150,746.06
Contract work on bridges			25,757.63
Work done by Grant & Co			15,670.00
Total			2,569,318.69

In the above calculation I have deducted the seventeen miles of rails laid by General Wilson, as this was all old and damaged iron.

The Chattanooga and Atlanta Railroad was relinquished as a military road and turned over to the State of Georgia, the original owner, September 25, 1865.

THE NASHVILLE AND CLARKSVILLE RAILROAD

Extends from Nashville to Clarksville, and is sixty-one miles long. It is composed of three links: First, the Louisville and Nashville Railroad from Nashville to Edgefield Junction, ten miles; second, the Edgefield and Kentucky Railroad to the State line, thirty-seven miles; and third, the Memphis, Clarksville and Louisville Railroad to Paris, fourteen miles. On the 4th of August, 1864, I received General Sherman's order directing this road to be opened so as to provide another avenue of supply to the depot at Nashville. Having made the necessary arrangements for carrying on the work at the front during my absence, I took the First Division of the Construction Corps, under L. H. Eicholtz, division engineer, and proceeded to Springfield, where we arrived on the 11th of August. I found the road had been repaired and put in running order from Edgefield Junction to this station by Capt. C. H. Irvin, assistant quartermaster, who was using it to haul lumber from his numerous saw-mills to Nashville. The portion from State line to Clarksville was in running order and being operated by the Louisville and Nashville Railroad Company. Putting the construction force to work at once, I made an examination of the line between Springfield and State line and found the work to be done consisted principally of bridging; the track had not been much damaged. Some of the cuts were so filled up that it required the removal of a good deal of material to clear the track. The bridges destroyed were of considerable magnitude and all the timber for their reconstruction had to be cut and prepared. The work was completed and the road opened through to Clarksville on the 16th of September. The construction force remained on the road until October 16, employed in getting out bridge timber and cross-ties, and grading and laying a track with sidings 6,765 feet long from main line to the levee at Clarksville. On the 25th of October I appointed W. R. Kingsley, division engineer, engineer of construction and repairs, and he continued to occupy this position while we held and operated the road. The cross-ties were badly decayed in places and many had to be taken out and replaced with new ones. On the 4th of March a freshet carried away the Red River bridge and it was rebuilt by the 25th of same month. Another freshet on the 7th of April again carried away this bridge and it was not rebuilt. Still another freshet occurred on the 20th of May, destroying the Sulphur Fork bridge and doing much additional damage to the road, all of which, however, was quickly repaired. The following tabular statement shows the amount of bridging and trestle-work on this road:

Name.	Height.	Length.	Remarks.
	Feet.	*Feet.*	
Springfield	44	410	
Sulphur Fork	60	433	Partly destroyed and rebuilt, 150 feet.
Spring Creek	60	560	
Red River	85	680	Partly destroyed and rebuilt, 300 feet.
Clarksville extension	6-20	900	
Total	....	2,983	

Add to this the amount rebuilt, 450 feet, and we have a total of 3,433 feet bridging and trestle on this road built by Government. The lumber consumed in these structures amounted to 890,000 feet, B. M.

Track laid.

	Feet, linear.
On Edgefield and Kentucky Railroad	2,484
On Clarksville extension	6,065
On side-tracks, Clarksville extension	700
	9,249

Or 1 mile 3,969 feet.

Cross-ties.

About 15,000 cross-ties were cut by the Construction Corps on the line of this road.

Statement of pay-rolls on the Nashville and Clarksville Railroad.

Month.	Number of men.	Amount of pay-rolls.
1864.		
August	502	$23,160.68
September	615	36,538.00
October	614	17,501.39
November	148	7,093.55
December	151	8,457.75
1865.		
January	160	7,878.93
February	206	10,504.46
March	226	13,667.68
April	153	9,151.60
May	91	2,870.00
June	81	3,713.83
July	70	4,360.60
August	73	2,908.30
September	45	649.15
Total	3,135	148,455.92

Summary of cost.

	Quantity.	Rate.	Total cost.
Materials:			
Iron rails ... tons	140	$120 per ton	$16,800.00
Chairs ... pounds	7,000	8 cents per pound	560.00
Spikes ... do	10,000	8½ cents per pound	850.00
			18,210.00
Labor			148,455.92
Total			166,665.92

The Nashville and Clarksville Railroad was relinquished as a military road and turned over to the owners September 25, 1865.

THE KNOXVILLE AND BRISTOL

Or East Tennessee and Virginia Railroad extends from Knoxville to Bristol, 130 miles, with a branch twelve miles long to Rogersville. This road was open during the greater part of 1864 between Knoxville and Strawberry Plains and at one time as far as Bull's Gap. On the 12th of March, 1865, orders were received from General Thomas to open this road to Bull's Gap "and put it in condition to sustain as heavy a business as was done on the Chattanooga and Atlanta line in the summer of 1864." The force sent to do this work reached Strawberry Plains on the 13th of March, and the road was opened to Bull's Gap on the 25th of same month. Orders were then received from

General Thomas to continue the work and open the road to Carter's Station, 110 miles from Knoxville. This point was reached on the 29th of April.

Track.

Extensive repairs were required over the whole distance and 12½ miles of main track and 5,755 feet of sidings were built.

Total track laid, 13 miles 3,115 feet.

Bridges.

Location.	Height.	Length.	Location.	Height.	Length.
	Feet.	*Feet.*		*Feet.*	*Feet.*
Flat Creek			Swan Pond	25	1,393
Strawberry Plains			Chucky Creek, No. 1	25	140
	10	30	Chucky Creek, No. 2	20	100
	12	30	Chucky Creek, No. 3	28	180
Mossy Creek	25	154	Road Crossing	16	75
Morristown		24	Culvert		30
		24			150
		24	Henderson	25	245
Russellville	22	150		35	137
Three miles beyond		40			20
Do		22	Limestone Creek	25	235
Bull's Gap	28	66			
Lick Creek	26	875	Total built by Government		4,168
		24			

Water stations.

Where built.	Number of tanks.
Friend's Station	2
Bull's Gap	2
Morristown	2
Chucky Creek	2
Total	8

The following tabular statement shows the cost of labor for construction and maintenance of way and the number of men in the Construction Corps employed each month:

Month.	Construction Corps.		Transportation Department.	Total.
	Number of men.	Amount of pay-rolls.	Amount of pay-rolls.	
1864.				
June			$2,845.67	$2,845.67
July			4,340.42	4,340.42
August			4,038.88	4,038.88
September			4,928.36	4,928.36
October			5,590.04	5,590.04
November			4,720.18	4,720.18
December			336.52	336.52
1865.				
January			6,808.62	6,808.62
February	875	$18,094.21	7,510.64	25,604.85
March	520	29,129.89	10,011.71	39,141.60
April	546	37,626.21	11,750.39	49,376.60
May	547	4,663.54	15,827.16	20,490.70
June			15,510.70	15,510.70
July			10,818.85	10,818.85
August			769.25	769.25
Total	2,488	89,513.85	105,807.39	195,321.24
Monthly average	622	22,378.43	7,053.82	13,021.41

Summary of cost.

	Quantity.	Rate.	Total cost.
Materials:			
Iron rails .... tons..	1,000	$120 per ton	$120,000.00
Chairs .... pounds..	54,000	8 cents per pound	4,320.00
Spikes .... do....	181,000	8½ cents per pound	15,385.00
Cross-ties	33,750	50 cents per tie	16,875.00
			156,580.00
Labor, as per tabular statement			195,321.24
Total			351,901.24

The East Tennessee and Virginia Railroad was relinquished as a military road and turned over to the company August 28, 1865.

The western end of the Memphis and Charleston Railroad was opened for a longer or shorter distance at various times during 1864 and 1865. Pocahontas Station, seventy-five miles from Memphis, was the farthest point east that was reached at any time. Forty-eight miles of the Mississippi Central Railroad from Grand Junction to Tallahatchie River was opened and used for a short time; but it was operated in connection with the Memphis and Charleston road, and the following statements of cost furnished by the general superintendent, Mr. A. F. Goodhue, includes both roads. But a small portion of the amount is properly chargeable to the Mississippi Central road:

Statement showing cost of labor for each month.

Month.	Amount.	Month.	Amount.
1864.		1865.	
February	$1,167.07	January	$1,499.67
March	1,186.19	February	1,786.68
April	688.54	March	1,789.96
May	738.55	April	5,166.40
June	2,254.33	May	6,439.25
July	3,954.18	June	9,616.34
August	5,115.95	July	10,399.25
September	2,509.50	August	8,492.98
October	2.354.07	September	2,547.57
November	1,540.97		
December	3,645.67	Total	72,893.12
		Monthly average	3,644.15

Summary of cost.

Labor	$72,893.12
Materials	134,194.77
Total	207,087.89

This part of the Memphis and Charleston Railroad was relinquished as a military road and restored to the company September 12, 1865.

The Mobile and Ohio Railroad was opened at the beginning of 1864 to Union City, but was abandoned about the 1st of May. It was reopened to Crockett, thirty-five miles from Columbus, Ky., in May, 1865.

The following statement of cost was furnished by Mr. Goodhue, general superintendent:

Statement showing cost of labor for each month.

Month.	Amount.	Month.	Amount.
1864.		1865.	
February	$389.02	January	$614.50
March	395.06	February	511.00
April	229.50	March	553.50
May	246.17	April	527.75
June	751.43	May	1,789.37
July	1,354.37	June	1,597.21
August	1,254.60	July	....
September	1,198.60	August	598.55
October	1,240.50		
November	1,714.25	Total	16,582.88
December	1,617.50	Monthly average	921.27

Summary of cost.

Labor	$16,582.88
Materials	3,762.44
Total	20,345.32

This road was relinquished as a military road and restored to the company August 25, 1865.

The Atlanta and Macon Railroad from Atlanta to Rough and Ready, eleven miles, was opened for a short time while we held Atlanta. The greater part of this iron was taken up and used for relaying the track destroyed by General Hood on the Chattanooga and Atlanta Railroad in October, 1864.

Recapitulation of cost of materials used and labor performed for construction and maintenance of way on the U. S. military railroads in the Military Division of the Mississippi.

Name of road.	From—	To—	Length.	Bridges built by Government.	Track laid by Government.			Cost.			
					Main track.	Sidings.	Total.	Materials.	Labor.	Contract work.	Total.
			Miles.	*Lin. feet.*	*Miles.*	*Miles.*	*Miles.*				
Nashville and Chattanooga	Nashville	Chattanooga	151	21,727	129.75	19.00	148.75	$1,747,741.00	$1,946,533.62	$385,216.71	$4,079,511.33
Shelbyville Branch *a*	Wartrace	Shelbyville	9								
McMinnville and Manchester *a*	Tullahoma	McMinnville	35								
Nashville and Decatur	Nashville	Decatur Junction	120	24,275	31.50	2.65	34.15	416,480.00	692,835.91	549,326.13	1,658,642.04
Mount Pleasant Branch	Columbia	Mount Pleasant	12								
Memphis and Charleston (Eastern Division).	Stevenson	Decatur Junction	80	4,943	3.50	1.07	4.57	75,685.00	216,308.18	88,442.33	380,435.51
Chattanooga and Knoxville	Chattanooga	Knoxville	112	4,002	35.00	3.38	38.38	542,030.50	506,554.45	161,990.26	1,210,575.21
Cleveland and Dalton Branch. *b*	Cleveland	Dalton	27								
Nashville and Northwestern	Nashville	Johnsonville	78	21,320	46.50	4.25	50.75	489,779.12	798,829.73	182,789.11	1,471,397.96
Chattanooga and Atlanta	Chattanooga	Atlanta	136	13,676	130.75	10.75	141.50	1,377,145.00	1,150,746.06	41,427.63	2,569,318.69
Rome Branch *c*	Kingston	Rome	17								
Atlanta and Macon *d*	Atlanta	Rough and Ready	11								
Nashville and Clarksville	Nashville	Clarksville	62	3,433	1.62	.13	1.75	18,210.00	148,455.92		166,665.92
Knoxville and Bristol	Knoxville	Bristol	110	4,168	12.50	1.09	13.59	156,580.00	195,321.24		351,901.24
Rogersville Branch *e*	Junction	Rogersville	12								
Memphis and Charleston (Western Division).	Memphis	Pocahontas	75					134,194.77	72,893.12		207,087.89
Mississippi Central *f*	Grand Junction	Tallahatchie River	48								
Mobile and Ohio	Columbus, Ky	Crockett, Tenn	35					3,762.44	16,582.88		20,345.32
Louisville City *g*	River landing	Louisville and Nashville Railroad Depot.	2								
Total			1,132	97,544	391.12	42.32	433.44	4,961,607.83	5,745,081.11	1,409,192.17	12,115,881.11

a Cost included in Nashville and Chattanooga Railroad.
b Cost included in Chattanooga and Knoxville Railroad.
c Cost included in Chattanooga and Atlanta Railroad.
d Used but a few days.
e Included in Knoxville and Bristol Railroad.
f Cost included in Memphis and Charleston Railroad (Western Division).
g Taken up by Government.

ROLLING-MILL.

Almost immediately on your arrival at Chattanooga in January, 1864, and even before the railroads in the Military Division of the Mississippi were formally placed in your charge, you advised the building of a Government rolling-mill at that point for the purpose of rerolling the large amount of old and damaged rails that would necessarily come into our possession if the contemplated military movements in that quarter should prove successful. General Grant, appreciating the importance of having an abundant supply of railroad iron, gave his order on the 17th of February for the mill to be built. Steps were at once taken to prepare the necessary materials, all of which were gotten out and the work on the building done by the Construction Corps. The mill was completed and went into operation about the last of March, 1865, which was as soon as the necessary machinery could be manufactured and transported from the North and set up at the works. The following is a statement of the total cost of the mill and buildings connected therewith, together with the railroad leading to it from the Nashville and Chattanooga Railroad. This statement gives the cost of all labor, but it is proper to say that much of this is not strictly chargeable to this work. We were compelled to keep a large force of mechanics and laborers on hand all the time so as to be prepared for any emergency that might arise, and it was only at times when this whole force was not required on the more important work of constructing and maintaining the many railroad lines in and coming into our possession that a portion of the force was detailed for work on the rolling-mill. Actually, the labor on the mill cost the Government nothing.

Cost of rolling-mill building, including engine and boiler house, coal-bin, trestle, tanks, wells, &c.

MATERIAL AND LABOR.

Main building, engine and boiler house, 198,500 feet lumber, B. M., at $30	$5,955.00
253,000 shingles, at $7	1,771.00
87 kegs nails, at $10	870.00
6 tons of strap bolts and suspension rods	900.00
200,000 bricks, at $16	3,200.00
2,500 bushels lime, at 40 cents	1,000.00
Glass and painting	500.00
Hauling stone, masonry, and blacksmithing	6,000.00
Labor—hauling timber, framing, raising, &c., from April 1, 1864, to April 1, 1865	39,957.00
Coal-bin, including trestle-work, 75,000 feet lumber, B. M., at $30	2,250.00
Labor on coal-bin, including bolts and spikes	4,915.00
Excavation of well, including cost of powder	7,430.00
Walling well, tank frame, &c	700.00
Building furnaces and stacks, setting up machinery, &c., including superintendence, to March 31, 1865, as per report of Mr. Yardley	40,905.81
18,000 rations, at 50 cents	9,000.00
	125,857.81

Cost of machinery.

Mr. Yardley's estimate of machinery	$100,000.00
Add 20 per cent. for transportation	20,000.00
	120,000.00

Cost of office buildings.

45,000 feet lumber, B. M., at $30	$1,350.00
30,000 shingles, at $7	210.00
Window frames and sash	100.00
Hardware, glass, &c	190.00
Labor	4,952.00
	6,802.00

Cost of mess-houses (sixteen in all).

95,000 feet lumber, B. M., at $30	$2,850.00
56,000 shingles, at $7	392.00
Hardware, nails, glass, &c	386.00
Labor	9,522.00
14 small houses, including materials, at $90	1,260.00
	14,410.00

Cost of branch railroad to mill, including Y and side-tracks; total length, one mile and two-thirds.

Graduation	$3,000.00
Trestle-work (600 linear feet)	2,000.00
118 tons iron rails	14,750.00
628 chairs (7½ pounds each)	329.70
60 kegs spikes (150 pounds each)	630.00
3,500 cross-ties	1,750.00
Track laying	800.00
	23,259.70

RECAPITULATION.

Rolling-mill building	$125,857.81
Machinery and transportation	120,000.00
Office buildings	6,802.00
Mess-houses	14,410.00
Railroad	23,259.70
Total cost	290,329.51

As previously stated, the mill went into operation about the last of March, or, say, the 1st day of April, and was sold by the Government to John A. Spooner for $175,000, and went into his possession on the 5th of October, 1865. It was therefore in operation a few days over six months while in possession of the Government. The entire amount of T-rail manufactured during this time was 3,818 tons 10 hundred-weight 2 quarters and 8 pounds. The amount of coal charged to these works shows a consumption of 145,897 bushels. This was not all used in manufacturing iron, but considerable of it was used for domestic purposes and in the quartermaster's shops. Charging, however, the whole amount to the cost of manufactured iron makes the entire cost of coal $36,474.25, or $9.55 for one ton of rails. The labor account as per pay-rolls from April 1 to October 5, inclusive, amounts to $98,776.39, or $25.87 per ton of finished rails, thus making the average cost of coal and labor per ton of new rails $35.42. Mr. T. W. Yardley superintended the erection of the mill, and has had charge as superintendent since it went into operation. The Government has been fortunate in securing the services of such a competent person for this position, and one who has so industriously and conscientiously attended to his duties.

NORTH CAROLINA.

On the 28th of December, 1864, while engaged in repairing [the Nashville] and Decatur Railroad, after the defeat of Hood's army at Nashville, I received your order to take one division of the Construction Corps and proceed to Savannah, Ga., to join General Sherman. The division selected for this purpose, together with a force of transportation men, left Nashville for Baltimore on the 4th of January, 1865, fully equipped for any kind of railroad work. They arrived in Baltimore on the 10th, but were detained there eight days, until a vessel could be furnished to take them to their destination. On the 28th they arrived at Hilton Head, but were not disembarked there because General Sherman's plans did not require the reconstruction of any of the railroads leading out of Savannah. On the 29th General Sherman gave me orders to proceed with my men to Morehead City, N. C., and "prepare to make railroad connection to Goldsborough by the middle of March." We left Hilton Head on the 3d and arrived off Morehead City on the 5th of February. The men and supplies were landed next day.

The Atlantic and North Carolina Railroad extends from Morehead City to Goldsborough and is ninety-five miles long. We found this road in running order to Batchelder's Creek, forty-four miles from Morehead City, and being operated by the Quartermaster's Department. As soon as the transfer could be made I took charge of it, and proceeded to put the main track in good repair, extend the sidings, build new water stations, and otherwise prepare for the heavy business which was expected to be done on the road. I appointed J. B. Van Dyne superintendent of transportation and William Cessford master mechanic; E. C. Smeed, division engineer, in charge of the Construction Corps. A small force of the Construction Corps from Virginia, under Mr. McAlpine, were at work on the road when we arrived. They had been sent there by order of General Grant, but considering himself relieved by our arrival, Mr. McAlpine at once returned with his men to Virginia. While here they repaired a few hundred yards of track and almost completed the bridge over Batchelder's Creek. With the exception of some little railroad iron and a few cross-ties, which Mr. McAlpine had brought with him, we found the road almost destitute of materials and tools necessary for the construction and repairs and for operating it. Accordingly requisitions for the necessary amount of these supplies, together with the probable additional amount of rolling-stock that would be required, were at once sent to your office at Washington. Although the railroad department was ready in one week from the time we landed to extend the road from Batchelder's Creek, the advance toward Goldsborough was not commenced until the 3d of March, after General Cox arrived and took command of the column to move from New Berne. The time was profitably employed, however, in the interim by the Construction Corps in getting out cross-ties and bridge timber and cutting wood. From a short distance beyond Batchelder's Creek to Kinston the track had been taken up and most of the rails removed and all the bridges and water stations destroyed. The construction of the railroad kept pace with the advance of the troops, and the supplies were moved by rail from camp to camp each day and unloaded from the main track. This mode of advance and movement of supplies was continued until we reached a point on the railroad opposite and near the battle-field of Wise's Cross-Roads. Here we made a temporary depot which was used until we reached Neuse

River on the 20th of March. The depot was then transferred to that point, from which General Schofield drew the necessary supplies for his army previous to his advance on Goldsborough. The Neuse River bridge was finished on the 23d, and pushing forward both night and day with the work beyond, we reached Goldsborough with the construction train late in the night of the 24th, but in consequence of having to repair a piece of track at the edge of town we did not reach the depot until 3 a. m. on the 25th. General Sherman's army had all reached the place of meeting on the previous day.

The amount of track laid on this road is as follows:

	Feet.	Feet.
Side-track on crib-work	1,000	
Side-track on new wharf	700	
Side-track to commissary store-house	500	
Total sidings at Morehead City		2,200
Siding at Carolina City		1,200
Siding at Wheeler's Station		500
Siding at Havelock Station		1,500
Siding at quartermaster's wood yard		5,280
Siding for crippled cars	500	
Siding to carpenter shop	1,000	
Total sidings at New Berne		1,300
Siding at Batchelder's Creek		1,500
Siding at Tuscarora		1,200
Siding at Core Creek		1,200
Siding at Dover Station		1,200
Siding at Neuse River		1,100
Siding at Goldsborough		2,000
Main line between Batchelder's Creek and Goldsborough, 17 miles and		2,300
Main line over bridges		1,288
Total, 21 miles		2,448

To this amount must be added one mile wide-gauge track for reception of five-feet gauge rolling-stock, which was not landed, making total 22 miles 2,448 feet, for which the Government furnished all the rails, chairs, and spikes, and also all the cross-ties, amounting to 111,100.

Bridges.

The following tabular statement shows the dimensions and amount of material in the bridges built on this line:

Name.	Number of spans.	Height.	Length.	Amount of timber.
		Feet.	*Feet.*	*Feet, B. M.*
Batchelder's Creek	1	17	70	10,500
Core Creek	1	17	100	15,000
Southwest Creek	1	18	85	12,750
Neuse River, No. 1	7	28	863	146,710
Falling Water Creek	1	20	70	10,500
Bear Creek	1	21	100	15,000
Total	......	......	1,288	210,460

Water stations were built at Havelock Station, Batchelder's Creek, Core Creek, Southwest Creek, Kinston Station, Moseley Hall Station, and Goldsborough.

Wharf.

A large wharf was constructed by General Sherman's order at Morehead City, which was of great service in the transshipping of freight for the army at that point. It covered an area of 53,682 square feet, or very nearly one acre and a quarter, and was of sufficient capacity for seven or eight vessels to lie alongside and discharge or receive freight at the same time. Any vessel that could cross the bar could come to the wharf; the depth of water on the bar is fourteen feet and a half. The cost of labor on this piece of work was $32,086, and the amount of lumber consumed 700,000 feet, B. M. A crib-work for an additional track alongside the causeway leading from the wharf to the mainland was built, in which was used 66,000 feet, B. M., of timber. The total cost of labor on the Atlantic and North Carolina Railroad up to June 30, 1865, was $362,366.30. This road was turned over to the company October 5, 1865.

WILMINGTON AND WELDON RAILROAD.

Immediately upon our arrival at Goldsborough the construction force was put to work on this road so as to open up communication with Wilmington, eighty-five miles distant from Goldsborough. This was accomplished on the 4th of April, and trains commenced running through on the same day. The portion of this road north of Goldsborough was not used for military purposes.

Track.

But a small amount of track other than that on the bridges which had been burned was destroyed.

	Feet.
Main track relaid	1,400
Side-track at Northeast	1,000
Total track laid	2,400

The following tabular statement shows the dimensions and the amount of material in the bridges built on this line:

Name.	Number of spans.	Height.	Length.	Amount of lumber.
		Feet.	*Feet.*	*Feet, B. M.*
Neuse River, No. 3	2	40	235	39,950
Northeast River	3	60	372	111,600
Smith's Creek	2	30	272	46,240
Total	......	......	879	197,790

The cost of labor on the Wilmington and Weldon Railroad up to June 30, 1865, amounted to $105,028.05. This road was turned over to the company August 27, 1865.

NORTH CAROLINA RAILROAD.

This road extends from Goldsborough to Charlotte, but we took possession of and used it only as far as Hillsborough, eighty-eight miles from Goldsborough. On the 10th of April General Sherman commenced his march on Raleigh, and on the same day we commenced the work of reconstruction on the railroad. We found the two principal bridges east of Raleigh destroyed and about eight miles of main track torn up, and ties burned, and rails bent in the usual manner. But in addition the enemy had filled up some of the principal cuts with earth, rocks, logs, and brush, hoping thus to prevent the work of reconstruction, or at least retard it so as to interfere with Sherman's plan of pursuit. But their efforts were unsuccessful, for on the 19th the work of reconstruction was completed and we ran into Raleigh on the evening of that day with the construction train, closely followed by two trains loaded with supplies for the army. During the negotiations for Johnston's surrender we ran trains to Durham's Station, and after the surrender we built Flat Creek bridge, ten miles beyond, thus opening the road to Hillsborough, to which point it was used during the time required to parole Johnston's army. The principal business done over it during this time was carrying subsistence stores to the enemy who had just surrendered.

Track.

The track laid is as follows:

	Feet.
Main track	37,960
Side-track at seventh mile post	200
Side-track at Boon Hill	1,500
Main track over bridges	564
Total	40,224

Or 7 miles 3,264 feet.

Bridges.

The following tabular statement shows the dimensions and the amount of material in the bridges on this line:

Name.	Number of spans.	Height.	Length.	Amount of lumber.
		Feet.	*Feet.*	*Feet, B. M.*
Little River	1	31	150	25,500
Neuse River, No. 2	2	38	314	62,800
Flat Creek	1	28	100	10,000
Total	......	......	564	98,300

Water stations

Were built at Little River and at Smithfield Station. The cost of labor on the North Carolina Railroad up to June 30, 1865, amounted to $162,433.86. The portion of this road west of Raleigh was relinquished to the company immediately after the dispersion of General Johnston's army, but the portion between Goldsborough and Raleigh, forty-eight miles in length, was held and operated by the Government until October 22, 1865, when it was also turned over to the company.

RALEIGH AND GASTON RAILROAD.

This road extends from Raleigh to Gaston, but only twenty-five miles of it, the portion from Raleigh to Cedar Creek, was in our possession and this but for a short time. By General Sherman's order I made an arrangement with Doctor Hawkins, the president of the road, for the use of four locomotives and forty cars for Government service as long as they might be required, and in consideration for this loan we built the Cedar Creek bridge. Johnston's surrender and the arrival of more rolling-stock from the North made it unnecessary for us to call on this company for the fulfillment of their part of the contract.

Track.

	Feet.
Main track laid (on Cedar Creek bridge)	600
Side-track (at Cedar Creek bridge)	200
Total	800

Cedar Creek bridge was in four spans, 74 feet high. Total length 532 feet, and contained 319,200 feet, B. M., of timber. This bridge was completed on the 3d of May, and the road never having been formally in our possession, was at once commenced to be operated by the company. The cost of labor on the Raleigh and Gaston Railroad amounted to $12,000.

The following tabular statement shows the cost of labor for construction and maintenance of way on the military railroads in the Department of North Carolina from February 1 to June 30, 1865. I have been unable to obtain a statement of expenses for maintenance of way after Colonel Boyd took charge, but I presume the receipts from passengers and freight were during his administration more than sufficient to pay them:

Month.	Amount.
1865.	
February	$128,377.69
March	191,131.11
April	176,433.86
May	95,740.87
June	50,144.68
Total	641,828.21
Monthly average	128,365.64

This amount is chargeable to the different roads in the following proportion:

Atlantic and North Carolina	$362,366.30
Wilmington and Weldon	105,028.05
North Carolina	162,433.86
Raleigh and Gaston	12,000.00
Total	641,828.21

The cost of materials used on the several roads is given below:

Atlantic and North Carolina Railroad.

	Quantity.	Rate.	Total cost.
Iron rails ... tons..	1,800	$120 per ton	$216,000.00
Chairs ... pounds..	90,000	8 cents per pound	7,200.00
Spikes ... do...	135,000	8½ cents per pound	11,475.00
Total			234,675.00

Wilmington and Weldon Railroad.

	Quantity.	Rate.	Total cost.
Iron rails ... tons..	40	$120 per ton	$4,800.00
Chairs ... pounds..	2,000	8 cents per pound	160.00
Spikes ... do...	3,000	8½ cents per pound	255.00
Total			5,215.00

North Carolina Railroad.

	Quantity.	Rate.	Total cost.
Iron rails ... tons..	620	$120 per ton	$74,400.00
Chairs ... pounds..	31,000	8 cents per pound	2,480.00
Spikes ... do...	46,500	8½ cents per pound	3,952.50
Total			80,832.50

Raleigh and Gaston Railroad.

	Quantity.	Rate.	Total cost.
Iron rails ....tons..	12	$120 per ton........	$1,440.00
Chairs ....pounds..	605	8 cents per pound........	48.40
Spikes ....do....	905	8½ cents per pound........	76.92
Total........	....	....	1,565.32

Recapitulation of cost of material used and labor performed for construction and maintenance of way on the U. S. military railroads in the Department of North Carolina.

Name of road.	From—	To—	Length.	Bridges built by Government.	Track laid by Government.		
					Main track.	Sidings.	Total.
			Miles.	*Lin. feet.*	*Miles.*	*Miles.*	*Miles.*
Atlantic and North Carolina.	Morehead City.	Goldsborough	95	1,288	17.68	4.78	22.46
Wilmington and Weldon.	Wilmington	....do	85	879	.26	.20	.46
North Carolina........	Goldsborough ..	Hillsborough.	88	564	7.30	.32	7.62
Raleigh and Gaston....	Raleigh........	Cedar Creek..	25	532	.10	.05	.15
Total........	....	....	293	3,263	25.34	5.35	30.69

Name of road.	From—	To—	Cost.		
			Materials.	Labor.	Total.
Atlantic and North Carolina.	Morehead City.	Goldsborough	$234,675.00	$362,366.30	$597,041.30
Wilmington and Weldon.	Wilmington	....do	5,215.00	105,028.05	110,243.05
North Carolina........	Goldsborough ..	Hillsborough.	80,832.50	162,433.86	243,266.36
Raleigh and Gaston....	Raleigh........	Cedar Creek..	1,565.32	12,000.00	13,565.32
Total........	....	....	322,287.82	641,828.21	964,116.03

GENERAL REMARKS.

The Construction Corps was an organization created by the necessities of the service. At the beginning of the war no one anticipated the important part that railroads were to play in the various military movements, and it was not until the spring of 1862 that the military railroad organization began to assume a useful shape. The first construction corps was composed of soldiers and was employed in opening the railroad from Aquia Creek to Fredericksburg, and afterward on the Orange and Alexandria Railroad. It was soon found, however, that soldiers were not well suited to this kind of service, and in their stead a small force of skilled civilian mechanics and laborers were employed. It was attempted, in the first place, to arm and drill these men, but after a time this was abandoned, as experience showed that men could not fight and work to advantage at the same time. The value and importance of this working corps was becoming fully known in the East when you took charge of the military railroads in the Southwest. You directed a portion of them to be sent to that new field of operations, and they thus formed the germ of the Construction Corps of the Military Division of the Mississippi, which at one time numbered nearly 6,000 men. The large field over which this corps had to operate and the extraordinary demands made upon the skill and endurance of its members rendered it necessary to make a more thorough organization than had existed in the East, and accordingly the following plan of organization was adopted for a division of the Construction Corps as it existed in the Military Division of the Mississippi:

The number of divisions was increased or diminished to suit the requirements of military movements. The greatest number of divisions at any one time was seven. Each division was under the command of a division engineer, and was divided into subdivisions or sections. A subdivision was under the command of a supervisor. The two largest and most important subdivisions in a division were the track-layers and bridge-builders. Subdivisions were composed of gangs, each under a foreman. Gangs were subdivided into squads, each under a sub-foreman.

Division engineer	1
Assistant engineer	1
Rodman	1
Clerk	1
Messengers	2
Total	6
Subdivision No. 1:	
Supervisor of bridges and carpenter work	1
Clerk and timekeeper	1
Commissary	1
Quartermaster	1
Surgeon	1
Hospital steward	1
Foremen (one for each fifty men)	6
Sub-foremen (one for each ten men)	30
Mechanics and laborers	300
Blacksmith and helper	2
Cooks	12
Total	356
Subdivision No. 2:	
Supervisor of track	1
Clerk and timekeeper	1
Commissary	1
Quartermaster	1
Surgeon	1
Hospital steward	1
Foremen (one for each fifty men)	6
Sub-foremen (one for each ten men)	30
Mechanics and laborers	300
Blacksmith and helper	2
Cooks	12
Total	356
Subdivision No. 3:	
Supervisor of water stations	1
Foreman	1
Mechanics and laborers	12
Cook	1
Total	15
Subdivision No. 4:	
Supervisor of masonry	1
Foreman	1
Masons and helpers	10
Cook	1
Total	13
Subdivision No. 5:	
Foreman of ox brigade	1
Ox drivers	18
Cook	1
Total	20
Train crew:	
Conductors	2
Brakemen	4
Locomotive engineers	2
Firemen	2
Cook	1
Total	11
Grand total	777

The commissaries had charge of drawing, caring for, and issuing rations. The quartermaster had charge of tools, camp equipage, &c. Each foreman was responsible for the tools and other Government property issued to his gang. Each supervisor reported the time made by the men in his subdivision through his division engineer to the chief timekeeper, who was stationed at the headquarters of the chief engineer. The surgeons were appointed by the chief engineer, and were paid out of a private fund voluntarily contributed by the men for hospital purposes. Sub-foremen were appointed by the foremen, subject to the approval of the division engineer. Foremen were appointed by the division engineer, subject to the approval of the chief engineer. Division and assistant engineers were appointed by the chief engineer, subject to the approval of the general manager. Under this organization each division was a complete whole in itself and was ready to move at a moment's notice to any point and do any kind of railroad work. In the early part of 1864 much difficulty was experienced in getting the requisite transportation for construction operations. The number of cars and locomotives was so limited that they were nearly all employed in carrying necessary supplies for the troops, and teams and wagons could not be furnished by the Quartermaster's Department. We were therefore compelled in many cases to carry or draw for long distances by hand bridge timber, cross-ties, and other heavy materials. In this dilemma Colonel Beckwith, chief commissary of subsistence Military Division of the Mississippi, came to our rescue and offered us the use of such cattle out of his droves of beef-cattle as we could train to work. We immediately made a lot of yokes and other necessary fixtures and rigged up several ox teams. The result was so satisfactory that we afterward drew a large number of cattle, and each division of the corps was furnished with about fifty yoke of work oxen. These were of great service in our future operations. And soon after the Atlanta campaign commenced our supply of rolling-stock had increased so much that we were able to get cars and locomotives enough for several construction trains, which were retained as long as wanted. As an instance of the facility with which the Construction Corps moved and its preparation for an emergency, I will mention the movement of the Second Division from Chattanooga to North Carolina via Baltimore, Md., and Savannah, Ga., in January, 1865. This division was at work on the Nashville and Chattanooga Railroad at the time the order was received, but within twenty-four hours it was ready to move, and after the long journey by land and sea in the dead of winter they commenced work on the Morehead City and Goldsborough Railroad within six hours after landing in North Carolina. In no railroad operations during the war was the efficiency of the military railroad organization more fully demonstrated than in North Carolina. We had but five weeks from the time of our arrival in this department in which to accomplish the work necessary to enable us to supply General Sherman's army at Goldsborough "by the middle of March." The various branches of the railroad service had to be thoroughly organized, the requisite men and materials procured from the North, the rolling-stock on hand repaired and put in serviceable condition, 22½ miles of track and 1,288 feet lineal of bridges built, a large wharf on piles built at Morehead City, and a vast amount of other work to be done. All was accomplished by the time appointed, and General Sherman's army more than fully supplied on the 9th of April, one day before the time he had fixed for moving from Goldsborough. The non-arrival of rolling-stock expected from the North left us with but a very limited supply for the large amount of transportation to be done, but by keeping every wheel we had moving night and day, and being so fortunate as not to have a single serious accident to our trains, we were enabled to get through. From the 25th of April to the 9th of May nearly 3,000 cars loaded with supplies of various kinds were forwarded from the coast to the army lying around Goldsborough. For this service we had up to April 1 five locomotives and eighty-seven cars, and after that date one more locomotive, but the same number of cars.

In conclusion, I again wish to bear full testimony to the valuable services rendered by my assistants, both in the Military Division of the Mississippi and in North Carolina. The following is a list of the principal officers: Military Division of the Mississippi—L. H. Eicholtz, division engineer, First Division, and acting chief engineer during my absence in North Carolina; Col. John Clark, in charge of construction Nashville and Northwestern Railroad; E. C. Smeed, division engineer, Second Division; John F. Burgin, division engineer, Fourth Division; W. R. Kingsley, division engineer, Fifth Division; Charles Latimer, division engineer, Seventh Division; William McDonald, assistant engineer, Third Division; M. E. Hart, chief clerk in chief engineer's office; M. B. Saul, chief timekeeper. North Carolina—J. B. Van Dyne, superintendent of transportation; E. C. Smeed, division engineer until May 1, 1865, and afterward resident engineer military railroads North Carolina; S. O. Bull, assistant engineer; William Cessford, master mechanic; H. M. Zook, chief clerk in office of chief engineer and general superintendent.

Several of the supervisors deserve special mention, and it gives me pleasure to name H. H. Rozelle, supervisor bridges, First Division; George Crisman, supervisor bridges, Second Division; G. J. Speer, supervisor, Third Division; A. R. Moore, supervisor carpenters, Fourth Division; H. E. Gray, supervisor track, First Division; O. W. Clough, supervisor track, Second Division; T. J. Bones, supervisor track, Third Division; I. N. Carroll, supervisor track, Seventh Division; H. J. Bradford, supervisor saw-mills; Frank McGorvin, supervisor wharf construction. To many of the officers of the Army I am indebted for valuable assistance and efficient co-operation in all our labors, but more especially to Generals Beckwith and Easton, chief commissary of subsistence and chief quartermaster, Military Division of the Mississippi.

I have the honor to be, very respectfully, your obedient servant,

W. W. WRIGHT,
Chief Engineer Military Railroads United States.

U. S. MILITARY RAILROADS, DIVISION OF THE MISSISSIPPI.

Report of lumber sawed at the mills operated by the Construction Corps.

MILL AT LOUDON.

Month.	Description of lumber.					Shingles.
	Plank.	Timber.	Boards.	Scantling.	Total.	
1864.	*Feet.*	*Feet.*	*Feet.*	*Feet.*	*Feet.*	*Number.*
June					*a* 29,000	
July	50,000	17,000	40,000		107,000	
August	68,000	23,000	12,400		103,400	
September	37,000	42,500	26,000		105,500	
October	38,332	58,000	87,632		183,964	
November	28,000	5,400	105,000		138,400	
December	8,500	4,100	85,400		98,000	
1865.						
January	17,000		65,000	15,000	97,000	
February	68,450	15,650	24,500		108,600	
March	1,000	39,477	17,000		57,477	
April	12,643		70,705		83,348	
May	13,689		83,153		96,842	
Total	342,614	205,127	616,790	15,000	1,208,531	

MILL AT LENOIR.

Month.	Plank.	Timber.	Boards.	Scantling.	Total.	Shingles.
1864.						
June					*a* 879,444	
July	60,000		65,903	2,662	128,565	87,250
August	134,366			16,943	151,309	86,500
September	76,305		30,798	19,583	126,686	133,250
October			85,353	21,558	106,911	142,405
November			75,539		75,539	191,950
December			80,348		80,348	260,250

a Assorted.

Report of lumber sawed at the mills operated by the Construction Corps—Cont'd.

MILL AT LENOIR—Continued.

Month.	Description of lumber.					Shingles.
	Plank.	Timber.	Boards.	Scantling.	Total.	
1865.	*Feet.*	*Feet.*	*Feet.*	*Feet.*	*Feet.*	*Number.*
January			76,683		76,683	144,750
February	23,430	15,643	32,266		71,339	113,500
March	21,750		50,465		72,215	108,500
April	22,000	13,765	23,366		59,131	157,000
May	14,116		61,194		75,310	122,000
Total	351,967	29,408	581,915	60,746	1,903,480	1,547,355

MILL AT CHARLESTON.

Month.	Plank.	Timber.	Boards.	Scantling.	Total.	Shingles.
1864.						
June					a 135,000	
July	14,000		35,000		49,000	
August	25,000		35,000		60,000	
September	24,000		34,000		58,000	
October			50,000		50,000	
November			51,873		51,873	
December	30,000		20,000		50,000	
1865.						
January	15,359		35,000	5,000	55,359	
February	8,000		12,000	6,729	26,729	
March	3,713	3,238	23,278		30,229	
April	7,735	3,031	22,891		33,657	
May	24,279		55,495		79,774	
Total	152,086	6,269	374,537	11,729	679,621	

MILL AT CHICKAMAUGA.

Month.	Plank.	Timber.	Boards.	Scantling.	Total.	Shingles.
1864.						
June					a 149,886	
July	50,000		40,000	15,000	105,000	
August	40,011		42,280	14,464	96,755	
September	41,000		43,000	15,000	99,000	
October			34,000	20,000	54,000	
November	11,916		36,194		48,110	
December	17,972		49,683	3,090	70,745	
1865.						
January	30,799		106,786	2,242	139,827	
February	30,476		31,754	72,519	134,749	
March	20,537		32,623	71,989	125,149	
April	14,019		36,955	58,336	109,310	
May	10,283		55,598	10,261	76,142	
Total	267,013		508,873	282,901	1,208,673	

MILL AT CHATTANOOGA.

Month.	Plank.	Timber.	Boards.	Scantling.	Total.	Shingles.
1864.						
November	12,543		35,488		48,031	
December	50,000	10,000	40,000	20,232	120,232	
1865.						
January	13,264		50,000	10,000	73,264	
February	20,000		15,000	5,850	40,850	
March	40,000		98,987		138,987	
April	40,514	300	68,839	3,000	112,653	
May	15,000	4,277	72,651	2,206	94,134	
Total	191,321	14,577	380,965	41,288	628,151	

a Assorted.

Report of lumber sawed at the mills operated by the Construction Corps—Cont'd.

RECAPITULATION.

Location of mill.	Description of lumber, &c.						
	Plank.	Timber.	Boards.	Scantling.	Assorted.	Total.	Shingles.
	Feet.	*Feet.*	*Feet.*	*Feet.*	*Feet.*	*Feet.*	*Number.*
Loudon	342,614	205,127	616,790	15,000	29,000	1,208,531	....
Lenoir	351,967	29,408	581,915	60,746	879,444	1,903,480	1,547,355
Charleston	152,086	6,269	374,537	11,729	135,000	679,621	....
Chickamauga	267,013	....	508,873	282,901	149,886	1,208,673	....
Chattanooga	191,321	14,577	380,965	41,288	....	628,151	....
Total	1,305,001	255,381	2,463,080	411,664	1,193,330	5,628,456	1,547,355

Cost of labor in manufacturing the above amount of lumber, $163,104.90.

Exhibit relative to the volunteer forces of the U. S. Army.

Department.	Remaining as per exhibit of March 27.			Since ordered mustered out.			Will remain when musters out as ordered shall have been completed.		
	White.	Colored.	Aggregate.	White.	Colored.	Aggregate.	White.	Colored.	Aggregate.
East *a*	791	....	791	490	....	490	301	....	301
Middle *a*	1,169	....	1,169	1,010	....	1,010	159	....	159
Washington *a*	1,714	739	2,453	1,421	27	1,448	293	712	1,005
Ohio *a*	1,285	843	2,128	1,126	....	1,126	159	....	159
Kentucky *b*	....	2,398	2,398	....	2,398	2,398	....	....	....
Missouri *c*	....	....	....	....	....	....	....	*d* 843	843
Virginia *e*	....	....	....	....	....	....	....	....	....
North Carolina *f*	870	806	1,676	....	....	....	870	806	1,676
South Carolina *f*	1,991	781	2,772	250	....	250	1,741	781	2,522
Georgia *g*	621	820	1,441	621	820	1,441	....	....	....
Mississippi *g*	1,071	3,712	4,783	1,071	3,712	4,783	....	....	....
Alabama *g*	2,450	721	3,171	2,450	721	3,171	....	....	....
Tennessee *g*	....	4,208	4,208	....	4,208	4,208	....	....	....
Arkansas *f*	....	2,908	2,908	....	....	....	....	2,908	2,908
Florida *f*	....	*h* 487	487	....	....	....	....	*h* 815	815
Louisiana *i*	1,422	4,660	6,082	871	197	1,068	551	4,463	5,014
Texas *i*	3,681	7,134	10,815	3,681	1,142	4,823	....	5,992	5,992
California / Columbia } *j*	....	....	....	....	....	....	2,000	....	2,000
Total	17,065	30,217	47,282	12,991	13,225	26,216	6,074	17,320	23,394

a Musters out completed. The white troops remaining are of the Veteran Reserve Corps and two and three years' men of Hancock's corps.
b Musters out completed.
c Musters out of number to be discharged. Statement of March 27 will be completed by June 10.
d Transferred from the Department of the Ohio.
e Completed.
f Completed so far as ordered.
g Musters out well advanced; will be completed, so far as now known, by June 5.
h Strength of 82d U. S. Colored Troops, that regiment having been kept instead of 99th (strength 487) as per report of March 27.
i Musters out will be completed by June 5.
j Dropped on return of March 27 and taken up on this, as it is believed circumstances have prevented the musters out.

THOMAS M. VINCENT,
Assistant Adjutant-General.

WAR DEPARTMENT, ADJUTANT-GENERAL'S OFFICE,
May 15, 1866.

OFFICE DIRECTOR AND GENERAL MANAGER
MILITARY RAILROADS UNITED STATES,
Washington, D. C., May 26, 1866.

Bvt. Maj. Gen. M. C. MEIGS,
Quartermaster-General U. S. Army, Washington, D. C.:

GENERAL: I have the honor to submit the following report upon the military railroads of the United States under my charge during the war:

On the 11th day of February, 1862, I received the following order:

WAR DEPARTMENT,
Washington City, D. C., February 11, 1862.

Ordered, That D. C. McCallum be, and he is hereby, appointed military director and superintendent of railroads in the United States, with authority to enter upon, take possession of, hold, and use all railroads, engines, cars, locomotives, equipments, appendages, and appurtenances that may be required for the transport of troops, arms, ammunition, and military supplies of the United States, and to do and perform all acts and things that may be necessary and proper to be done for the safe and speedy transport aforesaid.

By order of the President, Commander-in-Chief of the Army and Navy of the United States:

EDWIN M. STANTON,
Secretary of War.

Upon assuming the duties indicated by the above order I found only one railroad in possession of the Government—that from Washington to Alexandria, seven miles long, and in charge of Capt. R. F. Morley, acting assistant quartermaster.

Under an order from the War Department, dated January 10, 1862, the track had been relaid with new T-rails, the entire road bed repaired, and a track laid across Long Bridge over the Potomac River. Previously all passengers and freight had been transferred across the bridge by horse power. In Alexandria the tracks had been laid through the city to form a junction with the Orange and Alexandria Railroad. The road was used regularly and continuously without interruption from this time forward until the close of the war, and on the 7th day of August, 1865, was surrendered to the Alexandria, Washington and Georgetown Railroad Company. During the period of its military occupation the value of construction and repairs made upon it not properly chargeable to the cost of operation amounted to $107,328.88. The transportation from February 9, 1862, to August 7, 1865, three years five months twenty-eight days, was as follows: Number of engines run over the road for other than local construction purposes, 8,983; number of loaded cars, 30,457; number of empty cars, 20,699; total number of cars, 51,156.

In March, 1862, Major-General McClellan instructed me to have a line examined for a railroad from Winchester—the terminus of the Harper's Ferry and Winchester Railroad—to Strasburg, a station of the Manassas Gap Railroad, in the Shenandoah Valley, and to make an estimate of the cost. This was completed early in April, but the railroad was not built. March 14, 1862, General McClellan instructed me to have five locomotives and eighty cars loaded upon vessels in the harbor of Baltimore and held subject to his orders with a view to using them in his contemplated Peninsular campaign. They were purchased from Northern railroad companies, loaded as directed, and remained on the vessels until early in May, when they were sent to White House, Va., and placed upon the Richmond and York River Railroad. Another engine was added in June to the number, and all employed in transporting supplies between White House and the front, which, toward the close of June, was twenty miles from White House and four miles from Richmond. Upon the withdrawal of the Army of the Potomac to Harrison's Landing, June 28, all the rolling-stock was destroyed or damaged as far as practicable to prevent it from falling into the hands of the enemy.

Near the close of March, 1862, the Orange and Alexandria Railroad was opened to Manassas Junction, twenty-six miles from Alexandria, and in April to Warrenton Junction, thirty-nine miles. In August, after relaying six miles of track and bridging Rappahannock River, the road was open to Culpeper, sixty-one miles, which at the time was the main depot of supplies for the Army of Virginia. A few trains were run to the Rapidan River, eighty miles. Upon the retreat of General Pope in the last days of August the road was entirely abandoned, with the loss of 7 locomotives and 295 cars. In November it was reopened for a few days to Bealeton, forty-six miles, and to the town of Warrenton, to supply the Army of the Potomac on its march from Antietam to Fredericksburg.

The Manassas Gap Railroad was opened early in April, 1862, to Strasburg, sixty-one miles from Manassas and eighty-seven miles from Alexandria. It was operated only a very short time to Strasburg, but continued in use to Front Royal, fifty-one miles from Manassas, through May and part of June, when it was abandoned. In November, 1862, trains were run over it to Front Royal for a few days with supplies for General McClellan's army.

The Alexandria, Loudoun and Hampshire Railroad was opened in the spring of 1862 to Vienna, fifteen miles from Alexandria, and used for transporting supplies to the fortifications south of Washington and the camps along its line. During the first two weeks of September it was the principal line of supply for the Army of the Potomac when encamped near Washington after the second battle of Bull Run and previous to the Antietam campaign.

These four railroads comprise all that were operated as military lines from Alexandria and Washington. They were subsequently used more or less at various times, as will be mentioned hereafter, and continued to play an important part in the operations of the Army of the Potomac.

In April, 1862, the Richmond, Fredericksburg and Potomac Railroad was opened from Aquia Creek to Fredericksburg, fifteen miles, and operated to supply the forces stationed at Fredericksburg. The road was abandoned September 7, with the loss of one engine, fifty-seven cars, and a small quantity of material.

On the 18th of November repairs were again commenced, and the road was opened on the 28th to Falmouth, opposite Fredericksburg, and was used to supply the Army of the Potomac until June, 1863. A very large amount of work was required not only to the railroad, but to the wharves at Aquia Creek, all of which had been burned when this line was abandoned by our forces.

The limited accommodations for receiving and delivering freight and passengers at Aquia rendered an increase of wharf room and tracks necessary, and a new wharf, afterward named "Yuba Dam," was completed in February, one mile below Aquia Creek wharf, and the necessary tracks laid from the main road to it. Vessels drawing ten feet and a half of water could land at the new wharf at low tide, while there was only eight and a half feet at high water at the old one. This improvement proved to be a valuable acquisition to the means of supplying the army. The road continued to be used without interruption until June, 1863, when it was abandoned with small loss of material, but the bridges, buildings, and wharves were soon afterward burned by the enemy.

The eastern portion of the Norfolk and Petersburg Railroad was taken in charge July 22, 1862, and the gauge at once changed from five feet to four feet eight and one-half inches for forty-four miles. At Suffolk, twenty-three miles from Norfolk, this line crosses the Seaboard and Roanoke Railroad running from Portsmouth, opposite Norfolk. A connecting track was laid between the two roads in August, 1862, and these lines were afterward operated together.

In May, 1863, about fifteen miles of track was taken up on the Norfolk and Petersburg Railroad west of Suffolk by order of Major-General Dix, and about the same length on the Seaboard and Roanoke. The two roads were afterward operated to Suffolk until the close of the war, for local military purposes, and were not identified with any of the great military operations or campaigns. From July 22, 1862, to June 30, 1863, the transportation over them was as follows: Troops, 107,359 men; quartermaster's stores, 23,757 tons; subsistence stores, 9,043 tons; ordnance stores, 2,353 tons; total stores, 35,153 tons.

In April, 1863, the Orange and Alexandria Railroad was opened to Bealeton and used a few days to supply a force on the Rappahannock. The portion south of Bull Run was then abandoned, and about the 15th of June the whole road outside the defenses of Washington was evacuated.

July 18 repairs were recommenced and continued till the road was opened to Culpeper. Not having been much damaged by the enemy, the amount of work necessary to put it in running order was small. It was used until the 1st of October to supply the army of General Meade after its return to Virginia from the Gettysburg campaign.

Early in October it was again abandoned south of Bull Run, and was thoroughly destroyed by the enemy from Manassas Junction nearly to Brandy Station, about twenty-two miles. Repairs were commenced October 23, and the damaged road opened October 30 to Warrenton Junction, eleven miles, and to Culpeper November 16, to which point it was operated during the winter and until the final advance under Lieutenant-General Grant of the Army of the Potomac May 4, 1864, when it was abandoned beyond Burke's Station, fourteen miles from Alexandria.

Rappahannock River bridge, 625 feet long and 35 feet high, was rebuilt in nineteen working hours. The Army of the Potomac remained in winter quarters on the south side of the Rappahannock and received all its supplies for men and animals during the winter and spring over this single-track road.

The Manassas Gap Railroad was reopened to White Plains, twenty-three miles from Manassas, in August, 1863, and used for a few days to deliver supplies for General Meade's army on the march from Gettysburg to Culpeper.

On the 2d day of July, 1863, military possession was taken of the Western Maryland Railroad from Baltimore to Westminster, in Maryland, thirty-six miles, which, from its position, had become the line of supplies for the army of General Meade at Gettysburg. Sufficient locomotives, cars, fuel, supplies, and men to operate it were brought from the military railroads of Virginia, the equipment belonging to the road itself being wholly inadequate. The road was restored to the owners July 7, the army having moved to the line of the Baltimore and Ohio Railroad.

July 9, 1863, full military possession was taken of the railroad from Hanover Junction to Gettysburg, thirty miles, and it was operated as a military line until August 1 to remove the wounded from the field of battle to distant hospitals. During military occupation about 15,580 wounded men were transported over it. The equipment and men for this work were likewise furnished from the military railroads of Virginia.

During the rebel occupation of Central Pennsylvania in June all the bridges were destroyed by them on the Northern Central Railroad between Hanover Junction and Harrisburg, and several miles of track torn up on the Cumberland Valley and Franklin Railroads between Harrisburg and Hagerstown, Md. The Virginia military railroad construction corps rebuilt the bridges of the Northern Central Railroad. The materials for the same were furnished from the Government yard at Alexandria, Va. The railroad company afterward returned an equal quantity of material, the lumber amounting to 150,000 feet, B. M. The same construction corps also relaid a portion of the damaged track of the Cumberland Valley and Franklin Railroads.

As the war progressed the nature, capacity, and value of railroads were better understood on both sides, and more systematic and determined efforts were made by the enemy against the lines used for transporting supplies to our armies. The destruction of track and bridges was greater each subsequent time the roads passed within their military lines, and it became apparent that extraordinary preparations must be made to meet it. Early in 1863 a small construction corps was formed, consisting of about 300 men, which was the beginning of an organization afterward numbering in the East and West nearly 10,000. The design of the corps was to combine a body of skilled workmen in each department of railroad construction and repairs, under competent engineers, supplied with abundant materials, tools, mechanical appliances, and transportation. They were formed into divisions, gangs, and squads, in charge, respectively, of supervisors, foremen, and sub-foremen, furnished with tents and field equipment. Store-houses were established at principal points, with an ample stock of tools and materials.

With the opening of the campaign in Virginia in May, 1864, under Lieutenant-General Grant, the Alexandria railroads ceased to bear any important part. The Orange and Alexandria line was opened to Rappahannock River, fifty miles, between September 28 and October 2, 1864, but at once abandoned back to Manassas. It was operated to that station until November 10, when it was abandoned back to Fairfax, sixteen miles from Alexandria. It was operated for that distance until the close of the war, and June 27, 1865, was surrendered to the Board of Public Works of Virginia.

The Manassas Gap Railroad was opened from Manassas to Piedmont, thirty-four miles, between October 3 and 11, and operated until

October 27, 1864. Between that date and November 10 the rails were taken up between the above-named stations and carried to Alexandria.

On the 9th of May, 1864, repairs were again commenced on the railroad at Aquia Creek, and it was opened to Falmouth, fourteen miles, May 17. Potomac Creek bridge, seven miles from Aquia, 414 feet long and 82 feet high, was built ready for trains to pass in forty working hours. The road was operated until May 22 principally for removing the wounded of the battles at Spotsylvania Court-House. On that day it was abandoned and not afterward used as a military line.

The Richmond and York River Railroad was opened about the 1st of June from White House to Dispatch, fourteen miles, and operated until June 10, when it was finally abandoned, the track taken up by order of Lieutenant-General Grant, and the materials removed to Alexandria.

Rolling-stock for the Aquia Creek and York River Railroads was sent from Alexandria on barges prepared with tracks for the purpose and taken away in the same manner, without loss or injury, when the roads were abandoned.

Near the close of June, 1864, the City Point and Petersburg Railroad was occupied to Pitkin Station, eight miles from City Point. During the fall and winter of 1864–'65 eighteen miles of new railroad were built, passing around to the south and southwest of the city of Petersburg, by which the armies of General Grant were principally supplied.

The Richmond and Petersburg Railroad was opened April 4, 1865, from Petersburg to the south bank of James River, opposite Richmond, twenty-one miles, and was operated by this department until July 3, when it was turned over to the Virginia Board of Public Works.

The Petersburg and Lynchburg Railroad was repaired between April 4 and 11 to Burkeville, sixty-two miles from City Point, and used for a short time to supply the armies of General Meade and the paroled soldiers of General Lee's army. The gauge originally was five feet, but not having proper rolling-stock at hand it was changed to four feet eight inches and a half. It was operated as a military road until July 24, when it was turned over to the Board of Public Works.

Shortly after the surrender of General Johnston's army the Richmond and Danville Railroad was opened to Danville, 140 miles, and operated for military purposes until July 4, 1865, when it also was surrendered to the Board of Public Works.

The Winchester and Potomac Railroad was repaired from Harper's Ferry to Halltown, six miles, between August 14 and 19, 1864; to Stephenson's, twenty-eight miles, between November 2 and 24, and was used to supply the army of General Sheridan, operating in the Valley of Virginia. The iron used in the reconstruction of this line was principally that taken from the Manassas Gap Railroad. The bridges were all rebuilt. The road remained in charge of this department until January 20, 1866, when it was restored to the railroad company.

The railroads in Virginia, Maryland, and Pennsylvania used at any time during the war as military lines, the terminal stations on each while so used, and number of miles operated were as follows:

Names of lines.	Terminal stations.		Length.
	From—	To—	
			Miles.
Alexandria and Washington	Alexandria	Washington	7
Alexandria, Loudoun and Hampshire	....do	Vienna	15
Orange and Alexandria	....do	Mitchell's	68
Warrenton Branch	Warrenton Junction	Warrenton	9
Manassas Gap	Manassas	Strasburg	62
Richmond, Fredericksburg and Potomac	Aquia Creek	Fredericksburg	15
Richmond and York River	White House	Fair Oaks	20
Richmond and Petersburg	Manchester	Petersburg	22
Clover Hill Branch	Clover Hill	Coal Mines	18
Richmond and Danville	Manchester	Danville	140
South Side	City Point	Burkeville	62
Army Line and branches	Pitkin, &c	Humphreys, &c	18
Norfolk and Petersburg	Norfolk	Blackwater	44
Seaboard and Roanoke	Portsmouth	Suffolk	17
Winchester and Potomac	Harper's Ferry	Stephenson's	28
Western Maryland	Baltimore	Westminster	36
Hanover Branch and Gettysburg	Hanover Junction	Gettysburg	30
Total			611

The following tabular statements exhibit—

1. The number of persons employed, the greatest number employed in any one month of each year, the average monthly number for the year, and amount paid for their services.

2. The number of locomotive engines, how procured, number added each year, and final disposition made of them.

3. The number of cars, &c.

4. The length of bridges and track built or rebuilt.

1. *Number of persons employed and amount paid for services.*

Year ending—	Persons employed monthly.		Amount paid for services.
	Greatest number in one month.	Average number in one month.	
June 30, 1862	1,730	750	$345,743.50
June 30, 1863	2,721	1,974	777,628.31
June 30, 1864	3,160	2,378	1,277,968.34
June 30, 1865	4,542	3,060	2,296,145.73
Nine months ending March 31, 1866	1,360	417	162,475.07
Total	4,542	1,906	4,859,960.95

2. *Locomotive engines provided and final disposition made of them.*

Year.	Locomotives procured.				Locomotives disposed of.				
						Sold—			
	Purchased.	Built.	Captured.	Total.	Lost or destroyed in service or in transit.	For cash.	To Southern railroads under Executive orders of Aug. 8 and Oct. 14.	Returned to former owners.	Total.
1862	48	1	5	54	2	......	......	......	2
1863	18	......	......	18	......	3	......	......	3
1864	......	......	......	......	......	9	......	......	9
1865	......	......	......	......	......	51	......	3	54
1866	......	......	......	......	......	4	......	......	4
Total	66	1	5	72	2	67	......	3	72

3. *Cars provided and final disposition made of them.*

Year.	Cars procured.				Cars disposed of.				
						Sold—			
	Purchased.	Built.	Captured.	Total.	Lost or destroyed in service or in transit.	For cash.	To Southern railroads under Executive orders of Aug. 8 and Oct. 14.	Returned to former owners.	Total.
1862	503	......	13	516	458	......	......	......	458
1863	704	......	......	704	15	10	......	......	25
1864	68	30	......	98	57	126	......	......	183
1865	415	......	......	415	20	958	38	13	1,029
1866	......	......	......	......	......	38	......	......	38
Total	1,690	30	13	1,733	550	1,132	38	13	1,733

In addition to the rolling-stock belonging to the department, in cases of emergency the railroads north of Washington were freely drawn upon for a supply, particularly in the early part of the war.

4. *The length of bridges and track built or rebuilt.*

The total length of bridges built and rebuilt upon the Virginia railroads, including those rebuilt in 1863 in Maryland and Pennsylvania, was as follows:

Trestle or temporary bridges, 33,336 linear feet; truss or permanent bridges, 1,595 linear feet; total, 34,931 linear feet, or 6 miles 3,251 feet.

The total length of track laid upon the same railroads was 177 miles 2,961 feet. During the war and after its close 128 miles 5,163 feet were taken up.

The following is a list of the principal officers of military railroads of Virginia during the war:

1862.—J. H. Devereux, superintendent railroads running from Alexandria; E. L. Wentz, engineer of repairs railroads running from Alexandria; J. J. Moore, engineer of repairs railroads running from Alexandria; A. Anderson, engineer of repairs railroads running from Alexandria; W. W. Wright, engineer and superintendent Aquia Creek Railroad; E. L. Wentz, engineer and superintendent Richmond and York River Railroad; E. L. Wentz, engineer and superintendent Norfolk railroads.

1863.—J. H. Devereux, superintendent Alexandria railroads; J. J. Moore, engineer of repairs Alexandria railroads; W. W. Wright, engineer and superintendent Aquia Creek Railroad; E. L. Wentz, engineer and superintendent Norfolk railroads; A. Anderson, chief engineer military railroads of Virginia; J. B. Clough, construction engineer military railroads of Virginia.

1864.—E. L. Wentz, chief engineer and general superintendent military railroads of Virginia to November 1; J. J. Moore, chief engineer and general superintendent military railroads of Virginia after November 1; M. J. McCrickett, superintendent Alexandria railroads to October 10; P. McCallum, superintendent Alexandria railroads after October 10; P. McCallum, superintendent Norfolk railroads to October 10; H. F. Woodward, superintendent Norfolk railroads after October 10; G. M. Huntington, superintendent City Point railroads; C. L. McAlpine, engineer of repairs City Point railroads; J. G. Beggs, superintendent Harper's Ferry railroad (Winchester and Potomac).

1865.—J. J. Moore, chief engineer and general superintendent military railroads of Virginia; P. McCallum, superintendent Alexandria railroads to March 10; W. H. McCafferty, superintendent Alexandria railroads after March 10; G. M. Huntington, superintendent City Point railroads; C. L. McAlpine, engineer City Point railroads to May 1; T. D. Hays, engineer City Point railroads after May 1; H. F. Woodward, superintendent Norfolk railroads to March 1; P. B. Tompkins, superintendent Norfolk railroads after March 1; O. H. Dorrance, superintendent Harper's Ferry railroad to April 20; D. T. Shaw, superintendent Harper's Ferry railroad after April 20; O. H. Dorrance, superintendent Richmond and Danville Railroad.

MILITARY RAILROADS OF THE SOUTHWEST.

In obedience to War Department Special Orders, No. 562, dated December 19, 1863, paragraph 33, I proceeded to Tennessee and examined the condition of the railroad lines operated to supply the armies then encamped in the vicinity of Chattanooga, and submitted the following report:*

The following order was received on the 4th of February, 1864.†

Upon assuming the duties thus imposed I found most inadequate means to accomplish the purposes for which the railroads had been opened. The main army was at Chattanooga and in its vicinity, and all its supplies for men and food for its animals were received from Nashville, 151 miles distant, over the Nashville and Chattanooga Railroad. This road was necessarily the main line of supply during the subsequent campaigns from Chattanooga toward Atlanta, and from

*See Series I, Vol. XXXII, Part II, p. 143. †*Ibid.*, p. 329.

Knoxville toward Southwestern Virginia, and at this time was in the worst condition. The track was laid originally on an unballasted mud roadbed in a very imperfect manner, with a light U-rail on wooden stringers, which were badly decayed, and caused almost daily accidents by spreading apart and letting the engines and cars drop between them. The total length of the roads in use was as follows:

	Miles.
Nashville to Chattanooga	151
Nashville (south) to Dark's Mill	39
Stevenson to Huntsville	60
Chattanooga to Charleston	42
Total	292

Upon examination it was found there was on the above roads the following rolling-stock:

Forty-seven U. S. Military Railroad locomotives that could be made available, 3 locomotives borrowed from Louisville and Nashville Railroad; total, 50 locomotives, of which 11 were disabled and in the shop for repairs, leaving fit for service 39.

Four hundred and thirty-seven U. S. Military Railroad freight-cars, about 100 cars borrowed from Louisville and Nashville Railroad; total, 537 cars, of which 400 hundred were in running order, the remainder being disabled.

My attention was first directed to the most efficient organization of the men employed. Two distinct departments were projected—the "transportation department," embracing the operation and maintenance of all the lines in use, and the "construction corps," for the reconstruction of the railroads which might fall into our hands as the army advanced.

The following orders and instructions* were issued to the principal officers in charge of these respective organizations:

GENERAL ORDERS, No. 1. } OFFICE GEN. MGR. MIL. RAILROADS UNITED STATES, *Nashville, February 10, 1864.*

A. Anderson is hereby appointed general superintendent of transportation and maintenance of roads in use, and W. W. Wright chief engineer of construction, in the Military Division of the Mississippi. They will be respected accordingly.

D. C. McCALLUM,
Colonel, U. S. Army, General Manager Railroads United States.

Approved.

U. S. GRANT,
Major-General.

The transportation department embraced the following divisions of sub-departments:

First. Conducting transportation or managing the movements of trains.

Second. Maintenance of road and structures, or keeping the roadway, bridges, buildings, and other structures in repair; building new structures; rebuilding old ones when and where necessary.

Third. Maintenance of rolling-stock, keeping in order the locomotives and cars, and managing the shops where such work was done.

For conducting transportation each principal line was operated by a superintendent of transportation, who was held responsible for the movement of all trains and engines over it.

Subordinate to the superintendent were one or more masters of transportation, according to distance operated, who were constantly

*See McCallum to Anderson and McCallum to Wright, Series I, Vol. XXXII, Part II, pp. 371, 372.

moving over the road to see that the employés attended properly to their duties while out with their trains. At principal stations where locomotives were changed or kept in reserve an engine dispatcher was stationed to see that the locomotives were in good order for service; that they were properly repaired and cleaned when at the station; to supervise and control the engineers and firemen, and to assign the requisite crews to engines.

Maintenance of road and structures for each line was in charge of a superintendent of repairs, with the necessary supervisors, road-masters, foremen, &c.

Maintenance of rolling-stock was in charge, respectively, of the master machinist, who managed repairs of locomotives, and the master of car repairs, under whose charge all repairs to cars were made.

The above officers were independent of each other and reported directly to the general superintendent.

The maximum force employed at any one time in the transportation department of the Military Division of the Mississippi was about 12,000 men. The following is the organization in detail:

General superintendent's office—General superintendent, assistant general superintendent, chief clerk. Officers reporting to general superintendent—Superintendent Nashville and Chattanooga, Nashville and Northwestern, and Nashville and Clarksville lines; superintendent Nashville, Decatur, and Stevenson line; superintendent Chattanooga and Atlanta and Chattanooga and Knoxville lines; superintendent Knoxville and Bristol line; engineer and superintendent Memphis and Charleston, Mississippi Central, Mobile and Ohio, and Memphis and Little Rock lines; agent Louisville City line, chief master of transportation, general agent, engineers of maintenance and repairs, general machinist, master carpenter, superintendent of car repairs, general engine dispatcher, general train dispatcher, general freight agent, general fuel agent, general ticket agent, general car agent, general store-keeper, general lumber and timber inspector, surgeon in charge. Officers reporting to each superintendent—Master of transportation, train dispatchers, engine dispatchers, superintendents of road repairs, superintendents repairs bridges and buildings, station agent, freight agent, fuel agent, car agent. Officers reporting to general machinist—Master machinist Nashville shops, master machinist Huntsville shops, master machinist Chattanooga shops, master machinist Knoxville shops, master machinist Memphis shops. Officers reporting to superintendent car repairs—Master car repairs Nashville shops, master car repairs Chattanooga shops, master car repairs Knoxville shops, foreman car repairs Johnsonville shops, foreman car repairs Clarksville shops, foreman car repairs Huntsville shops, foreman car repairs Stevenson shops, foreman car repairs Atlanta shops, foreman car repairs Memphis shops, foreman car repairs Little Rock shops. Officers reporting to general agent—Station agents, conductors. Officers reporting to engineers of repairs—Assistant or division engineer, supervisors, road masters, foremen, sub-foremen, tie inspectors.

Allusion has already been made, in reviewing the Virginia railroads, to the circumstances under which the first construction corps originated. In the present case it was found to require a much broader development than it had previously received at the East in order to insure beyond contingency the prompt rebuilding in the shortest possible time of any length of road that might pass into our hands.

The Construction Corps of the Military Division of the Mississippi was organized in six divisions, under the general charge of the chief engineer, and at its maximum strength numbered nearly 5,000 men.

To give the corps entire mobility, enable it to move independently, and perform work at the same time at widely different points, each division was made a complete whole in itself and equipped with tools, camp equipage, and field transportation, in order that the whole or any part of the same might be moved at once in any direction where ordered, and by any mode of conveyance—by rail, with teams and wagons, or on foot.

The following is the organization of one division of the Construction Corps U. S. Military Railroads as it existed in the Military Division of the Mississippi:

The number of divisions was increased or diminished to suit the requirements of military movements.

Each division was under the command of a division engineer and was divided into subdivisions or sections. Each subdivision was under the immediate command of a supervisor. The two largest and most important subdivisions in a division were the track-layers and bridge-builders. A subdivision was composed of gangs, each under a foreman. Gangs were subdivided into squads, each under a sub-foreman.

A division completely organized was composed of the following-named officers and number of men:*

The commissaries had charge of drawing, caring for, and issuing rations.

The quartermaster had charge of tools, camp equipage, &c.

Each foreman was responsible for the tools and other Government property issued to his gang.

Each supervisor reported the time made by the men in his subdivision through his division engineer to the chief time-keeper, who was stationed at the headquarters of the chief engineer.

The surgeons were appointed by the chief engineer, and were paid out of a private fund voluntarily contributed by the men for hospital purposes.

Sub-foremen were appointed by the foremen, subject to the approval of the division engineer. Foremen were appointed by the division engineer, subject to the approval of the chief engineer.

Division and assistant engineers were appointed by the chief engineer, subject to the approval of the general manager.

After completing the organization of the working forces my attention was next directed to providing an adequate supply of locomotives and cars, with the necessary shops, tools, and materials to keep them in working order. In my report of January 19, 1864, I had estimated the rolling-stock necessary for the business anticipated on the lines that would probably be operated from Nashville at 200 locomotives and 3,000 cars, while only 47 available locomotives and 437 cars were on hand. From the imperative necessity of providing the additional equipment at the earliest possible time, the following order was given by the Honorable Secretary of War to the locomotive manufacturers of the country:

WAR DEPARTMENT,
Washington City, March 23, 1864.

GENTLEMEN: Col. Daniel C. McCallum, general manager of Government railways in the Department of the Cumberland, of the Ohio, and of the Tennessee,

* Here omitted; but see same statement with Wright's report, p. 969.

has been authorized by this Department to procure locomotives without delay for the railways under his charge.

In order to meet the wants of the military departments of the Government you will deliver to his order such engines as he may direct, whether building under orders for other parties or otherwise; the Government being accountable to you for the same. The urgent necessity of the Government for the immediate supply of our armies operating in Tennessee renders the engines indispensable for the equipment of the lines of communication, and it is hoped that this necessity will be recognized by you as a military necessity, paramount to all other considerations.

By order of the President:

EDWIN M. STANTON,
Secretary of War.

It is proper and just to state that the requisitions of this order were met by all in a spirit of zealous patriotism. The manufacturers at once placed all their available force at work upon the engines and cars ordered, which were completed and delivered in an unprecedented short time.

The following table shows the rate of delivery at Nashville of engines and cars from the manufacturers:

Month.	Received.		Month.	Received.	
	Locomotives.	Cars.		Locomotives.	Cars.
1864.			1864.		
February	13	158	December	1	101
March	7	183			
April	10	334	1865.		
May	23	244	January	......	85
June	24	132	February	......	85
July	26	182	March	......	78
August	8	267	April	......	100
September	8	231	May	......	66
October	19	195			
November	1	132	Total	140	2,573

Notwithstanding the large additions made to the rolling-stock in February, March, and April, it was still inadequate to supply the wants of the service, and it was necessary to use extraordinary measures to increase it. The gauge of the Tennessee railroads being five feet, and only the roads in Kentucky having a corresponding gauge, they were the only source from which rolling-stock could be obtained, and their engines and cars were temporarily impressed into the Government service and sent south of Nashville.

The following number of engines and cars were thus obtained, and used through May and during parts of April and June:

Railroads.	Engines.	Cars.
Louisville and Nashville	17	120
Louisville and Lexington	2	15
Kentucky Central	2	60
Total	21	195

The fifteen cars belonging to Louisville and Lexington Railroad and the sixty cars of the Kentucky Central Railroad were subsequently purchased by the Government.

To maintain the locomotives and cars in good working order extensive machine and car shops were built at Nashville and Chattanooga.

These shops were supplied with machinery partly seized or purchased in the country and partly obtained from Northern manufacturers.

The shops at Nashville, particularly, were on a large scale, as at times 100 engines and more than 1,000 cars were there at once, it being the main terminal station of 500 miles of road running from it east, south, and west. Extensive store-houses were also built at Nashville and Chattanooga, and kept supplied with all necessary materials to rebuild or repair track, bridges, buildings, engines, or cars to any reasonable extent.

The general intention was to make these two cities the great centers toward which all operations should converge; where supplies of all kinds could be obtained in case the roads were cut in their rear; where repairs of any kind or to any extent could be made, and in case communication was destroyed between them, operations could be conducted from either with facility in any direction.

The following tabular statement exhibits the development of these lines during the five months from February 4 to June 30:

U. S. MILITARY RAILROADS, MILITARY DIVISION OF THE MISSISSIPPI.

Statement of lines operated from February 4, 1864, to June 30, 1864.

IN USE FEBRUARY 4, 1864.

Name of line.	From—	To—	Length.
			Miles.
Nashville and Chattanooga	Nashville	Chattanooga	151
Nashville, Decatur and Stevenson	Nashville	Dark's Mill	39
Nashville, Decatur and Stevenson	Stevenson	Huntsville	60
Chattanooga and Knoxville	Chattanooga	Charleston	42
Total			292

IN USE JUNE 30, 1864.

Name of line.	From—	To—	Length.
Nashville and Chattanooga	Nashville	Chattanooga	151
Nashville, Decatur and Stevenson	Nashville	Stevenson	200
Nashville and Northwestern	Nashville	Tennessee River	78
Chattanooga and Knoxville	Chattanooga	Knoxville	112
Chattanooga and Atlanta	Chattanooga	Big Shanty	107
Cleveland and Dalton	Cleveland	Dalton	27
Rome Branch	Kingston	Rome	17
Louisville City	River Landing	L. & N. R. R. depot	2
Total			694

IN USE AT ANY TIME FROM FEBRUARY 4, 1864, TO JUNE 30, 1864.

Name of line.	From—	To—	Length.
Nashville and Chattanooga	Nashville	Chattanooga	151
Shelbyville Branch	Wartrace	Shelbyville	9
McMinnville and Manchester	Tullahoma	McMinnville	35
Nashville, Decatur and Stevenson	Nashville	Stevenson	200
Mount Pleasant Branch	Columbia	Mount Pleasant	12
Nashville and Northwestern	Nashville	Tennessee River	78
Chattanooga and Knoxville	Chattanooga	Knoxville	112
Knoxville and Bristol	Knoxville	Bull's Gap	56
Chattanooga and Atlanta	Chattanooga	Big Shanty	107
Cleveland and Dalton	Cleveland	Dalton	27
Rome Branch	Kingston	Rome	17
Louisville City	River Landing	L. & N. R. R. depot	2
Total			806

Besides the lines mentioned above, the Memphis and Charleston Railroad was opened from Memphis to Grand Junction, fifty-two miles, and the Mobile and Ohio Railroad had been used from Columbus to Union City, twenty-six miles. The operations in Western Tennessee and Kentucky and in North Mississippi were distinct and separate from those at Nashville; and although under the control of the general superintendent at the latter point, they required and received very little attention as compared with the lines leading to the front.

The Nashville and Chattanooga Railroad, 151 miles, was the great main line over which passed all the supplies for the Armies of the Cumberland, the Ohio, and the Tennessee through the campaigns which terminated with the occupation of Atlanta. Over this single line of railroad the provisions, clothing, and camp equipage of the men, forage for animals, arms, ammunition, and ordnance stores, re-enforcements, and all the varied miscellaneous supplies required for a great army engaged in an active campaign, were sent to the front, and by it were returned the sick, wounded, disabled, and discharged soldiers, refugees, and freedmen, captured prisoners and materials deemed advisable to send to the rear.

Portions of the road had been in use for military purposes since April, 1862, but I have not in my possession any data of the operations of this or any other military line of the Southwest prior to February, 1864.

About 115 miles of track were relaid with new iron, cross-ties, and ballast from February, 1864, to the close of the war. Sidings were put in at intervals to be not more than eight miles apart, each capable of holding from five to eight long freight trains, and telegraph stations were established at most of them. In all, nineteen miles of new sidings were added to this road and forty-five new water-tanks erected.

During the spring and summer of 1864 a few occasional guerrilla raids were made upon it, but they caused little damage to property or detention to transportation. About September 1, 1864, the rebel General Wheeler destroyed seven miles of the road between Nashville and Murfreesborough. In December General Hood destroyed seven miles and three-quarters of track and 530 feet of bridges between the same stations. In both cases the road was promptly repaired and trains were running in a few days.

The road was turned over to the company September 15, 1865.

The next railroad in importance for military purposes was the Western and Atlantic, from Chattanooga to Atlanta, 136 miles. It was opened to Ringgold, Ga., twenty-one miles from Chattanooga, in March, 1864. Early in May the work of reconstruction was commenced south from Ringgold, and kept pace with the movements of Sherman's army. The line was opened through to Atlanta in August, 1864, immediately after the evacuation of the town by the rebel army. In the reconstruction of this road 22½ miles of track and 4,081 linear feet of bridges were rebuilt.

The most important single structure was Chattahoochee bridge, 780 feet long and 92 feet high, which was completed by the Construction Corps in four and one-half days. While occupied as a military road this was more infested by guerrillas than any other during the war. Every device possible to apply was used to throw trains from the track; and though occasionally successful, the preparations to guard against such attempts were so complete that few of them caused loss of life or more than a few hours' detention.

Early in October, 1864, General Hood passed around General Sherman's army and fell upon the railroad at several points in its rear. He destroyed 35½ miles of track and 455 linear feet of bridges; but in thirteen days after he left the line it was repaired and trains were run over its entire length. Twenty-five miles of the track and 230 feet of bridges in one stretch between Tunnel Hill and Resaca were reconstructed in seven and a half days. This was accomplished by working from each end of the break, and at the same time working both ways from Dalton, which was reached by trains with material by way of Cleveland after relaying one mile and a half of track.

When General Sherman commenced his march to Savannah in November the road between Atlanta and Dalton, 100 miles, was abandoned. The track from Atlanta to Etowah River, forty-six miles, was torn up and destroyed, and from Resaca to Dalton, sixteen miles, the rails were taken up and carried to Chattanooga.

By order of Major-General Thomas the road from Dalton to Atlanta was reconstructed, and between May 10 and July 4, 1865, 66 miles of track were laid, 36 miles repaired, and 3,553 linear feet of bridges rebuilt.

On the 25th day of September, 1865, it was turned over to the State of Georgia, to which it originally belonged.

The East Tennessee and Georgia Railroad, from Chattanooga to Knoxville, 112 miles, was opened through in May, 1864, upon completion of Tennessee River bridge at Loudon. It had been used for three months previous by transshipping stores and passengers across the river in flat-boats. It was operated with great regularity during the entire military occupation of that region, except in August and September, 1864, when General Wheeler tore up twenty-five miles of track. It was speedily repaired and not molested afterward.

The Dalton branch, from Cleveland to Dalton, twenty-seven miles, was operated in connection with the main line, and was of great service on several occasions.

On the 28th day of August, 1865, the road and branch was restored to the company.

The East Tennessee and Virginia Railroad, from Knoxville to Bristol, was used and abandoned for short distances near Knoxville during 1864. The farthest point reached during the year was Bull's Gap, fifty-six miles from Knoxville.

By order of Major-General Thomas repairs were commenced near Knoxville March 4, 1865, and the road opened to Carter's Station, 110 miles, April 23. Between those dates 12 miles of track were rebuilt, 94 miles repaired, and 4,400 linear feet of bridges constructed. It was turned over to the company August 28, 1865.

Nashville, Decatur and Stevenson line, 200 miles.—This is formed of the Nashville and Decatur Railroad, 120 miles from Nashville south, to Decatur, on Tennessee River, together with the eastern portion of the Memphis and Charleston Railroad, from Decatur to Stevenson, eighty miles. Stevenson is at the junction of the latter railroad and the Nashville and Chattanooga, being 113 miles distant from Nashville. Although the distance via Decatur is eighty-seven miles greater than by the direct road, such was the pressure for transportation it was necessary to send return trains by that route from the front until the capacity of the Nashville and Chattanooga line was sufficiently increased to accommodate the business. In June, 1864, all through trains were transferred to the main line.

The Nashville, Decatur and Stevenson road was used for local purposes during the summer of 1864. About the 1st of September General Wheeler tore up several miles of the track between Nashville and Columbia, and late in September General Forrest destroyed several bridges and tore up a portion of the track between Athens and Pulaski. The whole length of track destroyed in the two raids was twenty-nine miles and a half. That between Nashville and Columbia was at once repaired, but between Pulaski and Athens it was not rebuilt until February, 1865. During Hood's Nashville campaign in November and December, 1864, all the bridges then standing between Nashville and Decatur were destroyed, with six miles of track. The work of reconstruction was commenced December 19, three days after the battle of Nashville, and completed to Pulaski February 10, 1865. In addition to relaying the track, 7,055 linear feet of bridges were built, consuming 1,045,675 feet timber, B. M.

Near the close of February and again in March most of these bridges were swept away by extraordinary floods, and were rebuilt, some of them twice and many of them three times, and they were finally replaced by permanent truss bridges.

The road from Stevenson to Decatur was restored to the company September 12, and between Nashville and Decatur September 15, 1865.

Nashville and Northwestern, seventy-eight miles.—At the beginning of the war this road had been completed to Kingston Springs, twenty-five miles from Nashville, and some work had been done upon it thence to Tennessee River.

It remained in this condition until after the following order was issued.*

On the 17th day of February, 1864, the supervision of the work of construction was placed in my charge by order of Major-General Grant. (Special Orders, No. 43, headquarters Military Division of the Mississippi, 1864.)

The road was connected through between Nashville and Tennessee River on the 10th day of May, 1865. On the 9th of August it was turned over to this department to be operated as a military line by an order of Major-General Sherman, issued by the authority of the President of the United States. At the terminus on Tennessee River, named Johnsonville, extensive arrangements were made to receive and transfer freight from steam-boat to cars. Ample buildings and platforms were erected and powerful hoisting machinery introduced. During the months of August, September, and October, the season of low water in the Cumberland River, large quantities of supplies for the army were received and shipped over this road. It was very much exposed to attacks from guerrillas, who at times inflicted considerable damage and interfered with its operation. On the 4th of November General Forrest planted batteries on the west bank of Tennessee River and succeeded in destroying all the valuable buildings at Johnsonville, with their contents.

On the 30th of November the road was entirely abandoned and the movable property on it taken to Nashville. During General Hood's occupation of the country, from December 1 to 16, all the bridges were destroyed. Repairs were commenced January 2 and the road was completed through by February 13; 2,200 linear feet of bridges being rebuilt. In February, March, and April most of these bridges

*See Special Order, War Department, October 22, 1863, Vol. III, this series, p. 910.

were swept away by floods and rebuilt—some of them three times. In May and June, 1865, all were replaced by permanent truss bridges.

On the 1st of September, 1865, the road was turned over to the railroad company.

Nashville and Clarksville, sixty-two miles.—This line was formed of the Edgefield and Kentucky Railroad, forty-seven miles from Nashville, and fifteen miles of the Memphis, Clarksville, and Louisville Railroad. It was repaired and opened in August, 1864, by order of Major-General Sherman, in order to have another railroad communication with water navigable in summer to aid in supplying the Nashville depot.

Important bridges were destroyed by floods at various times and rebuilt until in April, 1865, when its use as a military road was abandoned, except on the twenty-eight miles nearest Nashville. It was turned over to the company September 23, 1865.

After the war was closed the railroads leading south from Nashville were kept in active operation for some months transporting paroled prisoners to their homes and returning those who had been confined in camps north of the Ohio River, together with the movement of the Union troops to be mustered out or take up new positions in Tennessee and Georgia.

RAILROADS IN WESTERN TENNESSEE AND KENTUCKY.

In 1862 several lines and many miles of railroad were operated for military purposes from Memphis, Tenn., and Columbus, Ky., but no reports or statements of their business have been in my hands.

No part of the road was in operation from Memphis when I took charge, but during the years 1864 and 1865 the western portion of the Memphis and Charleston Railroad and a part of the Mississippi Central were operated as follows:

Date.		How operated.	Length.
1864.			*Miles.*
Feb.	26	Opened to Germantown	15
Mar.	26	Abandoned back to within five miles of Memphis	
June	11	Opened to White's Station	10
	29	Opened to Grand Junction	52
Aug.	2	Opened to Holly Springs	75
	6	Opened to Tallahatchie River	100
	18	Abandoned to Grand Junction	52
	23	Reopened to Tallahatchie River	100
	24	Abandoned to Grand Junction	52
Sept.	6	Abandoned to White's Station	10
Oct.	15	Abandoned entirely	
Dec.	20	Opened to Collierville	24
1865.			
Jan.	1	Abandoned entirely	
Feb.	28	Opened to Germantown	15
Mar.	4	Abandoned entirely	
	24	Opened to Collierville	24
Apr.	2	Opened to La Fayette	32
May	13	Opened to Moscow	39
	14	Opened to La Grange	49
	20	Opened to Grand Junction	52
June	30	Opened to Pocahontas	75
Sept.	12	Turned over to the company	

Each time it was abandoned it was badly damaged by the enemy—bridges, trestles, and cattle guards were burned and miles of track torn up.

At Columbus, Ky., I found the Mobile and Ohio Railroad open to Union City, twenty-six miles. It was abandoned about the 1st of

May, 1864, at the time of Forrest's raid upon Union City, and not afterward used, except in the immediate vicinity of Columbus, until May, 1865. It was reopened to Union City May 15, and to Crockett, thirty-five miles, May 31, and restored to the company August 25, 1865.

ARKANSAS.

The Memphis and Little Rock Railroad between Devall's Bluff and Little Rock, forty-nine miles, was the only line operated in this State. It did not come under my control until May 1, 1865. It was then in very bad condition, in consequence of the nature of the soil and neglect or want of skill in keeping up the necessary repairs.

It was operated as a military line until November 1, 1865, when it was restored to the company.

Statement of railroads operated in Tennessee, Georgia, Mississippi, Kentucky, and Arkansas.

Name of line.	Operated within the following periods.					Greatest distance operated.	Turned over to owners.
	1864.			1865.			
	Feb. 10.	June 30.	Dec. 31.	June 30.	Dec. 31.		
	Miles.	*Miles.*	*Miles.*	*Miles.*	*Miles.*	*Miles.*	1865.
Nashville and Chattanooga	151	151	151	151	151	151	Sept. 15
Nashville, Decatur and Stevenson	99	200	200	200	200	200	Do.
Nashville and Northwestern	......	......	78	78	78	78	Sept. 1
Nashville and Clarksville	......	......	62	62	28	62	Sept. 23
Shelbyville Branch	9	9	9	....	....	9	Sept. 15
McMinnville and Manchester	......	35	......	....	....	35	
Mount Pleasant Branch	......	12	......	....	....	12	Do.
Chattanooga and Knoxville	42	112	112	112	112	112	Aug. 28
Cleveland and Dalton	......	27	27	27	27	27	Do.
Knoxville and Bristol	......	56	17	110	110	110	Do.
Rogersville and Jefferson	......	......	......	12	12	12	
Chattanooga and Atlanta	......	107	136	136	136	136	Sept. 25
Rome Branch	......	17	17	17	17	17	
Atlanta and Macon	......	......	11	....	....	11	
Memphis and Charleston	......	52	52	75	75	75	Sept. 12
Mississippi Central	......	......	68	....	....	68	Do.
Mobile and Ohio	26	26	......	35	35	35	Aug. 25
Memphis and Little Rock	......	......	......	49	49	49	Nov. 1
Louisville City	2	2	2	2	2	2	
Total	329	806	942	1,066	1,032	1,201	

U. S. MILITARY RAILROADS, DIVISION OF THE MISSISSIPPI, EMBRACING THE ROADS IN TENNESSEE, GEORGIA, KENTUCKY, ALABAMA, MISSISSIPPI, AND ARKANSAS.

In the following tabular statements are given—

1. The greatest number of persons employed in any month of the year, average monthly number, and amount paid for services.
2. The number of locomotive engines, how procured, number added each year, and final disposition made of them.
3. The number of cars, &c.
4. The length of track and bridges built or rebuilt.

1. *Number of persons employed and amount paid for service.*

Year.	Persons employed monthly.		Amount paid for services.
	Greatest number in one month.	Average number per month.	
1864	16,364	11,586	$6,316,861.45
1865	17,035	10,061	6,513,384.15
Total	17,035	10,787	12,830,245.60

2. *Locomotive engines provided and final disposition made of them.*

Year.	Locomotives procured.			Locomotives disposed of.				
					Sold—			
	Purchased.	Captured.	Total.	Lost or destroyed in service or in transit.	For cash.	To Southern railroads under Executive orders of Aug. 8 and Oct. 14.	Returned to former owners.	Total.
1862	18	35	53					
1863	20	14	34					
1864	154	17	171	2				2
1865	2		2			161	63	224
1866					32		2	34
Total	194	66	260	2	32	161	65	260

3. *Cars provided and final disposition made of them.*

	Cars procured.			Cars disposed of.				
					Sold—			
	Purchased.	Built.	Total.	Lost or destroyed in service or in transit.	For cash.	To Southern railroads under Executive orders of Aug. 8 and Oct. 14.	Returned to former owners.	Total.
On hand February 1, 1864			755					
Year ending June 30—								
1864	1,081		1,081	160				160
1865	1,522	25	1,547	243				243
1866				32	536	2,311	101	2,980
Total	2,603	25	3,383	435	536	2,311	101	3,383

4. *The length of bridges and tracks built and rebuilt.*

The length of bridges built and rebuilt was 97,544 linear feet, or 18$\frac{2}{3}$ miles. The length of main track laid was 391.12 miles. The length of sidings laid was 42.32 miles, making a total of 433.44 miles.

The following list embraces the names of the general officers:

1864.—A. Anderson, general superintendent to November 1; E. L. Wentz, general superintendent after November 1; W. J. Stevens, superintendent railroads running from Nashville; Col. L. P. Wright, superintendent railroads from Chattanooga to July 1; W. C. Taylor, superintendent railroads from Chattanooga after July 1; A. F. Goodhue, engineer and superintendent railroads at Memphis, Tenn., and Columbus, Ky.; W. W. Wright, chief engineer of Construction Corps; L. H. Eicholtz, division engineer of First Division; E. C. Smeed, division engineer of Second Division; John F. Burgin, division engineer of Fourth Division; W. R. Kingsley, division engineer of Fifth Division; Col. John Clark, in charge of construction on the Nashville and Northwestern Railroad; William McDonald, assistant engineer; Charles Latimer, assistant engineer; John Trenbath, auditor; Col. John C. Crane, assistant quartermaster, disbursing officer; Capt. George S. Roper, commissary of subsistence.

1865.—W. J. Stevens, general superintendent; R. B. McPherson, assistant general superintendent; J. B. Van Dyne, chief master of transportation; A. W. Dickinson, superintendent Nashville railroads to July 25; George H. Hudson, superintendent Nashville railroads after July 25; W. R. Gifford, superintendent Nashville, Decatur and Stevenson Railroad; A. A. Talmadge, superintendent Chattanooga railroads; A. J. Cheeney, superintendent Knoxville and Bristol Railroad to September 1, superintendent of Chattanooga and Atlanta Railroad after September 1; A. Hebard, engineer of repairs Nashville railroads; A. F. Goodhue, engineer and superintendent of railroads West Tennessee, Kentucky, and Arkansas; Col. L. P. Wright, superintendent Memphis railroads; W. W. Wright, chief engineer of Construction Corps; L. H. Eicholtz, division engineer and acting chief engineer during the absence of the chief engineer in North Carolina; John F. Burgin, division engineer; W. R. Kingsley, division engineer on the Nashville and Northwestern Railroad; Charles Latimer, division engineer; John Trenbath, auditor; Capt. F. J. Crilly, chief quartermaster and disbursing officer; Capt. George S. Roper, commissary of subsistence; T. W. Yardley, superintendent of rolling-mill.

MISSOURI.

In October, 1864, orders were received to have the bridges rebuilt on the Pacific Railroad of Missouri and its southwestern branch, which had lately been destroyed by the rebels. This work required the construction of 1,680 linear feet of truss bridges and was completed early in April, 1865, at an expense of $170,564.65, including the cost of replacing trestles carried away by floods and other incidental expenses.

NORTH CAROLINA AND ATLANTIC COAST.

Under orders received from Major-General McClellan 4 locomotives and 100 freight cars were sent to Major-General Burnside at New Berne, N. C., in the months of June and July, 1862. On the passage two locomotives were lost with the vessel off Cape Hatteras and two others were afterward sent to replace them. One engine proving unserviceable was subsequently returned to Alexandria, Va., leaving

3 locomotives and 100 cars for service. The road was worked under orders and by officers appointed by the general commanding the department and did not come under my jurisdiction. I am therefore unable to give any account of its operation.

When it was ascertained to what point of the coast General Sherman was directing his march from Atlanta preparation was at once made to furnish him with railroad facilities. A portion of the Construction Corps from the Division of the Mississippi that had rebuilt the railroads during the Atlanta campaign were ordered in December, 1864, to proceed to Baltimore by railroad from Nashville and embark for Savannah. Upon reaching Hilton Head information was received that General Sherman would not use the railroads near Savannah, and orders were given to proceed to New Berne, N. C., and open the railroad to Goldsborough.

Eleven miles of the Savannah and Gulf Railroad were opened and operated with rolling-stock captured at Savannah for local military purposes and to supply the citizens of the town with fuel. The tracks and buildings of the Georgia Central Railroad within the city limits also were used. Five serviceable and 9 unserviceable locomotives and 213 cars, about one-half of them damaged and unfit for service, were captured at Savannah. On the 20th day of June, 1865, all the railroad property was restored to the original owners by order of the department commander.

A detachment of the Virginia Construction Corps was sent to North Carolina by order of General Grant, and landed at New Berne January 30, 1865. The railroad at that time was in charge of the depot quartermaster at New Berne, and was in operation between Morehead City and Batchelder's Creek, forty-four miles. This construction force at once commenced rebuilding the bridge over that stream. On the 6th day of February the detachment sent from the Military Division of the Mississippi landed at Morehead City and relieved the force from Virginia, which returned back to City Point.

The railroad was repaired as fast as the army advanced, and was opened to Goldsborough, ninety-five miles, March 25, the day following the arrival of General Sherman and his army from Savannah.

To provide another line of supplies the railroad from Wilmington to Goldsborough, eighty-five miles, was repaired and opened through April 4.

On the 10th of April movements were resumed toward the interior, and the railroad was opened April 19 to Raleigh, forty-eight miles from Goldsborough. It was opened soon after to Hillsborough and used until the parole of General Johnston's army was completed, when it was given up west of Raleigh.

The total length of railroads opened and used in this department was as follows:

Name of line.	Terminal stations.		Length.	Transferred to company.
	From—	To—		
			Miles.	1865.
Atlantic and North Carolina	Morehead City	Goldsborough	95	Oct. 25
Wilmington and Weldon	Wilmington	do	85	Aug. 27
North Carolina	Goldsborough	Hillsborough	88	Oct. 22
Raleigh and Gaston	Raleigh	Cedar Creek	25	May 3
Total			293	

On these roads, 25 miles 2,172 feet of main track were rebuilt, and 5 miles 1,460 feet side-track were laid, or 30 miles 4,632 feet of track in all. On the same roads 3,263 linear feet of bridges were built, consuming 825,750 feet timber, B. M. At Morehead City a wharf was built by the Construction Corps covering an area of 53,682 square feet, and consuming 700,000 feet timber, B. M.

In the following tabular statements are embraced the principal items of information in regard to these lines:

1. *Number of persons employed.*

The greatest number persons employed monthly in the year 1865 was 3,387.

2. *Locomotive engines provided and final disposition made of them.*

Year.	Locomotives procured.			Locomotives disposed of.				
					Sold—			
	Purchased.	Captured.	Total.	Lost or destroyed in service or in transit.	For cash.	To Southern railroads under Executive orders of Aug. 8 and Oct. 14.	Returned to former owners.	Total.
1862	5		5	2				2
1863	2		2					
1864								
1865	10	21	31		9	3	21	33
1866					3			3
Total	17	21	38	2	12	3	21	38

3. *Cars provided and final disposition made of them.*

Year.	Cars procured.			Cars disposed of.				
					Sold—			
	Purchased.	Captured.	Total.	Lost or destroyed in service or in transit.	For cash.	To Southern railroads under Executive orders of Aug. 8 and Oct. 14.	Returned to former owners.	Total.
1862	100	3	103	20				20
1863				38				38
1864								
1865	139	180	319	1		101	183	285
1866					79			79
Total	239	183	422	59	79	101	183	422

The following officers were directly in charge of operating the military railroads in North Carolina: W. W. Wright, chief engineer and general superintendent to July 1; Col. J. F. Boyd, general superintendent after July 1; J. B. Van Dyne, superintendent; E. C. Smeed, engineer of repairs.

RAILS AND ROLLING-MILL.

The greatest necessity, next to that of rolling-stock, was a supply of rails. These were obtained by purchase, manufacture, and by taking up lines unnecessary for military purposes.

The following roads were thus taken up entire for the distances specified:

Railroad.	From—	To—	Length.	
In Virginia.			*Miles.*	*Feet.*
Seaboard and Roanoke	Suffolk	Blackwater	14	
Norfolk and Petersburg	do	do	14	
Manassas Gap	Manassas	Piedmont	35	
Richmond and York River	White House	Chickahominy River	13	
In Military Division of the Mississippi.				
Winchester and Fayetteville	Decherd	Fayetteville	41	2,640
McMinnville and Manchester	Near Manchester	McMinnville	26	2,760
Mount Pleasant Branch	Columbia	Mount Pleasant	12	2,165

During the war the quantity of rails purchased and manufactured was as follows:

Year.	Quantity of rails— Purchased.		Manufactured at the Chattanooga Rolling-Mill.	
	Tons.	*Pounds.*	*Tons.*	*Pounds.*
1862	6,086	1,723		
1863	6,030	1,790		
1864	8,165	1,446		
1865	1,500	1,352	3,818	1,184
Total	21,783	831	3,818	1,184

The price paid for purchased rails varied from $40 per ton, the lowest price, paid in July, 1862, to $130 per ton, the highest price, paid in June, 1864.

Soon after taking charge of the railroads in the Military Division of the Mississippi the following communication was addressed to the commanding general:

OFFICE GENERAL MANAGER MILITARY RAILROADS UNITED STATES,
Nashville, Tenn., February 17, 1864.

Maj. Gen. U. S. GRANT,
Commanding Military Division of the Mississippi, Nashville, Tenn.:

GENERAL: When the track of the Nashville and Chattanooga Railroad is relaid we will have on hand 302 miles of old rails, weighing 11,864 gross tons. At present rates, new rails delivered at Chattanooga will cost $145 per ton.

There is at Chattanooga a rolling-mill, partially built by the rebels, which if completed—say at a cost of $30,000—these old rails can be rerolled at a cost of about $50 per ton, coal being contiguous and abundant. This would not only be a large saving to the Government, but, what in my opinion is of greater importance, the rails would be on hand ready for use when and where required. The following represents the case:

11,864 tons of new rails delivered at Chattanooga, at $145 per ton		$1,719,250
11,864 tons of old rails rerolled, at a cost of $50 per ton	$593,200	
Cost of mill (estimated)	30,000	
		623,200
In favor of rolling-mill		1,096,050

By advices recently received, the stock of railroad iron in the market is small and the demand large. In fact, should an emergency arise requiring a large amount of iron it is doubtful whether it could be had at any price. I therefore respectfully ask, unless military reasons forbid, your permission to complete the rolling-mill at Chattanooga.

I have the honor to be, very respectfully, your obedient servant,

D. C. McCALLUM,
Colonel, U. S. Army, General Manager Military Railroads United States.

The following order was the response to this letter:

SPECIAL ORDERS, No. 43. HDQRS. MILITARY DIVISION OF THE MISSISSIPPI, *Nashville, Tenn., February 17, 1864.*

Col. D. C. McCallum, general manager of military railroads within this military division, is hereby directed to proceed at once to complete and set at work the rolling-mill at Chattanooga, Tenn.

By order of Major-General Grant:

T. S. BOWERS,
Assistant Adjutant-General.

Upon a more extended and thorough examination it was found that many important parts of the machinery provided by the rebels for the rolling-mill were not at hand. They were, in fact, still within their lines, and no probability existed of obtaining them uninjured within any reasonable time, if at all; therefore it was decided to build entirely new machinery throughout, and to make it of the most improved pattern used in rolling-mills of the North.

The mill building, partially completed by the rebels, was declared by the military authorities too far from the fortifications at Chattanooga to be safe, and after careful investigation of the question the building was abandoned and a new one erected in a secure location. To reach the site selected and properly accommodate the mill required building one mile and two-thirds of railroad. Thus, instead of completing a partially built work an entirely new and very superior rolling-mill in point of machinery was the result.

The total cost of the mill complete and ready for work was as follows:

Rolling-mill building	$125,857.81
Machinery, including transportation	120,000.00
Quarters for workmen, officers, and other buildings	21,212.00
Railroad to mill, materials, and labor	23,259.70
Total	290,329.51

The mill, with its outbuildings and railroads, was built by the Construction Corps. Most of the timber used was got out by them, and nearly all the work was done at times when there was a lull in active operations in the field. As this force was necessarily kept on hand for emergencies, and their legitimate place was at the front, the work done by them in building the mill may be regarded as almost clear gain to the Government. More than $100,000 of the above sum was paid for labor thus expended.

Owing to the great pressure upon the manufacturers of machinery, the scarcity of labor, difficulty of obtaining proper materials, and of procuring transportation to Nashville on the over-crowded railroad lines of the North, the mill did not go into operation until April 1, 1865.

It was employed in manufacturing rails for the United States until October 5, 1865, when it was sold to the highest bidder, after two months' advertisement, for $175,000. It was in operation six months and five days, and in that time manufactured 3,818 tons and 1,184 pounds of new rails at a cost of—

For coal (145,897 bushels)	$36,474.25
For labor	98,776.39
Total	135,250.64

Average cost per ton, $35.42.

These were disposed of as follows:

	Tons.	Pounds.
To repair tracks	466	2,066
Sold to Southern railroads	3,351	1,358
Total	3,818	1,184

The quantity sold realized in cash the sum of $269,128.58.

ROLLING-STOCK.

In the preceding statements an account is given of the quantity of rolling-stock provided for each department and the final disposition made of it. Those statements embrace only the number in active service in each case. In the fall and winter of 1864 an additional supply was provided in view of probable wants for the spring campaign of 1865, but the close of the war rendered it unnecessary, and it was subsequently sold at the points where manufactured, or where it had been stored to await events. Thirty-five locomotives and 492 cars, of five-feet gauge, were built for the Military Division of the Mississippi and North Carolina; fifty cars, of four feet eight and a half inch gauge also were provided for Virginia and North Carolina. Ten platform cars, of four feet eight and a half inch gauge, had been purchased at an early day and used on the railroads of the Western States, to transport cars of the five-feet gauge from the manufacturers' works to Jeffersonville, opposite Louisville. Locomotives, five-feet gauge, provided but not used, 35. Cars—five-feet gauge, for Military Division of the Mississippi and North Carolina, 519; four feet eight and a half inch gauge, for Virginia and North Carolina, 50; four feet eight and a half inch gauge, for car transportation, 10; total, 579.

Of these engines and cars one of the ten cars was destroyed in service and all the rest were sold for cash.

The following tabular statements exhibit the entire rolling-stock of the military railroads during the war:

Locomotives.

Year delivered.	How obtained.			How disposed of.				
					Sold—			
	Purchased and built.	Captured.	Total.	Lost or destroyed.	For cash.	Under Executive orders of Aug. 8 and Oct. 14.	Returned to former owners.	Total.
1862	72	40	112	4				4
1863	40	14	54		3			3
1864	154	17	171	2	9			11
1865	47	35	82		95	164	101	360
1866					39		2	41
Total	313	106	419	6	146	164	103	419

Cars.

Fiscal year.	How obtained.					How disposed of.				
								Sold—		
	Purchased.	Built.	Captured.	On hand in Military Division of Mississippi Feb. 1, 1864.	Total.	Lost or destroyed.	Returned to former owners.	Under Executive orders of Aug. 8 and Oct. 14.	For cash.	Total.
1862	603		16		619	478				478
1863	704				704	53			10	63
1864	1,149	30		755	1,934	217			126	343
1865	2,655	25	393		3,073	265	213			478
1866						32	297	2,589	2,050	4,968
Total	5,111	55	409	755	6,330	1,045	510	2,589	2,186	6,330

The cars sold in the years 1863 and 1864 were damaged, disabled, and unfit for service.

In the above tables the rolling-stock borrowed and impressed into service from Northern railroads is not included.

In the general office of Military Railroads in Washington have been the following officers: W. H. Whiton, in charge April 1, 1862, to July 1, 1865; H. K. Cooper, in charge after July 1, 1865; J. A. Lawrence, accountant, to October 10, 1863; E. J. Kellogg, accountant, after October 10, 1863. Capt. (now Brevet Brigadier-General) H. L. Robinson, assistant quartermaster, has acted as disbursing and purchasing officer for the railroads in the East during the entire war.

GENERAL REMARKS.

With few exceptions the operations of military railroads have been conducted under orders issued by the Secretary of War or by army commanders in or out of the field.

It was made the duty of the director and general manager to arrange the military railroad organization upon a basis sufficiently comprehensive to permit the extension of the system indefinitely to perfect the modus operandi for working the various lines; to determine as to the number of men to be employed in the several departments, and the compensation to be paid therefor; the amount and kind of machinery to be purchased, and the direction as to the distribution of the same.

The following important order of the Secretary of War, the wisdom of which has been so abundantly vindicated by experience, is here inserted as defining in part the position of the military railroad organization, which seems not to have been clearly understood by many in and out of the service:

SPECIAL ORDERS, No. 337. } WAR DEPARTMENT, ADJUTANT-GENERAL'S OFFICE, *Washington, November 10, 1862.*

* * * * * * *

16. Commanding officers of troops along the U. S. military railroads will give all facilities to the officers of the roads and the quartermasters for unloading cars so as to prevent any delay. On arrival at depots, whether in the day or night, the cars will be instantly unloaded, and working parties will always be in readiness for that duty and sufficient to unload the whole train at once.

Commanding officers will be charged with guarding the track, sidings, wood, water-tanks, &c., within their several commands, and will be held responsible for the result.

Any military officer who shall neglect his duty in this respect will be reported by the quartermasters and officers of the railroad and his name will be stricken from the rolls of the Army.

Depots will be established at suitable points under the direction of the commanding general and properly guarded.

No officer, whatever may be his rank, will interfere with the running of the cars as directed by the superintendent of the road.

Any one who so interferes will be dismissed from the service for disobedience of orders.

By order of the Secretary of War:

E. D. TOWNSEND,
Assistant Adjutant-General.

The above order was given in consequence of several attempts having been made to operate railroads by army or department commanders, which had, without an exception, proved signal failures, disorganizing in tendency and destructive of all discipline. The great benefit resulting from this order was more especially exhibited during General Sherman's campaign from Chattanooga to Atlanta, and in this my final report I desire to put on record, for the benefit of those who may be called upon to conduct military railroad operations in the future, the following:

Having had a somewhat extensive railroad experience both before and since the rebellion, I consider this order of the Secretary of War to have been the very foundation of success. Without it the whole railroad system, which has proved an important element in conducting military movements, would have been not only a costly but ludicrous failure. The fact should be understood that the management of railroads is just as much a distinct profession as is that of the art of war, and should be so regarded.

The difficulty of procuring a sufficient force of competent railroad men, both in the construction and transportation departments, was almost insurmountable. Owing to the peculiar nature of the service and the rapid expansion of the railroad system, the supply of railroad operatives in the country has always been limited. Many had entered the Army in various positions, thus diminishing the actual number in civil life, while the stimulus imparted by the war to the business of Northern railroads had greatly enhanced the value of the services of those who remained at their posts, thus rendering the home demand for skillful labor far in advance of the supply. When the large number of men necessary to equip these military lines were sought for it was extremely difficult to induce those who were really valuable to leave secure positions and enter upon a new and untried field of action.

The difference between civil and military railroad service is marked and decided. Not only were the men continually exposed to great danger from the regular forces of the enemy, guerrillas, scouting parties, &c., but owing to the circumstances under which military railroads must be constructed and operated, what are considered the ordinary risks upon civil railroads are vastly increased on military lines.

The hardships, exposure, and perils to which train men especially were subjected during the movements incident to an active campaign were much greater than that endured by any other class of civil employés of the Government—equaled only by that of the soldier while engaged in a raid into the enemy's country. It was by no means unusual for men to be out with their trains from five to ten days without sleep, except what could be snatched upon their engines and cars while the same were standing to be loaded or unloaded, with but scanty food, or perhaps no food at all, for days together, while continually occupied in a manner to keep every faculty strained to its utmost. Many incidents during the war, but more especially during the Atlanta campaign, exhibited a fortitude, endurance, and self-devotion on the part of these men not exceeded in any branch of the service. All were thoroughly imbued with the fact that upon the success of railroad operations in forwarding supplies to the front depended in great part the success of our armies; that, although defeat might be the result even if supplies were abundantly furnished, it was evident there could be no advance without; and I hazard nothing in saying that should failure have taken place, either in keeping the lines in repair or in operating them, General Sherman's campaign, instead of proving, as it did, a great success, would have resulted in disaster and defeat; and the greater the army to supply the more precarious its position. Since the end of the rebellion I have been informed by railroad officers who were in the service of the enemy during the war that they were less surprised at the success of General Sherman in a military point of view than they were at the rapidity with which railroad breaks were repaired and the regularity with which trains were moved to the front; and it was only when the method of operating was fully explained that it could be comprehended.

In the beginning of the war military railroads were an experiment, and although some light as to their management had been gleaned by the operations of 1862 and 1863, yet so little progress had been made that the attempt to supply the army of General Sherman in the field, construct and reconstruct the railroad in its rear, and keep pace with its march was regarded by those who had the largest experience, and who had become most familiar with the subject, as the greatest experiment of all. The attempt to furnish an army of 100,000 men and 60,000 animals with supplies from a base 360 miles distant by one line of single-track railroad, located almost the entire distance through the country of an active and most vindictive enemy, is without precedent in the history of warfare, and to make it successful required an enormous outlay for labor and a vast consumption of material, together with all the forethought, energy, patience, and watchfulness of which men are capable.

This line, from the fact of its great length, was imperfectly guarded, as troops could not be spared from the front for that purpose. This rendered the railroad service one of great risk and hazard, and at times it was only by the force of military authority that men could be held to service. As an item showing the real danger attending military railroad operations, it may be stated that during the last six months of the fiscal year ending June 30, 1865, the wrecking train picked up and carried to Nashville 16 wrecked locomotives and 294 car-loads of car wheels, bridge iron, &c. These wrecks were caused by guerrillas and rebel raids.

The Chattanooga and Atlanta (or Western and Atlantic) Railroad extends from Chattanooga to Atlanta, 138 miles, with a branch from Kingston to Rome seventeen miles long.

The reconstruction and maintenance of this line was in many respects the most difficult of any military railroad operations during the war. By it the Confederate army under General Johnston made its retreat from Buzzard Roost to Atlanta; and in falling back from one strong position to another it did such damage to the road as was supposed would delay or prevent Sherman's pursuit, but in this it was unsuccessful. However great the damage done, it was so speedily repaired that General Sherman soon ceased to fear any delay from this cause, and made his advance movements with perfect confidence that the railroad in his rear would be "all right."

Being from the nature of the case entirely ignorant of the obstacles to be encountered at each advance, the construction force was at all times prepared for any emergency—either to build bridges of formidable dimensions, or lay miles of track, or perhaps push back to some point on the line and repair damages done by guerrillas or raiding parties. These attacks on the line to the rear were of such frequent occurrence, and often of so serious a character, that to insure speedy repairs it became necessary to station detachments of the Construction Corps at various points along the road, and also to collect supplies of construction materials, such as iron, rails, chairs, spikes, cross-ties, and bridge timber, at points where they would be comparatively safe and easily obtained when required. These precautionary measures proved to be of the utmost importance in keeping the road open.

The detachments stationed along the line were composed of bridge-builders and track-layers, with an ample supply of tools for all kinds of work. Each detachment was under the command of a competent engineer or supervisor, who had orders to move in either direction within certain limits as soon as a break occurred, and make the necessary repairs without delay, working day and night when necessary. Under this arrangement small breaks were repaired at once at any point on the line, even when the telegraph wires were cut and special orders could not be communicated to the working parties. When big breaks occurred one or more divisions of the Construction Corps were moved as rapidly as possible thereto, either from Chattanooga or the front. Construction trains loaded with the requisite tools and materials were kept ready at each end of the road to move at a moment's notice.

Guerrillas and raiding parties were more or less successful in destroying portions of the track during the whole time we held this line; but the crowning effort was made by the enemy in October, 1864, when Hood, getting to Sherman's rear, threw his whole army on the road, first at Big Shanty and afterward north of Resaca, and destroyed in the aggregate 35½ miles of track and 455 linear feet of bridges, killing and capturing a large number of our men. Fortunately, however, the detachments of the Construction Corps which escaped were so distributed that even before Hood had left the road two strong working parties were at work, one on each end of the break at Big Shanty, and this gap of ten miles was closed and the force ready to move to the great break of twenty-five miles in length north of Resaca as soon as the enemy had left it. The destruction by Hood's army of our depots of supplies compelled us to cut nearly all the cross-ties required to relay this track and to send a distance for rails.

The cross-ties were cut near the line of the road and many of them carried by hand to the track, as the teams to be furnished for hauling them did not get to the work until it was nearly completed. The rails used on the southern end of the break had to be taken up and brought from the railroads south of Atlanta, and those for the northern end were mostly brought from Nashville, nearly 200 miles distant.

Notwithstanding all the disadvantages under which the labor was performed, this twenty-five miles of track was laid and the trains were running over it in seven days and a half from the time the work was commenced.

The economy so commendable and essential upon civil railroads was compelled to give way to the lavish expenditure of war; and the question to be answered was not "How much will it cost?" but rather, "Can it be done at all at any cost?"

During February, 1862, I received the following important verbal order from the Secretary of War:

> I shall expect you to have on hand at all times the necessary men and materials to enable you to comply promptly with any order given, nor must there be any failure.

The greatest number of men employed at the same date during the war was:

In Virginia	4,542
In North Carolina	3,387
In Military Division of the Mississippi	17,035
Total	24,964

Total number of miles operated.

In Virginia	611
In North Carolina	293
In Military Division of the Mississippi	1,201
Total	2,105

Number of engines.

In Virginia	72
In North Carolina	38
In Military Division of the Mississippi	260
In Georgia	14
Provided but not used	35
Total	419

Number of cars.

In Virginia	1,733
In North Carolina	422
In Military Division of the Mississippi	3,383
In Georgia	213
Provided but not used	579
Total	6,330

Length of bridges built or rebuilt.

	Feet.
In Virginia	34,931
In North Carolina	3,263
In Missouri	1,680
In Military Division of the Mississippi	97,544
Total	137,418
Or 26 miles, 138 feet.	

Length of track laid or relaid.

	Miles.	Feet.
In Virginia	177	2,961
In North Carolina	30	4,632
In Military Division of the Mississippi	433	2,323
Total	641	4,636

The following statement exhibits the amount expended during the war in constructing and operating the U. S. military railroads, said sum having been furnished from the appropriation made for the expenditures of the Quartermaster's Department:

Virginia:		
For labor	$5,227,145.24	
For materials	4,920,317.27	
		$10,147,462.51
North Carolina:		
For labor	1,086,224.60	
For materials	1,510,435.45	
		2,596,660.05
Military Division of the Mississippi:		
For labor	16,792,193.05	
For materials	12,870,588.06	
		29,662,781.11
Department of the Gulf:		
For materials		55,238.88
Total		42,462,142.55
Property sold under Executive order August 8, 1865	7,428,204.96	
Property sold for cash	3,466,739.33	
Receipts for passengers and freight	1,525,493.04	
Receipts from hire of rolling-stock	103,528.50	
Property on hand (estimated)	100,000.00	
		12,623,965.83
Net expenditures		29,838,176.72

The U. S. military railroads were transferred, by Executive order of August 8, 1865, to the original owners.

The military railroad organization was designed to be a great construction and transportation machine for carrying out the objects of the commanding generals, so far as it was adapted to the purpose, and it was managed solely with a view to efficacy in that direction. It was the duty of the Quartermaster's Department to load all material upon the cars, to direct where such material should be taken, and to whom delivered. It then became the province of the railroad department to comply with said order in the shortest practicable time, and to perfect such arrangements as would enable it to keep the lines in repair under any and all circumstances. It was impossible for this department to keep an accurate account of the persons and material transported, as whole corps and even armies, with all their artillery and equipments, were moved upon verbal orders from commanders sometimes hundreds of miles, and frequently in face of the enemy. As an illustration, one of the largest movements of this character was that of the Fourth Army Corps in 1865 from Carter's Station, in East Tennessee, to Nashville, 373 miles, and which employed 1,498 cars.

Accompanying this report is a map showing the different lines operated in the United States by the Military Railroad Department during the war.*

In conclusion, permit me to say that the Government was peculiarly fortunate in securing the services of civilian officers of great nerve, honesty, and capability, to whom the whole country owes a debt of gratitude.

Among them I take the liberty of naming as principal assistants A. Anderson, chief superintendent and engineer; Col. W. W. Wright, chief engineer of the Military Division of the Mississippi, and chief engineer and general superintendent in the Department of North Carolina; J. J. Moore, general superintendent and chief engineer of railroads in Virginia; E. L. Wentz, general superintendent and chief engineer of railroads in Virginia, and afterward for a time general superintendent of railroads in the Division of the Mississippi; W. J. Stevens, general superintendent of U. S. Military Railroads, Division of the Mississippi; L. H. Eicholtz, acting chief engineer Military Division of the Mississippi during the absence of Col. W. W. Wright in North Carolina; A. F. Goodhue, engineer and superintendent military railroads, West Tennessee and Arkansas. Also the following commissioned officers: Bvt. Brig. Gen. H. L. Robinson, assistant quartermaster, Washington, D. C.; Bvt. Maj. F. J. Crilly, assistant quartermaster, Nashville, Tenn., and Capt. G. S. Roper, commissary of subsistence, Nashville, Tenn.

I have the honor to be, very respectfully, your obedient servant,

D. C. McCALLUM,

Brevet Brigadier-General, Director and General Manager U. S. Military Railroads.

---

* Inclosed in pocket at end of present volume.

Exhibit relative to the volunteer forces of the U. S. Army.

Department.	Remaining as per exhibit May 15.			Since ordered mustered out (white).	Will remain when musters out as ordered shall have been completed.		
	White.	Colored.	Aggregate.		White.	Colored.	Aggregate.
East *a*	301		301		301		301
Middle *a*	159		159		159		159
Washington *a*	293	712	1,005		293	712	1,005
Ohio *a*	159		159		159		159
Kentucky							
Missouri		843	843			*b* 843	843
Virginia							
North Carolina	870	806	1,676	*c* 870		806	806
South Carolina	1,741	781	2,522	*d* 1,741		781	781
Georgia							
Mississippi							
Alabama							
Tennessee							
Arkansas		2,908	2,908			2,908	2,908
Florida		815	815			815	815
Louisiana	551	4,463	5,014	*c* 551		4,463	4,463
Texas		5,992	5,992			5,992	5,992
California } Columbia }	2,000		2,000		*e* 2,000		2,000
Total	6,074		23,394	3,161	2,912	17,320	20,232

a Hancock's corps and independent companies Veteran Reserve Corps.
b Although no white volunteers appear, as in Department of the Missouri (they having been some time ago dropped on reports from General Pope that they would be out by a certain date), it is known that there are yet some 3,000 in the department, and General Pope, under date May 19, reported that the last would not be out until September 1.
c Musters out completed.
d Musters out will not be completed till last of this month.
e Have been under orders for discharge for a long time, and are being mustered out as rapidly as they can be relieved. Date when work will be completed unknown.

THOMAS M. VINCENT,
Assistant Adjutant-General.

WAR DEPARTMENT, ADJUTANT-GENERAL'S OFFICE,
June 11, 1866.

[JULY 26, 1866.—For Stanton to Colfax, transmitting report of the Quartermaster-General respecting railroad property in possession of the Government May 1, 1865, &c., see House Executive Document, No. 155, Thirty-ninth Congress, first session.]

GENERAL ORDERS, } WAR DEPT., ADJT. GENERAL'S OFFICE,
No. 70. } *Washington, August 25, 1866.*

The following proclamation is published for the information and guidance of the Army and of all concerned:

BY THE PRESIDENT OF THE UNITED STATES OF AMERICA:

A PROCLAMATION.

Whereas, a war is existing in the Republic of Mexico, aggravated by foreign military intervention;

And whereas, the United States, in accordance with their settled habits and policy, are a neutral power in regard to the war which thus afflicts the Republic of Mexico;

And whereas, it has become known that one of the belligerents in the said war—namely, the Prince Maximilian, who asserts himself to be Emperor in Mexico—has issued a decree in regard to the port of Matamoras and other Mexican ports which are in the occupation and possession of another of the said belligerents—namely, the United States of Mexico—which decree is in the following words:

"The port of Matamoras and all those of the northern frontier which have withdrawn from their obedience to the Government are closed to foreign and coasting traffic during such time as the empire of the law shall not be therein reinstated.

"ART. 2. Merchandise proceeding from the said ports, on arriving at any other where the excise of the Empire is collected, shall pay the duties on importation, introduction, and consumption; and on satisfactory proof of contravention shall be irremissibly confiscated. Our minister of the treasury is charged with the punctual execution of this decree.

"Given at Mexico the 9th of July, 1866."

And whereas, the decree thus recited, by declaring a belligerent blockade unsupported by competent military or naval force, is in violation of the neutral rights of the United States, as defined by the law of nations, as well as of the treaties existing between the United States of America and the aforesaid United States of Mexico:

Now, therefore, I, Andrew Johnson, President of the United States, do hereby proclaim and declare that the aforesaid decree is held, and will be held, by the United States to be absolutely null and void as against the Government and citizens of the United States; and that any attempt which shall be made to enforce the same against the Government or the citizens of the United States will be disallowed.

In witness whereof I have hereunto set my hand and caused the seal of the United States to be affixed.

Done at the city of Washington the seventeenth day of August, in the year of our Lord one thousand eight hundred and sixty-six, and of the Independence of the United States of America the ninety-first.

[SEAL.] ANDREW JOHNSON.

By the President:

WILLIAM H. SEWARD,
Secretary of State.

By order of the President of the United States:

E. D. TOWNSEND,
Assistant Adjutant-General.

GENERAL ORDERS, No. 84.

WAR DEPT., ADJT. GENERAL'S OFFICE,
Washington, October 4, 1866.

The following proclamations by the President are published for the information and government of the Army and all concerned:

I.

BY THE PRESIDENT OF THE UNITED STATES OF AMERICA:

A PROCLAMATION.

Whereas, by proclamations of the fifteenth and nineteenth of April, one thousand eight hundred and sixty-one, the President of the United States, in virtue of the power vested in him by the Constitution and the laws, declared that the laws of the United States were opposed, and the execution thereof obstructed, in the States of South Carolina, Georgia, Alabama, Florida, Mississippi, Louisiana, and Texas, by combinations too powerful to be suppressed by the ordinary course of judicial proceedings, or by the powers vested in the marshals by law;

And whereas, by another proclamation, made on the sixteenth day of August, in the same year, in pursuance of an act of Congress approved July thirteen, one thousand eight hundred and sixty-one, the inhabitants of the States of Georgia, South Carolina, Virginia, North Carolina, Tennessee, Alabama, Louisiana, Texas, Arkansas, Mississippi, and Florida (except the inhabitants of that part of the State of Virginia lying west of the Alleghany Mountains, and of such other parts of that State and other States before named as might maintain a loyal adhesion to the Union and the Constitution, or might be from time to time occupied and controlled by forces of the United States engaged in the dispersion of insurgents), were declared to be in a state of insurrection against the United States;

And whereas, by another proclamation of the first day of July, one thousand eight hundred and sixty-two, issued in pursuance of an act of Congress approved June seven, in the same year, the insurrection was declared to be still existing in the States aforesaid, with the exception of the certain specified counties in the State of Virginia;

And whereas, by another proclamation, made on the second day of April, one thousand eight hundred and sixty-three, in pursuance of the act of Congress of July thirteen, one thousand eight hundred and sixty-one, the exceptions named in the proclamation of August sixteen, one thousand eight hundred and sixty-one, were revoked, and the inhabitants of the States of Georgia, South Carolina, North Carolina, Tennessee, Alabama, Louisiana, Texas, Arkansas, Mississippi, Florida, and Virginia (except the forty-eight counties of Virginia designated as West Virginia, and the ports of New Orleans, Key West, Port Royal, and Beaufort, in North Carolina), were declared to be still in a state of insurrection against the United States;

And whereas, the House of Representatives, on the twenty-second day of July, one thousand eight hundred and sixty-one, adopted a resolution in the words following, namely:

"*Resolved by the House of Representatives of the Congress of the United States*, That the present deplorable civil war has been forced upon the country by the disunionists of the Southern States, now in revolt against the constitutional Government and in arms around the capital; that in this national emergency Congress, banishing all feelings of mere passion or resentment, will recollect only its duty to the whole country; that this war is not waged upon our part in any spirit of oppression nor for any purpose of conquest or subjugation, nor purpose of overthrowing or interfering with the rights or established institutions of those States, but to defend and maintain the supremacy of the Constitution, and to preserve the Union with all the dignity, equality, and rights of the several States unimpaired; and that as soon as these objects are accomplished the war ought to cease."

And whereas, the Senate of the United States, on the twenty-fifth day of July, one thousand eight hundred and sixty-one, adopted a resolution in the words following, to wit:

"*Resolved*, That the present deplorable civil war has been forced upon the country by the disunionsts of the Southern States, now in revolt against the constitutional Government and in arms around the capital; that in this national emergency Congress, banishing all feeling of mere passion or resentment, will recollect only its duty to the whole country; that this war is not prosecuted upon our part with any spirit of oppression nor for any purpose of conquest or subjugation, nor purpose of overthrowing or interfering with the rights or established institutions of those States, but to defend and maintain the supremacy of the Constitution and all laws made in pursuance thereof, and to preserve the Union with all the dignity, equality, and rights of the several States unimpaired; that as soon as these objects are accomplished the war ought to cease."

And whereas, these resolutions, though not joint or concurrent in form, are substantially identical, and as such may be regarded as having expressed the sense of Congress upon the subject to which they relate;

And whereas, by my proclamation of the thirteenth day of June last, the insurrection in the State of Tennessee was declared to have been suppressed, the authority of the United States therein to be undisputed, and such United States officers as had been duly commissioned to be in the undisturbed exercise of their official functions;

And whereas, there now exists no organized armed resistance of misguided citizens or others to the authority of the United States in the States of Georgia, South Carolina, Virginia, North Carolina, Tennessee, Alabama, Louisiana, Arkansas, Mississippi, and Florida, and the laws can be sustained and enforced therein by the proper civil authority, State or Federal, and the people of said States are well and loyally disposed, and have conformed, or will conform, in their legislation to the condition of affairs growing out of the amendment to the Constitution of the United States prohibiting slavery within the limits and jurisdiction of the United States;

And whereas, in view of the before-recited premises, it is the manifest determination of the American people that no State, of its own will, has the right or the power to go out of, or separate itself from, or be separated from, the American Union, and that therefore each State ought to remain and constitute an integral part of the United States;

And whereas, the people of the several before-mentioned States have, in the manner aforesaid, given satisfactory evidence that they acquiesce in this sovereign and important resolution of national unity;

And whereas, it is believed to be a fundamental principle of government that the people who have revolted, and who have been overcome and subdued, must either be dealt with so as to induce them voluntarily to become friends, or else they must be held by absolute military power, or devastated so as to prevent them from ever again doing harm as enemies, which last-named policy is abhorrent to humanity and to freedom;

And whereas, the Constitution of the United States provides for constituent communities only as States, and not as Territories, dependencies, provinces, or protectorates;

And whereas, such constituent States must necessarily be, and by the Constitution and laws of the United States are made equals, and placed upon a like footing as to political rights, immunities, dignity, and power with the several States with which they are united;

And whereas, the observance of political equality as a principle of right and justice is well calculated to encourage the people of the aforesaid States to be and become more and more constant and persevering in their renewed allegiance;

And whereas, standing armies, military occupation, martial law, military tribunals, and the suspension of the privilege of the writ of habeas corpus are, in time of peace, dangerous to public liberty, incompatible with the individual rights of the citizens, contrary to the genius and spirit of our free institutions, and exhaustive of the national resources, and ought not, therefore, to be sanctioned or allowed, except in cases of actual necessity, for repelling invasion or suppressing insurrection or rebellion;

And whereas, the policy of the Government of the United States, from the beginning of the insurrection to its overthrow and final suppression, has been in conformity with the principles herein set forth and enumerated:

Now, therefore, I, Andrew Johnson, President of the United States, do hereby proclaim and declare that the insurrection which heretofore existed in the States of Georgia, South Carolina, Virginia, North Carolina, Tennessee, Alabama, Louisiana, Arkansas, Mississippi, and Florida is at an end, and is henceforth to be so regarded.

In testimony whereof I have hereunto set my hand and caused the seal of the United States to be affixed.

Done at the city of Washington this second day of April, in the year of our Lord one thousand eight hundred and sixty-six, and of the Independence of the United States of America the ninetieth.

[SEAL.] ANDREW. JOHNSON.

By the President:

WILLIAM H. SEWARD,
Secretary of State.

II.

BY THE PRESIDENT OF THE UNITED STATES OF AMERICA:

A PROCLAMATION.

Whereas, by proclamations of the fifteenth and nineteenth of April, eighteen hundred and sixty-one, the President of the United States, in virtue of the power vested in him by the Constitution and the laws, declared that the laws of the United States were opposed, and the execution thereof obstructed, in the States of South Carolina, Georgia, Alabama, Florida, Mississippi, Louisiana, and Texas, by combinations too powerful to be suppressed by the ordinary course of judicial proceedings, or by the powers vested in the marshals by law;

And whereas, by another proclamation made on the sixteenth day of August, in the same year, in pursuance of an act of Congress approved July thirteen, one thousand eight hundred and sixty-one, the inhabitants of the States of Georgia, South Carolina, Virginia, North Carolina, Tennessee, Alabama, Louisiana, Texas, Arkansas, Mississippi, and Florida (except the inhabitants of that part of the State of Virginia lying west of the Alleghany Mountains, and except also the inhabitants of such other parts of that State, and the other States before named, as might maintain a loyal adhesion to the Union and the Constitution, or might be from time to time occupied and controlled by forces of the United States engaged in the dispersion of insurgents) were declared to be in a state of insurrection against the United States;

And whereas, by another proclamation of the first day of July, one thousand eight hundred and sixty-two, issued in pursuance of an act of Congress approved June 7, in the same year, the insurrection was declared to be still existing in the States aforesaid, with the exception of certain specified counties in the State of Virginia;

And whereas, by another proclamation made on the second day of April, one thousand eight hundred and sixty-three, in pursuance of the act of Congress of July thirteen, one thousand eight hundred and sixty-one, the exceptions named in the proclamation of August sixteen, one thousand eight hundred and sixty-one, were revoked, and the inhabitants of the States of Georgia, South Carolina, North Carolina, Tennessee, Alabama, Louisiana, Texas, Arkansas, Mississippi, Florida, and Virginia (except the forty-eight counties of Virginia designated as West Virginia, and the ports of New Orleans, Key West, Port Royal, and Beaufort, in North Carolina) were declared to be still in a state of insurrection against the United States;

And whereas, by another proclamation of the fifteenth day of September, one thousand eight hundred and sixty-three, made in pursuance of the act of Congress approved March third, one thousand eight hundred and sixty-three, the rebellion was declared to be still existing, and the privilege of the writ of habeas corpus was in certain specified cases suspended throughout the United States—said suspension to continue throughout the duration of the rebellion, or until said proclamation should, by a subsequent one to be issued by the President of the United States, be modified or revoked;

And whereas, the House of Representatives, on the twenty-second day of July, one thousand eight hundred and sixty-one, adopted a resolution in the words following, namely:

"*Resolved by the House of Representatives of the Congress of the United States*, That the present deplorable civil war has been forced upon the country by the disunionists of the Southern States, now in revolt against the constitutional Government and in arms around the capital; that in this national emergency Congress, banishing all feelings of mere passion or resentment, will recollect only its duty to the whole country; that this war is not waged upon our part in any spirit of oppression, nor for any purpose of conquest or subjugation, nor purpose of overthrowing or interfering with the rights or established institutions of those States, but to defend and maintain the supremacy of the Constitution, and to preserve the Union with all the dignity, equality, and rights of the several States unimpaired; and that as soon as these objects are accomplished the war ought to cease."

And whereas, the Senate of the United States, on the twenty-fifth day of July, one thousand eight hundred and sixty-one, adopted a resolution in the words following, to wit:

"*Resolved*, That the present deplorable civil war has been forced upon the country by the disunionists of the Southern States, now in revolt against the constitutional Government and in arms around the capital; that in this national emergency Congress, banishing all feeling of mere passion or resentment, will recollect only its duty to the whole country; that this war is not prosecuted upon our part in any spirit of oppression, nor for any purpose of conquest or subjugation, nor purpose of overthrowing or interfering with the rights or established institutions of those States, but to defend and maintain the supremacy of the Constitution and all laws made in pursuance thereof, and to preserve the Union with all the dignity, equality, and rights of the several States unimpaired; that as soon as these objects are accomplished the war ought to cease."

And whereas, these resolutions, though not joint or concurrent in form, are substantially identical, and as such have hitherto been and yet are regarded as having expressed the sense of Congress upon the subject to which they relate;

And whereas, the President of the United States, by proclamation of the thirteenth of June, 1865, declared that the insurrection in the State of Tennessee had been suppressed, and that the authority of the United States therein was undisputed, and that such United States officers as had been duly commissioned were in the undisturbed exercise of their official functions;

And whereas, the President of the United States, by further proclamation, issued on the second day of April, one thousand eight hundred and sixty-six, did promulgate and declare that there no longer existed any armed resistance of misguided citizens or others to the authority of the United States in any or in all the States before mentioned, excepting only the State of Texas, and did further promulgate and declare that the laws could be sustained and enforced in the several States before mentioned, except Texas, by the proper civil authorities, State or Federal, and that the people of the said States, except Texas, are well and loyally disposed, and have conformed, or will conform, in their legislation to the condition of affairs growing out of the amendment to the Constitution of the United States prohibiting slavery within the limits and jurisdiction of the United States;

And did further declare in the same proclamation that it is the manifest determination of the American people that no State of its own will has a right or power to go out of or separate itself from or be separated from the American Union, and that, therefore, each State ought to remain and constitute an integral part of the United States;

And did further declare in the same last-mentioned proclamation that the several aforementioned States, excepting Texas, had in the manner aforesaid given satisfactory evidence that they acquiesce in this sovereign and important resolution of national unity;

And whereas, the President of the United States, in the same proclamation, did further declare that it is believed to be a fundamental principle of government that the people who have revolted, and who have been overcome and subdued, must either be dealt with so as to induce them voluntarily to become friends, or else they must be held by absolute military power, or devastated so as to prevent them from ever again doing harm as enemies, which last-named policy is abhorrent to humanity and to freedom;

And whereas, the President did in the same proclamation further declare that the Constitution of the United States provides for constituent communities only as States and not as Territories, dependencies, provinces, or protectorates;

And further that such constituent States must necessarily be, and by the Constitution and laws of the United States are made equals, and placed upon a like footing as to political rights, immunities, dignity, and power with the several States with which they are united;

And did further declare that the observance of political equality as a principle of right and justice is well calculated to encourage the people of the before-named States, except Texas, to be and to become more and more constant and persevering in their renewed allegiance;

And whereas, the President did further declare that standing armies, military occupation, martial law, military tribunals, and the suspension of the writ of habeas corpus are in time of peace dangerous to public liberty, incompatible with the individual rights of the citizen, contrary to the genius and spirit of our free institutions, and exhaustive of the national resources, and ought not, therefore, to be sanctioned or allowed except in cases of actual necessity for repelling invasion or suppressing insurrection or rebellion;

And the President did further in the same proclamation declare that the policy of the Government of the United States from the beginning of the insurrection to its overthrow and final suppression had been conducted in conformity with the principles in the last-named proclamation recited;

And whereas, the President, in the said proclamation of the thirteenth of June, one thousand eight hundred and sixty-five,* upon the grounds therein stated and hereinbefore recited, did then and thereby proclaim and declare that the insurrection which heretofore existed in the several States before named, except in Texas, was at an end, and was henceforth to be so regarded;

And whereas, subsequently to the said second day of April, one thousand eight hundred and sixty-six, the insurrection in the State of Texas has been completely and everywhere suppressed and ended, and the authority of the United States has been successfully and completely established in the said State of Texas, and now remains therein unresisted and undisputed, and such of the proper United States officers as have been duly commissioned within the limits of the said State are now in the undisturbed exercise of their official functions;

And whereas, the laws can now be sustained and enforced in the said State of Texas by the proper civil authority, State or Federal, and the people of the said State of Texas, like the people of the other States before named, are well and loyally disposed and have conformed, or will conform, in their legislation to the condition of affairs growing out of the amendment of the Constitution of the United States prohibiting slavery within the limits and jurisdiction of the United States;

And whereas, all the reasons and conclusions set forth in regard to the several States therein specially named now apply equally and in all respects to the State of Texas, as well as to the other States which had been involved in insurrection;

And whereas, adequate provision has been made by military orders to enforce the execution of the acts of Congress, aid the civil authorities, and secure obedience to the Constitution and laws of the United States within the State of Texas, if a resort to military force for such purpose should at any time become necessary:

Now, therefore, I, Andrew Johnson, President of the United States, do hereby proclaim and declare that the insurrection which heretofore existed in the State of Texas is at an end, and is to be henceforth so regarded in that State, as in the other States before named, in which the said insurrection was proclaimed to be

* Error; should be April 2, 1866.

at an end by the aforesaid proclamation of the second day of April, one thousand eight hundred and sixty-six.

And I do further proclaim that the said insurrection is at an end, and that peace, order, tranquillity, and civil authority now exist in and throughout the whole of the United States of America.

In testimony whereof I have hereunto set my hand and caused the seal of the United States to be affixed.

Done at the city of Washington this twentieth day of August, in the year of our Lord one thousand eight hundred and sixty-six, and of the Independence of the United States of America the ninety-first.

[SEAL.] ANDREW JOHNSON.

By the President:

WILLIAM H. SEWARD,
Secretary of State.

By order of the Secretary of War:

E. D. TOWNSEND,
Assistant Adjutant-General.

ADJUTANT-GENERAL'S OFFICE,
Washington, October 20, 1866.

Hon. EDWIN M. STANTON,
Secretary of War:

SIR: * * * * * *

VOLUNTEER SERVICE.

The entire management of this branch of the duties of this office has continued under the immediate charge of Bvt. Brig. Gen. Thomas M. Vincent, assistant adjutant-general.

The number of volunteers borne on the returns of armies, military divisions, and departments on the 1st of May, 1865, was reported at 985,516. Subsequent to that date the number of white and colored troops taken up on the returns was 48,548, which, added to this first, made the entire number to be mustered out 1,034,064.

The number (48,548) was made up as follows:

State troops	5,844
First Corps	3,008
Veteran Reserve Corps	734
Colored troops	14,038
U. S. Volunteers	995
Volunteers for old and new organizations in rendezvous	10,938
Volunteers and drafted men en route to commands and not joined	6,524
Forces in transit dropped from returns of one command, and necessarily not taken up on that of the one for which destined	6,467
Total	48,548

MUSTERS OUT OF SERVICE.

The last annual report of the Adjutant-General brought down the operations of the Department in mustering out the Volunteer Army to the 15th of November, 1865, at which date 800,963 had been discharged.

The following is a statement of the numbers mustered out up to the dates set opposite them, showing the rapidity with which the work was continued after that time:

January 20, 1866	918,722
February 15, 1866	952,452
March 10, 1866	967,887
May 1, 1866	986,782
June 30, 1866	1,010,670
November 1, 1866	1,023,021

Leaving in service 11,043 volunteers, colored and white.

The following were the orders issued to complete the series necessary to take out of service all the remaining volunteer forces mentioned in the foregoing statement, amounting to 233,101:

December 11, 1865.—All white troops in the Departments of Georgia, Alabama, and Mississippi, leaving the aggregate force—including regulars—in the said departments 7,000 men.

December 30.—All volunteers in the Department of the East, all in the Middle Department except 1,500, and all in the Department of Virginia except 2,500.

December 30.—All troops in the Military Division of the Tennessee whose terms of service would expire in February, 1866, and, in addition, the force in the Department of the Tennessee to be reduced to 4,000 men.

December 30.—The force of white troops in the Military Division of the Gulf to be reduced to 10,000 men, and the force of black troops to 10,000.

In case of the public interest not warranting so great a reduction, the figures indicated to be approached as nearly as possible.

January 9, 1866.—All volunteer troops in the Department of Virginia.

March 15.—The force of colored troops in the Military Division of the Tennessee, so as to leave for the respective military departments as follows: Kentucky, two regiments; Tennessee, four regiments; Georgia, one regiment; Alabama, two regiments; Mississippi, four regiments.

March 15.—All colored troops in the Department of South Carolina except one regiment.

March 15.—All colored troops in the Department of Florida except one regiment.

March 15.—All colored troops in the Department of Washington except one regiment.

March 15.—All colored troops in the Military Division of the Mississippi except four regiments.

April.—All volunteers, both white and colored, in the Military Division of the Tennessee; this under discretionary authority given the commanding general of that division.

May 18.—All remaining white volunteers in the Military Division of the Gulf, Department of North Carolina, and Department of South Carolina.

July 11.—All the remaining officers and men of the First Army Corps (Hancock's).

From time to time, as the troops could be dispensed with, thirty-nine regiments in addition to the foregoing were ordered to be mustered out.

The movement homeward commenced May 29, 1865, and had it been possible to spare all the volunteers in service the entire number, 1,034,064, could easily have been disbanded and returned to their homes within three months from that date.

The annexed table, marked C, shows the whole force mustered out since May 1, 1865, properly classified.

The recruitment of white volunteers was under the exclusive control of the Adjutant-General from the first call for troops until May 1, 1863, when it was placed under the Provost-Marshal-General, who, being by law charged with the enrollment and draft, was charged also with enlistment, that the entire recruiting service for white volunteers might be under one head.

The regulations framed by this office for volunteer recruiting service remained in force with but slight modifications during the war.

The re-enlistment of veteran volunteers in the field and the recruitment of all colored volunteers was under the direction of the Adjutant-General.

The following statement shows the numbers recruited under his direction:

Militia (three and nine months) from April 15, 1861, to May 1, 1863	195,921
Volunteers from May 3, 1861, to May 1, 1863	1,149,719
Veteran volunteers re-enlisted in the field, 1863-'64	*138,251
Colored troops during the war	169,624
Total	1,653,515

making about two-thirds of the whole number furnished during the war.

The subject of organizing volunteer troops was under the charge of the Adjutant-General throughout the war. This involved—

First. The establishing and management of the general depots or rendezvous in the several States for collecting and instructing recruits.

Second. The care of all recruits (including those enlisted under the Provost-Marshal-General's Bureau) after arrival at general depot.

Third. The organization of the recruits, if for new commands, into regiments and companies.

Fourth. The forwarding of all troops, new organizations and detachments of recruits for old ones, to the field.

Fifth. The muster in of commissioned officers and enlisted men for all organizations already in the field, and for those serving not in the field, but under the control of commanding generals of departments. This important duty, in which many difficult questions arise, upon the solution of which depends the commencement of pay or date of rank, required at times a corps of 200 commissaries and assistant commissaries of musters, or one commissary for each military geographical division and department and each army, and one assistant for each division of troops.

Sixth. The mustering out and discharging all volunteers and militia and returning them to their homes.

Table D, giving two classifications—one by States, the other by calls—shows the number of new organizations organized and forwarded to the field under direction of this office during the war.

PROVOST-MARSHAL-GENERAL'S BUREAU.

Pursuant to the provisions of section 33 of the "Act to increase and fix the military peace establishment of the United States," approved July 28, 1866, the Bureau and office of the Provost-Marshal-General of the United States were discontinued on the 28th of August, and by General Orders, No. 66, War Department, Adjutant-General's Office, August 20, 1866, all business relating in any way to the Provost-Marshal-General's Bureau, or the raising of troops, with all the accounts and claims connected therewith, of whatever character or date or whensoever incurred, were transferred to the Adjutant-General of the Army, to whom all the records, papers, funds, and property were turned over. The Adjutant-General was authorized to retain such officers and clerks as were required, and directed to reduce the force from time to time as it could be done without detriment to the public service. The regulations and orders framed for the Provost-

*By credits subsequently allowed this number has been increased to 146,030.

Marshal-General's Bureau, in so far as they were applicable, were continued in force.

The transfer under these orders having been duly made, the business of the Bureau was consolidated into the "Enrollment" and "Disbursing" branches of the Adjutant-General's Office.

The Enrollment Branch is charged with answering calls for information from the Second Auditor, Pension Office, Paymaster-General, State and local authorities, and with miscellaneous business. In addition to this the work of consolidating and transferring the names of all men drafted into the service of the United States during the rebellion into books especially prepared and arranged by States and districts has been commenced, so that reference for information may be made easy. The number of names to be thus transferred is 776,829.

The Disbursing Branch is charged with all disbursements from the fund for "collecting, drilling, and organizing volunteers," and the "enrollment and draft fund;" also the business relating to all accounts and claims, of whatever character or date or whensoever incurred, connected with the raising of troops during the war.

Accounts relating to the current expenses of the mustering and disbursing offices in the respective States, such as rent, clerk hire, postage, telegrams, &c., are paid by chief mustering and disbursing officers from a limited supply of funds kept in their hands for that purpose.

All other accounts are forwarded, after a full examination by the chief mustering and disbursing officer, with his remarks and recommendation, and if proper are paid by the disbursing officer connected immediately with this office.

Of the records, those relating to the Veteran Reserve Corps and deserters have been merged into the "Roll and Return Division" of this office.

The Medical Branch was duly transferred, by order of the Secretary of War, to the charge of the Surgeon-General of the Army, with the view of complying with the requirements of the act approved July 28, 1866, in regard to the publication of the medical statistics of the Provost-Marshal-General's Bureau.

Prior to the transfer of the duties the Provost-Marshal-General had consolidated offices and reduced the force of his employés to the lowest limit consistent with the present prompt transaction of the public business.

Offices under the direction of a chief mustering and disbursing officer were continued at the following places:

State.	Station.	For what States, &c.
Vermont	Brattleborough	Vermont.
Massachusetts	Boston	Massachusetts, Maine, New Hampshire.
Connecticut	Hartford	Connecticut, Rhode Island.
New York	Albany	New York.
Pennsylvania	Philadelphia	Pennsylvania, New Jersey.
Maryland	Baltimore	Maryland, Delaware.
Ohio	Columbus	Ohio, West Virginia.
Indiana	Indianapolis	Indiana.
Kentucky	Louisville	Kentucky.
Illinois	Springfield	Illinois.
Missouri	Saint Louis	Missouri, Kansas, Dakota, Colorado, and Nebraska.
Iowa	Davenport	Iowa.
Minnesota	Saint Paul	Minnesota.
Wisconsin	Madison	Wisconsin.
Michigan	Detroit	Michigan.
Tennessee	Nashville	Tennessee.
New Mexico	Santa Fé	New Mexico.
California	San Francisco	California, Nevada, Oregon, and Washington Territory.

Measures have been adopted to obtain an accurate knowledge of the condition of the business in the respective States and Territories, with the view of closing all these offices at the earliest date it can be done without detriment to the public service, and collecting all the valuable papers and records at the seat of Government, where they will be filed in proper manner for future reference.

The Provost-Marshal-General's report of the operations of his Bureau, dated March 17, 1866, renders unnecessary reference in more detail to its business now under this office.

No appropriation of money will be required for this branch during the next fiscal year.

COLORED VOLUNTEERS.

For all information in relation to colored volunteer troops I beg leave to refer to the annexed report of Bvt. Col. C. W. Foster, assistant adjutant-general of volunteers, who organized and has continued in charge of that branch of the duties of this office.

In addition to the distinctive branches already referred to, there are four others immediately connected with this office, as follows:

1. The subject of commissions, under Bvt. Brig. Gen. J. C. Kelton, assistant adjutant-general. This branch embraces the preparation and issue of all letters of appointment and commissions to officers appointed by the President, and their accurate registry; the regulating of proper succession and promotion of officers; preparation of orders of promotion and army registers; ordnance-sergeants', hospital stewards', and sutlers' warrants; the solution of numerous questions of rank and of pay depending on dates of appointment and acceptance of commission, and of questions of organization of the Army under acts of Congress. Some little idea may be formed of the scope of this class of duties by the fact that over ten thousand commissions, brevets and other, have been issued since November 1, 1865, for regular and volunteer officers.

2. The preparation and distribution of all special orders, the measures for apprehension and trial of deserters, the miscellaneous correspondence with general and staff officers of the Regular and Volunteer Army, and regimental officers of the Regular Army, relating to leaves of absence, changes of station, &c., and the recruiting service for the Regular Army, details of which have been given above, have been under the immediate direction of Bvt. Brig. Gen. Robert Williams, assistant adjutant-general, who has arranged the detail and assignment of recruiting officers, the drawing of requisitions for funds to supply them, the assignment and forwarding of detachments from depots to regiments, the preparation of instructions to superintendents, and the correspondence with officers concerning accounts, returns, &c.

In addition to these duties, on the transfer of Brevet Brigadier-General Nichols, assistant adjutant-general, to the headquarters Division of the Missouri, General Williams was charged with correspondence on miscellaneous subjects, such as relate to reports of generals, claims, &c., which involves the investigation of all matters of a general nature upon which reports are to be made to the War Department and General-in-Chief, and with the proper filing of letters received.

3. Bvt. Brig. Gen. Samuel Breck, assistant adjutant-general, is charged with the preparation and distribution of all books of military

regulation and instruction which are used in the Army, and of all blank forms for muster-rolls, returns, &c.; with the custody and correction of returns, enlistments, and muster-rolls, showing the strength and military history of every soldier, together with the numerous questions requiring patient and laborious examination, and voluminous correspondence touching all that relates to soldiers, such as answering inquiries from the accounting, pension, and pay offices, and from relatives; removing charge of desertion; settling claims for horses lost; discharge of minors, &c.; the arrangement and care of old records collected from commands broken up, and the preparation, under a special act of Congress, of a register of every volunteer organization received into the U. S. service during the rebellion.

4. Bvt. Col. H. C. Wood, assistant adjutant-general, is charged with the preparation of all orders issued on court-martial cases, and of all business relating to them after they are reported upon by the Bureau of Military Justice, and with supervision over military prisoners, wherever confined. Also with the examination and auditing of accounts of regimental, post, and company funds, and also with the proper filing and copying of battle reports.

But a faint idea is conveyed in the foregoing of the vast amount of business daily transacted in this office, which is so made up of details as to be incapable of minute description.

It is only due to the officers, clerks, and employés in every branch to say that in intelligence, patient fidelity, accuracy, and neatness in keeping their records, they cannot, as a body, be surpassed.

DESERTERS.

From various causes arising out of the unsettled state of the Army there was a large number of desertions at the close of the war. To check this evil recruiting officers were instructed to apprehend and send to military posts for trial all deserters who could be found in the vicinity of their stations, and lists were sent from companies, with a description of deserters, to facilitate their arrest. The number apprehended under this system from February 1, 1866, to October 1, 1866, is 1,029.

As an inducement to return to their duty the President published an offer of pardon to all who would report themselves at a military post by the 15th of August, 1866. Three hundred and fourteen availed themselves of this act of clemency.

* * * * * * *

I have the honor to be, sir, very respectfully, your obedient servant,

E. D. TOWNSEND,

Assistant Adjutant-General.

TABLE C.—*Exhibit of volunteer troops mustered out and returned to their homes from May 1, 1865, to November 1, 1866.*

States.	Regiments.	Independent companies.	Batteries.	Aggregate strength—commissioned officers and enlisted men.
Alabama	1	......	......	667
Arizona	1	......	......	357
Arkansas	6	......	1	5, 186
California	9	10	......	6, 938
Colorado	2	......	1	1, 745
Connecticut	19	......	3	14, 169
Dakota	......	2	......	169
Delaware	5	......	2	2, 861
District of Columbia	1	......	......	1, 157
Florida	2	1	......	922
Georgia	......	2	......	147
Illinois	133	2	27	92, 567
Indiana	98	......	19	71, 209
Indian Nation	3	......	......	2, 017
Iowa	44	2	4	32, 173
Kansas	11	8	2	8, 496
Kentucky	24	......	5	14, 961
Louisiana	4	......	......	2, 642
Maine	17	24	7	19, 971
Maryland	14	3	3	11, 312
Massachusetts	39	12	21	34. 270
Michigan	44	1	2	38, 385
Minnesota	15	......	3	12, 437
Mississippi	......	5	......	355
Missouri	39	......	......	28, 266
Nebraska	......	8	......	508
Nevada	......	9	......	833
New Hampshire	16	......	......	10, 846
New Jersey	21	......	5	21, 153
New Mexico	2	......	......	1, 731
New York	163	......	24	136, 593
North Carolina	3	......	......	2, 224
Ohio	137	18	21	102, 398
Oregon	......	16	......	1, 124
Pennsylvania	116	5	9	107, 332
Rhode Island	8	1	......	5, 616
Tennessee	24	3	5	14, 659
Texas	2	......	......	1, 275
Vermont	12	2	3	9, 932
Virginia	......	1	......	85
Washington	......	3	......	253
West Virginia	15	3	5	12, 965
Wisconsin	49	......	10	38, 655
First Army Corps (Hancock's)	9	......	......	7, 406
U. S. Volunteers	6	......	......	5, 081
U. S. Colored Troops	124	1	10	111, 682
Veteran Reserve Corps	24	174	......	27, 291
Total	1, 262	316	192	1, 023, 021

THOMAS M. VINCENT,
Assistant Adjutant-General.

WAR DEPARTMENT, ADJUTANT-GENERAL'S OFFICE,
November 1, 1866.

TABLE D.—*Exhibit of the number of organizations—volunteers and militia—organized and mustered into the service of the United States during the rebellion.*

UNDER CALL OF APRIL 15, 1861, FOR 75,000 MILITIA.

States and Territories.	Infantry.			Cavalry.			Artillery.					
							Regiments.		Battalions.		Companies.	
	Regiments.	Battalions.	Independent companies.	Regiments.	Battalions.	Independent companies.	Light.	Heavy.	Light.	Heavy.	Light.	Heavy.
Alabama	......	......	......	......	......	......	......	......	......	......	......	......
Arizona	......	......	......	......	......	......	......	......	......	......	......	......
Arkansas	......	......	......	......	......	......	......	......	......	......	......	......
California	......	......	......	......	......	......	......	......	......	......	......	......
Colorado	......	......	......	......	......	......	......	......	......	......	......	......
Connecticut	3	......	......	......	......	......	......	......	......	......	......	......
Dakota	......	......	......	......	......	......	......	......	......	......	......	......
Delaware	2	......	......	......	......	......	......	......	......	......	......	......
District of Columbia	......	......	......	......	......	......	......	......	......	......	......	......
Florida	......	......	......	......	......	......	......	......	......	......	......	......
Georgia	......	......	......	......	......	......	......	......	......	......	......	......
Illinois	6	......	14	......	......	......	......	......	......	......	5	......
Indiana	6	......	......	......	......	......	......	......	......	......	......	......
Indian Territory	......	......	......	......	......	......	......	......	......	......	......	......
Iowa	1	......	......	......	......	......	......	......	......	......	......	......
Kansas	......	......	......	......	......	......	......	......	......	......	......	......
Kentucky	......	......	......	......	......	......	......	......	......	......	......	......
Louisiana	......	......	......	......	......	......	......	......	......	......	......	......
Maine	1	......	......	......	......	......	......	......	......	......	......	......
Maryland	......	......	......	......	......	......	......	......	......	......	......	......
Massachusetts	5	1	......	......	......	......	......	......	......	......	1	......
Michigan	1	......	......	......	......	......	......	......	......	......	......	......
Minnesota	1	......	......	......	......	......	......	......	......	......	......	......
Mississippi	......	......	......	......	......	......	......	......	......	......	......	......
Missouri	5	......	3	......	......	......	......	......	......	......	2	......
Nebraska	......	......	......	......	......	......	......	......	......	......	......	......
Nevada	......	......	......	......	......	......	......	......	......	......	......	......
New Hampshire	1	......	......	......	......	......	......	......	......	......	......	......
New Jersey	4	......	......	......	......	......	......	......	......	......	......	......
New Mexico	......	......	......	......	......	......	......	......	......	......	......	......
New York	17	......	......	......	......	......	......	......	......	......	......	......
North Carolina	......	......	......	......	......	......	......	......	......	......	......	......
Ohio	22	......	......	......	......	2	......	......	......	......	2	......
Oregon	......	......	......	......	......	......	......	......	......	......	......	......
Pennsylvania	25	......	......	......	......	......	......	......	......	......	......	......
Rhode Island	1	......	......	......	......	......	......	......	......	......	1	......
South Carolina	......	......	......	......	......	......	......	......	......	......	......	......
Tennessee	......	......	......	......	......	......	......	......	......	......	......	......
Texas	......	......	......	......	......	......	......	......	......	......	......	......
Vermont	1	......	......	......	......	......	......	......	......	......	......	......
Virginia	......	......	......	......	......	......	......	......	......	......	......	......
Washington Territory	......	......	......	......	......	......	......	......	......	......	......	......
West Virginia	1	......	......	......	......	......	......	......	......	......	......	......
Wisconsin	1	......	......	......	......	......	......	......	......	......	......	......
First Army Corps	......	......	......	......	......	......	......	......	......	......	......	......
U. S. Volunteers	......	......	......	......	......	......	......	......	......	......	......	......
U. S. Colored Troops	......	......	......	......	......	......	......	......	......	......	......	......
Total	104	1	17	......	......	2	......	......	......	......	11	......

UNDER CALL OF MAY 3, 1861, FOR THIRTY-NINE REGIMENTS OF INFANTRY AND ONE OF CAVALRY, AND ACTS OF JULY 22 AND 25, FOR 500,000 VOLUNTEERS.

States and Territories.	Infantry Regiments.	Infantry Battalions.	Infantry Independent companies.	Cavalry Regiments.	Cavalry Battalions.	Cavalry Independent companies.	Artillery Regiments Light.	Artillery Regiments Heavy.	Artillery Battalions Light.	Artillery Battalions Heavy.	Artillery Companies Light.	Artillery Companies Heavy.
Alabama	......	......	......	......	......	......	......	......	......	......	......	......
Arizona	......	......	......	......	......	......	......	......	......	......	......	......
Arkansas	......	......	......	......	......	......	......	......	......	......	......	......
California	......	......	......	......	......	......	......	......	......	......	......	......
Colorado	......	......	......	......	......	......	......	......	......	......	......	......
Connecticut	9	......	......	......	......	6	......	1	......	......	1	......
Dakota	......	......	......	......	......	......	......	......	......	......	......	......
Delaware	2	......	......	1	......	......	......	......	......	......	1	1
District of Columbia	......	......	......	......	......	......	......	......	......	......	......	......
Florida	......	......	......	......	......	......	......	......	......	......	......	......
Georgia	......	......	......	......	......	......	......	......	......	......	......	......
Illinois	58	......	......	13	......	......	......	......	......	......	25	......
Indiana	49	......	......	3	......	......	......	......	......	......	16	......

TABLE D.—*Exhibit of the number of organizations—volunteers and militia—organized and mustered into the service of the United States during the rebellion*—Continued.

UNDER CALL OF MAY 3, 1861, FOR THIRTY-NINE REGIMENTS OF INFANTRY AND ONE OF CAVALRY, AND ACTS OF JULY 22 AND 25, FOR 500,000 VOLUNTEERS—Continued.

States and Territories.	Infantry.			Cavalry.			Artillery.					
	Regiments.	Battalions.	Independent companies.	Regiments.	Battalions.	Independent companies.	Regiments.		Battalions.		Companies.	
							Light.	Heavy.	Light.	Heavy.	Light.	Heavy.
Indian Territory												
Iowa	16		3	5		2					3	
Kansas	3			5							2	
Kentucky	28			6							2	
Louisiana												
Maine	14		1	1							6	
Maryland	10		1	1		4					2	
Massachusetts	25		7	1				1			7	
Michigan	18		5	3		2					8	
Minnesota	4		2			3					2	
Mississippi												
Missouri	24		6	7	1	2	1	1			4	
Nebraska												
Nevada												
New Hampshire	7		3								1	
New Jersey	10			1							2	
New Mexico												
New York	89		4	12		1	2	4	3		14	
North Carolina												
Ohio	77		2	6		7	1				16	
Oregon												
Pennsylvania	77		4	11			1	1				1
Rhode Island	3				2		1	1				
South Carolina												
Tennessee												
Texas												
Vermont	7		3	1							2	
Virginia												
Washington Territory												
West Virginia	11			2							3	
Wisconsin	19		1	3		1					12	1
First Army Corps												
U. S. Volunteers												
U. S. Colored Troops												
Total	560		42	82	3	28	6	9	3		129	3

UNDER CALL OF JULY 2, 1862, FOR 300,000 VOLUNTEERS.

States and Territories.	Inf. Regiments.	Inf. Battalions.	Inf. Independent companies.	Cav. Regiments.	Cav. Battalions.	Cav. Independent companies.	Art. Regiments, Light.	Art. Regiments, Heavy.	Art. Battalions, Light.	Art. Battalions, Heavy.	Art. Companies, Light.	Art. Companies, Heavy.
Alabama												
Arizona												
Arkansas												
California												
Colorado												
Connecticut	7							1			1	
Dakota												
Delaware												
District of Columbia												
Florida												
Georgia												
Illinois	61			1							7	
Indiana	31			2							8	
Indian Territory												
Iowa	24		3	4							1	
Kansas	4										1	
Kentucky	4			9							2	
Louisiana												
Maine	4							1				
Maryland	4										1	
Massachusetts	11			2				1		1	6	
Michigan	12		1	8							6	
Minnesota	5											
Mississippi												
Missouri	7			3								

TABLE D.—*Exhibit of the number of organizations—volunteers and militia—organized and mustered into the service of the United States during the rebellion*—Continued.

UNDER CALL OF JULY 2, 1862, FOR 300,000 VOLUNTEERS—Continued.

States and Territories.	Infantry.			Cavalry.			Artillery.					
							Regiments.		Battalions.		Companies.	
	Regiments.	Battalions.	Independent companies.	Regiments.	Battalions.	Independent companies.	Light.	Heavy.	Light.	Heavy.	Light.	Heavy.
Nebraska												
Nevada												
New Hampshire	6											
New Jersey	5											
New Mexico												
New York	61		5	1				5			12	
North Carolina												
Ohio	44		8	6				2			10	
Oregon												
Pennsylvania	35		5	6				1				
Rhode Island	1			1								
South Carolina												
Tennessee												
Texas												
Vermont	2							1				
Virginia												
Washington Territory												
West Virginia	5		2	1							2	
Wisconsin	13											
First Army Corps												
U. S. Volunteers												
U. S. Colored Troops												
Total	346		24	44				12		1	57	

UNDER CALL OF AUGUST 4, 1862, FOR 300,000 MILITIA.

States and Territories.	Infantry Regiments.	Infantry Battalions.	Infantry Independent companies.	Cavalry Regiments.	Cavalry Battalions.	Cavalry Independent companies.	Artillery Regiments Light.	Artillery Regiments Heavy.	Artillery Battalions Light.	Artillery Battalions Heavy.	Artillery Companies Light.	Artillery Companies Heavy.
Alabama												
Arizona												
Arkansas												
California												
Colorado												
Connecticut	7											
Dakota												
Delaware	2											
District of Columbia												
Florida												
Georgia												
Illinois												
Indiana												
Indian Territory												
Iowa												
Kansas												
Kentucky												
Louisiana												
Maine	8											
Maryland												
Massachusetts	17										1	
Michigan												
Minnesota				1		4					1	
Mississippi												
Missouri												
Nebraska												
Nevada												
New Hampshire	2		3									
New Jersey	11											
New Mexico												
New York	2											
North Carolina												
Ohio												
Oregon												
Pennsylvania	15		2									
Rhode Island	2											
South Carolina												
Tennessee												
Texas												

TABLE D.—*Exhibit of the number of organizations—volunteers and militia—organized and mustered into the service of the United States during the rebellion*—Continued.

UNDER CALL OF AUGUST 4, 1862, FOR 300,000 MILITIA—Continued.

States and Territories.	Infantry.			Cavalry.			Artillery.					
							Regiments.		Battalions.		Companies.	
	Regiments.	Battalions.	Independent companies.	Regiments.	Battalions.	Independent companies.	Light.	Heavy.	Light.	Heavy.	Light.	Heavy.
Vermont	5											
Virginia												
Washington Territory												
West Virginia												
Wisconsin	1											
First Army Corps												
U. S. Volunteers												
U. S. Colored Troops												
Total	72		5	1		4					2	

UNDER CALL OF JUNE 15, 1863, FOR 100,000 SIX-MONTHS' MILITIA—FROM MARYLAND, PENNSYLVANIA, OHIO, AND WEST VIRGINIA.

States and Territories.	Infantry.			Cavalry.			Artillery.					
							Regiments.		Battalions.		Companies.	
	Regiments.	Battalions.	Independent companies.	Regiments.	Battalions.	Independent companies.	Light.	Heavy.	Light.	Heavy.	Light.	Heavy.
Alabama												
Arizona												
Arkansas												
California												
Colorado												
Connecticut												
Dakota												
Delaware												
District of Columbia												
Florida												
Georgia												
Illinois												
Indiana	4											
Indian Territory												
Iowa												
Kansas												
Kentucky												
Louisiana												
Maine												
Maryland	2					5					2	
Massachusetts												
Michigan												
Minnesota												
Mississippi												
Missouri												
Nebraska												
Nevada												
New Hampshire												
New Jersey												
New Mexico												
New York												
North Carolina												
Ohio	2					8						
Oregon												
Pennsylvania		3	2	3	1						3	
Rhode Island												
South Carolina												
Tennessee												
Texas												
Vermont												
Virginia												
Washington Territory												
West Virginia				1							1	
Wisconsin												
First Army Corps												
U. S. Volunteers												
U. S. Colored Troops												
Total	8	3	2	4	1	13					6	

TABLE D.—*Exhibit of the number of organizations—volunteers and militia—organized and mustered into the service of the United States during the rebellion*—Continued.

UNDER CALL OF OCTOBER 17, 1863, FOR 300,000 VOLUNTEERS.

States and Territories.	Infantry.			Cavalry.			Artillery.					
	Regiments.	Battalions.	Independent companies.	Regiments.	Battalions.	Independent companies.	Regiments.		Battalions.		Companies.	
							Light.	Heavy.	Light.	Heavy.	Light.	Heavy.
Alabama												
Arizona												
Arkansas												
California												
Colorado												
Connecticut	1		4									
Dakota												
Delaware												
District of Columbia												
Florida												
Georgia												
Illinois				1		9					1	
Indiana	6			5								
Indian Territory												
Iowa												
Kansas	1			2								
Kentucky											1	
Louisiana												
Maine	2											
Maryland												
Massachusetts	1											
Michigan												
Minnesota												
Mississippi												
Missouri				1			1					
Nebraska												
Nevada												
New Hampshire												
New Jersey	3			2							3	
New Mexico												
New York	3		4	7		2					2	
North Carolina												
Ohio				1								
Oregon												
Pennsylvania												
Rhode Island				1				1				
South Carolina												
Tennessee												
Texas												
Vermont	1										1	1
Virginia												
Washington Territory												
West Virginia												
Wisconsin												
First Army Corps												
U. S. Volunteers												
U. S. Colored Troops												
Total	18		8	20		11	1	1			8	1

UNDER CALLS OF FEBRUARY 1, 1864, FOR 500,000 MEN, AND MARCH 14, 1864, FOR 200,000 MEN.

States and Territories.	Infantry Regiments.	Infantry Battalions.	Infantry Independent companies.	Cavalry Regiments.	Cavalry Battalions.	Cavalry Independent companies.	Artillery Regiments Light.	Artillery Regiments Heavy.	Artillery Battalions Light.	Artillery Battalions Heavy.	Artillery Companies Light.	Artillery Companies Heavy.
Alabama												
Arizona												
Arkansas												
California												
Colorado												
Connecticut												
Dakota												
Delaware												
District of Columbia												
Florida												
Georgia												
Illinois						9						
Indiana												

TABLE D.—*Exhibit of the number of organizations—volunteers and militia—organized and mustered into the service of the United States during the rebellion*—Continued.

UNDER CALLS OF FEBRUARY 1, 1864, FOR 500,000 MEN, AND MARCH 14, 1864, FOR 200,000 MEN—Continued.

States and Territories.	Infantry.			Cavalry.			Artillery.					
							Regiments.		Battalions.		Companies.	
	Regiments.	Battalions.	Independent companies.	Regiments.	Battalions.	Independent companies.	Light.	Heavy.	Light.	Heavy.	Light.	Heavy.
Indian Territory												
Iowa												
Kansas				1								
Kentucky												
Louisiana												
Maine	2		2	1		8					1	
Maryland												
Massachusetts	5										3	
Michigan												
Minnesota				1		1						
Mississippi												
Missouri												
Nebraska												
Nevada												
New Hampshire				1								
New Jersey												
New Mexico												
New York	1			7				3				
North Carolina												
Ohio			15									
Oregon												
Pennsylvania												
Rhode Island												
South Carolina												
Tennessee												
Texas												
Vermont												
Virginia												
Washington Territory												
West Virginia												
Wisconsin	4										1	3
First Army Corps												
U. S. Volunteers												
U. S. Colored Troops												
Total	12		17	11		18		3			5	3

UNDER CALLS OF 1864 FOR 100-DAYS' TROOPS.

States and Territories.	Inf. Regiments.	Inf. Battalions.	Inf. Independent companies.	Cav. Regiments.	Cav. Battalions.	Cav. Independent companies.	Art. Regiments Light.	Art. Regiments Heavy.	Art. Battalions Light.	Art. Battalions Heavy.	Art. Companies Light.	Art. Companies Heavy.
Alabama												
Arizona												
Arkansas												
California												
Colorado												
Connecticut												
Dakota												
Delaware			3									
District of Columbia												
Florida												
Georgia												
Illinois	13		2									
Indiana	8											
Indian Territory												
Iowa	4	1										
Kansas	1											
Kentucky												
Louisiana												
Maine												
Maryland	2											
Massachusetts	5		9									
Michigan												
Minnesota												
Mississippi												
Missouri												

TABLE D.—*Exhibit of the number of organizations—volunteers and militia—organized and mustered into the service of the United States during the rebellion*—Continued.

UNDER CALLS OF 1864 FOR 100-DAYS' TROOPS—Continued.

States and Territories.	Infantry.			Cavalry.			Artillery.					
							Regiments.		Battalions.		Companies.	
	Regiments.	Battalions.	Independent companies.	Regiments.	Battalions.	Independent companies.	Light.	Heavy.	Light.	Heavy.	Light.	Heavy.
Nebraska												
Nevada												
New Hampshire												
New Jersey	1											
New Mexico												
New York	10		2								1	
North Carolina												
Ohio	42											
Oregon												
Pennsylvania	6	1	2			5			1		1	
Rhode Island												
South Carolina												
Tennessee												
Texas												
Vermont												
Virginia												
Washington Territory												
West Virginia												
Wisconsin	3											
First Army Corps												
U. S. Volunteers												
U. S. Colored Troops												
Total	95	2	18			5			1		2	

UNDER CALL OF JULY 18, 1864, FOR 500,000 MEN.

States and Territories.	Inf. Regiments.	Inf. Battalions.	Inf. Independent companies.	Cav. Regiments.	Cav. Battalions.	Cav. Independent companies.	Art. Regiments Light.	Art. Regiments Heavy.	Art. Battalions Light.	Art. Battalions Heavy.	Art. Companies Light.	Art. Companies Heavy.
Alabama												
Arizona												
Arkansas												
California												
Colorado												
Connecticut												
Dakota												1
Delaware												
District of Columbia												
Florida												
Georgia												
Illinois	2											
Indiana	2											
Indian Territory											1	
Iowa												
Kansas												
Kentucky	3			1								
Louisiana												
Maine			36									
Maryland			4									
Massachusetts			8					2				
Michigan	6											
Minnesota	1					2		1				
Mississippi												
Missouri	11											
Nebraska												
Nevada												
New Hampshire	1							1				
New Jersey	2											
New Mexico												
New York	8		41	2				1				
North Carolina												
Ohio	11											
Oregon												
Pennsylvania	13							2				
Rhode Island			5									

TABLE D.—*Exhibit of the number of organizations—volunteers and militia—organized and mustered into the service of the United States during the rebellion*—Continued.

UNDER CALL OF JULY 18, 1864, FOR 500,000 MEN—Continued.

States and Territories.	Infantry.			Cavalry.			Artillery.					
							Regiments.		Battalions.		Companies.	
	Regiments.	Battalions.	Independent companies.	Regiments.	Battalions.	Independent companies.	Light.	Heavy.	Light.	Heavy.	Light.	Heavy.
South Carolina												
Tennessee												
Texas												
Vermont												
Virginia												
Washington Territory												
West Virginia	1											
Wisconsin	5											
First Army Corps												
U. S. Volunteers												
U. S. Colored Troops												
Total	66		94	3		2		7			1	1

UNDER CALL OF DECEMBER 19, 1864, FOR 300,000 ONE, TWO, AND THREE YEARS' MEN.

States and Territories.	Infantry Regiments.	Infantry Battalions.	Infantry Independent companies.	Cavalry Regiments.	Cavalry Battalions.	Cavalry Independent companies.	Artillery Regiments Light.	Artillery Regiments Heavy.	Artillery Battalions Light.	Artillery Battalions Heavy.	Artillery Companies Light.	Artillery Companies Heavy.
Alabama												
Arizona												
Arkansas												
California												
Colorado												
Connecticut												
Dakota												
Delaware												
District of Columbia												
Florida												
Georgia												
Illinois	10		51									
Indiana	14											
Indian Territory												
Iowa												
Kansas											1	
Kentucky												
Louisiana												
Maine												
Maryland												
Massachusetts				2								
Michigan												
Minnesota	1		1									
Mississippi												
Missouri	1											
Nebraska												
Nevada												
New Hampshire												
New Jersey	1											
New Mexico												
New York	2		1									
North Carolina												
Ohio	14											
Oregon												
Pennsylvania	3		75									
Rhode Island												
South Carolina												
Tennessee												
Texas												
Vermont												
Virginia												
Washington Territory												
West Virginia												
Wisconsin	8											
First Army Corps												
U. S. Volunteers												
U. S. Colored Troops												
Total	54		128	2							1	

TABLE D.—*Exhibit of the number of organizations—volunteers and militia—organized and mustered into the service of the United States during the rebellion*—Continued.

UNDER SPECIAL CALLS AND OFFERS, 1861-'64, FOR VOLUNTEERS AND MILITIA.

States and Territories.	Infantry.			Cavalry.			Artillery.					
							Regiments.		Battalions.		Companies.	
	Regiments.	Battalions.	Independent companies.	Regiments.	Battalions.	Independent companies.	Light.	Heavy.	Light.	Heavy.	Light.	Heavy.
Alabama				2	1							
Arizona		1										
Arkansas	2	1		4							1	
California	8			2	1							
Colorado	1		1	3							1	
Connecticut												
Dakota						2						
Delaware												
District of Columbia	2		40		1	1						
Florida				2		1						
Georgia			2									
Illinois	5											
Indiana	18			1		1					1	
Indian Territory	3		2									
Iowa			18									
Kansas												
Kentucky	12			1							2	
Louisiana	4	1		2								
Maine			10									3
Maryland												
Massachusetts			15			7					1	8
Michigan												
Minnesota												
Mississippi				1								
Missouri	27	11	32	18	2						2	
Nebraska				2		1						
Nevada			3			6						
New Hampshire			4									2
New Jersey			11								1	
New Mexico	6			1								
New York	52					2						
North Carolina	4											
Ohio	6					1						
Oregon	1			1								
Pennsylvania	15	1	2	4		8			1		2	9
Rhode Island	2		1			2					1	
South Carolina												
Tennessee	16			12		3	1					
Texas				2		2						
Vermont						2						
Virginia	1		1									
Washington Territory			3									
West Virginia												
Wisconsin												
First Army Corps	9											
U. S. Volunteers	6											
U. S. Colored Troops	133		4	7				12			10	
Total	333	15	149	65	5	39	1	12	1		22	22

TABLE D.—*Exhibit of the number of organizations—volunteers and militia—organized and mustered into the service of the United States during the rebellion*—Continued.

RECAPITULATION.

States and Territories.	Infantry.			Cavalry.			Artillery.					
							Regiments.		Battalions.		Companies.	
	Regiments.	Battalions.	Independent companies.	Regiments.	Battalions.	Independent companies.	Light.	Heavy.	Light.	Heavy.	Light.	Heavy.
Alabama				2	1							
Arizona		1										
Arkansas	2	1		4							1	
California	8			2	1							
Colorado	1		1	3							1	
Connecticut	27		4			6		2			2	1
Dakota						2						
Delaware	6		3	1							1	1
District of Columbia	2		40		1	1						
Florida				2		1						
Georgia			2									
Illinois	155		67	15		18					38	
Indiana	138			11		1					26	
Indian Territory	3		2									
Iowa	45	1	24	9		2					4	
Kansas	9			8							4	
Kentucky	47			17							7	
Louisiana	4	1		2								
Maine	31		49	2		8		1			7	3
Maryland	18		5	1		9					5	
Massachusetts	69	1	39	5		7		4		1	19	8
Michigan	37		6	11		2					14	
Minnesota	12		3	2		10		1			3	
Mississippi				1								
Missouri	75	11	41	29	3	2	2	1			8	
Nebraska				2		1						
Nevada			3			6						
New Hampshire	17		10	1				1			1	2
New Jersey	37		11	3							6	
New Mexico	6			1								
New York	245		57	29		5	2	13	3		29	
North Carolina	4											
Ohio	218		25	13		18	1	2			28	
Oregon	1			1								
Pennsylvania	189	5	92	24	1	13	1	4	2		6	10
Rhode Island	9		6	2	2	2	1	2			2	
South Carolina												
Tennessee	16			12		3	1					
Texas				2		2						
Vermont	16		3	1		2		1			3	1
Virginia	1		1									
Washington Territory			3									
West Virginia	18		2	4							6	
Wisconsin	54		1	3		1					13	4
First Army Corps	9											
U. S. Volunteers	6											
U. S. Colored Troops	133		4	7				12			10	
Grand total	1,668	21	504	232	9	122	8	44	5	1	244	30

TABLE D.—*Exhibit of the number of organizations—volunteers and militia—organized and mustered into the service of the United States during the rebellion*—Continued.

RECAPITULATION—Continued.

Calls under which furnished.	Infantry.			Cavalry.			Artillery.					
							Regiments.		Battalions.		Companies.	
	Regiments.	Battalions.	Independent companies.	Regiments.	Battalions.	Independent companies.	Light.	Heavy.	Light.	Heavy.	Light.	Heavy.
Apr. 15, 1861	104	1	17	......	....	2	......	......	......	......	11	......
May 3 and acts of July 22 and 25, 1861	560	....	42	82	3	28	6	9	3	......	129	3
July 2, 1862	346	....	24	44	....	......	......	12	......	1	57	......
Aug. 4, 1862	72	....	5	1	....	4	......	......	......	......	2	......
June 15, 1863	8	3	2	4	1	13	......	......	......	......	6	......
Oct. 17, 1863	18	....	8	20	....	11	1	1	......	......	8	1
Feb. 1 and Mar. 14, 1864	12	....	17	11	....	18	......	3	......	......	5	3
1864, for 100-days' troops	95	2	18	......	....	5	......	......	1	......	2	......
July 18, 1864	66	....	94	3	....	2	......	7	......	......	1	1
Dec. 19, 1864	54	....	128	2	....	......	......	......	......	......	1	......
Special, 1861-'64	333	15	149	65	5	39	1	12	1	......	22	22
Grand total	1,668	21	504	232	9	122	8	44	5	1	244	30

THOMAS M. VINCENT,
Assistant Adjutant-General.

WAR DEPARTMENT, ADJUTANT-GENERAL'S OFFICE,
November 1, 1866.

ADJT. GEN.'S OFFICE, BUREAU FOR COLORED TROOPS,
October 20, 1866.

The ADJUTANT-GENERAL U. S. ARMY:

GENERAL: I have the honor to submit the following report of the operations of this Bureau for the past year:

On referring to the last annual report from this office it will be seen that there were at that time in service ninety-eight regiments and six light batteries of colored troops, numbering in all, officers and enlisted men, 85,024.

During the past year there have been mustered out of service seventy-nine regiments and six light batteries, which, with the incidental losses sustained during the year by the regiments still retained, gives an aggregate reduction of 72,039 officers and men, leaving in service at this date eighteen regiments of infantry and one of artillery, numbering in the aggregate 12,985. Of this force five regiments of infantry are now under orders for muster out of service, which will reduce the number in service, on or about the 1st of next November, to thirteen regiments of infantry and one of artillery, numbering about 10,000, commissioned and enlisted. The statistical table recently submitted will show when and where the several organizations were mustered out, where finally paid and discharged, and the numerical strength of each at date of discharge.

REMARKS UPON STATISTICAL TABLE, AND EXTRACTS THEREFROM.*

The statistical table to which reference has been made has required much labor in its preparation, and where doubts have arisen as to the

*The casualties embodied in the table here presented are still undergoing revision in the War Department and should not be accepted as conclusive.

fate of any officer or enlisted man the records have been carefully examined and compared and the facts elicited. The table is presented with the belief that it may be received as the nearest possible approximation to the truth. Some of the items contained therein are thought to be of sufficient general interest to warrant their presentation as below.

	Number.	Rate per thousand.
OFFICERS.		
Mustered out with their commands	3,412	490.65
Resigned and discharged	2,523	362.81
Dismissed and dropped	233	33.51
Died	194	27.90
Killed in action	91	13.09
Missing in action	4	0.58
Now in service	497	71.46
Appointed and mustered in during the rebellion	6,954	....
ENLISTED MEN.		
Mustered out	86,923	512.44
Discharged (principally for physical disability)	20,236	119.29
Died	31,866	187.86
Deserted	14,887	87.78
Killed in action	1,514	8.92
Missing in action	1,344	7.92
Transferred to Navy	366	2.17
Now in service	12,488	73.62
Mustered in during the rebellion	169,624	....

Of the officers it will be seen that the killed and missing in action constitute about 1.3 per cent. of the whole number in service. The loss sustained by the enlisted men from the same causes is about nine-tenths of one per cent. killed and nearly four-fifths of one per cent. missing.

About 2.7 per cent. of the officers and nearly 19 per cent. of the enlisted men died in service. The proportion of those who died from wounds cannot well be determined at this office.

Thirty-six per cent. of the officers were discharged before expiration of term of service and about 12 per cent. of the enlisted men—the latter principally in consequence of physical disability.

The number of enlisted men who deserted is about eight and three-fourths per cent.

COMMISSIONS UNDER THE ACTS APPROVED FEBRUARY 24, 1864, AND JULY 28, 1866.

The discontinuation of the commission for the State of Delaware, appointed by the Secretary of War under act of Congress approved February 24, 1864, was noted in my last annual report.

A synopsis of the transactions of the commission for the State of Maryland from the date of its organization to the date of the last annual report was therein presented. From that date up to November 30, 1865, at which time the commission was discontinued, 100 claims were presented, upon ninety-six of which the commission made awards amounting in the aggregate to $28,400. As the result of the labors of both commissions there are now on file in this office 804 claims, upon which awards have been made amounting in the aggregate to $235,683.

Under the act of Congress approved July 28, 1866, the payment of these claims, and all others that may hereafter be acted upon by like commissions, must be deferred until the final reports of all the commissions for the several States shall have been received.

For further details upon this subject, and also for an account of the money received and disbursed, attention is respectfully invited to the report of Bvt. Lieut. Col. A. F. Rockwell, disbursing officer for the Bureau, which is herewith, marked A.*

To my assistants, Bvt. Lieut. Col. F. W. Taggard and Bvt. Lieut. Col. A. F. Rockwell, and also to the clerical force employed in the office, I desire here to make due acknowledgments for able and efficient assistance cheerfully rendered and for constant and assiduous application to duty.

I have the honor to be, very respectfully, your obedient servant,

C. W. FOSTER,
Assistant Adjutant-General, U. S. Volunteers.

WAR DEPARTMENT,
Washington City, November 14, 1866.

MR. PRESIDENT: Disbandment of the volunteer forces in service at the time the rebel armies surrendered; collecting the arms, ordnance, and military stores scattered over the vast theater of war; the sale and disposition of unserviceable material; storing in arsenals, magazines, and depots that which might be used; settling and adjusting war claims; recruiting and organizing the Regular Army under the recent act; the establishment of posts and garrisons on the frontier and in the Indian country; testing the various improvements of breech-loading small-arms, and supplying them to the Army; practical experiments to determine the destructive power of projectiles and the comparative resisting qualities of materials; completing seaboard defenses and providing them with armaments; planning and carrying on harbor and river improvements—these, with the administration of the laws relating to refugees, freedmen, and abandoned lands, have constituted the chief operations of the War Department during the past year.

The entire number of volunteer troops to be mustered out was, on May 1, 1865, 1,034,064, and my last annual report recounted the operation of disbanding this force until November 15, 1865, when 800,963 troops had been transported, mustered out, and paid. The work was actively continued after that date, and on January 20, 1866, 918,722 volunteers had been mustered out; February 15, 952,452; March 10, 967,887; May 1, 986,782; June 30, 1,010,670; November 1, 1,023,021—leaving in service 11,043 volunteers, white and colored. The aggregate reduction of the colored troops during the year has been 75,024, and at this date one regiment of artillery and thirteen of infantry, numbering about 10,000 officers and enlisted men, remain in the service. Commenced in May, 1865, the work of discharging and returning to their homes 1,034,064 volunteers would have been completed within three months but for the necessity of retaining in service part of that force. Past experience shows that, should any national emergency require a larger force than is provided by the peace establishment, armies could be swiftly organized to at least the full strength of a million of men.

---

*Omitted.

The reduction of the Army has been attended by a corresponding reduction of material and retrenchment of expenditures. The advanced depots of the Quartermaster's Department, which had been established as bases of operations, have been broken up; the greater part of the material sold at advantageous rates or concentrated in five principal depots and arsenals, and all unnecessary employés discharged. From May 1, 1865, to August 2, 1866, over 207,000 horses and mules were sold for $15,269,075.54. About 4,400 barracks, hospitals, and other buildings have been sold during the year for $447,873.14. The sale of irregular and damaged clothing in store produced during the fiscal year the sum of $902,770.45. The fleet of 590 ocean transports in service on July 1, 1865, at a daily expense of $82,400, was reduced before June 30, 1866, to 53 vessels, costing $3,000 per diem, and most of these have since been discharged—ocean transportation being now almost entirely conducted by established commercial lines of steamers. Of 262 vessels which had been employed in inland transportation, at an expense of $3,193,533.28, none were remaining in service on June 30, 1866; sales of river transports, steamers, and barges during the year are reported as amounting to $1,152,895.92. The rates of wagon transportation in the Indian country have also been reduced by favorable contracts. The military railroads, which were operated during the war at a total expenditure of $45,422,719.15, and which are officially reported to have reached an extent of 2,630½ miles, and to have possessed 433 engines and 6,605 cars, have all been transferred to companies or boards of public works, upon condition of the adoption of loyal organizations of directors. Cash sales of railroad equipment to the amount of $3,466,739.33 are reported, and credit sales of $7,444,073.22. Upon the latter there have been paid, principal and interest, $1,200,085.18; leaving due to the United States on June 30, 1866, principal and interest, $6,570,074.05. The military telegraph, which attained an extent of 15,389 miles of lines constructed during the period of hostilities, with a total expenditure of $3,219,400 during the war, and $567,637 during the last fiscal year, has been discontinued, the material sold and disposed of, and the employés discharged, only a few confidential operators being still retained for cipher correspondence with commanders of important districts.

Such subsistence stores as could not be retained for supplying the reduced Army have for the most part been sold at satisfactory prices.

The sale of unserviceable and surplus stores pertaining to the Signal Corps has been effected; most of the officers have been mustered out and the employés discharged.

All the temporary ordnance depots established during the war, with the exception of that at Hilton Head, where the work is in progress but not completed, have been discontinued, and the supplies have been sent to arsenals for storage, or, when not worth the cost of transportation, have been sold. The expenditures at arsenals have been greatly diminished and their operations limited.

General hospitals, hospital transports and railroad trains, ambulance corps, and a number of medical purveying depots have been dispensed with, and all perishable articles of medicines and hospital supplies, in excesss of the requirements of a peace establishment, have been disposed of by public sale at advantageous rates, and the reserved supplies concentrated at five depots. The proceeds of old or surplus medical and hospital property amount to $4,044,261.59.

But the sale and disposition of these large amounts of unserviceable and perishable stores still leave on hand an adequate supply of war material to meet any emergency that can possibly arise. The stock of clothing, equipage, quartermaster's, subsistence, hospital, and ordnance stores, arms, ammunition, and field artillery is sufficient for the immediate equipment of large armies. The disbanded troops stand ready to respond to the national call, and, with our vast means of transportation and rapid organization developed during the war, they can be organized, armed, equipped, and concentrated at whatever points military emergency may require. While, therefore, the war expenses have been reduced to the footing of a moderate and economical peace establishment, the national military strength remains unimpaired and in condition to be promptly put forth.

While the reduction of the volunteer force and the advantageous disposition or concentration of war material were thus successfully accomplished without diminishing the military power of the country, recruiting and reorganizing the Regular Army favorably progressed. In consequence of the difficulty in procuring enlistments for the regular while so many men were required for the volunteer service 153 companies of the Regular Army, as then authorized, were unorganized on May 31, 1865, but in the middle of the following July these companies had been completed. Under the act of July 28, 1866, the Regular Army now comprises 10 regiments, or 120 companies, of cavalry, 5 regiments, or 60 companies, of artillery, and 45 regiments, or 450 companies, of infantry; of which 2 cavalry and 4 infantry regiments are composed of colored men, and 4 infantry regiments of men who were wounded in the line of their duty. One regiment of white cavalry had been fully recruited on September 15; the other regiment, assigned to the Pacific Coast, is very nearly completed. Forty-eight of the fifty-four companies required to convert into regiments the single battalions of the nine three-battalion regiments of the former organization have been completed and sent to their regiments. The four Veteran Reserve regiments have been assigned to districts where the men may be usefully employed in guarding store-houses and cemeteries and on similar duties. The colored regiments will be recruited, as far as possible, from the colored volunteers still in service. The law authorizes an assignment of 100 privates to a company as the maximum, fifty being the minimum, and the maximum strength of the Army is thus placed at 75,382, rank and file. The present strength of companies is fixed at 64 privates for cavalry, artillery, and infantry, and 122 privates for light batteries of artillery, making an aggregate strength of 54,302. As soon as the ranks shall be well filled it is designed to increase the efficiency of the military force by raising the standard of qualifications.

The troops in service were regularly paid, and the demands of those discharged and mustered out promptly met. During the fiscal year ending June 30, 1866, $10,431,004.42 were disbursed to the Army and Military Academy, $248,943,313.36 to volunteers; and in the disbursement of millions of dollars in small sums, and amid great difficulties and hazards, the total cost to the Government, in expenses of every character, is but a fractional portion of 1 per cent.

Every effort has been made to promote the comfort and health of the Army and to give the best medical treatment to the wounded and sick. Well-grounded apprehensions of the appearance of Asiatic cholera as an epidemic early in the present year required prompt action for the protection of our troops. A rigid military quarantine was established on the southern Atlantic Coast and sanitary precautions enforced. The adoption of these measures availed to control or eradicate the disease at the recruiting depots and forts where it appeared before it assumed its usual alarming epidemic form; and official recognition has been given to the meritorious services of medical officers whose fidelity, energy, and skillful administration succeeded in averting or diminishing the horrors of widespread pestilence. In other respects the general health of the troops has been good. Among white troops the proportion of deaths, from all causes, to cases treated has been one to every fifty-two. Among the colored troops the proportion of cases taken sick has been greater than with the white troops, and the mortality rate one death to every twenty-nine cases treated. There were remaining in general hospitals June 30, 1865, and admitted during the year 64,438 patients, of whom, on June 30, 1866, only ninety-seven remained under treatment. The comfort and proper medical treatment of the sick and wounded are secured in well-arranged post hospitals, of which there are at present 187, with a total capacity of 10,881 beds.

Measures have been adopted for the purpose of providing suitable shelter for the troops now stationed on the plains, and for those which may be ordered thither, and to prevent suffering during the winter. The Army has been well supplied with forage, about one-half the quantity having been supplied from the stock remaining on hand at the cessation of hostilities. The consumption for the year has been 3,300,000 bushels of oats, 5,061,000 bushels of corn, 136,000 tons of hay, 2,700 tons of straw.

Subsistence stores of good quality have been supplied to the Army, and though the larger part has been obtained at the principal market centers of the Northern States, yet the general return of the citizens, North and South, to the productiveness of peace, and the consequent reopening of the customary channels and sources of trade, have enabled a partial resumption of the course of procuring supplies at the points where they are to be consumed. Eighty-nine contracts for fresh beef have been made in the Southern States at a general average price of 11.06 cents per pound, and in the interior of those States other articles, to a small extent, have been purchased. The market at New Orleans is now so well furnished, and has so far resumed a healthful mercantile condition, as to render it possible to procure there, at satisfactory prices, most of the subsistence stores required in the Department of the Gulf. On the Pacific Coast, for several years after California was admitted to the Union, all the supplies for troops there stationed were required to be shipped from New York, but an ample and reliable market, comprising the products of California and Oregon and the foreign countries bordering upon the same ocean, is now found in San Francisco, and most of the subsistence stores for troops in the Division of the Pacific have been there obtained. In general the subsistence supplies purchased during the year have been procured upon contracts, concluded in pursuance of advertisements for sealed proposals, written proposals, and acceptances.

The importance of speedily providing the Army with breech-loading small-arms of the best pattern has been recognized and acted upon. By an order of January 3, 1866, a board of competent officers was convened for the purpose of examining, testing, and reporting on the various models of original breech-loaders, and the various plans for the conversion into breech-loaders of the arms heretofore borne by our troops. This board met on March 10 and continued in session until June 4, when its report was submitted, and directions have been given the Ordnance Department for the speedy manufacture of breech-loading arms. In view of the great number of small-arms on hand, it has been deemed advisable to convert Springfield rifle muskets, at a comparatively small cost, into efficient breech-loaders, rather than to incur the cost of the entire manufacture of new arms of that description, at a time, too, when the invention may not have been perfected. This alteration of the Springfield musket has been effected so successfully as to render it an arm believed to be better in all respects than the Prussian needle-gun, while its metallic ammunition is regarded as superior to that of the latter. The Department has already on hand breech-loaders of approved patterns adequate for the supply of the cavalry and mounted and light infantry.

Besides the measures that have been mentioned to provide for the comfort and promote the efficiency of the Army, stated monthly inspections have been made in every military command during the year, with a view to bring to notice and promptly remedy any irregularities and defects; and numerous special inspections have also been made throughout the whole country for the purpose of correcting abuses, suggesting improvements, and effecting retrenchment in the service. The inspection service has not been changed by the return to peace. The system developed during the war, meeting the requirements as nearly as practicable, is still continued.

The present organization of military departments and divisions is as follows:

The Department of the East, Maj. Gen. George G. Meade to command, to embrace the New England States, New York, New Jersey, Pennsylvania, and Fort Delaware. Headquarters at Philadelphia.

The Department of the Lakes, Brig. and Bvt. Maj. Gen. Joseph Hooker to command, to embrace the States of Ohio, Michigan, Indiana, Illinois, and Wisconsin. Headquarters at Detroit.

The Department of Washington, Brig. and Bvt. Maj. Gen. E. R. S. Canby to command, to embrace the District of Columbia, Alexandria and Fairfax Counties, Va., and the States of Maryland and Delaware, except Fort Delaware. Headquarters at Washington.

The Department of the Potomac, Brig. and Bvt. Maj. Gen. John M. Schofield to command, to embrace the States of Virginia, except Alexandria and Fairfax Counties, and West Virginia. Headquarters at Richmond.

The Department of the South, Maj. Gen. Daniel E. Sickles to command, to embrace the States of North and South Carolina. Headquarters at Charleston.

The Department of the Tennessee, Maj. Gen. George H. Thomas to command, to embrace the States of Kentucky, Tennessee, Georgia, Alabama, and Mississippi. Headquarters at Louisville.

The Department of the Gulf, Maj. Gen. Philip H. Sheridan to command, to embrace the States of Florida, Louisiana, and Texas. Headquarters at New Orleans.

The Department of the Arkansas, Brig. and Bvt. Maj. Gen. E. O. C. Ord to command, to embrace the State of Arkansas and Indian Territory, west. Headquarters at Little Rock.

The Department of the Missouri, Maj. Gen. Winfield S. Hancock to command, to embrace the States of Missouri and Kansas and the

Territories of Colorado and New Mexico. Headquarters at Fort Leavenworth.

The Department of the Platte, Brig. and Bvt. Maj. Gen. Philip St. George Cooke to command, to embrace the State of Iowa, the Territories of Nebraska and Utah, so much of Dakota as lies west of the one hundred and fourth meridian, and so much of Montana as lies contiguous to the new road from Fort Laramie to Virginia City, Mont. Headquarters at Omaha.

The Department of Dakota, Brig. and Bvt. Maj. Gen. A. H. Terry to command, to embrace the State of Minnesota and all the Territories of Dakota and Montana not embraced in the Department of the Platte. Headquarters at Fort Snelling.

The Department of California, Brig. and Bvt. Maj. Gen. Irvin McDowell to command, to embrace the States of California and Nevada and the Territory of Arizona. Headquarters at San Francisco.

The Department of the Columbia, Maj. Gen. Frederick Steele to command, to embrace the State of Oregon and the Territories of Washington and Idaho. Headquarters at Portland.

The principal movements of troops have been in Texas, on the Mexican frontier, and in the Territories, the details of which are given in the accompanying report of General Grant,* commanding the Armies of the United States, and the reports of division and department commanders, to which reference is made. General Grant reports that a military force has been kept in all the lately rebellious States for the purposes of insuring the execution of law and protecting life and property against the acts of those who as yet will acknowledge no law but force—a class smaller, in his opinion, than could have been expected after such a conflict as that through which we have passed, but sufficiently formidable to justify the course which has been pursued. Military movements have also been directed with a view to the protection of emigrants on their way to the mountain Territories against the hostility and opposition of the Indians.

Besides the operations thus recapitulated, of reduction, concentration, retrenchment, and reorganization of the military establishment, and payment, complete equipment, and disposition of the Army, other matters of national importance and interest have received the careful attention of the War Department.

The permanent defenses of the country have been strengthened. Their efficiency has already been much increased by substituting cannon of larger caliber and improved model for lighter guns, and wrought-iron for wooden gun carriages. This work is still in progress, and will be continued. Diligent and careful efforts, based upon the designs and recommendations of competent boards of engineers, have been made to adapt old works, as well as those in process of construction, to more powerful armaments. Construction has been suspended upon some works in order to await the completion of important experiments having in view the extensive use of iron shields or armor for the protection of guns and gunners. The results already attained give the promise of a practical and highly beneficial application of the knowledge obtained by these trials.

Surveys of the lakes have been continued, and progress has already been made in improving the harbors and rivers of the country. The work will be energetically prosecuted under the liberal appropriations made at the last session of Congress.

---

*See November 21, p. 1045.

Active and careful measures have been instituted for successfully and speedily carrying into effect the generous provisions of Congress for the benefit of surviving soldiers of the war for the Union. The subject of the payment of extra bounties to discharged soldiers and extra pay to discharged officers has received assiduous attention. The recent law devolving upon the War Department, instead of the accounting officers of the Treasury, the duties of examination and settlement of claims of this nature imposed a vast accumulation of labor and required the consideration of numerous acts of Congress and the regulations and practice of several bureaus. Upon the proper performance of these extraordinary labors depends the disbursement of nearly $80,000,000 among more than 1,000,000 claimants. Soon after the adjournment of Congress a competent board of officers was organized to prepare rules and regulations for the payment of the authorized bounties. Diligent application was given to the work, and the regulations, having been found to be in strict accordance with law, were promptly approved, published, and directed to be carried into effect. To the same board the subject of bounties for colored soldiers was also referred, with a view to provide any additional checks that might guard the bounty from fraudulent assignees and secure it to colored soldiers and protect the Treasury against fraud; and when the report was received payment of the bounties was ordered. As to the other class of bounties, the Paymaster-General regards it impracticable to make payment until all applications shall have been received and claims classified and registered by States and organizations, but by this preliminary process the ultimate payment of all will, it is believed, be greatly expedited. Attempted otherwise, probably the work would never be fully accomplished. Of the valuable public records by which the validity of the bounty claims is to be tested, there is in the archives of the Government but one copy, already much worn, for each period. An examination for each individual case would soon reduce them to illegible shreds.

The duty of the Government to the soldiers who have been maimed or have fallen in its defense has not been neglected. Much care has been taken, by precautions and practical tests, to secure for the former the most durable, useful, and comfortable artificial limbs. From July 16, 1862, the date of the act of Congress authorizing artificial limbs to be furnished, to July 1, 1866, there have been supplied to disabled soldiers 3,981 legs, 2,240 arms, 9 feet, 55 hands, 125 surgical apparatus, and it is supposed that not more than 1,000 limbs remain still to be supplied, at an estimated cost of $70,000. In order to include unfortunate cases in which, from the nature of the injury or operation, no limb or other surgical appliance can be advantageously adopted, the Surgeon-General has recommended that if the appropriation for this purpose shall be continued, the money value of an artificial limb, in lieu of an order for the apparatus, be given to the maimed soldier. Forty-one national military cemeteries have been established, and into these had already been gathered, on June 30, the remains of 104,526 Union soldiers. The sites for ten additional cemeteries have been selected, and the work upon them, for some time delayed by the climate and a threatened epidemic, is now in course of vigorous prosecution. Although it may not be desirable to remove the remains of those now reposing in other suitable burial grounds, it is estimated that our national cemeteries will be required to receive and protect the remains of 249,397 patriotic soldiers whose lives were sacrificed in defense of our national existence. The average cost of the removals and reinterments already accomplished is reported at $9.75, amounting in the aggregate to $1,144,791, and it is believed that an additional expenditure of $1,609,294 will be necessary. It is proposed, instead of the wooden headboards heretofore used, to erect at the graves small monuments of cast iron, suitably protected by zinc coating against rust. Six lists of the dead, containing 32,666 names, have been published by the Quartermaster-General, and others will be issued as rapidly as they can be prepared.

Documents submitted by the chiefs of bureaus and accompanying this report contain detailed information relative to the operations of the War Department and the requirements of its respective branches.

The total estimate of military appropriations for the fiscal year ending June 30, 1868, is $25,205,669.60.

The Adjutant-General's Office has immediate supervision of recruiting for the Regular Army and disbanding the volunteer force, and charge also of the records and unfinished business of the Provost-Marshal-General's Bureau, which, in accordance with act of July 28, 1866, was discontinued on August 28. Arrangements have been made for the prompt settlement of the undetermined questions formerly pertaining to that Bureau and for the removal to Washington of the records of its offices in the various States. The estimated appropriation required for the purposes of the Adjutant-General's Office is $300,000.

The officers of the Inspector-General's Department are now those of the regular establishment, and they are all engaged in their legitimate duties of stated and special inspections. No appropriation is required for this service.

In the Bureau of Military Justice during the past year 8,148 records of courts-martial and military commissions have been received, reviewed, and filed; 4,008 special reports made as to the regularity of judicial proceedings, the pardon of military offenders, the remission or commutation of sentences, and upon the miscellaneous subjects and questions referred for the opinion of the Bureau, including also letters of instruction upon military law and practice to judge-advocates and reviewing officers. The number of records of military courts received at this Bureau reached a minimum soon after the adoption of the recent Army act, and since that time has increased with the military force. The other business of the office, as an advisory branch of the War Department, will also, it is believed, continue to be augmented until the peace establishment shall be completely organized and the new Army fully recruited; and the fact that in a large number of important cases commanders of departments and armies are not authorized to execute sentences in time of peace, and that such cases can no longer be summarily disposed of without a reference to the Executive, will also require from the Bureau a very considerable number of reports which heretofore have not been called for. Its aggregate business will, it is thought, not be reduced in proportion to the reduction of the military force.

In the Quartermaster's Department the returns and accounts of officers responsible for clothing and equipage during the year have been examined and transmitted to the Treasury for final settlement. The erection of the fireproof warehouse at Philadelphia, for which Congress made an appropriation on July 28, will be commenced so soon as the proposals now invited by public advertisement shall have been received and compared, and authority is desired for the purchase of a site and erection of a similar structure at Jeffersonville, Ind. During the fiscal year ocean transportation has been furnished for 131,581 men; inland transportation for 1,016,300 persons, 138,389 animals, 10,370 wheeled vehicles, and 420,000 tons of stores of all kinds; and the greater part of the bills for transportation during the war have been settled and paid. Claims, principally under the act of July 4, 1864, have been filed during the year to the amount of over $11,000,000, upon which about $1,000,000 have been paid. No further appropriations are required for the regular service of the Quartermaster's Department, as it is believed that the balances now available and the sums received and to be received will suffice for the next fiscal year. For contingencies the sum of $100,000 is requested.

The Subsistence Department is engaged, under the joint resolution of July 25, 1866, in paying, upon certificates given by the Commissary-General of Prisoners, commutation of rations to those U. S. soldiers who were held as prisoners of war. Tobacco is now furnished to the enlisted men of the Army under proper regulations. The settlement of accounts of officers who have performed duty with the Subsistence Department has rapidly progressed. Claims under the act of July 4, 1864, which have been filed in the subsistence office, amount in the aggregate to $1,758,031.04, on which $85,343.10 have been allowed. Claims amounting to $1,021,123.70 await final examination and decision. The total amount of money drawn from the Treasury and disbursed by the Subsistence Department during the past fiscal year was $7,518,872.54, including payment of claims under the act of July 4, 1864. The amount disbursed during the fiscal years of the war was:

From July 1, 1861, to June 30, 1862	$48,799,521.14
From July 1, 1862, to June 30, 1863	69,537,582.78
From July 1, 1863, to June 30, 1864	98,666,918.50
From July 1, 1864, to June 30, 1865	144,782,969.41
From July 1, 1865, to June 30, 1866	7,518,872.54
Total amount	369,305,864.37

No appropriation is required for the next fiscal year.

Arrangements will soon be consummated by the Medical Department for the permanent security of its valuable mortuary records, including 16,000 folio volumes of hospital registers, 47,000 burial records, 16,000 hospital muster and pay rolls, alphabetical registers of the dead, containing 250,000 names of white and 20,000 of colored soldiers, and the pathological collection constituting the Army Medical Museum. During the year official evidence, obtainable from no other source, of cause of death, or of discharge for disability, has been furnished in 49,212 cases, and 210,027 discharges upon certificates of disability have been examined and classified. The total number of surgical cases classified and recorded is of wounds 133,952, and of operations 28,438. The preparation for publication of the medical and surgical history of the war has been prosecuted with energy, much of the manuscript and several of the illustrations for the first volume being completed. The Army Medical Museum continues to increase in value and usefulness, and the greater security and additional accommodations of the building to which it will be shortly removed admit of the addition of a great number of interesting and instructive specimens not hitherto available for want of space. A small appropriation will be required to continue the work of classification and preservation of this national collection. The number of casualties from the commencement of the war to the present time in the regular and volunteer medical staff is ascertained to be 336, including 29 killed in battle, 12 killed by accident, 10 died of wounds, 4 died in rebel prison, 7 died of yellow fever, 3 died of cholera, 270 died of other diseases. During the war 35 medical officers were wounded in battle. The distribution of troops in small bodies over so large an extent of country necessitates the employment of acting assistant surgeons temporarily, but the number of these has been reduced from 1,997 on July 1, 1865, to 264 on July 1, 1866, and will be still further diminished when existing vacancies in the grade of assistant surgeons, created by the act of Congress of July 28, 1866, are filled. A corresponding decrease in the number of hospital stewards for general service has also been effected, and in every branch of the Department reduction and retrenchment have been rigidly enforced. An aggregate expenditure of $267,391.92 was incurred by the Medical Department in furnishing officers and supplies to the Bureau of Refugees, Freedmen, and Abandoned Lands, which had under its control, during the fiscal year ending July 1, 1866, no appropriation applicable to the purpose; and though, under a decision of the Treasury Department, reimbursement was not made from subsequent appropriations for the Freedmen's Bureau, no embarrassment arose and no legislation is required. The funds at the disposal of the Medical and Hospital Department during the year ending June 30, 1866, were as follows:

Balance of appropriations remaining in the Treasury July 1, 1865	$1,161,181.24
Amount of Treasury draft No. 1,544, on war warrant 3,205, issued May 3, 1865, in favor of Asst. Surg. J. B. Brinton, lost in the mail and subsequently refunded	10,000.00
Proceeds of sales of old or surplus medical and hospital property	4,044,261.59
Amount refunded on account of supplies furnished for the use of prisoners of war	22,163.34
Amount refunded by the Subsistence Department, being apportionment of amount paid for board and care of sick soldiers in private hospitals	121,600.51
Amount received for board of officers in hospitals	14,298.96
Amount recovered on account of stores and furniture lost or damaged in transportation	4,597.42
Refunded from appropriation for care of destitute discharged soldiers, being for board of discharged soldiers while having artificial limbs fitted	6,955.24
Received from all other sources	1,005.94
Total	5,386,064.24

Of this amount there was disbursed during the same period—

For medical and hospital supplies (a great part of this sum expended in payment of debt of previous year)	$975,773.83
For pay of private physicians	926,584.05
For pay of nurses and other hospital employés	309,916.06
For purchase of artificial limbs for disabled soldiers	198,999.00
For board of sick soldiers in private hospitals	58,781.75
For expenses of hospitals for officers	23,158.51
For expenses of purveying depots, laboratories, repairs, &c	312,243.18
For miscellaneous expenses of the Medical Department	32,345.39
Total disbursements during the fiscal year	2,837,801.77
Balance in Treasury June 30, 1866	2,546,457.14
Refunded of amount advanced by disbursing officers during the previous year	1,805.33
	5,386,064.24

The estimated appropriation required for the Medical Department for the next fiscal year is $90,000.

The Pay Department remains without material change. In consequence of additional labors imposed upon this branch of the War Department by recent Congressional enactment, and in order to promptly pay the large issue of Treasury certificates, it was necessary to retain temporarily a number of additional paymasters. The financial summary exhibits—

A balance on hand at the beginning of the fiscal year	$120,106,999.32
Received from Treasury and other sources during the year	163,426,228.97
Total	283,533,228.29

Accounted for as follows:

Disbursements to Army and Military Academy	$10,431,004.42
Disbursements to volunteers	248,943,313.36
Unissued requisitions in Treasury	10,750,000.00
In hands of paymasters June 30	13,408,910.51
	283,533,228.29

The total disbursements of each class during the fiscal year is as follows:

To troops on muster out	$205,272,324.00
To troops in service	30,250,010.00
To referred claims	7,662,736.00
To payment of Treasury certificates	16,189,247.00
	259,374,317.00

The estimated appropriations of the Pay Department amount to $17,728,560.60 for pay of the Army for the next fiscal year.

The Corps of Engineers at the close of the fiscal year consisted of ninety-five officers, the battalion of engineer troops, and the Military Academy. Thirteen officers were on detached duty, serving in command of military departments, on special service connected with the levees of the Mississippi River, on the Light-House Board, with the Department of the Interior upon duties relating to the Pacific Railroad, on military surveys and staffs of the General-in-Chief and commanding general of the Military Division of the Gulf; the remainder were diligently engaged in the duties of their profession, officers of desirable experience and practice having direct supervision of the more important works. The engineer troops were distributed between the Military Academy and the two depots of engineer supplies located at Willets Point, N. Y., and at Jefferson Barracks, Mo. The condition of the battalion with regard to discipline and instruction is reported as satisfactory. At the two engineer depots much valuable war material has been collected from points where it had remained after the close of active operations in the field, and it is proposed to keep on hand a complete outfit on a moderate scale of such engineer, bridge, and siege equipage as would be most likely to come into requisition to supply unforeseen demands in the field. The Chief of Engineers suggests a modification of the act of June 23, 1866, in respect to the manner of procuring labor and material for improvements of harbors and rivers. The estimated appropriation required by the Engineer Bureau for the next fiscal year is $5,140,000.

The Ordnance Department now limits the operations at arsenals to the construction of wrought-iron sea-coast carriages and such ordnance supplies as are needed for immediate use; preservation of the ordnance stores left on hand at the close of the war; breaking up unserviceable ammunition, and completing unfinished buildings. Fireproof workshops have been completed at Watervliet, Frankford, and Alleghany Arsenals; three magazines, with a capacity for storing 15,000 barrels of gunpowder, have been built at Saint Louis Arsenal, and one of the same capacity at each of the arsenals at Washington City and Benicia. A board of officers is engaged in examining suitable sites for depositories of gunpowder provided for by an appropriation of the last session of Congress; and the erection of such magazines as will furnish secure and suitable storage for all our powder, ammunition, and niter will be commenced early next spring. The arsenals at the South which were seized by the rebels, having been retaken, are reoccupied, excepting the North Carolina Arsenal, which was destroyed; the Harper's Ferry Armory, the workshops of which were burned, and which has been used as an ordnance depot; the arsenal in Florida, which has been transferred temporarily to the Freedmen's Bureau, and the arsenal in Arkansas, which is occupied by troops of the line. The Chief of Ordnance is of opinion that it is not advisable to rebuild the North Carolina Arsenal or to re-establish the armory at Harper's Ferry, and the sale of both is recommended. All the small-arms and some of the other supplies which were collected at Baton Rouge, San Antonio, Augusta, Charleston, and Mount Vernon Arsenals have been removed, and the only supplies which have been sent to them were such as were required for immediate issue to troops. The commission appointed under the act of April 19, 1864, to examine and report the value of property on Rock Island taken by the United States by authority of that act has entered upon its duties. As soon as good titles to the property shall have been acquired the construction of the armory and arsenal, as required by law, will be hastened as fast as the appropriations will admit. It is important that this establishment should be built up as rapidly as possible, and a considerable sum has been estimated for that purpose during the next fiscal year. It is believed that all of it is necessary and can be judiciously and advantageously expended. The operations at the National Armory at Springfield, Mass., during the past year have been confined to cleaning and repairing arms used during the war, and to making the requisite preparations for converting the Springfield muskets into breech-loaders. The power and endurance of the 8-inch and 12-inch cast-iron rifle cannon have been subjected to practical tests, and the experiments will be continued. The ordnance returns for three consecutive years, including a period of active service and ordinary repairs, show an average duration of five years for cavalry carbines, of four years for cavalry pistols, sabers, and accouterments, of seven years for infantry muskets, and of six years for infantry accouterments. From January 1, 1861, to June 30, 1866, the Ordnance Department provided 7,892 cannon, 11,787 artillery carriages, 4,022,130 small-arms, 2,362,546 complete sets of accouterments for infantry and cavalry, 539,544 complete sets of cavalry horse equipments, 28,164 sets of horse artillery harness, 1,022,176,474 cartridges for small-arms, 1,220,555,435 percussion-caps, 2,862,177 rounds of fixed artillery ammunition, 14,507,682 cannon primers and fuses, 12,875,294 pounds of artillery projectiles, 26,440,054 pounds of gunpowder, 6,395,152 pounds of niter, and 90,416,295 pounds of lead. In addition to these there were immense quantities of parts provided for repairing and making good articles damaged, lost, or destroyed in the service. The fiscal resources of the Ordnance Bureau for the year amounted to $35,301,062.56, and the expenditures $16,551,677.58, leaving a balance of $18,749,385.18, of which $18,043,804.28 were undrawn balances in the Treasury, and $705,580.90 were to the credit of disbursing officers in the Government depositories on June 30, 1866. The estimated appropriation required by the Ordnance Office, including only such objects as require early attention, is $1,593,242.

In the office of the Commissary-General of Prisoners a reduced force has been engaged in receiving and completing the records relating to prisoners of war, in furnishing information required by the various bureaus, and in the investigation of claims for commutation of rations to U. S. soldiers while held as prisoners of war.

The clerical force at the office of the Signal Corps is employed in arranging and putting in durable form messages and reports which passed through or emanated from the corps during the war. The expenditures for the Signal Service during the year ending September 30, 1866, were $3,900.15; the total amount appropriated and still available for signal service September 30, 1866, was $252,565.97. No appropriation was requested of last Congress, and none will be required for the next fiscal year.

At the last examination the corps of cadets at the Military Academy numbered 228 members, and forty cadets of the graduating class completed the course of studies and were commissioned lieutenants in the Army. Under the provisions of the acts of Congress approved, respectively, July 13 and 28, 1866, the Military Academy was separated from the Corps of Engineers, which, together with certain professors and cadets, had heretofore constituted the institution, and the officers of which had exercised exclusive supervision and control over it. Bvt. Maj. Gen. Edmund Schriver, inspector-general, has been assigned as inspector, and Col. T. G. Pitcher, of the Forty-fourth Infantry, appointed superintendent. The report of the Board of Visitors for 1867 bears ample testimony to the usefulness and excellent condition of the academy, and recommends the increase of the number of cadets to 400. With the present number of cadets but one graduate can be supplied to each regiment every second year, after the ordinary demands of the staff corps are met. During the past session of Congress important measures were adopted respecting the academy, raising the standard of qualifications for admission, and requiring that appointments be hereafter made one year in advance of the date of admission. The inspector, from personal observation, reports the authorities of the institution as most assiduous in their efforts to advance the interests of the academy and its cadets. Its administration is characterized by economy and habits of frugality are inculcated. Excellent discipline is maintained and judiciously enforced. The estimated appropriation for the Military Academy is $243,867.

In the Bureau of Refugees, Freedmen, and Abandoned Lands the Commissioner reports that there is no material change of organization, but business is facilitated and vexed questions settled by the law of 1866. The jurisdiction of assistant commissioners coincides generally with department and district commands, but is distinct in

Maryland and the District of Columbia. Under the new law Maryland and Kentucky are embraced, and these States seem to require aid from the Bureau in promoting the interests of justice and education. In the Northern cities employment offices, of little expense to the Government, and not a source of revenue, have been established with a view to obtain work and homes for dependent freed people and to relieve crowded localities. The importance of self-support has been urged by proper means upon the laboring classes. Wages have been determined not by orders of Bureau officers, but by circumstances ordinarily affecting the price of labor in different localities. The education of freedmen and refugees has been carried on vigorously under the immediate patronage of benevolent societies. A superintendent of education, devoting his whole time to his work, is stationed at the Bureau headquarters in each State, and all Bureau officers co-operate with him. It is estimated that 150,000 freedmen and their children are now attending school in the Southern States. Schools for refugee white children are also established. Their formation is everywhere encouraged by the Bureau. There has been but little uniformity of action in different States in respect to the administration of justice. Assistant commissioners have been instructed to transfer military jurisdiction as rapidly as possible to State judicial tribunals. This has been done completely in some States, while in Virginia, Louisiana, and Texas Bureau courts are still in existence. A claim division, instituted in March last, and aided by officers and agents throughout the States, has sought to prevent frauds upon colored soldiers in their efforts to collect unpaid claims. One hundred and ninety-five claims were paid through the office of the Commissioner, 723 rejected at his office, 1,532 are in process of adjustment. The aggregate amount collected and paid is $10,539.09. Detailed reports are given of the operations of the Bureau in each State and the District of Columbia. Transportation is reported as furnished to 6,352 destitute freed people and 387 refugees. Thirteen million four hundred and twelve thousand two hundred and seventy-three rations were issued between June 1, 1865, and September 1, 1866. The average number per month to refugees and freedmen was 894,569; the average number per day, 29,819. The issue to whites increased until June 30, 1866, when issues to freedmen and refugees were about equal. From June 30, 1866, until September 1 the number supported of both classes has diminished. Rigid scrutiny has been exercised to prevent issues to any but the absolutely destitute, and parts of the ration not actually needed were cut off. Officers were directed to hold each plantation, county, parish, and town responsible for the care of its own poor, but to very little purpose, for with few exceptions the State authorities have failed to contribute to the relief of the class of persons supported by the Government. Owing to the failure of crops the requirements of Circular 10, of August 22, could not be rigidly enforced. Upon the application of State officials special issues are being made to certain States for the support of their pauper population. Rations are sold to teachers and agents of benevolent societies under the same rules that apply to such purchases made by commissioned officers. Bureau hospitals receive the usual freedmen's ration. The amount of land now in possession of the Bureau is 272,231 acres, to be increased by 228 tracts in Tennessee, of which the number of acres has not been reported. The aggregate number of parcels of town property, not included in the above, which have been in possession of the Bureau is 3,724, of which 2,605 have been restored, leaving a balance of 1,119 parcels of town property.

The balance on hand of the freedmen fund is		$282,383.52
The balance of district destitute fund		18,338.67
The balance of appropriation		6,856,259.30
		7,156,981.49
The estimated amount due Subsistence Department is	$297,000.00	
The transportation reported unpaid	26,015.94	
The transportation estimated due	20,000.00	
Estimated amount due Medical Department	100,000.00	
Estimated amount due Quartermaster's Department	200,000.00	
		643,015.94
Total balance for all purposes of expenditure		6,513,965.55

The Commissioner estimates the additional funds necessary for the next fiscal year as follows:

Salaries of assistant commissioners, sub-assistants, and agents	$147,500.00
Salaries of clerks	82,800.00
Stationery and printing	63,000.00
Quarters and fuel	200,000.00
Subsistence stores	1,500,000.00
Medical Department	500,000.00
Transportation	800,000.00
School superintendents	25,000.00
Buildings for schools and asylums (including construction, rental, and repairs)	500,000.00
Telegraphing and postage	18,000.00
Total	3,836,300.00

In compliance with recent enactments of Congress, commissioners to assess the value of slaves enlisted into the U. S. Army during the war have been appointed for Missouri, Maryland, Kentucky, and Tennessee, but their reports have not yet been received.

In conclusion it gives me pleasure to again express my obligations to the chiefs of bureaus and their subordinates, who, in reducing the War Department to a peace establishment, have evinced the same diligence, ability, and fidelity to the interests of the Government that distinguished them during the labors, anxiety, and vicissitudes of the war, and contributed so much to its successful termination.

EDWIN M. STANTON,
Secretary of War.

HEADQUARTERS ARMIES OF THE UNITED STATES,
Washington, November 21, 1866.

Hon. E. M. STANTON,
Secretary of War:

SIR: Since my report for 1865 the volunteer force then in service has been almost entirely replaced by the Regular Army, mostly organized under the act of Congress approved 28th July, 1866. The report of the Adjutant-General of the Army gives exact statistics on this subject.

Passing from civil war of the magnitude of that in which the United States has been engaged to government through the courts, it has been deemed necessary to keep a military force in all the lately rebellious States to insure the execution of law and to protect life and property against the acts of those who, as yet, will acknowledge no law but force. This class has proven to be much smaller than could have been expected after such a conflict. It has, however, been sufficiently formidable to justify the course which has been pursued. On the whole, the condition of the States that were in rebellion against the Government may be regarded as good enough to warrant the hope that but a short time will intervene before the bulk of the troops now occupying them can be sent to our growing Territories, where they are so much needed.

I respectfully refer you to the reports of Generals Sherman, Halleck, Meade, Sheridan, Thomas, Sickles, McDowell, Pope, and Steele, herewith, for full information of the condition of the States and Territories under their command.* The last of these reports is but this moment received. The time has passed when they should be in the hands of the printer to prepare them for presentation to Congress on its assembling. To make a full report I would have to get my facts from these reports. Time not permitting, I beg to refer to them in lieu of their condensation by me.

With the expiration of the rebellion Indian hostilities have diminished. With a frontier constantly extending and encroaching upon the hunting-grounds of the Indian, hostilities, opposition at least, frequently occur. To meet this and to protect the emigrant on his way to the mountain Territories troops have been distributed to give the best protection with the means at hand. Few places are occupied by more than two and many by but a single company. These troops are generally badly sheltered, and are supplied at great cost. During the past summer inspections were made by Generals Sherman, Pope, Ingalls, Sacket, and Babcock to determine the proper places to occupy to give the best protection to travel and settlements, and to determine the most economical method of furnishing supplies. The labor of putting up temporary quarters is performed by the troops intending to occupy them. In the course of the next season more permanent buildings will have to be erected, however, which will entail an expense for material at least. I would respectfully suggest, therefore, that an appropriation for this special purpose be asked.

The permanent peace establishment being much larger than has been heretofore provided for, an appropriation for building barracks, store-houses, &c., to meet present wants seems to be required. The reports of the heads of the staff departments of the Army, particularly that of the Quartermaster-General, may cover this point.

I would respectfully suggest for the consideration of Congress the propriety of transferring the Indian Bureau from the Interior to the War Department, and the abolition of Indian agencies, with the exception of a limited number of inspectors. The reason for this change seems to me both obvious and satisfactory. It would result in greater economy of expenditure and, as I think, diminution of conflict between the Indian and white races.

I have the honor to be, very respectfully, your obedient servant,

U. S. GRANT,
General.

---

*Reports omitted.

ADJUTANT-GENERAL'S OFFICE,
Washington, October 20, 1867.

General U. S. GRANT,
Commanding Armies of the United States:

GENERAL: I have the honor to submit herewith the annual returns of the Army.

* * * * * * *

MUSTERING AND DISBURSING FOR VOLUNTEERS.

The last annual report brought down the operations of the department, in mustering out the Volunteer Army, to November 1, 1866, at which date 1,023,021 volunteers had been discharged, leaving in service 11,043.

Of that number the following have since been mustered out:

U. S. Colored Troops	8,756
Perfected returns	1,303
Oregon Volunteers	65
New Mexican Volunteers	405
Officers of the general staff	168
Officers of the Veteran Reserve Corps	143

Thus leaving in service 203 commissioned officers and no enlisted men.*

Mustering and disbursing offices have been discontinued as rapidly as the public interest would permit. At the date of the last annual report there were eighteen offices, each under the charge of a commissioned officer. Of this number all have been closed except the following: At Albany, N. Y., for New York State; at Philadelphia, for Pennsylvania and New Jersey; at Columbus, Ohio, for Ohio and West Virginia.

The records of the offices closed have been transferred to this city, except those at Louisville, Ky., for Kentucky and Tennessee; at Saint Louis, Mo., for Missouri, Kansas, Dakota, Colorado, and Nebraska; at Santa Fé, N. Nex., for New Mexico; at San Francisco, Cal., for California, Nevada, Oregon, and Washington Territory; at which places, in consequence of the peculiar character of the business, they remain connected with military division or department headquarters.

No appropriation of money will be required for the volunteer disbursing branch during the next fiscal year.

COLORED TROOPS.

All the colored volunteers remaining in service at the date of the last report have been mustered out, except twelve commissioned officers, retained on duty in the Bureau of Refugees, Freedmen, and Abandoned Lands.

---

*It appears from the records on file in the War Department that the last white volunteer organization (Company B, 1st New Mexico Battalion) was mustered out of service November 18, 1867, and the last colored volunteer organization (One hundred and twenty-fifth U. S. Colored Infantry) was mustered out December 20, 1867. The last commissioned officer of volunteers (Maj. Calvin Holmes, additional paymaster) was mustered out July 1, 1869. The last enlisted man of volunteers (Private William Sadler, Company B, Ninth Veteran Reserve Corps) was discharged October 4, 1868, he having been retained on duty as a messenger in the War Department.

Under the joint resolution approved March 30, 1867, "suspending all proceedings in relation to payment for slaves drafted or received as volunteers in the military service of the United States," orders were issued by the Secretary of War the 4th of April, 1867, dissolving all the commissions appointed under previous laws, and the records of their proceedings have been collected and filed in this office.

* * * * * * *

I have the honor to be, general, very respectfully, your obedient servant,

E. D. TOWNSEND,
Assistant Adjutant-General.

ALTERNATE DESIGNATIONS

OF

ORGANIZATIONS MENTIONED IN THIS VOLUME

Alternate designation in black-faced type, the official designation, reference, or State to which organization belongs follows in *italics*.

Ahl's (G. W.) **Heavy Art.,** *Delaware.*
Bucktails, Inf., *150th Pa.*
Coast Guard, Inf., *Maine.*
Exempts Batt., Inf., *West Virginia.*
Mendel's (G. H.) **Engrs.,** *U. S. Regulars.*
Merrill's (W. E.) **Engrs.,** *1st U. S. Vet. Vols.*
New York, 1st Dragoons, *19th N. Y.*
Sloan's (T. S.) **Art.,** *Pennsylvania, Batty. E.*
Winegar's (C. E.) **Art.,** *1st N. Y., Batty. I.*

INDEX.

Brigades, Divisions, Corps, Armies, and improvised organizations are "Mentioned" under name of commanding officer; State and other organizations under their official designation.

* Subsequently designated 46th U. S. C. T.

*Subsequently designated 79th U. S. C. T.

*Subsequently designated 73d U. S. C. T.

*Subsequently designated 33d U. S. C. T.

O